GIVEN TO ME AS
A CHRISTMAS GIFT
FROM CHARLENE & CHRIS
LIVING IN PA.

12/24/2003

I SERVED IN THE NAVY
(ATLANTIC 6th FLEET)
FLAGSHIP USS FARGO/CL 106

1944 - 1945

The OFFICIAL
CHRONOLOGY of the U.S. NAVY
in WORLD WAR II

The OFFICIAL CHRONOLOGY of the U.S. NAVY in WORLD WAR II

ROBERT J. CRESSMAN

Naval Institute Press   Annapolis, Maryland

Naval Historical Center   Washington, D.C.

Naval Institute Press
291 Wood Road
Annapolis, MD 21402

First published by the Naval Institute Press in 2000

Library of Congress Cataloging-in-Publication Data

Cressman, Robert.
  The official chronology of the U.S. Navy in
World War II / Robert J. Cressman
        p.   cm.
  Includes bibliographical references (p.).
  ISBN 1–55750–149–1 (alk. paper)
  1. United States. Navy—History—World War,
1939–1945 Chronology.   2. World War, 1939–1945—
Naval operations, American Chronology.   I. Title.
D773. C74 1999
940.54′5973′0202—dc21   99-39136

07 06 05 04 03 02 01 00   9 8 7 6 5 4 3 2
First printing

CONTENTS

PREFACE AND ACKNOWLEDGMENTS

When I first came on board the Naval Historical Center Ship's History Branch in May 1976, I received a copy of the *United States Naval Chronology, World War II,* published by the Naval History Division in 1955. Copies of the book were so scarce that I was enjoined to keep it practically under lock and key. I used that well-worn volume often over the ensuing years. When I transferred to the Contemporary History Branch to write about the Navy's in-country operations during the Vietnam War, I little realized the detour I was about to take.

As the fiftieth anniversary of the end of World War II approached, Naval Historical Center staff, who knew of my interest in revising the work, asked me to undertake the task. The *United States Naval Chronology, World War II* was the shortest of those works produced by the major services and proved to be only a highly selective list of ship losses interspersed with cursory narrative noting significant events. The emphasis on commissioning dates for battleships and aircraft carriers served as a misleading yardstick for the growth of the Navy, especially when far more cruisers, destroyers, and amphibious ships and craft were commissioned or placed in service during World War II. In terms of coverage, the period between the onset of European hostilities in September 1939 and the attack on the Pacific Fleet at Pearl Harbor in December 1941 was conspicuous by its brevity.

While the original had served its purpose as a reference work, tremendous strides made in the research and writing of World War II naval history revealed that merely republishing the old work would not suffice. Readers who compare this chronology with the earlier edition will find many additions. The original alleged omission of lost U.S. naval vessels below the size of tank-landing ships (LSTs), but motor torpedo boats (much smaller than LSTs) were mentioned while larger amphibious ships—notably tank landing craft (LCT) and infantry landing craft (LCI)—were not. Likewise district craft were slighted.

The earlier edition only recounted losses of the major combatants of the Axis navies, skewing the outcome of naval battles in which enemy ships were damaged but not sunk. For this new edition, wherever it could be ascertained what enemy ships were damaged in encounters with American ships or planes, the enemy vessel is named. The U.S. Navy's operations against German blockade runners, largely omitted from the original, are also included. Reference to Vichy French naval vessels damaged or sunk by American submarines earned mention in the original, but the heavy losses suffered by the French in battle off Casablanca (November 1942) were not—an oversight rectified in this volume.

Because it was specifically a U.S. Navy chronology for World War II, the original editors made a conscious effort to not include the activities of merchant ships. But the continuation of trade by a neutral United States led to detention of U.S. merchantmen and the seizure of cargoes deemed contraband by belligerents. British interference with U.S. commerce during 1939 is important in comprehending the American attitude toward Great Britain at that point in the war. Incidents where U.S. merchantmen rescued British or French sailors from their torpedoed ships show that Americans sailed in dangerous seas carrying out their "business in great waters" before formal American entry into the conflict. Because historians have come to understand naval operations within the framework of a broader maritime perspective, U.S. merchant ship–related incidents have been included. While some might question broadening the scope, one cannot ignore those operations without doing disservice to the hazards faced by the oft-unsung officers and enlisted men who served in the U.S. Navy's Armed Guard detachments.

Likewise, the massive U.S. submarine campaign against Japanese merchant shipping originally was not addressed. Its omission in a U.S. Navy chronology is inexplicable when one considers that the war waged by the "Silent Service" played a significant role in disrupting Japan's logistics to its far-flung empire.

Another aspect that proved bothersome was the vague terminology. The word "collision" seemed ambiguous when one checked ships' war diaries and action reports, and often what was termed a "collision" was in effect no more than a nautical fender bender. Refueling at sea has always required seamanship of a high order, especially where conditions of wind and wave make it particularly hazardous. Ships occasionally come together during such encounters, as they would during reammunitioning or revictualing. Many of the collisions noted in the following text occurred during amphibious operations or in convoys. They reflect not only congested waters off busy beachheads but inclement weather such as sailors found in the often inhospitable climes of the Aleutians or the North Atlantic.

Verifying "accidental explosions" revealed incidents that ranged from a ship accidentally firing into herself, to a turret explosion, to bombs exploding onboard an aircraft that had just landed on a carrier flight deck. Wherever possible the reason for the damage is clarified. Vague references to "United States forces" scuttlings led to attempts to verify the cause. The

cumbersome "coastal defense guns" simply became "shore batteries" and "United States naval gunfire" became "friendly fire," where appropriate.

As much as possible, the nomenclature of enemy vessels (such as the replacement of "raider" with "auxiliary cruiser" or "armed merchant cruiser" and "armored ship" for "pocket battleship") has been rendered more accurately. Unless otherwise specified, naval vessels are designated with the nationality (Japanese destroyer, Japanese cargo ship, et cetera); where an army-chartered or civilian ship is referred to, the nationality plus either "army" or "merchant" is used to differentiate, as well as can be determined, those ships from naval vessels. Japanese surnames precede the given name.

Every effort was made to pinpoint the most exact location of each incident. Longitude/latitude coordinates are given whenever available from official reports. Varying details regarding the location of a specific place were encountered in source documents, especially for the Pacific theatre. For example, "Savo Island, Solomons" may be mentioned in some source documents and "Savo Island, Guadalcanal" mentioned in other source documents. Because either description will lead the reader to the area of action, no attempt was made to consistently identify the location of Savo Island, which is located in the southeast Solomon Islands group, northwest of Guadalcanal Island.

If coordinates are not given and the place name mentioned in the source document is not found in a standard dictionary, more detailed information has been added to direct the reader to the location. For example, "Menado" is identified as "Menado, Celebes" and "Chichi Jima" is identified as "Chichi Jima, Bonins."

Brief accounts are included of individuals who were awarded the Medal of Honor. This was done to bring a human dimension to the war, as well as to provide a context for these acts of bravery. While their circumstances differed, the common denominator was devotion to duty.

Inevitably one who compiles a chronology comes under fire for trying to be too exclusive or too inclusive. The decision of what to include in *The Official Chronology of the U.S. Navy in World War II* has been mine alone. There will be complaints that certain events have been omitted. Given the scope of the work, one has to try and do justice to an entire war. A book of this nature is very much a "work in progress."

Any errors of fact in the following pages are mine alone, and the opinions and interpretations contained herein do not necessarily represent the views of the Department of the Navy.

As is the case with any enterprise of this magnitude, there is a goodly company of people whose unique contributions I appreciate more than mere words can express. I particularly thank William S. Dudley, director of naval history (and his predecessor, Dean C. Allard), and Edward J. Marolda, senior historian, for asking me to undertake this project; William J. Morgan, historian emeritus at the Historical Center, for his insight and input; and Sandra J. Doyle and Wendy Karppi for their editorial assistance, as well as seemingly limitless patience, on numerous occasions. I especially thank the "band of brothers" in the Contemporary History Branch, Jeffrey G. Barlow, Richard A. Russell, John D. Sherwood, Robert J. Schneller, and Curtis A. Utz, for their insightful comments and unfailing good humor, as well as support and encouragement. Gary E. Weir, head of Contemporary History, deserves special acknowledgment for his unique contributions to this project. In addition the peer review he convened allowed me to benefit from the insights not only of the aforementioned scholars, but also Timothy Francis of the Center's Ship's History Branch; Lt. Col. Roger Cirillo, USA; Robert G. Browning Jr.; Scott T. Price; Sarandis Papadapoulis; and Roger Havern. Samuel L. Morison took the time to point out errors in the original edition. Richard B. Frank, Charles R. Haberlein, John B. Lundstrom, James T. Rindt, and James C. Sawruk read portions of the manuscript and offered helpful suggestions. Capt. Edward L. "Ned" Beach, USN (Ret.), proved a great help in calling attention to shortcomings of the original work during the formative stages of the revision.

No historian can perform his work without good source material. I would like to thank Bernard F. Cavalcante, head of the Operational Archives Branch, and his magnificent staff. Words of praise are too few to laud Kathleen M. Lloyd, Richard M. Walker, Regina T. Akers, John L. Hodges, and Ariana T. Jacob, who were never too busy to facilitate my research in what eventually amounted to hundreds of action reports, war diaries, command files, and biography files. I particularly appreciate their patient assistance when I called with yet another request in the midst of their own often hectic workday.

Another group of people who took my frequent visits in stride is the Navy Department Library staff: Jean Hort, Glenn Helm, Tonya Montgomery, David Brown, Davis Elliott, and Barbara Auman. Likewise my old friends in Ship's History, John C. Reilly Jr., James L. Mooney, Raymond A. Mann, Kevin Hurst, and Cherie Watson, cooperated cheerfully in allowing me to check pertinent files in the office that had been my professional home for more than a decade. Edwin Finney and Jack Green facilitated my research in the superbly organized Photographic Section of the Center's Curator Branch. Barry Zerby at the National Archives' College Park facility provided timely research assistance. Dana Bell of the National Air and Space Museum provided valuable input concerning USAAF operations during World War II. The Center's naval reservists, led by Capt. William Galvani, USNR, contributed to the project by putting the contents of the original chronology on diskette—a very necessary first step.

This chronology is dedicated to those men and women who served in the United States Navy during World War II, who continued to build upon the traditions of those who had served in the past, and who forged new traditions for the current generation.

I also dedicate this work to my wife, Linda; to my children, Christine and Bobby, who often put up with my bringing work home in the course of my career; and to my father, Lt. Cdr. Wilmer H. Cressman, USN (Ret.), who served in the transport *Susan B. Anthony* (AP 73) in the Mediterranean (1943) and in the attack cargo ship *Almaack* (AKA 10) in the Pacific (1944–1945), and who was an active participant in amphibious operations from Sicily to Iwo Jima. He and my mother (who died in 1988) provided me with a stable, loving, and nurturing home in my formative years as I grew to love naval history. I am also grateful to my friends (whether classmates or workplace colleagues) who have encouraged me from junior high school to the present to grow as a writer and as a historian—for this work is a product of their help as well.

The OFFICIAL
CHRONOLOGY *of the* U.S. NAVY
in WORLD WAR II

1939

SEPTEMBER

1 Friday

World War II begins as Germany invades Poland with a power and rapidity that convincingly demonstrates to the world the *blitzkrieg*, or "lightning war." Italy announces its neutrality. Ultimately, the global conflict set in motion on this late summer day will engulf much of the globe and wreak far-reaching changes in the world order.

The U.S. Navy in September 1939 is, for the most part, concentrated on the west coast of the United States, reflecting the nation's traditional interest in the Far East and its isolationist leanings away from Europe. Although the matter is discussed as hostilities loomed on the horizon late in August 1939, there are no plans to use U.S. naval vessels to repatriate American citizens except in "collecting small groups [of Americans] in the Mediterranean area for transportation to places where they can move to safe ports for embarkation."

Office of the Chief of Naval Operations sends dispatch to commanders in chief of U.S. and Asiatic Fleets, and commanders of Atlantic Squadron, Special Service Squadron, and Squadron 40-T: "Reliably informed [that] German submarines are set to operate on Atlantic trade routes and that a dozen German merchant vessels will operate as armed raiders [and that] neutral merchantmen may expect Great Britain may institute similar practices as in last war." Additional addressees to this warning include the three new warships on shakedown cruises: light cruiser *St. Louis* (CL 49) at Punta Delgada, Azores; destroyer *Anderson* (DD 411) at Montreal, Canada; and submarine *Spearfish* (SS 190) en route from New York City to Bahia, Brazil.

Hydrographic Office begins issuing, by dispatch and bulletin, special warnings of restrictions and dangers to navigation incident to the outbreak of hostilities between Germany and Poland. Special Warning No. 1 is that the German government has announced that Danzig Bay is a danger area due to military operations taking place there.

President Franklin Delano Roosevelt appoints Admiral William D. Leahy, who has recently retired as Chief of Naval Operations, as Work Projects Administrator for the Territory of Puerto Rico (see 11 September).

Light cruiser *Marblehead* (CL 12) transports marines from Chinwangtao, China, to Shanghai. The emergency movement is to bring the Fourth Marine Regiment to full strength in the event that the Japanese try to take advantage of the European war to force an incident at Shanghai.

German armored ship *Admiral Graf Spee*, which had left Wilhelmshaven, Germany, on 21 August for the South Atlantic, makes rendezvous with tanker *Altmark* southwest of the Canary Islands. The fuel oil carried in *Altmark*'s bunkers was obtained in August at Port Arthur, Texas. *Admiral Graf Spee*'s sister ship *Deutschland*, which had departed Wilhelmshaven on 24 August, is deployed to raid commerce in the North Atlantic.

3 Sunday

Great Britain and France declare war on Germany in accordance with their prewar pledges to Poland. Australia and New Zealand follow.

U.S. steamship *President Roosevelt* off-loads the Navy's first motor torpedo boat, the British-built Scott-Paine *PT 9*, onto crane barge *Colossus*, New York, 5 September 1939. (NHC, NH 44479)

to seek out and destroy German submarines: HMS *Ark Royal* off the northwestern approaches to the British Isles, HMS *Courageous* and HMS *Hermes* off the southwestern approaches (see 17 September).

U.S. freighter *Saccarappa*, with a cargo of phosphates and cotton, is seized by British authorities (see 8 September).

4 Monday

British passenger liner *Athenia* sinks as the result of damage sustained the previous day when torpedoed by German submarine *U 30*. After the sinking of *Athenia* is confirmed through radio intelligence and news broadcasts, the German Naval War Staff radios all U-boats at sea that the Führer has ordered that no hostile action be taken "for the present" against passenger ships, even if they are traveling in convoy (see 16 September).[2]

Office of the Chief of Naval Operations orders Commander Atlantic Squadron to establish, as soon as possible, a combined air and ship patrol to observe and report, in cipher, the movements of warships of warring nations, east from Boston along a line to 42°30′N, 65°00′W, then south to 19°N and around the seaward outline of the Windward and Leeward Islands, Trinidad.

European war again comes to the Americas: British light cruiser HMS *Ajax* intercepts German freighter *Carl Fritzen* 200 miles east-southeast of Rio Grande do Sul, Brazil, 33°22′S, 48°50′W, and sinks the merchantman with gunfire.

5 Tuesday

Captain Alan G. Kirk, U.S. Naval Attaché, and Commander Norman R. Hitchcock, Assistant Naval Attaché and Assistant Naval Attaché for Air, are flown to Galway, Ireland, where they interview *Athenia*'s surviving officers and men. The attachés' investigation concludes that *Athenia* was torpedoed by a submarine.

President Roosevelt proclaims the neutrality of the United States in the war between Germany and France, Poland, the United Kingdom, India, Australia, and New Zealand, and orders the Navy to form a Neutrality Patrol (see below).

Chief of Naval Operations (Admiral Harold R. Stark) directs Commander Atlantic Squadron (Rear Admiral Alfred W. Johnson) to maintain an offshore patrol to report "in confidential system" the movements of all foreign men-of-war approaching or leaving the east

Irish Free State, a British dominion, however, declares its neutrality.

German submarines (previously deployed to operating areas in late August) begin attacks on British shipping. During these early operations, *U 30* (*Kapitänleutnant* Fritz-Julius Lemp) torpedoes (without warning) British passenger liner *Athenia* south of Rockall Bank, 56°44′N, 14°05′W; 28 American citizens are among the dead. U.S. freighter *City of Flint*, Swedish yacht *Southern Cross*, Norwegian freighter *Knute Nelson*, and British destroyers HMS *Electra* and HMS *Escort* rescue survivors. Despite having been given strict orders that all merchant vessels are to be treated in accordance with naval prize law (giving a warning

before attacking), Lemp's torpedoing *Athenia* in the belief that she is an armed merchant cruiser gives the British the erroneous impression that Germany has commenced unrestricted submarine warfare (see 16 and 22 September and 7 November).[1]

European war comes to the Americas: Less than three hours after the British declaration of war on Germany, light cruiser HMS *Ajax* intercepts German freighter *Olinda*, outward bound from Montevideo, Uruguay, off the River Plate, 34°58′S, 53°32′W. Not having a prize crew available to seize the enemy merchantman, *Ajax* shells and sinks her (see 4 September).

British Home Fleet deploys aircraft carriers

coast of the United States and approaching and entering or leaving the Caribbean. U.S. Navy ships are to avoid making a report of foreign men-of-war or suspicious craft, however, on making contact or when in their vicinity to avoid the performance of unneutral service "or creating the impression that an unneutral service is being performed" (see 9 October). The patrol is to extend about 300 miles off the eastern coastline of the United States and along the eastern boundary of the Caribbean (see 6 September). Furthermore, U.S. naval vessels are to report the presence of foreign warships sighted at sea to the district commandant concerned.

Destroyers *Davis* (DD 395) and *Benham* (DD 397) (two 327-foot Coast Guard cutters will be assigned later) are designated as the Grand Banks Patrol. They are to render rescue and other neutral assistance in emergencies and to observe and report ("in confidential system") movements of all foreign warships. They are to patrol across existing steamer lanes to the southward of the Grand Banks and to approximately 50°W.

Maritime Commission (Hydrographic Office Special Warning No. 9) directs that all U.S. merchant ships en route to or from Europe are not to steer a zigzag course; are not to black out at night; are to paint the U.S. flag on each side of the hull, on hatches fore and aft, and on sundecks of passenger vessels; and are to illuminate the colors flying from the flagstaff at night. In Hydrographic Office Special Warning No. 12 (promulgated the same day), U.S. merchant vessels engaged in domestic, "near-by foreign," or transpacific trade are not required to paint the flag on hull, hatches, and decks but otherwise are to follow the other instructions contained in Special Warning No. 9.

U.S. freighter *Black Osprey*, bound for Rotterdam, Holland, and Antwerp, Belgium, is stopped by British warship off Lizard Head and ordered into the port of Weymouth, one of the five "contraband control bases" (the others are Ramsgate, Kirkwall, Gibraltar, and Haifa) established by the British government (see 13 September and 31 October). Freighter *Lehigh*, bound for Hamburg, Germany, is detained by the British (see 7 September).

Philippine motorship *Don Isidro*, on her maiden voyage en route from her builders' yard at Kiel, Germany, to Manila, P.I., clears the Suez Canal; U.S. government immediately protests British authorities having removed, at Port Said, Egypt, two German engineers (on

Rear Admiral Alfred W. Johnson (seen here at Guantánamo in February of 1939), Commander Atlantic Squadron, directed the initial deployment of the Navy's Neutrality Patrol in September 1939. (Author's Collection)

board "to guarantee construction and demonstrate proper manning" of the new vessel) from *Don Isidro* (which is under the American flag) as illegal and a violation of the neutral rights of the United States (see 29 April 1940).

U.S. steamship *President Roosevelt* off-loads British-built Scott-Paine–type motor torpedo boat *PT 9* at New York; *PT 9* will be the prototype for the motor torpedo boats constructed by the Electric Boat Company.

6 Wednesday
Commander Atlantic Squadron (Rear Admiral Alfred W. Johnson) begins to establish the offshore Neutrality Patrol. Small seaplane tenders *Gannet* (AVP 8) and *Thrush* (AVP 3) sail for San Juan, Puerto Rico, to establish a seaplane base there.

Rear Admiral Charles E. Courtney relieves Rear Admiral Henry E. Lackey as Commander Squadron 40-T on board light cruiser *Trenton* (CL 11), the squadron flagship, at Villefranche-sur-Mer, France. Squadron 40-T had been formed in 1936 to protect American lives and property during the Spanish Civil War; its ships operate directly under the control of the Chief of Naval Operations.

French authorities remove two seamen of German nationality from U.S. freighter *Exochorda* at Marseilles, France.

British Northern Patrol (7th and 12th Cruiser Squadrons) commences operation between Shetland and Faeroe Islands and Iceland. Light cruisers HMS *Caledon*, HMS *Calypso*, HMS *Diomede*, HMS *Dragon*, HMS *Effingham*, HMS *Emerald*, HMS *Cardiff*, and HMS *Dunedin* are the ships that undertake this work. The patrol stops 108 merchantmen over the next three weeks, ordering 28 into the port of Kirkwall, Orkneys, to have their cargoes inspected.

7 Thursday
Cruiser Division 7 (Rear Admiral Andrew C. Pickens) sails to establish patrol off the eastern seaboard between Newport, Rhode Island, and Norfolk, Virginia. Heavy cruisers *Quincy* (CA 39) and *Vincennes* (CA 44) depart first, *San Francisco* (CA 38) (flagship) and *Tuscaloosa* (CA 37) follow. The ships, burning running lights, are to observe and report the movements of foreign men-of-war, and, as required, render prompt assistance to ships or planes encountered.

British steamer *Olivegrove* is stopped, torpedoed, and sunk by German submarine *U 33*, 200 miles northwest of Spain, 49°05′N, 15°58′W; upon receiving *Olivegrove*'s distress signal, U.S. passenger liner *Washington*, en route to the British Isles to evacuate American citizens from the European war zone, alters course and increases speed to reach the scene. Meanwhile, *U 33*'s commanding officer, *Kapitänleutnant* Hans-Wilhelm von Dresky, treats the British survivors courteously, and aids in their rescue by having distress rockets fired to guide *Washington* to the two lifeboats containing the 33-man crew, which she picks up without loss.

U.S. freighter *Lehigh*, detained by British authorities since 5 September, is released; freighter *Warrior* is detained by the British (see 18 September).

U.S. passenger liner *Santa Paula* is hailed by British cruiser (unidentified) 30 miles off Curaçao, N.W.I., and ordered to stop; after a delay of 20 minutes, *Santa Paula* is allowed to proceed (see 8 September). Tanker *I. C. White* is challenged by cruiser (nationality unidentified) 15 miles off Baranquilla, Colombia, but is allowed to proceed without further hindrance.

Incident to the European war, the U.S. Naval Observatory is closed to all visitors except those specifically authorized by the Secretary of the Navy.

Light cruiser *Trenton* (CL 11), seen here at Madeira *circa* 1939, served as flagship for Squadron 40-T into 1940. (Author's Collection)

8 Friday

President Roosevelt proclaims a "limited national emergency" and orders enlisted strength of all armed forces increased—naval enlisted men from 110,813 to 145,000; Marine Corps from 18,325 to 25,000—and authorizes recall to active duty of officers, men, and nurses on retired lists of Navy and Marine Corps.

Undersecretary of State Sumner Welles and British Ambassador to the U.S. Lord Lothian have "off-the-record talk" (at the former's request) concerning the brief detention of U.S. passenger liner *Santa Paula* the day before. Lord Lothian is informed that *Santa Paula's* captain had been asked "to give formal assurances whether there were any German passengers on board, the implication being that if the captain had not given such assurances, the officers of the cruiser would have boarded [*Santa Paula*] to search for German passengers and possibly might have taken some off." Undersecretary Welles goes on to say that "any act by British cruisers affecting American ships in waters so close to the United States involving possible boarding of them and taking off of civilian passengers would create a very highly unfortunate impression upon American public opinion at this time and was something undesirable in itself, since if civilian passengers actually had been taken off, such act would be clearly counter to international

law." Lord Lothian agrees and promises to "take the necessary steps to prevent occurrences of this kind from happening."

Allies announce a long-range blockade of Germany (see 11 September).

Cargo (phosphates and cotton) is unloaded from U.S. freighter *Saccarappa,* detained since 3 September by British authorities; after the items deemed contraband are unloaded, the ship is released to continue on her voyage.

9 Saturday

U.S. freighter *Wacosta*, bound from Glasgow, Scotland, to New York, is stopped by German submarine (unidentified). *Wacosta* is detained for three hours while the Germans examine her papers and search her holds, but is permitted to proceed.

U.S. steamship *President Harding* is detained by French authorities and various items of her cargo (including 135 tons of copper and 34 tons of petroleum products) are seized as contraband. The ship is released promptly.

10 Sunday

Canada declares war on Germany.

U.S. freighter *Hybert* is detained for two hours by a U-boat (unidentified); *Hybert* is released, but the Germans warn the merchantman not to use her radio for 24 hours.

11 Monday

Germany announces counterblockade of Allies.

Admiral William D. Leahy, USN (Retired), former Chief of Naval Operations (1937–1939), takes office as Governor of Puerto Rico.

Navy charters barkentine *Bear of Oakland* for operations in the U.S. Antarctic Service and commissions her as auxiliary *Bear* (AG 29).[3] The expedition will be under the command of Rear Admiral Richard E. Byrd, USN (Retired). (Byrd was appointed commanding officer of the expedition on 13 July 1939.) Civilian sources provide scientific staff and dog drivers; sailors, marines, and soldiers perform the supporting aviation, radio, photography, commissary, carpentry, and mechanical duties, as well as operate tractors and light tanks and the Armour Institute of Technology's *Snow Cruiser*, the unique vehicle developed for polar exploration (see 22 November).

U.S. tanker *R. G. Stewart* is stopped by shot fired across her bow by German submarine *U 38* about 253 miles west of Ushant, France, 48°17′N, 11°16′W. Soon thereafter *U 38* shells, torpedoes, and sinks British motor tanker *Inverliffey*; *R. G. Stewart* rescues the tanker's crew and later transfers them to U.S. freighter *City of Joliet* for transportation to Antwerp, Belgium.

German armored ship *Admiral Graf Spee* provisions from tanker *Altmark*; security measure of launching the warship's AR 196 pays dividends, as British heavy cruiser HMS *Cumberland* is spotted closing the area. *Admiral Graf Spee* and her consort alter course and are thus not sighted.

12 Tuesday

USAAC 21st Reconnaissance Squadron (B-18s) (Major Howard Craig, USAAC) reports to Commander Atlantic Squadron for duty in connection with the Neutrality Patrol, based at Miami, Florida.

Instructions to Neutrality Patrol are modified to include covering the approaches to the Gulf of Mexico through the Yucatan Channel and the Straits of Florida.

U.S. freighter *Black Eagle* is detained by British authorities at the Downs, the roadstead in the English Channel off the coast of Kent (see 19 September).

13 Wednesday

Submarine *Squalus* (SS 192), which had accidentally sunk off Portsmouth, New Hampshire, on 23 May during a scheduled test dive (of her 59-man crew, 26 men perish and 33 are rescued by McCann Rescue Chamber), arrives under tow at Portsmouth Navy Yard for extensive repairs.[4]

U.S. freighter *Sea Arrow* is launched at Oakland, California, the first major ocean-going vessel of that type completed on the west coast since World War I.[5]

U.S. freighter *Black Osprey*, detained at Weymouth, England, by British authorities since 5 September, is released (see 31 October).

Norwegian motor vessel *Ronda* strikes mine off Terschelling Island, Netherlands, 54°10′N, 04°34′E; two U.S. citizens perish. Survivors (including four Americans) are subsequently rescued by Italian freighter *Providencia*.[6]

14 Thursday

Atlantic Squadron Neutrality Patrol assets deployed: Destroyers *Davis* (DD 395), *Jouett* (DD 396), *Benham* (DD 397), and *Ellet* (DD 398) operate between Halifax, Nova Scotia, and Placentia Bay, Newfoundland (Grand Banks Patrol); destroyers *Hamilton* (DD 141) and *Leary* (DD 158) operate off Georges Shoals; destroyers *Goff* (DD 247) and *Hopkins* (DD 249) and patrol squadron VP 54 (PBY-2s), supported by minesweeper (small seaplane tender) *Owl* (AM 2), operate out of Narragansett Bay, Rhode Island; destroyers *Decatur* (DD 341), *Barry* (DD 248), and *Reuben James* (DD 245) and auxiliary (high-speed transport) *Manley* (AG 28), with shore-based squadrons VP 52 and VP 53 (P2Y-2s), operate out of Chesapeake Bay; destroyers *Babbitt* (DD 128) and *Claxton* (DD 140) patrol the Florida Straits; heavy cruisers *San Francisco* (CA 38) and *Tuscaloosa* (CA 37), destroyers *Truxtun* (DD 229), *Simpson* (DD 221), *Broome* (DD 210), and *Borie* (DD 215), and patrol squadrons VP 33 (PBY-3s) and VP 51 (PBY-1s), supported by small seaplane tenders *Lapwing* (AVP 1), *Thrush* (AVP 3), and *Gannet* (AVP 8), watch the Caribbean and the Atlantic side of the Lesser Antilles; and heavy cruisers *Quincy* (CA 39) and *Vincennes* (CA 44) operate off Cape Hatteras, North Carolina. Held in reserve in Hampton Roads, Virginia, is a striking force consisting of carrier *Ranger* (CV 4) (her embarked air group consisting of squadrons VB 4, VF 4, VS 41, and VS 42) and battleships *New York* (BB 34) and *Texas* (BB 35). *Arkansas* (BB 33) and gunnery training ship (ex-battleship) *Wyoming* (AG 17) are carrying out training cruise for USNR midshipmen.[7]

U.S. freighter *City of Joliet* is detained by French authorities and her cargo examined (see 5 October).

Acting Secretary of the Navy Charles Edison, meeting with the press, Washington, D.C., 14 September 1939, warns belligerents that they "would be taking a long chance" attacking U.S. ships. To Edison's left are Lieutenant Bernard L. Austin (standing) and Commander Leland P. Lovette (seated), from the Public Relations section of the Office of Naval Intelligence. (NHC, NH 56939)

16 Saturday

Naval Attaché in Berlin reports that *Grössadmiral* Erich Raeder, Commander in Chief of the German Navy, has informed him that all submarine commanders had reported negatively concerning the sinking of British passenger liner *Athenia* (see 22 September and 7 November).

British Admiralty, reflecting the need to protect the Atlantic lifeline necessary to Britain's survival, announces establishment of convoy system for its merchant shipping; first Halifax–United Kingdom convoy (HX 1) sails—eighteen ships escorted by Canadian destroyers HMCS *St. Laurent* and HMCS *Saguenay*.

German submarine *U 31* inaugurates U-boat campaign against convoys when she attacks west-bound convoy OB 4, torpedoing and sinking British merchant steamer *Aviemore* in the North Atlantic, 49°11′N, 13°38′W.

U.S. freighter *Shickshinny* is detained at Glasgow, Scotland, by British authorities (see 18 September).

17 Sunday

USSR, its western border secure after its 23 August 1939 ceasefire with the Japanese along the Manchukuo-Mongolia frontier, invades eastern Poland.

British use of Home Fleet aircraft carriers to hunt German submarines, begun on 3 September, ends after *U 29* torpedoes and sinks HMS *Courageous* southwest of the British Isles, 50°10′N, 14°45′W. *Courageous* is the first capital ship lost by any of the warring powers. "A wonderful success," the German U-boat High Command War Diary exults, "and confirmation of the fact that the English defense forces are not as effective as they advertise themselves to be."

U.S. freighter *Black Condor* is detained by British authorities (see 24 September).

18 Monday

President Roosevelt authorizes Coast Guard to enlist 2,000 additional men and to build two training stations.

Heavy cruiser *San Francisco* (CA 38) arrives at San Juan, Puerto Rico, and reports that Dominican authorities are exercising proper precautions to learn promptly of the entry of any belligerent warship into Semana Bay, Dominican Republic.

U.S. freighter *Warrior*, detained by British

Destroyer *Downes* (DD 375) under way, 27 September 1939, painted as part of a Naval Research Laboratory (NRL) camouflage experiment. Ocean Gray replaces the standard navy gray overall scheme; hull numbers, usually white with black shadowing, are dark gray. (NHC, NH 63132)

authorities since 7 September, is released after her cargo of phosphates is requisitioned. Freighter *Shickshinny*, detained since 16 September at Glasgow, Scotland, is permitted to sail without unloading cargo deemed by British authorities to be contraband. *Shickshinny*, however, is to unload those items at Mersey, England.

U.S. freighter *Eglantine* is stopped by German submarine, ordered not to use her radio, and to send her papers to the U-boat for examination. The Germans allow *Eglantine* to proceed, but advise her not to use her radio for three hours.

19 Tuesday

VP 21 (PBYs), assigned to the Asiatic Fleet to provide aerial reconnaissance capability to safeguard the neutrality of the Philippines, departs Pearl Harbor for Manila, P.I. The squadron will fly via Midway, Wake, and Guam (see 25 September). Seaplane tender (destroyer) *Childs* (AVD 1) will provide support at Wake, the least developed place on the movement westward.

U.S. freighter *Black Hawk* is detained by British authorities (see 4 October); freighter *Black Eagle*, detained by the British since 12 September at the Downs, is released.

20 Wednesday

Squadron 40-T departs Villefranche, France; flagship, light cruiser *Trenton* (CL 11) (Rear Admiral Charles E. Courtney), and destroyer *Jacob Jones* (DD 130) head for Lisbon, Portugal; destroyer *Badger* (DD 126) heads for Marseilles, France (see 23 September).

U.S. freighters *Ethan Allen* and *Ipswich* are detained by British authorities (see 30 September).

21 Thursday

President Roosevelt asks for repeal of arms embargo provision of Neutrality Act of 1937 (see 4 November).

22 Friday

German submarine *U 30* arrives at Wilhelmshaven, Germany, where her commanding officer, *Kapitänleutnant* Fritz-Julius Lemp, informs Commander U-boats, in private, that he (Lemp) believes himself responsible for sinking British passenger liner *Athenia* (see 7 November).

U.S. freighter *Syros* is detained by French authorities (see 10 October).

23 Saturday

Squadron 40-T arrives at Lisbon, Portugal; en route, flagship, light cruiser *Trenton* (CL 11) (Rear Admiral Charles E. Courtney) intercepts distress signal from British freighter *Constant* which reports being pursued by what she believes to be a German U-boat. Rear Admiral Courtney sends destroyer *Jacob Jones* (DD 130) to provide water and provisions to the English merchantman.

24 Sunday

Seaplane tender *Langley* (AV 3) arrives at Manila, P.I., to serve as the flagship for Commander Aircraft Asiatic Fleet (Commander Arthur C. Davis) (see 25 September).

U.S. freighter *Black Condor*, detained by British authorities since 17 September, is released.

25 Monday

VP 21 arrives at Manila, P.I.; it will be tended by *Langley* (AV 3), which arrived the previous day.

26 Tuesday

German armored ships *Admiral Graf Spee* and *Deutschland*, poised to begin raiding Allied commerce in the South and North Atlantic, respectively, receive their orders to commence operations.

27 Wednesday

Warsaw falls; Poland surrenders unconditionally to Germany and the USSR. After the fall of Poland, the war on the western front degenerates into a stalemate, sometimes derisively called the *sitzkrieg* ("sitting war") after the *blitzkrieg* that had crushed Polish resistance in September.

Commandant of the Coast Guard informs Commander of the Boston Division that upon withdrawal of destroyers from the Grand Banks Patrol, the patrol will be maintained by two *Campbell*-class 327-foot cutters.

U.S. freighter *Executive* is detained by French authorities at Casablanca, French Morocco (see 29 September).

28 Thursday

Hawaiian Detachment, U.S. Fleet, is established in response to Japan's continuing undeclared war against China that has been under way since 7 July 1937. The establishment of the Hawaiian Detachment, to be based at Pearl Harbor, necessitates changing the schedules of the supply ships and oilers needed to provide logistics support.

29 Friday

Poland is partitioned by Germany and the Soviet Union.

U.S. freighter *Executive*, detained at Casablanca, French Morocco, since 27 September, is released by French authorities, provided that she proceed to Bizerte, Tunisia.

British warships operating on the Northern Patrol continue to stop neutral merchantman; between this date and 12 October, 63 vessels are stopped, of which 20 are detained at Kirkwall for the inspection of their cargoes.

Battleship *Arizona* (BB 39) engineering plant is sabotaged, San Pedro, California. A thorough FBI investigation into the occurrence concludes that the deed was done to embarrass certain ship's officers rather than cause serious damage.

30 Saturday

Rear Admiral Hayne Ellis relieves Rear Admiral Alfred W. Johnson as Commander Atlantic Squadron on board the squadron's flagship, battleship *Texas* (BB 35).

Vice Admiral Adolphus Andrews (Commander Scouting Force) assumes command of Hawaiian Detachment, breaking his flag in heavy cruiser *Indianapolis* (CA 35). Andrews will shift his flag to carrier *Enterprise* (CV 6) on 3 October prior to the detachment's move to its operating base (see 5 October).

European war again comes to the Americas: German armored ship *Admiral Graf Spee* stops and sinks British steamship *Clement* 75 miles southeast of Pernambuco, Brazil, 09°05′S, 34°05′W (see 1 and 5 October).

U.S. freighters *Ethan Allen* and *Ipswich*, detained by British authorities since 20 September, are released. Cargo destined for Bremen and Hamburg, Germany, however, is seized and taken off *Ipswich*.

OCTOBER

1 Sunday

As of this date, the U.S. Navy consists of 396 commissioned ships divided among the major U.S. Fleet commands afloat: Battle Force (Battleships, Cruisers, Destroyers, and Aircraft), Submarine Force, and Base Force; Scouting Force (Cruisers and Aircraft); Atlantic Squadron; Asiatic Fleet; Special Service Squadron; and Squadron 40-T. There are 175 district craft in service in the following naval districts: First (headquarters in Boston, Massachusetts), Third (New York, New York), Fourth (Philadelphia, Pennsylvania), Fifth (Norfolk, Virginia), Sixth, Seventh, and Eighth (Charleston, South Carolina), Ninth (Great Lakes, Illinois), Eleventh (San Diego, California), Twelfth (San Francisco, California), Thirteenth (Seattle, Washington), Fourteenth (Pearl Harbor, Territory of Hawaii), Fifteenth (Balboa, Canal Zone), and Sixteenth (Cavite, Philippine Islands). Vessels not in commission (but including those ordered recommissioned incident to the expansion of the fleet) number 151; five district craft are carried as not in service.[8]

Word of German armored ship *Admiral Graf Spee*'s sinking of British freighter *Clement* reaches British Admiralty, which begins disposition of ships to meet the threat posed by the surface raider in the South Atlantic (see 5 October).

2 Monday

Act of Panama is approved by Conference of Foreign Ministers of American Republics meeting in Panama City, establishing a Pan-American neutrality zone 300 miles wide off the coasts of the United States and Latin America.

German government notifies the United States that merchant vessels must submit to visit and search, and that neutral merchant vessels refrain from suspicious actions when sighting German men-of-war and that they stop when summoned to do so. Maritime Commission and State and Navy Departments representatives who meet to contemplate the request consider it proper and should be complied with.

Chief of Naval Operations instructs all planning agencies within the naval establishment to accord precedence to the preparation of ORANGE (Japan) war plans.

3 Tuesday

River gunboat *Tutuila* (PR 4) is damaged when she is accidentally rammed by Chungking Ferry Boat Co. *Ferry No. 2* at Chungking, China.

Norwegian motor vessel *Höegh Transporter* is sunk by mine off St. John Island, entrance to Singapore Harbor; the two Americans among the passengers survive, one is uninjured.

4 Wednesday

U.S. Naval Attaché in Berlin reports that *Grössadmiral* Erich Raeder, Commander in Chief of the German Navy, has informed him of a plot wherein U.S. passenger liner *Iroquois*, which had sailed from Cobh, Ireland, with 566 American passengers on 3 October, would be sunk (ostensibly by the British) as she neared the east coast of the United States under "*Athenia* circumstances" for the apparent purpose of arousing anti-German feeling. Raeder gives credence to his source in neutral Ireland

Vice Admiral Adolphus Andrews (Commander Hawaiian Detachment) (center, foreground), calls upon Major General Charles D. Herron, USA (Commander Hawaiian Department) at Fort Shafter, Oahu, *circa* October 1939, along with his type commanders: Rear Admirals John H. Newton, Royal E. Ingersoll, and Ralston S. Holmes. (NHC, NH 90928)

"944-39" Puget Sound Navy Yard, Bremerton, Washington. 9 October 1939.
U.S.S. WEST VIRGINIA.

Battleship *West Virginia* (BB 48) undergoes availability, Puget Sound (Washington) Navy Yard, 9 October 1939. Heavy cruiser *Chicago* (CA 29) is moored on opposite side of pier while light cruiser *Brooklyn* (CL 40) lies in background (right); both cruisers appear to be airing bedding. Structure visible beyond *Brooklyn*'s after superstructure is the unique airship mooring mast of oiler *Patoka* (AO 9). (Author's Collection)

as being "very reliable" (see 5, 8, and 11 October).

U.S. freighter *Black Hawk*, detained by British authorities since 19 September, is released.

5 Thursday

Hawaiian Detachment is formed and sent to its new operating base, Pearl Harbor, T.H.; carrier *Enterprise* (CV 6) (flagship), two heavy cruiser divisions, two destroyer squadrons and a light cruiser flagship, a destroyer tender, and a proportionate number of small auxiliaries make up the force.

Navy Department informs U.S. passenger liner *Iroquois* of word received late the previous day concerning the plot to sink the ship as she nears the east coast. "As a purely precautionary measure," President Roosevelt announces this day, "a Coast Guard vessel and several navy ships from the [neutrality] patrol will meet the *Iroquois* at sea and will accompany her to an American port" (see 8 and 11 October).

British Admiralty and French Ministry of Marine form eight "hunting groups" in the Atlantic and Indian Oceans to counter the

threat posed by German armored ship *Admiral Graf Spee*. That same day, the object of that attention, *Admiral Graf Spee*, captures British freighter *Newton Beech* in the South Atlantic at 09°35′S, 06°30′W.

U.S. freighter *Exeter* is detained by French authorities at Marseilles, France (see 6 October); freighter *City of Joliet*, detained by the French since 14 September, is released.

Secretary of State Cordell Hull requests Chargé d'Affaires ad interim in Germany, Alexander C. Kirk, to ascertain why German authorities have detained Swedish motorship *Korsholm* and Norwegian steamship *Brott* (at Swinemünde), and Estonian steamship *Minna* (at Kiel). All of the neutral merchantmen carry cargoes of wood pulp or wood pulp products consigned to various American firms. These are the first instances of cargoes bound for the United States held up for investigation by German authorities. While no U.S. ships are detained, cargoes bound for American concerns in neutral (Finnish, Estonian, Latvian, and Norwegian) merchant ships come under scrutiny by the Germans (see 10 October and 8 and 27 December).

6 Friday

Last organized Polish resistance ceases at Kock.

U.S. freighters *Black Gull* and *Black Falcon* are detained by British authorities (see 10 and 11 October and 17 October, respectively).

U.S. freighter *Exeter*, detained at Marseilles, France, the previous day, is released. She subsequently reports having been examined several times by French naval authorities.

7 Saturday

German armored ship *Admiral Graf Spee* stops and boards British freighter *Ashlea* in the South Atlantic at 09°00′S, 03°00′W, and after transferring her crew to *Newton Beech*, sinks *Ashlea* with demolition charges.

U.S. freighter *Black Heron* is detained by British authorities at Weymouth, England (see 16 October).

8 Sunday

Coast Guard cutter *Campbell* joins U.S. passenger liner *Iroquois*, followed later by destroyers *Davis* (DD 395) and *Benham* (DD 397). The four ships proceed in company to New York (see 11 October).

German armored ship *Admiral Graf Spee* takes on board crews of British freighters *Ashlea* and *Newton Beech* in the South Atlantic and sinks the latter with demolition charges.

9 Monday

President Roosevelt, in memorandum for the Acting Secretary of the Navy, expresses displeasure with "the slowness of getting the East Coast, Caribbean, and Gulf Patrol under way," the "lag between the making of contacts and the follow-up of the contact," and the weakness of the liaison between the Navy, the Coast Guard, and the State Department. The Chief Executive emphasizes that "in this whole patrol business time is of the essence and loss of contact with surface ships will not be tolerated." Roosevelt urges that patrol planes and naval or Coast Guard ships "may report the sighting of any submarine or suspicious surface ship in plain English" (see 20 October).

German armored ship *Deutschland* seizes U.S. freighter *City of Flint*, en route from New York to the United Kingdom, as "contraband carrier" and places a prize crew on board (see 21, 23, 24, 27, and 28 October and 3 November).

British Northern Patrol continues operations between the Shetlands, Faeroes, and Iceland; light cruiser HMS *Belfast* captures German passenger ship *Cap Norte*.

10 Tuesday

German armored ship *Admiral Graf Spee* stops and puts prize crew on board British freighter *Huntsman* in the South Atlantic at 08°30′S, 05°15′W.

U.S. freighter *Patrick Henry* is detained by British authorities (see 22 October). British authorities remove from freighter *Black Gull* (detained since 6 October) 293 sacks of American mail addressed to Rotterdam, Holland, and 10 to Antwerp, Belgium. This is among the first instances of the British removing mail addressed to neutral countries and opening and censoring sealed letter mail sent from the United States (see 11 October).

U.S. freighter *Syros*, detained by French authorities since 22 September, is released.

Norwegian freighter *Brott*, detained at Swinemünde, Germany, since early October with a cargo of wood pulp/wood pulp products, is released by German authorities to proceed on her voyage to the United States.

11 Wednesday

Submarine rescue vessel *Pigeon* (ASR 6), driven aground at Tsingtao, China, by a severe hurricane on 31 August, is refloated.

U.S. passenger liner *Iroquois* arrives safely in New York Harbor, having been accompanied for three days by Coast Guard cutter *Campbell* and destroyers *Davis* (DD 395) and *Benham* (DD 397).[9]

U.S. freighter *Sundance* is detained at London, England, by British authorities (see 25 October); freighter *Black Tern* is detained at Weymouth, England (see 12 and 28 October); and freighter *Black Gull*, detained by the British since 6 October, is released.

12 Thursday

German submarines attack convoys of French and British shipping; *U 48* shells and sinks French motor tanker *Emile Miguet* (from convoy KJ 2S) at 50°15′N, 14°50′W, and later torpedoes and sinks British freighter *Heronspool* (convoy OB 17S) at 50°13′N, 14°48′W. U.S. merchantmen rescue the survivors: freighter *Black Hawk* rescues *Emile Miguet*'s crew, passenger liner *President Harding* rescues *Heronspool*'s.

British warships operating on the Northern Patrol continue to stop neutral merchantman; between this date and 26 October, 112 vessels are stopped, of which 23 are detained at Kirkwall for the inspection of their cargoes.

British seizure of U.S. mail continues: Authorities at the contraband control station at Weymouth remove 94 sacks addressed to Rotterdam, 81 to Antwerp, and 184 to Germany, from U.S. freighter *Black Tern*, which had been detained the day before; authorities at the Downs remove 77 sacks of parcel post, 33 sacks of registered mail, and 156 sacks of regular mail addressed to the Netherlands, in addition to 65 sacks of mail addressed to Belgium, three to Luxembourg, three to Danzig, and 259 to Germany, from Dutch motorship *Zaandam*.

13 Friday

U.S. freighter *Iberville* is detained by British authorities (see 24 October); freighter *Oakman* is detained by the British (see 27 October).

German submarine *U 47* penetrates defenses of British fleet base at Scapa Flow, Orkney Islands, shortly before midnight and attacks. Her initial spread of torpedoes causes no damage to battleship HMS *Royal Oak* and aircraft repair vessel HMS *Pegasus* (see 14 October).

14 Saturday

German submarine *U 47* quickly carries out second attack in the confines of Scapa Flow, Orkney Islands, and torpedoes battleship HMS *Royal Oak*, 58°55′N, 02°59′W, which sinks in 13 minutes.

German armored ship *Deutschland* sinks Norwegian freighter *Lorentz W. Hansen* 420 miles east of Newfoundland, 49°05′N, 43°44′W.

U.S. freighter *Scanstates* is detained at Kirkwall, Orkneys, by British authorities; freighter *Exporter* is detained at Gibraltar by the British (see 20 October and 27 October, respectively).

U.S. freighter *Nashaba* is detained at Le Havre by French authorities (see 25 October).

15 Sunday

German armored ship *Admiral Graf Spee* meets tanker *Altmark* and refuels (see 17 October).

16 Monday

German tanker *Emmy Friedrich*, whose cargo includes refrigerants needed for the magazine cooling systems in armored ship *Admiral Graf Spee*, then on a raiding foray in the Atlantic, departs Tampico, Mexico. Neutrality Patrol assets, including carrier *Ranger* (CV 4) and heavy cruiser *San Francisco* (CA 38), are mobilized to locate and trail the ship if the need arises (see 24 October).

U.S. freighter *Gateway City* is detained by British authorities (see 31 October); freighter *Black Heron*, detained by the British at Weymouth, England, since 7 October, is released.

17 Tuesday

U.S. freighter *Cranford* is detained by British authorities (see 21 October); freighter *Black Falcon*, detained by the British since 6 October, is released.

German armored ship *Admiral Graf Spee* transfers crew of British freighter *Huntsman* to tanker *Altmark*; *Huntsman* is then sunk with demolition charges at 16°00′S, 17°00′W.

18 Wednesday

Naval landing force from gunboats *Asheville* (PG 21) and *Tulsa* (PG 22) and destroyer *Whipple* (DD 217) is withdrawn from Kulangsu, China, where it had been protecting the American Consulate and the Hope Memorial Hospital since 17 May.

U.S. freighter *West Hobomac* is detained by British authorities (see 25 October).

German armored ship *Admiral Graf Spee* transfers crews of British freighters *Newton Beech* and *Ashlea* to tanker *Altmark*. The two German ships then part company for a time (see 28 October).

19 Thursday

Gunboat *Erie* (PG 50) arrives off Manzanillo, Mexico, on neutrality patrol; she will monitor movements of German freighter *Havelland* until 11 December. Commander Special Service Squadron (Rear Admiral John W. Wilcox Jr.) commends the gunboat's work as "the outstanding event" of offshore patrol work conducted by the squadron.

20 Friday

Commander Atlantic Squadron informs his ships to use plain-language radio reporting of contacts.

U.S. freighter *Scanstates*, detained at Kirkwall, Orkneys, by British authorities since 14 October, is released.

21 Saturday

U.S. freighter *City of Flint*, under prize crew from German armored ship *Deutschland* since 9 October, puts in to Tromsö, Norway, for water. Norwegian government, however, orders the ship to leave; she sails for Soviet waters (see 23, 24, 27, and 28 October and 3 November).

U.S. freighter *Meanticut* is detained at Gibraltar by British authorities and ordered to proceed to Oran, Algeria, to discharge certain cargo earmarked for delivery to Italy (see 27 October).

U.S. freighter *Cranford,* detained by British authorities since 17 October, is released.

22 Sunday
U.S. freighters *Endicott* and *West Gambo* are detained by French authorities and portions of their cargo ordered ashore as contraband: 750 bales of carbon black from *West Gambo* and 2,276 bars of copper and 1,796 bags of carbon black from *Endicott* (see 2 November).

U.S. steamship *President Hayes* is detained by British naval authorities at Alexandria, Egypt, and searched for contraband (see 23 October); freighter *Patrick Henry,* detained by the British since 10 October, is released.

German armored ship *Admiral Graf Spee* stops British freighter *Trevanion,* embarks her crew, and sinks the ship at 19°40'S, 04°02'W.

23 Monday
U.S. freighter *City of Flint* arrives at Murmansk, Russia (see 24, 27, and 28 October and 3 November).

U.S. freighter *Tulsa* is detained at London by British authorities (see 9 November).

U.S. steamship *President Hayes,* detained by British naval authorities at Alexandria, Egypt, the previous day, is released, but not before a consignment of rubber earmarked for delivery to Genoa, Italy, is unloaded.[10]

24 Tuesday
British light cruiser HMS *Orion* and Canadian destroyer HMCS *Saguenay* locate German tanker *Emmy Friedrich* in the Yucatan Channel; British light cruiser HMS *Caradoc* subsequently intercepts *Emmy Friedrich,* whose crew scuttles her to avoid capture.

British steamships *Menin Ridge* and *Ledbury* are attacked and sunk by German submarine *U 37* (torpedoes and gunfire, respectively) at 36°01'N, 07°22'W. U.S. freighter *Crown City* rescues the only five survivors from the 27-man crew of *Menin Ridge* and *Ledbury*'s entire 33-man crew.

Soviet authorities intern U.S. freighter *City of Flint*'s German prize crew from armored ship *Deutschland* at Murmansk (see 27 and 28 October and 3 November).

U.S. freighter *Wacosta* is detained by British authorities (see 8 November); freighter *Iberville,* detained by the British since 13 October, is released after cargo due to be discharged at Antwerp and Rotterdam, Holland,

is seized as contraband. British authorities at Kirkwall remove 468 bags of U.S. mail destined for Gothenborg, Sweden, and 18 for Helsinki, Finland, from Finnish freighter *Astrid Thorden.*

25 Wednesday
U.S. freighter *Sundance,* detained at London, England, by British authorities since 11 October, is released; freighter *West Hobomac,* detained by the British since 18 October, is released.

U.S. freighter *Nashaba,* detained at Le Havre by French authorities since 14 October, is released.

26 Thursday
U.S. freighter *Black Eagle* is detained by British authorities (see 5 November).

U.S. Consul at Gibraltar William E. Chapman confers informally with British naval authorities there concerning protracted delays in detention of American merchantmen (see 27 October).

27 Friday
U.S. freighter *City of Flint* is again placed under German naval prize crew from armored ship *Deutschland* (see 28 October and 3 November).

U.S. Consul at Gibraltar William E. Chapman meets informally with British Colonial Secretary there, and objects to protracted delay in detention of U.S. merchantmen, especially freighter *Exporter,* which has on board diplomatic pouches bound for Athens, Greece. Consul Chapman's low-key approach bears fruit. *Exporter,* detained since 14 October, is released later that day, as are freighters *Oakman* (detained since 13 October) and *Meanticut* (detained since 21 October).

28 Saturday
U.S. freighter *City of Flint,* again under German control, sails from Murmansk for Norwegian waters. At no time during *City of Flint*'s enforced stay at Murmansk has the ship's master, Captain Joseph A. Gainard (an inactive USNR officer), been allowed to communicate with the U.S. Embassy in Moscow (see 3 November).

U.S. freighter *Black Tern,* detained at Weymouth, England, by British authorities since 11 October, is released.

German armored ship *Admiral Graf Spee* makes rendezvous with tanker *Altmark* near Tristan de Cunha, South Atlantic Ocean. The warship refuels from the auxiliary, and transfers British freighter *Trevanion*'s crew to her.

30 Monday
U.S. freighter *Scanpenn* is detained by British authorities at Kirkwall, Orkneys; freighter *Hybert* is detained by British authorities at the Downs the same day (see 11 November and 5 November, respectively).

31 Tuesday
U.S. freighter *Black Osprey* is detained at the Downs by British authorities; freighter *Gateway City,* detained by the British since 16 October, is released after cargo billed for delivery at Antwerp and Rotterdam, Holland, is seized as contraband.

NOVEMBER

1 Wednesday
U.S. freighter *Exminster* is detained at Gibraltar by British authorities (see 6 November).

2 Thursday
U.S. freighters *Endicott* and *West Gambo,* detained by French authorities since 22 October and portions of their cargo ordered ashore as contraband, are released and clear Le Havre, France.

3 Friday
U.S. freighter *City of Flint* is restored to U.S. control at Haugesund, Norway (see 1 January 1940).

4 Saturday
Neutrality Act of 1939 becomes law. It repeals the arms embargo and substitutes a policy of "cash and carry," prohibits U.S. vessels and citizens from entering combat zones, and establishes National Munitions Control Board composed of the Secretaries of State, Treasury, War, Navy, and Commerce.

President Roosevelt declares area around British Isles a combat zone.

5 Sunday
U.S. freighter *Black Condor* is detained by British authorities at Weymouth, England (see 17 November). Freighter *Scanmail* is detained by the British at Kirkwall, Orkneys; part of her cargo is seized (see 21 November). Steamship *President Polk* is detained by the British at Port Said, Egypt, and certain items of her cargo confiscated for inquiry; freighter *Black Eagle,* detained by the British since 26 October, is released.

U.S. freighter *Hybert,* detained by the British since 30 October, arrives at Rotterdam, Holland.

6 Monday

U.S. freighter *Exeter* is detained at Gibraltar by British authorities. She is released the same day after 700 bags of U.S. mail are removed from the ship (see 8 and 10 November). Freighter *Exminster*, detained at Gibraltar by the British since 1 November, is released without any confiscation of cargo.

7 Tuesday

Naval Attaché, Berlin, is informed by an official of the German Navy Ministry that it had been "definitely established that no German U-boat had torpedoed the *Athenia*." The German Navy considers the incident "closed as far as the Navy was concerned" and possesses only "an academic interest in how the ship was sunk."

8 Wednesday

U.S. freighter *Exeter* is detained by French authorities (see 10 November).

U.S. freighter *Express* is detained by British authorities at Gibraltar but is released the same day after her cargo is examined; freighter *Wacosta*, detained by the British since 24 October, is released after cargo billed for delivery to Rotterdam, Holland, is seized as contraband.

9 Thursday

U.S. freighter *Tulsa*, detained by British authorities at London since 23 October, is released.

10 Friday

U.S. freighter *Exeter*, detained by French authorities since 8 November, is released after 1,400 bales of cottonseed hulk consigned to a Swiss buyer are removed as contraband.

11 Saturday

U.S. freighter *Nishmaha* is detained by British authorities at Gibraltar (see 17 November); freighter *Yaka* is detained by the British and her cargo examined.

U.S. freighter *Scanpenn*, detained by the British at Kirkwall, Orkneys, since 30 October, is released.

12 Sunday

U.S. freighter *Express*, with cargo earmarked for Greece, Turkey, and Romania, is detained by British authorities at Malta (see 21 and 23 November).

13 Monday

British steamship *Sirdhana*, bound for Hong Kong, blunders into British minefield off Singapore; 10 U.S. citizens (a troupe of magicians) are among the survivors. There are no casualties.

U.S. freighter *Black Hawk* is detained by British authorities at Ramsgate, England.

15 Wednesday

Interior Department motorship *North Star* (U.S. Antarctic Service) departs Boston, Massachusetts, for the south polar regions (see 12 January 1940).

German armored ship *Admiral Graf Spee* stops and sinks British tanker *Africa Shell* 160 miles northeast of Lourenço Marques, 24°45'S, 35°00'E; Japanese freighter *Tihuku Maru* happens upon the scene of the action but is unmolested.

16 Thursday

U.S. freighter *Lafcomo* is detained by British authorities at Weymouth, England; freighter *West Harshaw* is detained by the British at Ramsgate.

German armored ship *Admiral Graf Spee* stops Dutch freighter *Mapia* in Indian Ocean but, since the latter is a neutral vessel, permits her to proceed.

17 Friday

U.S. freighter *Black Gull* is detained by British authorities.

U.S. freighter *Nishmaha*, detained at Gibraltar since 11 November, is given option of submitting to further detention or proceeding to Barcelona, Spain, and thence to Marseilles, France, to unload items seized by British authorities. *Nishmaha*'s master chooses the latter (see 23 November). On the same day the British allow *Nishmaha* to clear Gibraltar; however, they detain U.S. freighter *Examiner* and seize 11 bags of first-class mail (see 4 December). Freighter *Black Condor*, detained at Weymouth, England, since 5 November, is released after British authorities seize part of her cargo and 126 bags of mail.

20 Monday

U.S. freighter *Excambion* is detained at Gibraltar by British authorities (see 27 November).

21 Tuesday

"Navicert" system is instituted by the United States in an attempt to avoid incidents at sea. U.S. merchant ships are to obtain clearances for their cargoes (certificates of nonenemy origin for all items) prior to leaving port.

U.S. freighter *Express*, detained by British authorities at Malta since 12 November, is released and allowed to proceed on her voyage after declaring the nature of her cargo (see 23 November).

Freighter *Scanmail*, detained by British authorities at Kirkwall, Orkneys, is released and departs for the United States.

22 Wednesday

Auxiliary *Bear* (AG 29) departs Boston, Massachusetts, as part of the U.S. Antarctic Service. Rear Admiral Richard E. Byrd, USN (Retired), is to investigate and survey the land and sea areas of Antarctica (see 14 January 1940).

U.S. freighter *Exmouth* is detained at Gibraltar by British authorities (see 5 December).

23 Thursday

U.S. freighter *Express*, released from her detention at Malta on 21 November by British authorities, continues on her voyage to Greece, Turkey, and Romania.

U.S. Consul at Gibraltar William E. Chapman declines to consent to execute agreement wherein the master of freighter *Nishmaha* (detained since 11 November) will agree to proceed via Barcelona, Spain, to Marseilles to unload cargo deemed contraband by the Gibraltar Contraband Control Board (see 24 November). Secretary of State Cordell Hull subsequently (27 November) approves Consul Chapman's action. U.S. merchantmen that left the U.S. with cargoes prior to 4 November are not subject to the restrictions of the Neutrality Act.

24 Friday

U.S. freighter *Nishmaha*, her master having signed an agreement (see 23 November) under protest to proceed to Marseilles, France, via Barcelona, Spain, clears Gibraltar.

25 Saturday

Destroyer *Yarnall* (DD 143) drifts aground in Lynnhaven Roads, Virginia; refloated that same day, she enters the Norfolk (Virginia) Navy Yard for repairs on 26 November.[11]

26 Sunday

German armored ship *Admiral Graf Spee* and tanker *Altmark* rendezvous in South Atlantic (see 27 and 29 November).

27 Monday

U.S. freighter *Effingham* is detained at Ramsgate, England, by British authorities (see 7 December); freighter *Azalea City* is detained at London (see 11 December). Freighter *Excambion*, detained at Gibraltar by the British since 20 November, is released.

German armored ship *Admiral Graf Spee* refuels from tanker *Altmark* in South Atlantic (see 29 November).

28 Tuesday

USSR denounces its 1932 Non-Aggression Pact with Finland (see 30 November).

U.S. freighter *Winston Salem* is detained at Ramsgate, England, by British authorities (see 7 December).

29 Wednesday

Submarine *S 38* (SS 143) is damaged by explosion of after storage battery, Olongapo, P.I.; four sailors suffer injuries.

U.S. freighter *Nishmaha* is detained by French authorities at Marseilles; her cargo (cotton, paraffin, and beef casings) is held pending the decision of the Contraband Committee in London (see 8 December).

German armored ship *Admiral Graf Spee* reembarks from accompanying tanker *Altmark* all British merchant marine officers from the six ships that the "pocket battleship" has sunk up to that point. The officers are to be taken back to Germany; the crewmen remain imprisoned on board *Altmark* (see 16 February 1940).

30 Thursday

USSR invades Finland, which will receive not only American aid but British and French as well; the Finnish struggle (albeit against an initially inept Soviet invasion force) arouses the admiration of many (see 14 December).

Destroyer *Reuben James* (DD 245) is damaged by grounding, Lobos Cay, Cuba.

U.S. freighter *Extavia*, with cargo destined for Istanbul, Turkey, and the Piraeus, Greece, is detained at Gibraltar by British authorities (see 14 December).

DECEMBER

1 Friday

Submarine Division 14 arrives on the Asiatic Station, the first modern reinforcement received by the Asiatic Fleet in many years. Submarines in the division are *Pickerel* (SS 177) (flag), *Porpoise* (SS 172), *Perch* (SS 176), *Pike* (SS 173), *Tarpon* (SS 175), and *Permit* (SS 178).

2 Saturday

German armored ship *Admiral Graf Spee* stops British freighter *Doric Star*; the warship then torpedoes, shells, and sinks the merchantman at 19°15′S, 05°05′E.

3 Sunday

German armored ship *Admiral Graf Spee* stops British freighter *Tairoa*; the warship then sinks the merchantman at 21°30′S, 03°00′E. Ironically, the same day Commodore Commanding South Atlantic Station, Commodore Henry H. Harwood, RN, orders his three cruisers to concentrate off the River Plate estuary, between Uruguay and Argentina, on 12 December (see 13 December).

4 Monday

U.S. freighter *Examiner*, detained at Gibraltar since 17 November by British authorities, is released.

5 Tuesday

U.S. freighter *Exochorda* is detained at Gibraltar by British authorities, who maintain that the 45 tons of tin plate among the vessel's cargo is contraband. The latter maintain that the cargo must be taken to Marseilles and unloaded there; the manager of the shipping firm (Export Lines) maintains that the ship cannot proceed to a belligerent port without violating the Neutrality Act. Until the impasse is resolved, the merchantman remains at

Destroyer *Reuben James* (DD 245) aground off Lobos Cay, Cuba, 30 November 1939. (NA, 80-G-391561)

Gibraltar (see 13 December). Freighter *Exmouth*, detained at Gibraltar since 22 November, is released.

U.S. freighter *Yaka* is detained at the Downs by British authorities (see 6 December).

6 Wednesday

Light cruiser *Omaha* (CL 4) arrives at Havana, Cuba, from Guantánamo Bay, to take on board the remains of J. Butler Wright, the late U.S. Ambassador to Cuba who died 4 December in Havana. *Omaha* will proceed to Washington, D.C., via Quantico, Virginia (see 11 December).

U.S. freighter *Yaka*, detained at the Downs by British authorities the previous day, is released.

German armored ship *Admiral Graf Spee* refuels from tanker *Altmark* in South Atlantic, roughly 1,700 miles from Montevideo, Uruguay.

7 Thursday

Rear Admiral George J. Meyers, Commander Base Force, dies of coronary thrombosis on board his flagship, auxiliary *Argonne* (AG 31), San Pedro, California (see 28 December).

U.S. freighters *Effingham* and *Winston Salem*, detained at Ramsgate, England, by British authorities since 27 November and 28 November, respectively, are released; the latter proceeds to Rotterdam, Holland, where her cargo of 2,782 bales of cotton is seized by British authorities.

U.S. freighter *Exmoor* is detained at Gibraltar by British authorities (see 15 December).

German armored ship *Admiral Graf Spee* stops and sinks British freighter *Streonshalh* at 25°01'S, 27°50'W.

8 Friday

Duties of the former Technical Division, Office of Naval Operations, concerned with matters of research and invention, are transferred to Office of the Technical Aide to the Secretary of the Navy.

Secretary of State Cordell Hull urges U.S. Chargé d'Affaires in the United Kingdom Herschel V. Johnson to urge the Contraband Commission in London to release U.S. freighter *Nishmaha* (then at Marseilles, France). *Nishmaha* has been held 25 days, "a most unreasonable detention" (see 19 December).

U.S. Consul General in Hamburg Wilbur Keblinger reports that German prize control authorities are detaining more than 125 neutral ships in German ports: at least 40

Swedish, 12 Danish, five Norwegian, 40 Finnish, 14 Estonian, and 14 Latvian, comprising practically all neutral vessels clearing Baltic or Scandinavian ports with cargoes of goods that are on the German contraband list (see 27 December).

9 Saturday

U.S. freighter *Explorer* is detained at Gibraltar by British authorities (see 23 December).

German tanker *Nordmeer* sails from Curaçao, N.W.I. (see 5 January 1940).

10 Sunday

U.S. freighter *Steel Engineer* is detained at Gibraltar by British authorities (see 11 December).

11 Monday

Light cruiser *Omaha* (CL4) arrives at the Washington Navy Yard, bearing the remains of late U.S. Ambassador to Cuba J. Butler Wright, who died at his diplomatic post in Havana on 4 December.

U.S. freighter *Azalea City*, detained at London by British authorities since 27 November, is released to proceed to Antwerp and Rotterdam, Holland, after certain cargo is detained for guaranties. Freighter *Steel Engineer*, detained at Gibraltar by the British the previous day, is released.

13 Wednesday

British heavy cruiser HMS *Exeter*, light cruiser HMS *Ajax*, and New Zealand light cruiser HMNZS *Achilles* (Commodore Henry H. Harwood, RN, flag in *Ajax*), which had rendezvoused the previous day, engage German armored ship *Admiral Graf Spee* in the Battle of the River Plate, between Uruguay and Argentina. The "pocket battleship" knocks *Exeter* out of action and damages her consorts, but is compelled by the damage inflicted by her lesser-gunned adversaries (which are fought, as First Lord of the Admiralty Winston S. Churchill writes, "with the utmost resolution and skill") to retire toward Montevideo, Uruguay. *Exeter*, badly damaged, limps to the Falkland Islands (see 14 December ff.).[12]

U.S. freighter *Exochorda*, detained at Gibraltar by British authorities since 5 December, is released.

14 Thursday

League of Nations, in response to the Soviet invasion of Finland on 30 November, expels the USSR from its membership.

Heavy cruiser *Vincennes* (CA 44) and destroyers *Evans* (DD 78) and *Twiggs* (DD 127) (the latter destroyer having shadowed British destroyer HMS *Hereward* a short time before) trail Australian light cruiser HMAS *Perth*, which is prowling the Gulf of Yucatan waiting for the emergence of German passenger liner *Columbus*.[13]

German freighter *Arauca* departs Vera Cruz, Mexico, followed subsequently by passenger liner *Columbus*, the third largest ship in Germany's merchant marine. Destroyer *Benham* (DD 397), soon joined by destroyer *Lang* (DD 399), trails *Columbus*. A succession of U.S. ships will, over ensuing days, send out plain-language position reports (see 15–20 December).

German armored ship *Admiral Graf Spee* puts in to Montevideo, Uruguay, for repairs. British light cruiser HMS *Ajax* and New Zealand light cruiser HMNZS *Achilles* maintain patrol off the 120-mile wide River Plate estuary (between Uruguay and Argentina). British heavy cruiser HMS *Cumberland* reinforces *Ajax* and *Achilles* that night.

Interior Department motorship *North Star* (U.S. Antarctic Service), with the permission of the British government, visits Pitcairn Island to take on water and discovers the islanders in need of certain foodstuffs and medical supplies, which she provides.[14]

U.S. freighter *Extavia*, detained at Gibraltar by British authorities since 30 November, is released.

15 Friday

Destroyer *Jouett* (DD 396) relieves *Benham* (DD 397) at sea; the latter attempts to locate German freighter *Arauca*, while *Jouett* joins *Lang* (DD 399) in shadowing passenger liner *Columbus*.

British RFA oiler *Olynthus* refuels light cruiser HMS *Ajax* at Samborombon Bay, off the coast of Argentina; heavy cruiser HMS *Cumberland* covers the evolution should German armored ship *Admiral Graf Spee* attempt to sortie.

U.S. freighter *Exmoor*, detained at Gibraltar by British authorities since 7 December, is released.

16 Saturday

Destroyers *Schenck* (DD 159) and *Philip* (DD 76), soon joined by *Lea* (DD 118), relieve destroyers *Jouett* (DD 396) and *Lang* (DD 399) in trailing German passenger liner *Columbus* off Key West, Florida. *Jouett* and *Lang* steam to

Set afire by her crew to prevent her capture by British destroyer HMS *Hyperion*, German passenger liner *Columbus* burns, 19 December 1939. (Author's Collection)

join destroyer *Davis* (DD 395) in attempting to locate freighter *Arauca*. *Schenck* soon proceeds on other assigned duties.

British light cruiser HMS *Ajax*, heavy cruiser HMS *Cumberland*, and New Zealand light cruiser HMNZS *Achilles* patrol off River Plate estuary (between Uruguay and Argentina); *Ajax*'s Seafox reconnoiters the area.

17 Sunday

Destroyers *Ellis* (DD 154) and *Cole* (DD 155) relieve *Lea* (DD 118) and *Philip* (DD 76) of shadowing German passenger liner *Columbus*.

British RFA oiler *Olynthus* refuels New Zealand light cruiser HMNZS *Achilles* off Rouen Bank, the southernmost channel of the River Plate estuary (between Uruguay and Argentina). Light cruiser HMS *Ajax* and heavy cruiser HMS *Cumberland* cover the evolution.

German armored ship *Admiral Graf Spee*, her allotted time in neutral Uruguayan waters for repair of damage received in the Battle of the River Plate (between Uruguay and Argentina) having expired, and her crew transferred to freighter *Tacoma*, puts to sea from Montevideo, Uruguay, and is scuttled about five miles west-southwest of the entrance of Montevideo Harbor, 35°11′S, 56°26′W. The destruction of *Admiral Graf Spee* comes, as First Lord of the Admiralty Winston S. Churchill later declares, "like a flash of light and colour on the scene, carrying with it an encouragement to all who are fighting, to

ourselves, and to our Allies" (see 30 December and 1 January 1940).[15]

U.S. freighters *Meanticut* and *Excalibur* are detained by British authorities at Gibraltar (see 18 December and 31 December, respectively).

18 Monday

Destroyers *Greer* (DD 145) and *Upshur* (DD 144) relieve destroyers *Ellis* (DD 154) and *Cole* (DD 155) of shadowing German passenger liner *Columbus*. Later that same day, heavy cruiser *Tuscaloosa* (CA 37) replaces the destroyers in trailing the passenger ship.

U.S. freighter *Meanticut*, detained by British authorities at Gibraltar the previous day, is released.

19 Tuesday

British destroyer HMS *Hyperion* intercepts German passenger liner *Columbus* about 450 miles east of Cape May, New Jersey; the latter is scuttled to prevent capture. Two crewmen perish in the abandonment at 38°01′N, 65°41′W. Heavy cruiser *Tuscaloosa* (CA 37) rescues *Columbus*'s survivors (567 men and nine women stewardesses) and sets course for New York City, the only U.S. port that can handle such a large and sudden influx of aliens.

British light cruiser HMS *Orion* intercepts German freighter *Arauca* off Miami, Florida; the latter puts in to Port Everglades to avoid capture. Destroyer *Truxtun* (DD 229) has

trailed the merchantman at one point; destroyer *Philip* (DD 76) is present when *Arauca* reaches sanctuary. USAAC B-18 (21st Reconnaissance Squadron), however, witnesses the shot that *Orion* fires over *Arauca*'s bow (in the attempt to force the latter to heave-to) splashing *inside* American territorial waters off Hialeah, Florida. Learning of this incident, Secretary of State Cordell Hull instructs U.S. Ambassador to the Court of St. James Joseph P. Kennedy to remind the British Foreign Office that, as neutrals, the American republics are entitled to have their waters "free from the commission of any hostile act by any non-American belligerent nation."[16]

U.S. freighter *Nishmaha* is free to sail from Marseilles to continue her voyage, but port conditions and weather prevent her from sailing as scheduled.

20 Wednesday

Submarine tender *Bushnell* (AS 2), operating out of Tutuila, Samoa, as a survey ship under the auspices of the Hydrographic Office, completes Pacific Islands surveys, having covered a total of 76,000 nautical square miles since commencing that work on 1 July.

Heavy cruiser *Tuscaloosa* (CA 37) disembarks scuttled German passenger liner *Columbus*'s "distressed mariners" at Ellis Island, New York City.

Destroyer *Twiggs* (DD 127), on neutrality patrol in Yucatan Channel, relieves *Evans* (DD 78) of duty trailing British RFA tanker *Patella*.

German armored ship *Admiral Graf Spee*'s former commanding officer, Kapitan zur See Hans Langsdorff, commits suicide at Montevideo, Uruguay.

U.S. freighter *Exochorda* arrives at Naples with the 45 tons of tin plate condemned by the British prize court at Gibraltar among her cargo, having been permitted to sail by her master's agreeing to ship the 45 tons of tin to Marseilles from Genoa, Italy. Another 100 tons of tin, however, consigned to a Swiss buyer, are put on the "detained list" and held in Genoa at the disposal of the British consul. That turn of affairs prompts U.S. Ambassador in Italy William Phillips to take up the matter with the British Ambassador, who expresses his awareness of the "irritation and resentment . . . in American commercial and shipping circles" over the seemingly "arbitrary, careless, and casual" methods shown by the British contraband control people.

U.S. freighters *Oakwood*, bound for Genoa,

Italy, and *Executive*, bound for Greece, Turkey, and Romania, are detained by British authorities at Gibraltar (see 23 December and 3 January 1940, respectively).

21 Thursday

Destroyer *Twiggs* (DD 127), on neutrality patrol in Yucatan Channel, continues trailing British RFA tanker *Patella*.

22 Friday

Destroyer *Philip* (DD 76) relieves *Twiggs* (DD 127) of neutrality patrol duty trailing British RFA tanker *Patella* off east coast of Florida; while en route to Fort Lauderdale, *Twiggs* observes British light cruiser HMS *Orion* off Port Everglades and anchors to keep an eye on the British warship as the latter prowls the coast.

23 Saturday

Typhoon passes within 100 miles of Guam, M.I.; although the gale force winds cause little damage to Navy property, they cause widespread crop and property damage in the native quarters.

U.S. freighters *Explorer* (detained at Gibraltar since 9 December) and *Oakwood* (detained there since 20 December) are released by British authorities.

27 Wednesday

Department of State dispatches "vigorous protest" to British Foreign Office concerning the British practice of removing and censoring U.S. mail from British and U.S. and neutral ships (see 2 January 1940).

U.S. Consul General in Hamburg Wilbur Keblinger reports that German prize control authorities have released all but seven neutral vessels detained in German ports for the evaluation of cargo deemed contraband.

U.S. freighter *Oakwood*, en route from Gibraltar to Genoa, is intercepted by French naval vessel and diverted to Villefranche after boarding officer mistakes notation in log as an order to proceed to Marseilles. Once the mistake is realized, the ship is released to proceed on her way within a few hours.

28 Thursday

Rear Admiral William L. Calhoun assumes duty as Commander Base Force and breaks his flag in auxiliary *Argonne* (AG 31).

Rear Admiral Julius C. Townsend, Commandant Fourth Naval District and Commandant Philadelphia Navy Yard, dies of bronchial cancer at U.S. Naval Hospital, Brooklyn, New York.

U.S. freighter *Exilona* is detained at Gibraltar by British authorities.

29 Friday

U.S. steamship *President Adams* is detained at Port Said, Egypt, by British authorities. Cargo suspected of being contraband is discharged at Alexandria, Egypt.

30 Saturday

Uruguayan government gives German freighter *Tacoma* 24 hours to leave the port of Montevideo, deeming the ship an auxiliary war vessel since she had assisted various maneuvers of armored ship *Admiral Graf Spee* and embarked her crew when that warship was scuttled (see 1 January 1940).

31 Sunday

U.S. freighter *Excalibur*, detained at Gibraltar by British authorities since 17 December, is released.

1940

JANUARY

1 Monday

Tenth Naval District with headquarters at San Juan, Puerto Rico, is established; Commander Reuben L. Walker is the first commandant (see 26 February).

U.S. freighter *City of Flint*, her odyssey almost at an end, is damaged in collision with British steamship *Baron Blytheswood*. Repairs to *City of Flint* will keep her at Narvik, Norway, for another six days (see 7 January).

U.S. freighter *Exeter* is detained at Gibraltar by British authorities.

Uruguayan government interns German freighter *Tacoma* at Montevideo, Uruguay, as an auxiliary war vessel.

2 Tuesday

Charles Edison of New Jersey becomes Secretary of the Navy; he had been Acting Secretary since the death of Claude A. Swanson on 7 July 1939.

Department of State releases statement to the press telling of the delivery of "vigorous protest" (dated 27 December 1939) to the British Foreign Office concerning the British removal and censorship of U.S. mail from British, U.S., and neutral ships.

3 Wednesday

U.S. freighter *Mormacsun* is intercepted by British naval vessel and diverted to Kirkwall, Scotland, into the zone designated as a combat area. Freighter *Nashaba* is detained by British authorities at Gibraltar; freighter *Executive*, detained at Gibraltar since 20 December 1939, is released to proceed on her voyage to Greece, Turkey, and Romania.

4 Thursday

U.S. freighter *Exiria* is detained at Gibraltar by British authorities.

5 Friday

German tanker *Nordmeer* reaches Vigo, Spain, after her voyage from the Netherlands West Indies.

6 Saturday

Admiral James O. Richardson relieves Admiral Claude C. Bloch as Commander in Chief U.S. Fleet on board battleship *Pennsylvania* (BB 38) at Pearl Harbor, T.H.

Admiral Charles P. Snyder hoists flag as Commander Battle Force on board battleship *California* (BB 44).

U.S. passenger liner *Manhattan* is detained at Gibraltar by British authorities (see 7 January).

7 Sunday

U.S. freighter *City of Flint* departs Narvik, Norway, for Baltimore, Maryland. For his "skill, fine judgement [sic], and devotion to duty" during *City of Flint*'s unscheduled voyage, Captain Joseph A. Gainard, the merchantman's master, will receive the Navy Cross.

U.S. passenger liner *Manhattan*, detained at Gibraltar by British authorities the previous day, is released.

German freighter *Konsul Horn* escapes from Aruba, N.W.I., and, disguised as a Soviet merchantman, manages to deceive U.S. Navy patrol planes from the Neutrality Patrol and

British light cruiser HMS *Enterprise* (see 6 February).

9   Tuesday
U.S. freighter *Western Queen* is detained at Gibraltar for several hours by British authorities.

10   Wednesday
U.S. steamship *President Van Buren*, bound for Genoa, Italy, and New York, is detained at Port Said, Egypt, and subsequently discharges items of cargo, deemed as contraband, at Alexandria, Egypt, before being allowed to proceed.

11   Thursday
Fleet Landing Exercise (FLEX) No. 6 begins at Culebra, Puerto Rico (see 13 March). Lack of transports compels the Navy to substitute combatant ships in that role for purposes of the exercise; an important exception is the prototype high speed transport *Manley* (APD 1), converted from a World War I–emergency program "flush-deck, four-pipe" destroyer, which amply proves her worth.

Gunboat *Charleston* (PG 51) suffers damage when she runs aground at Colon, C.Z.

U.S. freighter *Tripp* is detained at Gibraltar by British authorities (see 13 January).

12   Friday
Interior Department motorship *North Star* (U.S. Antarctic Service) reaches Bay of Whales, Antarctica, and immediately begins discharging cargo to establish West Base. Ice conditions prohibit unloading at the original chosen site, King Edward VII Land.

13   Saturday
U.S. freighter *Narbo*, bound for Italy, Yugoslavia, and Greece, is detained at Gibraltar by British authorities (see 14 January). Freighter *Tripp*, detained at Gibraltar by the British since 11 January, is released, but not before some items of her cargo are seized as contraband.

14   Sunday
Auxiliary *Bear* (AG 29) reaches Bay of Whales, Antarctica. Along with Interior Department motorship *North Star*, *Bear* will establish the two bases to be used in the U.S. Antarctic Service's 1939–1941 expedition under Rear Admiral Richard E. Byrd, USN (Retired) (see 19 January).

British Minister in Panama Charles Dodd transmits response of British government to note sent by the President of Panama on behalf of the 21 American Republics concerning the violation of American neutrality that occurred in the Battle of the River Plate, between Uruguay and Argentina. The British "reserve their full belligerent rights in order to fight the menace presented by German action and policy and to defend that conception of law and that way of life, which they believe to be as dear to the peoples and Governments of America as they are to the peoples and Governments of the British Commonwealth of Nations." The British demonstrate their determination to assert "their full belligerant rights" less than one month later (see 12 February and 8 March).

U.S. freighter *Narbo,* detained at Gibraltar by British authorities the previous day, is released to continue her voyage to Italy, Yugoslavia, and Greece, but not before some items from her cargo are removed as contraband.

15   Monday
Joint amphibious exercise begins in the Monterey, California, area, to provide training for the Army and Navy in planning and executing joint operations, to train Army troops in embarking and disembarking, and to afford an opportunity for elements of the GHQ Air Force and Navy patrol squadrons to work together and with ground forces (see 22 January). Commander Battle Force (Admiral Charles P. Snyder) conducts the Navy portion of the exercise.

Japanese fishing schooner *No. 1 Seiho Maru* is stranded on reef off southeast coast of Guam, M.I. A detail of Guam Militia (12th Company) renders necessary assistance during salvage operations (see 21 January). Minesweeper *Penguin* (AM 33) rescues the 24-man crew.

17   Wednesday
U.S. passenger liner *Manhattan* and freighter *Excambion* are detained at Gibraltar by British authorities; the former is kept there for only a few hours before being allowed to proceed (see 23 January).

British Foreign Office replies to U.S. protest on treatment of mail, concluding that "His Majesty's Government find themselves unable to share the views of the United States government that their [the British] action in examining neutral mail in British or neutral shipping is contrary to their obligations under international law."

18   Thursday
British commence censorship of air mail passing through Bermuda; censor there removes through-bound mail for European destinations from Lisbon, Portugal–bound Pan American Airways Boeing 314 *American Clipper*. A written protest is lodged and no assistance in the unloading process is offered.

19   Friday
Auxiliary *Bear* (AG 29) steams eastward to begin flight operations in the vicinity of Biscoe Bay, Antarctica; the ship's embarked Barkley-Grow floatplane (Rear Admiral Richard E. Byrd, navigator) reconnoiters Sulzberger Bay to determine leads in the ice to permit *Bear*'s movement farther to the east (see 21 January).

20   Saturday
United States protests British treatment of American shipping in the Mediterranean.

U.S. freighter *Examelia* is detained at Gibraltar by British authorities (see 31 January); passenger liner *Washington*, bound for Genoa, is detained only a few hours before being allowed to proceed.

21   Sunday
Auxiliary *Bear* (AG 29) follows leads in the ice spotted on 19 January; the ship's Barkley-Grow floatplane flies over the northern limits of the Edsel Ford Mountains (see 25 January).

Minesweeper *Penguin* (AM 33) transfers 24 survivors of Japanese fishing schooner *No. 1 Seiho Maru*, stranded off the southeast coast of Guam, M.I., on 15 January, to Japanese freighter *Saipan Maru.*

British light cruiser HMS *Liverpool* stops Japanese passenger liner *Asama Maru* 35 miles off Nozaki, Chiba prefecture, Japan, and removes 21 Germans from the ship. All but nine are naval reservists, survivors of the scuttled passenger liner *Columbus*; the nine civilians are released. The incident further strains relations between Great Britain and Japan.

U.S. freighter *Nishmaha* is detained at Gibraltar by British authorities (see 22 January).

22   Monday
Joint amphibious exercise concludes in the Monterey, California, area, having afforded the Fleet profitable experience in joint planning. It also demonstrates interservice cooperation.

Light cruiser *Helena* (CL 50) arrives at Buenos Aires, Argentina, on her shakedown cruise (see 29 January).

Rear Admiral Adolphus E. Watson becomes Commandant Fourth Naval District and Commandant Philadelphia Navy Yard in the wake of the death of Rear Admiral Julius C. Townsend on 28 December 1939.

U.S. freighter *Excellency* is detained at Gibraltar by British authorities (see 23 January); freighter *Nishmaha*, detained there the previous day, is released.

23 Tuesday

Great Britain and France announce they will attack any German vessels encountered in Pan-American Safety Zone.

Destroyer *J. Fred Talbott* (DD 247) arrives at Wreck Bay, Galapagos Islands, to assist U.S. tuna boat *City of San Diego* (see 24 January).

U.S. freighter *Excambion*, detained at Gibraltar by British authorities since 17 January, is released to proceed on her voyage to Genoa, Italy, but not before 470 sacks of mail (bound for Germany and Italy) arc seized; freighter *Excellency*, detained at Gibraltar the previous day, is released.

24 Wednesday

Interior Department motorship *North Star* (U.S. Antarctic Service) departs Bay of Whales, Antarctica, for Valparaiso, Chile, for additional supplies and equipment to establish East Base. Construction of West Base commences immediately at the site chosen that lies at 78°29'06"S, 163°50'10"W, two miles from the edge of the ice barrier and five miles northeast of the site of Little America I and Little America II, the previous Byrd expedition bases. Until the main building is ready for habitation, the men live in regulation army tents (see 11 February).

Gunboat *Erie* (PG 50) joins destroyer *J. Fred Talbott* (DD 247) at Wreck Bay, Galapagos Islands, to assist U.S. tuna boat *City of San Diego*. The gunboat takes on board the craft's chief engineer (pneumonia) and sails the following day for Balboa, C.Z., where the man will be transferred ashore for medical attention.

25 Thursday

Auxiliary *Bear* (AG 29) (U.S. Antarctic Service) reaches 77°43'S, 143°52'W; it marks the deepest penetration by any ship into the Antarctic region (see 21 March).

26 Friday

United States–Japanese Trade Treaty of 1911 expires.

Minesweeper *Quail* (AM 15) arrives at Palmyra Island in the Central Pacific with first construction party to begin building a naval air station there.

27 Saturday

U.S. freighter *Cold Harbor*, bound for Odessa, Ukraine, is detained at Gibraltar by British authorities (see 30 January).

28 Sunday

U.S. freighter *Sarcoxic* is detained temporarily at Gibraltar for several hours by British authorities; freighter *Waban*, bound for Italy and Greece, is also held there briefly but is allowed to proceed after one item of cargo is seized as contraband and 34 detained for investigation.

29 Monday

British Admiralty orders that no American ships should, under any circumstances, be diverted into the war zone delineated by President Roosevelt in the provisions of the Neutrality Act.

Light cruiser *Helena* (CL 50) steams from Buenos Aires, Argentina, to Montevideo, Uruguay, on her shakedown cruise (see 2 February).

U.S. freighter *Exochorda* is detained at Gibraltar by British authorities (see 1 February).

30 Tuesday

U.S. freighter *Cold Harbor* (detained at Gibraltar since 27 January) is released by British authorities.

31 Wednesday

U.S. passenger liner *Washington* is detained for several hours at Gibraltar by British authorities, but is allowed to proceed the same day; freighter *Jomar* is also detained there (see 1 February). Freighter *Examelia*, detained at Gibraltar since 20 January, is released.

FEBRUARY

1 Thursday

President Roosevelt writes First Lord of the Admiralty Winston S. Churchill, concerning the detention of U.S. merchantmen, and frankly informs him of adverse American reaction to the British policy. "The general feeling is," Roosevelt informs Churchill, "that thc net benefit to your people and the French is hardly worth the definite annoyance caused to us."

U.S. freighter *Exminster* is detained by British authorities at Gibraltar (see 9 February); freighters *Exochorda* (detained since 29 January) and *Jomar* (detained since 31 January) are released.

2 Friday

Light cruiser *Helena* (CL 50), at Montevideo, Uruguay, on her shakedown cruise, sends party to inspect wreck of German armored ship *Admiral Graf Spee*.

U.S. passenger liner *Manhattan* is stopped by French auxiliary patrol vessel *Vaillant* about 25 miles southeast of Cape St. Vincent, Portugal, and ordered to proceed to Gibraltar for examination (see 3 and 4 February).

3 Saturday

Light cruiser *Helena* (CL 50) departs Montevideo, Uruguay, for Brazilian waters as her shakedown cruise continues (see 5 February).

U.S. passenger liner *Manhattan* is detained at Gibraltar by British authorities (see 4 February).

4 Sunday

U.S. passenger liner *Manhattan*, detained at Gibraltar the previous day, is released, but not before British authorities seize 390 sacks of German mail. American diplomatic mail pouches, however, are not disturbed.

5 Monday

Light cruiser *Helena* (CL 50) arrives at Santos, Brazil, on her shakedown cruise (see 10 February).

U.S. freighter *Exford* is detained at Gibraltar by British authorities (see 13 February).

6 Tuesday

German freighter *Konsul Horn*, which had departed Aruba on 7 January, reaches Norwegian waters having eluded or deceived the U.S. Neutrality Patrol as well as British and French warships.

8 Thursday

U.S. freighter *Scottsburg* is detained at Gibraltar by British authorities (see 9 February).

9 Friday

U.S. freighter *Scottsburg*, detained at Gibraltar by British authorities the previous day, is released. U.S. freighter *Exminster*, detained at Gibraltar since 1 February, is also released.

10 Saturday

Light cruiser *Helena* (CL 50) departs Santos, Brazil, winding up her shakedown cruise.

U.S. freighter *West Chatala* is detained for

several hours at Gibraltar by British authorities but is released to continue her voyage.

11 Sunday

U.S. Antarctic Service West Base main building is completed sufficiently to permit occupation. Over the next two months, the base—three buildings connected by an elaborate system of tunnels and caches—is finished by the time the sun sets for the winter on 21 April.

12 Monday

War again comes to the Americas: British heavy cruiser HMS *Dorsetshire* stops German freighter *Wakama* 12 miles off Cabo Frio, Brazil; *Wakama*'s crew scuttles her so that their ship will not fall into British hands (see 16 March).[17]

13 Tuesday

U.S. freighter *Exford*, detained at Gibraltar by British authorities since 5 February, is released.

14 Wednesday

U.S. passenger liner *Manhattan* is detained at Gibraltar for several hours by British authorities but allowed to proceed; not as fortunate is freighter *Exermont*, which is also detained there (see 16 February).

15 Thursday

President Roosevelt embarks in heavy cruiser *Tuscaloosa* (CA 37) at Pensacola, Florida, for a cruise to Panama and the west coast of Central America to discuss Pan-American defense and to inspect the Panama Canal.

Destroyer *Goff* (DD 247) collides with and sinks harbor tug *Wicomico* (YT 26) in Hampton Roads, off Naval Operating Base, Norfolk, Virginia. *Goff*, her bow damaged in the mishap, rescues *Wicomico*'s 11-man crew.

16 Friday

U.S. freighter *Excalibur* is detained for several hours by British authorities at Gibraltar but is released; freighter *Exermont*, detained since 14 February, is allowed to proceed as well.

British destroyer HMS *Cossack* violates Norwegian territorial waters, boards German tanker *Altmark* in Jössingfjord, Norway, and recovers 303 merchant seamen from ships destroyed by German armored ship *Admiral Graf Spee* during her commerce-raiding activities.

17 Saturday

U.S. freighter *Exhibitor* is detained by British authorities at Gibraltar (see 21 February).

Ten Consolidated P2Y-2s of VP 52, all but one bearing neutrality markings (red-centered blue and white star) on port and starboard sides of each flying boat's nose, share ramp space at the U.S. Coast Guard air station, Charleston, South Carolina, with two USCG Grumman JF-2s and a USCG Douglas RD-4, 27 February 1940. VP 52 had begun operating from the Coast Guard station on 3 October 1939. (Author's Collection)

21 Wednesday

U.S. freighter *Sahale* is detained by British authorities at Gibraltar (see 22 February); freighter *Exhibitor*, detained since 17 February, is allowed to proceed.

22 Thursday

U.S. freighter *Sahale*, detained by British authorities at Gibraltar the previous day, is released.

23 Friday

U.S. freighter *Lehigh* is detained for several hours at Gibraltar by British authorities, but is allowed to proceed the same day.

24 Saturday

U.S. freighter *Scottsburg* is detained for several hours at Malta by British authorities, but is allowed to proceed the same day.

25 Sunday

U.S. freighter *West Camargo* is stopped by unidentified French cruiser off north coast of Venezuela, 11°30′N, 66°20′W; French make no attempt to board but only request information "where from, where bound, and what

cargo" before allowing the merchantman to proceed after a 20-minute delay.

U.S. freighter *Exochorda* is detained for several hours at Gibraltar by British authorities, but is allowed to proceed.

26 Monday

Captain Raymond A. Spruance relieves Commander Reuben L. Walker as Commandant Tenth Naval District.

U.S. passenger liner *Washington* is detained at Gibraltar by British authorities.

27 Tuesday

U.S. freighter *Sundance* is detained at Gibraltar by British authorities.

29 Thursday

U.S. freighter *Cold Harbor* is detained at Gibraltar by British authorities.

MARCH

1 Friday

U.S. freighter *Exeter* is detained at Gibraltar by British authorities (see 4 March).

As the build-up of advanced bases in the Pacific continues apace, cargo ship *Sirius* (AK 15) steams past Bishop Point, Pearl Harbor, 21 March 1940, bound for Midway, pilings projecting over the side across her forward hatch and the non–self-propelled dump scow *YD 69*, laden with equipment, riding at a towline astern. (NHC, NH 96600)

2 Saturday

U.S. passenger liner *Manhattan* is detained at Gibraltar by British authorities, but is released the same day. Some 80 of 200 items of cargo, however, are detained subject to guarantees as to their destinations.

4 Monday

U.S. freighter *Exeter*, detained at Gibraltar by British authorities since 1 March, is released, but not before 155 sacks of mail for Germany are removed, as are 95 sacks for Italy and 59 for Switzerland. Some 140 sacks previously removed from other neutral ships, however, are brought on board and the ship is permitted to sail.

8 Friday

War again comes to the Americas: Canadian destroyer HMCS *Assiniboine* stops German freighter *Hannover* in Mona Passage, off the coast of the Dominican Republic, at which point the merchantman's crew sets fire to the ship and abandons her. Boarding party from British light cruiser HMS *Dunedin*, however, saves *Hannover* from destruction. Conflicting representations by British and German diplomats as to *Hannover*'s exact position prompt the Dominican government to drop the question of violation of territorial waters (see 24 May).[18] The effort expended to capture *Hannover*, however, allows German freighters *Mimi Horn* and *Seattle* to escape the Caribbean and make a break for Germany.[19]

9 Saturday

U.S. freighter *Exmoor* is detained at Gibraltar by British authorities (see 11 March).

10 Sunday

U.S. freighters *Explorer*, *Exchester*, and *West Cohas* are detained at Gibraltar by British authorities; all are released, however, after only several hours.

11 Monday

U.S. freighter *Exmoor*, detained at Gibraltar by British authorities since 9 March, is released.

12 Tuesday

Russo-Finnish War ends. Finnish desire to win back territory lost to Soviet encroachment (city of Viborg and areas along Finland's eastern borders) will push them closer toward the Axis.

13 Wednesday

Fleet Landing Exercise (FLEX) No. 6 concludes at Culebra, Puerto Rico. The Fleet Marine Force makes progress in developing techniques for rubber boat landings, getting heavy combat materiel ashore, and improving ship-to-shore supply.

16 Saturday

President of Panama transmits protest to King of England over British violation of Pan-American Neutrality Zone in the *Wakama* Incident that took place off the coast of Brazil on 12 February.

21 Thursday

Auxiliary *Bear* (AG 29) and Interior Department motorship *North Star* (U.S. Antarctic Service) depart Bay of Whales, Antarctica, for the United States. Staying behind are the men who will spend the long winter night at East and West Bases (see 5 June).

25 Monday

Heavy cruiser *Augusta* (CA 31) is damaged when she strikes an uncharted pinnacle in Coron Bay, P.I.

APRIL

2 Tuesday

U.S. Fleet departs West Coast for maneuvers in Hawaiian waters. Fleet Problem XXI is the last of the large prewar fleet exercises that mark the culmination of the training year. Conducted in two phases, Parts II and VI of the annual fleet exercises, it takes place in the waters of the Pacific in the vicinity of Hawaii to the westward. Part II exercises two fleets (the augmented Battle Force vs. the augmented Scouting Force) of approximately equal strength, one side concentrated and the other widely dispersed, in scouting, screening, and conducting major fleet engagements. Part VI exercises two fleets of approximately equal strength (the same opponents as in Part II), each dispersed, in scouting, screening, protecting convoys, seizing and defending advanced bases, and conducting major fleet engagements. The worsening world situation will prompt the cancellation of Fleet Problem XXII.

3 Wednesday

Destroyer *Crosby* (DD 164) accidentally sinks U.S. fishing boat *Lone Eagle* in collision in heavy seas off Point Arguello, California; *Crosby* rescues the seven-man crew.

4 Thursday

See photo and caption, top p. 21.

5 Friday

Operation WILFRED: British mining of Norwegian waters begins.

7 Sunday

Destroyer *J. Fred Talbott* (DD 247) departs Canal Zone to rendezvous at sea with Japanese steamship *Arimasan Maru* (see 13 April).

Destroyer *Twiggs* (DD 127), on neutrality patrol off the coast of Cuba, attempts to tow Norwegian freighter *Spind* off rocks six miles off Cape San Antonio, but is unsuccessful in two tries. Salvage tug *Warbler*, however, frees the merchantman from her predicament. *Twiggs* resumes her patrol.

8   Monday
Norway protests British minelaying operations off the Norwegian coast. Amid growing tensions in this region, U.S. freighter *Charles R. McCormick* arrives at Bergen, Norway, en route to her ultimate destination of Narvik. Freighter *Flying Fish* is also in Norwegian waters.

9   Tuesday
Operation WESERÜBUNG: Germany invades Denmark and Norway, claiming that they are only establishing a "protectorate." Norway, however, declares that a state of war exists with Germany.

Joint Planning Committee of the Joint Board submits a new general estimate of the world situation in relation to American defense and preparations for war. This is part of the revision of existing plans, and for developing or completing new plans of the RAINBOW series. Formulators of the RAINBOW plans envision multiple, simultaneous enemies instead of individual enemies, each designated by a single color (ORANGE, for example, stands for Japan).

Submarine tender *Bushnell* (AS 2), operating as a survey ship under the auspices of the Hydrographic Office, arrives in Venezuelan waters to commence hydrographic surveys of the Cape San Roman to Bahia Vela de Coro region (see 15 June).

Destroyer *Williams* (DD 108) transports hydrographic survey party to Palmetto Island, British West Indies.

10   Wednesday
President Roosevelt, acting under the Neutrality Act of 1939, issues proclamation extending the combat zone to include the northwestern part of the USSR on a line to the southern point of Svalbard, a Norwegian possession, to the northwestern tip of the combat zone issued in the President's proclamation of 4 November 1939.

11   Thursday
Rear Admiral Claude C. Bloch relieves Rear Admiral Orin G. Murfin as Commandant Fourteenth Naval District and Commandant Navy Yard Pearl Harbor, T.H.

Carrier *Saratoga* (CV 3) (right) launches a Douglas TBD-1 while heavy cruiser *Portland* (CA 33) steams in the carrier's screen (left), during Fleet Problem XXI, 4 April 1940. Broad black vertical stripe (adorned with an "E" and a hash mark) on *Saratoga's* stack distinguishes her from her nearly identical sister ship *Lexington* (CV 2). *Portland* carries Curtiss SOC floatplanes on her catapults and on her well-deck amidships. (NA, 80-CF-372-3)

12   Friday
Submarine rescue vessel *Falcon* (ASR 2) and U.S. freighter *El Oceano* are damaged when they collide in heavy fog in Buzzards Bay, Massachusetts, near Hen and Chickens Lightship.

13   Saturday
Destroyer *J. Fred Talbott* (DD 247) returns to Canal Zone after providing medical assistance to passenger on board Japanese steamship *Arimasan Maru*. The warship's medical officer remains with his patient until the Japanese vessel reaches Balboa.

15   Monday
Naval Reserve affairs pertaining to the administration of naval districts are transferred to the Naval Reserve Policy Division, Office of the Chief of Naval Operations, to prepare for expansion.

16   Tuesday
Captain Albert C. Read relieves Captain Aubrey W. Fitch as Commandant Naval Air Station, Pensacola, Florida.

Great Britain issues mobilization order for men who turn 27 years of age during the months of April and May 1940.

Iceland declares its independence and asks the United States to recognize it as such.

19   Friday
Japanese government informs the United States that Japan has no aggressive intentions toward the Netherlands East Indies.

20   Saturday
Captain George J. McMillin relieves Captain James T. Alexander as Governor of Guam and Commandant U.S. Naval Station, Guam.

U.S. freighters *Flying Fish* and *Charles McCormick* are reported safe at Norwegian ports; concern had been expressed over their safety in view of the German invasion of Norway. They had been shifted from Bergen to neighboring, safer places.

21   Sunday
U.S. Military Attaché Captain Robert E. Losey is killed in German bombing raid on Dombas, Norway. U.S. Minister to Sweden Frederick A. Sterling orders Naval Attaché (Lieutenant Commander Ole E. Hagen) to proceed to receive Captain Losey's remains.

24 Wednesday

U.S. Naval Attaché (Lieutenant Commander Ole E. Hagen) escorts party of American citizens evacuated from Oslo to the interior of Norway and thence across the border into Stockholm in neutral Sweden.

25 Thursday

President Roosevelt issues proclamation declaring that a state of war exists between Germany and Norway, and issues neutrality proclamation concerning same. In addition, he issues proclamation prohibiting Norwegian submarines from entering American waters.

29 Monday

Although the British explanation concerning the removal of German engineers from Philippine motorship *Don Isidro* at Port Said, Eygpt, on 5 September 1939 fails to satisfy the Department of State, the U.S. government nevertheless considers the incident closed "on the assumption that similar instances will not be permitted to occur in the future."

30 Tuesday

Fire and rescue party detailed by Commandant Sixth Naval District extinguishes blaze in Norwegian tanker *Willy* (loaded with aviation gasoline) lying in the Cooper River off Charleston, South Carolina. The sailors save the ship and the city's waterfront.

MAY

1 Wednesday

Naval Air Station, San Juan, Puerto Rico, is established effective this date, and designated as an activity of the Tenth Naval District. Captain Virgil C. Griffin Jr. is the first commanding officer.

3 Friday

Greenland, a crown colony of Denmark, seeks U.S. protection, so that Danish sovereignty can be maintained during the German occupation of the homeland.

7 Tuesday

President Roosevelt orders U.S. Fleet to remain in Hawaiian waters indefinitely as a deterrent to Japan (see 5 July and 7 October).

8 Wednesday

River gunboat *Tutuila* (PR 4) is damaged when she runs aground on a reef and becomes stranded as she shifts her anchorage at Chungking, China (see 13 May).

10 Friday

Germany invades the Netherlands, Belgium, and Luxembourg. The Netherlands and Belgium declare war on Germany.

British troops occupy Iceland.

British Prime Minister Neville Chamberlain resigns; First Lord of the Admiralty Winston S. Churchill becomes prime minister.

Secretary of State Cordell Hull reiterates that the United States will not stand for any country establishing a protectorate over the Netherlands East Indies. Japanese Foreign Minister indicates his country's desire to maintain the political and economic status quo in that region.

11 Saturday

President Roosevelt issues proclamations (1) recognizing the state of war that exists between Germany and Belgium, Luxembourg, and the Netherlands; (2) proclaiming American neutrality in the conflict; and (3) restricting belligerent submarines from using American ports and territorial waters, exclusive of the Panama Canal Zone.

British and French troops occupy Curaçao and Aruba, Netherlands West Indies. President Roosevelt announces that these actions are not contrary to the Monroe Doctrine.

13 Monday

River gunboat *Tutuila* (PR 4), stranded on a reef in the Yangtze River off Chungking, China, since 8 May, is refloated.

Dutch Royal Family and government flee to London, England.

14 Tuesday

German troops smash through French lines at Sedan and move toward the English Channel.

Dutch Army capitulates to Germany.

15 Wednesday

British Prime Minister Winston S. Churchill ("Former Naval Person") pleads for U.S. aid in a personal message to President Roosevelt. Churchill's request is six-fold. First, he requests the loan of 40 or 50 "older destroyers" to bridge the gap between what the Royal Navy has on hand and what is under construction; second, he asks for "several hundred" of the latest planes; third, he asks for antiaircraft "equipment and ammunition"; fourth, he asks that the United States continues to provide Britain with steel; fifth, he asks that a U.S. squadron visit Irish ports; and sixth, he intimates that the United States "keep that Japanese dog quiet in the Pacific, using Singapore in any way convenient" (see 16 May and 11 June).

U.S. Minister in Uruguay, Edwin C. Wilson reports to Secretary of State Cordell Hull that there has been an increase in "Nazi activities" in Uruguay. He notes "indifference and apathy . . . and in certain cases something worse" evidenced by the Uruguayan government. The situation, Wilson warns, "has serious possibilities" (see 20 May).

16 Thursday

President Roosevelt asks Congress to appropriate $546 million for the Army, $250 million for the Navy and Marine Corps, and $100 million for the President to provide for emergencies affecting the national security and defense. He also asks for authorizations for the Army, Navy, and Marine Corps to make contract obligations in the further sum of $186 million, and to the President an additional authorization to make contract obligations for $100 million. He also suggests that 50,000 planes a year be built.

President Roosevelt responds noncommittally to British Prime Minister Winston S. Churchill's telegram of the previous day. Addressing the possible loan of destroyers, Churchill's first concern, the President informs the "Former Naval Person" that such a step cannot be taken without "specific authorization of the Congress" and that U.S. defense requirements assumed priority. He also informs Churchill that the U.S. Fleet would remain concentrated in Hawaiian waters "at least for the time being."

17 Friday

President Roosevelt announces plans for recommissioning 35 more "flush-deck" destroyers to meet the requirements of fleet expansion and the Neutrality Patrol.

18 Saturday

British Prime Minister Winston S. Churchill, in a telegram to President Roosevelt, tells of British perseverance but suggests that "if American assistance is to play any part it must be available [soon]."

20 Monday

British Prime Minister Winston S. Churchill, in a telegram to President Roosevelt concerning the recent meeting of Lord Lothian (British Ambassador to the United States) with the Chief Executive, acknowledges U.S. difficulties but expresses continuing interest in destroyers. "If they were here in 6 weeks," Churchill states, "they would play an invaluable part."

President Roosevelt, in a memorandum to Undersecretary of State Sumner Welles, expresses concern over the situation in Uruguay as reported by U.S. Minister Edwin C. Wilson on 15 May. "Is there some way," Roosevelt asks Welles, "in which the Minister of Uruguay in Washington and Mr. Wilson in Montevideo can get word to the Uruguayan Government that the United States is concerned?" Undersecretary Welles, in his response to the President that same day, reports that the Uruguayan government has taken steps to investigate Nazi activities in Montevideo (see 26 May).

21 Tuesday

German troops reach the English Channel west of Abbeville, France, splitting the Allied armies and encircling their northern remnant.

24 Friday

President of Panama addresses diplomatic notes to the government of the Dominican Republic, supporting its position in the *Hannover* incident of 8 March, to the British and German governments, calling attention to their violation of the Pan-American Neutrality Zone, and to the Chairman of the Inter-American Neutrality Committee in Rio de Janeiro, Brazil, directing that body's attention to the case.

Allied Supreme Command decides to evacuate its forces from Norway.

25 Saturday

Minor Landing and Base Defense Exercise begins at San Clemente Island, California (see 1 June).

26 Sunday

U.S. Minister in Uruguay Edwin C. Wilson, in a telegram to Secretary of State Cordell Hull, reports tension between the Uruguayan and German governments over the former's searching homes and businesses of Germans and charges by the latter that the Uruguayan police were employing "rough methods" in their investigations (see 30 May).

Operation DYNAMO: Evacuation of British, French, and Belgian troops from Dunkirk, France, begins, aided by poor flying weather

that limits German aerial operations (see 4 June).

28 Tuesday

National Defense Advisory Committee is established, which includes in its membership former automobile manufacturer William S. Knudsen, corporate executive Edward R. Stettinius, labor leader Sidney Hillman, and economist Leon Henderson. There is, however, no head to this group that only serves to advise President Roosevelt on defense issues (see 7 January 1941).

Belgium surrenders to Germany.

Ambassador to France William C. Bullitt, through a telegram to Secretary of State Cordell Hull, urgently asks President Roosevelt to send a cruiser to Bordeaux, France, (1) to bring arms and ammunition urgently required by the French police to quell a feared "Communist uprising" as German forces near Paris and other industrial centers and (2) to take away the French and Belgian gold reserves. "If you cannot send a cruiser of the *San Francisco* [CA 38] class to Bordeaux," Bullitt implores, "please order the *Trenton* [CL 11] at Lisbon [Squadron 40-T flagship] to take on fuel and supplies at once for a trip to America and order her today to Bordeaux." Consequently, heavy cruiser *Vincennes* (CA 44) departs Hampton Roads, Virginia, in company with destroyers *Truxtun* (DD 229) and *Simpson* (DD 221), bound for the Azores on the first leg of the voyage undertaken in response to the ambassador's second concern (see 9 June).

Ambassador Bullitt also urges that the Atlantic Fleet be sent to the Mediterranean as "one of the surest ways" to obtain British and French cooperation in keeping German attacks away from the United States (see 30 May).

29 Wednesday

French auxiliary cruiser *Ville d'Oran* loads 200 tons of gold (French reserve) for shipment to Casablanca, French Morocco (see 9 June).

30 Thursday

President Roosevelt (through Secretary of State Cordell Hull) rejects Ambassador to France William C. Bullitt's request of 28 May to send the fleet to the Mediterranean. "The presence of the fleet in the Pacific at this time," Hull reminds the ambassador, "is a very practical contribution to the maintenance of peace in the Pacific."

U.S. Minister in Uruguay Edwin C. Wilson

reports "deteriorating" situation in Montevideo in a telegram to Secretary of State Cordell Hull. Wilson describes the Uruguayan government as "well meaning but weak, undecided and confused," with things "drifting" and "people . . . climbing on the Nazi band wagon." Wilson also warns that an "armed movement is a possibility" (see 31 May).

31 Friday

U.S. Ambassador to Argentina Norman Armour and U.S. Minister in Uruguay Edwin C. Wilson confer in Montevideo about the deteriorating situation in Uruguay, and jointly suggest (in a telegram to Secretary of State Cordell Hull) that "if the situation in the Far East permits," sending a "large U.S. naval force, 40 or 50 vessels . . . to the east coast of South America." A naval visit of that nature, the diplomats believe, "would strengthen the position of those who desire to combat Nazism, as well as restore the confidence of those who are now wavering" and that the stationing of a U.S. naval squadron "more or less permanently in these waters would be an added assurance that we are prepared to give effective and immediate assistance if required."

In reply to U.S. Minister in Uruguay Wilson's telegram of the previous day, Secretary of State Hull informs the envoy in Montevideo that President Roosevelt has ordered heavy cruiser *Quincy* (CA 39) to proceed immediately to Rio de Janeiro, Brazil, and thence directly to Montevideo for "friendly visits of courtesy" (see 12 June).

Chief of the Division of the American Republics (Laurence Duggan) of the State Department suggests to Undersecretary of State Sumner Welles that President Roosevelt's decision "to detach two or three cruisers to go down the east coast," of South America be made public "in order to put a little iron in the veins of our friends in those countries."

JUNE

1 Saturday

Undersecretary of State Sumner Welles, commenting on U.S. Minister in Uruguay Edwin C. Wilson's suggestion to send 40 or 50 naval vessels to South American waters, suggests "at least three or four heavy cruisers and a reasonable number of destroyers . . . on the East Coast [of South America] this summer." That same day, Welles informs U.S. Ambassador to Brazil Jefferson Caffery that heavy cruiser

Quincy (CA 39) is en route to Rio de Janeiro and Montevideo "to furnish a reminder of the strength and the range of action of the armed forces of the United States."

Battleship *Washington* (BB 56) is launched at the Philadelphia Navy Yard. She is the first American battleship to go down the ways since *West Virginia* (BB 48) on 19 November 1921.

Minor Landing and Base Defense Exercise at San Clemente Island, California, begun on 25 May, concludes; for the first time one of the newly organized USMC Defense Battalions carries out the mission of defending an advanced base against a landing force supported by aircraft and ships.

U.S. freighter *Charles R. McCormick*, the American flag displayed prominently, departs Bergen, Norway, for the United States.

2 Sunday

Chief of Naval Operations (Admiral Harold R. Stark) sends memorandum to President Roosevelt that addresses options concerning the situation in South America; of those proposed, the President believes that the only solution lies in dispatching one additional 8-inch gun cruiser to South America, continuing destroyer shakedown cruises to South American waters, and utilizing ships already in the Atlantic Squadron, thus not weakening the fleet in the Pacific.

U.S. steamship *President Roosevelt* departs Galway, Ireland, with 720 American citizens fleeing the European war zone. Passenger liner *Manhattan* departs Genoa, Italy, the same day with 1,905 passengers.

4 Tuesday

Operation DYNAMO, begun on 26 May, is completed; all told, some 848 vessels of every size and displacement take part in the extraction of 338,226 men (including 123,000 French).[20]

5 Wednesday

Auxiliary *Bear* (AG 29) arrives in Philadelphia, Pennsylvania, having proceeded from Antarctica via Valparaiso, Chile, the Panama Canal, and Key West, Florida (see 10 October).

9 Sunday

Allies complete evacuation of British, French, and Norwegian troops from Norway.

Heavy cruiser *Vincennes* (CA 44) and destroyers *Truxtun* (DD 229) and *Simpson* (DD 221) reach Casablanca, French Morocco, having touched briefly at Ponta Delgada,

Azores (4–6 June) en route. *Vincennes*'s mission is to load the 200 tons of gold brought to Casablanca by French auxiliary cruiser *Ville d'Oran*. The precious metal cargo (Bank of France gold reserves) will be transported to New York for deposit in U.S. banks (see 10 and 20 June).[21]

Destroyer *Dickerson* (DD 157), from Squadron 40-T, departs Casablanca with American nationals who desire passage on board U.S. passenger liner *Washington*, which is slated to leave Lisbon, Portugal, the next day for Ireland and the United States. *Washington* departs Bordeaux, France, for Lisbon with 813 U.S. citizens on board (see 10, 11, and 15 June).

10 Monday

Italy declares war on France and Great Britain; Italian troops invade France. President Roosevelt, in a speech at the University of Virginia, Charlottesville, proclaims that the Italian declaration of war on France is like "the hand that held the dagger has struck it in the back of its neighbor."

Norway capitulates to German forces.

Canada declares war on Italy.

Rear Admiral David M. LeBreton relieves Rear Admiral Charles E. Courtney as Commander Squadron 40-T on board light cruiser *Trenton* (CL 11) at Lisbon, Portugal.

Heavy cruiser *Vincennes* (CA 44), escorted by destroyers *Truxtun* (DD 229) and *Simpson* (DD 221), departs Casablanca, French Morocco, for New York (see 20 June).

U.S. passenger liner *Washington* arrives at Lisbon, Portugal, to embark American nationals desiring passage to the United States; destroyer *Dickerson* (DD 157) arrives the same day with her passengers who are to embark in the liner (see 11 and 15 June).

Destroyer *O'Brien* (DD 415) arrives at Bahia, Brazil, on her shakedown cruise (see 14 June).

11 Tuesday

Australia, New Zealand, and South Africa declare war on Italy.

President Roosevelt declares Mediterranean area and mouth of Red Sea to be combat zones in accordance with Neutrality Act.

British Prime Minister Winston S. Churchill, in a telegram to President Roosevelt sent via the British Embassy in Washington, D.C., again raises the need for destroyers with the Italian entry into the war and the possibility of having to deal with more submarines. "To this," Churchill declares, "the only counter is

destroyers. Nothing is so important as for us to have 30 or 40 old destroyers you have already had reconditioned."

U.S. passenger liner *Washington*, en route from Lisbon, Portugal, to Galway, Ireland, with 1,020 U.S. passengers, to embark more American citizens returning to the United States, is stopped by German submarine *U 101* at 42°12'N, 12°50'W. The submarine, mistakenly believing the ship to be a Greek vessel, orders *Washington* abandoned preparatory to being sunk. Blinker signals exchanged between the two ships soon result in the Germans' confirming *Washington*'s neutral identity and allowing her to proceed without further hindrance (see 15 June).

12 Wednesday

Navy Department awards contracts for 22 new warships.

Japan-Thailand Non-Aggression Pact is announced.

Heavy cruiser *Quincy* (CA 39) arrives at Rio de Janeiro, Brazil, for a port visit while she is en route to Montevideo, Uruguay (see 17 June).

13 Thursday

Rear Admiral William F. Halsey Jr. relieves Vice Admiral Charles A. Blakely as Commander Aircraft Battle Force, on board carrier *Yorktown* (CV 5) at Lahaina Roads, Maui, T.H., Halsey receives the temporary rank of vice admiral.

14 Friday

President Roosevelt signs "11% Naval Expansion Act" increasing the carrier, cruiser, and submarine tonnage of the Navy by 167,000 tons, auxiliary shipping by 75,000; and the useful number of authorized naval aircraft to 4,500 planes (see 15 June).

German troops occupy Paris, France.

Destroyer *O'Brien* (DD 415) departs Bahia, Brazil, on her shakedown cruise, bound for Buenos Aires, Argentina (see 20 June).

15 Saturday

Soviet forces, as allowed by the Nazi-Soviet pact, occupy Lithuania. The United States refuses to acknowledge this annexation or those of the two other Baltic states that the USSR will occupy two days later (see 17 June).

President Roosevelt approves Act of Congress to increase naval aviation to a strength of not more than 10,000 aircraft, overriding the 4,500 in the act signed the previous day.

British Prime Minister Winston S. Churchill,

in a telegram to President Roosevelt, again asks for destroyers, calling the matter one "of life and death." Britain will carry on the struggle "whatever the odds," the "Former Naval Person" declares to the President, "but it may well be beyond our resources unless we receive every reinforcement and particularly do we need this reinforcement on the sea."

Submarine tender *Bushnell* (AS 2) completes hydrographic surveys off the coast of Venezuela from Cape San Roman to Bahia Vela de Coro. Having begun on 9 April, she covered an area of 2,200 nautical square miles in the course of her work.

U.S. passenger liner *Washington* sails from Galway, Ireland, for the United States with an additional 852 American citizens, making a total of 1,872 U.S. passengers embarked. She will arrive at New York unmolested.

17 Monday

Soviet forces occupy Estonia and Latvia.

France sues for an armistice with Germany. France's collapse prompts concern for the disposition of the French fleet. French Minister for Foreign Affairs Paul Baudouin privately informs Deputy U.S. Ambassador to France Anthony J. Drexel Biddle Jr. that the fleet "would never be surrendered to Germany." To guarantee that pledge, Bauduoin informs Biddle that Admiral François Darlan has been appointed as Minister of Marine (see 18 June).

Chief of Naval Operations Admiral Harold R. Stark asks for $4 billion to construct the "Two-Ocean Navy."

Heavy cruiser *Quincy* (CA 39) departs Rio de Janeiro, Brazil, for Montevideo, Uruguay (see 20 June).

18 Tuesday

Secretary of State Cordell Hull directs Deputy U.S. Ambassador to France Anthony J. Drexel Biddle Jr. to inform the French government that if France fails to keep its fleet out of German hands, France would "permanently lose the friendship and goodwill of the Government of the United States." Although those sentiments "deeply pained" the French, Minister for Foreign Affairs Paul Baudouin reiterates that the French fleet "would never be surrendered to Germany."

U.S. Minister in Uruguay Edwin C. Wilson reports that Uruguayan government has arrested eight Nazi leaders and that Uruguay's Chamber of Deputies, in secret session the day before, has begun considering a report on Nazi activities in their country.

British steamship *Niagra* is sunk by a mine at 35°53'S, 174°54'E, while en route from Auckland, New Zealand, to Vancouver, British Columbia. All passengers, including nine Americans, and crew are rescued and taken to Auckland.

20 Thursday

Bureau of Ships is established with Rear Admiral Samuel M. Robinson as chief; Bureau of Construction and Repair and Bureau of Engineering are abolished.

Office of Undersecretary of the Navy is created for duration of emergency (see 22 August).

Heavy cruiser *Vincennes* (CA 44), escorted by destroyers *Truxtun* (DD 229) and *Simpson* (DD 221), arrives at New York Navy Yard and transfers the Bank of France gold reserves ashore for deposit in U.S. banks.

Destroyer *Herbert* (DD 160), attached to Squadron 40-T, departs Lisbon for French Morocco (see 21 June).

Heavy cruiser *Quincy* (CA 39) reaches Montevideo, Uruguay, as part of the American effort to counteract German propaganda in Latin America (see 21, 27, and 30 June).

Destroyer *O'Brien* (DD 415) reaches Buenos Aires, Argentina, as her shakedown cruise to Latin American ports continues (see 25 June).

Light cruiser *Phoenix* (CL 46) departs Lahaina, Maui, T.H., for the Panama Canal Zone, on the first leg of her goodwill cruise to the Pacific coast of South America (see 3 July).

Vichy France opens northern Indochina to Japanese military mission and supporting troops.

21 Friday

Heavy cruiser *Wichita* (CA 45), with Commander Cruiser Division 7 (Rear Admiral Andrew C. Pickens) embarked, arrives at Rio de Janeiro, Brazil, en route to join heavy cruiser *Quincy* (CA 39) at Montevideo, Uruguay (see 27 June).

Destroyer *Herbert* (DD 160) arrives at Casablanca, French Morocco (see 23 June).

Destroyer *Dickerson* (DD 157), attached to Squadron 40-T, departs Lisbon for Bilbao, Spain (see 22 June).

22 Saturday

Franco-German armistice is signed at Compiegne, France. France is divided: One zone is occupied by the Germans, the other administered by the French government from the city of Vichy. Free French government is estab-

lished in exile in England by General Charles DeGaulle. Among the terms of the armistice is the specification that the French fleet, except portions necessary to safeguard France's colonial interests, will be gathered in French metropolitan ports and demobilized and disarmed under German and Italian control.

Destroyer *Dickerson* (DD 157) arrives at Bilbao, Spain; she will remain there, safeguarding American interests, until 3 July.

Prince Konoye Fumimaro forms new Japanese cabinet with General Tojo Hideki as Minister of War and Matsuoka Yosuke as Minister of Foreign Affairs.

23 Sunday

Portuguese police arrest 30 sailors (three of whom are injured in the fracas) from light cruiser *Trenton* (CL 11) in street brawl in Santo Amaro Oerias, a suburb of Lisbon.

Destroyer *Herbert* (DD 160) proceeds from Casablanca, French Morocco, to Lisbon with American refugees.

24 Monday

Charles Edison, who had devoted himself to accelerating naval construction and to technical advances in the naval service, resigns as Secretary of the Navy. Lewis Compton, Assistant Secretary of the Navy since 9 February, becomes Acting Secretary. Edison will become Governor of New Jersey.

France signs armistice with Italy.

Japan requests that British close the Burma Road, thus severing the Allied supply line to China.

Rear Admiral Charles A. Blakely relieves Rear Admiral Joseph R. Defrees as Commandant Eleventh Naval District and Commandant Naval Operating Base, San Diego, California.

25 Tuesday

Franco-German armistice becomes effective and hostilities cease.

Act of Congress abolishes Construction Corps of the Navy; constructors are given line officer status designated for Engineering Duty Only (EDO). In addition, the status of those line officers who had previously been designated for Aeronautical Engineering Duty Only (AEDO) were redesignated EDO.

Destroyer *O'Brien* (DD 415) departs Buenos Aires, Argentina, for Rio Grande du Sol, Brazil (see 27 June).

27 Thursday

Romania yields to Soviet ultimatum and cedes Bessarabia and northern Bukovina.

President Roosevelt declares a national emergency and invokes Espionage Act of 1917 to exercise control over shipping movements in territorial waters and in vicinity of the Panama Canal.

President Roosevelt establishes eight-man National Defense Research Committee (Dr. Vannevar Bush, Carnegie Institution, Washington, D.C., chairman) to correlate and support scientific research on the mechanisms and devices of war; Rear Admiral Harold G. Bowen, Director of the Naval Research Laboratory, Anacostia Station, Washington, D.C., represents the U.S. Navy.

Heavy cruiser *Wichita* (CA 45), with Commander Cruiser Division 7 (Rear Admiral Andrew C. Pickens) embarked, departs Rio de Janeiro, Brazil, en route to join heavy cruiser *Quincy* (CA 39) at Montevideo, Uruguay (see 30 June).

Destroyer *O'Brien* (DD 415) reaches Rio Grande du Sol, Brazil, as her shakedown cruise to Latin American ports continues (see 29 June).

29 Saturday

Presidential yacht *Potomac* (AG 25), accompanied by auxiliary *Cuyahoga* (AG 26), departs Washington (D.C.) Navy Yard with President Roosevelt embarked, for a cruise down the Potomac River (see 30 June).

Destroyer *O'Brien* (DD 415) departs Rio Grande du Sol, Brazil, bound for Santos, Brazil, as her shakedown cruise to Latin American ports continues (see 1 July).

30 Sunday

Naval ships and district craft on hand (all types)—1,099. Personnel: Navy—160,997; Marine Corps—28,364; Coast Guard—13,766. Total personnel—203,127.

Heavy cruiser *Wichita* (CA 45), with Commander Cruiser Division 7 (Rear Admiral Andrew C. Pickens) embarked, reaches Montevideo, Uruguay, joining heavy cruiser *Quincy* (CA 39) to begin a tour of Latin American ports "to furnish a reminder of the strength and the range of action of the armed forces of the United States" (see 3 July).

Presidential yacht *Potomac* (AG 25), accompanied by auxiliary *Cuyahoga* (AG 26), returns to Washington (D.C.) Navy Yard with President Roosevelt embarked, after a cruise down the Potomac River.

JULY

1 Monday

Navy awards contracts for 44 ships.

Headquarters Marine Aircraft Wing, Fleet Marine Force (Brigadier General Ross E. Rowell, USMC) is established at the Marine Corps Base, San Diego, California.

U.S. Ambassador to France William C. Bullitt has lengthy private interview with the President of the French Council of Ministers, Marshal Henri Philippe Pétain, in which the latter informs the envoy that orders had been given "to every captain of the French Fleet to sink his ship rather than permit [it] to fall into German hands." The same day, Bullitt also has interview with Admiral François Darlan, who informs him that if the Germans should demand the fleet, it had orders to leave at once for Martinique and Guantánamo to place its ships in U.S. hands. He echoes Marshal Pétain's declaration that French ships had orders to scuttle if the Germans attempt to seize them.

Destroyer *O'Brien* (DD 415) reaches Santos, Brazil, as her shakedown cruise to Latin American ports continues (see 3 July).

2 Tuesday

Congress passes Export Control Act giving the President the power, whenever he deems "necessary in the interest of national defense," to prohibit or curtail the exportation of military equipment, munitions, tools, and materials.

3 Wednesday

Operation CATAPULT: British warships attack French naval vessels at Mers-el-Kebir, near Oran, Algeria, sinking battleship *Bretagne,* damaging battleship *Provence* and battle cruiser *Dunkerque,* and sinking seaplane tender *Commandant Teste* and destroyer *Mogadore*; French men-of-war in British ports (principally Portsmouth and Plymouth) are seized.

Heavy cruisers *Wichita* (CA 45) (Rear Admiral Andrew C. Pickens) and *Quincy* (CA 39) depart Montevideo, Uruguay, for Brazilian waters (see 5 July).

Light cruiser *Phoenix* (CL 46) reaches Balboa, C.Z. (see 5 July).

Destroyer *O'Brien* (DD 415) departs Santos, Brazil, for Pará, Brazil (see 9 July).

5 Friday

Vichy France breaks off diplomatic relations with Great Britain.

President Roosevelt invokes Export Control Act against Japan by prohibiting exportation, without license, of strategic minerals and chemicals, aircraft engines, parts, and equipment.

Admiral James O. Richardson arrives in Washington, D.C., for conferences with the President and Navy and State Department officials concerning the retention of the U.S. Fleet in Hawaiian waters. He will depart to return to the fleet on 17 July.

Light cruiser *Omaha* (CL 4) relieves light cruiser *Trenton* (CL 11) as flagship for Squadron 40-T (Rear Admiral David M. LeBreton) at Lisbon, Portugal.

Heavy cruisers *Wichita* (CA 45) (Rear Admiral Andrew C. Pickens) and *Quincy* (CA 39) reach Rio Grande du Sol, Brazil (see 11 July).

Light cruiser *Phoenix* (CL 46) departs Balboa, C.Z., for Valparaiso, Chile (see 12 July).

8 Monday

British launch two attacks to disable French battleship *Richelieu* at Dakar, French West Africa. In the first, four depth charges dropped over the side of a motor boat from carrier HMS *Hermes* fail to explode. In the second, FAA Swordfish TSR (torpedo spotting reconnaissance) planes (No. 814 Squadron) torpedo *Richelieu*, rendering her incapable of steaming at more than half power. Her main battery, however, is unaffected.

9 Tuesday

Destroyer *O'Brien* (DD 415) reaches Pará, Brazil, in the course of her shakedown cruise (see 12 July).

Coast Guard cutter *Campbell* arrives at Boston, Massachusetts, with U.S. Consul to Greenland James K. Penfield, Governor of North Greenland E. Brun, and a group of Danish officials to discuss commerce and trade of Greenland, due to the interruption of direct contact with Denmark, Greenland's mother country.

10 Wednesday

Battle of Britain begins with first concentrated German air attacks on British convoys in the English Channel.

11 Thursday

William Franklin (Frank) Knox of Illinois, publisher of the Chicago *Daily News*, takes office as Secretary of the Navy. President Roosevelt's choice of Knox, who had been the Republican Party's vice presidential nominee in the 1936 election, reflects the Chief Executive's desire for bipartisan support of his policies.

Heavy cruisers *Wichita* (CA 45) (Rear Admiral Andrew C. Pickens) and *Quincy* (CA 39) depart Rio Grande du Sol, Brazil, for Santos, Brazil (see 13 July).

Captain Laurence Wild relieves Captain Edward W. Hanson as Governor of American Samoa and Commandant of Naval Station, Tutuila, Samoa.

12 Friday

Light cruiser *Phoenix* (CL 46) reaches Valparaiso, Chile, for a six-day visit "to cultivate friendly relations" (see 18 July).

Destroyer *O'Brien* (DD 415) departs Pará, Brazil, for La Guaira, Venezuela (see 16 July).

Destroyers *Walke* (DD 416) and *Wainwright* (DD 419) reach Pará, Brazil, en route to Rio de Janeiro. Both destroyers are transporting marines to join the detachments in heavy cruisers *Wichita* (CA 45) and *Quincy* (CA 39).

U.S. passenger liner *Manhattan* departs Lisbon, Portugal, with approximately 800 American citizens and their families.

13 Saturday

Heavy cruisers *Wichita* (CA 45) (Rear Admiral Andrew C. Pickens) and *Quincy* (CA 39) reach Santos, Brazil (see 18 July).

Destroyers *Walke* (DD 416) and *Wainwright* (DD 419) depart Pará, Brazil, for Rio de Janeiro.

15 Monday

Light cruiser *Trenton* (CL 11) sails from Lisbon with members of the royal family of the Duchy of Luxembourg embarked (see 25 July).

16 Tuesday

Destroyer O'Brien (DD 415) arrives at La Guaira, Venezuela, completing her shakedown cruise to Latin American waters.

18 Thursday

Heavy cruisers *Wichita* (CA 45) (Rear Admiral Andrew C. Pickens) and *Quincy* (CA 39) depart Santos, Brazil, to pay a return call at Rio de Janeiro, Brazil (see 19 July).

Light cruiser *Phoenix* (CL 46) departs Valparaiso, Chile, for Callao, Peru (see 22 July).

19 Friday

President Roosevelt signs Naval Expansion ("Two-Ocean Navy") Act providing, among other things, for 1,325,000 tons of combatant shipping, 100,000 tons of auxiliary shipping, and 15,000 aircraft; this legislation will expand the fleet 70 percent.

William Franklin (Frank) Knox, former "Rough Rider," takes oath of office as Secretary of the Navy as President Roosevelt looks on, 11 July 1940. (NHC, NH 56976)

Presidential yacht *Potomac* (AG 25), with President Roosevelt embarked, departs Washington Navy Yard for a cruise in Chesapeake Bay, accompanied by auxiliary *Cuyahoga* (AG 26) (see 21 July).

Heavy cruisers *Wichita* (CA 45) (Rear Admiral Andrew C. Pickens) and *Quincy* (CA 39) reach Rio de Janeiro, Brazil; destroyers *Walke* (DD 416) and *Wainwright* (DD 419) arrive the same day and transfer their marine passengers; *Walke*'s to *Wichita* and *Wainwright*'s to *Quincy*.

20 Saturday

Destroyers *Walke* (DD 416) and *Wainwright* (DD 419) depart Rio de Janeiro for Rio Grande du Sol, Brazil (see 23 July).

21 Sunday

Presidential yacht *Potomac* (AG 25), with President Roosevelt embarked, returns to Washington Navy Yard after a cruise in Chesapeake Bay, accompanied by auxiliary *Cuyahoga* (AG 26).

22 Monday

Light cruiser *Phoenix* (CL 46) reaches Callao, Peru (see 26 July).

23 Tuesday

Destroyers *Walke* (DD 416) and *Wainwright* (DD 419) reach Rio Grande du Sol, Brazil (see 29 July).

25 Thursday

Heavy cruisers *Wichita* (CA 45) (Rear Admiral Andrew C. Pickens) and *Quincy* (CA 39) depart Rio de Janeiro, Brazil, for Bahia, Brazil (see 31 July).

Light cruiser *Trenton* (CL 11) arrives at Annapolis, Maryland, and disembarks members of the royal family of the Duchy of Luxembourg.

26 Friday

President Roosevelt invokes Export Control Act and prohibits exportation, without license, of aviation gasoline and certain classes of iron and steel scrap; this legislation halts flow of those important commodities to Japan.

Light cruiser *Phoenix* (CL 46) departs Callao, Peru, concluding her goodwill cruise to Chilean and Peruvian waters. She reaches Balboa, C.Z., on 30 July, and returns to the fleet at San Pedro, California, on 7 August.

27 Saturday

Presidential yacht *Potomac* (AG 25), with President Roosevelt, Secretary of the Navy William Franklin (Frank) Knox, and House

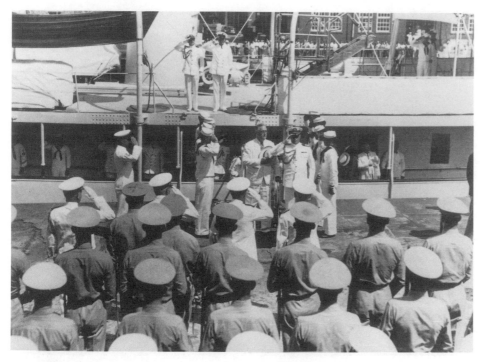

President Roosevelt, his naval aide (Captain Daniel J. Callaghan) at his side, disembarks from presidential yacht *Potomac* (AG 25) to inspect work in progress, Norfolk Navy Yard, 29 July 1940. (NHC, NH 96322)

Naval Affairs Committee Chairman Carl Vinson embarked, departs Washington Navy Yard for Norfolk Navy Yard, accompanied by auxiliary *Cuyahoga* (AG 26) (see 29 July).

29 Monday
Presidential yacht *Potomac* (AG 25), with President Roosevelt, Secretary of the Navy William Franklin (Frank) Knox, and House Naval Affairs Committee Chairman Carl Vinson embarked, reaches Norfolk (Virginia) Navy Yard, accompanied by auxiliary *Cuyahoga* (AG 26). Roosevelt and his guests inspect the yard and Naval Operating Base before reembarking in *Potomac* and traveling to Fortress Monroe, which the President inspects, as well as the USAAC Langley Field and the Newport News Ship Building and Drydock Company (see 30 July).

Destroyers *Walke* (DD 416) and *Wainwright* (DD 419) depart Rio Grande du Sol, Brazil, for Buenos Aires, Argentina (see 30 July).

30 Tuesday
Act of Havana, providing for the emergency establishment of a regime of provisional administration under specified conditions "when islands or regions in the Americas now under the possession of non-American nations are in danger of becoming the subject of barter of

territory or change of sovereignty" is signed by 21 nations at the Conference of Foreign Ministers of the American Republics.

Presidential yacht *Potomac* (AG 25), accompanied by auxiliary *Cuyahoga* (AG 26), returns to Washington Navy Yard with President Roosevelt embarked.

Destroyers *Walke* (DD 416) and *Wainwright* (DD 419) reach Buenos Aires, Argentina (see 3 August).

31 Wednesday
Heavy cruisers *Wichita* (CA 45) (Rear Admiral Andrew C. Pickens) and *Quincy* (CA 39) reach Bahia, Brazil (see 5 August).

British Prime Minister Winston S. Churchill, in a telegram sent from the U.S. Ambassador to the Court of St. James (Joseph P. Kennedy) to Secretary of State Cordell Hull, again asks President Roosevelt for the loan of destroyers. In the previous 10 days, the Royal Navy has suffered the loss of four of its destroyers and damage to seven. "If we cannot get reinforcement," Churchill states, "the whole fate of the war may be decided by this minor and easily remediable factor."

AUGUST

1 Thursday
Navy establishes Alaskan Sector as a military command within the Thirteenth Naval District.

2 Friday
President Roosevelt and his cabinet have "long discussion" in cabinet meeting concerning "ways and means to sell directly or indirectly" 50 or 60 destroyers to the British. There is no dissent "that the survival of the British Isles under German attack might very possibly depend on their [the British] getting these destroyers." All present agree that legislation to accomplish that goal is necessary.

3 Saturday
USSR annexes Lithuania as a Soviet Socialist Republic.

Rear Admiral H. Kent Hewitt relieves Rear Admiral John W. Wilcox Jr. as Commander Special Service Squadron on board gunboat *Erie* (PG 50).

Destroyers *Walke* (DD 416) and *Wainwright* (DD 419) depart Buenos Aires, Argentina, for Santos, Brazil (see 6 August).

5 Monday
Chief of Naval Operations establishes general ground rules to govern the exchange of scientific and technical information with the British mission under Sir Henry Tizard; arrival of the Tizard Mission begins the Anglo-American effort to jointly develop a wide range of weapons, sensors, and the technical equipment during the war.

Lord Lothian, British Ambassador to the United States, provides President Roosevelt with a note concerning the facilities that the British are prepared to "extend to the United States Government."

Rear Admiral John W. Greenslade and French Vice Admiral Georges A. M. J. Robert conclude agreement concerning status of Vichy French warships and aircraft in French West Indies. Ships in question are carrier *Bearn*, light cruiser *Emile Bertin*, training cruiser *Jeanne d'Arc*, and auxiliary cruisers *Esterelle*, *Quercy*, and *Barfleur*; aircraft are 44 SBC-4s, 15 Hawk 75s (export version of USAAC P-36), and six Belgian Brewster fighters (export version of USN F2A) (see 2 and 3 November).

Heavy cruisers *Wichita* (CA 45) (Rear Admiral Andrew C. Pickens) and *Quincy* (CA 39) depart Bahia for Pernambuco, Brazil (see 9 August).

6 Tuesday

U.S. Army transport *American Legion* reaches Petsamo, Finland, to embark American nationals returning to the United States from European countries (Finland, Estonia, Latvia, Lithuania, Sweden, Norway, Denmark, Germany, and the Netherlands) in which they had been residing (see 16 August).

Destroyers *Walke* (DD 416) and *Wainwright* (DD 419) reach Santos, Brazil (see 9 August).

9 Friday

Heavy cruisers *Wichita* (CA 45) (Rear Admiral Andrew C. Pickens) and *Quincy* (CA 39) reach Pernambuco, Brazil (see 13 August).

Gunboat *Erie* (PG 50) (Rear Admiral H. Kent Hewitt, Commander Special Service Squadron, embarked) departs Panama Canal Zone for a goodwill visit to Ecuador (see 12 August).

Destroyers *Walke* (DD 416) and *Wainwright* (DD 419) depart Santos, Brazil, for Rio de Janeiro (see 10 August).

10 Saturday

President Roosevelt inspects Portsmouth (New Hampshire) Navy Yard and then cruises in presidential yacht *Potomac* (AG 25), to Nahant, Massachusetts, escorted by destroyer *Mayrant* (DD 402), and then to Boston Navy Yard, which the Chief Executive inspects as well (see 11 and 12 August).

Destroyers *Walke* (DD 416) and *Wainwright* (DD 419) reach Rio de Janeiro, Brazil (see 14 August).

Japanese naval blockade of coast of China is extended to South China.

11 Sunday

Presidential yacht *Potomac* (AG 25) (with President Roosevelt embarked), escorted by destroyer *Mayrant* (DD 402), proceeds from Boston Navy Yard to Mattapoisett, Massachusetts (see 12 August).

12 Monday

Presidential yacht *Potomac* (AG 25) (with President Roosevelt embarked), escorted by destroyer *Mayrant* (DD 402), proceeds from Mattapoisett, Massachusetts, to Newport, Rhode Island. There the Chief Executive, accompanied by Secretary of the Navy William Franklin (Frank) Knox, Senator David I. Walsh, and Rear Admiral Edward C. Kalbfus, inspects the Torpedo Station and the Naval Training Station. Later the same day, the President reembarks in *Potomac* and cruises to the Submarine Base at New London, observing submarine operations en route. Roosevelt inspects the base and the nearby facilities of the Electric Boat Company before reembarking in *Potomac* for the final leg of the voyage to the Washington Navy Yard, which is reached later the same day.

Gunboat *Erie* (PG 50) (Rear Admiral H. Kent Hewitt, Commander Special Service Squadron, embarked) arrives at Guayaquil, Ecuador, for a goodwill visit.

13 Tuesday

President Roosevelt confers with Secretary of the Navy William Franklin (Frank) Knox, Secretary of War Henry L. Stimson, Secretary of the Treasury Henry Morgenthau, and Undersecretary of State Sumner Welles concerning the transfer of destroyers to Britain. Consequently, Roosevelt informs British Prime Minister Winston S. Churchill (in a telegram sent from Acting Secretary of State Welles to U.S. Ambassador to the Court of St. James Joseph P. Kennedy) that among other items previously sought "it may be possible to furnish to the British Government . . . at least 50 destroyers." Roosevelt states, though, that such aid could only be given provided that "the American People and the Congress frankly recognized in return . . . the national defense and security of the United States would be enhanced." The President thus insists that (1) should British waters be rendered untenable the British Fleet would be sent to other parts of the Empire (and neither turned over to the Germans nor sunk) and (2) that the British government would grant authorization to use Newfoundland, Bermuda, the Bahamas, Jamaica, St. Lucia, Trinidad, and British Guiana as naval and air bases, and to acquire land there through 99-year leases to establish those bases (see 15 August).

Commander in Chief Asiatic Fleet (Admiral Thomas C. Hart) shifts flag from heavy cruiser *Augusta* (CA 31) to submarine *Porpoise* (SS 172), Tsingtao, China, and travels to Shanghai, arriving the next day and transferring to yacht *Isabel* (PY 10). It is the first time a CINCAF (a submariner himself) has taken passage in a submarine in this fashion.

Heavy cruisers *Wichita* (CA 45) (Rear Admiral Andrew C. Pickens) and *Quincy* (CA 39)

depart Pernambuco, Brazil, for Montevideo, Uruguay (see 23 August).

14 Wednesday

Destroyers *Walke* (DD 416) and *Wainwright* (DD 419) depart Rio de Janeiro, Brazil, for Bahia (see 15 August).

15 Thursday

British Prime Minister Winston S. Churchill responds, encouraged and grateful, to President Roosevelt's telegram of 13 August; "the worth of every destroyer that you can spare to us is measured in rubies." The "moral value of this fresh aid from your Government and your people at this critical time will be very great and widely felt."

Assistant Chief of Naval Operations Rear Admiral Robert L. Ghormley, Major General Delos C. Emmons (USAAC), and Brigadier General George V. Strong (USA) arrive in London for informal staff conversations with British officers.

Naval Air Station, Miami, Florida, is established, Commander Gerald F. Bogan in command.

Destroyers *Walke* (DD 416) and *Wainwright* (DD 419) reach Bahia, Brazil (see 17 August).

16 Friday

President Roosevelt, in a press conference, announces that the U.S. government is discussing with the British government the acquisition of naval and air bases to defend the Western Hemisphere and the Panama Canal. Secrecy, however, continues to shroud the ongoing discussions concerning the transfer of destroyers to the British.

U.S. Army transport *American Legion* departs Petsamo, Finland, for New York; on board is Her Royal Highness Crown Princess Martha of Norway and her three children, who have been invited to come to the United States by President Roosevelt. The last neutral ship permitted to leave Petsamo, *American Legion* also carries a crated twin-mount 40-millimeter Bofors gun "with standard sights . . . spare parts, and 3,000 rounds of ammunition." Shipment of the gun, an almost Herculean effort that involved trucking the weapon the entire length of Sweden, has required the cooperation of the British, Swedish, and Finnish governments (see 28 August).

17 Saturday

German government establishes "total blockade" of the British Isles and warns that all ships will be sunk without warning.

Destroyers *Walke* (DD 416) and *Wainwright* (DD 419) depart Bahia, Brazil, for Pará, Brazil (see 21 August).

18 Sunday

President Roosevelt and Prime Minister W. L. MacKenzie King of Canada sign Ogdensburg Agreement, providing for Permanent Joint Board for the Defense of the United States and Canada (see 26 August).

21 Wednesday

Destroyers *Walke* (DD 416) and *Wainwright* (DD 419) reach Pará, Brazil (see 23 August).

22 Thursday

James V. Forrestal, former Administrative Assistant to the President and Wall Street broker, becomes first Undersecretary of the Navy. His office will become "the most important coordinating agency for procurement and materiel in the Navy Department."

23 Friday

Heavy cruisers *Wichita* (CA 45) (Rear Admiral Andrew C. Pickens Commander, Cruiser Division 7, embarked) and *Quincy* (CA 39) arrive at Montevideo, Uruguay (see 28 August).

Destroyers *Walke* (DD 416) and *Wainwright* (DD 419) wind up their shakedown/goodwill cruise in Latin American waters, departing Pará, Brazil, for Guantánamo Bay, Cuba.

26 Monday

Permanent Joint Board on Defense (United States and Canada), set up by President Roosevelt and Canadian Prime Minister W. L. MacKenzie King on 18 August, convenes in Ottawa, Canada. U.S. representatives are Fiorello H. LaGuardia (President, U.S. Conference of Mayors), Lieutenant General Stanley D. Embick, USA (Commanding Fourth Corps Area), Captain Harry W. Hill and Commander Forrest Sherman (War Plans Division, Office of the Chief of Naval Operations), Lieutenant Colonel Joseph T. McNarney, USAAC, and John D. Hickerson (Assistant Chief, Division of European Affairs, Department of State).

27 Tuesday

President Roosevelt signs joint resolution authorizing him to call Army Reserve components and National Guard into federal service for one year.

Legislation is enacted authorizing the appointment of naval aviators of the Navy and Marine Corps Reserves to the line of the regular Navy and Marine Corps, in order to augment the Naval Academy as a source of regular aviators.

President Roosevelt confers with Secretary of the Navy William Franklin (Frank) Knox, Secretary of War Henry L. Stimson, and Secretary of State Cordell Hull concerning a compromise to resolve the impasse that has arisen over the proposed destroyers-for-bases agreement. Subsequently, Roosevelt meets with Admiral Harold R. Stark (Chief of Naval Operations), Secretary of the Navy Knox, Secretary of State Hull, and British Ambassador Lord Lothian; these men review the proposal arrived at earlier that day. Admiral Stark certifies that the destroyers involved are no longer essential to the defense of the United States, thus clearing the way for their transfer.

Attorney General Robert H. Jackson delivers to President Roosevelt a ruling in which the legal framework for the transfer of destroyers to the British can be accomplished.

28 Wednesday

Destroyers *Biddle* (DD 151) and *Blakeley* (DD 150) escort U.S. Army transport *American Legion* on the final leg of her voyage from Petsamo, Finland, to New York City. The 40-millimeter Bofors gun she carries among her cargo is subsequently shipped to the Naval Proving Ground at Dahlgren, Virginia.

Heavy cruisers *Wichita* (CA 45) (Rear Admiral Andrew C. Pickens) and *Quincy* (CA 39) depart Montevideo, Uruguay, for Buenos Aires, Argentina (see 29 August).

29 Thursday

Heavy cruisers *Wichita* (CA 45) (Rear Admiral Andrew C. Pickens) and *Quincy* (CA 39) reach Buenos Aires, Argentina (see 3 September).

Rear Admiral John Downes relieves Rear Admiral William C. Watts as Commandant Ninth Naval District and Commanding Officer Naval Training Center, Great Lakes, Illinois.

30 Friday

Rear Admiral Charles S. Freeman relieves Rear Admiral Edward B. Fenner as Commandant Thirteenth Naval District and Commandant Puget Sound (Washington) Navy Yard.

Vichy France consents to Japanese military occupation of ports, airfields, and railroads in northern Indochina.

31 Saturday

President Roosevelt calls 60,000 National Guardsmen into federal service.

SEPTEMBER

2 Monday

Secretary of State Cordell Hull and British Ambassador Lord Lothian exchange notes, concluding the agreement to trade destroyers for bases; the United States will provide, by executive agreement, 50 over-age (World War I Emergency Program) destroyers in return for 99-year leases on bases in the Bahamas, Antigua, St. Lucia, Trinidad, Jamaica, and British Guiana. The British will provide bases at Newfoundland and Bermuda as outright gifts.

3 Tuesday

President Roosevelt announces the "destroyers-for-bases" agreement; Commander Destroyers Atlantic Squadron (Captain Ferdinand L. Reichmuth) is placed in charge of the transfer operation.

Heavy cruisers *Wichita* (CA 45) (Rear Admiral Andrew C. Pickens) and *Quincy* (CA 39) depart Buenos Aires, Argentina, for Rio de Janeiro, Brazil (see 6 September).

Light cruiser *St. Louis* (CL 49) sails from Norfolk, Virginia; embarked is an evaluation board, headed by Rear Admiral John W. Greenslade, which will evaluate base sites recently acquired from the British (see 5 September).

5 Thursday

Secretary of the Navy William Franklin (Frank) Knox and Commander Aircraft Scouting Force, Rear Admiral Arthur B. Cook, depart San Francisco, California, in XPB2Y-2 for Pearl Harbor, T.H. (see 6 September).

Light cruiser *St. Louis* (CL 49) arrives at Hamilton, Bermuda, with Greenslade Board embarked (see 8 September).

6 Friday

Destroyers *Aaron Ward* (DD 132), *Buchanan* (DD 131), *Crowninshield* (DD 134), *Hale* (DD 133), *Abel P. Upshur* (DD 193), *Welborn C. Wood* (DD 195), *Herndon* (DD 198), and *Welles* (DD 257) arrive at Halifax, Nova Scotia, along with destroyer *Russell* (DD 414), with Commander Destroyers Atlantic Squadron (Captain Ferdinand L. Reichmuth) embarked, and destroyer tender *Denebola* (AD 12). "By the long arm of coincidence" (as British Prime Minister Winston S. Churchill puts it) the

Royal Navy crews assigned to man the ships arrive simultaneously (see 9 September).[22]

Secretary of the Navy William Franklin (Frank) Knox and Commander Aircraft Scouting Force, Rear Admiral Arthur B. Cook, arrive at Pearl Harbor, T.H., in XPB2Y-2. Secretary Knox is visiting the fleet as it carries out operations in Hawaiian waters (see 9 September).

Heavy cruisers *Wichita* (CA 45) (Rear Admiral Andrew C. Pickens) and *Quincy* (CA 39) reach Rio de Janeiro, Brazil, the last port of call on their cruise to South America (see 10 September).

8 Sunday

Light cruiser *St. Louis* (CL 49) departs Hamilton, Bermuda, for Norfolk, Virginia, with Greenslade Board embarked (see 10 September).

9 Monday

Germany warns that all ships in war zones prescribed by Axis are subject to attack regardless of nationality.

First eight destroyers are transferred to Britain under destroyers-for-bases agreement at Halifax, Nova Scotia. *Aaron Ward* (DD 132) becomes HMS *Castleton*, *Buchanan* (DD 131) becomes HMS *Campbeltown*, *Crowninshield* (DD 134) becomes HMS *Chelsea*, *Hale* (DD 133) becomes HMS *Caldwell*, *Abel P. Upshur* (DD 193) becomes HMS *Clare*, *Welborn C. Wood* (DD 195) becomes HMS *Chesterfield*, *Herndon* (DD 198) becomes HMS *Churchill*, and *Welles* (DD 257) becomes HMS *Cameron*.

Navy awards contracts for 210 new-construction ships, including 12 aircraft carriers and seven battleships.

Aircraft carrier *Yorktown* (CV 5) and submarine *Shark* (SS 174) are damaged in collision, Hawaiian Operating Area.

Secretary of the Navy William Franklin (Frank) Knox breaks his flag in carrier *Enterprise* (CV 6) to observe operations; *Enterprise* is being used as fleet flagship for a trial period by Commander in Chief U.S. Fleet (Admiral James O. Richardson). Knox will fly in to Pearl Harbor in the *Enterprise* Air Group Commander's SBC to emphasize the rapid pace of modern naval operations.

10 Tuesday

Light cruiser *St. Louis* (CL 49) arrives at Norfolk, Virginia, with Greenslade Board embarked (see 12 September).

Heavy cruiser *Wichita* (CA 45) (Rear Admiral Andrew C. Pickens) and *Quincy* (CA 39)

Destroyers *Leary* (DD 158) and *Shubrick* (DD 268), New York Navy Yard, painted in navy gray with black-shadowed white hull numbers, 3 September 1940. *Shubrick*, deployed during the summer of 1940 in training naval reservists, will be one of the last group of destroyers turned over to the Royal Navy at Halifax, Nova Scotia, 26 November 1940. As HMS *Ripley*, she escorts convoys in the Atlantic for the remainder of her active service under the White Ensign; she will be scrapped in 1945. *Leary* will remain in USN service (see 24 December 1943). (NHC, NH 82138)

wind up their South American cruise. They depart Rio de Janeiro, Brazil, on this date and reach Norfolk, Virginia, on 24 September.

12 Thursday

Light cruiser *St. Louis* (CL 49) departs Norfolk, Virginia, with Greenslade Board embarked, bound for her ultimate destination on this leg of the voyage, St. John's, Newfoundland (see 16 September).

16 Monday

President Roosevelt signs Selective Training and Service Act, thus establishing the first peacetime draft in the history of the United States.

Light cruiser *St. Louis* (CL 49), with Greenslade Board embarked, arrives at St. John's, Newfoundland (see 18 September).

17 Tuesday

Special Service Squadron (Rear Admiral H. Kent Hewitt), consisting of gunboats *Erie* (PG 50) and *Charleston* (PG 51) and destroyers *J. Fred Talbott* (DD 156) and *Tattnall* (DD 125), is disbanded (see 21 September).

18 Wednesday

Second group of ships involved in the transfer to Britain—*Kalk* (DD 170), *Maddox* (DD 168), *Cowell* (DD 167), *Foote* (DD 169), *Hopewell* (DD 181), *Abbot* (DD 184), *Thomas* (DD 182), and *Doran* (DD 185)—arrives at Halifax, Nova Scotia (see 23 September).

Light cruiser *St. Louis* (CL 49), with Greenslade Board embarked, shifts from St. John's, Newfoundland, to Argentia (see 21 September).

19 Thursday

Battleship *Oklahoma* (BB 37) collides with U.S. tug *Goliah*, Puget Sound, Washington.

20 Friday

Third group of ships involved in the destroyers-for-bases agreement—*Mackenzie* (DD 175), *Haraden* (DD 183), *Williams* (DD 108), *Thatcher* (DD 162), *McCook* (DD 252), and *Bancroft* (DD 256)—arrives at Halifax, Nova Scotia (see 24 September).

21 Saturday

Rear Admiral H. Kent Hewitt hauls down his flag as Commander Special Service Squadron;

gunboat Erie (PG 50) is assigned to the Fifteenth Naval District and sister ship Charleston (PG 51) to the Thirteenth.

Light cruiser *St. Louis* (CL 49), with Greenslade Board embarked, departs Argentia, Newfoundland, for Boston, Massachusetts (see 23 September).

22 Sunday

Vichy France signs pact at Hanoi ceding airfields and agreeing to admit Japanese troops into northern Indochina.

23 Monday

Second group of ships involved in the transfer to Britain is turned over to Royal Navy crews at Halifax, Nova Scotia. *Kalk* (DD 170) becomes HMS *Hamilton*, *Maddox* (DD 168) becomes HMS *Georgetown*, *Cowell* (DD 167) becomes HMS *Brighton*, *Foote* (DD 169) becomes HMS *Roxborough*, *Hopewell* (DD 181) becomes HMS *Bath*, *Abbot* (DD 184) becomes HMS *Charlestown*, *Thomas* (DD 182) becomes HMS *St. Albans*, and *Doran* (DD 185) becomes HMS *St. Marys*.

Light cruiser *St. Louis* (CL 49), with Greenslade Board embarked, arrives at Boston, Massachusetts, but sails for Norfolk, Virginia, the same day (see 25 September).

24 Tuesday

Defense Communication Board is established; membership includes Director of Naval Communications (Rear Admiral Leigh Noyes).

Third group of ships involved in the destroyers-for-bases agreement is turned over to the Royal Canadian Navy at Halifax, Nova Scotia. *Mackenzie* (DD 175) becomes HMCS *Annapolis*, *Haraden* (DD 183) becomes HMCS *Columbia*, *Williams* (DD 108) becomes HMCS *St. Clair*, *Thatcher* (DD 162) becomes HMCS *Niagara*, *McCook* (DD 252) becomes HMCS *St. Croix*, and *Bancroft* (DD 256) becomes HMCS *St. Francis*.

Operation MENACE, the British–Free French attempt to take Dakar, French West Africa, commences (see 25 September).

25 Wednesday

Heavy cruiser *Louisville* (CA 28) departs Colón, C.Z., for Recife, Brazil, on the first leg of her goodwill cruise to Latin American ports.

Light cruiser *St. Louis* (CL 49), with Greenslade Board embarked, arrives at Norfolk, Virginia (see 29 September).

Operation MENACE, the British–Free French attempt to take Dakar, French West Africa, is abandoned as Vichy French resistance proves surprisingly vigorous.

French port of Nouméa, New Caledonia, sides with Free France.

27 Friday

Germany, Italy, and Japan sign Tripartite Pact at Berlin, thus establishing the Berlin-Rome-Tokyo Axis.

29 Sunday

Midway Detachment, Third Defense Battalion, Fleet Marine Force (Major Harold C. Roberts, USMC) arrives on Midway Island to begin construction of defenses. The marines are transported by cargo ship *Sirius* (AK 15) and light minelayers *Pruitt* (DM 22), *Sicard* (DM 21), and *Tracy* (DM 19).

Light cruiser *St. Louis* (CL 49), with Greenslade Board embarked, departs Norfolk, Virginia, for Guantánamo Bay, Cuba (see 2 October).

OCTOBER

1 Tuesday

Coast Guard cutter *Campbell* reports to Chief of Naval Operations for duty. She will then proceed to Lisbon, Portugal (see 18 and 22 October).

2 Wednesday

Light cruiser *St. Louis* (CL 49), with Greenslade Board embarked, arrives at Guantánamo Bay, Cuba (see 19 October).

5 Saturday

Secretary of the Navy William Franklin (Frank) Knox places all Organized Reserve divisions and aviation squadrons of the Organized Reserve on short notice for call to active duty and grants authority to call fleet reservists as necessary. Before this date, Naval Reserve personnel had been ordered to active duty on a voluntary basis only.

Fourth group of ships involved in the destroyers-for-bases agreement—*Branch* (DD 197), *Hunt* (DD 194), *Mason* (DD 191), *Satterlee* (DD 190), *Laub* (DD 263), *Aulick* (DD 258), *Edwards* (DD 265), and *McLanahan* (DD 264)—arrives at Halifax, Nova Scotia (see 6 October).

6 Sunday

Fourth group of ships involved in the destroyers-for-bases agreement is turned over to Royal Navy crews at Halifax. *Branch* (DD 197) becomes HMS *Beverley*, *Hunt* (DD 194) becomes HMS *Broadway*, *Mason* (DD 191) becomes HMS *Broadwater*, *Satterlee* (DD 190) be-

Rear Admiral Harry E. Yarnell, USN (Retired) (former Commander in Chief Asiatic Fleet, 1936–1939), Admiral Harold R. Stark (Chief of Naval Operations), Secretary of the Navy William Franklin (Frank) Knox, and Admiral James O. Richardson, Commander in Chief U.S. Fleet, meet in the Secretary of the Navy's office, Washington, D.C., 7 October 1940. (Author's Collection)

comes HMS *Belmont, Laub* (DD 263) becomes HMS *Burwell,* *Aulick* (DD 258) becomes HMS *Burnham,* *Edwards* (DD 265) becomes HMS *Buxton,* and *McLanahan* (DD 264) becomes HMS *Bradford.*

7   Monday

Admiral James O. Richardson arrives in Washington, D.C., for conferences with the President and Navy and State Department officials concerning the retention of the U.S. Fleet in Hawaiian waters as a deterrent to Japan. He will depart to return to the fleet on 11 October.

Heavy cruiser *Louisville* (CA 28) arrives at Recife, Brazil, as she begins her goodwill cruise to Latin American ports (see 14 October).

8   Tuesday

Legislation approved authorizes the appointment to commissioned rank in the Line of the Regular Navy of those Naval Reserve officers who receive their commissions upon graduation from the Naval Reserve Officer Training Corps.

United States advises American citizens to leave the Far East (see 14 October).

Japan protests U.S. embargo on aviation gasoline and scrap metal.

10   Thursday

Auxiliary *Bear* (AG 29) sails from Philadelphia, Pennsylvania, for Annapolis, Maryland, and the Panama Canal on the first leg of her voyage toward the Antarctic (see 10 January 1941).

12   Saturday

Commander Atlantic Squadron (Rear Admiral Hayne Ellis), in destroyer *Rhind* (DD 404), visits Port-au-Prince, Haiti.[23]

Carrier *Wasp* (CV 7), off the Virginia capes, launches 24 USAAC P-40s and nine O-47s to gather data on comparative takeoff runs of naval and army aircraft. For the first time army planes are flown off a navy carrier.

13   Sunday

Surveying ship *Bowditch* (AG 30) arrives at Placentia Harbor, Newfoundland, to make hydrographic surveys, having transported army engineers who will make a shore requirements survey.

14   Monday

Heavy cruiser *Louisville* (CA 28) departs Recife, Brazil, for Rio de Janeiro, as she continues "showing the flag" in Latin American waters (see 18 October).

USAAC Curtiss P-40s (8th Pursuit Group) and North American O-47s (3rd Observation Squadron) warm up on board carrier *Wasp* (CV 7), off the Virginia capes, in preparation for takeoff, 12 October 1940; plane guard destroyer astern (left) is either *Plunkett* (DD 431) or *Niblack* (DD 424). (NA, 80-G-66095)

Department of State announces that the U.S. passenger liners *Monterey, Mariposa,* and *Washington* are being sent to the Far East to repatriate American citizens from that region in view of prevailing "abnormal conditions" there. This move is made because of the shortage of accommodations on the ships already engaged in the Far East trade. *Monterey* is to go to Yokohama, Japan, and Shanghai, China; *Mariposa* will proceed to Shanghai and Chinwangtao, China, and Kobe, Japan.

15   Tuesday

Naval Air Station, Jacksonville, Florida is established, Captain Charles P. Mason in command.

16   Wednesday

Sixteen million men register for the draft under the Selective Training and Service Act.

Fifth group of ships involved in the destroyers-for-bases agreement—*Twiggs* (DD 127), *Philip* (DD 76), *Evans* (DD 78), *Wickes* (DD 75), *McCalla* (DD 253), *Rodgers* (DD 170), *Conner* (DD 72), *Conway* (DD 70), *Stockton* (DD 73), and *Yarnall* (DD 143)—arrives at Halifax, Nova Scotia (see 23 October).

18   Friday

Coast Guard cutter *Campbell* arrives at Lisbon, Portugal (see 22 October).

Heavy cruiser *Louisville* (CA 28) arrives at Rio de Janeiro, Brazil, as she continues "showing the flag" in Latin American waters (see 24 October).

19   Saturday

Light cruiser *St. Louis* (CL 49), with Greenslade Board embarked, departs Guantánamo Bay, Cuba, for San Juan, Puerto Rico (see 20 October).

20   Sunday

Oiler *Ramapo* (AO 12) delivers district patrol craft *YP 16* and *YP 17* at Apra Harbor to augment the local defenses at Guam.

Light cruiser *St. Louis* (CL 49), with Greenslade Board embarked, arrives at San Juan, Puerto Rico (see 21 October).

21   Monday

Light cruiser *St. Louis* (CL 49), with Greenslade Board embarked, departs San Juan, Puerto Rico, for return visit to Hamilton, Bermuda (see 24 October).

22 Tuesday

Squadron 40-T (Rear Admiral David M. Le-Breton) is disbanded. Coast Guard cutter *Campbell* assumes "to a certain extent the duties previously performed by Squadron 40-T."

23 Wednesday

Japan gives one-year notice of abrogation of North Pacific Sealing Convention of 1911.

Fifth group of ships involved in the destroyers-for-bases agreement is turned over to Royal Navy crews at Halifax, Nova Scotia. *Twiggs* (DD 127) becomes HMS *Leamington*, *Philip* (DD 76) becomes HMS *Lancaster*, *Evans* (DD 78) becomes HMS *Mansfield*, *Wickes* (DD 75) becomes HMS *Montgomery*, *McCalla* (DD 253) becomes HMS *Stanley*, *Rodgers* (DD 170) becomes HMS *Sherwood*, *Conner* (DD 72) becomes HMS *Leeds*, *Conway* (DD 70) becomes HMS *Lewes*, *Stockton* (DD 73) becomes HMS *Ludlow*, and *Yarnall* (DD 143) becomes HMS *Lincoln*.

24 Thursday

Heavy cruiser *Louisville* (CA 28) departs Rio de Janeiro, Brazil, for Montevideo, Uruguay, as she continues to "show the flag" in Latin American waters (see 28 October).

Light cruiser *St. Louis* (CL 49), with Greenslade Board embarked, arrives at Hamilton, Bermuda (see 25 October).

German freighter *Helgoland* sails from Puerto Colombia, Colombia; despite the efforts of destroyers *Bainbridge* (DD 246), *Overton* (DD 239), and *Sturtevant* (DD 240) to pursue her over the ensuing days, *Helgoland* will make good her attempt to escape the confines of the Caribbean (see 3 and 30 November).

25 Friday

Japanese naval land attack planes (13th *Kokutai*) raiding Chungking, China, follow a course that takes them directly over the U.S. Embassy and river gunboat *Tutuila* (PR 4). Due to what is later explained as a malfunctioning release mechanism, Japanese bombs fall north, east, and west of the embassy and the gunboat, the nearest falling 300 yards away. In response to American protests, Japanese naval authorities will advise the air commander in the region "to take necessary steps to prevent the recurrence of such incidents" (see 15 June and 30 July 1941).

Light cruiser *St. Louis* (CL 49), with Greenslade Board embarked, departs Hamilton, Bermuda, for Norfolk, Virginia (see 27 October).

27 Sunday

Light cruiser *St. Louis* (CL 49) arrives at Norfolk, Virginia, thus winding up her mission transporting the Greenslade Board to evaluate base sites acquired from the British in exchange for the provision of destroyers.

28 Monday

Italy invades Greece.

Heavy cruiser *Louisville* (CA 28) arrives at Montevideo, Uruguay, as she continues to "show the flag" in Latin American waters (see 3 November).

30 Wednesday

Because of delay in the arrival of crews assigned to the last of the destroyers to be transferred to the Royal Navy, Commander Destroyers Atlantic Squadron (Captain Ferdinand L. Reichmuth) departs Halifax, Nova Scotia, in destroyer tender *Denebola* (AD 12). Destroyer *Russell* (DD 414) accompanies the auxiliary.

31 Thursday

British forces occupy Crete in response to Italian invasion of Greece.

German auxiliary minelayer *Passat* begins laying mines in Bass Strait, the body of water between Australia and Tasmania (see 1, 7, and 8 November).

German freighter *Rio Grande* sails from Rio de Janeiro, Brazil; she eludes the Neutrality Patrol and ultimately reaches Bordeaux, France, six weeks later.

NOVEMBER

1 Friday

Atlantic Squadron (Rear Admiral Hayne Ellis) is renamed Patrol Force U.S. Fleet.

Submarine Force Scouting Force, ceases to exist; in its stead are two type commands: Submarines Scouting Force Pacific Fleet and Submarines Atlantic Fleet. Rear Admiral Wilhelm L. Friedell becomes Commander Submarines Scouting Force.

Naval Air Station, Alameda, California, is established, Captain Frank R. McCrary in command.

German auxiliary minelayer *Passat* completes laying barrage off Australian coast in Bass Strait (see 7 and 8 November).

2 Saturday

Rear Admiral John W. Greenslade arrives in Fort-de-France, Martinique, to confer with Vice Admiral Georges A. M. J. Robert on the economic distress afflicting Martinique and Guadeloupe, French West Indies, and on the status of French warships and aircraft there (see 3 November).

3 Sunday

Typhoon devastates Guam, M.I., rendering the U.S. Navy Yard at Piti a shambles, damaging the Marine Barracks, blowing away dwellings and poultry, destroying crops, and completely disrupting the lives of the native farmers; it also reduces the Pan American Airways hotel to "kindling wood." In addition, one of the recently arrived district patrol craft (*YP 16* or *YP 17*) is sunk; dredge *YM 13*, being used to dredge a channel near Sumay, Guam, is blown ashore. Greek freighter *Axios*, in the harbor for repairs, parts her moorings at the height of the typhoon, and despite the fact that she possesses neither harbor chart nor pilot miraculously escapes foundering on nearby reefs. Governor of Guam (Captain George J. McMillin) later praises the people of the island for their "cheerful willingness and unremitting effort . . . to repair or replace their homes" that reflected "character of which any group . . . might be proud."

Heavy cruiser *Louisville* (CA 28) departs Montevideo, Uruguay, for Buenos Aires, Argentina, as she continues to "show the flag" in Latin American waters (see 4 November).

Rear Admiral John W. Greenslade departs Fort-de-France, Martinique, after concluding talks with Vice Admiral Georges A. M. J. Robert. Among Admiral Greenslade's recommendations are that every effort be made to alleviate the distress of the inhabitants by easing restrictions on frozen assets to allow for purchase of food, medical supplies, and gasoline for automobiles and trucks; that the naval observer and U.S. vice consul maintain careful and complete liaison with Vice Admiral Robert; that a patrol plane make daily visits to Fort-de-France to improve communications and survey the situation from the air; and that the patrols off Martinique and Guadeloupe, French West Indies, be continued.

German freighter *Helgoland*, which had departed Colombian waters on 24 October, skirts the Antilles near St. Thomas, Virgin Islands, in her bid for freedom (see 30 November).

4 Monday

Heavy cruiser *Louisville* (CA 28) arrives at Buenos Aires, Argentina (see 12 November).

5 Tuesday

President Roosevelt, in his bid for a third term, defeats Republican challenger Wendell Willkie for the presidency.

7 Thursday

British freighter *Cambridge* is sunk by mine (laid by German auxiliary minelayer *Passat* on 31 October–1 November) off Wilson's Promontory, Australia (see 8 November).

8 Friday

Admiral Nomura Kichasaburo is appointed Japanese Ambassador to the United States.

U.S. freighter *City of Rayville* is sunk by a mine (laid by German auxiliary minelayer *Passat* on 31 October–1 November) east of Cape Otway, Bass Strait, Australia; *City of Rayville* is first U.S. merchant ship sunk in World War II. Third Engineer Mack B. Bryan, who drowns during the abandonment, is the first merchant marine casualty of World War II. The other 37 crewmen (one of whom is injured) reach safety at Apollo Bay.

11 Monday

Twenty-one FAA Swordfish TSR (torpedo spotting reconnaissance) planes, flown by 16 crews from carrier HMS *Illustrious* (No. 815 and No. 819 Squadrons) and five crews from HMS *Eagle* (No. 813 and No. 824 Squadrons), launched from *Illustrious,* begin night attack against Italian fleet at Taranto, Italy (Operation JUDGMENT) (see 12 November).

12 Tuesday

British attack (Operation JUDGMENT) against Italian fleet at Taranto concludes. At the cost of two Swordfish lost (one crew is captured), battleships *Littorio* and *Caio Duilio* are damaged and *Conte de Cavour* sunk; heavy cruiser *Trento* and destroyer *Libeccio* are hit by dud bombs. Battleships *Vittorio Veneto, Andrea Doria,* and *Julio Cesare* sail for Naples; heavy units of the Italian Fleet will not base at Taranto until May 1941. Word of the Taranto raid is received in the Navy Department with "great satisfaction." Secretary of the Navy William Franklin (Frank) Knox asks the Special Naval Observer in London, Rear Admiral Robert L. Ghormley, to "learn more details of how the attack was carried out, especially as to what extent aerial torpedoes were used." Secretary Knox tells Ghormley the successful operation "did not a little to promote a most optimistic attitude hereabouts."[24]

Heavy cruiser *Louisville* (CA 28) departs

Six Douglas B-18As (27th Reconnaissance Squadron) fly over San Juan, Puerto Rico, 5 November 1940. Ships in harbor beyond include destroyers *Moffett* (DD 362), *Rowan* (DD 405), and *Trippe* (DD 403), and small seaplane tender *Gannet* (AVP 8). (NASM 20330 A.C.)

Buenos Aires, Argentina, for Santos, Brazil, as she continues her goodwill cruise in Latin American waters (see 15 November).

13 Wednesday

Acting Secretary of State Sumner Welles, on the strength of a report that French battleships *Richelieu* (then at Dakar) and *Jean Bart* (then at Casablanca) were to be moved, perhaps to Toulon, France (within the German sphere of influence), requests the Chargé d'Affaires ad interim in Spain, H. Freeman Matthews, to let the appropriate French authorities know that the U.S. government would be prepared to contemplate purchase of both capital ships if the French government were willing to dispose of them with the agreement that they would not be used in the present war (see 16, 18, and 21 November).

15 Friday

Destroyer *Plunkett* (DD 431), on Neutrality Patrol off Tampico, Mexico, observes German freighter *Orinoco* and tanker *Phrygia* making preparations for sea (see 16 November).

Heavy cruiser *Louisville* (CA 28) arrives at Santos, Brazil, as she continues her goodwill cruise in Latin American waters (see 25 November).

16 Saturday

Destroyer *McCormick* (DD 223), on Neutrality Patrol off Tampico, Mexico, foils attempt by German freighter *Orinoco* to make a break for Europe. Destroyer *Plunkett* (DD 431), by her very presence, thwarts German tanker *Phrygia*'s bid for freedom; *Phrygia*'s crew scuttles her.

In accordance with Acting Secretary of State Sumner Welles's request of 13 November, Chargé d'Affaires ad interim H. Freeman Matthews meets with Marshal Henri Philippe Pétain concerning the possible move of French battleships *Richelieu* and *Jean Bart*. Pétain assures the U.S. envoy that the two capital ships would be used to defend French territory and would never be used against the British. "Under present circumstances," Pétain informs Matthews, "I have neither the right nor the possibility of selling them" (see 18 and 21 November).

17 Sunday

PBYs (VP 54) inaugurate flight operations from Bermuda; seaplane tender (destroyer) *George E. Badger* (AVD 3) provides support.

18 Monday

Acting Secretary of State Sumner Welles directs Chargé d'Affaires ad interim H. Freeman Matthews to communicate President Roosevelt's concern over the French battleships *Richelieu* and *Jean Bart* being moved to a port such as Toulon to Marshal Henri Philippe Pétain, and reiterate the U.S. offer to acquire those two ships "as well as any other vessels of the French Navy" (see 21 November).

20 Wednesday

Hungary joins the Axis.

21 Thursday

Sixth and last group of ships involved in the destroyers-for-bases agreement—*Bailey* (DD 269), *Meade* (DD 274), *Shubrick* (DD 268), *Swasey* (DD 273), *Claxton* (DD 140), *Fairfax* (DD 93), *Robinson* (DD 88), *Ringgold* (DD 89), *Sigourney* (DD 81), and *Tillman* (DD 135)—arrives at Halifax, Nova Scotia. Turnover of the last 10 ships is under the charge of Commander Destroyer Squadron 33 (Captain Schuyler F. Heim) (see 26 November).

Chargé d'Affaires ad interim H. Freeman Matthews meets with Marshal Henri Philippe Pétain concerning the French battleships *Richelieu* and *Jean Bart;* the French admiral responds immediately: "Then why not leave those vessels at Dakar and Casablanca where they now are? I shall keep them there and if there should be any change in this plan I will give you previous notice." This information, received in Washington, D.C., on the morning of 22 November, is communicated through channels by the President to the "Former Naval Person" (Prime Minister Winston S. Churchill) on 23 November.

23 Saturday

Romania joins the Axis.

Commander in Chief Asiatic Fleet (Admiral Thomas C. Hart) shifts his flag from heavy cruiser *Augusta* (CA 31) to sister ship *Houston* (CA 30) at Manila, P.I. *Augusta* departs this day to proceed to the United States via waters north of the Hawaiian chain to investigate reports of Japanese tankers operating in the region.

25 Monday

Heavy cruiser *Louisville* (CA 28) departs Santos, Brazil, for Rio Grande du Sol, continuing her goodwill cruise in Latin American waters (see 29 November).

26 Tuesday

Sixth and last group of ships involved in the destroyers-for-bases agreement is turned over to Royal Navy crews at Halifax, Nova Scotia. *Bailey* (DD 269) becomes HMS *Reading, Meade* (DD 274) becomes HMS *Ramsey, Shubrick* (DD 268) becomes HMS *Ripley, Swasey* (DD 273) becomes HMS *Rockingham, Claxton* (DD 140) becomes HMS *Salisbury, Fairfax* (DD 93) becomes HMS *Richmond, Robinson* (DD 88) becomes HMS *Newmarket, Ringgold* (DD 89) becomes HMS *Newark, Sigourney* (DD 81) becomes HMS *Newport,* and *Tillman* (DD 135) becomes HMS *Wells.*

27 Wednesday

Battle of Cape Spartivento: Two U.S. Naval Observers, Lieutenant Commander A. Dayton Clark in British battle cruiser HMS *Renown* and Lieutenant Commander Frederick P. Hartman in light cruiser HMS *Southampton,* witness the action that takes place between British and Italian forces off the coast of Sardinia.

29 Friday

Destroyers *Simpson* (DD 221) and *Broome* (DD 210), on Neutrality Patrol off Tampico, Mexico, trail German freighters *Idarwald* (see 8 December) and *Rhein* (see 11 December) as the latter ships make a bid for freedom.

Heavy cruiser *Louisville* (CA 28) arrives in Rio Grande du Sol, Brazil, as she continues her goodwill cruise in Latin American waters (see 3 December).

30 Saturday

United States lends $50 million to China for currency stabilization and grants an additional $50 million credit for purchase of supplies.

German freighter *Helgoland,* which has eluded the Neutrality Patrol, reaches St. Nazaire, France.

DECEMBER

1 Sunday

Headquarters for Alaskan units of Coast Guard is established at Ketchikan.

3 Tuesday

President Roosevelt embarks in heavy cruiser *Tuscaloosa* (CA 37) at Miami, Florida, to inspect base sites acquired from the British under the destroyers-for-bases agreement. During the cruise, he will broach the lend-lease concept that he will implement upon his return to Washington, D.C. (see 11 March 1941).

Heavy cruiser *Louisville* (CA 28) departs Rio Grande du Sol, Brazil, to pay a return call at Rio de Janeiro, as her goodwill cruise continues in Latin American waters (see 6 December).

4 Wednesday

Admiral William D. Leahy, USN (Retired), tenders his resignation as Governor of Puerto Rico effective the following day (see 5 December).

5 Thursday

Admiral William D. Leahy, USN (Retired), takes oath of office as Ambassador to Vichy France (see 23 December).

Seaplane tender (destroyer) *George E. Badger* (AVD 3) runs aground in high winds off Hamilton, Bermuda, but is refloated without damage.

6 Friday

Heavy cruiser *Louisville* (CA 28) returns to Rio de Janeiro, Brazil, as she continues to "show the flag" in Latin American waters (see 6 December).

8 Sunday

Destroyer *Sturtevant* (DD 240) stands by while British light cruiser HMS *Diomede* intercepts German freighter *Idarwald. Idarwald's* crew, however, scuttles their ship near the Yucatan Channel to prevent her capture by the British.

10 Tuesday

Naval Air Station, Tongue Point, Oregon, is established; although incomplete when placed in operation, it is being prepared for operation of patrol planes.

11 Wednesday

German freighter *Rhein,* having been trailed by destroyer *Simpson* (DD 221) and, later, *MacLeish* (DD 220), is intercepted by Dutch destroyer leader *Van Kinsbergen* near the Florida Straits, and is scuttled by her own crew to avoid capture. *MacLeish* and *McCormick* (DD 223) are present as the German ship's bid to escape fails.

12 Thursday

Rear Admiral John M. Smeallie, Commandant Sixteenth Naval District and Commandant Cavite Navy Yard, is hospitalized at Cañacao, P.I., after attempted suicide (see 27 December).[25]

Lord Lothian, British Ambassador to the United States, dies in Washington, D.C. President Roosevelt, at sea in heavy cruiser *Tuscaloosa* (CA 37), sends telegram to King George VI of England expressing his regrets at Lord Lothian's passing. "I am very certain," Roosevelt informs the King, "that if he had been allowed by Providence to leave us a last message he would have told us that the greatest of all efforts to retain democracy in the world must and will succeed."

15 Sunday

Headquarters, Eighth Naval District, is closed at Charleston, South Carolina, and established at New Orleans, Louisiana; Captain Thaddeus A. Thomson Jr. is Acting Commandant.

16 Monday

Patrol Wing 10 is formed in Asiatic Fleet organization.

Heavy cruiser *Louisville* (CA 28) departs Rio de Janeiro for Bahia, Brazil, as she continues her goodwill cruise in Latin American waters (see 18 December).

17 Tuesday

Rear Admiral Ernest J. King relieves Rear Admiral Hayne Ellis as Commander Patrol Force U.S. Fleet on board battleship Texas (BB 35).

18 Wednesday

Heavy cruiser *Louisville* (CA 28) arrives at Bahia, Brazil, as she continues to "show the flag" in Latin American waters (see 5 January 1941).

19 Thursday

Palmyra Island in the Central Pacific is placed under control of Secretary of the Navy.

20 Friday

President Roosevelt names a four-man defense board, to be headed by industrialist William S. Knudsen, to prepare defense measures and expedite aid to Great Britain.

23 Monday

Admiral William D. Leahy, USN (Retired), newly appointed Ambassador to Vichy France,

accompanied by his wife Louise, embarks in heavy cruiser *Tuscaloosa* (CA 37) at Norfolk, Virginia, for the transatlantic passage to take up his diplomatic post "at a very critical time in the relations between the United States and France." Destroyers *Madison* (DD 425) and *Upshur* (DD 144) escort *Tuscaloosa* on the initial stage of her voyage (see 30 December).

Naval Air Station, Key West, Florida, is established.

27 Friday

Captain Eugene T. Oates assumes temporary duty as Commandant Sixteenth Naval District and Commandant Cavite Navy Yard (see 11 January 1941).

30 Monday

Heavy cruiser *Tuscaloosa* (CA 37) arrives at Lisbon, Portugal, and disembarks Admiral and Mrs. Leahy, who will then proceed to Vichy via Madrid and Barcelona, Spain, and Montpellier, France (see 3 and 8 January 1941).

1941

JANUARY

3 Friday

Heavy cruiser *Tuscaloosa* (CA 37) departs Lisbon, Portugal, for Norfolk, Virginia, having transported Admiral William D. Leahy, USN (Retired), U.S. Ambassador to France, on the transatlantic leg of his journey to his diplomatic post (see 8 January).

5 Sunday

Heavy cruiser *Louisville* (CA 28) arrives at Simonstown, South Africa (see 6 January).

6 Monday

Heavy cruiser *Louisville* (CA 28) departs Simonstown, South Africa, for New York, having taken on board $148,342,212.55 in British gold for deposit in American banks (see 22 January).

7 Tuesday

Office of Production Management is established under industrialist William S. Knudsen, labor leader Sidney Hillman, Secretary of the Navy William Franklin (Frank) Knox, and Secretary of War Henry L. Stimson.

8 Wednesday

Admiral William D. Leahy, USN (Retired), presents his credentials as Ambassador to France at Vichy.

9 Thursday

Transport *William Ward Burrows* (AP 6) arrives at Wake Island with first increment of workmen (Contractors Pacific Naval Air Bases) to begin building a naval air station there.

10 Friday

Auxiliary *Bear* (AG 29) returns to Bay of Whales, Antarctica, to evacuate West Base; the evacuation is under the supervision of Commander Richard H. Cruzen, second-in-command of the U.S. Antarctic Service (see 24 January).

Operation EXCESS: British covering force for Malta-bound convoy comes under attack from German JU 87s in the Sicilian narrows. Carrier HMS *Illustrious* is badly damaged by bombs; Lieutenant Commander Kenneth P. Hartman, U.S. naval observer on board *Illustrious,* distinguishes himself in helping to fight fires and care for wounded men. He will later be commended for gallantry.

11 Saturday

Rear Admiral Harold M. Bemis relieves Captain Eugene T. Oates as Commandant Sixteenth Naval District and Commandant Navy Yard, Cavite, P.I. Captain Oates had been acting commandant since the incapacitation of Rear Admiral John M. Smeallie in December 1940.

16 Thursday

President Roosevelt asks Congress for immediate appropriation of $350 million for 200 new merchant ships.

17 Friday

Rear Admiral Thomas Withers relieves Rear Admiral Wilhelm L. Friedell as Commander Submarines Scouting Force on board light cruiser *Richmond* (CL 9) (force flagship) at Pearl Harbor, T.H.

Battle of Koh Chang: Vichy French retaliate against Thai moves against Cambodia.

French squadron (Rear Admiral Jules Terraux), consisting of light cruiser *Lamotte-Picquet,* colonial sloops *Amiral Charner* and *Dumont D'Urville,* and sloops *Tahure* and *Marne,* decisively defeats a Thai Navy force in a surface gunnery and torpedo action fought in the Gulf of Siam, sinking coast defense ship *Dhonburi* and torpedo boats *Cholbury* and *Songkhla* and damaging coast defense ship *Sri Ayuthia* and torpedo boat *Trat* in about two hours. *Lamotte-Picquet* suffers damage from own gun blast (see 23 January).

18 Saturday
German Consul General in San Francisco, California, displays the prescribed German Reich flag from the consular office in recognition of German national holiday. At noon this day the flag is taken down in the presence of what is described as "a large shouting throng of people" and torn to pieces. German Chargé d'Affaires Hans Thomsen makes "most emphatic protest" over the incident (see 19 January and 25 May).

19 Sunday
Secretary of State Cordell Hull responds to German Chargé d'Affaires Hans Thomsen's protest over the incident concerning the tearing down of the Reich flag over the consulate in San Francisco the previous day, promising a full investigation (see 25 May).

22 Wednesday
Heavy cruiser *Louisville* (CA 28) arrives at New York with $148,342,212.55 in British gold brought from Simonstown, South Africa, to be deposited in American banks.

23 Thursday
"S" operation: Japanese heavy cruisers *Suzuya, Mikuma, Mogami,* and *Kumano* depart Kure, Japan. Their voyage to Indochina waters is part of pressure brought to bear upon the Vichy French colonial government in the wake of the Battle of Koh Chang (see 28 January and 10 and 13 February).

24 Friday
Interior Department motorship *North Star* arrives at Bay of Whales, Antarctica, to take part in evacuating West Base of U.S. Antarctic Service (see 31 January).

25 Saturday
Keel of battleship *Wisconsin* (BB 64) is laid at the Philadelphia (Pennsylvania) Navy Yard.

Auxiliary *Bear* (AG 29) (right) lies moored at Bay of Whales, during preparations (10–31 January 1941) to evacuate the U.S. Antarctic Service's West Base, while civilian dog driver Jack Bursey pauses in his labors (left). (NHC, NR&L(M)-25691)

She will be the last battleship ever built by the U.S. Navy.

28 Tuesday
Japanese impose cease-fire to end Franco-Thai conflict; agreement is signed on board Japanese light cruiser *Natori* at Saigon, French Indochina (see 31 January).

29 Wednesday
U.S.-British-Canadian staff conversations begin in Washington, D.C., to determine joint strategy in case of U.S. involvement in the war.

30 Thursday
Germany announces that ships of any nationality bringing aid to Great Britain will be torpedoed.

31 Friday
Vice Admiral William S. Pye relieves Admiral Charles P. Snyder as Commander Battle Force.

Vice Admiral Walter S. Anderson becomes Commander Battleships Battle Force.

West Base, U.S. Antarctic Service, is closed (see 1 February).

Cease-fire ending Franco-Thai conflict goes into effect.

FEBRUARY

1 Saturday
Navy Department announces reorganization of U.S. Fleet, reviving old names Atlantic Fleet and Pacific Fleet; Asiatic Fleet remains unchanged.

Marine Corps expansion occurs as the First and Second Marine Brigades are brought up to division strength.

Rear Admiral H. Fairfax Leary relieves Rear Admiral Husband E. Kimmel as Commander Cruisers Battle Force.

Admiral Husband E. Kimmel relieves Admiral James O. Richardson as Commander in Chief U.S. Fleet on board battleship *Pennsylvania* (BB 38) at Pearl Harbor, T.H.

Vice Admiral Wilson Brown Jr. relieves Vice Admiral Adolphus Andrews as Commander Scouting Force.

Rear Admiral John H. Newton relieves Rear Admiral Gilbert J. Rowcliff as Commander Cruisers Scouting Force.

Auxiliary *Bear* (AG 29) and Interior Department motorship *North Star* depart Bay of Whales; they will proceed via different routes to rendezvous off Adelaide Island to evacuate Antarctic Service's East Base (see 24 February).

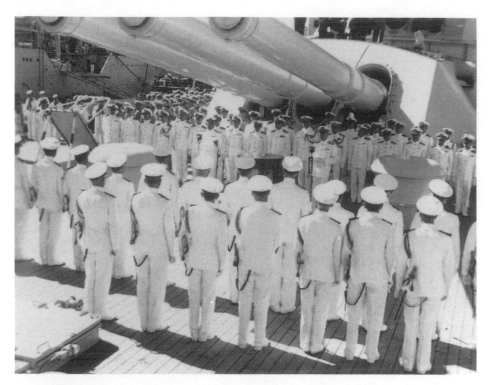

Beneath the 14-inch guns of Turret III of battleship *Pennsylvania* (BB 38), Admiral James O. Richardson (left) turns over command of the U.S. Fleet to Admiral Husband E. Kimmel (right), Pearl Harbor, T.H., 1 February 1941. (Paul C. Crosley Collection, NHF)

3 Monday

Navy Department General Order No. 143 creates three independent fleets, each commanded by an admiral. Admiral Husband E. Kimmel becomes Commander in Chief U.S. Pacific Fleet (and also Commander in Chief U.S. Fleet in the event that two or more fleets operate together); Patrol Force U.S. Fleet becomes U.S. Atlantic Fleet under command of Admiral Ernest J. King; and Admiral Thomas C. Hart continues as Commander in Chief U.S. Asiatic Fleet.

During routine exercises in Hawaiian Operating Area off Oahu, destroyers *Dale* (DD 353) and *Hull* (DD 350) contact what they believe is a submarine. With all U.S. boats accounted for, Commander Destroyers Battle Force orders *Lamson* (DD 367) to join *Dale* and *Hull*. The ships are to maintain contact and to take offensive action only if attacked. *Mahan* (DD 364) joins in search as well. With speculation that the only possible reason a submarine would be in those waters would be to obtain supplies or land agents, *Lamson* accordingly searches the shoreline east of Diamond Head (see 4 February).

4 Tuesday

Fleet Landing Exercise (FLEX) No. 7 begins in Culebra-Vieques, Puerto Rico, area, with all available ships of the Atlantic Fleet and elements of the First Marine Division and the U.S. Army's First Division, to train "Army and Navy Forces in the amphibious operations incident to a Joint Overseas Expedition." Unlike FLEX No. 6 in 1940, bona fide transports are available for, and participate in, the maneuvers.

Search for submarine off Oahu, begun the previous day, continues. After destroyers *Dale* (DD 353) and *Hull* (DD 350) return to Pearl Harbor, destroyers *Flusser* (DD 368) and *Drayton* (DD 366) join *Lamson* (DD 367) in the hunt. Ultimately, however, the search is called off.

7 Friday

U.S. Naval Academy class of 1941 graduates four months early because of national emergency.

10 Monday

"S" operation: Japanese heavy cruisers *Suzuya, Mikuma, Mogami,* and *Kumano* call at Bangkok, Thailand (see 13 February).

13 Thursday

Light cruisers *Brooklyn* (CL 40), *Philadelphia* (CL 41), and *Savannah* (CL 42) and stores issue ship *Antares* (AKS 3) arrive at Midway in the Central Pacific with the remainder of the Third Defense Battalion (Lieutenant Colonel Robert H. Pepper, USMC).

"S" operation: Japanese heavy cruisers *Suzuya, Mikuma, Mogami,* and *Kumano* call at Saigon, French Indochina.

14 Friday

Fleet Landing Exercise No. 7, which had begun on 4 February in Culebra-Vieques, Puerto Rico, area, concludes.

15 Saturday

Naval Air Station, Kaneohe Bay, Oahu, T.H., is established.

19 Wednesday

Rear Admiral William H. P. Blandy relieves Rear Admiral William R. Furlong as Chief of the Bureau of Ordnance.

Coast Guard Reserve is established.

21 Friday

Carrier *Enterprise* (CV 6) arrives off Oahu and launches 30 USAAC P-36s that will be based at Wheeler Field.

24 Monday

Auxiliary *Bear* (AG 29) and Interior Department motorship *North Star* rendezvous off Adelaide Island to begin evacuation of U.S. Antarctic Service East Base. Heavy pack ice south of this area, however, prevents the ships from reaching their destination. The two vessels retire north to Dallman Bay. The time spent in the Mechior Archipelago, however, is not unfruitful, as *North Star's* people conduct surveys, make soundings, and make a geological study of the island group, in addition to collecting further examples of flora and fauna. *Bear,* meanwhile, gets under way soon thereafter to attempt passage through the pack ice to reach East Base. She is unsuccessful. Amid growing concern as to whether or not a full or partial evacuation can take place since mid-March and the shortening of the polar days is approaching, *North Star,* running short of supplies and fuel, is sent to Punta Arenas, Chile, to replenish and return if required (see 22 March).

MARCH

1 Saturday

ATLANTIC. Support Force Atlantic Fleet (Rear Admiral Arthur L. Bristol), composed of destroyers and patrol plane squadrons and supporting auxiliaries, is established for protection of convoys in North Atlantic.

EUROPE. Bulgaria joins the Axis as German troops occupy the country.

3 Monday

PACIFIC. Heavy cruisers *Chicago* (CA 29) (Rear Admiral John H. Newton, Commander Cruisers Scouting Force) and *Portland* (CA 33); light cruisers *Brooklyn* (CL 40) and *Savannah* (CL 42); destroyers *Clark* (DD 361), *Conyngham* (DD 371), *Cummings* (DD 365), *Cassin* (DD 372), *Case* (DD 370), *Shaw* (DD 373), *Tucker* (DD 374), *Reid* (DD 369), and *Downes* (DD 375); and oiler *Sangamon* (AO 28) depart Pearl Harbor for Samoa (see 9 March).

7 Friday

ATLANTIC. Carrier *Wasp* (CV 7) encounters foundering U.S. lumber schooner *George E. Klinck* in storm off Cape Hatteras, North Carolina, and rescues her crew.

PACIFIC. Transport *William P. Biddle* (AP 15), escorted by light cruiser *Concord* (CL 10), arrives at Pago Pago, Samoa, and disembarks the Seventh Defense Battalion, the first unit of the Fleet Marine Force deployed to the Southern Hemisphere in World War II.

9 Sunday

PACIFIC. Heavy cruisers *Chicago* (CA 29) (Rear Admiral John H. Newton, Commander Cruisers Scouting Force) and *Portland* (CA 33), light cruisers *Brooklyn* (CL 40) and *Savannah* (CL 42), nine destroyers, and oiler *Sangamon* (AO 28), that had departed Pearl Harbor on 3 March, arrive at Samoa (see 12 March).

10 Monday

PACIFIC. Japan steps in to mediate undeclared war between France and Thailand; France cedes territory to Thailand and gives Japan monopoly of Indochinese rice crop and right to airfield at Saigon.

Rear Admiral Edward J. Marquart is detached as Commander Minecraft Battle Force.

11 Tuesday

UNITED STATES. Congress passes Lend-Lease Act; "cash and carry" provisions of Neutrality Act of 1939 are changed to permit transfer of munitions to Allies. Although criticized by isolationists, the act proves to be the primary means by which the United States will provide Great Britain, the USSR, and other belligerents with war materiel, food, and financial aid without the United States entering combat.

12 Wednesday

PACIFIC. Heavy cruisers *Chicago* (CA 29) (Rear Admiral John H. Newton, Commander Cruisers Scouting Force) and *Portland* (CA 33), accompanied by destroyers *Clark* (DD 361), *Conyngham* (DD 371), *Cassin* (DD 372), *Downes* (DD 375), and *Reid* (DD 369), depart Samoan waters for Sydney, Australia (see 20 March).

Light cruisers *Brooklyn* (CL 40) and *Savannah* (CL 42) and destroyers *Case* (DD 370), *Shaw* (DD 373), *Cummings* (DD 365), and *Tucker* (DD 374) depart Samoa for Auckland, New Zealand (see 17 March).

Oiler *Sangamon* (AO 28), which had accompanied the aforementioned cruisers and destroyers from Pearl Harbor, sails to return to Hawaiian waters.

UNITED STATES. Naval Air Station, Corpus Christi, Texas, is established.

17 Monday

PACIFIC. TG 9.2 (Captain Ellis S. Stone), comprising light cruisers *Brooklyn* (CL 40) and *Savannah* (CL 42) and destroyers *Case* (DD 370), *Cummings* (DD 365), *Shaw* (DD 373), and *Tucker* (DD 374), arrive at Auckland, New Zealand, beginning a three-day goodwill visit (see 20 March).

ATLANTIC. Heavy cruiser *Vincennes* (CA 44) arrives at Pernambuco, Brazil, en route to her ultimate destination of Simonstown, South Africa (see 20 March).

Coast Guard cutter *Cayuga* departs Boston, Massachusetts, with South Greenland Survey Expedition, composed of State, Treasury, War, and Navy Department representatives, embarked. The expedition's mission is to locate sites for airfields, seaplane bases, and radio and meteorological stations and aids to navigation on Greenland's soil (see 31 March).

18 Tuesday

PACIFIC. Rear Admiral William R. Furlong breaks his flag as Commander Minecraft Battle Force.

19 Wednesday

PACIFIC. Destroyers *Aylwin* (DD 355) and *Farragut* (DD 348) are damaged by collision during night tactical exercises in Hawaiian Operating Area, 23°35'N, 158°14'W. One man dies on board *Aylwin*.

20 Thursday

PACIFIC. Heavy cruisers *Chicago* (CA 29) (Rear Admiral John H. Newton, Commander Cruisers Scouting Force) and *Portland* (CA 33) and

destroyers *Clark* (DD 361), *Conyngham* (DD 371), *Reid* (DD 369), *Cassin* (DD 372) and *Downes* (DD 375) arrive at Sydney, Australia, beginning a three-day goodwill visit (see 23 March).

TG 9.2 (Captain Ellis S. Stone), comprising light cruisers *Brooklyn* (CL 40) and *Savannah* (CL 42) and destroyers *Case* (DD 370), *Cummings* (DD 365), *Shaw* (DD 373), and *Tucker* (DD 374), concludes its port visit to Auckland, New Zealand, and sails for Tahiti (see 25 March).

ATLANTIC. Heavy cruiser *Vincennes* (CA 44) departs Pernambuco, Brazil, for Simonstown, South Africa (see 29 March).

22 Saturday

ANTARCTIC. Emergency evacuation of U.S. Antarctic Service East Base, Marguerite Bay, is carried out. Two R4C flights (Aviation Chief Machinist's Mate Ashley C. Snow and Radioman First Class Earl B. Perce, Naval Aviation Pilots) bring out the entire complement of 24 people to Mikkelsen Island, the emergency landing field 25 miles northeast of Adelaide Island, whence they embark in *Bear* (AG 29), which soon sails for Punta Arenas, Chile, to rendezvous with Interior Department motorship *North Star* (see 1 April).

23 Sunday

PACIFIC. Heavy cruisers *Chicago* (CA 29) (Rear Admiral John H. Newton, Commander Cruisers Scouting Force) and *Portland* (CA 33) and destroyers *Clark* (DD 361), *Conyngham* (DD 371), *Reid* (DD 369), *Cassin* (DD 372), and *Downes* (DD 375) depart Sydney, Australia, for Brisbane (see 25 March).

25 Tuesday

PACIFIC. Heavy cruisers *Chicago* (CA 29) (Rear Admiral John H. Newton, Commander Cruisers Scouting Force) and *Portland* (CA 33) and destroyers *Clark* (DD 361), *Conyngham* (DD 371), *Reid* (DD 369), *Cassin* (DD 372), and *Downes* (DD 375) arrive at Brisbane, Australia, beginning a three-day goodwill visit (see 28 March).

TG 9.2 (Captain Ellis S. Stone), comprising light cruisers *Brooklyn* (CL 40) and *Savannah* (CL 42) and destroyers *Case* (DD 370), *Cummings* (DD 365), *Shaw* (DD 373), and *Tucker* (DD 374), arrive at Tahiti. (see 27 March).

27 Thursday

ATLANTIC. U.S.-British-Canadian staff discussions in Washington, D.C., end; ABC-1 Staff

OFFICIAL PHOTOGRAPH
NOT TO BE RELEASED FOR PUBLICATION

CONVERSION (AVG 1) No. 1
(Ex MORMACMAIL)
LOOKING Q. STD STERN
N.N.S. + ODCO. DATE 4-1-41

Illustrating the transition from plowshare to sword, *Long Island* (AVG 1) (ex–Moore-McCormack Lines' freighter *Mormacmail*) undergoes conversion from freighter to aircraft escort vessel, Newport News, Virginia, 1 April 1941. Note flight deck under construction and temporary retention of neutrality markings (the prominent U.S. flag) on her side, as well as her original name and hailing port on the stern: "MORMACMAIL, NEW YORK, N.Y." (NHC, NH 96711)

Agreement embodies the basic strategic direction of the war in the event of U.S. entry, making the defeat of Germany a priority and establishing a Combined Chiefs of Staff. U.S. Atlantic Fleet is to help the Royal Navy convoy ships across the Atlantic. The agreement inextricably links the U.S. Navy in the effort against Germany.

PACIFIC. TG 9.2 (Captain Ellis S. Stone), comprising light cruisers *Brooklyn* (CL 40) and *Savannah* (CL 42) and destroyers *Case* (DD 370), *Cummings* (DD 365), *Shaw* (DD 373), and *Tucker* (DD 374), departs Tahiti for Pearl Harbor, ending its goodwill cruise.

28 Friday

MEDITERRANEAN. Battle of Cape Matapan begins as British Force B (Rear Admiral Henry D. Pridham-Wippell, RN) (four light cruisers and four destroyers) encounters Italian Fleet's 3d Division (three heavy cruisers and three destroyers). Italian forces break off action but the British force interposes itself between the 3rd Division and the fleet flagship, battleship *Vittorio Veneto,* with its three screening destroyers. FAA Swordfish and Albacores from carrier HMS *Formidable* and RAF Blenheims from

Crete damage *Vittorio Veneto* and heavy cruiser *Pola* (from Italian Fleet's 1st Division), stopping the latter. Furious night action ensues as British Force A (Admiral Sir Andrew B. Cunningham, RN), formed around three battleships, engages *Pola* and her sister ships *Zara* and *Fiume*, sinking the latter two cruisers as well as two destroyers. British destroyers HMS *Jervis* and HMS *Nubian* finish off *Pola*. Lieutenant Commander Steadman Teller, U.S. naval observer, witnesses the night action from the bridge of HMS *Formidable*.

PACIFIC. Heavy cruisers *Chicago* (CA 29) (Rear Admiral John H. Newton, Commander Cruisers Scouting Force) and *Portland* (CA 33) and destroyers *Clark* (DD 361), *Conyngham* (DD 371), *Reid* (DD 369), *Cassin* (DD 372), and *Downes* (DD 375) depart Brisbane, Australia, for Suva, Fiji Islands (see 1 April).

29 Saturday

ATLANTIC. Heavy cruiser *Vincennes* (CA 44) arrives at Simonstown, South Africa (see 30 March).

Coast Guard receives report that crew of Italian motor tanker *Villarperosa*, interned at Wilmington, North Carolina, is sabotaging

the ship. The Coast Guard investigates reports that the crews of Italian and German vessels in American ports had received orders to "sabotage and disable" them (see 30 March).

30 Sunday

ATLANTIC. Heavy cruiser *Vincennes* (CA 44) departs Simonstown, South Africa, for New York, with a cargo of gold for deposit in the United States (see 16 April).

UNITED STATES. As the result of Coast Guard investigation of report that crew of Italian motor tanker *Villarperosa* was sabotaging its ship, United States takes protective custody of two German, 26 Italian, and 35 Danish ships in American ports; Coast Guardsmen take over the vessels. Executive order consequently imprisons 850 Italian and 63 German officers and men.

PACIFIC. Element of the First Defense Battalion (5-inch artillery, Detachment "A") arrives at Palmyra Island in stores issue ship *Antares* (AKS 3) to begin construction of defenses.

Elements of the First Defense Battalion (5-inch artillery, Detachment "B," and Machine Gun Battery, Detachment "A") arrive at Johnston Island in high-speed minesweeper *Boggs* (DMS 3) to begin construction of defenses.

31 Monday

ATLANTIC. South Greenland Survey Expedition, in Coast Guard cutter Cayuga, arrives at Godthaab, Greenland.

APRIL

1 Tuesday

PACIFIC. Heavy cruisers *Chicago* (CA 29) (Rear Admiral John H. Newton, Commander Cruisers Scouting Force) and *Portland* (CA 33) and destroyers *Clark* (DD 361), *Conyngham* (DD 371), *Reid* (DD 369), *Cassin* (DD 372), and *Downes* (DD 375) arrive at Suva, Fiji Islands (see 3 April).

ANTARCTIC. Interior Department motorship *North Star* and auxiliary *Bear* (AG 29) of the U.S. Antarctic Service, depart Punta Arenas, Chile; the former will proceed back to the United States via the west coast of South America, the latter via the east coast (see 5 May and 18 May, respectively).

3 Thursday

PACIFIC. Heavy cruisers *Chicago* (CA 29) and Portland (CA 33) and destroyers *Clark* (DD 361), *Conyngham* (DD 371), *Reid* (DD 369),

Cassin (DD 372), and *Downes* (DD 375) depart Suva, Fiji Islands, for Pearl Harbor (see 10 April).

6 Sunday

EUROPE. German troops invade Yugoslavia and Greece; Italy declares war on Yugoslavia.

7 Monday

ATLANTIC. Naval Operating Base, Bermuda, is established, Captain Jules James in command.

9 Wednesday

ATLANTIC. Battleship *North Carolina* (BB 55) is commissioned at New York Navy Yard, the first new U.S. Navy battleship to enter the fleet since *West Virginia* (BB 48) was commissioned in 1923.

Secretary of State Cordell Hull and Danish Minister to the United States Henrik de Kauffman sign Agreement Relating to the Defense of Greenland.

10 Thursday

ATLANTIC. President Roosevelt, equating the defense of the United Kingdom to the defense of the United States, authorizes, under Lend-Lease, the transfer of 10 *Lake*-class Coast Guard cutters to the Royal Navy. Coast Guardsmen will train the British crews in the waters of Long Island Sound (see 30 April, and, 2, 12, 20, and 30 May).

PACIFIC. Heavy cruisers *Chicago* (CA 29) and *Portland* (CA 33) and destroyers *Clark* (DD 361), *Conyngham* (DD 371), *Reid* (DD 369), *Cassin* (DD 372), and *Downes* (DD 375) arrive at Pearl Harbor, thus winding up the Australia–New Zealand goodwill cruise.

11 Friday

UNITED STATES. President proclaims that the Red Sea and Gulf of Aden are no longer combat areas and are open to U.S. shipping.

ATLANTIC. Destroyer *Niblack* (DD 424), while rescuing survivors of Dutch freighter *Saleier* (torpedoed and sunk by German submarine *U 52* the day before at 58°04′N, 30°48′W, after the dispersal of convoy OB 306) depth charges what she believes to be a German U boat off Iceland. A thorough investigation by the German navy, however, will conclude that none of their submarines are in the vicinity at the time of *Niblack*'s attack. The U.S. Navy's conclusion is that *Niblack* depth charged a false contact.

Officers and men salute the colors during the commissioning of new battleship *North Carolina* (BB 55), New York Navy Yard, 9 April 1941. (NHC, NH 44719)

13 Sunday

GENERAL. Soviet-Japanese Non-Aggression Pact is signed.

15 Tuesday

UNITED STATES. President Roosevelt signs executive order allowing Navy, Marine Corps, and Army Air Corps individuals to sign contracts with the Central Aircraft Manufacturing Company (CAMCO) in China for one year, after which time the men can rejoin their respective services with no loss in rank. This is the first step toward forming the American Volunteer Group (AVG), which will become known as the "Flying Tigers." Over half of the pilots in the AVG will be from the Navy and Marine Corps.

16 Wednesday

ATLANTIC. Heavy cruiser *Vincennes* (CA 44) arrives at New York, having transported gold from Simonstown, South Africa.

17 Thursday

EUROPE. Yugoslavia capitulates to Axis.

ATLANTIC. Egyptian steamship *Zamzam* is shelled and sunk by German auxiliary cruiser *Atlantis* (*Schiffe* 16) in South Atlantic; 138 Americans (including 21 ambulance drivers)

are among rescued passengers. Even U.S. citizens traveling in ostensibly neutral ships find themselves at risk.[26]

21 Monday

ATLANTIC. Battleship *Arizona* (BB 39) and destroyer *Davis* (DD 395) collide while fueling during exercises in Hawaiian Operating Area.

22 Tuesday

UNITED STATES. Authorized enlisted strength of regular navy is increased to 232,000.

23 Wednesday

MEDITERRANEAN. Greece signs armistice with Germany.

24 Thursday

ATLANTIC. Neutrality Patrol is extended east to 26°W.

25 Friday

ATLANTIC. Coast Guard cutter *Ingham* relieves sister ship *Campbell* at Lisbon, Portugal.

26 Saturday

ATLANTIC. Neutrality Patrol is ordered extended southward to 20°S. Accordingly, carrier task group patrols are inaugurated this date when carrier *Wasp* (CV 7) (embarked squadrons: VF 72, VS 71, and VS 72) departs Hampton Roads, Virginia, with heavy cruiser *Quincy* (CA 39) and destroyers *Livermore* (DD 429) and *Kearny* (DD 432). TG 2, as the force is designated, will steam 5,292 miles before it arrives at Bermuda on 12 May.

27 Sunday

PACIFIC. American-Dutch-British Conference at Singapore ends, having reached agreement on combined operating plan of local defense forces in the event of war with Japan; Captain William R. Purnell, Chief of Staff to Admiral Thomas C. Hart, Commander in Chief Asiatic Fleet, is senior U.S. representative.

30 Wednesday

ATLANTIC. First four *Lake*-class Coast Guard cutters are turned over to the Royal Navy. *Pontchartrain* becomes HMS *Hartland*, *Tahoe* becomes HMS *Fishguard*, *Mendota* becomes HMS *Culver*, and *Itasca* becomes HMS *Gorleston* (see 2, 12, 20, and 30 May).

MAY

1 Thursday

UNITED STATES. Office of Public Relations is established as an independent office directly under the Secretary of the Navy, "to serve as liaison between the people and their Navy and, within the limits of military security, to keep the public informed of the activities of the Navy."

2 Friday

ATLANTIC. Admiral Ernest J. King breaks his flag as Commander in Chief Atlantic Fleet in heavy cruiser *Augusta* (CA 31) at Newport, Rhode Island.

Fifth *Lake*-class Coast Guard cutter, authorized for transfer on 10 April under Lend-Lease, is turned over to the Royal Navy. *Chelan* becomes HMS *Lulworth* (see 12, 20, and 30 May).

5 Monday

ATLANTIC. Interior Department motorship *North Star* (U.S. Antarctic Service) reaches Boston, Massachusetts, winding up her work in support of the 1939–1941 expedition to the South Polar Region.

6 Tuesday

CANAL ZONE. Carrier *Yorktown* (CV 5) suffers slight damage (a long dent and scraped paint) when the ship's prominent "knuckle" rubs one side of Miraflores Lock, during night transit of Panama Canal.

9 Friday

ATLANTIC. TG 1, comprising carrier *Ranger* (CV 4) (VF 41, VS 41, and VS 42), heavy cruiser *Vincennes* (CA 44), and destroyers *Sampson* (DD 394) and *Eberle* (DD 430), sets out from Bermuda to begin a 4,675-mile neutrality patrol that will conclude at Bermuda on 23 May.

German submarine *U 110* is damaged in action with British destroyers HMS *Bulldog* and HMS *Broadway* [ex-U.S. destroyer *Hunt* (DD 194)] and corvette HMS *Aubretia*. Boarding party from *Bulldog* recovers a veritable cryptanalysis windfall, including an intact ENIGMA machine and important current codes. *Broadway* is damaged in the encounter by collision with *U 110*, which sinks the following day. *U 110*'s commanding officer, *Kapitänleutnant* Fritz-Julius Lemp (who had been in command of *U 30* when she had sunk British passenger liner *Athenia* on 3 September 1939), is not among the survivors.

12 Monday

UNITED STATES. Ambassador Nomura Kichisaburo presents Secretary of State Cordell Hull with Japanese proposal for establishment of "just peace in the Pacific."

ATLANTIC. Three *Lake*-class Coast Guard cutters, authorized for transfer on 10 April under Lend-Lease, are turned over to the Royal Navy. *Champlain* becomes HMS *Sennen*, *Sebago* becomes HMS *Walney*, and *Cayuga* becomes HMS *Totland* (see 20 and 30 May).

14 Wednesday

PACIFIC. Pacific Fleet Exercise No. 1 commences off coast of California. The maneuvers involve a landing on San Clemente Island and a bombardment exercise in which heavy cruisers and destroyers bombard shore targets (see 18 June).

15 Thursday

PACIFIC. During paratroop training at Camp Kearney, California, Second Lieutenant Walter A. Osipoff, USMC, becomes fouled in static cable and ripcord lines and dangles 100 feet to the rear of the R2D from which he was to jump. Efforts to bring him into the plane are unsuccessful. Seeing his plight, Lieutenant William W. Lowrey and Aviation Chief Machinist's Mate John R. McCants, test pilots at-

tached to the Naval Air Station, San Diego, California, take off in an SOC and effect a daring midair rescue.

18 Sunday

ATLANTIC. Auxiliary *Bear* (AG 29) reaches Boston, Massachusetts, her work in support of the U.S. Antarctic Service's 1939–1941 expedition coming to a close.

20 Tuesday

MEDITERRANEAN. German airborne troops invade Crete.

ATLANTIC. TG 2 (Rear Admiral Robert C. Giffen), comprising carrier *Wasp* (CV 7) (VF 71, VS 72, and VMB 2), heavy cruiser *Quincy* (CA 39), and destroyers *Livermore* (DD 429) and *Kearny* (DD 432), departs Bermuda to conduct a 4,170-mile neutrality patrol that will conclude at Bermuda on 3 June.

Ninth *Lake*-class Coast Guard cutter, authorized for transfer on 10 April under Lend-Lease, is turned over to the Royal Navy. *Shoshone* becomes HMS *Languard* (see 30 May).

21 Wednesday

ATLANTIC. Unarmed U.S. freighter *Robin Moor*, en route to South Africa and Mozambique, is stopped and sunk by German submarine *U 69* (torpedo and gunfire) about 700 miles off the west coast of Africa, 06°10′N, 25°40′W. *Robin Moor*—her nationality prominently reflected in the U.S. flags painted on her sides—is the first American merchantman sunk by a U-boat in World War II. There are no casualties among her 38-man crew and eight passengers, and *U 69*'s commanding officer, *Kapitänleutnant* Jost Metzler, provides rations to the Americans (see 3, 8, and 20 June).

24 Saturday

UNITED STATES. Construction or acquisition of 550,000 tons of auxiliary shipping for the Navy is authorized.

ATLANTIC. Battle of Denmark Strait: British battle cruiser HMS *Hood* is sunk and battleship HMS *Prince of Wales* is damaged by German battleship *Bismarck* (which is damaged by a shell from the latter) and heavy cruiser *Prinz Eugen*. British Home Fleet elements at sea then pursue the German battleship; carrier HMS *Victorious* launches FAA Swordfish that in the prevailing poor visibility conditions almost attacks Coast Guard cutter *Modoc*, which is in the vicinity searching for survivors of ships sunk in convoy HX 126.[27] *Bismarck*, although damaged by an aerial torpedo, eludes her shadowers and disappears, while detaching her consort, *Prinz Eugen,* to conduct independent operations.[28]

PBYs (VP 52) operating from seaplane tender *Albemarle* (AV 5) at Argentia, Newfoundland, and braving foul weather and dangerous flying conditions, search for *Bismarck* in the western Atlantic.

25 Sunday

UNITED STATES. State Department informs German Chargé d'Affaires Hans Thomsen that an investigation into the incident concerning the tearing down of the Reich flag over the German consulate in San Francisco, California, on 18 January has yielded the fact that the individual involved was a U.S. Navy enlisted man who was tried and found guilty by court-martial for the offense, and was serving "an appropriate sentence."

26 Monday

ATLANTIC. Naval observer Ensign Leonard B. Smith, USNR, flying an RAF Catalina (Coastal Command No. 209 Squadron) sights *Bismarck.* British fleet units alter course accordingly and converge on the lone German capital ship. The same day, another naval observer, Lieutenant James E. Johnson, flying another RAF Catalina (Coastal Command No. 240 Squadron) maintains contact with the German battleship as well (see 27 May).

27 Tuesday

ATLANTIC. President Roosevelt issues proclamation that an unlimited national emergency confronts the United States, requiring that American military, naval, air, and civilian defenses be readied to repel any and all acts or threats of aggression directed toward any part of the Western Hemisphere. In a separate address to the nation to acquaint it with the "cold, hard fact" that the conflict in Europe has developed into a "world war for world-domination," the President announces that the Atlantic Neutrality Patrol has been extended and that the Atlantic Fleet, greatly increased during the past year, is being constantly built up. He also mentions the dangers posed by "Nazi battleships of great striking-power" that pose "an actual military danger to the Americas," undoubtedly a reference to the recent operations of German battleship *Bismarck.* The President states the national policy is two-fold: active resistance "to every attempt by Hitler to extend his Nazi domination to the Western Hemisphere, or to threaten it" and his every attempt to gain control of the seas, and giving "every possible assistance to Britain and to all who, with Britain, are resisting Hitlerism or its equivalent with force of arms." The delivery of supplies to Britain, Roosevelt tells the nation, "is imperative. This can be done; it must be done; it will be done."

German battleship *Bismarck* is overwhelmed and sunk by British naval force, 300 nautical miles west of Ushant, France, 48°10′N, 16°12′W.

29 Thursday

ATLANTIC. In the event that Germany invades Spain and Portugal, the Joint Board (the oldest interservice agency, established in 1903 to facilitate Army-Navy planning) approves a plan for an occupation of the Portuguese Azores Islands; the joint Marine Corps–Army effort is to be headed by Major General Holland M. Smith, USMC (Commanding General First Marine Division).

TG 3, comprising carrier *Ranger* (CV 4) (VB 5, VF 5, and VS 5), heavy cruiser *Tuscaloosa* (CA 37), and destroyers *McDougal* (DD 358) and *Eberle* (DD 430), departs Bermuda for a 4,355-mile neutrality patrol that will conclude there on 8 June.

30 Friday

ATLANTIC. Last *Lake*-class Coast Guard cutter, authorized for transfer on 10 April under Lend-Lease, is transferred to the Royal Navy. *Itasca* becomes HMS *Gorleston.*

31 Saturday

ATLANTIC. TG 1 (Rear Admiral Arthur B. Cook), comprising *Yorktown* (CV 5) (VF 41, VS 41, VS 42, and VT 5), heavy cruiser *Vincennes* (CA 44), and destroyers *Sampson* (DD 394) and *Gwin* (DD 433), departs Bermuda for 4,550-mile neutrality patrol that will conclude at Hampton Roads, Virginia, on 12 June.

JUNE

1 Sunday

ATLANTIC. South Greenland Patrol (Commander Harold G. Belford, USCG) is established to operate from Cape Brewster to Cape Farewell to Upernivik; Coast Guard cutters *Modoc, Comanche,* and *Raritan,* together with unclassified auxiliary vessel *Bowdoin* (IX 50), make up the force.

MEDITERRANEAN. Crete capitulates to the Germans.

2 Monday

ATLANTIC. Rear Admiral Edward J. Marquart becomes Commandant New York Navy Yard.

Aircraft escort vessel *Long Island* (AVG 1) is commissioned at Newport News, Virginia. Converted from Maritime Commission C-3 type freighter *Mormacmail* in just 67 working days, *Long Island* is the first of a type of what come to be classified as "escort carriers" that will prove invaluable in the prosecution of the war in both Atlantic and Pacific theaters.

3 Tuesday

ATLANTIC. Cape Town, South Africa–bound British ship rescues 35 survivors of U.S. freighter *Robin Moor,* sunk by German submarine *U 69* on 21 May (see 8 June).

6 Friday

UNITED STATES. Bill is signed authorizing the government to requisition foreign merchant ships lying idle in U.S. ports.

PACIFIC. Naval Air Station, Balboa, Canal Zone, Panama, is established.

8 Sunday

ATLANTIC. Brazilian freighter *Osorio* rescues 11 survivors of U.S. freighter *Robin Moor,* sunk by German submarine *U 69* on 21 May.

9 Monday

ATLANTIC. Intelligence sources having indicated that Germany has no plans for invading Spain and Portugal, President Roosevelt suspends planning for the joint occupation of the Azores.

12 Thursday

UNITED STATES. All members of the U.S. Naval Reserve, not in a deferred status, are called to active duty.

14 Saturday

ATLANTIC. Central North Atlantic patrols commence with battleship/destroyer task groups; *Texas* (BB 35) and accompanying destroyers inaugurate these patrols (see 20 June).

15 Sunday

PACIFIC. Japanese land attack planes, bombing Chungking, China, drop their ordnance near river gunboat *Tutuila* (PR 4), U.S. military attaché's office, and U.S. Navy canteen. Japanese Admiral Shimada Shigetaro expresses regret over the incident and assures U.S. representatives that the bombing is "wholly unintentional." U.S. military and naval attachés privately concur, however, that the bombing "was either criminal carelessness or [with] deliberate intent to bomb Embassy and gunboat."

Naval Air Station, Kodiak, Alaska, is established.

ATLANTIC. TF 3 (Rear Admiral Jonas H. Ingram) begins patrol operations from Brazilian ports of Recife and Bahia; the force consists of four *Omaha* (CL 4)–class light cruisers and five destroyers.

16 Monday

UNITED STATES. State Department requests that the German government "remove from United States territory all German nationals in anywise connected with the German Library of Information in New York, the German Railway and Tourist Agencies, and the Trans-Ocean News Service," and that those agencies and their affiliates "shall be promptly closed." In addition, all German consular officers, agents, clerks, and employees thereof of German nationality shall be removed from American territory and that the consular establishments be promptly closed. The German government is given until 10 July to comply. This move is made because of suspicion that the agencies aforementioned "have been engaged in activities . . . of an improper and unwarranted character" and "wholly outside the scope of their legitimate duties."

ATLANTIC. Rear Admiral Joseph K. Taussig is detached as Commandant Fifth Naval District and Commander Naval Operating Base, Norfolk, Virginia.

18 Wednesday

PACIFIC. Pacific Fleet Exercise No. 1, which commenced off coast of California on 14 May, concludes.

19 Thursday

EUROPE / MEDITERRANEAN. Germany and Italy request closure of U.S. consulates.

20 Friday

ATLANTIC. President Roosevelt addresses message to Congress concerning the German sinking of U.S. freighter *Robin Moor* on 21 May. The President notes that *Robin Moor*'s destruction is a "warning that the United States may use the high seas of the world only with Nazi consent. Were we to yield on this we would inevitably submit to world-domination at the hands of the present leaders of the German Reich. We are not yielding," the President declares, "and we do not propose to yield." Un-

dersecretary of State Sumner Welles sends this message to the German Embassy for the information of the German government (see 24 June, 19 and 26 September, and 3 November).

Battleship *Texas* (BB 35) and destroyers *Mayrant* (DD 402), *Rhind* (DD 404), and *Trippe* (DD 403) are sighted by German submarine *U 203* within what the German navy regards as the war, or "blockade," zone in the Atlantic. The American force, however, unaware of the U-boat, outdistances the submarine and frustrates its attempted attack. In the wake of this incident, the commander in chief of the German navy (*Grössadmiral* Erich Raeder) orders that American warships can only be attacked if they cross the western boundary of the blockade area by 20 or more miles, or within the 20-mile strip along the western edge of the blockade zone.

TG 2.6, comprising carrier *Wasp* (CV 7) (VF 71, VS 72, and VMB 1), heavy cruiser *Tuscaloosa* (CA 37), and destroyers *Anderson* (DD 411) and *Rowan* (DD 405), departs Hampton Roads, Virginia, for a 4,320-mile neutrality patrol that will conclude at Bermuda on 4 July.

Submarines *O 6* (SS 67), *O 9* (SS 70), and *O 10* (SS 71) conduct deep submergence trials out of Portsmouth, New Hampshire; while *O 6* and *O 10* conduct their test dives without incident, *O 9*, the last boat to make hers, accidentally sinks (cause unknown) off the Isles of Shoals, southeast of Portsmouth, 42°59′48″N, 70°20′27″W. She is lost with all hands (33 men) (see 22 June).

21 Saturday

UNITED STATES. State Department requests closing of all Italian consulates in U.S. territory; the "continued functioning of Italian consular establishments in territory of the United States," Undersecretary of State Sumner Welles informs Italian Ambassador Don Ascanio dei principi Colonna, "would serve no desirable purpose." The Italian government is informed that such withdrawals and closures be effected before 15 July.

22 Sunday

EUROPE. Germany, Italy, and Romania declare war on the Soviet Union and invade along a front from the Arctic to the Black Sea.

ATLANTIC. After all hope of finding any survivors from the sunken submarine *O 9* (SS 70) is lost and with continued diving operations in the vicinity deemed hazardous, Secretary of the Navy William Franklin (Frank) Knox personally conducts memorial ceremony, held on

board submarine *Triton* (SS 201), over last known location of the lost boat.

24 Tuesday

UNITED STATES. German Chargé d'Affaires Hans Thomsen replies to Undersecretary of State Sumner Welles's 20 June note concerning the *Robin Moor* sinking. "I have the honor to advise you," Thomsen writes, "that I do not find myself in a position to pass on . . . the text of a message to Congress from the President of the United States for the information of my government" (see 19 and 26 September and 3 November).

25 Wednesday

EUROPE. Finland declares war on the Soviet Union.

ATLANTIC. TG 2.7, comprising light cruisers *Philadelphia* (CL 41) and *Savannah* (CL 42) and destroyers *Lang* (DD 399) and *Wilson* (DD 408), departs Hampton Roads, Virginia, for a 4,762-mile neutrality patrol that will conclude on 8 July at Bermuda.

27 Friday

EUROPE. Hungary declares war on the Soviet Union.

ATLANTIC. During German submarine attacks on convoy HX 133, Dutch steamship *Maasdam* is torpedoed and sunk by U 564 approximately 300 miles south of Iceland; among the survivors are marines under Major Walter L. Jordan, USMC, the advance detail for the Marine Detachment at the American Embassy in London.

28 Saturday

EUROPE. Albania declares war on the Soviet Union.

UNITED STATES. President Roosevelt issues executive order creating the Office of Scientific Research and Development (Dr. Vannevar Bush, chairman) that will replace the National Defense Research Committee. The new office will coordinate and supplement scientific research relating to the defense effort.

ATLANTIC. Destroyer *Madison* (DD 425) is damaged when she runs aground on the southeast tip of Moratties Shoal, Placentia Harbor, Argentia, Newfoundland.

29 Sunday

ATLANTIC. TG 2.8, comprising carrier *Yorktown* (CV 5) (VF 42, VS 42, VMO 1, and half of VMS 1), heavy cruisers *Quincy* (CA 39) and

Vincennes (CA 44), and destroyers *Wainwright* (DD 419), *Hammann* (DD 412), Mustin (DD 413), and *Stack* (DD 406), departs Hampton Roads, Virginia, for neutrality patrol. *Yorktown,* accompanied by *Wainwright* and *Stack,* departs the patrol on 10 July, returning to Hampton Roads on the 12th; *Quincy, Vincennes, Hammann,* and *Mustin* continue the cruise, putting in to Bermuda on 15 July.

30 Monday

UNITED STATES. Naval vessels on hand (all types)—1,899. Personnel: Navy—284,427; Marine Corps—54,359; Coast Guard—19,235. Total personnel—358,021.

EUROPE. Vichy France severs relations with the Soviet Union.

JULY

1 Tuesday

UNITED STATES. Naval Coastal Frontiers are established: North Atlantic, Southern, Caribbean, Panama, Pacific Southern, Pacific Northern, Hawaiian, and Philippine. Their commanders are responsible for the direction of local patrol, convoy escort, and antisubmarine warfare operations. Mobilization of all organized, fleet, and local defense divisions of the Naval Reserve is completed on this date.

ATLANTIC. Task forces are organized by Commander in Chief Atlantic Fleet (Admiral Ernest J. King) to support defense of Iceland and to escort convoys between the United States and Iceland: TF 1 (Rear Admiral David M. LeBreton) based at Narragansett Bay and Boston; TF 2 (Rear Admiral Arthur B. Cook) based at Bermuda and Hampton Roads, Virginia; TF 3 (Rear Admiral Jonas H. Ingram) based at San Juan, Puerto Rico, and Guantánamo; TF 4 (Rear Admiral Arthur L. Bristol) based at Narragansett Bay; TF 5 (Rear Admiral Richard S. Edwards), TF 6 and TF 8 (Rear Admiral Edward D. McWhorter), and TF 7 (Rear Admiral Ferdinand L. Reichmuth) based at Bermuda; TF 9 (Rear Admiral Randall Jacobs); and TF 10 (Major General Holland M. Smith, USMC).

Patrol Wing 7 (the redesignated Patrol Wing Support Force) (Captain Harold M. Mullinix) (TG 4.2) is established at Argentia, Newfoundland, for operations in North Atlantic.

Northeast Greenland Patrol (Commander Edward H. "Iceberg" Smith, USCG) (TG 6.5) is organized at Boston, Massachusetts, by the

Destroyer *Anderson* (DD 411), as seen from carrier *Wasp* (CV 7), 29 June 1941, still wears a peacetime navy gray paint scheme; prominent white/black-shadow hull numbers, as well as the ship's name, however, were painted out during her recent passage through the Panama Canal. (NA, 80-CF-2156-1)

Coast Guard; it consists of cutters *Northland* and *North Star,* and auxiliary Bear (AG 29).

2 Wednesday

PACIFIC. Japan recalls its merchant ships from Atlantic Ocean and calls up more than one million army conscripts.

4 Friday

ATLANTIC. PBYs (VP 72) begin operations based in seaplane tender (destroyer) *Goldsborough* (AVD 5), out of Reykjavik, Iceland, covering the movement of marines to Iceland (see 17 July).

5 Saturday

ATLANTIC. Destroyer *Charles F. Hughes* (DD 428) rescues 14 survivors (including four American Red Cross nurses) from the sunken Norwegian steamship *Vigrid,* which had been torpedoed while straggling from convoy HX 133 by German submarine *U 371* on 24 June, at 58°58′N, 36°35′W.[29]

6 Sunday

ATLANTIC. Transport *Munargo* (AP 20) and U.S. Army transport *Chateau Thierry* arrive at Tunugdliarfik Fjord, Greenland, to disembark

men and unload equipment to establish an air base there.

7 Monday

ATLANTIC. President Roosevelt announces to Congress that an executive agreement has been made with Iceland for U.S. troops to occupy that country; the Navy is ordered to take all steps necessary to maintain communications between the United States and Iceland. TF 19 (Rear Admiral David M. LeBreton) lands First Marine Brigade (Provisional) (Brigadier General John Marston, USMC) at Reykjavik, the Icelandic capital. The replacement of the British garrison frees those troops for combat duty elsewhere.

First Marine Aircraft Wing (Lieutenant Colonel Louis E. Woods, USMC) is established at Quantico, Virginia.

8 Tuesday

ATLANTIC. Patrol Wing 8 (Commander John D. Price) is established at Norfolk, Virginia.

10 Thursday

PACIFIC. Second Marine Aircraft Wing (Brigadier General Ross E. Rowell, USMC) is established at San Diego, California.

12 Saturday

UNITED STATES. Office of the Coordinator of Research and Development is established to unify the Navy's research activities and to evaluate the best ways of advising tactical officers of air, ground, and sea forces of the "latest applications of science to the problems of modern warfare."

ATLANTIC. Naval Air Station, Quonset Point, Rhode Island, is established.

15 Tuesday

ATLANTIC. Naval Air Station and Naval Operating Base, Argentia, Newfoundland, are established.

16 Wednesday

ATLANTIC. Transport *West Point* (AP 23) (former U.S. passenger liner *America*) sails from New York City with German and Italian consular officials and their families, bound for Lisbon, Portugal. British government has granted *West Point* safe-conduct for the voyage (see 24 and 26 July and 1 August).

TG 2.7, comprising light cruisers *Philadelphia* (CL 41) and *Savannah* (CL 42) and destroyers *Meredith* (DD 434) and *Gwin* (DD 433), departs Bermuda for 3,415-mile neutrality patrol that will conclude there on 25 July.

17 Thursday

ATLANTIC. VP 72 concludes its operations out of Reykjavik, Iceland, from seaplane tender (destroyer) *Goldsborough* (AVD 5).

18 Friday

PACIFIC. Prime Minister Prince Konoye Fumimaro forms new Japanese cabinet; Vice Admiral Toyoda Teijiro succeeds Matsuoka Yosuke as Minister of Foreign Affairs.

24 Thursday

ATLANTIC. Transport *West Point* (AP 23) disembarks German and Italian consular officials and their families at Lisbon, Portugal (see 26 July and 1 August).

PACIFIC. Japanese forces occupy northern French Indochina (see 26 July).

26 Saturday

PACIFIC. In response to the Japanese occupation of northern French Indochina on 24 July, President Roosevelt freezes Japanese and Chinese assets in the United States and cuts off the export of oil to Japan.

U.S. Army Forces Far East (Lieutenant General Douglas MacArthur) is organized; Philippine military forces are called into service with U.S. Army.

ATLANTIC. Transport *West Point* (AP 23), at Lisbon, Portugal, embarks American and Chinese consular staffs from Germany, German-occupied countries, and Italy, and sails for the United States. In addition, *West Point* embarks the 21 American ambulance drivers who had been passengers on board the Egyptian steamship *Zamzam* when she had been sunk by German auxiliary cruiser *Atlantis* on 17 April (see 1 August).

28 Monday

PACIFIC. Japan freezes U.S. assets.

29 Tuesday

PACIFIC. Japanese occupy southern French Indochina with French permission.

30 Wednesday

ATLANTIC. TG 2.5, comprising carrier *Yorktown* (CV 5) (VF 42, VS 41, and VT 5), light cruiser *Brooklyn* (CL 40), and destroyers *Roe* (DD 418), *Grayson* (DD 435), and *Eberle* (DD 430), departs Hampton Roads, Virginia, for 3,998-mile neutrality patrol that will conclude at Bermuda on 10 August.

PACIFIC. During Japanese bombing raid on Chungking, China, one bomb falls eight yards astern of river gunboat *Tutuila* (PR 4). While the bomb causes no damage to the ship, *Tutuila*'s motor boats are badly damaged and the motor sampan cut loose from its moorings. There are no casualties (see 31 July).

31 Thursday

UNITED STATES. Economic Defense Board is created.

PACIFIC. Japanese government assures U.S. government that the previous day's bombing of river gunboat *Tutuila* (PR 4) at Chungking, China, is "an accident 'pure and simple.'"

AUGUST

1 Friday

PACIFIC. Naval Air Station, Midway Island, is established.

ATLANTIC. Naval Operating Base, Trinidad, is established.

Transport *West Point* (AP 23) arrives at New York with American and Chinese passengers.

3 Sunday

ATLANTIC. President Roosevelt departs Washington, D.C., by train for Submarine Base, New London, Connecticut, where he arrives later the same day, boarding presidential yacht *Potomac* (AG 25) that evening. Accompanied by auxiliary *Calypso* (AG 35), *Potomac* sails for Point Judith, Rhode Island, where the ship anchors for the night.

4 Monday

ATLANTIC. New River, North Carolina, maneuvers begin with the First Marine Division and the First Infantry Division, U.S. Army, engaging in amphibious exercises. Aircraft escort vessel *Long Island* (AVG 1) participates and provides close air support in a test of that type of ship in that role.

Presidential yacht *Potomac* (AG 25), accompanied by *Calypso* (AG 35), proceeds to South Dartmouth, Massachusetts, where she embarks Her Royal Highness Crown Princess Martha of Norway and her party. After a day of fishing ("with some luck") President Roosevelt personally takes the helm of a Chris-Craft motorboat and transports his guests back to the place whence they came. That night, *Potomac*, again accompanied by *Calypso*, shifts to Menemsha Bight, Vineyard Sound, Massachusetts, where they join heavy cruisers *Augusta* (CA 31) and *Tuscaloosa* (CA 37) and five destroyers.

5 Tuesday

ATLANTIC. President Roosevelt transfers from presidential yacht *Potomac* (AG 25) to heavy cruiser *Augusta* (CA 31); soon thereafter, *Augusta* and *Tuscaloosa* (CA 37) and five destroyers sail for Argentia, Newfoundland. The President's flag, however, remains in *Potomac* and she, in company with *Calypso* (AG 35), will proceed via Cape Cod Canal to New England waters, maintaining a fiction of presidential presence (see 7 August). A suitably attired Secret Service agent impersonates the president.

PACIFIC. Heavy cruisers *Northampton* (CA 26) and *Salt Lake City* (CA 25) arrive at Brisbane, Australia, for a goodwill visit.

6 Wednesday

ATLANTIC. TF 16 (Rear Admiral William R. Monroe), formed around carrier *Wasp* (CV 7), battleship *Mississippi* (BB 41), heavy cruisers *Quincy* (CA 39) and *Wichita* (CA 45), and five destroyers, delivers U.S. Army troops, transported in transport *American Legion* (AP 35), stores ship *Mizar* (AF 12), and cargo ship *Al-maack* (AK 27), to Reykjavik, Iceland. Carrier *Wasp* flies off USAAF P-40s and PT-13s (33rd Pursuit Squadron) to Iceland to provide cover for the soldiers' arrival.

PACIFIC. Executive order transfers Coast Guard's Honolulu District from the Treasury Department to the Navy in the first step toward shifting the Coast Guard to naval control (see 11 September and 1 November).

7 Thursday

ATLANTIC. President Roosevelt arrives at Placentia Bay, Newfoundland, in heavy cruiser *Augusta* (CA 31); this day he fishes from the flagship's forecastle and inspects base development at Argentia (see 9 August).

8 Friday

PACIFIC. Japanese Ambassador Nomura Kichasaburo suggests conference between President Roosevelt and Japanese Prime Minister Prince Konoye Fumimaro.

9 Saturday

ATLANTIC. Atlantic Charter Conference begins: British battleship HMS *Prince of Wales*, with British Prime Minister Winston S. Churchill embarked, arrives at Placentia Bay, Newfoundland, escorted by destroyer HMS *Ripley* [ex-U.S. destroyer *Shubrick* (DD 268)] and Canadian destroyers HMCS *Restigouche* and *Assiniboine*. In this first meeting between the two men, Churchill calls upon President Roosevelt on board heavy cruiser *Augusta* (CA 31); the two confer over luncheon and dinner before the Prime Minister returns to *Prince of Wales*.

10 Sunday

ATLANTIC. Atlantic Charter Conference continues: President Roosevelt, transported in destroyer *McDougal* (DD 358), attends divine services on board British battleship HMS *Prince of Wales* as guest of Prime Minister Winston S. Churchill, Placentia Bay, Newfoundland. About 250 U.S. sailors and marines attend the service as well; hymns "O God, Our Help in Ages Past," "Onward, Christian Soldiers," and "Eternal Father, Strong to Save" (the Navy hymn) are sung by all hands.[30] After inspecting the topsides of the British battleship, the President returns in *McDougal* to heavy cruiser *Augusta* (CA 31); that night, the Chief Executive hosts the Prime Minister at dinner.

Marines wearing World War I–pattern M-1917A1 steel helmets splash through the North Carolina surf after disembarking from spoon-bowed Higgins landing boat from transport *Barnett* (AP 11) during the New River maneuvers, August 1941. Leatherneck at left carries a Hawley helmet in addition to his bedroll. (NA, USMC 504329)

11 Monday

ATLANTIC. Atlantic Charter Conference continues: President Roosevelt and British Prime Minister Winston S. Churchill confer twice on board heavy cruiser *Augusta* (CA 31).

12 Tuesday

ATLANTIC. Atlantic Charter Conference concludes as President Roosevelt confers with British Prime Minister Winston S. Churchill on board heavy cruiser *Augusta* (CA 31). Discussions have concerned British needs for support, joint strategy, and the political character of the postwar world. The Atlantic Charter, the joint declaration that results from the meetings, outlines goals in the war against Germany and emphasizes the principles of freedom, self-determination, peace, and cooperation. Roosevelt privately reassures Churchill that when the United States enters the war, it would accord the defeat of Germany first priority. He also pledges that U.S. warships would escort British merchant ships between the United States and Iceland. After the last meeting, Prime Minister Churchill embarks in battleship HMS *Prince of Wales* and departs Placentia Bay, Newfoundland. Soon thereafter, *Augusta*, accompanied by the same ships that had steamed with her to Newfoundland, sails for Blue Hill Bay, Maine, to rendezvous with presidential yacht *Potomac* (AG 25) and auxiliary *Calypso* (AG 35).

Maneuvers at New River, North Carolina, conclude.

13 Wednesday

PACIFIC. Heavy cruisers *Northampton* (CA 26) and *Salt Lake City* (CA 25), arrive at Port Moresby, Papua, Australian Territory of New Guinea, for a goodwill visit.

14 Thursday

ATLANTIC. President Roosevelt, on board heavy cruiser *Augusta* (CA 31), returning from the Atlantic Charter Conference, witnesses exhibition of flight operations by aircraft escort vessel *Long Island* (AVG 1) off Cape Sable, Nova Scotia. Roosevelt had been instrumental in championing conversion of merchant vessels to auxiliary aircraft carriers. *Long Island's* embarked scouting squadron (VS 201) is equipped with F2As and SOCs. That afternoon, *Augusta* reaches Blue Hill Bay, Maine, where the Chief Executive reembarks in presidential yacht *Potomac* (AG 25).

Submarine chaser *PC 457* is accidentally sunk in collision with U.S. freighter *Norluna* off Puerto Rico.

PACIFIC. During Japanese bombing raid on Chungking, China, Japanese planes approach the city from the east, passing directly over the U.S. Embassy chancery and the river gunboat *Tutuila* (PR 4). There is no repetition of the incident of 30 July.

15 Friday

PACIFIC. Naval Air Station, Palmyra Island, and Naval Air Facility, Johnston Island, are established.

ATLANTIC. TG 2.5, comprising carrier *Yorktown* (CV 5) (VF 42, VS 41, and VT 5), light

President Roosevelt bids farewell to Prime Minister Churchill after their final meeting on board heavy cruiser *Augusta* (CA 31), Argentia, Newfoundland, 12 August 1941. Roosevelt's sons, Franklin Jr. and Elliott, flank their father. (Author's Collection)

cruiser *Brooklyn* (CL 40), and destroyers *Roe* (DD 418), *Grayson* (DD 435), and *Eberle* (DD 430), departs Bermuda to begin 4,064-mile neutrality patrol that will conclude at Bermuda on 27 August.

President Roosevelt fishes (with "indifferent luck") off Deer Island from presidential yacht *Potomac* (AG 25); the ship anchors in Pulpit Harbor, Penobscot Bay, Maine, for the night.

16 Saturday

ATLANTIC. Presidential yacht *Potomac* (AG 25) reaches Rockland, Maine, and disembarks President Roosevelt and his party. The Chief Executive returns by train to Washington, D.C., the following morning.

PACIFIC. Heavy cruisers *Northampton* (CA 26) and *Salt Lake City* (CA 25) arrive at Rabaul, New Britain, British New Guinea, for a goodwill visit.

17 Sunday

UNITED STATES. President Roosevelt and Secretary of State Cordell Hull confer with Japanese Ambassador Nomura Kichasaburo and state conditions for resuming conversations or arranging a Pacific conference.

ATLANTIC. Panamanian (ex-Danish) freighter *Sessa* is torpedoed and sunk about 300 miles southwest of Iceland, 61°26′N, 30°50′W (see 6 September).[31]

18 Monday

UNITED STATES. President Roosevelt announces that the United States is ferrying combat aircraft to the British in the Near East via Brazil and Africa.

19 Tuesday

PACIFIC. Wake Detachment, First Defense Battalion, Fleet Marine Force (Major Lewis A. Hohn, USMC) arrives at Wake Island in cargo ship *Regulus* (AK 14) to begin work on defense installations.

22 Friday

ATLANTIC. Destroyer *Hughes* (DD 410) is damaged when accidentally rammed by British freighter *Chulmleigh* at Reykjavik, Iceland.

25 Monday

GENERAL. British and Soviet forces invade Iran from the south and north, respectively.

ATLANTIC. TG 2.6 (Rear Admiral H. Kent Hewitt), comprising *Wasp* (CV 7), light cruiser *Savannah* (CL 42), and destroyers *Meredith* (DD 434) and *Gwin* (DD 433), departs Hampton Roads, Virginia, on a neutrality patrol that will conclude at Bermuda on 10 September.

26 Tuesday

UNITED STATES. Ship Warrants Act is invoked by executive order, empowering President Roosevelt to direct Maritime Commission to establish cargo handling, ship repair, and maintenance priorities for merchant ships.

27 Wednesday

PACIFIC. Japan protests shipment of U.S. goods to Vladivostok, Soviet Far East, through Japanese waters.

ATLANTIC. German submarine *U 570*, attacked by an RAF Hudson (No. 269 Squadron), is captured intact by British surface force in the North Atlantic.[32]

28 Thursday

GENERAL. Supply, Priorities, and Allocations Board is established.

Hostilities in Iran cease.

ATLANTIC. TG 2.7, comprising aircraft escort vessel *Long Island* (AVG 1), light cruiser *Nashville* (CL 43), and destroyers *Livermore* (DD 429) and *Kearny* (DD 432), departs Bermuda. It will conclude the patrol—the first involving the prototype "escort carrier"—at Bermuda on 9 September.

SEPTEMBER

1 Monday

ATLANTIC. Navy assumes responsibility for transatlantic convoys from point off Argentia, Newfoundland, to meridian of Iceland. Commander in Chief Atlantic Fleet (Admiral Ernest J. King) designates Denmark Strait Patrol to operate between Iceland and Greenland.

PACIFIC. U.S. Consul General in Shanghai, China (Clarence Gauss), Commander Yangtze Patrol (Rear Admiral William A. Glassford Jr.), and Commanding Officer Fourth Marine Regiment (Colonel Samuel L. Howard, USMC) recommend that all naval forces in China (river gunboats and marines) be withdrawn.

4 Thursday

ATLANTIC. Destroyer *Greer* (DD 145), while tracking German submarine *U 652*, 175 miles southwest of Iceland, is attacked but not damaged. Soon thereafter, *Greer* damages the U-boat with depth charges (see 11 September).

6 Saturday

ATLANTIC. Destroyer *Lansdale* (DD 426) rescues only three survivors from Panamanian freighter *Sessa*, sunk on 17 August; 24 crewmen (one of whom is an American) perish.

7 Sunday

GULF OF SUEZ. Unarmed U.S. freighter *Steel Seafarer* (carrying cargo earmarked for the British Army in Egypt) is bombed and sunk by German plane (identified as a JU 88) off the

Grumman F4F-3s from VF 41, Beaumont, Texas, during Army GHQ maneuvers, September 1941. Color scheme is overall light gray with low-contrast white markings (plane in foreground is 41-F-3); white crosses are temporary markings applied to planes assigned to one of the "warring" forces. (Author's Collection)

Shadwan Islands; her 36-man crew is rescued unharmed.

9   Tuesday

UNITED STATES. Naval Coastal Frontier Forces are formed.

11   Thursday

ATLANTIC. President Roosevelt, in the wake of the *Greer–U 652* incident, announces order to Navy ("Shoot on Sight") to attack any vessel threatening U.S. shipping or ships under American escort. Roosevelt declares that if German or Italian vessels of war enter American-protected waters, they "do so at their own risk."

German submarines attack convoy SC 42; unarmed Panamanian freighter *Montana* is torpedoed and sunk by *U 105* at 63°40'N, 35°50'W.

UNITED STATES. Executive order provides that such additional Coast Guard vessels, units, or people should be transferred to the Navy as should be agreed upon between the Commandant of the Coast Guard and the Chief of Naval Operations (see 6 August and 1 November).

GULF OF SUEZ. Unarmed U.S. freighter *Arkansan* is damaged by antiaircraft shell fragments during heavy air raid on Port Suez; there are no reported casualties among the 38-man crew.

12   Friday

ATLANTIC. Coast Guard cutter *Northland*, assisted by cutter *North Star*, seizes Norwegian trawler *Buskoe* in MacKenzie Bay, Greenland, thwarting *Buskoe*'s mission of establishing and servicing German radio weather stations in that region. This is the first capture of a belligerent ship by U.S. naval forces in World War II.

14   Sunday

UNITED STATES. Army General Headquarters (GHQ) maneuvers commence in Louisiana. Army's neglect of aviation support for its ground troops during the interwar period compels it to ask the Navy to provide planes to take part. Five Navy (VB 2, VF 41, VF 72, VS 5, and VS 42) and four Marine Corps (VMF 111, VMO 151, VMSB 131, and VMSB 132) squadrons take part in the large-scale war games.

ATLANTIC. As TF 15 proceeds toward Iceland, destroyer *Truxtun* (DD 229) reports submarine emerging from the fog 300 yards away, but low visibility and uncertainty as to the position of *MacLeish* (DD 220), also in the screen of TF 15, prevents *Truxtun* from opening fire. After the submarine submerges, *Truxtun*, *MacLeish*, and *Sampson* (DD 394) make depth charge attacks with no verifiable result.

18   Thursday

ATLANTIC. U.S. Navy ships escort east-bound British transatlantic convoy for first time. TU 4.1.1 (Captain Morton L. Deyo), comprising destroyers *Ericsson* (DD 440), *Eberle* (DD 430), *Ellis* (DD 154), *Dallas* (DD 199), and *Up-*shur (DD 144), assumes ocean escort duties for convoy HX 150, 150 miles south of Newfoundland.

19   Friday

UNITED STATES. Secretary of State Cordell Hull sends note to German Chargé d'Affaires Hans Thomsen concerning settlement of the *Robin Moor* incident, citing reparations to the amount of $2,967,092.00. German Embassy acknowledges receipt of the note the same day (see 26 September).

20   Saturday

ATLANTIC. Army shore battery fires across the bow of destroyer *Charles F. Hughes* (DD 428) as TU 4.1.2 (Commander Fred D. Kirtland) enters Hvalfjordur, Iceland, in foggy weather conditions.

German submarines attack convoy SC 44; among the ships lost in the onslaught are Panamanian freighter *Pink Star* (ex-Danish *Landby*) and tanker *T. C. Williams*, torpedoed and sunk by *U 552* at 61°36'N, 35°07'W, and 61°34'N, 35°11'W, respectively.

24   Wednesday

ATLANTIC. Destroyer *Eberle* (DD 430), in TU 4.1.1, screening convoy HX 150, rescues crew of British freighter *Nigaristan*, which has suffered an engine room fire.

25   Thursday

ATLANTIC. U.S. Navy escorts (see 18 September) turn over convoy HX 150 to British escort vessels at the Mid-Ocean Meeting Point

(MOMP). All convoyed vessels reach port safely

26 Friday

ATLANTIC. Navy orders protection of all ships engaged in commerce in U.S. defensive waters—by patrolling, covering, and escorting and by reporting or destroying German and Italian naval forces encountered.

UNITED STATES. German Chargé d'Affaires Hans Thomsen replies to Secretary of State Cordell Hull's note of 19 September concerning reparations for the loss of *Robin Moor*. Referring to the notes of 20 June and 19 September 1941, Thomsen replies that "the two communications made are not such as to lead to an appropriate reply by my government" (see 3 November).

27 Saturday

UNITED STATES. First Maritime Commission EC-2 type freighter ("Liberty" ship), *Patrick Henry*, is launched at Baltimore, Maryland. This standardized type of ship is to be put into mass production in American shipyards to fulfill the need for merchant vessels in a wartime economy.

28 Sunday

UNITED STATES. Army GHQ maneuvers in Louisiana conclude.

30 Tuesday

ATLANTIC. TU 4.1.5 (Commander William K. Phillips) assumes escort duty for convoy HX 152. During the rough passage to the MOMP, which concludes on 9 October, all destroyers of the unit—*Mayo* (DD 422) (flagship), *Broome* (DD 210), *Babbitt* (DD 128), *Leary* (DD 158), and *Schenck* (DD 159)— suffer varying degrees of storm damage.

TU 4.1.3 (Commander Dennis L. Ryan) assumes escort duty for convoy ON 20 at the MOMP (see 2 October).

PACIFIC. Rear Admiral Harold M. Bemis, incapacitated by illness, is relieved as Commandant Sixteenth Naval District and Commandant Navy Yard, Cavite, P.I., by Captain Herbert J. Ray (see 5 November).

OCTOBER

1 Wednesday

EUROPE. United States, British, and Soviet representatives conclude three-day conference in Moscow on aid to the Soviet Union.

UNITED STATES. Secretary of the Navy William Franklin (Frank) Knox approves "popular" names for naval combat aircraft: "Avenger" (Grumman TBF), "Buccaneer" (Brewster SB2A), "Buffalo" (Brewster F2A), "Catalina" (Consolidated PBY), "Coronado" (Consolidated PB2Y), "Corsair" (Vought F4U), "Dauntless" (Douglas SBD), "Devastator" (Douglas TBD), "Helldiver" (Curtiss SB2C), "Kingfisher" (Vought OS2U/Naval Aircraft Factory OS2N), "Mariner" (Martin PBM), "Sea Ranger" (Boeing PBB patrol bomber), "Seagull" (Curtiss SO3C), and "Vindicator" (Vought SB2U). Names supplement the Navy's letter-number designations, which remain unchanged and continue to be used in correspondence.[33]

Sale of War Savings Bonds to naval personnel is inaugurated on this date; under the direction of a Coordinator for War Savings Bonds, supply corps officers are designated as issuing agents and assigned to 28 major shore activities. Actual sales of the bonds will amount to $61,000,000—over 50 percent in excess of the predicted sales.

ATLANTIC. Naval Air Station, Trinidad, is established.

2 Thursday

UNITED STATES. President Roosevelt rejects Japanese Prime Minister Konoye Fumimaro's request to meet and discuss Pacific and Far Eastern questions.

ATLANTIC. Destroyer *Winslow* (DD 359), in screen of convoy ON 20, is detached from TU 4.1.3 to proceed to the assistance of Dutch motor vessel *Tuva*, torpedoed by German submarine *U 575* at 54°16′N, 26°36′W. Although *Winslow* finds the freighter still afloat, the destroyer depth charges a "doubtful" submarine contact in the vicinity and upon her return is unable to locate any survivors. *Winslow* rejoins ON 20 the following morning.[34]

Coast Guard cutter *Campbell* scuttles irreparably damaged British tanker *San Florentino* (torpedoed by German submarine *U 575* at 52°50′N, 34°40′W, and 52°42′N, 34°51′W).

5 Sunday

ATLANTIC. Destroyer *Mayo* (DD 422), escorting convoy HX 152, after seeing Swedish motor vessel *Kaaparen* showing a string of lights for five minutes, thus jeopardizing the convoy, hails the offender and threatens to open fire if the practice is not stopped.

TIME IS SHORT

Beneath a banner bearing appropriate sentiments, Captain Arthur W. Radford (right) looks on during ceremonies activating NAS Trinidad, 1 October 1941. (NA, 80-G-463774)

7 Tuesday

ATLANTIC. TU 4.1.1 (Captain Marion Y. Cohen) assumes escort duty for convoy ON 22 at the MOMP. Although there are no U-boat attacks on the convoy, ships of TU 4.1.1 carry out depth charge attacks on suspicious contacts (see 8 and 9 October).

8 Wednesday

ATLANTIC. Destroyer *Dallas* (DD 199), in screen of convoy ON 22, depth charges a contact (later evaluated as "non-submarine") about 450 miles southwest of Reykjavik, Iceland, 58°54'N, 29°31'W.

Oiler *Salinas* (AO 19), with convoy HX 152, is damaged by heavy seas and is convoyed to Iceland by destroyer *Broome* (DD 210).

9 Thursday

ATLANTIC. Destroyer *Upshur* (DD 144), in screen of convoy ON 22, carries out depth charge attack (like *Dallas*'s the previous day, evaluated as "non-submarine") about 405 miles southeast of Cape Farewell, 56°47'N, 34°05'W.

10 Friday

ATLANTIC. TG 14.3 (Rear Admiral H. Kent Hewitt), comprising carrier *Yorktown* (CV 5), battleship *New Mexico* (BB 40), heavy cruiser *Quincy* (CA 39), light cruiser *Savannah* (CL 42), and Destroyer Divisions 3 and 16, sails from Argentia, Newfoundland, for Casco Bay, Maine. Encountering heavy weather en route, *Yorktown, New Mexico, Quincy, Savannah,* and destroyers *Rhind* (DD 404), *Hammann* (DD 412), *Anderson* (DD 411), *Sims* (DD 409), *Mayrant* (DD 402), *Rowan* (DD 405), *Hughes* (DD 410), and *Trippe* (DD 403) will all suffer varying degrees of topside damage before the force reaches Casco Bay on 13 October.

PACIFIC. Captain Lester J. Hudson relieves Captain Richard E. Cassidy as Commander South China Patrol on board river gunboat *Mindanao* (PR 8) at Hong Kong, B.C.C.

14 Tuesday

ATLANTIC. German submarine *U 553* encounters convoy SC 48 and summons help (see 15–18 October).

15 Wednesday

ATLANTIC. German submarine *U 553* begins onslaught against convoy SC 48, torpedoing and sinking British motorship *Silvercedar* at 53°36'N, 30°00'W, and Norwegian freighter *Ila* at 53°34'N, 30°10'W, before the U-boat is driven off by Canadian destroyer HMCS *Columbia* [ex-U.S. destroyer *Haraden* (DD 183)]. *U 432, U 502, U 558,* and *U 568,* followed by *U 73, U 77, U 101,* and *U 751* converge on the convoy, and one of these boats, *U 568,* torpedoes and sinks British steamer *Empire Heron* at 54°55'N, 27°15'W, before being driven off by British corvette HMS *Gladiolus.* Consequently, TU 4.1.4 (Captain Hewlett Thebaud), comprising four U.S. destroyers, is directed to proceed to SC 48's aid as the west-bound convoy it had been escorting, ON 24, is dispersed (see 16–18 October).

16 Thursday

ATLANTIC. Battle to protect convoy SC 48 continues. German submarines *U 502* and *U 568* reestablish contact before retiring upon arrival of TU 4.1.4 (Captain Hewlett Thebaud). Destroyer *Livermore* (DD 429) sweeps ahead of the convoy, depth charges *U 553;* destroyer *Kearny* (DD 432), sweeping astern, drops charges to discourage tracking submarines. Later, *U 502* and *U 568,* augmented by *U 432, U 553,* and *U 558,* renew attack upon SC 48. The U-boats commence a determined assault on SC 48 during the night of 16–17 October.

Destroyer *Charles F. Hughes* (DD 428), while escorting convoy HX 154, rescues the only seven survivors of British freighter *Hatasu* (torpedoed and sunk by German submarine *U 431* on 2 October, 600 miles east of Cape Race), at 51°56'N, 35°58'W.

PACIFIC. Destroyers *Peary* (DD 226) and *Pillsbury* (DD 227) are damaged in collision during night exercises in Manila Bay, P.I.

17 Friday

PACIFIC. General Tojo Hideki becomes Japanese Premier as Konoye Government resigns.

Commander in Chief Pacific Fleet (Admiral Husband E. Kimmel) sends two submarines to Midway and two to Wake on "simulated war patrols" (see 26 October).

Navy orders all U.S. merchant ships in Asiatic waters to put into friendly ports.

ATLANTIC. Battle to protect convoy SC 48 continues. SC 48 is the first U.S. Navy–escorted convoy to engage German submarines in battle, but despite the presence of the three modern U.S. destroyers, two flush-deckers—*Decatur* (DD 341) and HMCS *Columbia* [ex-U.S. destroyer *Haraden* (DD 183)]—and four Canadian corvettes, the enemy torpedoes six ships and an escort vessel in a total elapsed time of four hours and 47 minutes. *U 432* sinks Greek steamer *Evros* at 57°00'N, 24°30'W, and Panamanian steamer *Bold Venture* and Norwegian motor tanker *Barfonn* at 56°58'N, 25°04'W; *U 558* sinks British tanker *W. C. Teagle* at 57°00'N, 25°00'W, and Norwegian steamship *Rym* at 57°01'N, 24°20'W. *U 553* sinks Norwegian steamer *Erviken* at 56°10'N, 24°30'W, and conducts unsuccessful approach on destroyer *Plunkett* (DD 431). Destroyer *Kearny* (DD 432) is torpedoed by *U 568* southwest of Iceland, 57°00'N, 24°00'W; 11 of *Kearny*'s crew are killed and 22 injured (see 18 October). Soon thereafter, *U 101* torpedoes and sinks British destroyer HMS *Broadwater* [ex-U.S. destroyer *Mason* (DD 191)], at 57°01'N, 19°08'W.[35] Escorted by *Greer* (DD 145), the damaged *Kearny* limps to Hvalfjordur, Iceland.[36] Iceland-based PBYs (VP 73) arrive to provide air coverage for SC 48.

Destroyers *Charles F. Hughes* (DD 428) and *Gleaves* (DD 423), while screening convoy HX 154, depth charge suspicious contacts at 54°40'N, 33°59'W, and 54°40'N, 33°59'W (see 19 October).

18 Saturday

ATLANTIC. PBY (VP 73) drops package containing blood plasma and transfusion gear for use in treating the wounded on board damaged destroyer *Kearny* (DD 432); *Monssen* (DD 436) retrieves the package, but the gear becomes disengaged and sinks. PBM (VP 74) repeats the operation a few hours later; this time the drop is successful and *Monssen* retrieves the medical supplies intact. Destroyers *Plunkett* (DD 431), *Livermore* (DD 429), and *Decatur* (DD 341), meanwhile, make concerted depth charge attacks on sound contacts at 54°53'N, 33°08'W, with no visible results. German submarines break off operations against SC 48.

19 Sunday

ATLANTIC. Destroyers *Charles F. Hughes* (DD 428) and *Gleaves* (DD 423), while screening convoy HX 154, depth charge suspicious contacts at 59°58'N, 23°15'W; 60°00'N, 23°20'W; and 59°57'N, 22°41'W.

Unarmed U.S. freighter *Lehigh* is torpedoed and sunk by German submarine *U 126* about 75 miles off Freetown, Sierra Leone, 08°26'N, 14°37'W. While there are no fatalities, four men are slightly injured.

Destroyer *Kearny* (DD 432) lies careened alongside repair ship *Vulcan* (AR 4) at Hvalfjordur, Iceland, undergoing repairs to her damaged starboard side. (NA, 80-G-425654)

20 Monday

ATLANTIC. PBYs (VP 73) provide air coverage for convoy ON 26.

22 Wednesday

PACIFIC. Battleships *Oklahoma* (BB 37) and *Arizona* (BB 39) are damaged in collision in Hawaiian Operating Area.

25 Saturday

ATLANTIC. TF 14 (Rear Admiral H. Kent Hewitt), formed around carrier *Yorktown* (CV 5) (VF 42, VB 5, VS 5, and VT 5), battleship *New Mexico* (BB 40), light cruisers *Savannah* (CL 42) and *Philadelphia* (CL 41), and nine destroyers, departs Portland, Maine, to escort a convoy ("Cargo") of British merchantmen (see 2 November).

TU 4.1.3 (Commander Richard E. Webb) escorts convoy HX 156; destroyer *Hilary P. Jones* (DD 427) carries out depth charge attacks on suspicious contact but, after spying a school of porpoises, ceases fire.

South and Northeast Greenland Patrols are merged and renamed Greenland Patrol; it is designated as TG 24.8 of the Atlantic Fleet.

26 Sunday

PACIFIC. Submarines *Narwhal* (SS 167) and *Dolphin* (SS 169) arrive off Wake Island on simulated war patrols.

27 Monday

ATLANTIC. TU 4.1.6 (Commander George W. Johnson) screens convoy ON 28. During the day, destroyers *DuPont* (DD 152) and *Sampson* (DD 394) each carry out two depth charge attacks against suspected U-boat contacts.

Destroyer *Hilary P. Jones* (DD 427) is damaged by heavy seas while screening convoy HX 156.

29 Wednesday

ATLANTIC. TU 4.1.3 (Commander Richard E. Webb) escorts convoy HX 156; destroyer *Hilary P. Jones* (DD 427) carries out depth charge attack on suspicious contact.

TU 4.1.6 (Commander George W. Johnson) screens convoy ON 28. During the day, destroyers *Lea* (DD 118), *DuPont* (DD 152), *MacLeish* (DD 220), and *Sampson* (DD 394) depth charge suspected U-boat contacts.

30 Thursday

ATLANTIC. Oiler *Salinas* (AO 19), in convoy ON 28, is torpedoed by German submarine *U 106* about 700 miles east of Newfoundland. Only one of *Salinas*'s crew is injured. TU 4.1.6 (Commander George W. Johnson), screening ON 28, attacks sound contacts; destroyer *Bernadou* (DD 153) carries out five depth charge attacks and fires at what was most likely German submarine *U 67*, forcing her to

submerge; *Du Pont* (DD 152) carries out three depth charge attacks; *MacLeish* (DD 220) and *Sampson* (DD 394) one apiece. *Lea* (DD 118) escorts *Salinas*, which will reach port under her own power; they will be joined en route by Coast Guard cutter *Campbell* and tug *Cherokee* (AT 66).

TU 4.1.1 (Captain Marion Y. Cohen) contacts MOMP-bound convoy HX 157 at 45°43′N, 55°37′W. The convoy will not be attacked by U-boats (see 1 November).

31 Friday

ATLANTIC. Destroyer *Reuben James* (DD 245), while escorting 42-ship convoy HX 156, is torpedoed and sunk by German submarine *U 552* off western Iceland, 51°59′N, 27°05′W; 115 men are killed. No merchantmen in HX 156 are attacked. Despite the heavy oil slick in the vicinity and the need to investigate sound contacts, destroyer *Niblack* (DD 424) rescues 36 men (one of whom dies of wounds on 2 November); *Hilary P. Jones* (DD 427) picks up 10. The loss of *Reuben James*, the first U.S. naval vessel to be lost to enemy action in World War II, proves a temporary detriment to Navy recruiting efforts.

TU 4.1.6 (Commander George W. Johnson), screening ON 28, carries out vigorous attacks on sound contacts. Destroyer *Babbitt* (DD 128) carries out two, while *Buck* (DD 420), *DuPont* (DD 152) (which is attacked by U-boat but missed), *Leary* (DD 158), and *Sampson* (DD 394) carry out one attack apiece.

NOVEMBER

1 Saturday

UNITED STATES. Executive order places Coast Guard under jurisdiction of Department of the Navy for duration of national emergency.

PACIFIC. Pacific Escort Force is formed at Pearl Harbor to protect transports and certain merchant vessels carrying troops and valuable military cargoes between Hawaii and the Far East.

ATLANTIC. PBYs (VP 73) provide air coverage for convoy ON 30.

Destroyers *Dallas* (DD 199), *Ellis* (DD 154), and *Eberle* (DD 430), screening convoy HX 157, carry out depth charge attacks on sound contacts off St. John's, Newfoundland.

2 Sunday

ATLANTIC. TF 14 (Rear Admiral H. Kent Hewitt) (see 25 October for composition) reaches

MOMP and exchanges convoy "Cargo" for CT 5, eight British transports carrying 20,000 British troops earmarked for the Middle East. Convoy CT 5's first destination is Halifax, Nova Scotia.

PBMs (VP 74) provide air coverage for convoy ON 30.

3 Monday

UNITED STATES. Secretary of State Cordell Hull releases to the press the correspondence of June and September detailing the German refusal to pay reparations for sinking U.S. freighter *Robin Moor* on 21 May.

ATLANTIC. PBYs (VP 73) provide air coverage for convoy ON 31.

Destroyer *Upshur* (DD 144), escorting convoy HX 157, depth charges sound contact (later determined to be most likely a whale or blackfish) at 56°56′N, 49°21′W.

4 Tuesday

ATLANTIC. PBYs (VP 73) provide air coverage for convoy ON 31.

British RFA oiler *Olwen* reports German surface raider attack at 03°04′N, 22°42′W. Commander in Chief South Atlantic (Vice Admiral Algernon U. Willis, RN) orders heavy cruiser HMS *Dorsetshire* (accompanied by armed merchant cruiser HMS *Canton*) to investigate. Light cruiser HMS *Dunedin* and special service vessels HMS *Queen Emma* and *Princess Beatrix* are ordered to depart Freetown, Sierra Leone, to join in the search. *Dorsetshire* and *Canton* part company, with the former heading southeast and the latter steaming toward a position to the northwest, to be supported by TG 3.6, light cruiser *Omaha* (CL 4) and destroyer *Somers* (DD 381), which are at that time well to the northwest of the reported enemy position. Light cruiser *Memphis* (CL 13) and destroyers *Davis* (DD 395) and *Jouett* (DD 396), near to *Olwen*'s position, search the area without result; *Omaha* and *Somers* search unsuccessfully for survivors (see 5 and 6 November).

5 Wednesday

ATLANTIC. Oiler *Laramie* (AO 16) is rammed by Panamanian freighter *Montrose*, Tunugdliark Fjord, Narsarssuak, Greenland, but suffers no damage in the accidental encounter caused by stormy weather.

Search for German raider reported by British RFA oiler *Olwen* the previous day continues; Commander in Chief South Atlantic (Vice Admiral Algernon U. Willis, RN) in-

Sailors from light cruiser *Omaha* (CL 4) prepare to board the suspicious ship in the distance that is masquerading as U.S. freighter *Willmoto* but which is, in fact, German blockade runner *Odenwald*, 6 November 1941. Some of *Omaha*'s bluejackets are armed with Thompson submachine guns—.45-caliber weapons known to have excellent stopping power at short range. (NHC, NH 49938)

forms British ships of the unsuccessful efforts by the five U.S. ships (two light cruisers and three destroyers) involved in the search the previous day (see 6 November).

PACIFIC. Rear Admiral Francis W. Rockwell relieves Captain Herbert J. Ray as Commandant Sixteenth Naval District and Commander Philippine Naval Coastal Frontier. Ray had been acting in that capacity due to the illness of Rear Admiral Harold M. Bemis.

6 Thursday

ATLANTIC. Unsuccessful search for German raider reported by British RFA oiler *Olwen* on 4 November is not entirely fruitless. TG 3.6, light cruiser *Omaha* (CL 4) (Captain Theodore E. Chandler) and destroyer *Somers* (DD 381), en route to Recife, Brazil, returning from the 3,023-mile patrol, captures German blockade runner *Odenwald*, disguised as U.S. freighter *Willmoto*, in Atlantic equatorial waters, 00°40′N, 28°04′W. Boarding party from *Omaha* (Lieutenant George K. Carmichael) reaches *Odenwald* as Germans explode charges to scuttle the ship. *Omaha*'s sailors, however, joined by a diesel engine specialist from *Somers*, prevent *Odenwald*'s loss while the cruiser's SOCs and her accompanying de-

stroyer screen the operation. The three ships then proceed to Trinidad because of possible complications with the Brazilian government. In view of the precarious fuel state in the American ships, *Somers*'s crew ingeniously rigs a sail that cuts fuel consumption and allows her to reach her destination with fuel to spare. British RFA oiler *Olwen* subsequently reports that she had made the "raider" signal when what was probably a surfaced submarine had fired upon her at dawn on 4 November. Ten U.S. and British warships had searched for two days for a phantom enemy.

Destroyer *Madison* (DD 425), on the flank of convoy ON 39, carries out depth charge attack at 45°50′N, 40°40′W; investigation later proves their quarry to have been a whale.

7 Friday

ATLANTIC. Destroyers *Lansdale* (DD 426), *Charles F. Hughes* (DD 428), and *Gleaves* (DD 423), while in TU 4.1.2 escorting convoy ON 30, make depth charge attacks on sound contact. Destroyer *Madison* (DD 425) sights bleeding whale soon thereafter, leading to the conclusion that the warships had attacked a large marine mammal.

8 Saturday

ATLANTIC. Destroyer *Niblack* (DD 424) damages Norwegian freighter *Astra* in collision, Reykjavik, Iceland.

Naval Operating Base, Iceland, is established; Rear Admiral James L. Kauffman is the first commandant.

9 Sunday

ATLANTIC. TU 4.1.4 (Captain Alan G. Kirk) departs Argentia, Newfoundland, to screen 31-ship convoy HX 159. It is the first escort task unit that includes in its composition a Coast Guard cutter, *Campbell*. The convoy will not be attacked by U-boats, although the presence of whales and blackfish results in attacks on sound contacts on five occasions (see 11, 12, and 13 November).

10 Monday

ATLANTIC. U.S.-escorted convoy WS 12 (Rear Admiral Arthur B. Cook), formed around carrier *Ranger* (CV 4) and transporting more than 20,000 British soldiers (see 2 November) in six U.S. Navy transports, sails from Halifax, Nova Scotia.

Destroyer *Ericsson* (DD 440), screening convoy HX 157, depth charges sound contact later evaluated as a "doubtful" submarine.

PACIFIC. Commander in Chief Asiatic Fleet (Admiral Thomas C. Hart) receives permission to withdraw river gunboats from the Yangtze and USMC forces from China.

11 Tuesday

ATLANTIC. Destroyer *Edison* (DD 439), en route to rendezvous with convoy ON 34, depth charges sound contact.

Destroyer *Decatur* (DD 341), screening convoy HX 159, depth charges sound contact off the Grand Banks; it is later evaluated as a "doubtful" submarine.

12 Wednesday

ATLANTIC. TU 4.1.3 (Commander Richard E. Webb) assumes escort duty for convoy ON 34.

Destroyer *Decatur* (DD 341), screening convoy HX 159, twice depth charges sound contacts that are later evaluated as "non-submarine." Destroyer *Badger* (DD 126), depth charges sound contact that is later evaluated as perhaps *Decatur's* wake. Coast Guard cutter *Campbell* reports sound contact and conducts search; she is joined by destroyer *Livermore* (DD 429).

13 Thursday

ATLANTIC. Destroyer *Edison* (DD 439), screening convoy ON 34 southwest of Iceland, depth charges sound contact.

Destroyer *Decatur* (DD 341), screening convoy HX 159, depth charges sound contact; although it is regarded as a good contact, the ensuing search yields no evidence of a submarine.

14 Friday

PACIFIC. Marines are ordered withdrawn from Shanghai, Peiping, and Tientsin, China.

ATLANTIC. Destroyer *Benson* (DD 421) and *Niblack* (DD 424), screening convoy ON 34, depth charge sound contacts.

Destroyer *Edison* (DD 439), en route to MOMP in TU 4.1.1 to screen convoy ON 35, attacks a sound contact southwest of Iceland at 62°53′N, 24°30′W.

15 Saturday

UNITED STATES. Army GHQ maneuvers begin in North and South Carolina. Two U.S. Navy (VB 8 and VS 8) and two Marine Corps (VMF 111 and VMF 121) squadrons take part in the large-scale war games.

ATLANTIC. TU 4.1.1 (Captain Marion Y. Cohen) assumes escort duty for convoy ON 35 at the MOMP. There will be no U-boat attacks on the convoy, but nearly continuous heavy weather between 16 and 25 November results in 16 of the 26 ships straggling.

16 Sunday

ATLANTIC. TU 4.1.5 (Commander William K. Phillips) clears Argentia, Newfoundland, to assume escort duty for convoy HX 160; between 17 and 28 November, heavy seas will cause varying degrees of damage to destroyers *Mayo* (DD 422), *Nicholson* (DD 442), *Babbitt* (DD 128), *Leary* (DD 158), and *Schenck* (DD 159). The convoy will not be attacked by U-boats (see 18–20 and 27 November).

17 Monday

UNITED STATES. Congress amends the Neutrality Act of 1939 by Joint Resolution; U.S. merchant ships can now be armed and can enter war zones.

Bureau of Navigation directs that naval district personnel who received Armed Guard training be assigned to Little Creek, Virginia, or San Diego, California, for further instruction. They will be transferred to Armed Guard centers at New York, New York, and Treasure Island, California, for assignment to merchant ships.

Special Japanese envoy Kurusu Saburo arrives in Washington, D.C., and confers with Secretary of State Cordell Hull.

ATLANTIC. Destroyers *Benson* (DD 421) and *Edison* (DD 439), screening convoy ON 34, depth charge submarine contacts.

TU 4.1.5 (Commander William K. Phillips) intercepts and joins convoy HX 160; although none of the destroyers in the task unit will be damaged by enemy action, all—*Mayo* (DD 422), *Babbitt* (DD 128), *Leary* (DD 158), *Schenck* (DD 159), and *Nicholson* (DD 442)— will suffer storm damage of varying degrees between this date and 28 November.

German blockade runner *Odenwald*, captured by light cruiser *Omaha* (CL 4) and destroyer *Somers* (DD 381) on 6 November, is escorted into San Juan, Puerto Rico, by *Somers* and turned over to U.S. authorities.

19 Wednesday

ATLANTIC. Destroyer *Leary* (DD 158), with TU 4.1.5, escorting convoy HX 160, depth charges a sound contact.

20 Thursday

GENERAL. Ambassador Nomura Kichasaburo presents Japan's "final proposal" to keep peace in the Pacific.

ATLANTIC. Destroyer *Nicholson* (DD 442), with TU 4.1.5, escorting convoy HX 160, depth charges a sound contact at 50°30′N, 50°40′W.

21 Friday

UNITED STATES. Office of the Chief of Naval Operations mistakenly informs Naval Air Station, New York, of the imminent delivery of infantile paralysis serum from Navy Medical Supply Depot, Brooklyn, for further transport to Norfolk by 1000 on the following day and thence to Bermuda. It is soon discovered, however, that no such serum exists in Brooklyn or anywhere east of Milwaukee. Urgent ensuing search locates the needed serum in Milwaukee, whence it is flown to Chicago, where American Air Lines holds a plane to make the necessary connection for the flight to New York (see 22 November).

ATLANTIC. Lend-Lease is extended to Iceland.

PACIFIC. Destroyer *Shaw* (DD 373) and oiler *Sabine* (AO 25) are damaged in collision in Hawaiian Operating Area.

22 Saturday

UNITED STATES. Naval Air Station, New York, SNJ-2 delivers needed infantile paralysis serum to Norfolk, Virginia. It ultimately arrives in Bermuda on time.

23 Sunday

ATLANTIC. United States occupies Surinam, Dutch Guiana, pursuant to agreement with the Netherlands government to protect bauxite mines.

ATLANTIC. TU 4.1.6 (Commander Gilbert C. Hoover) assumes escort duty for convoy HX 161; the convoy will not be attacked by U-boats during its passage (see 24 November).

24 Monday

ATLANTIC. Destroyer *DuPont* (DD 152) in North Atlantic with TU 4.1.6, escorting convoy HX 161, is damaged in collision with Norwegian tanker *Thorshovdi*.

British light cruiser HMS *Dunedin* is torpedoed and sunk by German submarine *U 124* north of Pernambuco, Brazil, at approximately 03°00'S, 26°00'W (see 27 November).

25 Tuesday

PACIFIC. Japanese troop transports en route to Malaya are sighted off Formosa.

Submarines *Triton* (SS 201) and *Tambor* (SS 198) arrive off Wake Island on simulated war patrols.

26 Wednesday

UNITED STATES. Secretary of State Cordell Hull submits final proposal to Japanese envoys for readjustment of U.S.-Japanese relations.

PACIFIC. Japanese carrier task force (Vice Admiral Nagumo Chuichi), formed around six aircraft carriers, sails from remote Hittokappu Bay in the Kurils, its departure shrouded in secrecy. Its mission, should talks between the United States and Japan fail to resolve the diplomatic impasse over Far Eastern and Pacific questions, is to attack the U.S. Pacific Fleet wherever it is found in Hawaiian waters.

Tug *Sonoma* (AT 12) sails from Wake Island with Pan American Airways barges *PAB No. 2* and *PAB No. 4* in tow, bound for Honolulu.

27 Thursday

PACIFIC. Admiral Harold R. Stark, Chief of Naval Operations, sends "War Warning" message to commanders of the Pacific and Asiatic Fleets. General George C. Marshall, Army Chief of Staff, sends a similar message to his

While a depth bomb–armed Vought SB2U-2 Vindicator from carrier *Ranger* (CV 4) flies overhead on antisubmarine patrol, convoy WS ("Winston's Specials") 12 executes a turn as it steams toward Capetown, South Africa, 27 November 1941. Visible beyond are five of the six U.S. Navy transports carrying British troops: *West Point* (AP 23), *Mount Vernon* (AP 22), *Wakefield* (AP 21), *Leonard Wood* (AP 25), and *Joseph T. Dickman* (AP 26). Heavy cruisers *Quincy* (CA 39) and *Vincennes* (CA 44) are also visible. (NA, 80-G-464654)

Hawaiian and Philippine Department commanders.

U.S. passenger liner *President Madison,* chartered for the purpose, sails from Shanghai, China, with the Second Battalion, Fourth Marine Regiment (Lieutenant Colonel Donald Curtis, USMC) embarked, bound for the Philippines (see 30 November).

ATLANTIC. Destroyer *Babbitt* (DD 128), with TU 4.1.5, escorting convoy HX 160, depth charges a sound contact.

U.S. freighter *Nishmaha* rescues 72 survivors (five of whom succumb to their wounds) of British light cruiser HMS *Dunedin*, sunk by German submarine *U 124* on 24 November. *Nishmaha* transports the survivors to Trinidad.

28 Friday

PACIFIC. Carrier *Enterprise* (CV 6) sails for Wake Island in TF 8 (Vice Admiral William F. Halsey Jr.) to ferry USMC F4Fs (VMF 211) to the atoll. Occasioned by the "War Warning" of the previous day, the deployment is part of eleventh-hour augmentation of defenses at outlying Pacific bases. Halsey approves "Battle Order No. 1" that declares that *Enterprise* is operating "under war conditions." Supporting PBY operations will be carried out from advanced bases at Wake and Midway.

Seaplane tender *Wright* (AV 1), arrives at Wake Island, with Marine Aircraft Group 21 people to establish an advanced aviation base.

U.S. passenger liner *President Harrison,* chartered for the purpose, sails from Shanghai, China, with the First Battalion, Fourth Marine Regiment (Lieutenant Colonel Curtis T. Beecher, USMC) and regimental staff (Colonel Samuel L. Howard, USMC) embarked, bound for the Philippines. "Stirring scenes of farewell," U.S. Consul Edwin F. Stanton reports to Secretary of State Cordell Hull, accompany the marines' departure.

During their storm-fraught passage to rendezvous with the river gunboats proceeding from Shanghai to Manila, submarine rescue vessel *Pigeon* (ASR 6) experiences steering casualty; minesweeper *Finch* (AM 9), which loses both anchors in the tempest, stands by to render assistance, and eventually, after three tries, manages to take the crippled ship in tow the following day.

29 Saturday

PACIFIC. River gunboats *Luzon* (PR 7) and *Oahu* (PR 6) (Rear Admiral William A. Glassford Jr., Commander Yangtze Patrol, in *Luzon*) depart Shanghai for Manila.[37]

ATLANTIC. TU 4.1.2 (Commander Fred D. Kirtland), accompanied by salvage vessel *Redwing* (ARS 4) and oiler *Sapelo* (AO 11), assumes escort for convoy HX 162 (see 1 December).

TU 4.1.4 (Captain Alan G. Kirk) assumes escort duty for convoy ONS 39; the convoy will not be attacked by U-boats during its passage. ONS 39, however, will encounter considerable stormy weather that causes varying degrees of topside damage to destroyers *Plunkett* (DD 431), *Livermore* (DD 429), *Decatur* (DD 341), and *Cole* (DD 155).

Destroyer *Woolsey* (DD 437), screening convoy HX 161, despite having been hampered by propulsion problems during previous days, depth charges suspicious contact without result.

30 Sunday

PACIFIC. Japanese Foreign Minister Togo Shigenori rejects U.S. proposals for settling Far East crisis.

Small reconnaissance seaplane from Japanese submarine *I 10* reconnoiters Suva Bay, Fiji.

U.S. passenger liner *President Madison* arrives at Olongapo, P.I., and disembarks the Second Battalion, Fourth Marine Regiment (Lieutenant Colonel Donald Curtis, USMC). *President Madison* will then proceed on to Singapore.

River gunboats *Luzon* (PR 7) and *Oahu* (PR 6) (Rear Admiral William A. Glassford Jr., Commander Yangtze Patrol, in *Luzon*) rendezvous with submarine rescue vessel *Pigeon* (ASR 6) and minesweeper *Finch* (AM 9); they will remain in company until 3 December.

ATLANTIC. Destroyer *Decatur* (DD 341), in TU 4.1.4 (Captain Alan G. Kirk), escorting convoy ONS 39, carries out depth charge attack on suspicious contact, 59°24′N, 27°03′W.

UNITED STATES. Army GHQ maneuvers in North and South Carolina conclude.

DECEMBER

1 Monday

ATLANTIC. Patrol Wing 9 (Lieutenant Commander Thomas U. Sisson) is established at Quonset Point, Rhode Island.

German submarine *U 575* encounters and tracks unarmed U.S. tanker *Astral*, the latter en route from Aruba, N.W.I., to Lisbon, Portugal, with a cargo of 78,200 barrels of gasoline and kerosene. After seeing that *Astral* is unarmed and bears prominent neutrality markings, however, the U-boat's commanding officer, *Kapitänleutnant* Günther Heydemann, allows the American ship to pass unmolested. Subsequently, another submarine in the vicinity, *U 43*, encounters *Astral* and attacks her, but her torpedoes miss their mark (see 2 December).

TU 4.1.2 (Commander Fred D. Kirtland), accompanied by salvage vessel *Redwing* (ARS 4) and oiler *Sapelo* (AO 11), while escorting convoy HX 162, encounters heavy weather that scatters 35 merchantmen. Destroyers *Charles F. Hughes* (DD 428), *Madison* (DD 425), *Lansdale* (DD 426), *Wilkes* (DD 441), and *Sturtevant* (DD 240) all suffer storm damage of varying degrees (see 7 December).

Destroyer *Livermore* (DD 429), escorting convoy ONS 39, is dispatched to investigate darkened merchantman steaming on opposite course. *Livermore* trails her and after determining her to be Panamanian freighter *Ramapo*, en route to join convoy SC 56, allows her to continue her voyage after being warned not to radio a report of contact with a convoy.

PACIFIC. President Roosevelt orders a "defensive information patrol" of "three small ships" established off the coast of French Indochina; he specifically designates yacht *Isabel* (PY 10) (reserve flagship for Commander in Chief Asiatic Fleet) as one of the trio of vessels (see 3 and 6 December).[38]

U.S. passenger liner *President Harrison* arrives at Olongapo, P.I., with the remaining elements of the Fourth Marine Regiment (Colonel Samuel L. Howard, USMC) withdrawn from Shanghai. *President Harrison* soon sails to bring out the last marines from China (see 8 December).

As river gunboats *Luzon* (PR 7) and *Oahu* (PR 6) (Rear Admiral William A. Glassford Jr., Commander Yangtze Patrol, in *Luzon*), submarine rescue vessel *Pigeon* (ASR 6), and minesweeper *Finch* (AM 9) proceed toward Manila, they become the object of curiosity to Japanese forces in the vicinity; first a floatplane circles the formation, then seven warships of various types.

2 Tuesday

UNITED STATES. U.S. freighter *Dunboyne* receives first naval Armed Guard crew. By the end of World War II, the U.S. Navy will arm some 6,236 merchantmen; approximately 144,970 officers and enlisted men will defend these merchant vessels in every theater of the war.

ATLANTIC. German submarine *U 43* again attacks unarmed U.S. tanker *Astral* and this time torpedoes and sinks her at 35°40′N, 24°00′W. There are no survivors from the 37-man merchant crew.

Weather encountered by convoy ONS 39, being escorted by TU 4.1.4 (Captain Alan G. Kirk), worsens to the extent that the watch on board destroyer *Plunkett* (DD 431) cannot be relieved because officers and men cannot safely traverse the weather decks.

TU 4.1.5 (Commander William K. Phillips) clears Reykjavik, Iceland, to rendezvous with convoy ON 41, which due to poor weather will be 48 hours late to the MOMP. Over the ensuing period at sea, TU 4.1.5 battles "consistently severe" weather conditions that will cause varying degrees of damage to all of the ships in the task unit. Although ships of the unit carry out attacks (see 5, 9, and 11 December), there will be no U-boat attacks on the merchantmen under their protection.

TU 4.1.6 (Commander Gilbert C. Hoover), escorting convoy HX 161, encounters heavy weather. Destroyer *Bernadou* (DD 153) suffers storm damage; destroyers *Roe* (DD 418) and *Lea* (DD 118) each lose a man overboard. Neither sailor is recovered (see 4 December).

PACIFIC. Submarine *Trout* (SS 202) arrives off Midway Island on simulated war patrol.

3 Wednesday

ATLANTIC. Unarmed U.S. freighter *Sagadahoc* is torpedoed and sunk by German submarine *U 124* in South Atlantic, 21°50′S, 07°50′W. One man of the 37-man crew is lost.

Destroyer *Mayo* (DD 422), in TU 4.1.5 en route to MOMP and convoy ON 41, encounters two British ships, HMS *Tenacity* and merchantman *Meademere*, burning navigation lights south of Iceland; when they fail to answer challenge, *Mayo* illuminates them with starshells, at which point they darken ship and answer the challenge promptly.

PACIFIC. Yacht *Isabel* (PY 10) sails for coast of French Indochina, deployed in accordance with President Roosevelt's "defensive information patrol" order of 1 December.

Submarine *Argonaut* (SS 166) arrives off Midway Island on simulated war patrol.

4 Thursday

PACIFIC. River gunboats *Luzon* (PR 7) and *Oahu* (PR 6) (Rear Admiral William A. Glassford Jr., Commander Yangtze Patrol, in *Luzon*), followed later by submarine rescue vessel *Pigeon* (ASR 6) and minesweeper *Finch* (AM 9), reach Manila.

River gunboat *Mindanao* (PR 8) (Captain Lester J. Hudson, Commander South China Patrol, embarked) sails from Hong Kong, B.C.C., for Manila. She is the last U.S. Navy ship to depart Chinese waters prior to war. Luzon Stevedoring Company tug *Ranger* follows subsequently, carrying spare parts and 800 3-inch shells (previously stored ashore at Hong Kong) for *Mindanao*'s main battery. Only two U.S. naval vessels remain in Chinese waters: river gunboat *Wake* (ex-*Guam*) (PR 3) at Shanghai to maintain communications until a radio station is established at the Consulate General with Navy equipment, and river gunboat *Tutuila* (PR 4) at Chungking, where she furnishes essential services to the U.S. Embassy.

Carrier *Enterprise* (CV 6) ferries USMC F4Fs (VMF 211) to Wake Island; TF 8 (Vice Admiral William F. Halsey Jr.) then shapes a course to return to Pearl Harbor. TF 8 is slated to reach Pearl Harbor on 6 December. Heavy weather on 5 and 6 December, however, will result in a delay in fueling the force's destroyers and will push back the time of arrival in Pearl Harbor from the afternoon of the sixth to the morning of the seventh. That same day, a routine scouting flight from the carrier sights Honolulu-bound tug *Sonoma* (AT 12) with Pan American Airways barges *PAB No. 2* and *PAB No. 4* in tow.[39]

Japanese naval land attack plane (Chitose *Kokutai*) reconnoiters Wake Island undetected.

ATLANTIC. TU 4.1.5 (Commander William K. Phillips) reaches MOMP to escort convoy ON 41, which has been delayed by bad weather.

TU 4.1.6 (Commander Gilbert C. Hoover) encounters "mountainous" seas as it continues to escort convoy HX 161; destroyer *Roe* (DD 418) suffers two sailors hurt when torpedo breaks loose atop her after deckhouse.

5 Friday

PACIFIC. Japan assures the United States that her troop movements in French Indochina are only precautionary.

Admiral Sir Tom S. V. Phillips, RN, flies to Manila for a conference with Admiral Thomas C. Hart, Commander in Chief, Asiatic Fleet, to discuss possible detachment of destroyers to screen his capital ships (the recently arrived battleship HMS *Prince of Wales* and battle cruiser *Repulse*) in the event of hostilities (see 6 December).

Carrier *Lexington* (CV 2) in TF 12 (Rear Admiral John H. Newton) sails for Midway to ferry USMC SB2Us (VMSB 231) to that atoll. Like the TF 8's deployment to Wake, *Lexington*'s to Midway is in response to the "War Warning" of 27 November.

ATLANTIC. TU 4.1.3 (Commander George W. Johnson) assumes escort duty for convoy HX 163 in North Atlantic.

Destroyer *Babbitt* (DD 128), in TU 4.1.5 escorting convoy ON 41, depth charges suspected submarine contact without result.

6 Saturday

PACIFIC. Yacht *Isabel* (PY 10) is sighted by reconnaissance seaplane from Japanese seaplane carrier *Kamikawa Maru* at about 13°24′N, 112°21′E. Later in the day, *Isabel* receives orders to return to Manila.

Admiral Sir Tom S. V. Phillips, RN, departs Manila to return to Singapore when word is received of movement of Japanese troop convoys.

ATLANTIC. Destroyer *Decatur* (DD 341), in TU 4.1.4 (Captain Alan G. Kirk), escorting convoy ONS 39, carries out depth charge attack on suspicious contact, 51°54′N, 41°53′W.

7 Sunday

ATLANTIC. TU 4.1.2 (Commander Fred D. Kirtland), accompanied by salvage vessel *Redwing* (ARS 4) and oiler *Sapelo* (AO 11), while escorting convoy HX 162, reaches the MOMP; 21 of the 35 merchantmen scattered by the storm encountered on 1 December have rejoined by this time.

PACIFIC. Japanese guardboat seizes Panamanian steamship *Islas Visayas* off Nampang Island, interrupting the ship's voyage from Fort Bayard to Hong Kong and Macao. The boarding party removes parts of the ship's engines and wireless equipment.

Unarmed U.S. Army–chartered steam schooner *Cynthia Olson* is shelled and sunk by Japanese submarine *I 26* about 1,000 miles northwest of Diamond Head, Honolulu, T.H., 33°42′N, 145°29′W. She is the first U.S. merchantman to be sunk by a Japanese submarine in World War II. There are no survivors from the 33-man crew or the two Army passengers.

Japanese Type A midget submarine attempts to follow general stores issue ship *Antares* (AKS 3) into the entrance channel to Pearl Harbor; summoned to the scene by the auxiliary vessel, destroyer *Ward* (DD 139), on channel entrance patrol, with an assist from a PBY (VP 14), sinks the intruder with gunfire and depth charges. Word of the incident, however, works its way up the chain of command with almost glacial slowness.

Army radar station at Kahuku Point, Oahu, soon thereafter detects an unusually large "blip" approaching from the north, but the operator reporting the contact is told not to concern himself with the matter since a formation of USAAF B-17s is expected from the west coast of the United States. The army watch officer dismisses the report as "nothing unusual." The "blip" is the first wave of the incoming enemy strike.

Consequently, "like a thunderclap from a clear sky" Japanese carrier attack planes (in both torpedo and high-level bombing roles) and bombers, supported by fighters, totaling 353 planes from naval striking force (Vice Admiral Nagumo Chuichi) attack in two waves, targeting ships of the U.S. Pacific Fleet at Pearl Harbor, and nearby military airfields and installations. Japanese planes torpedo and sink battleships *Oklahoma* (BB 37) and *West Virginia* (BB 48) and auxiliary (gunnery training/target ship) *Utah* (AG 16). On board *Oklahoma*, Ensign Francis G. Flaherty, USNR, and Seaman First Class James R. Ward, as the ship is abandoned, hold flashlights to allow their shipmates to escape; on board *West Virginia*, her commanding officer, Captain Mervyn Bennion, directs his ship's defense until struck down and mortally wounded by a fragment from a bomb that hits battleship *Tennessee* (BB 43) moored inboard; on board *Utah*, Austrian-born Chief Watertender Peter Tomich remains at his post as the ship capsizes, securing the boilers and making sure his shipmates have escaped from the fireroom. Flaherty, Ward, Bennion, and Tomich are awarded the Medal of Honor posthumously.[40]

Japanese bombs also sink battleship *Arizona* (BB 39); the cataclysmic explosion of her forward magazine causes heavy casualties, among them Rear Admiral Isaac C. Kidd, Commander Battleship Division 1, who thus becomes the first U.S. Navy flag officer to die in combat in World War II. Both he and *Arizona*'s commanding officer, Captain Franklin van Valkenburgh, are awarded Medals of Honor posthumously. The ship's senior surviving officer on board, Lieutenant Commander Samuel G. Fuqua, directs efforts to

While launches and boats ply the waters of Pearl Harbor (left), battleship *Nevada* (BB 36) steams past 1010 Dock during the Japanese raid of 7 December 1941, in her bid for the open sea. In foreground lies the administration building for NAS Ford Island and small seaplane tender *Avocet* (AVP 4) (right, beyond smokestack); tank farms and submarine base in distance (left) will not be touched by the Japanese, nor will the Navy Yard, a part of which is visible at right, dominated by the hammerhead crane (right). (NA, 80-G-32559)

fight the raging fires and sees to the evacuation of casualties from the ship; he ultimately directs the abandonment of the doomed battleship and leaves in the last boat. He is awarded the Medal of Honor.

When *Arizona* explodes, she is moored inboard of repair ship *Vestal* (AR 4); the blast causes damage to the repair ship, which has already been hit by a bomb. *Vestal's* captain, Commander Cassin Young, earns the Medal of Honor by swimming back to his ship after being blown overboard by the explosion of *Arizona's* magazines, and directing her beaching on Aiea shoal to prevent further damage in the fires consuming *Arizona*.

Battleship *California* (BB 44), hit by both bombs and torpedoes, sinks at her berth alongside Ford Island; during the battle, Ensign Herbert C. Jones, USNR, organizes and leads a party to provide ammunition to the ship's 5-inch antiaircraft battery; he is mortally wounded by a bomb explosion. Gunner Jackson C. Pharris, leading an ordnance repair party, is stunned by concussion of a torpedo explosion early in the action but recovers to set up an ammunition supply train by hand; he later enters flooding compartments to save

shipmates. Chief Radioman Thomas J. Reeves assists in maintaining an ammunition supply party until overcome by smoke inhalation and fires; Machinist's Mate Robert R. Scott, although his station at an air compressor is flooding, remains at his post, declaring, "This is my station and I will stay and give them [the antiaircraft gun crews] air as long as the guns are going." Jones, Pharris, Reeves, and Scott receive the Medal of Honor (Jones, Reeves, and Scott posthumously).

Japanese bombs damage destroyers *Cassin* (DD 372) and *Downes* (DD 375), which are lying immobile in Drydock No. 1.

Minelayer *Oglala* (CM 4) is damaged by concussion from torpedo exploding in light cruiser *Helena* (CL 50) moored alongside, and capsizes at her berth; harbor tug *Sotoyomo* (YT 9) is sunk in floating drydock YFD 2.[41]

Battleship *Nevada* (BB 36), the only capital ship to get under way during the attack, is damaged by bombs and a torpedo before she is beached. Two of her men are later awarded the Medal of Honor: Machinist Donald K. Ross for his service in the forward and after dynamo rooms and Chief Boatswain Edwin J. Hill (posthumously) for his work in enabling

the ship to get under way and, later, in attempting to release the anchors during the effort to beach the ship.

Battleships *Pennsylvania* (BB 38), *Tennessee* (BB 43), and *Maryland* (BB 46), light cruiser *Honolulu* (CL 48), and floating drydock YFD 2 are damaged by bombs; light cruisers *Raleigh* (CL 7) and *Helena* (CL 50) are damaged by torpedoes; destroyer *Shaw* (DD 373), by bombs, in floating drydock YFD 2; heavy cruiser *New Orleans* (CA 32), destroyers *Helm* (DD 388) and *Hull* (DD 350), destroyer tender *Dobbin* (AD 3), repair ship *Rigel* (AR 11), and seaplane tender *Tangier* (AV 8) are damaged by near-misses of bombs; seaplane tender *Curtiss* (AV 4) is damaged by crashing carrier bomber; and garbage lighter YG 17 (alongside *Nevada* at the outset) is damaged by strafing and/or concussion of bombs.

Destroyer *Monaghan* (DD 354) rams, depth charges, and sinks Type A midget submarine inside Pearl Harbor proper, during the attack.[42]

Light minelayer *Gamble* (DM 15) mistakenly fires upon submarine *Thresher* (SS 200) off Oahu, 21°15′N, 159°01′W.[43]

Carrier *Enterprise* (CV 6) Air Group (CEAG, VB 6, and VS 6) search flight (Commander Howard L. Young, CEAG), in two-plane sections of SBDs, begins arriving off Oahu as the Japanese attack unfolds. Some SBDs meet their doom at the hands of Japanese planes; one (VS 6) is shot down by friendly fire. Another SBD ends up on Kauai where its radio-gunner is drafted into the local Army defense force with his single .30-caliber machine gun. Almost all of the surviving planes, together with what observation and scouting planes from battleship (VO) and cruiser (VCS) detachments, as well as flying boats (VP) and utility aircraft (VJ) that survive the attack, take part in the desperate, hastily organized searches flown out of Ford Island to look for the Japanese carriers whence the surprise attack had come.

Navy Yard and Naval Station, Pearl Harbor; Naval Air Stations at Ford Island and Kaneohe Bay; Ewa Mooring Mast Field (Marine Corps air facility); Army airfields at Hickam, Wheeler, and Bellows; and Schofield Barracks suffer varying degrees of bomb and fragment damage. Japanese bombs and strafing destroy 188 Navy, Marine Corps, and USAAF planes. At NAS Kaneohe Bay, Aviation Chief Ordnanceman John W. Finn mounts a machine gun on an instruction stand and returns the fire of strafing planes although wounded many times. Although ordered to leave his post to have his wounds treated, he returns to the squadron areas where, although in great pain, he oversees the rearming of returning PBYs. For his heroism, Finn is awarded the Medal of Honor.

Casualties. Killed or missing: Navy, 2,008; Marine Corps, 109; Army, 218; civilian, 68. Wounded: Navy, 710; Marine Corps, 69; Army, 364; civilian, 35.[44] Acts of heroism by sailors, marines, soldiers, and civilians (from telephone exchange operator to yard shop worker), in addition to those enumerated above, abound.[45]

Japanese losses amount to fewer than 100 men, 29 planes of various types, and four Type A midget submarines. A fifth Type A washes ashore off Bellows Field and is recovered; its commander (Ensign Sakamaki Kazuo) is captured, becoming U.S. prisoner of war no. 1.

Japanese Naval Aviation Pilot First Class Nishikaichi Shigenori, from the carrier *Hiryu*, crash-lands his Mitsubishi A6M2 Type 0 carrier fighter (ZERO) on the island of Niihau, T.H. He surrenders to the islanders who disarm him and confiscate his papers but, isolated as they are, know nothing of the attack on Pearl Harbor. "Peaceful and friendly," Nishikaichi is not kept in custody but is allowed to roam the island unguarded (see 9 and 12–14 December).

First night recovery of planes in World War II by the U.S. Navy occurs when *Enterprise* turns on searchlights to aid returning SBDs (VB 6 and VS 6) and TBDs (VT 6) that had been launched at dusk in an attempt to find Japanese ships reported off Oahu. Friendly fire, however, downs four of *Enterprise*'s six F4Fs (VF 6) (the strike group escort) that are directed to land at Ford Island. Other *Enterprise* SBDs make a night landing at Kaneohe Bay, miraculously avoiding automobiles and construction equipment parked on the ramp to prevent just such an occurrence.

Damage to the battle line proves extensive, but carriers *Enterprise* and *Lexington* (CV 2) are, providentially, not in port, having been deployed at the eleventh hour to reinforce advanced bases at Wake and Midway. *Saratoga* (CV 3) is at San Diego on this day, preparing to return to Oahu. The carriers will prove crucial in the coming months (see February–May 1942). Convinced that he has proved fortunate to have suffered as trifling losses as he has, Vice Admiral Nagumo Chuichi opts to set course for home, thus inadvertently sparing fuel tank farms, ship repair facilities, and the

submarine base that will prove invaluable to support the U.S. Pacific Fleet as it rebuilds in the wake of the Pearl Harbor disaster.

Midway Island is bombarded by Japanese Midway Neutralization Unit (Captain Kaname Konishi) consisting of destroyers *Ushio* and *Sazanami*; Marine shore batteries (Sixth Defense Battalion) return the fire, claiming damage to both ships. One of the submarines, *Trout* (SS 202), deployed on simulated war patrols off Midway, makes no contact with the enemy ships; the other, *Argonaut* (SS 166), is unable to make a successful approach and *Ushio* and *Sazanami* retire from the area. Subsequent bad weather will save Midway from a pounding by planes from the Pearl Harbor Attack Force as it returns to Japanese waters.

Damage control hulk *DCH 1* (IX 44), formerly destroyer *Walker* (DD 163), being towed from San Diego, California, to Pearl Harbor, by oiler *Neches* (AO 5), is cast adrift and scuttled by gunfire from *Neches* at 26°35′N, 143°49′W.

UNITED STATES. Japanese declaration of war reaches Washington, D.C., after word of the attack on Pearl Harbor has already been received in the nation's capital.

President Roosevelt orders mobilization.

8 Monday

UNITED STATES. United States declares war on Japan. In his address to the nation, President Roosevelt describes 7 December 1941 as "a date which will live in infamy."

Potomac River Naval Command with headquarters at Washington, D.C., and Severn River Naval Command with headquarters at Annapolis, Maryland, are established.

PACIFIC. Japanese submarine *I 123* mines Balabac Strait, P.I.; *I 124* mines the entrance to Manila Bay.

Striking Force Asiatic Fleet (Rear Admiral William A. Glassford Jr.) departs Iloilo, P.I., for Makassar Strait, N.E.I.

Seaplane tender (destroyer) *William B. Preston* (AVD 7) is attacked by fighters and attack planes from Japanese carrier *Ryujo* in Davao Gulf, P.I.; *William B. Preston* escapes, but two PBYs (VP 101) she is tending are strafed and destroyed on the water.

Japanese forces intern U.S. Marines and nationals at Shanghai, Tientsin, and Chinwangtao, China, and seize International Settlement, Shanghai. River gunboat *Wake* (PR 3), maintained at Shanghai as station ship and manned by a skeleton crew, is seized by Japa-

nese Naval Landing Force boarding party after attempt to scuttle fails.[46] British river gunboat HMS *Peterel*, however, moored nearby in the stream of the Whangpoo River, refuses demand to surrender and is sunk by gunfire from Japanese coast defense ship *Idzumo*. Japanese seize U.S. tugs *Meifoo No. 5*, *Mei Kang*, *Mei Nan*, *Mei Ying*, and *Mei Yun*, and Panamanian freighters *Folozu*, *Morazan*, and *Ramona*. They also take Panamanian freighters *Herleik* at Chinwangtao and *Needwood* at Tsingtao.

U.S. passenger liner *President Harrison*, en route to evacuate marines from North China, is intentionally run aground at Sha Wai Shan, China, and is captured by the Japanese.[47]

Port authorities at Yokohama, Japan, seize Panamanian freighter *Foch*.

Panamanian freighter *Essi* puts in to Hongay, French Indochina, to discharge her cargo (see 13 December).

Japanese forces land on Bataan Island, north of Luzon.

"E" operation: Japanese forces land on east coast of Malay Peninsula. RAF Hudsons bomb invasion shipping off Kota Bharu, Malaya, setting army cargo ship *Awajisan Maru* afire; destroyers *Ayanami* and *Shikinami* and submarine chaser *Ch 9* take off *Awajisan Maru*'s crew.

Japanese troops land at Patani and Singora, Thailand, and cross the Kra Isthmus; other Japanese forces invade Thailand from across the Indochina border, encountering only light resistance from the Thais.

Japanese planes bomb Hong Kong, Singapore, and the Philippine Islands. Extensive damage is inflicted on USAAF aircraft at Clark Field, Luzon, P.I. During Japanese bombing of shipping in Manila Bay, U.S. freighter *Capillo* is damaged by bomb, set afire, and abandoned off Corregidor (see 11 December).

Unarmed U.S. steamship *Admiral Cole* is bombed and strafed by Japanese flying boat in the Celebes Sea south of Zamboanga, Philippines, 04°50′N, 123°31′E, but is not damaged.

Japanese naval land attack planes (Chitose Kokutai) approach Wake Island undetected— the island has no radar— and bomb airfield installations on Wake Islet, causing heavy damage to facilities and remaining F4Fs on the ground. Pan American Airways Martin 130 *Philippine Clipper* (being prepared for a scouting flight with an escort of two VMF 211 F4Fs when the attack comes) in the aftermath of the disaster precipitately evacuates Caucasian airline staff and passengers only (Pan American's Chamorro employees are left behind).[48]

Japanese force slated to assault Wake Island

(Rear Admiral Kajioka Sadamichi) sails from Kwajalein, in the Marshall Islands.

Japanese reconnaissance seaplanes (18th *Kokutai*) bomb Guam, M.I., damaging minesweeper *Penguin* (AM 33) and miscellaneous auxiliary *Robert L. Barnes* (AG 27). *Penguin*, abandoned, is scuttled in deep water by her crew.[49]

ATLANTIC. Destroyers *Niblack* (DD 424), *Benson* (DD 421), and *Tarbell* (DD 142), part of TU 4.1.3 escorting convoy HX 163, depth charge sound contacts that are later classified as non-submarine.

9 Tuesday

PACIFIC. Japanese seize Tarawa and Makin, Gilbert Islands.

Japanese submarines *RO 63, RO 64,* and *RO 68* bombard Howland and Baker Islands in the mistaken belief that American seaplane bases exist there.

Transport *William Ward Burrows* (AP 6), en route to Wake Island, is re-routed to Johnston Island.

Japanese submarine *I 10* shells and sinks unarmed Panamanian motorship *Donerail* (en route from Suva to Vancouver, Canada), 200 miles southeast of Hawaii, 08°00′N, 152°00′W. There are only eight survivors of the 33-man crew; all seven passengers perish.

Japanese Naval Aviation Pilot First Class Nishikaichi Shigenori, from the carrier *Hiryu*, who had crash-landed his Mitsubishi A6M2 Type 0 carrier fighter on Niihau on 7 December, is placed under guard by the islanders; attempts this day and the next to transport him to Kauai are frustrated by bad weather (see 12–14 December).

Japanese naval land attack planes (Chitose *Kokutai*) bomb defense installations on the islets of Wilkes and Wake, Wake Island.

China declares war on Japan, Germany, and Italy.

Japanese carry out unopposed occupation of Bangkok, Thailand; Panamanian freighter *Gran* is seized.

River gunboat *Mindanao* (PR 8), en route from Hong Kong to Manila, encounters Japanese fishing vessel *No. 3 South Advance Maru*, stops her, and takes her 10-man Formosan crew prisoner. *Mindanao* leaves the craft adrift at 16°42′N, 118°53′E, and steams on, reaching her destination the following day.

Submarine *Swordfish* (SS 193), in initial U.S. submarine attack of the war, torpedoes Japanese ship 150 miles west of Manila at 14°30′N,

119°00′E. Her claim of a sinking, however, is not confirmed in enemy records.

ATLANTIC. TU 4.1.5 (Commander William K. Phillips) continues its escort duty with convoy ON 41; destroyers *Babbitt* (DD 128) and *Mayo* (DD 422) depth charge sound contacts, *Babbitt*'s at 57°19′N, 33°09′W. Destroyer *Schenck* (DD 159), operating independently from TU 4.1.5 while escorting U.S. freighter *Ozark*, carries out "well conducted" depth charge attack on sound contact at 52°19′N, 39°37′W.

10 Wednesday

ATLANTIC. PBYs (VP 52), supported by seaplane tender (destroyer) *Greene* (AVD 13) and small seaplane tender *Thrush* (AVP 3), begin antisubmarine patrols over the South Atlantic from Natal, Brazil, and thus inaugurate operations from Brazilian waters.

Battleship *New Mexico* (BB 40), en route to Hampton Roads, Virginia, accidentally rams and sinks U.S. freighter *Oregon*, bound for Boston, Massachusetts, south of Nantucket Lightship, 35°55′N, 69°45′W.

TU 4.1.1 (Captain Marion Y. Cohen) assumes escort duty for convoy HX 164; the ships will not be attacked by enemy submarines. While escorting oiler *Mattole* (AO 17) to join the main convoy, destroyer *Gleaves* (DD 423) carries out depth charge attack on sound contact at 45°50′N, 53°35′W. The contact is later classified as "doubtful" submarine.

PACIFIC. Cavite Navy Yard, P.I., is practically obliterated by Japanese land attack planes (Takao *Kokutai* and 1st *Kokutai*). Destroyers *Peary* (DD 226) and *Pillsbury* (DD 227), submarines *Seadragon* (SS 194) and *Sealion* (SS 195), minesweeper *Bittern* (AM 36), and submarine tender *Otus* (AS 20) suffer varying degrees of damage from bombs or bomb fragments; ferry launch *Santa Rita* (YFB 681) is destroyed by direct hit. Submarine rescue vessel *Pigeon* (ASR 6) tows *Seadragon* out of the burning wharf area; minesweeper *Whippoorwill* (AM 35) recovers *Peary*, enabling both warships to be repaired and returned to service. *Bittern* is gutted by fires. Antiaircraft fire from U.S. guns is ineffective. During bombing of Manila Bay area, unarmed U.S. freighter *Sagoland* is damaged. Land attack planes (Takao *Kokutai*) bomb Clark Field.

While flying to safety during the raid on Cavite, Lieutenant Harmon T. Utter's PBY (VP 101) is attacked by three Japanese Mitsubishi A6M2 Type 0 carrier fighters (ZERO) (3rd *Kokutai*); Chief Boatswain Earl D.

Payne, Utter's bow gunner, shoots down one, thus scoring the U.S. Navy's first verifiable air-to-air "kill" of a Japanese plane in the Pacific War.[50]

"M" Operation: Japanese forces land on Camiguin Island and at Gonzaga and Aparri, Luzon. Off Vigan, minesweeper *W.10* is bombed and sunk by USAAF P-35 at 17°32′N, 120°22′E; destroyer *Murasame* and transport *Oigawa Maru* are strafed; the latter, set afire, is beached to facilitate salvage. USAAF B-17s bomb and damage light cruiser *Naka* and transport *Takao Maru*; the latter is run aground at 17°29′N, 120°26′E (see 5 March 1942). Off Aparri, USAAF B-17s bomb invasion shipping: minesweeper *W.19* is run aground, damaged (total loss) at 18°22′N, 121°38′E; light cruiser *Natori* and destroyer *Harukaze* are also damaged by a B-17.[51]

British battleship HMS *Prince of Wales* and battle cruiser HMS *Repulse* (Admiral Sir Tom S. V. Phillips, RN) are sunk by Japanese land attack planes off Kuantan, Malaya. Destroyer Division 57—*Alden* (DD 211), *Whipple* (DD 217), *John D. Edwards* (DD 216), and *Edsall* (DD 219) (Commander William G. Lalor)—that had been sent to help screen Phillips's ships, having arrived at Singapore too late to sortie with the British force, search unsuccessfully for survivors before returning to Singapore.

Governor of Guam (Captain George J. McMillin) surrenders the island to Japanese invasion force (Rear Admiral Goto Aritomo). District patrol craft *YP 16* and *YP 17*; open lighters *YC 664, YC 665, YC 666, YC 667, YC 6687, YC 670, YC 671, YC 672, YC 673, YC 674, YC 685, YC 717,* and *YC 718;* dredge *YM 13;* water barges *YW 50, YW 55,* and *YW 58;* and miscellaneous auxiliary *Robert L. Barnes* (AG 27) are all lost to the Japanese occupation of that American Pacific possession.

SBD (CEAG) from carrier *Enterprise* (CV 6) sinks Japanese submarine *I 70* in Hawaiian Islands area, 23°45′N, 155°35′W.[52]

Japanese naval land attack planes (Chitose *Kokutai*) bomb Marine installations on Wilkes and Wake islets, Wake Island. During the interception of the bombers, Captain Henry T. Elrod, USMC, executive officer of VMF 211, shoots down a Mitsubishi G3M2 Type 96 land attack plane (NELL); this is the first USMC air-to-air "kill" of the Pacific War. Japanese submarines *RO 65, RO 66,* and *RO 67* arrive off Wake. Shortly before midnight, submarine *Triton* (SS 201), patrolling south of the atoll, encounters a Japanese warship, probably a picket for the oncoming assault force (see 11 December).

Unarmed U.S. freighter *Mauna Ala*, re-routed back to Portland, Oregon, because of Japanese submarines lurking off the U.S. west coast, runs aground off the entrance to the Columbia River; she subsequently breaks up on the beach, a total loss.

11 Thursday

GENERAL. Germany and Italy declare war on the United States.

United States declares war on Germany and Italy.

PACIFIC. Secretary of the Navy William Franklin (Frank) Knox arrives on Oahu to personally assess the damage inflicted by the Japanese on 7 December.

Submarine *Triton* (SS 201), patrolling south of Wake Island, attacks the Japanese ship encountered shortly before midnight; she is unsuccessful.

Wake Island garrison (Commander Winfield S. Cunningham) repulses Japanese invasion force (Rear Admiral Kajioka Sadamichi); marine shore battery gunfire (First Defense Battalion) straddles light cruiser *Yubari* (Kajioka's flagship), sinks destroyer *Hayate,* and damages destroyers *Oite, Mochizuki,* and *Yayoi* and *Patrol Boat No. 33* (high-speed transport); USMC F4Fs (VMF 211) bomb and sink destroyer *Kisaragi* and strafe and damage light cruiser *Tenryu* and armed merchant cruiser *Kongo Maru.* Later the same day, USMC F4F (VMF 211) bombs and most likely damages submarine *RO 66* south of Wake. U.S. submarines deployed off Wake, *Triton* to the south and *Tambor* (SS 198) to the north, take no active part in the battle. Following the abortive assault, Japanese naval land attack planes (Chitose *Kokutai*) bomb marine gun batteries on Peale islet.

Japanese submarine *I 9* shells unarmed U.S. freighter *Lahaina* about 800 miles northeast of Honolulu, T.H., 27°42′N, 147°38′W (see 12 and 21 December).

Japanese make landings at Legaspi, Luzon.

Unarmed U.S. freighter *Capillo*, damaged by bomb on 8 December 1941, is partially scuttled by U.S. Army demolition party, off Corregidor, P.I. (see 29 December). Freighter *Sagoland*, damaged by bombs the previous day, sinks in Manila Bay.

ATLANTIC. TU 4.1.5 (Commander William K. Phillips) detaches destroyers *Babbitt* (DD 128) and *Leary* (DD 158), low on fuel because of the delayed arrival of convoy ON 41 at the MOMP, to proceed to Argentia, Newfoundland. En route to Argentia, *Babbitt* depth charges sound contact without result at 51°37′N, 43°08′W.

TU 4.1.6 (Commander John S. Roberts) assumes escort duty at MOMP for convoy ON 43, which has been badly scattered by heavy weather conditions (see 13 and 15 December). Convoy HX 163, being escorted by TU 4.1.3 (Commander George W. Johnson), encounters same abominable weather.

12 Friday

UNITED STATES. Naval Air Transport Service (NATS) is established.

U.S. government seizes French ships in U.S. ports.

PACIFIC. Secretary of the Navy William Franklin (Frank) Knox departs Oahu after inspecting the damage done by the Japanese attack of 7 December.

Japanese flying boats (Yokohama *Kokutai*) bomb Wake Island in predawn raid. Later in the day, land attack planes (Chitose *Kokutai*) bomb Wake.

Unarmed U.S. freighter *Vincent* is shelled and sunk by Japanese armed merchant cruisers *Aikoku Maru* and *Hokoku Maru* about 600 miles northwest of Easter Island, 22°41′S, 118°19′E, and her entire crew captured.

Unarmed U.S. freighter *Lahaina*, shelled and torpedoed by Japanese submarine *I 9* the previous day, sinks (see 21 December).

Japanese Naval Aviation Pilot First Class Nishikaichi Shigenori begins, with aid of Harada Yoshio, a Japanese resident of Niihau, to terrorize the inhabitants of the island into returning papers confiscated on 7 December. In response to this campaign of intimidation, the islanders flee to the hills (see 13 December).

Submarine *S 38* (SS 143) mistakenly torpedoes and sinks Norwegian merchantman *Hydra II* west of Cape Calavite, Mindoro, P.I., believing her to be a Japanese auxiliary. *Hydra II* had been en route from Bangkok, Thailand, to Hong Kong, when she was diverted to Manila by the outbreak of war.

During Japanese bombing of shipping off Cebu, in the Visayan Sea, Philippine passenger vessel *Governor Wright* is sunk, 12°55′N, 123°55′E.

USAAF B-17 (19th Bombardment Group) bombs Japanese shipping off Vigan, P.I., damaging transport *Hawaii Maru*.

Dutch submarines operate off Malaya against Japanese invasion shipping. *K XII* torpedoes and sinks army cargo ship *Toro Maru* off Kota Bharu, 06°08′N, 102°16′E; *O 16* torpedoes and damages army cargo ships *Tozan Maru, Kinka Maru,* and *Asosan Maru* off Patani/Singora.

Panamanian freighters *Marion* and *Wawa* are scuttled in Hong Kong Harbor. *Marion* is subsequently renamed *Manryo Maru* (see 12 October 1944). *Wawa* became *Awa Maru* (see 14 July 1945).

Japanese minelayer/netlayer *Naryu* is damaged by marine casualty, Tomogashima Channel.

13 Saturday

UNITED STATES. Congress, to meet the demand for trained enlisted men, authorizes the retention of enlisted men in the Navy upon the expiration of their enlistments when not voluntarily extended.

PACIFIC. Japanese planes attack Subic Bay area and airfields in Philippines. During bombing of shipping in Manila Bay by naval land attack planes (Takao *Kokutai*), unarmed U.S. tankship *Manatawny* is damaged (see 11 January 1942).

Vichy French place guard on board Panamanian freighter *Essi,* Hongay, French Indochina; replaced by a Japanese guard on 22 December when the vessel is taken over to serve Japan.

Occupation of Niihau by Japanese Naval Aviation Pilot First Class Nishikaichi Shigenori ends. A party of Hawaiians sets out for Kauai to inform the outside world of events on Niihau; in the meantime, Nishikaichi burns his plane (it will not be until July 1942 that the U.S. Navy will be able to obtain an intact ZERO to study) and the house in which he believes his confiscated papers are hidden. Later, in a confrontation with a local Hawaiian, Benny Kanahele, a scuffle to grab the pilot's pistol ensues. Although Kanahele is shot twice, he picks up Nishikaichi bodily and dashes the pilot's head into a stone wall, killing him; Harada Yoshio, the Japanese resident of Niihau who has allied himself with the pilot, commits suicide. Kanahele survives his injuries. On the basis of the report by the islanders who have arrived on Kauai after a 15-hour trip, meanwhile, Commander Kauai Military District (Colonel Edward W. FitzGerald, USA) dispatches a squad from Company M, 299th Infantry in Coast Guard lighthouse tender *Kukui* to proceed from Kauai to Niihau (see 14 December).

Japanese cargo ship *Nikkoku Maru* is

stranded and wrecked off Hainan Island, 18°00'N, 110°00'E.

Gunboat *Erie* (PG 50) receives 50 Japanese POWs at Puntarenas, Costa Rica, from Costa Rican government and sends prize crew to take charge of motor vessel *Albert*.

ATLANTIC. Destroyer *Woolsey* (DD 437), sweeping astern of convoy ON 43, depth charges sound contact at 57°55'N, 32°05'W.

14 Sunday

PACIFIC. TF 11 (Vice Admiral Wilson Brown Jr.), comprising carrier *Lexington* (CV 2), three heavy cruisers, nine destroyers, and oiler *Neosho* (AO 23), sails for the Marshall Islands, to create a diversion to cover TF 14's attempt to relieve Wake Island (see 15 and 16 December).

Japanese flying boats (Yokohama *Kokutai*) bomb Wake Island. Later in the day, naval land attack planes (Chitose *Kokutai*) raid Wake, bombing airfield installations.

Destroyer *Craven* (DD 382) collides with heavy cruiser *Northampton* (CA 26) during underway refueling and is damaged. The ships are part of TF 8 operating north of Oahu.

Norwegian motorship *Höegh Merchant* is torpedoed and sunk by Japanese submarine *I 4* about 20 miles east-northeast of Oahu. All hands (35-man crew and five passengers) survive the loss of the ship.

Coast Guard lighthouse tender *Kukui* reaches Niihau with squad of soldiers from Company M, 299th Infantry (Lieutenant Jack Mizuha); the detachment learns of the denouement of the events that have transpired on Niihau since 7 December.

Japanese gunboat *Zuiko Maru*, wrecked and driven aground by storm, sinks off Matsuwa Jima, Kurils, 48°05'N, 153°43'E.

Gunboat *Erie* (PG 50), off coast of Costa Rica, boards and takes charge of motor vessel *Sea Boy*, and takes off a Japanese POW; she orders *Sea Boy* into Balboa the following day.

USAAF B-17s bomb and damage Japanese cargo ship *Ikushima Maru* and oiler *Hayatomo* off Legaspi, Luzon.

With its operating area rendered untenable by Japanese control of the air, Patrol Wing 10 (Captain Frank D. Wagner) departs Philippines for Netherlands East Indies. Seaplane tender (destroyer) *Childs* (AVD 1), with Captain Wagner embarked, sails from Manila.

Submarine *Seawolf* (SS 197) torpedoes Japanese seaplane carrier *San'yo Maru* off Aparri, P.I.; one torpedo hits the ship but does not explode.

Submarine *Swordfish* (SS 193), attacking Japanese shipping off Hainan Island, torpe-

does army transport *Kashii Maru*, 18°08'N, 109°22'E.

Navy boarding party (Lieutenant Edward N. Little), transported in commandeered yacht *Gem*, seizes French motor mail vessel *Marechal Joffre*, Manila Bay. Majority of the crewmen, pro-Vichy or unwilling to serve under the U.S. flag, are put ashore (see 17 and 18 December).

15 Monday

PACIFIC. Seaplane tender *Tangier* (AV 8), oiler *Neches* (AO 5), and four destroyers sail for Wake Island (see 16 December).

Japanese reconnaissance flying boats (Yokohama *Kokutai*) bomb Wake Island.

Johnston Island is shelled by Japanese submarine *I 22*; although one shell lands astern and another passes over her forecastle, transport *William Ward Burrows* (AP 6) is apparently unseen by the enemy submariners. She is not hit and escapes.

Kahului, Maui, T.H., is shelled by Japanese submarine from the Second Submarine Squadron.[53]

Philippine steamship *Vizcaya* is scuttled in Manila Bay, most likely to prevent potential use by the Japanese.

ATLANTIC. TU 4.1.2 (Commander Fred D. Kirtland) clears Reykjavik, Iceland, for the MOMP, escorting convoy ON 45; destroyer *Sturtevant* (DD 240), escorting cargo ship *Alchiba* (AK 23), depth charges sound contact at 62°05'N, 24°15'W (see 16 December).

Destroyer *Benson* (DD 421), detached from TU 4.1.3 and convoy HX 163 at the MOMP, searches for survivors of steamer *Nidardal*, reported sinking at 56°07'N, 21°00'W (later amended to 56°07'N, 23°00'W) (see 16 December).

Convoy ON 43, struggling through rough seas and high winds, being escorted by TU 4.1.6 (Commander John S. Roberts), is dispersed.

UNITED STATES. Admiral Ernest J. King is offered the post of Commander in Chief U.S. Fleet. He accepts (see 18, 20, and 30 December).

16 Tuesday

ATLANTIC. Carrier *Yorktown* (CV 5) departs Norfolk, Virginia, the first carrier reinforcement dispatched to the Pacific.

Convoy ON 45, escorted by TU 4.1.2 (Commander Fred D. Kirtland), is dispersed because of bad weather.

Destroyer *Benson* (DD 421) sights white dis-

tress rocket at 0241 and alters course in hopes of locating survivors of merchantman *Nidardal*; the intense darkness in which the search is being conducted renders it barely possible to see the surface of the ocean from the bridge, and the loudness of the wind makes it unlikely that a hail can be heard more than 50 to 100 feet from the ship. *Benson* searches throughout the daylight hours but finds no trace of the missing ship or her crew. She abandons the search at nightfall and proceeds to Reykjavik.

PACIFIC. TF 14 (Rear Admiral Frank Jack Fletcher), comprising carrier *Saratoga* (CV 3) (with VB3, VF3, VS3, VT3, and VMF221); heavy cruisers *Astoria* (CA 34) (flagship), *Minneapolis* (CA 36), and *San Francisco* (CA 38); and nine destroyers, sails from Pearl Harbor. These ships will overtake the force formed around seaplane tender *Tangier* (AV 8) and oiler *Neches* (AO 5) and their consorts that sortied the previous day. The objective of this combined force is to relieve Wake Island.

Japanese Pearl Harbor Attack Force (Vice Admiral Nagumo Chuichi) detaches carriers *Hiryu* and *Soryu*, heavy cruisers *Tone* and *Chikuma*, and two destroyers (Rear Admiral Abe Hiroaki) to reinforce second planned attack on Wake Island.

Japanese naval land attack planes (Chitose *Kokutai*) bomb Wake.

Submarine *Tambor* (SS 198), damaged by operational casualty, retires from the waters off Wake.

Submarine *Swordfish* (SS 193), attacking Japanese convoy south of Hainan Island, torpedoes army transport *Atsutasan Maru*, 18°06'N, 109°44'E.

Gunboat *Erie* (PG 50) boards Panamanian motor vessel *Santa Margarita* and orders her to proceed to Puntarenas, Costa Rica. Later the same day, the gunboat tows disabled motorboat *Orion* into Puntarenas.

17 Wednesday

PACIFIC. Vice Admiral William S. Pye, Commander Battle Force, becomes Acting Commander in Chief Pacific Fleet, pending the arrival of Rear Admiral Chester W. Nimitz, who is ordered on this date to relieve Admiral Husband E. Kimmel.

Small reconnaissance seaplane from Japanese submarine *I 7* reconnoiters Pearl Harbor.

Unarmed U.S. freighter *Manini* is torpedoed and sunk by Japanese submarine *I 175*, 180 miles south of Hawaii, 17°45'N, 157°03'E (see 27 and 28 December).

USMC SB2Us (VMSB 231), led by a plane-guarding PBY (VP 21) (no ships are available to plane-guard the flight), arrive at Midway, completing the longest over-water massed flight (1,137 miles) by a single-engine aircraft.[54]

Japanese submarine *RO 66* is sunk in collision with sister ship *RO 62* off Wake Island.

Philippine steamship *Corregidor*, crowded with about 1,200 passengers fleeing Manila for Mindanao, hits an army mine off Corregidor and sinks with heavy loss of life. Motor torpedo boats *PT 32*, *PT 34*, and *PT 35* pick up 282 survivors (196 by *PT 32* alone) and distribute them between Corregidor and the requisitioned French steamship *Si-Kiang;* seven of those rescued die of injuries suffered in the tragedy.[55]

Navy takes over French motor mail vessel *Marechal Joffre*, Manila Bay (see 18 December).

Japanese land at Miri, Sarawak, Borneo.

18 Thursday

UNITED STATES. President Roosevelt signs Executive Order No. 8984 that provides that Commander in Chief U.S. Fleet will take supreme command of the operating forces of all Navy fleets and Coastal Frontier commands, and be directly responsible to the President.

In another executive order, President Roosevelt directs a commission, to be headed by retired Supreme Court Chief Justice Owen J. Roberts (Roberts Commission), to "ascertain and report the facts relating to the attack made by the Japanese armed forces upon the Territory of Hawaii on December 7, 1941 . . . to provide bases for sound decisions whether any derelictions of duty or errors of judgment on the part of United States Army or Navy personnel contributed to such successes as were achieved by the enemy on the occasion mentioned; and if so, what these derelictions or errors were, and who were responsible therefor." In addition to Justice Roberts, the commission's membership includes Admiral William H. Standley, USN (Retired), Rear Admiral Joseph W. Reeves, USN (Retired), Major General Frank R. McCoy, USA (Retired), and Brigadier General Joseph T. McNarney, USA (see 23 January 1942).

Congress passes First War Powers Act.

CARIBBEAN. State Department announces that Rear Admiral Frederick J. Horne and Admiral Georges A. M. J. Robert, French High Commissioner at Martinique, French West Indies, have reached an agreement neutralizing French Caribbean possessions.

PACIFIC. French motor mail vessel *Marechal Joffre*, manned by a scratch crew that includes aviation personnel from Patrol Wing 10, departs Manila Bay for Borneo.[56]

Dutch Dornier 24 bombs and sinks Japanese destroyer *Shinonome* off Miri, Borneo.

19 Friday

PACIFIC. TF 8 (Vice Admiral William F. Halsey Jr.), formed around carrier *Enterprise* (CV 6), heavy cruisers, and destroyers, sails from Pearl Harbor proceeding to waters west of Johnston Island and south of Midway to cover TF 11 and TF 14 operations (see 14–16 December). Destroyer *Craven* (DD 382), in TF 8, is damaged by heavy sea soon after departure, however, and returns to Pearl Harbor for repairs.

Japanese naval land attack planes (Chitose Kokutai) bomb Wake Island, targeting installations on Wake and Peale islets.

Unarmed U.S. freighter *Prusa* is torpedoed and sunk by Japanese submarine *I 172* about 150 miles south of Hawaii, 16°45'N, 156°00'W; nine crewmen perish (see 27 December).

UNITED STATES. U.S. Naval Academy Class of 1942 is graduated six months early because of the national emergency.

20 Saturday

UNITED STATES. In the wake of the signing of Executive Order No. 8984, Admiral Ernest J. King is announced as the designated Commander in Chief U.S. Fleet (see 30 December).

PACIFIC. SBDs (VB 6 and VS 6) from carrier *Enterprise* (CV 6) accidentally bomb submarine *Pompano* (SS 181) twice, at 20°10'N, 165°28'W, and 20°15'N, 165°40'W.

PBY (VP 23) arrives at Wake Island to deliver information to the garrison concerning the relief efforts then under way (see 21 December).

Japanese troops land at Davao, Mindanao, P.I.

Unarmed U.S. tankship *Emidio* is shelled, torpedoed, and sunk by Japanese submarine *I 17* about 25 miles west of Cape Mendocino, California, 40°33'N, 125°00'W (see 21 December).

Unarmed U.S. tanker *Agwiworld* is shelled by Japanese submarine *I 23* off the coast of California, 37°00'N, 122°00'W.

Panamanian motor vessels *Florinha* and *Lindinha* are seized by the Japanese at Fort Bayard, Kwangchowan.

21 Sunday

PACIFIC. PBY (VP 23) departs Wake Island; Japanese concern over the potential presence of patrol planes at Wake, occasioned by the large amount of radio traffic that accompanies the sole PBY's arrival at the island, prompts advancing the date of the first carrier strikes. Consequently, planes from carriers *Soryu* and *Hiryu* bomb Wake Island for the first time. Later that day, land attack planes (Chitose Kokutai) bomb Wake.

Naval local defense forces in Philippine Islands (Rear Admiral Francis W. Rockwell) move headquarters to Corregidor.

Destroyer *Paul Jones* (DD 230) is damaged when her starboard propeller strikes a sunken object off Makassar, N.E.I.

Coast Guard cutter *Shawnee* rescues 31 survivors of U.S. tanker *Emidio*, sunk the previous day by *I 17* off Cape Mendocino, California, from Blunt's Reef Lightship.

Survivors of U.S. freighter *Lahaina* (sunk on 11 December by Japanese submarine *I 9*) land at Sprecklesville Beach, near Kahului, Maui, having lost four of their number during their ordeal in their one lifeboat.

ATLANTIC. Light cruiser *Omaha* (CL 4) and destroyer *Somers* (DD 381), operating out of Recife, Brazil, encounter darkened ship that acts suspicious and evasive when challenged. *Omaha* fires starshell and illuminates the stranger; *Somers* sends armed boarding party that learns that the merchantman nearly fired upon is Soviet freighter *Nevastroi*.

Destroyer *Edison* (DD 439), in TU 4.1.3 en route to MOMP to pick up convoy ON 47, depth charges sound contact without result.

22 Monday

GENERAL. President Roosevelt and British Prime Minister Winston S. Churchill open discussions (ARCADIA conference) in Washington, D.C., leading to establishment of Combined Chiefs of Staff. The ARCADIA conference, which lasts into January 1942, results in a formal American commitment to the "Germany First" strategy. In addition, the United States and Britain agree to form a Combined Chiefs of Staff as the supreme body for Allied war planning, to confer regularly in Washington (see 6 February 1942). The Anglo-American allies also agree that there should be one supreme commander directing operations in each theater.

PACIFIC. Japanese bombers and attack planes, covered by fighters, from carriers *Soryu* and *Hiryu*, bomb Wake Island for the second time;

the last two flyable USMC F4Fs (VMF 211) intercept the raid. One F4F is shot down, the other is badly damaged.

American troops (Task Force South Pacific) (Brigadier General Julian F. Barnes, USA) arrive at Brisbane in convoy escorted by heavy cruiser *Pensacola* (CA 24). This is the first U.S. Army troop detachment to arrive in Australia.

Japanese submarine *I 19* shells unarmed U.S. tanker *H. M. Storey* southwest of Cape Mendocino, California, 34°35′N, 120°45′W, but fails to score any hits and the American ship escapes.

Japanese commence invasion of Luzon, landing troops at Lingayen, P.I.; submarine *S 38* (SS 143) torpedoes and sinks Japanese army transport *Hayo Maru* in Lingayen Gulf, 16°00′N, 120°00′E.

USAAF B-17s bomb and damage Japanese army oiler *No. 3 Tonan Maru* off Davao, P.I.

ATLANTIC. TU 4.1.3 (Commander George W. Johnson) assumes escort duty at MOMP for convoy ON 47; the convoy is dispersed the following day.

23 Tuesday

GENERAL. U.S.-British War Council composed of President Roosevelt, British Prime Minister Winston S. Churchill, and their chief naval, military, and civilian advisers meets for the first time in Washington, D.C.

PACIFIC. Wake Island (Commander Winfield S. Cunningham) is captured by Japanese naval landing force (Commander Tanaka Mitsuo) that overcomes gallant resistance offered by the garrison that consists of marines, sailors, volunteer civilians (Contractors Pacific Naval Air Bases), and an army communications detachment. Japanese *Patrol Boat No. 32* and *Patrol Boat No. 33* (old destroyers converted to high-speed transports), intentionally run ashore to facilitate landing of troops, are destroyed by marine shore batteries (First Defense Battalion). Planes from carriers *Hiryu* and *Soryu*, as well as seaplane carrier *Kiyokawa Maru,* provide close air support for the invasion. Open cargo lighter *YCK 1* is lost to Japanese occupation of the atoll, as are civilian tugs *Pioneer* and *Justine Foss* and dredge *Columbia.*

Uncertainty over the positions and number of Japanese carriers and reports that indicate Japanese troops have landed on Wake Island compel Vice Admiral William S. Pye, Acting Commander in Chief Pacific Fleet, to recall TF 14 (Rear Admiral Frank Jack Fletcher) while it is 425 miles from its objective.

Palmyra Island is shelled by Japanese submarines *I 71* and *I 72.*

Unarmed U.S. tanker *Montebello* is torpedoed and sunk by Japanese submarine *I 21* about four miles south of Piedras Blancas Light, California, 35°30′N, 121°51′W. *I 21* machine guns the lifeboats, but miraculously inflicts no casualties. *I 21* later also shells unarmed U.S. tanker *Idaho* near the same location.

Japanese submarine *I 17* shells unarmed U.S. tanker *Larry Doheny* southwest of Cape Mendocino, California, 40°00′N, 125°00′W, but the American ship escapes.

USAAF B-17s bomb Japanese ships in Lingayen Gulf and off Davao, damaging minesweeper *W.17* and destroyer *Kuroshio* off the latter place. USAAF P-40s and P-35s strafe landing forces in San Miguel Bay, Luzon, damaging destroyer *Nagatsuki.*

Submarine *Seal* (SS 183) sinks Japanese army cargo ship *Soryu Maru* off Vigan, Luzon, 17°35′N, 120°12′E.

Japanese troops land at Kuching, Sarawak, Borneo. Off the invasion beaches, Dutch submarine *K XIV* torpedoes and sinks transport *Hokkai Maru* and army transport *Hiyoshi Maru,* and damages army cargo ship *Nichiran Maru* and transport *Katori Maru.*

ATLANTIC. TU 4.1.4 (Commander Richard E. Webb) assumes escort duty for convoy HX 166; the ships reach their destination without being attacked by U-boats.

24 Wednesday

PACIFIC. Unarmed U.S. freighter *Absaroka* is shelled by Japanese submarine *I 17* about 26 miles off San Pedro, California, 33°40′N, 118°25′W; although abandoned, she is later reboarded and towed to San Pedro.

Unarmed U.S. steamship *Dorothy Philips* is shelled by Japanese submarine *I 23* off Monterey Bay, California.

Seaplane tender *Wright* (AV 1) disembarks Marine reinforcements (Batteries "A" and "C," Fourth Defense Battalion) at Midway.

Second Marine Brigade (Colonel Henry L. Larsen, USMC) is formed at Camp Elliott, California, to defend American Samoa (see 6 and 20 January 1942).

Japanese land at Lamon Bay, Luzon.

Motor torpedo boat *PT 33* is damaged by grounding on reef five miles northwest of Cape Santiago, Luzon, 13°46′N, 120°40′E.

During Japanese bombing of shipping in Manila Bay by naval land attack planes (Takao *Kokutai* and 1st *Kokutai*), requisitioned French steamship *Si-Kiang* is set afire off Mariveles; of the eight-man USMC guard detachment on

board (from First Separate Marine Battalion), two marines are killed and three wounded. Tug *Napa* (AT 32) assists fire-fighting efforts.

Dutch submarine *K XVI* torpedoes and sinks Japanese destroyer *Sagiri* off Kuching, Sarawak, 01°34′N, 110°21′E.

25 Thursday

PACIFIC. Admiral Thomas C. Hart turns over all remaining naval forces in the Philippines to Rear Admiral Francis W. Rockwell (Commandant Sixteenth Naval District). After Japanese bombers destroy PBYs (VPs 101 and 102) earmarked to transport him and his staff south, Hart sails in submarine *Shark* (SS 174) (held in readiness for that eventuality) to establish new Asiatic Fleet headquarters in Java (see 1 January 1942). During Japanese bombing of shipping in Manila Bay, submarine *Sturgeon* (SS 187) is straddled but is not damaged.

British surrender Hong Kong. U.S. freighter *Admiral Y. S. Williams,* under repairs in that port for damage incurred in a grounding that had occurred on 24 September, is sabotaged to prevent use by the Japanese.[57] U.S. steamship (ex-yacht) *Hirondelle* (also under repairs in the Crown Colony when caught there by the outbreak of hostilities) and Philippine steamship *Argus* are captured.[58] Philippine steamship *Churruca* and Panamanian *Eldorado* are scuttled (the latter will be raised); Panamanian merchantman *Daylight* is captured.

Japanese land at Jolo, P.I.

Submarine *Sealion* (SS 195), damaged by bombs at Cavite, P.I. on 10 December, is scuttled by a demolition crew (Lieutenant Thomas J. E. Crotty, USCG), which also blows up other military and civilian establishments to prevent their falling into Japanese hands.

Carrier *Saratoga* (CV 3), diverted from the attempt to relieve Wake Island, flies off USMC F2As (VMF 221) to Midway. These will be the first fighter aircraft based there.

26 Friday

PACIFIC. Manila, P.I., is declared an open city, but Japanese bombing continues unabated. Japanese naval land attack planes (Takao *Kokutai* and 1st *Kokutai*) bomb shipping in Manila Bay; destroyer *Peary* (DD 226) is damaged by near-misses. Philippine freighter *Paz* is sunk. *Paz* will be salvaged and renamed *Hatsu Maru* (see 20 November 1944).

Motor torpedo boat *PT 33*, damaged by grounding on 24 December five miles northwest of Cape Santiago, Luzon, 13°46′N, 120°40′E, is burned to prevent capture.

Dutch Army planes bomb and sink Japanese minesweeper *W.6* and collier *No. 2 Unyo Maru* off Kuching, Sarawak, 01°34′N, 110°21′E.

Japanese destroyer *Murasame* and minesweeper *W.20* are damaged by marine casualties off Takao, Formosa.

Seaplane tender *Tangier* (AV 8), diverted from the attempt to relieve Wake Island, disembarks Battery "B," Fourth Defense Battalion and ground echelon of VMF 221 at Midway to augment that garrison's defenses.

ATLANTIC. Submarine chaser *PC 451* accidentally rams and sinks U.S. tug *Nancy Moran* off east coast of Florida.

27 Saturday

PACIFIC. Destroyer *Allen* (DD 66) rescues first of two groups of survivors from U.S. freighter *Manini* (sunk by Japanese submarine *I 175* on 17 December) at 21°29′N, 159°36′E.

Coast Guard cutter *Tiger* rescues 14 survivors of U.S. freighter *Prusa*, sunk by Japanese submarine *I 172* on 19 December. A second group of 11 survivors reaches safety after a 2,700-mile voyage, rescued by a Fijian government vessel and taken to Boruin, Gilberts.

Unarmed U.S. tanker *Connecticut* is shelled by Japanese submarine *I 25* about 10 miles west of the mouth of the Columbia River, between Washington and Oregon.

Submarine *Perch* (SS 176) torpedoes Japanese supply ship *Noshima* in South China Sea, 22°14′N, 115°13′E.

Six PBYs (VP 101) bomb Japanese shipping at Jolo, P.I. against heavy fighter opposition; four Catalinas are lost.

Japanese bomb shipping in Manila Bay and Pasig River (Takao *Kokutai* and 1st *Kokutai*). Philippine customs cutters *Arayat* and *Mindoro* and motor vessel *Ethel Edwards* are set afire, while lighthouse tender *Canlaon* is destroyed by a direct hit. Steamship *Taurus* is scuttled in the Pasig River (see 29 December).

28 Sunday

PACIFIC. Destroyer *Patterson* (DD 392) rescues second of two groups of survivors from U.S. freighter *Manini* sunk by Japanese submarine (*I 175*) on 17 December at 21°06′N, 161°55′E. at 21°06′N, 161°55′E.

Destroyer *Peary* (DD 226) is damaged when mistakenly bombed and strafed by RAAF Hudsons off Kina, Celebes, N.E.I.

Japanese bomb and sink Philippine freighter *Mauban* and lighthouse tender *Banahao*.

Japanese destroyer *Akikaze* and army cargo ships *Kamogawa Maru* and *Komaki Maru* are damaged by marine casualties east of Luzon.

29 Monday

PACIFIC. Corregidor is bombed for the first time by Japanese naval land attack planes (Takao *Kokutai* and 1st *Kokutai),* ending "normal" above-ground living there. During the bombings that day, submarine tender *Canopus* (AS 9) is damaged in Mariveles Harbor, 14°25′N, 120°30′E; river gunboat *Mindanao* (PR 8) is damaged by near-misses off Corregidor. Bombs also set fire to Philippine freighter *Don Jose* and the hulk of U.S. freighter *Capillo* off Corregidor. Minesweeper *Finch* (AM 9) puts out the blaze on board both ships; *Don Jose* is later moved to the south side of the island to ensure a clear shipping channel.[59] Philippine presidential yacht *Casiana* is bombed and sunk near the Fort Mills dock; Philippine steamship *Bicol* and motor vessel *Aloha* are scuttled in Manila Bay. *Finch* later assists Navy-commandeered tug *Trabajador* in dumping unused mines in Manila Bay, an operation these two ships will repeat the following day as well. Cable Censor, Manila (Lieutenant Frederick L. Worcester, USNR) clears Pasig River of interisland shipping and tugs and other ships that have drawn heavy bombing from Japanese planes, thus saving the area from further destruction and the shipping for use in maintaining communications between Bataan and Corregidor and in patrol work. This action is later praised as "commendable assumption of authority and action by nonnautical" district officers.

Japanese submarine *RO 60*, returning from the Wake Island operation, is irreparably damaged by grounding, Kwajalein Atoll, 09°00′N, 167°30′E.

ATLANTIC. TU 4.1.5 (Commander William K. Phillips) assumes guard for east-bound convoy HX 167. U.S. freighter *Stonestreet* is damaged by evaporator explosion; one man is killed and three injured. Destroyer *Simpson* (DD 221) puts medical officer and corpsman on board promptly to treat the injured; *Stonestreet* is directed to return to St. John's, Newfoundland; U.S. PBY provides cover. During the voyage to Iceland, HX 167 will not encounter any enemy submarines, but poor navigation by the convoy will result in a critical fuel state for the "shortlegged" flush-deck destroyers (see 3 January 1942).

30 Tuesday

UNITED STATES. Admiral Ernest J. King assumes duties as Commander in Chief U.S. Fleet. To avoid use of what he considers the pejorative acronym CINCUS ("Sink Us"), he institutes use of COMINCH ("Comm Inch").

PACIFIC. Japanese submarine *I 1* shells Hilo, Hawaii; seaplane tender (destroyer) *Hulbert* (AVD 6), moored to a pier adjacent to the one damaged by the bombardment, is not damaged.

Navy-commandeered tug *Ranger* lands volunteer raiding party on Sangley Point, Luzon, P.I. The sailors bring out diesel generators and diesel oil needed on Corregidor to provide auxiliary power.

31 Wednesday

PACIFIC. Admiral Chester W. Nimitz assumes command of Pacific Fleet in ceremonies on board submarine *Grayling* (SS 209) at Pearl Harbor.

Japanese submarines shell Kauai, Maui, and Hawaii.

While returning from attempting to aid destroyer *Peary* (DD 226), damaged on 28 December, small seaplane tender *Heron* (AVP 2) is damaged but fights off, over a seven-hour span, a series of attacks by Japanese flying boats (Toko *Kokutai*) and land attack planes off Ambon, N.E.I. *Heron* shoots down one flying boat whose crew refuses rescue.

Submarine rescue vessel *Pigeon* (ASR 6) transports armed party [Lieutenant (j.g.) Malcolm M. Champlin, USNR] to Sangley Point, Luzon, P.I., which brings out Luzon Stevedoring Company lighter loaded with 97 mines and eight truckloads of aerial depth charges; *Pigeon* then tows the barge to a point four and a half miles off Sangley Point and capsizes it in 11 fathoms of water. The sailors also destroy the aircraft repair shop at Cavite and one irreparable PBY.

Unarmed U.S. steamship *Ruth Alexander*, en route from Manila to Balikpapan, Borneo, is bombed and irreparably damaged by Japanese flying boat in Makassar Strait, N.E.I., 01°00′N, 119°10′W; one man is killed in the bombing.[60] Dutch Dornier 24 later rescues the 48 survivors and lands them at Tarakan, Borneo.

Japanese destroyer *Yamagumo* is damaged by mine off Lingayen, P.I.

Philippine steamships *Magellanes* and *Montanes* are scuttled, most likely at Manila, P.I., to prevent their use by the Japanese.

1942

JANUARY

1 Thursday

GENERAL. President Roosevelt and Prime Minister Winston S. Churchill sign the Joint Declaration of the United Nations; only the United States and Britain had discussed the document's creation, but ultimately representatives of 24 other nations, including the Soviet Union and China, will affix their signatures to it. There will be no separate peace agreements; the signatories pledge to fight until the Axis is defeated.

PACIFIC. Admiral Thomas C. Hart (Commander in Chief Asiatic Fleet) arrives in Surabaya, Java, N.E.I., after his passage from Manila, P.I., in submarine *Shark* (SS 174).

Unarmed U.S. freighter *Malama*, en route from Honolulu, T.H., to Manila, is bombed and sunk by floatplane from Japanese armed merchant cruiser *Aikoku Maru* at 26°21′N, 153°24′W. *Aikoku Maru* takes the 35-man crew and the eight passengers prisoner.[61]

Japanese army cargo ship *Teiun Maru* (ex-German *Bremerhaven*) is sunk by mine (U.S. or Japanese) off mouth of Lingayen Gulf, Luzon, P.I., 16°05′N, 120°20′E.

Japanese oiler *Toen Maru* is damaged by mine southwest of Hong Kong, B.C.C.

ATLANTIC. Admiral Royal E. Ingersoll succeeds Admiral Ernest J. King as Commander in Chief Atlantic Fleet.

2 Friday

PACIFIC. Japanese troops enter Manila.

3 Saturday

PACIFIC. Japanese freighter *Meiko Maru*, in Third Malaya Convoy, is sunk by accidental gasoline explosion south of Paracel Islands, 15°01′N, 112°48′E; escorting training cruiser *Kashii* rescues survivors.

Japanese collier *Moji Maru* is sunk by mine southwest of Hong Kong.

ATLANTIC. Critical fuel states in the "short-legged" flush-deck destroyers in the screen of convoy HX 167 prompts the adoption of the expedient of cargo ship *Delta* (AK 29) fueling destroyers *Babbitt* (DD 128) and *Schenck* (DD 159). Weather again worsens, however, preventing *Leary* (DD 158) from fueling; she is sent to Casco Bay, Maine, to refuel.

Light cruiser *Omaha* (CL 4) and destroyer *Somers* (DD 381), operating on patrol of shipping lanes between Brazil and Trinidad, encounter two ships in succession that fail to answer challenges; *Omaha* sends armed boarding party each time to obtain information. The vessels prove to be Greek freighter *Marika Protopapa* and Norwegian merchantman *Tercero*.

4 Sunday

PACIFIC. USAAF B-17s (Far East Air Force) bomb Japanese warships in Malalag Bay, Davao, P.I., and damage heavy cruisers *Myoko* (direct hit and near-misses) and *Nachi* (near-misses).

5 Monday

PACIFIC. Submarine tender *Canopus* (AS 9) is damaged by bombs, Lilimbom Cove, Mariveles, P.I.

Submarine *Pollack* (SS 180) torpedoes Japanese cargo ship *Heijo Maru* 80 miles east-

68

southeast of Tokyo Bay, Honshu, Japan, 34°15′N, 140°08′E.

6 Tuesday

PACIFIC. Second Marine Brigade (Brigadier General Henry L. Larsen, USMC), embarked in troop transports (former Matson Line passenger liners) *Lurline*, *Monterey*, and *Matsonia*, along with cargo ship *Jupiter* (AK 43) and ammunition ship *Lassen* (AE 3), sails from San Diego, California, for Pago Pago, American Samoa. Initial escort is provided by TF 17 (Rear Admiral Frank Jack Fletcher), formed around carrier *Yorktown* (CV 5) (see 20 January).

Japanese amphibious force lands at Brunei Bay, Borneo.

7 Wednesday

UNITED STATES. Navy's authorized aircraft strength is increased from 15,000 to 27,500.

PACIFIC. Submarine *Pollack* (SS 180) sinks Japanese collier *No. 1 Unkai Maru* south of Honshu, 34°27′N, 139°59′E.

8 Thursday

PACIFIC. Small reconnaissance seaplane from Japanese submarine *I 19* reconnoiters Pearl Harbor, T.H.

9 Friday

PACIFIC. Submarine *Pollack* (SS 180) sinks Japanese freighter *Teian Maru* (ex-Yugoslav *Tomislav*) 40 miles south-southwest of Inubo Saki, Japan, 35°00′N, 140°36′E.

10 Saturday

PACIFIC. Destroyer *Paul Jones* (DD 230) rescues survivors from Dutch steamships *Camphuijs* (sunk on 9 January by Japanese submarine *I 158* at 04°40′S, 111°47′E) and *Benkoelen* (also sunk on the ninth by *I 165* at 04°50′S, 112°50′E).

Submarine *Pickerel* (SS 177) sinks Japanese gunboat *Kanko Maru* at mouth of Davao Gulf, off Cape San Agustin, Mindanao, P.I., 06°19′N, 125°54′E.

Submarine *Stingray* (SS 186) sinks Japanese cargo ship *Harbin Maru* in South China Sea off the south coast of Hainan Island, 17°40′N, 109°20′E.

Dutch submarine *O 19* sinks Japanese army cargo ship *Akita Maru* and torpedoes freighter *Tairyu Maru* at the mouth of the Gulf of Siam, 07°40′N, 102°50′E.

11 Sunday

PACIFIC. Carrier *Saratoga* (CV 3) is torpedoed by Japanese submarine *I 6*, 500 miles southwest of Oahu, T.H., 19°00′N, 165°00′W.

Japan declares war on The Netherlands; invasion of Netherlands East Indies ("H" Operation) begins as Japanese Central Force (Vice Admiral Hirose Sueto) lands Army 56th Regimental Combat Group and 2nd Kure Special Landing Force at Tarakan, Borneo; naval paratroops (1st Yokosuka Special Landing Force) occupy Menado, Celebes. Eastern Force (Rear Admiral Kubo Kuji) then follows up the airborne assault on Menado with 1st Special Landing Force landing at Menado and Kema, Celebes. These operations will secure control of the northern approaches to the Java Sea.

U.S. Army transport *Liberty Glo* is torpedoed by Japanese submarine *I 166* about 10 miles southwest of Lombok Strait, 08°54′S, 115°28′E. Although destroyer *Paul Jones* (DD 230) and Dutch destroyer *Van Ghent* take the damaged ship in tow and beach her on the shores of Bali, *Liberty Glo* will be written off as a total loss.

U.S. tanker *Manatawny* sinks in Manila Bay as the result of damage received on 13 December 1941.

Naval Station Pago Pago, American Samoa, is shelled by Japanese submarine.

ATLANTIC. Operation PAUKENSCHLAG ("roll of the kettledrums") descends upon the unescorted (and sometimes unarmed) coastal shipping off the eastern seaboard of the United States like a "bolt from the blue." The first group of five German submarines takes up station off the U.S. east coast on this date. Over the next month, these boats (*U 66*, *U 109*, *U 123*, *U 125*, and *U 130*) will sink 26 Allied ships. Although the presence of the enemy in this area takes U.S. Navy antisubmarine forces by surprise at the outset, steady progress will be made in combating the menace and instituting coastal convoys and other effective countermeasures.

Destroyer *Sturtevant* (DD 240), in TU 4.1.2 (Commander Walter W. Webb), is damaged in collision with unidentified merchant ship in convoy HX 169 but is able to proceed (see 21 January).

12 Monday

UNITED STATES. Authorized enlisted strength of the U.S. Navy is increased to 500,000.

PACIFIC. Dutch army shore battery sinks Japanese minesweepers *W.13* and *W.14* off Tarakan, Borneo; destroyer *Asagumo* is damaged when she runs aground off Tarakan.[62]

Japanese submarine *I 121* mines Clarence Strait, the body of water connecting Van Diemen Gulf and the Timor Sea, off Australia's Northern Territory, at the approaches to Darwin, the Asiatic Fleet's main logistics base (see 16 January).

13 Tuesday

UNITED STATES. War Production Board (WPB) is established to supplant Office of Production Management (OPM); Donald M. Nelson is named chairman.

14 Wednesday

ATLANTIC. Panamanian tanker *Norness* is sunk by German submarine *U 123* at 40°26′30″N, 70°54′30″W. Destroyer *Ellyson* (DD 454) and Coast Guard cutter *Argo* (WPC 100) rescue 30 men; fishing boat *Malvina* picks up nine and brings them to Newport, Rhode Island.

15 Thursday

GENERAL. Third Conference of Foreign Ministers of the American Republics convenes at Rio de Janeiro, Brazil, to secure a unanimous and binding resolution for the American Republics to sever relations with the Axis powers (see 28 January).

PACIFIC. American-British-Dutch-Australian (ABDA) Supreme Command is established at the Grand Hotel, Lembang, Java. General Sir Archibald Wavell, British Army, assumes supreme command of all forces in area; Lieutenant General George H. Brett, USAAF, is deputy commander; and Admiral Thomas C. Hart is to command naval forces.

ATLANTIC. Storm with wind velocity of more than 80 knots and gusts of over 100 knots hits Hvalfjordur, Iceland; heavy cruiser *Wichita* (CA 45) is damaged in collisions with U.S. freighter *West Nohno* and British trawler HMS *Ebor Wyke*, and in grounding near Hrafneyri Light. Storm conditions last until 19 January and cause heavy damage among patrol planes based there and tended by seaplane tender *Albemarle* (AV 5).

Destroyer *Mayo* (DD 422) and British trawler HMS *Douglas* are damaged in collision in low visibility and heavy seas as TU 4.1.5 (Commander William K. Phillips) attempts to rendezvous with convoy ON 55 off Iceland; *Mayo* escorts the damaged *Douglas* to Iceland. Destroyer *Simpson* (DD 221), also in TU 4.1.5, suffers topside damage in the same heavy weather that disperses ON 55.

Sailors battle high winds and stinging spray to prevent further damage to a PBY-5A on board seaplane tender *Albemarle* (AV 5), Hvalfjordur, Iceland, 15 January 1942. (Author's Collection)

16 Friday

PACIFIC. Japanese submarines continue mining the approaches to Darwin, Northern Territory: *I 122* mines Clarence Strait, *I 123* Bundas Strait, and *I 124* the waters off Darwin itself (see 20 January).

Japanese cargo ship *Taishu Maru* is wrecked when she runs aground off Okushiri Island, Hokkaido, Japan, 42°00′N, 139°00′E.

During a routine search from carrier *Enterprise* (CV 6), TBD (VT 6) flown by Aviation Chief Machinist's Mate Harold F. Dixon (Naval Aviation Pilot) fails to return to the ship and force-lands at sea at about 04°20′S, 169°30′E, due to fuel starvation. Dixon and his two-man crew have no food and no water (see 19 February).

INDIAN OCEAN. Japanese invade Burma from Thailand.

17 Saturday

PACIFIC. Japanese submarine *I 60* is sunk by British destroyer HMS *Jupiter* 25 miles north-northwest of Krakatoa, Java, 06°00′S, 105°00′E.

Japanese transport *Fukusei Maru* is stranded and wrecked off Yangtze Estuary, 31°00′N, 122°00′E.

ATLANTIC. U.S. freighter *San Jose* is sunk in collision with freighter *Santa Elisa* off Atlantic City, New Jersey, 39°15′N, 74°09′W.

18 Sunday

GENERAL. Germany, Italy, and Japan sign new military pact in Berlin.

PACIFIC. River gunboat *Tutuila* (PR 4), stranded at Chungking by Sino-Japanese hostilities since 1937, is decommissioned and her crew flown out of China.[63]

Submarine *Plunger* (SS 179) sinks Japanese freighter *Eizan Maru* (ex-Panamanian *Aurora*) off mouth of Kii Strait, Honshu, 33°30′N, 135°00′E.

ATLANTIC. Unarmed U.S. freighter *Frances Salman* is sunk by German submarine *U 552* off St. John's, Newfoundland. There are no survivors from the 28-man crew.

Unarmed U.S. tanker *Allan Jackson* is sunk by German submarine *U 66* about 50 miles east of Cape Hatteras, North Carolina, 35°57′N, 74°20′W; destroyer *Roe* (DD 418) rescues the 13 survivors from the 35-man crew. Unarmed U.S. tanker *Malay* is shelled by *U 123* off Oregon Inlet, North Carolina, 35°25′N, 75°23′W. Freighter *Scania* provides fire-fighting assistance while the tanker's assailant pursues Latvian freighter *Ciltvaria*. Although *Malay* is torpedoed by *U 123* upon the U-boat's return and damaged further, the tanker reaches Hampton Roads, Virginia, safely the next day. One man perishes in the shelling; four drown when the ship is abandoned after she is torpedoed.

19 Monday

PACIFIC. Motor torpedo boat *PT 31* is damaged when her engines fail because of what is believed to be sabotaged gasoline and she runs aground on reef north of Mayagao Point, Bataan, P.I. (see 20 January).

ATLANTIC. Unarmed U.S. steamship *City of Atlanta* is sunk by German submarine *U 123* off the North Carolina coast at 35°42′N, 75°21′W; railroad ferry *Seatrain Texas* rescues the three survivors of the 46-man crew. *U 66* sinks Canadian steamer *Lady Hawkins* east by south of the Virginia capes, 35°00′N, 72°30′W (see 27 January).

20 Tuesday

PACIFIC. Second Marine Brigade (Brigadier General Henry L. Larson, USMC) arrives at Pago Pago, American Samoa, in transports *Lurline*, *Matsonia*, and *Monterey*, along with cargo ship *Jupiter* (AK 43) and ammunition ship *Lassen* (AE 3), to protect that portion of the important lifeline to Australia. Cover is provided by TF 8 formed around carrier *Enterprise* (CV 6) (Vice Admiral William F. Halsey Jr.) and TF 17 (Rear Admiral Frank Jack Fletcher) formed around carrier *Yorktown* (CV 5). The two task forces then set course for the Marshalls and Gilberts to carry out the initial raids on the Japanese defensive perimeter (see 1 February).

Motor torpedo boat *PT 31*, damaged by grounding the day before, is burned by crew to prevent capture, 14°45′N, 120°13′E.

Submarine *S 36* (SS 141) is damaged when she runs aground on Taka Bakang Reef, Makassar Strait, Celebes, N.E.I., 04°57′N, 118°31′E (see 21 January).

Oiler *Trinity* (AO 13) is attacked by what is most likely Japanese submarine *I 124* off Darwin, Australia. Destroyer *Alden* (DD 211) carries out unsuccessful depth charge attack. Later, destroyer *Edsall* (DD 219) and Australian minesweeper HMAS *Deloraine* sink *I 124* off Darwin.

Japanese gunboat *Aso Maru* and auxiliary minesweeper *No. 52 Banshu Maru* are sunk by mines, Subic Bay, Luzon, P.I., 14°45′N, 120°17′E.

Japanese merchant storeship *Sendai Maru* is damaged by unknown cause off mouth of Davao Gulf, P.I.

Japanese convoy is reported in Makassar Strait, bound for Balikpapan, Borneo (see 21 January).

21 Wednesday

PACIFIC. In response to the movement of the Japanese convoy sighted the previous day in Makassar Strait, a U.S. task force (Rear Admiral William A. Glassford Jr.), consisting of light cruisers *Boise* (CL 47) (flagship) and *Marblehead* (CL 12) and four destroyers sails from Koepang, Timor. En route, however, *Boise* steams across an uncharted pinnacle in Sape Strait, N.E.I., and suffers sufficient damage to eliminate her from the force. Turbine trouble limits *Marblehead* (the ship to which Glassford transfers his flag) to only 15 knots, so the admiral orders the destroyers (Commander Paul H. Talbot) ahead (see 24 January).

Submarine *S 36* (SS 141), damaged by grounding on 20 January, is scuttled by her crew in Makassar Strait.

ATLANTIC. TU 4.1.2 (Commander Walter W. Webb) reaches Londonderry, Northern Ireland, the first U.S. naval vessels to make port in the British Isles since the commencement of hostilities in December 1941.[64]

UNITED STATES. Donald M. Nelson, Chairman of the WPB, abolishes OPM and establishes six new divisions.

22 Thursday

PACIFIC. Japanese reinforcements land in Subic Bay area.

Japanese land on Mussau Island, north of New Ireland.

Allied forces evacuate Lae and Salamaua, New Guinea, as well as Rabaul, New Britain.

Dutch begin destruction of oil fields, Celebes, in anticipation of Japanese invasion.

TF 11 (Vice Admiral Wilson Brown Jr.), formed around carrier *Lexington* (CV 2), departs Oahu to raid Wake Island (see 23 January).

Destroyers *Gridley* (DD 380) and *Fanning* (DD 385) are damaged in collision 150 miles northwest of American Samoa as TF 8 proceeds toward the Marshalls and Gilberts.

Survey vessel *Sumner* (AG 32) arrives at Bora Bora, Society Islands, and commences survey work (see 29 January and 12 February).

ATLANTIC. Unarmed U.S. freighter *Norvana* is sunk by German submarine *U 123* south of Cape Hatteras, North Carolina. There are no

survivors, and pieces of wreckage from the ship when she explodes hit her attacker.

23 Friday

PACIFIC. Roberts Commission, whose work had begun on 18 December 1941, concludes its investigation to "ascertain and report the facts relating to the attack made by the Japanese armed forces upon the Territory of Hawaii on December 7, 1941." The exhibits gathered amount to 2,173 printed pages.

Oiler *Neches* (AO 5) is sunk by Japanese submarine *I 72*, west of Oahu, T.H., 21°01′N, 160°06′W. The loss of the oiler supporting TF 11 (Vice Admiral Wilson Brown Jr.) forces cancellation of the projected raid on Wake.

Japanese land at Balikpapan, Borneo, N.E.I. Dutch Martin 139s bomb invasion shipping, sinking transports *Nana Maru* and *Jukka Maru*, 00°10′N, 118°00′E (see 24 January).

"R" Operation: Japanese occupy Rabaul, New Britain (see 24 January), and land at Kieta, Bougainville, Solomons.

Japanese force lands on southwest coast of Bataan Peninsula; local U.S. Army commander inserts naval battalion of sailors and marines (Commander Francis J. Bridget) into the battle as a stopgap. It blocks enemy progress (see 24 January). Motor torpedo boat *PT 34* is damaged in action with Japanese armed launch while on patrol off Bataan Peninsula.

Destroyer *Edsall* (DD 219) is damaged by explosion of own depth charges during attack on submarine contact in Howard Channel, Clarence Strait, one of the approaches to Darwin, Australia.

Submarine *Seadragon* (SS 194) damages Japanese freighter *Fukuyo Maru* off the northern coast of French Indochina, 12°00′N, 109°00′E.

ATLANTIC. Unarmed U.S. collier *Venore* is sunk by German submarine *U 66* about 20 miles southeast of Cape Hatteras, North Carolina, 35°50′N, 75°20′W (see 25 January).

24 Saturday

PACIFIC. Battle of Makassar Strait: While Japanese light cruiser *Naka* and accompanying destroyers are hunting for Dutch submarine *K XVIII* (which will be damaged by submarine chaser *Ch 12*), Destroyer Division 59 (Commander Paul H. Talbot) attacks Borneo invasion convoy off Balikpapan. *John D. Ford* (DD 228) is damaged by gunfire (01°20′N, 117°01′E) but sinks transport *Tsuruga Maru*; *Parrott* (DD 218) sinks transport *Sumanoura*

Maru and torpedoes *Patrol Boat No. 37*, 00°10′N, 118°00′E; *Paul Jones* (DD 230) and *Pope* (DD 225) sink transport *Tatsukami Maru*; and *Paul Jones* sinks cargo ship *Kuretaki Maru*. *Naka* and destroyers *Minegumo* and *Natsugumo* pursue the retiring flush-deckers to no avail.

Naval battalion (Commander Francis J. Bridget) drives Japanese troops back to Longoskawayan and Quinauan Points on Bataan Peninsula.

Japanese force lands at Subic Bay, P.I.

Submarine tender *Canopus* (AS 9) is damaged by bombs, Lilimbom Cove, Mariveles, N.E.I.

Japanese land at Kendari, Celebes; submarine *Swordfish* (SS 193) sinks Japanese gunboat *Myoken Maru* north of Kema, Celebes, 01°26′N, 125°08′E.

"R" Operation: Japanese land at Kavieng, New Ireland.

GULF OF PANAMA. Submarine *S 26* (SS 131) is accidentally rammed and sunk by submarine chaser *PC 460*, 08°13′N, 79°21′E. *PC 460* rescues three survivors. Despite a search by the patrol craft and the other three submarines in company, *S 21* (SS 126), *S 29* (SS 134), and *S 44* (SS 155), no other survivors are found; 46 men lose their lives in the mishap.

25 Sunday

PACIFIC. Japanese submarine *I 73* shells Midway Island.

Japanese destroyer *Hatsuharu* is damaged by aircraft east of Kendari, Celebes.[65]

ATLANTIC. German submarine *U 125* attacks unarmed U.S. tanker *Olney* and forces her aground off Cape Lookout, North Carolina, 37°55′N, 74°56′W. *Olney* is subsequently removed from her predicament, however, and repaired and returned to service.

U.S. steamer *Tennessee* rescues one boatload of 21 survivors from U.S. collier *Venore*, sunk by German submarine *U 66* on 25 January; two survivors reach port in a second boat. U.S. tanker *Australia* rescues the only one surviving sailor the same day. Seventeen men of *Venore*'s crew perish.

26 Monday

ATLANTIC. First U.S. Expeditionary Force to Europe in World War II arrives in Northern Ireland.

U.S. freighter *West Ivis* is sunk by German submarine *U 125* off the eastern seaboard. There are no survivors from either the 36-man civilian crew or the nine-man Armed Guard.

27 Tuesday

PACIFIC. Submarine *Gudgeon* (SS 211) sinks Japanese submarine *I 73*, 240 miles west of Midway, 28°24′N, 178°35′E.

Submarine *Seawolf* (SS 197) delivers ammunition to Corregidor, P.I., and evacuates naval and army pilots.

USAAF B-17s bomb and damage Japanese seaplane carrier *Sanuki Maru* off Balikpapan, Borneo.

Naval Air Station, Puunene, Maui, T.H., is established.

ATLANTIC. Unarmed U.S. tanker *Francis E. Powell* is sunk by German submarine *U 130* about eight miles northeast of Winter Quarter Lightship, 37°45′N, 74°53′W; a Coast Guard boat from the Assateague Island station and U.S. tanker *W. C. Fairbanks* rescue the 28 survivors from the 32-man crew. U.S. tanker *Halo* is torpedoed by *U 130* about 17 miles northeast of Diamond Shoals Lightship, 35°33′N, 75°20′W.

U.S. steamship *Coamo* rescues 71 survivors of Canadian steamer *Lady Hawkins* that had been sunk by *U 66* on 19 January.

28 Wednesday

GENERAL. Third Conference of Foreign Ministers of the American Republics at Rio de Janeiro, Brazil, is concluded. Despite the efforts of Argentina and Chile, Pan-American unity is preserved; within days, all Latin American nations that had not already done so (except Argentina and Chile) sever ties with Germany, Italy, and Japan.

PACIFIC. Japanese land on Rossel Island off New Guinea.

ATLANTIC. PBO (VP 82), on an antisubmarine sweep astern of convoy HX 172, attacks a surfaced submarine off Newfoundland at 43°50′N, 53°50′E. Although pilot (Aviation Machinist's Mate First Class Donald F. Mason) reports "sighted sub, sank same" no U-boat is lost on this date.

29 Thursday

PACIFIC. British begin evacuation of civilian population from Singapore (see 30 January).

Japanese land at Badoeng Island and Mampawan, Celebes.

Minesweeper *Quail* (AM 15) bombards Japanese troop concentrations at Longoskawayan Point, Luzon.

Oiler *Ramapo* (AO 12) arrives at Bora Bora, Society Islands, to support survey operations being carried out by auxiliary *Sumner* (AG 32),

which had arrived on 22 January (see 12 February).

INDIAN OCEAN. Unarmed U.S. freighter *Florence Luckenbach* is sunk by Japanese submarine *I 64* about 15 miles east of Madras, India, 12°55′N, 80°33′E; there are no casualties among the 38-man crew and all hands reach Madras by lifeboat.[66]

ATLANTIC. Coast Guard cutter *Alexander Hamilton* (WPG 34) is torpedoed by German submarine *U 132* off Reykjavik, Iceland, 64°10′N, 22°56′W (see 30 January).

PBYs (VP 52) operating out of Natal, Brazil, are fired upon by British freighter *Debrett* owing to difficulty in mutual identification.

30 Friday

PACIFIC. Evacuation of civilians from Singapore proceeds apace as British troops withdraw to Singapore Island, after which time the causeway linking Kohore and Singapore is blown up. Japanese naval land attack planes (Genzan Kokutai) bomb Allied shipping at Keppel Harbor, Singapore, Straits Settlements; transport *Wakefield* (AP 21) is damaged, as are British transports (ex-passenger liners) *Duchess of Bedford* and *Empress of Japan* and freighter *Madura*. Transport *West Point* (AP 23), straddled and showered with fragments, suffers no damage; she provides medical assistance to *Wakefield*. Both U.S. transports embark passengers that include dockyard workers from Singapore and their families, in addition to Royal Navy officers and enlisted men and a small RAF contingent.[67]

ATLANTIC. Coast Guard cutter *Alexander Hamilton* (WPG 34), torpedoed by German submarine *U 132* the previous day, is scuttled by gunfire of destroyer *Ericsson* (DD 440) off Reykjavik, Iceland.

Unarmed U.S. tanker *Rochester* is torpedoed, shelled, and sunk by German submarine *U 106* off Chesapeake Lightship, 37°10′N, 73°58′W; three crewmen perish in the initial explosion. Destroyer *Roe* (DD 418) rescues 29 survivors.

31 Saturday

UNITED STATES. Office of Procurement and Material is established in the office of the Undersecretary of the Navy; Vice Admiral Samuel M. Robinson, Chief of the Bureau of Ships, is named director.

PACIFIC. TF 11 (Vice Admiral Wilson Brown Jr.), formed around carrier *Lexington* (CV 2),

departs Pearl Harbor to support TF 8 (Vice Admiral William F. Halsey Jr.) and TF 17 (Rear Admiral Frank Jack Fletcher) (see 1 February).

Japanese troops land on Amboina Island, N.E.I.

Destroyer *Helm* (DD 388) evacuates civilian radio operators and weather observers from Howland and Baker Islands; she is bombed by a Japanese flying boat (Yokohama Kokutai) off Baker, but is not damaged.

ATLANTIC. British tanker *San Arcadio* is sunk by German submarine *U 107* at 38°10′N, 63°50′W (see 11 February).

British tanker *Tacoma Star* is sunk by German submarine *U 109* at 37°33′N, 69°21′W; destroyer *Roe* (DD 418), on temporary duty with the Fifth Naval District defense forces due to the increase in ship sinkings off Cape Hatteras, North Carolina, is sent to rescue survivors.

FEBRUARY

1 Sunday

PACIFIC. TF 8 (Vice Admiral William F. Halsey Jr.), formed around carrier *Enterprise* (CV 6), and TF 17 (Rear Admiral Frank Jack Fletcher), formed around carrier *Yorktown* (CV 5), raid the Marshall and Gilbert Islands. TF 8 concentrates on Kwajalein and Wotje, with heavy cruiser *Chester* (CA 27) bombarding Maleolap Atoll; TF 17 targets enemy installations on Jaluit, Makin, and Mili. TF 11 (Vice Admiral Wilson Brown Jr.), formed around carrier *Lexington* (CV 2), operates in the vicinity of Christmas Island to cover the projected retirement of TF 8 and TF 17.

At Kwajalein, SBDs (VB 6 and VS 6) and TBDs (VT 6) from *Enterprise* sink transport *Bordeaux Maru* and damage light cruiser *Katori*, submarine *I 23*, minelayer *Tokiwa*, auxiliary netlayer *Kashima Maru*, auxiliary submarine chaser *No. 2 Shonan Maru*, submarine depot ship *Yasukuni Maru*, oiler *Toa Maru*, tanker *Hoyo Maru*, and army cargo ship *Shinhei Maru*; Rear Admiral Yatsushiro Sukeyoshi (Commander Sixth Base Force) becomes the first Imperial Navy flag officer to die in combat when an SBD scores a direct hit on his headquarters. Off Wotje, heavy cruisers *Northampton* (CA 26) and *Salt Lake City* (CA 25) sink gunboat *Toyotsu Maru*; destroyer *Dunlap* (DD 384) sinks auxiliary submarine chaser *No. 10 Shonan Maru*. Japanese retaliatory air attacks (Chitose Kokutai) on TF 8 cause damage to carrier *Enterprise* (near-miss of crash of land attack plane), 10°33′N, 171°53′E, and heavy cruiser *Chester* (by bomb dropped by carrier fighter), 08°45′N, 171°33′E.

Planes from *Yorktown* cause less damage, due to a paucity of targets at the objective; nevertheless, SBDs (VS 5) bomb and strafe gunboat *Nagata Maru* at Makin, while SBDs (VB 5) bomb and strafe cargo ship *Kanto Maru* at Jaluit. Rear Admiral Fletcher detaches three of his four destroyers to look for downed TBD (VT 5) reported in the water astern of TF 17. During the search, a Japanese flying boat (Yokohama *Kokutai*) attacks (but does not damage) destroyer *Sims* (DD 409). Soon thereafter, two F4Fs (VF 42) splash the flying boat. The TBD crew, however, is never found in the prevailing poor weather.

Motor torpedo boats and USAAF P-40s repulse Japanese landing attempt on southwest Bataan. *PT 32* damages Japanese minelayer *Yaeyama* off Subic Bay.

Naval Base, Sydney, Australia, is established.

ATLANTIC. Seventh Naval District with headquarters at Key West, Florida, is reestablished.

Naval Air Stations, St. Lucia, British West Indies, and British Guiana, and Naval Auxiliary Air Facility, Antigua, British West Indies, are established.

2 Monday

PACIFIC. Submarine *Seadragon* (SS 194) sinks Japanese army cargo ship *Tamagawa Maru* off Cape Bolinao, Luzon, P.I., 17°16′N, 119°48′E, but misses army cargo vessel *Nisshu Maru* in the same attack.

Japanese minesweeper *W.9* is sunk and minesweepers *W.11* and *W.12* are damaged by Dutch mines off Ambon, N.E.I., 03°42′S, 128°10′E.

ATLANTIC. Unarmed U.S. tanker *W. L. Steed* is sunk by German submarine *U 103* about 90 miles east of the mouth of the Delaware River, 38°25′N, 72°43′W. Exposure will eventually claim 34 of the 38-man crew who survive the loss of the ship at the outset (see 4, 6, and 12 February).

3 Tuesday

PACIFIC. Submarine *Trout* (SS 202) delivers ammunition to Corregidor, P.I., and removes gold, silver, securities, and mail. She uses the gold as ballast on the return voyage to Pearl Harbor.

Japanese naval land attack planes (Takao *Kokutai*) bomb ABDA operating base at Surabaya; other naval land attack planes (1st

Kokutai) bomb Malang, Java. These raids indicate for the first time that substantial Japanese air forces have been moved south. En route home from Malang, 1st *Kokutai* aircraft report presence of Allied naval force (Rear Admiral Karel W. F. M. Doorman, RNN) off Madoera (see 4 February).

ATLANTIC. Panamanian freighter *San Gil* is sunk by German submarine *U 103* approximately 15 miles south of Fenwick Island Light, 38°05′N, 74°40′W. Two crewmen perish in the attack; Coast Guard cutter *Nike* (WPC 112) rescues the 38 survivors.

4 Wednesday

PACIFIC. Australian–New Zealand naval command is established (Vice Admiral H. Fairfax Leary).

Japanese flying boats (Toko *Kokutai*) contact and shadow Allied force (Rear Admiral Karel W. F. M. Doorman, RNN) of four cruisers and accompanying destroyers (sighted the previous day by 1st *Kokutai* aircraft) attempting transit of Madoera Strait to attack Japanese Borneo invasion fleet. On the strength of that intelligence, naval land attack planes (Takao, Kanoya, and 1st *Kokutais*) bomb Doorman's ships, damaging heavy cruiser *Houston* (CA 30) (1st *Kokutai*) and light cruiser *Marblehead* (CL 12) (Kanoya *Kokutai*), 07°23′S, 115°47′E. Dutch light cruisers *De Ruyter* and *Tromp* are slightly damaged by near-misses (1st *Kokutai*). *Marblehead's* extensive damage (only by masterful seamanship and herculean effort does she reach Tjilatjap, Java) results in her being sent back to the United States via Ceylon and South Africa; despite the loss of turret III (one-third of her main battery), *Houston*, however, remains.

Asiatic Fleet (Admiral Thomas C. Hart) ceases to exist organizationally (not formally abolished). Units of Asiatic Fleet are organized into Naval Forces, Southwest Pacific Area (Vice Admiral William A. Glassford Jr.).

Submarine *Sculpin* (SS 191) torpedoes Japanese destroyer *Sukukaze* as the latter patrols off Staring Bay, south of Kendari, Celebes, 04°00′S, 123°00′E.

ATLANTIC. Destroyer *Lea* (DD 118), while escorting convoy HX 173, goes to assistance of Soviet steamer *Dvinoles*, after the latter is damaged in collision with Norwegian motor tanker *Havprins*. *Lea*, unable to tow the crippled Soviet vessel, takes off her crew and, leaving her adrift, transports the men to St. John's, Newfoundland.

Unarmed U.S. tanker *India Arrow* is sunk by German submarine *U 103* about 20 miles southeast of Cape May, New Jersey, 38°48′N, 73°40′W. Two of her men perish when the ship is shelled; 24 drown when two lifeboats are swamped. Fishing skiff *Gitana* rescues the 12 survivors 12 miles off Atlantic City, New Jersey.

British armed merchant cruiser HMS *Alcantara* comes across lifeboat from U.S. tanker *W. L. Steed* (sunk by German submarine *U 103* on 2 February) and rescues the three survivors she finds (see 6 and 12 February).

5 Thursday

PACIFIC. Submarine *Seadragon* (SS 194) evacuates a nucleus group of people from the naval communications/radio intelligence unit, and associated equipment, from Corregidor, to set up facilities on Java.

Japanese planes bomb Allied shipping off Soembawa Island, N.E.I.; after destroyer *Paul Jones* (DD 230) is damaged by near-miss, she then rescues survivors of Dutch motorship *Tidore*, which had run aground in an attempt to avoid Japanese bombs.

ATLANTIC. Naval Operating Base, Londonderry, Northern Ireland, is established to serve as a turnaround point for transatlantic convoys.

Destroyer *Bernadou* (DD 153), escorting convoy HX 173, rescues 10 survivors of Belgian freighter *Gandia* (sunk by German submarine *U 135* on 22 January) at 50°N, 46°W.

Unarmed U.S. tanker *China Arrow* is sunk by German submarine *U 103* off Winter Quarter Lightship, 37°44′N, 73°18′W (see 7 February).

UNITED STATES. National Naval Medical Center, Bethesda, Maryland, is established in this Washington, D.C., suburb.

6 Friday

UNITED STATES. Naval Coastal Frontiers—Eastern, Gulf, Caribbean, Panama, Hawaiian, Northwest, Western, Philippine—are redesignated as Sea Frontiers.

GENERAL. United States and Britain establish Combined Chiefs of Staff.

PACIFIC. Japanese land reinforcements at Lingayen Gulf, P.I.

Japanese artillery on the Cavite coast, near Ternate, bombards Corregidor and Fort Hughes, Fort Frank, Fort Drum, and Inshore Patrol anchorage, South Harbor, Corregidor. River gunboat *Luzon* (PR 7) is hit by a shell in her vacant admiral's quarters; there are no casualties.

ATLANTIC. Unarmed U.S. freighter *Major Wheeler*, en route from Fajardo, Puerto Rico, to Philadelphia, Pennsylvania, is sunk by German submarine *U 107*. There are no survivors from the 35-man crew.

British freighter *Hartlepool* comes across lifeboat from U.S. tanker *W. L. Steed* (sunk by German submarine *U 103* on 2 February) and rescues the two survivors she finds; one of them will die in the hospital on 10 February of exposure (see 12 February).

7 Saturday

UNITED STATES. President Roosevelt signs Executive Order No. 9054 establishing War Shipping Administration (WSA) to bring the control and operation of all U.S. merchant shipping under a single head. The WSA's most pressing task is to mobilize the shipping capacity of the country (the majority of which was still in private hands by the end of the year 1941) to bring it under single control so that vessels can be allocated more readily on the basis of overall shipping needs of the United States and its Allies (see 9 February).

PACIFIC. Commander Naval Forces Southwest Pacific Area (Vice Admiral William A. Glassford Jr.) establishes headquarters at the port of Tjilatjap, on Java's south coast.

Yacht *Isabel* (PY 10) rescues all 187 survivors from Dutch freighter *Van Cloon*, which had been torpedoed and shelled earlier that day by Japanese submarine *I 155* and beached in a sinking condition off Java, 06°25′S, 111°25′E.[68]

Small reconnaissance seaplane from Japanese submarine *I 25* reconnoiters Sydney, Australia.

Japanese submarines *RO 61* and *RO 62* are damaged in collision, Kwajalein, Marshall Islands.

ATLANTIC. U.S. freighter *West Jaffrey* is stranded off Halfbald Island, Nova Scotia, 43°36′N, 66°02′W, and wrecked. There are no casualties to either the merchant crew or the 14-man Armed Guard.

Coast Guard cutter *Nike* (WPC 112) rescues all 37 survivors of U.S. tanker *China Arrow*, sunk by German submarine *U 103* off Winter Quarter Lightship on 5 February.

U.S. freighter *Mary* is damaged in collision with freighter *Palimol* at 24°50′N, 66°00′W, and proceeds to San Juan, Puerto Rico, for repairs.

8 Sunday

PACIFIC. Japanese submarine *I 69*, which has been reconnoitering the atoll since 21 January, shells Midway.

Japanese troops land at Gasmata, New Britain.

Submarine *S 37* (SS 142) attacks Japanese convoy in Makassar Strait, and torpedoes destroyer *Natsushio* south of Makassar City, Celebes, 05°10′S, 119°24′E. *S 37* survives resultant depth charging (see 9 February).

Japanese infiltration force at Quinauan Point, Bataan, is mopped up, supported by armed motor launches from submarine tender *Canopus* (AS 9) (Lieutenant Commander Henry W. Goodall). Japanese planes, however, bomb and strafe the boats, killing three and wounding 15 (including Goodall).

British submarine HMS *Trusty* shells Japanese merchant coaster *Se Go* off Poulo Condore, French Indochina.

ATLANTIC. British freighter *Ocean Venture* is sunk by German submarine *U 108* off the Virginia capes, 37°05′N, 74°45′W (see 9 February).

9 Monday

UNITED STATES. Rear Admiral Emory S. Land, Chief of the Maritime Commission, is appointed Director of the War Shipping Administration. As WSA director, he is responsible only to the President.

Admiral William H. Standley, USN (Retired), former Chief of Naval Operations (1935–1937), is named Ambassador to the USSR.

PACIFIC. Twelve USAAF B-17s (TG 8.9) are released to Commander in Chief Pacific Fleet for operational control; they will cover the advance of TF 11 (Vice Admiral Wilson Brown Jr.) into the South Pacific.

Transport *St. Mihiel* (AP 32) is damaged by grounding off MacNamara Point, Alaska.

Submarine *Trout* (SS 202) sinks Japanese gunboat *Chuwa Maru* 53 miles off Keelung, Formosa, 25°30′N, 122°38′E.

Japanese carrier *Kaga* is damaged when she runs aground on an uncharted reef, Palau, Palau Islands.

Japanese transport *Kurama Maru* is sunk in the East China Sea, agent unknown, 28°25′N, 122°03′N.[69]

Japanese destroyer *Natsushio*, torpedoed by submarine *S 37* (SS 142) off Makassar the previous day, sinks.

Japanese planes bomb Batavia, Surabaya, and Malang in Java.

Japanese troops land on Singapore Island.

ATLANTIC. Transport *Lafayette* (AP 53) (ex-French liner *Normandie*) burns at New York City pier and capsizes at her berth.

Destroyer *Roe* (DD 418), at approximately 36°24′N, 74°34′W, rescues 14 survivors from British freighter *Ocean Venture*, sunk the previous day by German submarine *U 108*.

10 Tuesday

PACIFIC. USAAF LB-30s bomb and damage Japanese seaplane carrier *Chitose* in Makassar Strait south of Celebes.

Japanese submarine *I 69* shells Midway but is immediately bombed and damaged by USMC F2As (VMF 221).

ATLANTIC. Submarine *R 5* (SS 82) fires three torpedoes at what she later reports as a German U-boat at 35°00′N, 65°45′W, but the attack is not successful. By the time *R 5* has reloaded, the enemy is gone. While *R 5*'s captain is criticized for erring in judgment for failing to follow up his contact during darkness and continuing the attack, his inexperience (*R 5* is his first command) is considered, as is the fact that it is that commanding officer's first war patrol. *R 5*'s quarry may have been *U 564*, which sinks Canadian motor tanker *Victolite* at 36°12′N, 67°14′W, the same day.[70]

11 Wednesday

PACIFIC. Submarine *Shark* (SS 174) is sunk by Japanese destroyer *Yamakaze* about 120 miles east of Menado, Celebes, 01°45′N, 127°15′E. There are no survivors from *Shark*'s 58-man crew.

CARIBBEAN. U.S. Army troops (Colonel Peter C. Bullard, USA) arrive at Curaçao and Aruba, N.W.I., to assume occupation duty (with the cooperation of the British and Dutch governments) at this naval operating base. The primary mission will be port security, convoy routing, and protection of tankers transporting oil to U.S. ports.

ATLANTIC. Minesweeper *Brant* (AM 24) assists stranded Norwegian freighter *Anderson* at St. Shots Bay, Newfoundland (see 13 February).

PBM (VP 74) rescues nine survivors adrift in a lifeboat from British tanker *San Arcadio*, sunk by German submarine *U 107* on 31 January.

EUROPE. Admiral William D. Leahy, USN (Retired), Ambassador to France, receives instructions from President Roosevelt that the U.S. government has learned that French ships are to be used to transport war materiel between France and Tunisia, and that unless the French government gives assurances that no military aid would go forward to any Axis power, and that French ships would not be used in the furtherance of Axis acts of aggression in any theater of war, the ambassador would be recalled to the United States "for consultation in a determination of American future policy with regard to the government of Vichy" (see 20 and 21 February).

12 Thursday

PACIFIC. Destroyer *Whipple* (DD 217) is damaged in collision with Dutch light cruiser *De Ruyter*, Prigi Bay, Java.

USAAF B-17s (Far East Air Force) bomb Japanese shipping off Surumi, damaging transport *Kozui Maru* and merchant cargo vessel *Kinryu Maru*.

Auxiliary survey vessel *Sumner* (AG 32) completes survey work of Bora Bora, Society Islands, and publishes Hydrographic Office Field Chart No. 1 for those waters.

ATLANTIC. U.S. freighter *Dixie Sword* founders and sinks in Nantucket Sound, 41°35′N, 69°59′W.

British freighter *Raby Castle* comes across lifeboat from U.S. tanker *W. L. Steed*, sunk by German submarine *U 103* on 2 February, and rescues the one survivor she finds; sadly, he will die on board on 15 February, of exposure.

13 Friday

PACIFIC. Chartered U.S. passenger ship *President Taylor*, transporting 900 troops to occupy Canton Island runs aground on a reef off her destination, and becomes stranded.[71]

ATLANTIC. Destroyer *Ericsson* (DD 440) accidentally sinks Icelandic trawler *Greedir* in collision off Hvalfjordur, Iceland.

Minesweeper *Brant* (AM 24) transports survivors of stranded Norwegian freighter *Anderson* from St. Shots Bay to Argentia, Newfoundland.

14 Saturday

PACIFIC. Admiral Thomas C. Hart is relieved as Commander in Chief Allied Naval Forces in Southwest Pacific by Vice Admiral Conrad E. L. Helfrich, RNN.

Submarine *Sargo* (SS 188) delivers ammunition to Polloc Harbor, Mindanao, P.I., and evacuates USAAF ground crew (14th Bombardment Squadron).

Submarine *Swordfish* (SS 193) sinks Japanese transport *Amagisan Maru* off Davao, P.I., 06°45′N, 126°54′E.

Japanese army paratroopers assault Palembang, Sumatra. During ensuing Allied air attacks on Japanese invasion convoy, RAF Blenheims bomb and sink merchant ship *Inabasan Maru* off Palembang.

ABDA Float (headquarters of ABDA's naval component) orders task force (Rear Admiral Karel W. F. M. Doorman, RNN) to proceed and attack Japanese Palembang-bound expeditionary force. As Doorman's ships—two Dutch light cruisers, a Dutch flotilla leader, one British heavy cruiser, one Australian light cruiser, and four Dutch destroyers and six American—head toward their objective, Dutch destroyer *Van Ghent* runs aground on a reef north of Banka Island, N.E.I. Irreparably damaged, *Van Ghent* is scuttled; sister ship *Banckert* takes off her crew (see 15 February).

PBY (VP 73) accidentally bombs submarine *Thresher* (SS 200), returning from a war patrol, southwest of Oahu, T.H.

Japanese submarine *I 23* is last reported south of Oahu. She is not heard from again, and her fate is unknown.

INDIAN OCEAN. Light cruiser *Boise* (CL 47), at Ceylon en route to Bombay, India, for repairs following her grounding on 21 January, provides (on request from local British naval authorities) her two SOCs (VCS 9) to augment routine RAF Catalina searches from the seaplane station at Kogalla, Ceylon. *Boise*'s planes fly morning and evening search flights for the next three days.

15 Sunday

PACIFIC. Singapore surrenders to the Japanese.

Japanese army paratroops secure vital oil refineries at Palembang, on southeast Sumatra, N.E.I.; enemy capture of this territory establishes sea and air control of the Karimata Channel and Gaspar Strait.

ABDA striking force (Rear Admiral Karel W. F. M. Doorman, RNN), having proceeded through Gaspar Strait to the north of Banka, N.E.I., and failed to contact the Japanese force (which has already reached Banka Strait), is attacked by Japanese naval land attack planes (Genzan, Mihoro, and Kanoya *Kokutais*) as well as carrier attack planes from *Ryujo*. Australian light cruiser HMAS *Hobart* is straddled; near-misses damage destroyers *Barker* (DD 213) and *Bulmer* (DD 222), which will need to retire to Australia for repairs.

U.S. Army transport *Meigs*, U.S. freighters *Mauna Loa* and *Portmar*, and Australian coaster *Tulagi*, escorted by heavy cruiser *Houston* (CA 30), destroyer *Peary* (DD 226), and Australian corvettes HMAS *Swan* and HMAS *Warrego*, sail from Darwin, Australia, for Timor, N.E.I. (see 16 and 19 February).

ATLANTIC. Brazilian steamship *Buarque* is sunk by German submarine *U 432*, 30 miles southwest of Cape Henry, 36°35′N, 75°20′W (see 16 February).

U.S. tanker *Point Breeze* suffers explosion in engine room that damages steering gear, forcing the ship to go aground off Throggs Neck, New York; one man is killed and one is blown overboard. *Point Breeze* later floats free and is towed to New York for repairs.

16 Monday

CARIBBEAN. Operation NEULAND begins with simultaneous attacks on Dutch and Venezuelan oil ports to disrupt production and flow of petroleum products vital to the Allied war effort; German submarine *U 156* shells refinery on Aruba, N.W.I., and torpedoes U.S. tanker *Arkansas* as she lies alongside Eagle Dock; a second torpedo misses the ship and runs up on the beach. There are no casualties among the 37-man crew. The enemy does not emerge from the action unscathed, however, for the explosion of a shell prematurely in a gun barrel injures two men on board *U 156*, which will receive permission to put in to Martinique, French West Indies (see 20 and 21 February).

ATLANTIC. Minesweeper *Brant* (AM 24) assists British freighter *Kitty's Brook* off shoal at Argentia, Newfoundland.

Coast Guard cutter *Calypso* (WPG 104) rescues 42 survivors from Brazilian steamship *Buarque*, that had been sunk by German submarine *U 432* the day before (see 17 February).

Unarmed U.S. tanker *E. H. Blum* blunders into U.S. minefield off Cape Henry, Virginia, 36°57′N, 75°52′W, and is damaged by mine and breaks in half (see 17 February).

PACIFIC. Japanese planes bomb Timor-bound convoy, escorted by heavy cruiser *Houston* (CA 30) and destroyer *Peary* (DD 226); U.S. Army transport *Miegs* and U.S. freighter *Mauna Loa* are damaged by near-misses. On board the latter, one crewman is killed; of the 500 troops embarked, one is killed and 18 wounded. *Houston*'s heavy antiaircraft fire saves the convoy from destruction, but the imminent fall of Timor results in the recall of the convoy and its routing back to Darwin (see 19 February).

17 Tuesday

PACIFIC. "Seabees" (First Naval Construction Battalion) arrive at Bora Bora, Society Islands.

Submarine *Triton* (SS 201) sinks Japanese gunboat *No. 5 Shin'yo Maru* off Nagasaki, Japan, 32°14′N, 127°14′E.

Japanese destroyer *Ayanami* is damaged when she fouls an uncharted reef 2.4 nautical miles off Durai, Anambas Islands.

ATLANTIC. Coastal minesweeper *Detector* (AMc 75) is accidentally sunk in collision with U.S. tanker *Oswego* 300 yards east-northeast of Finn's Ledge Buoy, at the entrance to the north channel at Boston, Massachusetts. There are no casualties.

Coastal minesweeper *Paramount* (AMc 92) accidentally runs aground off Cape Hatteras, North Carolina, and is abandoned without loss. Coast Guard cutter *Dione* (WPG 107) provides assistance. *Paramount* is salvaged and returned to service.

Destroyer *Jacob Jones* (DD 130) rescues 16 men from Brazilian steamship *Buarque*, which had been sunk by German submarine *U 432* on 15 February; U.S. steamship *Eagle* rescues 16 more, accounting for all survivors.

Coast Guard cutter *Woodbury* (WPC 155) rescues all hands (40 men) from mined tanker *E. H. Blum*. Both halves of the ship are later salvaged and rejoined, and *E. H. Blum* returns to active service (see 29 December).

18 Wednesday

ATLANTIC. Destroyer *Truxtun* (DD 229) and stores issue ship *Pollux* (AKS 2) run aground during storm near Placentia Bay, Newfoundland, the former just east of Ferryland Point and the latter off Lawn Point. Minesweeper *Brant* (AM 24) arrives and sends rescue parties as well as brings medical officer and corpsmen from destroyer tender (Support Force flagship) *Prairie* (AD 15). The tragedy produces deep admiration for the lifesaving efforts of the local population. "Hardly a dozen men from both ships would have been saved," one observer writes later, "had it not been for the superb work of the local residents." Many men frequently jeopardize their own lives to save the American sailors. Several hang by lines over the cliffs to keep survivors from being dragged over sharp rocks as they are pulled up from the beach below; others go out in a dory, risking swamping several times in the rough waves. After working all day rescuing *Truxtun*'s men, some of the local inhabitants then toil all night rescuing *Pollux*'s with a stamina that defies description. Although poor, the men, women, and children of the town of St. Lawrence turn out to outfit the "survivors with blankets, warm clothes, boots, fed them, cleaned them up as best they could and turned them in in their own beds." Subsequently, they turn a deaf ear to offers to pay for food and clothing used in succoring the shipwrecked Americans. Destroyer *Wilkes* (DD 441) also runs aground off Lawn Head, 46°53'N, 55°28'W, but manages to free herself

from her predicament and escape the fates of *Truxtun* and *Pollux*.

Brazilian tanker *Olinda* is shelled, torpedoed, and sunk by German submarine *U 432* at 37°30'N, 75°00'W (see 19 February).

U.S. freighter *Mokihana* is torpedoed by German submarine *U 161* while at anchor at Port of Spain, Trinidad, 12°55'N, 80°33'E; there are no casualties among the 34-man merchant crew or eight-man Armed Guard. Subsequently, minesweeper *Partridge* (AM 16) and net tender (tug class) *Mankato* (YNT 8) tow the damaged ship to the Virgin Islands and thence to San Juan, Puerto Rico, for temporary repairs.

CARIBBEAN. U.S. freighter *Thompson Lykes* accidentally rams and sinks Free French submarine *Surcouf* approximately 75 miles northeast of Cristobal, C.Z., 10°40'N, 79°31'E.

19 Thursday

PACIFIC. Japanese forces land on Bali, N.E.I. Battle of Badoeng Strait occurs as Allied naval force (Rear Admiral Karel W. F. M. Doorman, RNN) of three cruisers and accompanying destroyers engages retiring Japanese occupation force (Rear Admiral Kubo Kyuji) in Badoeng Strait. Destroyer *Stewart* (DD 224) is damaged by gunfire from destroyers *Oshio* and *Asashio*, 07°18'S, 112°46'E. Dutch destroyer *Piet Hien* is sunk; 30 of her survivors find motor whaleboat jettisoned by destroyer *John D. Ford* (DD 228) and proceed otherwise unaided to Java. Dutch light cruisers *Java* and *Tromp* are damaged by Japanese gunfire. Japanese destroyers *Ushio* and *Michisio* are damaged by Allied gunfire.

Japanese carrier striking force (Vice Admiral Nagumo Chuichi) attacks Darwin, Australia. From carriers *Akagi, Kaga, Hiryu*, and *Soryu* 189 planes bomb shipping, airfields, and shore installations; carrier bombers sink destroyer *Peary* (DD 226), 12°30'S, 130°50'E, U.S. Army transport *Miegs,* and U.S. freighter *Mauna Loa* (on board the latter all hands—37-man crew and seven passengers—survive), and damage seaplane tender (destroyer) *William B. Preston* (AVD 7). U.S. freighter *Portmar* is damaged and beached (one of her 34-man crew is killed; two of the 300 embarked soldiers perish as well; 12 men are injured); freighter *Admiral Halstead* (carrying drummed gasoline) is damaged as well (she suffers no casualties). In related actions, U.S. freighter *Florence D*, under charter to the Army and carrying a cargo of ammunition, rescues eight-man PBY (VP 22) crew (Lieutenant Thomas H. Moorer) off north coast of

Australia, near Darwin, and later comes under attack by Japanese carrier aircraft that bomb and sink the ship (one man of Moorer's crew and three of the 37-man ship's complement are killed in action); Australian minesweeper HMAS *Warrnambool* and mission boat *St. Francis* rescue the survivors. Japanese carrier planes also bomb and sink Philippine motorship *Don Isidro* (chartered by the U.S. Army to run supplies to Corregidor) off northwest coast of Bathurst Island, 11°00'S, 130°00'E; 11 of the 67-man crew and one of the 16 embarked soldiers are killed. HMAS *Warrnambool* rescues the surviving crew and passengers. Japanese land attack planes (Kanoya and 1st *Kokutais*) bomb airfield at Darwin.

Submarine *S 37* (SS 142) is damaged by grounding off the northeast corner of Lembogan Island, Lombok Strait, N.E.I., but continues on patrol.

Aviation Chief Machinist's Mate Harold F. Dixon (Naval Aviation Pilot) and his two-man crew (VT 6), whose plane ditched due to fuel exhaustion on 16 January, reach Danger Islands, 10°48'S, 165°49'E, having spent 34 days at sea in their rubber boat. They have subsisted on occasional fish speared with a pocket knife, two birds, and rain water. While the straight line distance traveled measures 450 miles, the estimated track is approximately 1,200. Dixon is awarded the Navy Cross for his heroism, leadership, and resourcefulness.[72]

Submarine *Plunger* (SS 179) rolls off the Marine Railway at Pearl Harbor Navy Yard onto the floor of the carriage. Fortunately, neither the ship nor the marine railway suffers significant damage, and both are returned to service.

ATLANTIC. Destroyer *Dallas* (DD 199) rescues 46 survivors from Brazilian tanker *Olinda*, sunk the day before by German submarine *U 432*.

Unarmed U.S. tanker *Pan Massachusetts* is sunk by German submarine *U 128* about 20 miles off Cape Canaveral, Florida, 28°27'N, 80°08'W; Coast Guard lighthouse tender *Forward* (WAGL 160) and British tanker *Elizabeth Massey* rescue 18 survivors from the 38-man crew.

U.S. freighter *Lake Osweya* is sunk by German submarine *U 96* in the North Atlantic, 43°14'N, 54°45'W. Although *U 96* sees three lifeboats pull away from the ship, no survivors from the 30-man merchant complement or the seven-man Armed Guard are ever found.

CARIBBEAN. Transport *William P. Biddle* (AP 15) disembarks Ninth Defense Battalion, USMC, at Guantánamo Bay, Cuba.

20 Friday

UNITED STATES. Commander in Chief U.S. Fleet directs Atlantic and Pacific Fleets to establish Amphibious Forces.

PACIFIC. TF 11 (Vice Admiral Wilson Brown Jr.), en route to attack Rabaul, is spotted by Japanese flying boats (Yokohama *Kokutai*). Although the American strike is cancelled, Japanese land attack planes (4th *Kokutai*) sortie against TF 11, focusing their efforts on *Lexington* (CV 2). In the battle off Bougainville, combat air patrol F4Fs (VF 3) and SBDs (VS 2) (the latter utilized in the anti–torpedo plane role) and ships' antiaircraft fire annihilate the enemy. In the battle, Lieutenant Edward H. O'Hare (VF 3) shoots down four bombers and damages two, a phenomenal performance that earns him the Medal of Honor.

Submarine *Swordfish* (SS 193) embarks Philippine President Manuel Quezon, his wife, and two children; Vice President Sergio Osmeña; and other Philippine government officials off Mariveles (see 22 February).

Destroyer *Stewart* (DD 224), damaged by shellfire in the Battle of Badoeng Strait the previous night, suffers further damage when, improperly shored and placed on blocks, she rolls on her port side in a Dutch floating drydock at Surabaya, Java.

In the wake of the Japanese carrier strike the day before, Darwin, Australia, is abandoned as an Allied naval base. RAAF and USAAF air operations from the field outside the port, however, will continue.

Japanese invade Timor Island, N.E.I.

CARIBBEAN. U.S. freighter *Delplata* is torpedoed by German submarine *U 156* about 60 miles west of Martinique, 14°45′N, 62°10′W. Small seaplane tender *Lapwing* (AVP 1) rescues the 52 survivors (including the 13-man Armed Guard) and then scuttles the irreparably damaged merchantman with gunfire. German submarine *U 156* puts in to Martinique to put ashore one of the men wounded on 16 February (see 21 February).

ATLANTIC. Unarmed U.S. freighter *Azalea City* is sunk by German submarine *U 432* about 125 miles east-southeast of Ocean City, Maryland, 38°00′N, 73°00′W. There are no survivors from the 38-man crew.

EUROPE. Admiral William D. Leahy, USN (Retired), Ambassador to France, writes to President Roosevelt that he expects a recall "for consultation" since the French have not responded positively to Roosevelt's message of 11 February. Roosevelt, while sympathetic to Leahy's position, subsequently informs him

that "to hold the fort [in Vichy] is as important a military task as any other in these days." Leahy is thus retained in France.

21 Saturday

PACIFIC. Submarine *Triton* (SS 201) sinks Japanese merchant cargo vessel *Shokyu Maru* in East China Sea, 60 miles south of Quelpart Island, 32°10′N, 126°28′E.

ATLANTIC. Four destroyers of TU 4.1.4 (Commander Albert C. Murdaugh), accompanied by Canadian corvette HMCS *Algoma*, while escorting convoy ON 67, obtain sound contact in poor visibility conditions; destroyer *Edison* (DD 439) drops depth charges with no result; destroyer *Nicholson* (DD 442) reports whale in vicinity (see 22 February).

Unarmed U.S. tanker *J. N. Pew* is sunk by German submarine *U 67* about 225 miles west of Aruba, N.W.I., 12°40′N, 74°00′W; two survivors reach the coast of Colombia, 35 miles east of Riohacha (see 14 March).

Unarmed U.S. tanker *Republic* is torpedoed by German submarine *U 504* about three miles east of Jupiter Inlet, Florida, 27°05′N, 80°15′W; three crewmen perish in the initial explosion, while two drown in the abandonment. One lifeboat reaches shore unaided (18 men on board) while U.S. tanker *Cities Service Missouri* rescues six men from a second boat (see 23 February).

EUROPE. Admiral William D. Leahy, USN (Retired), Ambassador to France, receives instruction to see French Minister of Marine, Admiral François Darlan, immediately about German submarine *U 156*'s receiving assistance at Martinique. Unless the Vichy French can assure the U.S. government that no Axis ships or planes will be allowed to enter French ports or territory in the Western Hemisphere, and that unless such assurances are rigidly maintained, the United States "will take such action in the interest of security of the Western Hemisphere as it may judge necessary and in accordance with existing inter-American obligations." Leahy writes in his diary that everything points to his early recall to Washington, D.C., "for consultation" (see 16 April).

22 Sunday

PACIFIC. Submarine *Swordfish* (SS 193) disembarks Philippine President Manuel Quezon and his party at San Jose, Panay, P.I., to continue their journey out of the archipelago.

Japanese heavy cruiser *Chokai* is damaged by grounding on reef, Cape St. Jacques, French Indochina.

ATLANTIC. German submarine attacks convoy ON 67, which is escorted by TU 4.1.4 (Commander Albert C. Murdaugh). *U 155* sinks freighters *Sama* (Norwegian) and *Adellan* (British), 49°20′N, 38°15′W. Rescue vessel *Toward* picks up 12 survivors from *Adellan*; Canadian corvette HMCS *Algoma* rescues a survivor from *Sama*; and destroyer *Nicholson* (DD 442) rescues 19 *Sama* survivors (see 23 February).

U.S. tanker *Cities Service Empire* is sunk by German submarine *U 128*, 25 miles north of Bethel Shoals, 28°00′N, 80°22′W. Destroyer *Biddle* (DD 151) rescues survivors from life rafts while Coast Guard cutter *Vigilant* (WPC 154) goes alongside and rescues men directly from the burning ship. All told, three of the nine-man Armed Guard are lost, in addition to 11 of the 41-man civilian complement.

Unarmed U.S. tanker *W. D. Anderson* is sunk by German submarine *U 504* about 12 miles northeast of Jupiter Point Lighthouse, 27°09′N, 79°56′W. The sole survivor of the 36-man crew swims ashore at Stewart, Florida.

Unarmed U.S. freighter *West Zeda* is sunk by German submarine *U 129* about 125 miles southeast of Trinidad, B.W.I., 09°13′N, 69°04′W. Schooner *Emeralda* rescues the entire 35-man crew, who suffer no casualties in the encounter with the U-boat.

23 Monday

PACIFIC. Submarine *Tarpon* (SS 175) runs aground in Boling Strait, N.E.I., and becomes stranded (see 24 February).

Japanese submarine *I 17* shells oil refinery at Ellwood, California.

ATLANTIC. TU 4.1.4 (four U.S. destroyers) (Commander Albert C. Murdaugh) plus Canadian corvette HMCS *Algoma* continue to shepherd convoy ON 67; destroyer *Edison* (DD 439) carries out depth charge attack on sound contact; destroyers *Lea* (DD 118) and *Bernadou* (DD 153) make sweeps on convoy's beam, with the latter carrying out a depth charge attack (see 24 February).

Unarmed U.S. tanker *Republic*, torpedoed by German submarine *U 504* on 21 February, having drifted onto reefs off Hobe Sound, Florida, sinks.

CARIBBEAN. U.S. freighter *Lihue* is torpedoed by German submarine *U 161* about 275 miles west of Martinique, 14°30′N, 64°45′W; *Lihue*, damaged, engages *U 161* in a surface gunnery action before the freighter is subsequently abandoned and the crew rescued by British tanker *British Governor*. Canadian armed merchant cruiser HMCS *Prince Henry* places a salvage party on board in attempt to save *Lihue*. Minesweeper *Partridge* (AM 16) tries to tow *Lihue* to safety, but the crippled merchantman sinks short of St. Lucia, the intended destination. There are no casualties to either the 36-man merchant crew or the nine-man Armed Guard.

Unarmed U.S. tanker *Sun* is torpedoed by German submarine *U 502* about 54 miles north of Aruba, 13°02′N, 70°41′W, and although initially abandoned is reboarded. She is ultimately repaired and returned to service; there are no casualties among the 36-man crew.

24 Tuesday

PACIFIC. TF 16 (Vice Admiral William F. Halsey Jr.) raids Wake Island to destroy Japanese installations there. SBDs (VB 6 and VS 6) and TBDs (VT 6) from carrier *Enterprise* (CV 6) and SOCs (VCS 5) from heavy cruisers *Northampton* (CA 26) and *Salt Lake City* (CA 25) bomb installations on Wake. Bombardment unit consisting of *Northampton* and *Salt Lake City* and destroyers *Balch* (DD 363) and *Maury* (DD 401) (Rear Admiral Raymond A. Spruance) shells the atoll. Combined efforts of *Enterprise*'s planes (bombing and strafing) and ships' gunfire sink guardboats *No. 5 Fukyu Maru* and *No. 1 Miho Maru*. Fortunately,

the bombing and shelling of Wake harms none of the U.S. marines, sailors, and construction workers too badly wounded to have been evacuated in the initial group of POWs, nor the civilian workmen (Contractors Pacific Naval Air Bases) retained on the island to continue work on defenses. One SBD (VS 6) is lost, however, and its crew taken prisoner (see 13 March).

Small reconnaissance seaplane from Japanese submarine *I 9* reconnoiters Pearl Harbor.

Submarine *Swordfish* (SS 193) embarks U.S. High Commissioner to the Philippine Islands, Francis B. Sayre, and his party off Manila Bay. Their destination is Surabaya, Java (see 9 March).

Submarines *Pike* (SS 173) and *Pickerel* (SS 177) are sent to assist damaged submarine *Tarpon* (SS 175), stranded in Boling Strait, N.E.I.; in the event that they cannot free the grounded boat, *Pike* and *Pickerel* are to destroy her. Fortunately, *Tarpon*'s crew manages to work the boat free by removing anchors, torpedoes, oil, and ammunition.

Panamanian freighter *Snark* is mined while attempting to enter Nouméa, New Caledonia, without a pilot. Destroyer *Worden* (DD 352) tows the crippled ship out of the channel but has to abandon further salvage when the dam-

aged vessel drifts and grounds hard and fast onto a reef.

ATLANTIC. Convoy ON 67 again comes under attack by German submarines. TU 4.1.4 (Commander Albert C. Murdaugh), comprised of four U.S. destroyers and Canadian corvette HMCS *Algoma*, battles the onslaught. *U 558* torpedoes tankers *Inverarder* (British) and *Eidanger* (Norwegian); rescue vessel *Toward* takes on board survivors from both ships, which are abandoned but afloat (*Inverarder* sinks later). *U 158* and *U 162* fire torpedoes; one or the other damages British tanker *Empire Celt*. *U 158* torpedoes British tanker *Diloma*, but the merchantman survives and remains with the convoy while *U 158* submerges in a hurry to avoid counterattacks. *U 558* renders the coup de grâce to the abandoned and drifting *Eidanger*. Destroyer *Lea* (DD 118) makes persistent depth charge attacks on a submarine contact; although she claims destruction of her quarry, no U-boat is in fact lost. Destroyer *Edison* (DD 439), TU 4.1.4's flagship, also erroneously claims destruction of a U-boat (see 25 February).

25 Wednesday

UNITED STATES. Coast Guard assumes responsibility for U.S. port security.

PACIFIC. Japanese force lands from motor sailer on Bawean Island, 85 miles north of Surabaya, Java, and sets up a radio station (see 26 February).

Submarines *Perch* (SS 176) attacks what she identifies as a Japanese merchantman but is damaged by shellfire and is forced to break off action. *Perch* remains on patrol.

Japanese cargo ship *Fukushima Maru* runs aground on a reef and is wrecked, Katsura Bay, 35°09′N, 140°18′E.

ATLANTIC. TU 4.1.4 (Commander Albert C. Murdaugh) continues to conduct vigorous patrolling in wake of previous day's attacks upon convoy ON 67, which will undergo no more U-boat assaults. ON 67, however, is the first west-bound convoy under American command to sustain heavy losses.

26 Thursday

PACIFIC. Submarine *S 38* (SS 143) bombards Japanese radio station on Bawean Island, set up the previous day.

Small reconnaissance seaplane from Japanese submarine *I 25* reconnoiters Melbourne, Australia.

While destroyer *Edsall* (DD 219) stands by in background and her survivors look on in the foreground, seaplane tender *Langley* (AV 3) lists to port, 27 February 1942, her deck cargo (USAAF P-40s) destined never to reach Java, as seen from *Edsall*'s sister ship *Whipple* (DD 217). Both ships are most likely painted in the "Cavite home mix" blue gray. (NHC, NH 92472)

ATLANTIC. Unarmed U.S. bulk carrier *Marore* is torpedoed, shelled, and sunk by German submarine *U 432* off the North Carolina coast, 35°33′N, 74°58′W. U.S. tanker *John D. Gill* rescues 25 survivors; 15 more men land at Coast Guard Big Kinnakeet Lifeboat Station. There are no casualties.

U.S. tanker *R. P. Resor* is torpedoed by German submarine *U 578* five miles off Sea Girt, Delaware, 39°47′N, 73°26′W; of the 41-man merchant crew and eight Armed Guard sailors on board, only one civilian and one Armed Guard sailor are rescued by submarine chaser *PC 507*. Coast Guard cutters *Icarus* (WPC 110) and *Antietam* (WPC 128), yacht *Zircon* (PY 16), and coastal minesweeper *AMc 200* converge on the scene; Eagle Boat *PE 55* attacks sound contact in the vicinity without result (see 1 March).

U.S. tanker *Cassimir* is sunk in collision with U.S. freighter *Lara* 48 miles from Frying Pan Shoals (North Carolina coast), 33°28′N, 77°34′W.

27 Friday

PACIFIC. Seaplane tender *Langley* (AV 3), carrying 32 USAAF P-40s earmarked for the defense of Java, is bombed by Japanese naval land attack planes (Takao *Kokutai*) 75 miles south of Tjilatjap, Java, 08°58′S, 109°02′E. Irreparably damaged, the ship that had once been the U.S. Navy's first aircraft carrier (she had been converted to a seaplane tender in 1936) is shelled and torpedoed by destroyer *Whipple* (DD 217). Necessity to clear the area precludes seeing *Langley* sink.

U.S. freighter *Sea Witch* delivers 27 crated USAAF P-40s to Tjilatjap, Java, but the planes will be destroyed on the docks to deny their use by the victors.

Battle of the Java Sea: ABDA naval force (Rear Admiral Karel W. F. M. Doorman, RNN) of five cruisers and 11 destroyers engages Japanese support force (Rear Admiral Takagi Takeo) covering Java invasion convoy, in Java Sea off Surabaya. Japanese main battery gunfire proves ineffective, as heavy cruisers *Nachi* and *Haguro* expend 1,271 8-inch rounds but achieve only five hits. Of those five, four are duds: one each on heavy cruiser *Houston* (CA 30) (fighting without her Turret III) and British heavy cruiser HMS *Exeter*, and two on Dutch light cruiser *De Ruyter*. The only shell that does explode, however, reduces *Exeter*'s speed. Of the ABDA destroyers, Dutch *Kortenaer* is torpedoed and sunk by *Haguro*; HMS *Encounter* rescues survivors. Japanese de-

stroyer gunfire sinks HMS *Electra* (see 28 February), while HMS *Jupiter* is sunk by mine laid earlier that day by Dutch minelayer *Gouden Leeuw*. Allied gunfire damages Japanese destroyers *Asagumo* and *Minegumo*; U.S. destroyer torpedo attack proves ineffective (see 28 February).

Submarine *Narwhal* (SS 167) damages Japanese fleet tanker *Manju Maru* northwest of Chichi Jima, 28°55′N, 138°15′E.

GENERAL. Joint U.S.-Mexican Defense Commission is established.

28 Saturday

PACIFIC. Battle of the Java Sea, begun late the previous afternoon, concludes: Japanese heavy cruiser *Haguro* sinks Dutch light cruiser *De Ruyter* (Rear Admiral W. F. M. Karel Doorman, RNN, flagship, in which he is lost) while *Nachi* sinks Dutch light cruiser *Java*; remnants of the ABDA force flee to Surabaya, sheltering there briefly before trying to escape piecemeal to Australia. In the wake of the battle, submarine *S 37* (SS 142) encounters boat from the sunken *De Ruyter* and recovers two U.S. Navy sailors who had been serving in a liaison capacity in the Dutch ship. Before continuing on patrol, the U.S. submariners provide the Dutch seamen with rations. *S 37*'s sister ship *S 38* (SS 143) rescues survivors from sunken British destroyer HMS *Electra*. Destroyer Division 58 (Commander Thomas H. Binford) departs Surabaya for Australia (see 1 March).

Minesweeper *Whippoorwill* (AM 35), while searching waters south of Tjilatjap for survivors of seaplane tender *Langley* (AV 3), sunk the previous day, rescues crew of British freighter *City of Manchester*, which had just been torpedoed, shelled, and sunk by Japanese submarine *I 153* at 08°16′S, 108°52′E. Gunboat *Tulsa* (PG 22), in the vicinity on the same errand, takes on board and treats the wounded merchant sailors.

Japanese land on north coast of Java. Battle of Sunda Strait begins shortly before midnight as heavy cruiser *Houston* (CA 30) and Australian light cruiser HMAS *Perth* (Captain Hector M. L. Waller, RAN), attempting to retire from Java, encounter Japanese transport force and escorting ships (Rear Admiral Takagi Takeo) in Banten Bay, Java, and engage them (see 1 March).

ATLANTIC. German submarine *U 578* sinks destroyer *Jacob Jones* (DD 130) off the Delaware capes, 38°42′N, 74°39′W.

Destroyer *Edison* (DD 439), having just seen convoy ON 67 on the final leg of its passage,

accidentally fires upon British submarine HMS *Severn*, which is apparently looking for an escort to Halifax. *Edison* apologizes and provides the undamaged *Severn* the requisite directions.

Unarmed U.S. tanker *Oregon* is torpedoed, shelled, and sunk by German submarine *U 156* about 150 miles northeast of Mona Passage, 20°44′N, 67°52′W; *U 156* machine-guns the crew trying to launch one of the lifeboats, killing six men. One group of 26 survivors reaches Puerto Plata, Dominican Republic, on 4 March; U.S. tanker *Gulfpenn* rescues other group of four men the following day.

PBY (VP 73) mistakenly bombs and damages submarine *Greenling* (SS 213) outside submarine sanctuary off New London, Connecticut.

UNITED STATES. Navy Rescue Tug Service (NRTS) is organized; responsibility for rescue operations is delegated to the seagoing operating forces under Commander in Chief U.S. Fleet; responsibility for rescue operations in cases of vessels in distress 500 miles or less from land is delegated to the Sea Frontier's commanders. Borderline cases involving vessels approximately 500 miles from land will be the joint responsibility of Commanders in chief U.S. Fleet and commanders of Sea Frontiers.

MARCH

1 Sunday

ATLANTIC AND PACIFIC. Base Force Pacific Fleet is redesignated Service Force Pacific; Train Atlantic Fleet is redesignated Service Force Atlantic.

PACIFIC. Destroyer Division 58 (Commander Thomas H. Binford) encounters Japanese Bali Attack Unit (destroyers *Hatsuharu*, *Wakaba*, *Nenohi*, and *Hatsushimo*) in Bali Strait, N.E.I. None of the U.S. ships—destroyers *Alden* (DD 211), *Paul Jones* (DD 230), *John D. Edwards* (DD 216), and *John D. Ford* (DD 228)—are damaged in the brief night surface action that ends with Destroyer Division 58 continuing its voyage toward Australia.

Battle of Sunda Strait continues as heavy cruiser *Houston* (CA 30) and Australian light cruiser HMAS *Perth* (Captain Hector M. L. Waller, RAN), heading for Sunda Strait, are engaged by three Japanese cruisers and nine destroyers (Rear Admiral Takagi Takeo). In the melee, *Houston* (05°50′S, 105°55′E) and *Perth* are sunk by torpedoes and gunfire of heavy cruisers *Mogami* and *Mikuma*; *Houston*'s commanding officer, Captain Albert H. Rooks, killed while his ship is being abandoned, is awarded the Medal of Honor posthumously in recognition of his heroism, courage, gallantry, and distinguished service during the period between 4 and 27 February. Minesweeper *W.2*, landing ship *Shinshu Maru*, and transports *Tatsuno Maru*, *Sakura Maru*, and *Horai Maru* are all sunk by torpedoes fired by heavy cruiser *Mogami*. Destroyers *Shirakumo*, *Shirayuki*, and *Harukaze* are damaged by gunfire.[73] Japanese oiler *Tsurumi* is torpedoed by Dutch submarine *K XV* east of Nicholas Point, Banten Bay, Java.

Japanese heavy cruisers *Myoko*, *Ashigara*, *Haguro*, and *Nachi* engage three Allied ships (Captain Oliver L. Gordon, RN) fleeing Java, sinking British heavy cruiser HMS *Exeter* and destroyer HMS *Encounter*. U.S. destroyer *Pope* (DD 225), the third ship, escapes the cruisers but is located and bombed by aircraft from seaplane carriers *Chitose* and *Mizuho*. Damaged by one near-miss, *Pope* is then located by carrier attack planes from *Ryujo* and bombed; scuttling is in progress when *Myoko* and *Ashigara* deliver the coup de grâce with gunfire at 04°00′S, 111°30′E.[74]

Japanese naval forces sweep south of Java. Destroyer *Edsall* (DD 219) is sunk by gunfire from battleships *Hiei* and *Kirishima*, heavy cruisers *Tone* and *Chikuma*, and planes from carriers *Akagi* and *Soryu*; the number of main battery shells expended in the attempt to sink the U.S. ship comes to 297 15-inch and 844 8-inch. *Edsall*'s five enlisted survivors are later executed at Kendari, Celebes. Oiler *Pecos* (AO 6), with *Langley* (AV 3) survivors on board as well as evacuees from Java, is bombed and sunk by carrier bombers from *Akagi*, *Kaga*, *Hiryu*, and *Soryu*, south of Christmas Island, 14°27′S, 106°11′E.

Japanese naval land attack planes (Kanoya Kokutai) bomb Surabaya, Java; destroyer *Stewart* (DD 224), previously damaged on 19 and 20 February, is damaged again.[75]

Submarine *Perch* (SS 176) is depth charged and damaged by Japanese destroyers *Amatsukaze* and *Hatsukaze*, 73 miles west of Bawean Island, Java Sea, 06°30′S, 113°50′E (see 2 and 3 March).

Japanese invasion of Java proceeds: Allied planes (Dutch Martin 139s, RAF Blenheims and Vildebeests, and RNZAF Hudsons) bomb invasion shipping, damaging light cruiser *Kinu*, transport *Johore Maru*, and army cargo ship *Tokushima Maru*.

ABDA Command is dissolved as the fall of Java looms.

Small reconnaissance seaplane from Japanese submarine *I 25* reconnoiters Hobart, Tasmania.

ATLANTIC. PBO (VP 82), on an antisubmarine sweep, bombs and sinks German submarine *U 656* south of Newfoundland, 46°15′N, 53°15′W. *U 656* is the first U-boat sunk by U.S. Navy forces during World War II.

Tug *Sagamore* (AT 20) attempts to tow damaged U.S. tanker *R. P. Resor* (torpedoed by German submarine *U 578* on 26 February) to shallow water to permit salvage, but to no avail. The gutted ship sinks about 31 miles east of Barnegat, New Jersey.

2 Monday

PACIFIC. Japanese Main Body, Southern Force (Vice Admiral Kondo Nobutake) overtakes fleeing Allied ships southwest of Bali; heavy cruiser *Maya* and destroyers *Arashi* and *Nowaki* sink British destroyer HMS *Stronghold*. Heavy cruisers *Atago* and *Takao* engage what they initially identify as a *Marblehead*-class cruiser and sink her with gunfire; their quarry is actually destroyer *Pillsbury* (DD 227), which is lost with all hands at 14°30′S, 106°30′E.

Submarine *Perch* (SS 176) is depth charged and damaged by Japanese destroyer *Ushio*, Java Sea (see 3 March).

Submarine *S 38* (SS 143) attacks Japanese light cruiser *Kinu* off north coast of Java, N.E.I., but the latter evades all four torpedoes fired, 06°27′S, 112°12′E.

Submarine *Sailfish* (SS 192) sinks Japanese aircraft transport *Kamogawa Maru* north of Lombok Strait, 08°06′S, 115°57′E.

Japanese troops land at Zamboanga, Mindanao, P.I.

Bataan-based USAAF P-40s sink Japanese auxiliary submarine chaser *No. 11 Kyo Maru* in Subic Bay.

ATLANTIC. Antisubmarine Warfare Unit Atlantic Fleet is established at Boston, Massachusetts.

3 Tuesday

PACIFIC. Submarine *Perch* (SS 176), depth charged and irreparably damaged by Japanese destroyers *Ushio* and *Sazanami*, is scuttled by her crew in Java Sea. All hands (59 men) survive the boat's loss and are taken prisoner.[76]

Gunboat *Asheville* (PG 21) is sunk by gunfire of Japanese destroyers *Arashi* and *Nowaki* south of Java, 12°33′S, 111°35′E. *Asheville*'s sole survivor will perish in a POW camp in 1945.

ATLANTIC. Unarmed U.S. freighter *Mary* is sunk by German submarine *U 129* about 250

miles northeast of Paramaribo, Dutch Guiana, 08°25′N, 52°50′W (see 9 March).

4 Wednesday

PACIFIC. TG 16.5 (Vice Admiral William F. Halsey Jr.) raids Marcus Island; SBDs (VB 6 and VS 6) from carrier *Enterprise* (CV 6) bomb Japanese installations there.[77]

"K" Operation: Two Japanese flying boats (Yokosuka Kokutai), refueled by submarines *I 15* and *I 19* at French Frigate Shoals, T.H., bomb Oahu but cause no damage (see 10 March).

Submarine *Grampus* (SS 207) sinks Japanese tanker *No. 2 Kaijo Maru* 145 miles south of Truk, 00°56′N, 149°31′E.

Submarine *Narwhal* (SS 167) sinks Japanese army cargo ship *Taki Maru* off Amami-O-Shima, south of Kyushu, 28°37′N, 129°10′E.

Submarine *S 39* (SS 144) sinks Japanese oiler *Erimo* south of Billiton Island, 04°22′S, 108°23′E; light cruiser *Yura* rescues survivors.

Submarine *Sargo* (SS 188), while approaching Fremantle, Australia, is mistakenly attacked and damaged by an RAAF Hudson.

5 Thursday

PACIFIC. Submarine *Salmon* (SS 182) torpedoes Japanese transport *Taito Maru* north of Lombok, N.E.I., 05°35′S, 112°35′E.

Japanese transport *Takao Maru*, damaged and driven aground off Vigan, Luzon, on 10 December 1941, is destroyed by Filipino saboteurs.

ATLANTIC. Coastal yacht *Alabaster* (PYc 21) collides with unidentified merchant ship while patrolling off Cape May, New Jersey, but since the damage suffered by neither ship is serious enough to hamper their operations, both vessels continue on their way.

Unarmed U.S. freighter *Collamer*, straggling from convoy HX 178, is sunk by German submarine *U 404* off the coast of Nova Scotia, 44°18′N, 63°10′W. British freighter *Empire Woodcock* rescues the 24 survivors from the 31-man crew.

Unarmed U.S. freighter *Mariana* is sunk by German submarine *U 126* east of Nassau, Bahamas, 22°14′N, 71°23′W. There are no survivors from the 36-man crew.

6 Friday

ATLANTIC. German submarine *U 129* sinks unarmed U.S. freighter *Steel Age* about 130 miles northeast of Paramaribo, Dutch Guiana, 06°45′N, 53°15′W, and takes the sole survivor captive.

7 Saturday

PACIFIC. Submarine *Grenadier* (SS 210) torpedoes Japanese transport *Asahisan Maru* south of Shioya Saki, 36°27'N, 141°06'E.

ATLANTIC. Unarmed U.S. freighter *Barbara* is sunk by German submarine *U 126* approximately nine miles north-northwest of West Tortuga Island, Dominican Republic, 20°00'N, 73°56'W; a PBY rescues one group of survivors while the remainder reach shore. Later, *U 126* shells and sinks unarmed U.S. freighter *Cardonia* about five miles west-northwest of San Nicholas Mole, Haiti, 19°53'N, 73°27'W; 22 survivors reach safety at San Nicholas Mole less than five hours after the ship sinks (see 8 March).

U.S. freighter *Independence Hall*, straggling from convoy SC 73, founders and sinks off Sable Island, 43°55'N, 59°55'W. Ten of the 38-man merchant crew perish; there are no casualties among the nine-man Armed Guard.

Brazilian steamship *Arabutan* is sunk by German submarine *U 155* off the Virginia capes, 35°15'N, 73°55'W (see 8 March).

8 Sunday

PACIFIC. "SR" Operation: Japanese naval force (Rear Admiral Kajioka Sadamichi) occupies Lae and Salamaua, New Guinea.

Small reconnaissance seaplane from Japanese submarine *I 25* reconnoiters Wellington, New Zealand.

ATLANTIC. Net tender *Mulberry* (YN 22) rescues 14 survivors from U.S. freighter *Cardonia*, sunk by German submarine *U 126* the day before.

Coast Guard cutter *Calypso* (WPC 104) rescues 54 survivors from Brazilian steamship *Arabutan*, sinks their lifeboats as a hazard to navigation, and transports the men to Little Creek, Virginia.

9 Monday

PACIFIC. Submarine *Swordfish* (SS 193) disembarks U.S. High Commissioner to the Philippine Islands, Francis B. Sayre, and his party at Fremantle, Australia. The collapse of the ABDA Command has led to this change of destination.

Java surrenders to the Japanese.

ATLANTIC. Naval Air Transport Service Squadron (VR 1) is established at Norfolk, Virginia, for operations in Atlantic area.

U.S. freighter *Alcoa Scout* rescues survivors of U.S. freighter *Mary*, sunk by German submarine *U 129* on 3 March.

Submarine *Trout* (SS 202), her captain on the bridge, prepares to moor alongside light cruiser *Detroit* (CL 8), Pearl Harbor, 3 March 1942, with a cargo of gold bullion and securities brought out of the Philippines. Nests of destroyers undergoing upkeep are visible in the background. (Author's Collection)

Brazilian steamship *Cayru* is sunk by German submarine *U 94* off the Delaware capes, 39°10'N, 72°02'W (see 11 March).

10 Tuesday

PACIFIC. TF 11 (Vice Admiral Wilson Brown Jr.), which includes ships of TF 17 (Rear Admiral Frank Jack Fletcher), on the heels of initial raids by RAAF Hudsons, attacks Japanese invasion fleet (Rear Admiral Kajioka Sadamichi) off Lae and Salamaua, New Guinea. SBDs (VB 2, VS 2, VB 5, and VS 5) and TBDs (VT 2 and VT 5), supported by F4Fs (VF 3 and VF 42) from carriers *Lexington* (CV 2) and *Yorktown* (CV 5), sink armed merchant cruiser *Kongo Maru*, auxiliary minelayer *Ten'yo Maru*, and transport *Yokohama Maru* and damage light cruiser *Yubari*; destroyers *Yunagi*, *Asanagi*, *Oite*, *Asakaze*, and *Yakaze*; minelayer *Tsugaru*; seaplane carrier *Kiyokawa Maru*; transport *Kokai Maru*; and minesweeper *No. 2 Tama*

Maru. One SBD (VS 2) is lost to antiaircraft fire. USAAF B-17s and RAAF Hudsons conduct follow-up strikes but inflict no appreciable additional damage. In a message to British Prime Minister Winston S. Churchill, President Roosevelt hails the raid as "the best day's work we've had." The success of the U.S. carrier strike (the first time in which two carrier air groups attack a common objective) convinces Japanese war planners that continued operations in the New Guinea area will require aircraft carrier support, thus setting the stage for confrontation in the Coral Sea (see 4–8 May).

Japanese invade Finschhafen, New Guinea.

Japanese collier *Kosei Maru* is sunk by mine in Lingayen Gulf, P.I., 16°05'N, 120°20'E.

USMC F2As (VMF 221) from Midway shoot down Japanese flying boat (Yokosuka Kokutai) attempting to reconnoiter the atoll.[78]

ATLANTIC. U.S. tanker *Gulftrade* is sunk by German submarine *U 588* about two miles east of Barnegat, New Jersey, 39°50′N, 73°52′W; net tender *Larch* (YN 16) and Coast Guard cutter *Antietam* (WPC 128), along with Eagle Boat *PE 48* and Coast Guard motor lifeboats from the Barnegat station, are sent to the scene. *Larch* rescues seven survivors; *Antietam* rescues nine. *Larch's* part in the rescue is particularly noteworthy because circumstances (high winds and heavy seas) compel her to nose into the stern section of the tanker with the net tender's prominent "horns" lying across the sloping decks. *Larch's* sailors clamber onto the horns and help the tanker's survivors across; a slip means certain death from being crushed or lost overboard.

11 Wednesday

PACIFIC. Lieutenant General Douglas MacArthur and Rear Admiral Francis W. Rockwell depart Luzon for Mindanao, with their respective staffs, in motor torpedo boats *PT 32*, *PT 34*, *PT 35*, and *PT 41*. For his role in the evacuation, as well as other operations in the Philippines since the start of hostilities, Lieutenant John D. Bulkeley, Commander Motor Torpedo Boat Squadron 3, will receive the Medal of Honor (see 13 March).

Submarine *Pollack* (SS 180), operating in the East China Sea about 270 miles east of Shanghai, sinks Japanese freighter *Fukushu Maru*, 30°53′N, 126°20′E, and passenger-cargo ship *Baikal Maru*, 31°00′N, 126°32′E.

U.S. passenger ship *Mount McKinley* is stranded off Unimak Island, Aleutians; wrecked subsequently by heavy seas, the ship will be written off as a total loss.

ATLANTIC. Coastal minesweeper *AMc 202*, at 40°32′N, 71°40′W, rescues seven survivors from Brazilian steamship *Cayru*, sunk by German submarine *U 94* on 9 March, and transports them to New London, Connecticut.

Unarmed U.S. freighter *Texan* is sunk by German submarine *U 126* about 40 miles east of Nuevitas, Cuba, 21°32′N, 76°24′W; Cuban fishing boat *Yoyo* rescues survivors.

Unarmed U.S. freighter *Caribsea* is sunk by German submarine *U 158* about 14 miles east of Cape Lookout, North Carolina, 34°40′N, 76°10′W; U.S. freighter *Norlindo* rescues survivors.

12 Thursday

UNITED STATES. President Roosevelt combines duties of Commander in Chief U.S. Fleet and Chief of Naval Operations by executive order (see 26 March).

PACIFIC. U.S. Army troops (Brigadier General Alexander M. Patch, USA) arrive on New Caledonia to establish a base at Nouméa.

ATLANTIC. U.S. tanker *John D. Gill* is damaged by German submarine *U 158* off Frying Pan Shoals (North Carolina coast), 33°55′N, 77°39′W. Four of the seven-man Armed Guard are lost. Coast Guard cutter *CGC 186* and cutter *Agassiz* (WPC 126) rescue one group of survivors, tanker *Robert H. Colley* the remainder. *John D. Gill* sinks the next morning.

First British armed trawlers sent to augment U.S. Navy force efforts off the German submarine–plagued eastern seaboard, HMS *Wastwater* and HMS *Le Tigre*, begin operations in Third Naval District waters. They are assigned patrol areas off Atlantic City and Barnegat, New Jersey.

CARIBBEAN. German submarine *U 126* torpedoes unarmed U.S. freighters off the coast of Cuba, sinking *Olga* off Camaguey, 23°39′N, 77°00′W, and damaging *Colabee* about 10 miles off Cape Guajaba, 22°14′N, 77°35′W. *Colabee* drifts ashore and grounds on a shoal; Cuban ship *Oriente* rescues one group of survivors (and then tows the damaged ship off the shoal); tanker *Cities Service Kansas* rescues the other. Cuban Navy vessels later salvage the ship.

13 Friday

PACIFIC. Lieutenant General Douglas MacArthur and Rear Admiral Francis W. Rockwell, with their respective staffs, reach Cagayan, Mindanao, after a 560-mile voyage in heavy to moderate seas, in motor torpedo boats *PT 32*, *PT 34*, *PT 35*, and *PT 41*. *PT 32*, disabled during the operation, is scuttled by gunfire of submarine *Permit* (SS 178) one mile southwest of Taguayan Island, P.I., 10°58′N, 121°12′E.

Submarine *Gar* (SS 206) sinks Japanese victualling stores ship *Chichibu Maru* between six and 10 miles southwest of Mikura Jima, south of Tokyo Bay, Japan, 33°53′N, 139°29.5′E. Two American POWs perish.[79]

Small reconnaissance seaplane from Japanese submarine *I 25* reconnoiters Auckland, New Zealand.

Japanese minesweeper *No. 2 Tama Maru* sinks as the result of damage inflicted by U.S. Navy carrier-based planes on 10 March during the Lae-Salamaua, New Guinea, raid.

ATLANTIC. Unarmed U.S. schooner *Albert F. Paul* is sunk by German submarine *U 332* off the coast of Florida, 26°00′N, 72°00′W. There are no survivors.

Chilean freighter *Tolten* is sunk by German submarine *U 404* off Barnegat, New Jersey,

40°10′N, 73°50′W; subsequently, plane en route from Langley Field to Mitchell Field sights one survivor on a life raft at 39°50′N, 73°40′W; Coast Guard cutter *Antietam* (WPC 128) and coastal minesweeper *AMc 200* are sent to the scene. NAS Lakehurst dispatches three L-type blimps, one of which, *L 2*, ultimately sights the raft seen earlier. Net tender *Larch* (YN 16) rescues the only survivor of what had been a crew of between 16 and 21 men.

14 Saturday

ATLANTIC. Amphibious Force Atlantic Fleet (Rear Admiral Roland M. Brainard) is established.

Unarmed U.S. collier *Lemuel Burrows* is sunk by German submarine *U 404* off Atlantic City, New Jersey, 39°18′N, 74°16′W. Freighter *Sewalls Point* rescues one group of survivors, and freighter *James Elwood Jones* the other.

Panamanian motorship *Annetta I* rescues the last survivor of unarmed U.S. tanker *J. N. Pew*, sunk by German submarine *U 67* on 21 February; 33 of the 36-man crew are lost.

15 Sunday

ATLANTIC. German submarine *U 158* attacks two U.S. tankers. Unarmed *Ario* is sunk 11 miles southwest of Cape Lookout, North Carolina, 34°20′N, 76°39′W. Destroyer *DuPont* (DD 152) rescues the 29 survivors of the 36-man crew. *Olean* is sunk 15 miles south of Cape Lookout, 34°24′N, 76°29′W. Coast Guard motor lifeboats from Cape Lookout and Fort Mason stations rescue 33 survivors.[80]

PBO (VP 82), while providing coverage for convoy ON 74, sinks German submarine *U 503* east-southeast of Argentia, Newfoundland, 43°50′N, 48°45′W.

CARIBBEAN. Coast Guard lighthouse tender *Acacia* (WAGL 200) is sunk by German submarine *U 161* south of Haiti.

16 Monday

PACIFIC. Submarine *Permit* (SS 178) delivers ammunition to Corregidor and evacuates second increment of naval radio and communications intelligence people.

ATLANTIC. Unarmed U.S. tanker *Australia* is irreparably damaged by German submarine *U 332* off Diamond Shoals, North Carolina, 35°07′N, 75°22′W. U.S. freighter *William J. Salman* rescues survivors and transfers them to yacht *Ruby* (PY 21) for further transportation to Southport, North Carolina. *Australia*, sunk in shallow water, is written off as a total loss and her wreck demolished on 20 March.

British tanker *San Demetrio* is sunk by German submarine *U 404* at 37°03′N, 73°50′W (see 18 March).

17 Tuesday

GENERAL. The United States, in agreement with Allied governments, assumes responsibility for the strategic defense of entire Pacific Ocean.

PACIFIC. Submarine *Grayback* (SS 208) sinks Japanese collier *Ishikari Maru* six miles west of Port Lloyd, Chichi Jima, Bonins, 27°05′N, 142°05′E.

Submarine *Permit* (SS 178) is damaged by depth charges off Tayabas Bay, P.I., but remains on patrol.

UNITED STATES. Naval Forces Europe (Vice Admiral Robert L. Ghormley) is established.

ATLANTIC. Destroyer *Stack* (DD 406) and carrier *Wasp* (CV 7) are damaged in collision while en route from Casco Bay, Maine, to Norfolk, Virginia.

Unarmed U.S. tanker *Acme* is damaged by German submarine *U 124* west of Diamond Shoals, North Carolina, 35°06′N, 75°23′W; *U 124* later sinks Greek freighter *Kassandra Louloudi* four miles west-southwest of Diamond Shoals Gas Buoy. Coast Guard cutter *Dione* (WPC 107) rescues 20 survivors from *Acme* and 35 from *Kassandra Louloudi*; steamship *Beta* rescues 22 men from the latter ship.

Honduran freighter *Ceiba* is sunk by German submarine *U 124* at 35°43′N, 73°49′W (see 19 March).

18 Wednesday

PACIFIC. River gunboat *Tutuila* (PR 4), decommissioned at Chungking, China, on 18 January, is leased to the Chinese government for the duration of the war.[81]

Japanese freighter *Jumpo Maru* is sunk, agent unknown, off Tsushima Island.

ATLANTIC. U.S. tanker *E. M. Clark* is sunk by German submarine *U 124* about 22 miles southwest of Diamond Shoals, North Carolina, 34°50′N, 75°35′W. Venezuelan tanker *Catatumbo* rescues 23 of the tanker's complement. Unarmed U.S. tanker *Papoose* is torpedoed by German submarine *U 124* about 15 miles south of Cape Lookout, North Carolina, 34°17′N, 76°39′W (see 19 March).

Yacht *Tourmaline* (PY 20) and Coast Guard cutter *Cuyahoga* (WPC 157) rescue eight survivors of British tanker *San Demetrio*, sunk by *U 404* on 16 March.

Unarmed U.S. tanker *W. E. Hutton* is sunk by German submarine *U 332* about 20 miles southeast of Cape Lookout, North Carolina, 34°05′N, 76°40′W; 13 of the ship's complement of 36 merchant sailors perish in the attack (see 19 March).

19 Thursday

PACIFIC. Philippine President Manuel Quezon and 13 members of his party are transported from Dumaguete, Negros, to Oroquito, Mindanao, after a 240-mile voyage in motor torpedo boat *PT 41*.

Small reconnaissance seaplane from Japanese submarine *I 25* reconnoiters Suva, Fiji Islands.

ATLANTIC. Destroyer *Dickerson* (DD 157) rescues 14 of the 40-man crew of tanker *E. M. Clark*, sunk by *U 124* the previous day. Later, however, *Dickerson* is mistakenly fired upon and damaged by gunfire from U.S. freighter *Liberator* off Virginia capes; three men (including the ship's captain) are killed and six wounded. Later, *Liberator* is sunk by German submarine *U 332*, three miles west of the Diamond Shoals Buoy, 35°05′N, 75°30′W; five crewmen perish. Tug *Umpqua* (AT 25) rescues 26 merchant sailors and the four-man Armed Guard.

Destroyer *Hambleton* (DD 455), at 35°39′N, 71°10′W, rescues six survivors of Honduran freighter *Ceiba*, sunk by *U 124* on 17 March.

British motor vessel *Port Halifax* rescues the 23 survivors of U.S. tanker *W. E. Hutton*, sunk by German submarine *U 332* off Cape Lookout, North Carolina, the previous day.

High-speed transport *Stringham* (APD 6) rescues the 31 survivors of U.S. tanker *Papoose*, irreparably damaged the previous day by German submarine *U 124*. On report of the master, who believes his ship can be saved, tug *Kewaydin* (AT 24) is sent to investigate salvage possibilities. *Papoose*, however, is beyond saving, and sinks the next day; *Kewaydin* proceeds to assist *Acushnet* (see below).

Damaged U.S. tanker *Acme* (torpedoed by German submarine *U 124* on 17 March) is taken in tow by tug *Acushnet* (AT 63) and taken to Norfolk, Virginia.[82]

20 Friday

ATLANTIC. Unarmed U.S. tanker *Oakmar* is shelled by German submarine *U 71* at 36°21′N, 68°50′W, and abandoned; submarine *R 6* (SS 83) is sent to her assistance. *U 71* torpedoes *Oakmar* and shells her until she sinks. Six men perish in the abandonment; the remainder (30 men) are rescued by Greek steamship *Panos Pladelis*.

21 Saturday

ATLANTIC. Unarmed U.S. tanker *Esso Nashville* is torpedoed by German submarine *U 124* off Frying Pan Shoals (North Carolina coast), 33°35′N, 77°22′W. High-speed transport *McKean* (APD 5) rescues eight survivors from two lifeboats; Coast Guard cutters *Tallapoosa* (WPG 52) and *Agassiz* (WPC 126) recover the rest (21 men and eight men, respectively). After *Esso Nashville* breaks in two, tug *Umpqua* (AT 25) tows the after end of the vessel to Morehead City, North Carolina.[83] Later, *U 124* torpedoes tanker *Atlantic Sun* off Beaufort, North Carolina, but inflicts little damage; there are no casualties among the 40-man merchant complement or the five-man Armed Guard. *Atlantic Sun* reaches Beaufort without further incident.

22 Sunday

ATLANTIC. Unarmed U.S. tanker *Naeco* is torpedoed by German submarine *U 124* at 33°59′N, 76°40′W. Coast Guard cutter *Dione* (WPC 107) rescues 10 survivors from one lifeboat and two men from the sea, minesweeper *Osprey* (AM 56) rescues one survivor from a raft, and tug *Umpqua* (AT 25) takes off one man who had returned to the ship after she had been abandoned. All told, 24 men perish with the ship, which later breaks in half. The stern section sinks; destroyer *Roper* (DD 147) scuttles bow section with gunfire.

Unarmed U.S. tanker *Muskogee* is sunk by German submarine *U 123* at 28°00′N, 58°00′W. *U 123* draws near to the survivors on two rafts and questions them before clearing the area. None of the 34-man crew, however, are ever seen again.

23 Monday

PACIFIC. Submarine *Gato* (SS 212) is damaged when accidentally bombed by nonrigid airship *TC 13* off San Francisco Bay, California.

INDIAN OCEAN. "D" Operation: Japanese occupy Andaman Islands, Bay of Bengal.

24 Tuesday

PACIFIC. Japanese naval land attack planes (12th *Kokutai*) begin daily bombings of Corregidor.

25 Wednesday

ATLANTIC. Dutch tanker *Ocana* is sunk by German submarine *U 552* at 42°36′N, 64°25′W; destroyer *Mayo* (DD 422) rescues four survivors.

INDIAN OCEAN. "U" Operation: Japanese convoy lands troops (56th Infantry Division) at Rangoon, Burma (see 1 and 7 April).

26 Thursday

UNITED STATES. Admiral Ernest J. King relieves Admiral Harold R. Stark as Chief of Naval Operations and becomes Commander in Chief U.S. Fleet and Chief of Naval Operations; Vice Admiral Frederick J. Horne (Vice Chief of Naval Operations) and Vice Admiral Russell Willson (COMINCH Chief of Staff) are his principal assistants.

ATLANTIC. TF 39 (Rear Admiral John W. Wilcox Jr.), including battleship *Washington* (BB 56), carrier *Wasp* (CV 7), heavy cruisers *Wichita* (CA 45) and *Tuscaloosa* (CA 37), and eight destroyers, sails from Portland, Maine, for Scapa Flow, Orkney Islands, to reinforce the British Home Fleet (see 27 March).

Commander Eastern Sea Frontier is given operational control of certain USAAF units for antisubmarine patrol duty in the Atlantic. Unity of command over Navy and USAAF units operating over water to protect shipping and conduct antisubmarine warfare is thus vested in the Navy.

Antisubmarine vessel *Atik* (AK 101) is sunk with all hands (139 men) by German submarine *U 123* in the North Atlantic, 36°00′N, 70°00′W, after the gunfire from the "Q-ship" damages the U-boat in a spirited encounter. *Atik* is the only U.S. Navy warship disguised as a merchantman that is lost to enemy action during World War II. Sister ship *Asterion* (AK 100) will conduct a fruitless search for survivors (see 30 March).[84]

Unarmed U.S. tanker *Dixie Arrow*, bound for Paulsboro, New Jersey, is sunk by German submarine *U 71* about 12 miles off Diamond Shoals Lighted Buoy, North Carolina, 34°59′N, 75°33′W. The ship breaks in half and sinks. Destroyer *Tarbell* (DD 142), directed to the scene by a Coast Guard plane, rescues 22 survivors; 11 merchant sailors either drown or burn to death, however, as torpedo explosions set the ship's cargo of 86,136 barrels of crude oil afire.

Panamanian freighter *Equipoise* is sunk by German submarine *U 160* off the Virginia capes, 36°36′N, 74°45′W (see 27 March).

27 Friday

ATLANTIC. Commander TF 39 (Rear Admiral John W. Wilcox Jr.), taking an unaccompanied walk on deck of his flagship, battleship *Washington* (BB 56), is washed overboard and disappears in a heavy sea. Rear Admiral Robert C.

Giffen, in heavy cruiser *Wichita* (CA 45), becomes task force commander upon Wilcox's death.

Destroyer *Greer* (DD 145) proceeds to position indicated by Army plane and rescues five survivors from Panamanian freighter *Equipoise*, sunk the previous day by *U 160*; later, *Greer* picks up an additional eight survivors.

EUROPE. Operation CHARIOT: British raiding force begins attack on port facilities at St. Nazaire, France; destroyer HMS *Campbeltown* [ex-U.S. destroyer *Buchanan* (DD 131)], reconfigured to resemble a German *Möwe*-class torpedo boat and her bow packed with explosives, is to ram the caisson of the only drydock on the French coast capable of handling the battleship *Tirpitz* (see 28 March).

PACIFIC. Submarine *Gudgeon* (SS 211) sinks Japanese freighter *Nissho Maru* southeast of Kumun Island, 33°50′N, 127°33′E.

Japanese collier *Yubari Maru* is sunk by Dutch planes off Banjarmasin, Borneo, 03°05′S, 114°21′E.

Japanese transport *Kitano Maru* is sunk by Japanese mine off Mabilao, Lingayen Gulf, 16°10′N, 120°24′E.

28 Saturday

ATLANTIC. Operation CHARIOT concludes with British destroyer HMS *Campbeltown* successfully ramming the drydock caisson at St. Nazaire, France.

29 Sunday

PACIFIC. Fourth Defense Battalion, USMC, and VMF 212 arrive at Efate, New Hebrides.

ATLANTIC. U.S. steamship *City of New York* is torpedoed by German submarine *U 160* about 40 miles east of Cape Hatteras, North Carolina, 35°16′N, 74°25′W. Before the ship is torpedoed a second time, Armed Guard gunners, who man their stations promptly, manage to get 12 rounds off at the U-boat's periscope. A second torpedo sinks the ship, with the Armed Guard leaving only when the bridge is awash (see 30 and 31 March and 11 April).

U.S. tanker *Paulsboro* is damaged in heavy seas off Overfalls Lightship, Delaware; tug *Allegheny* (AT 19) is sent to her assistance.

U.S. freighter *Excelsior* suffers engine breakdown off Cape Hatteras, North Carolina; tug *Kewaydin* (AT 24) is sent to tow the ship to Norfolk, Virginia.

30 Monday

GENERAL. Pacific War Council representing the United States, Great Britain, Canada, Aus-

tralia, New Zealand, The Netherlands, and China is established in Washington, D.C., to plan war policy.

UNITED STATES. Joint Chiefs of Staff order Pacific Ocean divided into two commands: Pacific Ocean Areas (Admiral Chester W. Nimitz) and Southwest Pacific Area (Lieutenant General Douglas MacArthur, USA).

PACIFIC. Destroyer *Phelps* (DD 360), docked for repairs at Pearl Harbor Navy Yard, is damaged when a railroad crane falls into the drydock.

Submarine *Tambor* (SS 198) damages Japanese transport *Tatsuho Maru* off Eniwetok Atoll, 13°00′N, 157°30′E.

Submarine *Sturgeon* (SS 187) sinks Japanese transport *Choko Maru* off Makassar City, Celebes, N.E.I., 05°39′S, 119°00′E.

INDIAN OCEAN. "X" Operation: Japanese forces occupy Christmas Island (see 31 March and 1 April).

ATLANTIC. Debris sighted by plane at 34°52′N, 69°58′W includes five empty life rafts in the area of the last reported position of antisubmarine vessel *Atik* (AK 101), sunk on 26 March by German submarine *U 123*.

PBY search of area in which U.S. steamship *City of New York* was torpedoed the previous day proves negative (see 31 March and 11 April).

ARCTIC. U.S. freighter *Effingham*, straggling 90 miles astern of Murmansk-bound convoy PQ 13, is torpedoed and set afire by German submarine *U 435* at 70°28′N, 35°44′E. The ship explodes and sinks; two men drown in the abandonment (see 2 and 4 April).

31 Tuesday

INDIAN OCEAN. Submarine *Seawolf* (SS 197), operating against Japanese "X" Operation force off Christmas Island, attacks light cruisers *Naka* (once) and *Natori* (twice), but fails to score a hit; in turn, she is damaged by depth charges (destroyers *Natsukaze*, *Minegumo*, and *Amatsukaze* are among the screening ships), 10°26′S, 105°41′E (see 1 April).

CARIBBEAN. Commander of All Forces Aruba and Curaçao, Netherlands West Indies, is established (Rear Admiral Jesse B. Oldendorf).

ATLANTIC. German submarine *U 754* shells unarmed U.S. tug *Menominee* and the barges she has in tow—*Allegheny*, *Barnegat*, and *Ontario*—off the mouth of Chesapeake Bay, 37°34′N, 75°25′W, sinking *Menominee* and barges *Allegheny* and *Barnegat*. *Ontario*, remaining afloat, serves as a life preserver for the three men from each barge. Of the tug's

18-man crew, however, only two survive. Coast Guard lifeboat (Metomkin Inlet station) rescues the men from the barges; tanker *Northern Sun* rescues the tug's survivors. Later that day, *U 754* torpedoes unarmed Norfolk-bound U.S. tanker *Tiger*. One crewman dies in the initial explosion; the surviving 36 of the ship's complement, in addition to a six-man Navy gun crew riding the ship as passengers, abandon ship (see 1 and 2 April).

Unarmed U.S. tanker *T. C. McCobb*, en route to Caripito, Venezuela, is sunk by Italian submarine *Pietro Calvi* at 07°10′N, 45°20′W; one crewman drowns and one is killed by shellfire (see 8 and 10 April and 16 May).

Destroyer *Roper* (DD 147) and tug *Acushnet* (AT 63) rescue 124 survivors (including a newborn infant) of U.S. steamship *City of New York*, sunk by *U 160* off Cape Hatteras, North Carolina, on 29 March (see 11 April).

APRIL

1 Wednesday

INDIAN OCEAN. Submarine *Seawolf* (SS 197) torpedoes Japanese light cruiser *Naka* off Christmas Island, 10°00′S, 105°00′E.

PACIFIC. Naval Air Transport Service Squadron (VR) 2 is established at Alameda, California, for operations in the Pacific.

Japanese occupy Buka Island, Solomons.

British submarine HMS *Truant* attacks Japanese army transports returning from landing troops at Rangoon, Burma ("U" Operation), sinking *Yae Maru* and *Shunsei Maru* in Malacca Strait, 80 miles west-northwest of Penang, Malaya, 06°07′N, 99°12′E.

ATLANTIC. District patrol vessel *YP 52* rescues 42 survivors of U.S. tanker *Tiger*, torpedoed by German submarine *U 754* late the previous day. Coast Guard cutter *Jackson* (WPC 142) and vessel (NRTS) *Relief* take the damaged ship in tow (see 2 April).

2 Thursday

ATLANTIC. Unarmed U.S. tanker *Liebre* is shelled by German submarine *U 123* at 34°11′N, 76°08′W, and abandoned. Arrival of British motor torpedo boat *MTB 332*, however, compels *U 123* to withdraw before she can finish the work of destroying *Liebre*. Of the 34-man crew, 26 reboard the ship, which is towed by salvage vessel (NRTS) *Resolute* and British trawler HMS *St. Zeno* to Morehead City, North Carolina.[85]

Unarmed U.S. freighter *David H. Atwater* is shelled by German submarine *U 552* east of Chincoteague Inlet, Virginia, 37°37′N, 75°10′W; destroyers *Noa* (DD 343) and *Herbert* (DD 160), sent to the scene, arrive too late to be of assistance to the merchantman. The sudden and savage nature of *U 552*'s attack leaves *David H. Atwater*'s crew little or no time to take to lifeboats. Of the 25-man complement, only three are rescued by Coast Guard cutter *Legare* (WPC 144).

Despite the efforts of a salvage crew, U.S. tanker *Tiger*, torpedoed by German submarine *U 754* on 31 March and taken in tow the previous day, sinks short of her destination, Norfolk, Virginia.

ARCTIC. British minesweeper HMS *Harrier* rescues 17 men in lifeboat from U.S. freighter *Effingham*, sunk by German submarine *U 435* on 30 March; six of those rescued later die of exposure (see 4 April).

3 Friday

PACIFIC. Admiral Chester W. Nimitz is named Commander in Chief Pacific Ocean Areas (CINCPOA); his command encompasses the North, Central, and South Pacific. He retains his position as Commander in Chief Pacific Fleet (CINCPAC).

Light minelayers *Pruitt* (DM 22), *Preble* (DM 20), *Sicard* (DM 21), and *Tracy* (DM 19) mine French Frigate Shoals, T.H., to prevent Japanese submarines from using the area as a refueling point for flying boat raids on Oahu.

INDIAN OCEAN. U.S. freighter *Exhibitor* is bombed and damaged by Japanese reconnaissance flying boat near Calcutta, India, while proceeding to Colombo, Ceylon. The ship's gunfire drives off the enemy plane as it makes a second pass; only four of the men on board (43-man merchant complement and nine-man Armed Guard) are injured in the attack.

ATLANTIC. U.S. freighter *Otho*, en route to Philadelphia, Pennsylvania, from Takoradi, Gold Coast, is sunk by German submarine *U 754* about 200 miles east of Cape Henry, Virginia, 36°25′N, 71°57′W; survivors abandon ship in a raft and three boats (see 8 and 25 April).

U.S. freighter *West Irmo*, en route to Takoradi, Gold Coast, from Marshall, Liberia, is torpedoed by German submarine *U 505* at 02°10′N, 05°50′W, and abandoned. Ten longshoremen are lost in the explosion while the remainder of the ship's complement, 36 merchant seamen, the eight-man Armed Guard, and 55 longshoremen, are rescued by British escort vessel HMS *Copinsay* (see 4 April).

4 Saturday

ATLANTIC. U.S. tanker *Comol Rico* is sunk by German submarine *U 154* about 225 miles north of Puerto Rico, 20°46′N, 66°46′W; three merchant sailors perish in the explosion of the torpedo (see 7 April).

Unarmed U.S. tanker *Byron D. Benson* is torpedoed by German submarine *U 552* approximately eight miles off Currituck Inlet, North Carolina, 36°08′N, 75°32′W; fires, fed by the ship's cargo of 91,500 barrels of crude oil, consume nine of the 37-man crew. Nearby antisubmarine vessel *Asterion* (AK 100) reports the attack (see 5 April).

British escort vessel HMS *Copinsay* attempts to tow the damaged U.S. freighter *West Irmo*, torpedoed the previous day by German submarine *U 505*, but the merchantman proves beyond saving. *Copinsay* hastens *West Irmo*'s end with a depth charge.

ARCTIC. Soviet patrol boat rescues 11 men in a lifeboat from U.S. freighter *Effingham*, sunk by German submarine *U 435* on 30 March; four of those rescued later die of exposure. All told, 11 of the 34-man merchant crew perish, as does one of the nine-man Armed Guard.

5 Sunday

PACIFIC. Japanese naval force occupies Lorengau, Manus Island, Admiralty Islands, without opposition.

INDIAN OCEAN. "C" Operation: Japanese carrier striking force (Vice Admiral Nagumo Chuichi) raids Colombo, Ceylon. After reconnaissance seaplane from heavy cruiser *Tone* locates British heavy cruisers HMS *Cornwall* and HMS *Dorsetshire*, carrier bombers from *Akagi*, *Hiryu*, and *Soryu* sink both ships. Japanese Second Expeditionary Fleet, Malay Force (Vice Admiral Ozawa Jisaburo) is divided into three groups to disrupt Allied shipping in the Bay of Bengal (see 6 April).

ATLANTIC. U.S. tanker *Catahoula*, about 100 miles into her voyage from San Pedro de Macoris, Dominican Republic, to Wilmington, Delaware, is sunk by German submarine *U 154* at 19°16′N, 68°12′W; two merchant sailors perish in the explosion of the torpedo and five drown when the ship is abandoned (see 6 April).

Coast Guard cutter *Dione* (WPC 107) proceeds to the scene of the torpedoing of unarmed U.S. tanker *Byron D. Benson*, attacked by German submarine *U 552* the previous evening. High-speed minesweeper *Hamilton* (DMS 18) does likewise, and during the search for the submarine, rescues 27 survivors; British trawler HMS *Norwich City* picks up one man. *Byron D. Benson* sinks two days later.

6 Monday

INDIAN OCEAN. "C" Operation continues: Japanese Second Expeditionary Fleet, Malay Force (Vice Admiral Ozawa Jisaburo) raids Allied shipping off the east coast of India. Japanese Northern Group (Rear Admiral Kurita Takeo) attacks Allied convoy; unarmed U.S. freighter *Exmoor* is sunk by gunfire of heavy cruisers *Kumano* and *Suzuya* and destroyer *Shirakumo*, 19°53′N, 86°30′E (there are no casualties among the 37-man crew), as are British merchantmen *Silksworth*, *Autolycus*, *Malda*, and *Shinkuang*. Southern Group (Captain Sakiyama Shakao), consisting of heavy cruisers *Mogami* and *Mikuma* and destroyer *Amagiri*, sink British merchantmen *Dardanus*, *Gandara*, and *Indora*. Central Group, formed around carrier *Ryujo*, heavy cruiser *Chokai*, light cruiser *Yura*, and destroyers *Yugiri* and *Asagiri*, attacks shipping in a third area. After planes from *Ryujo* attack unarmed U.S. freighter *Bienville*, *Chokai* shells and sinks the merchantman at 17°50′N, 84°50′E. Japanese gunfire renders all lifeboats useless and kills 19 of the 41-man crew; five more crewmen die later of wounds. Lost with the ship is her cargo of 500 monkeys earmarked for infantile paralysis research in the United States. Seaplanes from *Chokai* bomb unarmed U.S. freighter *Selma City* (17°40′N, 83°20′E) and British freighter *Ganges*, sinking both. Two men wounded by bomb fragments constitute the only casualties on board *Selma City*; her 29-man crew reaches Vizagapatam later the same day by boat. *Yura* and *Yugiri*, meanwhile, sink Dutch motorships *Banjoewangi* and *Batavia* and British steamer *Taksang*. Planes from *Ryujo* bomb and sink British steamer *Sinkiang* and Dutch motorship *Van der Capellen* (the latter sinks on 8 April) and, at Vizagapatam, bomb and damage British motorship *Anglo Canadian*.

Unarmed U.S. freighter *Washingtonian*, en route from Suez to Ceylon, is sunk by Japanese submarine *I 5* at 07°25′N, 73°05′E; the 39 crewmen and two passengers survive the attack and reach the Maldives in less than a day's rowing.

PACIFIC. Advance elements of the U.S. Army 41st Division reach Melbourne, Australia.

River gunboats *Mindanao* (PR 8) and *Oahu* (PR 6) engage Japanese landing barges, claiming the destruction of at least four, in a night

surface action in Manila Bay; *Mindanao* is damaged by return fire.

ATLANTIC. Destroyer *Sturtevant* (DD 240), directed to the scene by a patrolling USAAF plane, rescues 31 merchant seamen and the seven-man Armed Guard from U.S. tanker *Catahoula*, sunk by *U 154* on 5 April.

Unarmed U.S. tanker *Bidwell*, bound from Corpus Christi, Texas, to New York City, is torpedoed by German submarine *U 160* about 30 miles east of Cape Lookout, North Carolina, 34°25′N, 75°57′W, but manages to reach Hampton Roads, Virginia, under her own power. One man of her 33-man crew is lost.

7 Tuesday

ATLANTIC. Destroyer *Wilkes* (DD 441) is damaged when accidentally rammed by British tanker *Davila*, in Boston, Massachusetts.

Destroyer *Sturtevant* (DD 240), directed to the scene by a USN patrol plane, rescues the 39 survivors (including the entire six-man Armed Guard detachment) of U.S. tanker *Comol Rico*, sunk by *U 154* on 4 April.

U.S. tanker *Pan Rhode Island*, off Cape Hatteras, North Carolina, rescues 29 survivors of Norwegian freighter *Lancing*, sunk by German submarine *U 552*, and 20 men from British tanker *British Splendour*, sunk by the same U-boat the same day.

INDIAN OCEAN. "U" Operation: Japanese convoy lands troops (18th Infantry Division) at Rangoon, Burma.

8 Wednesday

UNITED STATES. Hydrographic Office and Naval Observatory are transferred from the Bureau of Navigation to the Office of the Chief of Naval Operations.

PACIFIC. Submarine *Seadragon* (SS 194) delivers food to Corregidor, and evacuates the final increment of naval radio and communications intelligence people.

ATLANTIC. Submarine *Mackerel* (SS 204) is attacked by USAAF plane six miles south of Watch Hill Light, but is not damaged in the accidental encounter.

Unarmed U.S. tanker *Oklahoma*, en route from Port Arthur, Texas, to Providence, Rhode Island, is torpedoed by German submarine *U 123* about 12 miles off Brunswick, Georgia, 31°18′N, 80°59′W. *U 123* later torpedoes unarmed U.S. tanker *Esso Baton Rouge* about 15 miles off St. Simons Island, Georgia, 31°13′N, 80°05′W, before she returns to shell *Oklahoma*. Both tankers sink in shallow water; survivors (18 from *Oklahoma*'s 37-man crew

and 36 of *Esso Baton Rouge*'s 39 men) meet and proceed to Brunswick, aided by a Coast Guard boat. Both ships, however, are not lost to the war effort; they are refloated, repaired, and returned to service.

Yacht *Zircon* (PY 16) rescues 16 survivors (including one Armed Guard sailor) from U.S. freighter *Otho*, sunk by German submarine *U 754* on 3 April (see 25 April).

Panamanian merchantman *Santa Monica* rescues survivors from unarmed U.S. tanker *T. C. McCobb*, sunk by Italian submarine *Pietro Calvi* on 31 March (see 10 April and 16 May).

9 Thursday

PACIFIC. Luzon Force (Major General Edward King, USA) on Bataan Peninsula surrenders to Japanese. River gunboat *Mindanao* (PR 8) rescues soldiers escaping from Bataan to Corregidor. Navy facilities at Mariveles are demolished to prevent enemy use; submarine tender *Canopus* (AS 9), minesweeper *Bittern* (AM 36), tug *Napa* (AT 32), and drydock *Dewey* are scuttled. Ferry launches *San Felipe* (YFB 12), *Camia* (YFB 683), and *Dap Dap* (YFB 684) and *Canopus* motor launches evacuate men and equipment to Corregidor. Navy-commandeered tug *Henry Keswick* is shelled by Japanese artillery off Corregidor.

Submarine *Snapper* (SS 185) delivers food to Corregidor.

Motor torpedo boats *PT 34* and *PT 41* engage Japanese light cruiser *Kuma* and torpedo boat *Kiji* in a running fight off Cape Tanon, Cebu, P.I.; *Kuma* is hit by a dud torpedo and machine gun fire. Later that day, *PT 34* is bombed and strafed by floatplanes from Japanese seaplane carrier *Sanuki Maru* and beached off Cauit Island, P.I., 10°16′N, 123°52′E. A second bombing and strafing attack by *Sanuki Maru*'s planes destroys *PT 34*, which suffers two dead and three wounded from her six-man crew in the action.

INDIAN OCEAN. "C" Operation continues: Japanese carrier striking force (Vice Admiral Nagumo Chuichi) raids Trincomalee, Ceylon, which has been cleared of shipping in expectation of the attack. Notwithstanding the precautions taken by the British, Japanese carrier bombers attack the ships they find returning to Trincomalee. British carrier HMS *Hermes* is sunk, as is Australian destroyer HMAS *Vampire*, British corvette HMS *Hollyhock*, depot ship HMS *Athelstane*, and RFA oiler *British Sergeant*.

ATLANTIC. Motor torpedo boat *PT 59*, on practice run in upper Narragansett Bay,

Rhode Island, accidentally torpedoes cargo ship *Capella* (AK 13); tugs are on the scene immediately and anchor the damaged auxiliary in shoal water. Eight crewmen are injured in the mishap.

Unarmed U.S. freighter *Esparta*, en route from Honduras to New York, is sunk by German submarine *U 123* about 14 miles south of Brunswick, Georgia, 30°46′N, 81°11′W; one man perishes out of the merchantman's 40-man crew. Unarmed U.S. freighter *Malchace* is sunk by *U 160* about 50 miles off Cape Hatteras, North Carolina, 34°28′N, 75°56′W; Mexican freighter *Faja De Oro* rescues the 28 survivors (one crewman drowns when *Malchace* is abandoned). Unarmed U.S. tanker *Atlas* is sunk by *U 552* off Cape Hatteras, 34°27′N, 76°16′W; two of the 34-man crew die attempting to escape the fires fed by the cargo of 84,239 barrels of gasoline. Coast Guard cutter *CGC 462* rescues the 32 men who survive the inferno. *U 552* later torpedoes tanker *Tamaulipas* at 34°25′N, 76°00′W; British trawler HMS *Norwich City* rescues 35 survivors (two crewmen perish when the tanker is abandoned). *Tamaulipas*, gutted by fires, sinks the following morning.

Unarmed U.S. tanker *Eugene V. R. Thayer*, en route to Caripito, Venezuela, from Buenos Aires, Argentina, is pursued and shelled by Italian submarine *Pietro Calvi* at 02°20′S, 39°30′W; 11 of the tanker's crew are killed in the engagement that ends when *Eugene V. R. Thayer* is abandoned (see 10, 11, and 13 April).

10 Friday

PACIFIC. Pacific Fleet is reorganized into type commands: Battleships (Rear Admiral Walter S. Anderson), Aircraft Carriers (Vice Admiral William F. Halsey Jr.), Cruisers (Rear Admiral Frank Jack Fletcher), Destroyers (Rear Admiral Robert A. Theobald), Service Force (Vice Admiral William L. Calhoun), Amphibious Force (Vice Admiral Wilson Brown Jr.), Submarine Force (Rear Admiral Thomas Withers), and Patrol Wings (Rear Admiral John S. McCain). Old titles Battle Force and Scouting Force are abolished.

Submarine *Snapper* (SS 185) embarks military evacuees from Corregidor.

Minesweeper *Finch* (AM 9) is sunk by aerial bombs off Luzon, 14°22′N, 120°35′E.[86]

Crews of river gunboats *Oahu* (PR 6), *Luzon* (PR 7), and *Mindanao* (PR 8) are transferred ashore to man U.S. Army guns at Fort Hughes, Manila Bay.

Japanese troops land on Cebu (see 12 April).

Submarine *Thresher* (SS 200) sinks Japanese (ex-Portuguese) freighter *Sado Maru* six miles north of Oshima, near the entrance to Tokyo Bay, Honshu, Japan, 34°59′N, 139°29′E.

ATLANTIC. U.S. tanker *Gulfamerica*, silhouetted by the lights of Jacksonville, Florida, is torpedoed and shelled by German submarine *U 123* at 30°14′N, 81°18′W. Some of the tanker's crew perish in the torpedo explosion or gunfire when *U 123* shells the vessel; others drown as the ship is abandoned. Of the 41-man crew, 17 perish; two of the seven-man Armed Guard die in the attack. District patrol vessel *YP 32* aids in rescue of survivors. *Gulf-america* capsizes and sinks on 16 April.

Norwegian freighter *Marpesia*, off Surinam, Dutch Guiana, rescues 19 survivors from U.S. tanker *T. C. McCobb*, sunk by Italian submarine *Pietro Calvi* on 31 March (see 16 May).

Seaplane recovers 13 survivors from U.S. tanker *Eugene V. R. Thayer*, shelled on 9 April by Italian submarine *Pietro Calvi* (see 11 and 13 April).

11 Saturday

PACIFIC. Submarine *Trout* (SS 202) torpedoes Japanese fleet tanker *Nisshin Maru* west of Shiono Misaki, Japan, 33°26′N, 135°38′E.

USAAF A-20s (5th Air Force) attack Japanese shipping off Lae, New Guinea, damaging cargo vessel *Taijun Maru*, 06°49′S, 147°02′E. *Taijun Maru*, deemed irreparable, is later scuttled.

ATLANTIC. Unarmed U.S. tanker *Harry F. Sinclair Jr.* is torpedoed by German submarine *U 203* seven miles south of Cape Lookout, North Carolina, 34°25′N, 76°30′W. Intense fires, fed by the tanker's 66,000 barrels of gasoline, consume the amidships section of the vessel; 10 of the 36-man crew perish. British armed trawler HMS *Hertfordshire* rescues 24 survivors, destroyer *Herbert* (DD 160) rescues two. British (ex-French) armed trawler HMS *Senateur Duhamel* tows *Harry F. Sinclair Jr.* into Morehead City, North Carolina.[87] British steamship *Ulysses* is sunk by German submarine *U 160* off the Virginia capes, 34°23′N, 75°35′W; high-speed transport *Manley* (APD 1) rescues all hands (195 crew and 95 passengers).

British trawler HMS *St. Cathan* (one of the Royal Navy patrol vessels operating off the eastern seaboard) and Dutch freighter *Hebe* collide at 38°40′N, 73°00′W; both ships sink. District patrol vessel *YP 22* rescues seven survivors from *St. Cathan* and 31 from *Hebe*; yachts *Azurlite* (PY 22) and *Beryl* (PY 23) participate in rescue efforts and between them

later transport the survivors (*Hebe's* entire 31-man crew and nine of the 39-man crew of *St. Cathan*) to Charleston, South Carolina.

After a patrol plane sights lifeboat at 38°40′N, 73°00′W, Coast Guard cutter *CGC 455* proceeds from Cape May, New Jersey, to the reported position, and there rescues last nine survivors of U.S. steamship *City of New York*, sunk by *U 160* off Cape Hatteras on 29 March, and transports them to Lewes, Delaware. All told, one Armed Guard sailor, 16 crewmen, and seven passengers have perished in the loss of the ship.[88]

Second group of 13 survivors from U.S. tanker *Eugene V. R. Thayer*, shelled on 9 April by Italian submarine *Pietro Calvi*, reaches the Brazilian coast north of Aracati (see 13 April).

12 Sunday

PACIFIC. Motor torpedo boat *PT 35*, undergoing repairs on marine railway at the Cebu Shipyard and Engineering Works, is destroyed by crew as Japanese capture Cebu, 10°18′N, 123°54′E.

RAAF Hudsons bomb Koepang, Timor; Japanese transport *No. 3 Hino Maru* is damaged in the raid.

ATLANTIC. U.S. freighter *Delvalle*, en route from New Orleans, Louisiana, to Buenos Aires, Argentina, via St. Thomas, Virgin Islands, is sunk by German submarine *U 154* at 16°51′N, 72°25′W. One man from the 54-man crew drowns when the ship is abandoned; there are no casualties among the five passengers or the four-man Armed Guard. Canadian armed merchant cruiser HMCS *Prince Henry* rescues some of the survivors, the rest reach Jacmel, Haiti, via motor launch.

Panamanian motor tanker *Stanvac Melbourne* is sunk by German submarine *U 203* about 15 miles off Frying Pan Shoals (North Carolina coast), 33°53′N, 77°29′W; Coast Guard cutter *CGC 186* rescues 41 merchant seamen and the seven-man Armed Guard.

Unarmed U.S. tanker *Esso Boston*, en route from Venezuela to Nova Scotia, is torpedoed and shelled by German submarine *U 130* at 21°42′N, 60°00′W, and abandoned. The Germans question the survivors, offer food and water, and provide directions to the nearest land (see 13 April).

U.S. freighter *Leslie* is sunk by German submarine *U 123* approximately three miles southeast of Hetzel Shoals Gas Buoy, 28°37′N, 80°25′W; 27 survivors from the 31-man crew, and one passenger, reach the coast of Florida just north of Cape Canaveral. U.S. tanker *Esso*

USAAF North American B-25, bound for Tokyo, strains skyward over a whitecap-flecked sea as it lifts off from the spray-slicked flight deck of carrier *Hornet* (CV 8), 18 April 1942. (Author's Collection)

Bayonne rescues one other surviving crewman; he goes ashore at Key West the next day.

Coast Guard cutter *Vigilant* (WPC 154) runs aground during search for submarine off St. Lucie's Inlet, 27°03′N, 80°05′W, but emerges from the incident with only minor damage.

13 Monday

PACIFIC. Submarine *Grayling* (SS 209) sinks Japanese freighter *Ryujin Maru* off southwest tip of Shikoku, Japan, 31°51′N, 132°50′E. Destroyer *Minazuki* drives off *Grayling* with depth charges.

ATLANTIC. Unarmed U.S. tanker *Esso Boston*, torpedoed and shelled by German submarine *U 130* the previous day, sinks; the entire 37-man crew is rescued by destroyer *Biddle* (DD 151) and taken to San Juan, Puerto Rico.

Abandoned U.S. tanker *Eugene V. R. Thayer*, shelled on 9 April by Italian submarine *Pietro Calvi*, sinks off coast of Brazil.

14 Tuesday

ATLANTIC. Destroyer *Roper* (DD 147) sinks German submarine *U 85* off Virginia capes, 35°55′N, 75°13′W.

British freighter *Empire Thrush* is sunk by German submarine *U 203* about eight miles north of Diamond Shoals, North Carolina, 35°12′N, 75°14′W. Antisubmarine vessel

Asterion (AK 100), masquerading as freighter *Evelyn* (her original mercantile name), picks up all hands and the captain's dog. Canine silence being assured, the rescued men are enjoined not to reveal the fact that they were rescued by a "Q-ship" and to keep secret *Asterion*'s true identity. As far as can be ascertained, they do.

Unarmed U.S. freighter *Margaret* is sunk by German submarine *U 571* off the eastern seaboard while bound for New York from San Juan, Puerto Rico. Although the Germans see the crew lower a boat and put rafts over the side, none of the 29 sailors from *Margaret*'s complement are ever seen again.

15 Wednesday

PACIFIC. Last remaining motor torpedo boat in the Philippines, *PT 41*, torpedoes expended and lacking gasoline, is transferred to the Army to be moved overland to Lake Lanao. She is slated for service as a machine gun boat. The rapid Japanese advance across Mindanao, however, compels the Army to destroy *PT 41* to prevent her capture.

Submarine bases at Kodiak and Dutch Harbor, Alaska, and naval air station at Barbers Point, Oahu, T.H., are established.

ATLANTIC. Unarmed U.S. freighter *Robin Hood*, en route to Boston, Massachusetts, from Trinidad, B.W.I., is sunk by German sub-

marine *U 575* about 500 miles off Nantucket, 38°39′N, 66°38′W; three merchant sailors perish in the torpedo explosion while 11 men go down with the ship (see 23 April).

16 Thursday

PACIFIC. Submarine *Tambor* (SS 198) sinks Japanese stores ship *Kitami Maru* 50 miles southeast of Kavieng, New Ireland, 03°00′S, 152°00′E.

ATLANTIC. Unarmed U.S. freighter *Alcoa Guide*, en route from New York to Guadeloupe, French West Indies, is shelled by German submarine *U 123* (which expended her last torpedo on 12 April) at 35°34′N, 70°08′W; *Alcoa Guide* tries to ram the U-boat without success. *U 123* pauses to allow the crew to abandon ship and then sinks the freighter with gunfire once the merchant sailors (two of whom die of wounds suffered in action) have gotten away safely (see 19 April and 18 May).

EUROPE. Admiral William D. Leahy, USN (Retired), Ambassador to France, receives cable from Washington, D.C., with information that his recall "for consultation" will be announced shortly after the formation of a new Vichy government (see 17 and 18 April).

17 Friday

PACIFIC. Submarine *Searaven* (SS 196) begins rescue of stranded Australian sailors, airmen, and soldiers from Japanese-occupied Timor, N.E.I.

ATLANTIC. Argentine tanker *Victoria*, en route from Buenos Aires to New York, is torpedoed by German submarine *U 201* at 36°41′N, 68°48′W, and abandoned (see 18 April).

EUROPE. Admiral William D. Leahy, USN (Retired), Ambassador to France, receives word that Washington will publicly announce that Leahy has been "directed to return to Washington for consultation upon the appointment of (Pierre) Laval to a dominant position in the Vichy government."

18 Saturday

PACIFIC. Halsey-Doolittle Raid: TF 16 (Vice Admiral William F. Halsey Jr.), formed around carriers *Enterprise* (CV 6) and *Hornet* (CV 8), approaches to within 650 miles of Japan. Discovery by Japanese guardboat *No. 23 Nitto Maru*, however, compels Vice Admiral Halsey to order *Hornet* to launch 16 USAAF B-25s (Lieutenant Colonel James H. Doolittle) earlier than planned. B-25s bomb targets in Tokyo, Yokosuka, Yokohama, Kobe, and Nagoya; one B-25 bombs and damages carrier *Ryuho* (being converted from submarine depot ship *Taigei*) at Yokosuka. Of the 16 B-25s launched, however, 15 are lost in occupied China, where brutal reprisals by Japanese against Chinese populace (Chekiang province) ensue; one B-25 lands intact at Vladivostok where it and its crew are interned by the Soviets. SBDs (VB 3 and VB 6) and F4Fs (VF 6) from *Enterprise*, meanwhile, attack many small Japanese naval vessels serving as an early warning screen, damaging armed merchant cruiser *Awata Maru* and guardboats *Chokyu Maru*, *No. 1 Iwate Maru*, *No. 2 Asami Maru*, *Kaijin Maru*, *No. 3 Chinyo Maru*, *Eikichi Maru*, *Kowa Maru*, and *No. 26 Nanshin Maru*. Guardboats *No. 23 Nitto Maru* and *Nagato Maru*, also damaged by SBDs and F4Fs from *Enterprise*, are sunk by gunfire of light cruiser *Nashville* (CL 43) (see 19 April). While the material damage inflicted is small, the psychological effect of an air raid on the Japanese capital (not to mention the threat to the Emperor's safety) is great. Most important, the Halsey-Doolittle Raid ends all debate within the Japanese high command whether or not a thrust against the important U.S. advanced naval base at Midway should be attempted.

Carrier *Lexington* (CV 2), in TF 11 (Rear Admiral Aubrey W. Fitch), ferries USMC F2As (VMF 211) to Palmyra Island.

Submarine *Searaven* (SS 196) completes rescue of Australians from Japanese-occupied Timor, begun the previous evening.

USAAF B-26s (5th Air Force) sink Japanese aircraft transport *Komaki Maru* in Rabaul Harbor, 04°12′S, 152°10′E.

Japanese troops land at Panay, Visayan Islands.

ATLANTIC. Minesweeper *Owl* (AM 2) locates abandoned Argentine tanker *Victoria*, torpedoed the previous day by German submarine *U 201*, and places salvage crew on board; *Owl* later rescues the vessel's crew and returns them to their ship. Escorted by destroyers *Nicholson* (DD 442) and *Swanson* (DD 443), *Owl* will bring *Victoria* into New York on 21 April.

Unarmed U.S. tanker *Axtell J. Byles*, in a coastal convoy, is torpedoed by German submarine *U 136* off Cape Hatteras, North Carolina, 35°32′N, 75°19′W, but reaches Hampton Roads, Virginia, the next day; there are no injuries to any of the 39-man crew.

EUROPE. Change of government in Vichy France: Pierre Laval becomes Chief of Government, Minister of Interior, Foreign Affairs and Information.

19 Sunday

PACIFIC. Japanese guardboat *No. 21 Nanshin Maru*, damaged by *Enterprise* (CV 6) planes on 18 April, is scuttled by gunfire of light cruiser *Kiso*, 37°12′N, 151°15′E; guardboat *No. 1 Iwate Maru* sinks as the result of damage inflicted by *Enterprise* planes on 18 April. Submarine *I 74* rescues *No. 1 Iwate Maru*'s crew and ultimately transfers them to *Kiso* on 22 April.

CARIBBEAN. German submarine *U 130* shells oil installations at Curaçao, N.W.I.

ATLANTIC. U.S. freighter *Steel Maker* is sunk by German submarine *U 136* west of Bermuda, 33°05′N, 70°36′W; all hands save one (36 crewmen, the nine-man Armed Guard, and one passenger) survive. "I am sorry to have to sink you and do this to you," one German officer says apologetically after the enemy has questioned the survivors about the ship, its cargo, and destination, "but this is war." He promises to send *Steel Maker*'s position to enable the Americans to be rescued (see 22 and 29 April and 18 May).

Destroyer *Broome* (DD 210) rescues 27 survivors from U.S. freighter *Alcoa Guide*, sunk by German submarine *U 123* on 16 April (see 18 May).

20 Monday

MEDITERRANEAN. Operation CALENDAR: Escorted by British Home Fleet Force "W" formed around battle cruiser HMS *Renown* (Commodore Charles S. Daniel, RN), and screened by two U.S. and four British destroyers, carrier *Wasp* (CV 7), as part of the effort to reinforce fighter defenses of the embattled British island of Malta, launches 47 RAF Spitfires. Within four days, however, heavy German bombing raids on the besieged isle's airfields reduce the number of flyable Spitfires to six, necessitating a second ferry mission (see 9 May).

ATLANTIC. Unarmed U.S. freighter *West Imboden*, her presence advertised by an accidental fire in her stack, is torpedoed by German submarine *U 752* about 200 miles off Nantucket Lightship, 41°14′N, 65°54′W, and abandoned as she is being shelled by the U-boat. *U 752* nears one of the lifeboats and asks about casualties. "That's good," one German officer responds when told that the American merchant sailors have come through unharmed (see 22 April).

21 Tuesday

ATLANTIC. U.S. freighter *Pipestone County*, en route from Trinidad, B.W.I., to Boston, Massa-

chusetts, is torpedoed by German submarine *U 576* at 37°35′N, 66°20′W, and abandoned by all hands (36-man merchant complement and the nine-man Armed Guard). *U 576* provisions one of the sunken freighter's four lifeboats after questioning some of the survivors (see 22 April and 7 and 8 May).

Unarmed U.S. freighter *San Jacinto*, en route to San Juan, Puerto Rico, is torpedoed and shelled by German submarine *U 201* at 31°10′N, 70°45′W, and abandoned. Lost with the ship are five merchant sailors and nine passengers; 74 crewmen and 95 passengers survive (see 23 April).

EUROPE. Louise Leahy, wife of Admiral William D. Leahy, USN (Retired), Ambassador to France, dies at Vichy of an embolism. Her death, on the eve of departure from Vichy, is a "crushing emotional shock" to the admiral, "beyond the understanding of anyone who has not had an identical experience."

22 Wednesday

ATLANTIC. Destroyer *Bristol* (DD 453) rescues all 35 survivors of U.S. freighter *West Imboden*, sunk by German submarine *U 752* on 20 April.

Destroyer *Rowan* (DD 405) rescues 13 merchant seamen and five Armed Guard sailors from U.S. freighter *Steel Maker*, sunk by German submarine *U 136* on 19 April (see 29 April and 18 May).

British steamship *Tropic Star* rescues two lifeboats full of survivors from U.S. freighter *Pipestone County*, sunk by German submarine *U 576* on 21 April (see 7 and 8 May).

23 Thursday

ATLANTIC. Destroyer *Greer* (DD 145) rescues 24 survivors of U.S. freighter *Robin Hood*, sunk on 15 April by German submarine *U 575*, and transports them to Hamilton, Bermuda.

Destroyer *Rowan* (DD 405) rescues surviving crew and passengers from U.S. freighter *San Jacinto*, sunk by German submarine *U 201* on 21 April.

U.S. tanker *Connecticut*, bound for Cape Town, South Africa, is torpedoed by German motor torpedo boat LS 4 (*Esan*), from auxiliary cruiser *Michel* (Schiffe 28) in the South Atlantic, 23°00′S, 15°00′W. The second torpedo ignites the 84,200 barrels of gasoline and airplane engine and heating oils that *Connecticut* is carrying as cargo; the ensuing inferno engulfs two lifeboats as the crew abandons the burning ship. *Michel* picks up the survivors, who will ultimately end up in a POW camp at Fukuoka, Japan.

U.S. freighter *Lammont Du Pont*, bound for New York, is torpedoed by German submarine *U 125* at 27°10′N, 57°10′W; four men perish from among the combined 46-man merchant complement and the nine-man Armed Guard (see 25 April and 16 May).

24 Friday

PACIFIC. Submarine *Trout* (SS 202) torpedoes Japanese merchant transport *Tachibana Maru* south of Kii Strait, 33°31′N, 135°29′E.

25 Saturday

PACIFIC. Submarine *Spearfish* (SS 190) torpedoes Japanese army transport *Toba Maru* off northwestern Luzon, 17°01′N, 120°15′E.

ATLANTIC. Norwegian motor vessel *Gallia* rescues one merchant sailor and five of the 10-man Armed Guard from U.S. freighter *Otho*, sunk by German submarine *U 754* on 3 April. All told, 23 of the 36-man merchant complement, four of the 10-man Armed Guard, and four of seven passengers perish.

Swedish motor vessel *Astri* rescues 15 survivors from U.S. freighter *Lammont Du Pont*, sunk by German submarine *U 125* on 23 April (see 16 May). These men are subsequently transferred to light cruiser *Omaha* (CL 4).

26 Sunday

PACIFIC. Submarine *Pickerel* (SS 177) damages Japanese hospital ship *Takasugo Maru* in Manipa Strait, Malay Archipelago, 03°00′S, 127°00′E.

Japanese transport *No. 2 Nankai Maru* is damaged by aircraft (nationality unspecified), Shortland Island, Solomons.

ATLANTIC. Destroyer *Sturtevant* (DD 240) is sunk by mine off Marquesas Key, Florida.

CARIBBEAN. Unarmed U.S. freighter *Alcoa Partner* is torpedoed by German submarine *U 66* approximately 80 miles northeast of Bonaire, N.W.I., at 13°32′N, 67°57′W; the ship's bauxite ore cargo causes the ship to sink before the men on board have time to launch boats. One boat floats free, however, and 25 men gather in it. Nine crewmen and a workaway, however, drown in the wake of the ship's loss. The survivors reach Bonaire the next day.

28 Tuesday

ATLANTIC. TF 99 (Rear Admiral Robert C. Giffen), consisting of battleship *Washington* (BB 56), heavy cruisers *Wichita* (CA 45) and *Tuscaloosa* (CA 37), and four U.S. destroyers, sails from Scapa Flow, Orkney Islands, as part of mixed U.S.-British force (Force "Distaff"); British fleet units include battleship HMS *King George V*, carrier HMS *Victorious*, light cruiser HMS *Kenya*, and five destroyers. The force steams to the waters northeast of Iceland to provide cover for Russia-bound convoy PQ 15.

District patrol vessel *YP 77* is sunk in collision off Atlantic coast.

29 Wednesday

PACIFIC. "MO" Operation: Japanese naval force (3rd Kure Special Landing Force) occupies former RAAF seaplane base at Tulagi, Solomons (see 2 and 4 May).

Japanese seize Parang and Cotabato, Mindanao.

ATLANTIC. First coastal convoy leaves New York City for the Delaware River.

Off Frying Pan Shoals (North Carolina coast), British steamship *Pacific Exporter* rescues 27 survivors (including the remaining four Armed Guard sailors) from U.S. freighter *Steel Maker*, sunk by German submarine *U 136* on 19 April (see 18 May).

U.S. tanker *Mobiloil*, proceeding alone, is sunk by German submarine *U 108* about 350 miles northwest of Turks Island at 26°10′N, 66°15′W; all hands (43-man merchant crew and nine-man Armed Guard) survive the loss of the ship (see 2 May).

CARIBBEAN. Unarmed U.S. tanker *Federal*, bound for Banes, Cuba, is sunk by German submarine *U 507* at 21°13′N, 76°05′W; heavy close-range fire from the U-boat's guns kills four crewmen and mortally wounds one of the 33-man merchant complement, as well as destroying one lifeboat and preventing the tanker's crew from launching a second. U.S. Army transport *Yarmouth* arrives on the scene soon thereafter but only circles the area; fishing boats from Gibara, Cuba, rescue *Federal*'s survivors from rafts while the one boat that was launched follows the Cuban boats to shore.

30 Thursday

PACIFIC. PBYs evacuate military and civilian personnel from Corregidor.

Submarine *Greenling* (SS 213) torpedoes Japanese ammunition ship *Seia Maru* west-northwest of Ponape, Carolines, 09°32′N, 156°03′E.

EUROPE. Admiral Harold R. Stark assumes command of U.S. Naval Forces Europe.

MAY

1 Friday

EUROPE. Admiral William D. Leahy, USN (Retired), deeply grieved by the loss of his wife Louise, ends service as U.S. Ambassador to Vichy France.

PACIFIC. Submarine *Grenadier* (SS 210) mistakenly sinks Soviet merchant ship *Angarstroi* about 90 miles west-southwest of Nagasaki, Japan, 32°00′N, 129°25′E.

Submarine *Triton* (SS 201) sinks Japanese army cargo ship *Calcutta Maru* about 180 miles north-northeast of Formosa, 28°06′N, 123°47′E.

Eighth Defense Battalion, USMC, arrives on Wallis Island, from Tutuila, Samoa.

ATLANTIC. During covering operations for convoy PQ 15, British battleship HMS *King George V* accidentally collides with, and sinks, destroyer HMS *Punjabi* off Iceland; battleship *Washington* (BB 56), unable to maneuver to clear the wreckage, has to steam through it. *Punjabi*'s exploding depth charges cause some concussion damage to *Washington*'s fire control systems. Heavy cruiser *Tuscaloosa* (CA 37) leaves formation to assist in rescue of *Punjabi*'s survivors.

Naval Base and Naval Auxiliary Air Facility, Great Exuma, Bahama Islands, and Naval Base, Grand Cayman, British West Indies, are established.

2 Saturday

PACIFIC. Admiral Chester W. Nimitz, Commander in Chief Pacific Fleet, conducts informal visit to Midway to inspect defenses and present decorations. He will leave the following day.[89]

SBDs (VS 5) and TBDs (VT 5) from carrier *Yorktown* (CV 5) bomb Japanese submarine *I 21* in the Coral Sea. *I 21* reports being attacked by planes, but fails to specify whether or not her assailants are land- or carrier-based; TF 17's approach to the Solomons thus remains undetected.

"MO" Operation: Japanese special landing force (3rd Kure Special Landing Force) lands on Florida Island, Solomons.

River gunboat *Mindanao* (PR 8) is scuttled off South Harbor, Corregidor.

Submarine *Drum* (SS 228) sinks Japanese seaplane carrier *Mizuho* off south coast of Honshu, 34°26′N, 138°14′E; heavy cruiser *Takao* rescues survivors.

Submarine *Trout* (SS 202) sinks Japanese freighter *Uzan Maru* off southeast coast of Honshu, 33°26′N, 135°52′E.

ATLANTIC. Yacht *Cythera* (PY 26) is sunk by German submarine *U 402* off the coast of North Carolina; 66 men perish with the ship. *U 402* rescues the two survivors and transports them back to Germany as POWs.

Submarine chaser *PC 490* rescues all 52 survivors of U.S. tanker *Mobiloil*, sunk on 29 April by German submarine *U 108*.

3 Sunday

PACIFIC. Submarine *Spearfish* (SS 190) evacuates naval and military officers (including nurses) from Corregidor. These evacuees will be the last to leave "The Rock" by this method.

Japanese land on northern Mindanao.

Light cruiser *Nashville* (CL 43) departs Pearl Harbor under orders to fuel at Midway and then proceed on a foray into the Japanese fishing grounds off the Kamchatka Peninsula, Kurils. Submarines *S 34* (SS 139) and *S 35* (SS 140) are to operate in support.

4 Monday

UNITED STATES. Commander in Chief U.S. Fleet (Admiral Ernest J. King) directs Coast Guard Auxiliary to organize civilian small craft as coastal pickets.

PACIFIC. Battle of the Coral Sea opens as TF 17 (Rear Admiral Frank Jack Fletcher) attacks Japanese Tulagi Invasion Force (Rear Admiral Shima Kiyohide) at Tulagi, Solomons, where elements of the Japanese 3rd Kure Special Landing Force have gone ashore (as well as on neighboring Gavutu) to establish defenses ("MO" Operation). SBDs and TBDs (VB 5, VS 5, and VT 5), supported by F4Fs (VF 42) from carrier *Yorktown* (CV 5), sink destroyer *Kikuzuki*, minesweeper *Tama Maru,* and auxiliary minesweepers *Wa 1* and *Wa 2* and damage destroyer *Yuzuki*, minelayer *Okinoshima*, transport *Azumasan Maru*, and cargo ship *Kozui Maru*. Lieutenant John J. Powers of VB 5 participates in all three strikes, receiving credit for one direct hit, two close-misses, and a persistent low-level strafing attack (see 7 and 8 May). Destroyer *Hammann* (DD 412) rescues two downed F4F pilots (VF 42) from Guadalcanal; destroyer *Perkins* (DD 377), however, sent to retrieve the pilot and radio-gunner of a downed TBD (VT 5) south of the island, does not locate them.[90]

Japanese transports sail from Rabaul, bound for Port Moresby, New Guinea ("MO" Operation).

Minesweeper *Tanager* (AM 5) is sunk by Japanese shore battery, Corregidor.

Submarine *Greenling* (SS 213) sinks Japanese gunboat *Kinjosan Maru* near Truk, Carolines, 08°44′N, 150°56′E.

Submarine *Trout* (SS 202) sinks Japanese gunboat *Kongosan Maru* off southeast coast of Honshu, Japan, 33°32′N, 136°05′E.

ATLANTIC. Unarmed U.S. freighter *Eastern Sword* is torpedoed by German submarine *U 162* approximately 12 miles off Georgetown, British Guiana, 07°10′N, 57°58′W (see 5 and 6 May).

Unarmed U.S. tanker *Norlindo* is torpedoed by German submarine *U 507* approximately 200 miles northeast of Havana, Cuba, 24°57′N, 84°00′W, and sinks, taking five crewmen with her (see 6 May). Eight hours later, *U 507* torpedoes and shells tanker *Munger T. Ball* at 25°17′N, 83°57′W; flames, fed by the ship's cargo of 65,000 barrels of gasoline, trap many crewmen. Only four sailors of the 34-man crew survive the inferno to be rescued by Norwegian motor vessel *Katy* later the same day. Before the day is over, *U 507* attacks a third tanker, the unarmed *Joseph M. Cudahy*, and torpedoes her approximately 74 miles northwest of the Dry Tortugas, 25°57′N, 83°57′W. Of the ship's 37-man complement, 27 perish in the attack (see 5 and 7 May).

Unarmed U.S. freighter *Delisle* is torpedoed by German submarine *U 564*, 15 miles off Jupiter Inlet, Florida, 27°02′N, 80°03′W, and abandoned by the 34 survivors (30 crewmen and four workaways) of the 36 men that had been on board at the time of the attack. They row to shore, but return to the ship the following day to rig the ship for tow. Subsequently repaired, *Delisle* is returned to service.

CARIBBEAN. Unarmed U.S. freighter *Tuscaloosa City* is sunk by German submarine *U 125* at 18°25′N, 81°35′W; the latter's officers, after questioning the survivors, give them directions to the nearest land and wish them well. U.S. steamship *Falcon* rescues all hands (34 men) and transports them to Cartagena, Colombia.

5 Tuesday

PACIFIC. Japanese troops (61st Infantry Regiment and supporting units) land on Corregidor, initially opposed by the First Battalion, Fourth Marines. Submarine rescue vessel *Pigeon* (ASR 6) is bombed and sunk, 14°23′N, 120°36′E; tug *Genesee* (AT 55) and harbor tug *Vaga* (YT 116) are scuttled off Corregidor, 14°25′N, 120°30′E.[91]

Japanese Imperial General Staff orders the Combined Fleet to assist in Army operations against Midway ("MI" Operation) and the Aleutian Islands, Alaska ("AL" Operation).

U.S. freighter *John Adams* is sunk by Japanese submarine *I 21*, 85 miles from Amadee Lighthouse, Nouméa, New Caledonia, 23°11′S, 165°08′E; five of the 11-man Armed Guard drown when the ship is abandoned (see 10 May).

ATLANTIC. Unarmed U.S. freighter *Afoundria* is sunk by German submarine *U 108* about eight miles north of Le Male Light, Haiti, 20°00′N, 73°30′W. There are no casualties among the 38-man crew and eight passengers (see 6 May).

U.S. tanker *Java Arrow* is torpedoed by German submarine *U 333* at 27°30′N, 80°08′W, and abandoned, with the 39 survivors of the 41-man merchant complement, together with the six-man Armed Guard, taking to two lifeboats. Submarine chaser *PC 483* and a Coast Guard boat rescue the men. The ship is later reboarded and believed reparable. Subsequently, civilian tugs *Ontario* and *Bafshe* tow *Java Arrow* to Port Everglades, Florida.[92]

Twelve survivors of U.S. freighter *Eastern Sword*, torpedoed by German submarine *U 162* the previous day, reach Georgetown, British Guiana (see 6 May).

PBYs rescue the 10 survivors of U.S. tanker *Joseph M. Cudahy*, attacked by German submarine *U 507* the day before (see 6 May).

6 Wednesday

PACIFIC. Corregidor and Manila Bay forts surrender to the Japanese. River gunboats *Oahu* (PR 6) and *Luzon* (PR 7) and minesweeper *Quail* (AM 15) are scuttled off Corregidor, 14°23′N, 120°35′E.[93] Fitted out with weapons, ammunition, provisions, and clothing scrounged from abandoned Navy-commandeered tug *Ranger*, *Quail*'s commanding officer (Lieutenant Commander John H. Morrill), one other officer, and 16 men in 36-foot motor launch (from *Quail*) escape Manila Bay.[94]

Lost to Japanese occupation of the Philippines are district patrol vessel *YP 97*; ash lighters *YA 52, YA 59*, and *YA 65*; miscellaneous district auxiliaries *YAG 2, YAG 3*, and *YAG 4*; open lighters *YC 178, YC 181, YC 537, YC 643, YC 644, YC 646, YC 647, YC 648, YC 649, YC 652, YC 653, YC 654, YC 669, YC 683, YC 714, YC 715,* and *YC 716*; floating derricks *YD 19, YD 47, YD 56,* and *YD 60*; covered lighters *YF 177, YF 178, YF 179, YF 180, YF 181, YF 212, YF 223, YF 224, YF 230,* and *YF 317*; ferry launches *San Felipe* (YFB 12), *Rosal* (YFB 682), *Camia* (YFB 683), *Dap Dap* (YFB 684), *Rivera* (YFB 685), *Magdalena* (YFB 687), and *Yacal* (YFB 688); dredge *YM 4*; fuel oil barge *YO 64*[95]; pile driver *YPD 22*; salvage pontoons *YSP 41, YSP 42, YSP 43, YSP 44, YSP 45, YSP 46, YSP 47, YSP 48, YSP 49,* and *YSP 50*; sludge removal barge *YSR 2*; harbor tugs *Banaag* (YT 104), *Iona* (YT 107), and *Mercedes* (YT 108); and water barge *YW 54*.

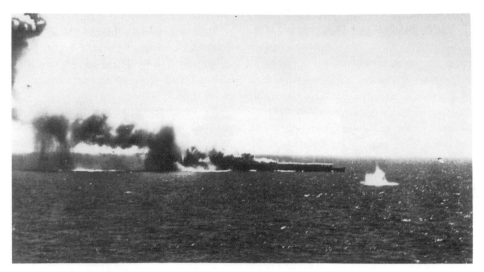

Japanese small carrier *Shoho* under attack at Coral Sea, 7 May 1942, as seen from a Douglas TBD-1 Devastator from the *Lexington* (CV 2) Air Group. Another TBD-1 is visible at right, just having fired its torpedo. (NA, 80-G-17024)

Submarine *Skipjack* (SS 184) sinks Japanese merchant passenger-cargo ship *Kanan Maru* about 26 miles northeast of Cam Ranh Bay, French Indochina, 12°33′N, 109°30′E.

Submarine *Triton* (SS 201), attacking Japanese convoy north-northeast of Keelung, Formosa, sinks cargo ship *Taiei Maru*, 28°42′N, 123°50′E, and transport/cargo ship *Taigen Maru*, 28°19′N, 123°28′E.

Naval Auxiliary Air Facility, Nawiliwili, Kauai, T.H., is established.

ATLANTIC. Auxiliary *Semmes* (AG 24) is damaged when she accidentally rams and sinks British (ex-French) armed trawler HMS *Senateur Duhamel* off Cape Lookout, North Carolina, 34°32.7′N, 75°35.6′W.

Net tender *Mulberry* (YN 22) rescues all 46 survivors from U.S. freighter *Afoundria*, sunk by German submarine *U 108* on 5 May.

Unarmed U.S. tanker *Halsey* is torpedoed by German submarine *U 333*, northeast of Jupiter Inlet, Florida, 27°14′N, 80°03′W, and abandoned by all hands (32 men). The ship explodes and breaks in two. Submarine chaser *PC 451* proceeds to the survivors' assistance but breaks off her efforts to conduct an unsuccessful pursuit of *U 333*. Local fishing boats ultimately tow *Halsey's* two lifeboats to the Gilbert Bar Lifeboat Station.

Fishing boat *Ocean Star* rescues last survivor of U.S. freighter *Eastern Sword*, torpedoed by German submarine *U 162* on 4 May.

Steamship *San Blas* rescues 23 survivors of U.S. tanker *Norlindo*, sunk by German submarine *U 507* on 4 May.

Yacht *Coral* (PY 15) scuttles fire-gutted U.S. tanker *Joseph M. Cudahy*, attacked by German submarine *U 507* on 5 May, as a menace to navigation.

GULF OF MEXICO. Unarmed U.S. freighter *Alcoa Puritan* is shelled by German submarine *U 507* at 28°40′N, 88°22′W, and abandoned by all hands (47-man crew and seven passengers). After the U-boat delivers the coup de grâce to *Alcoa Puritan* with a torpedo, the submarine comes to within 100 yards of the survivors. Coast Guard cutter *Boutwell* (WPC 130) rescues *Alcoa Puritan's* survivors later the same day.

CARIBBEAN. Unarmed U.S. freighter *Green Island* is torpedoed by German submarine *U 125*, while en route from New Orleans, Louisiana, to Aruba, N.W.I., 18°25′N, 81°30′W, and abandoned by her 22-man crew. Although her men reboard her later in the day, *Green Island* is beyond salvage and sinks (see 7 May).

7 Thursday

PACIFIC. Battle of the Coral Sea: Support Group (Rear Admiral John G. Crace, RN), detached to intercept Port Moresby Invasion Force (Rear Admiral Abe Koso), is attacked by Japanese land attack planes carrying torpedoes (4th *Kokutai*) or bombs (Genzan *Kokutai*); destroyer *Farragut* (DD 348) is damaged by friendly fire. Later, mistaken for Japanese Port Moresby Invasion Force, Crace's ships are bombed by USAAF B-26s. Australian heavy cruiser HMAS *Australia* (flagship) is straddled; heavy cruiser *Chicago* (CA 29) and destroyer *Perkins* (DD 377) are near-misses.

SBDs and TBDs (VB 2, VB 5, VS 2, VS 5, VT 2, and VT 5) from carriers *Yorktown* (CV 5) and *Lexington* (CV 2) attack Japanese Close Support Force (Rear Admiral Goto Aritomo) and sink small carrier *Shoho* off Misima Island, 10°29′S, 152°55′E. During the action off Misima, Lieutenant John J. Powers (VB 5) and Lieutenant (j.g.) William E. Hall, USNR (VS 2), exhibit skill and determination in pressing home their attacks (see 8 May). That night, Powers, VB 5's gunnery officer, lectures his Bombing Five shipmates on point of aim and diving technique. He advocates a low-level release point to ensure accuracy, a philosophy he had demonstrated in the attack on *Shoho*.

Mistaken at the outset for a carrier and a cruiser, oiler *Neosho* (AO 23) and destroyer *Sims* (DD 409) are attacked by Japanese planes, although the enemy recognizes the mistake in time to avoid expending torpedoes. *Neosho* is damaged by bombs and crashing carrier bomber, 15°35′S, 155°36′E, and *Sims* is sunk by bombs, 15°10′S, 158°05′E. On board the damaged oiler, Chief Watertender Oscar V. Peterson, although badly wounded, risks his life and closes bulkhead stop valves, receiving severe burns (see 11 and 21 May).

Japanese attempt to find U.S. force in waning daylight runs afoul in bad weather. Operational losses incurred by the enemy's brush with the weather, gunfire, and fighters (TF 17) limit the size of the strike that can be launched the next day.

Japanese occupy Hollandia, New Guinea.

INDIAN OCEAN. Small reconnaissance seaplane from Japanese submarine *I 30* reconnoiters Aden.

ATLANTIC. Coast Guard cutter *Calypso* (WPC 104) rescues one boatload of survivors from U.S. freighter *Pipestone County*, sunk by German submarine *U 576* on 21 April (see 8 May).

CARIBBEAN. British merchantman *Fort Qu'Appelle* rescues all 22 survivors of U.S. freighter *Green Island*, sunk by German submarine *U 125* the previous day.

8 Friday

PACIFIC. Battle of the Coral Sea concludes: Carrier *Lexington* (CV 2) SBD (VS 2) sights Japanese carrier striking force (Vice Admiral Takagi Takeo) formed around *Shohaku* and *Zuikaku*. As VB 5 pilots leave the ready room on board *Yorktown* (CV 5), Lieutenant John J. Powers exhorts his shipmates: "Remember the folks back home are counting on us. I am going to get a hit if I have to lay it [his bomb] on their flight deck." SBDs from *Lexington* and *Yorktown* (CV 5) damage *Shokaku* and force her retirement. Lieutenant Powers scores a hit on *Shokaku*, pressing home his attack to a perilously low altitude of 200 feet; he is last seen attempting, unsuccessfully, to recover from his dive. For his heroism on this day as well as on the previous day and on 4 May, Powers is awarded the Medal of Honor posthumously.

Almost simultaneously, Japanese carrier bombers and attack planes strike TF 17. The comparatively few fighters on hand compel the continuation of stopgap use of SBDs as anti–torpedo plane patrol. Lieutenant William E. Hall, USNR (VS 2), whose performance of duty the previous day had elicited favorable notice, distinguishes himself further in attacking the Japanese planes pressing home their assault against *Lexington*. Although Hall is badly wounded, he brings his damaged SBD back to his ship, having participated in the destruction of at least three carrier attack planes. Hall's bravery and skill are rewarded with the Medal of Honor.

Japanese planes, however, manage to get through and damage carriers *Lexington* (bombs and torpedoes) and *Yorktown* (bombs) (14°35′S, 155°15′E). On board *Yorktown*, Lieutenant Milton E. Ricketts, in charge of an engineering repair party, is mortally wounded when a bomb passes through and explodes just beneath his compartment, killing, stunning, or wounding all of his men. Ricketts, despite his wounds, opens the valve on a nearby fire plug, partially leads out the hose, and directs water into the burning compartment before he drops dead. For his extraordinary heroism, he is awarded the Medal of Honor posthumously. *Lexington* is further damaged when gasoline vapors are ignited as repairs are being carried out, triggering massive explosions that lead to her abandonment. She is then scuttled by destroyer *Phelps* (DD 360), 15°12′S, 155°27′E.

The Battle of the Coral Sea is the first engagement in naval history in which opposing warships do not exchange a shot; all damage is inflicted by carrier aircraft. *Zuikaku*'s air group suffers heavy losses. Damage to *Shokaku*, as well as to *Zuikaku*'s air group, prevents the use of those two carriers for several months and renders them unavailable for immediate operations. The temporary unavailability of *Zuikaku* and *Shokaku*, however, is tempered by the Japanese' erroneous belief that both *Yorktown* and *Lexington* have been sunk. In halting the Japanese push southward and blunting the seaborne thrust toward Port Moresby, Coral Sea is a strategic U.S. victory (see 10 May).

Light cruiser *Nashville* (CL 43) is damaged when she runs aground at Midway Island. Necessity of returning to Pearl Harbor for repairs

Supermarine Spitfire Mk. V, painted in standard European temperate camouflage, takes off past the island of carrier *Wasp* (CV 7), bound for Malta, 9 May 1942. Curious onlookers are an inevitable feature of carrier operations. (Author's Collection)

postpones *Nashville*'s raiding cruise to Kamchatka.

Submarine *Grenadier* (SS 210) attacks Japanese convoy about 120 miles southwest of Kyushu, Japan, and sinks army transport *Taiyo Maru*, 30°40′N, 127°54′E; *Grenadier* survives persistent attacks by enemy antisubmarine forces the following day. *Taiyo Maru* carries to their deaths many technical experts bound for the East Indies to work on resuming oil production.

Submarine *Porpoise* (SS 172) is damaged by depth charges off Ceram, Moluccas, 03°50′N, 129°57′E, but remains on patrol.

Submarine *Skipjack* (SS 184) attacks Japanese convoy about 125 miles east of Cam Ranh Bay, French Indochina, and sinks army cargo ship *Bujun Maru*, 12°18′N, 111°13′E.

GULF OF ADEN. Small reconnaissance seaplane from Japanese submarine *I 30* reconnoiters Djibouti.

ATLANTIC. U.S. freighter *Greylock* is torpedoed by German submarine *U 588* off Halifax, Nova Scotia, 44°14′N, 63°33′W; there are, however, no casualties among the 41-man merchant crew or the 11-man Armed Guard and the ship reaches Halifax unaided.

Unarmed U.S. freighter *Ohioan* is torpedoed by German submarine *U 564* four and a half miles off the coast of Florida, 26°31′N, 79°58′W, and sinks so quickly that no lifeboats can be launched. Coast Guard boats rescue the 22 survivors from the 37-man crew.

Fishing boat *Irene and May* rescue last boatload of survivors from U.S. freighter *Pipestone County*, sunk by German submarine *U 576* on 21 April. All hands (36-man merchant complement and nine-man Armed Guard) have come through the ordeal unhurt.

9 Saturday

MEDITERRANEAN. Operation BOWERY: In the second attempt to bolster fighter strength on besieged Malta, carrier *Wasp* (CV 7), again covered by British Home Fleet Force "W" (Commodore Charles S. Daniel, RN), launches 47 RAF Spitfires; British carrier HMS *Eagle* accompanies *Wasp* and launches 17 additional Spitfires. The success of the American carrier's second ferry mission prompts British Prime Minister Winston S. Churchill to observe: "Who said a *Wasp* couldn't sting twice?" Unlike in Operation CALENDAR, the Spitfires are speedily serviced and readied for action, and take a heavy toll of Axis bombers this day and the next. "Daylight raiding," Malta's war diary notes laconically, "was brought to an abrupt end."

ATLANTIC. Coast Guard cutter *Icarus* (WPC 110) sinks German submarine *U 352* off Cape Lookout, North Carolina, 34°12′N, 76°35′W.

10 Sunday

ATLANTIC. Carrier *Ranger* (CV 4), in TF 36, launches 68 USAAF P-40 fighters off Accra, Gold Coast of Africa. She had transported them from Naval Air Station Quonset Point, Rhode Island.

GULF OF MEXICO. U.S. motor tanker *Aurora* is torpedoed and shelled by German submarine *U 506* approximately 40 miles off Southwest Pass, Louisiana, 28°35′N, 90°00′W, and abandoned. Coastal yacht *Onyx* (PYc 5) and district patrol vessel *YP 157* rescue the 38 merchant seamen (one of whom dies later of wounds) and the 12-man Armed Guard. Coast Guard harbor tug *Tuckahoe* (WYT 89) arrives on the scene to tow the damaged ship, and upon her arrival provides a fire and rescue party with hoses and extinguishers. *Onyx* and *YP 157* convoy *Tuckahoe* and *Aurora* toward Southwest Pass (see 11 May).

PACIFIC. "MO" Operation, the Japanese seizure of Port Moresby, New Guinea, is cancelled.

Submarine *Silversides* (SS 236) engages Japanese guardboat *No. 5 Ebisu Maru* in a surface gunnery action 540 miles north of Marcus Island, 33°14′N, 150°58′E, and sets her afire. As *Silversides* closes in to finish off her pugnacious adversary, however, machine gun fire from *No. 5 Ebisu Maru* (which reaches port in a heavily damaged condition) kills one submariner.

Survivors (39-man crew and six of the 11-man Armed Guard) of U.S. freighter *John Adams*, sunk by Japanese submarine *I 21* on 5 May, are rescued. One boat with survivors is recovered at sea; two boats reach Nouméa, New Caledonia.

11 Monday

PACIFIC. Oiler *Neosho* (AO 23), damaged and adrift since 7 May and deemed beyond salvage, is scuttled by torpedoes and gunfire of destroyer *Henley* (DD 391), which rescues survivors from *Neosho* and *Sims* (DD 409) (see 21 May). Among those men is the injured Chief Watertender Oscar V. Peterson, who dies of his wounds. For the extraordinary heroism he displayed on 7 May, Peterson is awarded the Medal of Honor posthumously.

Submarine *S 42* (SS 153) torpedoes Japanese minelayer *Okinoshima* west of Buka, Solomons, 05°06′S, 153°48′E (see 12 May).

Japanese freighter *Oridono Maru* is sunk by Japanese mine near Surabaya, Java, 07°00′S, 112°40′E.

GULF OF MEXICO. U.S. motor tanker *Aurora*, torpedoed and shelled by German submarine *U 506* the previous day, is brought to Southwest Pass, Louisiana, under tow of Coast Guard harbor tug *Tuckahoe* (WYT 89). Civilian tug *Robert W. Wilmot* aids *Tuckahoe*, but *Aurora* drifts onto a shoal at the entrance of the pass. Subsequently, however, *Aurora* is salvaged and returns to service as *Jamestown*.[96]

12 Tuesday

PACIFIC. Submarine *S 44* (SS 155) sinks Japanese repair ship *Shoei Maru* en route to attempt salvage of minelayer *Okinoshima*, damaged the previous day by submarine *S 42*, 15 miles southwest of Cape St. George, 05°06′S, 152°30′E, and survives counterattacks by her victim's escort. Transport *Kinryu Maru* and destroyer *Mochizuki* attempt to save *Okinoshima*, but fail. The minelayer sinks in Queen Carola Bay, on the west coast of Buka. Japanese heavy cruiser *Kako*, covering the operation, is stranded accidentally on reef in Queen Carola Bay. She is refloated the following day.

GULF OF MEXICO. Unarmed U.S. tanker *Virginia* is torpedoed by German submarine *U 507* as the former lies-to approximately one and a half miles off Southwest Pass, Louisiana, 28°53′N, 89°29′W, awaiting the arrival of a pilot. The explosion of the second and third torpedoes ignites the tanker's cargo (150,000 barrels of gasoline) and the rapid spread of the fire prevents the crew from launching boats or rafts. Of *Virginia's* 41-man crew, 27 perish in the inferno. Motor torpedo boat *PT 157* rescues the 14 survivors.

ATLANTIC. U.S. tanker *Esso Houston* is torpedoed by German submarine *U 162* approximately 150 miles east of Barbados, 12°12′N, 57°24′W, and abandoned. After the U-boat has administered the coup de grâce to the tanker, she surfaces nearby and her commanding officer offers assistance, helpfully informing the ship's master that one of the lifeboats is sinking. Survivors (38-man civilian complement and four-man Armed Guard) congregate in two lifeboats (see 14 and 17 May).

13 Wednesday

UNITED STATES. Bureau of Navigation, its technical functions having been largely transferred to other bureaus, is renamed Bureau of Naval Personnel.

PACIFIC. Submarine *Drum* (SS 228) sinks Japanese freighter *Shonan Maru* northeast of Mikimoto, Honshu, 34°00′N, 139°00′E.

RAAF Hudsons bomb Japanese shipping off Ambon, N.E.I., sinking auxiliary *Taifoku Maru* and damaging gunboat *Taiko Maru*.

Japanese merchant cargo vessel *Nagasaki Maru* is sunk by Japanese mine off Nagasaki, Japan.

ATLANTIC. Vichy French agree to immobilize aircraft carrier *Béarn*, light cruiser *Emile Bertin*, and training cruiser *Jeanne D'Arc* at Martinique, French West Indies.

Unarmed U.S. freighter *Norlantic* is shelled by German submarine *U 69* while en route to Puerto La Cruz, Venezuela, from Pensacola, Florida, 12°13′N, 66°30′W; *U 69* continues to shell the freighter as the latter's crew abandons ship. *U 69* then torpedoes *Norlantic* and sinks her. Six of the freighter's 29-man crew perish in the attack (two below in the engine room and four trying to launch boats under fire); one sailor will die of wounds (see 16 and 24 May and 19 June).

GULF OF MEXICO. Unarmed U.S. tanker *Gulfprince* is attacked by German submarine *U 506* approximately six miles south of the Ship Shoals Sea Buoy, Louisiana, 28°32′N, 91°00′W, but *Gulfprince* is skillfully handled and evades the first two torpedoes. The second pair only strike a glancing blow and *Gulfprince* escapes to New Orleans without further incident. Later, *U 506* sinks unarmed tanker *Gulfpenn* at 28°29′N, 89°12′W; 12 men die in the initial explosion or perish with the ship. Of the 26 survivors, one dies of his injuries. Coast Guard plane directs Honduran freighter *Telde* toward the position of the survivors, and the merchantman rescues them. Still later, *U 506* torpedoes U.S. freighter *David McKelvy* approximately 35 miles south of the mouth of the Mississippi, 28°30′N, 89°55′W; an explosion ignites the ship's cargo of 81,000 barrels of crude oil and forces the crew to abandon ship. *U 506* retires without expending further torpedoes, apparently thinking the freighter doomed. Coast Guard cutter *Boutwell* (WPC 130) rescues 19 merchant sailors and four of the Armed Guard. Sixteen civilians and one Armed Guard sailor perish (see 14 and 29 May).

14 Thursday

ATLANTIC. German submarine *U 213* mines the waters off St. John's, Newfoundland.

Norwegian motor tanker *Havprins* rescues 18 survivors of U.S. tanker *Esso Houston*, sunk by German submarine *U 162* on 12 May;

Havprins will transfer these men to Latvian freighter *Everagra* for transportation to St. Thomas, Virgin Islands (see 17 May).

GULF OF MEXICO. Norwegian merchantman *Norsol* rescues two survivors from U.S. freighter *David McKelvy*, sunk the day before by German submarine *U 506*.

15 Friday

PACIFIC. Submarine *Tuna* (SS 203) sinks Japanese transport *Toyoharu Maru* 65 miles off Sohuksando, Korea, 33°34′N, 125°09′E.

ARCTIC. German planes bomb Allied shipping at Murmansk, USSR; U.S. freighter *Yaka* suffers a direct hit that causes extensive damage but no casualties to the 38-man merchant crew or the 11-man Armed Guard. The ship is beached to prevent loss.

ATLANTIC. U.S. freighter *Nicarao* is sunk by German submarine *U 751* north of San Salvador, Bahamas, 25°20′N, 74°19′W; eight of the 35-man merchant crew perish as they abandon ship. The four-man Armed Guard survives intact (see 16 May).

16 Saturday

PACIFIC. Submarine *Tautog* (SS 199) torpedoes Japanese fleet tanker *Goyo Maru* west of Truk, 07°00′N, 152°00′E. *Tautog*'s first "fish" circles, forcing her to go deep at once.

ATLANTIC. Last three survivors from unarmed U.S. tanker *T. C. McCobb*, sunk by Italian submarine *Pietro Calvi* on 31 March, land at Surinam, Dutch Guinea. Two of the three men, however, later die of exposure.

Destroyer *Tarbell* (DD 142) rescues 23 survivors from U.S. freighter *Lammont Du Pont*, sunk by German submarine *U 125* on 23 April. There are originally 31 men on the raft spotted by the destroyer; eight have perished in the interval between the loss of the ship on 23 April and *Tarbell*'s appearance on 16 May.

U.S. tanker *Esso Augusta* rescues the 27 merchant seamen and four Armed Guard sailors who have survived the loss of freighter *Nicarao*, sunk by German submarine *U 751* the previous day.

GULF OF MEXICO. U.S. tanker *Sun*, en route to Beaumont, Texas, is torpedoed by German submarine *U 506* at 28°41′N, 90°19′W, but escapes to reach New Orleans, Louisiana, under her own power. *Sun* suffers no casualties among the 37-man merchant crew and five-man Armed Guard. Later the same day, *U 506* torpedoes and shells U.S. tanker *William C. McTarnahan* approximately 35 miles east of

Lieutenant John D. Bulkeley, former commander of Motor Torpedo Boat Squadron 3 in the Philippines in the early months of the war, exhorts workers at the New York Navy Yard, 15 May 1942. (NA, 80-G-17730)

Ship Shoals Light, Louisiana, 28°52′N, 90°20′W, but retires without finishing off her quarry; 18 of the 38-man merchant crew perish in the attack. The 20 merchant seamen and the seven Armed Guard sailors survive to be rescued by shrimp boats *Defender*, *Pioneer*, and *Viscali* and a fourth (unnamed) craft. Coast Guard harbor tug *Tuckahoe* (WYT 89), assisted by civilian tug *Baranca*, tows the damaged tanker to Southwest Pass; she will subsequently return to service. Still later, *U 506* sinks U.S. tanker *Gulfoil* approximately 75 miles southwest of the mouth of the Mississippi, 28°08′N, 89°46′W; the tanker sinks so rapidly that the crew have no time to launch boats. Of the 36-man merchant complement and four-man Armed Guard, only 19 merchant seamen survive to reach two life rafts that float free when the ship sinks (see 18 May).

CARIBBEAN. Unarmed U.S. freighter *Ruth Lykes* is attacked by German submarine *U 103* at 16°37′N, 82°27′W; after the U-boat scores a hit with a dud torpedo she surfaces to shell her quarry, killing five sailors. *U 103* rescues one sailor and transfers him into a lifeboat, after which *Kapitänleutnant* Werner Winter, the submarine's commanding officer, apologizes: "You can thank Mr. Roosevelt for this. I am sorry." The U-boat also gives the Americans bandages and cigarettes before departing (see 17 May).

Dutch schooners *India* and *Mississippi* sight lifeboats of U.S. freighter *Norlantic*, sunk by German submarine *U 69* on 13 May. The latter tows the boats into Bonaire, N.W.I., the following day (see 24 May and 19 June).

17 Sunday

PACIFIC. Submarine *Grampus* (SS 207) is damaged by gunfire of Japanese patrol craft off Truk, 08°02′N, 151°03′E.

Submarine *Silversides* (SS 236) damages Japanese transport *Tottori Maru* and freighter *Thames Maru* off Shiono Misaki, southern Honshu, 33°28′N, 135°33′E.

Submarine *Skipjack* (SS 184) sinks Japanese army transport *Taizan Maru* near the mouth of the Gulf of Siam, 06°22′N, 108°36′E.

Submarine *Tautog* (SS 199) sinks Japanese submarine *I 28* north of Rabaul, 06°30′N, 152°00′E.

Submarine *Triton* (SS 201) sinks Japanese submarine *I 64* southeast of Kyushu, Japan, 29°25′N, 134°06′E.

ATLANTIC. Destroyer *Hambleton* (DD 455) is damaged in collision with destroyer *Ellyson* (DD 454) while in TF 36, en route to the United States from the Gold Coast of Africa.

British tanker *San Victorio* is sunk by German submarine *U 155* at 11°40′N, 62°33′W; the sole survivor is rescued by yacht *Turquoise* (PY 19). U.S. freighter *Challenger*, en route to

Trinidad for voyage repairs, is also sunk by *U 155* at 12°11′N, 61°18′W; five merchant seamen, two Armed Guard sailors, and one passenger perish. *Turquoise* picks up the 36 merchant seamen, nine Armed Guard sailors, and 11 passengers who survive *Challenger*'s loss, and puts them ashore at Trinidad the next day.

Unarmed U.S. fishing trawler *Foam* is shelled by German submarine *U 432* approximately 85 miles south of Halifax, Nova Scotia, 43°20′N, 63°08′W, and abandoned by her 21-man crew (one of whom dies of wounds) (see 18 and 19 May).

CARIBBEAN. Twenty-three survivors of U.S. tanker *Esso Houston*, sunk by German submarine *U 162* on 12 May, reach St. Vincent, British Windward Islands. One Armed Guard sailor perishes of wounds suffered in the attack five days previous; he is the only casualty.

Norwegian motor vessel *Somerville* rescues 27 survivors (one of whom dies of his wounds after being picked up) from U.S. freighter *Ruth Lykes*, sunk by German submarine *U 103* the previous day, and transports them to Key West, Florida.

18 Monday

UNITED STATES. Office of Naval Inspector General (Admiral Charles P. Snyder) is established.

ARCTIC. U.S. freighter *Deer Lodge*, anchored in Kola Inlet, Murmansk, is bombed by German planes, and damaged by near-misses. There are no casualties among the 34-man merchant complement or among the 11-man Armed Guard sailors, and the ship is moved to another anchorage.

ATLANTIC. Brazilian steamship *Commandante Lyra* is torpedoed by Italian submarine *Barbarigo* at 02°59′S, 34°10′W; light cruisers *Milwaukee* (CL 5) and *Cincinnati* (CL 6) rescue survivors. Small seaplane tender *Thrush* (AVP 3) tows the damaged ship to Fortaleza, Brazil, while PBYs (VP 83) provide cover.

Unarmed U.S. freighter *Quaker City* is sunk by German submarine *U 156* approximately 300 miles east of Barbados, 15°47′N, 53°12′W; 10 men perish (one will subsequently die of wounds). The 30 survivors take to four lifeboats. *U 156* surfaces and questions the survivors as to the name of the ship and her cargo and destination; the Germans then provide the Americans with directions to Barbados (see 22, 24, and 26 May).

British steamship *Hororata* rescues raft with the last survivor from U.S. freighter *Alcoa Guide*, sunk by German submarine *U 123* on

16 April. A total of six have perished from *Alcoa Guide*'s 34-man complement.

Rescue craft (not specified) recovers last survivor from U.S. freighter *Steel Maker*, sunk by German submarine *U 136* on 19 April. This man, the radio operator, had pooled supplies from several rafts in his vicinity after the ship sank and "lived comfortably" until rescued.

Lifeboat with 17 survivors of unarmed U.S. fishing trawler *Foam*, attacked by German submarine *U 432* the previous day, reaches Sambro Lightship, whence they are transported to Halifax, Nova Scotia, by a Canadian patrol craft (see 19 May).

GULF OF MEXICO. Unarmed U.S. tanker *Mercury Sun* is sunk by German submarine *U 125* at 20°02′N, 84°25′W, and abandoned; six merchant seamen perish in the attack (see 19 May).

Unarmed U.S. freighter *William J. Salman* is sunk by German submarine *U 125* at 20°08′N, 83°47′W, as the merchantman proceeds to Antigua, B.W.I.; six men perish (see 19 May).

U.S. tanker *Benjamin Brewster* rescues 19 survivors from tanker *Gulfoil*, sunk by *U 506* on 16 May, and transports them to Galveston, Texas.

19 Tuesday

PACIFIC. Light cruiser *Nashville* (CL 43) sails independently from Midway, bound for the western Aleutians.[97]

Small reconnaissance seaplane from Japanese submarine *I 21* reconnoiters Suva Bay, Fiji.

INDIAN OCEAN. Small reconnaissance seaplane from Japanese submarine *I 30* reconnoiters Zanzibar and Dar-es-Salaam.

ATLANTIC. U.S. freighter *Ironclad*, at Hvalfjordur, Iceland, experiences disturbance among the crew, occasioned by some of the merchant seamen having broken into a quantity of liquor consigned to Admiral William H. Standley, USN (Retired), U.S. Ambassador to the USSR. *Ironclad*'s armed guard officer reports the trouble, and battleship *Washington* (BB 56) provides marines from her shipboard detachment to restore order and bring the rowdies under control. Consequently, *Ironclad* is withdrawn from the list of ships in convoy PQ 16 so the incident can be investigated.

Last three survivors of unarmed U.S. fishing trawler *Foam*, attacked by German submarine *U 432* on 17 May, are rescued by Canadian corvette HMCS *Halifax*.

GULF OF MEXICO. U.S. steamship *Howard* rescues the 29 survivors of U.S. tanker *Mercury Sun*, sunk by German submarine *U 125* the

previous day; she transfers one to a Coast Guard boat at the Tampa Sea Buoy for medical attention and transports the rest to Mobile, Alabama.

U.S. freighter *Heredia* is sunk by German submarine *U 506* two miles south of the Ship Shoals Buoy, Louisiana, 27°32′N, 91°00′W; the rapidity with which the vessel sinks gives the crew no time to launch boats. Of the 62 men on board (48-man merchant crew, six-man Armed Guard, and eight passengers), 36 (30 crewmen, five Armed Guard sailors, and one passenger) perish. Shrimp boats *Papa Joe*, *Conquest*, *J. Edwin Treakle*, and *Shellwater* rescue 23 survivors; a seaplane rescues three.

U.S. freighter *Ogontz* is sunk by German submarine *U 103* near the Yucatan Channel, 23°30′N, 86°37′W; 17 merchant seamen and two Armed Guard sailors perish in the attack, the majority of the casualties caused when a mast falls across a lifeboat when the ship is being abandoned. *U 103* questions two survivors on board before returning them to their shipmates. The Germans provide medical assistance and cigarettes before leaving (see 20 May).

CARIBBEAN. Unarmed U.S. freighter *Isabela* is torpedoed, shelled, and sunk by German submarine *U 751*, 35 miles south of Navassa Island Light, 17°50′N, 75°00′W; three crewmen perish. Survivors subsequently reach Cape Briton, Haiti, in two lifeboats.

Latvian freighter *Kegums* rescues the 22 survivors of U.S. freighter *William J. Salman*, sunk by German submarine *U 125* the previous day, and takes them to Key West, Florida.

20 Wednesday

PACIFIC. Air Force South Pacific Area (Rear Admiral John S. McCain) is established.

ATLANTIC. District patrol vessel *YP 387* is sunk in collision off the coast of Delaware, 39°00′N, 75°00′W.

GULF OF MEXICO. Unarmed U.S. tanker *Halo* is sunk by German submarine *U 506* approximately 50 miles from Southwest Pass, Louisiana, 28°42′N, 90°08′W; 23 survivors from a merchant complement of 42 men initially survive the loss of the ship (see 25 and 27 May).

U.S. freighter *George Calvert* is sunk by German submarine *U 752* near the Yucatan Channel, 22°55′N, 84°26′W; three Armed Guard sailors perish in the attack. Fifty-one merchant seamen and seven surviving Armed Guard sailors abandon ship in three boats, in which they reach the coast of Cuba, going ashore the following day.

U.S. tanker *Esso Dover* rescues 20 merchant sailors and two Armed Guard sailors, survivors of freighter *Ogontz*, sunk by German submarine *U 103* the previous day.

CARIBBEAN. U.S. freighter *Clare* is sunk by German submarine *U 103* approximately 40 miles off the south coast of Cuba, 21°35′N, 84°43′W; the 33-man merchant complement and seven-man Armed Guard (all hands) survive, abandoning ship in one boat and three rafts.[98] Later the same day, *U 103* sinks U.S. freighter *Elizabeth* at 21°36′N, 84°48′W; six of the 35 merchant seamen perish and the remainder, along with the seven-man Armed Guard, reach the coast of Cuba the following day.

21 Thursday

PACIFIC. North Pacific Force (Rear Admiral Robert A. Theobald) is established for operations in Alaskan sector.

Destroyer *Helm* (DD 388) rescues four survivors from *Neosho* (AO 23) that had abandoned ship when the oiler was damaged on 7 May.

ATLANTIC. Unarmed U.S. freighter *Plow City*, en route from Trinidad to New York, mistakes lifeboat from British motorship *Peisander* (sunk by German submarine *U 653* on 17 May) for U-boat conning tower and flees, her smoke attracting the attention of *U 588*, which sinks *Plow City* at 39°08′N, 69°57′W. One crewman dies in the attack. *U 588* briefly interrogates one crewman on board the submarine before returning him to his shipmates with rum and cigarettes; U-boat sailors also help the Americans right a capsized lifeboat (see 26 May).

22 Friday

GENERAL. Mexico declares war on Germany, Italy, and Japan.

CARIBBEAN. Unarmed U.S. tanker *William Boyce Thompson*, en route to Curaçao, N.W.I., is torpedoed by German submarine *U 558* at 16°26′N, 76°55′W; there are no casualties among the 37 merchant seamen and two Navy signalmen, and the ship reaches port under her own power.

ATLANTIC. Destroyer *Blakeley* (DD 150), at 15°01′N, 57°38′W, rescues seven survivors from U.S. freighter *Quaker City*, sunk by German submarine *U 156* on 18 May (see 24 and 26 May).

Admiral William D. Leahy, USN (Retired), boards Swedish passenger liner *Drottningholm* at Lisbon, Portugal, for passage home to the United States. He will arrive in New York on 1 June.

PACIFIC. Submarine *Tautog* (SS 199) damages Japanese transport *Sanko Maru* southwest of Truk, 07°00′N, 151°00′E.

Submarine *Silversides* (SS 236) damages Japanese transport *Asahisan Maru* at the mouth of Kii Strait, between Ichiyo Saki and Shiono Misaki, Honshu, 33°30′N, 135°27′N. Counterattack by Japanese seaplane (Maizuru *Kokutai*) is unsuccessful.

23 Saturday

PACIFIC. District patrol vessel *YP 277* is destroyed by fire after striking U.S. mine at French Frigate Shoals, T.H.

Small reconnaissance seaplane from Japanese submarine *I 29* reconnoiters Sydney, Australia.

CARIBBEAN. U.S. tanker *Samuel Q. Brown* is torpedoed by German submarine *U 103* south of the Yucatan Channel, 20°15′N, 84°38′W; two merchant seamen die at the outset. After the U-boat surfaces and the Germans ask the identity of the ship and her cargo, the survivors (37 merchant seamen and the 16-man Armed Guard) gather in two lifeboats. Later that day, a Navy plane from the Canal Zone rescues five wounded men (see 24 and 25 May).

24 Sunday

PACIFIC. Submarine *Pompano* (SS 181) sinks Japanese merchant fishing boat *Kotoku Maru*, 25°16′N, 122°41′E.

Small reconnaissance seaplane from Japanese submarine *I 21* reconnoiters Auckland, New Zealand.

CARIBBEAN. Unarmed U.S. freighter *Beatrice* is torpedoed by German submarine *U 558* at 17°23′N, 76°58′W, but the torpedo fails to explode. *U 558* then surfaces to shell the ship, which is abandoned under fire with the loss of one man. PBY arrives on the scene and drives off the submarine. Of the 30 survivors, 21 men in a lifeboat reach Pigeon Island, Jamaica; British patrol craft *Hauken* rescues the remaining nine sailors. *Beatrice* sinks the next morning.

Steamship *Marpesia* rescues two survivors on a raft from U.S. freighter *Norlantic*, sunk by German submarine *U 69* on 13 May (see 19 June).

Destroyer *Goff* (DD 247) rescues 48 survivors of U.S. tanker *Samuel Q. Brown*, torpedoed by German submarine *U 103* the previous day (see 25 May).

ATLANTIC. Fifteen survivors from U.S. freighter *Quaker City*, sunk by German submarine *U 156* on 18 May, reach safety at Barbados (see 26 May).

25 Monday

PACIFIC. Light cruiser *St. Louis* (CL 49) arrives at Midway and disembarks Companies "C" and "D," Second Marine Raider Battalion, and 37-millimeter gun battery of the Third Defense Battalion.

Submarine *Drum* (SS 228) sinks Japanese freighter *Kitakata Maru* east of Nojima Saki, Honshu, Japan, 34°00′N, 139°00′E.

Submarine *Permit* (SS 178) damages Japanese transport *Senko Maru* in Makassar Strait, 00°20′N, 118°20′N.

Submarine *Pompano* (SS 181) sinks Japanese merchant tanker *Tokyo Maru* about 70 miles west of Naha, Okinawa, Japan, 27°03′N, 127°03′E.

Submarine *Tautog* (SS 199) sinks Japanese transport *Shoka Maru* about 385 miles southwest of Ulithi, Carolines, 04°07′N, 143°32′N.

Small reconnaissance seaplane from Japanese submarine *I 9* reconnoiters Kiska and Amchitka, Aleutians.

ATLANTIC. Destroyer *Blakeley* (DD 150) is torpedoed by German submarine *U 156* off Martinique, French West Indies.

ARCTIC. German planes attack convoy PQ 16 as it proceeds toward Murmansk, USSR, from Reykjavik, Iceland; U.S. freighter *Carlton* is damaged by near-misses. She leaves the convoy under tow of British trawler HMS *Northern Spray*. There are no casualties among *Carlton*'s 35-man merchant crew or 11-man Armed Guard (see 26 May).

GULF OF MEXICO. Unarmed U.S. freighter *Alcoa Carrier* is torpedoed and shelled by German submarine *U 103* at 18°45′N, 79°50′W, and abandoned. *U 103* surfaces and her commanding officer asks the Americans for the name and speed of their ship, and if all of her men have been accounted for, before he provides them with cigarettes. *Alcoa Carrier* sinks early the following morning, after which time the U-boat departs (see 30 May).

Mexican freighter *Oaxaca* rescues three survivors from U.S. tanker *Halo*, sunk by German submarine *U 506* on 20 May; two of the men recovered, however, will die of their wounds (see 27 May).

CARIBBEAN. Destroyer *Goff* (DD 247) scuttles the hulk of U.S. tanker *Samuel Q. Brown*, torpedoed by German submarine *U 103* on 23 May.

As salvage efforts proceed in the distance on battleship *West Virginia* (BB 48), Admiral Chester W. Nimitz, Commander in Chief Pacific Fleet, decorates heroes of the opening battles of the war in ceremonies on board carrier *Enterprise* (CV 6), 27 May 1942. Awaiting his turn is African-American Mess Attendant Second Class Doris Miller, who will receive a Navy Cross for his heroism on board the ship that is in process of being salvaged in the background. (NA, 80-G-80431)

26 Tuesday

GENERAL. Anglo-American air conference opens in London to discuss allocation of aircraft; U.S. Navy representative is Rear Admiral John H. Towers, Chief of the Bureau of Aeronautics.

PACIFIC. Aircraft ferry *Kitty Hawk* (AKV 1) arrives at Midway with reinforcements for Marine Air Group 22, as well as the 3-inch antiaircraft group (Third Defense Battalion) and a light tank platoon earmarked for a mobile reserve.

Submarine *Salmon* (SS 182) sinks Japanese repair ship *Asahi* about 180 miles south-southeast of Cam Ranh Bay, French Indochina, 10°00′N, 110°00′E.

Small reconnaissance seaplane from Japanese submarine *I 9* reconnoiters Kiska.

ATLANTIC. Eight survivors from U.S. freighter *Quaker City*, sunk by German submarine *U 156* on 18 May, reach safety on Dominica, B.W.I.

Coastal yacht *Sapphire* (PYc 2) rescues the 30 survivors of U.S. freighter *Plow City*, sunk by German submarine *U 588* on 21 May.

ARCTIC. U.S. freighter *Syros*, in convoy PQ 16, is sunk by German submarine *U 703* approximately 200 miles southwest of Bear Island, 72°35′N, 05°30′E. Of the 39 souls on board (37 merchant seamen and two Navy signalmen), 27 civilians and one signalman survive, rescued by British minesweeper HMS *Hazard*.

German planes attack Reykjavik, Iceland–bound U.S. freighter *Carlton* (detached from convoy PQ 16 for repairs), under tow of British trawler HMS *Northern Spray*, but cause no additional damage. As in the previous day's attack, there are no casualties.

GULF OF MEXICO. Unarmed U.S. tanker *Carrabulle* is sunk by German submarine *U 106* at 26°18′N, 89°21′E. Reportedly, the submarine's commanding officer, *Kapitänleutnant* Herman Rasch, asks survivors if all men are clear of the ship. When told no, he laughs and orders a second torpedo launched that strikes the ship directly beneath a lifeboat as it is being lowered, killing 22 of the 24 men in it. U.S. freighter *Thompson Lykes* rescues the 18 survivors. Later the same day, *U 106* shells U.S. freighter *Atenas* at 25°50′N, 89°05′E, but accurate Armed Guard gunfire drives off the U-boat before she can cause much damage. There are no casualties on board *Atenas*

among the 54-man crew, eight-man Armed Guard, and 10 passengers.

27 Wednesday

PACIFIC. "MI" Operation: Japanese forces begin heading for Midway. Chief among them is First Mobile Force, Carrier Strike Force (Vice Admiral Nagumo Chuichi), which departs home waters on this date.

Japanese submarine *I 19* prepares to launch her small reconnaissance seaplane off the northern side of Bogoslof Island, Aleutians, but sights what she identifies as a U.S. destroyer and submerges hurriedly, irreparably damaging the aircraft.

Small reconnaissance seaplane from Japanese submarine *I 25* reconnoiters Kodiak, Alaska.

Marines and Seabees occupy Wallis Island, South Pacific Ocean.

ATLANTIC. Destroyer tender *Prairie* (AD 15) and gunboat *Spry* (PG 64) are damaged by fire, Argentia, Newfoundland.

ARCTIC. German bombers attack convoy PQ 16, hitting four U.S. freighters: *Alamar* is sunk approximately 100 miles southeast of Bear Island, USSR. British corvette HMS *Starwort*, tug HMS *St. Elstan,* and submarine HMS *Trident* rescue all hands (36 merchant seamen and nine Armed Guard sailors); *Trident* torpedoes and scuttles the irreparably damaged freighter as a hazard to navigation. *Mormacsul* is sunk by a direct hit and three near-misses; three of the ship's crew perish in the attack. The survivors (36 merchant seamen and the nine-man Armed Guard) abandon ship and are rescued by HMS *Starwort* and a British tug. *Alcoa Banner* is damaged by near-misses 200 miles southwest of Bear Island; there are no casualties to the 44-man merchant complement or the two Armed Guard sailors. *City of Joliet* is damaged by near-misses; her pumps fight a losing battle against in-rushing water, but there are no casualties among the 37 merchant seamen or the 11-man Armed Guard (see 28 May).

GULF OF MEXICO. British tanker *Orina* rescues two survivors from U.S. tanker *Halo*, sunk by German submarine *U 506* on 20 May.

CARIBBEAN. Unarmed U.S. freighter *Alcoa Pilgrim*, en route to Mobile, Alabama, from Trinidad, is sunk by German submarine *U 502* at 16°28′N, 67°37′W. The rapidity with which the ship sinks prevents the crew from launching boats, and 31 men of the 40-man complement are lost with the ship (see 2 June).

28 Thursday

PACIFIC. "MI" Operation: Japanese First Fleet, Main Body (Admiral Yamamoto Isoroku in battleship *Yamato*) allocated to the Midway operation sorties from home waters. The Second Fleet, Escort Force (Rear Admiral Tanaka Raizo), whose composition includes 15 transports, sails from Saipan; Second Fleet, Occupation Support force (Rear Admiral Kurita Takeo) sorties from Guam.

TF 16 (Rear Admiral Raymond A. Spruance, who replaces Vice Admiral William F. Halsey Jr. at this key juncture because of the latter's suffering from shingles), formed around carriers *Enterprise* (CV 6) (VB 6, VF 6, VS 6, and VT 6) and *Hornet* (CV 8) (VB 8, VF 8, VS 8, and VT 8), departs Pearl Harbor to take up position northeast of Midway.

Submarine *Salmon* (SS 182) sinks Japanese freighter *Ganges Maru* in the South China Sea about 250 miles south-southeast of Cam Ranh Bay, French Indochina, 09°00′N, 111°00′E.

Submarine *Seal* (SS 183) damages Japanese army cargo ship *Tatsufuku Maru* at western entrance to Balabac Strait, 07°27′N, 116°17′E.

U.S. troops (500 men drawn from the garrison at Efate) arrive at Espíritu Santo, New Hebrides.

ARCTIC. In the aftermath of German air attacks on convoy PQ 16, U.S. freighter *City of Joliet*, damaged by near-misses the previous day, is abandoned in Barents Sea, 73°41′N, 21°58′E. All hands (including the 11-man Armed Guard) reach safety on board British tug HMS *St. Elstan* and Free French corvette *Roselys*.

CARIBBEAN. U.S. tanker *New Jersey* is sunk by German submarine *U 103* about 90 miles southwest of Grand Cayman Island, 18°32′N, 82°28′W. There are no casualties among the 36 merchant seamen and five Armed Guard sailors, and all hands abandon ship in two lifeboats (see 29 May and 1 June).

29 Friday

PACIFIC. Seaplane tender (destroyer) *Thornton* (AVD 11) arrives at French Frigate Shoals, T.H., to relieve light minelayer *Preble* (DM 20). Japanese submarine *I 123* arrives the same day to find the Americans already there. The presence of ships such as *Preble* and *Thornton* at French Frigate Shoals prevents the Japanese from repeating "K" Operation utilizing submarine-refueled flying boats to reconnoiter Pearl Harbor. The enemy has thus missed detecting the departure of TF 16 (28 May), and will not detect the sailing of TF 17 on 30 May.[99]

Seaplane tender (destroyer) *Ballard* (AVD 10) arrives at Midway along with 11 motor torpedo boats from Motor Torpedo Boat Squadron 1 (Lieutenant Clinton McKellar Jr.); the latter are assigned to local defense forces of Midway (Captain Cyril T. Simard).[100] Four district patrol vessels also arrive at Midway to patrol outlying areas: *YP 284* is allocated to Lisianski, *YP 290* to Laysan, *YP 345* to Gardner's Pinnacles, and *YP 350* to Necker.

PBYs (VP 71) and RAAF Catalinas bomb Japanese base at Tulagi, Solomons.

Small reconnaissance seaplane from Japanese submarine *I 21* reconnoiters Sydney, Australia (see 31 May).

Submarine *Swordfish* (SS 193) sinks Japanese army cargo ship *Tatsufuku Maru* at the southwestern entrance to Balabac Strait, 07°33′N, 116°18′E.

CARIBBEAN. Destroyer *Tattnall* (DD 125) rescues 26 survivors (including three Armed Guard sailors) of U.S. tanker *New Jersey*, sunk on 28 May by German submarine *U 103* (see 1 June).

Net tender *Mulberry* (YN 22) rescues the only six survivors of the 30-man crew of British freighter *Western Head*, which had been sunk the previous day by German submarine *U 107*, 20 miles south-southwest of Cape Maisi, Cuba, 20°N, 74°W.

GULF OF MEXICO. Salvage crew boards abandoned U.S. freighter *David McKelvy*, torpedoed by German submarine *U 506* on 13 May; beached, the merchantman is deemed a total loss.

30 Saturday

PACIFIC. TF 17 (Rear Admiral Frank Jack Fletcher), formed around carrier *Yorktown* (CV 5) (VB 3, VB 5, VF 3, and VT 3), departs Pearl Harbor to join TF 16 northeast of Midway.[101]

Submarine *Pompano* (SS 181) sinks Japanese army transport *Atsuta Maru* in East China Sea east of Okinawa, 26°07′N, 129°06′E, and survives counterattack by escort vessel.

INDIAN OCEAN. Small reconnaissance seaplane from Japanese submarine *I 10* reconnoiters Diego Suarez, Madagascar.

ATLANTIC. Unarmed U.S. freighter *Alcoa Shipper*, en route to New York from Trinidad, is sunk by German submarine *U 404* at 37°49′N, 65°15′W; three men die in the initial explosion. The rapidity with which the ship sinks prevents the crew from launching boats, and four men are lost with the ship. *U 404* provides

the 25 survivors with rum, cigarettes, and (for one ill-clad sailor) a pair of dungarees (see 1 June).

GULF OF MEXICO. Thirty-five survivors of U.S. freighter *Alcoa Carrier*, sunk by German submarine *U 103* on 25 May, are rescued by Cuban gunboat and Navy patrol plane.

31 Sunday

PACIFIC. Japanese Type A midget submarines from submarines *I 22*, *I 24*, and *I 27* penetrate the harbor defenses of Sydney, Australia. Torpedoes near-miss heavy cruiser *Chicago* (CA 29) but sink RAN accommodation ship *Kuttabul* and damage Dutch submarine *K IX* beyond economical repair. All three Japanese midget submarines are lost.

Submarine *Pollack* (SS 180) sinks Japanese auxiliary submarine chaser *No. 5 Shunsei Maru* off Murotosan, 31°38′N, 133°45′E.

INDIAN OCEAN. Small reconnaissance seaplane from Japanese submarine *I 10* reconnoiters Diego Suarez (see 1 June).

CARIBBEAN. Submarine *Grunion* (SS 216) rescues survivors of U.S. Army–chartered freighter *Jack*, sunk by German submarine *U 155* about 100 miles southwest of Port Saluit, Haiti, 17°36′N, 74°42′W. Three of the nine-man Armed Guard are lost.

Panamanian freighter *Bush Ranger* is sunk by German submarine *U 107* while en route from St. Thomas, Virgin Islands, to Key West, Florida, 19°15′N, 81°25′W (see 8 and 12 June).

JUNE

1 Monday

INDIAN OCEAN. Small reconnaissance seaplane from Japanese submarine *I 10* again reconnoiters Diego Suarez.

ATLANTIC. Light cruiser *Omaha* (CL 4) rescues survivors from British freighter *Charlbury*, which had been en route from Cardiff, Wales, to Buenos Aires, Argentina, when sunk by Italian submarine *Barbarigo* at 06°22′N, 29°44′W.

Destroyers *Ludlow* (DD 438) and *Bernadou* (DD 153) rescue survivors of British freighter *Fred W. Green* (en route from New York to Freetown, Sierra Leone), which was sunk the previous night by German submarine *U 506* at 30°20′N, 62°00′W.

U.S. freighter *West Notus* is shelled by German submarine *U 404* off Cape Hatteras, North Carolina, 34°10′N, 68°20′W; four of the 35-man merchant complement are killed in the attack. The 36 survivors (31 merchant seamen and the five-man Armed Guard) are divided among two lifeboats (see 2–4 June).

U.S. freighter *Illinois* is torpedoed by German submarine *U 172* at 24°00′N, 60°00′W; only six of the 38-man crew survive the loss of the ship (see 7 June).

Norwegian merchantman *Margrethe Bakke* rescues the 25 survivors from U.S. freighter *Alcoa Shipper*, sunk by German submarine *U 404* on 30 May.

GULF OF MEXICO. Unarmed U.S. freighter *Hampton Roads* is sunk by German submarine *U 106* in the Yucatan Channel at 23°00′N, 85°42′W; five men perish. The 23 survivors are rescued by U.S. freighter *Alcoa Pathfinder*.

CARIBBEAN. U.S. freighter *Knoxville City* is sunk by German submarine *U 158* south of the Yucatan Channel at 21°15′N, 83°50′W; two men perish. The survivors (35 merchant seamen, 14-man Armed Guard, and four passengers) abandon ship into two lifeboats (see 3 June).

Destroyer *Biddle* (DD 151) rescues 15 survivors (including two Armed Guard sailors) of U.S. tanker *New Jersey*, sunk on 28 May by German submarine *U 103*.

2 Tuesday

PACIFIC. TF 17 (Rear Admiral Frank Jack Fletcher) and TF 16 (Rear Admiral Raymond A. Spruance) rendezvous about 350 miles northeast of Midway; Rear Admiral Fletcher is officer in tactical command of a force that consists of three carriers, seven heavy cruisers, one light cruiser, 16 destroyers, and two oilers. After fueling, the task force will detach the oilers and prepare for battle. As part of the force deployed to meet the Japanese, 25 fleet submarines of TF 7 (Rear Admiral Robert H. English) are deployed around Midway.

INDIAN OCEAN. Japanese freighter *Kofuku Maru* is sunk by mine off Rangoon, Burma.

ATLANTIC. German submarine *U 404* sinks U.S. freighter *West Notus* (which she had shelled the day before) with explosive charge off Cape Hatteras, North Carolina (see 3 and 4 June).

Unarmed U.S. freighter *City of Alma* is sunk by German submarine *U 159* about 400 miles northeast of San Juan, Puerto Rico, 23°00′N, 62°30′W; district patrol vessel *YP 67* rescues the 10 survivors from the 36-man merchant complement.

CARIBBEAN. U.S. freighter *Domino* is machine gunned by unidentified submarine off Nuevitas, Cuba; the ship suffers no casualties.

U.S. merchantman *Thomas Nelson* rescues nine survivors from U.S. freighter *Alcoa Pilgrim*, sunk by German submarine *U 502* on 27 May.

3 Wednesday

PACIFIC. In the preliminaries for the Battle of Midway, Midway-based aircraft locate and attack Japanese transports in the Second Fleet Escort Force about 600 miles west of Midway. USAAF B-17s inflict no damage. Four PBYs set out to attack the approaching Occupation Force. Japanese forces bearing down on Midway ("MI" Operation) are under the personal direction of Admiral Yamamoto Isoroku, Commander in Chief Combined Fleet, who wears his flag in battleship *Yamato*.

"AL" Operation: Japanese Second Strike Force (Rear Admiral Kakuta Kikuji) attacks Dutch Harbor, Alaska; planes from carriers *Ryujo* and *Junyo* bomb U.S. installations. In an event whose importance only becomes clear later, one Mitsubishi A6M2 Type 0 carrier fighter (ZERO) from *Ryujo*'s air unit, most likely damaged by antiaircraft fire over Dutch Harbor, makes an emergency landing on Akutan Island. The pilot, however, is fooled by the flat surface upon which he is landing; it turns out to be a bog and the ZERO flips over, killing the pilot (see 10 July).

Coastal minesweeper *Bunting* (AMc 7) is sunk in collision with submarine chaser *PC 569*, San Francisco Bay, California.

ATLANTIC. U.S. tanker *M. F. Elliott* is sunk by German submarine *U 502* off the Florida Keys, 11°58′N, 63°33′W; 13 of the 38-man civilian complement perish. Navy PBY keeps in contact with the survivors (25 merchant seamen and the seven-man Armed Guard) into the following day (see 4 June). *U 502* takes two survivors on board for interrogation before the arrival of a Navy patrol plane compels the U-boat to submerge in a hurry with the Americans still on board. When the danger has passed, the Germans release the U.S. sailors and provide them with a life raft and provisions (see 8 June).

German submarine *U 432* encounters unarmed U.S. fishing boats *Ben and Josephine* and *Aeolus* as they are en route from Gloucester, Massachusetts, to Sea Island, Nova Scotia. The Germans allow the fishermen to leave their boats, then shell and sink the craft at 43°07′N, 66°51′W (see 5 June).

Greek steamship *Constantinos H* rescues 18 survivors from U.S. freighter *West Notus*, attacked by German submarine *U 404* on 1 June (see 4 June).

CARIBBEAN. Survivors of U.S. freighter *Knoxville City*, sunk by German submarine *U 158* on 1 June, reach La Calina, Cuba, aided by Cuban gunboat *Donativo*.

ARCTIC. U.S. freighter *Steel Worker* is mined at Kola Inlet, Murmansk; there are no casualties among the 36 merchant seamen or two Navy signalmen.

4 Thursday

PACIFIC. Battle of Midway opens as PBYs attack Occupation Force northwest of Midway; one PBY (VP 24) torpedoes fleet tanker *Akebono Maru*.

Japanese carrier bombers and attack planes, supported by fighters, from *Akagi*, *Kaga*, *Soryu*, and *Hiryu* bomb installations on Sand and Eastern Islands, Midway. Although defending USMC F2As and F4Fs (VMF 221) suffer disastrous losses, damage to facilities on Midway is comparatively slight. Motor torpedo boat *PT 25* is damaged by strafing Midway lagoon.

Japanese carrier fighters and antiaircraft fire annihilate the USMC SBDs and SB2Us (VMSB 241), Navy TBFs (VT 8 detachment), and USAAF torpedo-carrying B-26s sent out to attack the Japanese carriers. USAAF B-17s likewise bomb the Japanese enemy force without success.

TBDs (VT 8, VT 6, and VT 3) from U.S. carrier striking force (Rear Admiral Frank Jack Fletcher) from *Hornet* (CV 8), *Enterprise* (CV 6), and *Yorktown* (CV 5) attack the enemy carriers. Although mauled by the defending combat air patrol (only VT 3 has fighter cover) and antiaircraft fire, they draw off the former and leave the skies open for SBDs from *Enterprise* and *Yorktown*. In attempting to defend VT 3, VF 3's pilots, led by Lieutenant Commander John S. Thach, inaugurate use of a defensive fighting tactic that will later bear his name, the "Thach Weave." SBDs from *Enterprise* (VB 6 and VS 6) sink carrier *Kaga*, 30°20′N, 179°17′W, and bomb *Akagi* (Vice Admiral Nagumo Chuichi's flagship); SBDs from *Yorktown* (VB 3) sink carrier *Soryu*, 30°38′N, 179°13′W. Submarine *Nautilus* (SS 168) torpedoes *Kaga*, but her "fish" do not explode. The one carrier that escapes destruction that morning, *Hiryu*, launches planes that bomb and temporarily disable *Yorktown*, forcing Rear Admiral Fletcher to transfer his flag to heavy cruiser *Astoria* (CA 34) and turn over tactical command to Rear Admiral Raymond A. Spruance. Before SBDs from *Enterprise* (VS 6, joined by VB 3, which is unable to operate from the immobilized *Yorktown*) can reach her, though, *Hiryu* launches torpedo-carrying carrier attack planes that stop *Yorktown* a second time. *Yorktown*, listing dangerously, is abandoned (see 5–7 June). During the defense of TF 17, destroyer *Benham* (DD 397) is damaged by friendly fire.

Ultimately, destruction of his carrier force compels Admiral Yamamoto Isoroku to abandon Midway invasion plans ("MI" Operation), and the Japanese Fleet retires westward.

Japanese destroyer *Arashi* picks up a TBD pilot (VT 3), *Makigumo* an SBD crew (VS 6). After interrogation, all three Americans are subsequently murdered. A fourth U.S. naval aviator, a TBD pilot (VT 8), however, escapes detection and recovery by the enemy. He is rescued subsequently by a PBY.

British submarine HMS *Trusty* sinks Japanese freighter *Toyohashi Maru* in Strait of Malacca, 07°14′N, 98°06′E.

ATLANTIC. Swiss steamship *Saentis* rescues 18 survivors from U.S. freighter *West Notus*, attacked by German submarine *U 404* on 1 June.

Destroyer *Tarbell* (DD 142) rescues 30 survivors of U.S. tanker *M. F. Elliott*, sunk by German submarine *U 502* on 3 June (see 8 June).

CARIBBEAN. U.S. freighter *Velma Lykes* is sunk by German submarine *U 158* south of the Yucatan Channel, 21°21′N, 86°36′W; the rapidity with which the ship sinks prevents lifeboats from being launched. Of the ship's 28-man merchant complement, 15 perish; the four-man Armed Guard survives intact (see 6 and 10 June).

5 Friday

GENERAL. U.S. declares war on Bulgaria, Hungary, and Romania.

PACIFIC. Battle of Midway continues: TF 16 (Rear Admiral Raymond A. Spruance) pursues Japanese fleet, now without its central core of carriers, westward, while efforts proceed to try and salvage the crippled carrier *Yorktown* (CV 5). Motor torpedo boats from Midway fail to locate "burning Japanese carrier" reported earlier by Midway-based planes; USMC SB2Us (VMSB 241) likewise fail to make contact.

Japanese carrier *Akagi*, damaged on 4 June, is scuttled by destroyers *Nowaki*, *Arashi*, and *Hagikaze*, 30°30′N, 178°40′W; carrier *Hiryu* is scuttled by destroyers *Kazegumo* and *Yugumo*, 31°27.5′N, 179°23.5′W (see 19 June).

Heavy cruisers *Mogami* and *Mikuma* are damaged in collision while turning to avoid shadowing submarine *Tambor* (SS 198), while retiring from Midway. Later attack on cruisers

by SB2Us (VMSB 241) is unsuccessful (see 6 June).

"AL" Operation: Planes from Japanese carriers *Ryujo* and *Junyo* reprise their attack on U.S. installations at Dutch Harbor, Alaska. Attu Occupation Force (Rear Admiral Omori Sentaro) seizes Attu, Aleutians, without opposition.

CARIBBEAN. U.S. tanker *L. J. Drake* is sunk with all hands (35 merchant seamen and a six-man Armed Guard) by German submarine *U 68* at 17°30′N, 68°20′W, one day's steaming from Aruba, N.W.I.

ATLANTIC. Unarmed U.S. freighter *Delfina* is sunk by German submarine *U 172* at 22°22′N, 67°08′W; four crewmen perish. Submarine chaser *PC 67* rescues 12 survivors from two rafts; the remainder (15 men in a lifeboat) reach the port of Montecristi, Dominican Republic.

Eight survivors from U.S. fishing boat *Ben and Josephine* and six from *Aeolus*, their craft sunk by German submarine *U 432* on 3 June, reach Mt. Desert Coast Guard Light Station, Maine.

EUROPE. Operation HARPOON, the resupply of Malta, commences as convoy WS 19Z (Force "X") sails from the River Clyde, Scotland; two of the five freighters, U.S. motorship *Chant* and Dutch *Tanimbar*, have U.S. Navy Armed Guard crews on board (see 12 June).

6 Saturday

PACIFIC. Battle of Midway concludes: SBDs (VB 3, VS 5, VB8, and VS 8) from carriers *Enterprise* (CV 6) and *Hornet* (CV 8) bomb heavy cruisers *Mikuma* (which sinks later at approximately 29°22′N, 176°34′E) and *Mogami*; SBDs (VB 8 and VS 8) also near-miss destroyers *Asashio* and *Arashio*. At Rear Admiral Raymond A. Spruance's direct order (because of the destruction of three torpedo squadrons on 4 June), TBDs (VT 6, the only squadron with operable aircraft remaining) that accompany the strike do not attack because of the antiaircraft fire from the Japanese ships. After recovering planes, TF 16 changes course to eastward to refuel and breaks contact with the enemy.

Japanese submarine *I 168* interrupts salvage operations on *Yorktown* (CV 5), which is under tow of tug *Vireo* (AT 144) and screened by destroyers, torpedoing the carrier and destroyer *Hammann* (DD 412) as the latter lies alongside (30°36′N, 176°34′W) supporting the salvors. *Hammann* sinks, but *Yorktown* remains afloat. Screening destroyers depth charge *I 168*, but the Japanese boat, although damaged, escapes. *Vireo* is damaged by concussion of depth charge explosions.

Submarine tender *Fulton* (AS 11), sent out from Pearl Harbor, embarks 2,015 *Yorktown*

Beneath a somber sky, carrier *Yorktown* (CV 5), painted in an unmodified Measure 12 camouflage, prepares for flight operations on the morning of 4 June 1942. (Author's Collection)

(CV 5) survivors; light minelayer *Breese* (DM 18) embarks 84, and destroyer *Allen* (DD 66) 94.

Submarine *Grayling* (SS 209) is accidentally bombed by USAAF B-17s about 450 to 500 miles west by south of Midway.

The Battle of Midway, one of the most decisive battles in naval history, marks the turning point of the Pacific War. In the wake of the battle, efforts to locate downed aviators persist over the ensuing days. These not only yield American aviators but also enemy sailors (see 9 and 19 June). For the Japanese, the failure of the "MI" Operation, so close on the heels of the cancellation of the "MO" Operation, results in the cancellation of the proposed invasion of Fiji and Samoa ("FS" Operation) projected for July 1942. It also focuses attention on the need to convert and build aircraft carriers.

INDIAN OCEAN. U.S. freighter *Melvin H. Baker* is torpedoed by Japanese submarine *I 10* off the coast of Mozambique, 21°44'S, 36°38'W; all hands abandon ship. British steamship *Twickenham* rescues the 48 men: 34 merchant seamen, six-man Armed Guard, and eight passengers (six of whom had survived the loss of freighter *Bienville* on 6 April).

ATLANTIC. Panamanian tanker *Stanvac Calcutta* battles German auxiliary cruiser *Stier* (*Schiffe 23*) about 500 miles off the coast of Brazil. Two of the nine-man Armed Guard are wounded by shrapnel during the action; *Stier* rescues the survivors, ultimately transferring 26 merchant seamen and nine Armed Guard sailors to Japanese custody. One man is sent to prison camp in Germany.

U.S. freighter *George Cylmer*, disabled by a broken main shaft and drifting, is torpedoed by German motor torpedo boat *Esan*, launched from auxiliary cruiser *Michel* (*Schiffe 28*) at 14°28'S, 18°37'W; one crewmen perishes below. *George Cylmer* is abandoned (see 7 and 8 June).

CARIBBEAN. British motor vessel *Ardenvour* rescues 17 survivors (13 merchant seamen and four Armed Guard sailors) from U.S. freighter *Velma Lykes*, sunk by German submarine *U 158* on 4 June (see 10 June).

7 Sunday

UNITED STATES. Command of naval forces is reallocated: Atlantic and Pacific Fleets, Sea Frontiers, and Special Task Forces are placed directly under Commander in Chief U.S. Fleet and Chief of Naval Operations; Naval Local Defense Forces, Naval Transportation Service,

Special Duty Ships, and Naval District Craft are made responsible to Vice Chief of Naval Operations.

Carrier *Yorktown* (CV 5) sinks as the result of heavy damage received on 4 and 6 June, 30°36'N, 176°34'W.

Submarine *Grouper* (SS 214) is bombed (but not damaged) by USAAF B-17s north-northwest of Midway.

"AL" Operation: Japanese Kiska Occupation Force (Captain Ono Takeji) seizes Kiska, Aleutians, without opposition.

U.S. freighter *Coast Trader* is sunk by Japanese submarine *I 26* off Cape Flattery, Washington, 48°19'N, 125°40'W. Coast Guard PBY (V-206) guides Canadian corvette HMCS *Edmundston* to the scene; *Edmundston* and fishing boat *Virginia I* rescue survivors, who include the 37-man crew and 19-man Armed Guard. One crewman dies of exposure before the survivors can be picked up.

ATLANTIC. Small seaplane tender *Gannet* (AVP 8) is sunk by German submarine *U 652* off Bermuda, 35°50'N, 65°38'W.

U.S. tanker *Esso Montpelier* rescues the six survivors from freighter *Illinois*, sunk by German submarine *U 172* on 1 June.

Damaged U.S. freighter *George Cylmer*, torpedoed the day before, is reboarded by her crew (see 8 June).

CARIBBEAN. Unarmed U.S. freighter *Edith* is sunk by German submarine *U 159*, 14°33'N, 74°35'W. Two crewmen perish in the attack, the remainder (29 men) gather on board one lifeboat and two rafts. *U 159* conducts a brief interrogation of the survivors, provides them with directions to the nearest land, and gathers floating supplies before departing. Within a week's time, *Edith*'s survivors reach Black River, Jamaica.

Unarmed U.S. freighter *Suwied* is sunk by German submarine *U 107* southeast of the Yucatan Channel, 20°00'N, 84°48'W; 26 of the 32-man crew, and the ship's one passenger, survive the sinking (see 8 June).

8 Monday

PACIFIC. Tug *Vireo* (AT 144) is damaged by grounding, Midway.

ATLANTIC. British armed merchant cruiser HMS *Alcantara* embarks survivors from damaged U.S. freighter *George Cylmer*; attempts to scuttle the freighter prove futile and *Alcantara* must leave on 12 June with the American ship still stubbornly afloat.

Brazilian tanker *Santa Maria* rescues the two sailors from U.S. tanker *M. F. Elliott* who

had been held briefly as prisoners of war when their ship had been sunk by German submarine *U 502* on 3 June.

CARIBBEAN. U.S. tanker *Franklin K. Lane*, en route to Aruba, N.W.I., in convoy TA 5, is torpedoed by German submarine *U 502* approximately 35 miles northeast of Cape Blanco, 11°22'N, 69°38'W. Four crewmen perish in the attack; 31 merchant seamen and the six-man Armed Guard survive to be rescued by British destroyer HMS *Churchill* [ex-U.S. destroyer *Herndon* (DD 198)] (see 9 June).

Coast Guard cutter *Nemesis* (WPC 111) rescues the 27 survivors of U.S. freighter *Suwied*, sunk by German submarine *U 107* on 7 June.

Navy plane (type and squadron unspecified) rescues four survivors of Armed Guard crew from Panamanian freighter *Bush Ranger*, sunk by German submarine *U 107* on 31 May (see 12 June).

9 Tuesday

PACIFIC. Submarine *Trout* (SS 202) picks up two enlisted survivors from Japanese heavy cruiser *Mikuma*, sunk on 6 June.

Lieutenant Commander Lyndon B. Johnson, USNR, in the South Pacific theater on a congressional inspection tour, is to accompany USAAF bombing mission scheduled to attack Japanese installations at Lae, New Guinea. Johnson is to go along as a passenger in a B-26 (19th Squadron, 22nd Bomb Group). Engine trouble, however, compels the pilot of Johnson's Marauder ("Heckling Hare") to abort the mission; the plane never sees combat. Inexplicably, however, Johnson receives Silver Star for "gallantry." He goes on to become the 36th President of the United States.

Naval Operating Base, Kodiak, Alaska, is established.

CARIBBEAN. U.S. freighter *Merrimack* is sunk by German submarine *U 107* about 60 miles north of Cozumel Island, off the Honduran coast, 19°47'N, 85°55'W. Of the 51 men on board at the time of the attack (nine of whom comprise the Armed Guard), only 10 (including one Navy man) survive (see 15 June).

British destroyer HMS *Churchill* [ex-U.S. destroyer *Herndon* (DD 198)] scuttles damaged U.S. tanker *Franklin K. Lane*, torpedoed by German submarine *U 502* the previous day, as a menace to navigation.

10 Wednesday

PACIFIC. Carrier *Saratoga* (CV 3) in TF 11 (Rear Admiral Aubrey W. Fitch) makes rendezvous with TF 16 to transfer planes to bring carriers *Enterprise* (CV 6) and *Hornet* (CV 8) up to strength in the wake of the Battle of Midway. Poor weather, however, forces a postponement of the evolution (see 11 June).

ATLANTIC. U.S. tanker *Hagan*, en route to Havana, Cuba, is sunk by German submarine *U 157* at 22°00′N, 77°30′W. Six of the 35-man merchant complement perish in the attack, but all nine Armed Guard sailors survive. The survivors reach the Cuban coast by lifeboat the following day.

CARIBBEAN. Unarmed U.S. freighter *American*, en route to New Orleans, Louisiana, is torpedoed by German submarine *U 157* at 17°58′N, 84°28′W. Three of the 41-man crew perish in the initial explosion. Steamship *Kent* rescues the 38 survivors, one of whom dies of his wounds, and transports them to Cristobal, C.Z.

British motor vessel *Ardenvour* is sunk by German submarine *U 68*; among the souls on board are the 13 merchant seamen and four Armed Guard sailors who have already survived the loss of their ship, U.S. freighter *Velma Lykes,* on 4 June. They survive the loss of a second ship less than a week after the first.

11 Thursday

PACIFIC. Carrier *Saratoga* (CV 3) in TF 11 (Rear Admiral Aubrey W. Fitch) transfers planes to bring carriers *Enterprise* (CV 6) and *Hornet* (CV 8) up to strength. Losses in torpedo planes have been especially heavy; *Saratoga* transfers TBDs (VT 5) to *Enterprise*, TBFs (VT 8) to *Hornet*, and SBDs to both ships.

ATLANTIC. German submarine *U 87* mines the waters off Boston, Massachusetts; *U 373* mines the waters off Delaware Bay (see 24 June).

Unarmed U.S. tanker *F. W. Abrams*, en route to New York from Aruba, blunders into minefield off Cape Hatteras, North Carolina, and fouls two mines, at 34°55′N, 75°50′W. Her 36-man crew abandons ship and reaches shore near Morehead City, North Carolina. Salvage vessel (NRTS) *Relief* attempts salvage (see 15 June).

12 Friday

PACIFIC. USAAF B-24s (11th Air Force) bomb Japanese shipping off Kiska, damaging destroyer *Hibiki* by close near-misses.

Submarine *Plunger* (SS 179) is damaged when emergency identification flare explodes as she signals friendly aircraft; she suffers no serious injuries and remains on patrol.

Submarine *Swordfish* (SS 193) sinks Japanese freighter *Burma Maru* northwest of Pulo Wai, in the Gulf of Siam, 10°08′N, 102°34′E.

ATLANTIC. German submarine *U 701* mines the waters off Cape Henry, Virginia.

GULF OF MEXICO. U.S. tanker *Cities Service Toledo*, bound for Portland, Maine, with a cargo of 84,000 barrels of crude oil, is torpedoed by German submarine *U 158*, 20 miles east of Trinity Shoals Gas Buoy, 29°02′N, 91°59′W, and explodes; 11 of the 36-man merchant complement perishes in the inferno, as do four of the nine-man Armed Guard. Norwegian tanker *Belinda*, U.S. tanker *Gulf King*, and steamship *San Antonio* rescue the 30 survivors from among the merchant seamen and bluejackets.

CARIBBEAN. Gunboat *Erie* (PG 50), at 10°12′N, 80°14′30″W, rescues master and 45 other survivors of British steamship *Fort Good Hope*, which had been sunk by German submarine *U 159* at 10°19′N, 80°16′W. After salvaging the lifeboats, *Erie* joins with a patrol plane in prosecuting a submarine contact, ultimately dropping six charges with no result. Later, *Erie* transfers *Fort Good Hope*'s survivors and their boats to submarine chaser *PC 209*.

U.S. steamship *Sixaola* is sunk by German submarine *U 159* off the coast of Panama, 09°54′N, 81°25′W. Of the 87-man crew, 29 perish in the attack. The 58 surviving crewmen, together with the six-man Armed Guard and the 108 passengers, take to five boats and six rafts. U.S. steamship *Carolinian* rescues 32 survivors and transfers them to motor torpedo boat tender *Niagara* (PG 52); *Niagara* herself rescues 75 more. Army tug *Shasta* picks up 23 (see 16 June).

Coast Guard cutter *Nike* (WPC 112) rescues 19 more survivors of Panamanian freighter *Bush Ranger*, sunk by German submarine *U 107* on 31 May, and transports them to Key West, Florida.

MEDITERRANEAN. Operation HARPOON: Convoy WS 19Z (Force "X") transits the Straits of Gibraltar. The ships are soon detected by German reconnaissance aircraft. Escort (Acting Captain Cecil C. Hardy, RN) for the five freighters (two of which, U.S. motorship *Chant* and Dutch *Tanimbar*, have U.S. Navy Armed Guards on board) and one tanker is provided by antiaircraft cruiser HMS *Cairo* (flag), nine destroyers (eight British and one Polish), four minesweepers, and six motor gunboats. Cover is provided by Force "W," composed of battleship HMS *Malaya*, aircraft carriers HMS *Argus* and HMS *Eagle*, light cruisers HMS *Kenya* (flagship for Vice Admiral Alban T. B. Curteis, RN), HMS *Charybdis,* and HMS *Liverpool*, and eight destroyers. A second convoy, MW 11

(Operation VIGOROUS), sets out from Alexandria and Port Said, Egypt, and Haifa (see 13 June).

13 Saturday

ARCTIC. U.S. freighter *Yaka* is damaged by near-misses when German aircraft bomb Allied shipping at Murmansk, USSR. There are no casualties among the 38 merchant seamen or 11-man Armed Guard.

MEDITERRANEAN. Operation HARPOON: Convoy WS 19Z (Force "X") stands toward Malta, detected by Axis reconnaissance aircraft. Italian torpedo bombers flying from Sardinia fail to make contact, however, and Italian fleet units that sortie from Cagliari put into Palermo, Sicily, when their presence is reported by British submarines (see 14 and 16 June).

ATLANTIC. German submarine *U 584* puts four agents ashore at Amagansett, Long Island, New York. Coast Guard beach patrolman, however, detects the landing and FBI agents capture the would-be saboteurs (see 17 June and 8 August).

Coast Guard cutter *Thetis* (WPC 115) sinks German submarine *U 157* north of Cuba, 24°13′N, 82°03′W.

CARIBBEAN. U.S. freighter *Solon Thurman* is sunk by German submarine *U 159* off the Panama Canal Zone, 10°45′N, 80°24′W. The 44 merchant seamen and nine Armed Guards all abandon ship; *U 159*'s officers query the survivors and offer them aid before departing (see 14 June).

14 Sunday

PACIFIC. First echelon of First Marine Division (Major General Alexander A. Vandegrift, USMC) arrives at Wellington, New Zealand.

Japanese cargo ship *Taizan Maru* is stranded and sinks off southwest coast of Korea, 35°00′N, 125°00′E.

PBYs bomb Japanese ships southwest of Kiska, near-missing light cruiser *Tama*.

CARIBBEAN. U.S. bulk carrier *Lebore* is sunk by German submarine *U 172* about 200 miles north of Cristobal, C.Z., 12°53′N, 80°40′W (see 15 and 16 June).

U.S. freighter *Scottsburg* is sunk by German submarine *U 161* at 11°51′N, 62°56′W; five men are killed in the attack (see 15 and 16 June).

Colombian schooners *Envoy* and *Zamora* rescue the 53 survivors from U.S. freighter *Solon Thurman*, sunk by German submarine *U 159* on 13 June. One crewman, however, drowns when he falls overboard from schooner *Envoy*.

MEDITERRANEAN. Operation HARPOON continues as WS 19Z (Force "X") is attacked by Italian planes. Dutch motor vessel *Tanimbar* is torpedoed by an SM 79 and sunk, but not before the U.S. Navy Armed Guard gunners display "great courage and skill" and splash one of the attackers. British light cruiser HMS *Liverpool* is also torpedoed by another SM 79, and is towed to Gibraltar (see 15 and 16 June).

15 Monday

PACIFIC. Submarine *Seawolf* (SS 197) sinks Japanese gunboat *Nampo Maru* off Corregidor, 14°00'N, 120°00'E.

MEDITERRANEAN. Operation HARPOON: Convoy WS 19Z (Force "X") is attacked by Italian light cruisers *Eugenio di Savoia* and *Raimondo Montecuccoli* and five destroyers. In this surface action, British destroyer HMS *Bedouin* is sunk and HMS *Partridge* damaged, but the screen for WS 19Z proves impenetrable and the Italians retire. At the same time, however, German JU 87s dive-bomb the convoy, damaging tanker *Kentucky* (she is later scuttled). U.S. freighter *Chant* suffers two direct hits, catches fire, and is abandoned, 36°25'N, 11°40'E. British minesweeper HMS *Rye* rescues *Chant's* survivors: 49 of the 52-man merchant complement, 10 of 11 Armed Guards, and 25 British Navy and Army sailors and soldiers embarked to man the antiaircraft battery.[102]

ATLANTIC. Destroyer *Borie* (DD 215) rescues nine survivors (including the sole Armed Guard sailor to emerge from the ordeal) from U.S. freighter *Merrimack* at 20°48'N, 85°30'W, which had been sunk on 9 June by U 107. Earlier that same day, merchant ship *Argentina* had rescued the only other man to survive *Merrimack's* loss.

Salvage vessel *Relief* (NRTS) finds tanker *F. W. Abrams*, mined off Cape Hatteras, North Carolina, on 11 June, beyond salvage. The wreck is scuttled with demolition charges.

U.S. freighter *Kahuku* rescues 46 survivors (35 merchant seamen and the 11-man Armed Guard) from freighter *Scottsburg*, sunk by German submarine U 161 the day before, and 17 from Panamanian steamer *Cold Harbor*, sunk by U 502 the day before. Later that same day, however, *Kahuku* is torpedoed by U 126 at 11°54'N, 63°07'W (see 16 June).

U.S. freighter *West Hardaway* is sunk by German submarine U 502 northwest of Trinidad, 11°50'N, 62°15'W, and is abandoned by all hands without loss (see 17 June).

U.S. tanker *Robert C. Tuttle*, in convoy KN 109, strikes mine laid by German submarine U 701 off Virginia Beach, Virginia, 36°51'20"N, 75°51'15"W; one merchant seaman is blown overboard and lost. Survivors (40-man merchant complement, a six-man Armed Guard, and a Navy signalman) take to lifeboats, which are taken in tow by submarine chaser PC 474. U.S. tanker *Esso Augusta*, also in convoy KN 109, strikes mine laid by German submarine U 701, a half mile south of the Chesapeake Bay entrance lighted whistle buoy, 36°52'N, 75°51'30"W; she suffers no casualties among the 44-man merchant complement or the 13-man Armed Guard. *Esso Augusta* ultimately returns to service.[103]

U.S. tanker *Cherokee*, in convoy XB 25, is sunk by German submarine U 87 approximately 50 miles east of Boston, Massachusetts, 42°11'N, 69°25'; 65 of the 103-man crew, as well as one of the 11-man Armed Guard and 20 of 46 passengers, perish in the attack. Freighter *Norlago* rescues 44 survivors; Coast Guard cutter *Escanaba* (WPG 77) rescues 39 more.

CARIBBEAN. Gunboat *Erie* (PG 50), off St. Andrews Island, rescues master and 22 survivors of U.S. bulk carrier *Lebore*, which had been sunk by German submarine U 172 the day before. *Erie* embarks the merchant sailors at 12°39'N, 81°20'W, and then sinks their lifeboat with gunfire as a menace to navigation.

U.S. freighter *Tillie Lykes* is torpedoed (most likely) by German submarine U 502 approximately 150 miles east-southeast of Punta Herrero, Mexico, 19°00'N, 85°00'W; there are no survivors from the 29-man merchant crew and four-man Armed Guard.

Unarmed U.S. freighter *Arkansan* is sunk by German submarine U 126 west of Grenada, 12°07'N, 62°51'W; four of the ship's 40-man complement are lost (see 16 June).

16 Tuesday

CARIBBEAN. Gunboat *Erie* (PG 50) and destroyer *Tattnall* (DD 125), south of St. Andrews Island, rescue survivors of U.S. bulk carrier *Lebore*, which had been sunk by German submarine U 172 on 14 June. Among those rescued are the eight Armed Guard sailors from *Lebore* and the 49 survivors of the Dutch steamship *Crijnssen*, which *Lebore* had rescued on 11 June when U 504 had sunk the Netherlands-flag ship at 18°14'N, 85°11'W.

Submarine chaser PC 460 rescues 42 survivors from U.S. steamship *Sixaola*, sunk by German submarine U 159 off the coast of Panama on 12 June.

Provision stores ship *Pastores* (AF 16) rescues 36 survivors of U.S. freighter *Arkansan*, sunk by German submarine U 126 the day before.

ATLANTIC. U.S. freighter *Kahuku*, torpedoed by U 126 the previous day, sinks; six of her 36-man crew as well as three of her 10-man Armed Guard perish in the attack. Lost as well are nine passengers: six of the 46 survivors from U.S. freighter *Scottsburg*, sunk by U 161 on 15 June, and three of the 17 survivors of Panamanian steamer *Cold Harbor*, sunk by U 502 the same day. Coastal yacht *Opal* (PYc 8) and district patrol vessel YP 63 rescue the 91 survivors from the three ships.

MEDITERRANEAN. Operation HARPOON: Of the six ships in convoy WS 19Z, only two reach Malta; two escorting destroyers are lost, while a light cruiser, three destroyers, and a minesweeper suffer varying degrees of damage.

17 Wednesday

ATLANTIC. German submarine U 202 puts four agents ashore on Ponte Vedra Beach, south of Jacksonville, Florida; fishermen discover the landing. Subsequently, FBI agents capture the Germans (see 8 August).

U.S. freighter *Columbian* is attacked by what she believes is a German submarine at 07°18'N, 41°03'W; although the ship is damaged by shell fragments and machine gun fire, Armed Guard gunfire drives off her attacker without further incident. *Columbian* suffers no casualties among her 42-man merchant complement or 17-man Armed Guard.

U.S. freighter *Millinocket* is sunk by German submarine U 129 off the north coast of Cuba, 23°12'N, 79°58'W; nine of 29 merchant seamen perish, as do two of the six-man Armed Guard. U 129's captain briefly questions the survivors and then provides the Americans with a first aid kit for the wounded (see 18 June).

U.S. collier *Santore*, in convoy KS 511, strikes mine laid by German submarine U 701 off Virginia Beach, Virginia, 36°52'N, 75°51'W; three merchant seaman are lost. Survivors (34 merchant sailors and the nine-man Armed Guard) are rescued by the Coast Guard.

CARIBBEAN. Survivors (37 merchant seamen and 13 Armed Guard sailors) from U.S. freighter *West Hardaway*, sunk by German submarine U 502 on 15 June, reach Margarita Island, Venezuela.

18 Thursday

PACIFIC. USAAF B-17s, B-24s, and an LB-30 (11th Air Force) bomb Japanese shipping in

Kiska Harbor, sinking fleet tanker *Nissan Maru*, 51°58′N, 177°40′E.

Japanese cargo ship *Tairyu Maru* is stranded and wrecked off Gyoji Island, Korea, 34°33′N, 125°53′E.

ATLANTIC. U.S. freighter *Seattle Spirit* is torpedoed by German submarine *U 124* at 50°23′N, 42°25′W; four merchant seamen perish in the attack. Survivors (33 merchant sailors, the 11-man Armed Guard, and seven passengers) are rescued by steamship *Perth* and Canadian corvette HMCS *Agassiz*. *Agassiz* scuttles the irreparably damaged merchantman with gunfire.

Cuban boats rescue survivors of U.S. freighter *Millinocket*, sunk by German submarine *U 129* the previous day.

Naval Air Facility, La Fe, Cuba, is established.

19 Friday

PACIFIC. Vice Admiral Robert L. Ghormley assumes command of South Pacific Area and South Pacific Force with headquarters at Auckland, New Zealand.

Submarine *S 27* (SS 132) runs aground off St. Makarius Point, Amchitka, Aleutians; all hands reach safety ashore. Crew, provisions, clothing, guns, and medical supplies are ferried ashore by rubber boat (see 20 June).

Seaplane tender (destroyer) *Ballard* (AVD 10), directed to the scene by a PBY (VP 11), rescues 35 survivors (one of whom dies shortly after rescue) from Japanese carrier *Hiryu* that had been scuttled on 5 June. They had been members of the engineering department, left below for dead in the abandonment of the ship.

USAAF B-17s (5th Air Force) bomb harbor facilities and airfield at Rabaul, New Britain; water carrier *Wayo Maru* is damaged in the raid.

ATLANTIC. District patrol vessel *YP 389* is sunk by German submarine *U 701* five to six miles northeast of Buoy No. 4, Cape Hatteras mine area, North Carolina.

CARIBBEAN. U.S. schooner *Cheerio* is shelled by German submarine *U 161* approximately eight miles southeast of Mona Island, Puerto Rico, 18°02′N, 67°40′W; patrol plane interrupts *U 161*'s attack but not in time to prevent the U-boat from inflicting irreparable damage. All hands (nine men) survive the attack; Coast Guard cutter *CG 459* rescues them with the help of a second patrol plane that arrives on the scene.

Tug *Crusader Kingston* rescues the last three survivors from a raft from U.S. freighter *Norlantic*, sunk by German submarine *U 69* on 13 May.

20 Saturday

PACIFIC. Japanese submarine *I 26* shells Estevan Point, Vancouver Island, British Columbia.

Submarine *S 27* (SS 132) crew reaches deserted village at Constantine Harbor, Amchitka, Aleutians, and inhabit it until rescue comes (see 23 June).

ATLANTIC. U.S. freighter *West Ira* is sunk by German submarine *U 128* about 120 miles southeast of Barbados, 12°04′N, 57°35′W. One man of *West Ira*'s merchant complement of 48 is killed; there are no casualties among the 10-man Armed Guard. Survivors are for the most part rescued between three and five days later; the last survivor comes ashore on 1 July at Barbados.

21 Sunday

PACIFIC. PBY (VP 24) recovers two-man crew from *Enterprise* (CV 6) TBD (VT 6) 360 miles north of Midway. Their plane had to land in the water on 4 June; these are the last survivors of the Battle of Midway to be recovered.

Submarine *S 44* (SS 155) sinks Japanese gunboat *Keijo Maru* 12 miles west of Gavutu, Solomons, 09°00′S, 160°00′E.

Japanese submarine *I 25* shells Fort Stevens, Oregon.

ARCTIC. U.S. freighter *Alcoa Cadet* is mined in Kola Inlet, Murmansk, USSR, and breaks in two. Ships in the vicinity rescue the survivors (33 merchant seamen and 10 passengers).

22 Monday

CARIBBEAN. Unarmed U.S. tanker *E. J. Sadler* is shelled by German submarine *U 159* about 175 miles south of the Windward Passage, 15°36′N, 67°52′W, and abandoned. After the 36 survivors take to their lifeboats, a boarding party from *U 159* sinks the tanker with demolition charges (see 23 June).

GULF OF MEXICO. Unarmed U.S. tanker *Rawleigh Warner* is torpedoed by German submarine *U 67* approximately 40 miles south of South Pass, Louisiana, 28°53′N, 89°15′W; ignition of the ship's cargo of 38,909 barrels of gasoline incinerates the ship and her crew. There are no survivors from the 33-man complement of merchant seamen.

23 Tuesday

PACIFIC. PBY on routine search spots submarine *S 27* (SS 132) crew at Constantine Harbor, Amchitka; 15 men are transported out (see 24 June).

CARIBBEAN. Destroyer *Biddle* (DD 151), directed to the scene by PBYs, rescues the 36 survivors of U.S. tanker *E. J. Sadler*, sunk the day before by German submarine *U 159*.

24 Wednesday

PACIFIC. Three PBYs bring out remainder of submarine *S 27* (SS 132)'s crew from Constantine Harbor, Amchitka.

ATLANTIC. British freighter *Port Darwin* runs aground off Fenwick Island Shoal; tug *John R. Williams* (Navy Rescue Tug Service) refloats the ship and, her task complete, shapes course for Cape May, New Jersey. En route, however, *John R. Williams* is sunk by mine (laid by German submarine *U 373* on 11 June) at 38°45′N, 74°55′W. District patrol vessel *YP 334* rescues the four survivors of the 14-man crew and transports them to Lewes, Delaware.[104]

U.S. freighter *Manuela* is torpedoed by German submarine *U 404* at 34°30′N, 75°40′W, and abandoned. Three of the 36-man merchant complement perish in the attack. The survivors, 33 merchant seamen and the six-man Armed Guard, are rescued by British armed trawler HMS *Norwich City* and Coast Guard cutter *CGC 483*. *Manuela* sinks the following day while being towed to Morehead City, North Carolina, by tug *P. F. Martin* (Navy Rescue Tug Service).

25 Thursday

GENERAL. President Roosevelt and British Prime Minister Winston S. Churchill conclude conference in Washington, D.C.; decision is reached for combined U.S.-British research and development of the atomic bomb.

PACIFIC. Carrier *Saratoga* (CV 3) ferries 25 USAAF P-40s (73rd Fighter Squadron) to Midway to provide fighter defense for the atoll, after the heavy losses suffered by VMF 221 during the Battle of Midway on 4 June. *Saratoga* also brings in 18 SBDs to bring VMSB 241 (also badly battered on 4–5 June) up to strength.

Submarine *Nautilus* (SS 168) sinks Japanese destroyer *Yamakaze* southeast of Yokosuka, Japan, 34°34′N, 140°26′E.

Submarine *Grouper* (SS 214) damages Japanese oiler *No. 3 Tonan Maru* east of the Ryukyus, 28°46′N, 136°36′E.

PBYs (VP 71) bomb Japanese base at Tulagi, Solomons; Rear Admiral John S. McCain (Commander Aircraft South Pacific Force) is present in one of the flying boats to observe operations.

EUROPE. U.S. Army establishes European Theater of Operations under Major General Dwight D. Eisenhower.

ATLANTIC. Norwegian freighter *Tamesis* is torpedoed by German submarine *U 701* off Cape Hatteras, North Carolina, 34°59′N, 75°41′W; tug *P. F. Martin* (NRTS) and salvage vessel *Relief* (NRTS) beach the damaged merchantman off Okracoke Inlet; she is later salvaged.

26 Friday
ATLANTIC. Naval Auxiliary Air Station (Lighter-than-Air), San Julian, Cuba, is established.

Germany announces unrestricted submarine warfare off U.S. Atlantic Coast.

27 Saturday
PACIFIC. Submarine *Nautilus* (SS 168) sinks Japanese auxiliary minesweeper *Musashi Maru* east of Nojima Saki, Japan, 34°38′N, 140°08′E.

ATLANTIC. Unarmed U.S. freighter *Polybius* is torpedoed by German submarine *U 128* at 11°00′N, 57°30′W; 10 crewmen perish. *U 128*'s officers briefly question the survivors before the submarine departs. The 34 survivors are rescued over the next three days: by Dutch steamship *Dracos* on 28 June; an unidentified Allied ship on the 29th; and British steamship *Clarona* on the 30th.

U.S. freighter *Potlatch* is torpedoed by German submarine *U 153* at 19°20′N, 53°18′W; six crewmen perish. Of the 39-man crew, 33 survive, as do the 16 Armed Guard sailors. *U 153* briefly questions the survivors and provides them with cigarettes before departing (see 29 July).

28 Sunday
PACIFIC. Submarine *Nautilus* (SS 168) is damaged by depth charges off central Honshu, 34°34′N, 140°13′E.

Submarine *Stingray* (SS 186), attacking Japanese convoy, sinks gunboat *Saikyo Maru* about 190 miles north of Yap, Carolines, 12°41′N, 136°22′E; cargo ship *Meiten Maru* fires at *Stingray*'s periscope without effect.

PBYs (VP 14) bomb Japanese base at Tulagi.

ATLANTIC. Unarmed U.S. freighter *Raphael Semmes* is sunk by German submarine *U 332* at 29°30′N, 64°30′W; 18 men from the 35-man crew, and one of the two passengers, perish. *U 332* remains in the vicinity of the sinking, providing medical assistance and supplies to the survivors before departing (see 16 July).

U.S. freighter *Sam Houston* is sunk by German submarine *U 203* at 19°21′N, 62°22′W; three crewmen perish. *U 203* briefly embarks the freighter's master for questioning but returns him to a lifeboat before departing (see 30 June).

U.S. tanker *William Rockefeller* is sunk by German submarine *U 701* approximately 16 miles northeast of Diamond Shoals, North Carolina, 35°07′N, 75°07′W; escorting Coast Guard cutter *CGC 470*, which attacks the U-boat without success, rescues all hands: 44 merchant seamen and the six-man Armed Guard.

U.S. freighter *Sea Thrush*, en route to Cape Town, South Africa, is sunk by German submarine *U 505* at 22°40′N, 61°26′W. All hands survive the loss of the ship: 42-man crew, 11-man Armed Guard, and 14 passengers (see 30 June).

U.S. freighter *Ruth* is sunk by German submarine *U 153* about 100 miles north of Cape Maysi, Cuba, 21°44′N, 74°05′W. *U 153* rescues one survivor and places him on a raft with three of his shipmates; they are the only survivors from a crew of 34 men. There are no survivors from the four-man Armed Guard unit (see 4 July).

29 Monday
ATLANTIC. U.S. freighter *Thomas McKean*, en route to Cape Town, South Africa, is sunk by German submarine *U 505* at 22°00′N, 60°00′W. Three Armed Guard sailors are killed in the shelling and torpedoing. *U 505* provides medical attention to the wounded in the lifeboats before departing (see 4, 12, and 14 July).

30 Tuesday
UNITED STATES. Naval ships and craft on hand (all types)—5,612. People: Navy—640,570; Marine Corps—143,528; Coast Guard—58,998. Total—843,096.

PACIFIC. Submarine *Plunger* (SS 179) sinks Japanese freighter *No. 5 Unkai Maru* off the China coast near approaches to Shanghai, 30°04′N, 122°54′E.

XPBS-1 transporting Admiral Chester W. Nimitz, Commander in Chief Pacific Fleet, and his staff to San Francisco crashes upon landing off Alameda, California. Nimitz suffers scratches and abrasions in the mishap but remains topside on the wreckage to direct rescue operations, refusing to leave that post until the wrecked flying boat has been searched for survivors.

Coastal minesweeper *Hornbill* (AMc 13) is sunk in collision with U.S. lumber schooner *Esther Johnson* in San Francisco Bay, California.

District patrol vessel *YP 270* sinks after running aground at Boca, Santo Domingo, while en route from San Diego, California, to the Panama Canal Zone, 25°30′N, 112°06′W.

District patrol vessel *YP 128* sinks after running aground in heavy weather three miles northeast of Monterey, California.

INDIAN OCEAN. U.S. freighter *Express*, en route from Bombay, India, to Cape Town, South Africa, is sunk by Japanese submarine *I 10* at 23°30′S, 37°30′E; one lifeboat is swamped when the ship is abandoned, and two Armed Guard sailors and 11 merchant seamen are lost. Forty-one survivors reach Mozambique six days later; one survivor is rescued by a Dutch tanker and disembarks at Cape Town.

ATLANTIC. PBM (VP 74) sinks German submarine *U 158* west-southwest of Bermuda, 32°50′N, 67°28′W.

U.S. steamship *City of Birmingham*, en route to Bermuda, is sunk by German submarine *U 202* about 250 miles east of Cape Hatteras, North Carolina, 35°04′N, 61°01′W; six of the 113-man crew and two of 263 passengers are lost in the sinking. Escorting high-speed minesweeper *Stansbury* (DMS 8), after depth charging *U 202*, rescues 107 merchant seamen (one of whom dies of his injuries), 261 passengers, and the five-man Armed Guard.

Coastal minesweeper *Courier* (AMc 72) rescues 30 merchant seamen (four wounded men have perished in the lifeboats) and the nine-man Armed Guard from U.S. freighter *Sam Houston*, sunk by German submarine *U 203* on 28 June. One crewman dies of wounds subsequently. *Courier* transports the survivors to St. Thomas, Virgin Islands.

Gunboat *Surprise* (PG 63) rescues survivors from U.S. freighter *Sea Thrush*, sunk by German submarine *U 505* on 28 June. A second group of survivors reaches St. Thomas, Virgin Islands, on 3 July.

JULY

1 Wednesday
PACIFIC. Submarine *Sturgeon* (SS 187) sinks Japanese transport *Montevideo Maru* about 65 miles west of Cape Bojeador, Luzon, 18°37′N, 119°29′E. Unbeknown to the submariners, *Montevideo Maru* is transporting 1,050 Allied POWs to Hainan Island.

ARCTIC. Convoy PQ 17 sails from Seidisfjord, Iceland, bound for North Russia. Among the U.S. naval vessels in the close covering force that had departed Reykjavik, Iceland, the previous day are heavy cruisers *Wichita* (CA 45) and *Tuscaloosa* (CA 37) and destroyers *Wainwright* (DD 419) and *Rowan* (DD 405) (see 4 July).

ATLANTIC. U.S. freighter *Warrior* is sunk by German submarine *U 126* just north of Trinidad, 10°54′N, 61°01′W; three of the 42-man crew and four of the 14-man Armed Guard are lost. Survivors are rescued and transported to Trinidad.

GULF OF MEXICO. U.S. freighter *Edward Luckenbach* blunders into U.S. minefield off Smith Shoal, Florida, and strikes two mines, 24°56′N, 81°53′W; one of the 42-man merchant complement perishes in the incident. The ship sinks with the superstructure above water. The 41 merchant seamen and the 12-man Armed Guard reboard the ship the next day and are transported to Key West by patrol craft.

2 Thursday

PACIFIC. Submarine *Plunger* (SS 179), attacking Japanese convoy off the mouth of the Yangtze, sinks army cargo ship *No. 3 Unyo Maru*, 30°44′N, 123°09′E.

Japanese guardboats *No. 1 Kaiyo Maru* and *No. 2 Kaiyo Maru* are wrecked (cause unknown) off Guadalcanal.

3 Friday

PACIFIC. USAAF B-24s (11th Air Force) bomb and damage Japanese seaplane carriers *Kamikawa Maru* and *Kimikawa Maru* and transport *Fujisan Maru* off Agattu Island, Aleutians.

British submarine HMS *Truant* sinks Japanese army cargo ship *No. 1 Tamon Maru* in Strait of Malacca, 3°14′N, 99°48′E.

ATLANTIC. U.S. tanker *Gulfbelle* is torpedoed by German submarine *U 126* about 21 miles north of Tobago, 11°43′N, 60°35′W, and is abandoned. Two crewmen perish on board in the explosion. The U-boat surfaces after torpedoing her quarry, but after the Armed Guard (eight men, all have remained on board) lobs one shell over *U 126*, the enemy boat submerges and departs. British destroyer HMS *Warwick* subsequently tows the damaged *Gulfbelle* to Trinidad.

U.S. freighter *Alexander Macomb*, in convoy BA 2, is sunk by German submarine *U 215* at 41°40′N, 66°52′W; four of the ship's 41-man crew and six of the 25-man Armed Guard are killed in the attack. British trawler HMS *Le Tiger* rescues 31 survivors; Canadian corvette HMCS *Regina* rescues 25.

Unarmed U.S. freighter *Norlandia*, steaming from San Juan, Puerto Rico, to Nuevitas, Cuba, is sunk by German submarine *U 575* at 19°33′N, 68°39′W; nine crewmen lose their lives. *U 575*'s commander, *Kapitänleutnant* Günther Heydemann, apparently genuinely solicitous of the needs of the survivors of the ship he has just torpedoed, gives them a bottle of brandy before departing (see 4 and 5 July).

4 Saturday

PACIFIC. Submarine *Triton* (SS 201) torpedoes Japanese destroyer *Nenohi* off Cape Sabak, off southeast tip of Agattu, Aleutians, 52°15′N, 173°51′E.

Japanese Second Reinforcement Convoy, formed around seaplane carrier *Chiyoda* (carrying floatplanes and midget submarines) and transport *Argentina Maru*, reaches Kiska; fog forces escorting destroyers to anchor in Salmon Lagoon (see 5 July).

ARCTIC. Convoy PQ 17 is ordered to scatter as fears of a German surface ship sortie from Norwegian waters prompts the detachment of major escort vessels to deal with the threat that does not materialize. German torpedo-carrying HE 111s attack PQ 17, 200 miles northeast of Bear Island, USSR. U.S. freighter *William Hooper* is torpedoed (75°57′N, 27°14′E) and abandoned; three crewmen lose their lives. The survivors (36 merchant seamen and the 15-man Armed Guard) are picked up by British rescue ships *Rathlin* and *Zamalek*. Attempted scuttling by escort vessel fails; German submarine *U 334* torpedoes and sinks *William Hooper* later the same day. As the convoy disperses, freighter *Christopher Newport* is torpedoed by HE 115 (75°49′N, 22°15′E); three crewmen are killed. *Christopher Newport* is abandoned, with the 36 merchant seamen and 11-man Armed Guard picked up by rescue ship *Zamalek*. British escort vessel's attempt to scuttle the damaged freighter fails (see 5 July). Freighter *Washington* is damaged by near-misses, but there are no casualties among her crew or Armed Guard.

ATLANTIC. Destroyer *Corry* (DD 463) rescues four survivors of U.S. freighter *Ruth*, sunk by German submarine *U 153* on 28 June.

Twenty-nine survivors from U.S. freighter *Thomas McKean*, sunk by German submarine *U 505* on 29 June, reach St. Thomas, Virgin Islands (see 12 and 14 July).

Fourteen survivors from U.S. freighter *Norlandia*, sunk by German submarine *U 575* the previous day, reach Samana, Dominican Republic (see 5 July).

EUROPE. First USAAF raid on Western Europe: USAAF aircrew flying American-built Bostons participate in low-level RAF raid on German airfields in The Netherlands, starting fires at installations at Haanstead and strafing dispersed fighters at Daltonburg.

5 Sunday

PACIFIC. Submarine *Growler* (SS 215) torpedoes Japanese destroyers in Salmon Lagoon, off Kiska, sinking *Arare* and damaging *Kasumi* and *Shiranui*, 52°00′N, 177°40′E. *Growler* is damaged by depth charges but remains on patrol.

Submarine *Sturgeon* (SS 187) damages Japanese oiler *San Pedro Maru* south of Palauig, Luzon, 16°07′N, 119°13′E.

ATLANTIC. Seven survivors from U.S. freighter *Norlandia*, sunk by German submarine *U 575* on 3 July, reach Samana, Dominican Republic.

ARCTIC. German air and submarine attacks on the dispersed convoy PQ 17 continue. Submarine *U 457* sinks abandoned U.S. freighter *Christopher Newport*, torpedoed the previous day. *U 88* sinks U.S. freighter *Carlton*, 72°50′N, 24°35′E, killing two crewmen (see 13, 14, and 24 July). Freighter *Peter Kerr*, steaming in company with steamship *Earlston Smiles*, suffers three direct bomb hits, 74°30′N, 35°00′E; the burning ship is abandoned by the 35 merchant seamen and the 11-man Armed Guard (see 12 July). Freighter *Daniel Morgan*, steaming in company with four other ships for mutual protection that proves largely illusory, is bombed and is damaged by 30 near-misses; although emerging battered from the bombing, she does not escape *U 88*, which torpedoes and sinks her, 75°08′N, 44°10′E. *Daniel Morgan*'s survivors (37 of 39 merchant seamen, one of whom dies later of his injuries, and the 15-man Armed Guard) are rescued later by Soviet tanker *Donbass* and ultimately reach Archangel, USSR. Nearby freighter *Fairfield City* is also bombed, 74°40′N, 39°45′E; eight men die when one bomber scores a direct hit on the merchantman's bridge. Irreparably damaged, *Fairfield City* is abandoned by the 28 merchant seamen and the six-man Armed Guard (see 9 and 12 July). Freighter *Washington*, steaming in company with Dutch *Paulus Potter* and British *Bolton Castle*, is attacked by JU-88s 175 miles east-northeast of Bear Island, 76°25′N, 33°41′E; after attacking the other two vessels, the Germans direct their efforts at *Washington*, and near-misses cause further

While her lifeboats pull away (left), U.S. freighter *Carlton* sinks by the bow in the Barents Sea, 5 July 1942, as seen from German submarine *U 88*. (NHC, NH 71304)

damage to hull plates weakened the day before. The 36-man crew and nine-man Armed Guard abandon ship in lifeboats, and decide to take their chances in the boats instead of being taken on board freighter *Olopana*, which arrives in response to *Washington*'s call for help (see 7 and 12 July). Freighter *Honomu*, steaming alone, is sunk by *U 456*, 75°05'N, 38°00'E; the latter takes the ship's master prisoner and provides rations for the survivors (34 crewmen, four British armed guard sailors, and two Navy signalmen) before departing (see 18 and 22 July). Freighter *Pan Kraft*, steaming alone, is bombed by German planes, 76°50'N, 38°00'E, and is abandoned; one crewman dies during the abandonment, a second dies of wounds later. British corvette HMS *Lotus* rescues the 34 merchant seamen and the 11-man Armed Guard, but fails in her attempt to scuttle the merchantman, which ultimately explodes and sinks between nine and 36 hours after she is abandoned (see 6 July and 22 September).

Convoy QP 13, meanwhile, groping its way through poor visibility conditions, blunders into a British minefield in Denmark Strait. U.S. freighter *Richard Henry Lee* is damaged but suffers no casualties among her 34-man crew and nine-man Armed Guard. U.S. freighter *Massmar* sinks; 17 of the ship's

36-man crew and five of her nine-man Armed Guard perish, as do 26 (22 merchant seamen and four Armed Guard sailors) of the 45 passengers she is carrying—survivors of freighter *Alamar* (sunk in convoy PQ 16 on 27 June). Free French corvette *Roselys* rescues survivors. U.S. freighter *Hybert* is abandoned and as all hands (39-man crew, 11-man Armed Guard, and 26 passengers from *Syros*, which was sunk on 26 June) abandon ship, the merchantman drifts into a second mine. British armed trawler HMS *Lady Madeleine* and *Roselys* rescue the survivors. U.S. freighter *John Randolph* breaks in two; five of the 38-man crew perish in the incident, but none of the 12 passengers or the 12-man Armed Guard are lost. Other ships in QP 13 rescue the survivors. *John Randolph*'s bow section is recovered and salvaged; the stern section sinks. U.S. freighter *Heffron* is abandoned; one crewman dies in the abandonment. *Roselys* rescues the 36 crewmen, two Navy signalmen, and 23 passengers. *Heffron* sinks very early the next morning.

6 Monday
ARCTIC. Ordeal of dispersed convoy PQ 17 to German submarines and planes continues. U.S. freighter *John Witherspoon*, having emerged unscathed from the German aerial attacks the previous several days, is sunk by

German submarine *U 255* approximately 20 miles off Novaya Zemlya, USSR, 72°05'N, 48°30'E, and abandoned with the loss of one merchant seaman. Survivors (38 merchant seamen and 11 Armed Guard sailors) gather in three lifeboats and a raft; *U 255* surfaces and conducts a brief interrogation of some of the survivors before clearing the area (see 8 and 9 July 1942). Freighter *Pan Atlantic*, hastily painted white to camouflage her against the ice floes through which she is fleeing to Archangel, USSR, is bombed and sunk with the loss of 18 (of 37) merchant seamen and seven (of 11) Armed Guard sailors. German submarines *U 88* and *U 703* salvage provisions from the freighter's flotsam; one of the enemy submarines conducts brief interrogation of survivors before departing. British corvette HMS *Lotus* rescues *Pan Atlantic*'s surviving merchant and naval complement and transports them, along with *Pan Kraft*'s survivors, to Archangel (see 22 September).

7 Tuesday
PACIFIC. Japanese freighter *Haruna Maru* founders and sinks near Omae Saki, Japan.

ATLANTIC. Naval Air Facility, Reykjavik, Iceland, is established.

USAAF A-29 sinks German submarine *U 701* off North Carolina coast, 34°50'N, 74°55'W—the first submarine "kill" by a USAAF plane in World War II.

GULF OF MEXICO. U.S. tanker *Paul H. Harwood* is torpedoed by German submarine *U 67* off Southwest Pass, Louisiana, 29°26'N, 88°38'W; there are no casualties among the 40-man crew or 16-man Armed Guard, and the ship puts into Burrwood, Louisiana, under her own power. She returns to service in September.

ARCTIC. Ordeal of dispersed USSR-bound convoy PQ 17 to German submarines and planes continues. U.S. freighter *Olopana* is torpedoed by German submarine *U 255* about 10 miles west of Novaya Zemlya, 72°10'N, 51°00'E, and abandoned; five merchant seamen and two Armed Guard sailors perish in the attack. *U 255* then surfaces and shells the ship, after which time the Germans conduct a brief interrogation of some of the survivors before clearing the area (see 9 July). U.S. freighter *Alcoa Ranger* is torpedoed by German submarine *U 255* at 71°38'N, 49°35'E, and abandoned by the 34-man crew and the six-man Armed Guard. *U 255* surfaces and conducts a brief interrogation of some of the survivors, as she had done in the case of *John*

Witherspoon and *Olopana* earlier, before the U-boat shells and sinks the ship. Two of three lifeboats from *Alcoa Ranger* reach Novaya Zemlya later that day (see 14 July).

8 Wednesday

PACIFIC. Submarine *S 37* (SS 142) sinks Japanese transport *Tenzan Maru* about 30 miles west of Rabaul, 04°00'S, 151°50'E. Escorting submarine chaser *Ch 30* depth charges *S 37* without success.

ARCTIC. Ordeal of dispersed USSR-bound convoy PQ 17 to German submarines and planes continues. Nineteen survivors (16 merchant seamen and three Armed Guard sailors) of U.S. freighter *John Witherspoon* (sunk by German submarine *U 255* on 6 July) are rescued by Panamanian freighter *El Capitan*. German bombers, however, attack the latter and sink her. British armed trawler HMS *Lord Austin* rescues the 19 *John Witherspoon* men and takes them to Archangel, USSR.

ATLANTIC. U.S. tanker *J. A. Moffett Jr.* is torpedoed by German submarine *U 571* three miles south by west of Tennessee Reef, Florida Straits, 24°47'N, 80°42'W; and is run aground on Tennessee Reef to prevent the ship's loss. The ship's master is the only fatality; the survivors (36 merchant seamen and the six-man Armed Guard) are rescued by Coast Guard auxiliary crafts *Mary Jane* and *Southbound* and cutter *Nike* (WPC 112). Later salvaged, *J. A. Moffett Jr.* is written off as a total loss.

9 Thursday

PACIFIC. Submarine *Sailfish* (SS 192) damages Japanese army cargo ship *Aobasan Maru* off the coast of French Indochina, 11°31'N, 109°21'E.

Submarine *Thresher* (SS 200) sinks Japanese torpedo recovery vessel *Shinshu Maru* at entrance to Kwajalein Atoll, Marshalls, 08°43'N, 167°33'E. *Thresher* is damaged by bombs and depth charges and is briefly hooked by a grapnel trailed by the searching Japanese, but escapes and remains on patrol.

GULF OF MEXICO. U.S. tanker *Benjamin Brewster* is torpedoed by German submarine *U 67* approximately 60 miles west of Southwest Pass, Louisiana, 29°05'N, 90°05'W, and a good portion of the ship's cargo of 70,578 barrels of aviation gasoline and lubricating oil catches fire. In the resulting conflagration, 25 crewmen die. Survivors (10 merchant seamen and the five-man Armed Guard) are rescued the following morning by fishing boat, whence they are transferred to the Coast Guard.

ATLANTIC. U.S. freighter *Santa Rita* is torpedoed by German submarine *U 172* approximately 700 miles northeast of Puerto Rico, 26°11'N, 55°40'W, and abandoned; three men are killed in the torpedoing, a fourth drowns during the abandonment. *U 172* then shells the ship, makes the master a POW, and sends a boarding party to scour her victim for provisions before shelling and sinking her. Destroyers *Livermore* (DD 429) and *Mayo* (DD 422) and a crash boat rescue the 48 merchant seamen, two passengers, and the nine-man Armed Guard who survive the loss of the vessel.

ARCTIC. Ordeal of dispersed USSR-bound convoy PQ 17 to German submarines and planes continues. U.S. freighter *Hoosier* is straddled by bombs and damaged irreparably, 69°45'N, 39°35'E. The 42-man crew and 11-man Armed Guard abandon ship and are rescued by British corvette HMS *Poppy*. Corvette HMS *La Malouine* takes the crippled merchantman in tow, but discontinues the operation and recovers her salvage party put on board the freighter earlier when the escort vessel sights German submarine *U 255* trailing four miles away. *La Malouine*'s attempt to scuttle the freighter fails. *U 376* later finishes off *Hoosier* with a torpedo, and the latter sinks early the following morning. Survivors from U.S. freighters *Fairfield City* (sunk on 5 July) and *Olopana* (sunk on 7 July) reach Novaya Zemlya (see 12 July). *La Malouine* rescues 22 merchant seamen and eight Armed Guards, survivors from U.S. freighter *John Witherspoon* (sunk by German submarine *U 255* on 6 July).

10 Friday

PACIFIC. PBYs (VP 14) attempt to bomb Japanese bases at Tulagi and Gavutu in the Solomons, but bad weather prompts cancellation of the mission (see 13 July).

PBY (VP 41), returning from a routine patrol, sights Mitsubishi A6M2 type 0 carrier fighter upside-down in a bog on Akutan Island, Aleutians, where it has been since its forced landing on 3 June (see 12 July).

12 Sunday

PACIFIC. Submarine *Seadragon* (SS 194) sinks Japanese freighter *Nichizan Maru* off Cam Ranh Bay, French Indochina, 13°47'N, 109°33'E.

Salvage party from VP 41, transported to Akutan Island, Aleutians, in district patrol vessel *YP 151*, begins salvage of ZERO fighter discovered on 10 July. Initial efforts reveal more work will be required (see 15 July).

ATLANTIC. Twelve survivors from U.S. freighter *Thomas McKean*, sunk by German submarine *U 505* on 29 June, reach Antigua (see 14 July).

U.S. freighter *Andrew Jackson* is sunk by German submarine *U 84* approximately 20 miles off Cardenas, Cuba, 23°32'N, 81°02'W. Three of the 38-man crew perish; there are no casualties among the 11-man Armed Guard (see 13 July).

CARIBBEAN. U.S. freighter *Tachira*, en route to New Orleans, Louisiana, is sunk by German submarine *U 129* at 18°15'N, 81°54'W. Four of the 32-man crew perish, as does one of the six-man Armed Guard; *U 129* briefly interrogates survivors and then provides medical assistance and directs them toward the nearest land (see 16 July).

ARCTIC. Survivors from U.S. freighter *Peter Kerr* (sunk on 5 July) are rescued by Soviet motor torpedo boat and taken to Murmansk. Soviet whaler rescues survivors of U.S. freighter *Washington* (also sunk on 5 July). Toward the end of their journey by lifeboat, *Washington*'s survivors (one of whom dies of exposure on 28 July at Archangel, USSR) had subsisted on rations scrounged from U.S. freighter *Winston-Salem* that had been beached by her crew and abandoned on the shores of Novaya Zemlya. British armed trawler HMS *Ayrshire* rescues survivors from U.S. freighter *Fairfield City* (sunk on 5 July) from Novaya Zemlya.

13 Monday

PACIFIC. Submarine *Seadragon* (SS 194) sinks Japanese auxiliary vessel *Shinyo Maru* 10 miles northeast of Cape Varella, French Indochina, 13°05'N, 109°29'E.

PBYs (VP 71) attempt daylight bombing of Japanese bases at Tulagi and Gavutu in the Solomons, but bad weather forces a second straight cancellation of the mission.

Japanese transport *No. 3 Mikage Maru* is sunk in collision three miles south of Tsuru Jima, Japan, 33°00'N, 133°00'E.

Japanese Combined Fleet is reorganized in the wake of the disastrous defeat suffered at Midway; Vice Admiral Nagumo Chuichi (formerly commander of the First Air Fleet) becomes commander of the newly reconstituted Third Fleet.

CARIBBEAN. Submarine *S 16* (SS 121) is accidentally damaged by USAAF plane off coast of Panama.

German submarine *U 153*, damaged by submarine chaser *PC 458* and USAAF plane off coast of Panama, is sunk by destroyer *Lansdowne* (DD 486), 09°56'N, 81°29'W.

Naval Air Facility, Grand Cayman, British West Indies, is established.

ATLANTIC. Unarmed U.S. freighter *Oneida*, straggling from convoy NG 359, is sunk by German submarine *U 166* approximately two miles north of Cape Maysi, Cuba, at 20°17′N, 74°06′W. Six crewmen perish; the 23 survivors reach the Cuban coast in two life rafts.

Survivors from U.S. freighter *Andrew Jackson*, sunk by German submarine *U 84* the day before, reach Vavendero, Cuba, by lifeboat.

GULF OF MEXICO. U.S. tanker *R. W. Gallagher* is sunk by German submarine *U 67* approximately 80 miles from Southwest Pass, Louisiana, 28°32′N, 90°59′W, and abandoned. Eight of the ship's 40-man merchant complement die in the attack, as do two of the 12-man Armed Guard. Coast Guard cutter *Boutwell* (WPC 130) rescues survivors; two men later die of their injuries.

ARCTIC. Survivors of U.S. freighter *Carlton* (sunk by *U 88* on 5 July) receive rations dropped by a British plane (see 14 and 24 July).

14 Tuesday

ATLANTIC. Last 13 survivors (a 14th had perished in the interval between the loss of the ship and the survivors making landfall) from U.S. freighter *Thomas McKean*, sunk by German submarine *U 505* on 29 June, reach the Dominican Republic.

ARCTIC. German submarine *U 376* comes upon survivors of U.S. freighter *Carlton* (sunk by *U 88* on 5 July). While the German offer of medical help is turned down, the enemy sailors give the Americans rations, blankets, and cigarettes (see 24 July).

One boat full of survivors of U.S. freighter *Alcoa Ranger*, sunk by *U 255* on 7 July, reaches Cape Kanin, USSR. Soviet patrol craft subsequently take the men to Archangel.

PACIFIC. Unarmed U.S. freighter *Arcata*, steaming from Bethel, Alaska, to Seattle, Washington, is sunk by Japanese submarine *I 7* at 53°35′N, 157°40′W. Seven of the 29-man crew perish; three Navy and one civilian passenger survive the attack. *I 7* machine guns the life rafts; one sailor suffers mortal wounds. Destroyer *Kane* (DD 235) rescues 11 survivors; fishing boat *Yukon* rescues 14.

15 Wednesday

UNITED STATES. Naval Air Transport Service Squadron (VR 3) is established at Kansas City, Kansas, for operations in the United States.

PACIFIC. Submarine Base, Midway Island, is established.

Submarine *Grunion* (SS 216) sinks Japanese submarine chasers *Ch 25* and *Ch 27* west of Sredni Point, Kiska, Aleutians, 52°02′N, 177°42′E.

Salvage party, transported to Akutan Island, Aleutians, in district patrol vessel *YP 72*, continues salvage of ZERO fighter discovered on 10 July.

ATLANTIC. German submarine *U 576* attacks convoy KS 520, torpedoing U.S. bulk carrier *Chilore* about 20 miles east of Okracoke Inlet, North Carolina, 34°45′N, 75°29′W, as well as Panamanian freighter *J. A. Mowinkel* and Nicaraguan merchantman *Bluefield*. *Chilore* later blunders into a U.S. minefield, fouling two mines and receiving further damage. Two of her 42-man crew are lost when a lifeboat capsizes; there are no casualties among the nine-man Armed Guard. *U 576*'s time to savor her triple triumph, however, is short, for an OS2U (VS 9) and U.S. merchant vessel *Unicoi* combine to sink that U-boat off the North Carolina coast, 34°51′N, 75°22′W. *Chilore* later capsizes and sinks at the mouth of Chesapeake Bay. Tug *P. F. Martin* (Navy Rescue Tug Service) tows *J. A. Mowinkel* through the minefields off Cape Hatteras (see 19 July).

GULF OF MEXICO. U.S. tanker *Pennsylvania Sun* is torpedoed by German submarine *U 571* about 125 miles west of Key West, Florida, 24°05′N, 83°42′W; the crew (42 merchant seamen and the 17-man Armed Guard) abandon the burning ship. Destroyer *Dahlgren* (DD 187) rescues the survivors and transports them to Key West (see 16 July).

16 Thursday

PACIFIC. Submarine *Seadragon* (SS 194), attacking Japanese convoy off coast of French Indochina, sinks freighter *Hakodate Maru* north of Cape Varella, 12°55′N, 109°29′E.

ATLANTIC. Advanced Group, Amphibious Force, Atlantic Fleet (Rear Admiral Andrew C. Bennett) is established to conduct amphibious training in Great Britain.

Unarmed U.S. fishing boat *Gertrude* is sunk (demolition charge or gunfire) by German submarine *U 166* approximately 30 miles northeast of Havana, Cuba, 23°32′N, 82°00′E (see 19 July).

U.S. freighter *William F. Humphrey* battles German auxiliary cruiser *Michel* (Schiffe 28) about 800 miles west of the mouth of the Congo River, 05°37′S, 00°56′E, but is sunk by

gunfire and torpedoes, the latter fired by motor torpedo boat *Esan* (LS 4) after a gallant fight. Of the seven-man Armed Guard, two sailors are killed while a third is wounded; *Michel* recovers 26 merchant seamen and three Armed Guard sailors, but the rest of the survivors manage to avoid capture (see 22 July).

U.S. steamship *Fairport*, in Persian Gulf–bound convoy AS 4, is sunk by German submarine *U 161* at 27°12′N, 64°30′W; destroyer *Kearny* (DD 432) rescues all hands: 43-man crew, 16-man Armed Guard, and 66 passengers.

Survivors (17 crewmen and one passenger) from unarmed U.S. freighter *Raphael Semmes*, sunk by German submarine *U 332* on 28 June, are rescued by U.S. freighter *Explorer*.

GULF OF MEXICO. U.S. tanker *Pennsylvania Sun*'s master, three of his officers, and a salvage party reboard their ship (torpedoed the previous day by *U 571*) and, aided by salvage vessel *Willet* (ARS 12), quell the remaining fires and save the ship, which is towed to port by tug *Thomas E. Moran* (Navy Rescue Tug Service). *Pennsylvania Sun* subsequently returns to service.

CARIBBEAN. Survivors of U.S. freighter *Tachira*, sunk by German submarine *U 129* on 12 July, reach Punta Herrera, Mexico.

18 Saturday

PACIFIC. Amphibious Force, South Pacific Area (Rear Admiral Richmond Kelly Turner) is established.

ARCTIC. British minesweeper and escort vessel rescue 22 survivors from U.S. freighter *Honomu*, sunk on 5 July (see 22 July).

19 Sunday

ATLANTIC. Carrier *Ranger* (CV 4), in TF 22, ferries 72 USAAF P-40s (earmarked for ultimate delivery to Burma) to Accra off the Gold Coast of Africa.

With the successful operation of convoys off the east coast of the United States, Admiral Karl Doenitz orders the last U-boats deployed there (*U 89*, *U 132*, *U 402*, *U 458*, and *U 754*) reassigned to other hunting grounds.

Unarmed U.S. tug *Keshena* (Navy Rescue Tug Service) is sunk by U.S. mine east of Okracoke Island, North Carolina, 35°00′N, 75°45′E, while engaged in salvage work on damaged Panamanian tanker *J. A. Mowinkel*. Two men perish in the explosion, but the surviving crew (14 men and one woman) is rescued by a launch and taken to the Coast Guard station at Okracoke.[105]

Three-man crew of U.S. fishing boat *Gertrude*, sunk by German submarine *U 166* on 16 July, reaches safety at Whale Harbor.

20 Monday

UNITED STATES. Admiral William D. Leahy, USN (Retired), reports to President Roosevelt as Chief of Staff to the Commander in Chief of the Army and Navy.

PACIFIC. Naval Operating Base and Naval Air Facility, Dutch Harbor, Alaska, are established.

ATLANTIC. German submarine *U 66* mines the waters off Castries, St. Lucia.

21 Tuesday

PACIFIC. "RI" Operation: Japanese naval force begins landing 2,000 troops at Gona, west of Buna, New Guinea. This move, which preempts Allied Operation PROVIDENCE, is the first step of a transmontane campaign to take Port Moresby, the enemy having been twice frustrated in the attempt to capture that objective by sea (first at Lae-Salamaua and then at the Battle of the Coral Sea).

U.S. freighter *Coast Farmer* is sunk by Japanese submarine *I 11* in the Tasman Sea south of Sydney, Australia, 35°23'S, 151°00'E. RAAF crash boat rescues the 40 survivors, which includes the seven-man Armed Guard.

GULF OF MEXICO. U.S. freighter *William Cullen Bryant*, in convoy TAW 4J, is torpedoed by German submarine *U 84* in the Straits of Florida, 24°08'N, 82°23'W; all hands (40-man crew, 12-man Armed Guard, and two USN signalmen) abandon ship but later reboard the freighter; salvage vessel *Willet* (ARS 12) and civilian tug *Thomas E. Moran* (Navy Rescue Tug Service) tow *William Cullen Bryant* to Key West, Florida. She subsequently returns to service.

22 Wednesday

PACIFIC. USAAF B-17s and B-26s (5th Air Force) bomb Japanese shipping off Buna, New Guinea, damaging destroyer *Uzuki* and sinking army transport *Ayatosan Maru*, 08°50'S, 148°50'E.

U.S. freighter *William Dawes* is torpedoed by Japanese submarine *I 24* off the coast of Australia at 36°47'S, 150°16'E; four of the 15-man Armed Guard and one of five Army passengers are killed in the attack, but there are no casualties among the 40 merchant seamen who make up the ship's complement. Survivors row toward the coast, where fishing boats tow them the remainder of the way. The burning *William Dawes* sinks the next day.

ATLANTIC. Unarmed U.S. freighter *Honolulan* is sunk by German submarine *U 582* off the west coast of Africa at 08°41'N, 22°12'W. *U 582* provides the Americans with cigarettes and questions them briefly before departing. There are no casualties among the 39-man crew and one stowaway (see 28 July).

Norwegian freighter *Triton* rescues survivors from U.S. freighter *William F. Humphrey*, sunk by German auxiliary cruiser *Michel* (*Schiffe 28*) in the South Atlantic on 16 July.

ARCTIC. German submarine rescues last survivors from lifeboat from U.S. freighter *Honomu*, sunk on 5 July. Nine of the 19 men in the lifeboat have perished of exposure during their ordeal.

23 Thursday

ATLANTIC. Unarmed U.S. freighter *Onondaga*, bound for Havana, Cuba, is sunk by German submarine *U 129* five miles north of Cayo Guillermo, 22°40'N, 78°40'W. Nineteen of the 33-man crew die in the attack, as does the sole passenger, the former master of U.S. freighter *Thomas McKean* (sunk by *U 505* on 29 June). Cuban fishing boat *Laventina* rescues the 14 survivors.

24 Friday

PACIFIC. Submarine *Narwhal* (SS 167) sinks Japanese guardboat *No. 83 Shinsei Maru*, Utasutsu Bay, Hokkaido, 44°53'N, 147°09'E, and freighters *Nissho Maru* off Etorofu, Kurils, 45°09'N, 147°31'E, and *Kofuji Maru* off Oito, 45°14'N, 147°31'E.

ARCTIC. Survivors of U.S. freighter *Carlton* (sunk by *U 88* on 5 July) reach North Cape, Norway, where they become POWs. During the ordeal in the lifeboat, one man dies shortly before they make landfall.

26 Sunday

PACIFIC. Destroyer *Worden* (DD 352) and oiler *Platte* (AO 24) rescue survivors of Dutch motorship *Tjinegara*, which had been sunk by Japanese submarine *I 169* about 75 miles southeast of Nouméa, New Caledonia, 23°10'S, 165°00'E, on 25 July.

27 Monday

UNITED STATES. Army-Navy Petroleum Board is established.

PACIFIC. TF 8 approaches Kiska to bombard Japanese positions, but limited surface visibility results in the operation being postponed. During the retirement, however, high-speed minesweeper *Lamberton* (DMS 2) accidentally

rams high-speed minesweeper *Chandler* (DMS 9). While investigating that collision, destroyer *Monaghan* (DD 354) and high-speed minesweeper *Long* (DMS 12) collide; both ships suffer damage.

Light cruiser *Boise* (CL 47) departs Pearl Harbor to proceed, via Midway, toward the Japanese home islands to emit enough radio traffic to create the impression of an approaching American task force, as well as to locate and destroy small patrol vessels operating off Honshu (see 5 August).

Submarine *Spearfish* (SS 190) damages Japanese submarine depot ship *Rio de Janeiro Maru* 95 miles east of Cam Ranh Bay, French Indochina, 11°28'N, 110°52'E.

Dutch submarine *O 23* damages Japanese coaster *No. 2 Shofuku Maru* south of Penang, Malaya, 05°07'N, 98°50'E.

USAAF B-26s (5th Air Force) damage Japanese transport *Kotoku Maru* off Buna, New Guinea (see 8 August).

ATLANTIC. U.S. freighter *Stella Lykes* is torpedoed and shelled by German submarine *U 582* off the west coast of Africa at 06°46'N, 24°55'W, and abandoned with no casualties. *U 582* takes two POWs, provides the Americans with cigarettes and medical supplies, and then scuttles her quarry with demolition charges before departing (see 6 August).

GULF OF MEXICO. German submarine *U 166* completes mining the waters off the Mississippi River Passes (see 30 July and 1 August).

28 Tuesday

ATLANTIC. Unarmed U.S. fishing trawler *Ebb* is shelled and sunk by German submarine *U 754*, 45 miles east of Cape Sable, Nova Scotia, 43°18'N, 63°50'W; five of the 17-man crew are killed and seven are wounded. British destroyer HMS *Witherington* rescues the 12 survivors.

British merchantman *Winchester Castle* rescues the 40 survivors of U.S. freighter *Honolulan*, sunk by German submarine *U 582* on 22 July.

ARCTIC. U.S. freighter *Winston Salem*, the last straggler from convoy PQ 17, arrives at the port of Molotovsk, USSR. PQ 17, which sailed from Seidisfjord, Iceland, on 1 July, has lost 24 ships in the course of its ordeal.

29 Wednesday

PACIFIC. PBYs (VP 23) bomb Japanese bases at Tulagi and Gavutu in the Solomons.

ATLANTIC. Survivors (47 in number, two merchant seamen having died during the 32-day ordeal in the 25-foot lifeboat) from U.S.

freighter *Potlatch*, sunk by German submarine *U 153* on 27 June, reach Great Inagua Island, Bahamas; their search for water will take them thence to Little Inagua, and then to Aklins Island. Ultimately picked up by steamship *Vergermere*, they reach Nassau on 1 August.

30 Thursday

UNITED STATES. Women's Naval Reserve (WAVES; *Women Accepted for Volunteer Emergency Service*) is established (see 2 August).

PACIFIC. Submarine *Grenadier* (SS 210) torpedoes Japanese tanker *San Clemente Maru* off Truk, 07°02′N, 151°15′E.

GULF OF MEXICO. German submarine *U 166* attacks convoy TAW 7 about 25 miles southeast of the mouth of the Mississippi River, and sinks U.S. passenger ship *Robert E. Lee*, 28°40′N, 88°30′W. Submarine chasers *PC 566* and *SC 519*, and civilian tug *Underwriter* rescue survivors; none of the six-man Armed Guard are lost (see 1 August).

ATLANTIC. U.S. freighter *Cranford* is sunk by German submarine *U 155* about 250 miles east-southeast of Barbados, 12°17′N, 55°11′W. *U 155* treats two injured Americans and then provides the survivors with navigational information, matches, a line, and water. Running short of provisions, *U 155* can spare none. *Cranford*'s surviving complement (including six of eight Armed Guard sailors) are eventually picked up later the same day by Spanish tanker *Castillo Alemenara*.

31 Friday

PACIFIC. Submarine *Grunion* (SS 216) torpedoes Japanese transport *Kashima Maru* off Kiska, Aleutians, but is sunk by gunfire from her quarry, 10 miles north of Segula Island.

PBYs attempt to bomb Japanese bases at Tulagi and Gavutu in the Solomons is aborted because of bad weather.

ATLANTIC. German submarine *U 751* lays mines off Charleston, South Carolina.

AUGUST

1 Saturday

PACIFIC. Vice Admiral Robert L. Ghormley, Commander South Pacific Force, establishes his headquarters afloat on board auxiliary *Argonne* (AG 31) at Nouméa, New Caledonia.

Submarine *Narwhal* (SS 167), attacking Japanese shipping south of Shiraya Saki, sinks

freighter *Meiwa Maru*, 41°12′N, 141°36′E, and oiler *Koan Maru*, 41°03′N, 141°28′E.

Naval Base, Galapagos Islands, and Naval Auxiliary Air Facility and Motor Torpedo Boat Base, Salinas, Ecuador, are established.

ATLANTIC. Naval Station, Taboga Island, Canal Zone, Panama, is established.

GULF OF MEXICO. Coast Guard J4F bombs and sinks German submarine *U 166* south of New Orleans, Louisiana, 28°31′N, 90°45′W.

2 Sunday

UNITED STATES. Lieutenant Commander Mildred H. McAfee, who received the first WAVES commission, becomes the first WAVES commandant.

PACIFIC. Dutch submarine *O 23* sinks Japanese army cargo ship *Zenyo Maru* off Penang, Malaya, 05°36′N, 99°53′E.

3 Monday

PACIFIC. Light minelayers *Gamble* (DM 15), *Breese* (DM 18), and *Tracy* (DM 19) lay minefield off western entrance of Segond Channel, Espíritu Santo, New Hebrides (see 4 August and 26 October).

Submarine *Gudgeon* (SS 211) sinks Japanese transport *Naniwa Maru* west-southwest of Truk, 07°37′N, 150°11′E.

4 Tuesday

PACIFIC. Destroyer *Tucker* (DD 374), uninformed of its presence, is sunk in U.S. minefield laid the previous day in Segond Channel, Espíritu Santo, New Hebrides.

Submarine *Narwhal* (SS 167) sinks Japanese freighter *Fukuyama Maru* off northern Honshu, 40°26′N, 141°50′E.

CARIBBEAN. Submarine *S 17* (SS 122) is damaged when bombed accidentally by USAAF B-18 off Cristobal, Canal Zone.

5 Wednesday

PACIFIC. Light cruiser *Boise* (CL 47), in the course of her deception mission, launches two SOCs to search the area. Despite repeated efforts to do so, however, the planes do not find the ship upon their return. Radio silence is broken, thus compromising the operation, and the ship returns to Pearl Harbor, but the Japanese believe that a major U.S. task force is close to the homeland.

Submarine *Greenling* (SS 213), attacking Japanese shipping about 150 miles north-northwest of Truk, sinks transport *Brazil Maru*, 09°50′N, 150°38′E, and merchant passenger-cargo ship *Palau Maru*, 09°04′N, 150°54′E.

6 Thursday

PACIFIC. Submarine *Tautog* (SS 199) sinks Japanese army transport *Ohio Maru* in South China Sea about 250 miles east-northeast of Cam Ranh Bay, French Indochina, 13°51′N, 113°15′E.

ATLANTIC. Unarmed U.S. schooner *Wawaloam*, en route to St. John's, Newfoundland, is sunk by shellfire of German submarine *U 86* at 39°18′N, 55°44′W, but suffers no casualties to the six-man crew and the sole passenger (see 12 August).

Fifty survivors of U.S. freighter *Stella Lykes*, sunk by German submarine *U 582* on 27 July, reach Portuguese Guinea.

7 Friday

PACIFIC. Operation WATCHTOWER: First Marine Division (Major General Alexander A. Vandegrift, USMC) lands on Florida, Tulagi, Gavutu, Tanambogo, and Guadalcanal, in the first American land offensive of the war. Amphibious Force, South Pacific (Rear Admiral Richmond Kelly Turner) lands the leathernecks under cover of naval surface and air forces (Vice Admiral Frank Jack Fletcher). Landings are supported by carrier and shore-based aircraft (Rear Admiral Leigh Noyes and Rear Admiral John S. McCain). Overall commander is Vice Admiral Robert L. Ghormley, Commander South Pacific Force; officer in tactical command is Vice Admiral Fletcher. During Japanese air attacks on the transport force and its escorts off Guadalcanal, destroyer *Mugford* (DD 389) is damaged by carrier bomber (2nd *Kokutai*), 09°00′S, 160°00′E. Following shore bombardment operations in Tulagi Bay, light cruiser *San Juan* (CL 54) is damaged by explosion in one of her forward 5-inch gun mounts.

TG 8.6 (Rear Admiral William W. Smith), consisting of two heavy cruisers, three light cruisers, and four destroyers, bombards Japanese installations at Kiska, Aleutians. High-speed minesweeper *Elliot* (DMS 4), sweeping ahead of light cruiser column, is straddled by shore battery fire and showered with fragments.

Submarine *Tambor* (SS 198) sinks Japanese auxiliary netlayer *Shofuku Maru* off Wotje, Marshalls, 09°25′N, 170°11′E.

8 Saturday

PACIFIC. Marines wrest control of Tulagi, Gavutu, and Tanambogo in the Solomons from tenacious Japanese resistance. Unfinished airstrip on Guadalcanal is occupied and named "Henderson Field" in honor of the late Major Lofton R. Henderson, USMC, who was killed while leading VMSB 241 in the gallant but unsuccessful attack on Japanese carrier *Hiryu* at Midway on 4 June. Coastwatchers report incoming raid. During fierce Japanese aerial assault by land attack planes (4th and Misawa *Kokutais*) on invasion shipping, destroyer *Jarvis* (DD 393) and transport *George F. Elliott* (AP 13), 09°10′S, 160°10′E, are torpedoed. The latter, also crashed by a Japanese plane, is later scuttled by destroyer *Hull* (DD 350). Another crashing bomber damages transport *Barnett* (AP 11), 09°13′S, 160°01′E.

Two of three RAAF Hudsons based at Fall River, Milne Bay, New Guinea, sight Japanese force of four heavy cruisers, three light cruisers, and a destroyer (Vice Admiral Mikawa Gunichi), steaming to disrupt Operation WATCHTOWER. Delays in transmission of the sighting reports (that are made in timely fashion by the RAAF crews), as well as underestimation of the composition of the enemy, result in an error in gauging the threat to the ongoing unloading operations at Tulagi (see 9 August).

Submarine *Narwhal* (SS 167) sinks Japanese crab boat *Bifuku Maru* southeast of Shiriya Saki, 41°14′N, 141°32′E.

Submarine *S 38* (SS 143), despite presence of escorting minesweeper *W.21*, sinks Japanese transport *Meiyo Maru* at southern entrance of St. George Channel, between New Britain and New Ireland, 04°52′S, 152°42′E.

Submarine *Silversides* (SS 236), attacking Japanese convoy emerging from Kobe Harbor, torpedoes and sinks freighter *Nikkei Maru* in Kii Strait, 33°33′N, 135°23′E.

USAAF B-26s (5th Air Force) bombing Japanese targets of opportunity in vicinity of Salamaua, New Guinea, irreparably damage cargo vessel *Kotoku Maru*, 08°43′S, 148°28′E.

Destroyer *Mustin* (DD 413) and *Morris* (DD 417) are damaged in collision during night maneuvers in Hawaiian Operating Area.

ATLANTIC. German submarine *U 98* mines waters off Jacksonville, Florida.

U.S. freighter *Kaimoku*, en route to Liverpool in convoy SC 94, is torpedoed, shelled, and sunk by German submarine *U 379* at 56°32′N, 32°15′W. Two of the 36-man crew die in the attack, as do two of the 14-man Armed Guard. Canadian corvette HMCS *Battleford* rescues survivors.

UNITED STATES. Military trial of eight German agents, landed by submarine on 13 and 17 June, concludes. Six of the men receive the

Consolidated PBY-5A Catalina, assigned to Commander South Pacific Force, taxis on Henderson Field, 10 August 1942, the first plane to land on the recently captured airstrip. (NA, USMC 50844)

death sentence, one receives life imprisonment, and one receives a 30-year sentence.

9 Sunday

PACIFIC. Battle of Savo Island: Japanese warships (Vice Admiral Mikawa Gunichi) sighted by RAAF Hudsons the previous day, evade patrolling destroyer *Blue* (DD 387) off Savo Island, Solomons, and engage forces screening the transports and cargo ships unloading off Tulagi. In the initial phase of the action, the southern force (Captain Howard D. Bode), consisting of heavy cruiser *Chicago* (CA 29), Australian heavy cruiser HMAS *Canberra,* and destroyers *Patterson* (DD 392) and *Bagley* (DD 386), bears the brunt of the enemy's onslaught. *Chicago* is damaged by torpedo from heavy cruiser *Kako* and gunfire, and *Patterson* by gunfire from light cruisers *Yubari* and *Tenryu*. HMAS *Canberra* is hit by at least one torpedo (perhaps accidentally from *Bagley*) and Japanese gunfire (see below). Gunfire from *Chicago* and *Patterson* damages *Tenryu*. *Chicago*, however, provides no warning for the northern group (Captain Frederick L. Riefkohl) (three heavy cruisers and two destroyers), which is similarly mauled. Heavy cruiser *Astoria* (CA 34) is sunk by gunfire of heavy cruisers *Chokai, Aoba, Kinugasa,* and *Kako*.[106] *Quincy* (CA 39) is sunk by gunfire of heavy cruisers *Aoba, Kako, Furutaka* and light cruiser *Tenryu*

and is torpedoed by light cruiser *Yubari*. Gunfire from *Astoria* and *Quincy*, however, damages Mikawa's flagship *Chokai; Quincy*'s shellfire also damages *Aoba*. The third heavy cruiser in the northern force, *Vincennes* (CA 44), is sunk by gunfire and torpedo from *Chokai*, and gunfire from *Kako, Aoba, Kinugasa,* and *Yubari*. Before *Vincennes*'s demise, however, she scores one 8-inch hit (the shell, however, proves to be a dud) that damages *Kinugasa*. *Ralph Talbot* (DD 390), guarding the opposite side of Savo Island from *Blue*, is damaged by gunfire of *Furutaka, Yubari,* and *Tenryu*, as well as that of most likely *Helm* (DD 388) and/or *Wilson* (DD 408), the two U.S. destroyers attached to the *Vincennes* group, as the Japanese retire. *Chicago* and *Patterson* exchange gunfire briefly (and, fortunately, ineffectively). Subsequently, *Canberra*, deemed beyond salvage, is scuttled by destroyer *Selfridge* (DD 357). The Japanese, however, despite having inflicted one of the worst defeats ever administered to the U.S. Navy, do not press their advantage; the vulnerable transports and cargo ships are unmolested. Withdrawal of the U.S. carrier force (plagued by heavy losses in fighter aircraft) providing cover for the landings, however, results in the auxiliaries being withdrawn, too, for the time being. The Japanese Navy temporarily controls the waters around Guadalcanal.

Destroyer *Jarvis* (DD 393), damaged the previous day, is mistaken for an *Achilles*-class cruiser and attacked by Japanese land attack planes (Misawa *Kokutai*) and torpedoed 200 nautical miles southeast of Tulagi, 09°42′S, 158°59′E. *Jarvis* puts up a stout fight, splashing two of the attacking planes (a third ditches due to battle damage) but is sunk with all hands.

ATLANTIC. German submarine *U 98* completes laying mines off mouth of St. Johns River, east of Jacksonville, Florida.

10 Monday

PACIFIC. Submarine *S 44* (SS 155) torpedoes and sinks Japanese heavy cruiser *Kako* near Kavieng, 02°15′S, 152°15′E, as *Kako* retires from the Battle of Savo Island.

MEDITERRANEAN. Operation PEDESTAL: British convoy, WS 21S, formed around 13 transports and cargo ships (which include U.S. freighters *Almeria Lykes* and *Santa Elisa*) and one tanker, transits Straits of Gibraltar, bound for Malta. Royal Navy cover and escort forces include a total of two battleships, four aircraft carriers, seven light cruisers, and 25 destroyers (see 11–13 August).

11 Tuesday

MEDITERRANEAN. Operation PEDESTAL: Large British convoy (which includes in its composition U.S. freighters *Almeria Lykes* and *Santa Elisa*), bound for Malta, its presence determined by Axis aerial reconnaissance, comes under attack from *Luftwaffe* JU 88s and HE 111s (see 12 and 13 August).

12 Wednesday

ATLANTIC. Light cruiser *Cleveland* (CL 55), on her shakedown cruise in Chesapeake Bay, tests the newly developed proximity-fused antiaircraft projectiles for the first time under simulated combat conditions; she destroys all three target drones with four proximity bursts.

Seven survivors of U.S. schooner *Wawaloam*, sunk by German submarine *U 86* on 6 August, are rescued by steamship *Irish Rose*, which transfers them subsequently to British corvette HMS *Campanula*.

MEDITERRANEAN. Operation PEDESTAL: Attacks by German and Italian aircraft continue on large British convoy (which includes within its composition U.S. freighters *Almeria Lykes* and *Santa Elisa*), bound for Malta (see 13 August).

PACIFIC. Submarine *Pickerel* (SS 177) is damaged by depth charges off the Marianas, 16°19′S, 145°23′E, but remains on patrol.

USAAF B-17s (5th Air Force) bomb Japanese shipping at Rabaul, damaging oiler *Matsumoto Maru.*

13 Thursday

GULF OF MEXICO. U.S. tanker *R. M. Parker Jr.*, en route to Port Arthur, Texas, is sunk by German submarine *U 171* at 28°37′N, 90°48′W. There are no casualties, and Coast Guard auxiliary cutter *Pioneer* rescues all 37 merchant seamen and the seven-man Armed Guard.

ATLANTIC. U.S. freighter *Cripple Creek* is sunk by German submarine *U 171* at 04°55′N, 18°30′W; one crewman is killed. The survivors take to three lifeboats (see 16 August).

U.S. freighter *Delmundo*, in convoy TAW 12, is sunk by German submarine *U 600* in the Windward Passage, 19°55′N, 73°49′W; five of the 41-man crew perish, as do three of the eight passengers. The survivors, including the nine-man Armed Guard, are rescued by British destroyer HMS *Churchill* [ex-U.S. destroyer *Herndon* (DD 198)].

MEDITERRANEAN. Operation PEDESTAL: German and Italian motor torpedo boats attack Malta-bound convoy before dawn; German *S 30* and *S 36*, and Italian *MAS 554* and *MAS 557* sink British merchantman *Wairangi* and damage *Rochester Castle* (which will eventually reach Malta although she is damaged further by *Luftwaffe* JU 87s and JU 88s). U.S. freighter *Almeria Lykes* is torpedoed and abandoned, 36°40′N, 11°35′E. The ship remains afloat, but is sunk by scuttling charge after daybreak. British destroyer HMS *Somali* rescues all hands: 51 merchant seamen, 15-man Armed Guard, and 39 passengers. Freighter *Santa Elisa* is torpedoed in the same attack, approximately 20 miles southeast of Cape Bon, 36°48′N, 11°23′E, and is abandoned when her cargo of aviation gasoline catches fire. Four of the 33 embarked army passengers are killed, but the 56-man merchant complement and the 11-man Armed Guard suffer no fatalities. British destroyer HMS *Penn* rescues the survivors and transports them to Malta; three Armed Guard sailors will be hospitalized there for burns suffered in the attack. *Santa Elisa* is finished off by bombs later that day. Three surviving British transports and the one tanker will reach Malta later in the day; a fourth transport will reach the island on 14 August.

14 Friday

PACIFIC. Submarine *S 39* (SS 144) is damaged when she strikes submerged reef off Rossel Island, Louisiade Archipelago (see 16 August).

Submarine *Seawolf* (SS 197) sinks Japanese merchant passenger-cargo ship *Hachigen Maru* (ex-British *Wenchow*) in Sibitu Passage, 05°07′N, 119°37′E.

EUROPE. Lieutenant General Dwight D. Eisenhower, USA, Commanding General, European Theater of Operations, is appointed Commander in Chief of Allied Expeditionary Forces; Admiral Sir Andrew B. Cunningham, RN, is appointed Allied Naval Commander.

ATLANTIC. Unarmed U.S. freighter *California* is sunk by Italian submarine *Reginaldo Giuliani* at 09°24′N, 33°02′W; all hands (38 men) abandon the sinking ship under fire (see 4, 5, and 14 September).

15 Saturday

PACIFIC. Naval Air Station, Whidbey Island, Washington, is established.

Marine Aircraft Wings, Pacific (Major General Ross E. Rowell, USMC) is established at San Diego, California.

CARIBBEAN. Naval Auxiliary Air Facility, Jamaica, British West Indies, is established.

ATLANTIC. U.S. freighter *Balladier*, in convoy SC 95, is sunk by German submarine *U 705* (one of 13 boats deployed to intercept Allied transatlantic convoys) approximately 550 miles southeast of Iceland at 55°00′N, 25°00′W; 11 of the 34-man crew and two of the 11-man Armed Guard die in the attack. Merchantman *Norluna* rescues survivors.

Patrol Wing 11 (Commander Stanley J. Michael) is established at San Juan, Puerto Rico, for operations in Caribbean Sea Frontier.

16 Sunday

PACIFIC. Submarine *S 39* (SS 144), irreparably damaged by striking reef off Rossel Island on 14 August, is abandoned.

Airship *L 8* (ZP 32) is damaged upon return from patrol off California coast, landing at Dale City, California. The airship, however, is unmanned; the fate of its two-man crew remains a mystery.

ATLANTIC. Surviving 38 merchant seamen and the 13-man Armed Guard of U.S. freighter *Cripple Creek*, sunk by German submarine *U 171* on 13 August, are rescued by British armed trawler HMS *St. Wistan* and transported to Sierra Leone.

17 Monday

PACIFIC. Companies "A" and "B," Second Raider Battalion, USMC (Lieutenant Colonel Evans F. Carlson, USMCR) are put ashore by

TG 7.15 (Commander John M. Haines), consisting of submarines *Nautilus* (SS 168) and *Argonaut* (SS 166), on Makin Island, Gilberts. *Nautilus* provides gunfire support. Surf conditions, however, thwart the planned efforts to withdraw the marines (see 18 August).

Submarine *Gudgeon* (SS 211) damages Japanese oilers *Shinkoku Maru* and *Nichiei Maru* northwest of Truk, 07°43′N, 151°13′W.

ATLANTIC. U.S. tanker *Louisiana* is sunk by German submarine *U 108* approximately 200 miles from Paramaribo, Dutch Guiana, 07°24′N, 52°33′W; although *U 108* sees three men escape from the burning ship, they are never found. There are no survivors from the 41 merchant sailors and the eight-man Armed Guard.

18   Tuesday

PACIFIC. Japanese destroyers *Kagero*, *Hagikaze*, *Maikaze*, *Urakaze*, *Isokaze*, and *Hamikaze* begin landing over 900 troops under Colonel Ichiki Kiyonao (Ichiki Detachment) on Guadalcanal (see 19–21 August).

TG 7.15 (Commander John M. Haines), consisting of submarines *Nautilus* (SS 168) and *Argonaut* (SS 166), evacuates Second Raider Battalion (Lieutenant Colonel Evans F. Carlson, USMCR) from Makin Island, Gilberts. The relative ease with which the assault has been carried out, however, inspires the Japanese to bolster defenses in the region.[107]

CARIBBEAN. Convoy TAW 13, steaming south of Cuba, comes under attack from German submarine *U 553*, which torpedoes and sinks Swedish merchantman *Blankaholm* and British freighter *Empire Bede*; *U 553* also torpedoes and sinks U.S. freighter *John Hancock* at 19°27′N, 76°48′W. All 38 merchant sailors and the 11-man Armed Guard survive the loss of the ship; the men are rescued by British corvette HMS *Pimpernel*.

Convoy TAW (S), 15 ships escorted by gunboat *Courage* (PG 70), British corvette HMS *Clarkia*, two Coast Guard cutters, and four submarine chasers, is attacked by German submarine *U 162*, which torpedoes unarmed U.S. freighter *West Celina* off Grenada, 11°45′N, 62°30′W (see 19, 21, and 22 August).

19   Wednesday

PACIFIC. USAAF B-17s (South Pacific Force), flying from Espíritu Santo, bomb Japanese destroyers *Kagero*, *Hagikaze*, and *Maikaze* off Guadalcanal, damaging *Hagikaze* off Tulagi.

Small reconnaissance seaplane from Japanese submarine *I 29* reconnoiters the Seychelles.

CARIBBEAN. German submarine *U 162* continues stalking convoy TAW (S), attacked the previous day, and again torpedoes unarmed U.S. freighter *West Celina*, which is abandoned by the 39-man crew and the convoy commodore's staff of four men; the convoy commodore, however, is lost (see 21 and 22 August). German submarine *U 564* attacks the convoy as well, torpedoing and sinking two British ships: tanker *British Consul* and freighter *Empire Cloud*. Escorting ships, however, will frustrate further attacks by the U-boats.

20   Thursday

PACIFIC. First USMC planes arrive at Guadalcanal. Auxiliary aircraft carrier *Long Island* (ACV 1) ferries 19 F4Fs (VMF 223) and 12 SBDs (VMSB 232) to Henderson Field. Although Japanese flying boat (14th *Kokutai*) sights *Long Island*, screened by light cruiser *Helena* (CL 50) and destroyers *Aylwin* (DD 355) and *Dale* (DD 353), the U.S. ships prove to be out of range of enemy land-based air and retire from the area unmolested.

Small seaplane tender *Mackinac* (AVP 13) is damaged when mistakenly bombed by SBDs (VS 71) from carrier *Wasp* (CV 7) off Ndeni Island, Santa Cruz Islands.

Japanese launch first major counterattack against Henderson Field under Colonel Ichiki Kiyonao. Over 900 troops begin to try and forge across the Ilu River toward the marine-held airstrip (see 21 August).

ATLANTIC. PBY-5A (VP 73) sinks German submarine *U 464*, North Atlantic Area, 61°25′N, 14°40′W.

21   Friday

PACIFIC. Marines hold Henderson Field against the assault by the Japanese Ichiki Detachment, which suffers over 700 casualties (including Colonel Ichiki Kiyonao himself).

Submarine *Cuttlefish* (SS 171) damages Japanese ammunition ship *Nichiro Maru* off southern tip of Kyushu, 31°00′N, 130°00′E.

Submarine *Tambor* (SS 198) sinks Japanese collier *No. 6 Shinsei Maru* off Ponape Island, 06°45′N, 158°10′E.

Motor vessel *Lakatoi*, commissioned at Nouméa, New Caledonia, on 15 August and manned by a crew made up of survivors of transport *George F. Elliott* (AP 13), sinks in storm off Efate, 18°55′S, 167°40′E.

CARIBBEAN. One group of 19 survivors from U.S. freighter *West Celina*, torpedoed by German submarine *U 162* on 18 and 19 August,

reaches Manzanillo Bay, Venezuela (see 22 August).

22   Saturday

GENERAL. Brazil declares war on Germany and Italy.

PACIFIC. First USAAF planes (five P-400s from the 67th Fighter Squadron) arrive at Henderson Field, Guadalcanal.

Destroyers *Blue* (DD 387) and *Henley* (DD 391) off Savo Island, Solomons, in advance of arrival of supply convoy, encounter Japanese destroyer *Kawakaze*, which has just completed landing troops. *Kawakaze* torpedoes *Blue* off Guadalcanal and retires; *Henley* tows *Blue* to Tulagi (see 23 August). SBDs (VS 3) on morning search from carrier *Saratoga* (CV 3) strafe and damage *Kawakaze* 75 miles north of Tulagi.

Submarine *Haddock* (SS 231) torpedoes and sinks Japanese transport *Tatsuho Maru* off China coast, near Foochow, 26°07′N, 121°29′E.

ATLANTIC. Destroyer *Ingraham* (DD 444) is sunk in collision with oiler *Chemung* (AO 30) off Nova Scotia, 42°34′N, 60°05′W; *Chemung* is damaged. Destroyer *Buck* (DD 420) is damaged in collision with British transport *Awatea*, 42°34′N, 60°05′W.

CARIBBEAN. USAAF plane (45th Bombardment Squadron) sinks German submarine *U 654* north of Panama, 12°00′N, 79°56′W.

Second group of 23 survivors from U.S. freighter *West Celina*, torpedoed by German submarine *U 162* on 18 and 19 August, reaches Manzanillo Bay, Venezuela.

23   Sunday

ARCTIC. Operation EUROPE: Heavy cruiser *Tuscaloosa* (CA 37), escorted by destroyers *Rodman* (DD 456) and *Emmons* (DD 457) and British destroyer HMS *Onslaught*, arrives at Murmansk, Russia, and disembarks men and unloads equipment from two RAF squadrons. The ships depart the following day to return to Scapa Flow, Orkney Islands.

PACIFIC. Japanese light cruiser *Yubari*, accompanied by four destroyers and supporting ships, shells Nauru Island, Gilberts, in preparation for landings there.

Destroyer *Blue* (DD 387), torpedoed by Japanese destroyer *Kawakaze* on 22 August, is scuttled by her crew off Florida Island, 09°17′S, 160°02′E.

Submarine *Skipjack* damages Japanese oiler *Hayatomo* southwest of Ambon, N.E.I., 03°52′N, 127°54′E.

PBY (VP 23) attacks Japanese heavy cruiser *Furutaka*, as the latter is en route from Shortland to Kieta, Solomons.

24 Monday

PACIFIC. Battle of the Eastern Solomons: TF 61 (Vice Admiral Frank Jack Fletcher), the combined TF 11 (Vice Admiral Fletcher) and TF 16 (Rear Admiral Thomas C. Kinkaid), engages Japanese First Carrier Division, Third Fleet (Vice Admiral Nagumo Chuichi). Planes from Japanese carrier *Ryujo* bomb U.S. positions on Lunga Point, but SBDs (VB 3) and TBFs (VT 8) from carrier *Saratoga* (CV 3) sink *Ryujo* at 06°10′S, 160°50′E. Carrier *Enterprise* (CV 6), however, is damaged by carrier bombers from *Shokaku* (carrier bomber from *Zuikaku* achieves a near-miss) at 08°38′S, 163°30′E; dive-bombing attacks against battleship *North Carolina* (BB 55) by both Japanese carriers' planes are unsuccessful. Destroyer *Grayson* (DD 435) is damaged by strafing and near-miss. Later, SBDs (VB 3) from *Saratoga* damage Japanese seaplane carrier *Chitose*; USAAF B-17s bomb but miss destroyer *Maikaze* (see 25 August).

Submarine *Saury* (SS 189) torpedoes Japanese army transport *Otowasan Maru* west of Luzon, 14°15′N, 120°19′E.

Submarine *Guardfish* (SS 217) sinks Japanese merchant passenger-cargo ship *Seikai Maru* off entrance to Sendai Harbor, 38°12′N, 141°30′E.

Japanese transport *Cuba Maru*, stranded south of Sakhalin Island, Kurils, sinks, 48°00′N, 142°30′E.

25 Tuesday

PACIFIC. While U.S. and Japanese carrier forces retire after the Battle of the Eastern Solomons, Japanese Guadalcanal-bound reinforcement convoy (Rear Admiral Tanaka Raizo), comes under attack by planes from Henderson Field (Major Richard C. Mangrum, USMC). USMC SBD (VMSB 232) damages light cruiser *Jintsu* north of Malaita Island, forcing Rear Admiral Tanaka to shift his flag to destroyer *Kagero*; SBD (VB 6) damages armed merchant cruiser *Kinryu Maru* north of Guadalcanal, 07°47′N, 160°13′E. USMC SBD (VMSB 232) damages transport *Boston Maru*. USAAF B-17s flying from Espíritu Santo sink destroyer *Mutsuki* off Santa Isabel, Solomons, as she stands by the foundering *Kinryu Maru*. "[Major Richard C.] Mangrum's strike," John Lundstrom writes of this battle, "transformed an indecisive clash of carriers into an Allied

tactical victory." The Japanese retire, their mission unaccomplished.

Submarine *Growler* (SS 215) sinks Japanese gunboat *Sen-Yo Maru* 20 miles south of Takao, Formosa, 22°33′N, 120°10′E, and survives several ensuing depth chargings by escort vessels.

Submarine *Seawolf* (SS 197) sinks Japanese cargo ship *Showa Maru* off northeast coast of Borneo, 03°55′N, 118°59′E.

"RE" Operation: Japanese troops land on Rabi Island after invasion convoy has been attacked by RAAF P-40s and a Hudson that damage Japanese transport *Nankai Maru* and destroyer *Urakaze*. After initial success, Japanese suffer reversal, though, as Australian forces counterattack and wipe them out.

Japanese also occupy Nauru, Gilberts, and Goodenough Island, off southeast coast of New Guinea; the latter is occupied by Sasebo 5th Special Landing Force (Tsukioka Unit) to seek out communications and weather stations (see 11 September and 3 and 26 October).

26 Wednesday

PACIFIC. Japanese land at Milne Bay, New Guinea. USAAF B-17s, B-25s, B-26s, P-40s, along with RAAF Hudsons, attack beaches and transports, destroying supplies brought ashore during the landings. A second convoy puts ashore more troops after nightfall.

Japanese destroyers land 350 soldiers east of Taivu Point, Guadalcanal (see 27 August).

Japanese occupy Ocean Island.

SBDs (VS 71) from carrier *Wasp* (CV 7) damage Japanese submarine *I 17* west of Malaita, Solomons, 09°25′N, 162°47′E.

Submarine *Haddock* (SS 231) sinks Japanese freighter *Teishun Maru* off China coast, about 100 miles north-northwest of Keelung, Formosa, 26°27′N, 121°23′E.

Seaplane tender (destroyer) *Williamson* (AVD 2) is damaged off Dutch Harbor, Alaska, when bombs are jarred loose from the wings of a downed PBY that the ship is attempting to take in tow.

27 Thursday

ATLANTIC. German submarine *U 165* attacks convoy SG 6 off Belle Isle Strait, Newfoundland, torpedoing oiler *Laramie* (AO 16) at 51°44′N, 55°40′W; four sailors are killed. *U 165* also torpedoes U.S. freighter *Arlyn* at 51°53′N, 55°48′W; 12 of the 34-man crew perish (see 28 August).

German submarine *U 517* attacks convoy SG 6F off Belle Isle Strait, torpedoing U.S. Army transport *Chatham* at 51°51′N, 55°49′W;

seven of the 106-man crew perish, as do seven of the 428 passengers. There are no casualties among the 28-man Armed Guard. The majority of the men who survive the sinking pull ashore in a dozen lifeboats; the remainder, who embark in nine rafts, are rescued by destroyer *Bernadou* (DD 153), Coast Guard cutter *Mojave* (WPG 47), and Canadian corvette HMCS *Trail*.

CARIBBEAN. German submarine *U 511* attacks convoy TAW 15 (see 28 August).

PACIFIC. Japanese destroyers land 128 soldiers northwest of Taivu Point, Guadalcanal.

28 Friday

PACIFIC. Japanese increase efforts to transport reinforcements (Kawaguchi Detachment) to Guadalcanal. USMC and Navy SBDs (VMSB 232 and VS 5), however, attack the initial convoy, bombing three destroyers. *Asagiri* is sunk off Santa Isabel, Solomons, and *Shirakumo* and *Yugiri* are damaged. A fourth destroyer, *Amagiri*, takes *Shirakumo* in tow and proceeds back to Shortland Island. A second reinforcement convoy, however, escorted by five destroyers, reaches its destination, Taivu Point, and disembarks troops unmolested.

Light minelayer *Gamble* (DM 15) sinks Japanese submarine *I 123* off Florida Island, Solomons, 09°21′S, 160°43′E.

ATLANTIC. U.S. freighter *Topa Topa*, bound for the Gold Coast, is sunk by German submarine *U 66* at 10°16′N, 51°30′W; 18 of the 42-man crew perish, as do seven of the 15-man Armed Guard. All three passengers survive. British merchantman *Clan MacInnes* rescues the 35 survivors and transports them to Trinidad.

Freighter *Harjurand* rescues some of the survivors from U.S. freighter *Arlyn*, torpedoed by *U 165* the day before; the rest row to shore. A total of 22 merchant sailors, the 14-man Armed Guard, and the sole passenger survive *Arlyn*'s loss. *U 517* finishes off the abandoned *Arlyn* with a torpedo at 51°53′N, 55°48′W.

CARIBBEAN. PBY (VP 92) and Canadian corvette HMCS *Oakville* sink German submarine *U 94* at 17°54′N, 74°36′W. Destroyer *Lea* (DD 118) and *Oakville* pick up survivors.

U.S. tanker *Esso Aruba*, in convoy TAW 15, is torpedoed by German submarine *U 511* approximately 120 miles south-southeast of Guantánamo Bay, 17°54′N, 74°47′W; *U 511* also torpedoes British tanker *San Fabian* and Dutch tanker *Rotterdam*, both of which sink. *Esso Aruba*, however, suffers no casualties (convoy commodore and his five-man staff,

41-man merchant complement, and 13-man Armed Guard), remains in convoy, and reaches her destination the same day without further incident.

29 Saturday

PACIFIC. Transport *William Ward Burrows* (AP 6) is damaged when she runs aground on Sylvia Reef off Tulagi, Solomons, 09°07′S, 160°10′E.

Australian destroyer HMAS *Arunta* sinks Japanese submarine *RO 33* ten miles southeast of Port Moresby, New Guinea, 09°36′S, 147°06′E.

30 Sunday

PACIFIC. Japanese land attack planes (Kizarazu and Misawa *Kokutais*) bomb shipping off Kukum Point, Guadalcanal, sinking high-speed transport *Colhoun* (APD 2), 09°24′S, 160°01′E. High-speed transport *Little* (APD 4) and chartered freighter *Kopara* emerge undamaged from the attack.

Small reconnaissance seaplane from Japanese submarine *I 19* reconnoiters Santa Cruz Island, Solomons.

TG 8.8 lands Army occupation forces on Adak, Aleutians, to begin construction of an air and naval base.

ATLANTIC. U.S. tanker *Jack Carnes*, bound for Aruba, is shelled by German submarine *U 705*. After Armed Guard gunfire compels the Germans to submerge, *U 705* torpedoes the tanker, 42°00′N, 28°05′E; 24 merchant seamen and four Armed Guard sailors man one lifeboat, while 18 merchant sailors (including the ship's master) and 10 Armed Guard sailors take to the other (see 31 August and 5 September).

U.S. freighter *Star of Oregon*, bound for Trinidad, is torpedoed by German submarine *U 162*, and abandoned; one workaway sailor is killed in the attack. *U 162* then shells and sinks the freighter, 11°48′N, 59°45′E, before questioning the crew and then leaving the area. The entire 38-man crew and 14-man Armed Guard sailors survive the loss of the ship; a U.S. patrol boat (unidentified) rescues them.

U.S. freighter *West Lashaway* is sunk by German submarine *U 66* approximately 375 miles east of Trinidad, 10°30′N, 55°10′E; the rapidity with which the ship sinks prevents boats from being launched. Of the 56 people on board (including a woman missionary and four children among the passengers), 42 manage to reach four rafts (see 2, 13, 18, and 24 September).

31 Monday

PACIFIC. Eight Japanese destroyers put ashore 1,000 troops under Major General Kawaguchi Kiyotake (Kawaguchi Detachment) on Guadalcanal. This same day, the Japanese Army assigns priority to Guadalcanal campaign over that of Papua New Guinea, thus largely dooming the latter effort.

Carrier *Saratoga* (CV 3) is torpedoed by Japanese submarine *I 26*, 260 miles southeast of Guadalcanal, 10°34′S, 164°18′E.

Destroyer *Reid* (DD 369) and PBYs (VP 42 and VP 43) sink Japanese submarine *RO 61* off Atka, Aleutians, 52°36′N, 173°57′W.

Submarine *Growler* (SS 215) sinks Japanese freighter *Eifuku Maru* in Formosa Strait, 25°43′N, 122°38′E.

ATLANTIC. Storm separates the two lifeboats with survivors from U.S. tanker *Jack Carnes*, sunk by German submarine *U 705* the previous day (see 5 September).

SEPTEMBER

1 Tuesday

PACIFIC. Japanese Premier Tojo Hideki also becomes Foreign Minister as Togo Shigenori resigns.

Air Force, Pacific Fleet (Vice Admiral Aubrey W. Fitch) is established.

Cargo ship *Betelgeuse* (AK 28) disembarks 6th Naval Construction Battalion (Seabees), the first to serve in a combat area, at Lunga Point, Guadalcanal.

USAAF B-17s bomb and damage Japanese flying boat support ship *Akitsushima* and destroyer *Akikaze* off Buka Island, Solomons.

ATLANTIC. PBY (VP 73) bombs and sinks German submarine *U 756* southwest of Iceland, 57°30′N, 29°00′W.

2 Wednesday

PACIFIC. Transport *William Ward Burrows* (AP 6) is damaged by grounding on Southern Cross Reef, off Tulagi, Solomons.

Submarine *Flying Fish* (SS 229) is damaged by depth charges off Truk, 07°46′N, 151°57′E, and ends her patrol.

Submarine *Guardfish* (SS 217) sinks Japanese freighter *Teikyu Maru* (ex-Danish *Gustav Diederickson*) 13 miles southeast of Chikyu Misaki, Hokkaido, Japan, 42°08′N, 141°15′E.

USAAF B-17 (South Pacific Force) damages Japanese minelayer *Tsugaru* off north coast of Santa Isabel Island, Solomons, 07°16′N, 158°33′E.

ATLANTIC. Storm separates the four rafts upon which survivors of U.S. freighter *West Lashaway* (sunk by German submarine *U 66* on 30 August) have gathered (see 13, 18, and 24 September).

3 Thursday

ATLANTIC. Transport *Wakefield* (AP 21) is extensively damaged by fire while en route from River Clyde to New York in convoy TA 18. Light cruiser *Brooklyn* (CL 40) and destroyers *Mayo* (DD 422), *Madison* (DD 425), *Niblack* (DD 424), and *Charles F. Hughes* (DD 428) provide assistance; all hands (1,500 men) are saved. *Niblack* stands by with a salvage party. Tugs *Kalmia* (AT 23) and *Iuka* (AT 37) are sent from Casco Bay, Maine; *Wandank* (AT 26) from Boston; *Sagamore* (AT 20) and salvage vessel *Relief* (NRTS) from New York; and civilian tugs *Foundation Aranmore* from Cape Cod Bay and *Foundation Franklin* from Halifax. *Wakefield* will be towed to Halifax where initial repairs will be effected.[108]

PACIFIC. Submarine *Seal* (SS 183) damages Japanese merchant passenger-cargo ship *Kanju Maru* southeast of Cape Padaran, French Indochina, 11°00′N, 109°00′E.

4 Friday

PACIFIC. High-speed transports *Gregory* (APD 3) and *Little* (APD 4) land marines (First Raider Battalion) on Savo Island, Solomons. A sweep reveals no Japanese installations there. The operation completed too late to permit return to Tulagi, the two ships disembark the raiders at Lunga Point and patrol off that place (see 5 September).

Submarine *Growler* (SS 215) sinks Japanese ammunition ship *Kashino* in Formosa Straits, about 50 miles northeast of Keelung, Formosa, 25°43′N, 122°38′E.[109]

Submarine *Guardfish* (SS 217), operating off northeast coast of Honshu, sinks freighters *Kaimei Maru* and *Chita Maru* at 40°14′N, 141°51′E, and passenger-cargo ship *Tenyu Maru* at 40°12′N, 141°49′E, off Kuji Bay.

Submarine *Pompano* (SS 181) sinks guardboat *No. 27 Nanshin Maru* northeast of Honshu, Japan, 35°22′N, 151°40′E.

Japanese freighter *Suki Maru* is sunk by mine in Bangka Strait, N.E.I.

ATLANTIC. Unidentified German U-boat comes across one boat containing 19 survivors of U.S. freighter *California*, sunk by Italian submarine *Reginaldo Giuliani* on 13 August, and provides rations and navigational assistance before departing (see 5 and 14 September).

5 Saturday

PACIFIC. Japanese destroyers *Yudachi*, *Murakumo*, and *Hatsuyuki* bombard U.S. positions on Guadalcanal. High-speed transports *Gregory* (APD 3) and *Little* (APD 4), patrolling off Lunga Point, are mistakenly illuminated by a flare dropped by a PBY. Destroyer *Yudachi* sinks both ships, 09°20′S, 160°01′E.

Submarine *Seal* (SS 183) sinks Japanese merchant passenger-cargo ship *Kanju Maru* southeast of Cam Ranh Bay, French Indochina, 11°00′N, 109°32′E.

Japanese troops are withdrawn from their tenuous beachhead at Milne Bay, New Guinea.

ATLANTIC. British steamship *City of Capetown* rescues 19 survivors of U.S. freighter *California*, sunk by Italian submarine *Reginaldo Giuliani* on 13 August (see 14 September).

Lifeboat with 28 survivors of U.S. tanker *Jack Carnes*, sunk by German submarine *U 705* on 30 August, reaches Terceira, Azores. The other 28 survivors (18 merchant seamen and 10 Armed Guard sailors) are never recovered.

6 Sunday

PACIFIC. Battleship *South Dakota* (BB 57) is damaged when she fouls a coral reef in Lahai Passage, Tonga Islands.

District patrol vessel *YP 74* is sunk by collision with merchant vessel *Derblay* off Unimak Island, Aleutians, southwest of Unimak Strait, 54°23′N, 164°10′W.

7 Monday

GENERAL. U.S. and Cuba conclude agreement for naval and military cooperation.

PACIFIC. Submarine *Growler* (SS 215) sinks Japanese freighter *Taika Maru* 20 miles northwest of Keelung, Formosa, 25°31′N, 121°38′E.

8 Tuesday

PACIFIC. Japanese floatplanes bomb transport *Fuller* (AP 14) and cargo ship *Bellatrix* (AK 20) as they unload off Tulagi, Solomons; the auxiliaries emerge undamaged (see 9 September).

9 Wednesday

PACIFIC. Small reconnaissance seaplane from Japanese submarine *I 25* drops incendiary bombs on forest near Mount Emily, 10 miles northeast of Brookings, Oregon, in an attempt to ignite forest fires. It is the first time that the continental United States is bombed during World War II. The bombing is reported by a forest ranger (see 29 September).

Japanese submarine *I 30* reaches Penang, Malaya, having successfully run the Allied blockade of Lorient, France (see 13 October).

District patrol vessel *YP 346* is sunk by Japanese light cruiser *Sendai* and three destroyers off Guadalcanal.

Japanese land attack planes bomb transport *Fuller* (AP 14) and cargo ship *Bellatrix* (AK 20) off Tulagi, Solomons; the auxiliary vessels again suffer no damage.

ATLANTIC. Coast Guard weather ship *Muskeget* (WAG 48) is sunk by German submarine *U 755* between Norfolk, Virginia, and Iceland.

10 Thursday

ATLANTIC. German submarine *U 69* lays mines at mouth of Chesapeake Bay.

U.S. freighter *American Leader* is shelled, torpedoed, and sunk by German auxiliary cruiser *Michel* (*Schiffe 28*) approximately 800 miles west of the Cape of Good Hope, 34°26′S, 02°00′E. *Michel* recovers the survivors, 39 of 49 merchant seamen and eight of nine Armed Guard sailors, and ultimately transports them to Singapore where they are turned over to the Japanese. Of that group, 14 will perish as POWs.

11 Friday

PACIFIC. Submarine *Saury* (SS 189) sinks Japanese aircraft transport *Kanto Maru* in Makassar Strait, approximately 30 miles off the west coast of the Celebes, 03°15′S, 118°27′E.

On board submarine *Seadragon* (SS 194), en route to conduct a war patrol in the South China Sea, Pharmacist's Mate First Class Wheeler B. Lipes performs successful appendectomy on Seaman First Class Darrell D. Rector, USNR.[110]

USAAF B-17s (5th Air Force) and RAAF Hudsons attack Japanese destroyers *Yayoi* and *Isokaze*, attempting to reach Goodenough Island to extract the Tsukioka Unit, about 15 miles northeast of Normanby Island, D'Entrecasteaux Islands. *Yayoi* is sunk and *Isokaze* near-missed; 83 of the former's survivors reach Normanby (see 25 September).

12 Saturday

GENERAL. Brazil places its naval forces under U.S. Navy operational control.

ATLANTIC. U.S. tanker *Patrick J. Hurley*, en route to Belfast, Ireland, is shelled by German submarine *U 512* at 22°59′N, 46°15′E, and abandoned after Armed Guard gunfire proves unavailing in the tanker's defense (see 19 September and 2 October).

Laconia Incident: German submarine *U 156* torpedoes and sinks British transport *Laconia*, which has 1,800 Italian POWs on board, northeast of Ascension Island, 05°05′S, 11°38′W; the U-boat immediately commences rescue operations and dispatches plain-language request for help. In addition, diplomatic channels are utilized to seek aid from Vichy French naval units in West African waters (see 16–18 September).

13 Sunday

ARCTIC. German aerial and submarine attacks begin against convoy PQ 18, bound for Archangel, USSR, approximately 100 miles southwest of Spitsbergen, Norway. U.S. freighter *Oliver Ellsworth* is torpedoed by German submarine *U 589* at 75°52′N, 07°55′E, and abandoned; one Armed Guard sailor is killed in the attack. Survivors (42 merchant seamen and 27 Armed Guard) are rescued by merchantman *Copeland* and British armed trawler HMS *St. Kenan;* the latter scuttles the crippled *Oliver Ellsworth* with gunfire. Later that day, German planes attack, torpedoing freighter *John Penn* at 75°52′N, 07°55′E; three of the 40-man merchant crew are killed. British destroyer HMS *Eskimo* and minesweeper HMS *Harrier* rescue the survivors, including the 25-man Armed Guard; *John Penn* is scuttled by escort vessels. Shortly thereafter, freighter *Oregonian* is also torpedoed at 76°00′N, 09°30′E; escort vessels rescue 21 of the 40-man crew, in addition to eight of the 14-man Armed Guard.

ATLANTIC. Plane drops rations to one raft containing 19 survivors from U.S. freighter *West Lashaway* (sunk by German submarine *U 66* on 30 August) (see 18 and 24 September).

14 Monday

PACIFIC. USAAF B-17s (5th Air Force) damage Japanese heavy cruiser *Myoko* as she is en route from Truk, Carolines, to carry out support operations off Guadalcanal.

USAAF B-24s and B-17s, escorted by P-38s and P-39s (11th Air Force), raid Japanese shore installations and shipping at Kiska, Aleutians. Ammunition ship *Nojima Maru* is sunk; P-39s strafe and damage submarines *RO 63* and *RO 64*.

ARCTIC. German torpedo planes continue attacks upon Archangel, USSR–bound convoy PQ 18, sinking U.S. freighter *Mary Luckenbach* about 600 miles west of North Cape, Norway, 76°00′N, 16°00′E; she is lost with all hands (41 merchant seamen and a 24-man Armed Guard). The violent explosion of *Mary Lucken-*

bach's ammunition cargo rains debris on nearby freighter *Nathanael Greene*, 76°00'N, 16°00'E, injuring 11 men (five of whom are transferred to British destroyer HMS *Onslaught* for medical attention), but the merchantman makes port under her own power. Concussion from the explosion also disables U.S. freighter *Wacosta*, which is later sunk about 400 miles northeast of Jan Mayen Island, 76°05'N, 10°00'E; she suffers no casualties. British light cruiser HMS *Scylla* and minesweeper HMS *Harrier* rescue all of *Wacosta*'s 38 merchant sailors and her 11 man Armed Guard.

ATLANTIC. Norwegian steamship *Talisman* rescues 18 survivors (one of the original 19 has succumbed to exposure during the 32-day ordeal) of U.S. freighter *California*, sunk by Italian submarine *Reginaldo Giuliani* on 13 August.

15 Tuesday

PACIFIC. TF 18 (Rear Admiral Leigh Noyes), covering reinforcement convoy carrying the Seventh Marines from Espíritu Santo to Guadalcanal, is attacked by Japanese submarine *I 19*, which torpedoes carrier *Wasp* (CV 7) southwest of the Solomons, 12°25'S, 164°08'E. Irreparably damaged and being consumed by gasoline fires and exploding ammunition, *Wasp* is scuttled by destroyer *Lansdowne* (DD 486). Remarkably, *I 19*, in the same spread of torpedoes, also damages battleship *North Carolina* (BB 55) and destroyer *O'Brien* (DD 415) (see 19 October).

Japanese destroyer *Fumizuki* is damaged by grounding in Formosa Strait.

ATLANTIC. Light cruiser *Philadelphia* (CL 41) and transport *Edward Rutledge* (AP 52) are damaged in collision in Hampton Roads, Virginia.

16 Wednesday

PACIFIC. Japanese overland assault on Port Moresby, New Guinea, "grinds to a halt" at Ioribaiwa.

Japanese forces evacuate Attu, Aleutians.

ATLANTIC. TF 23 (Vice Admiral Jonas H. Ingram) is designated South Atlantic Force, Atlantic Fleet.

Patrol Wing 12 (Captain William G. Tomlinson) is established at Key West, Florida, for operations in Gulf Sea Frontier.

U.S. freighter *Commercial Trader* is sunk by German submarine *U 558* east of Trinidad, 10°30'N, 60°16'W; seven of the 29-man crew perish in the attack, as do three of the nine-man Armed Guard. The survivors, in one lifeboat, reach Tobago later the same day.

Laconia Incident: USAAF B-24 from Ascension Island bombs German submarine *U 156* (see 12 September), which, along with *U 506* and *U 507* and Italian submarine *Capellini*, is engaged in rescuing survivors of the torpedoed British transport *Laconia* (see 17 September).

17 Thursday

ATLANTIC. *Laconia* Incident: In the wake of the attack by USAAF B-24 upon German submarines *U 156*, *U 506*, and *U 507* and Italian submarine *Capellini*, engaged in rescuing survivors of the torpedoed British transport *Laconia*, Admiral Karl Doenitz issues orders forbidding U-boats from rescuing survivors of sunken ships (the "*Laconia* Order"). Vichy French light cruiser *Gloire*, colonial sloop *Dumont D'Urville*, and second class sloop *Annamite* rescue 1,041 people from lifeboats and the German submarines that have picked them up (see 18 September).

U.S. freighter *Mae* is torpedoed, shelled, and sunk by German submarine *U 515* approximately 41 miles north of Georgetown, British Guiana, 08°03'N, 58°13'W; one crewman is killed. Norwegian merchantman *Sorwangen* rescues the 31 surviving merchant crewmen and the nine-man Armed Guard, and transfers them to Canadian merchantman *Gypsum King*, which takes them to Georgetown.

18 Friday

PACIFIC. Seventh Marine Regiment arrives on Guadalcanal.

ATLANTIC. German submarine *U 455* lays mines off Charleston, South Carolina.

British destroyer HMS *Vimy* is detached from convoy to investigate raft containing survivors from U.S. freighter *West Lashaway* (sunk by German submarine *U 66* on 30 August). *Vimy*, believing the hoisted sail to be part of the disguise of a U-boat, opens fire on the raft. Her gunnery, however, is fortunately bad, and the survivors (who hurriedly strike the sail) are rescued. This group includes among them the woman missionary and four children (see 24 September).

Laconia Incident: Vichy French colonial sloop *Dumont D'Urville* takes on board 42 survivors from sunken British transport *Laconia* that had been rescued by Italian submarine *Capellini*.

ARCTIC. German torpedo planes continue attacks upon Archangel, USSR–bound convoy PQ 18, sinking U.S. freighter *Kentucky* approximately 35 miles west of Cape Kanin, USSR. Two British minesweepers rescue all 38 merchant seamen and the 16-man Armed Guard.

19 Saturday

PACIFIC. Submarine *Amberjack* (SS 219) sinks Japanese transport *Shirogane Maru* at northern entrance of Bougainville Strait, 06°33'S, 156°05'E.

Destroyer *Hughes* (DD 410), in TF 17, rescues surviving crewmen of USAAF B-17 that had made a forced landing in the Coral Sea one week before.

ATLANTIC. U.S. freighter *Wichita* is sunk by German submarine *U 516* about 300 miles northeast of Barbados, 15°00'N, 54°00'W. There are no survivors from either the 40-man merchant complement or 10-man Armed Guard.[111]

Swedish steamship *Etna* rescues 22 survivors from lifeboat from U.S. tanker *Patrick J. Hurley*, sunk by German submarine *U 512* on 12 September (see 2 October).

20 Sunday

PACIFIC. Naval Operating Base, Auckland, New Zealand, is established.

ARCTIC. U.S. freighter *Silver Sword*, in convoy QP 14, is sunk by German submarine *U 225* at 75°41'N, 03°12'E; rescue ships *Rathlin* and *Zamalek* pick up all 32 merchant seamen (one of whom dies later of his injuries), the 11-man Armed Guard, and 18 passengers (crewmen from freighters *Peter Kerr* and *Honomu*, sunk on 5 July in PQ 17).

21 Monday

PACIFIC. Submarine *Grouper* (SS 214) sinks Japanese army cargo ship *Tone Maru* east of Shanghai, China, 31°18'N, 123°27'E.

Submarine *Trout* (SS 202) sinks Japanese auxiliary netlayer *Koei Maru* south of Truk, 06°54'N, 151°51'E.

22 Tuesday

PACIFIC. Submarine *Amberjack* (SS 219), en route to patrol off Kieta, Bougainville, is damaged when she runs aground on an uncharted coral head off Oema Island, 06°31'31"S, 155°59'E. The damage, however, does not hinder her from continuing her patrol.

INDIAN OCEAN. U.S. freighter *Paul Luckenbach* is sunk by Japanese submarine *I 29* approximately 800 miles from the coast of India, 10°03'N, 63°42'E; although the four lifeboats containing the entire 44-man complement and 17-man Armed Guard become separated during the 16- and 21- day voyages, all hands reach safety.

ATLANTIC. U.S. tanker *Esso Williamsburg* is sunk by German submarine *U 211* approximately 500 miles south of Cape Farewell, Greenland, 53°12′N, 41°00′W; there are no survivors from the 42-man crew and 18-man Armed Guard.

ARCTIC. U.S. freighter *Bellingham*, in convoy QP 14, is sunk by German submarine *U 435* approximately 45 miles west of Jan Mayen Island, 71°23′N, 11°03′E; escort vessels rescue the 39 merchant seamen, 10-man Armed Guard, and 26 passengers (survivors from freighters *Pan Kraft* and *Pan Atlantic*, sunk in PQ 17 on 5 and 6 July, respectively, and who are being transported home).

23 Wednesday

ATLANTIC. U.S. freighter *Antinous* is torpedoed by German submarine *U 515* off Georgetown, British Guiana, 08°58′N, 59°33′W; Armed Guard gunfire forces *U 515* to submerge. All hands abandon *Antinous*; a volunteer crew returns to the ship to try and get her under way (see 24 September).

U.S. freighter *Penmar*, straggling from convoy SC 100 and steering toward Cape Farewell, is sunk by German submarine *U 432* at 58°12′N, 34°35′W. One man dies as the ship is being abandoned, but 38 merchant sailors and the 22-man Armed Guard are rescued by Coast Guard cutter *Bibb* (WPG 31) and transported to Iceland.

24 Thursday

PACIFIC. Japanese land on Maiana, Gilberts.

SBDs (VMSB 231 and VS 3) from Henderson Field, Guadalcanal, damage Japanese destroyer *Umikaze* while the ship engages in resupply operations.

USAAF B-17 (South Pacific Force) damages Japanese seaplane carrier *Sanuki Maru* off Shortland Island, Solomons.

INDIAN OCEAN. U.S. freighter *Losmar* is sunk by Japanese submarine *I 165* about 250 miles west of Cape Comorin, India, 07°40′N, 74°15′E; of the ship's nine-man Armed Guard detachment, three are lost when she sinks. British ship *Louise Moller* will rescue 14 survivors on 5 October; seven survivors will reach the west coast of Ceylon by boat on 17 October.

ATLANTIC. U.S. freighter *John Winthrop*, straggling from convoy ON 131, is sunk by German submarine *U 619* at 56°00′N, 31°00′W. There are no survivors from the 39-man merchant complement or the 13-man Armed Guard.

U.S. freighter *West Chetac* is sunk by German submarine *U 175* north of British Guiana, 08°06′N, 58°12′W; only 17 of the 39-man crew and two of the 11-man Armed Guard reach the rafts that float free of the ship as she sinks in heavy seas. *U 175* conducts a brief interrogation of the survivors before departing (see 1 October).

U.S. freighter *Antinous*, torpedoed the previous day, is reboarded by the rest of the crew and is taken in tow by British rescue tug HMS *Zwarte Zee*. Soon thereafter, however, *Antinous* is torpedoed by *U 512*. Again, *Antinous* is abandoned, and all hands are picked up by *Zwarte Zee* and HMS *Busy*. The freighter sinks later that day.

West Indian fishing boat rescues last two survivors (one of whom subsequently dies of exposure) of U.S. freighter *West Lashaway* (sunk by German submarine *U 66* on 30 August). All told, only 12 of the 38-man merchant complement, one of the 9-man Armed Guard, and five of nine passengers survive *West Lashaway*'s loss.

25 Friday

PACIFIC. Submarine *Sargo* (SS 188) sinks Japanese freighter *Teibo Maru* (ex-Danish *Nordbo*) off coast of French Indochina, 180 miles east of Saigon, 10°31′N, 109°31′E.

Japanese land on Beru, Gilberts.

USAAF B-17s damage Japanese light cruiser *Yura* off Shortland Island.

Japanese submarine *I 5* is damaged by gunfire off Guadalcanal.

Japanese destroyers *Isokaze* and *Mochizuki* rescue survivors of destroyer *Yayoi*, sunk on 11 September, from Normanby Island, D'Entrecasteaux Islands.

USAAF P-39s (11th Air Force) damage Japanese submarine *RO 67* off Kiska, Aleutians.

26 Saturday

PACIFIC. Japanese submarine *I 33* accidentally sinks while undergoing voyage repairs at Truk, Carolines.

Japanese weather observation ship *No. 6 Kyoei Maru* is sunk by RAAF Beaufighters and a Hudson off Woodlark Island off the southeastern coast of New Guinea.

27 Sunday

PACIFIC. First Battalion, Seventh Marines (Lieutenant Colonel Lewis B. Puller, USMC) withdraws from Matanikau River, Guadalcanal, covered by destroyer *Monssen* (DD 436) and USMC SBD (VMSB 231). All available Higgins boats (24) are sent to extract the

marines, under Signalman First Class Douglas A. Munro, USCG. Munro, with a volunteer crew, interposes his boat to draw fire away from the five craft that are embarking marines. Munro is killed; two of his three-man crew are wounded (one mortally). Succeeding in his mission, although at the cost of his own life, Munro is awarded the Medal of Honor posthumously.[112]

Japanese land on Kuria, Gilberts.

ATLANTIC. U.S. freighter *Stephen Hopkins* engages German auxiliary cruiser *Stier* (*Schiffe 23*) and supply ship *Tannenfels* in a surface gunnery action in the central South Atlantic on the shipping lane between Capetown, South Africa, and Paramaribo, Dutch Guiana. *Stier* sinks *Stephen Hopkins*, but the German raider sinks after having received heavy damage inflicted by the freighter's Armed Guard (Lieutenant [j.g.] Kenneth M. Willett, USNR) and civilian volunteer (Cadet Midshipman Edwin J. O'Hara) gunners, 28°08′S, 20°01′W. *Tannenfels* rescues *Stier*'s survivors (see 27 October). Lieutenant Willett will receive a posthumous Navy Cross.[113]

28 Monday

PACIFIC. Submarine *Nautilus* (SS 168) torpedoes and sinks Japanese freighter *No. 6 Tamon Maru* east of Japan, 40°35′N, 141°50′N.

Submarine *Sculpin* (SS 191) torpedoes Japanese seaplane carrier *Nisshin* east of Kokoda Island; the submarine is damaged by depth charges off New Britain, 03°47′S, 151°36′E, but continues her patrol.

Submarine *Trout* (SS 202) torpedoes Japanese escort carrier *Taiyo* east of Truk, 06°59′N, 151°45′E.

ATLANTIC. U.S. freighter *Alcoa Mariner* is sunk by German submarine *U 175* approximately 20 miles off the mouth of the Orinoco River, 08°57′N, 60°08′W; all hands survive the loss of the ship. Canadian motorship *Turret Cape* rescues 41 merchant seamen and the 13-man Armed Guard.

29 Tuesday

PACIFIC. Small reconnaissance seaplane from Japanese submarine *I 25* drops incendiary bombs on a forest in southern coastal Oregon—the second and last time a Japanese aircraft will bomb the continental United States during World War II in an attempt to ignite forest fires.

Cargo ship *Alhena* (AK 26) is torpedoed by Japanese submarine *I 4*, 20 miles south of San Cristobal Island, Solomons, 10°47′S, 161°16′E.

ATLANTIC. Open lighters *YC 898* and *YC 899* sink off Key West, Florida, while in tow en route from New Orleans, Louisiana, to Key West.

30 Wednesday

PACIFIC. Heavy cruiser *San Francisco* (CA 38) and light minelayer *Breese* (DM 18) are damaged in collision during night illumination exercises east of Espíritu Santo, New Hebrides, 15°39′S, 167°39′E. Destroyer *Farragut* (DD 348) tows the damaged *Breese* to Espíritu Santo.

Admiral Chester W. Nimitz, Commander in Chief Pacific Fleet, arrives on Guadalcanal in a USAAF B-17, to personally ascertain whether or not the island can be held, and to present decorations. He will leave the following day.

OCTOBER

1 Thursday

PACIFIC. Submarine *Grouper* (SS 214) torpedoes and sinks Japanese army transport *Lisbon Maru* 20 miles north of Chushan Island, 29°57′N, 122°56′N. Unbeknown to the submariners, *Lisbon Maru* has on board 1,800 British prisoners of war. Few survive the sinking.

Submarine *Kingfish* (SS 234) torpedoes and sinks freighter *Yomei Maru* off eastern shore of Kii Strait, Honshu, Japan, 33°31′N, 135°26′E.

Submarine *Nautilus* (SS 168) sinks freighter *Tosei Maru* east of Shiriya Saki, Honshu, Japan, 41°20′N, 141°35′E.

Submarine *Sturgeon* (SS 187) torpedoes and damages Japanese aircraft transport *Katsuragi Maru* off Cape St. George, New Ireland, 05°51′S, 153°18′E, and survives counterattacks by escorting destroyer *Hakaze*.

ATLANTIC. Advanced Group, Amphibious Forces, Atlantic Fleet becomes Amphibious Forces, Europe under Commander U.S. Naval Forces Europe.

Destroyer *Roe* (DD 418), 20 miles off the coast of Trinidad, rescues 17 merchant seamen and two Armed Guard sailors who have survived the loss of U.S. freighter *West Chetac* (sunk by German submarine *U 175* on 24 September) and transports them to Port of Spain.

2 Friday

PACIFIC. Fifth Defense Battalion, USMC, occupies Funafuti, Ellice Islands.

Transport *St. Mihiel* (AP 32) is damaged when she strikes uncharted underwater object off Turn Island, Alaska.

USAAF B-17s (5th Air Force) bomb Japanese shipping and installations at Rabaul, damaging light cruiser *Tenryu*.

ATLANTIC. USAAF B-18 (99th Bombardment Squadron) sinks German submarine *U 512* off French Guiana, 06°50′N, 52°25′W.[114]

U.S. freighter *Alcoa Transport* is sunk by German submarine *U 201* about 100 miles southeast of Trinidad, 09°03′N, 60°10′W. Submarine chaser *PC 490* rescues the surviving 31 merchant seamen (three crewmen are killed; a fourth dies of wounds later) and five-man Armed Guard sailors.

British steamship *Loch Dee* rescues 23 survivors from lifeboat from U.S. tanker *Patrick J. Hurley*, sunk by German submarine *U 512* on 12 September. All told, 31 of 44 merchant seamen and 14 of 18 Armed Guard sailors survive the loss of *Patrick J. Hurley*.

3 Saturday

PACIFIC. SBDs (VS 71, VMSB 141, VMSB 231, and VS 3) and TBFs (VT 8) from Henderson Field attack Japanese supply convoy en route to Guadalcanal, damaging seaplane carrier *Nisshin*. RAAF Beauforts attack Japanese shipping at Faisi, Bougainville.

Submarine *Greenling* (SS 213) sinks Japanese freighter *Kinkai Maru* off northeast coast of Honshu, 38°46′N, 142°02′E.

Submarine *Trout* (SS 202) is damaged by Japanese aerial bomb off Truk, Carolines, forcing the submarine to end her patrol.

Japanese submarine *I 1* extracts 71 men of the Tsukioka Unit from east side of Goodenough Island, off southeast coast of New Guinea (see 26 October).

4 Sunday

PACIFIC. Destroyers *Drayton* (DD 366) and *Flusser* (DD 368) are damaged in collision during exercises in Hawaiian Operating Area.

Submarine *Greenling* (SS 213) sinks Japanese freighter *Setsuyo Maru* off northeast coast of Honshu, 39°48′N, 142°08′E.

U.S. tanker *Camden* is torpedoed by Japanese submarine *I 25* off the coast of Oregon, 43°42′N, 124°52′W, and is abandoned. One crewman drowns as the men leave the ship. Swedish motorship *Kookaburra* rescues the 38 merchant seamen and the nine Armed Guard sailors (see 5 October).

CARIBBEAN. U.S. freighter *Caribstar* is sunk by German submarine *U 175* off the mouth of the Orinoco River, 08°30′N, 59°37′W. The 29-man merchant crew suffers four dead and 13 wounded (two of whom later die of their wounds); there are no casualties among the six-man Armed Guard. Submarine chaser *PC 469* rescues survivors.

ATLANTIC. U.S. tanker *Robert H. Colley*, in convoy HX 209, is torpedoed by German submarine *U 254* at 59°06′N, 28°18′W, and breaks in two, with the forward part sinking first. Twenty of the 44-man merchant complement perish, as do eight of the 17 Armed Guard sailors (see 5 October).

5 Monday

PACIFIC. TF 17 (Rear Admiral George D. Murray), formed around carrier *Hornet* (CV 8), attacks "Tokyo Express" staging areas: Japanese installations in Buin-Tonolei area and Faisi, Bougainville, Solomons. SBDs (VS 8) damage destroyers *Minegumo* and *Murasame* and near-miss seaplane carriers *Sanuki Maru* and *Sanyo Maru*. TF 17's raid forces temporary postponement of planned resupply run by seaplane carrier *Nisshin*.

SBDs (VS 3, VS 71, and VMSB 141) from Henderson Field, Guadalcanal, attack Japanese convoy.

PBY (Commander Aircraft South Pacific) sinks Japanese submarine *I 22* near Indispensable Strait, Solomons.[115]

Submarine *Trigger* (SS 237) damages Japanese transport *Shinkoku Maru* north of Haha Jima, 31°40′N, 142°06′E.

U.S. tanker *Camden*, torpedoed by Japanese submarine *I 25* the previous day and abandoned, is taken in tow by tug *Kenai* (see 10 October).

ATLANTIC. PBY (VP 73) sinks German submarine *U 582* south of Iceland at 58°52′N, 21°42′W.

German submarine *U 175* torpedoes, shells, and sinks U.S. freighter *William A. McKenney* about 50 miles east of Corocoro Island, Venezuela, 08°35′N, 59°20′W; one man is killed. Destroyer *Blakeley* (DD 150) rescues 30 merchant seamen and the four-man Armed Guard.

British corvette HMS *Borage* rescues the 24 merchant seamen and nine Armed Guard sailors from the after section of U.S. tanker *Robert H. Colley* (the ship had been torpedoed by German submarine *U 254* the previous day). *Borage* scuttles the stern section of the ship with gunfire and depth charges.

6 Tuesday

PACIFIC. U.S. tanker *Larry Doheny* is torpedoed by Japanese submarine *I 25* off the coast of Oregon, 42°20′N, 125°02′W, and abandoned. Two of the ship's 34-man merchant complement die in the attack, as do four of the eight-man Armed Guard. Small seaplane tender *Coos Bay* (AVP 25) rescues the survivors. *Larry Doheny* sinks the next morning.

7 Wednesday

PACIFIC. Submarine *Amberjack* (SS 219) sinks Japanese supply ship *Senkei Maru* northwest of Kapingamarangi Atoll, 01°55′N, 153°01′E.

Submarine *Sculpin* (SS 191) sinks Japanese army transport *Naminoue Maru* northwest of Rabaul, 03°14′S, 150°01′E. Although damaged by counterattacking destroyer *Takanami*, *Sculpin* continues her patrol.

Japanese freighter *Midori Maru* founders and sinks above Woosung, China, 31°00′N, 122°30′E.

ATLANTIC. U.S. freighter *Chickasaw City* is sunk by German submarine *U 172* approximately 85 miles south-southwest of Cape Town, South Africa, 34°00′S, 17°16′E; five of the 37-man crew, one of the 11-man Armed Guard, and the sole passenger perish in the attack (see 8 October and 2 November).

U.S. freighter *John Carter Rose* is attacked by German submarine *U 201*; one dud torpedo fails to damage the merchantman and Armed Guard gunfire drives off the ship's assailant (see 8 October).

8 Thursday

PACIFIC. Submarine *Drum* (SS 228) attacks Japanese convoy off southern tip of Honshu, and sinks freighter *Hague Maru*, 34°06′N, 136°22′E.

Japanese guardboat *Toyohama Maru* is wrecked (cause unspecified), Wotje Atoll, Marshall Islands.

INDIAN OCEAN. U.S. tanker *Swiftsure* is torpedoed by German submarine *U 68* approximately 25 miles southeast of the Cape of Good Hope, 34°40′S, 18°25′E, and after firefighting efforts prove futile, is abandoned. There are no casualties among the 31-man crew, and all hands are rescued by a British minesweeper that comes out from Cape Town, South Africa (see 2 November).

ATLANTIC. U.S. freighter *John Carter Rose* is torpedoed by German submarine *U 202* at 10°27′N, 45°37′W; fires triggered by the explosions make abandoning ship difficult. Five of the 45-man crew perish, as do three of the 20-man Armed Guard. *U 201* returns, but a second dud torpedo fails to damage the merchantman. The U-boat then shells *John Carter Rose*, after which time the Germans provide the survivors with cigarettes, medical supplies, and food (see 13 October).

British corvette HMS *Rockrose* picks up 42 survivors (32 merchant seamen and 10 Armed Guard sailors) of U.S. freighter *Chickasaw City*,

sunk the previous day by German submarine *U 172* (see 2 November).

9 Friday

PACIFIC. TG 62.6 (Rear Admiral Richmond Kelly Turner), consisting of transports *McCawley* (AP 10) and *Zeilin* (AP 9) and eight high-speed transports, sails from Nouméa, New Caledonia, for Guadalcanal with the U.S. Army 164th Infantry Regiment embarked.

Auxiliary aircraft carrier *Copahee* (ACV 12) ferries 20 USMC F4Fs (VMF 121) to Henderson Field, Guadalcanal.

Small reconnaissance seaplane from Japanese submarine *I 7* reconnoiters Espíritu Santo, New Hebrides.

Submarine *Drum* (SS 228) sinks Japanese freighter *Yawatasan Maru* off Oshima Island, southern Honshu, close to the easternmost entry to Kii Strait, 33°27′N, 136°01′E.[116]

ATLANTIC. U.S. freighter *Coloradan* is sunk by German submarine *U 159* approximately 214 miles southwest of Cape Town, South Africa, 35°47′S, 14°34′E; six crewmen are killed in the attack. Survivors (who include 33 merchant seamen and the 15-man Armed Guard) divide themselves between two lifeboats; the men in no. 1 lifeboat are questioned by the Germans and are given a course to Cape Town (see 11 and 19 October and 2 November).

German submarine *U 505* is damaged by aircraft off Trinidad, B.W.I.[117]

U.S. freighter *Examelia* is sunk by German submarine *U 68* 20 miles south of the Cape of Good Hope, 34°52′S, 18°30′E; U-boat officers question the survivors before the enemy submersible leaves the area. U.S. freighter *John Lykes* subsequently rescues the survivors (30 of 38 merchant sailors and 10 of the 13-man Armed Guard) (see 2 November).

10 Saturday

PACIFIC. Submarine *Amberjack* (SS 219) damages Japanese transport *Tenryu Maru* (see 25 December 1943) and auxiliary *No. 2 Tonan Maru* (see 22 August 1944) off Kavieng, New Ireland, 02°36′S, 150°48′E.

Submarine *Seadragon* (SS 194) sinks Japanese transport *Shigure Maru* in Makassar Strait, off Balikpapan, Borneo, 01°01′S, 117°22′E.

Submarine *Wahoo* (SS 238) sinks Japanese collier *Kamoi Maru* off Bougainville, Solomons.

Submarine chaser *Ch 14* is damaged by planes (USAAF B-24s and B-17s, accompanied by P-38s, bomb shipping in Trout Lagoon and

off South Head) (11th Air Force) off Kiska, Aleutians.

U.S. tanker *Camden*, torpedoed by Japanese submarine *I 25* on 4 October, catches fire and sinks off the mouth of the Columbia River, 46°46′38″N, 124°31′15″W.

11 Sunday

PACIFIC. Japanese transport force (Rear Admiral Joshima Koji), formed around seaplane carriers *Chitose* and *Nisshin* and six destroyers, reaches Tassafaronga, Guadalcanal, to disembark elements of the Japanese Army's 2nd Infantry Division. Three heavy cruisers and two destroyers (Rear Admiral Goto Aritomo, his flag in heavy cruiser *Aoba*) are to provide cover by shelling Henderson Field. Shortly before midnight, however, the Battle of Cape Esperance begins when TG 64.2 (Rear Admiral Norman Scott) bars Goto's way. Heavy cruiser *Salt Lake City* (CA 25) and light cruiser *Boise* (CL 47) are damaged (the latter by shellfire from Japanese heavy cruiser *Kinugasa*), but combine to cripple heavy cruiser *Furutaka*; destroyers *Duncan* (DD 485) and *Farenholt* (DD 491) are also damaged by Japanese gunfire, the latter possibly by friendly fire from either *Boise* or *Helena* (CL 50) as well. American cruiser and destroyer gunfire sinks Japanese destroyer *Fubuki*, 09°06′S, 159°38′E, and damages heavy cruiser *Aoba* (Rear Admiral Goto is killed on board his flagship) and destroyer *Hatsuyuki* (see 12 October).

Submarine *Searaven* (SS 196) torpedoes German blockade runner *Regensburg* in Sunda Strait, N.E.I.

Japanese submarine *I 25*, homeward bound from her deployment off the U.S. West Coast, torpedoes and sinks Soviet submarine *L 16* (bound from Dutch Harbor, Alaska, to San Francisco, California), 46°41′N, 138°56′E.

Japanese cargo vessel *Nichiei Maru* is sunk in collision with merchantman *Yugumo Maru* west of Korea, 35°00′N, 125°00′E.

ATLANTIC. British destroyer HMS *Active* rescues 23 survivors from no. 2 lifeboat from U.S. freighter *Coloradan*, which had been sunk by German submarine *U 159* on 9 October (see 19 October).

U.S. freighter *Steel Scientist*, en route to Paramaribo, Dutch Guiana, is sunk by German submarine *U 514*, 05°48′N, 51°39′W; one crewman is killed in the attack. Survivors (who include 37 merchant seamen and the nine-man Armed Guard) take to a gig and three lifeboats (see 19 and 20 October).

12 Monday

PACIFIC. As the result of damage received in the Battle of Cape Esperance the previous day, Japanese heavy cruiser *Furutaka* sinks, 09°02′30″S, 159°33′30″E; destroyer *Hatsuyuki* recovers *Furutaka*'s survivors; and destroyers *Murakumo* and *Shirayuki* rescue survivors from *Fubuki*. Despite efforts of a salvage party from destroyer *McCalla* (DD 488), destroyer *Duncan* (DD 485) sinks as the result of battle damage. *McCalla* also conducts unsuccessful attempt to sink Japanese submarine *I 2* off Guadalcanal.

SBDs (VS 71) sink Japanese destroyer *Natsugumo* off Savo Island; destroyer *Murakumo*, after being damaged by TBFs (VT 8), Navy and USMC SBDs (VS 3, VS 71, and VMSB 141), and USMC F4Fs (VMF 121, VMF 212, and VMF 224) off New Georgia, Solomons, is scuttled by destroyer *Shirayuki*. Destroyers *Gwin* (DD 433), *Nicholas* (DD 449), and *Sterett* (DD 407) shell Japanese artillery positions on Guadalcanal.

Submarine *Nautilus* (SS 168) is damaged by depth charges off northern Honshu, 41°05′N, 141°58′E, but remains on patrol.

High-speed minesweepers *Southard* (DMS 10) and *Hovey* (DMS 11) tow motor torpedo boats *PT 38, PT 46, PT 48,* and *PT 60* to a point 300 miles south of Tulagi, then release them to proceed to Tulagi under their own power.

Transport *Mount Vernon* (AP 22) is stranded by storm in Sydney, Australia, harbor, but is not damaged in the accidental grounding.

ATLANTIC. U.S. freighter *Pan Gulf*, in convoy TAG 18S, blunders into U.S. minefield at 10°01′N, 61°50′W; she returns to Trinidad under her own power. There are no casualties among the 38-man merchant complement and 21-man Armed Guard.

13 Tuesday

PACIFIC. TG 62.6 (Rear Admiral Richmond Kelly Turner) arrives at Kukum, Guadalcanal, where transports *McCawley* (AP 10) and *Zeilin* (AP 9) disembark U.S. Army's 164th Infantry Regiment. These soldiers, the first major infusion of troops to arrive at Guadalcanal, will reinforce the First Marine Division.

High-speed minesweepers *Hovey* (DMS 11) and *Trever* (DMS 16) rescue 113 Japanese survivors of the Battle of Cape Esperance.

Small reconnaissance seaplane from Japanese submarine *I 7* reconnoiters Espíritu Santo.

Japanese submarine *I 30* is sunk by mine, three miles east of Singapore.

ATLANTIC. U.S. freighter *Susana*, in convoy SC 104 and bound for Cardiff, Wales, is sunk by German submarine *U 221*, 53°41′N, 41°23′W; 27 of the 42-man crew perish with the ship, as do 10 of the 16-man Armed Guard. British rescue ship *Gothland* rescues the six Armed Guard survivors and the 15 merchant seamen who survive *Susana*'s loss.

U.S. freighter *West Humhaw* rescues 18 survivors of freighter *John Carter Rose*, sunk by *U 201* and *U 202* on 8 October. Argentinian tanker *Santa Cruz* picks up the remainder of those who survive the merchantman's loss.

14 Wednesday

PACIFIC. Motor torpedo boats *PT 60, PT 38, PT 46,* and *PT 48* (Lieutenant Commander Alan R. Montgomery) engage Japanese surface force (Rear Admiral Kurita Takeo), composed of battleships *Haruna* and *Kongo*, light cruiser *Isuzu*, and seven destroyers, bombarding Henderson Field, Guadalcanal. Destroyer *Naganami* turns back the motor torpedo boats; bombardment destroys 48 of 90 planes at the field, putting the facility temporarily out of action. *PT 60* is damaged by grounding on coral reef off Guadalcanal.

SBDs (Guadalcanal-based VS 3) attack six-ship Japanese convoy escorted by eight destroyers heading southward toward Guadalcanal between Santa Isabel and Florida Islands, 08°50′S, 160°00′E, but inflict no damage.

Submarine *Finback* (SS 230), attacking Japanese convoy, sinks army transport *Teison Maru* about 20 miles off Tansui Harbor, on northwest tip of Formosa, 25°20′N, 121°25′E.

Submarine *Grampus* (SS 207) lands Australian coastwatchers on Vella Lavella, Solomons (see 19 October).

Submarine *Greenling* (SS 213) sinks Japanese army cargo ship *Takusei Maru* six miles off Todo Saki, off northeast coast of Honshu, 39°33′N, 142°15′E.

Submarine *Sculpin* (SS 191) sinks Japanese army cargo ship *Sumiyoshi Maru* 75 miles southwest of Kavieng, New Ireland, 03°51′S, 151°21′E.

Submarine *Skipjack* (SS 184) sinks Japanese army cargo ship *Shunko Maru* about 450 miles west-southwest of Truk, 05°35′N, 144°25′E.

Japanese submarine *I 7* shells Espíritu Santo.

15 Thursday

PACIFIC. Japanese heavy cruisers *Chokai* and *Kinugasa* (Vice Admiral Mikawa Gunichi) bombard Henderson Field, covering the movement of six destroyers and eleven transports to Tassafaronga, Guadalcanal. Planes from Henderson Field, including USMC and Navy SBDs (VMSB 141, VB 6, and other unidentified units), USAAF B-17s and P-39/P400s, Navy F4Fs (VF 5), and USMC PBY (personal flag plane of Commanding General First Marine Aircraft Wing), conduct a succession of attacks upon Japanese supply convoy off Tassafaronga undamaged by VS 3's strike the previous day. USAAF B-17s damage transport *Azumasan Maru* that, along with freighter *Kyushu Maru*, is run aground, where uncontrollable fires destroy both ships. Air attacks also sink *Sasago Maru* and damage destroyer *Samidare*.[118]

TU 62.4.5 (Captain William F. Dietrich) is proceeding toward Guadalcanal when it receives word of Japanese air strike headed in its direction. Consequently, cargo ship *Alchiba* (AK 23) casts loose its tow, Pan American Airways barge *PAB No. 6* (see 23 October). Carrier bombers from *Zuikaku* attack the convoy. Cargo ship *Bellatrix* (AK 20) is damaged by near-misses; *Alchiba* is damaged by own gunfire and near-missed by bombs as well. Bombs also near-miss escorting destroyer *Nicholas* (DD 449). Gunboat *Jamestown* (PG 55), which aids in the antiaircraft barrage, is not attacked.

TU 62.4.6 (Commander Harry E. Hubbard) prepares for air attack: Destroyer *Meredith* (DD 434) takes on board crew of tug *Vireo* (AT 144) off San Cristobal, Solomons, but before *Meredith* can scuttle the tug with a torpedo to prevent her from falling into enemy hands, the destroyer is overwhelmed and sunk by bombs and aerial torpedoes dropped by planes from Japanese carrier *Zuikaku*, 11°53′S, 163°20′E; *Vireo* and her tow (Pan American Airways barge *PAB No. 4*), having been abandoned, drift off unmolested. Some *Meredith* survivors reach safety on board the tug (see 18 October).

Heavy cruiser *Portland* (CA 33) bombards Japanese shipping and installations at Tarawa, Gilberts.

Submarine *Skipjack* (SS 184) attacks Japanese auxiliary *Kifuku Maru* east of the Palaus, 04°36′N, 146°59′E. *Skipjack*'s torpedoes miss; *Kifuku Maru* returns fire with her guns and escapes into a rain squall.

Submarine Base, Fremantle-Perth, Australia, is established.

Patrol Wing 14 (Captain William M. McDade) is established at San Diego, California, for operations in Western Sea Frontier.

16 Friday

PACIFIC. Japanese surface force (Rear Admiral Omori Sentaro), with heavy cruisers *Maya* and *Myoko*, light cruiser *Isuzu*, and seven destroyers (Rear Admiral Tanaka Raizo), shells Henderson Field, Guadalcanal.

TF 17, formed around carrier *Hornet* (CV 8) (Rear Admiral George D. Murray), attacks Japanese troop concentrations on Guadalcanal, and seaplane base at Rekata Bay, Santa Isabel, Solomons. TBFs (VT 6) bomb transport *Azumasan Maru*, damaged the previous day and grounded between Cape Esperance and Lunga Point.

Seaplane tender (destroyer) *McFarland* (AVD 14) is damaged by Japanese carrier bombers (31st *Kokutai*), Lunga Roads, Guadalcanal, 09°24′S, 160°02′E. The attack on *McFarland* ends just as a ferry flight (F4Fs, SBDs, and R4Ds) reaches Guadalcanal. Marine Lieutenant Colonel Harold W. Bauer, in an F4F (VMF 212), attacks the retiring enemy formation and quickly splashes three Type 99s, a display of good shooting that will figure in the subsequent award to Bauer of the Medal of Honor (posthumously). District patrol vessel *YP 239* tows *McFarland* to Tulagi.

After attacks by Navy PBYs fail, USAAF B-26s (11th Air Force) sink Japanese destroyer *Oboro* about 20 miles northeast of Sirius Point, Kiska, 52°17′N, 178°08′E, and damage destroyer *Hatsuharu*.

Submarine *Thresher* (SS 200) mines the approaches to Bangkok, Thailand, in the first U.S. Navy submarine mine plant of World War II.

ATLANTIC. U.S. freighter *Winona*, in convoy bound for Rio de Janeiro, Brazil, is torpedoed by German submarine *U 160* at 11°00′N, 61°10′W, and veers out of line, grazing the stern of steamship *Austvangen*. One merchant seaman and two Armed Guard sailors suffer injuries in the attack, but there are no fatalities among the 42-man crew or 15-man Armed Guard (see 17 October).

17 Saturday

PACIFIC. Submarine *Trigger* (SS 237) sinks Japanese freighter *Holland Maru* close inshore near the mouth of Bungo Strait, off Kyushu, 32°21′N, 132°04′E.

ATLANTIC. U.S. freighter *Angelina*, straggling from New York–bound convoy ON 137, is torpedoed by German submarine *U 618* at 49°39′N, 30°20′W (see 18 October).

U.S. freighter *Winona*, torpedoed the day before by German submarine *U 160*, arrives at Port of Spain, Trinidad, under her own power.

18 Sunday

PACIFIC. Vice Admiral William F. Halsey Jr. relieves Vice Admiral Robert L. Ghormley as Commander South Pacific Area and South Pacific Force, on board auxiliary *Argonne* (AG 31) at Nouméa, New Caledonia.

Submarine *Grampus* (SS 207) torpedoes Japanese light cruiser *Yura* off Choiseul, 07°47′S, 157°19′E, but the one "fish" that strikes the enemy ship fails to explode.

Submarine *Greenling* (SS 213) sinks Japanese transport *Hakonesan Maru* close inshore off northeast coast of Honshu, 38°46′N, 142°03′E.

Tug *Seminole* (AT 65), pushing on after finding tug *Vireo* (AT 144) adrift (see 21 October), recovers Pan American Airways barge *PAB No. 4*, which has been adrift since 15 October, and takes it in tow, arriving at Guadalcanal the following day. The arrival of the 100,000-gallon cargo of aviation gasoline on board the barge proves timely. *Seminole* is retained at Guadalcanal to handle barges and damaged ships (see 25 October).

ATLANTIC. U.S. freighter *Angelina*, straggling from New York–bound convoy ON 137, is again torpedoed by German submarine *U 618* at 49°39′N, 30°20′W, and abandoned; "exceptionally heavy sea" claims 33 crewmen and 13 Armed Guards. British rescue ship *Bury* rescues six men (one of whom dies later) from a raft and three from a lifeboat. Only four merchant seamen and four Armed Guards thus survive the ship's loss. U.S. freighter *Steel Navigator*, also straggling from ON 137, takes on 40-degree list as her sand ballast shifts; Armed Guard volunteers shovel ballast for 30 hours without relief (reducing the list to 12 degrees) until financial bonus offered by ship's master induces reluctant merchant sailors to lend a hand in the arduous work (see 19 October).

19 Monday

PACIFIC. SBDs (VS 71, VMSB 141, and VB 6) from Henderson Field attack three Japanese destroyers north of Guadalcanal, damaging *Uranami*.

Destroyer *O'Brien* (DD 415), damaged by submarine torpedo on 15 September, breaks in two and sinks en route to United States for repairs, 53 miles north-northwest of Tutuila, Samoa, 13°30′S, 171°18′E.

Submarine *Amberjack* (SS 219) arrives at Espíritu Santo, New Hebrides, assigned temporarily to Commander Aircraft South Pacific

for duty. Over the next three days, two of the submarine's fuel tanks will be cleaned and converted to carry aviation gasoline. She will also take on board 100-pound bombs and embark USAAF enlisted ground crew for transportation to Guadalcanal.

Submarine *Grampus* (SS 207) lands Australian coastwatchers on Choiseul Island, Solomons.

Small reconnaissance seaplane from Japanese submarine *I 19* reconnoiters Nouméa, New Caledonia.

ATLANTIC. U.S. freighter *Steel Navigator*, straggling from convoy ON 137, is attacked by German submarine *U 610*; *Steel Navigator* briefly drives off the shadower with 5-inch gunfire, but the U-boat returns and torpedoes and sinks the freighter at 49°20′N, 32°00′W. Hastily launched motor boat swamps in heavy seas; no. 3 lifeboat swamps as the ship plunges and spills its 35 occupants into the sea. *U 610* surfaces and approaches the survivors' boats and rafts; when questions shouted by the submarine's commander fail to get answers, the enemy threatens to cut a raft in two. After answers are given in the brief interrogation, the Germans refuse to provide a course to the nearest land and depart. Subsequently, survivors right no. 3 lifeboat and redistribute themselves; the boats become separated (see 27 October).

Fishing boat (nationality unspecified) tows no. 1 lifeboat, with 25 men on board, from U.S. freighter *Coloradan*, which had been sunk by German submarine *U 159* on 9 October, into Thorne Bay, South Africa; the Americans reach Cape Town the next day (see 2 November).

Master and radio operator in gig from U.S. freighter *Steel Scientist*, sunk by German submarine *U 514* on 11 October, reach Tarlogie, British Guiana (see 20 October).

20 Tuesday

PACIFIC. Heavy cruiser *Chester* (CA 27) is torpedoed by Japanese submarine *I 176*, 120 miles southeast of San Cristobal, Solomons, 13°31′S, 163°17′E.

Submarine *Drum* (SS 228), attacking Japanese convoy off southern Honshu, sinks freighter *Ryunan Maru*, 34°09′N, 136°46′E.

Submarine *Finback* (SS 230), attacking Japanese convoy off west coast of Formosa, damages army passenger-cargo ship *Africa Maru* and cargo ship *Yamafuji Maru*, 24°26′N, 120°25′E. Both sink the next morning.

Submarine *Gar* (SS 206) mines the approaches to Bangkok, Thailand.

Submarine *Tautog* (SS 199) sinks Japanese trawler *Nanshin Maru* in Sulu Sea, off northern Borneo, 06°59′N, 119°20′E.

ATLANTIC. Remainder of crew (35 merchant seamen and nine Armed Guard sailors) from U.S. freighter *Steel Scientist*, sunk by German submarine *U 514* on 11 October, reaches Paramaribo, Dutch Guiana, in three lifeboats.

21 Wednesday

PACIFIC. Destroyers *Grayson* (DD 435) and *Gwin* (DD 433) locate abandoned but undamaged tug *Vireo* (AT 144); *Grayson* is damaged by rolling into *Vireo* during recovery operations, 12°08′S, 161°04′E. Salvage party from *Grayson* ultimately brings the tug (abandoned on 15 October) safely into Espíritu Santo.

Japanese carrier *Hiyo* is damaged by engine room fire after departing Truk; she thus cannot participate in the Battle of Santa Cruz Islands (see 26 October).

Submarine *Guardfish* (SS 217) sinks Japanese freighter *Nichiho Maru* about 120 miles north-northeast of Formosa, 27°03′N, 122°42′E.

Submarine *Gudgeon* (SS 211), attacking Japanese convoy in the Bismarck Sea, sinks transport *Choko Maru* about 110 miles west-northwest of Rabaul, 03°30′S, 150°30′E.

MEDITERRANEAN. Major General Mark W. Clark, USA; Brigadier General Lyman M. Lemnitzer, USA; two additional Army officers; and Navy Captain Jerauld Wright are landed at Cherchel, Algeria, from British submarine HMS *Seraph* to meet with a French military delegation to ascertain French attitudes toward impending Allied invasion of North Africa. Among issues discussed is the French request for an American submarine to evacuate General Henri-Honoré Giraud from occupied France. Since none is available, a British submarine under temporary U.S. command will be substituted (see 5 November).

22 Thursday

PACIFIC. Destroyers *Mahan* (DD 364) and *Lamson* (DD 367), detached from TF 16 to "shoot up the Japanese picket boat line" west of the Gilberts, sink gunboat *Hakkaisan Maru* southwest of Tamana, 03°30′S, 175°15′E.

Naval Air Facility, Otter Point, Alaska, is established.

23 Friday

PACIFIC. High-speed minesweeper *Hovey* (DMS 11) recovers drifting and undamaged Pan American Airways barge *PAB No. 6*, released from its tow 15 October. The latter is

subsequently turned over to tug *Vireo* (AT 144), which has been returned to service.[119]

Submarine *Kingfish* (SS 234) sinks Japanese gunboat *Seikyo Maru* at entrance to Kii Strait, Honshu, 33°20′N, 135°27′E.

USAAF B-17s (5th Air Force) bomb Japanese shipping at Rabaul, New Britain; submarine chasers *Ch 31* and *Ch 32* are damaged in the raid.

Japanese submarine *I 7* shells Espíritu Santo.

ATLANTIC. U.S. freighter *Reuben Tipton*, bound for Trinidad, is sunk by German submarine *U 129*; three merchant seamen are killed in the attack (see 25 and 26 October).

24 Saturday

PACIFIC. Submarine *Nautilus* (SS 168) sinks Japanese freighter *Kenun Maru* about 20 miles east of Shiriya Saki, Honshu, 41°24′N, 141°50′E.

Submarine *Trigger* (SS 237) damages Japanese oiler *Nissho Maru* in Bungo Strait, 32°06′N, 132°34′E.

25 Sunday

PACIFIC. Submarine *Whale* (SS 239) lays mines off Honshu, Japan, at entrance to Inland Sea.

Motor torpedo boats *PT 37*, *PT 39*, *PT 45*, and *PT 61*, the second division of Motor Torpedo Boat Squadron 3, arrive at Tulagi.

Tug *Seminole* (AT 65) and district patrol vessel *YP 284* are sunk off Lunga Point, Guadalcanal, by Japanese destroyers *Akatsuki*, *Ikazuchi*, and *Shiratsuyu*, which are on their way to shell marine positions. Submarine *Amberjack* (SS 219), which has arrived that morning to deliver her cargo and disembark her passengers at Tulagi, is unable to attain a firing position to help *Seminole* and *YP 284*. Later, high-speed minesweeper *Zane* (DMS 14) is damaged by the same trio of enemy warships in Sealark Channel. The Japanese destroyers, however, do not emerge from the day's action unscathed. USMC F4Fs (VMF 121) strafe *Akatsuki* and *Ikazuchi*; USAAF P-39s damage *Samidare* and *Akizuki*. USMC shore batteries also do their part to hurry the destroyers on their way. *Amberjack* later disembarks USAAF enlisted men (67th Fighter Squadron and 347th Fighter Group), 200 100-pound bombs, and 9,000 gallons of aviation gasoline at Tulagi. Released from duty under Commander Air Force South Pacific, *Amberjack* sets course for Brisbane, Australia.

Japanese light cruiser *Yura* and four destroyers (Rear Admiral Takama Tamotsu),

proceeding through Indispensable Strait (ultimately to shell Henderson Field), are attacked by SBDs (VS 71 and VMSB 141), two of which (one SBD from each squadron) score direct hits on *Yura*. Attacks continue, by SBDs (VB 6, VS 71, and VMSB 141) and USAAF P-39s; the last strike is escorted by F4Fs (VF 71 and VMF 121). *Yura* receives three more direct hits and is abandoned. After destroyer *Murasame* takes off the light cruiser's survivors, *Harusame* and *Yudachi* scuttle *Yura* west of Cape Astrolabe, Malaita Island, 08°15′S, 159°57′E, with torpedoes and gunfire.

USAAF B-17s (5th Air Force) bomb Japanese shipping at Rabaul; auxiliary minelayer *Kotobuki Maru* is sunk.

Dutch submarine *O 23* damages Japanese army cargo ship *Shinyo Maru* off Penang, Malaya, 05°28′N, 99°56′E.

ATLANTIC. Master and one merchant seaman from U.S. freighter *Reuben Tipton*, sunk by German submarine *U 129* on 23 October, are recovered by PBM and transported to Trinidad (see 26 October).

CARIBBEAN. U.S. freighter *Daniel Boone* strikes mine while off coast of Panama; there are no casualties to the 42-man crew and 11-man Armed Guard, and the ship reaches port under her own power.[120]

26 Monday

PACIFIC. Battle of Santa Cruz Island: TF 61 (Rear Admiral Thomas C. Kinkaid), the combined TF 16 (Rear Admiral Kinkaid) and TF 17 (Rear Admiral George D. Murray), engage a numerically superior Japanese force (Vice Admiral Nagumo Chuichi). In the fourth and last carrier battle of 1942, *Enterprise* (CV 6) is damaged by planes from carriers *Junyo* and *Shokaku*, while *Hornet* (CV 8) is damaged by planes from *Junyo*, *Shokaku*, and *Zuikaku*. Battleship *South Dakota* (BB 57) and light cruiser *San Juan* (CL 54) are damaged by planes from *Junyo*; heavy cruiser *Portland* (CA 33) is hit by three aerial torpedoes that do not explode. Destroyer *Smith* (DD 378) is damaged by a crashing carrier attack plane from *Zuikaku*; while fighting *Hornet*'s fires and taking off her survivors, destroyer *Hughes* (DD 410) is damaged in collision with the doomed carrier (as well as by friendly fire earlier in the action). The attempt to scuttle the irreparably damaged *Hornet*, by gunfire and torpedoes from destroyers *Mustin* (DD 413) and *Anderson* (DD 411), fails (see 27 October). Destroyer *Porter* (DD 356) is torpedoed accidentally by battle-damaged and ditched TBF (VT 10), and,

Carrier *Hornet* (CV 8) heels to starboard as she turns at high speed as Japanese planes approach during the Battle of Santa Cruz, 26 October 1942; light cruiser *Juneau* (CL 52) is visible just beyond *Hornet*'s stern. Both ships are painted in the highly individualistic Measure 12 (Modified) camouflage. (Author's Collection)

deemed beyond salvage, is scuttled by destroyer *Shaw* (DD 373). SBDs (VS 10) from *Enterprise*, however, damage carrier *Zuiho*; SBDs (VB 8 and VS 8) from *Hornet* damage carrier *Shokaku* and destroyer *Terutsuki*; and SBDs from *Hornet* damage heavy cruiser *Chikuma*, 07°25′S, 163°30′E. Although the Japanese achieve a tactical victory at Santa Cruz, the failure of their 17th Army to take Henderson Field means that they cannot exploit the victory at sea to its fullest. The battle has also taken a heavy toll of Japanese carrier planes.

U.S. liner *President Coolidge*, chartered for use as a troop transport, blunders into U.S. minefield (laid on 3 August) in Segond Channel, Espíritu Santo, New Hebrides; the ship is beached to facilitate salvage, but slips into deep water and sinks. Four of the 5,050 Army troops are lost in the accident, as is one of the 290-man merchant complement. There are no casualties among the 51-man Armed Guard.[121]

Submarine *S 31* (SS 136) sinks Japanese transport *Keizan Maru* off Paramushir, Kurils, 50°10′N, 155°36′E.

Japanese light cruiser *Tenryu* extracts the remainder of the Tsukioka Unit from Goodenough Island, off the southeast coast of New Guinea.

INDIAN OCEAN. U.S. freighter *Anne Hutchinson* is torpedoed and shelled by German submarine *U 504* some 90 miles off East London,

South Africa, 33°12′S, 29°03′E; three crewmen are killed in the attack. The rest of the ship's complement (37 merchant sailors and the 17-man Armed Guard) take to two lifeboats (see 27, 28, and 31 October).

ATLANTIC. British motor torpedo boat rescues 39 merchant seamen and the 10-man Armed Guard from U.S. freighter *Reuben Tipton*, sunk by German submarine *U 129* on 23 October, and are transported to Barbados.

27 Tuesday

PACIFIC. Battleship *South Dakota* (BB 57) and destroyer *Mahan* (DD 364) are damaged in collision while retiring from the Battle of Santa Cruz.

Carrier *Hornet* (CV 8), damaged by bombs and torpedoes and attempted scuttling the previous day, is sunk by Japanese destroyers *Akigumo* and *Makigumo*, 08°38′S, 166°43′E.

Striking force (three radar-equipped PBYs from Espíritu Santo) hunts for the retiring Japanese carrier force. One PBY (VP 91) bombs and damages destroyer *Terutsuki*, 05°25′S, 164°35′E; a second PBY (VP 51) attacks carrier *Junyo* with a torpedo but misses, 06°51′S, 165°06′E.

ATLANTIC. German submarines attack convoy HX 212 as it heads toward the British Isles. U.S. tanker *Gurney E. Newlin* is torpedoed by

U 436; three crewmen are killed. The rest of the 37-man crew and the 19-man Armed Guard abandon ship into three boats and two rafts. Canadian corvette HMCS *Alberni* rescues six merchant seamen and six Armed Guard sailors; Canadian tanker *Bic Island* picks up 31 merchant seamen and 13 Armed Guard sailors (see 28 and 29 October).

U.S. freighter *Stephen Hopkins*'s survivors reach Itabopoano, Brazil; 32 of 40 merchant sailors, as well as nine of the 15-man Armed Guard, have perished either in battle or from exposure during the month-long ordeal in the lifeboat.

Survivors (10 merchant seamen and six Armed Guard sailors) from U.S. freighter *Steel Navigator*, sunk by German submarine *U 610* on 19 October, are rescued by British destroyer HMS *Decoy*. The other lifeboat containing the remaining 17 survivors is never found.

INDIAN OCEAN. Ten survivors from U.S. freighter *Anne Hutchinson*, who had abandoned their damaged ship on 26 October, are rescued by U.S. freighter *Steel Mariner* (see 28 and 31 October).

28 Wednesday

INDIAN OCEAN. Thirty-seven survivors from U.S. freighter *Anne Hutchinson*, who had abandoned their damaged ship on 26 October, are rescued by fishing trawler and taken to Port Alfred, South Africa. Aircraft sight the drifting freighter, now broken into two pieces, at 34°13′S, 26°55′E (see 31 October).

ATLANTIC. German submarines continue to stalk British Isles–bound convoy HX 212. U.S. tanker *Gurney E. Newlin*, abandoned after being torpedoed the previous day by German submarine *U 436*, is given the coup de grâce by *U 606* and sinks (see 29 October).

29 Thursday

PACIFIC. Submarine *Grenadier* (SS 210) lays mines in Tonkin Gulf off Haiphong, French Indochina.

PBY (VP 11) sinks Japanese submarine *I 172* west of San Cristobal Island, Solomons, 13°01′S, 162°45′E.

ATLANTIC. German submarine attacks on convoy HX 212 continue. U.S. tanker *Pan New York* is torpedoed by *U 624* about 550 miles west of Northern Ireland, 54°58′N, 23°56′W, and her cargo of aviation gasoline catches fire, virtually incinerating the ship. Of the 56 men on board (39 merchant seamen and a 17-man

Armed Guard), only 15 (13 crewmen and one Armed Guard sailor) are rescued by Canadian corvettes: HMCS *Rosthern* picks up 13 (one of whom dies after being rescued); HMCS *Summerside* picks up two. Escort vessels shell and depth charge the doomed ship. *U 224* torpedoes Canadian tanker *Bic Island* as it straggles from the convoy at 55°05'N, 23°27'E, and sinks her with all hands (including the 44 men rescued from U.S. tanker *Gurney E. Newlin* on 27 October).

U.S. freighter *West Kebar* is sunk by German submarine *U 129*, 14°57'N, 53°37'E, while en route from Freetown, Sierra Leone, to St. Thomas, Virgin Islands; three merchant seamen are killed. The survivors take to two lifeboats and one raft (see 8, 10, and 18 November).

30 Friday

PACIFIC. TG 64.2 (Rear Admiral Norman Scott), composed of light cruiser *Atlanta* (CL 51) and four destroyers, bombards Japanese positions at Point Cruz, Guadalcanal.

Small reconnaissance seaplane from Japanese submarine *I 9* reconnoiters Nouméa, New Caledonia.

Japanese land second invasion force at Attu, Aleutians.

ATLANTIC. Auxiliary aircraft carrier *Santee* (ACV 29), en route to North Africa to take part in Operation TORCH, is damaged when depth bomb accidentally falls free of an SBD (VGS 29) being catapulted, rolls off the flight deck, and explodes just under the starboard bow. *Santee* sustains no hull damage, but her radar and homing antennae (among other items of equipment) require repairs.

31 Saturday

PACIFIC. Submarine *Grayback* (SS 208) damages Japanese army cargo ship *Noto Maru* off Rabaul, 04°37'S, 152°30'E.

District patrol vessel *YP 345* is lost without a trace (cause unknown) about 80 miles northeast of Laysan Island, while en route from French Frigate Shoals, T.H., to Midway.

INDIAN OCEAN. South African naval forces board the forward portion of U.S. freighter *Anne Hutchinson*, abandoned on 26 October; British tug HMS *David Haigh* tows the bow portion (the after part has sunk in the meantime) to Port Elizabeth, South Africa.

NOVEMBER

1 Sunday

UNITED STATES. Patrol Wings are redesignated Fleet Air Wings.

ATLANTIC. U.S. freighter *George Thatcher*, bound for French Equatorial Africa, is torpedoed by German submarine *U 126*, 01°45'S, 07°30'E, and abandoned; five crewmen and five Armed Guard sailors, as well as eight soldier passengers, perish in the attack. Free French corvettes rescue the survivors (34 merchant seamen, 10 Armed Guard sailors, and four army passengers) and transport them to their original destination, Port Noire (see 3 November).

District patrol vessel *YP 205* is lost after grounding off Saba Island, 18°30'N, 65°00'W.

PACIFIC. Japanese freighter *Biwa Maru* is lost (cause unknown) off coast of French Indochina, 13°30'N, 109°21'E.

2 Monday

PACIFIC. Fleet Air Wing 6 (Captain Douglass P. Johnson) is established at Seattle, Washington, for multi-engine aircraft training.

Destroyer *Conyngham* (DD 371) and transport *Fuller* (AP 14) are damaged in collision in Sealark Channel, Guadalcanal.

Submarine *Seawolf* (SS 197) sinks Japanese water tender *Gifu Maru* west-southwest of Cape San Agustin, Mindanao, P.I., 06°14'N, 126°07'E.

Submarine *Tambor* (SS 198) lays mines in Hainan Strait, Tonkin Gulf.

Submarine *Tautog* (SS 199) sows mines south of Cape Padaran, French Indochina.

USAAF B-17s (5th Air Force) bomb Japanese shipping northeast of Buna, New Guinea, sinking army cargo ship *Yasukawa Maru*, 08°41'S, 148°27'E.

Small reconnaissance seaplane from Japanese submarine *I 8* reconnoiters Efate Island, New Hebrides.

ATLANTIC. Dutch motorship *Zaandam* is sunk by German submarine *U 174* at 01°25'N, 36°22'W. Lost with the ship are men who have survived the loss of four U.S. freighters: 18 (12 merchant seamen and six Armed Guard sailors) from *Chickasaw City* (sunk 7 October), 15 from *Swiftsure* (8 October), six from *Coloradan* (9 October), and 15 from *Examelia* (9 October) (see 24 January 1943).

3 Tuesday

PACIFIC. Submarine *Haddock* (SS 231) sinks freighter *Tekkai Maru* in the East China Sea between Shanghai and Korea, 32°02'N, 126°13'E.

Submarine *Seawolf* (SS 197) sinks Japanese transport *Sagami Maru* off Davao, P.I., 07°02'N, 125°33'E.

Submarine *Tambor* (SS 198) sinks freighter *Chikugo Maru* in Tonkin Gulf, northwest of Hainan Island, 21°18'N, 108°39'E.

ATLANTIC. U.S. tanker *Hahira*, in convoy SC 107, is sunk by German submarine *U 521* approximately 400 miles south of Cape Farewell, 54°15'N, 41°57'E; two crewmen and one Armed Guard sailor are killed in the attack. British rescue ship *Southport* rescues the 36 surviving crewmen and 17 Armed Guard sailors.

U.S. freighter *East Indian* is sunk by German submarine *U 181*, 300 miles southwest of the Cape of Good Hope; 17 of the 47-man crew and six of the 12 passengers perish (see 16 November).

U.S. freighter *George Thatcher*, torpedoed by German submarine *U 126* on 1 November and abandoned, eventually sinks.

4 Wednesday

PACIFIC. TG 65.4 cruisers and destroyers bombard Japanese positions near Koli Point, Guadalcanal.

Small reconnaissance seaplane from Japanese submarine *I 31* reconnoiters Suva, Fiji Islands; small reconnaissance seaplane from *I 9* reconnoiters Nouméa, New Caledonia.

Japanese submarine *RO 65* is sunk when she accidentally dives into a reef while seeking to avoid attack, Kiska Harbor, 51°58'N, 177°33'E.

ATLANTIC. Submarines *Shad* (SS 235), *Gunnel* (SS 253), *Herring* (SS 233), *Barb* (SS 220), and *Blackfish* (SS 221) are deployed to reconnoiter French North African waters off Rabat, Fedala, Casablanca, Safi, and Dakar, in advance of Operation TORCH.

ARCTIC. U.S. freighter *John H. B. Latrobe*, proceeding independently from Reykjavik, Iceland, to Archangel, USSR, is attacked by HE 115s at 74°37'N, 02°00'E. Withering Armed Guard gunfire disrupts the attack by the enemy floatplanes and none of the seven torpedoes launched strike home; strafing, however, slightly damages the merchantman, and three of the 25-man Armed Guard are wounded. *John H. B. Latrobe* returns to Reykjavik for repairs.

U.S. freighter *William Clark*, proceeding independently from Hvalfjordur, Iceland, to Murmansk, is sunk by German submarine *U 354* at 71°05′N, 13°20′W. Survivors abandon ship into three lifeboats (see 7 November).

5 Thursday

MEDITERRANEAN. British submarine HMS *Seraph*, under the temporary command of U.S. Navy Captain Jerauld Wright, embarks French General Henri-Honoré Giraud and a party of French officers in the Gulf of Lyons. The general will transfer to a Catalina on 7 November for further transportation to Gibraltar.

ATLANTIC. PBY (VP 84) sinks German submarine *U 408* off Iceland, 67°40′N, 18°32′W.

CARIBBEAN. U.S. tanker *Meton*, en route to Cienfuegos, Cuba, in convoy TAG 18, is sunk by German submarine *U 129* at 12°25′N, 69°20′W; one merchant seaman dies in the attack. Dutch motor torpedo boat *MTB 23* rescues the survivors (37 merchant seamen and the 12-man Armed Guard).

6 Friday

PACIFIC. Submarine *Grayling* (SS 209) is damaged by Japanese aerial bombs off Truk, 06°44′N, 151°25′E.

Submarine *Haddock* (SS 231) damages Japanese army cargo ship *France Maru*, 33°46′N, 127°28′E.

7 Saturday

PACIFIC. SBDs (VMSB 132), TBFs (VT 8), Marine F4Fs, and USAAF P-39s from Henderson Field, Guadalcanal, attack Japanese convoy, damaging destroyers *Naganami* and *Takanami*.

Miscellaneous auxiliary *Majaba* (AG 43) is torpedoed by Japanese midget submarine *Ha.11* (launched from submarine *I 20*) off Lunga Point, Guadalcanal, and is beached two miles east of Lunga Point to facilitate salvage. Destroyers *Lansdowne* (DD 486) and *Lardner* (DD 487) depth charge *I 20*, but the submarine escapes; *Ha.11* is scuttled.

MEDITERRANEAN. Transport *Thomas Stone* (AP 59), en route to Algiers to participate in Operation TORCH, is torpedoed by German submarine *U 205* in the western Mediterranean, 37°32′N, 00°01′E.

Italian submarine *Antonio Sciesa* is sunk by USAAF aircraft off coast of Libya, 32°05′N, 23°59′E.

ATLANTIC. U.S. freighter *La Salle* is sunk with all hands (including 13 Armed Guards) by German submarine *U 159* about 350 miles southeast of the Cape of Good Hope, South Africa, 40°00′S, 21°30′E. When the merchantman, which is carrying ammunition, explodes, the cataclysmic blast rains debris on her assailant's decks nearby, wounding three German submariners.

U.S. freighter *West Humhaw*, en route from Freetown, Sierra Leone, to Takoradi, Gold Coast, is sunk by German submarine *U 161* at 04°21′N, 02°42′W. There are no casualties among the 39-man merchant crew, the 16-man Armed Guard, and the five passengers. British *ML 281* rescues all hands and transports them to Takoradi.

U.S. freighter *Nathaniel Hawthorne*, en route to New York in convoy TAG 19, is sunk by German submarine *U 508* at 11°34′N, 63°26′W; the merchantman sinks with a rapidity that does not allow lifeboats to be launched. For his bravery as he directs his men to safety, Lieutenant Kenneth Muir, the Armed Guard commander, is awarded the Navy Cross posthumously (see 9 November).

British trawlers rescue two boatloads of survivors from U.S. freighter *William Clark*, sunk by German submarine *U 354* on 4 November. HMS *St. Elstan* rescues 26; HMS *Cape Palliser* rescues 15. The third boat, with 23 men, is never seen again; 18 of 41 merchant seamen are lost, as are 13 of the 30-man Armed Guard.

As TG 34.10 (Rear Admiral Lyal A. Davidson) approaches Safi, French Morocco, destroyer *Mervine* (DD 489) is damaged in collision with Spanish fishing vessel. The latter is diverted from the area in which amphibious operations are soon to begin (see 8 November).

8 Sunday

PACIFIC. Motor torpedo boats *PT 61*, *PT 39*, and *PT 37* engage two Japanese destroyers south of Savo Island, Guadalcanal; *PT 61*, *PT 39*, and *Mochizuki* are damaged in the encounter.

Submarine *Seawolf* sinks Japanese gunboat *Keiko Maru* off Cape San Agustin, Mindanao, P.I., 06°22′N, 126°03′E.

U.S. freighter *Edgar Allen Poe* is torpedoed by Japanese submarine *I 21* in a spirited fight 56 miles southeast of Amadee Light, Nouméa, New Caledonia, 22°14′S, 166°30′E, during which two crewmen are killed. A part of the crew (including the 14-man Armed Guard) remains on board while New Zealand minesweeper HMNZS *Matai* and corvette HMNZS *Kiwi* tow the vessel to Nouméa, where she will be declared a total loss (see 9 November).

ATLANTIC/MEDITERRANEAN. Operation TORCH, the invasion of French North Africa, by Allied Expeditionary Force under the supreme command of Lieutenant General Dwight D. Eisenhower, USA, begins.

Allied naval force (Admiral Sir Andrew B. Cunningham, RN) is composed of three principal parts: Western Naval Task Force (TF 34) (Rear Admiral H. Kent Hewitt), which lands troops (Major General George S. Patton, USA) near Casablanca; Center Naval Task Force (Commodore Thomas H. Troubridge, RN), which lands troops (Major General Lloyd R. Fredendall, USA) at Oran; and Eastern Naval Task Force (Rear Admiral Sir Harold M. Burrough, RN), which puts troops (Major General Charles W. Ryder, USA) ashore at Algiers.

MEDITERRANEAN. Attempt to force the entrance to Oran Harbor meets disaster. Cutters HMS *Hartland* (ex-USCGC *Ponchartrain*) and HMS *Walney* (ex-USCGC *Sebago*) with combined American-British antisabotage party embarked, encounter fierce gunfire. *Walney* is sunk by Vichy French destroyer *Tramontane* and large destroyer *Epervier*; U.S. naval contingent (Lieutenant Commander George D. Dickey) (five officers, 22 enlisted men, and six marines) is embarked in *Hartland*, which is sunk by the combined fire of Vichy French destroyer *Typhon*, two submarines (second class boats *Ariane*, *Danae*, and *Diane* are in port), and shore batteries. Casualties are heavy on board both ships. The objective is not achieved.

German planes bomb Allied shipping off Algiers. U.S. freighter *Exceller* is damaged by near-misses; there are no casualties among the 32 merchant seamen and the 19-man Armed Guard.

ATLANTIC. TG 34.8 (Mehdia–Port Lyautey in French Morocco): Destroyer *Dallas* (DD 199), with Army raider detachment (Third Battalion) embarked, attempts twice to enter the Sebou River (French Morocco), but is driven off by Vichy French artillery (see 10 November).

TG 34.9 (Casablanca–Cape Fedala): High-speed minesweeper *Hogan* (DMS 6) is attacked by Vichy French auxiliary patrol boat *Victoria* as the enemy vessel is escorting a small convoy rounding Cape Fedala, French Morocco. U.S. destroyer gunfire disables the enemy craft; a prize crew is placed on board. Minesweeper *Auk* (AM 57) escorts *Victoria* to the transport area off Fedala. French merchantman *Lorraine* is also boarded by a prize crew; remainder of convoy anchors peaceably between Casablanca and Fedala. Unaware that gunfire from destroyer *Ludlow* (DD 438) has compelled the French defenders to surrender Fort Blondin, light cruiser *Brooklyn* (CL 40) mistakenly fires upon friend (Seventh Infantry) and foe alike, causing fatalities on both sides before the enemy guns are again silenced and the French can arrange a surrender. French shore battery fire, however, damages destroyers *Ludlow* and *Murphy* (DD 603). Heavy cruiser *Augusta* (CA 31) duels French shore batteries at Fedala; destroyer *Wilkes* (DD 441) silences French guns on northeast side of Cape Fedala.

Minesweeper *Auk* and destroyer *Tillman* (DD 641) encounter coastal convoy escorted by Vichy French surveying vessel *Estafette* off Fedala. In the ensuing action, *Estafette* is damaged by *Tillman*'s gunfire and, along with three of the six vessels being convoyed by her, is beached; the remaining three, *Simon Duhamel*, *Foudroyant*, and *Loup de Mer*, are boarded by U.S. prize crews and brought to the transport area. *Loup de Mer* will later be used to transport U.S. troops.

TBFs (VGS 27) bomb and sink Vichy French second class submarines *Oréade*, *Amphitrite*, and *La Psyché* at their moorings in Casablanca Harbor; surviving boats sortie, followed by surface force (Rear Admiral Gervais de Lafonde in large destroyer *Milan*) that makes a valiant attempt to disrupt the landings off Casablanca. *Augusta* and *Brooklyn* engage the French ships as they emerge; the latter is damaged by small caliber fire in the action that turns back the initial attempt. Battleship *Massachusetts* (BB 59) and heavy cruisers *Wichita* (CA 45) and *Tuscaloosa* (CA 37) come up to assist *Augusta* and *Brooklyn*. French large destroyer *Milan* is damaged by gunfire from either *Wichita* or *Tuscaloosa* (both of which are using green dye–loaded shells). *Milan* is later damaged further by carrier-based planes.

Second French attempt to disrupt landings meets defeat: Heavy cruisers *Wichita* or *Tuscaloosa* sink destroyer *Fougueux* and damage large destroyer *Milan* (a second time) and destroyer *Frondeur*. *Augusta* sinks destroyer *Boulonnaise* at 33°40′N, 07°34′W, and, in concert with *Brooklyn*, damages destroyer *Brestois*. French light cruiser *Primauguet* is damaged by U.S. cruiser gunfire, as is destroyer *Albatros*, which is towed in to Casablanca Harbor where she is beached and further damaged by carrier-based planes. Surviving French ships limp back to Casablanca: *Primauguet*, beached, is further damaged by bomb; *Brestois* and

Frondeur later capsize and sink as the result of damage received earlier that morning. French colonial sloop *La Grandiere* and second class sloops *Commandant Delage* and *La Gracieuse* sortie that afternoon and pick up survivors from the ships sunk that morning; *La Grandiere* is damaged by carrier-based aircraft. Submarine *Sidi-Ferruch* is sunk by planes (VGS 27) from auxiliary aircraft carrier *Suwanee* (AVG 27); submarine *Meduse* is bombed by planes (VGS 29) from auxiliary aircraft carrier *Santee* (ACV 29) (see 9 and 10 November). French second class submarine *Amazone* attacks *Brooklyn* without success; second class submarine *La Sybille* is lost off Casablanca on this date as well. French destroyers *Tempete* and *Simoun*, damaged in a previous collision and undergoing repairs at the time of commencement of TORCH, take no part in the battle and receive no further damage.

Battleship *Massachusetts* shells Casablanca, damaging Vichy French battleship *Jean Bart* and large destroyer *Le Malin* and sinking merchant passenger liner *Savoie Marseille* and cargo ship *Ile de Edienruder*; carrier-based planes sink passenger liner *Porthos*, tanker *Ouessant*, and freighter *Lipari*.

French shore batteries damage *Massachusetts*, *Wichita*, and *Brooklyn*, as well as high-speed minesweeper *Palmer* (DMS 5) off Casablanca. High-speed minesweeper *Stansbury* (DMS 8) is damaged by mine; transport *Leedstown* (AP 73) is damaged by German aerial torpedo.

Minelayer *Miantonomah* (CM 10) lays defensive minefield off Casablanca to cover northern flank of the invasion beaches. The field is not extensive, however, and fails to prevent German submarines from attacking amphibious shipping (see 11 and 12 November).

TG 34.10 (Safi): To secure the port of Safi, French Morocco, to serve as unloading point for heavy tanks in mechanized artillery transport *Lakehurst* (APM 9), destroyers *Bernadou* (DD 153) and *Cole* (DD 155), each transporting a company of the 47th Infantry specially trained in night operations, stand toward the harbor. Battleship *New York* (BB 34) and light cruiser *Philadelphia* (CL 41) bombard French guns (*Batterie Railleuse*), which respond by straddling *New York*, *Philadelphia*, and the destroyers *Mervine* (DD 489) and *Beatty* (DD 640) but not hitting them. Although Safi's defenders are alert, *Bernadou* and *Cole* succeed in landing their embarked troops that secure their objectives, and, joined by *Mervine*, silence harbor defenses. *Bernadou* is damaged

by grounding. *New York* and *Philadelphia* ultimately succeed in silencing *Batterie Railleuse*; the latter ship destroys another battery in concert with her SOCs (VCS 8), which drop depth charges and bombs.

Submarine *Herring* (SS 233) torpedoes Vichy French freighter *Ville du Havre* off French Morocco, 33°34′N, 07°52′W.

British patrol boat rescues 34 survivors of U.S. freighter *West Kebar*, sunk on 29 October by German submarine *U 129*, and transports them to Barbados, B.W.I. (see 10 and 18 November).

9 Monday

MEDITERRANEAN. Operation TORCH: Transport *Leedstown* (AP 73), bombed and torpedoed by German planes, is sunk by German submarine *U 331* near Algiers.

ATLANTIC. Operation TORCH continues: SOC (VCS 8) from *Philadelphia* (CL 41) bombs and damages French submarine *Meduse* near Cape Mazagan, French Morocco, at 32°45′N, 09°10′W (see 10 November). SBD (VGS 29) from auxiliary aircraft carrier *Santee* (ACV 29) also attacks a surfaced submarine.

Destroyer *Biddle* (DD 151) rescues survivors (three of 10 Armed Guard sailors, 10 of the 40-man merchant crew, and one of the two passengers) from U.S. freighter *Nathaniel Hawthorne*, sunk by German submarine *U 508* on 7 November.

INDIAN OCEAN. U.S. freighter *Marcus Whitman*, proceeding independently to Dutch Guiana from Cape Town, South Africa, is torpedoed by Italian submarine *Leonardo da Vinci* at 05°45′S, 32°40′W, and abandoned without loss. *Leonardo da Vinci* then finishes off the merchantman with gunfire (see 11 November).

PACIFIC. Destroyer *Russell* (DD 414) rescues that portion of the crew of U.S. freighter *Edgar Allen Poe* who abandoned ship after she was torpedoed by *I 21* the night before.

10 Tuesday

PACIFIC. Light cruiser *Raleigh* (CL 7), patrolling along the 175th meridian, encounters no Japanese patrol activity estimated to be in those waters west of the Ellice Islands.

High-speed minesweeper *Southard* (DMS 10) sinks Japanese submarine *I 15* five miles off Hada Bay, the northwest point of San Cristobal Island, Solomons, 10°13′S, 161°09′E. Presence of the Japanese boat in that vicinity, however, prompts the rerouting of TF 67 (en route to Guadalcanal) to the south of San Cristobal.

Heavy cruiser *Augusta* (CA 31) off Casablanca, 10 November 1942; shell splashes ahead of her are from 15-inch shells fired by French battleship *Jean Bart*. (Author's Collection)

ATLANTIC. Operation TORCH continues. TG 34.8 (Mehdia–Port Lyautey in French Morocco): Demolition party from tug *Cherokee* (AT 66) and salvage vessel *Brant* (ARS 32) destroy cable blocking Sebou River, enabling destroyer *Dallas* (DD 199) to make third and successful attempt to head up the river, some of which literally sees the ship plowing through the muddy shallows. Guided by a Free French pilot (who will receive a Navy Cross for the exploit), *Dallas* presses upriver and lands rangers to occupy the airfield at Port Lyautey. *Dallas* engages Vichy French shore battery, which is later silenced by depth bombs dropped by SOC (VCS 8) from light cruiser *Savannah* (CL 42). Chartered steamer *Contessa* follows *Dallas* upriver with supplies but runs aground (she proceeds to the airport the following morning); minesweepers *Raven* (AM 55) and *Osprey* (AM 56) resupply the occupation force. Auxiliary aircraft carrier *Chenango* (ACV 28) ferries in USAAF P-40s to be based on the newly captured field. Light cruiser *Savannah* and destroyers shell French positions; planes from battleship *Texas* (BB 35) bomb and strafe French troop columns (one OS2U, in a novel use of a depth charge, destroys three tanks).

Vichy French submarines conduct unsuccessful attacks against U.S. task force off North Africa; carrier *Ranger* (CV 4), battleship *Massa-* chusetts (BB 59), and heavy cruiser *Tuscaloosa* (CA 37) escape the attentions of *Le Tonnant, Meduse,* and *Antiope,* respectively.

Vichy French second class sloops *Commandant Delage* and *La Gracieuse* sortie and shell U.S. positions (Seventh Infantry) near Roches Noires. Heavy cruiser *Augusta* (CA 31) and destroyers *Tillman* (DD 641) and *Edison* (DD 439) engage the two enemy ships and drive them back to Casablanca, damaging *Commandant Delage* in the encounter. Soon thereafter, French battleship *Jean Bart* straddles *Augusta; Jean Bart* is bombed by planes from carrier *Ranger* and heavily damaged. SOC (VCS 8) from light cruiser *Philadelphia* (CL 41) bombs French submarine *Meduse,* which is aground off Cape Blanco, French Morocco, 33°05′N, 08°35′W; landing party from destroyer *Doran* (DD 634) verifies identity of the beached boat.

German submarine *U 608* lays mines off New York City, east of Ambrose Light.

Minelayer *Salem* (CM 11) is damaged when she is accidentally rammed by British landing craft HMS *LCI(L) 166,* South Brooklyn, New York.

Eight survivors of U.S. freighter *West Kebar,* sunk on 29 October by German submarine *U 129,* reach Guadeloupe, French West Indies.

CARIBBEAN. Naval Station, Puerto Castillo, Honduras, is established.

MEDITERRANEAN. Oran, Algeria, surrenders to U.S. forces.

11 Wednesday

PACIFIC. Small reconnaissance seaplane from Japanese submarine *I 7* reconnoiters Vanikoro, Solomons; small reconnaissance seaplane from *I 21* reconnoiters Nouméa, New Caledonia; and small reconnaissance seaplane from *I 9* reconnoiters Espíritu Santo, New Hebrides.

Japanese planes bomb Henderson Field and the recently arrived TG 62.4 (Rear Admiral Norman Scott) off Lunga Point, Guadalcanal. Transport *Zeilin* (AP 9) is damaged, 09°24′S, 160°02′E; near-misses damage cargo ships *Libra* (AK 53) and *Betelgeuse* (AK 28). Destroyer *Lardner* (DD 487) escorts the battered *Zeilin* as the latter is sent to Espíritu Santo.

Submarine *Haddock* (SS 231) sinks Japanese freighter *Venice Maru* in Yellow Sea, between China and Korea, 35°36′N, 123°44′E.

Submarine *Tautog* (SS 199) is damaged by depth charges in Makassar Strait, 01°22′N, 119°31′E, and is forced to terminate her patrol.

Japanese transport *Kobe Maru* is sunk in collision with army cargo ship *Tenzan Maru* 87 miles off the Yangtze River estuary; *Tenzan Maru* then founders and sinks.

BAY OF BENGAL. Japanese armed merchant cruiser *Hokoku Maru* is sunk by Indian Navy minesweeper RINS *Bengal* and Dutch merchant tanker *Ondina* south-southwest of Cocos Islands, 20°00′S, 93°00′E.

ATLANTIC. Casablanca surrenders to U.S. forces. Allied-French armistice is signed.

Mechanized artillery transport *Lakehurst* (APM 9) is damaged when accidentally rammed by cargo ship *Titania* (AK 55) in Safi Harbor, French Morocco.

In attack on convoy UGF 1 in Fedala Roads, French Morocco, German submarine *U 173* torpedoes and sinks transport *Joseph Hewes* (AP 50), 35°10′N, 04°00′W, and torpedoes oiler *Winooski* (AO 38), 33°45′N, 07°22′W, and destroyer *Hambleton* (DD 455), 33°40′N, 07°35′W (see 12 November). Tug *Cherokee* (AT 66) stands by the damaged destroyer.

MEDITERRANEAN. German troops occupy France, south to the Mediterranean Sea; Italian troops land on Corsica and move into France.

Naval Operating Base, Oran, Algeria, is established.

INDIAN OCEAN. First survivors from U.S. freighter *Marcus Whitman*, sunk by Italian submarine *Leonardo da Vinci* on 9 November, reach coast of Natal, South Africa, in the merchantman's motor lifeboat; the remainder will arrive within the next few hours. All hands (41-man merchant complement and the 11-man Armed Guard) reach safety.

12 Thursday

PACIFIC. Naval Battle of Guadalcanal: TF 67 (Rear Admiral Richmond Kelly Turner) disembarking troops and unloading cargo in Lunga Roads, Guadalcanal, under the protection of air and surface forces, is attacked by Japanese land attack planes (705th, 703rd, and 707th *Kokutais*). Heavy cruiser *San Francisco* (CA 38) is damaged when hit by a crashing bomber; destroyer *Buchanan* (DD 484) is hit by friendly fire.

Light cruiser *Helena* (CL 50) and destroyers *Barton* (DD 599) and *Shaw* (DD 373) destroy Japanese shore batteries firing upon unloading operations of TF 67 off Kukum Point, Guadalcanal, followed later by destroyers *Buchanan* (DD 484) and *Cushing* (DD 376).

Submarine *Grenadier* (SS 210) damages Japanese army cargo vessel *Hokkai Maru* off the south coast of French Indochina, 11°18′N, 109°02′E.

USAAF B-17s bomb Japanese shipping off Buin and airfield at Kahili, Bougainville; oiler *Naruto* is damaged.

ATLANTIC. German submarine *U 130* attacks convoy UGF 1 in Fedala Roads, French Morocco, and torpedoes and sinks transports *Tasker H. Bliss* (AP 42), *Hugh L. Scott* (AP 43), and *Edward Rutledge* (AP 52), 33°40′N, 07°35′W.

Prize crew from battleship *New York* (BB 34) takes over Vichy French auxiliary patrol boat *Victoria*; prize crew from battleship *Texas* (BB 35) places scuttled Dutch freighter *Export* in service, and makes great strides in readying merchantmen *Paco*, *Nyhorn*, and *Fortunato* for operation. Small seaplane tender *Barnegat* (AVP 10) proceeds up Sebou River (French Morocco) to Port Lyautey and establishes base there (see 13 November). Destroyer *Quick* (DD 490) places prize crew on board French merchantman *Nancern*.

Naval Operating Base, Casablanca, Morocco, is established.

Submarine chaser *SC 330* accidentally collides with, and sinks, merchant vessel *Rogist* seven miles southeast of Cape Charles, Virginia, Lighthouse.

Damaged destroyer *Hambleton* (DD 455) moored alongside transport *Dorothea Dix* (AP 57) at Fedala, 12 November 1942; torpedo damage amidships is plainly visible. (NA, 80-G-21886)

CARIBBEAN. Gunboat *Erie* (PG 50) is torpedoed by German submarine *U 163*, 12°03′N, 68°58′W, and is beached northwest of Willemstad, Curaçao, N.W.I., to prevent sinking (see 28 November and 5 December).

13 Friday

PACIFIC. Naval Battle of Guadalcanal continues: TG 67.4, consisting of two heavy cruisers, three light cruisers, and eight destroyers (Rear Admiral Daniel J. Callaghan), encounters Japanese Bombardment Force (Rear Admiral Abe Hiroaki), which includes battleships *Hiei* and *Kirishima*, steaming to bombard Henderson Field, Guadalcanal, shortly after midnight on 12 November; a savage nocturnal naval action ensues. Abe's force inflicts heavy damage on TG 67.4 before it retires northward; Rear Admirals Callaghan and Norman Scott are killed on board their respective flagships, heavy cruiser *San Francisco* (CA 38) and light cruiser *Atlanta* (CL 51). Both Callaghan and Scott are awarded Medals of Honor posthumously. On board *San Francisco*, Lieutenant Commanders Herbert E. Schonland and Bruce McCandless prove instrumental in saving their ship, and Boatswain's Mate First Class Reinhardt J. Keppler performs a succession of heroic acts in fighting fires and removing wounded during the thick of the battle. Those three men (Keppler posthumously) also earn the nation's

highest award for bravery. "These splendid ships and determined men," Rear Admiral Richard Kelly Turner writes later of TG 67.4's gallantry, "won a great victory against heavy odds. Had this battle not been fought and won, our hold on Guadalcanal would have been gravely endangered."[122] TF 16 (Rear Admiral Thomas C. Kinkaid), formed around carrier *Enterprise* (CV 6), the last operational fleet carrier in the Pacific, nears the battle area and launches air search and attacks against the enemy (see 14 November).[123]

Light cruiser *Atlanta*, irreparably damaged by Japanese naval gunfire and torpedo as well as by friendly fire from heavy cruiser *San Francisco*, is scuttled by demolition charges three miles off Lunga Point; light cruiser *Juneau* (CL 52), damaged by gunfire, is sunk by Japanese submarine *I 26*, 10°34′S, 161°44′E, as *Juneau* retires toward Espíritu Santo. Loss of life is heavy.[124] Also sunk are destroyers *Cushing* (DD 376) and *Monssen* (DD 436) to gunfire, *Laffey* (DD 459) to gunfire and torpedo, and *Barton* (DD 599) to two torpedoes. Heavy cruiser *Portland* (CA 33) suffers torpedo damage; *San Francisco*, light cruiser *Helena* (CL 50), and destroyer *Aaron Ward* (DD 483) are damaged by gunfire. Friendly fire damages destroyer *O'Bannon* (DD 450).

The Japanese, however, do not emerge unscathed from the brutal slugfest. Battleship

Hiei, damaged by gunfire from heavy cruisers *Portland* and *San Francisco* and destroyers *Cushing*, *Laffey*, and *O'Bannon*, is sunk by TBFs (VT 8) from carrier *Enterprise* and USMC SBDs (VMSB 142) and TBFs (VMSB 131) from Henderson Field. Destroyer *Akatsuki* is sunk by *San Francisco* and *Atlanta* near Savo Island, 09°17'S, 159°56'E. Destroyer *Yudachi*, damaged by gunfire, is sunk by *Portland* southeast of Savo Island, 09°14'S, 159°52'E. Destroyers *Murasame*, *Ikazuchi*, and *Amatsukaze* are damaged by gunfire; light cruiser *Nagara* is straddled by gunfire from *San Francisco*. Destroyers *Yukikaze* and *Michisio* are damaged by aircraft, the former off Guadalcanal, and the latter off Shortland Island.

In the aftermath of the action of 12–13 November, Admiral Yamamoto Isoroku orders Vice Admiral Kondo Nobutake to form the "Volunteer Attack Force" and shell Henderson Field.

On the night of 13 November, heavy cruisers *Suzuya* and *Maya* approach Guadalcanal to shell Henderson Field, intending to render it inoperable the following morning.

ATLANTIC. PBYs (VP 73) arrive at Port Lyautey, French Morocco, to begin operations from that place, supported by small seaplane tender *Barnegat* (AVP 10).

Unarmed U.S. schooner *Star of Scotland* is shelled and sunk by German submarine *U 159* while en route from Cape Town, South Africa, to Paranagua, Brazil, 26°30'S, 00°20'W; one sailor of the 17-man crew drowns when the ship is abandoned (see 1 December).

INDIAN OCEAN. U.S. freighter *Excello*, proceeding independently from Port Said, Egypt, to Cape Town, South Africa, is sunk by German submarine *U 181* at 32°23'S, 30°07'E; one Armed Guard sailor and one merchant seaman perish in the attack (see 14, 15, and 20 November).

14 Saturday

PACIFIC. Naval Battle of Guadalcanal continues as bombardment of Henderson Field by heavy cruisers *Suzuya* and *Maya* fails to achieve the desired effect, prompting the postponement of the landing of troops from the 11 transports poised to proceed down the "Slot" toward Guadalcanal. Japanese heavy cruisers *Chokai* and *Kinugasa*, light cruiser *Isuzu*, and two destroyers (Vice Admiral Mikawa Gunichi) and heavy cruisers *Maya* and *Suzuya*, light cruiser *Tenryu*, and four destroyers (Rear Admiral Nishimura Shoji) come under attack by planes from carrier *Enterprise* (CV 6) and

from Henderson Field. *Kinugasa* is sunk by USMC and Navy SBDs (VMSB 132 and VB 10), 15 nautical miles northwest of Rendova, 08°45'S, 157°00'E. *Maya* (crashed by a crippled VB 10 SBD) and *Isuzu* are damaged south of New Georgia Island; *Chokai*, *Tenryu*, and destroyer *Ayanami* are also damaged.

That afternoon, USMC and Navy land-based F4Fs, SBDs, and TBFs, as well as USAAF B-17s (11th Bombardment Group) and P-39s (339th Fighter Squadron), attack Japanese convoy off Guadalcanal, sinking transports *Arizona Maru* and *Canberra Maru* and freighters *Brisbane Maru* (VS 10 and VMSB 141), *Kumagawa Maru* (VMSB 130), *Nagara Maru* (VT 10), *Nako Maru*, and *Shinano Maru*; cargo ship *Sado Maru* is damaged.

Beginning shortly before midnight, TF 64 (Rear Admiral Willis A. Lee Jr.), composed of battleships *Washington* (BB 56) and *South Dakota* (BB 57) and four destroyers, engages the Japanese "Volunteer Attack Force" (Vice Admiral Kondo Nobutake), composed of battleship *Kirishima*, heavy cruisers *Atago* and *Takao*, light cruisers *Sendai* and *Nagara*, and nine destroyers. Japanese gunfire sinks destroyers *Preston* (DD 379) (by light cruiser *Nagara*) and *Walke* (DD 416) (see 15 November).

INDIAN OCEAN. First boatload of survivors from U.S. freighter *Excello*, sunk by German submarine *U 181* the previous day, make landfall at Port St. John, South Africa.

15 Sunday

PACIFIC. Naval Battle of Guadalcanal ends as TF 64 (Rear Admiral Willis A. Lee Jr.) repulses Japanese "Volunteer Attack Force" (Vice Admiral Kondo Nobutake). Battleship *South Dakota* (BB 57) is damaged by gunfire of Japanese battleship *Kirishima* and heavy cruisers *Atago* and *Takao*; destroyer *Benham* (DD 397), damaged by torpedo, is scuttled by destroyer *Gwin* (DD 433) in Savo Sound, Solomons; *Gwin* is damaged by gunfire. Gunfire from Admiral Lee's flagship, battleship *Washington* (BB 56), sinks *Kirishima* and destroyer *Ayanami* southeast of Savo Island, 09°10'S, 159°52'E.

Navy SBDs (VS 10) and TBFs (VT 10), USMC SBDs (VMSB 132), USMC and Army coast artillery, and gunfire from destroyer *Meade* (DD 602) sink four Japanese transports off the northern coast of Guadalcanal: *Kinugasa Maru*, *Hirokawa Maru*, *Yamazuki Maru*, and *Yamura Maru*. *Meade* also rescues survivors from sunken destroyers *Walke* (DD 416) and *Preston* (DD 379).

Although the U.S. Navy suffers the greater loss in warships in the savagely fought series of engagements on 12–15 November, the Japanese withdraw and never again send naval forces formed around capital ships into the confined waters around Guadalcanal.

USAAF B-17s (5th Air Force) bomb Japanese shipping at Rabaul, sinking supply ship *No. 3 Unkai Maru*, 04°12'S, 152°00'E, and damaging transport *Azuma Maru*.

ATLANTIC. German submarines attack Allied shipping involved in the ongoing operations in North Africa. *U 155* attacks convoy MK 1, torpedoing cargo ship *Almaack* (AK 27), 36°19'N, 07°52'W; *U 155* also torpedoes and sinks British escort carrier HMS *Avenger* and transport *Ettrick* from the same convoy. Elsewhere, *U 173* torpedoes cargo ship *Electra* (AK 21), 34°00'N, 07°24'W; minesweeper *Raven* (AM 55) is damaged alongside *Electra* during salvage operations, but succeeds in saving the crippled auxiliary.

Vichy French submarine *Le Tonnant*, having been damaged by U.S. warships off Casablanca, is scuttled off Cadiz, Spain.

CARIBBEAN. Unarmed U.S. schooner *Lucy Evelyn* is shelled by what she believes to be an enemy submarine at approximately 12°00'N, 75°00'W; apparently undamaged, she reaches Baranquilla, Colombia, soon thereafter, having suffered no casualties among the seven-man crew.

INDIAN OCEAN. Second boat of survivors from U.S. freighter *Excello*, sunk by German submarine *U 181* on 13 November, makes landfall at Port St. John, South Africa.

16 Monday

PACIFIC. U.S. Army 32nd Division and Australian 7th Division land south of Buna, New Guinea.

Submarine *Haddock* (SS 231) sinks Japanese freighter *Nichinan Maru* west-southwest of Kyushu, 31°52'N, 126°14'E.

Submarine *Seal* (SS 183) sinks Japanese army cargo ship *Boston Maru* off the Palaus, 06°18'N, 135°20'E. Just 12 seconds after firing her torpedoes at the cargo ship, *Seal* is rammed by another enemy vessel; the damage leads to termination of her patrol.

Japanese destroyer *Harukaze* is damaged by mine off Surabaya, Java.

ATLANTIC. Destroyers *Woolsey* (DD 437), *Swanson* (DD 443), and *Quick* (DD 490) sink German submarine *U 173* off Casablanca, French Morocco.

Minelayers *Terror* (CM 5), *Monadnock* (CM 9), and *Miantonomah* (CM 10) lay minefield to protect approaches to Casablanca.

British steamship *Durando* rescues the 19 survivors (13 of the 47-man crew, four of the 15-man Armed Guard, and two of the 12 passengers) (one of whom dies later of his injuries) from U.S. freighter *East Indian*, sunk on 3 November by *U 181*. The remainder of those who survived the loss of the ship 13 days before (18 crewmen, 11 Armed Guards, and three passengers) and managed to reach four rafts, are never found.

17   Tuesday

PACIFIC. Submarine *Searaven* (SS 196) sinks Japanese transport *Nissei Maru* in Flying Fish Cove, off Christmas Island, 10°24′S, 105°41′E.

Submarine *Salmon* (SS 182), attacking Japanese convoy off west coast of Luzon, sinks repair ship *Oregon Maru* about 65 miles northwest of Manila, 14°16′N, 119°44′E.

Japanese convoy, escorted by five destroyers, brings in troops and supplies to Buna, New Guinea.

ATLANTIC. Naval Air Station, De Land, Florida, is established.

18   Wednesday

PACIFIC. Japanese convoy, escorted by three destroyers, reaches Buna, New Guinea, and disembarks troops and unloads supplies; USAAF B-17s (5th Air Force) bomb shipping at that port, damaging destroyers *Umikaze* and *Kawakaze*.

USAAF B-17s (5th Air Force) sink Japanese freighter *Havana Maru* off Kahili airfield, Bougainville.

British submarine HMS *Trusty* sinks Japanese army cargo ship *Columbia Maru* off Penang, Malaya.[125]

ATLANTIC. German submarines attack westbound convoy ONS 144. U.S. freighter *Parismina* is sunk by *U 624* at 54°07′N, 38°26′W; of the 75 souls on board, 20 are lost with the ship: 15 crewmen, two Armed Guard sailors, and three passengers. British rescue ship *Perth* and Dutch-manned corvette *Rose* rescue the 55 survivors between them. U.S. freighter *Yaka* also falls victim to *U 624*, at 54°25′N, 38°52′W, and is abandoned; all hands (41 merchant seamen and a 11-man Armed Guard) are rescued by Canadian corvette HMCS *Vervain*. German submarine *U 522* torpedoes and finishes off *Yaka*.

U.S. tanker *Brilliant*, in convoy SC 109, is torpedoed by German submarine *U 43* at 50°45′N, 45°53′E; an intense fire breaks out. Although ship's master and six merchant seamen and two Armed Guard sailors take to a lifeboat, apparently intending to remain nearby, the boat swamps, drowning two men; British corvette HMS *Bury* rescues the survivors and retains them on board for medical treatment. The ship's junior third officer, J. Cameron, meanwhile, takes command; the crew puts out the fire. Lieutenant John R. Borum, USNR, the Armed Guard officer, instills confidence by the casual attitude he displays when things are the worst (see 19 November).

Spanish tanker *Campares* rescues nine survivors (including six Armed Guard sailors) from U.S. freighter *West Kebar*, sunk by German submarine *U 129* on 29 October.

19   Thursday

CARIBBEAN. District patrol vessel YP 26 is destroyed by explosion of undetermined origin while on marine railway, Cristobal, C.Z.

ATLANTIC. U.S. tanker *Brilliant*, damaged by *U 43* the previous day, proceeds back toward Newfoundland, obtaining her true position from passing warships (see 21 November).

20   Friday

PACIFIC. Japanese submarine *I 175* is damaged when she runs aground at Truk, Carolines.

ATLANTIC. District patrol vessel YP 405 burns and sinks off Smith Shoal, Florida.

INDIAN OCEAN. U.S. freighter *Pierce Butler* is sunk by German submarine *U 177* off the coast of South Africa at 29°40′S, 36°35′E. All hands (41-man merchant complement and 21-man Armed Guard) abandon ship in four lifeboats (see 21 November).

British hospital ship *Atlantis* rescues the last 13 survivors from U.S. freighter *Excello*, sunk by German submarine *U 181* on 13 November.

ATLANTIC. Damaged U.S. tanker *Brilliant* encounters auxiliary schooner *Isabel H.*, whose master pilots the ship to Musgrave Harbor, Newfoundland, where she anchors to await an escort to St. John's (see 21 November).

21   Saturday

PACIFIC. Submarine *Stingray* (SS 186) torpedoes Japanese seaplane carrier *San'yo Maru* off Shortland Island, 06°32′S, 156°05′E.

INDIAN OCEAN. Survivors from U.S. freighter *Pierce Butler*, sunk by German submarine *U 177* off the coast of South Africa the previous day, are rescued by British destroyer HMS *Forward* and transported to Durban, South Africa.

U.S. freighter *Alcoa Pathfinder* is sunk by German submarine *U 181* approximately six miles off the coast of Portuguese East Africa, 26°41′S, 33°08′E; five merchant seamen are lost. Survivors row ashore (see 22 November).

ATLANTIC. Destroyer *Somers* (DD 381) intercepts German blockade runner *Anneliese Essberger* in the South Atlantic. The German ship is scuttled by her crew.

Damaged U.S. tanker *Brilliant* sails from Musgrave Harbor, Newfoundland, for St. John's (see 22 November).

22   Sunday

ATLANTIC. Damaged U.S. tanker *Brilliant* arrives at St. John's, Newfoundland, completing a 300-mile voyage under the command of the ship's junior third officer (see 18 December).

PACIFIC. USAAF B-25s and P-40s (10th Air Force) on shipping strike sink Vichy French ship *Khai Dinh* east of Haiphong Harbor, French Indochina, 20°58′N, 106°40′E.

INDIAN OCEAN. Survivors from U.S. freighter *Alcoa Pathfinder*, sunk the previous day by German submarine *U 181*, row ashore, reaching land about 12 miles north of Oro Point, Portuguese East Africa, whence they walk to lighthouse and to airfield. Entire 15-man Armed Guard unit survives, as do 55 of the 61-man crew and the solitary passenger.

23   Monday

ATLANTIC. Auxiliary aircraft carriers *Sangamon* (ACV 26) and *Chenango* (ACV 28), en route back to the United States after participating in Operation TORCH, are damaged by heavy seas, North Atlantic.

U.S. tanker *Caddo*, en route from Baytown, Texas, to Iceland, is sunk by German submarine *U 518* at 42°25′N, 48°27′E, and abandoned, with the 58 men on board (42-man merchant complement and 17-man Armed Guard) taking to three lifeboats. *U 518* briefly interrogates survivors, takes the ship's master and another officer as prisoners, and departs after the German offer of cigarettes is refused (see 7 and 8 December).

24   Tuesday

PACIFIC. Japanese forces land at Munda Point, New Georgia, Solomons.

Submarine *Snapper* (SS 185) is damaged by aerial bombs and depth charges off northern Solomons, 07°58′S, 156°12′E, but remains on patrol.

USAAF B-17s and B-25s (5th Air Force) and RAAF Beaufighters sink Japanese destroyer

Heavy cruiser *Minneapolis* (CA 36) lies at Tulagi, 1 December 1942, after the Battle of Tassafaronga; the work of cutting away her damaged bow lies ahead. (NA, 80-G-211215)

Hayashio in Huon Gulf between Lae and Finschhafen, New Guinea, 07°00′S, 147°30′E, and damage torpedo boats *Otori* and *Hiyodori* east of Lae.

USAAF B-17s (South Pacific Force) damage Japanese seaplane carrier *Sanuki Maru*, Shortland Island, Solomons.

MEDITERRANEAN. Transport *Thomas Stone* (AP 59) is damaged by horizontal bomber off Algiers, 36°48′N, 03°10′E.

25 Wednesday

PACIFIC. USAAF B-25s and P-40s (10th Air Force) damage Japanese freighter *Ryokusei Maru* at Canton, China.

Japanese submarine *I 17* lands 11 tons of supplies at Kamimbo Bay, Guadalcanal. Submarine missions to supply the beleaguered Japanese garrison on Guadalcanal will continue through the end of November.

MEDITERRANEAN. Transport *Thomas Stone* (AP 59), damaged by grounding off Algerian coast, is left beached and abandoned, 36°49′N, 03°07′E.

26 Thursday

PACIFIC. USAAF B-26s (11th Air Force) damage Japanese freighter *Cheribon Maru* off Attu, Aleutians.

27 Friday

PACIFIC. USAAF B-26s (11th Air Force) sink Japanese army cargo ship *Kachosan Maru* off Attu, Aleutians.

MEDITERRANEAN. Vichy French Fleet at Toulon is scuttled to prevent it from falling into German hands. Naval vessels immobilized in this manner include three battleships, four heavy cruisers, three light cruisers, an aircraft depot ship, 30 destroyers, three torpedo boats, 16 submarines, and 11 gunboats and auxiliaries.

ATLANTIC. U.S. freighter *Jeremiah Wadsworth* is sunk by German submarine *U 178* approximately 270 miles south of Cape Agulhas, South Africa, 39°25′S, 22°23′E; there are no casualties among the 43-man merchant crew and the 14-man Armed Guard (see 5 and 6 December).

28 Saturday

UNITED STATES. "Cocoanut Grove" nightclub in Boston, Massachusetts, catches fire. Ensign Jackson G. Akin Jr., USNR, of the office of the Inspector of Naval Materiel, Boston, makes quick investigation when he learns of the general fire alarm and discovers that the club is in the immediate vicinity of his office. He joins in the efforts to rescue the living and carry out the dead. Ensigns George W. Carlson and Mac A. Cason, SC-V(P), USNR, driving through the city at that hour, respond immediately when they see flames issuing from the burning building. Exhibiting courage, leadership, and resourcefulness, Ensigns Carlson and Cason, who organize rescue parties from enlisted men they see in the gathering crowd, are later deemed "the cause of saving more lives than any other single agency." Despite rescuers' efforts, however, 492 people perish in the tragedy.

PACIFIC. Cargo ship *Alchiba* (AK 23) is torpedoed by Japanese midget submarine *Ha.10* (from submarine *I 16*) 3,000 yards northeast of Lunga Point, Guadalcanal (see 7 December).

USAAF B-17s attack Japanese convoy en route from Munda, New Georgia, to Guadalcanal, and damage cargo vessel *Chihaya Maru*.

CARIBBEAN. Gunboat *Erie* (PG 50), torpedoed by German submarine *U 163* on 12 November, is moved into the inner harbor at Willemstad, Curaçao, N.W.I., to prevent her from sinking and to facilitate salvage (see 5 December).

ATLANTIC. Auxiliary aircraft carrier *Chenango* (ACV 28), en route back to the United States after participating in Operation TORCH, is damaged by heavy seas, North Atlantic.

U.S. freighter *Alaskan* is torpedoed, shelled, and sunk by German submarine *U 172* about 400 miles north of St. Paul's Rocks, 03°58′N, 26°19′W; six merchant seamen and one Armed Guard sailor are killed in the attack (see 13 and 15 December and 5 January 1943).

29 Sunday

PACIFIC. USAAF B-17s (5th Air Force) bomb Japanese convoy of four destroyers bound for Buna. Destroyers *Shiratsuyu* (transporting troops) and *Makigumo* are damaged in Vitiaz Strait; the two retire to Rabaul. *Kazagumo* and *Yugumo*, which survive the attacks, reach Buna with minimal supplies.

Aircraft from Henderson Field sink Japanese cargo ships *Azusa Maru* and *Kiku Maru*, Wickham Anchorage, New Georgia.

INDIAN OCEAN. U.S. freighter *Sawokla* is sunk by torpedo and gunfire of German auxiliary cruiser *Michel* (*Schiffe 28*) at approximately 28°00′S, 54°00′E, about 400 miles southeast of Madagascar, while en route from Colombo, Ceylon, to Cape Town, South Africa; 16 of the 41-man crew are killed in the attack, as are four of the 13 Armed Guard sailors. *Michel* rescues 25 crewmen, five Armed Guard sailors, and the five passengers (see 30 November).

30 Monday

PACIFIC. Battle of Tassafaronga: TF 67 (Rear Admiral Carlton H. Wright), consisting of four heavy cruisers, one light cruiser, and six destroyers, surprises Japanese destroyers (Captain Sato Torajiro) off Tassafaronga Point, Guadalcanal. The enemy presses on to jettison supply containers to sustain Japanese troops ashore, while torpedoes launched from destroyers *Kagero, Makinami, Kuroshio, Oyashio, Kawakaze,* and *Naganami* wreak havoc on Wright's ships, damaging heavy cruisers *Pensacola* (CA 24), *Northampton* (CA 26), *New Orleans* (CA 32), and *Minneapolis* (CA 36). Japanese destroyer *Takanami* is damaged by cruiser and destroyer gunfire off Tassafaronga (see 1 December).

German auxiliary cruiser *Thor* (*Schiffe 10*) is sunk by explosion of supply ship *Uckermark,* moored alongside, Yokohama, Japan. The blast also sinks German prize ship *Leuthen* and Japanese harbor craft in the vicinity.

Japanese cargo ship *No. 3 Unkai Maru* is lost (cause unknown) off Yokosuka, 35°17'N, 139°41'E.

INDIAN OCEAN. USAAF B-24s (India Air Task Force) bomb Japanese torpedo boat *Kari* off Port Blair, Andaman Island, in a strike that inaugurates attacks on the sea approaches to Burma.

German auxiliary cruiser *Michel* (*Schiffe 28*) rescues four additional Armed Guard sailors who have survived the sinking of U.S. freighter *Sawokla* the previous day (see 18 February 1943).

DECEMBER

1 Tuesday

PACIFIC. Heavy cruiser *Northampton* (CA 26) sinks at 09°12'S, 159°50'E, in the wake of the Battle of Tassafaronga; Japanese destroyer *Takanami* goes down about 10 miles southsouthwest of Savo Island, 09°18'S, 159°56'E.

Submarine *Peto* (SS 265) sinks Japanese transport *Konei Maru* north of the Bismarck Archipelago.

USAAF B-17s, B-24s, and B-25s (5th Air Force) attack four Japanese destroyers off coast of New Guinea between Buna and Gona; although the bombers score no direct hits, *Isonami* is damaged by near-misses. The Japanese land troops at the mouth of the Amboga River instead of at Gona (see 2 December).

ATLANTIC. Fleet Air Wing 15 (Captain George A. Seitz) is established at Norfolk, Virginia, for service at Port Lyautey, French Morocco.

Sixteen survivors from unarmed U.S. schooner *Star of Scotland,* shelled and sunk by German submarine *U 159* on 13 November, reach Angola after an open-boat voyage of 1,040 miles.

2 Wednesday

ATLANTIC. Naval Operating Base and Naval Air Facility, Rio de Janeiro, Brazil, are established.

U.S. steamship *Coamo* is sunk by German submarine *U 604* off Bermuda; some survivors from the 186 men on board manage to escape on rafts (see 3 December).

PACIFIC. USAAF B-17s, B-25s, A-20s, and P-400s (5th Air Force) again attack the four Japanese destroyers bombed the day before off the coast of New Guinea; no hits are scored.

3 Thursday

PACIFIC. SBDs and TBFs from Henderson Field, Guadalcanal, attack a Japanese Reinforcement Unit, 10 ships strong, en route to Guadalcanal and damage destroyer *Makinami.* The Japanese put some 1,500 supply canisters in the water for their troops on Guadalcanal, but only 310 reach the intended recipients.

ATLANTIC. Gale sweeps area in which U.S. steamship *Coamo* has been sunk by German submarine *U 604* off Bermuda the previous day; the survivors who managed to reach safety on rafts most likely perish on this and/or subsequent days. No survivors from the 133-man crew, the 37 Armed Guard sailors, or the 16 Army passengers are ever found.

4 Friday

MEDITERRANEAN. USAAF B-24s (9th Air Force) conduct first U.S. bombing raid on Italy, targeting the port of Naples. Light cruiser *Muzio Attendolo* is sunk; light cruisers *Raimondo Montecuccoli* and *Eugenio di Savoia* and four destroyers are damaged.

ATLANTIC. New tank landing ship *LST 389* runs aground off Norfolk, Virginia, but is freed from her predicament by commercial tug *Cumco* (Navy Rescue Tug Service).

5 Saturday

PACIFIC. Tug *Grebe* (AT 134) sinks after running aground south of Fiji, 19°49'S, 178°13'W.

VCS Detachment RINGBOLT is established at Tanambogo, Solomons, composed of planes (SOCs/SONs) from heavy cruisers *Pensacola* (CA 24), *Northampton* (CA 26), *New Orleans* (CA 32), and *Minneapolis* (CA 36) and light cruiser *Honolulu* (CL 48). Operations of the

new unit commence immediately, taking precedence over setting up camp. Two SOCs patrol this night with PT boats. Lack of equipment and communication difficulties handicap operations that are carried out on moonless nights in rain squalls. Only facility provided is a flashlight on the beach to guide returning planes through reef passage after landing.

Japanese freighter *Mansei Maru* founders and sinks in storm in Formosa Strait, 23°30'N, 119°34'E.

CARIBBEAN. Gunboat *Erie* (PG 50), damaged on 12 November and moved to facilitate salvage on 28 November, capsizes and sinks at her moorings at Willemstad, Curaçao, N.W.I.

ATLANTIC. U.S. freighter *John Lykes* rescues 19 survivors from freighter *Jeremiah Wadsworth,* sunk by German submarine *U 178* on 27 November; an unidentified Allied ship rescues 20 more of *Jeremiah Wadsworth*'s men the same day.

6 Sunday

ATLANTIC. British armed merchant cruiser HMS *Alcantara* rescues 18 survivors from freighter *Jeremiah Wadsworth,* sunk by German submarine *U 178* on 27 November.

Harbor tug *Bomazeen* (YT 238) assists commercial tug *Cumco* (Navy Rescue Tug Service) in freeing grounded freighter *Santa Marta* off Norfolk, Virginia.

7 Monday

PACIFIC. USMC SBDs (VMSB 132) from Henderson Field attack Japanese Reinforcement Unit (Captain Sato Torajiro), 12 ships strong, carrying reinforcements and supplies to Guadalcanal, and damage destroyers *Nowaki* and *Arashi.*

Cargo ship *Alchiba* (AK 23) is torpedoed by Japanese midget submarine *Ha.38* (from submarine *I 24*) off Lunga Point, Guadalcanal.

Submarine *Kingfish* (SS 234) sinks Japanese transport *No. 3 Hino Maru* west of the Bonins, 23°59'N, 138°43'E.

ATLANTIC. U.S. freighter *James McKay,* attempting to join convoy HX 217 in heavy seas east of Newfoundland, is sunk by German submarine *U 600* at 57°50'N, 23°10'W; although *U 600* notes two boats clearing the ship's side containing survivors, none of the 48-man merchant complement or the 14-man Armed Guard are ever found.

Lifeboat from U.S. tanker *Caddo,* sunk on 23 November by German submarine *U 518,* capsizes twice; seven of the 13 occupants drown.

Of the 17 men who originally occupied the boat, four had already perished at sea (see 8 December).

8 Tuesday

PACIFIC. Motor torpedo boats *PT 36*, *PT 37*, *PT 40*, *PT 43*, *PT 44*, *PT 48*, *PT 59*, and *PT 109* turn back eight Japanese destroyers (Captain Sato Torajiro) attempting to reinforce Guadalcanal. Richard B. Frank in his magnificent study, *Guadalcanal*, lauds this "night's work" as "perhaps the greatest individual success of American PT boats during the war."

Submarine *Gar* (SS 206) sinks Japanese cargo ship *Heinan Maru*, Makassar Strait, 00°52′N, 118°54′E.

USAAF B-17s and B-24s damage Japanese destroyers *Asashio* and *Isonami* off Buna, New Guinea.

ATLANTIC. Spanish motorship *Motomar* rescues the only six survivors (three merchant seamen and three Armed Guard sailors) from U.S. tanker *Caddo*, sunk on 23 November by German submarine *U 518*, at 38°10′N, 35°24′W. The other two lifeboats with their occupants from *Caddo* are never seen again.[126]

9 Wednesday

PACIFIC. Major General Alexander A. Vandegrift, USMC, is relieved by Major General Alexander M. Patch, USA, as commander of Marine and Army troops, Guadalcanal.

Aircraft from Henderson Field, Guadalcanal, begin what become daily attacks on Japanese installations at Munda, New Georgia.

Motor torpedo boat *PT 59* sinks Japanese submarine *I 3*, engaged in a resupply mission to Guadalcanal, three miles northeast of Kamimbo Bay, 09°12′S, 159°42′E.

10 Thursday

PACIFIC. Submarine *Halibut* (SS 232) sinks Japanese freighter *Kosei Maru* and damages Japanese transport *Uyo Maru*, off Hachinoihe, 40°40′N, 141°58′E.

Submarine *Stingray* (SS 186) is damaged by bombs off northern Solomons, 07°58′S, 156°12′E.

Submarine *Wahoo* (SS 238) sinks Japanese collier *Kamoi Maru* off Buin, Bougainville, 04°06′S, 154°58′E.

USAAF B-17s damage Japanese oilers *Fujisan Maru* and *Toa Maru* off Buin, Bougainville.

ATLANTIC. PBY (VP 84) sinks German submarine *U 611* south of Reykjavik, Iceland, 58°09′N, 22°44′W.

11 Friday

PACIFIC. SBDs and USAAF P-39/P-400s from Henderson Field attack 11 Japanese destroyers (Rear Admiral Tanaka Raizo) on a resupply mission to Guadalcanal, north of New Georgia, without success.

Submarine *Seadragon* (SS 194) damages cargo ship *Johore Maru* off Cape St. George, New Ireland, 04°55′S, 152°44′E.

12 Saturday

PACIFIC. Five motor torpedo boats attack 11 Japanese destroyers (Rear Admiral Tanaka Raizo) off Cape Esperance, Guadalcanal. Motor torpedo boats *PT 37* and *PT 40* sink *Terutsuki*, but *Kawakaze* and *Suzukaze* sink *PT 44* off Savo Island, 09°10′S, 159°45′E.

Submarine *Drum* (SS 228) torpedoes Japanese aircraft carrier *Ryuho* off Hachijo Jima, 32°04′N, 142°30′E.

Submarine *Halibut* (SS 232) sinks Japanese freighter *Gyokusan Maru* off northeast coast of Honshu, 40°37′N, 142°40′E.

13 Sunday

ATLANTIC. Spanish tanker *Cilurum* rescues 11 crewmen and three Armed Guard sailors from U.S. freighter *Alaskan*, sunk by German submarine *U 172* on 28 November, and transports them to Las Palmas, Canary Islands (see 15 December and 5 January 1943).

PACIFIC. USAAF B-17s (5th Air Force) bomb Japanese reinforcement convoy of five destroyers off Buna, New Guinea; *Isonami* is damaged. The Japanese Navy will make no more organized attempts to reinforce the troops at Buna and Gona.

14 Monday

PACIFIC. Fleet Air Command, Nouméa, New Caledonia (Rear Admiral Marc A. Mitscher), is established.

Submarine *Sunfish* (SS 281) lays mines in entrance to Iseno Umi Bay, Japan. She continues these mining operations in those waters on 15, 16, and 17 December.

On board submarine *Grayback* (SS 208), on war patrol in the Bismarck Archipelago, appendectomy commences (2300) by Pharmacist's Mate First Class Harry B. Roby, USNR, on Torpedoman First Class W. R. Jones (see 15 December).

ATLANTIC. U.S. freighter *Alcoa Rambler* is sunk by German submarine *U 174* while en route from Port of Spain, Trinidad, to Santos, Brazil, 03°51′S, 33°08′W; one merchant seaman

drowns when the ship is abandoned (see 17 December).

15 Tuesday

ATLANTIC. Coast Guard cutter *Ingham* (WPG 35) sinks German submarine *U 626* roughly south-southwest of Iceland, 56°46′N, 27°12′W.

Twelve Armed Guard sailors (one of whom dies later of his wounds) and 17 merchant seamen from U.S. freighter *Alaskan*, sunk by German submarine *U 172* on 28 November, reach Salinas, Brazil, by lifeboat (see 5 January 1943).

PACIFIC. Appendectomy is completed (0200) on board submarine *Grayback* (SS 208), by Pharmacist's Mate First Class Harry B. Roby, USNR, on Torpedoman First Class W. R. Jones. This is the second of three such procedures that will be performed on board U.S. submarines during the war.

16 Wednesday

PACIFIC. Submarine *Halibut* (SS 232) sinks Japanese freighter *Shingu Maru* off Shiraya Saki, Honshu, 41°18′N, 141°32′E; in the confusion that attends *Halibut*'s attack upon *Shingu Maru*, cargo ship *Genzan Maru* is run aground, stranded, and abandoned, 41°10′N, 141°32′E.

17 Thursday

PACIFIC. Submarine *Drum* (SS 228) mines the Bungo Strait, Japan.

Submarine *Grouper* (SS 214) sinks Japanese army passenger-cargo ship *Bandoeng Maru* about 15 miles northwest of Cape Henpan, Buka Island, Solomons, 04°54′S, 154°17′E, and survives counterattack by submarine chaser *Ch 29*.

ATLANTIC. Coast Guard cutter *Natsek* (WPG 170) sinks after foundering in Belle Isle Strait off Newfoundland.

Twenty-five survivors from U.S. freighter *Alcoa Ranger*, sunk by German submarine *U 174* on 14 December, reach Natal, Brazil, by lifeboat.

18 Friday

PACIFIC. USAAF B-17s (5th Air Force) bomb Japanese invasion force steaming toward Madang, New Guinea, to land troops (5th Infantry Division), damaging armed merchant cruiser *Gokoku Maru*, 05°10′S, 145°57′E. While the landings proceed, submarine *Albacore* (SS 218) sinks light cruiser *Tenryu* off Madang Harbor, 05°12′S, 145°56′E, and survives counterattacks by escorting destroyer (*Sukukaze* or *Isonami*).

Submarine *Sunfish* (SS 281) damages Japanese transport *Kyowa Maru* off Daio Saki, Japan, 34°10′N, 136°52′E.

ATLANTIC. U.S. tanker *Brilliant*, torpedoed on 18 November by *U 43*, sets out from St. John's, Newfoundland, but is forced by heavy seas to return the next day (see 20 January 1943).

19 Saturday

PACIFIC. USAAF B-24s (5th Air Force) bomb Japanese warships north of New Britain, damaging destroyer *Mochizuki* with near-misses.

20 Sunday

PACIFIC. Submarine *Amberjack* (SS 219) is damaged by depth charges off northern Solomons, 07°10′S, 155°21′E, but remains on patrol.

Submarine *Trigger* (SS 237) lays mines off Inubo Saki, Honshu; one immediately sinks Japanese freighter *Mutsuki Maru* south of Daio Saki, Japan, 35°45′N, 140°55′E, as the enemy freighter happens by in the midst of the submarine's minelaying operation.

Light minelayer *Gamble* (DM 15) lays mines to reinforce minefield laid at Espíritu Santo, New Hebrides, on 3 August.

Gunboat *Tulsa* (PG 22) is damaged when she runs aground in Milne Bay, New Guinea, 10°15′S, 149°27′E.

21 Monday

PACIFIC. Submarine *Seadragon* (SS 194) sinks Japanese submarine *I 4* between New Britain and New Ireland, 05°02′S, 152°33′E, while *I 4* is engaged in a resupply mission to Guadalcanal.

Submarine *S 35* (SS 140) is damaged by electrical fire while on patrol off Amchitka, Aleutians.

Japanese army cargo ship *Hakuyo Maru* is sunk by aircraft (nationality unspecified) near Rabaul.

22 Tuesday

PACIFIC. Submarine *Greenling* (SS 213), attacking Japanese convoy, sinks *Patrol Boat No. 35* about 70 miles north-northeast of Kieta, Bougainville, 05°05′S, 156°04′E.

Submarine *S 35* (SS 140) is again plagued by electrical fires; on this day and the one previous, however, other than cases of smoke inhalation, exposure, and exhaustion, the boat suffers no casualties.

On board submarine *Silversides* (SS 236), submerged in the shipping channel off

Rabaul, New Britain, Pharmacist's Mate First Class Thomas A. Moore performs successful appendectomy on Fireman Second Class George M. Platter. This is the third of three such procedures that will be performed on board U.S. submarines during the war.

Submarine *Trigger* (SS 237) damages Japanese freighter *Yoshu Maru* south of the entrance to Tokyo Bay, 34°52′N, 139°49′E. *Trigger* clears the area without seeing her quarry sink.

USAAF B-24 (5th Air Force) sinks Japanese freighter *Takasaka Maru* off Gasmata, New Britain.

Japanese freighter *Kaiyo Maru* is lost, Inland Sea, Japan.

24 Thursday

PACIFIC. Henderson Field, Guadalcanal–based SBDs, P-40s, and F4Fs attack 13 Japanese troop-laden barges bound for Munda, New Georgia, sinking nine of the enemy craft.

Japanese netlayer *Koa Maru* is sunk by aircraft (possibly a USAAF B-24 heavy bomber), Marcus Bay, New Britain. USAAF B-17s and B-24s (5th Air Force) bomb Japanese shipping at Gasmata, New Britain, damaging transport *No. 2 Tama Maru*, 06°18′S, 150°16′E.

Submarine *Silversides* (SS 236) is bombed (tumbling the convalescing appendectomy patient "out of his bunk on the wardroom transom") by Japanese plane off Rabaul. Damage sustained in the attack does not prevent *Silversides* from continuing her patrol.

Submarine *Triton* (SS 201) sinks Japanese water tanker *No. 1 Amakusa Maru* south of Wake Island, 19°16′N, 166°36′E.

ATLANTIC. Transports *Florence Nightingale* (AP 70) and *Thurston* (AP 77) are damaged in collision off Fedala, French Morocco, 34°41′N, 07°25′W.

25 Friday

PACIFIC. Submarine *Seadragon* (SS 194) torpedoes Japanese transport *Nankai Maru* off Cape St. George, New Britain, 05°05′S, 152°28′E; escorting destroyer *Uzuki*, after depth charging *Seadragon* (and claiming destruction of her quarry), is then damaged in collision with the holed *Nankai Maru*. Despite the enemy destroyermen's optimism, *Seadragon* emerges to fight another day.

Submarine *Tautog* (SS 199) sinks Japanese army cargo ship *No. 2 Banshu Maru* about 15 miles north of Dili, Timor, 08°40′S, 124°30′E.

Submarine *Thresher* (SS 200) sinks Japanese army transport *No. 1 Tokiwa Maru* off north coast of Java, N.E.I., 06°38′S, 112°44′E.

USAAF B-17s damage Japanese transport *Kagu Maru* and freighter *Kozan Maru* at Rabaul.

ATLANTIC. Philippine motorship *Dona Aurora* is sunk by Italian submarine *Enrico Tazzoli* about 200 miles off the coast of Brazil, 02°02′S, 35°17′W; *Enrico Tazzoli* takes two passengers and one Armed Guard sailor prisoner and leaves the rest afloat in a boat and three rafts (see 27 December and 3 and 24 January 1943).

26 Saturday

PACIFIC. Henderson Field, Guadalcanal–based SBDs, F4Fs, and P-38s attack Japanese transports at Wickham Anchorage, New Georgia, sinking freighters *Takashima Maru* and *Iwami Maru*.

USAAF B-24 (5th Air Force) bombs Japanese shipping in St. George Channel, Solomons, and damages destroyer *Ariake* as she escorts transport *Nankai Maru*, damaged by submarine *Seadragon* (SS 194) the previous day, and destroyer *Uzuki*.

USAAF B-17s (5th Air Force) bomb Japanese shipping off Rabaul, New Britain, damaging destroyer *Tachikaze* (see 27 December).

Mine laid by submarine *Trigger* (SS 237) sinks Japanese freighter *Teifuku Maru* four miles northeast of Inubo Saki, Japan, 35°45′N, 140°55′E.

RAAF Beaufighters strafe Japanese shipping, troop concentrations, and supply dumps at Laivai, Timor; this strike may be the one responsible for the loss of freighter *Izumi Maru* in the "South Seas area."

ATLANTIC. Submarine *Barb* (SS 220) mistakenly torpedoes neutral Spanish tanker *Campomanes* off Cape Finisterre, Spain.

27 Sunday

PACIFIC. USAAF B-17s (5th Air Force) bomb Japanese shipping off Rabaul, New Britain, sinking freighters *Italy Maru* and *Tsurugisan Maru*, 04°21′S, 142°17′E.

ATLANTIC. Minelayers *Keokuk* (CM 8), *Salem* (CM 11) and *Weehawken* (CM 12) begin mining approaches to Casablanca, French Morocco (see 28 December).

British freighter *Testbank* rescues 50 survivors from Philippine motorship *Dona Aurora*, sunk by Italian submarine *Enrico Tazzoli* on 25 December (see 3 January 1943).

28 Monday

PACIFIC. Submarine *Kingfish* (SS 234) sinks Japanese freighter *Choyo Maru* off northwest coast of Formosa, 24°46′N, 120°40′E.

Submarine *Triton* (SS 201) sinks Japanese merchant passenger-cargo ship *Omi Maru* between Truk and Ponape, Carolines, 06°24′N, 160°18′E.

Japanese army cargo ship *No. 8 Tokiwa Maru* is sunk by mine off north coast of Java, 06°50′S, 112°47′E.

Japanese minelayer *Nichiyu Maru* is damaged (cause unknown) off Kiska, Aleutians.

ATLANTIC. Minelayers *Keokuk* (CM 8), *Salem* (CM 11), and *Weehawken* (CM 12) complete mining approaches to Casablanca, French Morocco.

29 Tuesday

PACIFIC. High-speed minesweeper *Wasmuth* (DMS 15) is sunk by explosion of two of her own depth charges during a gale, 35 miles off Scotch Cape, the southwest point of Unimak Island, Aleutians. In a masterful display of seamanship, oiler *Ramapo* (AO 12) comes alongside in the heavy sea and rescues *Wasmuth's* crew.

Mine laid by submarine *Tambor* (SS 198) on 2 November sinks Japanese freighter *Fukken Maru* off northwest coast of Hainan, 20°04′N, 109°18′E.

ATLANTIC. Coastal yacht *Mentor* (PYc 37) is disabled by engine trouble off Sea Isle City, New Jersey; commercial tug *Samson* is sent to her assistance. When *Mentor* is able to proceed under her own power, *Samson* is rerouted to assist *E. H. Blum*, which has run aground two miles south of Fenwick Isle shoals. Salvage vessel *Accelerate* and tug *Allegheny* (AT 19) also proceed to the tanker's assistance. *E. H. Blum*, however, breaks in two; *Samson* takes the 39 survivors to Lewes, Delaware.

30 Wednesday

PACIFIC. Submarine *Greenling* (SS 213) attacks Japanese convoy about 180 miles northeast of Manus, Admiralties, sinking army cargo ship *Hiteru Maru* and damaging cargo ship *Ryufuku Maru*, 00°41′N, 148°52′E.

Submarine *Searaven* (SS 196) lands agents on south coast of Ceram Island, N.E.I.

Submarine *Thresher* (SS 200) sinks Japanese freighter *Hachian Maru* (ex-British *Kinshan*) about 120 miles west of Mata Siri Island, off southeast tip of Borneo, 04°45′N, 113°54′E.

Japanese coastal minesweeper *M 2* is sunk by mine, Surabaya Harbor, Java.

USAAF B-17s (5th Air Force) bomb Japanese shipping in Simpson Harbor, Rabaul, sinking freighter *Tomiura Maru*, 04°14′S, 152°11′E.

31 Thursday

PACIFIC. Japanese Imperial Headquarters in Tokyo decides to begin the evacuation of Guadalcanal.

USAAF B-24s (11th Air Force), covered by P-38s, bomb Japanese shipping in Kiska Harbor, Aleutians, damaging freighter *Urajio Maru*.

1943

JANUARY

1 Friday

PACIFIC. Salvage vessel *Rescuer* (ARS 18) sinks after running aground off Scotch Cape, Aleutians.

Submarine *Nautilus* (SS 168) evacuates 29 civilians from Teop Island, Solomons.

Submarine *Porpoise* (SS 172), in attack on Japanese convoy, sinks freighter *Renzan Maru* off northeastern coast of Honshu, Japan, 39°11′N, 142°02′E.

Submarine *Trigger* (SS 237) damages Japanese transport *Shozan Maru* off Nojima Saki, Honshu, 35°55′N, 140°55′E.

Japanese army cargo ship *Osaka Maru* is damaged by mine, 16 miles off Ambon, N.E.I.

MEDITERRANEAN. German submarine *U 73* sinks U.S. freighter *Arthur Middleton* off Oran, Algeria, 35°45′N, 00°45′W; of the 81 souls on board (11 of whom are from the crew of tank landing craft *LCT 21*, which is also lost) three sailors of the 27-man Armed Guard detachment are the only survivors.

2 Saturday

PACIFIC. USAAF B-17s (South Pacific Force), escorted by P-38s, bomb 10 Japanese supply-carrying destroyers (Rear Admiral Koyanagi Tomiji) south of Shortland Island, Solomons, but achieve no success; SBDs, escorted by F4Fs, later attack same force southwest of Munda, damaging *Sukukaze*. Eleven motor torpedo boats later attack the force off Cape Esperance without success.

U.S. Army I Corps (Lieutenant General Robert L. Eichelberger) captures Buna, New Guinea, significantly reducing the threat to Port Moresby.

Submarine *Argonaut* (SS 166) sinks Japanese guardboat *Ebon Maru*, Bismarck Sea, 04°30′S, 151°30′E.

Submarine *Spearfish* (SS 190) damages Japanese army cargo ship *Akagisan Maru* off New Ireland, Bismarck Archipelago, 03°30′S, 151°30′E.

MEDITERRANEAN. USAAF B-17s, escorted by P-38s (12th Air Force), bomb La Goulette Harbor, Tunisia, damaging two merchant vessels.[127]

3 Sunday

PACIFIC. SOCs (VCS Detachment RINGBOLT) bomb footbridge and probable Japanese bivuoac near Kukumbona, Guadalcanal.

ATLANTIC. U.S. freighter *Samuel Livermore* goes aground three miles east of Key West Sea Buoy, Florida. Efforts of tug *Apache* (AT 67), harbor tug *YT 160*, salvage vessel *Willet* (ARS 12), and tug *Nancy Moran* bear fruit the following day when the merchantman is floated free.

Small seaplane tender *Humboldt* (AVP 21) rescues 10 survivors from Philippine motorship *Dona Aurora*, sunk by Italian submarine *Enrico Tazzol* on 25 December 1942.

EUROPE. USAAF B-17s and B-24s (8th Air Force) bomb German U-boat base at St. Nazaire, France; it is the heaviest effort to date (68 bombers participate) and the first against that base since 23 November 1942.

Submarine *Peto* (SS 265) sits high and dry in a floating drydock during her 1,500-mile journey down the Mississippi from her builder's yard in Manitowoc, Wisconsin, to New Orleans for fitting out. She arrives at her destination on 7 January 1943. (Author's Collection)

4 Monday

ATLANTIC. Submarine *Shad* (SS 235) sinks German minesweeper *M 4242* (ex-French trawler *Odet II*) in Bay of Biscay, 43°55′N, 02°42′W.

5 Tuesday

PACIFIC. TG 67.2 (Rear Admiral Mahlon S. Tisdale) bombards airfield and installations at Munda, New Georgia, Solomons. Submarine *Grayback* (SS 208) serves as reference vessel; "Black Cat" PBYs serve as spotters. After the rest of TF 67 (Rear Admiral Walden L. Ainsworth) joins TG 67.2, Japanese planes at-

tack the force, near-missing light cruiser *Honolulu* (CL 48) and damaging New Zealand light cruiser HMNZS *Achilles*, 18 miles south of Cape Hunter, Guadalcanal. During that action, light cruiser *Helena* (CL 50) becomes the first U.S. Navy ship to use Mk. 32 proximity-fused projectiles in combat, downing a Japanese Aichi Type 99 carrier bomber (VAL) with her second salvo.

ATLANTIC. Tug *Allegheny* (AT 19) is sent to bring in disabled coastal minesweeper *Roller* (AMc 52), drifting about 17 miles south-southeast of Five Fathom Bank, 38°30′N, 74°23′W. *Allegheny*, however, suffers a steering gear ca-

sualty but manages to reach port under her own power. Salvage tug *Samson* tows *Roller* to Cape May, New Jersey.

Last nine survivors (including the Armed Guard unit commander) of U.S. freighter *Alaskan*, sunk by German submarine *U 172* on 28 November 1942, utilizing a bailed-out lifeboat, reach Cayenne, French Guiana.

6 Wednesday

PACIFIC. In the Aleutians, motor torpedo boats *PT 22* and *PT 24* are damaged in collision during storm, Dora Harbor, Unimak Island. In attacks against Japanese shipping, PBY sinks freighter *Montreal Maru* near Kiska, 53°28′N, 177°52′E; USAAF B-24s (11th Air Force) sink freighter *Kotohira Maru* off Holtz Bay, Attu, 53°00′N, 173°10′E.

USAAF B-17s and B-24s (5th Air Force) bomb Japanese shipping at Rabaul, New Britain, sinking army cargo vessel *Keifuku Maru* and damaging destroyer *Tachikaze* and cargo vessel *Kagu Maru*.

RAAF Hudsons damage Japanese torpedo boat *Tomozuru* off Kai Island, Banda Sea. She is taken in tow the next day to be brought to Ambon, N.E.I., for repairs (see 9 January).

ATLANTIC. PBY-5A (VP 83) sinks German submarine *U 164* off Brazil, 01°58′S, 39°23′W.

District patrol vessels *YP 613* and *YP 492* collide off Mayport, Florida; the latter, abandoned, is deemed beyond economical repair. *YP 492*'s service to the war effort, however, is not over, for her hulk is set up on shore for use as a preliminary training boat for recruits.

7 Thursday

PACIFIC. USAAF B-17s, B-24s, B-25s, and B-26s, supported by P-38s and P-40s (5th Air Force) and RAAF or RNZAF Hudsons and RAAF Catalinas, set upon Japanese convoy bound for New Guinea. During these attacks, army cargo ship *Nichiryu Maru* is sunk off Lae, 06°30′S, 149°00′E, and army cargo ship *Myoko Maru* is forced aground south of Arawe, 06°49′S, 147°04′E (see 8 January).

MEDITERRANEAN. German planes attack convoy KMS 7 off Bougie, Algeria, bombing U.S. freighter *William Wirt*; there are no casualties among the ship's complement (including the 21-man Armed Guard).

8 Friday

PACIFIC. USAAF B-17s, B-24s, B-25s, and A-20s, supported by P-38s (5th Air Force), attack Japanese convoy unloading off Lae, New Guinea, and complete the destruction of army cargo ship *Myoko Maru*, forced aground south of Arawe the previous day.

ATLANTIC. Shortly before midnight, submarine *U 124* attacks 12-ship Rio de Janeiro, Brazil–bound convoy TB 1, torpedoing U.S. tanker *Broad Arrow* at 07°21N, 55°43′W, and freighter *Birmingham City* at 07°12′N, 55°37′W. On board *Broad Arrow*, the initial explosion kills seven of the eight-man Armed Guard; the surviving crewmen abandon the blazing ship (which is illuminating the entire convoy) without orders. *Birmingham City* sinks in three minutes (see 9 January).

MEDITERRANEAN. USAAF B-17s (12th Air Force) bomb naval base at Ferryville, Tunisia; ex-French first class sloop *Ypres* is sunk.

9 Saturday

PACIFIC. Submarine *Gar* (SS 206) damages Japanese oiler *Notoro* in Makassar Strait, 01°46′N, 119°01′E.

Submarine *Nautilus* (SS 168) survives depth charge attack by Japanese transport *Yoshinogawa Maru* just east of Kieta, Bougainville, 06°13′S, 156°00′E, and then sinks her tormentor.

Submarine *Searaven* (SS 196) damages Japanese army cargo ship *Yubae Maru* southwest of the Palaus, 07°38′N, 134°12′E.

Submarine *Tautog* (SS 199) torpedoes Japanese light cruiser *Natori* (proceeding to sea to cover the arrival of damaged torpedo boat *Tomozuru*) southeast of Ambon, 04°07′S, 128°32′E (see 21 January).

ATLANTIC. German submarine *U 384* attacks Belfast, Ireland–bound U.S. freighter *Louise Lykes* in the North Atlantic at 58°55′N, 23°40′W; although the U-boat will ultimately destroy the merchantman, Armed Guard gunfire nearly turns the tables on the enemy. Sadly, none of *Louise Lykes*'s people (including the 24-man Armed Guard) survive.

German submarine *U 124* continues assault on convoy TB 1, begun shortly before midnight the day before, about 100 miles northeast of Paramaribo, Dutch Guiana. *U 124* torpedoes U.S. freighters *Collingsworth* and *Minotaur* at 07°12′N, 55°37′W; each ship sinks four minutes after being struck (see 10 January). Tanker *Broad Arrow* sinks as the result of damage received in *U 124*'s initial attack. Submarine chaser *PC 577* rescues survivors from all four ships sunk by the U-boat. Of the Armed Guards on the four merchantmen, only one sailor of the eight-man guard on board *Broad Arrow* survives, five of the 18-man Armed Guard perish in the abandonment of *Birmingham City*, and *Collingsworth*'s detach-

Destroyer *Worden* (DD 352) in extremis (left) off Amchitka, 12 January 1943; sister ship *Dewey* (DD 349) stands by. (NA, 80-G-75598)

ment loses four of 24 men. *Minotaur*'s 15-man Armed Guard, however, survives intact.

10 Sunday

PACIFIC. Transport submarine *Argonaut* (APS 1), attacking a Japanese convoy southeast of New Britain, is sunk by aircraft (582nd *Kokutai*) and destroyers *Isokaze* and *Maikaze*, 05°40′S, 152°02′E.

Destroyer *Shaw* (DD 373) is damaged by grounding, Bulari Passage, New Caledonia.

Motor torpedo boats *PT 27* and *PT 28* are damaged by storm, Dora Harbor, Unimak Island, Aleutians (see 14 January).

Submarine *Trigger* (SS 237) sinks Japanese destroyer *Okikaze* off Yokosuka, Japan, 35°02′N, 140°12′E.

RAAF Hudsons and Catalinas damage Japanese army cargo ship *Brazil Maru* off Lae, New Guinea.

ATLANTIC. U.S. freighter *Norwalk* is sunk in collision with Norwegian freighter *Nidareid* north of Cuba, 28°18′N, 80°00′W. While one of the 30-man merchant crew perishes in the accident, none of the 14-man Armed Guard are hurt.

Norwegian freighter *Dalvanger* rescues 21 men from U.S. freighter *Collingsworth*, torpe-

doed and sunk by *U 124* the previous day while in convoy TB 1.

11 Monday

PACIFIC. Nine motor torpedo boats operating from Tulagi, Solomons, directed to the scene by a PBY, attack Japanese Reinforcement Unit (Captain Koyanagi Tomiji), eight destroyers strong, off Cape Esperance, Guadalcanal; destroyer *Hatsukaze* is damaged.[128] Motor torpedo boat *PT 112* is sunk and *PT 43* is damaged by destroyer gunfire, 09°15′S, 159°42′E (see 12 January).

Submarine *Trout* (SS 202) damages Japanese oiler *Kyokuyo Maru* off Miri, 04°24′N, 113°51′E.

12 Tuesday

PACIFIC. TF 8 (Rear Admiral Thomas C. Kinkaid) covers unopposed landing of Army troops (Brigadier General Lloyd E. Jones) to occupy Amchitka, Aleutians. Destroyer *Worden* (DD 352) founders and sinks after running aground south of Kirilof Point, at entrance to Constantine Harbor. Motor torpedo boat *PT 28* is damaged by grounding during storm, Dora Harbor, Unimak Island.

Submarine *Guardfish* (SS 217) sinks *Patrol*

Boat No. 1 about 10 miles southwest of the Tingwon Islands, located just southwest of the northern tip of New Hanover, Bismarck Archipelago, 02°51'S, 149°43'E.

New Zealand corvette scuttles hulk of motor torpedo boat *PT 43*, damaged on 11 January, off Guadalcanal.

District patrol vessel *YP 183* sinks after running aground off west coast of Hawaii, T.H.

13 Wednesday

PACIFIC. Transport *Arthur Middleton* (AP 55) is damaged when she runs aground at western end of Constantine Harbor, Amchitka, Aleutians.[129]

Submarine *Triton* (SS 201) damages Japanese oiler *Akebono Maru* north of the St. Matthias Island group, 00°26'S, 148°40'E.

Submarine *Whale* (SS 239) sinks Japanese collier *Iwashiro Maru* about 40 miles north of Kwajalein, Marshall Islands, 09°54'N, 167°07'E.

ATLANTIC. PBY-5As (VP 83) sink German submarine *U 507* off Brazil, 01°38'S, 39°52'W.

14 Thursday

GENERAL. Casablanca (SYMBOL) Conference begins. President Roosevelt, British Prime Minister Winston S. Churchill, and their respective staffs meet to plan future operations against the Axis powers.

PACIFIC. Submarine *Gudgeon* (SS 211) lands men and equipment near Catmon Point, Negros, P.I., to establish a radio station there.

Submarine *Nautilus* (SS 168) hits Japanese *Toa Maru* with dud torpedo off Bougainville, Solomons, 05°13'S, 155°09'E.

Submarine *Pike* (SS 173) is damaged by bombs and depth charges off Ichie Saki, Honshu; she is forced to terminate her patrol.

Submarine *Searaven* (SS 196) attacks Japanese convoy northwest of the Palaus, sinking the sole escort, auxiliary submarine chaser *No. 1 Ganjitsu Maru*, and army cargo ship *Shiraha Maru*, 09°12'N, 130°38'E.

Motor torpedo boat *PT 28*, damaged by storm on 10 January, is abandoned, Dora Harbor, Unimak Island, Aleutians.

SOCs (VCS Detachment RINGBOLT) locate and illuminate Guadalcanal-bound Japanese destroyers for PT boats; the planes also bomb and strafe the enemy ships (see 15 January).

15 Friday

PACIFIC. SBDs from Henderson Field, Guadalcanal, escorted by F4Fs, attack nine Japanese destroyers (Rear Admiral Tanaka Raizo) that were harassed by SOCs (VCS Detachment RINGBOLT) the previous night. Tanaka's ships, attacked northeast of New Georgia, Solomon Islands, are bringing in 600 troops to cover the evacuation of Japanese forces from Guadalcanal; the SBDs damage *Arashi*, *Tanikaze*, *Urakaze*, and *Hamakaze*.

Japanese attempt to reinforce their troops in the northern Solomons begins as Section A (three transports accompanied by destroyer *Shigure*) departs Truk, Carolines, for Bougainville. The soldiers are being transferred from China (see 17, 19, and 20 January).

ANDAMAN SEA. USAAF B-24s (10th Air Force) bomb Japanese convoy, sinking army cargo ship *Nichimei Maru* and damaging army cargo ship *Moji Maru*, about 200 miles south-southwest of Rangoon, Burma, 13°30'N, 97°30'E. Unknown to the aviators, *Nichimei Maru* is transporting Allied POWs, 500 of whom are lost.

MEDITERRANEAN. USAAF B-24s, escorted by P-40s (9th Air Force), bomb Tripoli Harbor, Libya, to destroy wrecked shipping and thus prevent it from being used to block the harbor entrance. Missions of this nature are flown 16 through 21 January (see 23 January).

16 Saturday

PACIFIC. Submarine *Greenling* (SS 213) sinks Japanese transport *Kimposan Maru* west of Kavieng, New Ireland, 02°47'S, 149°10'E, and survives depth charging by submarine chaser *Ch 17*, which, after she drives the U.S. boat deep, rescues *Kimposan Maru*'s survivors.

Submarine *Growler* (SS 215) attacks Japanese convoy, sinking army passenger-cargo ship *Chifuku Maru* 11 miles north of Waton Island, 04°00'S, 151°55'E, and survives escorts' counterattacks.

17 Sunday

PACIFIC. Section B of Japanese Solomons reinforcement convoy sails from Truk, bound for Shortland Island (see 21 January).

Submarine *Finback* (SS 230) damages Japanese freighter *Yachiyo Maru* off Tanega Jima, 30°33'N, 132°25'E.

Submarine *Searaven* (SS 196) torpedoes Japanese cargo ship *Gokoku Maru* just off Palau, 07°52'N, 134°02'E, but the "fish" that hits proves a dud.

Submarine *Whale* (SS 239) damages Japanese troopship *Heiyo Maru* northeast of Truk, 10°13'N, 151°25'E.

SOC (VCS Detachment RINGBOLT) on night patrol locates Japanese submarine by lightning flash and attacks her, but the bomb fails to detonate.

Naval Base and Naval Air Station, Brisbane, Australia, are established.

18 Monday

PACIFIC. Submarine *Greenling* (SS 213) damages Japanese ammunition ship/survey vessel *Soya* in Queen Carola Channel, 02°04'S, 150°37'E.

Submarine *Silversides* (SS 236) sinks Japanese fleet tanker *Genyo Maru* about 90 miles southwest of Truk, 06°19'N, 150°15'E, but is damaged by depth charges from escorting warship and is forced to terminate her patrol.

USAAF B-24 (5th Air Force) sinks Japanese transport *Senzan Maru* off Kavieng, 03°29'S, 149°02'E; submarine chaser *Ch 16* rescues survivors.

USAAF B-17s, escorted by P-39s (13th Air Force), bomb and sink Japanese cargo vessel *Yamafuku Maru* off Shortland Island.

Japanese collier *Tokachi Maru* is sunk by Japanese mine west of Surabaya, Java, N.E.I., 06°50'S, 112°12'E.

U.S. tanker *Mobilube* is torpedoed by Japanese submarine *I 21* off coast of New South Wales, Australia, 33°57'S, 157°20'E; Australian minesweeper HMAS *Kapunda* provides assistance as the tanker remains afloat. Other than three men killed in the initial explosion, no other members of the ship's complement (including the 11-man Armed Guard) perish. *Mobilube* is towed to Sydney by salvage tug *St. Aristell*, but is eventually declared a total loss.

19 Tuesday

PACIFIC. Submarine *Swordfish* (SS 193) encounters Section A of the Japanese Solomons reinforcement convoy and sinks army cargo ship *Myoho Maru*, 05°38'S, 156°20'E. Section C of the convoy, meanwhile, departs Truk (see 20 January).

Submarine *Greenling* (SS 213) damages Japanese army cargo ship *Shinai Maru* north of Rabaul, 01°35'S, 150°57'E.

Submarine *Haddock* (SS 231) attacks Japanese convoy off south coast of Honshu, damaging transport *Shunko Maru*, 34°13'N, 136°59'E.

Submarine *Nautilus* (SS 168) damages Japanese destroyer *Akizuki* 270 miles west of Tulagi, 05°55'S, 156°20'E.

Submarine *Spearfish* (SS 190), en route to Pearl Harbor after completing her patrol, is damaged by aerial bombs off the Gilberts, 04°44'N, 175°28'E.

ATLANTIC. Carrier *Ranger* (CV 4) launches USAAF P-40s off Accra, Gold Coast, for further transfer to the North African theater.

20 Wednesday

PACIFIC. Submarine *Silversides* (SS 236), encountering Section C of Japanese Solomons reinforcement convoy, torpedoes two army transports, sinking *Meiu Maru* and irreparably damaging *Surabaya Maru*, 286 miles from Truk, 03°52'N, 153°26'E. Submarine chaser *Ch 11* and gunboat *No. 2 Choan Maru* rescue survivors; destroyer *Asagumo* arrives from Truk and scuttles *Surabaya Maru*.

First destroyer escort type ship, *Brennan* (DE 13), is commissioned at Mare Island, California, Navy Yard.

MEDITERRANEAN. German planes attack United Kingdom–bound convoy MKS 6 off coast of Algeria; U.S. freighter *Walt Whitman* is torpedoed at 36°55'N, 03°07'E. Four sailors of the 17-man Armed Guard are blown overboard by the explosion but are recovered by an escort vessel within a quarter-hour. There are no casualties, and the ship ultimately reaches Algiers under her own power.

ATLANTIC. Submarine chaser *SC 997* is blown ashore near Ponce de Leon Inlet, Florida; salvage vessels *Willet* (ARS 12) and *Harjurand* are sent to succor the subchaser (see 24 January).

U.S. tanker *Brilliant* departs St. John's, Newfoundland, under tow, bound for Halifax, Nova Scotia, but breaks up in storm (see 24 January).

21 Thursday

PACIFIC. Rear Admiral Robert H. English, Commander Submarines Pacific Fleet, is killed in the accidental crash of the Pan American Airways Martin 130 *Philippine Clipper* in California.

Submarine *Gato* (SS 212) encounters Section B of Japanese Solomons reinforcement convoy and damages army transport *Kenkon Maru* just east of Kieta, Bougainville, 06°12'S, 155°51'E; escorts scuttle the ship to hasten her sinking.

Submarine *Pollack* (SS 180) sinks Japanese freighter *Asama Maru* off Kushiro, Japan, 42°41'N, 145°37'E.

USAAF B-24s (5th Air Force) bomb concentration of Japanese shipping at Ambon, N.E.I.; light cruiser *Natori* (undergoing repairs for damage received on 9 January) is damaged by near-miss.

Naval Base and Naval Auxiliary Air Facility, Corinto, Nicaragua, are established.

22 Friday

PACIFIC. Papua New Guinea campaign ends as Australian 18th Brigade eliminates last pocket of Japanese resistance west of Sananda.

Submarine *Tautog* (SS 199) sinks Japanese army cargo ship *Yashima Maru* (ex-Dutch passenger-cargo ship *Mijer*), five miles east of Salier Strait, Celebes, N.E.I., 05°40'S, 120°30'E.

USAAF B-17s (5th Air Force), in low-level attack on Japanese shipping in Rabaul Harbor, sink freighter *Tetsuzan Maru*; 30 landing craft on board are lost, 04°15'S, 152°10'E.

U.S. freighter *Peter H. Burnett* is torpedoed by Japanese submarine *I 21* about 500 miles east of Newcastle, Australia, 32°54'S, 159°32'E, and abandoned; other than one sailor of the 26-man Armed Guard who dies of injuries received in the explosion, there are no casualties. When *I 21* withdraws, the freighter is reboarded (see 24 January).

23 Saturday

GENERAL. Casablanca (SYMBOL) Conference ends. Major accomplishments of the talks include the decision to invade Sicily in June or July 1943; to maintain a U.S.-British bombing campaign from bases in the United Kingdom against the European continent; to have U.S. forces advance toward the Philippines through the central and southwestern Pacific; and to build up American forces in the China-Burma-India theater. President Roosevelt and British Prime Minister Winston S. Churchill declare that the Allies will pursue a policy of "Unconditional Surrender" of the Axis.

UNITED STATES. District patrol vessel *YP 577* is destroyed by explosion of undetermined origin, Great Lakes, Illinois.

PACIFIC. Submarine *Guardfish* (SS 217) sinks Japanese destroyer *Hakaze* south of Steffen Strait, between New Ireland and New Hanover, 02°47'S, 156°38'E.

Japanese submarine *I 8* bombards Canton Island (see 31 January).

Japanese planes bomb U.S. shipping in Milne Bay, New Guinea; fragments from near-misses damage freighter *Stephen Johnson Field*. One Armed Guard sailor and one merchant crewman are injured; there are no other casualties among the 23-man Armed Guard and 43 merchant seamen.

ATLANTIC. German submarine *U 175* sinks U.S. freighter *Benjamin Smith* off Cape Palmas, Liberia, 04°05'N, 07°50'W. The 23-man Armed Guard detachment (as well as the 43-man merchant complement) survives intact; all hands reach Sassandra, French Ivory Coast, the next day.

MEDITERRANEAN. British forces occupy Tripoli,

South Atlantic patrol: Destroyer *Eberle* (DD 430) prepares to come alongside auxiliary aircraft carrier *Suwanee* (ACV 29), 19 January 1943. Light cruiser *Savannah* (CL 42) is in background (right). Less than two months later, *Eberle* sends a boarding party on board German blockade runner *Karin* (see 10 March). (NA, 80-G-64925)

Libya. Investigation discloses the following wrecked vessels in the harbor, possibly destroyed by USAAF B-24s (9th Air Force) between 16 and 21 January: Italian freighters *Giulia*, *Marocchino*, *San Giovanni Battista*, *Sirio*, and *Penseveranza* and German freighter *Galilea*.

24 Sunday

PACIFIC. TF 67 (Rear Admiral Walden L. Ainsworth), consisting of four light cruisers and eight destroyers, bombards Japanese fuel and munitions dumps and staging areas in the Vila-Stanmore area, Kolombangara, Solomons; spotting is provided by radar-equipped PBYs ("Black Cats"). TF 11 (Rear Admiral DeWitt C. Ramsey) operates in support from south of Rennell Island. Later that same day, USAAF B-17s bomb Japanese airfield at Munda; TBFs, SBDs, and F4Fs from carrier *Saratoga* (CV 3) air group, operating from Henderson Field, Guadalcanal, bomb the same Vila-Stanmore area shelled earlier by TF 67.

Submarine *Wahoo* (SS 238) damages Japanese destroyer *Harusame* 11 miles west of Wewak, New Guinea, 03°23′S, 143°34′E.

High-speed minesweeper *Zane* (DMS 14) recovers one boatload of crewmen from freighter *Peter H. Burnett*, torpedoed by *I 21* on 22 January, and then proceeds to aid the stricken merchantman. *Zane* then tows the freighter to Sydney, Australia, for repairs.

ATLANTIC. Submarine chaser *PC 576* rescues Seaman First Class Basil D. Izzi, USNR, and two Dutch seamen from Dutch motorship *Zaandam* at 08°39′N, 58°46′W. *Zaandam* had been sunk by German submarine *U 174* on 2 November 1942. The three survivors have spent 83 days on the small raft, subsisting on raw fish, fowl, and rainwater.

Submarine chaser *SC 997*, which went aground off Ponce de Leon Inlet, Florida, on 20 January, is floated free by salvage vessel *Willet* (ARS 12).

Survivors of U.S. tanker *Brilliant*, which had broken in two on 20 January, are rescued by Canadian minesweeper from the after portion of the ship. Of the 54 men on board, 31 merchant seamen are saved; 13 of the Armed Guard survive.[130]

After 30 days on a raft, five survivors from Philippine motorship *Dona Aurora*, sunk by Italian submarine *Enrico Tazzoli* on 25 December 1942, reach the mouth of the Pacatuba River, Brazil; one man, however, drowns trying to swim ashore.

25 Monday

ATLANTIC. Submarine *Shad* (SS 235) encounters east-bound German blockade runners (ore transports) in Bay of Biscay. *Shad* attacks *Nordfels*, 43°28′N, 02°59′W, but the torpedo fails to explode. Ore transport *Livadia* remains out of range; *Nordfels* returns to Bilbao, Spain. German antisubmarine trawlers hunt for *Shad* without success. The submarine's presence in the area, however, causes a temporary suspension in the ore traffic.

German submarine *U 575* sinks U.S. freighter *City of Flint*, straggling from Casablanca-bound convoy UGS 4, about 300 miles south of the Azores, 34°47′N, 31°40′W; four of 24 Armed Guard sailors are lost (see 28 January).

26 Tuesday

PACIFIC. Submarine *Flying Fish* (SS 229) damages Japanese transport *Tokai Maru* at Apra, Guam, 13°27′N, 144°37′E.

Submarine *Grayling* (SS 209) sinks Japanese freighter *Ushio Maru* in Verde Island Passage, north of Mindoro, P.I., 13°26′N, 121°16′E.

Submarine *Gudgeon* (SS 211) is damaged by depth charges in the Banda Sea, 03°59′S, 127°54′E, but remains on patrol.

Submarine *Wahoo* (SS 238) attacks Japanese convoy about 270 miles north of Dutch New Guinea and sinks army cargo ships *Buyo Maru* and *No. 2 Fukuei Maru*, 02°00′N, 139°14′E. After dispatching the freighters, which are serving as transports, *Wahoo* (Lieutenant Commander Dudley W. Morton) surfaces to recharge her batteries and mans her guns. Firing her 4-incher at the largest of the craft draws Japanese return fire from automatic weapons. As Morton later writes, "We then opened fire with everything we had." Subsequently, *Wahoo* pursues and torpedoes armed merchant cruiser *Ukishima Maru*, 02°37′N, 139°42′E, and army cargo ship *Pacific Maru*, 02°30′N, 139°44′E (see 27 January).

27 Wednesday

PACIFIC. Japanese gunboat *No. 2 Choko Maru* rescues almost 1,000 survivors of army cargo ship *Buyo Maru*, sunk the previous day by submarine *Wahoo* (SS 238).

Submarine *Whale* (SS 239) damages Japanese transport *Shoan Maru* west of Rota, Saipan, 14°24′N, 153°30′E; towed to Saipan and grounded to facilitate salvage, *Shoan Maru* performs no more active service.

Japanese destroyer *Karukaya* is damaged off Takao, Formosa, by marine casualty.

Submarine *I 27* is damaged by marine casualty off Penang, Malaya.

ATLANTIC. U.S. freighter *Cape Decision*, steaming independently from Charleston, South Carolina, to Freetown, Sierra Leone, is torpedoed and sunk by German submarine *U 105* at 23°00′N, 46°40′W; all 45 merchant sailors, 26-man Armed Guard, and six passengers survive the sinking (see 5 and 10 February).

U.S. freighter *Charles C. Pinckney*, a straggler from convoy UGS 4, is torpedoed by German submarine *U 514* about 200 miles southwest of the Azores, 36°37′N, 30°55′W. When *U 514* surfaces nearby, Armed Guard gunners hold fire until well within range, at which point they open up and score hits on their assailant, driving her off for the time being (see 28 January).

28 Thursday

ATLANTIC. German submarines continue operations against stragglers from convoy UGS 4. *U 514* resumes attack on freighter *Charles C. Pinckney*. The freighter is abandoned for a second time, after which time *U 514*'s officers question the survivors. The U-boat then sinks *Charles C. Pinckney* with gunfire; a storm separates the four boatloads of survivors (see 8 February). *U 442* sinks freighter *Julia Ward Howe* about 175 miles south of the Azores, 35°29′N, 29°10′W, one of the 29-man Armed Guard is lost with the ship (see 29 January).

Portuguese destroyer *Lima* rescues 48 survivors from U.S. freighter *City of Flint*, sunk by *U 575* on 25 January; British destroyer HMS *Quadrant* rescues 10.

29 Friday

PACIFIC. Battle of Rennell Island begins as Japanese land attack planes (701st and 705th *Kokutais*) attack TF 18 (Rear Admiral Robert C. Giffen), cruisers and destroyers covering the movement of transports (TG 62.8) toward Guadalcanal. Japanese land attack planes (701st *Kokutai*) torpedo heavy cruisers *Chicago* (CA 29) and *Louisville* (CA 28); *Chicago* is disabled, but the "fish" that hits *Louisville* proves a dud. In the retirement from the area, *Louisville*, in a masterful piece of seamanship, takes her damaged sister ship in tow in complete darkness.

New Zealand corvette HMNZS *Kiwi* attacks Japanese submarine *I 1* off Kamimbo Bay, Guadalcanal, 09°13′S, 159°40′E, and forces her to the surface with two depth charge attacks. *Kiwi* then rams *I 1* three times, suffering damage in so doing; corvette HMNZS *Moa* assists *Kiwi* in keeping up a withering fire that forces their bigger adversary to abandon ship.

Submarine *Gato* (SS 212) sinks Japanese

army cargo ship *Nichiun Maru* off southeast tip of Bougainville, Solomons, 06°22′S, 156°04′E, despite proximity of escorting submarine chaser *Ch 22*.

ATLANTIC. Portuguese destroyer *Lima* recovers survivors from U.S. freighter *Julia Ward Howe*, sunk by German submarine *U 442* on 28 January, about 350 miles southwest of the Azores.

30 Saturday

PACIFIC. Battle of Rennell Island ends as F4Fs (VF 10) engage Japanese land attack planes (751st *Kokutai*) attacking the retiring TF 18. Heavy cruiser *Chicago* (CA 29), under tow of tug *Navajo* (AT 64), is torpedoed (again), as is destroyer *LaVallette* (DD 448). Consequently, *Chicago* sinks 30 miles east of Rennell Island, 11°26′S, 160°56′E.

Japanese submarine *I 10* sinks U.S. freighter *Samuel Gompers* 115 miles from Amadee Lighthouse, New Caledonia, 24°28′S, 166°20′E; one of the 17-man Armed Guard dies and three of the 43-man merchant complement perish in the sinking. French fishermen and U.S. Army crash boat *P 111* rescue the survivors.

Floating drydock *YFD 20* founders and sinks in heavy weather off California coast.

Naval Station, Akutan Harbor, Fox Island, Alaska, is established.

MEDITERRANEAN. USAAF B-17s (12th Air Force), escorted by P-38s, bomb harbor installations and shipping at Ferryville, Tunisia; Italian torpedo boat *Unie* and cargo vessel *Noto* are sunk.

ATLANTIC. *Grössadmiral* Karl Doenitz succeeds *Grössadmiral* Erich Raeder as Commander in Chief of the German Navy.

31 Sunday

PACIFIC. USMC SBDs (VMSB 233), TBFs, and F4Fs and USAAF P-39s (13th Air Force), flying from Guadalcanal, sink Japanese transport *Toa Maru* between Vella Lavella and Kolombangara, 07°50′S, 156°50′E. Torpedo boat *Hiyodori* and minelayer *Kamime*, damaged in the air attacks, rescue survivors and transport them to Kolombangara.

Japanese submarine *I 8* again bombards Canton Island, China.

MEDITERRANEAN. USAAF B-17s (12th Air Force) bomb shipping and harbor installations at Bizerte, Tunisia; ex-French submarines *Calypso* and *Nautilus* are sunk.

FEBRUARY

1 Monday

PACIFIC. High-speed transport *Stringham* (APD 6) and five tank landing craft (LCTs) land U.S. Army Second Battalion, 132nd Infantry, at Verahue, Guadalcanal, to the rear of Japanese positions at Cape Esperance, covered by four destroyers. Although the landing itself is unopposed, three LCTs, escorted by destroyers *Nicholas* (DD 449) and *DeHaven* (DD 469), come under attack from Japanese planes about three miles south of Savo Island. *DeHaven* is sunk by three bombs, 09°09′S, 159°52′E, while *Nicholas* is damaged by near-misses. Tank landing craft *LCT 63* and *LCT 181*, aided by SOCs (VCS Detachment RINGBOLT), rescue 146 *DeHaven* sailors, including 38 wounded.

Light minelayers *Tracy* (DM 19), *Montgomery* (DM 17), and *Preble* (DM 20) sow 255 mines to deny the Japanese "Tokyo Express" access to the channel between Savo Island and Cape Esperance. The three ships clear the area as Japanese men-of-war are only 12,000 yards away and closing (see 2 February).

Two waves of aircraft from Henderson Field (TBFs, SBDs, and F4Fs and USAAF P-38s, P-39s, and P-40s of the 13th Air Force) attack Japanese destroyers (Rear Admiral Hashimoto Shintaro) en route to begin "KE" Operation, the evacuation of Japanese troops from Guadalcanal, damaging *Makinami* (Hashimoto's flagship). U.S. motor torpedo boats later attack the Japanese, but in that action *PT 111* and *PT 37* are sunk by gunfire from destroyer *Kawakaze*; a Japanese reconnaissance seaplane sinks *PT 123*. Hashimoto's force extracts 4,935 soldiers.

Submarine *Tarpon* (SS 175) sinks Japanese merchant passenger-cargo ship *Fushimi Maru* about 20 miles south of Omai Saki, 34°08′N, 138°11′E.

ANDAMAN SEA. USAAF B-24s (10th Air Force) bomb targets in Rangoon, Burma; Japanese torpedo boat *Kari* is damaged during the raid.

2 Tuesday

PACIFIC. Japanese destroyer *Makigumo* is damaged by mine laid by light minelayers *Tracy* (DM 19), *Montgomery* (DM 17), and *Preble* (DM 20) off Cape Esperance the previous night; she is scuttled by destroyer *Yugumo*, 09°10′S, 159°45′E. Admiral William F. Halsey Jr., Commander South Pacific Force, lauds the success of the mining mission as resulting from "bold execution of a sound plan," while Admiral

Chester W. Nimitz, Commander in Chief Pacific Fleet, calls it a "splendidly conducted operation . . . carried out by old ships, inadequate in speed and gun power."

USAAF B-17s and P-39s (13th Air Force) sink Japanese cargo vessel *Keiyo Maru* off Shortland Island, Solomons.

USAAF B-24s (5th Air Force) sink Japanese cargo vessel *Kenkoku Maru* while en route from Kokope to New Guinea, between Lolobau Island and New Britain, 04°58′S, 151°12′E.

ATLANTIC. German submarine *U 456* attacks convoy HX 224 in the North Atlantic and torpedoes U.S. freighter *Jeremiah Van Rensselaer* at 54°50′N, 28°55′W; 10 of the 28-man Armed Guard are lost. The ship is scuttled by escorts later the same day.

3 Wednesday

MEDITERRANEAN. Command designated U.S. Naval Forces Northwest African Waters is established with headquarters at Algiers.

CARIBBEAN. Open lighters *YC 886* and *YC 887* founder and sink in heavy weather, Guantánamo, Cuba.

PACIFIC. Submarine *Tunny* (SS 282) damages Japanese army transport *No. 1 Shinto Maru* in the South China Sea, 22°03′N, 114°23′E.

ATLANTIC. German submarine *U 223* attacks Greenland-bound supply convoy SG 19, escorted by Coast Guard cutters *Tampa* (WPG 48), *Escanaba* (WPG 77), and *Comanche* (WPG 76), and sinks War Department–chartered transport *Dorchester* about 150 miles west of Cape Farewell, Greenland, 59°22′N, 48°42′W, and damages Norwegian freighter *Biscaya*. Casualties on board *Dorchester* are heavy, 675 men (including 15 of 24 Armed Guard sailors) are lost. Four Army chaplains, representing four different faiths, bravely give up their lifebelts to soldiers who have none; all four perish with the ship.

ARCTIC. German submarine *U 255* attacks convoy RA 52, 600 miles northeast of Iceland, torpedoing U.S. freighter *Greylock*, 70°50′N, 00°48′W; there are no casualties. British escort trawler HMS *Lady Madeleine* rescues all hands.

4 Thursday

PACIFIC. "KE" Operation continues: SBDs, TBFs, and F4Fs and USAAF P-40s from Henderson Field attack Japanese destroyers (Rear Admiral Hashimoto Shintaro) en route to evacuate troops from Guadalcanal, damaging *Shirayuki* (Hashimoto's flagship), *Maikaze*,

Kuroshio, and *Kawakaze*. Hashimoto's force, however, extracts 3,921 soldiers. SOC (VCS Detachment RINGBOLT) sights, tracks, and illuminates the Japanese ships.

Submarine *Tunny* (SS 282) damages Japanese transport *Tatsuwa Maru* in South China Sea, 21°30'N, 113°42'E.

ATLANTIC. German submarines attack convoy SC 118; Coast Guard cutter *Bibb* (WPG 31) pinpoints location of *U 187*, which is sunk by British destroyers HMS *Vimy* and HMS *Beverley* [ex-U.S. destroyer *Branch* (DD 197)], 50°12'N, 36°34'W. *Bibb* later participates in driving off the four U-boats that try to close the convoy during the night.

Destroyer *Stevenson* (DD 645) is damaged in collision with freighter *Berwindale* off Newport, Rhode Island. Local district craft assist the disabled warship into port; tug *Sagamore* (AT 20) is diverted to stand by. Salvage tug *Resolute* (NRTS), meanwhile, proceeds to aid *Berwindale*, which is beached off Potters Cove, Narragansett Bay.

5 Friday

PACIFIC. USAAF B-24s (5th Air Force) sink Japanese cargo vessels *Hoshikawa Maru* off Talasea, New Britain, and *Shunko Maru* off Finschhafen, New Guinea.

ATLANTIC. Battle to protect convoy SC 118 continues; destroyers *Babbitt* (DD 128) and *Schenck* (DD 159) and Coast Guard cutter *Ingham* (WPG 35) arrive to reinforce the harried escorts. German submarine *U 413* sinks U.S. freighter *West Portal*, a straggler from SC 118, in the North Atlantic, 52°00'N, 33°00'W. There are no survivors (12 Armed Guard sailors lost among them).

Forty survivors in boat from U.S. freighter *Cape Decision*, sunk by *U 105* on 27 January, reach safety at Barbados, B.W.I. (see 10 February).

6 Saturday

PACIFIC. Submarine *Flying Fish* (SS 229) damages transport *Nagizan Maru* off Tinian, Marianas.

USAAF B-24 (5th Air Force) sinks Japanese cargo ship *Gisho Maru* off north coast of New Britain, 04°30'S, 151°30'E.

ATLANTIC. Efforts to protect SC 118 continue; *Babbitt* (DD 128) helps prevent attacks by three U-boats attempting to close the convoy.

MEDITERRANEAN. North African Theater of Operations (Lieutenant General Dwight D. Eisenhower) is established.

7 Sunday

PACIFIC. "KE" Operation continues: SBDs, escorted by F4Fs and P-40s from Henderson Field, attack 18 Japanese destroyers (Rear Admiral Hashimoto Shintaro) on the final mission to evacuate Japanese troops from Guadalcanal, damaging *Isokaze* and near-missing *Urakaze*.

Submarine *Growler* (SS 215) is damaged by accidental ramming of Japanese stores ship *Hayasaki* and gunfire from the same vessel, 70 miles northwest of Rabaul, 03°34'S, 151°09'E. During this action, *Growler's* commanding officer, Commander Howard W. Gilmore, is mortally wounded. Rather than further hazard his ship, he orders *Growler* taken down. For his gallantry, Gilmore is awarded the Medal of Honor posthumously. *Hayasaki* is damaged in the encounter; *Growler* is forced to terminate her patrol.

Submarine *Swordfish* (SS 193) is damaged when mistakenly attacked by USAAF B-17, 150 miles north of New Ireland, 00°12'N, 152°00'E, and terminates her patrol as a result.

Submarine *Trout* (SS 202) damages Japanese tanker *Nisshin Maru* off Miri, 04°31'N, 114°52'E.

ATLANTIC. During continued fight to defend SC 118, Coast Guard cutter *Bibb* (WPG 31) drives off *U 402*, only to battle that submarine and *U 456* later the same day. *U 402*, however, sinks U.S. tanker *Robert E. Hopkins* about 650 miles west of Northern Ireland, 55°14'N, 26°22'W. Only one of the 19-man Armed Guard detachment is lost; survivors are rescued by British corvette HMS *Mignonette*. *U 402* also sinks U.S. passenger ship *Henry R. Mallory* at 55°30'N, 29°33'W; 49 of the 77-man merchant crew perish, as do 15 of the 34-man Armed Guard and 208 of 283 embarked passengers, primarily to exposure. Coast Guard cutters *Bibb* and *Ingham* (WPG 35) rescue 227 men, five of whom die of their injuries.

8 Monday

PACIFIC. "KE" Operation ends: Japanese destroyer force (Rear Admiral Hashimoto Shintaro) completes the evacuation of 1,796 troops from Guadalcanal.

Submarine *Tunny* (SS 282) sinks Japanese freighter *Kusuyama Maru* off southwest coast of Formosa about 55 miles west of Takao, 22°40'N, 119°12'E.

Japanese cargo ship *Shotoku Maru* is sunk by storm near Hino Misaki, Honshu, 35°26'N, 132°38'E.

ATLANTIC. During continued efforts by German submarines against SC 118, *U 608* unsuccessfully attacks destroyer *Schenck* (DD 159).

Swiss freighter *Caritasi* rescues 14 survivors of U.S. freighter *Charles C. Pinckney*, sunk on 28 January by *U 514*; eight of the 27-man Armed Guard survive their ordeal, as do six merchant sailors.

German submarine *U 160* sinks U.S. freighter *Roger B. Taney*, en route to Bahia, Brazil, 22°00'S, 07°00'W. Three crewmen perish in the explosion of the initial torpedo, but the rest of the 47-man merchant complement and the sole passenger survive, in addition to the 17-man Armed Guard (see 21 February and 20 March).

9 Tuesday

PACIFIC. Organized Japanese resistance on Guadalcanal ends, thus concluding the bitter six-month struggle for Guadalcanal and other islands in the southern Solomons.

Submarine *Tarpon* (SS 175) sinks Japanese transport *Tatsuta Maru* 42 miles east of Mikura Jima, 33°45'N, 140°25'E.

Japanese submarine *I 21* sights U.S. freighter *Starr King* one day out of Sydney, Australia, and begins pursuit of the freighter (see 10 February).

ATLANTIC. Destroyer *Boyle* (DD 600) rescues 54 survivors of U.S. freighter *Pan Royal*, which sinks at 36°40'N, 67°20'W, after being accidentally rammed by motor vessel *Evita* and freighter *George Davis*, while proceeding in convoy UGS 5. Eight merchant sailors are lost in the mishap; there are no casualties to the 26-man Armed Guard.

Tugs *Allegheny* (AT 19) and *Carrabassett* (WAT 55) reach disabled Brazilian freighter *Recifeloid*, which had run out of fuel on 6 February 145 miles southeast of Cape Henry, Virginia; *Allegheny* begins towing the merchantman toward Newport, Rhode Island (see 12 February).

10 Wednesday

PACIFIC. Submarine *Pickerel* (SS 177) sinks Japanese freighter *Amari Maru* off Sanriku, 40°10'N, 142°04'E.

Japanese submarine *I 21* continues pursuit of U.S. freighter *Starr King* and torpedoes her, 34°15'S, 154°20'E; there are no casualties among the merchant crew or Armed Guard. Australian destroyer HMAS *Warramunga* rescues survivors but has to abandon attempt to tow the crippled freighter when a line fouls her port screw. *Starr King*, however, sinks that night.

ATLANTIC. USAAF B-24 (2nd Antisubmarine Squadron) sinks German submarine *U 519* northwest of Spain, 47°05′N, 18°34′W.

Thirty-seven survivors in boat from U.S. freighter *Cape Decision*, sunk by *U 105* on 27 January, reach St. Barthelemy, French West Indies.

11 Thursday

PACIFIC. Destroyer *Fletcher* (DD 445) and SON (VCS 9) from light cruiser *Helena* (CL 50) sink Japanese submarine *I 18* in Coral Sea, 14°15′S, 161°53′E.

Submarine *Grayling* (SS 209) damages Japanese army cargo ship *Hoeizan Maru* off Corregidor, P.I.,14°16′N, 120°28′E.

ATLANTIC. Infantry landing craft *LCI 234* and *LCI 235* run aground three-quarters of a mile off Barnegat, New Jersey. Commercial tugs refloat the former; salvage vessel *Accelerator* the latter.

12 Friday

PACIFIC. Submarine *Grampus* (SS 207) sails from Brisbane, Australia, for her sixth war patrol. U.S. forces never hear from her again.[131]

ATLANTIC. Oiler *Salamonie* (AO 26) is damaged in collision with merchant vessel *Uruguay* east-northeast of Bermuda, 36°54′N, 49°29′W.

Tug *Wandank* (AT 26), accompanied by coastal yacht *Captor* (PYc 40) and salvage tug *Samson* (NRTS), relieves *Allegheny* (AT 19) of towing disabled Brazilian merchantman *Recifeloid*; when *Wandank*'s towing engine becomes disabled later this day, *Samson* takes over the task (see 15 February).

14 Sunday

PACIFIC. Submarine *Amberjack* (SS 219) is probably sunk by combined efforts of Japanese reconnaissance seaplane (JAKE) or observation seaplane (PETE) (both of which equip the 958th *Kokutai*), torpedo boat *Hiyodori,* and submarine chaser *Ch 18* off Cape St. George, New Britain, 05°05′S, 152°37′E.[132]

Submarine *Runner* (SS 275) unsuccessfully attacks Japanese cargo vessel *Tokyo Maru* north of Biak, New Guinea, 07°31′N, 134°21′E.

Submarine *Thresher* (SS 200) damages Japanese submarine *I 62* off the Lesser Sundas, 06°05′S, 105°47′E.

Submarine *Trout* (SS 202) engages Japanese gunboat *Hirotama Maru* at south entrance to Makassar Strait, 04°11′S, 117°45′E; return fire from the enemy warship in the last phases of the action fought on the surface wounds seven sailors before *Trout* sinks her adversary.

PB4Ys (VB 101) bomb and strafe Japanese ammunition ship *Hitachi Maru* off Buin, Bougainville, 06°48′S, 155°50′E.

15 Monday

PACIFIC. Joint air command designated Aircraft, Solomons (Rear Admiral Charles P. Mason) is established with headquarters at Guadalcanal.

Submarine *Gato* (SS 212) sinks Japanese stores ship *Suruga Maru* in Bougainville Strait, 06°27′S, 156°02′E.

Submarine *Pickerel* (SS 177) attacks Japanese convoy, sinking cargo vessel *Tateyama Maru* off the east coast of Honshu, 39°18′S, 142°08′E.

USAAF B-24 (5th Air Force) sinks Japanese cargo ship *Kokoku Maru* in Stettin Bay, New Britain, 05°32′S, 150°09′E.

ATLANTIC. U.S. tanker *Atlantic Sun*, straggling from convoy ON 165, is torpedoed and sunk by German submarine *U 607*, 150 miles off Cape Race, 51°00′N, 41°00′W; other than one deckhand rescued by *U 607*, all hands (45 merchant sailors, a 19-man Armed Guard, and one passenger) perish with the ship.

Heavy seas and high winds cause towline from tug *Samson* (Navy Rescue Tug Service) to disabled Brazilian freighter *Recifeloid* to part, but *Samson* puts out new line and tows the ship via Long Island Sound to City Island, New York.

16 Tuesday

PACIFIC. Submarine *Flying Fish* (SS 229) sinks Japanese stores ship *Hyuga Maru* 24 miles off Pagan, Marianas, 18°30′N, 145°57′E.

Submarine *Triton* (SS 201) departs Brisbane, Australia, for her sixth war patrol. She will never be seen again (see 6 March).

ATLANTIC. Fleet Air Wing 16 (Captain Rossmore D. Lyon) is established at Norfolk, Virginia.

INDIAN OCEAN. U.S. freighter *Deer Lodge* is torpedoed by German submarine *U 607* about 60 miles east of Port Elizabeth, South Africa, and abandoned (see 17 and 20 February).

EUROPE. USAAF B-17s (8th Air Force) bomb German submarine installations at St. Nazaire, France.

17 Wednesday

PACIFIC. Japanese torpedo-carrying land attack planes (701st *Kokutai*) engage TU 62.7.2

(Captain Ingolf N. Kiland) northeast of San Cristobal, Solomons. The four transports (carrying the U.S. Army 169th Infantry to Guadalcanal) and one oiler are screened by six destroyers; the task unit suffers neither loss nor damage in turning away the attackers.

Submarine *Sawfish* (SS 276) accidentally sinks Soviet cargo ship *Ilmen* off east coast of Kyushu, 30°56′N, 135°30′E.

ATLANTIC. Moroccan Sea Frontier (Rear Admiral John L. Hall Jr.) is established.

INDIAN OCEAN. U.S. freighter *Deer Lodge*, torpedoed by German submarine *U 607* about 60 miles east of Port Elizabeth, South Africa, the previous day, sinks at 33°46′S, 26°57′E. Two merchant seamen are lost with the ship, but the survivors (37 civilians and an 18-man Armed Guard) are rescued by South African minesweeper *Africana* (13 men) and British trawler *Havorn* (32 men) (see 20 February).

18 Thursday

PACIFIC. TG 8.6 (Rear Admiral Charles H. McMorris), consisting of light cruiser *Richmond* (CL 9), heavy cruiser *Indianapolis* (CA 35), and four destroyers, bombards Japanese installations at Holtz Bay and Chichagof Harbor, Attu, Aleutians.

TF 44.3, consisting of Australian heavy cruiser HMAS *Australia* and three U.S. destroyers, operates south of Australia to cover passage of five-ship convoy transporting the 30,000 troops of the 9th Australian Division to Sydney.

Submarine *Grampus* (SS 207) damages Japanese transport *Keiyo Maru* off coast of New Britain, 05°04′S, 152°18′E.

German auxiliary cruiser *Michel* (*Schiffe* 28) arrives at Singapore; the next day she turns over to the Japanese the merchant and Armed Guard sailors captured when she sank U.S. freighter *Sawokla* on 29 November 1942.

19 Friday

PACIFIC. TU 8.6.2, consisting of heavy cruiser *Indianapolis* (CA 35) and destroyers *Coghlan* (DD 606) and *Gillespie* (DD 609), intercepts Japanese army cargo ship *Aragane Maru* bound for the Aleutians and engages her northwest of Attu, Aleutians (see 20 February).

Submarine *Gato* (SS 212) torpedoes Japanese ammunition ship *Hibari Maru* off eastern Bougainville, 06°27′S, 156°05′E. *Hibari Maru* is beached off Buin (see 28 February).

Submarine *Grampus* (SS 207) torpedoes Japanese transport/aircraft ferry *Keiyo Maru* off coast of New Britain, 04°55′S, 152°26′E.

Submarine *Runner* (SS 275) is damaged by aerial bomb off the Palaus, 07°35′N, 134°25′E, and is forced to terminate her patrol.

USAAF B-17s (5th Air Force), in coordination with attack by RAAF Catalinas on Japanese airfield installations at Kahili, bomb enemy shipping off Buin, Bougainville, damaging transport *Tokai Maru*, 06°45′S, 155°50′E.

ATLANTIC. Submarine *Blackfish* (SS 221) sinks German patrol vessel *P 408* (ex-trawler *Haltenbank*), 43°30′N, 002°54′W, but is damaged by depth charges from *P 408*'s sister ship, and is forced to terminate her patrol.

20 Saturday

PACIFIC. Submarine *Albacore* (SS 218) sinks Japanese destroyer *Oshio* about 140 miles north-northwest of Manus, Admiralty Islands, 00°50′S, 146°06′E, and survives depth charging by another enemy warship.[133]

Submarine *Halibut* (SS 232) sinks Japanese transport *Shinkoku Maru* about 450 miles north of Ponape, Carolines, 15°09′N, 159°30′E.

Japanese auxiliary patrol vessel *Yoshida Maru* is damaged by mine, probably laid by submarine *Sunfish* (SS 281) between 14 and 17 December 1942, at 34°28′N, 137°20′E.

Japanese army cargo ship *Aragane Maru* sinks as the result of damage inflicted by gunfire from heavy cruiser *Indianapolis* (CA 35) and destroyers *Coghlan* (DD 606) and *Gillespie* (DD 609) off Attu, 53°05′N, 171°22′E.

Motor minesweeper *YMS 133* founders and sinks, Coos Bay, Oregon.

ATLANTIC. German submarines sight New York–bound convoy ON 166, which is escorted by Coast Guard cutters *Spencer* (WPG 36) and *Campbell* (WPG 32) and one British and four Canadian corvettes. During the night of 20–21 February, Coast Guard cutter *Spencer* depth charges *U 604*.

USAAF B-24 locates German prize tanker *Hohenfriedberg* 500 nautical miles southwest of Cape Finisterre, Spain; consequently, British heavy cruiser HMS *Sussex* intercepts and sinks the Axis vessel.

INDIAN OCEAN. Hospital ship *Atlantis* rescues the last 10 survivors of U.S. freighter *Deer Lodge*, torpedoed by German submarine *U 607* about 60 miles east of Port Elizabeth, South Africa, on 16 February.

21 Sunday

PACIFIC. Operation CLEANSLATE: Marines (Third Raider Battalion, USMC, and 10th Defense Battalion detachment) and Army troops (elements of the 43rd Division) occupy Russell Islands in the inaugural movement through the central Solomons. Supported by TU 62.7.2 (Captain Ingolf N. Kiland), the landings are made with no opposition. Four light cruisers and four destroyers of TF 68 (Rear Admiral Aaron S. Merrill) and Henderson Field, Guadalcanal-based carrier *Saratoga* (CV 3) air group provide cover.

Submarine *Sawfish* (SS 276) damages Japanese oiler *Ose* off Oagari Jima, 29°29′N, 132°48′E.

Submarine *Thresher* (SS 200) attacks Japanese convoy northeast of Soembawa Island, N.E.I., damaging army cargo ship *Kuwayama Maru*, 07°53′N, 119°13′E (see 22 February).

Dutch submarine *O 24* sinks Japanese merchant motor vessel *Bandai Maru* off Salang Island, 07°50′N, 098°09′E.

ATLANTIC. Battle to protect ON 166 from German submarines begins as *U 332* and *U 603* torpedo and sink Norwegian motor tanker *Stigstad*; *U 92* torpedoes British steamer *Empire Trader* (she will be scuttled by Canadian corvette HMCS *Dauphin*). Coast Guard cutter *Campbell* (WPG 32), British corvette HMS *Dianthus*, and Canadian corvette *Dauphin*, aided by flying boats, temporarily drive off *U 332*, *U 454*, and *U 753* threatening the merchantmen. Coast Guard cutter *Spencer* (WPG 36) sinks German submarine *U 225* at 51°25′N, 27°28′W.

U.S. freighter *Rosario*, steaming in convoy ON 167, is torpedoed and sunk by German submarine *U 664* at 50°13′N, 24°48′W. Fourteen of the 17-man Armed Guard, and 14 of 44 merchant crewmen are picked up by British rescue ship *Rathlin*; the rest perish with the ship.

British merchantman *Penrith Castle* rescues 15 merchant seamen and 13 Armed Guard sailors, survivors of freighter *Roger B. Taney*, which had been sunk by *U 160* on 8 February (see 20 March).

22 Monday

ATLANTIC. Battleship *Iowa* (BB 61) is commissioned at New York City, the first of a four-ship class that will be the last American battleships ever built.

Battle to protect convoy ON 166 in the North Atlantic continues. British rescue ship *Stockport* rescues *Empire Trader*'s survivors; German submarine *U 92* torpedoes Norwegian motor tanker *Nielson Alonso* (which is again torpedoed by *U 92* and then by *U 753*, but is eventually scuttled by Polish destroyer *Burza*). *U 606* torpedoes a trio of merchantmen: U.S. freighters *Chattanooga City* at 46°54′N, 34°30′W, and *Expositor* at 46°52′N, 34°26′W, as well as British steamer *Empire Redshank*. *Chattanooga City* sinks. Canadian corvette HMCS *Trillium* rescues all hands (including the 21-man Armed Guard) from *Chattanooga City* as well as 34 of 41 merchant sailors (two of whom die of their wounds) and the entire 21-man Armed Guard from *Expositor*. *Trillium* scuttles *Empire Redshank*. *U 606*'s opportunity to savor her triple play is short-lived, for Canadian corvette HMCS *Chilliwack* and Polish destroyer *Burza* depth charge *U 606* and drive her to the surface, where Coast Guard cutter *Campbell* (WPG 32) rams and sinks her at 47°44′N, 33°43′W. *Campbell*, damaged in the encounter, is taken in tow by *Burza*.

German submarines locate Curaçao, N.W.I.–bound convoy UC 1; four U.S. destroyers operate as part of the escort force (see 23 February).

PACIFIC. District patrol vessel *YP 72* sinks after grounding off Spruce Cape entrance to Kodiak, Alaska.

Japanese army cargo ship *Kuwayama Maru* sinks off Soembawa Island as the result of damage inflicted by submarine *Thresher* (SS 200) the previous day, 07°53′N, 119°13′E.

23 Tuesday

ATLANTIC. Battle to protect convoy ON 166 continues as German submarines continue the onslaught. After Canadian corvette HMCS *Trillium*'s attempt to scuttle U.S. freighter *Expositor* (torpedoed the previous day by *U 606*) with depth charges fails, it falls to German submarine *U 303* to administer the coup de grâce to the hardy American merchantman. *U 186* then sinks U.S. freighter *Hastings* at 46°30′N, 36°23′W, as well as British motor tanker *Eulima*; from *Hastings*, nine merchant sailors (of the 41-man civilian complement) perish, but all 20 Armed Guards and the ship's sole passenger survive, rescued by Canadian corvette HMCS *Chilliwack*. *U 707* sinks straggling U.S. freighter *Jonathan Sturges* at 46°15′N, 38°11′W; no. 1 lifeboat (with 19 survivors) from *Jonathan Sturges* encounters one from torpedoed Dutch motorship *Madoera* (three men on board) and transfers eight men to the Dutch lifeboat to equalize the number of survivors in each craft. *Jonathan Sturges*'s no. 3 lifeboat (nine men) locates one merchant sailor in the no. 2 boat and four Armed Guards from the ship; that second group of survivors is then divided between boats no. 2 and no. 3 to distribute them evenly (see 12 March and 6 April).

German submarines attack Curaçao, N.W.I.–bound convoy UC 1, which is shepherded by four U.S. destroyers, two British frigates, and three corvettes. Despite the proximity of the Anglo-American escort force, *U 382* torpedoes Dutch motor tanker *Murena*; *U 202* torpedoes British tankers *Empire Norseman* and *British Fortitude* and U.S. tanker *Esso Baton Rouge*, the last-named ship at 31°15′N, 27°22′W. British sloop HMS *Totland* (ex-U.S. Coast Guard cutter *Cayuga*) rescues *Esso Baton Rouge*'s survivors, including 24 of the 25-man Armed Guard and 41 of the 43-man merchant complement.

Destroyer *DuPont* (DD 152) fouls Ambrose Channel Buoy No. 11; salvage tug *Eugene F. Moran* (NRTS) assists the damaged warship to Todd's Erie Basin yard, New York, for repairs.

District patrol vessel *YP 336* sinks after running aground, Delaware River.

24 Wednesday

PACIFIC. Naval Air Facility, Amchitka, Alaska, is established.

MEDITERRANEAN. U.S. freighter *Nathanael Greene*, en route to join Algiers-bound convoy MKS 8, is first torpedoed by German submarine *U 565* about 40 miles northeast of Oran, 35°56′N, 00°05′N, and then is hit with an aerial torpedo during an air attack, forcing her abandonment. British minesweeper HMS *Brixham* takes on board 26 survivors directly from the sinking ship, and plucks others from the water. *Brixham* tows the ship out of further danger, transferring the tow to rescue tug *Restive*, which beaches *Nathanael Greene* off Oran, where salvage vessel *Redwing* (ARS 4) saves 400 of the 1,300 tons of cargo. *Nathanael Greene* will be written off, however, as a total loss. Of her complement, four merchant sailors die in the initial explosion, but the Armed Guard (16 men) survives intact.

ATLANTIC. Carrier *Ranger* (CV 4) launches USAAF P-40s off Accra, Gold Coast, for further transfer to the North African theater in her second such ferry mission of 1943.

PBM (VP 74) sights Italian submarine *Barbarigo* attacking Spanish merchantman *Monte Igueldo*, 04°46′S, 31°55′N, and attacks the enemy submersible, which comes to the surface and fights it out with the flying boat. Neither side, however, inflicts damage on the other.

Defense of convoy ON 166 continues. German submarine *U 604* is damaged by depth charges from Coast Guard cutter *Spencer* (WPG 36) or corvettes HMCS *Chilliwack*, HMCS *Rosthern*, or HMCS *Trillium. U 621* conducts unsuccessful attack on *Spencer*.

25 Thursday

ATLANTIC. Battle to protect convoy ON 166 comes to a close. *U 92* and *U 600* conduct unsuccessful attacks on Coast Guard cutter *Spencer* (WPG 36); *U 628* sinks British steamer *Manchester Merchant* at 45°10′N, 43°23′W. The enemy loses contact with the convoy this evening.

26 Friday

ANDAMAN SEA. Japanese auxiliary minesweeper *No. 3 Kyo Maru* is mined and sunk off Rangoon, Burma, 15°36′N, 96°15′E.

27 Saturday

PACIFIC. SBDs, escorted by F4Fs, attack Japanese convoy off northeast coast of Vella Lavella, Solomons, damaging transport *Kirikawa Maru* despite efforts of escorting minesweeper *W.22* and submarine chaser *Ch 26*, one of which scuttles the burning ship.

Submarine *Grampus* (SS 207) possibly damages Japanese minesweeper *W.22* off Kolombangara, Solomons.

Submarine *Plunger* (SS 179) torpedoes Japanese oiler *Iro* 130 miles west of Jaluit, 06°09′N, 167°18′E; *Katori Maru* tows the crippled ship to Kwajalein for repairs.

ANDAMAN SEA. USAAF B-24s (10th Air Force) sink Japanese cargo vessel *Asakasan Maru* 95 miles southeast of Rangoon, Burma, 15°53′N, 97°40′E.

28 Sunday

PACIFIC. TBF (VGS 11) bombs Japanese shipping at Buin, Bougainville, and completes destruction of ammunition ship *Hibari Maru*, previously damaged on 19 February.

Japanese cargo ship *Kashii Maru* is sunk in collision with *Kasagisan Maru* off Shimoda, Honshu, 34°39′N, 138°58′E.

MEDITERRANEAN. U.S. freighter *Daniel Carroll*, in convoy TE 16, is torpedoed by German submarine *U 371* off the coast of Algeria, 37°05′N, 04°02′30″E, but is towed by a British tug to Algiers, arriving there the following day; she suffers no casualties to her merchant crew, 27-man Armed Guard, or 30 passengers.

ATLANTIC. U.S. freighter *Wade Hampton*, straggling from convoy HX 227, is torpedoed and sunk by German submarine *U 405* at 59°55′N, 35°55′E; British corvette HMS *Vervain* rescues 41 merchant seamen and 26 Armed Guard sailors (see 3 March). Lost with *Wade Hampton* are Soviet motor torpedo boats *RPT 1* (ex-*PT 85*) and *RPT 3* (ex-*PT 87*), lend-lease craft being carried as deck cargo.

MARCH

1 Monday

PACIFIC. USAAF B-24 (5th Air Force) on reconnaissance flight spots Japanese convoy of eight transports and cargo vessels (with soldiers of the 51st Division embarked) in a convoy (Captain Matsumoto Kametaro), escorted by eight destroyers (Rear Admiral Kimura Masatomi, flag in *Shirayuki*), moving southwestward along the north coast of New Britain under cover of a westward-moving weather front. USAAF B-24 attacks convoy; B-17s drop flares (see 2–5 March).

Japanese submarine *I 10* torpedoes U.S. tanker *Gulfwave* at 22°30′S, 174°45′E; *Gulfwave* reaches Suva, Fiji, under her own power and suffers no casualties to either her merchant crew or the Armed Guard.

Naval Auxiliary Air Facility, Annette Island, Alaska, is established.

ATLANTIC. Atlantic Convoy Conference meets in Washington, D.C.

U.S. freighter *Fitz John Porter*, in Bahia, Brazil–to–Trinidad convoy BT 6, is torpedoed by German submarine *U 518*, 12°25′S, 36°55′E, and abandoned. While there are no casualties among the merchant sailors, one Armed Guard seaman is blown overboard and lost. Brazilian minelayer *Carioca* rescues the survivors, and *Fitz John Porter* sinks the following evening.

2 Tuesday

PACIFIC. Battle of the Bismarck Sea opens: USAAF B-17s and B-24s (5th Air Force) carry out succession of attacks on the convoy consisting of eight Japanese transports and cargo vessels (with soldiers of the 51st Division embarked), escorted by eight destroyers (Rear Admiral Kimura Masatomi, flag in *Shirayuki*), bound for Lae, New Guinea (Captain Matsumoto Kametaro), beginning at the northern entrance of Dampier Strait, off the southern tip of New Britain, 05°05′S, 148°28′E. Army cargo ship *Kyokusai Maru* is sunk; destroyers *Yukikaze* and *Asagumo* rescue the survivors, steam ahead to Lae to disembark them, and then rejoin the convoy. During the attacks this day, army cargo ship *Kembu Maru* and transport *Teiyo Maru* are damaged; army cargo ships *Oigawa Maru* and *Shinai Maru* are near-missed. RAAF Catalina tracks the convoy as it passes through Vitiaz Strait during the night and into the next morning (see 3–5 March).

Submarine *Permit* (SS 178) damages Japanese army cargo ship *Tsurushima Maru* off northeast coast of Honshu, 39°00′N, 141°54′E.

Submarine *Thresher* (SS 200) sinks Japanese fleet tanker *Toen Maru* in Makassar Strait, 03°29′S, 117°17′E.

ATLANTIC. German submarine *U 759*'s attack on U.S. freighter *Meriwether Lewis*, straggling from convoy HX 227, fails, but *U 634*, summoned to the scene by *U 759*, torpedoes the U.S. merchantman at 62°10′N, 28°25′W. After *Meriwether Lewis* breaks in two, *U 634* sinks the after part of the ship with gunfire. Despite a two-day search by Coast Guard cutter *Ingham* (WPG 35), however, no trace of the freighter's crew (44 merchant sailors and a 25-man Armed Guard) is ever found.

U.S. salvage tug *Wellfleet*, en route to Norfolk, Virginia, to be turned over to the British Ministry of War Transport, is accidentally rammed and sunk off Cape Hatteras, North Carolina, by U.S. tanker *Edward L. Doheny*; submarine chaser *SC 686* rescues *Wellfleet*'s 17-man crew and takes them to Morehead City, North Carolina.

Submarine chaser *SC 1024* is sunk in collision off North Carolina.

3 Wednesday

PACIFIC. Battle of the Bismarck Sea continues: RAAF Catalina continues tracking the Japanese convoy attacked the previous day. RAAF Beaufort spots the ships at 07°10′S, 148°20′E, about 60–70 miles east-southeast of Lae, New Guinea. USAAF B-17s and B-25s (5th Air Force), escorted by P-38s, carry out high-level bombing attacks, while B-25s and A-20s and RAAF Beaufighters and Bostons carry out relentless low-level skip- and mast-head bombing attacks and strafing runs against the enemy ships. Rear Admiral Kimura Masatomi is wounded on board his flagship, destroyer *Shirayuki*. Due to the nature of the battle, wartime analysts deemed it neither "possible from the pilots' accounts to determine which ships were hit by which bombs" nor "possible to determine exactly how and when each vessel was sunk." In any event, destroyers *Asashio*, *Tokitsukaze*, and *Shirayuki* are all sunk southeast of Finschhafen, 07°15′S, 148°30′E; a fourth destroyer, *Arashio*, is abandoned and left in sinking condition (see 4 March). Supply ship *Noshima*, damaged by aircraft and collision with *Arashio*, sinks southeast of Finsch-

hafen, New Guinea, 07°15′S, 148°30′E. Army cargo vessels *Aiyo Maru*, *Shinai Maru*, *Taimei Maru*, and *Kembu Maru*, and transport *Teiyo Maru* (the latter two ships damaged the day before) are sunk by U.S. and RAAF aircraft, 07°15′S, 148°30′E; army cargo ship *Oigawa Maru* is damaged and abandoned. That night, motor torpedo boats *PT 143* and *PT 150*, searching for damaged ships in Huon Gulf, sink *Oigawa Maru* at 06°58′S, 148°16′E (see 4 and 5 March).

Submarine *Halibut* (SS 232) torpedoes Japanese naval auxiliary *Nichiyu Maru* about 170 miles south of Guam, 10°25′N, 145°25′E. *Nichiyu Maru* reaches Apra under tow, but is deemed beyond salvage by 17 June and never resumes active service (see 12 and 25 June 1944).

Japanese land attack planes bomb shipping at Tulagi, Solomons; cargo ship *Carina* (AK 74) is damaged by near-misses.

PB4Y sinks Japanese guardboat *Choei Maru* off Vella Lavella, Solomons.

INDIAN OCEAN. U.S. freighter *Harvey W. Scott*, bound for Iran in convoy DN 21, is torpedoed by German submarine *U 160* off the coast of South Africa, 31°54′S, 30°37′E; first boatload of survivors (there are no casualties among the 42 merchant sailors or the 19-man Armed Guard) reaches shore (see 4 March).

ATLANTIC. British destroyer HMS *Beverley* [ex-U.S. destroyer *Branch* (DD 197)] rescues last survivor of freighter *Wade Hampton*, sunk by German submarine *U 405* on 28 February.

U.S. freighter *Staghound*, proceeding independently from New York to Rio de Janeiro, Brazil, is torpedoed and sunk by Italian submarine *Barbarigo* off the coast of Brazil, 16°44′S, 36°33′E (see 4 March).

4 Thursday

PACIFIC. Battle of the Bismarck Sea continues: USAAF B-17s and B-25s (5th Air Force) bomb and sink hulk of abandoned destroyer (most likely *Arashio*, 07°15′S, 148°30′E). The attack by B-25s on that warship terminates the efforts against the major vessels of the convoy; only strafing missions against boats and rafts remain to be carried out (see 5 March).

Japanese freighter *Hokuto Maru* is sunk by mine south of Muroran, 39°30′N, 142°08′E.[134]

INDIAN OCEAN. U.S. freighter *Harvey W. Scott*, torpedoed by German submarine *U 160* the previous day, sinks; a second boatload of survivors reaches shore safely (see 6 March).

ATLANTIC. Destroyer *DuPont* (DD 152) fouls

the chain of Gedney Channel Buoy No. 5 in a propeller shaft. As in *DuPont*'s mishap on 23 February, tug *Eugene F. Moran* again frees her from her predicament the following morning.

Survivors from U.S. freighter *Staghound*, sunk by Italian submarine *Barbarigo* the previous day, are rescued by Argentine steamship *Rio Colorado*. There are no casualties among the 59-man merchant complement or the 25-man Armed Guard.

5 Friday

PACIFIC. Battle of the Bismarck Sea concludes: RAAF Beaufighters strafe Japanese landing barges and lifeboats crammed with survivors of the ships sunk on 3 March ("grim and bloody work for which the crews had little stomach") in Huon Gulf. U.S. motor torpedo boats destroy barges in the vicinity of those attacked by the Australian planes. Failure of the convoy to reach its destination, Japanese naval officers admit later, proves "the impossibility of surface transport in the Lae area." Of the sixteen ships that sailed for Lae, all eight transports are sunk, as are four of the escorting destroyers. Motor torpedo boats *PT 143* and *PT 150*, patrolling 25 miles northeast of Cape Ward Hunt, New Guinea, encounter a Japanese submarine rescuing survivors of the engagement and force her down.[135]

Submarine *Tambor* (SS 198) lands party of men (Lieutenant Commander Charles Parsons, USNR), two tons of ammunition, and $10,000 in currency at Labangan, Pagadian Bay, Mindanao, P.I.

ATLANTIC. Auxiliary aircraft carrier *Bogue* (ACV 9) begins escorting convoys in North Atlantic, marking the first time a ship of her type undertakes antisubmarine operations as primary duty; she supports convoy HX 228 until 14 March.

Panamanian freighter *Aristides* is disabled approximately 57 miles southeast of Cape May, New Jersey (see 6 March).

ARCTIC. German submarine *U 255* attacks Loch Ewe, Scotland–bound convoy RA 53, torpedoing U.S. freighters *Executive* and *Richard Bland* at 72°45′N, 11°40′E; the former is abandoned without orders, with the survivors (one Armed Guard sailor and four merchant seamen are lost with the ship) being rescued by British trawlers HMS *St. Elstan* and HMS *Northern Pride*. *Executive* is scuttled. *Richard Bland*, although damaged by a dud torpedo that nevertheless passes through the ship, remains with the convoy; she suffers no casualties (see 10 March).

6 Saturday

PACIFIC. TF 68 (Rear Admiral Aaron S. Merrill), composed of three light cruisers and seven destroyers, bombards Vila and Munda, Solomons, and sinks Japanese destroyers *Minegumo* and *Murasame* in Kula Gulf, 08°05′S, 157°15′E.

Submarine *Sawfish* (SS 276) damages Japanese army cargo ship *Clyde Maru* southeast of Toi Saki, 31°04′N, 131°48′E.

Submarine *Triton* (SS 201) sinks Japanese army cargo ship *Kiriha Maru* about 145 miles northwest of the Admiralties, 00°37′N, 145°30′E. *Triton*, which reports this success on 11 March, is never heard from again.[136]

INDIAN OCEAN. Last boatload of survivors from U.S. freighter *Harvey W. Scott*, torpedoed by German submarine *U 160* off the coast of South Africa on 3 March, reaches shore safely.

ATLANTIC. German submarines locate convoy SC 121; escort group (Commander Paul R. Heineman) consists of Coast Guard cutter *Spencer* (WPG 36), destroyer *Greer* (DD 145), two Canadian corvettes, a British corvette, and a rescue ship. Operations against this convoy will continue until 11 March.

Tug *Allegheny* (AT 19) reaches Panamanian freighter *Aristides,* disabled the previous day, and takes her in tow; tug *Sciota* (AT 30) relieves *Allegheny* of the tow that same afternoon. Both auxiliaries assist the crippled merchantman into port the next day.

7 Sunday

PACIFIC. Submarine *Permit* (SS 178) damages Japanese merchant fishing vessel *Shoshin Maru* off northeastern Honshu, 41°55′N, 143°50′E.

Submarine *Tautog* (SS 199) lays mines off southeast coast of Borneo.

ATLANTIC. U.S. freighter *Alcoa Guard*, in convoy UGS 6 en route to Casablanca, French Morocco, accidentally collides with and sinks Norwegian freighter *Tamesis* about 190 miles from Bermuda. Destroyer *Tillman* (DD 641) stands by the damaged *Alcoa Guard*; freighter *Richard A. Alvey* rescues 57 survivors from *Tamesis* and 19 from *Alcoa Guard*. Tug *Owl* (AT 137) proceeds from Bermuda and makes contact but proves unable to control the disabled *Alcoa Guard* under the prevailing weather conditions (see 13 March).

8 Monday

PACIFIC. Submarine *Permit* (SS 178), attacking Japanese convoy off northern Honshu, sinks freighter *Hisashima Maru*, 41°16′N, 142°27′E.

ATLANTIC. PBY-5 (VP 53) sinks German submarine *U 156* east-northeast of Trinidad, 12°18′N, 54°39′W.

INDIAN OCEAN. U.S. freighter *James B. Stephens*, independently bound for Durban, is torpedoed by German submarine *U 160* off the coast of South Africa, 28°53′S, 33°18′E; one Armed Guard sailor drowns in the abandonment after the ship breaks in two. The forward half ultimately sinks while under tow toward Durban; the after half is scuttled with gunfire (see 11 and 14 March).

9 Tuesday

PACIFIC. TBFs and SBDs, escorted by F4Fs, bomb Japanese installations at Munda, Solomons. Bombing of this area becomes a regular occurrence.

Submarine *S 32* (SS 137) is damaged by Japanese depth charges off Holtz Bay, Attu Island, Aleutians.

ATLANTIC. Battle to protect convoy SC 121 continues (see 6 March) as Coast Guard cutters *Bibb* (WPG 31) and *Ingham* (WPG 35) and destroyer *Babbitt* (DD 128) reinforce the escorts. *Babbitt* proves her worth this day as she helps keep U-boats down. Despite the efforts of the escorts, however, German submarine *U 409* torpedoes U.S. freighter *Malantic* at 59°30′N, 24°00′W, which is abandoned in a gale; 19 merchant seamen, five Armed Guard sailors, and the ship's sole passenger perish in the attempt to reach British rescue vessel *Melrose Abbey*. *Malantic* will sink the next day.

German submarine *U 510* carries out series of attacks on ships of convoy BT 6, which is escorted by destroyer *Borie* (DD 215), gunboats *Courage* (PG 70) and *Tenacity* (PG 71), and two submarine chasers, off Cayenne, French Guiana. *U 510* torpedoes U.S. freighters *George G. Meade*, *Mark Hanna*, *James Smith*, *Thomas Ruffin,* and *James K. Polk* at 07°11′N, 52°30′W. *George G. Meade* suffers no casualties to either her merchant crew or the Armed Guard and returns to service. *Mark Hanna* is abandoned by most of the crew, submarine chaser *PC 592* rescuing the men while a portion of the complement remains on board to prepare the ship to be towed; after repairs, she returns to active service. *James Smith* suffers the loss of six merchant sailors and five Armed Guard seamen in the initial explosion and is partially abandoned, with submarine chaser *PC 592* rescuing a portion of the crew. The ship, however, will be towed to Trinidad by British tug *Zwarte Zee* and will eventually re-enter active service. *Thomas Ruffin* is par-

tially abandoned, with *Courage* and *PC 592* rescuing crewmen (four of the ship's merchant complement and two of the 15-man Armed Guard are killed); the ship will eventually be written off as a total loss. *James K. Polk* (one Armed Guard sailor is killed when the ship is torpedoed—the only casualty) is partially abandoned, with *PC 592* serving as the rescuing agent; the master and a volunteer crew rig tarpaulins and with those makeshift sails proceed some 360 miles. Eventually towed to Trinidad and thence to Mobile, Alabama, *James K. Polk* will be written off as a total loss.

ARCTIC. U.S. freighter *Puerto Rican*, straggling from convoy RA 53, is torpedoed and sunk by German submarine *U 586* at 66°44′N, 10°41′W; of the 40-man merchant complement and 25-man Armed Guard, only one man of the former will survive the abandonment in the below-freezing environment (see 12 March).

10 Wednesday

PACIFIC. Motor torpedo boat *PT 114*, acting on intelligence that 18 Japanese in a lifeboat (survivors from the Battle of the Bismarck Sea) had drifted ashore on Kiriwina in the Trobriand Islands, captures the enemy soldiers and takes them to Milne Bay, New Guinea, the following day.

USAAF B-24 (5th Air Force) damages Japanese fleet tanker *Kaijo Maru* south of Boeton Passage, Celebes, 04°45′S, 123°10′E; *Kaijo Maru* is run aground on Landaila Reef, where she is abandoned (see 17 March).

ATLANTIC. Light cruiser *Savannah* (CL 42) and destroyer *Eberle* (DD 430) intercept German blockade runner *Karin* (ex-Dutch *Kota Nopan*) in the South Atlantic 400 miles west northwest of Ascension Island, 07°00′S, 21°00′W. Boarding party from *Eberle*, while attempting to retrieve intelligence documents, suffers seven killed and two wounded when scuttling charges explode. *Savannah* takes on board the German survivors as POWs.

German submarine *U 185* attacks convoy KG 123, torpedoing U.S. tanker *Virginia Sinclair* at 20°11′N, 74°04′W, and freighter *James Sprunt* at 19°49′N, 74°38′W. Submarine chaser *SC 742* rescues all but seven of *Virginia Sinclair*'s complement, but *James Sprunt*, laden with general cargo and explosives, disintegrates, killing all hands (44 merchant sailors and the 25-man Armed Guard) and showering nearby ships with debris.

German submarines attack convoy HX 228; *U 221* torpedoes U.S. freighter *Andrea F. Luck-*

enbach at 51°04′N, 29°40′W. Explosion of the after magazine blows off the stern and kills 10 of the 28-man Armed Guard outright. British oiler *Appleleaf* rescues 17 Armed Guard sailors and 46 of the 55-man merchant complement. *U 444* torpedoes freighter *William C. Gorgas* at 51°35′N, 28°30′W; British destroyer HMS *Harvester* rescues the 27-man Armed Guard and 33 of the 43-man merchant complement, but is herself later torpedoed and sunk by *U 432*. Ultimately, only four Armed Guard sailors and eight merchant seamen from *William C. Gorgas* survive *Harvester's* loss, rescued by Free French–manned British corvette HMS *Aconit*. *U 757* administers the coup de grâce to *William C. Gorgas*.

Tank landing ship *LST 380* runs aground at Barnegat, New Jersey, breakwater; salvage tug *Resolute* (NRTS) refloats *LST 380* and tows her to New York for repairs.

Open lighter *YC 1278* is destroyed in experimental bombing tests off Atlantic coast.

ARCTIC. German submarine *U 255* torpedoes U.S. freighter *Richard Bland*, straggling from convoy RA 53, at 66°48′N, 14°15′W; the ship breaks in two. During the abandonment in rough seas, 17 of the 26-man Armed Guard and 19 of the 42-man merchant complement perish. Survivors are rescued (27 by British destroyer HMS *Impulsive*); the forward portion of the ship is eventually towed to Iceland and salvaged.

INDIAN OCEAN. German submarine *U 182* torpedoes U.S. freighter *Richard D. Spaight* in the Mozambique Channel, 28°00′S, 37°00′E; after the freighter is abandoned, the U-boat completes the work of destruction with gunfire, then questions and aids the crew before clearing the area. Two boats of survivors (42 of 43 merchant sailors and the entire 24-man Armed Guard survive) reach Richards Bay, South Africa (within three days), Cape St. Lucia, and Cuanalobi Beach (five days later).

British light cruiser HMS *Nigeria* rescues 30 survivors of U.S. freighter *James B. Stephens*, torpedoed by German submarine *U 160* off the coast of South Africa on 8 March; British trawler HMS *Norwich City* rescues 19 (see 14 March).

12 Friday

PACIFIC. Submarine *Plunger* (SS 179) sinks Japanese water carrier *Taihosan Maru* off Ponape, Carolines, 07°15′N, 159°10′E.

ATLANTIC. German submarines begin gathering to attack convoy UGS 6, which is being shepherded by seven U.S. destroyers (Captain

Charles Wellborn Jr.). *Champlin* (DD 601) sinks *U 130* (which had first sighted UGS 6), 37°10′N, 40°21′W.

Destroyer *Belknap* (DD 251) rescues seven Armed Guard sailors, survivors from freighter *Jonathan Sturges*, along with three Dutch seamen from torpedoed motorship *Madoera*, both merchantmen the victims of *U 707* on 23 February (see 6 April).

ARCTIC. Sole survivor of U.S. freighter *Puerto Rican*, sunk on 9 March by German submarine *U 586* as the former straggled from convoy RA 53, is rescued by British trawler HMS *St. Elstan*.

13 Saturday

PACIFIC. Submarine *Grayback* (SS 208) damages Japanese transport *Noshiro Maru* 100 miles northwest of Bismarck Archipelago, 00°10′S, 151°06′E.

Submarine *Sunfish* (SS 281) sinks Japanese freighter *Kosei Maru* near Tokara Jima, Ryukyus, 29°04′N, 129°17′E.

USAAF B-17s (5th Air Force) bomb Japanese convoy off Wewak, New Guinea, sinking cargo vessel *Momoyama Maru*; submarine *Greenling* (SS 213) witnesses attacks.

ANDAMAN SEA. Dutch submarine *O 21* sinks Japanese cargo ship *No. 2 Kasuga Maru* off Port Blair, Andaman Islands, 11°40′N, 92°50′E.

ATLANTIC. U.S. salvage vessel *Relief* (NRTS) arrives to assist tug *Owl* (AT 137) in towing U.S. freighter *Alcoa Guard* (damaged in collision on 7 March) to Bermuda.

MEDITERRANEAN. German submarine *U 172* torpedoes U.S. freighter *Keystone*, straggling from convoy UGS 6, at 38°10′N, 37°58′W. The initial explosion kills one Armed Guard sailor and a merchant seaman; these are the only casualties suffered by the ship, which is abandoned. Portuguese steamship *Sines* rescues the survivors.

CARIBBEAN. German submarine *U 68* attacks Aruba-bound convoy GAT 49, and torpedoes U.S. tanker *Cities Service Missouri*, at 14°10′N, 74°40′W. Destroyer *Biddle* (DD 151) rescues survivors, including the 11-man Armed Guard.

14 Sunday

ATLANTIC. Fleet Operational Training Command, Atlantic Fleet (Rear Admiral Donald B. Beary) is established.

INDIAN OCEAN. Off Durban, South Africa, SAAF crash boat rescues 13 survivors of U.S. freighter *James B. Stephens*, torpedoed by German submarine *U 160* on 8 March.

15 Monday

UNITED STATES. Commander in Chief establishes numbered fleet system; fleets in the Pacific will have odd numbers and those in the Atlantic even.

PACIFIC. Submarine *Trigger* (SS 237) attacks Japanese convoy about 150 miles northwest of the Admiralties, damaging transport *Florida Maru*, 00°00′N, 145°00′E, and sinking army cargo ship *Momoha Maru*, 00°02′S, 145°05′E.

Naval Auxiliary Air Facility, French Frigate Shoals, T.H., is established.

16 Tuesday

PACIFIC. Four U.S. destroyers (Commander Francis X. McInerney) shell Japanese positions at Vila, Solomons.

Submarine *Flying Fish* (SS 229) sinks Japanese victualling stores ship *Hyuga Maru* west of the Marianas.

Submarine *S 32* (SS 137) damages Japanese submarine *RO 103* off Silipuaka Island, 52°54′N, 173°13′E.

MEDITERRANEAN. Vice Admiral H. Kent Hewitt becomes Commander Naval Forces Northwest African Waters.

ATLANTIC. German submarine *U 172*, stalking convoy UGS 6, torpedoes U.S. freighter *Benjamin Harrison* at 39°09′N, 24°15′W. Precipitately abandoned, the ship is scuttled by gunfire of destroyer *Rowan* (DD 405), which rescues three survivors. Freighter *Alan A. Dale* rescues the remainder. Other attacks by *U 172* and *U 524* fail, including one that misses destroyer *Rhind* (DD 404).

German submarines attack convoy HX 229 as it proceeds toward the British Isles. *U 758* torpedoes U.S. freighter *James Oglethorpe* at 50°00′N, 36°00′W; 13 merchant seamen, 15 Armed Guard sailors, and two passengers are rescued by British corvette HMS *Pennywort*. *U 435* torpedoes freighter *William Eustis* at 49°57′N, 37°06′W; British destroyer HMS *Volunteer* rescues the entire crew, which includes a 30-man Armed Guard. Both "Liberty" ships remain afloat (see 17 March).

17 Wednesday

PACIFIC. Submarine *Kingfish* (SS 234) damages Japanese transport *Tenryugawa Maru* in Formosa Strait, 24°32′N, 120°15′E.

Submarine *Tautog* (SS 199) inflicts further damage to Japanese fleet tanker *Kaijo Maru*, driven aground and abandoned on 10 March.

Motor torpedo boats *PT 67* and *PT 119* are destroyed by an explosion of an undetermined origin off eastern New Guinea, 09°02′S, 149°20′E.

ATLANTIC. Destroyer *Upshur* (DD 144), from convoy ON 170, having joined the escort force for convoy SC 122 the previous day, helps turn away U-boats attempting to stalk the merchantmen.

German submarine *U 167* attacks convoy UGS 6 and damages U.S. freighter *Molly Pitcher* about 500 miles west of Lisbon, Portugal, 38°21′N, 19°54′W; destroyer *Champlin* (DD 601), along with destroyer *Rowan* (DD 405) and merchantman *William Johnson,* rescues survivors. *Champlin* attempts, unsuccessfully, to scuttle the crippled freighter with a torpedo; *U 521* finishes off *Molly Pitcher* later the same day. Two of the 24-man Armed Guard and two merchant seamen perish in the sinking.

German U-boat operations against convoy HX 229 continue. *U 91* administers the coup de grâce to U.S. freighters *James Oglethorpe,* torpedoed by *U 758* the previous day, and the abandoned *William Eustis,* torpedoed the day before by *U 435.* Lost with the former are the 31 men who had remained on board. *U 91* also sinks U.S. freighter *Harry Luckenbach* at 50°38′N, 34°46′W; British corvette HMS *Pennywort* is the only escort vessel that sights *Harry Luckenbach*'s survivors but, already crammed with 108 men retrieved from other sunken ships from HX 229, is unable to recover them. *Harry Luckenbach* is thus lost with all hands (54 merchant sailors and 26-man Armed Guard). *U 600* torpedoes freighter *Irénée Du Pont* at 50°36′N, 34°30′W, with the loss of six of the 26-man Armed Guard, one of nine Navy passengers, and six of the 49-man merchant complement. Dutch merchantman *Tekoa* rescues 55 survivors; Canadian destroyer HMS *Mansfield* [ex-U.S. destroyer *Evans* (DD 78)] rescues 16 (one of whom dies of wounds). British corvette HMS *Anemone* fails to scuttle *Irénée Du Pont* with gunfire and a depth charge; it thus falls to *U 91* to finish off the battered "Liberty" ship.

U.S. freighter *Katrina Luckenbach* runs aground in dense fog five miles east of Fire Island Inlet, Long Island, N.Y.; Coast Guard cutter *Kimball* (WPC 143), salvage tug (NRTS) *Resolute,* and two commercial tugs, as well as salvage vessel (NRTS) *Relief,* proceed to the merchantman's assistance. She is ultimately refloated on 22 March.

18 Thursday

ATLANTIC. As German operations against Allied convoys continue, destroyer *Babbitt* (DD 128) reinforces the escort for HX 229 and Coast Guard cutter *Ingham* (WPG 35) reinforces SC 122. *U 221* attacks HX 229 and torpedoes U.S. freighter *Walter Q. Gresham* at 53°39′N, 27°53′W; British corvettes HMS *Pennywort* and HMS *Anemone* rescue 42 survivors (23 merchant seamen and five of the 26-man Armed Guard perish with the ship).

19 Friday

PACIFIC. Submarine *Kingfish* (SS 234) sinks Japanese army hospital ship *Takachiko Maru* in Formosa Strait, 26°00′N, 122°18′E.

Submarine *Sawfish* (SS 276) damages Japanese guardboat *Shinsei Maru,* southeast of Japan, 32°54′N, 152°11′E.

Submarine *Wahoo* (SS 238), operating in the Yellow Sea, sinks Japanese freighter *Zogen Maru* just east of Dairen, Kwantung Peninsula, Manchukuo, 38°29′N, 122°19′E, and damages freighter *Kowa Maru,* 38°27′N, 122°18′E.

USAAF B-25s (5th Air Force) damage Japanese submarine *I 176* as she is unloading cargo at Lae, New Guinea. *I 176,* however, is able to continue her voyage to Rabaul.

ATLANTIC. German U-boat onslaught against Atlantic convoys continues. U.S. freighter *Mathew Luckenbach* departs convoy HX 229, believing her chances greater of completing the voyage independently than in company with other ships, but runs afoul of *U 527* in the vicinity of SC 122. *U 527* torpedoes *Mathew Luckenbach* at 54°20′N, 25°07′W; Coast Guard cutter *Ingham* (WPG 35) rescues the freighter's entire complement (42 merchant sailors and 26-man Armed Guard). Subsequently, *U 523* administers the coup de grâce to *Mathew Luckenbach.* With the loss of *Mathew Luckenbach* and Greek freighter *Carras* (a straggler from SC 122) to *U 533* on this date, German U-boats will break off operations against SC 122 and HX 229 and conclude what is regarded as the largest convoy battle of the war. Despite the valiant efforts of the escorts, the merchantmen suffer heavy losses.

MEDITERRANEAN. Axis planes bomb shipping in Oran Harbor, Algeria; U.S. freighter *Examiner* is damaged by near-misses that kill one Armed Guard sailor and wound six (an additional Armed Guard sailor is killed on shore during the raid). Merchant casualties amount to three crewmen wounded on board ship and one killed while ashore.

20 Saturday

ATLANTIC. Brazilian merchantman *Baje* rescues 27 survivors of freighter *Roger B. Taney,* sunk by *U 160* on 8 February.

District patrol vessel *YP 438* sinks after running aground on submerged breakwater at entrance to Port Everglades, Florida.

PACIFIC. Submarine *Sawfish* (SS 276) sinks Japanese guardboat *Shinsei Maru* north-north-west of Marcus Island, 32°55′N, 152°11′E.

Submarine *Scamp* (SS 277) damages Japanese freighter *Seinan Maru* off Tomari, 41°06′N, 141°26′E.

Submarine *Trigger* (SS 237) damages Japanese gunboat *No. 2 Choan Maru* off the Admiralties, 03°44′N, 144°12′E, with a dud torpedo.

21 Sunday

ATLANTIC. Submarine *Herring* (SS 233) sinks German submarine *U 163,* Bay of Biscay, 44°13′N, 08°23′W.[137]

PACIFIC. Submarine *Finback* (SS 230) damages Japanese transport (ex-seaplane carrier) *Sanuki Maru* south of the Carolines, 07°40′N, 139°48′E.

Submarine *Scamp* (SS 277) damages Japanese transport *Manju Maru* off east coast of Honshu, 41°45′N, 142°14′E.

Submarine *Wahoo* (SS 238), operating in the Yellow Sea off Korea, sinks Japanese freighters *Hozan Maru,* 38°11′N, 124°33′E, and *Nittsu Maru,* 38°05′N, 124°33′E.

22 Monday

PACIFIC. Submarine *Gudgeon* (SS 211) attacks Japanese convoy 30 miles north of Surabaya, Java, sinking army cargo ship *Meigen Maru,* 06°31′S, 112°47′E, and survives the resultant depth charging by escort vessels.

Submarine *Tambor* (SS 198) damages Japanese transport *Bugen Maru* in the Sulu Sea, off Negros, P.I., 08°58′N, 123°08′E.

ATLANTIC. USAAF aircraft (1st Antisubmarine Squadron) sink German submarine *U 524* north of the Canary Islands, 30°15′N, 18°13′W.

USAAF B-17s and B-24s (8th Air Force) bomb Wilhelmshaven, Germany, U-boat pens, sinking German tanker *Eurosee.*

23 Tuesday

PACIFIC. Submarine *Kingfish* (SS 234) is damaged by depth charges off Formosa, 26°20′N, 121°55′E, and is forced to terminate her patrol.

Submarine *Whale* (SS 239) sinks Japanese transport *Ken'yo Maru* about 130 miles northwest of Saipan, 17°20′N, 145°00′E; one of *Whale*'s torpedoes circles back toward her, forcing the boat to "go deep" but then heads back and hits the target.

Open lighter *YC 869* sinks after grounding off Imperial Beach, California.

Destroyer escort *Pettit* (DE 253), goes down the ways at Brown Shipbuilding Company, Houston, Texas, 28 April 1943; restricted inland waters compelled builders to adopt novel methods of launching ships. *Pettit* honors the late Radioman First Class Robert L. Pettit, awarded a posthumous Navy Cross for heroism on board a PBY in the attack on Japanese shipping at Jolo, P.I., 27 December 1941. (NA, 80-G-50585)

ATLANTIC/MEDITERRANEAN. Naval Station and Naval Air Facility are established at Arzeu, Algeria; Advanced Amphibious Training Bases are established at Port Lyautey, Morocco, and at Nemours, Tenes, Beni Saf, and Mostaganem in Algeria.

24 Wednesday

MEDITERRANEAN. USAAF B-17s, escorted by P-38s (Northwest African Air Forces), bomb naval base at Ferryville, Tunisia; Italian cargo vessel *Citta di Savona* and ex-French large destroyer *L'Audacieux* are sunk.[138]

25 Thursday

PACIFIC. Operating in the Yellow Sea near Port Arthur, submarine *Wahoo* (SS 238) sinks Japanese merchant passenger-cargo ship *Teisho Maru* at 39°01′N, 122°25′E, cargo ship *Takaosan Maru* at 38°13′N, 123°24′E, and cargo ship *Satsuki Maru* at 38°10′N, 123°26′E.

26 Friday

PACIFIC. Battle of the Komandorski Islands: TG 16.6 (Rear Admiral Charles H. McMorris), composed of one heavy cruiser, one light cruiser, and four destroyers, outfights and re-pulses a Japanese force of two heavy cruisers, two light cruisers, and four destroyers (Vice Admiral Hosogaya Boshiro) escorting two transports with reinforcements for Kiska, Aleutians. In this daylight surface action, heavy cruiser *Salt Lake City* (CA 25) is damaged by gunfire from heavy cruisers *Maya* and *Nachi* and light cruiser *Abukuma*, 52°47′N, 172°45′E, but damages *Nachi* in return. Light cruiser *Richmond* (CL 9) (flagship) is straddled but not hit; destroyers *Bailey* (DD 492) and *Coghlan* (DD 606) are also damaged by gunfire, 53°20′N, 168°36′E.

PBYs and USAAF B-24s (13th Air Force) bomb Nauru Island, South Pacific; Japanese cargo vessel *Asaka Maru* reports being bombed by two PBYs.

ATLANTIC. Auxiliary aircraft carrier *Bogue* (ACV 9) operates in support of convoy SC 123; her aircraft keep *U 443* and *U 415* down and prevent their attacking the convoy.

U.S. freighter *Lillian Luckenbach* is accidentally rammed and sunk in collision with U.S. freighter *Cape Henlopen* in Chesapeake Swept Channel, 36°58′33″N, 75°25′05″W. Tug *Acushnet* (AT 63) and harbor tug *Bomazeen* (YT 238), assisted by submarine chaser *SC 682*, take the damaged *Cape Henlopen* in tow. *Lillian Luckenbach*'s survivors are brought to Little Creek, Virginia (see 28 March).

Naval Operating Facility, Belem, Brazil, is established.

27 Saturday

ATLANTIC. Naval Air Facility, Natal, Brazil, and Naval Operating Facilities at Victoria, Florianopolis, Fortaleza, Maceio, Recife, Rio Grande do Sul, Santos, and Sao Luiz, Brazil, are established.

Coast Guard cutter *CGC 85006* (ex-motor boat *Catamount*) is sunk by explosion off Long Island, New York.

28 Sunday

PACIFIC. Submarine *Tunny* (SS 282) damages Japanese troopship *Suwa Maru* off Wake Island, 19°13′N, 166°34′E; to prevent her from sinking, *Suwa Maru* is run aground off Wake's southern shore (near the wrecks of two patrol boats beached there on 23 December 1941) (see 5 April and 27 July).

Japanese cargo ship *Funakawa Maru* is stranded off Shiraya Saki, Honshu, and sinks, 41°22′N, 141°22′E.

ATLANTIC. U.S. freighter *Cape Henlopen*, damaged in collision with freighter *Lillian Luckenbach* on 26 March, goes aground off Cape Henry, Virginia; salvage tug *Resolute* (NRTS) is dispatched from New York. The merchantman is refloated the next day.

29 Monday

PACIFIC. Submarine *Gato* (SS 212) evacuates military and civilian people (including nine women, three nuns, and 27 children) from Teop Island, Solomons.

Submarine *Gudgeon* (SS 211) sinks Japanese fleet tanker *Toho Maru* in Makassar Strait, 00°00′N, 118°18′E, and damages tanker *No. 2 Kyoei Maru*, 00°54′N, 119°01′E.

Submarine *Wahoo* (SS 238) sinks Japanese auxiliary cable ship *Yamabato Maru* south of Kyushu, 30°26′N, 129°41′E.

ATLANTIC. German submarine *U 160* torpedoes U.S. freighter *William Pierce Frye*, straggling from convoy HX 230, at 56°57′N, 26°15′W. Heavy seas have previously damaged most of her lifeboats, and the only serviceable one is swamped; life rafts and floats drift away from the ship. One tank landing craft (LCT) being carried as deck cargo breaks free as the ship sinks, but only seven men reach it (see 3 April).

U.S. tanker *Esso Manhattan* breaks in two in

Ambrose Swept Channel; Navy Rescue Tug Service assets are mobilized. Coast Guard cutter *Kimball* (WPC 143) rescues all hands; while blimps cover the operation, tug *Sagamore* (AT 20) and salvage vessel *Accelerate* (ARS 30) proceed to the scene along with four commercial tugs and salvage vessel (NRTS) *Relief*. Both sections of the tanker are taken in tow (bow by tug *Nancy Moran* and stern by *Relief*) and towed to the Standard Oil Company plant, Bayonne, New Jersey.

30 Tuesday

PACIFIC. Submarine *Tuna* (SS 203) attacks Japanese convoy north of Manus, Admiralty Islands, sinks army cargo ship *Kurohime Maru*, 00°22′S, 147°46′E, and survives the resultant depth charging by escort vessels.

31 Wednesday

PACIFIC. Japanese cargo ship *Nanshin Maru* is sunk in collision with *Ona Maru* west of O-Shima, off Hakata, Honshu, 34°13′N, 133°06′E.

APRIL

1 Thursday

PACIFIC. Submarine *Gato* (SS 212) is damaged by depth charges off New Ireland, 03°08′S, 153°00′E, and is forced to terminate her patrol.

USAAF B-24s and B-17s (5th Air Force) bomb Japanese convoy off Kavieng, New Ireland, sinking freighter *Kokoko Maru*.

ATLANTIC. Submarine *Shad* (SS 235) torpedoes Italian blockade runner *Pietro Orseolo*, 44°37′N, 02°18′W, shortly after the Italian ship has reached the Bay of Biscay and her escort of four German destroyers.

Naval Operating Facility, Grondal, Greenland, is established.

GULF OF MEXICO. District patrol vessel *YP 235* is sunk by explosion of undetermined origin, Gulf of Mexico.

UNITED STATES. Naval Air Station, Patuxent River, Maryland, is established.

2 Friday

PACIFIC. Submarine *Tunny* (SS 282) sinks Japanese transport *No. 2 Toyo Maru* west of Truk, 07°23′N, 149°13′E.

3 Saturday

PACIFIC. Submarine *Haddock* (SS 231) sinks Japanese fleet tanker *Arima Maru* north of Palau, 10°26′N, 135°00′E.

Submarine *Pickerel* (SS 177) sinks Japanese submarine chaser *Ch 13* southeast of Shiriya Saki, Japan, 40°03′N, 141°58′E, but is afterward sunk by minelayer *Shirakami* and auxiliary subchaser *Bunzan Maru* off northern Honshu.

USAAF B-17s (5th Air Force) bomb Japanese shipping off Kavieng, New Ireland, sinking transport *Florida Maru*, 02°35′S, 150°49′E, and damaging heavy cruiser *Aoba* and destroyer *Fumizuki*.

Japanese destroyer *Kazagumo* is damaged by mine, Kahili Bay, Bougainville.

ATLANTIC. German submarine *U 155* sinks U.S. tanker *Gulfstate* off Key West, Florida, 24°22′N, 80°27′W. USCG plane rescues three survivors; district patrol vessel *YP 351* rescues 15. Thirty-four merchant seamen and nine Armed Guard sailors perish with the ship.

British destroyer HMS *Shikari* rescues seven survivors (five merchant seamen and two Armed Guard sailors) from U.S. freighter *William Pierce Frye*, sunk by German submarine *U 160* on 29 March. Thirty-five merchant seamen have perished, as have 22 of the 24-man Armed Guard.

4 Sunday

PACIFIC. Submarine *Haddock* (SS 231), damaged by depth charges off Palaus, 09°31′N, 133°39′E, is forced to terminate her patrol.

Submarine *Porpoise* (SS 172) sinks Japanese whaling ship *Koa Maru* near Eniwetok, 13°10′N, 162°05′E.

5 Monday

PACIFIC. Destroyer *O'Bannon* (DD 450) sinks Japanese submarine *RO 34* near Russell Island, Solomons, 08°15′S, 158°58′E.

Submarine *Finback* (SS 230) inflicts further damage upon Japanese troopship *Suwa Maru*, previously damaged by *Tunny* (SS 282) on 28 March and beached, off Wake Island, 19°20′N, 166°35′E (see 27 July).

ATLANTIC. German submarine *U 563* torpedoes U.S. tanker *Sunoil*, a straggler from convoy HX 231, at 58°16′N, 38°00′W. Armed Guard gunfire forces the attacker to submerge, but *U 563* torpedoes and finishes off the ship later the same day. British destroyer HMS *Vidette*, sent from HX 231 in response to the tanker's summons, locates no survivors; *Sunoil* is lost with all hands (43 merchant seamen and 26-man Armed Guard).

6 Tuesday

MEDITERRANEAN. USAAF B-17s (Northwest African Air Forces) bomb Axis convoy off Bizerte, Tunisia, sinking German freighter *San Diego* and damaging Italian transport *Rovereto*; the latter is beached to prevent her sinking.

ATLANTIC. German submarine *U 336* picks up six survivors (four merchant seamen and two Armed Guard sailors) from U.S. freighter *Jonathan Sturges*, sunk by *U 707* on 23 February. These men (who will ultimately be interned at a POW camp near Bremen, Germany) will be the last of *Jonathan Sturges*'s survivors to be rescued.

GULF OF MEXICO. German submarine *U 185* attacks Mobile, Alabama–bound convoy GTMO 83, sinking U.S. freighter *John Sevier* at 20°35′N, 74°00′W. Destroyer *Bennett* (DD 473) rescues all hands (39 merchant seamen, 17-man Armed Guard, and one passenger).

7 Wednesday

PACIFIC. "I" Operation: last major Japanese air offensive in the Solomons. Carrier bombers (VALs), supported by fighters (ZEROs), strike U.S. and Allied shipping off the east coast of Guadalcanal, off Koli Point, and off Tulagi, damaging destroyer *Aaron Ward* (DD 483) and sinking New Zealand corvette HMNZS *Moa* and damaging oilers *Kanawha* (AO 1) and *Tappahannock* (AO 43) and tank landing ship *LST 449* (the latter two ships by near-misses). Submarine rescue vessel *Ortolan* (ASR 5) and tug *Vireo* (AT 144) attempt to beach *Aaron Ward*, but the destroyer sinks as the result of bomb damage at 09°10′S, 160°12′E. Destroyer *Farenholt* (DD 491) is near-missed by at least three bombs. Tug *Rail* (AT 139) is damaged by friendly fire as motor torpedo boat tender *Niagara* (AGP 1), moored alongside, fires through the former's rigging. *Rail* fire party boards abandoned *Kanawha* and, assisted by minesweeper *Conflict* (AM 85), attempts to put out the raging fires until told to withdraw. Later, *Rail*, tug *Menominee* (AT 73), and net tender *Butternut* (YN 9), tow *Kanawha* into Tulagi Harbor, where the damaged oiler is beached. *Rail* suffers further damage alongside *Kanawha* (see 8 April). Elsewhere off Tulagi, destroyer *Sterett* (DD 407) is damaged by friendly fire from adjacent ships (six men are wounded), while attack cargo ship *Libra* (AKA 12), off Lunga Point, is near-missed. *Adhara* (AK 71), loading cargo off the Tenaru River, is damaged by near-misses and suffers one dead and eight wounded. Of the freighters, two bombs land near *William Williams*, *Louis Joliet* is strafed, and *Dona Nati* is shaken by two near-misses; none of these three ships suffer casualties.

Submarine *Grayling* (SS 209) unsuccessfully attacks Japanese cargo ship *Lima Maru* off Mindoro, 13°20′N, 121°33′E.

Submarine *Trout* (SS 202) lays mines off Sarawak, Borneo.

Submarine *Tunny* (SS 282), despite presence of escort vessel, torpedoes Japanese victualling stores ship *Kosei Maru* about 250 miles northwest of Truk, 08°50′N, 147°06′E. Attempt to tow the damaged vessel fails, and *Kosei Maru* sinks en route to Truk.

Submarine *Pickerel* (SS 177) sinks Japanese cargo ship *Fukuei Maru* near Shiriya Saki, Honshu, 41°00′N, 142°00′E.

8 Thursday

PACIFIC. Oiler *Kanawha* (AO 1), damaged the day before and beached off Tulagi by tugs *Rail* (AT 139) and *Menominee* (AT 73), sinks.

9 Friday

UNITED STATES. Rank of Commodore, U.S. Navy, is reestablished.

PACIFIC. Submarine *Drum* (SS 228) attacks Japanese convoy, sinking army cargo ship *Oyama Maru* about 180 miles north-northwest of Kavieng, New Ireland, 00°32′N, 150°05′E.

Submarine *Grayling* (SS 209), in attack on Japanese convoy off Mindoro, sinks army cargo ship *Shanghai Maru* about 10 miles east of Dumali Point, 13°11′N, 121°45′E.

Submarine *Tautog* (SS 199) attacks Japanese convoy in Buton Passage, off southeastern Celebes, sinking army cargo ship *Penang Maru*, 05°31′S, 123°06′E. *Tautog* then sinks destroyer *Isonami* as the enemy warship tries to rescue *Penang Maru*'s survivors, 05°26′S, 123°04′E.

10 Saturday

MEDITERRANEAN. USAAF B-17s (9th Air Force) bomb Italian fleet units at La Maddalena, Sardinia, sinking heavy cruiser *Trieste* and motor torpedo boats *MAS 501* and *MAS 503* and damaging heavy cruiser *Gorizia*. *Gorizia* will be towed to La Spezia for repairs.

ATLANTIC. U.S. freighter *Edward B. Dudley*, straggling from United Kingdom–bound convoy HX 232, is torpedoed by German submarine *U 615* in the North Atlantic, 53°00′N, 38°00′W, but the torpedo that hits the freighter is a dud (see 11 April).

11 Sunday

ATLANTIC. U.S. freighter *Edward B. Dudley* is sunk by German submarine *U 615* in the North Atlantic, 53°00′N, 39°00′W. Debris

from the explosion that follows the coup de grâce damages *U 615*'s conning tower. Survivors of the 42 merchant sailors and the 25-man Armed Guard who manage to lower boats are never recovered.

U.S. freighter *James W. Denver*, straggling from convoy UGS 7, is sunk by German submarine *U 195* west of the Canary Islands, 28°46′N, 25°40′W. All hands (42 merchant seamen, one passenger, and 25 Armed Guards) survive the loss of the ship and set sail for the coast of Africa (see 18 and 24 April and 4, 6, and 16 May).

U.S. freighter *Matt W. Ransom*, steaming in Casablanca-bound convoy UGS 6A, is mined at 33°59′N, 07°51′W. All hands (42 merchant seamen, two passengers, and 28 Armed Guard sailors) abandon ship and are rescued by submarine chasers *PC 471* and *PC 481*; the master and six men, however, return to the damaged ship and take her to Gibraltar under her own power.[139]

12 Monday

PACIFIC. Submarine *Flying Fish* (SS 229) sinks Japanese freighter *No. 12 Sapporo Maru* off Shiriya Saki, Honshu, 41°23′N, 141°30′E.

USAAF B-17s and B-24s (5th Air Force) bomb Japanese shipping in Hansa Bay, sinking army cargo ship *Sydney Maru*, 03°18′S, 143°38′E.

14 Wednesday

PACIFIC. Submarine *Pike* (SS 173) damages Japanese army cargo ship *Madras Maru* north of the Admiralties, 01°25′N, 148°22′E.

USAAF B-17s and B-24s (5th Air Force) bomb Japanese shipping in Hansa Bay, sinking army cargo ship *India Maru*, 03°18′S, 143°38′E.

15 Thursday

PACIFIC. Submarine *Seawolf* (SS 197) sinks Japanese transport *Kaihei Maru* about 275 miles south-southwest of Marcus Island, 21°15′N, 152°00′E.

USAAF B-17s (5th Air Force) bomb Japanese shipping at Wewak, New Guinea, damaging destroyer *Tachikaze*.

Sino-American Cooperative Organization (SACO) is established; it is headed by Lieutenant General Tai Li, Chief of the Bureau of Investigation and Statistics of the [Chinese] Military Council. Commander Milton E. Miles, USN, is Li's deputy. By war's end, SACO will have trained Chinese guerrillas and saboteurs, established a medical organization, reported weather, collected intelligence information, and established a coastwatcher network.

ATLANTIC. PBY (VP 83) sinks Italian submarine *Archimede* off coast of Brazil, 03°23′S, 30°28′W.

German submarine *U 262* makes contact with convoy HX 233, whose escort (Commander Paul R. Heineman) includes Coast Guard cutters *Spencer* (WPG 36) and *Duane* (WPG 33), a Canadian destroyer, and two Canadian and three British corvettes. Escorts will drive off *U 262* the next day.

District patrol vessel *YP 453* sinks after grounding on Bahamas Bank.

17 Saturday

PACIFIC. Submarine *Flying Fish* (SS 229) sinks Japanese army cargo ship *Amaho Maru* off Erimo Saki, Hokkaido, 42°04′N, 143°22′E.

Japanese transport *Shinnan Maru* is sunk by mine (laid by USN TBFs on 30 March), near Buin, Bougainville, 06°50′N, 155°45′E.

Japanese ex-whale factory ship *No. 2 Nissho Maru* is sunk by unknown agent about 160 miles east of Formosa, 23°36′N, 124°18′E.[140]

ATLANTIC. Coast Guard cutter *Spencer* (WPG 36), while escorting convoy HX 233, attacks German submarine *U 175*, which had located the convoy on the night of 16–17 April after *U 262* had been driven off, and sinks her at 48°50′N, 21°20′W.

18 Sunday

PACIFIC. Admiral Yamamoto Isoroku, Commander in Chief Combined Fleet, is killed when the land attack plane (BETTY) (705th *Kokutai*) in which he is traveling is shot down by USAAF P-38s (339th Fighter Squadron) off Bougainville. Interception of Yamamoto, who is on an inspection trip of the forward areas to inspire those under his command, is brought about through signals intelligence. A second BETTY is splashed by the P-38s, but its high-ranking passenger, Vice Admiral Ugaki Matome, Yamamoto's chief of staff, survives (see 21 April).

Submarine *Drum* (SS 228) sinks Japanese ammunition ship *Nisshun Maru* about 200 miles north-northwest of Mussau Island, Bismarck Archipelago, 01°55′N, 148°24′E. Submarine chaser *Ch 18* rescues survivors, including a number of Army prostitutes among them.

ATLANTIC. Spanish merchantman *Cabo Huertas* rescues 11 survivors from U.S. freighter *James W. Denver*, sunk by German submarine *U 195* on 11 April (see 24 April and 4, 6, and 16 May).

Open lighter *YC 891* founders and sinks while in tow of harbor tug *Mauvila* (YT 328) off Key West, Florida.

ARCTIC. German planes bomb Allied shipping at Murmansk, USSR, damaging U.S. freighter *Thomas Hartley*.

19 Monday

PACIFIC. Submarine *Scorpion* (SS 278) mines waters off Kashima Nada, Japan.

Submarine *Seawolf* (SS 197) sinks Japanese depot ship *No. 5 Banshu Maru* off the Bonins, 26°15′N, 139°35′E.

TBFs bomb Japanese shipping in Tonolei Harbor, Bougainville, damaging cargo vessel *Shirogare Maru*.

ATLANTIC. U.S. freighter *Elmer E. Sperry* runs aground off Savannah, Georgia; tug *Umpqua* (AT 25) and salvage vessel *Warbler* (ARS 11) proceed to the scene (see 21 April).

20 Tuesday

PACIFIC. Submarine *Runner* (SS 275) mines waters near Hong Kong.

Submarine *Scorpion* (SS 278) sinks Japanese gunboat *No. 1 Meiji Maru* off east central coast of Honshu, 37°10′N, 141°25′E.

USAAF B-17s (5th Air Force) bomb Japanese shipping off Wewak, sinking cargo ship *Kosei Maru*, 03°30′S, 143°30′E.

USAAF B-24s, B-25s, P-38s, and P-40s (11th Air Force) attack Japanese installations and shipping at Kiska, Aleutians; during these raids, cargo ship *Nojima Maru* is sunk.

Japanese transport-cargo ship *Sumerusan Maru* is sunk by accidental explosion, Surabaya, Java, 03°30′S, 143°30′E.

MEDITERRANEAN. U.S. freighter *Michigan*, steaming in convoy UGS 7, is torpedoed and sunk by German submarine *U 565* off Oran, Algeria, 36°01′N, 01°25′W. All hands (37 merchant seamen, 23 Armed Guards, and the one passenger) survive; some remain in the boats to help rescue survivors (Senegalese soldiers) from French steamship *Sidi-Bel-Abbes*, also torpedoed and sunk by *U 565*, thus preventing the toll in human life from the loss of that Allied vessel from being much larger. *Michigan*'s survivors are rescued by British escort trawlers HMS *Stella Carina* and HMS *Foxtrot*, and then transferred to sloop HMS *Felixstowe*, which transports them to Oran.

21 Wednesday

PACIFIC. Submarine *Grenadier* (SS 210) is damaged by Japanese reconnaissance seaplane (JAKE) (936th *Kokutai*) near Strait of Malacca (see 22 April).

Submarine *Stingray* (SS 186) mines waters off Wenchow, China (see 22 April).

Admiral Koga Mineichi is appointed Commander in Chief Japanese Combined Fleet.

ATLANTIC. Destroyer *Swanson* (DD 443) drives German submarine *U 129* away from NG convoy in the Greater Antilles.

Tug *Umpqua* (AT 25) and salvage vessel *Warbler* (ARS 11) refloat U.S. freighter *Elmer E. Sperry* from her 19 April predicament off Savannah, Georgia.

INDIAN OCEAN. U.S. freighter *John Drayton* is torpedoed by Italian submarine *Leonardo da Vinci* off the coast of South Africa, 34°00′S, 34°40′E, and abandoned. *Leonardo da Vinci* then surfaces, finishes off the freighter with gunfire, and temporarily detains a member of the crew on board for questioning before returning him to his shipmates (see 23 and 27 April and 21 May).

22 Thursday

PACIFIC. Submarine *Grenadier* (SS 210) is scuttled off Penang, Malaya, 06°30′N, 97°40′E, after having been damaged by Japanese reconnaissance seaplane (JAKE) (936th *Kokutai*) the previous day.

Submarine *Stingray* (SS 186) continues mining waters off Wenchow, China.

Dutch submarine *O 21*, despite presence of escort vessel, sinks Japanese army cargo ship *Yamazato Maru* in Strait of Malacca, 03°28′N, 99°47′E.

Japanese land attack planes (NELLs) (755th *Kokutai*) commence bombing airfield at Funafuti, Ellice Islands (see 23 April).

ATLANTIC. PBYs (VP 84), flying from bases in Iceland and Greenland, drive off German U-boats threatening convoy HX 234.

23 Friday

PACIFIC. Submarine *Pike* (SS 173) is damaged by depth charges off central Carolines, 04°20′N, 152°02′E, and is forced to terminate her patrol.

Submarine *Seawolf* (SS 197) sinks Japanese *Patrol Boat No. 39* off east central coast of Formosa, 23°45′N, 122°45′E, while the enemy warship is screening the towing of the wrecked *No. 2 Nisshin Maru*.

Japanese land attack planes (NELLs) (755th *Kokutai*) conclude bombing attack on airfield at Funafuti, Ellice Islands; two USAAF B-24s (7th Air Force) are destroyed, five are damaged.

District patrol vessel *YP 422* founders after grounding on Tumbo Reef, three miles southeast of entrance to North Bulari Passage, New Caledonia.

ATLANTIC. U.S. freighter *Robert Gray*, straggling from convoy HX 234, is sunk by German submarine *U 306* in the North Atlantic at 57°30′N, 43°00′W, with all hands (39-man merchant complement and 19-man Armed Guard).

U.S. freighter *Santa Catalina*, bound for Basra, Iraq, is sunk by German submarine *U 129* at 30°59′N, 70°57′W, and abandoned (see 24 April).

INDIAN OCEAN. Swedish merchantman *Oscar Gorthon* rescues 11 survivors from U.S. freighter *John Drayton*, sunk by Italian submarine *Leonardo da Vinci* on 21 April (see 27 April and 21 May).

24 Saturday

PACIFIC. Submarine *Flying Fish* (SS 229) sinks Japanese merchant passenger-cargo ship *Kasuga Maru* in Tsugaru Strait, 41°44′N, 141°21′E.

Submarine *Runner* (SS 275) damages Japanese army hospital ship *Buenos Aires Maru* south of Hong Kong, 21°41′N, 116°24′E.

USAAF B-24s (7th Air Force) bomb Japanese airfield at Tarawa, Gilberts.

ATLANTIC. British freighter *Campana* rescues 15 survivors from U.S. freighter *James W. Denver*, sunk by German submarine *U 195* on 11 April (see 4, 6, and 16 May).

Swedish motor vessel *Venezia* rescues all hands (57 merchant seamen, 28-man Armed Guard, and 10 passengers) from U.S. freighter *Santa Catalina*, sunk by German submarine *U 129* the previous day.

25 Sunday

ATLANTIC. District patrol vessel *YP 481* founders after running aground off Charleston, South Carolina.

MEDITERRANEAN. U.S. freighter *Samuel Parker* is damaged by fire on board gasoline lighter moored alongside Tripoli Harbor, Libya. There are no casualties to the merchant crew, Armed Guard, or Egyptian stevedores working cargo.

26 Monday

PACIFIC. TG 16.6, three light cruisers and six destroyers (Rear Admiral Charles H. McMorris), bombards Japanese installations at Attu, Aleutians.

ATLANTIC. District patrol vessel *YP 47* is sunk in collision with motor minesweeper *YMS 110* in Ambrose Channel, off Staten Island, New York.

MEDITERRANEAN. Naval Station, Mers el Kebir, Morocco, is established.

27 Tuesday

PACIFIC. Submarine *Scorpion* (SS 278) attacks Japanese convoy, sinking freighter *Yuzan Maru* off east coast of Honshu, 38°08′N, 143°03′E.

U.S. freighter *Lydia M. Child* is sunk by Japanese submarine *I 178* about 100 miles east of Sydney, Australia, 33°08′S, 153°24′E; Australian corvette HMAS *Warrnambool* and minesweeper HMAS *Deloraine* rescue the entire crew, including the 21-man Armed Guard.

ATLANTIC. PV-1 (VB 125), providing coverage for convoy SC 128 off Halifax, Nova Scotia, sinks German submarine *U 174*, 43°35′N, 56°18′W.

INDIAN OCEAN. British destroyer HMS *Relentless* rescues 14 survivors from U.S. freighter *John Drayton*, sunk by Italian submarine *Leonardo da Vinci* on 21 April (see 21 May).

28 Wednesday

PACIFIC. Submarine *Gudgeon* (SS 211) sinks Japanese transport-hospital ship *Kamakura Maru* 30 miles southwest of Naso Point, Panay, P.I., 10°18′N, 121°44′E.

ATLANTIC. Escort group formed around auxiliary aircraft carrier *Bogue* (ACV 9) and four destroyers drives off five German submarines deploying against convoy HX 235. Another group of U-boats threatens convoy ONS 5, which is protected by British escort vessels and PBYs (VP 84) (see 29 April).

29 Thursday

PACIFIC. Submarine *Gato* (SS 212) lands coastwatchers at Teop Island, Solomons, and evacuates missionaries.

ATLANTIC. German submarine *U 404* attacks carrier, misidentified as *Ranger* (CV 4), in screen of convoy ONS 4. Although *U 404*'s *Korvettenkapitän* Otto von Bulow claims to have heard four detonations, leading the German Navy to credit him with *Ranger*'s destruction, *U 404*'s intended victim, however, is British escort carrier HMS *Biter*, which emerges unscathed from the encounter. To paraphrase Mark Twain, rumors of *Ranger*'s demise are greatly exaggerated; she will prove, much to the Germans' distress, a very potent adversary (see 4 October).

PBY (VP 84) damages German submarine *U 528* as she threatens convoy ONS 5; U.S. freighter *McKeesport*, however, is torpedoed by *U 258* at 60°52′N, 34°20′W, and abandoned. British trawler HMS *Northern Gem* rescues all hands: 43 merchant seamen (one of whom dies subsequently) and the 25-man Armed Guard. British frigate HMS *Tay* scuttles *McKeesport* with gunfire.

30 Friday

PACIFIC. Submarine *Gudgeon* (SS 211) lands four men and three tons of equipment near Libertad, on coast of Panay, P.I., 4.3 miles east of Pucio Point.

Submarine *Scorpion* (SS 278) attacks Japanese convoy east of Honshu and sinks guardboat *No. 5 Ebisu Maru*, 37°24′N, 154°40′E.

Submarine *Snook* (SS 279) lays mines off Saddle Island, China.

U.S. freighter *Phoebe A. Hearst* is torpedoed and sunk by Japanese submarine *I 19* about 240 miles southeast of Suva, Fiji Islands, 19°48′S, 176°44′E (see 1, 5, and 14 May).

ATLANTIC. Atlantic Fleet turns over responsibility for convoys between Halifax, Nova Scotia, and United Kingdom to British and Canadian naval forces.

MAY

1 Saturday

PACIFIC. Submarine *Pogy* (SS 266), in attack on Japanese convoy, sinks gunboat *Keishin Maru* off Iwaki, Japan, 37°04′N, 141°06′E.

PBY rescues eight survivors from U.S. freighter *Phoebe A. Hearst*, sunk by Japanese submarine *I 19* the previous day (see 5 and 14 May).

ATLANTIC. Tug *P. F. Martin* (NRTS) tows disabled district patrol vessel *YP 429* to Section Base, Morehead City, North Carolina.

2 Sunday

PACIFIC. Submarine *Gar* (SS 206) sinks Japanese guardboat *No. 12 Jimbo Maru* in Makassar Strait, 00°41′S, 117°50′E.

Submarine *Stingray* (SS 186) attacks Japanese convoy off Wenchow, China, sinking army transport *Tamon Maru* about 12 miles off Nanki Shan, 27°18′N, 121°38′E.

U.S. freighter *William Williams* is torpedoed by Japanese submarine *I 19* near Suva, Fiji Islands, 20°09′S, 178°04′W. There are no casualties among the 40-man merchant crew and the 15-man Armed Guard; the latter remains on board with a fire-fighting crew to battle the blaze in two compartments (see 4 and 7 May).

ATLANTIC. U.S. tanker *Livingston Rowe*, loaded with aviation gasoline, catches fire at Recife, Brazil, near warehouses containing ammunition and dynamite; prompt fire-fighting efforts by crews of U.S. and British naval vessels in the harbor, from U.S. Navy and U.S. Army shore establishments, and from Brazilian army, naval, and civilian organizations prevent a catastrophe.

Coastal yacht *Alabaster* (PYc 21), directed to the scene by blimp *K 4*, rescues two survivors from U.S. schooner *Rebecca R. Douglas*, which had gone down on 28 April while en route from New York to Brazil, at 38°17′N, 71°46′W. Coast Guard lighthouse tender *Laurel* (WAGL 291) finds only an overturned lifeboat. Remainder of search proves negative.

Coast Guard cutter *CGC 58012* is destroyed by explosion off Manomet Point, Massachusetts.

3 Monday

PACIFIC. Oiler *Neches* (AO 47) is damaged when she accidentally runs aground at entrance to Cold Bay, Aleutians.

MEDITERRANEAN. Tank landing craft *LCT 23* is destroyed by explosion of undetermined origin off Algiers.

ATLANTIC. U.S. Army transport *Oneida* sinks off Virginia capes, 37°13′N, 74°17′W. Coast Guard cutters *Jackson* (WPC 142) and *CGC 83324*, tug *Sciota* (AT 30), submarine chaser *SC 1290*, salvage vessel *Relief* (NRTS) are dispatched to assist; provision stores ship *Ariel* (AF 23) and gunboat *Temptress* (PG 62) are alerted; and district patrol vessel *YP 261*, in the vicinity, is ordered to search (see 5 May).

4 Tuesday

PACIFIC. Submarine *Gudgeon* (SS 211) sinks Japanese merchant trawler *Naku Maru* west of Panay, P.I., 10°11′N, 121°43′E.

Submarine *Seal* (SS 183) attacks Japanese convoy, sinking fleet tanker *San Clemente Maru* about 50 miles southeast of Palau, 06°30′N, 130°30′E.

Net tender *Catalpa* (YN 5) begins towing damaged U.S. freighter *William Williams*, torpedoed by Japanese submarine *I 19* on 2 May (see 7 May).

ATLANTIC. German submarine attacks on ships of convoy ONS 5 continue. U.S. freighter *West Maximus* is torpedoed and sunk by *U 264* at 55°00′N, 43°00′W; during the abandonment, one sailor of the 21-man Armed Guard drowns, while five of the 39-man merchant complement are lost with the ship. British trawler HMS *Northern Spray* rescues the survivors, including two Army passengers.

Portuguese fishing trawler *Albufeira* rescues 11 survivors from U.S. freighter *James W. Denver*, sunk by German submarine *U 195* on 11 April (see 6 and 16 May).

Panamanian tanker *Panam* is sunk by German submarine *U 129*, 30 miles southeast of Cape Lookout, North Carolina, 34°11′N, 76°12′W; submarine chaser *SC 664* rescues 50 survivors from the 52-man crew and takes them to Morehead City, North Carolina.

5 Wednesday

PACIFIC. Submarine *Permit* (SS 178) damages Japanese transport *Tokai Maru*, Apra, Guam, 13°27′N, 144°35′E.

Submarine *Sawfish* (SS 276), despite proximity of escort vessel, sinks Japanese gunboat *Hakkai Maru* off Ise Wan, Honshu, Japan, 34°11′N, 137°41′E.

Submarine *Snook* (SS 279) attacks Japanese merchant shipping in the Yellow Sea, sinking freighters *Kinko Maru*, 38°39′N, 122°35′E, and *Taifuku Maru*, 38°38′N, 122°39′E.

Twenty-three survivors from U.S. freighter *Phoebe A. Hearst*, sunk by Japanese submarine *I 19* on 30 April, reach Tofua Island; motor minesweeper *YMS 89* picks them up and transfers them to Tongatabu, Tonga Islands, in the southwest Pacific (see 14 May).

ATLANTIC. German submarine attacks on ships of convoy ONS 5 continue. U.S. freighter *West Madaket* is torpedoed by *U 707* at 54°47′N, 44°12′W, and abandoned. British frigate HMS *Pink* rescues the 39-man merchant complement and the 22-man Armed Guard and then scuttles the crippled vessel with depth charges.

Destroyer escort *Andres* (DE 45), at 37°24′N, 72°20′W, rescues 31 survivors from the 62-man crew of U.S. Army transport *Oneida*, which sank off the Virginia capes on 3 May. Coast Guard cutter *Jackson* (WPC 142) and submarine chaser *SC 1290*, aided by aircraft, continue the search for survivors to no avail.

6 Thursday

PACIFIC. Submarine *Gar* (SS 206) sinks Japanese freighter *Kotoku Maru* in Makassar Strait off Tarakan, Borneo, 03°14′N, 117°58′E.

ATLANTIC. U.S. freighter *Samuel Jordan Kirkwood*, bound for Bahia, Brazil, is torpedoed by German submarine *U 195* in the South Atlantic at 15°00′S, 07°00′W, and abandoned (see 7 May).

Fourteen survivors from U.S. freighter *James W. Denver*, sunk by German submarine *U 195* on 11 April, reach Port Etienne, French West Africa (see 16 May).

Covered lighter *YF 575* founders after grounding off Atlantic City, New Jersey.

7 Friday

PACIFIC. TG 36.5, composed of light minelayers *Gamble* (DM 15), *Preble* (DM 20), and *Breese* (DM 18), covered by destroyer *Radford* (DD 446), mines Blackett Strait, western approaches to Kula Gulf, Solomons (see 8 May).

Submarine *Snook* (SS 279) sinks Japanese freighters *Tosei Maru* and *No. 3 Shinsei Maru* in the Yellow Sea, 36°05′N, 123°21′E.

Submarine *Wahoo* (SS 238) sinks Japanese transport *No. 5 Tamon Maru* off Benten Saki, Honshu, 40°05′N, 141°53′E.

Net tender *Catalpa* (YN 5), escorted by minesweeper *Dash* (AM 88), brings damaged U.S. freighter *William Williams*, torpedoed by Japanese submarine *I 19* on 2 May, into Suva, Fiji Islands.[141]

Vichy French steamship *Gouverneur Général Pasquir* is sunk by mine off coast of French Indochina, 20°14′N, 107°00′E.

ATLANTIC. U.S. freighter *Samuel Jordan Kirkwood*, torpedoed by German submarine *U 195* in the South Atlantic the previous day, sinks (see 16 May).

8 Saturday

PACIFIC. Japanese destroyer *Kuroshio* is sunk by mine laid by TG 36.5 on 7 May, Blackett Strait, Solomons; destroyer *Oyashio*, damaged by mine off Rendova, is sunk by SBDs; destroyer *Kagero*, damaged by mine off Rendova, is sunk by USMC aircraft; destroyer *Michisio* is damaged by SBDs in Blackett Strait.

Submarine *Plunger* (SS 179) sights Japanese Saipan-bound convoy about 60 miles northwest of Truk (see 10 and 11 May).

USAAF B-25s (5th Air Force) sink Japanese freighter *Tomioka Maru* and army cargo ship *Sumida Maru*, Madang Harbor, New Guinea, 05°12′S, 145°50′E.

MEDITERRANEAN. U.S. freighter *Pat Harrison* is mined in Gibraltar Bay; she is later written off as a total loss. One merchant seaman dies in the incident, but there are no casualties among the 26-man Armed Guard or the two Army security officers.

Allied forces occupy Sfax, Tunisia, capturing Italian water tanker *Pro Patria*.

9 Sunday

PACIFIC. Submarine *Gar* (SS 206) sinks Japanese gunboat *Aso Maru* southeast of Cagayan Island, 09°09′N, 122°50′E.

Submarine *Pogy* (SS 266) damages Japanese transport *Uyo Maru* off Iwaki, Japan, 37°05′N, 141°06′E.

Submarine *Wahoo* (SS 238) sinks Japanese freighters *Takao Maru* and *Jimmu Maru* off Kone Saki, Honshu, Japan, 38°57′N, 141°49′E.

ATLANTIC. Light cruiser *Marblehead* (CL 12), on patrol in the South Atlantic, rescues the crew of a crashed USAAF B-26, 06°42′S, 21°35′W.

MEDITERRANEAN. Organized German and Italian resistance in North Africa ceases. Although resistance on land has ended, aerial opposition continues. Axis planes bomb Allied shipping in harbor at Bône, Algeria. A fragment from a near-miss ignites a portion of the cargo (7,000 tons of drummed gasoline) on board U.S. freighter *Daniel Huger*; although the efforts to fight the blaze (initially conducted by two Merchant Marine cadet midshipmen and a volunteer) are ultimately successful (aided by efforts of a well-equipped British fire-fighting party), one merchant sailor and one of the 27-man Armed Guard perish in the attack.

10 Monday

PACIFIC. Destroyer *MacDonough* (DD 351) and light minelayer *Sicard* (DM 21) are damaged in collision about 100 miles north-northwest of Holtz Bay, Attu, Aleutians, 54°34′N, 173°58′E.

Submarine *Plunger* (SS 179) attacks Japanese transports in convoy tracked since 8 May, sinking *Tatsutake Maru* and damaging *Kinai Maru* about 200 miles east of Saipan, 14°29′N, 149°00′E; the latter is abandoned. Torpedo boat *Hiyodori* is damaged in collision with *Tatsutake Maru* and *Kinai Maru*, probably during the rescue of survivors.

11 Tuesday

PACIFIC. Operation LANDCRAB: U.S. Army troops (Seventh Division) land on Attu Island, Aleutians; TF 16 (Rear Admiral Thomas C. Kinkaid) and TF 51 (Rear Admiral Francis W. Rockwell) cover the landing. Submarine *Nautilus* (SS 168) and *Narwhal* (SS 167) land scouts on Attu Island.

Submarine *Grayback* (SS 208) attacks Japanese convoy, sinking collier *Yodogawa Maru* about 125 miles northwest of Kavieng, 00°47′S, 149°02′E.

Submarine *Plunger* (SS 179) finishes off abandoned Japanese transport *Kinai Maru*, damaged the day before east of Saipan, 14°29′N, 149°00′E.

12 Wednesday

PACIFIC. Battleship *Pennsylvania* (BB 38) neutralizes Japanese positions on the west arm of Holtz Bay, Attu Island, while battleship

Nevada (BB 36) renders Japanese positions at head of Massacre Bay, Attu, ineffective. Japanese submarine *I 31* attacks *Pennsylvania* nine miles northeast of Holtz Bay, but the torpedoes miss their mark; *I 35* likewise conducts an unsuccessful attack against light cruiser *Santa Fe* (CL 60). Destroyer *Edwards* (DD 619), assisted by destroyer *Farragut* (DD 348), subsequently sinks *I 31* about five miles northeast of Chichagof Harbor, Attu, 53°00′N, 173°21′E.

Submarine *Gudgeon* (SS 211), despite her quarry's being skillfully camouflaged and moored close inshore, sinks Japanese army cargo ship *Sumatra Maru* off Bulusan, Luzon, 12°43′N, 124°08′E.

Submarine *Steelhead* (SS 280) lays mines off Erimo Saki, Japan.

MEDITERRANEAN. Advanced Amphibious Training Base, Bizerte, Tunisia, is established.

ATLANTIC. U.S. freighter *Cape Neddick*, bound for Suez, via Durban, South Africa, is torpedoed by German submarine *U 195* in the South Atlantic at 23°21′S, 01°22′W; she eventually reaches Walvis Bay, South Africa, under her own power. There are no casualties among the 51-man merchant complement or the 25-man Armed Guard.

13 Thursday

PACIFIC. TF 18 (Rear Admiral Walden L. Ainsworth) bombards Munda and Vila, Solomons, while minelayers (TG 36.5) sow a field across the northwestern approaches to Kula Gulf. Light cruiser *Nashville* (CL 43), 08°28′S, 158°49′E, and destroyers *Chevalier* (DD 451) and *Nicholas* (DD 449), 08°30′S, 158°01′E, are all damaged by gun mount explosions.

Battleship *Idaho* (BB 42) and destroyer *Phelps* (DD 360) silence enemy batteries on Attu, permitting U.S. Army artillery units to move up at Holtz Bay.

ATLANTIC. German submarine *U 176* attacks convoy DM 69 in the Greater Antilles, sinking U.S. tanker *Nickeliner* and Cuban-registry tanker *Mambi*, 21°25′N, 76°40′W, and eludes destroyer escort *Brennan* (DE 13), eight submarine chasers, and a blimp. There are no casualties on board *Nickeliner* (23 merchant sailors, seven Armed Guards, and one passenger); the survivors are rescued by a Cuban submarine chaser.

MEDITERRANEAN. USAAF B-17s, B-25s, and B-26s, escorted by P-38s (Northwest African Air Forces), bomb railroad yards, dock facilities, and submarine base at Cagliari, Sardinia. During this raid, Italian submarine *Mocenigo* is sunk.

Enemy resistance in North Africa ends with unconditional surrender of German and Italian forces in Tunisia.

14 Friday

PACIFIC. Motor torpedo boats *PT 150* and *PT 152* sink Japanese submarine *RO 102* in Vitiaz Strait, New Guinea, 06°55′S, 147°34′E.

USMC TBFs (VMSB 143) damage Japanese army cargo ship *Houn Maru* and force her aground off Tonolei, Bougainville, 06°48′N, 155°49′E, a total loss.

Minesweeper *Dash* (AM 88) rescues 25 survivors from U.S. freighter *Phoebe A. Hearst*, sunk by Japanese submarine *I 19* on 30 April. With this recovery, all hands from the lost freighter (including the 16-man Armed Guard) are accounted for.

Japanese land attack planes (751st *Kokutai*) bomb Allied port facilities at Oro Bay and Port Harvey, New Guinea, destroying a bitumen dump and a gasoline barge. Japanese submarines *I 5* and *I 6* rescue aircrew from BETTYs that force-land due to battle damage.

ATLANTIC. PBY (VP 84) sinks German submarine *U 657* threatening convoy ONS 7, southwest of Iceland, 60°10′N, 31°52′W.

EUROPE. USAAF B-17s and B-24s (8th Air Force) bomb submarine building yards, Kiel, Germany, destroying *U 235*, *U 236*, and *U 237*.

15 Saturday

GENERAL. TRIDENT Conference begins, with President Roosevelt, British Prime Minister Winston S. Churchill, and the Combined Chiefs of Staff meeting in Washington, D.C.

PACIFIC. Submarine *Gar* (SS 206) attacks Japanese convoy, screened by escort vessel *Matsuwa*, at eastern entrance of Verde Island Passage, and sinks army cargo ships *Meikai Maru* and *Indus Maru* between Dumali Point, Mindoro, and Marinduque Island, P.I., 13°07′N, 121°49′E.

USAAF B-24s (7th Air Force), flying from Midway, bomb Wake Island.

Naval Advanced Base and Naval Air Facility, Russell Islands, Solomons, are established.

Naval Air Station, Adak, Aleutians, is established.

ATLANTIC. OS2U/OS2N (VS 62) and Cuban *Submarine Chaser 13* sink German submarine *U 176* off Cuba, 23°21′N, 80°18′W.

16 Sunday

ATLANTIC. Destroyer *MacKenzie* (DD 614) sinks German submarine *U 182* west of Madeira, 33°55′N, 20°35′W.

Spanish sailing ship *Juan* rescues 18 survivors from U.S. freighter *James W. Denver*, sunk by German submarine *U 195* in the North Atlantic on 11 April; two of the ship's 42-man merchant complement perish of exposure.

USAAF crash boat spots boatloads of survivors (41-man merchant complement, 25-man Armed Guard, and four passengers) of U.S. freighter *Samuel Jordan Kirkwood*, which had sunk on 7 May as the result of damage inflicted by German submarine *U 195* on 6 May, and tows them to Ascension Island.

PACIFIC. Submarine *Grayback* (SS 208) damages Japanese destroyer *Yugure* northwest of Kavieng, 01°00′S, 148°44′W.

U.S. freighter *William K. Vanderbilt* is torpedoed by Japanese submarine *I 19* southwest of Suva, Fiji Islands, 18°41′S, 175°07′E, and abandoned by the 41-man merchant complement. The 16-man Armed Guard remains on board to the last, but abandons after a second torpedo splits the ship in twain. *I 19* then fires upon one lifeboat and two rafts, and questions the ship's master before departing; throughout the ordeal only the ship's chief engineer is killed (see 17 May).

17 Monday

PACIFIC. Submarine *Grayback* (SS 208) attacks Japanese convoy, sinking army cargo ship *England Maru* about 60 miles northwest of Mussau Island, 01°00′S, 148°40′E.

Minesweeper *Dash* (AM 88) rescues 56 survivors from U.S. freighter *William K. Vanderbilt*, sunk by Japanese submarine *I 19* the previous day southwest of Suva.

Japanese cargo ship *Woosung Maru* strikes reef and sinks off Chiba Prefecture, southern Honshu, 35°00′N, 140°00′E.

ATLANTIC. PBM (VP 74) damages German submarine *U 128* in South Atlantic, at 11°02′S, 35°35′W; destroyers *Moffett* (DD 362) and *Jouett* (DD 396) then sink *U 128* at 11°08′S, 35°38′W.

18 Tuesday

PACIFIC. Submarine *Pollack* (SS 180) sinks Japanese gunboat *Terushima Maru* southwest of Maleolap Atoll, Marshalls, 08°00′N, 171°00′E.

U.S. tanker *H. M. Storey* is torpedoed by Japanese submarine *I 25* while en route from Nouméa, New Caledonia, to San Pedro, California, 17°30′S, 173°02′E, and abandoned by the 48-man civilian complement (two merchant seamen are lost when the ship is hit), two passengers, and 15-man Armed Guard.

I 25 then hastens the sinking by shelling the burning ship. Destroyer *Fletcher* (DD 445) subsequently rescues *H. M. Storey*'s survivors and takes them to Efate, New Hebrides.

19 Wednesday

PACIFIC. Submarine *Gar* (SS 206) sinks Japanese guardboat *Asuka Maru* in Makassar Strait, 01°02′N, 119°08′E.

MEDITERRANEAN. Axis planes bomb Allied shipping in Oran Harbor, Algeria, damaging U.S. freighters *Samuel Griffin* and *Luther Martin*; the former suffers 15 men injured among her complement of 44 merchant seamen and 26 Armed Guards; the latter suffers no injuries. Both ships are repaired and returned to service.

20 Thursday

ATLANTIC. Tenth Fleet with headquarters in Washington, D.C., is established under Commander in Chief U.S. Fleet (Admiral Ernest J. King) to control U.S. antisubmarine operations in the Atlantic.

PACIFIC. Submarine *Pollack* (SS 180) sinks Japanese armed merchant cruiser *Bangkok Maru* southeast of Jaluit, Marshalls, 06°47′N, 169°42′E. *Pollack* is damaged by depth charges during counterattacks by what she describes as a "*Chidori*-class torpedo boat," but remains on patrol.

21 Friday

ATLANTIC. TBFs (VC 9) from auxiliary aircraft carrier *Bogue* (ACV 9) damage German submarine *U 231*; destroyer *Osmond Ingram* (DD 255) and Canadian destroyer HMCS *St. Laurent* drive off U-boats menacing ON 184.

MEDITERRANEAN. Destroyer *Nields* (DD 616) sinks Italian submarine *Gorgo* as she attacks a U.S. convoy off Algeria, 36°01′N, 00°34′W.

INDIAN OCEAN. Last eight survivors from U.S. freighter *John Drayton*, sunk by Italian submarine *Leonardo da Vinci* on 21 April, are rescued. Originally, 24 men had been in the boat found this date; only the eight remain. A total of 21 merchant seamen and six Armed Guard sailors perish in the loss of *John Drayton*.

22 Saturday

PACIFIC. Japanese land attack planes (752nd *Kokutai*) attack gunboat *Charleston* (PG 51) and destroyer *Phelps* (DD 360) off Attu, Aleutians; both ships emerge unscathed and splash one BETTY.

ATLANTIC. Battle to protect ON 184 in the North Atlantic continues. TBFs (VC 9) from auxiliary aircraft carrier *Bogue* (ACV 9) sink German submarine *U 569*, 50°40′N, 35°21′W,[142] and damage *U 305*.

MEDITERRANEAN. Advanced Amphibious Training Base, Tunis, Tunisia, is established.

23 Sunday

PACIFIC. Motor torpedo boat tender *Niagara* (AGP 1), damaged by horizontal bomber while en route from Tulagi to New Guinea, is scuttled by motor torpedo boat *PT 147*, 11°00′S, 163°00 E.

Motor torpedo boats *PT 165* and *PT 173* are lost on board U.S. tanker *Stanvac Manila* when Japanese submarine *I 17* torpedoes the tanker (which is transporting the boats) 100 miles south of Nouméa, New Caledonia, 23°45′S, 166°30′E.[143]

Japanese heavy cruiser *Mogami* is damaged in collision with fleet tanker *Toa Maru* in Tokyo Bay.

ATLANTIC. British Swordfish from escort carrier HMS *Archer* irreparably damage German submarine *U 752* in the North Atlantic with rocket projectiles in the first use of those particular weapons during World War II. *U 752* is scuttled to prevent capture.

25 Tuesday

GENERAL. TRIDENT Conference ends. President Roosevelt and British Prime Minister Winston S. Churchill reaffirm earlier decisions to accord first priority to defeating Germany and agree to step up the strategic bombing of Germany and occupied Europe as a preliminary for a cross-channel invasion; to sever Italy from the axis following the capture of Sicily (Operation HUSKY); to bomb the Ploesti (Romania) oil fields from bases in the Mediterranean; to increase aid to, and communication with, China; and to plan the invasion of northwestern Europe to take place on 1 May 1944 (Operation OVERLORD). General approval is accorded the U.S. plan for advancing across the Central Pacific toward Japan.

ATLANTIC. PBY (VP 84) sinks German submarine *U 467* south-southeast of Iceland, 62°25′N, 14°52′W.

MEDITERRANEAN. USAAF B-17s and B-24s (Northwest African Air Forces) bomb harbor installations at Messina, Italy, sinking Italian torpedo boat *Groppo*.

26 Wednesday

PACIFIC. "KE GO" Operation (first phase) begins: Japanese commence evacuation of troops from Kiska, Aleutians, to Paramushir, Kurils, via submarines. Between 26 May and 21 June, 13 boats will be involved in the operation that will eventually extricate 820 men. Three boats, however, will be sunk (see 10, 13, and 22 June) and three (*I 2, I 155,* and *I 157*) damaged.

Gunboat *Charleston* (PG 51) bombards Japanese positions in the Chichagof area, Attu, Aleutians, starting numerous fires.

Submarine *Pogy* (SS 266), in attack on Japanese convoy, sinks freighter *Tainan Maru* off Shioya Saki, Honshu, 37°03′N, 141°09′E.

Submarine *Saury* (SS 189) attacks Japanese convoy south of Kyushu, sinking transport *Kagi Maru* some 10 miles north of the Nansei Shoto, 28°49′N, 129°40′E.

Submarine *Trout* (SS 202) lands party of men, $10,000 in currency, and equipment on Basilan Island, P.I., to set up an intelligence unit in the Sulu Archipelago and at Zamboanga, to set up a coastwatcher network in the area and to conduct surveys, and to arrange for the delivery of further supplies to guerrilla units.

Submarine *Whale* (SS 239) sinks Japanese gunboat *Shoei Maru* (transporting men of the Guam Base Detachment) about 17 miles north-northwest of Rota, Marianas, 14°17′N, 144°54′E.

Japanese merchant tanker *Palembang Maru* is damaged by mine, possibly laid by *Trout* (SS 202) on 7 April, off coast of Borneo, 02°00′N, 109°15′E.

27 Thursday

PACIFIC. Submarine *Finback* (SS 230) sinks Japanese army cargo ship *Kochi Maru* about 75 miles northwest of Palau, 08°23′N, 134°06′E.

Submarine *Runner* (SS 275) departs Midway for her third war patrol. She is never heard from again.[144]

ATLANTIC. German submarine *U 154* attacks Brazil-to-Trinidad convoy BT 14 at 03°56′S, 36°43′W, torpedoing three U.S. merchantmen: motor tanker *Florida*, freighter *Cardinal Gibbons*, and freighter *John Worthington*. Submarine chaser *PC 592* rescues *Florida*'s crew; there are no casualties among the 52-man merchant complement or the 27-man Armed Guard. Gunboat *Saucy* (PG 65) takes the seriously damaged tanker in tow and brings her to Fortaleza, Brazil. Salvage vessel *Crusader* (ARS 2) subsequently tows *Florida* to Puerto Rico for repairs.

Naval Station, Coco Solo, Canal Zone, is established.

28 Friday

PACIFIC. Submarine *S 41* (SS 146) sinks Japanese barkentine *Asuka Maru* off Paramushir, Kurils, 50°38′N, 155°15′E.

Submarine *Saury* (SS 189) sinks Japanese fleet tanker *Akatsuki Maru* about 90 miles northwest of Okinawa, 27°32′N, 126°08′E. Although early in the battle *Akatsuki Maru* responds to the submarine's attack with depth charges and gunfire, and later claims to have sunk her assailant, her efforts at self-defense prove unavailing and *Saury* emerges the victor.

Submarine *Trigger* (SS 237) damages Japanese merchant tanker *Koshin Maru* off Iro Saki, Japan, 34°33′N, 138°50′E.

ATLANTIC. German submarine *U 177* attacks convoy CD 20 and sinks U.S. freighter *Agwimonte*, 34°57′S, 19°33′E; there are no casualties among the 46-man merchant complement or 23-man Armed Guard and South African Navy whaler *Vereeniging* rescues most of *Agwimonte*'s crew. An army crash boat rescues the remainder of the men the next day.

29 Saturday

PACIFIC. Submarine chaser *SC 669* sinks Japanese submarine *I 178*, 30 miles west of Espíritu Santo, New Hebrides, 15°35′S, 166°17′E.

Submarine *Gar* (SS 206) sinks Japanese gunboat *Aso Maru* southeast of Cayagan, Sulu Sea, 09°09′N, 121°50′E.

Submarine *Scamp* (SS 277) sinks Japanese seaplane carrier *Kamikawa Maru* north of Kavieng, New Ireland, 01°36′S, 150°24′E, and survives attacks by one of the submarine chasers escorting her, *Ch 12* or *Ch 37*.

Submarine *Tambor* (SS 198) sinks Japanese freighter *Eisho Maru* (ex-Panamanian *Folozu*) in South China Sea about 60 miles southeast of Hainan Island, 17°30′N, 110°55′E.

Submarine *Tinosa* (SS 283) unsuccessfully attacks Japanese cargo vessel *Shinto Maru* off east coast of Kyushu, 32°00′N, 131°51′E.

30 Sunday

PACIFIC. Organized Japanese resistance ends on Attu, Aleutians.

Submarine *Saury* (SS 189) attacks Japanese convoy, sinking freighter *Hakozaki Maru* and army cargo ship *Takamisan Maru* about 150 miles east-southeast of Shanghai, China, 30°07′N, 124°32′E.

Submarine *Steelhead* (SS 280) lays mines off Erimo Saki, Japan.

ATLANTIC. German submarine *U 126* torpedoes U.S. freighter *Flora McDonald* off the west coast of Africa, 07°20′N, 13°15′W; escorting trawler HMS *Fandango* rescues *Flora McDonald*'s survivors and proceeds to Freetown, Sierra Leone. British tug HMS *Zwarte Zee*, escorted by British sloop HMS *Milford* and corvettes HMS *Woodruff* and HMS *Tamarisk*, proceed to the blazing freighter's assistance (see 1 June).

MEDITERRANEAN. Tank landing craft *LCT 28* is sunk by mine, Mediterranean Sea.

31 Monday

ATLANTIC. Light cruisers *Milwaukee* (CL 5) and *Omaha* (CL 4) are damaged in collision off the coast of Brazil.

JUNE

1 Tuesday

PACIFIC. Submarine *Trigger* (SS 237) sinks Japanese merchant collier *Noborikawa Maru* off Kominato, southern Honshu, 35°02′N, 140°14′E.

ATLANTIC. U.S. freighter *Flora McDonald*, torpedoed by German submarine *U 126* off the west coast of Africa on 30 May, is beached at Freetown, Sierra Leone, to facilitate salvage. She burns for 16 days, however (part of her cargo includes rubber), and she is subsequently written off as a total loss.

U.S. freighter *John Morgan* and U.S. tanker *Montana* collide in Norfolk Swept Channel, 36°59′N, 75°78′W; *John Morgan* explodes and sinks immediately while fires break out on board *Montana*. Salvage vessel (NRTS) *Relief* and fleet tug *Choctaw* (AT 70) tow *Montana* to Smith Island Shoal, where she is beached; the fire is extinguished the following day.

2 Wednesday

PACIFIC. Submarine *Tambor* (SS 198) sinks Japanese transport *Eika Maru* (ex-Portuguese *Wing Wah*) in Tonkin Gulf off coast of French Indochina, 20°29′N, 107°57′E.

ATLANTIC. Submarine chaser *PC 565* sinks German submarine *U 521* off Virginia capes, 37°43′N, 73°16′W.

3 Thursday

INDIAN OCEAN. U.S. freighter *Montanan* is torpedoed and sunk by Japanese submarine *I 27* off the Arabian coast, 17°58′N, 58°09′E. Six of the 42-man merchant complement and two of the 23-man Armed Guard are lost. Dhow *Naranpasha* comes across one boatload of survivors and transfers them to Indian Navy trawler RINS *Baroda*, which eventually transports them to Port Okah, India; the remaining three boatloads of survivors reach shore on Masirah Island, off Oman.

4 Friday

PACIFIC. Submarine *Silversides* (SS 236) mines Steffen Strait between New Hanover and New Ireland.

ATLANTIC. TBFs (VC 9) from auxiliary aircraft carrier *Bogue* (ACV 9) damage German submarines *U 228*, *U 603*, and *U 641* west by north of the Canary Islands, 31°50′N, 43°25′W.

MEDITERRANEAN. Submarine chaser *PC 496* is sunk by mine off Bizerte, Tunisia, 37°23′N, 09°52′E.

5 Saturday

PACIFIC. TBFs and SBDs, covered by F4Us and USAAF P-40s and P-38s, bomb Japanese shipping, Bougainville; army cargo ship *Shintoku Maru* is sunk southwest of Buin, 07°00′S, 155°33′E.

ATLANTIC. TBF (VC 9) from auxiliary aircraft carrier *Bogue* (ACV 9) sinks German submarine *U 217* west by north of the Canary Islands, 30°18′N, 42°50′W.

6 Sunday

PACIFIC. Submarine *S 30* (SS 135) sinks Japanese freighter *No. 3 Nagashige Maru* south of Kamchatka, 50°45′N, 156°56′E.

Submarine *Tautog* (SS 199) sinks Japanese army cargo ship *Shinei Maru* in Moro Gulf, off Zamboanga, 07°00′N, 123°37′E.

INDIAN OCEAN. U.S. tanker *William King* is sunk by German submarine *U 198* off the South African coast, 30°34′S, 33°56′E; while six of the 42-man merchant complement perish in the sinking, there are no casualties among the 23-man Armed Guard. *U 198* surfaces and brings the lifeboats alongside, however, and takes ship's master Owen H. Reed prisoner before departing (see 8 and 12 June).[145]

8 Tuesday

PACIFIC. Submarine *Finback* (SS 230) attacks Japanese convoy, sinking auxiliary minelayer *Kahoku Maru* about 100 miles north of Palau, 08°14′N, 134°18′E.

Naval Air Facility, Attu, Aleutians, is established.

Japanese battleship *Mutsu* is sunk by accidental explosion, Hiroshima Bay, Japan, 34°05′N, 132°20′E.

INDIAN OCEAN. British trawler HMS *Northern Chief* rescues survivors from U.S. tanker

William King, sunk by German submarine *U 198* off the South African coast on 6 June (see 12 June).

ATLANTIC. TBF (VC 9) from auxiliary aircraft carrier *Bogue* (ACV 9) damages German submarine *U 758* west by south of the Canary Islands, 29°19′N, 33°05′W.[146]

9   Wednesday

PACIFIC. Submarine *Greenling* (SS 213) damages Japanese oiler *Akebono Maru* en route to Truk, 02°17′N, 145°38′E.

UNITED STATES. Naval Academy Class of 1944 is graduated one year early because of the national emergency.

10   Thursday

PACIFIC. Submarine chaser *PC 487* is damaged when she rams and sinks Japanese submarine *I 24* (engaged in "KE GO" Operation), 40 miles north-northeast of Shemya Island, Aleutians, 53°16′N, 174°24′E.

Submarine *Flying Fish* (SS 229) unsuccessfully attacks Japanese cargo vessel *Fujikawa Maru* off Iwo Jima, 24°55′N, 145°36′E.

Submarine *S 30* (SS 135) sinks Japanese freighter *Jimbu Maru* off Paramushir, Kurils, 50°23′N, 155°36′E.

Submarine *Tinosa* (SS 283) damages Japanese oiler *Iro* 30 miles off Fuka Island, Kyushu, 31°14′N, 132°44′E. Although damaged by depth charges during enemy counterattacks, the submarine remains on patrol.

Submarine *Trigger* (SS 237) damages Japanese carrier *Hiyo* 18 miles off Iro Saki, 34°13′N, 139°50′E.

Japanese river gunboat *Atami* is damaged by Chinese aircraft near Tung Ting Lake, China.

ATLANTIC. U.S. tanker *Esso Gettysburg*, en route from Port Arthur, Texas, to Philadelphia, Pennsylvania, is sunk by German submarine *U 66* at 31°02′N, 79°15′E; intense fires, fed by the ship's cargo of crude oil, prevent boats from being launched, and only seven of the 27-man Armed Guard and eight of the 45-man merchant complement survive the inferno that consumes the ship. For his heroism in ordering the forward gun manned and opening fire on the attacking U-boat, Ensign John S. Arnold II, USNR, commanding the Armed Guard, will receive the Navy Cross. Steamship *George Washington* rescues the few survivors.

German submarine *U 118* is attacked by a TBF from auxiliary aircraft carrier *Bogue* (ACV 9), 12 June 1943; large splash is from a depth bomb, small splashes from machine gun fire. German sailors take shelter on the starboard side of the conning tower; note the prominent mine chutes forward. (NA, 80-G-68694)

11   Friday

PACIFIC. Submarine *Finback* (SS 230) attacks Japanese Palau-bound convoy just west of Babelthuap, sinking army cargo ship *Genoa Maru*, 07°36′N, 134°17′E. *Patrol Boat No. 46*'s counterattack fails to inflict damage, and *Finback* escapes.

Submarine *Runner* (SS 275) perhaps (see 27 May) sinks Japanese freighter *Seinan Maru* off Monomi Saki, Honshu, 41°00′N, 141°30′E.

Submarine *S 30* (SS 135) sinks Japanese merchant cargo vessel *Jimbu Maru*, anchored in Kakumabetsu Wan, Paramushir, Kurils, 50°23′N, 155°36′E.

Submarine *Silversides* (SS 236) attacks Japanese convoy about 270 miles south of Truk, sinking transport *Hinode Maru* north of New Ireland, 02°43′N, 152°00′E.

12   Saturday

PACIFIC. Submarine *Trout* (SS 202) lands men and supplies on Mindanao, P.I.

ATLANTIC. TBF (VC 9) from auxiliary aircraft carrier *Bogue* (ACV 9) sinks German submarine *U 118* west by north of the Canary Islands, 30°49′N, 33°49′W.

Submarine *R 12* (SS 89) sinks (cause unknown) off Key West, Florida, 24°24.30′N, 81°38.30′W.

INDIAN OCEAN. British destroyer HMS *Relentless* rescues last survivors from U.S. tanker *William King*, sunk by German submarine *U 198* off the South African coast on 6 June.

13   Sunday

PACIFIC. Destroyer *Frazier* (DD 607) sinks Japanese submarine *I 9* (engaged in "KE GO" Operation) east of Sirius Point, Kiska, Aleutians, 52°08′N, 177°38′E.

Submarine *Guardfish* (SS 217) sinks Japanese army cargo ship *Suzuya Maru* off the southwest coast of New Ireland, 03°08′S, 151°24′E.

Submarine *Sargo* (SS 188) attacks Japanese convoy 250 miles south of Yap, Carolines, sinks army transport *Konan Maru*, 06°08′N, 138°28′E, and although damaged by depth charges, 06°40′N, 136°59′E, remains on patrol.

ATLANTIC. Coast Guard cutter *Escanaba* (WPG 77) is sunk by explosion off Ivigtut, Greenland, 60°50′N, 52°00′W. An investigation into *Escanaba*'s loss yields no concrete findings. Investigators conclude the "most

During June 1943, destroyer *Greer* (DD 145) escorted two Atlantic convoys, UGS 8 east-bound and GUS 8 west-bound. In this view, she encounters some of the frequently rough seas often common to that area of the world; discernible are some of the modifications made to the venerable "flush-deckers" to suit them for escort work: depth charge projectors ("K"-guns), 3-inch/.50-caliber antiair-craft guns amidships, and in foreground, the after mount replaces one bank of torpedo tubes. The 26-foot motor whaleboat is swung out in the "ready" position. (NA, 80-G-42021)

probable explanation" is "mine, torpedo, or internal explosion of magazine and depth charges." The evidence, however, proves "not sufficiently conclusive to attach cause directly or even remotely" to those causes. The German U-boat high command war diary records no submarine attacks against the convoy being escorted by *Escanaba* at the time of her loss.

14 Monday

PACIFIC. Submarine *Sargo* (SS 188) is damaged by depth charges off the Palaus, 06°40′N, 136°59′E, but remains on patrol.

ATLANTIC. U.S. freighter *William H. Webb* is mined while en route from Baltimore, Maryland, to Casablanca, French Morocco, and returns whence she had come for repairs. There are no casualties among the 42-man merchant complement, the sole passenger, and the 30-man Armed Guard.

15, Tuesday

PACIFIC. Submarine *Gunnel* (SS 253) sinks Japanese merchant passenger-cargo ship *Koyo Maru* in Tsushima Strait, 33°55′N, 127°38′E.

Submarine *Sailfish* (SS 192) sinks Japanese freighter *Shinju Maru* south of Todo Saki, Honshu, 39°00′N, 142°00′E.

Submarine *Trout* (SS 202) damages Japanese oiler *Sanraku Maru* in the Celebes Sea, off Sibitu, 05°09′N, 119°38′E; *Sanraku Maru* is eventually scuttled, 04°45′N, 119°48′E.

16 Wednesday

PACIFIC. In the largest raid since 7 April, Japanese aircraft attack ships off Guadalcanal. While a large number of enemy planes are shot down, tank landing ship *LST 340*, damaged by dive bombers, is beached off Lunga Point, 09°26′S, 160°05′E; cargo ship *Celeno* (AK 76) is also damaged, 09°24′S, 160°02′E.

17 Thursday

PACIFIC. Submarine *Drum* (SS 228) attacks Japanese convoy, sinking transport *Myoko Maru* about 175 miles east-northeast of Kavieng, New Ireland, 02°03′S, 153°44′E.

Submarine chaser *SC 740* sinks after running aground off northeastern coast of Australia, 15°32′S, 147°06′E.

MEDITERRANEAN. Tank landing ships *LST 6* and *LST 326* are damaged in collision off Algerian coast, 37°18′N, 09°51′E.

18 Friday

PACIFIC. Submarine *S 33* (SS 138) damages two Japanese fishing craft off Paramushir, Kurils, 50°25′N, 155°02′E.

19 Saturday

PACIFIC. Submarine *Guardfish* (SS 217) is damaged by depth charges north of Bismarck Archipelago, 02°00′N, 148°14′E, but remains on patrol.

Submarine *Growler* (SS 215), in attack on Japanese convoy on the Palau-to-Rabaul route, sinks army cargo ship *Miyadono Maru* about 200 miles north-northwest of Mussau Island, 01°38′N, 148°14′E.

Submarine *Gunnel* (SS 253) damages Japanese gunboat *Hong Kong Maru* (ex-Philippine *Argus*) and sinks freighter *Tokiwa Maru*, off Shirase, Japan, 32°40′N, 126°37′E, and coastal minesweeper *Tsubame*, 32°31′N, 126°17′E.

Submarine *Sculpin* (SS 191) sinks Japanese guardboat *No. 1 Miyasho Maru* and army cargo ship *Sagami Maru* off Inubo Saki, Japan, 37°11′N, 142°30′E.

INDIAN OCEAN. U.S. freighter *Henry Knox*, en route from Fremantle, Australia, to Bandar Shahpur, Iran, is torpedoed and sunk by Japanese submarine *I 37* at 00°05′S, 69°50′E. Although *I 37* surfaces and conducts an extensive questioning of the survivors in one boat, the Japanese take no action against the men, who begin sailing toward the Maldives, 200 miles distant, upon the enemy's departure (see 27, 28, and 30 June).

20 Sunday
PACIFIC. Submarine *Seawolf* (SS 197) sinks Japanese freighter *Shojin Maru* in Formosa Strait, 24°39′N, 118°58′E.

Submarine *Tautog* (SS 199) sinks Japanese transport *Meiten Maru* west of the Marianas, 15°57′N, 140°55′E.

ATLANTIC. PBY (VP 84) sinks German submarine *U 388* south-southwest of Iceland, 57°36′N, 31°20′W, in the first use of homing torpedo (FIDO) and damages *U 420*.

U.S. freighter *Santa Maria* is damaged by mine laid by German submarine *U 214* five miles off Dakar, French West Africa, 14°34′18″N, 17°28′23″W, and is towed back to Dakar by French tugs. While there are no casualties among the merchant complement, one sailor of the 30-man Armed Guard is blown overboard and lost.

Covered lighter *YF 401* founders in heavy weather off Virginia capes, 35°7′N, 69°00′W.

MEDITERRANEAN. Tank landing craft *LCT 208* founders after grounding off coast of Algeria.

21 Monday
PACIFIC. Fourth Raider Battalion, USMC, lands at Segi Point, New Georgia, Solomons.

Submarine *Harder* (SS 257) damages Japanese oiler *No. 3 Kyoei Maru* east of Daio Saki, Japan, 34°30′N, 137°32′E.

Submarine *Hoe* (SS 258) attacks Japanese vessel *Koyo Maru* west-northwest of Palau, 08°58′N, 131°13′E; although *Hoe* claims a sinking, *Koyo Maru* survives the encounter with no damage.

Japanese gunboat *Hong Kong Maru* sinks as the result of damage inflicted by submarine *Gunnel* (SS 253) off Shirase, Japan, on 19 June.

22 Tuesday
PACIFIC. While engaged in "KE GO" Operation, Japanese submarine *I 7* is damaged by destroyer *Monaghan* (DD 354) 10 miles south of Cape Hita and runs aground, irreparably damaged, 12 miles south-southwest of Kiska, Aleutians, 51°49′N, 177°20′E.[147]

Submarine *Grayling* (SS 209) damages Japanese merchant oiler *Eiyo Maru* off coast of Malaya, 04°03′N, 103°57′E.

Submarine chaser *SC 751* sinks after grounding off western Australia, 21°56′S, 113°53′E.

ATLANTIC. Planes from auxiliary aircraft carrier *Santee* (ACV 29) attack German submarine *U 572*, limiting the damage the latter can inflict on convoy UGS 10.

MEDITERRANEAN. Tank landing ships *LST 333* and *LST 387* (both carrying landing pontoons) are torpedoed by German submarine *U 593* about five miles east of Dellys, Algeria, 36°59′N, 04°02′E. *LST 333* is beached; *LST 387* is towed to Dellys by tank landing craft *LCT 294* and *LCT 431*. Damaging of these two particular LSTs hampers training for the forthcoming invasion of Sicily (Operation HUSKY).

23 Wednesday
PACIFIC. Japanese submarine *RO 103* sinks cargo ship *Aludra* (AK 72) and torpedoes cargo ship *Deimos* (AK 78) while both are in convoy en route to Guadalcanal, 11°26′S, 162°01′E. *Deimos*, irreparably damaged, is scuttled by destroyer *O'Bannon* (DD 450), 11°26′S, 162°01′E.

Submarine *Harder* (SS 257) damages Japanese seaplane carrier *Sagara Maru* off southern Honshu, 33°45′N, 138°10′E (see 4 July).[148]

SBDs and TBFs, with F4F escort, bomb Japanese antiaircraft positions at Rekata Bay; this attack may have been responsible for the sinking of Japanese guardboat *Nikka Maru* north of Bougainville, 05°34′N, 155°07′E. TBFs and USAAF B-25s (13th Air Force), escorted by F4Us, bomb Buki village, Ganongga Island, New Georgia.

USAAF B-24s (5th Air Force) bomb Makassar, N.E.I., hitting port area and shipping; during the raid, light cruiser *Kinu* is damaged by near-misses.

24 Thursday
PACIFIC. Submarine *Snook* (SS 279) damages Japanese oiler *Ose* west of Amami-O-Shima, 28°50′N, 126°56′E.

ATLANTIC. PBY (VP 84) sinks German submarine *U 200* southwest by south of Iceland, 59°00′N, 26°18′W.

Harbor tug *YT 211* is damaged by storm off Casablanca, 33°38′N, 07°32′W.

25 Friday
PACIFIC. Submarine *Sailfish* (SS 192) attacks Japanese convoy, sinking army collier *Iburi Maru* off northeast coast of Honshu, 39°00′N, 142°00′E.

ATLANTIC. U.S. tanker *Eagle*, en route to Bahia, is torpedoed by German submarine *U 513* about eight miles southeast of Cape Frio, Brazil, at 31°02′N, 79°15′E; Armed Guard gunfire keeps the U-boat submerged while the ship returns to Rio de Janeiro for repairs. There are no casualties among the 41 merchant sailors or the 12-man Armed Guard.

26 Saturday
PACIFIC. Submarine *Jack* (SS 259) attacks Japanese convoy, sinking transports *Shozan Maru* and *Toyo Maru* off Hachijo Jima, southern Honshu, Japan, 33°22′N, 138°56′E. Although damaged by a Japanese aerial bomb during enemy counterattacks, *Jack* continues on patrol.

Submarine *Runner* (SS 275) perhaps (see 27 May) sinks Japanese army cargo ship *Shinryu Maru* off Matsuwa Island, Kurils, 48°06′N, 153°15′E.

27 Sunday
MEDITERRANEAN. Salvage vessel *Redwing* (ARS 4) is sunk by underwater explosion (possibly an enemy mine) off coast of North Africa, 37°19′N, 09°56′E.

INDIAN OCEAN. U.S. freighter *Sebastian Cermeno*, en route from Mombasa, Kenya, to Bahia, Brazil, is torpedoed and sunk by German submarine *U 511* at 29°00′S, 50°10′E; after *U 511* surfaces to question the survivors, the enemy submarine submerges and retires from the area (see 8, 13, 14, 23, and 27 July).

First group of survivors of U.S. freighter *Henry Knox*, sunk by Japanese submarine *I 37* on 19 June, reaches the Maldives (see 28 and 30 June).

28 Monday
PACIFIC. Submarine *Peto* (SS 265) sinks Japanese hydrographic-meteorological research ship *Tenkai No. 2* northeast of Mussau Island, 01°47′N, 151°46′E.

Submarine *Tunny* (SS 282) sinks Japanese gunboat *Shotoku Maru* off west coast of Rota, Marianas, 14°10′N, 145°03′E.

INDIAN OCEAN. Second group of survivors of U.S. freighter *Henry Knox*, sunk by Japanese submarine *I 37* on 19 June, reaches the Maldives (see 30 June).

29 Tuesday

PACIFIC. Submarine *Gurnard* (SS 254) unsuccessfully attacks Japanese convoy, 07°34′N, 134°26′E.

Japanese cargo vessel *No. 8 Mikage Maru* is sunk in collision with *Nikko Maru* 30 miles west of Iwanni, northern coast of Hokkaido, 45°04′N, 142°03′E.

Naval Auxiliary Air Facility, Shemya, Alaska, is established.

30 Wednesday

GENERAL. Naval ships and craft on hand (all types): 18,493. People: Navy—1,741,750; Marine Corps—310,994; Coast Guard—154,976; total—2,207,720.

PACIFIC. Beginning shortly before midnight on 29 June, four cruisers and four destroyers of TU 36.2.1 (Rear Admiral Aaron S. Merrill) bombard Vila-Stanmore on Kolombangara and Buin-Shortland, Bougainville, Solomons; TU 36.2.2—light minelayers *Preble* (DM 20), *Gamble* (DM 15), and *Breese* (DM 18)—sow mines off Shortland Harbor, Bougainville, between Alu and Munda Islands. *Gamble* also lays mines off New Georgia.

Operation TOENAILS: TF 31 (Rear Admiral Richmond Kelly Turner), supported by land-based aircraft (Vice Admiral Aubrey W. Fitch) and destroyer gunfire, lands New Georgia Occupation Force (Major General John H. Hester, USA). Army troops (172nd Infantry, 43rd Division) go ashore on Rendova without opposition. Marines (Fourth Raider Battalion, USMC) land on New Georgia and begin move toward Viru Harbor (see 1 July). Destroyer *Gwin* (DD 433) is damaged off Munda by Japanese shore battery. Attack transport *McCawley* (APA 4) (Rear Admiral Turner's flagship) is damaged by Japanese torpedoes from land attack planes (702nd or 705th *Kokutais*) off New Georgia. Turner transfers his flag to destroyer *Farenholt* (DD 491); destroyer *Ralph Talbot* (DD 390) removes all unnecessary crew and wounded while attack cargo ship *Libra* (AKA 12) takes the damaged transport in tow. Destroyer *McCalla* (DD 488) removes remainder of crew; tug *Pawnee* (AT 74) relieves *Libra* of tow. *McCawley*, however, is later accidentally torpedoed by U.S. motor torpedo boat and sinks, 08°25′S, 157°28′W. High-speed minesweeper *Zane* (DMS 14) is damaged by grounding off Onaiavisi Island, 08°30′S, 157°25′E, but is towed off the beach by tug *Rail* (AT 139).

Operation CHRONICLE: TF 76 (Rear Admiral Daniel E. Barbey) lands troops on Woodlark and Kiriwina Islands, off southeastern coast of New Guinea, the former from tank landing ships (LST), and the latter from infantry landing craft (LCI). Airstrip construction soon begins on Woodlark (see 23 July).

Seaplane tender (destroyer) *Hulbert* (AVD 6) is damaged by grounding off Alexai Point, Massacre Bay, Aleutians.[149]

INDIAN OCEAN. Last survivors of U.S. freighter *Henry Knox*, sunk by Japanese submarine *I 37* on 19 June, reaches the Maldives. From *Henry Knox's* complement, 13 of 42-man merchant sailors perish, as do 13 of the 25-man Armed Guard.

ATLANTIC. Coast Guard cutter *CGC 83421* is sunk, and submarine chaser *SC 1330* damaged in collision en route to Miami, Florida.

JULY

1 Thursday

PACIFIC. Submarine *Gar* (SS 206) lands commandoes on south coast of Timor, N.E.I.

Submarine *Gurnard* (SS 254) unsuccessfully attacks Japanese landing craft/aircraft transport *Akitsu Maru* east of the Palaus, 07°39′N, 134°20′E.

Submarine *Thresher* (SS 200) attacks Japanese convoy off the northwest coast of Celebes, in Makassar Strait, damaging destroyer *Hokaze*, 00°43′N, 119°34′E, and sinking army cargo ship *Yoneyama Maru*, 00°20′N, 119°32′E, 38 miles from Balikpapan. *Hokaze* is grounded in Sibaya Harbor, Celebes, to facilitate salvage.

Motor torpedo boat *PT 162*, operating out of Rendova, is damaged by Japanese plane, south of Mbalumbala Island.

Marines of Fourth Raider Battalion, USMC, landed on New Georgia Island the day before by TF 31, seize their objective, Viru Harbor.

Naval Operating Base, Espíritu Santo, New Hebrides, is established.

2 Friday

PACIFIC. Japanese naval and army aircraft bomb Rendova, New Georgia, Solomons; light cruiser *Yubari* and nine destroyers bombard the beachhead. Motor torpedo boats *PT 156*, *PT 157*, and *PT 161* engage the enemy, but inflict no damage; *PT 153* and *PT 158*, damaged by grounding off Kolombangara, 08°20′S, 157°15′E, are beached and abandoned.

Submarine *Flying Fish* (SS 229) sinks Japanese merchant troopship *Canton Maru* off China coast, about 80 miles northeast of Amoy, 25°07′N, 119°18′E.

Submarine *S 35* (SS 140) sinks Japanese crab-catcher *No. 7 Banshu Maru* off the west coast of the Kamchatka Peninsula, 52°30′N, 156°12′E.

Submarine *Trout* (SS 202) sinks Japanese army cargo ship *Isuzu Maru* off north coast of Marinduque Island, P.I., 13°36′N, 121°49′E.

USAAF B-25 (13th Air Force), covered by F4Us, sink Japanese auxiliary minelayer *Kashi Maru* off Bairoko Harbor, New Georgia.

ATLANTIC. U.S. tanker *Bloody Marsh*, en route from Houston, Texas, to New York City, is torpedoed and sunk by German submarine *U 66* at 32°45′N, 78°45′W; three merchant sailors are lost in the initial explosion (see 3 July).

3 Saturday

PACIFIC. Submarine *Scorpion* (SS 278) attacks Japanese convoy in the Yellow Sea and sinks freighters *Anzan Maru* and *Kokuryu Maru*, 38°20′N, 124°25′E.

ATLANTIC. U.S. freighter *Elihu B. Washburne* is torpedoed and sunk by German submarine *U 513* off the coast of Brazil at 24°05′S, 45°25′W; all hands survive the attack (see 4 July).

Submarine chaser *SC 1048* rescues survivors (previously sighted by Navy blimp) from tanker *Bloody Marsh*, torpedoed and sunk by German submarine *U 66* the previous day.

4 Sunday

PACIFIC. Submarine *Jack* (SS 259) attacks Japanese convoy off Honshu, sinking army cargo ship *Nikkyu Maru* east-southeast of Omae Saki, 34°33′N, 138°37′E.

Submarine *Pompano* (SS 181) sinks Japanese seaplane carrier *Sagara Maru*, previously damaged by *Harder* (SS 257) on 23 June, west-southwest of Omae Saki, Honshu, 34°38′N, 137°53′E.

Submarine *Snook* (SS 279) attacks Takao, Formosa–bound Japanese convoy in the East China Sea, damaging transport *Atlantic Maru* and sinking army cargo ships *Liverpool Maru* and *Koki Maru* about 250 miles north-north-east of Keelung, 28°40′N, 124°10′E.

MEDITERRANEAN. Destroyer *Wilkes* (DD 441) is damaged by grounding off Bizerte, Tunisia, 37°18′N, 09°51′E.

ATLANTIC. Survivors (42 merchant sailors, three passengers, and the 25-man Armed Guard) of U.S. freighter *Elihu B. Washburne*, sunk by German submarine *U 513* the previous day, reach safety on the island of São Sabastião, Brazil.

5 Monday

PACIFIC. TG 36.1 (Rear Admiral Walden L. Ainsworth) bombards Vila, Kolombangara, and Bairoko Harbor, New Georgia, Solomons. That night, shortly before midnight, Rear Admiral Ainsworth's ships engage a force of Japanese destroyers (Rear Admiral Akiyama Teruo) in the Battle of Kula Gulf. Destroyer *Strong* (DD 467) is sunk by Japanese destroyer torpedo (fired by *Niizuki, Yunagi,* or *Nagatsuki*), 08°05′S, 157°15′E.

Marines (First Marine Raider Battalion) and Army troops land at Rice Anchorage, New Georgia, Solomons.

Japanese light cruiser *Yubari* is damaged by mine (laid by TBF in March/May) off Buin, Bougainville, but manages to reach Rabaul under her own power.

RAAF Beaufighters sink Japanese auxiliary sailing vessel *No. 12 Koyo Maru*, chartered to carry fuel, 35 miles west of Dobo, Tanahbesar Island, en route to Ambon, N.E.I.

CARIBBEAN. U.S. freighter *Maltran*, in convoy GTMO 134 and en route from Guantánamo Bay, Cuba, to Ponce, Puerto Rico, is torpedoed and sunk by German submarine *U 759* at 18°11′N, 74°57′W; submarine chaser *SC 1279* rescues all hands (35 merchant sailors and the 12-man Armed Guard).

ATLANTIC. Motor torpedo boat *PT 250* is damaged when accidentally grounded off Looe Key, Florida, 24°33′N, 81°25′E.

INDIAN OCEAN. U.S. freighter *Alcoa Prospector*, in convoy PA 44 and en route from Abadan, Iran, to Montevideo, Uruguay, is torpedoed by Japanese submarine *I 27* at 24°26′N, 58°20′E; Royal Indian Navy minesweeper RINS *Bengal* takes on board the survivors (see 6 July).

6 Tuesday

PACIFIC. Battle of Kula Gulf: TG 36.1 (Rear Admiral Walden L. Ainsworth), composed of three light cruisers and four destroyers, engages seven Japanese destroyers (Rear Admiral Akiyama Teruo), four of which (*Amagiri, Hatsuyuki, Nagatsuki,* and *Satsuki,* are carrying troops and supplies to Kolombangara, Solomons. Light cruiser *Helena* (CL 50) is sunk by *Suzukaze* and *Tanikaze,* 07°46′S, 157°11′E, but *Niizuki* is sunk by gunfire of a "*Brooklyn*-class light cruiser," what is most likely light cruiser *Honolulu* (CL 48), 07°50′S, 157°15′E; *Nagatsuki,* damaged by gunfire, is grounded and abandoned on the southeastern coast of Kolombangara. Gunfire from what is most likely *St. Louis* (CL 49) and *Honolulu* damages *Suzukaze;* gunfire damages *Amagiri;* gunfire

from *Honolulu* and what is most likely destroyers *Nicholas* (DD 449) and *O'Bannon* (DD 450) damage *Hatsuyuki;* and *Tanikaze* is hit by a dud shell. In the wake of the battle, while engaged in rescuing some of *Helena's* survivors, *Nicholas* and *Radford* (DD 446) engage *Amagiri* and *Hatsuyuki,* damaging both. Still later, SBDs, TBFs, and F4Fs bomb the beached *Nagatsuki* (see 10 July).

TG 16.7 (Rear Admiral Robert C. Giffen), consisting of three heavy cruisers, one light cruiser, and four destroyers, conducts unopposed bombardment of Kiska, Aleutians.

Submarine *Gurnard* (SS 254) is damaged by aerial bombs and depth charges off Palau, 07°33′N, 134°26′E, but remains on patrol.

Submarine *Permit* (SS 178) sinks Japanese freighter *No. 33 Banshu Maru* off west coast of Hokkaido, 43°35′N, 140°21′E.

PB4Y-1 (VB 102) attacks Japanese installations at Greenwich Island, but during the daring, low-level operation the plane is shot down by observation seaplanes (PETEs) (902nd *Kokutai*). Nevertheless, for his "conspicuous gallantry and intrepidity" displayed this day, the PB4Y's commander, Lieutenant Commander Bruce A. Van Voorhis, is awarded a Medal of Honor posthumously.

INDIAN OCEAN. U.S. freighter *Alcoa Prospector*, torpedoed by Japanese submarine *I 27* the previous day, is reboarded by the crew, as Royal Indian Navy RINS *Bengal* stands by (see 9 and 10 July).

ATLANTIC. U.S. freighter *Langdon Cheves* runs aground on Parramore Bank, about 30 miles north of Cape Henry, Virginia; while accompanying freighter *Joseph Lecorte* and submarine chaser *SC 717* stand by, tug *Sciota* (AT 30) and salvage vessel (NRTS) *Relief* proceed from Norfolk, Virginia. *Langdon Cheves* is refloated before the day is over.

7 Wednesday

PACIFIC. Motor torpedo boat *PT 161*, operating out of Rendova, is damaged by Japanese plane off Banieta Point.

Destroyer *Waller* (DD 466) fires upon and depth charges unidentified Japanese submarine off New Georgia, 08°00′S, 158°05′E.

Submarine *Permit* (SS 178) sinks Japanese freighter *Showa Maru* off Otaru, Hokkaido, Japan, 43°14′N, 139°53′E.

Submarine *Peto* (SS 265) damages Japanese oiler *Shinkoku Maru* north-northeast of the Admiralties, 00°35′N, 148°00′E.

Submarine *Plunger* (SS 179) damages Japanese freighter *Anzan Maru* in the Sea of Japan, 37°14′N, 132°57′E.

ATLANTIC. German submarine *U 185* carries out two attacks on convoy BT 18 off the coast of Brazil, torpedoing U.S. freighter *James Robertson* and tanker *William Boyce Thompson* at 04°00′S, 36°00′W, in the first assault. *James Robertson* careens through the columns of the convoy, colliding in succession with U.S. freighter *Alcoa Banner* and Brazilian *Cotazaloide* before she is abandoned. Submarine chaser *PC 575* rescues 21 men. *William Boyce Thompson,* which loses three men in the initial explosion (a fourth dies subsequently of his injuries), is abandoned, with the survivors being picked up by gunboat *Surprise* (PG 63) and a boat from the torpedoed *James Robertson.* A Brazilian ship subsequently rescues the latter as well as the remainder of that ship's survivors (but not before one Armed Guard sailor from *James Robertson* drowns) (see 9 July). *William Boyce Thompson* is later scuttled with gunfire and depth charges by escorts. In the second attack on BT 18, *U 185* torpedoes U.S. tanker *S. B. Hunt* and freighter *Thomas Sinnickson* at 03°51′S, 36°22′W. The former suffers no casualties to either the 37-man merchant complement or the 11-man Armed Guard, and ultimately makes port at Trinidad for temporary repairs; the latter loses one of the 27-man Armed Guard in the initial explosion but no casualties from its 43-man merchant complement, and remains afloat into the night while gunboat *Surprise* stands by and takes off 18 men (see 8 July).[150]

USAAF B-24 sinks German submarine *U 951* west of Cape St. Vincent, Portugal, 37°40′N, 15°30′W.

8 Thursday

PACIFIC. SBDs and TBFs, covered by F4Us, bomb Vila, Kolombangara, Solomons.

Submarine *Seal* (SS 183) is damaged by bombs and depth charges off northern Honshu, 39°53′N, 142°10′E, and is forced to terminate her patrol.

ATLANTIC. USAAF aircraft (2nd Antisubmarine Squadron) sink German submarine *U 232* off coast of Portugal, 40°37′N, 13°41′W.

U.S. freighter *Thomas Sinnickson,* torpedoed the previous day during German submarine *U 185*'s attack on convoy BT 18, defies the valiant efforts of her crew and continues to sink. Gunboat *Surprise* (PG 63), which has remained close at hand during the attempted salvage, takes off the remainder of the crew and Armed Guard and scuttles the irreparably damaged freighter.

German submarine *U 510* attacks convoy TJ 1 about 150 miles northeast of Cayenne,

French Guiana, 05°50′N, 50°20′W, and sinks U.S. freighter *Eldena*. Submarine chaser *PC 495* rescues all hands (including the 26-man Armed Guard).

MEDITERRANEAN. Tank landing craft *LCT 222* is disabled by mine off Bizerte, Tunisia.

INDIAN OCEAN. One group of survivors of freighter *Sebastian Cermeno*, sunk by German submarine *U 511* on 27 June, reaches safety at Madagascar (see 13, 14, 23, and 27 July).

9 Friday

PACIFIC. Destroyer *Aylwin* (DD 355), on Kiska blockade patrol, bombards Japanese positions in the Gertrude Cove area, drawing light and inaccurate return fire.

Four U.S. destroyers bombard Lambert Plantation near Munda, New Georgia, Solomons; TBFs and SBDs bomb the same area later the same day.

Submarine *Permit* (SS 178), believing her quarry to be a Japanese trawler, shells Soviet oceanographic vessel *Seiner No. 20* 27 miles off Kaiba To. Once the mistake is realized, *Permit* comes alongside the blazing vessel and rescues the survivors before the Russian craft sinks. The Soviet sailors are taken to Akutan, Alaska.

Submarine *Thresher* (SS 200) lands men, stores, and ammunition on west coast of Negros, P.I.

ATLANTIC. PBY (VP 94) sinks German submarine *U 590* at mouth of Amazon River, Brazil, 03°22′N, 48°18′W.

Two boats of survivors from freighter *James Robertson*, torpedoed and sunk by German submarine *U 185* on 7 July, reach the Brazilian coast, one at Fortaleza and the other at Cascavel.

MEDITERRANEAN. Ensign John J. Parle, USNR, officer-in-charge of small boats from tank landing ship *LST 375* off the island of Sicily, as preparations for Operation HUSKY proceed, becomes aware of the accidental ignition of a smoke pot in one of *LST 375*'s landing craft. Although fully aware of the hazards, Parle enters the boat, extinguishes a burning fuse, and when unable to put out the burning smoke pot, seizes it and throws it over the side, thus saving the ship from serious damage and preventing the premature disclosure of the impending landings. For his bravery, Ensign Parle, who succumbs to his injuries on 17 July, is awarded the Medal of Honor posthumously.

INDIAN OCEAN. Royal Indian Navy RINS *Bengal* fails in attempt to tow damaged freighter *Alcoa Prospector*, torpedoed by Japanese submarine *I 27* on 5 July (see 10 July).

U.S. freighter *Samuel Heintzelman*, en route from Fremantle, Australia, to Colombo, Ceylon, is torpedoed and sunk by German submarine *U 511* at 09°00′S, 81°00′E. There are no survivors from the 42-man merchant complement, the 27-man Armed Guard, and six passengers.

10 Saturday

PACIFIC. Submarine *Halibut* (SS 232) damages Japanese transport (ex-armed merchant cruiser) *Aikoku Maru* north-northwest of Truk, 10°27′N, 150°50′E.

Submarine *Pompano* (SS 181) damages Japanese oiler *Kyokuyo Maru* south of Shio Saki, 33°34′N, 136°07′N.

Submarine *Steelhead* (SS 280) damages Japanese escort carrier *Un'yo* north-northeast of Truk, 10°00′N, 150°48′E.

USAAF B-25s bomb wreck of beached Japanese destroyer *Nagatsuki* on southeastern coast of Kolombangara, Solomons.

MEDITERRANEAN. Operation HUSKY: Invasion of Sicily begins as troops land under cover of naval gunfire and aircraft. The overall commander is General Dwight D. Eisenhower, USA; naval commander is Admiral of the Fleet Sir Andrew B. Cunningham, RN. Western Naval Task Force (Vice Admiral H. Kent Hewitt) lands the U.S. Seventh Army (Lieutenant General George S. Patton, USA), and Eastern Naval Task Force (Vice Admiral Sir Bertram H. Ramsay, RN) lands British Eighth Army (British General Sir Bernard L. Montgomery). Naval gunfire will support the forces ashore throughout the Sicilian campaign. Off Sicily, Axis planes bomb invasion shipping and screening ships, sinking destroyer *Maddox* (DD 622), 36°52′N, 13°56′E; tank landing ship *LST 313*, 37°01′N, 14°15′E; and minesweeper *Sentinel* (AM 113), 37°06′N, 13°55′E. Collisions in the crowded waters off the beaches account for damage to destroyers *Roe* (DD 418) and *Swanson* (DD 443) at 37°03′N, 13°36′E, and *LST 345* and submarine chaser *PC 621* at 37°02′N, 14°15′E. Tank landing craft *LCT 242* is damaged by shore battery fire.

German submarine *U 371* attacks convoy off the Algerian coast, torpedoing U.S. freighter *Matthew Maury* at 37°00′N, 05°00′E, and tanker *Gulfprince* at 37°13′N, 05°12′E. There are no casualties on board the former (including the 28-man Armed Guard), which is towed to the port of Bougie and subsequently returns to service. The latter is abandoned by the 36-man merchant complement and 28-man Armed Guard, the survivors being rescued by British trawler HMS *Sir Gareth* and freighter *Empire Commerce*; one Armed Guard sailor dies of his wounds on board the latter. A salvage crew later boards *Gulfprince* and the ship is towed to Algiers by British salvage tugs HMS *Weazel* and HMS *Hudson*; she subsequently is chartered by the Navy for use as a mobile storage facility in North African waters.

INDIAN OCEAN. Anglo-Iranian oil company tugs tow damaged freighter *Alcoa Prospector*, torpedoed by Japanese submarine *I 27* on 5 July, into Bandar Abbas, Iran. Although there were no casualties inflicted by *I 27*'s attack, one merchant seaman dies of pneumonia.

U.S. freighter *Alice F. Palmer*, bound for Durban, South Africa, is torpedoed by German submarine *U 177* at 26°30′S, 44°10′E, and abandoned by the 43 merchant seamen and the 25-man Armed Guard. After the Germans question the survivors, *U 177* hastens the freighter's sinking by shelling her before she clears the area (see 13, 25, 26, and 30 July).

11 Sunday

PACIFIC. Destroyer *Monaghan* (DD 354) bombards Japanese positions at Gertrude Cove, Kiska Island, Aleutians.

Submarine *Flying Fish* (SS 229) sinks Japanese guardboat *No. 8 Takatori Maru* between Okino Daito Jima and Kazan Retto, 24°00′N, 135°25′E.

Submarine *Gurnard* (SS 254) attacks Japanese convoy, sinking army cargo ship *Taiko Maru* about 375 miles northeast of Palau, 13°08′N, 132°00′E.

PBYs attack Japanese guardboats off Kamchatka, sinking *Seiun Maru* and damaging *Koshin Maru*.

USAAF B-24s (14th Air Force) damage Vichy French customs vessel *Albert Sarraut* and Japanese cargo vessel *No. 3 Kiri Maru* 45 miles east of Haiphong, French Indochina.

MEDITERRANEAN. U.S. cruiser and destroyer gunfire stops German tank attack on landing beaches near Gela, Sicily; Army observers report 13 of the 50 tanks that make the attack are destroyed. Off the invasion beaches, enemy air attacks account for damage to tank landing ship *LST 158* off Licata (she is then beached and abandoned), 37°05′N, 13°55′E (*LST 318*, beached adjacent to her burning sister ship, retracts immediately to avoid damage from exploding ammunition and gasoline); attack transport *Barnett* (APA 5); and transport

Orizaba (AP 24). Near-misses damage transport *Monrovia* (AP 64), 37°02′N, 14°15′E, and attack transport *Joseph T. Dickman* (APA 13); attack transport *William P. Biddle* (APA 8) and *LST 382* are damaged in collision, 36°41′N, 14°23′E. Off Gela, U.S. freighter *Robert Rowan* is set afire by bomb and is abandoned. Once the blaze reaches her ammunition cargo, the freighter explodes. Destroyer *McLanahan* (DD 615) attempts to sink *Robert Rowan* with gunfire to extinguish the flames from the burning vessel that are illuminating all ships within miles, but the attempt is frustrated because the water is too shallow and the abandoned merchantman will not sink. Navy landing craft and transport *Orizaba*, however, rescue all hands: 41-man merchant complement, 32-man Armed Guard, and 348 troops.

ATLANTIC. Destroyer *Hilary P. Jones* (DD 427) grounds off Hoffman Island, New York, but she refloats herself at high tide and proceeds to her destination.

As seen from a Coast Guard–manned transport off Sicily in July 1943, bombs splash among the Allied ships unloading off the invasion beaches. Note 20-millimeter Oerlikon guns in action at right and 3-inch/.50-caliber at left. (NA, 26-G-1790)

12 Monday

PACIFIC. TG 36.9 (four light cruisers and two destroyers) (Rear Admiral Aaron S. Merrill) bombards Munda, New Georgia, Solomons.

Coast Guard cutter *Taney* (WPG 37), reconnoitering Baker Island, is bombed, but not damaged, by Japanese flying boat.

Destroyer *Taylor* (DD 468) sinks Japanese submarine *RO 107* east of Kolombangara, Solomons, 08°00′S, 157°19′E.

Submarine *Mingo* (SS 261) stalks Japanese convoy northwest of the Admiralties, but her attack, principally directed against cargo vessel *Ryoyo Maru*, is not successful, 00°54′N, 143°01′E. Two of the ships of Submarine Chaser Division 23 (*Ch 22*, *Ch 23*, and *Ch 24*), which are escorting *Ryoyo Maru* and two other merchantmen, are not successful in their attacks upon *Mingo*.

Submarine *Plunger* (SS 179) sinks Japanese freighter *Niitaka Maru* in the Sea of Japan, west of Hokkaido, 43°02′N, 140°00′E.

Submarine *Spearfish* (SS 190) damages Japanese destroyer *Kawakaze* off Eniwetok, 11°12′N, 161°50′E.

USAAF B-24s (14th Air Force) bomb Japanese shipping in Dulong Bay, 18 miles east of Haiphong, French Indochina, and sink cargo ships *Chikuzan Maru* (ex–*Ariadne Moller*) and *Tairyu Maru*, 20°52′N, 106°41′E.

ATLANTIC. USAAF B-24 (1st Antisubmarine Squadron) sinks German submarine *U 506* off coast of Portugal, 42°30′N, 16°30′W.

U.S. freighter *African Star* is torpedoed and sunk by German submarine *U 172* off the coast of Brazil at 25°46′S, 40°35′W. One of the 31-man Armed Guard is lost in the initial explosion, but the 56-man merchant complement survives intact. *U 172* surfaces after sinking the ship, questions a few of the survivors, and then provides them with directions to the nearest land before she retires (see 13 July).

MEDITERRANEAN. German air attacks against invasion shipping off Sicily continue. U.S. freighter *Joseph G. Cannon* is struck by a bomb and sinks in shallow water; she suffers no casualties to the 40-man merchant complement or the 25-man Armed Guard, although a number of British soldiers on board perish when the bomb hits the ship.

13 Tuesday

PACIFIC. Battle of Kolombangara: TG 36.1 (three light cruisers and 10 destroyers) (Rear Admiral Walden L. Ainsworth) engage Japanese light cruiser *Jintsu* and five destroyers (Rear Admiral Izaki Shunji) escorting troop-carrying destroyers. Japanese torpedoes damage U.S. light cruisers *Honolulu* (CL 48), 07°31′S, 157°19′E, and *St. Louis* (CL 49), 07°37′S, 157°16′E; and New Zealand light cruiser HMNZS *Leander*, which has replaced the lost *Helena* (CL 50). Destroyer *Gwin*

(DD 433), damaged by torpedo, is scuttled by *Ralph Talbot* (DD 390), 07°41′S, 157°27′E. Destroyers *Woodworth* (DD 460) and *Buchanan* (DD 484) are damaged by collision, 07°40′S, 157°14′E. Japanese light cruiser *Jintsu* is sunk by cruiser gunfire and destroyer torpedo, 07°38′S, 157°06′E, and destroyer *Yukikaze* is damaged. Rear Admiral Izaki is lost with his flagship, *Jintsu*.

INDIAN OCEAN. Second group of survivors of freighter *Sebastian Cermeno*, sunk by German submarine *U 511* on 27 June, reaches Durban, South Africa (see 14, 23, and 27 July).

RAF Catalina rescues one group of survivors from U.S. freighter *Alice F. Palmer*, torpedoed, shelled, and sunk by German submarine *U 177* on 10 July, 60 miles southeast of Madagascar (see 25, 26, and 30 July).

ATLANTIC. TBF (VC 13) from auxiliary aircraft carrier *Core* (ACV 13) sinks German submarine *U 487*, 720 miles south-southwest of Fayal, Azores, 27°15′N, 34°18′W.

Brazilian destroyer *Maranhao* rescues survivors of U.S. freighter *African Star*, torpedoed and sunk by German submarine *U 172* off the coast of Brazil the previous day.

MEDITERRANEAN. German air attacks continue on invasion shipping off the beaches at

Sicily; off Avola, freighter *Timothy Pickering*, hit by a bomb, catches fire. The blaze spreads with a rapidity that denies escape to those on board: 127 of 128 embarked British troops perish, as do 22 of the 43-man crew and 16 of the 23-man Armed Guard. *Timothy Pickering* is scuttled by a torpedo from a British destroyer.

Naval Advanced Base, Gela, Sicily, is established.

14 Wednesday

PACIFIC. Destroyer *Monaghan* (DD 354) bombards Japanese positions at Gertrude Cove, Kiska Island, Aleutians. She repeats the bombardment on 15 July. On neither occasion do enemy guns reply.

Japanese land attack plane (NELL) (755th *Kokutai*) sights small seaplane tender *Chincoteague* (AVP 24) as she tends patrol planes at Saboe Bay, Vanikoro, Solomons (see 16 and 17 July).

Japanese submarine *I 179* sinks, accidentally, off Aki Saki, Japan, 33°40'N, 132°40'N.

Naval Operating Base, Adak, Aleutians, is established.

INDIAN OCEAN. Third group of survivors of freighter *Sebastian Cermeno*, sunk by German submarine *U 511* on 27 June, is located by U.S. freighter *Theodore Parker* and taken to Durban, South Africa (see 23 and 27 July).

U.S. freighter *Robert Bacon* is torpedoed and sunk by German submarine *U 178*, 35 miles off Mozambique Light, 15°25'S, 41°13'E. *U 178* surfaces after sinking the ship, questions the survivors, provides them with directions to the nearest land, and then retires. Two of the 44-man merchant complement perish in the attack, but the 27-man Armed Guard survives intact (see 16, 27, and 28 July and 3 and 27 August).

ATLANTIC. TBF and F4F (VC 29) from auxiliary aircraft carrier *Santee* (ACV 29) sink German submarine *U 160* south of Azores, 34°02'N, 26°02'W.[151]

MEDITERRANEAN. Light cruiser *Brooklyn* (CL 40) is damaged by mine off Licata, Sicily, 36°57'N, 14°06'E; tank landing craft *LCT 19* is sunk by aircraft off Salerno, Italy.

15 Thursday

PACIFIC. Submarine *Narwhal* (SS 167) shells airfield on Matsuwa Island, Kurils.

Submarine *Tinosa* (SS 283) attacks Japanese transport (ex-armed merchant cruiser) *Aikoku Maru* north of Truk, 10°16'N, 151°27'E.

USAAF B-25s, P-40s, and P-38s (13th Air Force) bomb small Japanese cargo vessels west of Canongga Island, 08°03'S, 156°35'E, damaging *Wada Maru*.

Japanese light cruiser *Nagara* is damaged by mine (laid by RAAF Catalina) at Kavieng, 02°36'S, 150°34'E.

ATLANTIC. PBY (VP 92) and British destroyer HMS *Rochester* and frigates HMS *Mignonette* and HMS *Balsam* sink German submarine *U 135* west of the Canary Islands, 28°20'N, 13°17'W.

TBF (VC 29) from escort carrier *Santee* (CVE 29) sinks German submarine *U 509* south of Azores, 34°02'N, 26°02'W.[152]

CARIBBEAN. PBM (VP 32) sinks German submarine *U 159* south of Haiti, 15°58'N, 73°44'W.

MEDITERRANEAN. Minesweeper *Staff* (AM 114) is damaged by mine off Port Empedocle, Sicily, 37°17'N, 13°30'E; sister ship *Skill* (AM 115) enters the minefield and tows *Staff* to safety.

ATLANTIC. Panamanian tanker *Calliope* is disabled at 25°19'N, 74°26'W; tug *Umpqua* (AT 25) proceeds to her assistance (see 17 July).

16 Friday

PACIFIC. Small seaplane tender *Chincoteague* (AVP 24) is bombed by Japanese land attack planes (NELLs) (755th *Kokutai*) off Vanikoro, Solomons, but suffers no damage (see 17 July).

High-speed transports *Waters* (APD 8) and *Dent* (APD 9) rescue last two groups of survivors from light cruiser *Helena* (CL 50), sunk on 6 July, from Japanese-held Vella Lavella.

ATLANTIC. TBFs (VC 13) from escort carrier *Core* (CVE 13) sink German submarine *U 67* in mid-Atlantic, 30°05'N, 44°17'W.

U.S. freighter *Richard Caswell* is torpedoed and sunk by German submarine *U 513* about 200 miles off the coast of Brazil, 28°10'S, 46°30'E. *U 513* surfaces, questions the survivors, provides them with cigarettes, and then retires. Nine of the 42-man merchant complement perish in the attack; there are no casualties among either the 24-man Armed Guard or the two passengers (see 19 and 22 July).

MEDITERRANEAN. German planes bomb Allied shipping in Algiers Harbor. U.S. freighters *John H. Eaton* and *Stephen C. Foster* are damaged by falling debris and concussion when nearby Allied merchantmen are destroyed by bombs. There are no casualties to either the merchant complements or the Armed Guards on board either U.S. vessel.

German planes bomb Allied shipping off Sicily; U.S. freighter *William T. Coleman* is damaged by near-miss.

INDIAN OCEAN. First group of survivors from U.S. freighter *Robert Bacon*, sunk by German submarine *U 178* on 14 July, arrives at Mozambique (see 27 and 28 July and 3 and 27 August).

17 Saturday

PACIFIC. Navy and USMC SBDs (VB 11 and VMSB 132), Navy TBFs (VT 11 and VT 21), escorted by USMC F4Us (VMF 122, VMF 211, and VMF 221) (other F4U-equipped units also participate), and USAAF B-24s, escorted by USAAF P-39s and P-40s and RNZAF P-40s, attack Japanese shipping at Buin, Bougainville, Solomons. The pilots press home their strikes in the face of heavy fighter opposition and sink destroyer *Hatsuyuki* and damage destroyers *Hatsukaze* and *Yunagi* and auxiliary minesweeper *W.15*, 06°50'S, 155°46'E.

Small seaplane tender *Chincoteague* (AVP 24) is bombed and damaged by Japanese land attack planes (NELLs) (755th *Kokutai*) off Vanikoro, Solomons; seaplane tender (destroyer) *Thornton* (AVD 11), high-speed minesweeper *Trever* (DMS 18), and destroyer *Jenkins* (DD 447) render timely assistance to save the crippled ship.

ATLANTIC. Tug *Umpqua* (AT 25) takes disabled Panamanian tanker *Calliope* in tow; she reaches Jacksonville, Florida, the following day.

18 Sunday

PACIFIC. USN and USMC SBDs and TBFs, and USAAF B-24s (13th Air Force), attack Japanese shipping in the Buin-Kahili area, Bougainville, Solomons, and damage destroyer *Mochizuki*.

Tank landing ship *LST 342* is sunk by Japanese submarine *RO 106*, Solomons, 09°03'S, 158°11'E.[153]

ATLANTIC. Airship *K 74* is shot down by German submarine *U 134* in the Florida Straits (only naval airship lost to enemy action during World War II), but *U 134* is also damaged in the encounter.

Covered lighter *YF 487* is lost in the Caribbean Sea.

MEDITERRANEAN. Submarine chaser *PC 562* is damaged by mine off Port Empedocle, Sicily, 37°10'N, 12°35'E.

19 Monday

PACIFIC. Japanese naval land attack planes (NELLs) (755th *Kokutai*) bomb U.S. airfield at Funafuti, Ellice Islands.

Submarine *Porpoise* (SS 172) sinks Japanese transport *No. 20 Mikage Maru* 50 miles south of Wake Island, 18°45′N, 166°04′E; vessels of Submarine Chaser Division 32 (*Ch 28*, *Ch 29*, and *Ch 30*) carry out unsuccessful counterattacks.

ATLANTIC. PBM (VP 74) sinks German submarine *U 513* off Santos, Brazil, 27°17′S, 47°32′W; small seaplane tender *Barnegat* (AVP 10) rescues survivors.[154] Ironically, this same day two boatloads of survivors from U.S. freighter *Richard Caswell*, sunk by *U 513* on 16 July, are rescued by Argentine steamship *Mexico* (see 22 July).

MEDITERRANEAN. German planes bomb shipping off Avola, Sicily; U.S. freighter *Samuel Parker* is straddled and damaged by near-misses, but suffers no casualties to either the merchant complement or the Armed Guard.

20 Tuesday

PACIFIC. Searching PBY detects movement of Japanese surface force (Rear Admiral Nishimura Shoji) through the "slot" between Vella Lavella and Choiseul. TBFs from Henderson Field attack Nishimura's ships, sinking destroyer *Yugure* and damaging heavy cruiser *Kumano* (TBF from VMTB 131) and destroyer *Minazuki*. After a second wave of American planes (TBFs and USAAF B-25s) attack the enemy ships without success, a third wave (B-25s) sinks destroyer *Kiyonami*.

USAAF B-25s, unaware of friendly naval vessels in their patrol area, mistakenly sink motor torpedo boat *PT 166* (08°15′S, 156°53′E) and damage *PT 164* and *PT 168* in Ferguson Passage, Solomons.

Submarine *Pompano* (SS 181) damages Japanese transport *Uyo Maru*, east of Miki Saki, 33°55′N, 136°26′E.

ATLANTIC. USAAF aircraft (19th Antisubmarine Squadron) sink German submarine *U 558* in Bay of Biscay, 45°10′N, 09°42′W.

MEDITERRANEAN. German planes bomb Allied shipping off Augusta, Sicily; U.S. freighter *William T. Coleman* is damaged when British tanker *Fort Pelly*, moored to same buoy, is set afire by direct hits. Getting under way, *William T. Coleman* runs aground, and while thus immobile, is menaced by burning oil from *Fort Pelly*, which then explodes, further damaging the freighter by flying debris.

21 Wednesday

PACIFIC. Destroyers *Monaghan* (DD 354) and *Aylwin* (DD 355) carry out an unopposed

bombardment of Japanese positions in the Gertrude Cove area, Kiska Island.

Tank landing ship *LST 343* is damaged by Japanese bomb off Rendova; among the casualties is Captain Elphege M. Gendreau, Pacific Fleet Medical Officer.

Japanese naval land attack planes (NELLs) (755th *Kokutai*) again bomb U.S. airfield at Funafuti, Ellice Islands.

Submarine *Haddock* (SS 231) sinks Japanese army transport *Saipan Maru* (whose passenger list includes 180 geishas) and survives counterattacks by torpedo boat *Hato* west by north of Guam, 16°18′N, 134°04′E.

ATLANTIC. PBY (VP 94) sinks German submarine *U 662* off mouth of Amazon River, Brazil, 03°36′N, 48°46′W.

22 Thursday

PACIFIC. TG 16.21 (Rear Admiral Robert C. Giffen) and TG 16.22 (Rear Admiral Robert M. Griffin), consisting of two battleships, three heavy cruisers, one light cruiser, and nine destroyers, bombard Kiska, Aleutians. Enemy return fire proves ineffective. USAAF B-25s, P-38s, P-40s, and F5As (P-38s modified for photo reconnaissance) also bomb the Japanese positions.

Three waves of Navy and USAAF planes, including B-17s and B-24s, attack Japanese resupply convoy off Cape Friendship; SBDs and TBFs sink seaplane carrier *Nisshin*.

USAAF B-24s (5th Air Force) raid Surabaya, Java, targeting refineries, dock areas, and railroad yards; auxiliary submarine chaser *Cha 111* is damaged in the attack on harbor facilities.

Submarine *Sawfish* (SS 276) damages Japanese ammunition ship *Seia Maru* east-southeast of Kyushu, 30°54′N, 125°15′E.

ATLANTIC. U.S. tanker *Cherry Valley*, proceeding independently from New York to Aruba, N.W.I., is torpedoed by German submarine *U 66* at 25°10′N, 68°35′W. *U 66*'s second torpedo attack fails, and as she surfaces to shell her quarry and finish her off in that fashion she finds herself hotly engaged by Armed Guard gunfire. The 28-man Armed Guard serves its weapons efficiently; *Cherry Valley* escapes her assailant and reaches San Juan, Puerto Rico, under her own power and with no casualties.

Third boatload of survivors from U.S. freighter *Richard Caswell*, torpedoed and sunk by German submarine *U 513* off the coast of Brazil on 16 July, reaches safety at Florianopolis. Small seaplane tender *Barnegat* (AVP 10), which had ironically rescued survivors from *U 513* (which had sunk *Richard Caswell*) when

the enemy submarine had been sunk on 19 July, rescues the last of *Richard Caswell*'s survivors from a raft.

MEDITERRANEAN. During German air attack upon shipping off Avola, Sicily, U.S. freighter *Samuel Parker* is straddled and damaged by near-misses of bombs, as well as strafed. The latter attacks result in the death of two Armed Guard sailors.

23 Friday

ATLANTIC. VP 63, equipped with PBYs, the first U.S. naval aircraft squadron to operate from the United Kingdom, arrives in South Wales for antisubmarine patrol duty over the Bay of Biscay.

Destroyer *George E. Badger* (DD 196) sinks German submarine *U 613* (en route to mine the waters off Jacksonville, Florida) south of Azores, 35°32′N, 28°36′W.

TBFs (VC 9) from escort carrier *Bogue* (CVE 9) break up a rendezvous between German submarines *U 527* and *U 648* south of the Azores. *U 527* is sunk at 35°25′N, 27°56′W, but *U 648* escapes.

PB4Ys (VB 107) sink German submarine *U 598* off Brazil, 04°05′S, 33°23′W.

PACIFIC. USAAF P-39s (67th Fighter Squadron) begin operation from airfield at Woodlark Island, off southeastern coast of New Guinea.

INDIAN OCEAN. Fourth group of survivors of freighter *Sebastian Cermeno*, sunk by German submarine *U 511* on 27 June, reaches Durban, South Africa, on board a British corvette (see 27 July).

24 Saturday

PACIFIC. Destroyers bombard Bairoko Harbor, New Georgia, Solomons, and Kolombangara; later that day, TBFs and SBDs, accompanied by USAAF P-40s, bomb Japanese installations in the Bairoko area.

Submarine *Tinosa* (SS 283) attacks Japanese oiler *No. 3 Tonan Maru* west of Truk, 06°56′N, 147°52′E. *Tinosa* fires 15 torpedoes; 13 hit, but only two explode. The incident highlights torpedo exploder problems that have plagued the submarine force since the beginning of the war. An investigation into the performance of the Mk. XIV torpedo will result. *No. 3 Tonan Maru*, meanwhile, is towed to Truk by light cruiser *Isuzu* and will be utilized as a floating oil storage tank.

Japanese army cargo ship *Mie Maru* is sunk by mine, Babo Harbor, 02°31′S, 133°26′E.

Famous Naval Sayings "Damm Those Torpedoes - Period."

Fist-tightening frustration felt by submarine skippers, such as *Tinosa* (SS 283)'s, on 24 July 1943 is aptly mirrored in this variation on Farragut's "Damn the Torpedoes, Full Speed Ahead." This cartoon by William C. Eddy (USNA '26) reflected a grim truth: sometimes American torpedoes simply did not work. (USN, *General Instructions for Commanding Officers*)

ATLANTIC. USAAF B-17s (8th Air Force) bomb nitrate works and aluminum and magnesium plants at Heroya, Norway, 70 miles southwest of Oslo, and port area of Trondheim, pounding naval installations, quays, and shipping; German submarine *U 622* is sunk in the latter attack, 63°27'N, 10°23'E.

TBF and F4F (VC 29) from escort carrier *Santee* (CVE 29) damage German submarine *U 373* about 130 miles west of Madeira Islands, 33°10'N, 19°54'W.[155]

USAAF B-24s damage German submarine *U 466* off Cayenne, French Guiana, 07°30'N, 50°15'W.

25 Sunday

PACIFIC. Destroyers shell Japanese installations at Munda, New Georgia, Solomons; over 250 Allied planes bomb Munda (USAAF B-24s, B-25s, and B-17s and Navy/USMC SBDs and TBFs, covered by fighters).

Submarine *Pompon* (SS 267) damages Japanese transport *Kinsen Maru* and sinks army cargo ship *Thames Maru* north-northeast of the Admiralties, 02°46'N, 148°35'E.

"KE GO" Operation (second phase): As Japanese evacuation force awaits favorable weather off Kiska, escort vessel *Kunashiri* accidentally collides with light cruiser *Abukuma*. In the resultant chain reaction among the destroyers, *Hatsushimo* accidentally rams *Wakaba* and is then rammed by *Naganami* (see 27 July).

INDIAN OCEAN. Second group of survivors from U.S. freighter *Alice F. Palmer*, sunk by German submarine *U 177* on 10 July, reaches safety at Mozambique (see 26 and 30 July).

26 Monday

PACIFIC. "Battle of the Pips": TG 16.7 (Rear Admiral Robert C. Giffen) and TG 16.17 (Rear Admiral Robert M. Griffin) engage radar targets 90 miles southwest of Kiska. The contacts, however, prove to be phantom echoes on the U.S. radar screens.

INDIAN OCEAN. Third group of survivors from U.S. freighter *Alice F. Palmer*, sunk by German submarine *U 177* on 10 July, reaches safety at Mozambique (see 30 July).

CARIBBEAN. PBM (VP 32) sinks German submarine *U 759* off Haiti, 18°06'N, 75°00'W.

MEDITERRANEAN. Off Palermo, Sicily, destroyer *Mayrant* (DD 402) is bombed and damaged by German horizontal bomber, 38°16'N, 13°20'E; minesweeper *Skill* (AM 115) helps tow the damaged destroyer into port where she can be repaired. Motor torpedo boat *PT 202* is damaged by gunfire from German F-lighter.[156]

27 Tuesday

PACIFIC. Submarine *Sawfish* (SS 276) damages Japanese minelayer *Hirashima* off Kyushu, Japan, 32°32'N, 127°41'E.

Submarine *Scamp* (SS 277), south-southwest of Truk, sinks Japanese submarine *I 168*, 02°50'S, 149°01'E, and damages oiler *Kazahaya*, 02°38'S, 149°20'E.

Submarine *Seadragon* (SS 194) inflicts further damage on Japanese transport *Suwa Maru*, previously damaged on 28 March and 5 April, off Wake Island, 19°15'N, 166°30'E.

Japanese freighter *Teikin Maru* is sunk by mine, laid by submarine *Tambor* (SS 198) on 2 November 1942, off Hainan Island, 19°57'N, 109°05'E.

"KE GO" Operation (second phase) continues: Evacuation of Kiska, Aleutians (Vice Admiral Kawase Shiro), undetected by U.S. forces, concludes. Light cruiser *Kiso* evacuates 1,189 men, *Abukuma* 1,202. The remainder are taken out on accompanying destroyers, a total of 5,183 men. Among the materiel wrecked by the evacuating enemy are three midget submarines.

INDIAN OCEAN. Last group of survivors of freighter *Sebastian Cermeno*, sunk by German submarine *U 511* on 27 June, reaches Durban, South Africa, on board a British destroyer. From the 42-man merchant complement, five passengers, and 27-man Armed Guard, five of the crew perish in the initial attack or die of their wounds or from exposure in the lifeboats.

Second and third groups of survivors from U.S. freighter *Robert Bacon*, sunk by German submarine *U 178* on 14 July off Mozambique Light, are rescued from their boats, one by British steamship *English Prince*, the other by British tanker *Steaua Romana*. Three rafts with survivors are still at sea (see 28 July and 3 and 27 August).

28 Wednesday

PACIFIC. Destroyer *Farragut* (DD 348) on Kiska blockade patrol sinks an empty Japanese landing craft (perhaps cast adrift by the evacuating enemy garrison) four miles east of Sobaka Rock, off the south coast of Kiska.

Japanese submarine *RO 103* is last reported on this date; subsequent attempts to contact her are unsuccessful and she never returns to her base at Rabaul. Her fate is uncertain; she may have been mined.

USAAF B-25s sink Japanese destroyers *Ariake* and *Mikazuki* off Cape Gloucester, New Britain.

ANDAMAN SEA. USAAF B-24s sink Japanese army cargo vessel *Tamishima Maru* off Tavoy Island, 13°53′N, 97°40′E.

INDIAN OCEAN. Fourth group of survivors from U.S. freighter *Robert Bacon*, sunk by German submarine *U 178* on 14 July off Mozambique Light, reaches safety after two weeks at sea (see 3 and 27 August).

ATLANTIC. USAAF (4th Antisubmarine Squadron) and British (RAF No. 224 Squadron) aircraft sink German submarine *U 404* in Bay of Biscay, 45°53′N, 09°23′W.

U.S. freighter *John A. Poor*, straggling from convoy BX 65 in a heavy fog, fouls mine laid by German submarine *U 119* at 42°51′N, 64°55′W, but reaches port under tow; there are no casualties among the 42-man merchant complement or the 28-man Armed Guard.

MEDITERRANEAN. Naval Operating Base, Palermo, Sicily, is established.

CARIBBEAN. PBY (VP 32) sinks German submarine *U 359* south-southwest of Puerto Rico, 15°57′N, 68°30′W.

29 Thursday

PACIFIC. Submarine *Tuna* (SS 203) is mistakenly bombed by RAAF Catalina off Woodlark Island, 08°02′S, 152°07′E, and is forced to terminate her patrol.

USAAF B-25s and P-38s bomb wreck of Japanese destroyer *Mikazuki* (see 28 July), off Cape Gloucester.

ANDAMAN SEA. RAF or RAAF Liberators damage Japanese guardboat *No. 1 Kyo Maru* off Ross Island, Andamans.

ATLANTIC. Advanced Amphibious Training Base, Appledore, England, is established.

MEDITERRANEAN. Motor torpedo boat *PT 218* is damaged by Italian MAS boat.

30 Friday

PACIFIC. Destroyers *Farragut* (DD 348) and *Hull* (DD 350), unaware that the Japanese garrison has been evacuated, bombard the Gertrude Cove and main camp areas on Kiska Island.

ATLANTIC. German submarine *U 230* lays mines off entrance to Chesapeake Bay.

PV-1 (VB 127), providing coverage for convoy TJ 2, sinks German submarine *U 591* off Pernambuco, Brazil, 08°36′S, 34°34′W.

PV-1 (VB 129) attacks German submarine *U 604*, South Atlantic (see 3 and 11 August).

TBFs and F4Fs (VC 29) from escort carrier *Santee* (CVE 29) sink German submarine *U 43* in mid-Atlantic, 34°57′N, 35°11′W, thus breaking up a rendezvous between *U 43* and *U 403* and preventing *U 43* from sowing mines off Lagos, Nigeria.

MEDITERRANEAN. Submarine chaser *PC 624* sinks German submarine *U 375* off Tunisia, 36°40′N, 12°28′E.

INDIAN OCEAN. U.S. freighter *William Ellery*, en route from Basra, Iraq, to Durban, South Africa, is torpedoed by German submarine *U 197* some 300 miles from her destination, 32°00′S, 36°00′E, but reaches it under her own power; there are no casualties among the 39-man merchant complement and the 27-man Armed Guard.

Fourth and last group of survivors from U.S. freighter *Alice F. Palmer*, sunk by German submarine *U 177* on 10 July, reaches safety at Mozambique. All hands survive the ordeal of the loss of the ship and the ensuing open boat voyages.

31 Saturday

PACIFIC. Submarine *Finback* (SS 230) sinks Japanese army cargo ship *Ryuzan Maru* in Java Sea, off north coast of Java, 06°30′S, 111°30′E.

Submarine *Grayling* (SS 209) lands supplies and equipment at Pucio Point, Panay.

Submarine *Guardfish* (SS 217) lands survey party on west coast of Bougainville, Solomons.

Submarine *Pogy* (SS 266) sinks Japanese aircraft transport *Mogamigawa Maru* northwest of Truk, 11°08′N, 153°18′E.

Submarine *Saury* (SS 189), at periscope depth, is rammed by Japanese destroyer and damaged west of the Bonins, 27°03′N, 135°27′E; consequently, *Saury* terminates her patrol.

ATLANTIC. PBM (VP 74) and Brazilian A-28 and Catalina sink German submarine *U 199* off Rio de Janeiro, Brazil, 23°45′S, 42°57′W. Small seaplane tender *Barnegat* (AVP 10) rescues German survivors.

AUGUST

1 Sunday

PACIFIC. Rendova-based motor torpedo boats patrolling off Vanga Vanga and Gatere, Solomons, encounter Japanese destroyers in Blackett Strait off Kolombangara (see 2 August).

Japanese planes bomb motor torpedo boats, Rendova Harbor. *PT 117*, damaged off Lumbari Island, 08°24′S, 157°19′E, is beached and abandoned; *PT 164* is sunk, 08°25′S, 157°20′E.

Submarine *Finback* (SS 230) damages Japanese transport *Atlas Maru* in Java Sea off south coast of Borneo, 04°10′S, 112°10′E.

Submarine *Mingo* (SS 261) bombards Sorol Island, Carolines.

Submarine *Steelhead* (SS 280) attacks same Japanese convoy harassed by *Pogy* (SS 266) the previous day and damages auxiliary vessel *Seiko Maru* as she tries to reach Truk, 11°20′N, 153°30′E.

ATLANTIC. Naval Station, Roosevelt Roads, Puerto Rico, is established.

Gunboat *Brisk* (PG 89) attacks German submarine *U 732*, driving her away from Guantánamo-bound convoy NG 376.

MEDITERRANEAN. Minesweeper *Skill* (AM 115) is damaged by horizontal bomber off Sicily.

Operation TIDALWAVE: USAAF B-24s (Northwest African and 8th Air Forces) carry out low-level mass bombing of oil fields at Ploesti, Romania, from Libyan airfields.

2 Monday

PACIFIC. TG 16.6 (Rear Admiral Wilder D. Baker) and TG 16.17 (Rear Admiral Howard F. Kingman), consisting of two battleships, two heavy cruisers, three light cruisers, and nine destroyers, bombard Kiska, Aleutians. Kiska is bombarded 10 times between 2 and 15 August. Also in preparation for the impending assault on Kiska, USAAF planes (11th Air Force) begin daily bombings of the island.

Motor torpedo boats continue to engage Japanese destroyers off Kolombangara; motor torpedo boat *PT 109* is rammed and sunk by Japanese destroyer *Amagiri*, Blackett Strait, Solomons, 08°03′S, 156°58′E (see 6 August).[157] *Amagiri* is damaged in the collision.

USAAF B-25s (5th Air Force) strike Japanese shipping off Lae, New Guinea, and sink motor torpedo boats *Gyoraitei No. 112* and *Gyoraitei No. 113*, 07°00′N, 147°00′E.

RAAF Catalinas damage Japanese destroyer *Akikaze* south of Rabaul, 06°50′N, 151°10′E.

ATLANTIC. USAAF aircraft (4th Antisubmarine Squadron) sink German submarine *U 706* north-northwest of the coast of Spain, 46°15′N, 10°25′W.

3 Tuesday

ATLANTIC. PBM (VP 205) sinks German submarine *U 572*, north of Dutch Guiana, 11°33′N, 54°05′W.

TBF and F4F (VC 1) from escort carrier *Card* (CVE 11) damage German submarine *U 66* about 457 miles west-southwest of Flores Island, Azores (see 8 August).

PB4Ys (VB 107) and destroyer *Moffett* (DD 362) damage German submarine *U 604*, South Atlantic. (see 11 August).

In the nocturnal action, *Moffett* is accidentally damaged by PB4Y (VB 107), approximately 09°40′S, 30°07′W (see 7 August).

PACIFIC. German auxiliary cruiser *Michel* (*Schiffe 28*) sights transport *Hermitage* (AP 54) off Pitcairn Island, but does not attack (see 7 August).

INDIAN OCEAN. Fifth group of survivors from U.S. freighter *Robert Bacon*, sunk by German submarine *U 178* on 14 July off Mozambique Light, reaches safety after 20 days at sea (see 27 August).

MEDITERRANEAN. Destroyer *Buck* (DD 420) sinks Italian submarine *Argento* off Tunisia, 36°52′N, 12°08′E.

U.S. tanker *Yankee Arrow*, in convoy KMS 20, is mined as she nears Bizerte, Tunisia, 37°10′N, 11°06′E; two of the 25-man Armed Guard perish, as do five merchant sailors. The ship reaches port under her own power, but is adjudged unfit for further service.

4 Wednesday

PACIFIC. Radar-equipped PBY carries out predawn bombing of submarine base and main Japanese camp area on Kiska. The Catalina also drops 92 empty beer bottles (for the disconcerting whistling effect they produce) on those targets.

U.S. motor torpedo boats engage Japanese guardboats off Vanga Vanga, Kolombangara, sinking *No. 3 Matsue Maru* and driving *No. 2 Banyo Maru* ashore, damaged.

Submarine *Finback* (SS 230) sinks Japanese army cargo ship *Kaisho Maru* in Java Sea off north coast of Java, N.E.I., 05°18′S, 111°50′E.

Submarine *Seadragon* (SS 194) damages Japanese transport *Kembu Maru* east of Ponape, 07°33′N, 161°12′E.

MEDITERRANEAN. Destroyer *Shubrick* (DD 639) is damaged by dive bomber off Palermo, Sicily, 38°06′N, 13°20′E.

U.S. freighter *Harrison Grey Otis*, anchored in Gibraltar Harbor, is irreparably damaged by Italian limpet mine. Of the ship's 45-man merchant complement, one man dies and eight are injured; there are no casualties among the 23-man Armed Guard.

5 Thursday

PACIFIC. U.S. Army XIV Corps captures Munda airfield, New Georgia, the main objective of the campaign in the central Solomons, after almost a fortnight of jungle fighting.

Submarine *Pike* (SS 173) sinks Japanese transport *Shoju Maru* west of Marcus Island, 24°30′N, 158°50′E.

Submarine *Silversides* (SS 236) torpedoes Japanese minelayer *Tsugaru* north-northeast of Rabaul, 01°53′N, 153°52′E.

USAAF B-25 (13th Air Force) and USN/USMC F4Us sink Japanese fishing boat *No. 9 Kaiyo Maru* off Kolombangara, Solomons.

ATLANTIC. Destroyer *Black* (DD 666) is damaged when accidentally rammed by ferry boat *Staten* (YFB 36) at New York Navy Yard.

Gunboat *Plymouth* (PG 57) is torpedoed and sunk by German submarine *U 566*, 120 miles southeast of Cape Henry, Virginia, 36°17′N, 74°29′W.

6 Friday

PACIFIC. Battle of Vella Gulf is joined shortly before midnight, as six destroyers of TG 36.2 (Commander Frederick Moosbrugger) attack four Japanese destroyers attempting to bring troops and supplies to Kolombangara, Solomons, in Vella Gulf; *Dunlap* (DD 384), *Craven* (DD 382), and *Maury* (DD 401) sink *Kawakaze*, *Hagikaze*, and *Arashi*, 07°50′S, 156°47′E. U.S. force suffers no damage.

Submarine *Pike* (SS 173) unsuccessfully attacks Truk-bound Japanese aircraft carrier *Taiyo*, 21°23′N, 153°31′E.

Motor torpedo boat *PT 157*, assisted by *PT 171*, rescues the 11 survivors of *PT 109*, sunk in collision with Japanese destroyer *Amagiri* on 2 August.

CARIBBEAN. PV-1 (VB 130), PBMs (VP 204 and VP 205), and USAAF B-18 sink German submarine *U 615* off coast of Venezuela, 12°53′N, 64°54′W.

MEDITERRANEAN. Tank landing ship *LST 3* is damaged by horizontal bomber off Sicily, 38°01′N, 14°20′E.

7 Saturday

ATLANTIC. Destroyer *Moffett* (DD 362) is again accidentally damaged by a PB4Y (VB 107) while both are hunting for German submarine *U 604*, approximately 09°00 S, 26°00′W.

TBF and F4F (VC 1) from escort carrier *Card* (CVE 11) sink German submarine *U 117* west of the Azores, 39°32′N, 38°21′W.[158]

PACIFIC. Japanese planes bomb concentration of large infantry landing craft beached in Rendova Harbor; *LCI(L) 66* and *LCI(L) 328* are damaged by near-misses.

German auxiliary cruiser *Michel* (*Schiffe 28*) again sights transport *Hermitage* (AP 54) off Pitcairn Island, but, again, does not attack.

8 Sunday

PACIFIC. Motor torpedo boat *PT 113*, damaged by grounding, eastern New Guinea, 09°12′S, 146°29′E, is beached and abandoned.

Submarine *Salmon* (SS 182) unsuccessfully attacks Japanese vessel *No. 2 Shinko Maru* off Karafuto, 46°50′N, 144°40′E.

Submarine *Whale* (SS 239) sinks Japanese ammunition ship *Naruto Maru* northwest of the Marianas, 24°12′N, 142°52′E, and survives counterattack by destroyer *Asanagi*. *Asanagi* then rescues *Naruto Maru*'s survivors.

Japanese gunboat *Tozan Maru* is wrecked in a storm on the south coast of Hokkaido, 42°25′N, 143°20′E.

ATLANTIC. F4F (VC 1) from escort carrier *Card* (CVE 11) damages German submarine *U 262*, North Atlantic. *U 262* unsuccessfully attacks destroyer *Borie* (DD 215); *U 664* conducts unsuccessful attack on *Card*. VC 1 fliers find *U 664* on the surface but do not damage the U-boat (see 9 August).

9 Monday

PACIFIC. Submarine *Sculpin* (SS 191) sinks Japanese merchant passenger cargo ship *Sekko Maru* off west coast of Formosa, 24°55′N, 122°00′E.

Japanese freighter *Esutoru Maru* is damaged by mine laid off coast of Honshu by submarine *Scorpion* (SS 278) on 19 April, 36°05′N, 140°45′E.

ATLANTIC. TBF (VC 1) from escort carrier *Card* (CVE 11) sinks German submarine *U 664*, 570 miles west of Fayal, Azores, 40°12′N, 37°29′W.

MEDITERRANEAN. Tank landing ship *LST 318* is damaged by dive bomber off Sicily, 38°04′N, 14°30′E (see 10 August).

LCT 311 founders in heavy weather off Bizerte, Tunisia.

10 Tuesday

PACIFIC. Motor torpedo boat *PT 161*, operating from Rendova, is damaged by Japanese floatplane off Gatere. Other motor torpedo boats engage Japanese craft (Korean fishing boats) in Blackett Strait, sinking *Suiko Maru*.

Submarine *Salmon* (SS 182) sinks Japanese merchant fishing boat *Wakanoura Maru* off Karafuto, 46°55′N, 143°30′E.

Submarine *Tullibee* (SS 284) is damaged when rammed by Japanese cargo ship during the submarine's attack on a three-ship convoy on the Saipan-Truk route.

USAAF B-24 damages (with a near-miss) Japanese auxiliary sailing vessel *No. 5 Shinsei Maru* west of Cape St. George, 04°50′S, 152°55′E.

MEDITERRANEAN. Off Sicily, tank landing ship *LST 318*, damaged by dive bomber on 9 August, 38°04′N, 14°30′E, is beached and abandoned; salvage vessel *Brant* (ARS 32) is damaged by friendly fire from destroyer *Benson* (DD 421), 36°49′N, 13°27′E.

11 Wednesday

PACIFIC. Submarine *Finback* (SS 230) damages Japanese auxiliary vessel *Tatsumiya Maru*, bound for Singapore, at 05°30′S, 120°48′E, and survives counterattack by auxiliary submarine chaser *Toseki Maru*.

U.S. freighter *Matthew Lyon* is torpedoed by Japanese submarine *I 11* as the ship proceeds toward Espíritu Santo, 13°42′S, 165°59′E, but reaches her destination under her own power. Of the 59 men on board, 41 merchant sailors and an 18-man Armed Guard, only one is injured in the attack.[159]

USAAF B-24 attacks Japanese convoy 30 miles west of Mussau Island, 01°20′S, 148°55′E; escorting minesweeper *W.22* is not damaged.

ATLANTIC. TBF and F4F (VC 1) from escort carrier *Card* (CVE 11) sink German submarine *U 525* about 376 miles west-southwest of Corvo Island, Azores, 41°29′N, 38°55′W.

German submarine *U 60*—previously damaged by PV-1s (VB 129) on 30 July and by PB4Ys (VP 107) and destroyer *Moffett* (DD 362) on 3 August in South Atlantic, 05°00′S, 20°00′W—is scuttled. Her crew, embarked in *U 185*, will be further divided between *U 185* and *U 172* for the voyage home.

12 Thursday

PACIFIC. TU 16.6.1 (Rear Admiral Wilder D. Baker), consisting of two heavy cruisers, two light cruisers, and five destroyers, bombards Kiska.

Motor torpedo boat *PT 168*, operating from Rendova, is damaged by Japanese aircraft off Sandfly Harbor and Ferguson Passage.

Advance party is landed on Barakoma to mark channels and beaches to be used by landing craft in impending occupation of Vella Lavella, and to select bivouac and dispersal areas, as well as beach defense positions. The advance party also includes men from forces at Rendova to take custody of a large number of Japanese POWs held by the natives. The party learns, however, that instead of a few prisoners in hand there are several hundred survivors of the Battle of Vella Lavella at large, reportedly armed. Reinforcements are sought (see 14 August).

MEDITERRANEAN. Submarine chaser *SC 526* is damaged by grounding off Sicily, 38°01′N, 13°27′E.

13 Friday

PACIFIC. Japanese carrier attack planes (KATEs) raid shipping at Guadalcanal, torpedoing and sinking attack transport *John Penn* (APA 23), 09°23′S, 160°30′E.

Motor torpedo boat *PT 181*, operating out of Rendova, is attacked by Japanese aircraft and is damaged by near-miss of bomb, off Hunda Cove.

Submarine *Paddle* (SS 263) damages Japanese transport *Hidaka Maru* off southeast coast of Honshu, 34°42′N, 136°13′E.

Submarine *Sunfish* (SS 281) sinks Japanese gunboat *Edo Maru* 180 miles from Chichi Jima, 24°04′N, 142°21′E.

U.S. freighter *M. H. De Young* is torpedoed by Japanese submarine *I 19* as the ship proceeds toward Espíritu Santo, 21°50′S, 175°10′E, but though damaged remains afloat due to barge pontoons stowed in each hold. The 25-man Armed Guard remains on board along with the master and two merchant marine officers while the crew and passengers linger nearby (see 14 August).

U.S. aircraft sink Japanese guardboat *No. 15 Dai Nippon Maru* in Bismarck Archipelago.

MEDITERRANEAN. German HE 111s attack convoy MKS 21 off the coast of Algeria, strafing and holing U.S. freighters *Jonathan Elmer*, 36°07′N, 03°07′E, and *Anne Bradstreet*, 36°19′N, 02°18′E; one man is wounded on board the latter. Freighter *Francis W. Pettygrove* is torpedoed at 36°08′N, 02°14′E; partially abandoned, the survivors that clear the ship are taken on board British minesweeper HMS *Hythe*. The rest of the crew and Armed Guard remain on board to prepare the ship for tow (see 14 August).

14 Saturday

PACIFIC. Motor torpedo boats land troops at Vella Lavella to reinforce the advance party landed on 12–13 August (see 15 August).

Japanese planes bomb concentration of large infantry landing craft beached in Rendova Harbor but do not inflict any damage.

Submarine chaser *SC 67* makes rendezvous with damaged U.S. freighter *M. H. De Young*, torpedoed by Japanese submarine *I 19* the previous day, and takes off wounded men to transport to Tongatabu, Tonga Islands, in the southwest Pacific. *M. H. De Young* is subsequently towed to that port by Canadian steamship *Quebec* two days later.

USAAF B-24s (5th Air Force) bomb oil refineries at Balikpapan, Borneo; this strike may account for the damage to Japanese auxiliary submarine chaser *Cha 109* off that port.

USAAF B-25s sink three Japanese fishing craft, Iboki, 05°33′S, 149°08′E.

Open lighter *YC 970* sinks in Puget Sound, Washington, while employed by Puget Sound Bridge and Dredge.

MEDITERRANEAN. U.S. freighter *Francis W. Pettygrove*, torpedoed by German plane while in convoy MKS 21 the previous day, is taken in tow by British minesweeper HMS *Hythe*.[160]

15 Sunday

PACIFIC. TF 31 (Rear Admiral Theodore S. Wilkinson) lands USN (58th Construction Battalion and Naval Base Group), USMC (Fourth Defense Battalion), and U.S. Army (35th Combat Team) force (Brigadier General Robert B. McClure, USA) on Vella Lavella, Solomons, thus bypassing enemy positions on Kolombangara, Solomons. Japanese air attacks follow. Destroyer *Cony* (DD 508) (Rear Admiral Wilkinson's flagship) is near-missed by bombs, as is tank landing ship *LST 395*.

Operation COTTAGE: Forces under Commander North Pacific Force (Vice Admiral Thomas C. Kinkaid) land U.S. Army and Canadian troops at Kiska, Aleutians. They find Kiska had been evacuated by the Japanese on 28 July. Only casualties in the unopposed operation occur because of accidents or friendly fire incidents.

Submarine *Wahoo* (SS 238), operating off west coast of Hokkaido, damages Japanese fleet tanker *Terukawa Maru*, 43°15'N, 140°03'E, and merchant fishery mother ship *Ryokai Maru*, 43°12'N, 140°00'E.

16 Monday

MEDITERRANEAN. U.S. freighter *Benjamin Contee* is hit by aerial torpedo 16 miles north of Bône, Algeria; while the explosion kills 264 and injures 142 of the 1,800 Italian POWs on board, there are no casualties to the 43-man merchant complement, 27-man Armed Guard, 26 British guards, and seven Army security people. Italian-speaking crewmen reassure the anxious captives that the ship is in no danger of sinking; *Benjamin Contee* ultimately returns to service.

17 Tuesday

GENERAL. QUADRANT Conference at Quebec, Canada, begins with President Roosevelt, British Prime Minister Winston S. Churchill, and the Combined Chiefs of Staff to discuss worldwide strategy, with the principal concern to eliminate Italy from the war.

PACIFIC. Destroyers destroyers *Waller* (DD 466) and *Philip* (DD 498) are damaged by collision off Barakoma, 08°11'S, 156°43'E, while defending convoy against Japanese air attack, as occupation of Vella Lavella proceeds.

USAAF B-24s (5th Air Force) bomb installations and facilities at Balikpapan, Borneo; Japanese cargo vessel *Amagisan Maru* is damaged.

ATLANTIC. Portugal agrees to grant bases in the Azores to Great Britain.

MEDITERRANEAN. Army troops enter Messina, terminating the campaign in Sicily. Commander Motor Torpedo Boat Squadron 15 (Lieutenant E. A. Dubose, USNR), after unopposed landings from motor torpedo boats *PT 215*, *PT 216*, and *PT 217* on islands of Lipari and Stromboli, accepts the unconditional surrender of the Lipari Islands (Alicudi, Filicudi, Vulcano, Stromboli, Salina, and Lipari). Destroyer *Trippe* (DD 403) covers the operation.

Infantry landing craft *LCI 1* is sunk by aircraft off Bizerte, Tunisia.

18, Wednesday

PACIFIC. Commander TF 31 dispatches task group composed of four destroyers (Captain Thomas J. Ryan) to intercept Japanese warships that are approaching to either interrupt the landings at Barakoma, Vella Lavella, or reinforce Bougainville. Consequently, *Nicholas* (DD 449), *Chevalier* (DD 451), *O'Bannon* (DD 450), and *Taylor* (DD 468) sink auxiliary submarine chasers *Cha 5* and *Cha 12* north of Vella Gulf. There is no damage to U.S. forces.

In the first step toward acquiring airfields in the Ellice Islands to support projected operations in the Marshalls and Gilberts, an advanced survey party moves onto Nanomea Atoll, Ellice Islands.

During operations supporting the occupation of Vella Lavella, tank landing ship *LST 396*

is sunk by explosion (believed to have been caused accidentally by own ship's force), en route to Barakoma, 08°18'S, 156°55'E.

Destroyer *Abner Read* (DD 526) is damaged by mine off Conquer Point, Kiska Island, Aleutians, 52°01'N, 177°26'E.

Submarine *Plunger* (SS 179) damages Japanese freighter *Okuni Maru* in Uchiura Wan, Hokkaido, 43°30'N, 140°30'E.

ATLANTIC. Advanced Amphibious Training Base, St. Mawes, Cornwall, England, is established.

MEDITERRANEAN. Light cruisers *Philadelphia* (CL 41) and *Boise* (CL 47) and four destroyers shell Gioia Tauro and Palmi on Italian mainland.

19 Thursday

PACIFIC. OS2N (VS 57) and New Zealand corvette HMNZS *Tui* sink Japanese submarine *I 17* off eastern Australia, 23°26'S, 166°50'E.

Submarine *Finback* (SS 230) sinks Japanese auxiliary submarine chaser *Cha 109* (ex-Dutch patrol vessel *Kawi*) off east coast of Celebes, 03°01'S, 125°50'E.

ATLANTIC. TBF (VC 25) from escort carrier *Croatan* (CVE 25) attacks German submarine *U 134* northwest of the Azores, but the latter escapes.

20 Friday

PACIFIC. Destroyer *Pringle* (DD 477) is damaged by Japanese strafing and near-miss of bombs while transiting Gizo Strait, Solomons, en route to Vella Lavella. During Japanese bombing of beached tank landing ships off Barakoma, *LST 354* and *LST 398* are damaged by near-misses.

Submarine *Gar* (SS 206) sinks Japanese transport *Seizan Maru* at northern end of Makassar Strait, off coast of Borneo, 01°00'N, 119°00'E.

Submarine *Pompano* (SS 181) departs Midway on her seventh war patrol. She is never heard from again.[161]

Submarine *Plunger* (SS 179) sinks Japanese freighter *Seitai Maru* off southwest coast of Hokkaido, 42°15'N, 139°58'E.

Submarine *Wahoo* (SS 238) sinks Japanese merchant sampan *No. 1 Inari Maru* west of the Kurils, 45°50'N, 146°22'E.

Dutch submarine *O 24* sinks Japanese gunboat *Chosa Maru* south of Penang, Malaya, 05°09'N, 100°10'E.

ATLANTIC. Naval Base, Rosneath, Scotland, is reestablished.

Destroyers *O'Bannon* (DD 450), *Chevalier* (DD 451), and *Taylor* (DD 468), as seen from sister ship *Nicholas* (DD 449), bones in teeth, steam toward Vella Lavella, 15 August 1943. (NA, 80-G-58800)

21 Saturday

PACIFIC. Motor torpedo boats *PT 181* and *PT 183*, operating from Rendova, are damaged by strafing of Japanese floatplane, northwest of Turovilu Island.

MEDITERRANEAN. U.S. freighter *Cape Mohican* is damaged (most likely by drifting mine) while in convoy MKF 22, off coast of North Africa, 33°42′N, 16°43′E, but reaches Malta under tow. There are no fatalities among the complement of 41 merchant sailors and a 24-man Armed Guard.

22 Sunday

PACIFIC. Marines (Second Airdrome Battalion) begin occupation of Nukufetau Atoll, Ellice Islands, as efforts proceed to acquire airfields to support the projected operations in the Marshalls and Gilberts (see 27 and 28 August).

Submarine *Pike* (SS 173) damages Japanese army cargo ship *Toun Maru* west-southwest of Iwo Jima, 21°22′N, 137°50′E.

Submarine *Plunger* (SS 179) sinks Japanese merchant fishery mother ship *Ryokai Maru* northwest of La Pérouse Strait, 42°40′N, 139°48′E.

Submarine *Swordfish* (SS 193) sinks Japanese army cargo ship *Nishiyama Maru* off Palau, 02°53′N, 136°21′E.

Submarine *Tullibee* (SS 284) sinks Japanese transport *Kaisho Maru* northwest of Truk, 10°09′N, 147°25′E, and survives depth charge attack by *Ikazuchi*.

23 Monday

PACIFIC. Coastal minesweeper *Crow* (AMc 20) is sunk by erratic-running friendly aircraft torpedo, Puget Sound, Washington.

Submarine *Grayling* (SS 209) delivers two tons of supplies and equipment to Filipino guerrilla forces at designated spot near Libertad, Panay.

Submarine *Paddle* (SS 263) sinks Italian merchant passenger-cargo ship *Ada* off Hamamatsu, Japan, 34°37′N, 137°53′E.[162]

ANDAMAN SEA. USAAF B-24s sink Japanese transport *Heito Maru* east of Car Nicobar, Andaman Islands.

MEDITERRANEAN. Tug *Narragansett* (AT 88) is damaged and submarine chasers *SC 694* and *SC 696* are sunk by German JU-88s off Palermo, Sicily, 38°08′N, 13°22′E.

U.S. freighter *Pierre Soule*, en route from Sicily to Bizerte, Tunisia, is torpedoed by German submarine *U 380*, 38°21′N, 12°50′E. Tug *Nauset* (AT 89) tows the damaged freighter to Bizerte, arriving the following morning. There are no casualties.

24 Tuesday

GENERAL. QUADRANT Conference ends. President Roosevelt and British Prime Minister Winston S. Churchill agree to intensify the war against Japan without relaxing the effort against Germany in Europe, and to intensify the war against Italy. Additionally, steps will be taken to include the Soviets to a greater degree in the western Allies and to recognize General Charles DeGaulle's French Committee of National Liberation as representative of the Free French.

PACIFIC. New Georgia, Solomons, campaign ends as U.S. Army troops occupy Bairoko Harbor.

Motor torpedo boats *PT 175*, *PT 176*, and *PT 164*, operating from Rendova, are damaged by Japanese floatplanes, Gizo Strait.

Submarine *Whale* (SS 239) damages Japanese fleet tanker *San Diego Maru* in East China Sea southwest of Nagasaki, 31°30′N, 128°35′E.

Small reconnaissance seaplane from Japanese submarine *I 25* reconnoiters Espíritu Santo.

ATLANTIC. TBFs (VC 13) from escort carrier *Core* (CVE 13) sink German submarines *U 84* at 27°09′N, 37°03′W, and *U 185* at 27°00′N, 37°06′W, southwest of the Azores.[163]

MEDITERRANEAN. German planes bomb U.S. tanker *Esso Providence* off Port Augusta, Sicily; there are no fatalities among the ship's merchant and Armed Guard complement.

25 Wednesday

PACIFIC. Rear Admiral Marc A. Mitscher is relieved as Commander Aircraft, Solomons, by Major General Nathan F. Twining, USAAF.

TG 34.9, covered by four destroyers (Destroyer Division 41), sows mines off Wilson Cove, western Kolombangara; the latter draw attacks by Japanese planes, thus diverting attention from the mining operation. Light minelayers *Montgomery* (DM 17) and *Preble* (DM 20) are heavily damaged in collision as they retire from the area, 09°01′S, 159°50′E, but excellent seamanship and damage control enable both ships to return to Tulagi under their own power.

Destroyer *Patterson* (DD 392) sinks Japanese submarine *RO 35*, 170 miles southeast of San Cristobal Island, Solomons, 12°57′S, 164°23′E.

USAAF B-24 damages Japanese vessel *Mito Maru* 60 miles west-northwest of Mussau Island, Bismarck Archipelago.

26 Thursday

PACIFIC. Submarine *Tunny* (SS 282) attacks Japanese convoy consisting of transport *Amagisan Maru* and oiler (ex-seaplane carrier) *Tsurumi*, escorted by submarine chaser *Ch 4*, off Palaus, 07°30′N, 134°20′E. *Tunny*'s attack is unsuccessful, but *Ch 4* damages the submarine and forces her to terminate her patrol.

USAAF B-24s bomb Japanese destroyers attempting to reach Buin, 45 miles from Buka, damaging *Hamakaze* and forcing her to put into Rabaul for repairs.

MEDITERRANEAN. German submarine *U 410* attacks convoy UGS 14 off the coast of Algeria, torpedoing U.S. freighters *John Bell*, 37°11′30″N, 08°21′E, and *Richard Henderson*, 37°12′N, 08°21′E; one of the 43-man merchant complement perishes on board the former while there are no casualties on board the latter. Both ships, irreparably damaged, sink the next morning. British motor minesweeper HMS *BYMS 23* and South African armed whaler *Southern Maid* rescue *John Bell*'s survivors; *Southern Maid* participates in rescuing *Richard Henderson*'s survivors as well.

27 Friday

PACIFIC. Marines (Second Airdrome Battalion) and Seabees (16th Construction Battalion) complete occupation of Nukufetau, Ellice Islands. Army troops (RCT 172 of 43rd Infantry Division) are landed on Arundel Island, Solomons.

Submarine *Drum* (SS 228) damages Japanese transport *Yamagiri Maru* north-northeast of the Admiralties, 01°31′S, 148°41′E.

Submarine *Grayling* (SS 209) sinks Japanese army cargo ship *Meizan Maru* in South China Sea, off Mindoro, P.I., 13°35′N, 120°45′E.

Submarine *Pollock* (SS 180) sinks Japanese army cargo ship *Taifuku Maru* off Kyushu, 32°28′N, 132°23′E; although minesweeper *W.17* arrives on the scene in time to open fire on *Pollock*, the submarine escapes.

Submarine *Snapper* (SS 185) inflicts further damage on Japanese transport *Tokai Maru*, previously damaged on 26 January, at Apra, Guam, 13°31′N, 144°37′E.

USAAF B-17s and B-24s, escorted by P-38s, bomb Japanese installations in the Hansa Bay area, New Guinea, damaging small cargo vessel *No. 8 Manryu Maru*.

USAAF B-24s bomb Japanese shipping off western tip of New Hanover, Bismarck Archipelago, damaging army cargo ship *No. 18 Shinsei Maru*.

Grumman TBF-1c Avenger, with burning Japanese installations on Marcus Island visible in the background beyond, 31 August 1943. (Author's Collection)

USAAF B-25s (13th Air Force) bomb Japanese shipping and installations at Choiseul, Solomons, damaging fishing vessel *Kokusei Maru*.

Tank landing craft *LCT 319* sinks after running aground, Kiska, Aleutians.

INDIAN OCEAN. Last group of survivors from U.S. freighter *Robert Bacon*, torpedoed and sunk by German submarine *U 178* on 14 July off Mozambique Light, reaches safety after 44 days at sea. Only one survivor perishes from exposure.

ATLANTIC. TBF (VC 1) from escort carrier *Card* (CVE 11) attacks German submarine *U 508*, but the enemy escapes; TBF and F4Fs sink *U 847*, mid-Atlantic area, 28°19′N, 37°58′W.

28 Saturday

PACIFIC. Marines (Seventh Defense Battalion, USMC) occupy Nanomea, Ellice Islands.

Submarine *Tarpon* (SS 175) damages Japanese stores ship *Shinsei Maru* south of Honshu, 33°39′N, 138°28′E.

PBY attacks Japanese minelayer *Hoko* off Buka, Solomons; although the Catalina crew claims damage, the enemy auxiliary escapes unscathed.

USAAF B-25s (5th Air Force) bomb Japanese installations at Hansa Bay, New Guinea, sinking fishing vessels *Owaru Maru* and *Seio Maru*.

29 Sunday

EUROPE. During turmoil in Denmark following the Danish government's refusal to yield to German demand for the death penalty for saboteurs, the Danish government resigns and the Danish Army is disarmed. The Danish fleet (coast defense ship, nine submarines, a tender, three minesweepers, five patrol boats, five small minesweepers, and four minelayers) is scuttled at Copenhagen; one coast defense ship is scuttled at Isefjord. Germans capture three minesweepers and two patrol boats, but one patrol boat, three motor minesweepers, and nine small auxiliary vessels escape to Sweden.

PACIFIC. German auxiliary cruiser *Michel* (*Schiffe 28*) eludes light cruiser *Trenton* (CL 11) off the coast of Chile.

30 Monday

PACIFIC. Submarine *Halibut* (SS 232) sinks Japanese cargo ship *Taibun Maru* in La Pérouse Strait, 41°50′N, 141°13′E.

31 Tuesday

PACIFIC. TBFs, SBDs, and F6Fs from TF 15 (Rear Admiral Charles A. Pownall), consisting of carriers *Essex* (CV 9) and *Yorktown* (CV 10) and small carrier *Independence* (CVL 22), screened by one battleship, two light cruisers, and 11 destroyers, and supported by an oiler, bomb Marcus Island. TBFs from *Independence*

sink three Japanese small craft. Submarine *Snook* (SS 279) operates in support of TF 15.

Submarine *Seawolf* (SS 197) damages Japanese torpedo boat *Sagi* and sinks army cargo ship *Shoto Maru* and freighter *Kokko Maru* in the East China Sea north-northeast of Formosa, 28°30′N, 123°05′E.

U.S. tanker *W. S. Rheem* is torpedoed by Japanese submarine *I 20* near Espíritu Santo, 15°51′S, 167°02′E, but reaches port under her own power; there are no casualties to either the 49-man merchant complement or the 25-man Armed Guard.

USAAF P-40s (14th Air Force) sink small Japanese coastal vessel *Shirogane Maru* between Amoy and Hong Kong, 22°13′N, 114°10′E.

MEDITERRANEAN. Tank landing craft *LCT 154* capsizes while under tow and is lost off Bizerte, Tunisia, 37°8′N, 10°58′E. Scuttled by gunfire.

SEPTEMBER

1 Wednesday

PACIFIC. Army occupation troops (804th Aviation Battalion) land on Baker Island, supported by TF 11 (Rear Admiral Willis A. Lee Jr.), formed around small carriers *Princeton* (CVL 23) and *Belleau Wood* (CVL 24). *Ashland* (LSD 1) in this operation pioneers the use of the dock landing ship.

Destroyer *Wadsworth* (DD 516) sinks Japanese submarine *I 182* off Espíritu Santo, New Hebrides, 15°38′N, 166°57′E.

Submarine *Pompano* (SS 181) sinks Japanese merchant vessel *Nankai Maru* off Miyako Jima.

Naval Air Station, Kahului, Maui, T.H., is established.

ATLANTIC. Navy assumes full responsibility for airborne antisubmarine operations by U.S. forces in Atlantic.

2 Thursday

MEDITERRANEAN. Convoy UGF 10 (Algiers-Bizerte section) comes under attack from enemy aircraft off Algerian coast; destroyer *Kendrick* (DD 612) is damaged by aerial torpedo, 36°42′N, 00°47′E; she reaches Oran under her own power, escorted by destroyers *Benson* (DD 421) and *McLanahan* (DD 615).

PACIFIC. Convoy (TU 32.45) is attacked by submarine about 100 miles west of Espíritu Santo at 13°20′S, 165°00′E. Destroyer *Lansdowne* (DD 486) hunts for the submarine while the convoy proceeds to its destination, Guadalcanal (see 3 September).

Submarine *Seawolf* (SS 197) sinks Japanese army cargo ship *Fusei Maru* east of Formosa, 31°28′N, 127°24′E.

Submarine *Snapper* (SS 185) sinks Japanese escort vessel *Mutsure*, 85 miles north-north-west of Truk, Carolines, 08°40′N, 151°31′E.

USAAF B-25s escorted by P-38s (5th Air Force) pound Japanese convoy off Wewak, New Guinea, sinking army cargo ships *Nagato Maru* and *Hankow Maru*, and damaging *Nagano Maru*.

3 Friday

PACIFIC. Destroyer *Ellet* (DD 398), which has relieved *Lansdowne* (DD 486) of hunter-killer operations off Espíritu Santo, sinks Japanese submarine *I 25* at 13°10′S, 165°27′E.

Submarine *Pollack* (SS 180) sinks Japanese transport *Tagonoura Maru* off Mikura Jima, 33°38′N, 140°07′E.

Submarine *Pompano* (SS 181) sinks Japanese freighter *Akama Maru* southeast of Hokkaido, 41°00′N, 144°34′E

MEDITERRANEAN. Operation BAYTOWN: British troops, with naval and air support, land on the Italian mainland at Calabria. Italian government signs short-term armistice with Allies to become effective on 8 September.

4 Saturday

PACIFIC. Operation POSTERN: TF 76 (Rear Admiral Daniel E. Barbey) lands Australian 9th Division on Huon Peninsula near Lae, New Guinea. In Japanese retaliatory air strikes by naval land attack planes (BETTYs) (702nd *Kokutai*) and carrier bombers (VALs), escorted by ZERO fighters, destroyer *Conyngham* (DD 371) is damaged, 07°28′S, 147°44′E, as are tank landing ships *LST 471* (aerial torpedo) and *LST 473* (bombs), 07°45′S, 148°01′E. During the attack on *LST 473*, as the order comes down for full right rudder to avoid a torpedo, a bomb hits the pilot house, blowing the helmsman clear. Mortally wounded in the blast, Seaman First Class Johnnie D. Hutchins grabs the wheel and executes the order, thus saving the ship. For his gallantry, Hutchins is awarded the Medal of Honor posthumously. Elsewhere off the beach, large infantry landing craft *LCI(L) 30* is damaged during the air attack; *LCI(L) 338* is damaged by near-miss; and *LCI(L) 339* is damaged by direct bomb hit and abandoned. *LCI(L) 341* is damaged and temporarily abandoned; the crew lives ashore in foxholes and helps put out fires on board

LCI(L) 339. *LCI(L) 343* and *LCI(L) 338* are damaged in collision. *LCI(L) 343* is damaged by mortar fire, *LCI(L) 344* by machine gun fire.

Japanese planes attack four Rendova-based U.S. motor torpedo boats off Meresu Cove, damaging *PT 124* and *PT 125*.

Submarine *Albacore* (SS 218) sinks Japanese gunboat *Heijo Maru* southwest of Ponape, Carolines, 05°25′N, 156°37′E.

Submarine *Pargo* (SS 264) torpedoes Japanese fleet tanker *Ryuei Maru* in East China Sea, 30°06′N, 128°02′E.

Submarine *Sunfish* (SS 281) sinks Japanese army cargo ship *Kozan Maru* in southern Formosa Strait, 22°06′N, 119°50′E.

Submarine *Tarpon* (SS 175) sinks Japanese guardboat *Yulin Maru* west of Honshu, 35°56′N, 157°59′E.

5 Sunday

PACIFIC. Submarine *Albacore* (SS 218) torpedoes Japanese transport *Hokusho Maru* south-southwest of Ponape, 03°50′N, 160°20′E, but both "fish" that hit are duds.

Submarine *Swordfish* (SS 193) sinks Japanese army transport *Tenkai Maru* north-northeast of Hollandia, 01°35′N, 141°45′E.

District patrol vessel *YP 279* founders in heavy weather off Townsville, Australia.

Japanese salvage vessel *Yusho Maru* is sunk by mine in Makassar Strait, 05°00′S, 119°00′E.

6 Monday

PACIFIC. Submarine *Halibut* (SS 232) sinks Japanese freighter *Shogen Maru* in Uchiura Bay, Hokkaido, 42°13′N, 142°00′E, and later torpedoes heavy cruiser *Nachi* off Ominato, 40°07′N, 142°20′E. The torpedo that hits *Nachi*, however, proves to be a dud, and the enemy warship proceeds on her way (she is bound for Paramushir, Kurils) without further incident.

Submarine *Seahorse* (SS 304) is damaged by depth charges off the Palaus, 07°31′N, 134°21′E, shortly after attacking a convoy, but remains on patrol.

RAAF Beauforts sink small Japanese cargo vessel *Seicho Maru* 21 nautical miles east of Garove Island, 04°39′S, 152°59′E.

7 Tuesday

PACIFIC. Japanese land attack plane (755th *Kokutai*) bombs Nanomea, Ellice Islands.

Rendova-based motor torpedo boats *PT 118* and *PT 172*, damaged by grounding off Tambama Bay, Solomons, are burned to prevent capture.

INDIAN OCEAN. U.S. freighter *Lyman Stewart*, en route to Durban, South Africa, from Colombo, Ceylon, is attacked by Japanese submarine *I 27* at 03°30′N, 75°00′E, and slightly damaged by a dud torpedo. *I 27*'s gunfire attack proves equally ineffective, and *Lyman Stewart* proceeds on her way. There are no casualties on board the freighter.

8 Wednesday

PACIFIC. Submarine *Drum* (SS 228) sinks Japanese army cargo ship *No. 13 Hakutetsu Maru* off Hollandia, 02°44′S, 141°36′E.

Japanese land attack planes (755th *Kokutai*) bomb Nanomea, Ellice Islands.

MEDITERRANEAN. General Dwight D. Eisenhower announces from Algiers that an armistice has been concluded with the Italian government. German forces in Italy, however, remain in place; among other actions, they occupy harbors along the Tyrrhenian Sea, as well as Sardinia and Corsica (see 9 September).

Operation SLAPSTICK: Light cruiser *Boise* (CL 47), withdrawn temporarily from the bombardment force being massed for Operation AVALANCHE, transports British troops from Bizerte and is the only U.S. Navy ship to participate in the British occupation of Taranto, Italy.

Convoy FSS 1, bound for Salerno to participate in Operation AVALANCHE, is attacked by German JU 88s; large infantry landing craft *LCI(L) 87* is damaged by near-misses. German planes bomb TG 85.1; tank landing ship *LST 375* is damaged by direct hit and near-misses.

ARCTIC. Operation SIZILIEN: German battleship *Tirpitz*, accompanied by a destroyer flotilla, shells Barentsburg, Spitsbergen, Norway; battleship *Scharnhorst* and two destroyer flotillas land troops (349th Grenadier Regiment) that destroy facilities at Grönfjord and Advent Bay before reembarking. The German force returns to its Norwegian bases unhindered.

9 Thursday

PACIFIC. Submarine *Grayling* (SS 209) is sunk, possibly rammed by Japanese transport *Hokuan Maru* in the South China Sea west of Luzon.[164]

Submarine *Harder* (SS 257) sinks Japanese freighter *Koyo Maru* off entrance of Sagami Wan, Honshu, 35°30′N, 140°40′E.

Submarine *Permit* (SS 178) torpedoes Japanese cargo vessel *Tateyama Maru* off Kwajalein, 09°00′N, 168°40′E.

On board light cruiser *Savannah* (CL 42), a sailor trains a fire hose through the roof of Turret III, which had taken a direct hit from a German rocket bomb off Salerno, 11 September 1943, while his shipmates treat casualties on the deck beside Turret II; the shrouded body in right background reflects one who is beyond help. (NA, 80-G-54357)

Submarine *Pompano* (SS 181) torpedoes Japanese army cargo ship *Nanking Maru* off northeastern Honshu, 40°12′N, 141°55′E.

Tank landing craft *LCT 366* founders and sinks in heavy weather west of the Aleutians, 53°01′N, 152°00′W.

GULF OF PANAMA. German submarine *U 214* lays mines off Colón, C.Z.

MEDITERRANEAN. Italian fleet departs La Spezia, Genoa, and Taranto. German DO 217s attack utilizing radio-guided bombs; battleship *Roma* is sunk and *Italia* damaged west of the Straits of Bonifacio. German shore batteries take destroyers *Da Noli* and *Vivaldi* under fire in the Straits; the former is sunk by gunfire, the latter by a mine. With the exception of Italian warships that rescue the survivors of the ships sunk (which put into Port Mahon, Balaeric Islands, where they are interned), the bulk of the fleet reaches Malta.

Operation AVALANCHE: Under protection of TF 80 (Western Naval Task Force) (Vice Admiral H. Kent Hewitt, USN), the Allied Fifth Army (Lieutenant General Mark W. Clark, USA) lands on the assault beaches in the Gulf of Salerno against mounting opposition. German bombing sinks tug *Nauset* (AT 89) at 40°38′N, 14°38′E; U.S. tug *Intent* is damaged by bomb and by explosion of *Nauset*. Tank landing ships *LST 336*, *LST 357*, and *LST 385* (40°40′N, 14°44′E) are damaged by shellfire; *LST 375* is bombed; and *LST 386* is mined, as is British monitor HMS *Abercrombie*.[165] Infantry landing craft *LCI 42* is damaged by shelling, as is tank landing craft *LCT 221*. Naval gunfire support, initially suffering from communication difficulties incident to the heavy opposition at the beaches, will grow in effectiveness as AVALANCHE proceeds, delivering a great volume of counterbattery, interdiction, and neutralization fire, and will become (as even Axis propagandists state) one of the decisive factors in holding the Salerno beachhead.

10 Friday

PACIFIC. TG 76.2 (four high-speed transports) begins antisubmarine and antibarge sweep off New Guinea coast between Lae and Salamaua; off Lae, the ships are straddled in engagement with Japanese shore battery but emerge undamaged (see 11 September).

11 Saturday

PACIFIC. TG 76.2 completes its sweep of the New Guinea coast, shelling shore battery at Lae; high-speed transport *Humphreys* (APD 12) is damaged by operational casualty (damaged recoil cylinder of no. 1 gun).

Submarine *Harder* (SS 257) sinks Japanese transport *Yoko Maru* south of Mikura Jima, 33°48′N, 139°37′E.

Submarine *Narwhal* (SS 167) sinks Japanese transport *Hokusho Maru* five miles northwest of Nauru, 00°30′S, 166°50′E.

Submarine *Spearfish* (SS 190) torpedoes Japanese army transport *Tsuyama Maru* south of Kyushu, 30°56′N, 132°47′E.

USAAF B-24s and B-25s (11th Air Force) bomb Japanese shipping off Paramushir, Kurils; light cruiser *Abukuma* is damaged by near-misses.

USAAF B-24s sink Japanese minesweeper *W.16* in bombing raid on Makassar, Celebes, 06°08′S, 119°20′E.

Tank landing craft *LCT 71* founders and sinks in heavy weather east of the Aleutians, 53°38′N, 146°05′W.

ATLANTIC. German submarine *U 107* lays mines off Charleston, South Carolina.

MEDITERRANEAN. Destroyer *Rowan* (DD 405) engages German motor torpedo boats (3rd Motor Torpedo Boat Flotilla) off Salerno and is sunk by torpedo, 40°07′N, 14°18′E; destroyer *Bristol* (DD 453) rescues survivors. German DO 217s attack shipping; light cruiser *Savannah* (CL 42) takes a direct hit from a rocket bomb at 40°21′N, 14°55′E; light cruiser *Philadelphia* (CL 41) is near-missed at 40°24′N, 14°51′E.

12 Sunday

MEDITERRANEAN. In predawn air raid off Salerno, small seaplane tender (amphibious command ship) *Biscayne* (AVP 11) is near-missed by bombs.[166] A near-miss by a rocket bomb near British ammunition ship *Lyminge* sets that vessel afire and prompts her abandonment. Fire and rescue party from *Biscayne*, however, boards the vessel and controls the flames before salvage tugs arrive. Later this day, British hospital ship *Newfoundland* (with U.S. nurses embarked) is bombed and abandoned, 40°14′N, 13°20′E.

U.S. freighter *William B. Travis* is damaged (most likely by mine) about 25 miles north of Bizerte, Tunisia, 37°17′N, 10°30′E, but reaches port under her own power. While there are no casualties among the 47-man merchant complement or the 27-man Armed Guard, one of the 41 passengers perishes in the explosion.

PACIFIC. Tank landing ship *LST 455* is damaged by dive bomber off Buna, New Guinea, 08°59′S, 149°10′E.

Tug *Navajo* (AT 64), en route from Tutuila, Samoa, to Espíritu Santo and towing gasoline barge *YOG 42*, is sunk by Japanese submarine *I 39*, 150 miles east of her destination; motor minesweeper *YMS 266* picks up the survivors.

Submarine *Permit* (SS 178) torpedoes Japanese aircraft transport *Fujikawa Maru* off Kwajalein, 08°23′N, 165°12′E (see 13 September).

ATLANTIC. U.S. freighter *Benjamin Franklin* runs aground off Black Fish Bank; from Norfolk, Virginia, tug *Sciota* (AT 30), harbor tug *Bomazeen* (YT 238), and salvage vessel *Warbler* (ARS 11) proceed to the merchantman's assistance and refloat her so that she can proceed under her own power.

13 Monday

PACIFIC. Submarine *Permit* (SS 178) torpedoes Japanese fleet tanker *Shiretoko* off Kwajalein, 08°33′N, 164°40′E, but misses light cruiser *Naka*, which has been sent out from Truk to protect the oiler.

Submarine *Snook* (SS 279) sinks Japanese army transport *Yamato Maru* in East China Sea, east of Hangchow Bay, 30°08′N, 123°32′E, and although escorting destroyer *Shiokaze* claims her destruction, *Snook* emerges from the encounter to fight again.

Japanese land attack planes (755th *Kokutai*) bomb Nanomea, Ellice Islands.

MEDITERRANEAN. German planes bomb Allied shipping off Salerno. U.S. freighter *James W. Marshall* is damaged by bomb and resultant fire. There are, however, no casualties among the crew. Submarine chaser *SC 666* is damaged by collision in Gulf of Salerno, 40°40′N, 14°44′E.

14 Tuesday

MEDITERRANEAN. German aircraft bomb invasion shipping off Salerno. U.S. freighter *Bushrod Washington* is set afire by a direct hit and is abandoned; tug *Hopi* (AT 71) assists boats with the latter's survivors. One Armed Guard sailor, four merchant seamen, and 10 stevedores perish in the explosion and fires (see 15 September).

PACIFIC. Motor torpedo boat *PT 219* is blown aground in storm off Attu, Aleutians. Small seaplane tender *Casco* (AVP 12) pulls the PT off the rocks, but the battered boat fills with water and sinks (see 20 September).

Expanded opportunities for women in the naval service included communications; here Ensign Beulah Wheeler, USNR, works at district headquarters, Spokane, Washington, 16 September 1943, with Lieutenant Commander Louis J. Malnati, USNR. Malnati will distinguish himself as Officer in Charge of Commander Seventh Fleet Communication Center, handling large volumes of radio traffic incident to the landings at Morotai and Leyte, and the Battle of Leyte Gulf. (NA, 80-G-207702)

15 Wednesday

MEDITERRANEAN. German air attacks on Allied shipping off Salerno continue. U.S. freighter *James W. Marshall* is damaged by rocket bomb; tank landing craft *LCT 19* alongside catches fire and the resultant blaze compels the abandonment of the freighter. Thirteen of the ship's merchant complement perish, as do 50 Army stevedores working cargo. LCM tows *LCT 19* from alongside the burning "Liberty" ship; beyond salvage, the LCT is later scuttled by British destroyer HMS *Hambledon*. Small seaplane tender (amphibious command ship) *Biscayne* (AVP 11) provides aid for survivors. U.S. freighter *William Bradford* is strafed by German planes; there are no casualties among the freighter's merchant or Armed Guard complements. *LCT 241* is sunk by aerial bomb; *LCT 209* is destroyed when freighter *Bushrod Washington* explodes when the uncontrolled fires (started the previous day when the ship suffers a direct hit) reach the 500-pound bombs stowed forward.

PACIFIC. Fleet Air Wing 17 (Commodore Thomas S. Combs) is established in Brisbane, Australia, for operations in southwestern Pacific.

Destroyer *Saufley* (DD 465) and PBY (VP 23) sink Japanese submarine *RO 101*, 100 miles east of San Cristobal, Solomons, 10°57′S, 163°56′E.

Submarine *Haddock* (SS 231) sinks Japanese collier *Sansei Maru* north of Truk, 09°32′N, 150°38′E.

16 Thursday

PACIFIC. Japanese gunboat *Seikai Maru* is sunk by mine, laid by submarine *Silversides* (SS 236) on 4 June, off Kavieng, New Ireland, 02°36′N, 150°34′E.

PBY sinks small Japanese cargo vessel *No. 2 Taira Maru* en route to Hansa Bay, 04°10′S, 144°55′E.

ATLANTIC. Salvage vessel *Weight* (ARS 35), in convoy UGS 18, suffers damage to steering gear at 35°47′N, 70°55′W, and returns to Norfolk, Virginia, for repairs.

MEDITERRANEAN. German planes again bomb shipping off the Salerno beachhead, scoring direct hits and near-misses on British battleship HMS *Warspite*; tugs *Moreno* (AT 87) and *Hopi* (AT 71) assist the damaged dreadnought.

German planes bomb Allied shipping off Bizerte, Tunisia. U.S. freighter *Edward P. Costigan* is damaged by near-miss of bomb; there are no casualties to either merchant or Armed Guard complements.

17 Friday

PACIFIC. Submarine *Gudgeon* (SS 211) battles Japanese minelayer *No. 2 Fumi Maru* in an inconclusive surface gunnery action off Rota, Marianas, 13°50′N, 145°02′E (see 28 September).

Motor torpedo boat *PT 136* runs aground on an uncharted reef while patrolling Vitiaz Strait, 05°55′S, 148°01′E, and is destroyed by gunfire from *PT 142* to prevent capture.

18 Saturday

PACIFIC. USAAF B-24s (7th Air Force) (TG 15.7), flying from Canton, China, and Funafuti, Ellice Islands, bomb Japanese installations on Tarawa. That same day, TF 15 (Rear Admiral Charles A. Pownall) attacks Tarawa, Makin, and Abemama, Gilberts, to destroy Japanese aircraft and airfield facilities on Tarawa, to decrease pressure on the Ellice Islands (in the wake of the air raids on Nanomea on 7, 8, and 13 September), and to provide operational training. During the attack on Tarawa, TBFs, SBDs, and F6Fs from carrier *Lexington* (CV 16) and small carriers *Princeton* (CVL 23) and *Belleau Wood* (CVL 24) sink Japanese motor torpedo boats *Gyoraitei No. 2* and *Gyoraitei No. 3*. Submarine *Steelhead* (SS 280) supports TF 15 (see 19 September).

Submarine *S 42* (SS 153) torpedoes Japanese gunboat *Chowa Maru* off Paramushir, Kurils, 50°22′N, 155°43′E.

Submarine *Scamp* (SS 277) attacks Japanese convoy north of New Guinea, sinking army cargo ship *Kansai Maru*, 00°41′N, 146°28′E. Although damaged by depth charges (perhaps dropped by submarine chasers *Ch 38* and/or *Ch 16*, which rescue survivors) *Scamp* remains on patrol.

Submarine *Spearfish* (SS 190) damages Japanese torpedo boat *Sagi* (premature explosion of two torpedoes) west of Tokara Gunto, 29°08′N, 134°29′E.

Submarine *Trigger* (SS 237) sinks Japanese freighter *Yowa Maru* northwest of Okinawa, Japan, 27°20′N, 126°53′E.

ATLANTIC. U.S. freighter *William Pepperell* is attacked by German submarine *U 260*, 55°02′N, 29°27′E, but the torpedo detonates in the ship's torpedo streamer, causing only minor damage to the freighter herself; there are no casualties to either the 42-man merchant complement or the 26-man Armed Guard (see 20 September).

Destroyer *Gillespie* (DD 609) is slightly

damaged in collision with destroyer escort *Wyffels* (DE 6) at Gibraltar.

MEDITERRANEAN. German planes again bomb shipping off Salerno; submarine chaser *SC 508* is damaged by near-miss.

19 Sunday

PACIFIC. USAAF B-24s (7th Air Force) (TG 15.7) provides cover for retirement of TF 15 from the Gilberts in the wake of the carrier strike bombing Tarawa the previous day.

Submarine *Harder* (SS 257) sinks Japanese freighter *Kachiyama Maru* off mouth of Kii Strait, Honshu, 33°25′N, 135°38′E.

Motor torpedo boats *PT 121* and *PT 133* receive superficial damage from machine gun and small-arms fire during engagement with Japanese barge off Langemak Bay, New Guinea.

20 Monday

PACIFIC. Submarine *Haddock* (SS 231) torpedoes Japanese fleet tanker *Notoro* east of the Palaus, 07°23′N, 150°11′E; auxiliary submarine chaser *No. 2 Takunan Maru* conducts fruitless search for *Haddock*.

Submarine *S 28* (SS 133) sinks Japanese gunboat *No. 2 Katsura Maru* 165 miles southwest of Paramushir, Kurils, 49°05′N, 151°45′E.

Motor torpedo boat *PT 219*, sunk in storm at Attu, Aleutians, after unsuccessful salvage attempt by small seaplane tender *Casco* (AVP 12), is raised by seaplane wrecking derrick *YSD 26* and placed in a floating drydock for repairs.[167]

USAAF B-25s, escorted by P-40s, bomb Kiukiang, China; Japanese repair ship *Hayase* is sunk.

Covered lighter *YF 579* springs leaks while under tow; salvage attempts are unsuccessful and the lighter is blown up and sinks off San Francisco, California.

ATLANTIC. U.S. freighter *William Pepperell* is again attacked by German submarine *U 260*, but with the same result as two days before. Again, there are no casualties and the ship ultimately reaches port under her own power.

German submarine *U 238* attacks New York–bound convoy ON 202, torpedoing U.S. freighters *Frederick Douglass*, 57°03′N, 28°08′W, and *Theodore Dwight Weld*, 57°03′N, 28°12′W. British rescue ship *Rathlin* rescues all hands (40-man merchant complement, 29-man Armed Guard, and one female stowaway) from *Frederick Douglass*, which remains afloat until finished off later the same day by *U 645*. *Theodore Dwight Weld* sinks so quickly

that 20 of the 42-man merchant complement and 13 of the 28-man Armed Guard perish. *Rathlin* rescues the survivors.

MEDITERRANEAN. Motor torpedo boats *PT 209* and *PT 204* conduct daylight reconnaissance of Bay of Naples to investigate German shore battery activity on the Sorento Peninsula. Although the boats are showered with water from near-misses, they are not hit, and the position of enemy guns is charted before the PTs lay smoke and retire.

21 Tuesday

PACIFIC. Submarine *Haddock* (SS 231) torpedoes Japanese collier *Shinyubari Maru* westnorthwest of Truk, 08°53′N, 148°30′E.

Submarine *Trigger* (SS 237) sinks Japanese fleet oilers *Shiriya* and *Shoyo Maru* and freighter *Argun Maru,* and torpedoes fleet oiler *No. 1 Ozura Maru* north of Keelung, Formosa, 26°27′N, 122°40′E.

Submarine *Wahoo* (SS 238) sinks Japanese merchant fishing vessel *Hokusei Maru* east of Etorofu, Kurils, 45°45′N, 145°46′E.

USAAF B-24 (5th Air Force) aircraft sink Japanese transport *No. 6 Takashima Maru* in Bismarck Sea, 03°45′S, 149°20′E.

MEDITERRANEAN. U.S. freighter *William W. Gerhard*, in Salerno-bound convoy, is torpedoed by German submarine *U 238* at 40°07′N, 14°43′E, and abandoned by the 46-man crew, 29 of the 30-man Armed Guard (one man perishes in the initial explosion), and 191 Army troops. After the crew returns to the ship to prepare her for towing, tug *Moreno* (AT 87) takes the torpedoed merchantman in tow and heads for Salerno. Fires break out on board, however, and after unavailing efforts by the crew, aided by tug *Narragansett* (AT 88) and British rescue tug HMS *Weazel*, the crew abandons ship a second time, transferring to *Moreno. William W. Gerhard* explodes that night and breaks in two; the bow section sinks immediately (see 22 September). German shore battery shells Allied shipping, scoring direct hit on British tank landing craft HMS *LCT 584*. As shipping gets under way without orders, the vessel to which the tank landing craft is moored, British freighter *Lambrook*, proceeds to sea. Large infantry landing craft *LCI(L) 10*, in a display of good seamanship, goes alongside and provides needed medical assistance to the wounded on board *LCT 584*.

INDIAN OCEAN. U.S. freighter *Cornelia P. Spencer* is torpedoed by German submarine *U 188* at 02°08′N, 50°10′E; when the U-boat surfaces to finish off the merchantman, however, the

Armed Guard gunfire proves so accurate that the U-boat submerges and torpedoes the ship again (the explosion kills two merchant sailors). *Cornelia P. Spencer* is then abandoned. Torpedoed a third time she sinks soon thereafter. The survivors (39 merchant sailors and the 27-man Armed Guard) are divided among four lifeboats (see 22 September and 6 October).

22 Wednesday

PACIFIC. TF 76 (Rear Admiral Daniel E. Barbey) lands 20th Australian Brigade at Finschhafen, New Guinea. Large infantry landing craft *LCI(L) 343* and *LCI(L) 344* lose ramps during beaching operations; *LCI(L) 343* is damaged by mortar fire.

Submarine *Harder* (SS 257) sinks Japanese merchant tanker *Daishin Maru* and cargo ship *Kowa Maru* south of Honshu, 34°46′N, 140°55′E.

Submarine *Hoe* (SS 258) attacks Japanese fleet tanker *Gen'yo Maru* north-northwest of Truk, 10°08′N, 147°01′E. Although *Hoe* claims two hits on her quarry, *Gen'yo Maru* carries out a rigorous schedule of operations soon thereafter, indicating that she sustains little, if any, damage in *Hoe's* attack.

Submarine *Snook* (SS 279) sinks Japanese freighter *Katsurahama Maru*, 39°00′N, 124°20′E, and torpedoes freighter *Hakutetsu Maru* off Dairen, Manchuria, 39°15′N, 123°30′E.

Submarine *Trigger* (SS 237) torpedoes Japanese army cargo ship *Gyoku Maru* northeast of Keelung, Formosa, 26°27′N, 122°40′E.

German auxiliary cruiser *Michel* (Schiffe 28) sights U.S. convoy escorted by submarine chasers *SC 1042* and *SC 1045* on the Panama-Australia route but, overestimating its composition, refrains from attacking.

Gunboat *Charleston* (PG 51) is damaged when accidentally rammed by U.S. freighter *Sam Jackson*, Kuluk Bay, Adak, Alaska.

Coastal transport *APc 35*, irreparably damaged by grounding en route to Renard Sound, New Georgia, 08°48′S, 157°46′E, is beached and abandoned.

MEDITERRANEAN. U.S. freighter *Richard Olney*, in convoy KMS 26, is mined off Bizerte, Tunisia, 37°25′N, 09°54′E; two of the 43-man merchant complement perish in the explosion. There are no casualties among the 31-man Armed Guard or among the 143 troop passengers. Although *Richard Olney* reaches Bizerte under tow of British (ex–Coast Guard) cutter HMS *Landguard*, the freighter will be written off as a total loss.

Tugs *Moreno* (AT 87) and *Narragansett* (AT 88) and British rescue tug HMS *Weazel* scuttle the stern section of U.S. freighter *William W. Gerhard,* broken in two on 21 September, with gunfire off Salerno, Italy.

INDIAN OCEAN. British destroyer HMS *Relentless* rescues 34 survivors from two boats from U.S. freighter *Cornelia P. Spencer*, torpedoed by German submarine *U 188* the day before. Freighter *Sandown Castle* rescues 16 men from a third boat (see 6 October).

23 Thursday

PACIFIC. Submarine *Trout* (SS 202) sinks Japanese transport *Ryotoku Maru* and freighter *Yamashiro Maru* northwest of the Marianas, 20°45′N, 142°10′E, and eludes counterattacks of auxiliary minesweeper *Keinan Maru*.

Submarine *Tuna* (SS 203) attacks Japanese cargo vessel *Shinwa Maru* in the East China Sea north-northwest of the Anambas Islands, 04°50′N, 105°50′E.

ATLANTIC. U.S. freighter *Steel Voyager*, in convoy ONS 202, is torpedoed by German submarine *U 952* at 53°30′N, 40°40′W, and abandoned. Although reboarded when Canadian corvette HMCS *Morden* and Free French corvette *Renoncule* arrive to provide assistance, *Steel Voyager* is abandoned a second time when it becomes obvious that the ship cannot be gotten under way. All hands (39-man merchant complement and 27-man Armed Guard) are taken on board the two corvettes.

24 Friday

PACIFIC. Submarine *Cabrilla* (SS 288) attacks Japanese carrier *Taiyo*, escort carrier *Chuyo*, and destroyer *Shimakaze* (en route from Truk to Yokosuka) northeast of Chichi Jima, torpedoing *Taiyo* at 28°00′N, 146°10′E. *Chuyo* tows the disabled carrier to Yokosuka. *Taiyo* is saved from worse damage because two of the three torpedo warheads that hit the ship (of the six fired by *Cabrilla*) detach upon impact.

USAAF B-24 sinks small Japanese cargo vessel *Shonan Maru* south of Mussau Island, 00°27′S, 147°43′E.

INDIAN OCEAN. U.S. freighter *Elias Howe* is torpedoed and sunk by Japanese submarine *I 10* about 75 miles southeast of Aden, 11°40′N, 44°35′E. Subsequently, British seaplanes rescue one boatload of survivors and those on board two rafts; British trawler HMS *Aiglon* rescues the remainder. Two of the 42-man merchant complement are killed in the initial explosion; the 18-man Armed Guard survives intact.

25 Saturday

PACIFIC. Tank landing ship *LST 167* is damaged by dive bomber off Vella Lavella, Solomons, 07°45′S, 156°30′E.

Submarine *Bluefish* (SS 222) torpedoes Japanese freighter *Akashi Maru* off Labuan, Borneo, 06°23′S, 118°55′E, and survives counterattack by auxiliary minesweeper *Wa 4* (see 29 September).

Submarines *Bowfin* (SS 287), *Billfish* (SS 286), and *Bonefish* (SS 223) attack Japanese convoy; *Bowfin* sinks tanker *Kirishima Maru* 220 nautical miles north of Nha Trang, French Indochina, 09°50′N, 112°03′E. None of the other attacks, however, prove successful, and the enemy ships continue their passage to Manila.

MEDITERRANEAN. Minesweeper *Skill* (AM 115) is sunk by German submarine *U 593* in Gulf of Salerno, 40°19.5′N, 14°35.5′E. Sister ship *Speed* (AM 116) rescues the few survivors, screened by *Seer* (AM 112). *Pilot* (AM 104) conducts a follow-up search for survivors without success.

26 Sunday

ATLANTIC. Naval Operating Facility, Natal, Brazil, is established.

27 Monday

PACIFIC. Submarine *Bluefish* (SS 222) sinks Japanese torpedo boat *Kasasagi* south of Kabaena Island, 05°45′S, 121°50′E.

Submarine *Bonefish* (SS 223) sinks Japanese army transport *Kashima Maru*, and torpedoes cargo ship *Chihaya Maru* off Cape Padaran, French Indochina, 10°10′N, 109°40′E.

USAAF B-24s and P-38s (5th Air Force) bomb Japanese shipping at Wewak, New Guinea, sinking transport *Taisei Maru* and cargo vessels *Sakihana Maru, Taisho Maru, Fuji Maru,* and *Kiri Maru.*

Malayan saboteurs, promised a livelihood after the British reoccupy Malaya, sink Japanese cargo ship *Hakusan Maru* and damage cargo ship *Kizan Maru* at Singapore. Efforts to salvage the latter are eventually abandoned and the ship is written off as a total loss.

ATLANTIC. PBMs (VP 74) sink German submarine *U 161* off Brazil, 12°30′S, 35°35′W.

28 Tuesday

PACIFIC. Submarine *Cisco* (SS 290) is sunk, probably by Japanese observation seaplane (PETE) (954th *Kokutai*) and gunboat *Karatsu* [ex-U.S. river gunboat *Luzon* (PR 7)] in Sulu Sea off Panay Island, 09°47′N, 121°44′E.

Naval armed guard crew of the "Liberty" ship *William J. Worth* fires the merchantman's 4-inch/.50-caliber gun at gunnery practice, probably during her 15–26 September 1943 passage from New York to San Juan, Puerto Rico, via Guantánamo Bay, Cuba. (NA, 80-G-104069)

Submarine *Grouper* (SS 214) lands men and supplies on south coast of New Britain.

Submarine *Gudgeon* (SS 211) sinks Japanese freighter *Taian Maru* off Saipan, Marianas, 15°22′N, 145°38′E, and survives counterattack by minelayer *No. 2 Fumi Maru* (which *Gudgeon* had engaged on 17 September) as *Gudgeon* and *No. 2 Fumi Maru* encounter each other for the second time in a fortnight.

MEDITERRANEAN. Salvage vessel *Brant* (ARS 32) is damaged when she is accidentally rammed by British landing craft HMS *LCF 16* during a gale in the Gulf of Salerno.

29 Wednesday

PACIFIC. Destroyers *Patterson* (DD 392) and *McCalla* (DD 488), during a sweep to destroy Japanese barge traffic north of Kolombangara, are damaged in collision, 07°36′S, 157°12′E.

Submarine *Bluefish* (SS 222) sinks Japanese freighter *Akashi Maru* in the Banda Sea, 06°11′S, 126°00′E.

Submarine *Gudgeon* (SS 211) torpedoes Japanese gunboat *Santo Maru* off Saipan, 15°28′N, 145°57′E.[168] Transport *Kenryu Maru* tows the damaged ship to Saipan.

MEDITERRANEAN. Severe gale hits Salerno area. Tank landing craft *LCT 342* sinks after

running aground; *LCT 537*, *LCT 553*, *LCT 556*, *LCT 583*, *LCT 603*, *LCT 605*, *LCT 606*, *LCT 614*, *LCT 616*, *LCT 618*, *LCT 621*, and *LCT 626* are all damaged when the storm strands them off Salerno's south beaches. Some 58 LCMs and LCVPs are broached on the beaches as well.

30 Thursday

PACIFIC. Tank landing ship *LST 334* is damaged by dive bombers off Vella Lavella, Solomons, 07°43′S, 156°40′E.

Four U.S. motor torpedo boats are strafing Japanese landing barges between Tuki and Ropo Points, Kolombangara, when three USMC F4Us approach; two of the friendly planes recognize standard recognition signals. One F4U (VMF 213), however, strafes and damages *PT 126*, 07°50′S, 157°05′E. The Corsair is shot down by PT gunfire.

Motor torpedo boat *PT 68* is damaged by grounding off Vincke Point, Huon Peninsula, eastern New Guinea, 05°56′S, 147°18′E (see 1 October).

Submarine *Bowfin* (SS 287) delivers supplies, officer mail, stores, and currency; leaves what of her own stores, ammunition, cigarettes, and clothing she can spare; and embarks nine evacuees from Siquijor Island, P.I. During the course of carrying out her mis-

sion, *Bowfin* also sinks small Japanese cargo ship *Mitake Maru*, 05°17′N, 121°57′E.

Submarine *Harder* (SS 257) sinks Japanese auxiliary submarine chaser *No. 3 Shosei Maru* south of Honshu, 34°10′N, 150°45′E.

Submarine *Pogy* (SS 266) sinks Japanese army transport *Maebashi Maru* 300 miles east of Palau, 06°01′N, 139°08′E.

USAAF B-25s and P-40s (14th Air Force) sink Japanese auxiliary minesweeper *Chikushi Maru* in Kwangchow Bay, China, 21°12′N, 110°24′E; the vessel is later salvaged, however, and resumes active service.

ATLANTIC. Coast Guard cutter *Wilcox* (WYP 333) founders and sinks 94 miles off Nags Head, North Carolina.

OCTOBER

1 Friday

PACIFIC. Motor torpedo boat *PT 68*, damaged by grounding off Vincke Point, Huon Peninsula, eastern New Guinea, the previous day, 05°56′S, 147°18′E, is scuttled by motor torpedo boat *PT 191* to prevent capture.

Eight U.S. destroyers conduct sweep near Kolombangara to disrupt Japanese barge traffic, sinking 20 of an estimated 35. Japanese "snoopers," however, carry out constant harassment of the U.S. force; destroyer *Saufley* (DD 465) is damaged by near-miss, 07°42′S, 160°14′E.

Submarine *Peto* (SS 265) sinks Japanese transport *Tonei Maru* and Japanese army cargo ship *Kinkasan Maru* southwest of Truk, 04°00′N, 143°50′E.

Submarine *Wahoo* (SS 238) sinks Japanese freighter *Masaki Maru* in Sea of Japan.

Tank landing ship *LST 448* is damaged by horizontal bomber south of Vella Lavella, 07°45′S, 156°30′E (see 5 October).

Mobile degaussing barge *YDG 4* sinks nine miles southeast of Bulari Passage, after running aground off New Caledonia.

ATLANTIC. Naval forces under Commander Naval Forces Europe (Admiral Harold R. Stark) are designated the Twelfth Fleet.

Escort carrier *Block Island* (CVE 21) and destroyer *Black* (DD 666) are damaged in collision in Elizabeth River Channel, Norfolk, Virginia.

PV-1s (VB 128) attack German submarines *U 402* and *U 448* as the latter seek (unsuccessfully) convoy HX 258 in the North Atlantic.

Naval Air Facility, Recife, Brazil, is established.

MEDITERRANEAN. U.S. freighter *Metapan*, in convoy UGS 15, is mined and sunk at 37°20′N, 10°35′E. Fuel oil barge *Syncline* (YO 63) rescues the 50-man merchant complement, the 23-man Armed Guard, and the one passenger.

2 Saturday

PACIFIC. Submarine *Kingfish* (SS 234) lays mines off southern Celebes, N.E.I.

Tank landing ship *LST 203* is damaged by grounding near Nanomea, Ellice Islands.

Japanese minesweeper *W.28* is damaged by mine, laid by submarine *Silversides* (SS 236) on 4 June, off Kavieng, 02°36′S, 150°34′E.

3 Sunday

PACIFIC. Japanese complete evacuation of Kolombangara, Solomons.

Destroyer *Henley* (DD 391) is sunk by Japanese submarine *RO 108* off eastern New Guinea, 07°40′S, 148°06′E.

Japanese hospital ship *Hikawa Maru* is damaged by mine, Surabaya, Java.

4 Monday

ATLANTIC. Operation LEADER, the only U.S. Navy carrier operation carried out in northern European waters during World War II, causes "appreciable losses" to two convoys off the Norwegian coast and to shipping in the harbor of Bodø, Norway. TBFs (VT 4), SBDs (VB 4), and F4Fs (VF 4) from carrier *Ranger* (CV 4) sink Norwegian steamer *Vagan* and damage Norwegian steamer *Topeka*; sink German steamers *Kaguir*, *LaPlata*, and *Rabat* and transport *Skramstad*; and damage German tanker *Schleswig* and steamers *Kerkplein* and *Ibis*. German steamer *Malaga* is damaged by a dud bomb. Only two German planes approach the task force: both (JU 88 and HE 115) are shot down by combat air patrol F4Fs (VF 4).

TBF and F4Fs (VC 9) from escort carrier *Card* (CVE 11) attack three German submarines—*U 264*, *U 422*, and *U 455*—rendezvousing with a milch cow, *U 460*, north of the Azores. *U 460* and *U 422* are sunk, 43°13′N, 28°58′W, and 43°18′N, 28°58′W, respectively. This action in the Central Atlantic allows convoy UGS 19 to pass through the vicinity unmolested by the enemy.

PV-1s (VB 128) sink German submarine *U 336* southwest of Iceland, 60°40′N, 26°30′W, during operations to protect convoy ONS 204.

MEDITERRANEAN. German bombers attack convoy UGS 18; a near-miss damages U.S. freighter *Hiram S. Maxim* about 12 miles northwest of Cape Tenes, Algeria, 36°42′N,

Splashes from bombs and machine gun bullets straddle merchantman *Saar* as she steams in the waters off Bodo, Norway, during the attack by *Ranger* (CV 4) planes on that port in Operation LEADER, 4 October 1943. (NHC, NH 84254)

01°17′E; abandoned by all but a skeleton crew of seven merchant seamen and six Armed Guard sailors, the ship is towed to Algiers for repairs. Freighters *Leslie M. Shaw* and *Harry Lane* rescue the remainder of the crew (33 merchant and 22 Armed Guard). There are no casualties.

5 Tuesday

PACIFIC. TF 14 (Rear Admiral Alfred E. Montgomery), including three carriers, three small carriers, three heavy cruisers, four light cruisers, 24 destroyers, and two oilers, pounds Wake Island. Fearing that the strikes portend a landing and that an escaped POW could communicate the weakness of his garrison, Rear Admiral Sakaibara Shigematsu, the Japanese island commander, orders the execution of the 98 remaining civilians (Contractors Pacific Naval Air Bases) captured on 23 December 1941. He personally decapitates the last man himself (see 6 October).

Tank landing ship *LST 448*, damaged on 1 October, sinks while in tow of tug *Bobolink* (AT 131) south of Vella Lavella, Solomons, 08°03′S, 156°43′E.

Submarine *Wahoo* (SS 238) sinks Japanese army transport *Konron Maru* in Tsushima Straits, 34°00′N, 129°00′E. Loss of *Konron Maru*,

of the Shimonoseki-to-Fusan ferry line, prompts the cancellation of night ferry trips across Tsushima Straits. Because of heavy seas, only 72 people, of the 616 on board, are rescued.

MEDITERRANEAN. German bombers attack convoy UGS 18; a near-miss damages U.S. freighter *Cotton Mather* about 15 miles north of Cape Tenes, Algeria, 36°00′N, 01°00′E. There are no casualties among the 53-man merchant complement and the 27-man Armed Guard; the ship reaches Algiers under her own power.

6 Wednesday

PACIFIC. TF 14 (Rear Admiral Alfred E. Montgomery) again pounds Japanese installations on Wake Island. Submarine *Skate* (SS 305), lifeguarding for the strikes, is strafed and damaged by Japanese aircraft off the atoll, but remains on patrol.

Battle of Vella Lavella: Three U.S. destroyers (Captain Frank R. Walker) intercept nine Japanese ships (Vice Admiral Ijuin Masuji) (convoying some 20 barges) evacuating troops from Vella Lavella, in what proves to be the last surface engagement in the central Solomons. All three U.S. ships are damaged: *O'Bannon* (DD 450) in collision with *Chevalier* (DD 451), 07°30′S, 156°15′E; *Selfridge*

(DD 357) by torpedo fired from either *Shigure* or *Samidare*, 07°27′S, 156°13′E; and *Chevalier* by torpedo from *Yugumo*. *Chevalier* is scuttled by destroyer *LaVallette* (DD 448), 07°30′S, 156°14′E. Torpedoes from *Chevalier* and *Selfridge* sink *Yugumo*.

Submarine *Kingfish* (SS 234) lands men and supplies on northeast coast of Borneo.

Submarine *Steelhead* (SS 280) damages Japanese fast fleet tanker *Kazuhaya*, 10°30′N, 146°37′E; *Tinosa* (SS 283) later finishes off *Kazuhaya* 240 nautical miles northwest of Truk, 10°30′N, 148°20′E.

Submarine *Wahoo* (SS 238) sinks Japanese army cargo ship *Kanko Maru* in the Sea of Japan off the east coast of Korea, 37°18′N, 129°33′E.

Submarine chaser *PC 478* and tank landing ship *LST 451* are damaged in collision while en route from Adak to Amchitka, Aleutians.

ATLANTIC. Submarine *Dorado* (SS 248) departs New London, Connecticut, for the Panama Canal. She is never heard from again.[169]

INDIAN OCEAN. Last boatload (16 men) from U.S. freighter *Cornelia P. Spencer*, torpedoed by German submarine *U 188* on 21 September, reach safety on the coast of Somalia.

7 Thursday

PACIFIC. Japanese complete evacuation of Vella Lavella, Solomons.

Light cruiser *Concord* (CL 10) is damaged by on-board explosion (leaking gasoline tank) off Nukahiva Island, Marquesas.

Submarine *S 44* (SS 155) is sunk by Japanese escort destroyer *Ishigaki* north-northeast of Araito Island, east of the Kamchatka Peninsula, Kurils.

Japanese guardboat *No. 20 Inari Maru* is destroyed by accidental fire off Wake Island.

Japanese transport *Kikukawa Maru* is destroyed by accidental fire at Truk.

MEDITERRANEAN. Tank landing craft *LCT 216* breaks in half in heavy sea while in tow to Palermo, Italy; *LCT 196* breaks in half in heavy sea; the after section is scuttled by British surface ship but the forward section is towed to Bizerte, Tunisia.

ATLANTIC. U.S. freighter *Yorkmar*, in convoy SC 143, is torpedoed and sunk by German submarine *U 645* at 56°48′N, 20°30′W. Of the 39-man merchant complement, 11 drown in the abandonment; two of the 28-man Armed Guard perish as well. Canadian corvette HMCS *Kamloops* and British frigate HMS *Duckworth* rescue the survivors.

8 Friday

PACIFIC. Submarine *Gato* (SS 212) damages Japanese cargo ship *Amagisan Maru* with dud torpedo southeast of Truk, 05°34′N, 152°10′E, and survives ensuing hunter-killer operations by escorting torpedo boat *Hiyodori*.

Submarine *Guardfish* (SS 217) sinks Japanese army cargo ship *Kashu Maru* north-northwest of the Admiralties, 00°20′S, 146°17′E.

Submarine *Gurnard* (SS 254) sinks Japanese army cargo ship *Taian Maru* and transport *Dainichi Maru* off northern tip of Luzon, 18°48′N, 119°21′E.

ATLANTIC. Naval Air Facility, Dakar, French West Africa, is established.

9 Saturday

PACIFIC. Submarine *Guardfish* (SS 217) attacks Japanese stores ship *Manko Maru* en route to Davao, 01°04′N, 146°08′E. Although *Guardfish* claims that one of four torpedoes fired hits the target, none do.

Submarine *Kingfish* (SS 234) torpedoes Japanese oiler *Hayamoto* in Sibitu Channel, 05°09′N, 119°18′E.

Submarine *Puffer* (SS 268) torpedoes Japanese tanker *Kumagawa Maru* in Makassar Strait, 01°08′N, 119°31′E, but is damaged by depth charges (possibly dropped by auxiliary submarine chasers *Cha 37* and *Cha 41*, summoned to the scene as escorts for *Shoyo Maru*, which will tow *Kumagawa Maru* to Balikpapan) and is forced to terminate her patrol.

Submarine *Rasher* (SS 269) sinks Japanese army cargo ship *Kogane Maru* 28 miles from Ambon, 03°30′S, 127°45′E.

Submarine *Wahoo* (SS 238) sinks Japanese cargo ship *Hankow Maru* off Oga Peninsula, 37°18′N, 129°33′E.

MEDITERRANEAN. Destroyer *Buck* (DD 420) is torpedoed and sunk by German submarine *U 616* in Gulf of Salerno, 39°57′N, 13°28′E.

10 Sunday

PACIFIC. Japanese planes attack three Lambu Lambu–based U.S. motor torpedo boats north of Vella Lavella, damaging *PT 168* and *PT 179*.

Submarine *Bonefish* (SS 223) sinks Japanese army cargo ship *Isuzugawa Maru* and merchant transport *Teibi Maru* off Cam Ranh Bay, French Indochina, 14°49′N, 110°10′E.

Submarine *Grayback* (SS 208) attacks Japanese troopship *Hakozaki Maru* northwest of the Bonins, 28°41′N, 138°32′E; although the submariners believe one of the four torpedoes fired hits the ship, all four in fact miss.

Submarine *Kingfish* (SS 234) lays mines off Cape Pepe, Makassar Strait, Celebes.

USAAF B-24 sinks Japanese army cargo ship *No. 5 Hino Maru* 20 miles southwest of Buka Passage, Solomons.

11 Monday

PACIFIC. Submarine *Skipjack* (SS 184) damages Japanese transport *Matsutani Maru* five miles off Kwajalein, 06°25′N, 171°40′E.

Submarine *Wahoo* (SS 238) is sunk by Japanese naval aircraft, submarine chasers *Ch 15* and *Ch 43*, and minesweeper *W.18*, in La Pérouse Strait, 45°13′N, 141°56′E.[170]

Japanese planes attack U.S. shipping off Koli Point, Guadalcanal, torpedoing freighters *George H. Himes* and *John H. Couch*; tug *Menominee* (AT 73) beaches *George H. Himes* (which suffers no casualties among the 41-man merchant complement, 27-man Armed Guard, and 20 CB stevedores) to save the ship's cargo of lumber, shells, and bombs. Three men perish on board *John H. Couch* (a merchant seaman, one Armed Guard sailor, and a CB stevedore), whose cargo of gasoline and diesel oil catches fire at the initial explosion. Fire-fighting efforts by two destroyer escorts prove as unsuccessful as the crew's efforts in putting out the blaze, and the ship is abandoned by the 42 merchant seamen, 25 Armed Guards, 28 troop passengers, and 99 stevedores (see 13 October).

USAAF B-25s attack small Japanese cargo vessels off Bougainville, sinking *Sanwa Maru* and damaging *Muyo Maru* with a near-miss.

ATLANTIC. Advanced Amphibious Training Base, Falmouth, Cornwall, England, is established.

12 Tuesday

PACIFIC. USAAF B-24s, B-25s, and P-38s and RAAF Beaufighters raid Rabaul, pounding Japanese shipping, town, harbor, and airfields in the vicinity, sinking transports *Keisho Maru* and *Kosei Maru*, cargo lighters *No. 1 Wakamatsu Maru* and *Kurogane Maru*, and guardboat *Mishima Maru* and damaging destroyers *Mochizuki*, *Minazuki*, and *Tachikaze*, submarines *I 177*, *I 180*, and *RO 105*, special service ship *Tsukushi*, oiler *Naruto*, and auxiliary sailing vessels *Tenryu Maru* and *Koan Maru*.

Submarine *Cero* (SS 225) torpedoes Japanese stores ship *Mamiya* off Chichi Jima, 28°39′N, 137°28′E; collier *Asakaze Maru* tows the damaged vessel to Saeki, Japan.

ATLANTIC. TBFs (VC 9) from escort carrier *Card* (CVE 11) break up another German

U-boat refueling rendezvous when they attack *U 488* about 600 miles north of Flores Island, Azores, and damage *U 731*.

13 Wednesday

GENERAL. Italy declares war on Germany.

PACIFIC. Japanese planes attack four Lambu Lambu–based U.S. motor torpedo boats southwest of Choiseul, Solomons; PT boaters shoot down attacking Japanese floatplane, an event that proves "the greatest lift" to the sailors who tangle almost nightly (and heretofore largely without success) with nocturnal enemy aircraft in that theater.

Submarine *Rasher* (SS 269) attacks Japanese convoy proceeding from Ambon to Kendari, sinking cargo ship *Kenkoku Maru*, 03°47′S, 127°41′E.

Submarine *Seadragon* (SS 194) attacks Kwajalein-bound Japanese ammunition ship *Soya*, escorted by auxiliary submarine chaser *No. 6 Shonan Maru*, 08°50′N, 167°50′E, but damages neither enemy ship. *No. 6 Shonan Maru*'s attacks on *Seadragon* prove equally unsuccessful.

Tug *Pawnee* (AT 74) tows gutted U.S. freighter *John H. Couch*, torpedoed by Japanese planes on 11 October off Koli Point, Guadalcanal, to a point two miles east of that place, where the merchantman capsizes.

USAAF B-25s (14th Air Force) bomb Japanese shipping in Amoy Harbor, China, sinking auxiliary submarine chaser *Kongo Maru*.

Japanese auxiliary minesweeper *Wa 101* is damaged by mine near Madoera Island, N.E.I., 07°11′S, 112°45′E.

ATLANTIC. TBF (VC 9) from escort carrier *Card* (CVE 11) sinks German submarine *U 402* north-northwest of the Azores, 48°56′N, 29°41′E.

MEDITERRANEAN. Destroyer *Bristol* (DD 453) is torpedoed and sunk by German submarine *U 371*, 70 miles west-northwest of Bône, Algeria, 37°25′N, 06°20′E.

14 Thursday

PACIFIC. Japanese planes attack six Lambu Lambu–based U.S. motor torpedo boats off Choiseul Bay, Solomons, damaging *PT 183*.

Submarine *Grayback* (SS 208) sinks Japanese fleet tanker *Kozui Maru* west-northwest of Okinawa, 27°35′N, 127°30′E, and eludes hunter-killer operations carried out by aviation supply ship *Takasaki*.

ATLANTIC. Airship *K 96* reports U.S. tanker *Chapultepec* disabled at 36 58′N, 73 04′W; tug *Sciota* (AT 30) takes the merchantman in tow

and brings her to Norfolk, Virginia, the following day.

Coast Guard Cutter *Dow* (WYP 353) runs aground off Mayaguez, Puerto Rico, and is abandoned.

Naval Air Facility, Igarape Assu, Brazil, is established.

15 Friday

PACIFIC. Submarine *Tullibee* (SS 284) attacks 10-ship Japanese convoy in Formosa Strait, sinking transport *Chicago Maru*, 24°35′N, 120°30′E.

ATLANTIC. U.S. freighter *James Russell Lowell*, in convoy GUS 18, is torpedoed by German submarine *U 371* at 37°18′15″N, 07°10′30″E, and abandoned. British whaler HMS *Southern Sea* rescues the 41-man merchant complement and the 28-man Armed Guard. With hopes high for saving the ship, the merchant crew reboards the ship and *Southern Sea* takes *James Russell Lowell* in tow. As weather conditions worsen, however, all but the master and two men abandon ship once more (see 16 October).

Advanced Amphibious Training Base, Fowey, Cornwall, England, is established.

16 Saturday

PACIFIC. USAAF B-24 (5th Air Force) sinks Japanese auxiliary submarine chaser *Cha 31* off Cape Lambert, New Britain, 04°00′N, 145°45′E.

Submarine *Mingo* (SS 261) attacks Japanese escort carrier *Chuyo* north-northwest of Truk, 11°02′N, 151°21′E. Although *Mingo* claims two damaging hits, the carrier emerges from the encounter unscathed; destroyer *Hatsukaze* depth charges *Mingo* but does not damage her.

ATLANTIC. U.S.-built destroyer escorts (the British classify them as "frigates") transferred under Lend-Lease to Great Britain (HMS *Byard*, HMS *Bentinck*, HMS *Berry*, HMS *Drury*, and HMS *Bazely*) enter combat for the first time as escorts for convoy ONS 20. *Byard* will sink *U 841* on 17 October.

Coastal yacht *Moonstone* (PYc-9) sinks in collision with destroyer *Greer* (DD 145), off the Delaware capes.

MEDITERRANEAN. U.S. freighter *James Russell Lowell*, torpedoed by German submarine *U 371* the day before, is beached off Colla, Algeria, by British tug. The ship breaks in twain and sinks two weeks later, a total loss.

17 Sunday

PACIFIC. Small reconnaissance seaplane from Japanese submarine *I 36* reconnoiters Pearl Harbor.

Submarine *Tarpon* (SS 175) sinks German auxiliary cruiser *Michel* (*Schiffe No. 28*) off Chichi Jima, Bonins, 33°42′N, 140°08′E.

USAAF B-24s damage Japanese troopship *Hakusan Maru* 80 miles from Kavieng, New Ireland.

ATLANTIC. Minesweeper *Tide* (AM 125) is detached from convoy UGS 21 to escort freighter *African Sun* to Bermuda for repairs to her refrigeration plant to save the latter's cargo, which consists entirely of frozen turkeys for the Thanksgiving dinners of American forces in North Africa and Italy. They rejoin UGS 21 on 21 October.

18 Monday

PACIFIC. Small carrier *Cowpens* (CVL 25) and destroyer *Abbot* (DD 629) are damaged in collision during maneuvers in Hawaiian Operating Area.

Submarine *Flying Fish* (SS 229) attacks Yokosuka-bound Japanese escort carrier *Chuyo*, 19°27′N, 145°20′E. Although *Flying Fish* claims one hit, the enemy flattop bears a charmed life, having survived an attack by *Mingo* (SS 261) on 16 October, and continues on to her destination on schedule.

Submarine *Lapon* (SS 260) sinks Japanese freighter *Taichu Maru* south-southeast of Shiono Misaki, 33°59′N, 136°24′E, and scores two dud hits on auxiliary minesweeper *No. 2 Keijin Maru*.

Submarine *Silversides* (SS 236) sinks Japanese army cargo ship *Tairin Maru* northwest of the Admiralties, 00°22′N, 143°23′E.

19 Tuesday

GENERAL. Moscow Conference, attended by Secretary of State Cordell Hull, British Foreign Minister Anthony Eden, and Soviet Foreign Minister Vyacheslav Molotov, convenes to discuss how to shorten hostilities and cooperate in the postwar world.

ATLANTIC. Heavy cruiser *Tuscaloosa* (CA 37), accompanied by one U.S. and three British destroyers, transports Norwegian troops and equipment to Spitsbergen, Norway, to reestablish bases destroyed in the German raid of 8 September. A second allied force, with carrier *Ranger* (CV 4) included, provides cover for the operation.

U.S. freighter *Delisle*, in convoy WB 65, fouls mine laid by German submarine *U 220* as the merchantman lies to, 15 miles out of St. John's, Newfoundland, rescuing survivors of British freighter *Penolver*. *Delisle* suffers no casualties and is abandoned by the 32-man crew and seven-man Armed Guard, and three sailors from *Penolver*. British trawler HMS *Miscou* rescues the survivors.

20 Wednesday

PACIFIC. Submarine *Gato* (SS 212) sinks Japanese transport *Tsunushima Maru* north-north-east of the Admiralties, 01°26′N, 148°36′E.

Submarine *Kingfish* (SS 234) sinks Japanese freighter *Sana Maru* off Banbon Bay, French Indochina, 12°36′N, 109°30′E.

ATLANTIC. TBFs (VC 13) from escort carrier *Core* (CVE 13), escorting convoy UGS 20, sink German submarine *U 378* north of the Azores, 47°40′N, 28°27′W.

Destroyer *Cowie* (DD 632), assigned to fast troop convoy UT 4, is damaged in collision with U.S. steamship *Craigsmere* in New York Harbor. *Cowie's* place in the escort is taken by *Quick* (DD 490).

MEDITERRANEAN. USAAF B-25s and RAF Beaufighters attack German convoys north of Crete, sinking transport *Sinfra*, which, unbeknown to the attackers, is transporting Allied POWs.

21 Thursday

PACIFIC. Submarine *Steelhead* (SS 280) damages Japanese aircraft transport *Goshu Maru* southeast of Ulithi, Carolines, 08°16′N, 141°53′E.

RAAF Beauforts attack Japanese light cruisers *Kiso* and *Tama* and destroyer *Uzuki* 53 miles from Cape St. George, 04°23′S, 153°11′E. *Kiso* is damaged by direct hit; *Tama* by near-misses. *Uzuki*, undamaged, screens *Tama* as she tows the disabled *Kiso* to Rabaul.

Japanese cargo ship *No. 11 Chofuku Maru* is sunk by mine while en route from Surabaya to Penang; cargo ship *Rakuto Maru* is damaged by mine off Padamarang Island.

ATLANTIC. Destroyer *Murphy* (DD 603), detached from convoy UT 4 to investigate strange ship, is cut in two (her forward section sinks) when she is accidentally rammed by U.S. tanker *Bulkoil* 265 miles east-southeast of Ambrose Lightship, 39°39′N, 72°34′W. Tugs *Sagamore* (AT 20) and *Rescue* (NRTS) are sent from New York; *Allegheny* (AT 19) is sent from Cape May. Coast Guard cutters *Cartigan* (WPC 132) and *Kimball* (WPC 143) and submarine chaser *PC 1262* search the area for survivors, as do *Glennon* (DD 620) and *Jeffers* (DD

621). The two destroyers rescue survivors; the former initially takes *Murphy's* stern in tow. *Rescue* and *Sagamore* bring *Murphy's* stern into New York while *Allegheny* takes part in the search for survivors.

TBF (VC 13) from escort carrier *Core* (CVE 13) damages German submarine *U 271* north of the Azores.

MEDITERRANEAN. German planes attack convoy MKS 28, strafing and torpedoing U.S. freighter *Tivives* about 15 miles off Cape Tenes, Algeria; one of 48 merchant seamen and one of the 25-man Armed Guard perish in the ensuing abandonment as the ship sinks swiftly. British corvette HMS *La Malouine* rescues the survivors, including the six-man staff of the convoy commodore and one passenger.

22 Friday

PACIFIC. Submarine *Grayback* (SS 208) sinks Japanese transport *Awata Maru* in the East China Sea, west of Okinawa, 26°40′N, 125°00′E.

Submarine *Shad* (SS 235) attacks Japanese light cruisers *Naka* and *Isuzu*, en route from Shanghai to Rabaul, 28°40′N, 124°10′E. Although *Shad* claims to have damaged both, neither enemy warship is hit.

23 Saturday

PACIFIC. Submarine *Silversides* (SS 236) sinks Japanese fleet tanker *Tennan Maru* and army cargo ships *Johore Maru* and *Kazan Maru*, 02°30′N, 144°45′E (see 24 October).

USAAF B-24 damages Japanese cargo vessel *No. 1 Kinpo Maru* off Greenwich Island, 01°01′N, 154°08′E.

Japanese transport *Kyowa Maru* is sunk by aircraft (type unspecified) northwest of Buka, Solomons; auxiliary submarine chaser *Cha 23* rescues survivors.

MEDITERRANEAN. German planes raid shipping off Naples, Italy; U.S. freighter *James Iredell* is hit by three bombs that set alight the ship's gasoline cargo. Although the ship is abandoned and the fire burns for 64 hours until it is ultimately put out, there are no casualties among the 44-man merchant crew, the 28-man Armed Guard, or the 28 passengers.[171]

24 Sunday

PACIFIC. Japanese army cargo ship *Kazan Maru* sinks as the result of damage inflicted by *Silversides* (SS 236) the previous day; attempt by submarine chaser *Ch 24* to scuttle the immobilized *Johore Maru* fails. *Silversides* later finishes off *Johore Maru* herself.

PBY sinks Japanese destroyer *Mochizuki* south of Jacquinot Bay, 05°35′N, 151°35′E; destroyer *Uzuki*, her starboard propeller disabled, takes survivors on board and transports them to Rabaul.

USAAF B-24 (5th Air Force) sinks Japanese cargo vessel *Nagaragawa Maru* off Manokwari, New Guinea.

Japanese destroyer *Satsuki* is damaged by grounding off Utano Island, 05°31′S, 149°14′E (see 26 and 30 October).

25 Monday

PACIFIC. Submarine *Tullibee* (SS 284) attacks Japanese transport *Teisho Maru* (ex-German *Havenstein*), escorted by auxiliary minesweeper *No. 11 Misago Maru* 12 miles off Oshima, 26°05′N, 121°03′E. Although *Tullibee* claims damage to the larger vessel, *Teisho Maru* survives unscathed. *No. 11 Misago Maru* carries out counterattacks to no avail.

ATLANTIC. Destroyers *Parrott* (DD 218) and *Paul Jones* (DD 230), in TG 21.16, formed around escort carrier *Block Island* (CVE 21), attack German submarine *U 488*. Although *Parrott* damages *U 488*, the U-boat escapes *Paul Jones's* depth charge attacks.

Submarine chaser *SC 1472* runs out of fuel off Barnegat, New Jersey, 39°50′N, 73°50′W, while escorting U.S. freighter *James L. Couper*; motor minesweeper *YMS 359*, in the vicinity, is diverted to the scene while tug *Rescue* (NRTS) puts to sea from New York as weather worsens (see 26 October).

26 Tuesday

PACIFIC. PBY damages Japanese destroyer *Satsuki*, previously damaged on 24 October, 15 miles east of Teop Harbor, 05°34′S, 155°06′E.

USAAF B-25s (14th Air Force) bomb Japanese shipping off Kiungshan, 20°05′N, 110°05′E, sinking transport *Yamatogawa Maru*, army cargo vessels *No. 3 Shinwa Maru* and *Hokuzan Maru*, and freighter *Hachiman Maru*.

USAAF P-38s (13th Air Force) damage auxiliary submarine chaser *Cha 20*, transporting troops and cargo, five miles off Buka, Solomons.

ATLANTIC. Severe northeast storm strikes eastern seaboard between Cape May, New Jersey, and Nantucket, Massachusetts, forcing ships aground in the gale, including U.S. freighters *F. J. Luckenbach* (off Belmar, New Jersey), *James H. Longstreet*, and *Exilona* and British freighter *Fort Douglas* (the latter three ships all off Sandy Hook). In addition, Norwegian motor vessel *Thordis* runs aground in East Chester Bay, U.S. schooner *Lucy Evelyn* at

Vineyard Haven. Of all the aforementioned merchantmen, only *Exilona* succeeds in freeing herself from her predicament, the rest require assistance over ensuing days. Motor minesweeper *YMS 359* is unable to put a line on board disabled submarine chaser *SC 1472* in the prevailing weather conditions and contact is lost before tug *Rescue* (NRTS) reaches the area (see 27 October).

27 Wednesday

PACIFIC. New Zealand troops (8th Brigade Group, 3rd Division, Brigadier General R. A. Row) land on Mono and Stirling Islands in the Treasury Island Group, Solomons; preinvasion bombardment and covering for the landings are provided by U.S. naval vessels and aircraft. TG 39.3 (Captain Andrew G. Shepard) (two light cruisers and Destroyer Squadron 23) and aircraft from South Pacific Air Force provide cover for the landings. During Japanese retaliatory air strikes, destroyer *Cony* (DD 508) is damaged by bombs 15 miles north of Mono, Treasury Islands, 07°23′S, 155°27′E. Tank landing ships *LST 399* and *LST 485* are damaged by mortar fire, 07°25′S, 155°34′E.

Diversionary raid by Second Paratroop Battalion, USMC (Lieutenant Colonel Victor H. Krulak) is carried out against Choiseul Island, Solomons.

Submarine *Flying Fish* (SS 229) sinks Japanese transport *Nanman Maru* west-northwest of Yap, 12°02′N, 134°28′E.

Submarine *Shad* (SS 235) and *Grayback* (SS 208) attack same convoy off the Ryukyus within a few hours of each other; they sink Japanese freighter *Fuji Maru*, 28°20′N, 128°05′E, and torpedo cargo vessel *Kamo Maru*. Transport *Oryoko Maru* is hit by a dud torpedo.

ATLANTIC. PBY-5A (VP 73) on antisubmarine patrol out of Agadir, French Morocco, is attacked by what is identified as a "CR 42" fighter that had taken off from Gando, Gran Canaria. In response, Commander Fleet Air Wing 15 deploys two PV-1s (VB 127) from Port Lyautey to Agadir to carry out antisubmarine sweeps in place of the PBY-5As "in order to have aircraft better suited to repel such an attack should it recur" (see 28 October).

Canadian minesweeper HMCS *Guysborough* locates submarine chaser *SC 1472* (adrift in stormy weather since 25 October), off Brigantine Shoals and takes her in tow, bringing her into New York.

28 Thursday

PACIFIC. Submarine *Flying Fish* (SS 229) sinks Japanese fleet oiler *Koryu Maru* west-northwest of Yap, 12°54′N, 134°06′E.

District patrol vessel *YP 88* sinks after running aground off Cape Amchitka, Aleutians.

ATLANTIC. TBF and FM (VC 1) from escort carrier *Block Island* (CVE 21) sink German submarine *U 220* east of Newfoundland, 48°53′N, 33°30′W. *U 256* is attacked at the same time, but escapes unharmed.

PV-1s (VB 127) temporarily operating from Agadir, French Morocco, are attacked by what is most likely a Spanish HS-132L (license-built Fiat CR-32) (29th *Grupo*) off Gran Canaria, 27°56′N, 15°21′W. The two PV-1s meet the attack "aggressively and skilfully" with fixed and turret guns, and the HS-132L breaks off action. "It is unfortunate that the engagement did not last longer," VB 127's commanding officer writes, "to deduct some conclusions of the fighter qualities of the PVs." While the PVs are not damaged, the HS-132L is seen force-landing on the beach at Gran Canaria.

29 Friday

PACIFIC. Submarine *Seawolf* (SS 197) sinks Japanese freighter *Wuhu Maru* off Swatow, 22°30′N, 115°25′E.

Navy or USMC F4Us damage small Japanese cargo vessel *No. 16 Kiku Maru* near Tonolei, 06°47′S, 155°53′E.

30 Saturday

GENERAL. Moscow Conference ends. Groundwork is laid for conference of President Roosevelt, British Prime Minister Winston S. Churchill, and Soviet Premier Joseph Stalin at Teheran, Iran. Other agreements include the decision that China should join the alliance as the fourth major power and that a postwar organization to keep peace should be established. The latter will be the future United Nations.

PACIFIC. Navy planes, as well as B-25s and P-39s (13th Air Force), strike targets of opportunity near Kieta, Bougainville, sinking Japanese transport *Ujigawa Maru*, 06°20′S, 155°45′E.

USAAF B-24 attacks Japanese destroyer *Satsuki*, damaged on 24 and 26 October, 20 miles south of Mussau, 04°40′S, 149°20′E.

31 Sunday

PACIFIC. Submarine *Rasher* (SS 269) sinks Japanese oiler *Koryu Maru* in Makassar Strait, 00°25′N, 119°45′E.

ATLANTIC. TBF (VC 9) from escort carrier *Card* (CVE 11) sinks German submarine *U 584* about 580 miles north of Flores Island, Azores, 49°14′N, 31°55′W. Other VC 9 aircraft attack *U 91* at the same rendevous point, but she escapes unharmed.

Destroyer *Borie* (DD 215) damages German submarine *U 256* north of the Azores.

U.S. airship *K 94*, en route from Guantánamo Bay, Cuba, to San Juan, Puerto Rico, catches fire and crashes 35 miles north of Cape Borinquen, Puerto Rico.

NOVEMBER

1 Monday

PACIFIC. TF 31 (Rear Admiral Theodore S. Wilkinson) lands First Marine Amphibious Corps (Lieutenant General Alexander A. Vandegrift, USMC) at Cape Torokina, Bougainville, Solomons; assault by Third Marine Division (Major General Allen H. Turnage, USMC) is covered by TBFs and destroyer gunfire. During Japanese retaliatory air strikes that cause delays in unloading cargo, destroyer *Wadsworth* (DD 516) is damaged by near-miss of bomb.[172]

TF 39 (Rear Admiral Aaron S. Merrill) (light cruisers and destroyers) shells Japanese airfields and installations in Buka-Bonis area, Solomons. TF 39 later blasts airfields on Shortland Island. Japanese return fire damages destroyer *Dyson* (DD 572). That same day, TF 38 (Rear Admiral Frederick C. Sherman) attacks the fields in the Buka-Bonis area; TBFs, SBDs, and F6Fs from carrier *Saratoga* (CV 3) and small carrier *Princeton* (CVL 23) carry out two air strikes (see 2 November).

Destroyer *Fullam* (DD 474) is damaged by grounding off west coast of Bougainville, 06°25′S, 154°53′E.

Submarine *Haddock* (SS 231) attacks Japanese cable-layer *Tateishi* and trawler *Kitagami Maru* off Rokutei Island, 09°02′N, 150°43′E. Although *Haddock* claims damage to both ships, neither is actually hit.

F4Us strafe bivouac area and shipping off Shortland Island; Japanese auxiliary submarine chaser *Cha 13* is sunk west of the island, 07°00′S, 155°30′E.

Light minelayers *Tracy* (DM 19) and *Pruitt* (DM 22) begin sowing field in the first mining operation of a series designed to render the southern Bougainville area "completely useless to the Japanese." They complete the first operation early the following morning.

Increasing Allied command of the air meant that Japanese men-of-war could not be safe even in port. Seen from a USAAF B-25 on a low-level pass over Rabaul, 2 November 1943, is heavy cruiser *Haguro*, damaged earlier that morning in the Battle of Empress Augusta Bay, with auxiliary vessel *Hakusan Maru* in the background. (NHC, NH 95558)

ATLANTIC. Destroyer *Borie* (DD 215) sinks German submarine *U 405* north of the Azores, 49°00'N, 31°14'W, but is damaged in the battle (see 2 November).

2 Tuesday

ATLANTIC. Destroyer *Borie* (DD 215), damaged in engagement with *U 405* the previous day (during which the destroyer had rammed the U-boat), 1,000 miles east of Cape Race, Newfoundland, is scuttled by TBF (VC 9) from escort carrier *Card* (CVE 11), 50°12'N, 30°48'W, after attempt to scuttle *Borie* with gunfire by sister ship *Barry* (DD 248) fails.

PACIFIC. Battle of Empress Augusta Bay: TF 39, composed of four light cruisers and eight destroyers (Rear Admiral Aaron S. Merrill), intercepts and turns back a Japanese force of two heavy and two light cruisers and six destroyers (Rear Admiral Omori Sentaro) steaming to attack U.S. transports off Bougainville ("RO" Operation). Light cruiser *Denver* (CL 58) is damaged by 8-inch gunfire, destroyer *Foote* (DD 511) by torpedo, and destroyer *Spence* (DD 512) by gunfire and collision with sister ship *Thatcher* (DD 514). *Foote* is towed to safety, initially by sister ship *Claxton* (DD 571) and then by tug *Sioux* (AT 75). *Charles Ausburne* (DD 570), *Spence*, *Dyson* (DD 572), *Claxton*, and *Stanly* (DD 478) sink Japanese destroyer *Hatsukaze* (previously damaged in collision with heavy cruiser *Myoko*); U.S. gunfire sinks light cruiser *Sendai*, 06°10'S, 154°20'E, and damages heavy cruisers *Myoko* and *Haguro*. Destroyers *Shiratsuyu* and *Samidare* are damaged in collision during this night surface action. Japanese planes attack TF 39 during its retirement from the scene of battle, damaging light cruiser *Montpelier* (CL 57). Japanese destroyers and submarine *RO 104* pick up *Sendai*'s survivors.

TF 38 (Rear Admiral Frederick C. Sherman) reprises attacks on Japanese airfields and facilities at Buka and Bonis, Solomons; TBFs, SBDs, and F6Fs from carrier *Saratoga* (CV 3) and small carrier *Princeton* (CVL 23) carry out two strikes. These and the ones the day before prevent the Japanese from launching aerial attacks against the unfolding operations at Empress Augusta Bay.

USAAF B-25s, escorted by P-38s (5th Air Force), carry out low-altitude raid on airfields and harbor at Rabaul, New Britain, sinking Japanese stores ship *Manko Maru* and inflicting further damage upon heavy cruisers *Haguro* and *Myoko* and destroyer *Shiratsuyu* (three of the four warships damaged during the pre-dawn Battle of Empress Augusta Bay), stores ship *Hayasaki*, and minesweeper *W.26*.

Submarine *Haddock* (SS 231) engages Japanese submarine chaser *Ch 28* north of Truk, 09°12'N, 150°13'E, but neither side damages the other.

Submarines *Seahorse* (SS 304), *Halibut* (SS 232), and *Trigger* (SS 237), each operating independently of the other, attack Japanese convoy south of Honshu; *Seahorse* sinks transport *Chihaya Maru*, 29°31'N, 134°50'E, and army cargo ship *Yawata Maru*, 28°30'N, 135°35'E; *Halibut* sinks army cargo ship *Ehime Maru*, 28°40'N, 135°35'E; and *Trigger* sinks army transport *Delagoa Maru*, 28°30'N, 135°35'. *Seahorse* or *Trigger* sinks army cargo ship *Ume Maru*, 28°40'N, 135°35'E.

3 Wednesday

PACIFIC. PB4Ys sink Japanese stores ship *Minato Maru* 19 miles off Ocean Island, 00°53'S, 169°35'E.

USAAF B-24s (13th Air Force) bomb Japanese ships en route to Rabaul, but score no damage upon their targets, transport (ex-armed merchant cruiser) *Gokoku Maru* and destroyer *Urakaze*.

Battleship *Oklahoma* (BB 37), sunk at Pearl Harbor on 7 December 1941 by Japanese aerial torpedoes, is refloated after months of arduous effort.

4 Thursday

PACIFIC. Submarine *Seawolf* (SS 197) sinks Japanese freighter *Kaifuku Maru* 90 miles south-southwest of Hong Kong, 21°22'N, 113°20'E.

USAAF B-24s (13th Air Force) bomb Japanese convoy off central New Ireland, damaging transport (ex-armed merchant cruiser) *Kiyozumi Maru*, 02°00'S, 151°30'E; light cruiser *Isuzu* takes the damaged ship in tow. Later that day, however, the Japanese ships foul the minefield newly sown by submarine *Silversides* (SS 236) off New Ireland. Surveying ship *Tsukushi* and transport *Ryuosan Maru* are sunk; light cruiser *Isuzu* and destroyer *Isokaze* are damaged.[173]

Submarine *Tautog* (SS 199) unsuccessfully attacks Japanese convoy northwest of the Palaus, 07°45'N, 134°09'E.

TBFs (VMTB 143) and SBDs bomb antiaircraft positions at Kahili airfield, Solomons, escorted by F4Us. Escorting fighters, upon retirement from objectives, strafe Japanese cargo vessel *Giyu Maru* in Matchin Bay, Bougainville, 05°28'S, 154°45'E (see 10 November). Japanese auxiliary submarine chaser *Cha 30* is sunk, most likely by F4Us, off Kieta, Bougainville, 06°10'S, 155°35'E.

USAAF B-25s (14th Air Force) sink Japanese cargo ship *Chinko Maru*, Swatow Harbor, China, 23°20'N, 116°50'E; *Chinko Maru* carries down with her 100,000,000 *Yuan* in Central Reserve Bank notes.

USAAF B-24s (5th Air Force) damage Japanese cargo vessel *Nissho Maru*, in company with destroyer *Amatsukaze*, north of Mussau Island, 00°20'N, 150°40'E.

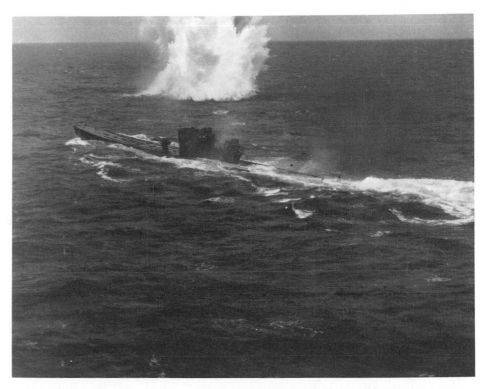

Southwest of Ascension Island, German Type IXD2 submarine *U 848* vainly attempts to escape attacking Consolidated PB4Y-1 of VB 107 commanded by Lieutenant Charles R. Baldwin, USNR, 5 November 1943; *U 848* carries the 20-millimeter quadruple machine gun mount fitted to give the *unterseeboote* at least a fighting chance if caught on the surface. (NA, 80-G-208282)

5 Friday

PACIFIC. TF 38 (Rear Admiral Frederick C. Sherman) carries out an "all out" attack on Japanese fleet units (Rear Admiral Takagi Takeo) concentrated in Simpson Harbor, Rabaul. TBFs, SBDs, and F6Fs from carrier *Saratoga* (CV 3) and small carrier *Princeton* (CVL 23) press home attacks through heavy antiaircraft fire from batteries ringing the harbor, from five adjacent airfields, and from the enemy ships themselves in a "bold and highly successful attack" that damages heavy cruisers *Atago*, *Takao*, *Maya*, *Chikuma*, and *Mogami*; light cruisers *Noshiro* and *Agano*; and destroyers *Fujinami* and *Amagiri*. The strike not only removes the threat from this quarter to ongoing operations at Empress Augusta Bay, but signals the beginning of the end for Rabaul as a major Japanese fleet base.

Submarine *Halibut* (SS 232) torpedoes Japanese carrier *Junyo* (returning from transferring her air group ashore to operate out of Rabaul in "RO" Operation) in Bungo Strait, 32°19'N, 132°58'E; heavy cruiser *Tone* tows the damaged ship to Kure.

USAAF B-24s sink Japanese fishing vessel *No. 1 Kanto Maru* north of Kieta, 06°15'S, 155°25'E.

ATLANTIC. PB4Ys (VB 107) and USAAF B-25s (1st Composite Squadron) sink German submarine *U 848*, 480 miles southwest of Ascension Island, 10°09'S, 18°00'W.

Open cargo lighter *YCK 2*, adrift in a sinking condition off Nova Scotia, is sunk by tug *Pinto* (AT 90) as hazard to navigation, 45°47'N, 58°57'W.

6 Saturday

PACIFIC. Japanese torpedo planes attack infantry landing craft (gunboat) *LCI(G) 70* and motor torpedo boat *PT 167* as the U.S. ships retire from Cape Torokina to the Treasury Islands. Dud torpedoes damage both *LCI(G) 70* and *PT 167*, the latter is hit by a torpedo that passes clean through the bow, leaving an entrance and an exit hole.

Transported by 21 barges, 475 Japanese troops land near the mouth of the Laruma River, northwest of Cape Torokina, Bougainville, in the first counterlanding against the newly established beachhead. Ground forces counterattack, however, supported by aircraft, and on 7 and 8 November kill over 250 enemy troops and scatter the rest into the jungles.

Submarine *Haddock* (SS 231) attacks Japanese Truk-to-Singapore convoy, consisting of fleet tankers *Gen'yo Maru* and *Hoyo Maru* and escorting destroyer *Yakaze*, roughly west-northwest of Truk, 08°04′N, 150°04′E. *Haddock* torpedoes *Hoyo Maru* at 08°08′N, 149°45′E, and during evasive maneuvers *Yakaze* is damaged when she accidentally rams *Gen'yo Maru*. Despite the damage, *Yakaze* counterattacks *Haddock*. Submarine *Scorpion* (SS 278) torpedoes fleet tanker *Hoyo Maru*, 07°54′N, 150°06′E.

USAAF B-25s (13th Air Force) attack Japanese shipping west of Buka, Solomons, sinking submarine chaser *Ch 11*, auxiliary submarine chaser *No. 9 Asahi Maru*, cargo vessel *Asayama Maru*, and water tanker *Chozan Maru*. Small cargo vessel *No. 3 Nissen Maru* is sunk in the same general area.

MEDITERRANEAN. German planes attack Naples-bound convoy KMF 25A; destroyer *Beatty* (DD 640) is sunk by aerial torpedo 32 miles northwest of Phillippeville, Tunisia, 37°10′N, 06°00′E. Troop transport *Santa Elena* is also torpedoed about 27 miles off Phillippeville, 37°13′N, 06°21′E, and abandoned. Transport *Monterey* takes on board the 1,870 Canadian troops (and nurses) traveling in *Santa Elena*; the crew and Armed Guard return to the ship (see 7 November).

7 Sunday

PACIFIC. USAAF B-25s (14th Air Force) bomb Japanese shipping in Amoy Harbor, China, sinking army cargo ships *No. 28 Nagata Maru* and *No. 6 Inushima Maru* and auxiliary sailing vessel *Kanlu*.

MEDITERRANEAN. Troop transport *Santa Elena*, struck by aerial torpedo while in convoy KMF 25A the previous afternoon, suffers further damage when accidentally rammed by damaged Dutch transport *Marnix Van St. Aldegonde* (then under tow). The cumulative damage from the torpedo and the collision nullifies the efforts to tow the crippled *Santa Elena* to port and she sinks. Four of the 133-man merchant crew perish in the abandonment; the 44-man Armed Guard survives intact.

8 Monday

PACIFIC. Japanese carrier planes from their temporary base at Rabaul and land-based naval aircraft (land attack planes from the 751st *Kokutai* are among those involved) attack U.S. ships transporting the second wave of assault troops (U.S. Army 37th Infantry Division) off Cape Torokina, Bougainville. Light cruiser *Birmingham* (CL 62), 06°00′S, 154°00′E, is damaged, as are attack transports *Fuller*

(APA 7) and *President Jackson* (APA 18), 06°15′S, 155°05′E.

Destroyers *Anthony* (DD 515) and *Hudson* (DD 475) accidentally engage motor torpedo boats *PT 163*, *PT 169*, and *PT 170*; fortunately, neither side suffers any damage in the mistaken encounter.

Submarine *Bluefish* (SS 222) sinks Japanese army tanker *Kyokuei Maru* in South China Sea off northwestern coast of Luzon, 17°00′N, 116°19′E. Although *Bluefish* claims the destruction of five more ships, none are damaged; escort vessel *Tsushima* counterattacks unsuccessfully.

Submarine *Rasher* (SS 269) sinks Japanese merchant tanker *Tango Maru* in Makassar Strait, 00°25′N, 119°45′E, and survives counterattacks by auxiliary submarine chaser *Cha 41*.

ATLANTIC. Advanced Amphibious Training Base, Plymouth, England, is established.

9 Tuesday

PACIFIC. Submarine *Rasher* (SS 269) unsuccessfully attacks Balikpapan-bound Japanese fleet oiler *Toa Maru* in Makassar Strait, 00°34′N, 118°59′E.

Submarine *Sargo* (SS 188) sinks Japanese army cargo ship *Taga Maru* east of Luzon Strait, 21°40′N, 131°12′E.

Submarine *Seawolf* (SS 197) unsuccessfully attacks Japanese cargo vessel *Hokuriku Maru* in South China Sea, west of Luzon Strait, 20°38′N, 118°33′E.

10 Wednesday

PACIFIC. Submarine *Albacore* (SS 218) is accidentally damaged by U.S. four-engine bomber (possibly a 5th Air Force B-24) off New Ireland, 03°08′S, 150°17′E, but remains on patrol.

Submarine *Barb* (SS 220) engages Japanese Keelung-to-Sasebo convoy, unsuccessfully attacking cargo ships *Yamahagi Maru* and damaging *Nishi Maru*. Escorting auxiliary minesweeper *No. 7 Toshi Maru* counterattacks, but does not damage *Barb*.

Submarine *Scamp* (SS 277) torpedoes Japanese transport *Tokyo Maru* south by west of Truk, 03°30′N, 150°10′E; transport *Mitakesan Maru* takes the crippled ship in tow (see 12 November).

British submarine HMS *Tally Ho* sinks Japanese water carrier *Kisogawa Maru* in Malacca Strait, 06°12′N, 99°25′E.

Japanese cargo vessel *Giyu Maru*, damaged on 4 November, sinks in Matchin Bay, 05°33′S, 154°45′E.

ATLANTIC. PB4Y-1s (VB 103, VB 105, and VB 110), RAF No. 311 (Czechoslovakian) Squadron Liberator, and an RAF Wellington sink German submarine *U 966* in Bay of Biscay off northwest Spain, 44°00′N, 08°30′W; Spanish fishing trawlers rescue the survivors.

11 Thursday

PACIFIC. TF 38 (Rear Admiral Frederick C. Sherman) launches carrier air strike on Rabaul from the eastern side of the Solomons, TG 50.3 (Rear Admiral Alfred E. Montgomery) from the western. TBFs, SBDs, and F6Fs from three carriers and two small carriers attack Japanese ships, according priorities to cruisers, destroyers, tankers, and merchant shipping. Poor weather forces TF 38 and TG 50.3 planes to attack only ships under way off Simpson Harbor. Despite the Japanese managing to find cover in rain squalls, destroyer *Suzunami* is sunk; light cruisers *Yubari* and *Agano* and destroyers *Naganami*, *Urakaze*, and *Wakatsuki* are damaged. USAAF B-24s follow up the carrier strikes, but achieve no hits. Japanese retaliatory air strike against TG 50.3 is likewise unsuccessful.

Submarine *Capelin* (SS 289) sinks Japanese army cargo ship *Kunitama Maru* northwest of Ambon, 03°08′S, 127°30′E.

Submarine *Drum* (SS 228) engages Japanese Truk-to-Rabaul convoy, unsuccessfully attacking submarine depot ship *Hie Maru*, 00°19′N, 149°40′E (see 17 November). Later that day, a USAAF B-24 bombs the same convoy, damaging *Hie Maru*. Despite those attacks, the enemy ships reach Rabaul the following day.

Submarine *Sargo* (SS 188) sinks Japanese transport *Kosei Maru* east of the Nansei Shoto, 27°40′N, 130°24′E.

U.S. freighter *Cape San Juan*, bound for Townsville, Australia, is torpedoed by Japanese submarine *I 21* at 22°11′S, 178°03′W; 16 of the 1,348 embarked troop passengers are killed in the initial explosion and a further 114 drown during the abandonment. U.S. freighter *Edwin T. Meredith* begins picking up survivors, joined later by Allied planes, destroyer *McCalla* (DD 488), destroyer escort *Dempsey* (DE 26), and motor minesweeper *YMS 241*. *Edwin T. Meredith* attempts to scuttle *Cape San Juan* with gunfire, but the ship will remain afloat for another two days. Submarine chaser *SC 1048* comes across the ship the next day and sends a boarding party that subsequently buries at sea the six bodies they find on board.

12 Friday

ATLANTIC. President Roosevelt embarks in battleship *Iowa* (BB 61) at the start of his journey that will include his presence at conferences at Teheran and Cairo.

PACIFIC. "RO" Operation ends as Japanese carrier aircraft are withdrawn from Rabaul (planes from carriers had been moved there during the build-up of forces to oppose the Bougainville landings). Losses of carrier aircraft during the "RO" Operation hamper immediate resumption of full-scale operations.

Submarine *Harder* (SS 257) attacks Japanese convoy north-northwest of Pagan Island, Marianas, sinking auxiliary minesweeper *No. 11 Misago Maru*, 21°40′N, 144°40′E, and damaging motor sailing vessel *Hei Maru*.

Submarine *Scamp* (SS 277) torpedoes Truk bound Japanese light cruiser *Agano* (damaged the previous day by TF 38's strike), 01°03′N, 149°15′E.

Submarine *Thresher* (SS 200) sinks Japanese transport *Muko Maru* north of Truk, 09°02′N, 152°46′E, but is damaged by depth charges and terminates her patrol.

Japanese transport *Tokyo Maru*, damaged by *Scamp* (SS 277) on 10 November, sinks while under tow between Kavieng and Truk, 05°42′N, 151°09′E. Destroyer *Suzutsuki* rescues survivors.

USAAF B-24s (5th Air Force) bomb Japanese naval base at Surabaya, Java, damaging submarine chasers *Ch 6* and *Ch 10*.

ATLANTIC. PB4Y-1 (VB 103) sinks German submarine *U 508* in Bay of Biscay, 46°00′N, 07°30′W.

Open lighter *YC 857* sinks after grounding off Cape Cod, Massachusetts.

13 Saturday

PACIFIC. U.S. carrier and land-based aircraft begin daily bombings of Japanese positions in the Gilbert and Marshall Islands as preliminaries to Operation GALVANIC.

Japanese naval land attack planes (702nd and 751st *Kokutais*) attack TF 39 (Rear Admiral Aaron S. Merrill) off Empress Augusta Bay, Bougainville, Solomons; light cruiser *Denver* (CL 58) is damaged by aerial torpedo, 06°45′S, 154°15′E.

British submarine HMS *Taurus* sinks Japanese submarine *I 34,* 30 miles south of Penang, Malaya, 05°17′N, 100°05′E.

Submarine *Narwhal* (SS 167) lands two parties of men and 46 tons of cargo, ammunition, and stores on west beach of Paluan Bay, Mindoro, P.I. (see 14 November).

Submarine *Scorpion* (SS 278) damages Japanese oiler *Shiretoko* northwest of the Marianas, 18°22′N, 142°50′E.

Submarine *Trigger* (SS 237) sinks Japanese transport *Nachizan Maru* in East China Sea, 32°55′N, 124°57′E; although damaged by depth charges, she remains on patrol.

14 Sunday

PACIFIC. Submarine *Apogon* (SS 308) attacks Truk-bound Japanese convoy consisting of transports *Akibasan Maru* and *Okitsu Maru*, escorted by destroyers *Asanagi* and *Inazuma*, 08°20′N, 154°15′E; although she claims one damaging hit on a transport, she is unsuccessful.

Submarine *Narwhal* (SS 167) delivers 46 tons of ammunition and stores, disembarks Lieutenant Commander Charles Parsons at Nasipit, Mindanao, and embarks 32 evacuees (including eight women, two children, and a baby) who will be transported to Darwin, Australia (see 2 December).

ATLANTIC. During battle drills, destroyer *William D. Porter* (DD 579) inadvertently fires a live torpedo at battleship *Iowa* (BB 61), in which President Roosevelt is traveling. Fortunately, the destroyer signals the battleship in time and a catastrophe is avoided.

15 Monday

PACIFIC. Submarine *Crevalle* (SS 291) sinks Japanese army cargo ship *Kyokko Maru* off San Antonio, Zambales province, 14°53′N, 119°56′E.

Advanced Naval Base and Naval Auxiliary Air Facility, Funafuti, Ellice Islands, are established.

16 Tuesday

PACIFIC. Destroyer Squadron 23 (Captain Arleigh A. Burke), consisting of five destroyers (three from Destroyer Division 45 and two from Destroyer Division 46), bombards Japanese airfield at Buka, Bougainville, Solomons; Destroyer Squadron 23 remains in the area to cover transport operations.

Submarine *Corvina* (SS 216) is sunk by Japanese submarine *I 176* south of Truk, 05°05′N, 151°10′E.[174]

Joint USN-USMC-USAAF-RNZAF aerial mining of waters off Buka, Solomons, begins. Planes earmarked to take part include PV-1s (VB 140), Venturas (RNZAF), and TBFs (VC 38, VC 40, VMTB 143, and VMTB 233). USAAF B-25s (42nd Bombardment Group) and B-24s (13th Air Force) are to strafe and bomb known antiaircraft positions and conduct diversionary high-level strike to draw searchlights and antiaircraft fire, respectively. TBFs mine the western entrance to Ramun Bay, and the channel between the east coast of Madehas Island and the shoals southwest of Minan Island. Hampered by materiel failures, however, the PV-1s (both USN and RNZAF) fail to reach Buka Passage. This results in a second operation (see 17 November).

PBYs attack Japanese shipping off New Guinea, sinking cargo vessel *No. 2 Kyoritsu Maru*, 03°51′S, 153°20′E.

USAAF B-24s (7th Air Force) bomb Japanese shipping at Jaluit and Imidj Atolls in the Marshalls.

Japanese minelayer *Ukishima* is lost to unknown cause, 11 miles off Hatsushima, Japan, 34°28′N, 137°20′E.[175]

17 Wednesday

PACIFIC. Japanese land attack planes (702nd and 751st *Kokutais*) and torpedo planes engage Echelon 5 convoy (eight tank landing ships, and eight high-speed transports, escorted by six destroyers) carrying USMC reinforcements to Bougainville. High-speed transport *McKean* (APD 5) is sunk by aerial torpedo 19 miles southwest of Cape Torokina, 06°31′S, 154°52′E; destroyers *Ralph Talbot* (DD 390), *Sigourney* (DD 643), and *Waller* (DD 466), in the face of determined torpedo attacks, rescue survivors.

Submarine *Capelin* (SS 289) departs Darwin, Australia, for Molucca and Celebes Seas. She is never heard from again (see 23 November).[176]

Submarine *Drum* (SS 228) sinks Japanese submarine depot ship *Hie Maru* (which had eluded *Drum* on 11 November) north-northwest of New Ireland, 01°45′N, 148°20′E.

Joint USN-USMC-USAAF-RNZAF aerial mining of waters off Buka, Solomons, is completed as PV-1s (VB 140) and Venturas (RNZAF) mine previously designated waters of Buka Passage.

18 Thursday

PACIFIC. TG 50.4 (Rear Admiral Frederick C. Sherman) planes attack Nauru in support of the unfolding operations to capture the Gilberts.

Submarine *Bluefish* (SS 222) sinks Japanese destroyer *Sanae* and damages oiler *Ondo* 90 miles south of Basilan Island, 05°00′N, 122°00′E. *Ondo* engages the submarine with gunfire.

Submarine *Crevalle* (SS 291) attacks Japa-

Marines, some with bayonets fixed, scramble forward past shell- and bomb-shattered palms to assault a Japanese stronghold on Betio Island, Tarawa, during the battle to take the island (20–23 November 1943). (NA, USMC 63458)

nese landing ship/aircraft transport *Akitsu Maru*, escorted by torpedo boat *Tomozuru* in South China Sea off entrance to Manila Bay, 15°10′N, 119°40′E; although *Crevalle* claims destruction of her quarry, *Akitsu Maru* survives.

19 Friday

PACIFIC. Submarine chaser *SC 1067* founders and sinks in Massacre Bay, Attu, Aleutians.

Motor torpedo boat *PT 147*, damaged by grounding off Japoanese-held Sio, New Guinea, 05°55′S, 147°20′E, is destroyed by crew so that it will not fall into enemy hands.

Submarine *Harder* (SS 257) attacks Japanese convoy escorted by escort vessel *Fukue* and destroyer *Yuzuki*, sinking transports *Hokko Maru* and *Udo Maru*, 22°28′N, 147°22′E (see 20 November).

Submarine *Nautilus* (SS 168), en route from an observation mission off Tarawa, Marshalls, to land a reconnaissance party on Abemama, Gilberts, is damaged by friendly fire from light cruiser *Santa Fe* (CL 60) and destroyer *Ringgold* (DD 500) off Tarawa, 01°05′N, 173°03′E. *Nautilus*'s presence is unknown to the task force commander, and lest the task force be discovered by the enemy, "attack without challenge" had been authorized.

Submarine *Sculpin* (SS 191) is damaged by

Japanese destroyer *Yamagumo* about 154 miles north of Truk, Carolines, 00°00′N, 152°50′E, and is scuttled. Captain John P. Cromwell, the embarked submarine squadron commander in *Sculpin*, familiar with secret details of impending Operation GALVANIC, decides to go down with the ship rather than risk capture and undergo the inevitable interrogation. For his sacrifice, Cromwell is awarded the Medal of Honor posthumously.

20 Saturday

PACIFIC. Operation GALVANIC: The occupation of the Gilbert Islands begins under overall command of Commander Central Pacific Force (Vice Admiral Raymond A. Spruance). Task forces that carry out the operation are the assault force, TF 54 (Rear Admiral Richmond Kelly Turner); the carrier force, TF 50 (Rear Admiral Charles A. Pownall); and the defense forces/shore-based air, TF 57 (Rear Admiral John H. Hoover). TF 54 lands Fifth Amphibious Corps (Major General Holland M. Smith, USMC), the Second Marine Division (Major General Julian C. Smith, USMC), units of the 27th Army (Major General Ralph C. Smith, USA), USMC and Army Defense Battalions, and other service units. Strong and tenacious opposition develops on Tarawa de-

spite heavy preinvasion shelling and bombing. During operations supporting GALVANIC, four ships are damaged: battleship *Mississippi* (BB 41) by turret explosion, 03°10′N, 172°58′E; small carrier *Independence* (CVL 22) by aerial torpedo, 01°30′N, 172°40′E; destroyer *Ringgold* (DD 500) by shore battery, 01°24′N, 172°58′E; and destroyer *Dashiell* (DD 659) by grounding, 01°00′N, 173°00′E.

Submarine *Harder* (SS 257) continues stalking convoy attacked the previous day and sinks Japanese transport *Nikko Maru* northeast of the Marianas, 23°20′N, 147°30′E.

PBYs sink Japanese cargo vessel *Naples Maru* off New Ireland, 03°22′S, 151°45′E; submarine chasers *Ch 17* and *Ch 18* rescue survivors.

Naval Base, Cairns, Australia, is established.

ATLANTIC. U.S. tanker *Altair* collides with Panamanian tanker *Bostonian* off the Delaware capes, 38°17′N, 74°08′W; fire breaks out on board *Altair* and compels the ship to be abandoned, with *Bostonian* taking on board the survivors. Tug *Christine Moran* (NRTS) proceeds to *Altair*'s assistance; tug *Sciota* (AT 30), after embarking a fire-fighting party at Norfolk, Virginia, proceeds to the scene, as do tugs *Acushnet* (AT 63) and *Bomazeen* (YT 238) (the latter has embarked a fire-fighting party from Naval Operating Base, Norfolk). *Sciota*'s firefighters control the blaze, and *Altair* is taken in tow to be anchored inside the Delaware breakwater on 23 November where tugs provided by the owners take over.

21 Sunday

PACIFIC. Submarine *Nautilus* (SS 168) lands USMC reconnaissance company on Abemama, Gilberts. Marines find the natives very helpful; the latter provide abundant water, coconuts, and intelligence on the whereabouts and strength of the Japanese garrison (see 24 November).

Submarine *Trigger* (SS 237) sinks Japanese freighter *Eizan Maru* in Yellow Sea off southwest coast of Korea, 36°40′N, 125°31′E.

USAAF B-24s and B-25s (5th Air Force) strike Japanese shipping and installations in Aroe Islands and off Manokwari, New Guinea, sinking transport *Shinwa Maru* off the latter, 02°24′S, 134°36′E. Transport *Nichii Maru* is sunk by USAAF B-24 northeast of Kavieng, New Ireland, 02°00′S, 149°15′E.

Dutch Mitchells and RAAF Beaufighters sink Japanese fishing vessel *Shinko Maru* off Taberfane, 06°11′S, 134°07′E.

RAAF Bostons sink small Japanese cargo

vessel *No. 2 Suisan Maru* off south coast of New Britain, 06°03′S, 151°14′E.

22   Monday

GENERAL. President Roosevelt, British Prime Minister Winston S. Churchill, and Chinese Generalissimo Chiang Kai-shek meet in Cairo, Egypt, for talks (SEXTANT Conference).

PACIFIC. Destroyer *Frazier* (DD 607) is damaged when she intentionally rams Japanese submarine *I 35*; the I-boat is sunk by *Frazier* and destroyer *Meade* (DD 602) off Tarawa, 01°22′N, 172°47′E.

Submarine *Drum* (SS 228) is damaged by depth charges north of New Guinea, 02°53′N, 141°36′E, and is forced to terminate her patrol.

Submarine *Seahorse* (SS 304) sinks Japanese freighter *Taishu Maru* south of Tsushima Strait, 33°41′N, 128°35′E.

Submarine *Tinosa* (SS 283) sinks Japanese army cargo ships *Kiso Maru* and *Yamato Maru* off Palau, 07°09′N, 134°32′E; although damaged by depth charges, 07°09′N, 134°34′E, she remains on patrol.

Japanese cargo ship *Kinyamasan Maru*, 01°00′N, 149°20′E, which escaped damage the previous day, is sunk by USAAF B-24 (5th Air Force) north of Mussau, 01°00′N, 149°20′E; destroyer *Asanagi* continues on to Truk with survivors of *Nichii Maru*, sunk the previous day, and *Kinyamasan Maru*.

Japanese army repair ship *Kashima Maru* is sunk by mine (laid by USAAF B-24 on 16 November) off Macao.

CARIBBEAN. U.S. tanker *Elizabeth Kellogg*, bound for Puerto Barrios, Guatemala, is torpedoed by German submarine *U 516* north of the Canal Zone, 11°10′N, 80°43′W, and abandoned (see 24 November).

23   Tuesday

PACIFIC. Betio, Tarawa Atoll, and Makin are declared secured.

Cruiser and destroyer force (Rear Admiral Aaron S. Merrill) bombards Buka-Bonis area, Bougainville, Solomons.

Destroyers *Waller* (DD 466) and *Renshaw* (DD 499) bombard Japanese positions on Magine Islands.

Motor torpedo boat *PT 322*, damaged by grounding off coast of eastern New Guinea, 06°09′S, 147°36′E, is scuttled to prevent capture.

Submarine *Blackfish* (SS 221) sinks Japanese transport *No. 2 Yamato Maru* between New Guinea and Palau, 02°28′N, 140°06′E.

Submarine *Capelin* (SS 289) possibly sinks Japanese army cargo ship *Kizan Maru* west of

Halmahera, 01°50′N, 127°55′E (see 17 November).

Submarine *Gudgeon* (SS 211) attacks Takao, Formosa–bound Japanese convoy, sinking Japanese escort vessel *Wakamiya* and army transport *Nekka Maru*, East China Sea, 28°38′N, 122°00′E, and damaging fleet tankers *Ichiyo Maru* and *Goyo Maru*.

24   Wednesday

PACIFIC. Escort carrier *Liscome Bay* (CVE 56) is sunk by Japanese submarine *I 175* southeast of Makin Island, Gilberts, 02°34′N, 172°30′E. *I 175* undergoes six hours of counterattacks by *Liscome Bay*'s escorts; of the 34 depth charges counted, six explode close enough to damage *I 175* so that she cannot "go deep." Lost with *Liscome Bay* is Rear Admiral Henry M. Mullinnix, Commander, Carrier Division 24.[177]

Submarine *Nautilus* (SS 168) and destroyer *Gansevoort* (DD 608) shell Japanese positions on Abemama Atoll, Gilberts. Abemama falls with negligible resistance as the bombardment (and suicide) accounts for the small enemy garrison. Construction of an airfield begins two days later.

In successive separate attacks, USAAF B-24s and Navy PBYs damage Japanese light cruiser *Yubari*, 04°20′S, 150°00′E, and 03°41′S, 150°15′E, respectively, as she attempts to transport soldiers and supplies to Garove, New Britain. Damage to the ship prompts cancellation of her mission.

USAAF B-25s (14th Air Force) damage Japanese lighthouse tender *Heicho Maru*, Amoy, China.

MEDITERRANEAN. USAAF B-17s (15th Air Force) bomb Toulon Harbor, sinking light cruiser *Jeanne de Vienne*, destroyer *Aigle*, and sloop *SG.21* (ex–second class sloop *Chamois*).

CARIBBEAN. U.S. freighter *Melville E. Stone* is torpedoed and sunk by German submarine *U 516* about 100 miles northwest of Cristobal, C.Z., 10°29′N, 80°20′W; 12 of the 42-man merchant complement lose their lives, as do two of the 23-man Armed Guard and one of the 23 embarked passengers. Submarine chasers *SC 662* and *SC 1023* rescue survivors.

Survivors of U.S. tanker *Elizabeth Kellogg*, torpedoed by *U 516* on 22 November, are rescued by submarine chaser *SC 1017* and Army tanker *Y 10*. Eight of the tanker's 36-man merchant complement and two of the 12-man Armed Guard perish with the ship.

25   Thursday

PACIFIC. Battle of Cape St. George is fought during the early hours as the five ships of Destroyer Squadron 23 (Captain Arleigh A. Burke) intercept five Japanese destroyers (Captain Kagawa Kiyoto) off Cape St. George, New Ireland. *Charles Ausburne* (DD 570), *Claxton* (DD 571), and *Dyson* (DD 572) sink *Onami* with torpedoes and *Yugiri* with gunfire; the same three U.S. ships, joined by *Spence* (DD 512) and *Converse* (DD 509), sink *Makinami* with torpedoes and gunfire and damage *Uzuki*. Destroyer Squadron 23 suffers no damage.

Destroyer *Radford* (DD 446) sinks Japanese submarine *I 19* north of the Gilberts, 03°10′N, 171°55′E.

Submarine *Albacore* (SS 218) sinks Japanese army cargo ship *Kenzan Maru* west-northwest of Manus, 00°46′N, 144°50′E.

Submarine *Searaven* (SS 196) sinks Japanese fleet tanker *Toa Maru* north of Ponape, 08°22′N, 158°00′W.

Japanese submarine *RO 100* is sunk by mine two miles west of Omai Island, outside north channel to Buin, Bouganville.

USAAF B-24s (7th Air Force) bomb Japanese installations at Taroa, Marshalls, damaging guardboat *Takeura Maru*.

ATLANTIC. PB4Y (VB 107) sinks the Indian Ocean–bound German submarine *U 849*, South Atlantic, 06°30′S, 05°40′W.

Destroyer escort *Harveson* (DE 316) is damaged when she is accidentally rammed by Canadian fishing vessel *O. K. Service* off Bermuda, B.W.I.

Advanced Amphibious Base, Salcombe, Devonshire, England, is established.

26   Friday

GENERAL. First Cairo (SEXTANT) Conference between President Roosevelt, British Prime Minister Winston S. Churchill, and Chinese Generalissimo Chiang Kai-shek ends.

PACIFIC. Submarine *Bowfin* (SS 287) sinks Japanese army tanker *Ogurasan Maru* and freighter *Tainan Maru* off coast of French Indochina, 13°00′N, 109°30′E.

Submarine *Raton* (SS 270) torpedoes Japanese ammunition ship *Onoe Maru* northeast of the Admiralties, 00°40′N, 148°20′E; submarine chaser *Ch 40* counterattacks but is damaged by the explosion of her own depth charges.

Submarine *Ray* (SS 271) carries out unsuccessful attacks on Japanese cargo vessel *Sumiyoshi Maru* south-southwest of Truk, 02°32′N, 148°56′E, but sinks transport *Nikkai*

Maru southwest of that major enemy base, 04°12′N, 148°20′E.

Submarine *Tinosa* (SS 283) attacks Japanese army cargo ships off Peleliu, sinking *Shini Maru* and damaging *Taiyu Maru*, 07°08′N, 134°48′E.

PV-1 (VP 138) attacks what is most likely Japanese submarine *I 177*, engaged in rescuing survivors of the Battle of Cape St. George, New Ireland. *I 177* rescues approximately 200 Japanese sailors in the wake of the engagement.[178]

USAAF B-25s (14th Air Force) sink Japanese auxiliary minesweeper *Genchi Maru* off Canton, China, 21°33′N, 112°00′E.

ATLANTIC. Naval Air Facilities are established at Amapa, Aratu, and Belem, Brazil; Naval Air Facilities (Lighter than Air) are established at Fernando de Noronha, Fortaleza, and Ipitanga, Brazil.

27 Saturday

PACIFIC. Submarine *Bowfin* (SS 287) sinks Vichy French cargo ship *Van Vollenhoven* off coast of French Indochina, 13°13′N, 109°27′E.

Submarine *Seahorse* (SS 304) sinks Japanese fleet tanker *San Ramon Maru* in East China Sea, 33°36′N, 128°57′E.

USAAF B-24s (13th Air Force) sink Japanese army hospital ship *Buenos Aires Maru* in Steffen Strait, 02°40′S, 149°20′E.

USAAF B-25s (14th Air Force) attack Japanese convoy in northern part of Formosa Strait, sinking transport *Hakone Maru* and damaging torpedo boat *Tomozuru*, 25°20′N, 120°00′E.

28 Sunday

GENERAL. Teheran (EUREKA) Conference begins in Teheran, Iran, between President Roosevelt, British Prime Minister Winston S. Churchill, and Soviet Premier Joseph Stalin.

PACIFIC. Submarine *Bowfin* (SS 287) sinks Japanese army cargo ship *Sydney Maru* and freighter *Tonan Maru* off central Philippines, 12°45′N, 109°41′E, but is damaged by Japanese gunfire and is forced to terminate her patrol.

Submarines *Pargo* (SS 264) and *Snook* (SS 279) attack Japanese transport convoy escorted by destroyer *Oite* and auxiliary submarine chaser *No. 2 Choan Maru* northwest of the Marianas (see 29 November). *Snook* sinks *Yamafuku Maru*, 18°21′N, 140°08′E.

Submarines *Raton* (SS 270) sinks Japanese army cargo ships *Hokko Maru* and *Yuri Maru* north of Hollandia, 01°40′N, 141°25′E.

29 Monday

PACIFIC. First Marine Parachute Battalion is landed before dawn about six miles east of Cape Torokina from 27 LCVPs and LCMs, covered by two LCI(G)s and a motor torpedo boat; heavy Japanese opposition (including mortar, artillery, and sniper fire) at daybreak, however, compels order to withdraw the landing force. Destroyer *Fullam* (DD 474) is detached from a southbound convoy, near New Georgia, to provide support, as are *Lardner* (DD 487) and *Lansdowne* (DD 486) from the vicinity of the Treasury Islands. Japanese gunfire twice forces the LCI(G)s and the landing craft to draw off; *Fullam*'s arrival, however, soon turns the tide. Together with F4Us that bomb and strafe the enemy positions, *Fullam* silences the troublesome batteries and allows the successful extraction of the beleaguered marines. *Lardner* and *Lansdowne* join *Fullam* in patrolling the area during the night (see 30 November).

TG 74.2 (Captain Frank R. Walker), two U.S. destroyers and two Australian destroyers (HMAS *Arunta* and HMAS *Warramunga*), shell Japanese positions on Gasmata, New Britain.

Destroyer *Perkins* (DD 377) is sunk in collision with Australian troop ship *Duntroon* off eastern New Guinea, 09°39′S, 150°04′E.

Submarine *Bonefish* (SS 223) sinks Surabaya-bound Japanese army cargo ship *Suez Maru* off Kangean Island, north of Bali, 06°57′S, 115°42′E. Unbeknown to the submariners, *Suez Maru* has on board 546 British POWs. Minesweeper *W.12* rescues survivors.

Submarine *Paddle* (SS 263) attacks Japanese fleet tanker *Nippon Maru* 19 miles off Eniwetok, Marshalls, 11°30′N, 162°15′E.

Submarines *Pargo* (SS 264) and *Snook* (SS 279) continue attacks against Japanese transport convoy northwest of the Marianas. *Pargo* sinks *Manju Maru*, 18°36′N, 140°04′E; *Snook* sinks *Shiganoura Maru*, 18°38′N, 139°35′E. Destroyer *Oite* and auxiliary submarine chaser *No. 2 Choan Maru* counterattack to no avail.

Submarine *Snapper* (SS 185) sinks Japanese transport *Kenryu Maru* off Hachijo Jima, 33°16′N, 139°35′E.

ATLANTIC. TBF (VC 19) from escort carrier *Bogue* (CVE 9), from convoy UGS 24, sinks German submarine *U 86* about 385 miles east of Terceira, Azores, 39°33′N, 19°01′W; *U 238* and *U 764* survive air attacks (see 30 November).

30 Tuesday

PACIFIC. TU 76.6.5 (four destroyers) shells Japanese barge hideouts, gun emplacements,

and ammunition dumps at Madang, New Guinea; *Shaw* (DD 373) is damaged by machine gun fire.

Destroyers *Lardner* (DD 487) and *Lansdowne* (DD 486), having patrolled the area in the vicinity of the successful extraction of the First Marine Parachute Battalion carried out late the previous afternoon, bombard Japanese positions along the length of Empress Augusta Bay, Bougainville, Solomons.

Submarine *Gato* (SS 212) sinks Japanese army transport *Columbia Maru* northwest of the Admiralties, 01°54′N, 143°26′E; and survives counterattacks by escorting submarine chaser *Ch 24*.

Submarine *Skate* (SS 305) attacks Japanese carrier *Zuiho* north-northwest of Truk, 09°10′N, 151°30′E, which, along with carrier *Un'yo* and escort carrier *Chuyo* and escort vessels, is proceeding back to Japan. Although *Skate* claims one damaging hit, none of her four torpedoes strikes home.

PBY sinks Palau-bound Japanese cargo ship *Himalaya Maru* six nautical miles south of New Hanover, Bismarck Archipelago.

ATLANTIC. FM and TBFs (VC 19) from escort carrier *Bogue* (CVE 9) damage German submarine *U 238* east of the Azores, 41°21′N, 18°19′W.

DECEMBER

1 Wednesday

UNITED STATES. Naval Air Ferry Command is established.

PACIFIC. Submarine *Bonefish* (SS 223) sinks Japanese transport *Nichiryo Maru* in Celebes Sea, 01°02′N, 120°52′E.

Submarine *Pargo* (SS 264) sinks Japanese transport *Shoko Maru* north of Ulithi, 14°24′N, 140°40′E.

Submarine *Peto* (SS 265) sinks Truk-bound Japanese transport *Konei Maru*, 01°16′N, 146°45′E, and survives counterattack by torpedo boat *Otori*.

USAAF B-25s (14th Air Force) bomb Taikoo dockyard, Hong Kong, damaging Japanese transport *Teiren Maru* (ex–Vichy French *Gouverneur General A. Varenne*). Subsequently, the ship is written off as a total loss.

USAAF B-24s (5th Air Force) pound Japanese installations at Wewak, New Guinea; among the heavy damage inflicted, small cargo vessel *No. 16 Yoshitomo Maru* is sunk.

2 Thursday

GENERAL. Teheran (EUREKA) Conference ends.

PACIFIC. Submarine *Narwhal* (SS 167) delivers

90 tons of ammunition and stores, and lands party of two U.S. Army officers and nine enlisted men at Butuan Bay, Mindanao. *Narwhal* then embarks Lieutenant Commander Charles Parsons and seven evacuees (two soldiers, three civilians, one woman, and an eight-year-old girl) (see 5 December).

USAAF B-24 damages Japanese cargo ship *Shinyu Maru* off New Hanover, Bismarck Archipelago.

Japanese cargo vessel *Koki Maru* is sunk by mine, laid by USAAF B-24 on 16 November, off Macao.

ANDAMAN SEA. RAAF Beaufighters damage Japanese paddle steamer *Assam* in Irrawaddy River in Burma (near Rangoon) (see 3 December).

MEDITERRANEAN. Tank landing craft *LCT 242* is sunk by circling torpedo off Naples, Italy.

ADRIATIC. German planes bomb Allied shipping at Bari, Italy, sinking and damaging a number of U.S. freighters moored there. *John M. Schofield* and *Grace Abbott* are damaged by flying fragments (the latter also by a dud bomb); the former suffers no casualties among the 44-man merchant complement, 28-man Armed Guard, and an indeterminate number of British Army stevedores on board to work cargo while the latter has only one merchant seaman wounded from among her 41-man civilian and 28-man Armed Guard complement. *Samuel J. Tilden* is hit by two bombs and catches fire; 17 of the 209 embarked troops perish as the soldiers abandon ship. The 41-man merchant crew and the 28-man Armed Guard remain at their posts to battle the blaze that eventually burns out of control and forces her crew off the ship. Ten of the ship's civilian complement die in the conflagration (see 3 December). *John L. Motley*, carrying a cargo of ammunition, is hit by at least three bombs. Direct hits and near-misses set nearby *John Bascom* afire; four of 44 merchant seamen perish, as do 10 of 28 Armed Guard sailors. The survivors, in addition to one passenger, abandon ship as the flames burn out of control. Her mooring lines burnt through, *John Bascom* drifts near the burning *John L. Motley*, which explodes, killing all on board (42 of the 46-man merchant complement and 22 of the 29-man Armed Guard). The only survivors are on shore at the time of the attack and thus escape the fate of their shipmates. Debris from *John L. Motley* damages gasoline tanker *Aroostook* (AOG 14), 41°06′N, 16°52′E, and sets fire to *Lyman Abbott*. *John Harvey*, moored originally between *John L. Motley* and *Joseph Wheeler*, is showered by burning debris, and catches fire herself, drifting into the harbor where she explodes, showering debris on the unfortunate *Lyman Abbott*. Tragically, *John Harvey*'s cargo includes mustard gas, which subsequently kills and injures many of the local inhabitants, in addition to harming many among the 42 merchant seamen and 29 Armed Guards on board *Lyman Abbott*. Consequently, two of the ship's civilian crew and one Armed Guard sailor, in addition to the ship's sole passenger, succumb to shrapnel wounds or mustard gas burns. *Joseph Wheeler* is hit by one bomb that touches off her ammunition cargo and the ship disintegrates, killing all on board; 15 of 41 merchant seamen and 13 of the 28-man Armed Guard, in addition to the single passenger, perish in the cataclysmic blast. Fifteen Armed Guard sailors and 26 merchant sailors escape the fate of their shipmates only because they were away from the ship, on shore, when she explodes.

3 Friday

GENERAL. Second Cairo Conference begins, attended by President Roosevelt, British Prime Minister Winston S. Churchill, and Chinese Generalissimo Chiang Kai-shek.

PACIFIC. Submarine *Guardfish* (SS 217) is damaged in collision with unidentified tanker during exercises off the coast of Australia.

Submarine *Tinosa* (SS 283) sinks Palau-bound Japanese fleet tanker *Azuma Maru* northwest of Sonserol, 06°34′N, 131°35′E.

USAAF B-24s bomb Japanese fishing boats off Garove, New Britain, sinking *No. 13 Sansei Maru*.

ANDAMAN SEA. USAAF B-25s sink Japanese paddle steamer *Assam*, immobilized the day before by RAAF Beaufighters, in the Irrawaddy River in Burma (near Rangoon).

ADRIATIC. Abandoned U.S. freighter *Samuel J. Tilden*, damaged in the German air raid on Bari, Italy, the night before, is scuttled by two torpedoes from British warships.

ATLANTIC. U.S. tanker *Touchet* is torpedoed twice (the second torpedo is a dud) by German submarine *U 193* at 25°15′N, 86°15′W, and abandoned by most of the 50-man merchant complement and 30-man Armed Guard. The latter's commander and nine men, however, stay with the ship, manning the 5-inch gun aft. *U 193*'s third torpedo finishes off the tanker, though, and she sinks, taking nine of the 10 Armed Guards who manage to reach a raft (they are swept off as the ship goes under), as well as the detachment commander, down with her (see 5 and 6 December).

Naval Air Facility, São Luíz, Brazil, is established.

4 Saturday

PACIFIC. TF 50 (Rear Admiral Charles A. Pownall) attacks Japanese installations on Kwajalein and Wotje Atolls, Marshalls. SBDs and TBFs from carriers *Yorktown* (CV 10) and *Lexington* (CV 16) and small carrier *Independence* (CVL 22) sink collier *Asakaze Maru*, cargo ship *Tateyama Maru*, auxiliary submarine chaser *No. 7 Takunan Maru*, and guardboat *No. 5 Mikuni Maru* and damage light cruisers *Nagara* and *Isuzu*, stores ship *Kinezaki*, auxiliary vessel *Fujikawa Maru*, and transports *No. 2 Eiko Maru*, *Kembu Maru*, and *No. 18 Mikage Maru*. During Japanese retaliatory air strikes, three U.S. ships suffer damage: carrier *Lexington* by aerial torpedo (752nd or 753rd *Kokutais*), 13°30′N, 171°25′E; light cruiser *Mobile* (CL 63) when one of her 5-inch mounts accidentally fires into one of her own 40-millimeter mounts, 12°47′N, 170°57′E; and destroyer *Taylor* (DD 468) by friendly fire from light cruiser *Oakland* (CL 95), 10°00′N, 170°00′E.

Submarine *Apogon* (SS 308) sinks Japanese gunboat *Daido Maru* northeast of Ponape, 08°22′N, 159°02′E.

Submarine *Gunnel* (SS 253) sinks Japanese transport *Hiyoshi Maru* northeast of Haha Jima, 29°436′N, 145°54′E, and survives counterattacks by destroyer *Inazuma*.

Submarine *Sailfish* (SS 192) sinks Yokosuka-bound Japanese escort carrier *Chuyo* southeast of Honshu, 32°27′N, 143°49′E. Unbeknown to *Sailfish*, *Chuyo* is carrying survivors from sister ship *Sculpin* (SS 191).

Japanese transport (ex-seaplane carrier) *Sanuki Maru* is damaged by mine, Pomelaa, as she sails for Singapore.

5 Sunday

PACIFIC. U.S. destroyers bombard Choiseul Bay area, Choiseul Island, Solomons.

Submarine *Narwhal* (SS 167) embarks nine evacuees (two men, three women, and four children) at Alubijid, Masacalar Bay, and then sinks Japanese cargo ship *Himeno Maru* (ex-Philippine *Dos Hermanos*) off Camiguin Island, 09°09′N, 124°29′E.

INDIAN OCEAN. "RYU I-GO" Operation: Japanese land attack planes (BETTYs) (705th *Kokutai*), escorted by carrier fighters (ZEROs) (331st *Kokutai*), bomb dockyards at Calcutta, India; U.S. freighter *William Whipple* is straddled and holed with fragments. There are no casualties among the 42-man merchant crew, but one man of the 28-man Armed Guard is injured. Japanese Army planes take part in the raid as well.

ATLANTIC. Norwegian freighter *Lillemor* rescues 43 survivors from U.S. tanker *Touchet*, sunk by German submarine *U 193* on 3 December; shortly thereafter, destroyer escort *Falgout* (DE 324) picks up 11 more men from the lost ship (see 6 December).

6 Monday

EUROPE. General Dwight D. Eisenhower, USA, is named commander of Allied Expeditionary Force for invasion of Europe.

ATLANTIC. Minesweeper *Raven* (AM 55) rescues 16 survivors from U.S. tanker *Touchet*, sunk by German submarine *U 193* on 3 December. All told, the entire merchant complement of 50 men survives *Touchet*'s loss, but 10 of the 30-man Armed Guard are lost with the ship.

7 Tuesday

GENERAL. Second Cairo Conference ends.

BAY OF BENGAL. Operation RATCHET: Tank landing ships *LST 208* and *LST 209* unload British tanks at Regu Creek, Burma.

PACIFIC. Submarine *Pogy* (SS 266) sinks Japanese collier *Soyo Maru* north of Truk, 14°03′N, 152°20′E.

Submarine *Sailfish* (SS 192) is attacked by Japanese plane off Kyushu, Japan, 31°21′N, 134°10′E, but although damaged by aerial bomb, remains on patrol.

8 Wednesday

PACIFIC. TG 50.8 (Rear Admiral Willis A. Lee Jr.), comprised of battleships and destroyers, shells Nauru Island, Gilberts; destroyer *Boyd* (DD 544) is damaged by shore battery fire. OS2Us (VO 6 and VO 9) from the battleships strafe and photograph barracks area upon completion of bombardment.

Submarine *Sawfish* (SS 276) sinks Japanese transport *Sansei Maru* southwest of Chichi Jima, 25°19′N, 141°44′E.

TBFs sink Rabaul-bound Japanese fishing boats *No. 3 Yusho Maru*, *No. 7 Fukuei Maru*, *No. 2 Takatori Maru*, and *No. 1 Hoko Maru*, 00°20′N, 152°10′E.

9 Thursday

ATLANTIC. Following the Teheran and Cairo Conferences, President Roosevelt reembarks in battleship *Iowa* (BB 61) at Dakar, French West Africa, for the return voyage to the United States.

10 Friday

PACIFIC. Destroyer *Sigourney* (DD 643) is damaged by grounding off west coast of Bougainville, Solomons, 06°21′S, 155°10′E.

11 Saturday

PACIFIC. Submarine *Bonefish* (SS 223) damages small Japanese cargo vessel *Toyohime Maru* in Celebes Sea, off Tarakan, Borneo, 04°03′N, 118°22′E.

MEDITERRANEAN. German U-boats *U 223*, *U 593* (see 13 December), and *U 73* attack convoy KMS 34 in the Mediterranean; they achieve a minor success against the British escort vessels, but no results with the merchantmen.

ATLANTIC. U.S. collier *Suffolk* founders and sinks in storm at 40°43′N, 71°58′W. Auxiliary *Semmes* (AG 24) proceeds from Block Island, submarine rescue ship *Falcon* (ASR 2) from New London, tug *Kewaydin* (AT 24) from Newport, and tug *Fire Island* from New York; destroyer escorts *Scott* (DE 214), *Burke* (DE 215), *Weber* (DE 675), *Schmitt* (DE 676), and *Frament* (DE 677), operating in the vicinity, proceed to the stricken ship's assistance. The destroyer escorts will search to no avail until directed to return to port on 12 December. The search for *Suffolk*'s survivors will be abandoned on 13 December.

12 Sunday

PACIFIC. Submarine *Tuna* (SS 203) sinks Japanese transport *Tosei Maru* north of Halmahera, 02°44′N, 126°14′E.

ATLANTIC. TBF (VC 19) from escort carrier *Bogue* (CVE 9) damages German submarine *U 172* south-southwest of the Canary Islands, 26°27′N, 29°44′W; *U 219* escapes.

U.S. fishing vessel *St. Peter* is disabled about 105 miles east-northeast of Cape Henry; tug *Sciota* (AT 30) proceeds from Norfolk, Virginia, to assist (see 13 December).

13 Monday

PACIFIC. Submarine *Pogy* (SS 266) damages Japanese army cargo ship *Fukkai Maru* off Palaus, 07°06′N, 134°30′E, but is damaged by depth charges, 07°06′N, 134°31′E, and forced to terminate her patrol.

Submarine *Pompon* (SS 267) lays mines off Poulo Condore, southwest of French Indochina.

Submarine *Puffer* (SS 268) unsuccessfully attacks Japanese transport *Teiko Maru* (ex–Vichy French steamship *D'Artagnan*) in South China Sea off entrance to Manila Bay, 14°29′N, 119°59′E.

Submarine *Sailfish* (SS 192) sinks Japanese army cargo ship *Totai Maru* east of Tokara Strait, 30°15′N, 132°30′E.

PBY sinks Japanese cargo vessel *Tokiwa Maru* in Bismarck Sea off New Ireland, 03°30′S, 151°30′E.

ATLANTIC. Destroyer *Osmond Ingram* (DD 255) is damaged by gunfire of German submarine *U 172*, 660 miles west-southwest of the Canary Islands, 26°19′N, 29°58′W, but takes part in sinking *U 172*, along with *George E. Badger* (DD 196), *Clemson* (DD 186), and FMs (VC 19) from escort carrier *Bogue* (CVE 9).

Aerial reconnaissance locates disabled U.S. fishing vessel *St. Peter* east-northeast of Cape Henry; tug *Sciota* (AT 30) takes her in tow and brings her into Norfolk, Virginia, the following day.

Open cargo lighter *YCK 8*, under tow of Army tug *LT 4*, sinks 2.7 miles off Key West, Florida.

EUROPE. USAAF B-17s and B-24s (8th Air Force) bomb Kiel, Germany, sinking torpedo boat *T 15* and minesweeper *R 306*, among other shipping.

MEDITERRANEAN. German submarine *U 593* is sunk by destroyer *Wainwright* (DD 419) and British frigate HMS *Calpe*, 150 miles northeast of Algiers, 37°38′N, 05°58′E.

14 Tuesday

PACIFIC. Faulty fuel pump ignites gasoline dump that in turn explodes ammunition dump; resultant fire destroys motor torpedo boat *PT 239*, Lambu Lambu Cove, Vella Lavella, Solomons, 07°42′S, 156°47′E.

Submarine *Herring* (SS 233) sinks Japanese freighter *Hakozaki Maru* in Yellow Sea northeast of the Yangtze estuary, 33°01′N, 124°01′E.

ATLANTIC. Naval Air Facility, Maceio, Brazil, is established.

15 Wednesday

PACIFIC. Operation DIRECTOR: TF 76 (Rear Admiral Daniel E. Barbey) lands U.S. Army troops (112th Cavalry Regiment) on Arawe Peninsula, New Britain. Japanese planes attack flagship, destroyer *Conyngham* (DD 371), but score no hits.

USAAF B-25s (14th Air Force) sink Japanese cargo ship *Senko Maru* in Gulf of Tonkin, 21°05′N, 108°30′E.

RAAF Beaufighters sink Japanese army cargo ship *Wakatsu Maru* and Dutch Mitchells sink cargo ship *Genmei Maru* off Timor, N.E.I.

Naval Operating Base, Treasury Island, Solomons, is established.

16 Thursday

PACIFIC. Submarine *Flying Fish* (SS 229) sinks Japanese freighter *Ginyo Maru* southwest of the Ryukyus, 22°18′N, 119°52′E.

USAAF B-24 sinks small Japanese cargo vessel *No. 6 Heiei Maru* 150 miles northeast of Wewak, New Guinea.

MEDITERRANEAN. German submarine *U 73* attacks convoy GUS 24 off the Algerian coast, torpedoing U.S. freighter *John S. Copley* at 46°00′N, 22°16′W. Partially abandoned, *John S. Copley* is deemed salvageable, and rescue tug *ATR 47* takes the damaged ship in tow, bringing her into Oran. Submarine chasers *PC 546* and *SC 977* pick up the men who have abandoned ship; only two from among the 44-man merchant complement, 28-man Armed Guard, and Army Security officer are injured. Subsequently, destroyers *Trippe* (DD 403), *Woolsey* (DD 437), and *Edison* (DD 439) sink *U 73*, 35 miles north-northwest of Oran, 36°07′N, 00°50′W.

ATLANTIC. U.S. freighter *Blue Jacket*, mistaken for a German blockade runner while proceeding toward her destination of Cardiff, Wales, is engaged in a running surface gunnery action by three British frigates. Armed Guard gunfire keeps the "friendly" ships at bay, saving the American merchantman. Once the mistake is realized, one of the erstwhile adversaries provides medical assistance; of the 56 merchant seamen and 33 Armed Guards, only seven men are hurt. There are no fatalities.

U.S. tanker *McDowell*, en route from New York to Aruba, N.W.I., is torpedoed and sunk by German submarine *U 516* at 13°08′N, 70°02′W. Later that day, U.S. tanker *Fairfax* rescues 63 survivors; motor minesweeper *YMS 56* picks up eight. Two of the 45-man merchant complement drown in the abandonment; a third dies subsequently of injuries. There are no casualties to the 28-man Armed Guard.

Destroyer escort *Harveson* (DE 316) is damaged in collision with U.S. merchantman *William T. Barry* off the Virginia capes, 36°47′N, 74°33′W; tug *Sciota* (AT 30) brings the damaged destroyer escort into port.

District patrol vessel *YP 426* runs aground in heavy weather off Savannah, Georgia, and sinks, 31°59′N, 80°48′W.

17 Friday

PACIFIC. Coastal transport *APc 21* is sunk by dive bomber, 06°15′S, 149°01′E, and motor minesweeper *YMS 50* is damaged by horizontal bomber, 06°12′S, 149°03′E, off New Britain.

18 Saturday

PACIFIC. Submarine *Aspro* (SS 309) attacks Japanese convoy in Sakishima Gunto, damaging fleet tankers *Sarawak Maru* and *Tenei Maru* at about 24°10′N, 124°40′E, and escapes counterattacks by destroyer *Shiokaze*.

Submarine *Cabrilla* (SS 288) lays mines off Saracen Bay, Cambodia, French Indochina.

Submarine *Grayback* (SS 208) sinks Japanese freighter *Gyokurei Maru* east-northeast of Naha, Okinawa, 26°30′N, 128°19′E, and escapes counterattacks by destroyer *Numakaze* (see 19 December).

19 Sunday

PACIFIC. Submarine *Grayback* (SS 208) sinks Japanese destroyer *Numakaze*, 50 miles east-northeast of Naha, Okinawa, 26°30′N, 128°26′E.

USAAF B-24 and USN PBYs sink Japanese cargo ship *Kaito Maru* southwest of Kavieng, 03°17′S, 151°18′E.

PBY damages Japanese merchant cargo vessel *Shoei Maru*, Kwajalein; *Shoei Maru* sinks the next day.

20 Monday

PACIFIC. Destroyers *Charles Ausburne* (DD 570) and *Dyson* (DD 572) conduct unopposed bombardment of Japanese positions (Tinputs Harbor, Ruri Bay, and Tsundawan) on northern coast of Bougainville, Solomons. The two ships are the first U.S. naval vessels to circumnavigate that island.

Submarine *Gato* (SS 212) sinks Japanese transport *Tsuneshima Maru*, East China Sea, 01°26′N, 148°36′E, and although damaged by depth charges dropped by torpedo boat *Otori*, remains on patrol.

Submarine *Puffer* (SS 268) sinks Japanese destroyer *Fuyo* 60 miles west of Manila, 14°45′N, 119°54′E, but the submarine's attack on cargo ship *Gozan Maru* is not successful.

PBYs sink Japanese transport *Alaska Maru* 30 miles north of northwestern Gazelle Peninsula, 03°43′S, 151°30′E.

ATLANTIC. TBF (VC 19) from escort carrier *Bogue* (CVE 9) attacks Indian Ocean–bound German submarine *U 850*, which responds with antiaircraft fire and fights it out on the surface. TBFs and FMs (VC 19) reinforce the TBF on station and sink *U 850* as the U-boat attempts (too late) to submerge, 530 miles southwest of Fayal, Azores, 32°54′N, 37°01′W.

CARIBBEAN. Coast Guard cutter *Bodega* (WYP 342) is damaged when she runs aground off Margarita Point, C.Z. (see 21 December).

UNITED STATES. Naval Air Training Command is established at Naval Air Station, Pensacola, Florida.

21 Tuesday

PACIFIC. PBYs from Attu, Aleutians, bomb Shimushu, Paramushir Strait, Kurils.

Coastal transport *APc 2* is damaged by dive bomber off New Britain, 06°12′S, 149°03′E.

Submarine *Grayback* (SS 208) sinks Japanese auxiliary netlayer *Kashiwa Maru* and merchant passenger-cargo ship *Konan Maru* south-southwest of Kagoshima, Japan, 30°26′N, 129°58′E.

Submarine *Sailfish* (SS 192) sinks Japanese transport *Uyo Maru* off Miya Saki, 32°38′N, 132°04′E.

Submarine *Skate* (SS 305) sinks Japanese fleet tanker *Terukawa Maru* northwest of Truk, Carolines, 09°45′N, 151°56′E.

USAAF B-25s sink small Japanese cargo vessel *Matsushima Maru* off Wewak, New Guinea.

CARIBBEAN. Coast Guard cutter *Bodega* (WYP 342), damaged by grounding on 20 December off Margarita Point, C.Z., is abandoned.

22 Wednesday

PACIFIC. Submarine *Gurnard* (SS 254) damages German cargo ship *Havelland* east of Kashino Saki, 33°30′N, 135°57′E; the ship never returns to active service.

USAAF A-24s and P-39s (7th Air Force), escorted by F6Fs, raid Mili Atoll, Marshalls, sinking Japanese transport *No. 2 Nankai Maru*, 06°05′N, 171°43′E (see 24 December).

USAAF B-25s (14th Air Force) sink Japanese merchant cargo vessel *Ginrei Maru* in South China Sea, south of Hong Kong, 20°12′N, 113°40′E.

23 Thursday

PACIFIC. USAAF B-25s (14th Air Force) sink Japanese gunboat *Nan-Yo* 35 miles south of Formosa Straits, 25°30′N, 119°30′E.

ATLANTIC. Escort carrier *Card* (CVE 11) and destroyer *Decatur* (DD 341) are attacked unsuccessfully by German submarine *U 415* as they steam toward Horta, Azores, after escorting convoy GUS 24. Destroyer *Schenck* (DD 159), in *Card*'s screen, attacks and probably damages another enemy boat in the vicinity, *U 645* (see 24 December). FM from *Card* locates blockade runner *Osorno*, bound for the Gironde Estuary (see 25 December).

German submarine *U 471* unsuccessfully attacks battleship *Arkansas* (BB 33), screening convoy TU 5, in the North Atlantic, 300 miles west of Rockall Bank.

24 Friday

PACIFIC. TF 39 (Rear Admiral Aaron S. Merrill), consisting of three light cruisers and four destroyers, bombards Buka-Bonis area and islands off the coast of Buka, Solomons. "Black Cat" PBYs spot for the ships; shore battery response is weak and no shells land anywhere near the U.S. ships.

Destroyer escort *Griswold* (DE 7) sinks Japanese submarine *I 39* off Koli Point, Guadalcanal, 09°23'S, 160°09'E.

Submarine *Gurnard* (SS 254) sinks Japanese transport *No. 2 Seizan Maru* 27 nautical miles east of Miki Saki, 33°57'N, 136°19'E, and auxiliary minesweeper *Naruo Maru*, 34°17'N, 136°55'E.

Submarine *Raton* (SS 270) torpedoes Japanese transport *Heiwa Maru* in Kaoe Bay, Halmahera, N.E.I., 02°57'N, 127°32'E; *Heiwa Maru* is intentionally run aground in shallow water to prevent her sinking.

USAAF B-24s (7th Air Force) damage Japanese cargo ship *Kensho Maru* off Kwajalein; A-24s and P-39s attack Mili, bombing wreck of transport *No. 2 Nankai Maru,* sunk 22 December.

ATLANTIC. Escort carrier *Card* (CVE 11) screen continues to battle concentration of U-boats northeast of the Azores. Destroyer *Schenck* (DD 159) sinks German submarine *U 645* at 45°20'N, 21°40'W. *Leary* (DD 158) is torpedoed and sunk by *U 275* and *U 382*, 585 miles west-northwest of Cape Finisterre, Spain, 45°00'N, 22°00'W.

Advanced Amphibious Base, Dartmouth, England, is established.

25 Saturday

PACIFIC. TG 50.2 (Rear Admiral Frederick C. Sherman) attacks Japanese ships at Kavieng, New Ireland. Planes from aircraft carrier *Bunker Hill* (CV 17) and small aircraft carrier *Monterey* (CVL 26) sink transport *Tenryu Maru*, 02°36'S, 150°49'E, and damage minesweepers *W.21* and *W.22* and transport (ex-armed merchant cruiser) *Kiyozumi Maru*.

Submarine *Skate* (SS 305) torpedoes Japanese battleship *Yamato* northeast of Truk, Carolines, 10°05'N, 150°32'E.

USAAF B-25s (14th Air Force) damage Japanese *Patrol Boat No. 14* south of Hong Kong.

ATLANTIC. German blockade runner *Osorno* arrives off the Gironde estuary on the west coast of France, met by six destroyers and six torpedo boats. Although *Osorno* has avoided damage from her foes, she cannot escape friendly wreckage. She fouls sunken German auxiliary vessel *Sperrbrecher 21*, necessitating the blockade runner's being beached.

U.S. freighter *Powder River*, in convoy TU 5, is battered by storm that causes varying degrees of damage to all ships in the convoy; destroyer *Jeffers* (DD 621) stands by the crippled merchantman.

26 Sunday

PACIFIC. Operation BACKHANDER: TF 76 (Rear Admiral Daniel E. Barbey) lands First Marine Division (Major General William H. Rupertus, USMC) at Cape Gloucester, New Britain. TF 74 (Rear Admiral Victor A. C. Crutchley, RN) provides shore bombardment support. This operation marks the first time that the Seventh Amphibious Force employs control officers to guide landing craft through reefs to designated beaches. During retaliatory Japanese air attacks, destroyer *Brownson* (DD 518) is sunk, 05°20'S, 148°25'E, while destroyers *Lamson* (DD 367), *Shaw* (DD 373), and *Mugford* (DD 389), tank landing ship *LST 66,* and coastal transport *APc 15* are damaged.

CARIBBEAN. U.S. tanker *Chapultepec*, en route from Aruba, N.W.I., to Cristobal, C.Z., is torpedoed by German submarine *U 530* at 10°33'N, 79°10'W. While there are no fatalities among the 53-man merchant complement or the 28-man Armed Guard, two of that aggregate total are injured. The ship reaches her destination under her own power and discharges her cargo of fuel oil. Subsequently, U.S. tanker *Esso Buffalo*, en route from Aruba to the Canal Zone (ultimate destination: Melbourne, Australia), most likely accidentally rams *U 530* at 10°25'N, 78°28'W.

27 Monday

PACIFIC. TF 38 (Rear Admiral Walden L. Ainsworth), consisting of two light cruisers and four destroyers, bombards east coast of Bougainville, Solomons, to harass the Japanese evacuation operations and increase Japanese suspicions that a landing is taking place on that island.

Submarine *Flying Fish* (SS 229) sinks Japanese fleet tanker *Kyuei Maru* in South China Sea west of Luzon Strait, 21°25'N, 118°05'E.

Submarine *Gurnard* (SS 254) damages Japanese transport (ex-armed merchant cruiser) *Gokoku Maru* south of Honshu, 34°23'N, 138°24'E.

Submarine *Ray* (SS 271) sinks Japanese fleet tanker *Kyoko Maru* (ex-Dutch *Semiramis*) west of the Celebes, 05°00'S, 121°22'E.

Submarine *Tautog* (SS 199) damages Japanese seaplane carrier *Kimikawa Maru* off Shiono Misaki, 33°25'N, 135°33'E.

INDIAN OCEAN. U.S. freighter *Jose Navarro*, bound for Calcutta, India, is torpedoed by German submarine *U 178* at 08°20'N, 73°35'E. A volunteer crew returns to the ship after she is abandoned in hopes of saving her but go over the side before *U 178* finishes off the freighter in a second attack. There are no fatalities among the 46-man merchant complement, the 34-man Armed Guard, or the 86 embarked troops (only one man of that aggregate total is injured) (see 28 December).

28 Tuesday

PACIFIC. Submarine *Muskallunge* (SS 262) unsuccessfully attacks Japanese convoy west of Truk, 08°50'N, 147°20'E.

PV-1 attacks Japanese net tender *Katsura Maru* off Kwajalein.

USAAF B-25s and P-51s (14th Air Force) sink Japanese merchant cargo vessels *Heizan Maru, Unyo Maru,* and *Koka Maru* in Yangtze River at Chihchow, 30°40'N, 117°30'E.

Amphibious Training Base, Kamaole, Maui, T.H., is established.

INDIAN OCEAN. U.S. freighter *Robert F. Hoke*, en route from Abadan, Iran, to Mombasa, Kenya, is torpedoed by Japanese submarine *I 26* at 20°05'N, 59°58'E, and abandoned by all but the 27-man Armed Guard, who remain at their guns and fire upon the I-boat's periscope to keep the enemy down. *I 26* abandons any further attacks and retires while *Robert F. Hoke* remains afloat. The crew reboards the ship but is not able to get her under way and she is abandoned a second time. RAF crash boat rescues all hands (41 merchant sailors and the Armed Guard), and the abandoned freighter is later towed to Aden by British rescue tug HMS *Masterful*. *Robert F. Hoke*, later towed to Suez, never returns to active service and is written off as a total loss.

Indian Navy minesweeper RINS *Rajputana* rescues the survivors of U.S. freighter *Jose Navarro*, sunk by German submarine *U 178* the previous day, and transports them to Cochin.

ATLANTIC. PB4Y (VB 105), on patrol over Bay of Biscay, sights five German destroyers and six torpedo boats returning from attempt to rendezvous with blockade runner *Alsterfurer*, sunk the day before by an RAF No. 311 (Czechoslovakia) Squadron Liberator. Of 15 PB4Ys dispatched as a strike force, six (five from VB 105 and one from VB 103) attack the enemy force. Contact reports by Navy planes, meanwhile, draw British light cruisers HMS *Glasgow* and HMS *Enterprise* to the scene, resulting in the sinking of German destroyer *Z 27* and torpedo boats *T 25* and *T 26*, the survivors of which are rescued by the British ships, an Irish steamer, and four Spanish destroyers.

29 Wednesday

PACIFIC. Submarine *Silversides* (SS 236), operating off Palau, sinks Japanese transport *Tenposan Maru*, 08°09′N, 133°51′E, army cargo ship *Shichisei Maru*, 08°00′N, 133°51′E, and freighter *Ryuto Maru*, 08°03′N, 134°04′E, and damages army cargo ship *Bichu Maru*.

"B-24" (possibly a PB4Y) attacks Truk-bound Japanese cargo ship *Katori Maru*, 06°12′N, 167°45′E.

USAAF B-25s (14th Air Force) sink Japanese freighter *Kakuzan Maru* and transport *Daitei Maru* in the Yangtze River southwest of Wuhu, China.

30 Thursday

PACIFIC. Submarine *Bluefish* (SS 222) sinks Japanese oiler *Ichiyu Maru*, Java Sea, 02°45′S, 109°10′E.

USAAF B-24s (13th Air Force) bomb Japanese shipping off Rabaul; during this raid, guardboat *Ukui Maru* is sunk.

31 Friday

PACIFIC. Four PBY-5As from Attu, Aleutians, bomb Shimushu and Kashiwabara, Kurils.

Submarine *Greenling* (SS 213) sinks Japanese transport *Shoho Maru* southeast of Ponape, 05°40′N, 160°20′E, and evades counterattacks by submarine chaser *Ch 30*.

Submarine *Herring* (SS 233) attacks Japanese convoy northwest of Chichi Jima, 31°46′N, 138°22′E (see 1 January 1944).

ATLANTIC. Destroyer *Lea* (DD 118) is damaged when she is accidentally rammed by U.S. freighter *Elihu Yale* east of Bermuda, 33°29′30″N, 48°12′30″W.

1944

JANUARY

1 Saturday

PACIFIC. TG 37.2 (Rear Admiral Frederick C. Sherman) attacks Japanese convoy off Kavieng, New Ireland. Planes from carrier *Bunker Hill* (CV 17) and small carrier *Monterey* (CVL 26) bomb shipping escorted by cruisers and destroyers, damaging light cruisers *Oyodo* and *Noshiro*.

Destroyers *Smith* (DD 378) and *Hutchins* (DD 476) are damaged in collision off eastern New Guinea, 05°00′S, 146°00′E.

Tank landing ship *LST 446* is damaged by accidental explosion off south coast of Bougainville, Solomons, 06°15′S, 155°02′E.

Submarine *Balao* (SS 285) damages Japanese transport *Kiyozumi Maru* south of Truk, Caroline Islands, 04°32′N, 147°23′E.

Submarine *Herring* (SS 233), pursuing Japanese convoy spotted the previous day, sinks aircraft transport *Nagoya Maru* 220 miles south-southwest of Tokyo Bay, 32°10′N, 138°37′E, and survives counterattacks by destroyer *Ikazuchi*.

Submarine *Puffer* (SS 268), in attack on Japanese convoy at the western entrance of the Mindanao Sea, sinks army cargo ship *Ryujo Maru* about 40 miles south of Negros Island, 08°36′N, 122°52′E.

Submarine *Ray* (SS 271) sinks Japanese gunboat *Okoyo Maru* at mouth of Ambon Bay, N.E.I., 03°51′S, 128°04′E.

PBYs sink Japanese cargo ship *Kanaiyama Maru* near Lorengau, Admiralties, 02°03′S, 147°27′E.

Aerial minelaying operations in the Marshalls begin. Four PB4Y-1s (VB 108), flying from Abemama in the Gilberts, mine Enijun Channel, Maleolap; flying from Tarawa, three PV-1s (VB 137) mine the waters off Jaluit; and two PBY-5s (VP 72) mine Jabor Anchorage, Jaluit.

Naval Air Facility, Honolulu, Oahu, T.H., is established.

2 Sunday

ATLANTIC. Succession of PB4Ys (VB 107) sight and track German blockade runner *Weserland* (disguised as British freighter *Glenbank*), en route from Japan to Germany, 595 miles south-southwest of Ascension Island. Gunfire from the German ship damages one of the PB4Ys. Destroyer *Somers* (DD 381) intercepts *Weserland* and opens fire (see 3 January).

PACIFIC. Operation MICHAELMAS: TF 76 (Rear Admiral Daniel E. Barbey) lands U.S. Sixth Army troops (126th RCT, 32nd Division, Reinforced) at Saidor, New Guinea. Insertion of American troops at Saidor leap-frogs the Japanese garrison at Sio, 75 miles to the east. U.S. cruisers and destroyers provide cover.

Submarine *Finback* (SS 230) sinks Japanese merchant tanker *Isshin Maru* in East China Sea about 30 miles northwest of Takara Jima, Nansei Shoto, 29°30′N, 128°50′E.

Aerial minelaying operations in the Marshalls continue. Flying from Tarawa, five PV-1s (VB 137) and one PBY-5 (VP 72) mine Jabor Anchorage, Jaluit.

INDIAN OCEAN. U.S. freighter *Albert Gallatin* is torpedoed and sunk by Japanese submarine *I 26* about 60 miles off the Arabian coast, 21°21′N, 59°58′E; there are no casualties among the complement (including the 28-man Armed Guard, who remain at their posts until the ship literally sinks beneath them). Norwegian tanker *Britannia* rescues the survivors.

3 Monday

PACIFIC. Submarine *Bluefish* (SS 222) lays mines off eastern Malayan coast.

Submarine *Kingfish* (SS 234) attacks Japanese convoy northwest of Miri, Sarawak, Borneo, and sinks fleet tankers *Bokuei Maru*, 06°58′N, 112°02′E, and *Ryuei Maru*, 08°06′N, 112°30′E.

Submarine *Raton* (SS 270) damages Japanese fleet tanker *Akebono Maru* east of Mindanao, P.I., 08°18′N, 129°59′E.

Submarine *Scorpion* (SS 278) departs Midway for her fourth war patrol. She will rendezvous with *Herring* (SS 233) on 5 January, but will never be seen again.[179]

Submarine *Tautog* (SS 199) sinks Japanese transport *Saishu Maru* south of Honshu, 33°44′N, 136°02′E.

Aerial minelaying operations in the Marshalls continue. Seven PB4Y-1s (VB 108 and VB 109), flying from Abemama in the Gilberts, mine the waters northwest of Enijun Island, off west side of Taroa, and outside lagoon off Kumaru Island, and strafe shipping anchored off Taroa; four PV-1s (VB 137), flying from Tarawa, mine southeast pass, Jaluit.

Japanese land attack planes (752nd or 753rd *Kokutai*) bomb advanced base on Abemama Atoll, demolishing one PB4Y; exploding ammunition in the burning bomber damages two additional PB4Ys.

ATLANTIC. Destroyer *Somers* (DD 381) sinks German blockade runner *Weserland*, 14°55′S, 21°39′W, and recovers 130 survivors (see 13 January).

Destroyer *Turner* (DD 648) is sunk by internal explosion, three miles north of Ambrose Lightship, New York Harbor. During efforts to help the injured, a Coast Guard helicopter transports needed blood plasma in the Navy's first operational use of the helicopter in treating casualties.

4 Tuesday

PACIFIC. TG 37.2 (Rear Admiral Frederick C. Sherman) planes bomb Japanese shipping at Kavieng, New Ireland, damaging destroyers *Fumizuki* and *Satsuki* in Steffen Strait.

Motor torpedo boat *PT 145*, damaged by grounding off Mindiri, 05°34′S, 146°10′E, is scuttled by motor torpedo boat *PT 370*. The

German blockade runner *Burgenland* burns, set afire by her crew after she has been intercepted in the South Atlantic by light cruiser *Omaha* (CL 4) and destroyer *Jouett* (DD 396), 5 January 1944. (NHC, NH 75616)

latter suffers damage during the attempt to tow *PT 145* out of the area.

Submarines *Bluefish* (SS 222) and *Rasher* (SS 269) attack Japanese convoy off coast of French Indochina. *Bluefish* sinks merchant tanker *Hakku Maru*, 07°10′N, 108°28′E; *Rasher* damages tanker *Kiyo Maru* (ex-Norwegian *Vigrid*), 06°44′N, 108°43′E (see 5 January). Third ship in convoy, *Konsan Maru*, escapes unharmed. *Rasher* also carries out mining operation in waters off Cochin China the same day.

Submarine *Cabrilla* (SS 288) sinks Japanese freighter *No. 8 Tamon Maru* off Cape Padaran, French Indochina, 11°05′N, 109°10′E.

Submarine *Tautog* (SS 199), despite presence of two escort vessels, sinks Japanese freighter *Usa Maru* off southern Honshu, 34°09′N, 136°50′E.

Aerial minelaying operations in the Marshalls continue. Two PV-1s (VB 137) and one PBY-5 (VP 72), flying from Tarawa, mine southeast pass, Jaluit.

Japanese land attack planes (752nd *Kokutai*) bomb U.S. advanced bases at Tarawa, Makin, and Abemama in the Gilberts; they achieve only minor damage at the last place.

USAAF B-25s (5th Air Force), covered by RAAF Beaufighters, attack Japanese shipping

in Tenau Harbor, Timor, sinking army cargo ship *Heimei Maru*, 10°10′S, 123°35′E.

Escort carrier *Tripoli* (CVE 64) is damaged by accidental gasoline fire, Naval Repair Base, San Diego, California.

ATLANTIC. Light cruiser *Omaha* (CL 4) and destroyer *Jouett* (DD 396) intercept German blockade runner *Rio Grande* about 55 miles northeast of the coast of Brazil, 06°41′S, 25°36′W. Gunfire and scuttling charges sink *Rio Grande* (see 8, 11, and 13 January).

5 Wednesday

PACIFIC. Submarine *Rasher* (SS 269) sinks Japanese tanker *Kiyo Maru* (ex-Norwegian *Vigrid*) in South China Sea, 05°46′N, 108°36′E.

Aerial minelaying operations in the Marshalls continue. One PBY-5 (VP 72), flying from Tarawa, mines Schischmarov Strait, Wotje.

Japanese land attack planes (753rd *Kokutai*) bomb U.S. advanced base at Tarawa.

ATLANTIC. PBM-3S (VP 203) sights German blockade runner *Burgenland* and summons light cruiser *Omaha* (CL 4) and destroyer *Jouett* (DD 396). Gunfire and scuttling charges sink *Burgenland*, 07°29′S, 25°37′W, the last of the German surface vessels used to run the Allied blockade (see 7, 8, and 13 January).

6 Thursday

PACIFIC. Aerial minelaying operations in the Marshalls continue. One PBY-5 (VP 72), flying from Tarawa, mines Schischmarov Strait, Wotje; a second Catalina, vexed by engine trouble, brings its mines back and does not carry out the mission.

ATLANTIC. Gunboat *St. Augustine* (PG 54) is sunk in collision with U.S. tanker *Camas Meadows*, 73 miles south-southwest of Cape May, New Jersey, 38°12′N, 74°10′W. Tug *Allegheny* (AT 19) and civilian tug *Point Judith* (NRTS) proceed from Cape May and assist in the search for survivors.

MEDITERRANEAN. U.S. freighter *William S. Rosecrans* drags anchor during storm south of Naples, Italy, and strikes a mine that starts a fire that dooms the ship. She sinks later that afternoon, but there are no casualties to either the merchant complement or the 27-man Armed Guard, who are rescued by British naval vessels.

7 Friday

PACIFIC. Small carrier *Belleau Wood* (CVL 24) and destroyer *Dunlap* (DD 384) are damaged in collision during exercises off Oahu, T.H.

Submarine *Kingfish* (SS 234) attacks Japanese convoy southwest of Palawan, sinking merchant tanker *No. 3 Fushimi Maru*, 09°27′N, 117°36′E.

PB4Y-1s (VB 108 and VB 109), flying from Abemama in the Gilberts, encounter bad weather that forces cancellation of their minelaying mission to the Marshalls.

USAAF B-25s sink Vichy French merchant ship *Kai Ping*, Ben Thuy, French Indochina.

Japanese cargo vessel *Katsuragisan Maru* is sunk by Japanese mine in northwest channel, Truk, 07°30′N, 151°50′E.

ATLANTIC. Tug *Carib* (AT 82) proceeds to sea from Bahia, Brazil. She stops and boards Spanish merchant ship *Monte Amiboto,* removes a stowaway (an alleged German internee in Argentina from the armored ship *Admiral Graf Spee*), and returns to Bahia, where her passenger is turned over to local authorities.

Destroyer *Davis* (DD 395) rescues 21 survivors of German blockade runner *Burgenland,* sunk on 5 January, 08°06′S, 26°45′W.

8 Saturday

PACIFIC. TF 38 (Rear Admiral Walden L. Ainsworth), consisting of two light cruisers and five destroyers, bombards Japanese shore installations on Faisi, Poporang, and Shortland Islands, Solomons.

Aerial minelaying operations in the Marshalls continue. Eight PB4Y-1s (VB 108 and VB 109), flying from Abemama in the Gilberts, mine the waters off Wotje and then strafe enemy facilities on the island and shipping offshore; seven PBY-5s (VP 72), flying from Tarawa, mine Wotje anchorage and Schischmarov Strait.

Japanese land attack planes (753rd *Kokutai*) harass U.S. advanced base at Tarawa.

ATLANTIC. Light cruiser *Marblehead* (CL 12) rescues 72 survivors of German blockade runner *Rio Grande*, sunk on 4 January, 07°45′S, 33°00′W.[180] Destroyer *Winslow* (DD 359) rescues 35 survivors of German blockade runner *Burgenland*, sunk on 5 January, 08°14′S, 29°22′W.

9 Sunday

PACIFIC. District patrol vessel *YP 281* founders in heavy weather west of the Society Islands, 16°53′S, 177°18′W, and is scuttled by submarine chaser *PC 1134*.

USAAF B-25s strafe Japanese barge base at Gali Point; P-40s and P-38s sweep over northeast coast of New Guinea, silencing gun positions and destroying Japanese fishing boats *Yawata Maru, Kenichi Maru, Kosei Maru,* and *Kaiun Maru* at Ulingan Harbor.

10 Monday

PACIFIC. Motor minesweeper *YMS 127* sinks after running aground, Aleutian Islands.

Submarine *Seawolf* (SS 197) begins series of attacks on Japanese convoy about 70 miles north of Naha, Okinawa, sinking army cargo ship *Asuka Maru*, 27°30′N, 127°45′E, and freighter *Getsuyo Maru* at 27°10′N, 127°28′E (see 11 January).

Submarine *Steelhead* (SS 280), in the midst of a "full-fledged typhoon," attacks Japanese convoy south of Honshu, sinking repair ship *Yamabiko Maru*, 31°28′N, 137°44′E.

Aerial minelaying operations in the Marshalls continue. Two PBY-5s (VP 72), flying from Tarawa, mine Meichen Channel and Legediak Strait, Wotje.

Japanese land attack plane (753rd *Kokutai*) bombs U.S. advanced base at Tarawa.

MEDITERRANEAN. U.S. freighter *Daniel Webster* is damaged by German aerial torpedo during air attack on convoy KMS 37 while en route from Gibraltar to Augusta and Naples, 36°04′N, 00°14′W (see 11 January).

11 Tuesday

PACIFIC. Submarine *Seawolf* (SS 197) concludes operations against Japanese convoy attacked the previous day, sinking army cargo ship *Yahiko Maru* about 50 miles north of Naha, Okinawa, 27°10′N, 127°28′E.

Submarine *Sturgeon* (SS 187) attacks Japanese convoy in approaches to Bungo Strait, sinking army cargo ship *Erie Maru* about 20 miles east of Saeki, Kyushu, 32°56′N, 132°02′E, and survives ensuing depth charging by escorts.

Submarine *Tautog* (SS 199) damages Japanese ammunition ship *Kogyo Maru* off Honshu, 34°10′N, 136°56′E.

British submarine HMS *Tally Ho* sinks Japanese light cruiser *Kuma* 10 miles northwest of Penang, Malaya, 05°26′N, 99°52′E. Destroyer *Uranami* rescues survivors.

Aerial minelaying operations in the Marshalls continue. Four PBYs (VP 72), flying from Tarawa, mine Meichen Channel and Schischmarov Strait, Wotje, and Enibin and Torappu Channels, Maleolap.

Japanese land attack planes (753rd or 752nd *Kokutai*) conduct nuisance attack on U.S. advanced bases at Tarawa and Abemama, Gilberts.

ATLANTIC. Brazilian 10th Military Region forces take custody of 22 survivors of German blockade runner *Rio Grande,* sunk on 4 January, who reach Fortaleza, Brazil.

MEDITERRANEAN. U.S. freighter *Daniel Webster*, damaged by German aerial torpedo the previous day, reaches Oran, Algeria, under escort of British frigate HMS *Barle*; rescue tug *ATR 47* brings *Daniel Webster* into port where she is subsequently written off as a total loss. There are no fatalities among the ship's complement, which includes a 29-man Armed Guard.

12 Wednesday

PACIFIC. PB4Ys (VB 108 and VB 109) bomb Japanese shipping in Kwajalein lagoon, sinking gunboat *Ikuta Maru*, 08°42′N, 167°44′E. USAAF B-25Gs strike Japanese shipping and installations at Maleolap and Wotje in the Marshalls, damaging destroyer *Ushio*. PB4Ys pound ground installations.

Aerial minelaying operations continue in the Marshalls as five PBY-5s, flying from Tarawa, mine Tokowa and Torappu Channels and the south entrance to Maleolap; one Catalina goes on to bomb Jabor but is forced down by antiaircraft fire six miles east of Jaluit (see 14 January).

Japanese land attack planes (753rd or 752nd *Kokutai*) bomb advanced base at Tarawa, destroying a machine shop, igniting gasoline stores, and causing light casualties at Mullinnix and Hawkins fields.

Submarine *Albacore* (SS 218) sinks Japanese gunboat *No. 2 Choko Maru* about 350 miles southwest of Truk, 03°30′N, 147°27′E; she also damages motor gunboat *Hayabusa-Tei No. 4*, under tow of *No. 2 Choko Maru*, so badly that the smaller craft has to be scuttled, 03°37′N, 147°27′E.

Submarine *Hake* (SS 256) sinks Japanese aircraft transport *Nigitsu Maru* about 300 miles southeast of Okinawa, 23°15′N, 133°49′E.

Japanese army cargo vessel *Kanjo Maru* is sunk by USAAF mine in Takao Harbor, Formosa, 22°37′N, 120°15′E.

ATLANTIC. Naval Air Station, Port Lyautey, French Morocco, is established.

13   Thursday

PACIFIC. Submarine *Swordfish* (SS 193) is damaged by depth charges off central Honshu, 33°16′N, 139°30′E, but remains on patrol.

USAAF B-24 (5th Air Force) sinks Japanese transport *Haguro Maru* 35 miles northwest of New Hanover, 02°43′N, 149°25′E.

Thai ship *Valaya* is sunk by mine in Menam River, Thailand.

ATLANTIC. Brazilian minelayer *Camocim*, while escorting convoy JT 19, picks up the last 34 survivors (26 German and 8 Italian) of the three German blockade runners sunk on 3, 4, and 5 January.

14   Friday

PACIFIC. Submarine *Scamp* (SS 277) attacks Japanese convoy about 400 miles east-southeast of the Palaus, sinking fleet tanker *Nippon Maru* south of Sorol Island, 05°02′N, 140°50′E; *Albacore* (SS 218), nearby, sinks destroyer *Sazanami*, 05°30′N, 141°34′E. *Guardfish* (SS 217) attacks same convoy attacked earlier by *Scamp* and sinks fleet tanker *Ken'yo Maru* 520 miles southeast of Palau, 05°23′N, 141°57′E.

Submarine *Seawolf* (SS 197) attacks Japanese convoy approximately 300 miles northeast of Okinawa, sinking fleet tanker *Yamazuru Maru*, 25°00′N, 132°00′E.

Submarine *Swordfish* (SS 193) attacks Japanese convoy, sinking transport *Yamakuni Maru* off Hachijo Jima, 33°16′N, 139°30′E.

SBDs and TBFs, supported by Allied fighters, bomb Japanese shipping in Simpson Harbor, Rabaul, damaging destroyer *Matsukaze* and fleet tanker *Naruto*.

PBY-5 (VP 72) shot down attacking Jabor on 12 January is located and its crew rescued about 40 miles southwest of Jaluit.

Fuel oil barge *YO 159*, under tow of U.S.

tanker *Gulf Star*, is torpedoed by Japanese submarine *RO 42*, 250 miles east of Espíritu Santo, New Hebrides, 15°27′S, 171°28′E (see 15 January).

USAAF B-25s strike Japanese shipping and installations at Wotje Atoll, Marshalls, sinking guardboat *Tama Maru*.

USAAF B-24s (14th Air Force) sink army cargo ship *Gyoei Maru* in South China Sea, 20°35′N, 113°44′E, and damage guardboat *No. 17 Banshu Maru* at 20°00′N, 114°00′E.

ATLANTIC. Destroyers *Bulmer* (DD 222) and *Parrott* (DD 218) damage German submarine *U 382*, 560 miles west-northwest of Cape Finisterre, Spain.

15   Saturday

PACIFIC. Service Squadron 10 (Captain Worrall R. Carter) is activated at Pearl Harbor to provide mobile logistics support for a projected advanced major fleet anchorage in the Central Pacific Area.[181]

Submarine *Crevalle* (SS 291) lays mines east of Saigon, French Indochina.

Submarine *Thresher* (SS 200) attacks Japanese convoy, sinking army cargo ship *Toho Maru* and merchant tanker *Tatsuno Maru* about 75 miles north of Luzon, 20°00′N, 120°51′E.

Fuel oil barge *YO 159*, torpedoed the previous day by Japanese submarine *RO 42*, is scuttled by gunfire of submarine chaser *PC 1138*.

USAAF B-25 sinks Vichy French coastal patrol craft *Ping Sung* off Hongay, French Indochina.

ANDAMAN SEA. British submarine HMS *Tally Ho* sinks Japanese army cargo ship *Ryuko Maru* south of Port Blair, Andaman Islands, 10°03′N, 93°05′E.

16   Sunday

PACIFIC. Submarine *Blackfish* (SS 221) attacks Japanese convoy and sinks transport *Kaika Maru* about 275 miles southwest of Truk, 04°03′N, 148°41′E.

Submarine *Flier* (SS 250) runs aground as she transits channel at Midway Island; submarine rescue vessel *Macaw* (ASR 17) becomes stranded as she attempts to assist the damaged fleet boat (see 22 January and 12 February).

Submarine *Redfin* (SS 272) damages Japanese destroyer *Amatsukaze* 250 miles north of the Spratly Islands, 14°40′N, 113°50′E.

Submarine *Seahorse* (SS 304) sinks Japanese freighter *Nikko Maru* southeast of the Marianas, 12°49′N, 150°19′E.

Submarine *Sturgeon* (SS 187) damages Japa-

nese destroyer *Suzutsuki* in Bungo Strait, 32°15′N, 132°29′E, but fails to hit the destroyer's charge, cargo vessel *Azaki Maru*.

Submarine *Swordfish* (SS 193), despite presence of escort vessel, sinks Japanese gunboat *Delhi Maru* off Honshu, 34°04′N, 139°56′E.[182]

Submarine *Whale* (SS 239) attacks Japanese convoy and sinks army cargo ship *Denmark Maru* about 400 miles southeast of Okinawa, 23°09′N, 135°14′E; *Seawolf* (SS 197), nearby, damages transport *Tarushima Maru*, 23°00′N, 135°00′E, which *Whale* later finishes off, 22°50′N, 135°40′E.

PBYs attack Rabaul-bound Japanese convoy O 905, sinking army cargo ships *Shunko Maru*, 02°30′S, 149°42′E, and *Hozugawa Maru* and transport *Meisho Maru* about 45 miles northwest of New Hanover, 02°20′S, 149°42′E. *Kosei Maru* (see 17 January) and escorting submarine chasers *Ch 24* and *Ch 29* emerge unscathed.

Japanese submarine *I 181* is sunk by U.S. forces in St. George Strait.

Japanese land attack planes (753rd or 752nd *Kokutai*) bomb U.S. advanced base at Tarawa (see 17 January).

ATLANTIC. TBF (VC 13) from escort carrier *Guadalcanal* (CVE 60) sinks German submarine *U 544* in mid-Atlantic, 40°30′N, 37°20′W.[183]

U.S. freighter *Sumner I. Kimball*, straggling from New York–bound convoy ON 219, is torpedoed and sunk by German submarine *U 960* in the North Atlantic, 52°35′N, 35°00′W. There are no survivors from either the 40-man merchant complement or the 29-man Armed Guard.

17   Monday

PACIFIC. SBDs and TBFs, covered by fighters, bomb Japanese shipping at Rabaul, sinking repair ship *Hakkai Maru*, transport *Kenshin Maru* (ex-British *Celebes*), and army cargo ship *Kosei Maru* (which had escaped damage the previous day), and damaging aircraft transport *Lyon Maru*. *Kosei Maru* sinks with 14 landing barges still on board, 04°13′S, 152°11′E.

RAAF Beaufighters bomb villages on Tanimbar Island, N.E.I., and sink Japanese guardboat *No. 6 Shinko Maru*.

USAAF B-24s (5th Air Force) sink Japanese freighter *Chiburi Maru* 80 miles east of Manus, 02°27′S, 148°58′E, and *No. 9 Fukei Maru* at 02°00′S, 149°00′E.

USAAF P-39s, using night intruder tactics, down Japanese land attack planes (753rd or 752nd *Kokutai*) (the same planes that had carried out the nuisance raid on Tarawa the night before) before dawn over Mille, Marshalls; later that day, USAAF A-24s, P-39s, and P-40s bomb and strafe installations at Mille.

ATLANTIC. Airship *K 36* crashes in a fog on the lee side of Ilha de Cabo Frio, Brazil.

18 Tuesday

PACIFIC. Tropical hurricane batters Nouméa, New Caledonia, damaging high-speed transport *Noa* (APD 24), district patrol vessel *YP 239*, district auxiliary (miscellaneous) *YAG 25*, and a crane barge.

Submarine *Bowfin* (SS 287) sinks Japanese merchant tanker *Shoyu Maru* off west coast of Palawan, 00°18′N, 118°37′E.[184]

Submarine *Flasher* (SS 249) sinks Japanese oiler *Yoshida Maru* about 140 miles west-southwest of Marcus Island, 23°50′N, 151°28′E.

PB4Y-1 (VB 108), to simulate minelaying operations, sows unfused 100-pound bombs in Mellu, Gegibu, and Onemak Channels, Kwajalein.

Japanese land attack planes (752nd *Kokutai*) bomb U.S. advanced base at Tarawa.

USAAF A-24s and P-40s bomb Japanese installations at Jaluit, sinking merchant tanker *No. 1 Nanyu Maru*.

19 Wednesday

PACIFIC. Submarine *Haddock* (SS 231) torpedoes Japanese carrier *Unyo* 140 miles east-southeast of Guam, 12°50′N, 146°23′E.

USAAF B-24 (5th Air Force) sinks Japanese cargo vessel *Kaishu Maru* at Manus, Admiralties.

20 Thursday

PACIFIC. Submarine *Batfish* (SS 310) attacks Japanese convoy off southern Honshu, sinking transport *Hidaka Maru* south of Shiono Misaki, 31°28′N, 134°52′E.

Submarine *Gar* (SS 206) attacks Japanese convoy on the New Guinea–to–Palau route, sinking army cargo ship *Koyo Maru* about 50 miles south-southwest of Palau, 06°40′N, 134°17′E.

Submarine *Seadragon* (SS 194) damages Japanese stores ship *Irako* northwest of Truk, 08°04′N, 152°40′E.

Submarine *Tinosa* (SS 283) lands men and equipment in northeast Borneo.

USAAF B-24s (14th Air Force) sink Japanese transports *Menado Maru* and *Kuzan Maru* 140 miles southeast of Swatow, China, 22°10′N, 118°15′E.

USAAF B-25s sink transport *Ogashima Maru* at Namu Atoll, Marshalls, 08°07′N, 168°00′E.

USAAF planes sink Japanese dredge *Jintsu Maru* at 03°04′S, 142°10′E.

Japanese land attack planes (752nd *Kokutai*) bomb U.S. advanced base at Tarawa.

ATLANTIC. Tank landing ship *LST 228* sinks after running aground off the Azores, 38°39′N, 27°12′W.

U.S. freighter *Leland Stanford* runs aground on Hen and Chicken Shoals, off Cape Henlopen, Delaware. While assisting the stricken merchantman, tug *Allegheny* (AT 19) is damaged (steering gear) when she goes aground herself. Refloated by district patrol vessel *YP 221* and Army tug *ST 248*, *Allegheny* continues to assist *Leland Stanford* while Navy Rescue Tug Service assets are ordered to the scene: salvage tug *Resolute* from New York and tug *Nancy Moran* from the Delaware breakwater (see 21 and 23 January).

21 Friday

PACIFIC. PBY-5As, flying from Attu, Aleutians, bomb and photograph Japanese installations in the Kurabu Saki area, south Paramushir, Kurils, and in the Musashi Wan–Otomaye area, south coast of Paramushir; PV-1s bomb and photograph enemy installations in the north Paramushir area.

Submarine *Seahorse* (SS 304) attacks Japanese convoy on the Palau–Hollandia, New Guinea, track, sinking army transport *Ikoma Maru* and cargo ship *Yasukuni Maru* 280 miles east-southeast of Palau, 03°19′N, 137°02′E.

British submarine HMS *Tally Ho* sinks Japanese cargo ship *No. 67 Daigen Maru* at 03°15′N, 100°40′E.

ATLANTIC. U.S. tanker *Plattsburg Socony* and freighter *Charles Henderson* collide about two and a half miles east of Cape Henlopen, Delaware; the former catches fire. Coast Guard fire-fighting parties are sent out in craft from Cape May while tug *Allegheny* (AT 19) and tug *Nancy Moran* (NRTS) are both diverted from assisting U.S. freighter *Leland Stanford,* grounded the previous day. Fire-fighting party from *Allegheny* extinguishes the blaze on board *Plattsburg Socony*; *Nancy Moran* tows the damaged tanker to Cape May.

22 Saturday

PACIFIC. Submarine *Flier* (SS 250), run aground on 16 January, is refloated and taken in tow by submarine rescue vessel *Florikan* (ASR 9); submarine rescue vessel *Macaw* (ASR 17), however, remains stranded at Midway (see 12 February).

Oiler *Cache* (AO 67) is torpedoed by Japa-

nese submarine *RO 37* about 155 miles southeast of San Cristobal, Solomons, 12°08′S, 164°33′E. Destroyer *Buchanan* (DD 484), proceeding independently from Purvis Bay to Espíritu Santo, is directed to the scene of the torpedoing of *Cache*. *Buchanan* sinks *RO 37* about 130 miles east-southeast of San Cristobal, 11°47′S, 164°17′E.

Submarine *Tinosa* (SS 283) attacks Japanese convoy, sinking merchant tankers *Seinan Maru* and *Koshin Maru* about 120 miles north of Labuan, Borneo, 07°22′N, 115°05′E.

USAAF B-25s, escorted by P-38s, attack Japanese shipping in Lorengau Harbor, Manus, Admiralties, sinking auxiliary submarine chaser *Cha 40*, 01°50′S, 147°20′E, and damaging cargo vessel *No. 3 Kurebame Maru*.

ATLANTIC. Tank landing craft *LCT 582* sinks after running aground, Azores.

MEDITERRANEAN. Operation SHINGLE: Elements of the British First Army and U.S. Third Army (Major General Lucian K. Truscott, USA) land on the Italian coast at Anzio; naval commander is Rear Admiral Frank K. Lowry. Initial landings progress as scheduled with little opposition, and the troops are landed with small loss. Enemy opposition, however, will mount over the ensuing weeks, and naval gunfire support will prove crucial to troops holding the beachhead. Off Anzio, minesweeper *Portent* (AM 106) is sunk by mine, 41°24′N, 12°44′E; large infantry landing craft *LCI(L) 20* is sunk by aircraft.

23 Sunday

PACIFIC. PBY-5As and PV-1s, flying from Attu, bomb Japanese installations on the west and south coasts of Paramushir, Kurils.

Submarine *Gar* (SS 206), in attack on Japanese convoy, sinks transport *Taian Maru* about 75 miles south of Palau, 05°45′N, 134°45′E.

Submarine *Snook* (SS 279) sinks Japanese gunboat *Magane Maru* about 175 miles north-northwest of Chichi Jima, 29°49′N, 140°08′E.

USAAF B-25s (14th Air Force) attack Japanese convoy off Foochow, China, sinking army cargo ship *Panama Maru*, 27°15′N, 120°45′E.

ANDAMAN SEA. USAAF B-24s (10th Air Force) sink Japanese cargo ship *Seikai Maru* in Mergui Harbor, 12°26′N, 98°36′E.

ATLANTIC. U.S. freighter *Leland Stanford*, aground since 20 January off Cape Henlopen, Delaware, is refloated with aid of tug *Allegheny* (AT 19) and tugs *Nancy Moran* and *Resolute* (NRTS).

24 Monday

PACIFIC. USMC TBFs, supported by large concentration of USN, USMC, USAAF, and RNZAF fighters, attack Japanese shipping at Rabaul, sinking water tanker *Koan Maru*, aircraft transport *Lyon Maru* (previously rendered unnavigable on 17 January), and army cargo ships *Taisho Maru* and *Yamayuri Maru*, 04°13′S, 152°11′E.

PB4Ys damage cargo ship *Ogashima Maru* south of Kwajalein, 08°14′N, 168°02′E; deemed beyond salvage, *Ogashima Maru* is scuttled by auxiliary minesweeper *No. 5 Tama Maru*. PB4Ys also sink auxiliary submarine chaser *Cha 14* 70 miles east-southeast of Eniwetok, 11°10′N, 163°25′E.

USAAF B-25s bomb Japanese shipping and harbor facilities at Manus, sinking transport *Heiwa Maru* and auxiliary minelayer *Tatsu Maru*, and damaging auxiliary minelayer *Matsu Maru*.

USAAF B-25s (14th Air Force) sink Japanese ship *Liu Hsing* in Lishen Bay, China, 26°58′N, 120°04′E.

Submarine *Sturgeon* (SS 187) attacks Japanese convoy in eastern approaches to Bungo Strait, sinking army cargo ship *Chosen Maru*, 32°28′N, 132°23′E.

Japanese planes bomb U.S. shipping in Dreger Bay, New Guinea, damaging freighter *John Muir* at 06°32′08″N, 147°53′05″E, with one direct hit and at least four near-misses that injure two of 42 merchant sailors, one of the 28-man Armed Guard, and 13 of the 40 Construction Battalion stevedores embarked to work cargo.

MEDITERRANEAN. German planes attack invasion shipping off Anzio, Italy. Destroyer *Plunkett* (DD 431), 41°15′N, 12°37′E, and minesweeper *Prevail* (AM 107), 41°00′N, 12°00′E, are damaged by bombs; destroyer *Mayo* (DD 422) is damaged by aerial torpedo, 41°24′N, 12°43′E.

During German air raid on Allied shipping at Naples, Italy, U.S. freighter *F. A. C. Muhlenberg* is damaged by direct hit and near-miss; ship's crew and port fire-fighting crews extinguish the fires thus started. Of the ship's complement, six of 46 merchant sailors die; one of the 31-man Armed Guard perishes in the blaze.

Tank landing craft *LCT 185* founders and sinks in heavy weather off Bizerte, Tunisia.

ARCTIC. German submarines attack Murmansk, Russia–bound convoy JW 56A. U.S. freighter *Penelope Barker* is torpedoed and sunk by *U 278* about 115 miles from North Cape,

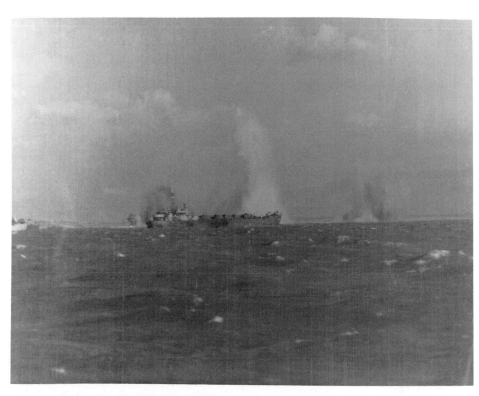

A tank landing ship (LST), her upper deck packed with what appear to be two and a half ton trucks, stands toward the beachhead at Anzio as bombs from German planes fall thick in the vicinity, as seen from the destroyer escort *Frederick C. Davis* (DE 136), 22 January 1944. (NA, 80-G-223439)

Norway, 72°23′N, 23°10′E; 10 merchant sailors and five Armed Guard men (of the 43-man merchant complement and the 28-man Armed Guard, respectively) perish in the explosions. British destroyer HMS *Savage* rescues the survivors (see 26 January).

25 Tuesday

PACIFIC. Escort carrier *Sangamon* (CVE 26) is damaged by fire following a TBM (VC 37) barrier crash, en route to the Marshalls.

Japanese cargo ship *Nanshin Maru* sinks after running aground on a shoal off Miyagi Peninsula, 35°31′N, 133°09′E.

MEDITERRANEAN. Off Anzio, motor minesweeper *YMS 30* is sunk by mine, 41°23′N, 12°45′E; submarine chaser *PC 676* is damaged by near-miss of bomb.

26 Wednesday

PACIFIC. TG 74.2 (Rear Admiral Russell S. Berkey), consisting of two light cruisers and three destroyers, bombards Japanese installations in Madang-Alexischafen area of New Guinea.

Motor torpedo boat *PT 110* is sunk by depth charge explosion following collision with motor torpedo boat *PT 114*, Ablingi Harbor, New Britain, 06°17′S, 150°09′E; *PT 114* is damaged.

Escort carriers *Suwanee* (CVE 27) and *Sangamon* (CVE 26) are damaged in collision while operating in support of TF 53 during operations in the Marshalls campaign.

Submarine *Crevalle* (SS 291) sinks Japanese gunboat *Busho Maru* in South China Sea, about 175 miles southeast of Cape St. Jacques, French Indochina, 08°30′N, 109°10′E.

Submarine *Hake* (SS 256) sinks Japanese auxiliary netlayer *Shuko Maru* off Ambon, N.E.I., 05°50′N, 126°00′E.

Submarine *Skipjack* (SS 184) sinks Japanese destroyer *Suzukaze* 140 miles northwest of Ponape, Carolines, 09°00′N, 157°27′E, and transport *Okitsu Maru* 150 miles northwest of Ponape, 09°22′N, 157°26′E.

British submarine HMS *Templar* damages Japanese light cruiser *Kitakami* southwest of Penang, Malaya, 04°54′N, 98°28′E.

MEDITERRANEAN. Off Anzio, mines sink large infantry landing craft *LCI(L) 32* and damage tank landing ship *LST 422*. During German air raid on shipping off the invasion beaches, U.S. freighter *John Banyard* is damaged by near-miss of aerial bomb. While there are no casualties to those on board (including the 27-man

Armed Guard), the ship will later be written off as a total loss. Off Nettuno, a German fighter plane crashes into freighter *Hilary A. Herbert* shortly before the freighter is further damaged by the near-miss of a bomb. Beached to prevent her loss, *Hilary A. Herbert* is later repaired and returned to service.

ARCTIC. German submarines continue attacks against Murmansk-bound convoy JW 56A. U.S. freighter *Andrew G. Curtin* is torpedoed and sunk by *U 716*, 73°25′N, 25°16′E; two of the merchant crew and one Armed Guard sailor (of the 43-man merchant complement and the 28-man Armed Guard, respectively) perish. British destroyer HMS *Inconstant* rescues the survivors.

INDIAN OCEAN. U.S. freighter *Walter Camp* is torpedoed and sunk by German submarine *U 532* at 10°00′N, 71°40′E; all hands (40 merchant crew, 28 Armed Guards, and one passenger) survive. British light cruiser HMS *Danae* rescues them four and a half days later.

27 Thursday

PACIFIC. Submarine *Swordfish* (SS 193), in attack on Japanese convoy about 130 miles south of Tokyo Bay, sinks gunboat *Kasagi Maru*, 33°31′N, 139°36′E.

Submarine *Thresher* (SS 200) attacks Japanese convoy, sinking transport *Kosei Maru* and freighter *Kikuzuki Maru* about 70 miles southwest of Formosa, 22°11′N, 119°12′E.

MEDITERRANEAN. German air opposition to landings at Anzio begins to intensify; submarine chaser *SC 534* is damaged by near-miss of bomb. Adverse weather conditions cause damage to one LCI(L) (large infantry landing craft) and 11 LCTs (tank landing craft).

28 Friday

PACIFIC. Submarine *Bowfin* (SS 287) damages Japanese oiler *Kamoi* off Makassar, N.E.I., 03°25′S, 118°15′E.

USAAF B-24 (13th Air Force) and USN PBYs sink Japanese transport *Neikai Maru* south of Kavieng, 03°45′S, 150°38′E; midget submarine *Ha.49*, carried on board *Neikai Maru*, is lost as well.

ATLANTIC. PB4Y-1 (VB 103) sinks German submarine *U 271* off Limerick, Eire, 53°15′N, 15°52′W.

MEDITERRANEAN. Off Anzio, motor torpedo boat *PT 201*—with Lieutenant General Mark W. Clark, Commanding General of the U.S. Fifth Army, on board—is damaged by friendly fire from minesweeper *Sway* (AM 120); sub-

marine chaser *SC 534* is damaged by near-miss of bomb.

29 Saturday

PACIFIC. TF 58 (Rear Admiral Marc A. Mitscher) begins series of strikes to destroy Japanese air power and shipping in the Marshalls. Planes from TG 58.1 sink Japanese auxiliary netlayer *Uji Maru*. Attacks continue daily until 6 February.

Submarine *Bowfin* (SS 287) lays mines off southeastern coast of Borneo.

Submarine *Tambor* (SS 198) attacks Japanese convoy in the Nansei Shoto, sinking freighter *Shuntai Maru* north of Okinawa, 27°51′N, 128°24′E.

During Japanese bombing raid on U.S. shipping off Cape Cretin, New Guinea, freighter *George Sterling* is damaged by near-miss, 06°41′S, 147°52′E. There are no fatalities among the complement, including the 26-man Armed Guard.

MEDITERRANEAN. German planes bomb U.S. shipping off the invasion beaches at Anzio and Nettuno; off the former place, rescue tug *ATR 1* is damaged by near-miss of bomb, 41°27′N, 12°40′E. Freighter *Alexander Martin* is damaged by strafing, but there are no fatalities among the ship's complement (including the 24-man Armed Guard). Off Nettuno, freighter *Samuel Huntington* is sunk by bombs; three merchant sailors die in the explosions and one will die of wounds later. Her survivors are rescued by tank landing craft *LCT 277*. There are no casualties among the 39-man Armed Guard; the ship will later be written off as a total loss. *LCT 198* rescues survivors from British light cruiser HMS *Spartan*.

30 Sunday

PACIFIC. PB2Ys (VP 13 and VP 102) from Midway Island carry out nocturnal bombing raid on Wake Island to neutralize Japanese airfield installations there that could threaten the imminent Marshalls operations. Motor torpedo boats *Gyoraitei No. 5* and *Gyoraitei No. 6* are sunk during the raid. The strike marks the first time that Coronados are used as bombers, and strikes are repeated on the nights of 4, 8, and 9 February.

During preinvasion bombardment of Wotje, Marshalls, destroyer *Anderson* (DD 411) is damaged by shore battery, 09°33′N, 170°18′E.

TG 52.8 SBDs and F6Fs, from carriers *Enterprise* (CV 6), *Yorktown* (CV 10), and *Bunker Hill* (CV 17) and small carrier *Belleau Wood*

(CVL 24), attack Japanese shipping in the Marshalls, sinking auxiliary submarine chasers *Cha 18* and *Cha 21* and guardboat *No. 6 Shonan Maru* at Kwajalein; sinking *Cha 14*, *Cha 19*, and *Cha 28* at Mille; and damaging cargo vessel *Katsura Maru* at Eniwetok. Destroyer *Phelps* (DD 360) subsequently finishes off the crippled *Katsura Maru*.

Battleships *Washington* (BB 56), *Indiana* (BB 58), and *Massachusetts* (BB 59) and destroyers *Ingersoll* (DD 652), *Knapp* (DD 653), *Caperton* (DD 650), and *Cogswell* (DD 651) bombard Japanese installations at Kwajalein. Battleship *North Carolina* (BB 55) sinks transport *Eiko Maru* off west coast of Roi, 09°10′N, 167°20′E (see 14 February). Destroyer *Burns* (DD 588) sinks Japanese transport *Akibasan Maru* and guardboat *Nichiei Maru* off Ujae. Japanese naval vessels that will be accounted for in the preinvasion shelling and bombing at Kwajalein include auxiliary submarine chaser *No. 11 Fuji Maru* and guardboats *Kikyo Maru*, *Meiho Maru*, *Palau Maru*, *Takeura Maru*, and *Yamashiro Maru*.

SBDs and TBFs, supported by Allied fighters, bomb Japanese shipping at Rabaul, sinking water supply ship *Iwata Maru* and damaging auxiliary vessel *Juzan Maru*, 04°12′S, 152°12′E.

TG 31.8 (four destroyers, three high-speed transports, and two motor torpedo boats) lands 30th New Zealand Battalion and U.S. Navy personnel on the Green Islands, north of Bougainville, to locate areas suitable for airstrips and landing beaches. The reconnoitering force is recovered the next day.

Submarine *Seahorse* (SS 304) attacks Japanese convoy on the Palau-Rabaul track, sinking army cargo ship *Toko Maru* southeast of Palau, 06°10′N, 138°14′E.

Submarine *Spearfish* (SS 190) attacks Japanese convoy, sinking transport *Tamashima Maru* about 400 miles north-northeast of Saipan, 21°15′N, 149°18′E.

31 Monday

PACIFIC. Operation FLINTLOCK: Marines and Army troops (Major General Holland M. Smith, USMC) land on atolls of Kwajalein and Majuro in the Marshalls. The operation is under the overall command of Commander Central Pacific. TF 50 (Vice Admiral Raymond A. Spruance) assault force includes Southern Attack TF 51 (Rear Admiral Richmond Kelly Turner), Northern Attack TF 53 (Rear Admiral Richard L. Conolly), and Reserve Force and Majuro Attack Group TF 51.2

(Rear Admiral Harry W. Hill). Landings are supported by carrier-based aircraft TF 58 (Rear Admiral Marc A. Mitscher) and land-based aircraft TF 57 (Rear Admiral John H. Hoover).

TG 58.3 (Rear Admiral Frederick C. Sherman) planes bomb aircraft and airfield facilities at Engebi Island, Eniwetok, Marshalls. Attacks by this carrier group continue on the first three days of February and afterward by TG 58.4 (Rear Admiral Samuel P. Ginder) through 7 February. TG 58.3 aircraft and destroyer *Harrison* (DD 573) sink Japanese auxiliary netlayer *Katsura Maru* off Eniwetok.

U.S. air strike on Nauru, in support of the Marshalls operations, sinks Japanese auxiliary submarine chasers *Cha 25* and *Cha 33*.

Cargo ship *Enceladus* (AK 80) is damaged by storm south of New Georgia, Solomons, 08°09′S, 157°38′E.

Submarine *Trigger* (SS 237) sinks Japanese auxiliary submarine depot ship *Yasukuni Maru* northwest of Truk, 09°21′N, 147°02′E, and damages destroyer *Michisio*, 09°50′N, 147°06′E.

Submarine *Tullibee* (SS 284) sinks Japanese auxiliary netlayer *Hiro Maru* north-northwest of Saipan, 15°23′N, 145°35′E.

USAAF B-24 sinks Japanese guardboat *Seisho Maru* off Celebes, N.E.I.

Japanese plane carries out high-level bombing raid on U.S. shipping in Langemak Bay, New Guinea; freighter *Stephen Crane* is damaged by bomb that glances off her stack and explodes in the water nearby. One Army passenger is killed; 22 men (including one merchant seaman and one of the 29-man Armed Guard) are injured.

FEBRUARY

1 Tuesday

PACIFIC. Command designated Amphibious Forces, Pacific Fleet, with headquarters at Pearl Harbor, is established. Vice Admiral Richmond Kelly Turner, Commander Fifth Amphibious Force, is ordered to assume this command as additional duty.

Invasion of the Marshalls continues as Marines land on Roi and Namur and Army troops land on Kwajalein under cover of heavy naval gunfire from battleships, cruisers, and destroyers. Heavy cruiser *Louisville* (CA 28) is damaged by richocheting 8-inch shell fired by heavy cruiser *Indianapolis* (CA 35), 09°00′N, 167°00′E; destroyer *Anderson* (DD 411) is damaged when she runs aground in northern Kwajalein lagoon, 09°10′N, 167°25′E; de-

Marines disembark from a tracked landing vehicle (LVT) off Namur, 1 February 1944, while their prone comrades (right) watch; the leathernecks in this photo are equipped with either the M-1 Garand rifle or the M-1 carbine. (NA, USMC Photo 72411)

stroyer *Haggard* (DD 555) is damaged by accidental explosion off northwestern end of Kwajalein, 09°00′N, 167°00′E; destroyer *Colahan* (DD 658) is damaged when she fouls a coral reef at the north end of Enubuj Island, Kwajalein, 08°52′N, 167°38′E; battleships *Washington* (BB 56) and *Indiana* (BB 58), operating in TG 58.1, are damaged in collision, 07°00′N, 167°00′E; and minesweeper *Chief* (AM 135) is damaged by grounding off northwestern end of Kwajalein, 09°00′N, 167°00′E.

Destroyers *Guest* (DD 472) and *Hudson* (DD 475) sink Japanese submarine *I 171*, 15 miles west of Buka, Solomons, 05°37′S, 154°14′E.

Submarine *Guardfish* (SS 217) attacks Japanese convoy heading for Truk's south pass and sinks destroyer *Umikaze*, 07°11′N, 151°44′E.

Submarine *Hake* (SS 256) sinks Japanese army cargo ship *Nanka Maru* and transport *Tacoma Maru* off northeast coast of Halmahera, N.E.I., 01°32′N, 128°50′E.

Submarine *Seahorse* (SS 304) attacks Japanese convoy on the Palau-Rabaul track, sinking transport *Toei Maru* about 175 miles south of Woleai, 04°24′N, 143°15′E.

USAAF B-24s damage Japanese ship *Hakka Maru*, 02°43′S, 141°28′E, as she is en route from Hollandia to Aitap, New Guinea.

Naval Base, Finschhafen, New Guinea, is established.

MEDITERRANEAN. German planes carry out torpedo attack on convoy UGS 30; U.S. freighter *Richmond P. Hobson* is damaged at 36°40′N, 01°10′E. There are no casualties among the crew (including the Armed Guard), and the ship reaches Port Said, Egypt, on 10 February. Freighter *Edward Bates* is torpedoed 65 miles from Oran, 36°34′N, 01°14′E, and is abandoned; one of the 46-man merchant complement is killed, but there are no casualties among the 38-man Armed Guard or the seven passengers.

2 Wednesday

PACIFIC. Roi and Namur Islands in the Marshalls are secured.

Destroyer *Walker* (DD 517) sinks Japanese submarine *RO 39*, 10 miles east of Wotje, Marshalls, 09°24′N, 170°32′E.

Submarine *Plunger* (SS 179) attacks Japanese convoy south of Honshu and sinks freighters *No. 5 Toyo Maru* and *No. 8 Toyo Maru* off Kushimoto, 33°29′N, 135°59′E, and survives resultant depth charging.

Japanese transport *Katsura Maru* sinks after running aground off Futsing, China, 25°37′N, 119°47′E.

3 Thursday

PACIFIC. Cruiser and destroyer gunfire supports landing of Army troops on Ebeye, Kwajalein Atoll, Marshalls.

Submarine *Tambor* (SS 198) attacks Japanese convoy in East China Sea, sinking fleet tanker *Goyo Maru* and merchant tanker *Ariake Maru* about 200 miles southeast of Shanghai, 28°53′N, 124°19′E. Although damaged by depth charges from escort vessels, the submarine remains on patrol.

PBYs and USAAF B-25s (5th Air Force) attack Japanese convoy west of New Hanover and sink cargo ship *Nichiai Maru*, 03°27′S, 149°32′E.

ATLANTIC. Destroyer escort *J. R. Y. Blakeley* (DE 140) is damaged when accidentally rammed by U.S. freighter *Franklin P. Mall* while in Norfolk, Virginia–to–Casablanca, French Morocco, convoy UGS 32, but reaches her destination under her own power.

EUROPE. USAAF planes (8th Air Force) bomb German naval base at Wilhelmshaven, sinking accommodation ship *Monte Pasqual* and damaging minesweepers *M 18* and *M 19*.

4 Friday

PACIFIC. TG 94.6 cruisers and destroyers (Rear Admiral Wilder D. Baker) bombard Japanese installations at Paramushir, Kurils, damaging cargo ship *Kokai Maru*.

Destroyers bombard Sarine Plantation, northwest coast of Bougainville, Solomons; destroyer *Claxton* (DD 571) is damaged by return fire from Japanese shore battery, 05°49′S, 154°39′E.

Destroyer *Charrette* (DD 581) and destroyer escort *Fair* (DE 35) sink Japanese submarine *I 175*, 100 miles north of Jaluit, Marshalls, 06°48′N, 168°08′E.

PV-1s sink Japanese water tanker *Goryu Maru* off Emidj Island, Jaluit, 06°00′N, 169°44′E.

USMC PB4Ys (VMD 154) reconnoiter Truk in the first general reconnaissance of that important Japanese fleet base by U.S. planes.

5 Saturday

PACIFIC. Submarine *Flasher* (SS 249) sinks Japanese army cargo ship *Taishin Maru* about 60 miles west of Mindoro, 13°09′N, 120°24′E. Accompanying sampan *Ise Maru* is sunk and *Kanhoku Maru* runs aground off the west coast of Mindoro while fleeing. *Tokai Maru* rescues survivors and heads for Manila.

Submarine *Narwhal* (SS 167) lands 45 tons of ammunition and cargo to support Filipino guerrilla operations at Libertad, Panay, P.I.,

and embarks six evacuees (five servicemen and a British subject) (see 7 February).

British submarine HMS *Stonehenge* sinks Japanese ship *No. 2 Koryu Maru* north of Sumatra.

USAAF B-24s and B-25s (14th Air Force) attack convoy in South China Sea, sinking gunboat *Rozan Maru* and freighters *Lushan Maru* and *Seikyo Maru* off Swatow, China, 22°00′N, 116°00′E.

USAAF B-25s sink *Fatsumi Maru* off Wewak.

6 Sunday

PACIFIC. USAAF A-20s and P-40s sink Japanese ships *Kaiyo Maru* and *Takegiku Maru* and damage *Torihime Maru* off Wewak, New Guinea.

ATLANTIC. PB4Y-1 (VB 107) sinks German submarine *U 177* west of Ascension Island, 10°35′S, 23°12′W.

7 Monday

PACIFIC. Kwajalein Atoll is declared secured.

Submarine *Narwhal* (SS 167) delivers 45 tons of cargo near Balatong Point, Negros, P.I., and embarks 28 evacuees (eight women, nine children, five civilian men, and six servicemen). These people, together with the ones embarked on 5 February, will be transported to Darwin, Australia.

Escort carrier *White Plains* (CVE 66) and destroyer *Caldwell* (DD 605) are damaged in collision while transferring people at sea off the Marshalls.

Light cruiser *Birmingham* (CL 62) is damaged in collision with merchant vessel *Manukai*, San Francisco, California.

MEDITERRANEAN. Destroyer *Ludlow* (DD 438) is damaged by dud shell from German shore battery off Anzio, Italy.

8 Tuesday

PACIFIC. Submarine *Snook* (SS 279), in attack on Japanese convoy off the west coast of Kyushu, sinks transport *Lima Maru* about 30 miles southeast of Goto Retto, 31°05′N, 127°37′E, damages army cargo ship *Shiranesan Maru*, and survives depth charging by one or more of the convoy's escorts that include *Patrol Boat No. 38*, auxiliary submarine chaser *No. 5 Kyoei Maru*, and torpedo boat *Sagi*.

ATLANTIC. Light cruiser *Marblehead* (CL 12) rescues the survivors of German submarine *U 177*, sunk by PB4Y (VB 107) on 6 February.

Tug *Acushnet* (AT 63) assists disabled fishing vessel *Manchonock* off the Virginia capes, 37°03′N, 74°04′W, and tows the craft to Norfolk, arriving the following day.

MEDITERRANEAN. Destroyer *Ludlow* (DD 438)

is damaged by shore battery fire off Anzio, 41°28′N, 12°30′E.

9 Wednesday

PACIFIC. Submarine *Bonefish* (SS 223) damages Japanese merchant tanker *No. 2 Tonan Maru* off French Indochina, 11°30′N, 109°10′E.

10 Thursday

PACIFIC. TG 58.4 (Rear Admiral Samuel P. Ginder) planes bomb Japanese installations on Eniwetok Atoll, Marshalls; similar strikes are made on 11 and 12 February.

Tank landing ship *LST 170* is damaged by horizontal bomber, off eastern New Guinea, 08°39′S, 148°27′E.

Submarine *Hake* (SS 256) attacks Japanese mine/netlayer *Wakatake*, escorting a convoy to Manokwari, New Guinea, 01°43′N, 129°30′E, without success, and survives depth charging by her quarry.

Submarine *Pogy* (SS 266) attacks Japanese MOTA 01 convoy and sinks destroyer *Minekaze* and freighter *Malta Maru* 85 miles northeast of Formosa, 23°20′N, 121°30′E.

Submarine *Spearfish* (SS 190) damages Japanese transport *Tatsuwa Maru* southwest of Formosa, 21°53′N, 119°13′E.

PBY sinks Japanese fishing boat *No. 8 Inawa Maru* off Wewak, New Guinea.

Japanese cargo ship *Waka Maru* is sunk by "sea trouble" near Bokai Bay, western Korea, 35°40′N, 126°20′E.

ANDAMAN SEA. Japanese fishing vessel *Kirishima Maru* is damaged by mine off Moulmein, Burma.

11 Friday

PACIFIC. Motor torpedo boat *PT 279* is sunk in collision with *PT 282* off Buka, Solomons, 05°30′S, 154°15′E.

Submarine *Gudgeon* (SS 211) sinks Japanese freighter *Satsuma Maru* (previously damaged by Chinese B-25s off Wenchow, China, at 28°01′N, 121°30′E), 27°38′N, 121°15′E.

ATLANTIC. British freighter *Empire Knight*, en route from St. John, New Brunswick, to New York in a "nor'easter," runs aground on Boon Island Ledge. The heavy snowstorm forces the Coast Guard motor lifeboats that set out from Isles of Shoals and Portsmouth, New Hampshire, to return to port, but minesweeper *Firm* (AM 98) (diverted from patrol), submarine rescue vessel *Falcon* (ASR 2) (from Portsmouth), netlaying ship *Gumtree* (AN 18) (from Portland, Maine), and Coast Guard tender *Cactus* (WAGL 270) (from Rockland,

Maine) arrive on the scene. Tug *Wandank* (AT 26) is dispatched from Newport, Rhode Island, and salvage tug *Resolute* (NRTS) from New York. Rough seas, however, prevent any of the four ships standing by the stricken freighter from being able to venture alongside to take off the crew (see 12 February).

Tugs *Acushnet* (AT 63) and *Sciota* (AT 30) proceed to the assistance of U.S. tanker *Vacuum*, which has suffered a steering gear casualty off the Virginia capes, 34°20′N, 73°45′W; the tugs take the tanker in tow the following day and bring her into Norfolk on 15 February.

CARIBBEAN. Navy blimp (ZP 51) locates Army launch adrift in Gulf of Paria. Choppy seas and the onset of darkness compel the airship to take the boat in tow, "thereby accomplishing a unique and effective rescue."

12 Saturday

PACIFIC. Marines land on Arno Atoll, beginning a series of "mopping-up" operations in the minor atolls of the Marshalls.

Japanese flying boats bomb and destroy supply concentrations on Roi Island, Marshalls; tank landing craft *LCT 346* and *LCT 347* are damaged.

Submarine rescue vessel *Macaw* (ASR 17), stranded at entrance to Midway Channel since 16 January, slips off the reef and sinks.

Submarine *Tambor* (SS 198) sinks Japanese merchant tanker *Ronsan Maru* in East China Sea about 40 miles southwest of Amami-O-Shima, 27°45′N, 128°42′E.

British submarine HMS *Stonehenge* sinks Japanese netlayer *Choko Maru* off west coast of Malaya, 05°46′N, 99°52′E.

USAAF B-25s aircraft attack Japanese fishing boats operating in Tonkin Gulf, sinking *No. 12 Kainan Maru* and *No. 11 Kainan Maru*, 20°44′N, 107°02′E.

ATLANTIC. British freighter *Empire Knight*, grounded the previous day, remains aground on Boon Island Ledge in heavy snowstorm, while minesweeper *Firm* (AM 98), submarine rescue vessel *Falcon* (ASR 2), netlaying ship *Gumtree* (AN 18), and Coast Guard tender *Cactus* (WAGL 270) stand by, unable to go alongside due to rough seas. Shortly after *Empire Knight* launches a lifeboat (that capsizes), the merchantman breaks in two, the stern falling clear of the ledge and drifting away while the bow remains aground. All ships quickly devote their efforts to picking up the survivors from the wintry sea. Tugs *Kalmia* (AT 23) and *Wandank* (AT 26) and tugs *Christine Moran* and

Resolute (NRTS) subsequently search, without success, for the after part of the ship.

UNITED STATES. Secretary of the Navy William Franklin (Frank) Knox initiates an inquiry to be conducted by Admiral Thomas C. Hart, USN (Retired), "for an examination of witnesses and the taking of testimony pertinent to the Japanese attack on Pearl Harbor." Hart is to record and preserve this testimony to prevent its loss "by death or unavoidable absence" (see 15 June).

13 Sunday

PACIFIC. Submarine *Permit* (SS 178) is damaged by depth charges off western Carolines, 07°42′N, 148°18′E, but remains on patrol.

Submarine *Robalo* (SS 273) conducts unsuccessful attack on Japanese army cargo ships *Minryu Maru* and *Sekino Maru* off the coast of Luzon (see 14 February).

USAAF A-20s (5th Air Force) sink Japanese army cargo ship *Yoshino Maru* and motor sailboat *Tokun Maru* (in tow of the cargo ship) off Aitape, 03°10′S, 142°31′E.

USAAF B-25s (14th Air Force) sink Japanese cargo ship *Shoka Maru* and damage *Kokoku Maru* off Hainan Island, 18°35′N, 108°30′E.

Japanese motor sailer *No. 7 Sakura Maru* is sunk by accidental fire, Surabaya, Java, N.E.I.

USAAF and Chinese aircraft sink fishing vessel *Meiji Maru* off the China coast, 26°40′N, 121°40′E.

MEDITERRANEAN. Tank landing craft *LCT 220* founders in heavy weather and sinks off Anzio.

14 Monday

PACIFIC. Command designated Central Pacific Forward Area (Rear Admiral John H. Hoover) is established; Rear Admiral Hoover flies his flag in seaplane tender *Curtiss* (AV 4).

Light cruiser *St. Louis* (CL 49), covering the unopposed landing at Pakonian Plantation, west side of Green Island, is damaged by bomb dropped by Japanese dive bomber, 06°15′S, 153°29′E.

Submarine *Flasher* (SS 249) attacks Japanese convoy escorted by *Patrol Boat No. 103* [ex-U.S. minesweeper *Finch* (AM 9)] and minesweeper *W.7*, sinking army cargo ship *Minryu Maru*, which had escaped submarine *Robalo* (SS 273) the day before, off Cape Santiago, Luzon, 13°43′N, 120°39′E, and tanker *Hokuan Maru*, 13°44′N, 120°29′E.

Submarine *Snook* (SS 279) sinks Japanese freighter *Nittoku Maru* southwest of Tsushima, Japan, 33°48′N, 128°50′E.

British submarine HMS *Tally Ho* sinks German submarine *UIT 23* (ex-Italian *Reginaldo Giuliani*) off Penang, Malaya, 04°25′N, 100°09′E.

PBY damages Japanese cargo ship *Mitsu Maru* and forces her aground east of Sepik, New Guinea. Allied air attacks subsequently destroy *Mitsu Maru*.

USAAF B-25 sinks Japanese ship *Satsuma Maru* off Wenchow, 28°00′N, 121°30′E.

Salvage of *Eiko Maru* (sunk on 30 January) by U.S. Navy divers yields a large number of Japanese charts of the Pacific area and other intelligence material.

ATLANTIC. Tank landing ship *LST 560* runs aground off Barnegat Inlet, New Jersey; tug *Allegheny* (AT 19) assists in refloating the vessel, towing her to Cape May soon thereafter.

15 Tuesday

PACIFIC. TF 31 (Rear Admiral Theodore S. Wilkinson) lands Third New Zealand Division (Major General H. E. Barraclough) on Green Island, east of New Ireland. TF 38 (Rear Admiral Walden L. Ainsworth) (two light cruisers and five destroyers) covers the operation from the south and TF 39 (Rear Admiral Aaron S. Merrill) (two light cruisers and five destroyers) from the north and east; Solomons-based aircraft also operate in support. During Japanese air attack on invasion shipping, tank landing ship *LST 486* is damaged by near-miss of bomb.

Lieutenant (j.g.) Nathan G. Gordon, USNR, commanding a PBY (VP 34), makes four hazardous landings in the face of point-blank antiaircraft fire at Kavieng, New Ireland; he and his crew rescue 15 USAAF men, crews of three B-25s shot down in an earlier raid. For his "gallantry and intrepidity," Gordon is awarded the Medal of Honor.

Naval aircraft from Abemama, Gilberts, bomb Wake Island.

Submarine *Aspro* (SS 309) sinks Japanese submarine *I 43* (then engaged in transporting sailors of the Sasebo Special Landing Force to Truk) 280 miles east-southeast of Guam, 10°23′N, 150°23′E.

Submarine *Gato* (SS 212) sinks Japanese guardboat *No. 3 Taiyo Maru* off Rabaul, New Britain, 04°00′N, 150°10′E.

Submarine *Snook* (SS 279) sinks Japanese freighter *No. 2 Hoshi Maru* off south coast of Korea, 34°23′N, 128°23′E.

Submarine *Steelhead* (SS 280) damages Japanese cargo ship *Enju Maru* 110 miles from Chichi Jima, Bonins.

Submarine *Tinosa* (SS 283) attacks Japanese convoy H 17, escorted by *No. 2 Kyo Maru*, east of Mindanao, P.I., sinking army cargo ship *Odatsuki Maru* east of Dinagat Island, 09°30′N, 127°00′E (see 16 February).

USAAF B-25s and A-20s sink Japanese auxiliary netlayer *Matsu Maru* at Rabaul.

USAAF B-25s (14th Air Force) sink Vichy French patrol craft *Ping Sang* off Hongay, French Indochina, 21°00′N, 107°22′E.

Mine laid by 14th Air Force B-24s on 10 February sinks Japanese freighter *Ryoka Maru* off entrance to Yangtze River, 31°16′N, 121°46′E; *Hokkai Maru* picks up survivors.

Japanese freighter *Hoshi Maru* is sunk by mine off south coast of Korea, 34°27′N, 128°45′E.

MEDITERRANEAN. Off Anzio, Italy, destroyer escort *Herbert C. Jones* (DE 137) is damaged by radio-controlled bomb, 41°27′N, 12°35′E, and large infantry landing craft *LCI(L) 2* is damaged by mine, 41°24′N, 12°43′E. Bomb holes U.S. freighter *Elihu Yale*; the explosion starts fires that spread to tank landing craft *LCT 35* alongside, destroying that vessel as well. Firefighting efforts by tug *Hopi* (AT 71) ultimately prove successful, but *Elihu Yale* is later written off as a total loss. Two of the 40-man Armed Guard perish in the attack, as do three of the 45-man merchant complement and seven of the 182 stevedores working cargo. Tank landing craft *LCT 152* rescues survivors from *Elihu Yale* and *LCT 35*.

ATLANTIC. U.S. freighters *Haym Solomon* and *Samforth* collide while in Norfolk–to–Casablanca convoy UGS 32; damage sustained by each vessel in the maritime accident does not prevent them from reaching Casablanca under their own power.

16 Wednesday

PACIFIC. TG 58.4 (Rear Admiral Samuel P. Ginder) planes bomb Eniwetok, Marshalls.

Destroyer *Phelps* (DD 360) and minesweeper *Sage* (AM 111) sink Japanese submarine *RO 40*, 45 miles northwest of Kwajalein, Marshalls, 09°50′N, 166°35′E.

Submarine *Skate* (SS 305) sinks Japanese light cruiser *Agano* 170 miles north of Dublon Island, Truk, 10°10′N, 151°40′E.

Submarine *Tinosa* (SS 283) continues pursuit of convoy H 17 engaged the previous day, and sinks Japanese army cargo ship *Chojo Maru* off Sarangani Island, 09°15′N, 127°05′E.

USAAF B-25s (38th and 345th Bomb Groups) carry out succession of attacks on Japanese convoy off New Hanover and Kavieng, damaging submarine chaser *Ch 39* (which is intentionally run aground) and sinking auxiliary submarine chaser *Cha 16* and transport *Sanko Maru* (which is apparently transporting a midget submarine), 02°24′S, 150°06′E. Auxiliary netlayer *No. 16 Kashi Maru* is badly damaged and intentionally grounded to facilitate salvage. Neither *Ch 39* nor *No. 16 Kashi Maru*, however, are refloated.

MEDITERRANEAN. Destroyer *Hilary P. Jones* (DD 427) is damaged by near-miss of bomb off Anzio.

17 Thursday

PACIFIC. Operation HAILSTONE: TF 58 (Vice Admiral Raymond A. Spruance), which includes nine carriers and six battleships, strikes Japanese installations and shipping at Truk, inflicting massive damage. SB2Cs and TBFs from carrier *Bunker Hill* (CV 17) and TBFs from small carrier *Cowpens* (CVL 25) sink light cruiser *Naka* 35 miles west of Truk, 07°15′N, 151°15′E, while heavy cruisers *Minneapolis* (CA 36) and *New Orleans* (CA 32) and destroyers *Bradford* (DD 545) and *Burns* (DD 588) sink training cruiser *Katori* northwest of Truk, 07°48′N, 151°32′E, after she had been torpedoed by TBFs from carrier *Intrepid* (CV 11). *Minneapolis*, *New Orleans*, *Bradford*, and *Burns* also sink destroyer *Maikaze* 40 miles northwest of Truk, 07°45′N, 151°20′E. *Burns*, detached from TG 50.9, engages and sinks submarine chaser *Ch 24* west of Truk, 07°24′N, 150°30′E. TF 58 planes sink destroyer *Oite* (carrying survivors of light cruiser *Agano* sunk the day before), 07°40′N, 151°45′E; destroyer *Tachikaze*, 07°40′N, 151°55′E; armed merchant cruiser *Akagi Maru*, 07°54′N, 151°25′E; auxiliary submarine depot ship *Heian Maru*; aircraft transport *Fujikawa Maru*; transports *Rio de Janeiro Maru*, *Kiyozumi Maru*, *Aikoku Maru*, *Gosei Maru*, *Hanakawa Maru*, *Hokuyo Maru*, *Amagisan Maru*, and *Kensho Maru*; *Matsutani Maru*, 07°23′N, 151°05′E; *Momokawa Maru*, 07°20′N, 151°53′E; *Reiyo Maru*, 07°25′N, 151°45′E; *San Francisco Maru*, 07°22′N, 151°54′E; *Seiko Maru*, 07°22′N, 151°45′E; *Taiho Maru*, 07°22′N, 151°34′E; *Zukai Maru*, 07°46′N, 150°27′E; *No. 6 Unkai Maru*; *Yamagiri Maru*, 07°23′N, 151°51′E; fleet tankers *Fujisan Maru*, *Hoyo Maru*, *Shinkoku Maru*, and *No. 3 Tonan Maru*; water carrier *Nippo Maru*, 07°20′N, 151°40′E; auxiliary vessel *Yamakisan Maru*, 07°25′N, 151°45′E; army cargo ships *Nagano Maru* and *Yubai Maru*; freighter *Taikichi Maru*; and motor torpedo boat *Gyoraitei No. 10*, 07°31′N, 151°59′E. TF 58 planes damage destroyers *Shigure* and *Matsukaze*, submarines *I 10* and *RO 37*, target ship *Hakachi*, repair ship *Akashi*, ammunition ship *Soya*, seaplane tender *Akitsushima*, and auxiliary submarine chaser *Cha 20*. Japanese retaliatory air attacks accomplish little: Carrier *Intrepid* is damaged by aerial torpedo, 07°23′N, 153°32′E.

Destroyer *Nicholas* (DD 449) sinks Japanese submarine *I 11* northwest of the Marshalls, 10°34′N, 173°31′E.

Submarine *Cero* (SS 225) sinks Japanese transport *Jozan Maru* between Truk and New Ireland, 00°53′N, 146°26′E.

Submarine *Sargo* (SS 188), in attack on Japanese convoy about 150 miles northeast of Palau, sinks ammunition ship *Nichiro Maru* and damages oiler *Sata*, 08°50′N, 135°40′E.

Submarine *Tang* (SS 306) attacks Japanese convoy 3206, sinking army cargo ship *Gyoten Maru* and merchant tanker *Kuniei Maru* about 130 miles west-northwest of Truk, 08°00′N, 149°17′E, and survives depth charging by one or more of the escorts, which include escort vessel *Amakusa*, submarine chaser *Ch 31*, auxiliary submarine chaser *Cha 24*, and auxiliary minesweeper *Hagoromo Maru*.

SBDs and TBFs bomb Japanese shipping in Keravia Bay, near Rabaul, sinking minesweeper *W.26* (which had been damaged on 2 November 1943 and had been beached at that time to prevent her loss), guardboat *No. 2 Fuku Maru*, and army cargo ship *Iwate Maru*.

USAAF B-25s attack Japanese ships going to the aid of convoy attacked north of New Hanover the day before, damaging *Kashi Maru* and forcing her to be run aground to prevent sinking.

USAAF A-24s, P-40s, and P-39s attack Japanese shipping at Jaluit; P-39s damage cargo ship *Chosen Maru*. Cargo vessel *Goryu Maru*, aground since the previous December, receives further damage.

Japanese merchant tanker *Zuiho Maru* is damaged by mine downstream from Woosung, China.

Fifth Amphibious Corps Reconnaissance Company, USMC, lands on islands east of Engebi, Eniwetok Atoll; Scout Company "D" lands on islands to the west (see 18 February).

18 Friday

PACIFIC. Operation CATCHPOLE: After preliminary reconnaissance/scout landings had been made the previous day, TG 51.11 (Rear Admiral Harry W. Hill) supports seizure of Engebi Island, Eniwetok (see 19 February).

TF 58 (Vice Admiral Raymond A. Spruance) repeats strike on Japanese installations and vessels at Truk; TF 58 planes sink destroyer *Fumizuki*, 07°24'N, 151°44'E and submarine chaser *Ch 29*, 07°25'N, 151°45'E.

Destroyer Squadron 23 (TG 39.4) (Captain Arleigh A. Burke) bombards Japanese positions at Kavieng, New Ireland; Destroyer Squadron 12 (Captain Rodger W. Simpson) shells Rabaul, Japanese installations on the Crater Peninsula, and bivouac and supply areas at Vunapope and Cape Gazelle.

USAAF B-25s (14th Air Force) sink Japanese transport *Shinsoku Maru* south of Takhow Island, Wenchow, China, 28°23'N, 121°51'E.

U.S. aircraft sink Japanese auxiliary submarine chaser *Cha 17* off Kavieng, 02°30'S, 150°30'E.

Japanese cargo ship *Gokenzan Maru* is stranded and sunk off northwestern Hokkaido, 44°01'N, 141°38'E.

ANDAMAN SEA. British submarine HMS *Trespasser* sinks Japanese gunboat *Eifuku Maru* off Burma, 07°55'N, 93°03'E.

MEDITERRANEAN. Heavy German air attacks, as well as artillery fire, continue on beachhead at Anzio on an almost daily basis; harbor tug *YT 198* is sunk by mine off Anzio, 41°27'N, 12°38'E. Elsewhere in the Mediterranean theater, tank landing craft *LCT 205* capsizes in Gulf of Tunis while being towed; tank landing craft *LCT 340* is stranded by heavy weather at Pantelleria, Italy. Heavy weather also damages large infantry landing craft *LCI(L) 211*, resulting in her being towed to Palermo, Sicily, and minesweeper *Pilot* (AM 104) is accidentally rammed by U.S. merchant ship *Samuel Ashe* and damaged off Naples, 40°48.7'N, 14°16.5'E.

19   Saturday

PACIFIC. TG 51.11 (Rear Admiral Harry W. Hill) lands expeditionary force (Brigadier General Thomas E. Watson, USMC) on Eniwetok Island, Eniwetok Atoll, Marshalls (see 21 February).

USAAF, USN, and USMC land-based aircraft bomb airfield and other Japanese installations at Rabaul. The area has been repeatedly pounded, and after this date the Japanese largely abandon air defense of Rabaul.

Submarine *Cero* (SS 225) conducts unsuccessful attack on Japanese cargo ship *No. 18 Shinsei Maru* while en route to Palau, 03°34'N, 136°36'E.

Submarine *Grayback* (SS 208) attacks Japanese convoy TAPA 02, sinking army cargo ship *Taikei Maru* southwest of Takao, Formosa, 21°48'N, 119°50'E. Subsequently, *Grayback* sinks army cargo ship *Toshin Maru*, 21°46'N,

120°06'E, which had arrived on the scene and rescued *Taikei Maru*'s survivors. Destroyer *Harukaze* rescues the survivors of both ships.

Submarine *Jack* (SS 259) attacks Japanese convoy of six tankers shepherded by escort vessel *Shimushu* in South China Sea about 300 miles west of Luzon, sinking *Kokuei Maru* and *Nanei Maru*, 14°34'N, 114°11'E; *Nichirin Maru*, 15°40'N, 115°48'E; and *Ichiyo Maru*, 15°46'N, 115°57'E. *Shimushu* rescues survivors.

USAAF B-25s (5th Air Force) sink auxiliary submarine chaser *Cha 34* west of Kavieng, 02°45'S, 150°47'E; B-25s, A-20s, and P-38s (5th Air Force) wipe out Japanese convoy O 902 off Kavieng, sinking submarine chasers *Ch 22* and *Ch 40*, 03°04'S, 150°42'E, and cargo vessels *No. 1 Shinto Maru* and *Shinkiku Maru*, 02°46'N, 150°42'E.

USAAF B-24s and B-25s sink Japanese cargo vessel *Ebon Maru* at Kusaie, Carolines.

USAAF B-24s (14th Air Force) sink Japanese cargo ship *Tairyu Maru* and damage auxiliary submarine chaser *Chikuzen Maru* in Formosa Strait, 25°25'N, 121°30'E. Destroyer *Tsuga* emerges from the action unscathed.

Japanese cargo ship *Kogen Maru* is sunk in collision in Kii Strait, 35°00'N, 135°00'E.

MEDITERRANEAN. Motor torpedo boats engage German convoy southeast of island of Elba off Italy.

Light cruiser *Philadelphia* (CL 41) arrives off Anzio to provide gunfire support; she is thrice under shore battery fire but suffers no damage in the encounters.

Destroyer *Madison* (DD 425) conducts unsuccessful hunt for enemy submarine believed off Anzio.

20   Sunday

PACIFIC. TG 58.1 (Rear Admiral John W. Reeves Jr.) planes bomb Japanese installations on Jaluit Atoll, Marshalls.

Submarine *Pogy* (SS 266) sinks Japanese cable layer *Nanyo Maru* about 100 miles east of Formosa, 24°12'N, 123°20'E, and freighter *Taijin Maru* northeast of Formosa, 24°14'N, 123°17'E.

USAAF B-24 damages Japanese cargo vessel *Tasmania Maru* northwest of Wewak, New Guinea.

MEDITERRANEAN. Tank landing ship *LST 348* is sunk by German submarine *U 410*, 40 miles south of Naples, Italy, 40°57'N, 13°14'E.

LCT 340 founders and sinks in heavy weather off coast of Algeria, 36°49'N, 01°55'E.

21   Monday

PACIFIC. Eniwetok Island is formally secured.

SBDs and TBFs bomb antiaircraft positions at Lakunai airfield and shore installations at Rabaul, sinking guardboat *No. 2 Yawata Maru*.

USAAF B-25s (5th Air Force) strike Japanese five-ship convoy O 003 (evacuating 751st *Kokutai* maintenance people to Japan, via Palau) off New Hanover, sinking auxiliary submarine chasers *Cha 38* and *Cha 48*, 02°30'S, 149°55'E; transport *Kokai Maru* and gunboat *Kowa Maru*, 02°30'S, 150°15'E; and damaging tug *Nagaura*, which, after effecting repairs, rescues some of the survivors of the two *Marus* and continues on her voyage north (see 22 February).

Submarine *Cero* (SS 225) damages Japanese army cargo ship *Hasshu Maru* north of New Guinea, 00°10'S, 139°45'E.

British submarine HMS *Tally Ho* sinks Japanese army cargo ship *No. 6 Taigen Maru* in Strait of Malacca, 04°00'N, 101°00'E.

22   Tuesday

PACIFIC. TF 58 (Rear Admiral Marc A. Mitscher) planes bomb Saipan, Tinian, Rota, and Guam, in first strike against the Marianas. TF 58 planes sink Japanese transport *Shoan Maru* off Saipan, 15°15'N, 145°42'E; planes from TG 58.2 and TG 58.3 sink transport *Seizan Maru* off Saipan, 15°00'N, 145°30'E.

Marines (22nd Regiment) land on Parry Island, covered by naval gunfire and carrier-based planes; this operation completes U.S. control of Eniwetok Atoll. Infantry landing craft *LCI 365*, *LCI 440*, and *LCI 442*, on the right flank of the boat waves, are damaged by friendly fire.

TG 39.4 (Captain Arleigh A. Burke) bombards Japanese airstrips, pier area, and anchorages at Kavieng. Destroyers *Charles Ausburne* (DD 570), *Dyson* (DD 572), and *Stanly* (DD 478) sink Japanese minelayer *Natsushima* off New Ireland, 02°40'S, 149°40'E; the same three destroyers, joined by *Converse* (DD 509) and *Spence* (DD 512), sink tug *Nagaura* about 160 miles northwest of Kavieng, 00°54'S, 148°38'E. Other Japanese ships sunk during this action include auxiliary submarine chaser *No. 8 Tama Maru* and small cargo vessels *Choryu Maru* and *No. 9 Tokuyama Maru*, and auxiliary netlayer *Kyosei Maru* in Isabel Channel, New Hanover.

Submarine *Gato* (SS 212) sinks Japanese repair ship *Yamashiro Maru* off Truk, 07°13'N, 151°38'E.

Submarine *Narwhal* (SS 167) attempts to deliver stores and ammunition and disembark two naval officers, one Army officer, and four Filipinos (USA) at designated point on Mautabuan Island (05°00′N, 120°30′E) but sees no security signal from shore. No such signals the following day result in the cancellation of this part of *Narwhal's* mission (see 2 March).

Submarine *Puffer* (SS 268), despite presence of escort vessel, sinks Japanese army transport *Teiko Maru* (ex-French passenger liner *D'Artagnan*) about 120 miles northwest of Kuching, Borneo, 03°10′N, 109°15′E.

Submarine *Ray* (SS 271) lays mines off Saigon, French Indochina.

Submarine *Tang* (SS 306), in attack on Japanese convoy, sinks gunboat *Fukuyama Maru* about 60 miles southwest of Saipan, 15°14′N, 144°55′E.

Japanese auxiliary submarine chaser *Cha 29* is sunk by mine, possibly laid by submarine *Silversides* (SS 236) on 4 June 1943, near Kavieng, New Ireland.

SBDs and TBFs pound Japanese shipping in Keravia Bay, Rabaul, sinking guardboats *No. 2 Fuku Maru* and *No. 2 Tenjin Maru*, army cargo ship *Taisho Maru*, and merchant tanker *Takatori Maru* and damaging minelayer *Nasami*.

Vichy French river gunboat *Francis Garnier* is sunk by mine sown by USAAF planes (14th Air Force) in South China Sea off Cape St. Jacques, French Indochina, 10°30′N, 108°00′E.

ATLANTIC. Motor torpedo boat *PT 200* collides with unknown object off Long Island, New York, 41°23′N, 71°01′W; *PT 141* and *PT 486* attempt to tow the damaged (but rapidly sinking) boat. Tug *Wandank* (AT 26), sent out from Newport, Rhode Island, is unable to make a line fast. Meanwhile, salvage tug *Resolute* (NRTS) is sent out from New York to try her hand at saving the foundering craft (see 23 February).

MEDITERRANEAN. Five German E-boats approach Anzio beachhead during the night, but all are driven off without inflicting any damage. Submarine chaser *PC 621* claims destruction of one E-boat and drives another ashore.

German submarine *U 969* attacks convoy GUS 31 off the coast of Algeria, irreparably damaging U.S. freighters *Peter Skene Ogden* and *George Cleeve*, 37°18′N, 06°59′E; other than one fatality on board the former, there are no casualties to the American ships. Both ships are towed and beached to facilitate salvage: *Peter Skene Ogden* to Herbillon and *George Cleeve* to Bône, Tunisia. Both are later written off as total losses.

23 Wednesday

PACIFIC. During strikes on Japanese shipping in Tanapag Harbor, Saipan, F6Fs, TBFs, and SBDs from carriers *Essex* (CV 9) and *Yorktown* (CV 10) (in TG 58.2) damage cargo ship *Shoan Maru*, 15°15′N, 145°45′E; planes from carrier *Bunker Hill* (CV 17) (in TG 58.3) sink cargo vessel *Seizan Maru* off Tinian, 15°00′N, 145°30′E.

Submarine *Balao* (SS 285), in attack on Japanese convoy about 35 miles north of Biak, New Guinea, sinks army cargo ship *Nikki Maru*, 00°11′S, 135°00′E.

Submarine *Cod* (SS 224) sinks Japanese fleet tanker *No. 3 Ogura Maru* off Halmahera, 04°23′N, 129°05′E.

Submarine *Plunger* (SS 179), in attack on Japanese convoy, sinks transport *Kimishima Maru* about 200 miles northwest of Chichi Jima, 30°11′N, 140°49′E.

Submarine *Pogy* (SS 266) attacks Japanese convoy, damaging freighter *Horei Maru*, 26°20′N, 126°11′E, and merchant tanker *Teikon Maru*, 26°22′N, 126°16′E, about 60 miles west of Okinawa. *Shonan Maru* tows the crippled *Horei Maru* to Naha, Okinawa, where she sinks as the result of damage inflicted by *Pogy*.

Submarine *Snook* (SS 279) attacks Japanese convoy, sinking transport *Kayo Maru* about 120 miles north-northwest of Chichi Jima, 28°49′N, 141°13′E.

Submarine *Sunfish* (SS 281) and planes from carrier *Yorktown* (CV 10) sink Japanese collier *Shinyubari Maru* about 40 miles west of Saipan, 15°23′N, 145°03′E.

Submarine *Tang* (SS 306) sinks Japanese repair ship *Yamashimo Maru* west of Saipan, 14°45′N, 144°32′E. The cataclysmic explosion of the enemy auxiliary damages *Tang*, but not enough to prevent the boat from remaining on patrol.

Japanese gunboat *Eiko Maru* is sunk by aircraft north of Saipan, 15°12′N, 144°52′E, as she proceeds to the position of the loss of *Fukuyama Maru*, sunk by *Tang* (SS 306) on 22 February.

Japanese cargo ship *Gyoko Maru* is destroyed by accidental explosion in Naha Harbor, Okinawa, 26°13′N, 127°40′E.

INDIAN OCEAN. U.S. tanker *E. G. Seubert*, in convoy PA 69, is torpedoed and sunk by German submarine *U 510* about 200 miles from Aden, 13°45′N, 48°56′E; three of the 27-man Armed Guard (including its commander) perish, as do three of the ship's merchant complement. Australian minesweeper HMAS *Tamworth* and Indian Navy corvette RINS *Orissa* rescue survivors.

ATLANTIC. Salvage tug *Resolute* (NRTS) attempts to tow motor torpedo boat *PT 200*, damaged the previous day, to shallow water off Brenton Reef Light, Rhode Island, but the line slips free and the boat sinks into 60 feet of water.

24 Thursday

PACIFIC. Destroyers *Buchanan* (DD 484) and *Farenholt* (DD 491) are damaged by shore battery, north of New Ireland, 02°20′S, 151°02′E.

Submarine *Grayback* (SS 208) sinks Japanese oiler *Nanho Maru* about 20 miles east of Formosa, 24°20′N, 122°25′E, damages transport *Asama Maru*, 24°15′N, 122°19′E, and survives escort vessel *Shimushu's* counterattacks.

Submarine *Pogy* (SS 266) bombards phosphate plant on Rasa Island, Okino Daito Jima.

Submarine *Sand Lance* (SS 381) is damaged by ice and heavy seas, Kurils.

Submarine *Tang* (SS 306), in attack on Japanese convoy west of Saipan, sinks freighter *Echizen Maru*, 15°45′N, 143°29′E.

USAAF B-25s, P-40s, and P-38s hit targets of opportunity along the Yangtze, damaging Japanese guardboat *Yoko Maru*.

U.S. aircraft sink Japanese transport *No. 2 Shunzan Maru* off Kusaie, Carolines, 05°20′N, 162°58′E.

British submarine HMS *Tally Ho* damages Japanese torpedo boat *Kari* (transporting ground crew of the 331st *Kokutai* from Sabang, N.E.I., to Singapore) in Strait of Malacca, and survives the ensuing depth charge attack.

ATLANTIC. PBY-5As (VP 63), employing Magnetic Anomaly Detection (MAD) gear, and a PV-1 (VB 127), together with RAF Catalina (No. 202 Squadron), bomb German submarine *U 761* as she attempts to transit the Straits of Gibraltar, 35°55′N, 05°45′W. British destroyers HMS *Anthony* and HMS *Wishart* rescue the survivors who abandon their badly damaged U-boat after scuttling her to avoid capture. *U 761* is the first U-boat destroyed through the employment of MAD equipment.

Open lighter *YC 523* sinks after grounding off Portsmouth, New Hampshire.

25 Friday

PACIFIC. Destroyer Division 90 (Commander Edmund B. Taylor) bombards Rabaul.

Destroyer Squadron 12 (Captain Rodger W. Simpson), en route to bombard Kavieng and its airstrips, shipping, and fortifications, encounters Japanese army cargo ship *Tatsugiko Maru*. In the ensuing action, destroyers *Farenholt* (DD 491), *Buchanan* (DD 484), *Lansdowne* (DD 486), *Woodworth* (DD 460), and *Lardner* (DD 487) sink the enemy freighter at 02°46′N, 150°42′E. Japanese shore batteries subsequently give Destroyer Squadron 12 a warm reception, damaging *Buchanan* and *Farenholt*, 02°20′S, 151°02′E.

Submarine *Hoe* (SS 258) attacks Japanese convoy at the mouth of Davao Gulf, sinking fleet tanker *Nissho Maru*, 05°50′N, 126°00′E, and damaging fleet tanker *Kyokuto Maru*, 05°38′N, 126°00′E.

Submarine *Rasher* (SS 269) sinks Japanese army cargo ship *Ryusei Maru*, 07°55′S, 115°15′E, and freighter *Tango Maru*, 07°41′S, 115°10′E, off north coast of Bali.

Submarine *Tang* (SS 306) continues pursuit of Japanese convoy engaged the previous day, and sinks fleet tanker *Choko Maru* west of Saipan, 15°46′N, 144°10′E.

MEDITERRANEAN. Tank landing craft *LCT 26* founders and sinks in heavy weather off Anzio, 41°04′N, 13°30′E.

26 Saturday

PACIFIC. Submarine *Gato* (SS 212) attacks Japanese convoy Wewak No. 20 as it proceeds along the Palau-Hollandia track, and sinks transport *No. 3 Daigen Maru* about 140 miles northwest of Hollandia, 01°51′N, 139°00′E. *Narita Maru*, along with submarine chaser *Ch 35* and a sister ship, rescues over 700 of the 1,200 troops being transported in *No. 3 Daigen Maru*.

Submarine *Grayback* (SS 208) is damaged by land-based Japanese naval aircraft, East China Sea, 25°47′N, 128°45′E.[185]

Motor torpedo boat *PT 251* runs aground during action with Japanese barges in southern Empress Augusta Bay and is then sunk by shore battery, Solomons, 06°30′S, 155°10′E.

USAAF B-25s (14th Air Force) attack shipping in port of Tourane, French Indochina, sinking Vichy French surveying vessel *Astrolabe* and dredging ship *Gilmot*, 16°04′N, 108°13′E. Vichy naval officials consider *Astrolabe* a total loss, given the absolute impossibility of raising her with the means available in that isolated French possession.

MEDITERRANEAN. Tank landing ship *LST 349* sinks after running aground off south coast of Italy, 40°55′N, 12°58′E; *LCT 36* sinks after grounding off Naples.

27 Sunday

PACIFIC. Submarine *Cod* (SS 224) sinks Japanese army cargo ship *Taisoku Maru* west of Halmahera, 02°00′S, 127°40′E.

Submarine *Trout* (SS 202) sinks Japanese cargo ship *Aki Maru* east of Formosa, 131°50′E.

Submarine *Grayback* (SS 208) sinks Japanese cargo ship *Ceylon Maru* in the East China Sea, 31°50′N, 127°45′E.

Large infantry landing craft *LCI(L) 24* covers unopposed Army occupation of the Magine Islands.

MEDITERRANEAN. Light cruiser *Philadelphia* (CL 41) carries out seven gunfire support missions off Anzio.

28 Monday

PACIFIC. Destroyer *Abner Read* (DD 526) is damaged by grounding off eastern New Guinea, 08°44′S, 148°27′E.

Submarine *Balao* (SS 285), in attack on Japanese convoy, sinks army cargo ship *Akiura Maru* and transport *Shoho Maru* about 90 miles northwest of Manokwari, New Guinea, 00°06′N, 132°53′E.

Submarine *Sand Lance* (SS 381) sinks Japanese transport *Kaiko Maru* just east of Musashi Wan, off Paramushir, Kurils, 50°20′N, 155°26′E, but is later damaged when she runs aground off Paramushir.

29 Tuesday

PACIFIC. Operation BREWER: TG 76.1 (Rear Admiral William M. Fechteler), composed of nine destroyers and three high-speed transports, lands Army troops (First Cavalry Division) on Los Negros Island, Admiralty Islands, continuing the strategic encirclement of Rabaul. The two light cruisers and four destroyers of TF 74 provide cover and bombard Japanese positions on Los Negros and Manus.

Destroyer Division 44 (Commander James R. Pahl) bombards wharf areas and installations at Rabaul.

PB4Y-1s (VB 108, VB 109, and VD 3), flying from Abemama, Gilberts, and staging through Kwajalein and Roi, carry out low-level bombing raid on Japanese installations on Wake Island.

Submarine *Rock* (SS 274), while making a night surface attack on a convoy of three Japanese freighters, is damaged by surface gunfire off the Nansei Shoto, 25°33′N, 130°42′E, and is forced to terminate her patrol.

Submarine *Sargo* (SS 188) attacks Japanese convoy and damages army cargo ship *Uchide*

Maru about 120 miles west of Palau, 08°57′N, 132°52′E (see 1 and 2 March).

Submarine *Trout* (SS 202) attacks Guam-bound Japanese convoy about 625 miles east of Formosa. She sinks army transport *Sakito Maru* southeast of Okinawa, 22°40′N, 131°50′E, and damages transport *Aki Maru*, but *Trout* is later sunk, most probably by Japanese destroyer *Asashimo*, 22°40′N, 131°45′E.[186]

USAAF B-25s sink Japanese merchant tow boat *Choka Maru* on the Yangtze near Chiuhsienchen.

USAAF B-24s damage Japanese cargo ship *Narita Maru* 45 miles east of Hollandia, New Guinea.

MEDITERRANEAN. Tank landing ship *LST 197* is damaged by shore battery off Anzio.

MARCH

1 Wednesday

PACIFIC. Naval Base, Milne Bay, New Guinea, and Naval Auxiliary Air Facility, Tanaga, Alaska, are established.

Japanese army cargo ship *Uchide Maru*, damaged by submarine *Sargo* (SS 188) the previous day, is abandoned. Her crew transfers to torpedo boat *Sagi* and *Patrol Boat No. 31* (see 2 March).

ATLANTIC. Destroyer escort *Bronstein* (DE 189) sinks German submarine *U 603* in the North Atlantic, 48°55′N, 26°10′W, and teams with destroyer escorts *Thomas* (DE 102) and *Bostwick* (DE 103) to sink *U 709* at 49°10′N, 26°00′W.

Tug *Wandank* (AT 26), assisted by tug *Sagamore* (AT 20) and Coast Guard tug *Kaw*, tows Norwegian freighter *Tercero* (damaged in collision earlier in the day with U.S. freighter *Casimir Pulaski* about 11 miles northeast of Race Point, Massachusetts) to Boston.

2 Thursday

PACIFIC. Submarine *Narwhal* (SS 167) delivers 70 tons of ammunition and supplies at Butuan Bay, Nasipit, Mindanao, and embarks 28 evacuees (20 servicemen and eight civilians, the latter including two women) (see 5 March).

Submarine *Burrfish* (SS 312) attacks Japanese army cargo ship *Shinkyo Maru* without success. Submarine *Picuda* (SS 382), however, sinks *Shinkyo Maru* about 200 miles southwest of Truk, 06°22′N, 148°27′E, and survives escort vessel *Amakusa*'s counterattack.

Japanese army cargo ship *Uchide Maru* sinks as the result of damage inflicted by submarine *Sargo* (SS 188) on 29 February.

SBDs and TBFs damage small Japanese cargo vessel *Ransei Maru* south of Keravia, Rabaul.

ATLANTIC. Destroyer escort *Alexander J. Luke* (DE 577) runs aground on Rams Head, off Boston, Massachusets; tug *Wandank* (AT 26) is sent out from Boston to assist, while salvage tug *Resolute* (NRTS) is diverted from ongoing efforts to raise the sunken *PT 200* off Long Island, New York.

3 Friday

UNITED STATES. President Roosevelt announces that the Italian Fleet will be distributed among the United States, Great Britain, and Soviet Union.

PACIFIC. TF 94 (Rear Admiral Wilder D. Baker), comprising light cruiser *Richmond* (CL 9) and eight destroyers, begins two-day sweep of the Kurils. Adverse weather, however, not only results in the cancellation of the scheduled bombardments of Japanese positions in the Musashi Wan area but causes varying degrees of damage to the ships (see 4 March). The poor weather in the region accords the enemy no favors: Japanese mine-layer *Shirakami* is sunk in collision with army transport *Nichiran Maru* in a gale south of Urup Island, 45°30'N, 150°00'E; supply ship *No. 2 Ten-Yo Maru* is sunk by storm south of Paramushir, 50°17'N, 155°55'E.

Submarine *Narwhal* (SS 167) torpedoes Japanese gunboat *Karatsu* [ex-U.S. river gunboat *Luzon* (PR 7)] in Sulu Sea, 08°55'N, 123°20'E; ironically, *Karatsu* had been engaged in hunting a submarine at the time.[187]

Submarine *Rasher* (SS 269) attacks Japanese convoy in Celebes Sea, sinking army transport *Nittai Maru* about 290 miles northwest of Wasile, Halmahera, 03°18'N, 123°56'E. Ironically, one of the convoy escorts is *Patrol Boat No. 103* [ex-U.S. minesweeper *Finch* (AM 9)].

Submarine *Sand Lance* (SS 381) attacks Japanese Ominato, Honshu–to–Paramushir ("HA") convoy and sinks transport *Akashisan Maru* west of Uruppu, Japan, 46°00'N, 149°10'E; later that same day, however, the submarine accidentally sinks Soviet cargo ship *Belorussia* at 46°28'N, 149°18'E, mistaking the ship for earlier victim *Akashisan Maru*.

British submarine HMS *Sea Rover* sinks Japanese army cargo vessel *No. 1 Matsu Maru* in Strait of Malacca, 04°56'N, 100°17'E.

4 Saturday

PACIFIC. USAAF and USN land-based planes bomb Japanese installations on Choiseul Island, Solomons.

TF 74 (Rear Admiral Victor A. C. Crutchley, RN), composed of Australian heavy cruiser HMAS *Shropshire*, U.S. light cruisers *Phoenix* (CL 46) and *Nashville* (CL 43), and four U.S. destroyers, bombards Japanese shore batteries and positions on Hauwei and Norilo Islands in the Admiralty Islands (see 6 and 7 March).

Light cruiser *Richmond* (CL 9) and destroyers *Luce* (DD 522), *Kimberly* (DD 521), *Isherwood* (DD 520), *Sproston* (DD 577), *Wickes* (DD 578), *Picking* (DD 685), *William D. Porter* (DD 579), and *Young* (DD 580) are all damaged by heavy weather during sweep of the Kurils.

Submarine *Bluefish* (SS 222) attacks Japanese convoy in the South China Sea, sinks oiler *Ominesan Maru* about 300 miles west of Miri, Sarawak, 05°29'N, 108°46'E, and survives ensuing depth charging by escorts.

Submarine *Peto* (SS 265) attacks Japanese convoy, sinks army cargo ship *Kayo Maru* 75 miles west-northwest of Hollandia, 01°28'S, 138°40'E, and survives depth charge attack by escorts (one of which is submarine chaser *Ch 34*).

Japanese submarine *I 10* is damaged by depth charges (attacker unknown), 06°10'N, 177°50'E.

Japanese army transport *Ryuyo Maru* is damaged when struck by a huge wave and driven aground off Matsuwa Jima, Kurils, 48°04'N, 153°16'E (see 2 May).

5 Sunday

PACIFIC. Submarine *Narwhal* (SS 167) delivers ammunition and stores and evacuates eight people from Tawi Tawi, P.I. Presence of Japanese forces in the area, however, interrupts *Narwhal*'s mission and compels her to jettison the balance of unloaded cargo. After departure, *Narwhal*'s sailors discover two stowaways on board. All passengers (authorized and unauthorized) will be disembarked at Darwin on 11 March.

Submarine *Rasher* (SS 269), pursuing same Japanese convoy attacked on 3 March, damages cargo ship *Ryuwa Maru*.

6 Monday

PACIFIC. TF 74 (Rear Admiral Victor A. C. Crutchley, RN) repeats shelling of Japanese shore batteries and positions on Hauwei and Norilo Islands, Admiralties. Enemy guns at the mouth of Seeadler Bay damage destroyer *Nicholson* (DD 442), operating in TG 76.1, 02°00'S, 147°00'E (see 7 March).

Submarine *Nautilus* (SS 168), in attack on Japanese convoy about 420 miles north-north-west of Saipan, sinks transport (ex-hospital ship) *America Maru*, 22°19'N, 143°54'E, and survives counterattack by torpedo boat *Otori*.

MEDITERRANEAN. Convoy UGS 33, bound from New York to Alexandria, Egypt, strays into Allied minefield off Tunis. U.S. freighter *Daniel Chester French* is sunk by mines at 37°18'N, 10°22'E; four Armed Guard sailors (of the 28-man detachment), nine of the merchant crew (of 44 men), and 24 of the 86 Army passengers perish with the ship. British rescue tug *Charon*, steamer *Thelma*, and tug *Rescue* pick up the surviving crew and passengers. Freighter *Virginia Dare* is irreparably damaged at approximately 37°18'N, 10°22'E; there are no casualties among the ship's complement, including the 28-man Armed Guard (see 8 March).

7 Tuesday

PACIFIC. TF 74 (Rear Admiral Victor A. C. Crutchley, RN), as the result of the Japanese shore battery damaging destroyer *Nicholson* (DD 442) the day before, repeats shelling of enemy guns on Hauwei and Norilo Islands, Admiralties.

Japanese shore battery sinks motor torpedo boat *PT 337*, Hansa Bay, New Guinea, 04°09'S, 144°50'E (see 11 March).

USAAF B-24s (10th Air Force) mine waters off Koh Chang, Thailand; Japanese freighter *Juyo Maru* is sunk, 13°10'N, 100°50'E.

ATLANTIC. U.S. freighter *Herman Winter* runs aground off Gay Head, Martha's Vineyard; Coast Guard cutter *General Greene* (WPC 140) and tug *Kaw*, and commercial tug *Elizabeth Moran* (NRTS) are dispatched to assist, as is salvage vessel *Accelerate* (ARS 30) (see 8 March).

8 Wednesday

PACIFIC. Japanese planes bomb Engebi Island, Eniwetok, destroying ammunition, petroleum products, and distillation units but leaving the airstrip undamaged.

Submarine *Lapon* (SS 260), in attack on Japanese convoy southeast of Hong Kong, damages freighter *Hokoku Maru* in South China Sea, 19°21'N, 116°09'E; freighter *Nicherei Maru* takes the damaged merchantman in tow (see 9 March).

British submarine HMS *Sea Rover*, in attack on Japanese convoy, sinks transport *Shobu Maru* in Strait of Malacca, 03°38'N, 99°12'E.

PBY sinks Japanese fishing boat *No. 5 Ebisu Maru* off Tadji, 03°10'S, 142°13'E.

USAAF P-38s sink Japanese fishing boat *No. 38 Taigyo Maru* off Aitape, New Guinea.

U.S. aircraft sink Japanese guardboat *No. 2 Nanshu Maru* off Duke of York Isle, St. George Channel, 04°12′S, 152°30′E.

MEDITERRANEAN. U.S. freighter *Virginia Dare*, irreparably damaged by Allied mine on 6 March off Tunis, breaks up after encountering heavy weather; she is subsequently written off as a total loss.

ATLANTIC. Submarine chaser *SC 1053* takes off the crewmen from stranded U.S. freighter *Herman Winter*, aground off Martha's Vineyard, and transports them to Newport, Rhode Island. Subsequent salvage efforts fail, however, and after the removal of cargo, *Herman Winter* is stripped and the wreck abandoned.

Tug *Sagamore* (AT 20) assists disabled U.S. freighter *Medina* off the Delaware capes, 40°25′N, 73°52′W, and tows her to New York.

9 Thursday

PACIFIC. Submarine *Lapon* (SS 260), continuing her pursuit of Japanese convoy engaged the previous day in the South China Sea, sinks freighters *Hokoku Maru*, 19°21′N, 116°09′E, and *Nicherei Maru* (the ship that was towing her) 19°21′N, 116°09′E, and survives counterattack by gunboat *Peking Maru*.

PBYs bomb Japanese shipping off Hollandia, sinking small cargo ships *Yashima Maru* and *No. 12 Genei Maru*, and damaging *Tenryu Maru*.

USAAF B-25s bomb Japanese installations and dock area, Simpson Harbor, Rabaul, sinking small cargo vessels *Mankei Maru* and *Kinka Maru*.

USAAF B-24 sinks small Japanese cargo vessel *No. 1 Kissho Maru* off Kapingamarangi (Greenwich) Atoll.

INDIAN OCEAN. "SA No. 1" Operation (Rear Admiral Sakonju Naomasa): Raiding the Australia-Aden shipping lane, Japanese heavy cruiser *Tone* sinks British freighter *Behar* south of Cocos Island, 20°32′S, 87°10′E, and captures crew and passengers (108 men, four of whom are mortally wounded). *Behar*'s transmitting a distress call, however, results in the cancellation of "SA No. 1" before it proceeds further.[188]

ATLANTIC. Destroyer escort *Leopold* (DE 319) is torpedoed by German submarine *U 255*, 650 miles west of Scotland (see 10 March).

Naval Air Facility (Lighter than Air), Santa Cruz, Brazil, is established.

MEDITERRANEAN. Destroyer *Edison* (DD 439) sinks German submarine *U 450* off Anzio, 41°11′N, 12°27′E.

U.S. freighter *Clark Mills* is damaged by mine off North African coast, 37°18′N, 10°13′E; beached off Bizerte, the ship is later written off as a total loss. There are no casualties to the merchant crew, passengers, or the 42-man Armed Guard.

10 Friday

PACIFIC. Submarine *Bowfin* (SS 287), in attack on Japanese convoy in Tabalai Strait, damages army cargo ship *Tsukikawa Maru* at 01°28′S, 128°12′E, and survives counterattacks by escorts.

Submarine chaser *SC 700* is destroyed and fuel oil barge *YO 44* is damaged by fire, Vella Lavella, Solomon Islands.

PBY bombs and sinks Japanese army cargo ship *Hasshu Maru*, previously damaged on 21 February, off Hollandia, New Guinea.

ATLANTIC. Destroyer escort *Leopold* (DE 319), irreparably damaged by German submarine *U 255* 650 miles west of Scotland the previous day, is scuttled by sister ship *Joyce* (DE 317).

MEDITERRANEAN. U.S. freighter *William B. Woods* is torpedoed and sunk by German submarine *U 952* approximately 47 miles off Palermo, Sicily, 38°43′N, 13°50′E; one of the 28-man Armed Guard and 51 of the 407 Army troops being transported in the ship perish. There are no casualties among the 43-man merchant complement. Escorting Italian destroyer escort *Aretusa* provides no help.

11 Saturday

PACIFIC. Submarine *Bowfin* (SS 287) sinks Japanese army cargo ship *Tsukikawa Maru*, west of Halmahera Island, 01°25′S, 128°14′E, and survives counterattacks by minelayer *Wakatake* and army aircraft. *Bowfin*'s attack on *Asaka Maru*, which is rescuing *Tsukikawa Maru*'s survivors, is unsuccessful.

Japanese cargo ship *Daitoku Maru* is sunk in collision with cargo ship *No. 6 Daiboshi Maru*, Sea of Japan, 40°10′N, 137°41′E.

PBY (VP 34) rescues survivors of motor torpedo boat *PT 337*, sunk in Hansa Bay, New Guinea, by Japanese shore battery fire on 7 March.

INDIAN OCEAN. Japanese submarine *RO 110* is sunk by Indian Navy sloop HMIS *Jumna* and Australian minesweepers HMAS *Ipswich* and HMAS *Launceston* 17 miles south of Vizagapatam, 17°25′N, 83°21′E.

MEDITERRANEAN. Commander Cruiser Division 8 (Rear Admiral Lyal A. Davidson) breaks flag in French light cruiser *Emile Bertin* at Oran, Algeria, and takes operational com-

mand of *Emile Bertin*, *Gloire*, *Georges Leygues*, and *Duguay-Trouin* for training purposes (see 24 March).

USAAF aircraft sink German submarines *U 380* and *U 410*, Toulon, France.

12 Sunday

PACIFIC. Submarine *Flying Fish* (SS 229) sinks Japanese freighter *Taijin Maru* about 10 miles northwest of Daito Jima, approximately 175 miles southeast of the Ryukyus, 25°53′N, 131°19′E.

Submarine *Gato* (SS 212) sinks Japanese army cargo ship *No. 3 Okinoyama Maru* north of New Guinea, 01°15′S, 133°20′E.

PBYs attack Japanese convoy en route to Hollandia, sinking motor sailboat *Hosho Maru*.

MEDITERRANEAN. Light cruisers *Philadelphia* (CL 41) and *Brooklyn* (CL 40) provide gunfire support off Anzio; they repeat the missions on 13 March. On both occasions they encounter shore battery fire without damage.

Submarine chaser *PC 624* is damaged when she runs aground three miles east of Palermo, Sicily.

13 Monday

PACIFIC. Submarine *Sand Lance* (SS 381) attacks Japanese Saipan-bound convoy East Matsu No. 2 off Honshu, sinking light cruiser *Tatsuta* and cargo ship *Kokuyo Maru* 150 miles south-southwest of Yokosuka, 32°52′N, 139°12′E. Following those attacks, Japanese escort vessels drop 105 depth charges and keep *Sand Lance* at deep submergence for 18.5 hours.

Submarine *Tautog* (SS 199) sinks Japanese army cargo ship *Ryua Maru* and transport *Shojin Maru* about 20 miles west of Rashuwa Island, Kurils, 47°38′N, 152°38′E.

PBYs bomb Japanese shipping off Pelillo Island, 02°09′S, 140°19′E, sinking small cargo ship *Hara Maru*.

INDIAN OCEAN. U.S. tanker *H. D. Collier* is torpedoed and shelled by Japanese submarine *I 26* at 21°30′N, 66°11′E, and abandoned; of the 28-man Armed Guard, 12 perish in the action (see 16 and 17 March).

ATLANTIC. TBF (VC 95) from escort carrier *Bogue* (CVE 9), along with destroyer *Hobson* (DD 464), destroyer escort *Haverfield* (DE 393), Canadian armed merchant cruiser HMCS *Prince Rupert*, and RAF Flying Fortress (No. 220 Squadron), sink German submarine *U 575*, North Atlantic, 46°18′N, 27°34′W.

14 Tuesday

PACIFIC. USAAF B-24 damages Japanese hospital ship *Tachibana Maru*, en route from Wewak to Palau, 02°14'S, 142°37'E.

Japanese seaplane carrier *Sanuki Maru* is damaged by mine off Cape St. Jacques, French Indochina.

Japanese cargo ship *Fuki Maru* is sunk, by stranding, off east coast of Honshu, near Fukushima, 37°29'N, 141°35'E.

15 Wednesday

ATLANTIC. Destroyer escort *McAnn* (DE 179), coordinating her operations with USN and USAAF planes, rescues survivors of a crashed B-17 off coast of Brazil, 01°31'N, 32°35'W.

PACIFIC. USAAF B-25s sink small Japanese cargo vessel *Konpira Maru* off Hollandia.

MEDITERRANEAN. U.S. freighter *China Mail* is damaged by bomb fragments during German air raid on Naples, Italy. There are no casualties among the ship's complement, which includes 13 Armed Guard sailors.

16 Thursday

PACIFIC. Submarine *Flying Fish* (SS 229) attacks Japanese convoy in the Nansei Shoto, sinking freighter *Anzan Maru* about 20 miles north of Okinoeradu Jima, 27°38'N, 128°38'E, and unsuccessfully attacks tanker *Teikon Maru* (ex-German *Winnetou*).

Submarine *Lapon* (SS 260) unsuccessfully attacks Japanese seaplane tender *Kunikawa Maru*, 18°14'N, 117°44'E.

Submarine *Silversides* (SS 236) attacks Japanese convoy and sinks army cargo ship *Kofuku Maru* about 225 miles southeast of Palau, 05°00'N, 136°46'E.

Submarine *Tautog* (SS 199) sinks Japanese destroyer *Shirakumo* and army cargo ship *Nichiren Maru* off east coast of Hokkaido, southeast of Kushiro Harbor, 42°18'N, 145°11'E, and survives counterattacks by destroyers *Kamikaze* and *Namikaze*.

PBYs (and later USAAF B-24s) attack Japanese convoy north of Hollandia, damaging submarine chaser *Ch 35* and cargo ships *Taiei Maru*, *Yakumo Maru*, and *Teshio Maru* (see 19 March).

INDIAN OCEAN. U.S. tanker *H. D. Collier*, damaged by Japanese submarine *I 26* on 13 March, sinks; British freighter *Empire Raja* rescues 14 survivors (see 17 March).

MEDITERRANEAN. PBY-5As (VP 63) employ MAD gear to detect German submarine *U 392* as the enemy boat attempts to transit the Straits of Gibraltar; the PBYs bomb the

U-boat, and British frigate HMS *Affleck* and destroyer HMS *Vanoc* depth charge her. *Affleck* delivers the coup de grâce to sink *U 392* at 35°55'N, 05°41'W.

17 Friday

PACIFIC. Motor torpedo boat *PT 283* is sunk by friendly fire from destroyer *Guest* (DD 472) off Choiseul Island, Solomons, 06°27'S, 155°08'E.

USAAF B-24s bomb Surabaya, Java, naval base; Japanese guardboats *No. 8 Kaho Maru* and *No. 4 Matsu Maru* may have been damaged during this raid.

MEDITERRANEAN. Destroyers *Madison* (DD 425) and *Eberle* (DD 430) make sound contact 25 miles southwest of Anzio; five-hour search yields no result. Tank landing craft *LCT 277* is damaged in air raid.

During German air raid on the port of Naples, Italy, U.S. freighter *James Guthrie* is damaged by bomb; there are no casualties among the ship's company.

German submarine *U 371* attacks Naples-bound convoy SNF 17 about 30 miles northeast of Bougie, Algeria, and torpedoes U.S. freighter *Maiden Creek*, 37°08'N, 05°27'E. Initially, the ship is abandoned, but is reboarded and prepared for towing. *U 371* again torpedoes *Maiden Creek*, the resulting explosion kills six merchant seamen and two of the 29-man Armed Guard (see 18 March).

Destroyer *MacKenzie* (DD 614) joins three British escort vessels for submarine hunt off Philippeville, Tunisia, with no results.

INDIAN OCEAN. Last survivors of U.S. tanker *H. D. Collier*, torpedoed and shelled by Japanese submarine *I 26* on 13 March, are rescued by steamship *Karagola*.

ATLANTIC. TBFs (VC 6) from escort carrier *Block Island* (CVE 21), along with destroyer *Corry* (DD 463) and destroyer escort *Bronstein* (DE 189), sink German submarine *U 801* west of the Cape Verdes, 16°42'N, 30°26'W.

18 Saturday

PACIFIC. TG 50.10 (Rear Admiral Willis A. Lee Jr.), formed around carrier *Lexington* (CV 16) and battleships *Iowa* (BB 61) and *New Jersey* (BB 62), screened by seven destroyers, pounds Japanese installations on Mille Island in the Marshalls; *Iowa* is damaged by shore battery off Mille.

TG 74.5 (Captain Kenmore M. McManes) commences bombardment of Japanese installations in Wewak area, New Guinea (see 19 March).

Submarine *Lapon* (SS 260) attacks Japanese convoy HI 48, sinking transport *Hokoroku Maru* about 250 miles southwest of Hong Kong, 19°24'N, 116°50'E.

Submarine *Rock* (SS 274) is damaged by depth charges off North Borneo, 07°25'N, 115°20'E, but remains on patrol.

Submarine *Picuda* (SS 382) conducts unsuccessful attack against Japanese cargo ship *Kasuga Maru* north-northeast of Ulithi, 12°33'N, 141°08'E.

Large infantry landing craft *LCI(L) 330* is accidentally rammed by freighter *Richard Moszowski* off Koli Point, Guadalcanal. The latter suffers damage in the encounter.

USAAF B-25s bomb Japanese installations on Ponape, Carolines, sinking small cargo vessel *No. 2 Kasuga Maru*.

Japanese cargo ship *Shinten Maru* is damaged by mine off Kaimana, 03°40'S, 133°47'E.

ANDAMAN SEA. Japanese motor torpedo boats *Gyoraitei No. 402* and *Gyoraitei No. 153* are sunk by British aircraft off Boronga, Burma.

MEDITERRANEAN. U.S. freighter *Maiden Creek*, torpedoed the previous day by German submarine *U 371* about 30 miles north-northeast of Bougie, Algeria, is towed into Bougie where she is beached to facilitate salvage. Subsequently, however, she is swept off the beach by a storm and breaks up in the heavy weather, a total loss.

ATLANTIC. U.S. tanker *Seakay*, in Avonmouth, England–bound convoy CU 17, is torpedoed by German submarine *U 311* at 51°10'N, 20°20'W, and abandoned. One Armed Guard sailor perishes in the abandonment; destroyer escort *Reeves* (DE 156) rescues survivors. Escort ships scuttle the irreparably damaged tanker with shells and depth charges.

19 Sunday

PACIFIC. TG 74.5 concludes its bombardment of Japanese positions in Wewak area, during which destroyer *Daly* (DD 519) sinks auxiliary submarine chaser *Cha 10* off Mushu, 03°33'S, 143°38'E.

USAAF B-24s, B-25s, A-20s, and P-38s (5th Air Force) wipe out Japanese convoy 50 miles northwest of Wewak, sinking cargo ships *Yakumo Maru* and *Taiei Maru* and their escorts, auxiliary submarine chasers *Cha 47* and *Cha 49*, 02°55'S, 143°40'E (see 20 March).

USAAF B-25s (14th Air Force) sink Japanese ship *Kaen Maru* off Wuhu, China.

U.S. freighter *Oriental* is damaged by mine east of Espíritu Santo, New Hebrides, 15°31'36"S, 167°17'49"E, but makes port under own power; there are no casualties among the ship's complement, which includes a 28-man Armed Guard.

INDIAN OCEAN. U.S. freighter *John A. Poor* is torpedoed and sunk by German submarine *U 510* at 13°58′N, 70°30′E; 25 of the 43-man merchant complement perish with the ship, as do nine of the 30-man Armed Guard (see 20 March).

ATLANTIC. TBF and FM-2 (VC 6) from escort carrier *Block Island* (CVE 21) sink German submarine *U 1059* west-southwest of Dakar, 13°10′N, 33°44′W.

MEDITERRANEAN. Submarine chaser *PC 545*, on patrol west of Anzio, sinks a German E-boat.

20 Monday

PACIFIC. TG 31.2 (Commodore Lawrence F. Reifsnider) lands Fourth Marine Division (Brigadier General Alfred H. Noble, USMC) on undefended Emirau Island, Bismarck Archipelago, thus cutting the Japanese supply line from Rabaul to Kavieng, New Ireland.

TF 37, including four battleships, two escort carriers, and destroyers (Rear Admiral Robert M. Griffin), bombards Kavieng.

Submarine *Picuda* (SS 382) sinks Japanese victualling stores ship *Hoko Maru* about 40 miles north of Yap, Carolines, 10°09′N, 138°10′E.

Submarine *Pollack* (SS 180) sinks Japanese auxiliary netlayer *Hakuyo Maru* about 30 miles northeast of Torishima, 30°53′N, 140°42′E, and survives counterattack by submarine chaser *Ch 44*.

Japanese submarine chaser *Ch 35*, sent out from Hollandia to rescue survivors of cargo ships *Yakumo Maru* and *Taiei Maru* and auxiliary submarine chasers *Cha 47* and *Cha 49*, sunk by USAAF planes the previous day, finds no trace of them.

USAAF B-24 sinks Japanese auxiliary submarine chaser *Cha 62*, 130 nautical miles east of Hollandia, New Guinea, 02°55′S, 143°40′E; cargo vessel *Atsushi Maru* may have also been sunk in this attack.

U.S. aircraft sink Japanese guardboats *Kaiun Maru* and *No. 2 Taiho Maru* off southern tip of Rabaul.

INDIAN OCEAN. Survivors (including 21 Armed Guard sailors) of U.S. freighter *John A. Poor,* sunk by German submarine *U 510* the previous day, are rescued by British freighter *Fort Worth.*

21 Tuesday

PACIFIC. Submarine *Angler* (SS 240) completes evacuation of 58 U.S. citizens, including women and children, from the west coast of Panay, P.I.

Submarine *Bashaw* (SS 241) torpedoes Japanese salvage vessel *Urakami Maru* in the Palaus, 06°55′N, 136°29′E. Destroyer *Minazuki* takes the damaged vessel in tow; *Yuzuki* screens the evolution.

22 Wednesday

PACIFIC. Submarine *Growler* (SS 215) carries out unsuccessful attack on Japanese cargo vessel *Teizui Maru* east-northeast of Okinawa, 27°55′N, 129°15′E.

Submarine *Tunny* (SS 282) damages Japanese tanker *Iro* west of the Palaus, 07°22′N, 132°08′E.

23 Thursday

PACIFIC. Destroyers *Franks* (DD 554) and *Haggard* (DD 555) bombard Japanese installations on Mussau Island in the St. Matthias group, Bismarck Archipelago.

Tank landing craft *LCT 315* is sunk by explosion of undetermined origin, Eniwetok. The blast levels buildings and tents nearby.

Submarine *Tunny* (SS 282) sinks Japanese submarine *I 42* six miles southwest of Angaur, Palaus, 06°40′N, 134°03′E.

Japanese freighter *Hokko Maru* runs aground off Inubo Saki, Japan, and sinks. Fishing boats rescue the survivors.

ATLANTIC. Naval Air Facility, Dunkeswell, England, is established.

District patrol vessel *YP 331* founders and sinks in heavy weather off Key West, Florida, 24°56′30″N, 81°57′35″W.

24 Friday

PACIFIC. Submarine *Bowfin* (SS 287) attacks Japanese convoy about 15 miles off the south coast of Mindanao and approximately 95 miles south of Davao, sinks transport *Shinkyo Maru,* 05°38′N, 125°50′E, and army cargo ship *Bengal Maru,* 05°37′N, 125°58′E, and survives counterattack by minesweeper *W.30.*

USAAF B-24s bomb Wake Island, sinking Japanese motor torpedo boat *Gyoraitei No. 4.*

MEDITERRANEAN. Commander Cruiser Division 8 (Rear Admiral Lyal A. Davidson) reports results of his inspection of French naval vessels. He considers *Emile Bertin, Montcalm,* and *Georges Leygues* ready for independent or joint duty; *Duguay-Trouin,* however, an older ship, is deemed as needing repairs. French bat-

tleship *Lorraine,* also inspected, is deemed in very good material condition; with a brief period of training and target practice, she is deemed ready for combatant service. The French specifically desire that *Lorraine* be employed on active service against the enemy "as an aid to the morale of the entire French fleet." These ships will later participate in the invasion of Southern France, taking active part in the liberation of their homeland.

25 Saturday

PACIFIC. Destroyer escort *Manlove* (DE 36) and submarine chaser *PC 1135* sink Japanese submarine *I 32,* 50 miles south of Wotje, 08°30′N, 170°10′E.

Submarine *Pollack* (SS 180) attacks Japanese "East Matsu No. 3" convoy and sinks submarine chaser *Ch 54* (one of 10 escorts) about 50 miles north of Muko Jima, Bonins, 28°44′N, 141°45′E.

ATLANTIC. Oiler *Salamonie* (AO 26) is accidentally rammed by U.S. tug *Joseph O'Brien,* and damaged, off the Naval Supply Depot, Bayonne, New Jersey.

26 Sunday

PACIFIC. Submarine *Tullibee* (SS 284) is sunk by circular run of own torpedo, north of the Palaus, 134°45′E, 09°30′N.

USAAF B-25s (5th Air Force) attack Japanese shipping off Mapia Island, Dutch New Guinea, sinking guardboat *No. 3 Tenjin Maru,* 02°00′N, 135°00′E.

Japanese army cargo ship *Shimotsuki Maru* is sunk by mine off Muroto Saki, Japan.

27 Monday

PACIFIC. Destroyer *Hoel* (DD 533) encounters and sinks outrigger canoe bound from Mussau, St. Matthias Group, Bismarck Archipelago, to Tingwon Island, part of the effort to evacuate the Mussau garrison by any means available.

Motor torpedo boats *PT 121* and *PT 353* are mistakenly sunk by friendly bomber, Bismarck Archipelago, 05°17′S, 151°01′E.

Submarine *Hake* (SS 256) sinks Japanese merchant tanker *Yamamizu Maru* about 75 miles south of Borneo, 03°53′S, 109°42′E.

Submarine *Rasher* (SS 269), in attack on Japanese convoy in the Java Sea, sinks army cargo ship *Nichinan Maru* about 50 miles north of Bali, 07°27′S, 115°55′E.

RAAF Catalinas sink Japanese merchant cargo vessel *Shinsei Maru* in Banda Sea north of Dowalger Island, 07°44′S, 130°02′E.

MEDITERRANEAN. Destroyer *Livermore* (DD 429) provides gunfire support at Anzio.

Motor torpedo boat *PT 207* is damaged by naval gunfire off Anzio-Nettuno, Italy, 41°27′N, 12°40′E.

Allied force of American and British motor torpedo boats and British motor gunboats (Commander Robert A. Allan, RNVR) destroys six German ferry barges off Vada Rocks, Corsica. U.S. motor torpedo boats *PT 208*, *PT 214,* and *PT 218* participate in the battle.

28 Tuesday

PACIFIC. Destroyers of Destroyer Division 94 bombard Japanese positions on Kapingamarangi (Greenwich) Atoll, demolishing a radio and meteorological station.

Submarine *Barb* (SS 220) sinks Japanese freighter *Fukusei Maru* off Rasa Island, 24°25′N, 131°11′E.

Submarine *Silversides* (SS 236) sinks Japanese cargo ship *Kairyu Maru* off Manokwari, New Guinea.

British submarine HMS *Truculent*, in attack on Japanese convoy, sinks army cargo ship *Yasushima Maru* in Strait of Malacca, 03°38′N, 100°50′E.

29 Wednesday

PACIFIC. Submarine *Haddo* (SS 255) torpedoes Japanese army cargo ship *Nichian Maru* in South China Sea, 17°42′N, 109°57′E.

Submarine *Tunny* (SS 282) torpedoes Japanese battleship *Musashi* off Palau, 07°30′N, 134°30′E.

Motor gunboat *PGM 8* is damaged when she runs aground off Kundu Kundu Island.

INDIAN OCEAN. U.S. freighter *Richard Hovey* is torpedoed by Japanese submarine *I 26* at 16°40′N, 64°30′E, and abandoned. *I 26* then surfaces and after shelling the ship and setting her afire (*Richard Hovey* sinks subsequently), fires upon the lifeboats and rafts, killing one Armed Guard sailor. The Japanese submarine then rams and sinks one of the boats before taking four POWs and clearing the area (see 2 and 14 April).

MEDITERRANEAN. Destroyer *John D. Ford* (DD 228) is damaged when accidentally rammed by British armed trawler HMS *Kingston Agate* while departing Gibraltar, B.C.C.

Destroyers *Ericsson* (DD 440) and *Kearny* (DD 432), along with submarine chasers *PC 626*, *PC 556*, and *PC 558* and British destroyers HMS *Laforey*, HMS *Tumult*, HMS *Hambledon,* and HMS *Blencathra*, begin submarine

hunt 30 miles northeast of Palermo, Sicily. Their efforts culminate in the sinking of German submarine *U 223* at 38°48′N, 14°10′E.

30 Thursday

PACIFIC. TF 58 under Commander Fifth Fleet (Admiral Raymond A. Spruance) begins intensive pounding of Japanese airfields, shipping, fleet servicing facilities, and other installations at Palau, Yap, Ulithi, and Woleai in the Carolines. During these attacks (that continue until 1 April), TBFs and TBMs from carriers *Lexington* (CV 16), *Bunker Hill* (CV 19), and *Hornet* (CV 12) sow extensive minefields in and around the channels and approaches to the Palaus in the first tactical use of mines laid by carrier aircraft. TF 58 planes sink destroyer *Wakatake*; fleet tankers *Ose, Sata, Iro, Akebono Maru,* and *Amatsu Maru*; submarine chaser *Ch 6*; auxiliary submarine chasers *Cha 22, Cha 26, Cha 53,* and *No. 5 Showa Maru*; Patrol Boat *No. 31*; netlayer *No. 5 Nissho Maru*; aircraft transport *Goshu Maru*; transports *Gozan Maru, Nagisan Maru, Raizan Maru, Ryuko Maru,* and *No. 18 Shinsei Maru*; tankers *Amatsu Maru* and *Asashio Maru*; guardboats *Ibaraki Maru* and *No. 2 Seiei Maru*; salvage vessel *Urakami Maru* and repair ship *Akashi*; torpedo transport and repair ship *Kamikaze Maru*; army cargo ships *Chuyo Maru, Kibi Maru,* and *Shoei Maru*; army tanker *No. 2 Unyo Maru*; and army cargo ships *Bichu Maru* (outside Palau Harbor) and *Teisho Maru* (in the channel west of Palau). At Angaur, small craft *No. 3 Akita Maru, Chichibu Maru, Yae Maru, Toku Maru, Kiku Maru, Hinode Maru, Yamato Maru, Ume Maru,* and *Akebono Maru* are sunk. Submarine chaser *Ch 35*, netlayer *Shosei Maru*, tanker *No. 2 Hishi Maru,* and army cargo ship *Hokutai Maru* are damaged.

Submarine *Tunny* (SS 282), while on lifeguard duty off the Palaus, is attacked accidentally by TBF from carrier *Yorktown* (CV 10) 07°40′N, 134°00′E. Damage suffered in the friendly fire encounter forces *Tunny* to terminate her patrol.

Submarine *Darter* (SS 227), despite presence of one escort vessel, sinks Japanese army cargo ship *Fujikawa Maru* about 175 miles northwest of Manokwari, New Guinea, 01°50′N, 133°00′E.

Submarine *Picuda* (SS 382) attacks Japanese convoy and sinks transport *Atlantic Maru* about 90 miles south-southwest of Guam, 12°20′N, 145°55′E.

Submarine *Stingray* (SS 186) attacks Japanese convoy and sinks transport *Ikushima Maru* about 350 miles north-northwest of Saipan, 20°43′N, 143°04′E.

TBFs and SBDs bomb airfield facilities at Vunakanau, Rabaul, New Britain; B-25s and P-38s (13th Air Force) attack other targets in adjacent areas; one of these strikes most likely damages Japanese minelayer *Nasami* off Rabaul (see 1 April).

MEDITERRANEAN. Destroyer *Eberle* (DD 430) provides gunfire support off Anzio.

31 Friday

PACIFIC. Japanese Admiral Koga Mineichi, Commander in Chief of the Combined Fleet, en route to establish a new fleet headquarters at Davao, P.I., in the wake of the devastating U.S. carrier raids on the Carolines the day before, is lost when the flying boat (EMILY) (852nd *Kokutai*) in which he is traveling disappears without a trace. Accompanying EMILY (802nd *Kokutai*), carrying a party of officers that includes his chief of staff, Vice Admiral Fukudome Shigeru, makes a forced landing off Cebu, P.I., where Fukudome is captured (along with invaluable intelligence documents) by Filipino guerrillas. Vice Admiral Takaso Shiro becomes interim Commander in Chief, Combined Fleet, until the Navy Ministry can appoint a successor to Admiral Koga (see 5 May).

TF 58 aircraft sink Japanese guardboat *Hakko Maru*, Palaus.

APRIL

1 Saturday

PACIFIC. TU 57.10.9, composed of destroyer escort *Sanders* (DE 40), tank landing ship *LST 127*, and infantry landing craft (gunboat) *LCI(G) 346* and *LCI(G) 449* carry out unopposed occupation of Ailuk Atoll, Marshalls.

Submarine *Flying Fish* (SS 229) sinks Japanese cargo ship *Minami Maru* at Kaito Daito Jima, 25°57′N, 131°19′E.

Japanese submarines *I 46* and *RO 46* are damaged in underwater collision southwest of Kominase Shima in the northern Inland Sea, Japan.

Japanese minelayer *Nasami* sinks as the result of damage suffered off Rabaul, New Britain, on 30 March.

MEDITERRANEAN. Convoy UGS 36 is attacked by German torpedo bombers off Algiers; tank landing ship *LST 526* is damaged when low-flying enemy plane knocks off radio antenna. U.S. freighter *Jared Ingersoll* is torpedoed; destroyer escort *Mills* (DE 383) and British tug *Mindful* rescue the crew (including the 29-man Armed Guard) from the sinking ship. After one attempt to quell the fires consuming the ship fails, *Mills* places a fire-fighting party on board that succeeds in its attempt; the destroyer escort then assists in towing *Jared Ingersoll* out of danger. Beached off Algiers, the freighter is subsequently returned to service.

2 Sunday

PACIFIC. Submarine *Greenling* (SS 213) begins reconnoitering the Marianas, taking photographs, obtaining tidal data, and making soundings. She will be engaged in that work until 29 April. Simultaneously, submarine *Salmon* (SS 182) will reconnoiter the western Carolines, spending about a week at three successive places: Ulithi, Yap, and Woleai.

Submarine *Hake* (SS 256) attacks Japanese convoy HI 55 in South China Sea and damages tanker *Tarakan Maru*, 01°58'N, 106°20'E.

TU 57.10.9, composed of destroyer escort *Sanders* (DE 40), tank landing ship *LST 127*, and infantry landing craft (gunboat) *LCI(G) 346* and *LCI(G) 449*, occupies Mejit Island, Marshalls. The small Japanese force that opposes the occupation is wiped out by gunfire from the LCI(G)s.

USAAF B-24s (13th Air Force) (7th Air Force B-24s, flying from Eniwetok, also bomb Truk during 1 and 2 April) bomb Dublon Island, Truk, targeting warehouses and dock areas; Japanese cargo vessel *No. 3 Akebono Maru* is most likely destroyed during this attack.

ATLANTIC. Tug *Allegheny* (AT 19), dispatched from Cape May, New Jersey, takes U.S. tanker *Fort Meigs* (disabled the day before by a casualty to her propeller shaft) in tow and heads for New York. Tug *Rescue* (NRTS) takes over the tow from *Allegheny* the following morning.

MEDITERRANEAN. Submarine chaser *PC 621* is damaged by aerial mine, and harbor tug *YT 207* is damaged by near-miss from shore battery off Anzio.

INDIAN OCEAN. British freighter *Samcalia* rescues 25 survivors of U.S. freighter *Richard Hovey*, sunk by Japanese submarine *I 26* on 29 March (see 14 April).

3 Monday

PACIFIC. Submarine *Pollack* (SS 180), in attack on Japanese convoy, sinks army cargo ship *Tosei Maru* about 325 miles south of Yokohama, Japan, 30°14'N, 139°44'E.

USAAF B-25s (13th Air Force) bomb Japanese installations in northeastern section of Rabaul, New Britain; Taiwan fishing boat *Kojin Maru* is set afire and sunk.

Transport *Kenmore* (AP 162) is damaged by grounding, Nawiliwili, T.H.

4 Tuesday

PACIFIC. Destroyer *Hall* (DD 583) is damaged by shore battery off Wotje, 09°30'N, 170°00'E.

PB4Ys bomb Japanese shipping and harbor installations at Truk. Submarine *I 169* is sunk (accidental flooding) during the raid; efforts to save trapped crewmen (the last of whom live until 7 April) prove unsuccessful. Provision ship *Sapporo Maru* is damaged irreparably by near-misses.

5 Wednesday

PACIFIC. Harbor tug *YT 247* founders and sinks while in tow of tug *Sunnadin* (ATO 28) en route from Pearl Harbor to Palmyra, 425 miles south by west of Oahu, 14°14'N, 158°59'W.

PB4Y (VB 109) sinks Japanese auxiliary submarine chaser *Cha 46* off Wake Island.

TBMs and FM-2s (VC 66) damage Japanese submarine *I 45*, 650 miles northeast of Majuro, 14°27'N, 176°37'E.

USAAF B-24s, B-25s, A-20s, and P-38s (5th Air Force) attack Hollandia; during the bombing of dock areas there, Japanese army cargo ships *Choun Maru* and *Iwakuni Maru* are sunk.

ATLANTIC. Minesweeper *Curlew* (AM 69) rescues crew of foundering fishing vessel *Spring Chicken* off Cape Hatteras, North Carolina, 36°51'N, 75°11'W.

6 Thursday

PACIFIC. RAAF Beaufighters sink small Japanese tanker *Myosho Maru* in Koepang, Timor, harbor.

Japanese cargo vessel *Arabia Maru* is damaged by mine off Takao, Formosa.

Japanese transport *Hsing Yun Maru* is sunk by USAAF mine in the Yangtze River near Chinkiang, 32°05'N, 119°56'E.

MEDITERRANEAN. Infantry landing craft (gunboat) *LCI(G) 34* is damaged by shore battery off Anzio.

U.S. motor torpedo boats engage German E-boats and a flak ship south of Vada Rocks, Corsica, sinking one E-boat; flak ship later explodes as the result of gunfire damage. Enemy shore batteries take the motor torpedo boats under fire but inflict no damage.

7 Friday

PACIFIC. Destroyer *Saufley* (DD 465) sinks Japanese submarine *I 2*, 50 miles west-north-west of New Hanover, 02°17'S, 149°14'E.

Submarine *Pampanito* (SS 383) is damaged by depth charges off the Marianas, 12°46'N, 143°49'E, but remains on patrol.

Submarine *Scamp* (SS 277) is damaged by bomb from Japanese floatplane off Mindanao, 05°02'N, 126°07'E, and is forced to terminate her patrol.

ATLANTIC. Destroyer *Champlin* (DD 601) is damaged when she intentionally rams German submarine *U 856*, 380 miles southeast of Cape Sable, 40°18'N, 62°22'W; *Champlin* and destroyer escort *Huse* (DE 145) team to sink *U 856*.

8 Saturday

PACIFIC. Submarine *Seahorse* (SS 304) attacks Japanese convoy seven miles off Guam, torpedoing ammunition ship *Aratama Maru*; debris from explosion damages escorting destroyer *Asakaze*. Destroyer *Akikaze* and guardboat *Mifuku Maru* are ordered to search for *Seahorse*. *Seahorse* also torpedoes water tanker *Kizugawa Maru*, 13°16'N, 145°11'E. After destroyer *Minazuki* and submarine chaser *Ch 30* conduct unsuccessful pursuit of the submarine, *Minazuki* tows *Kizugawa Maru* to port while the crippled *Aratama Maru*, burning, drifts ashore, where she explodes and sinks the next day.

Submarine *Trigger* (SS 237) attacks TOSHO No. 4 convoy off the Marianas, but counterattacking escorts drop depth charges, 19°06'N, 142°36'E. Although damaged, *Trigger* remains on patrol (see 9 April).

9 Sunday

PACIFIC. Submarine chaser *SC 984* is damaged by grounding, Cooks Reef, near Mai Island, New Hebrides. She is abandoned the following day, a total loss.

Submarine *Seahorse* (SS 304) attacks Japanese Matsu No. 4 convoy, and sinks transport *Misaku Maru* about 40 miles west of Saipan, 15°32'N, 145°00'E; destroyer *Ikazuchi* and minelayer *Sokuten* are dispatched to carry out countermeasures and rescue survivors.

Submarine *Trigger* (SS 237) is again damaged by depth charges off the Marianas, 19°03'N, 142°31'E, but, as before, remains on patrol.

Submarine *Whale* (SS 239) sinks Japanese army cargo ship *Honan Maru* off northwestern coast of Kyushu, 33°45'N, 128°42'E.

USAAF B-25s (14th Air Force) sink Japanese freighter *Hokurei Maru* off southern tip of Hainan Island, 19°00'N, 110°00'E.

Japanese hospital ship *Takasago Maru* is damaged by mine off Palau.

ATLANTIC. TBMs and FM-2s (VC 58) from escort carrier *Guadalcanal* (CVE 60), together with destroyer escorts *Pillsbury* (DE 133), *Pope*

(DE 134), *Flaherty* (DE 135), and *Chatelain* (DE 149), sink German submarine *U 515* off Madeira Island, 34°35'N, 19°18'W.

MEDITERRANEAN. Destroyer *Hilary P. Jones* (DD 427) provides gunfire support off Anzio.

10 Monday

PACIFIC. Small seaplane tender *Chincoteague* (AVP 24) is damaged by grounding near entrance to Funafuti Channel, Ellice Islands.

Navy plane (possibly a PB4Y) bombs Japanese shipping off Woleai, Carolines, damaging transport *No. 18 Nissho Maru.*

ATLANTIC. TBMs and FM-2s (VC 58) from escort carrier *Guadalcanal* (CVE 60) sink German submarine *U 68* off Madeira Island, 33°25'N, 18°59'W.

MEDITERRANEAN. Convoy UGS 37 transits Straits of Gibraltar (60 merchantmen and six tank landing ships), escorted by TF 65 (Commander William R. Headden): four destroyers, eight destroyer escorts, and British anti-aircraft cruiser HMS *Delhi* and frigate HMS *Nadder*, in addition to radar-jamming ships, destroyer *Lansdale* (DD 426) and British corvette HMS *Jonquil* (see 11 April). Escorts keep German submarines *U 421*, *U 471*, and *U 969* at bay.

11 Tuesday

PACIFIC. Submarine *Cero* (SS 225) is bombed by USAAF B-24 (5th Air Force) northeast by east of Biak, 01°00'N, 139°20'E. Although *Cero* suffers minor damage, she continues on her war patrol.

Submarine *Redfin* (SS 272) sinks Japanese destroyer *Akigumo* in eastern entrance to Basilan Strait, 06°43'N, 122°23'E.

PB4Y sinks Japanese auxiliary net tender *Shosei Maru* off Vanimo on the northern coast of New Guinea.

MEDITERRANEAN. German planes begin attack on convoy UGS 37. Destroyer escort *Holder* (DE 401) is damaged by aerial torpedo 35 miles northeast of Algiers, 37°03'N, 03°58'E, as she lays smoke ahead of the convoy. Freighter *Charles Piez* is damaged by strafing, 37°10'N, 03°45'E; her crew (including a 28-man Armed Guard), however, suffers no casualties. Aerial torpedoes narrowly miss destroyer escorts *Stanton* (DE 247) and *Swasey* (DE 248) (see 12 April).

Increased German aerial mining activities are noted off Anzio.

12 Wednesday

PACIFIC. Motor torpedo boat *PT 135*, damaged by grounding one-half mile north of Crater Point, New Britain, 05°21'S, 152°09'E, is scuttled by crew and motor torpedo boat *PT 137.*

Submarine *Halibut* (SS 232), despite presence of at least three escort vessels, sinks Japanese army passenger-cargo ship *Taichu Maru* about 20 miles southwest of the Nansei Shoto, 28°08'N, 128°57'E.

USAAF B-24s, B-25s, B-26s, and P-38s (5th Air Force) bomb Japanese installations and shipping at Hollandia, sinking army cargo ship *Narita Maru* and fishing vessels *Aiko Maru*, *Kompira Maru*, and *Kyoei Maru*. USAAF A-20s (5th Air Force) sink army cargo ship *Narita Maru* in Humboldt Bay, Hollandia, 02°30'S, 140°52'E.

ATLANTIC. Rescue tug *ATR 98* is sunk in collision with tug *Abnaki* (AT 96) off the Azores, 44°04.8'N, 24°08'W.

MEDITERRANEAN. German air attack, which began shortly before midnight, on convoy UGS 37 concludes west of Algiers. U.S. freighter *Horace H. Lurton* is damaged by friendly fire; five men from the 44-man crew and 28-man Armed Guard are injured. Destroyer *Breckinridge* (DD 148) provides medical assistance.

13 Thursday

PACIFIC. Submarine *Bashaw* (SS 241), operating in an area in which no bombing of submarines is permitted under any circumstances, is mistakenly bombed by USAAF B-24 southwest of Truk, 04°30'N, 147°26'E. *Bashaw* is not damaged and proceeds toward her assigned patrol area.

Submarine *Harder* (SS 257) sinks Japanese destroyer *Ikazuchi* 180 miles south-southwest of Guam, 10°13'N, 143°51'E.

Japanese cargo vessel *Kumano Maru* is sunk by mine, Mergui Harbor.

14 Friday

MEDITERRANEAN. Three U.S. motor torpedo boats and two British Fairmile "D" patrol craft brave intense German shore battery fire to carry out two torpedo attacks on north-bound German F-lighters off San Vincenzio, Italy. No hits are observed.

INDIAN OCEAN. British freighter *Samuta* rescues 38 survivors of U.S. freighter *Richard Hovey*, sunk by Japanese submarine *I 26* on 29 March.

15 Saturday

PACIFIC. Alaskan Sea Frontier (Vice Admiral Frank Jack Fletcher) with headquarters at Adak, Aleutians, and Seventeenth Naval District (Rear Admiral Francis E. M. Whiting) with temporary headquarters at Adak and permanent headquarters at Kodiak, Alaska, are established.

Submarine *Redfin* (SS 272), in attack on Japanese convoy southwest of Mindanao, damages army cargo ship *Shinyo Maru*, 06°22'N, 123°42'E (see 16 April).

USAAF B-25s attack Ponape, Carolines, and Japanese convoy approaching the island; guardboat *Hakuo Maru* and two fishing boats are sunk.

Japanese freighter *Sumida Maru* is sunk by Japanese mine off southern Hokkaido, 42°04'N, 142°22'E.

Naval Base, Abemama, Gilbert Islands, is established.

ANDAMAN SEA. British submarine HMS *Storm* sinks Japanese minesweeper *W.7* about 30 miles east of Port Blair, Andaman Islands, 11°34'N, 93°08'E.

16 Sunday

PACIFIC. Submarine *Paddle* (SS 263) attacks Japanese convoy and sinks Japanese army transport *Mito Maru* and freighter *No. 1 Hino Maru* in the Ceram Sea, 02°25'S, 127°24'E.

Submarine *Redfin* (SS 272) continues to pursue the convoy attacked the previous day, sinking army cargo ship *Yamagata Maru* in Moro Gulf, southwest of Mindanao, 06°52'N, 123°47'E.

PB2Ys and PB4Ys operating from Eniwetok begin mining the principal entrance channels to Truk; between this date and 20 April, these aircraft will carry out 19 successful sorties.

RAAF Catalinas mine the principal entrances to Woleai, Carolines, to prevent the Japanese from using them during the projected Hollandia operations. The evolution is repeated on 18 and 19 April.

Movement of Japanese TAKE No. 1 convoy, deploying elements of the 32nd and 35th Divisions to reinforce garrisons in the Halmaheras and in northwestern New Guinea, gets under way as four transports and escorts depart Pusan, Korea (see 18 April).

Battleship *Colorado* (BB 45) runs aground on Kuia Shoal, off Kahoolawe, T.H., but suffers no serious damage.

ATLANTIC. Battleship *Wisconsin* (BB 64)—the last battleship in the U.S. Navy—is commissioned at Philadelphia, Pennsylvania.

U.S. tanker *Pan Pennsylvania*, in United Kingdom–bound convoy CU 1, is torpedoed by German submarine *U 550*, 150 miles east of Ambrose Light, 40°05′N, 69°40′W, and abandoned. Ten of the 31-man Armed Guard sailors perish in the action, as do 15 of the 50-man merchant complement; survivors are picked up by destroyer escorts *Joyce* (DE 317) and *Peterson* (DE 152). Later, destroyer escort *Gandy* (DE 764) is damaged when she intentionally rams German submarine *U 550* off Nantucket Shoals, 40°09′N, 69°44′W, and teams with *Peterson* and *Joyce* to sink the U-boat. During the action, shells from the destroyer escorts set afire *Pan Pennsylvania*'s abandoned wreck. Net tender *Hazel* (YN 24) and Coast Guard cutter *General Greene* (WPC 140) are sent from Newport, Rhode Island, with fire-fighting parties (see 17 April).

Destroyer escort *Enright* (DE 216) is damaged in collision with Portuguese freighter *Thome*, 37°58′N, 69°50′W (see 17 April).

MEDITERRANEAN. German submarine *U 407* attacks convoy UGS 37 about 17 miles off Derna, Libya, torpedoing U.S. freighters *Meyer London* and *Thomas G. Masaryk*, 32°51′N, 23°00′E; the latter, out of control at one point, nearly rams *Meyer London*. There are no casualties on board either ship (including the 27-man Armed Guard in each freighter). British corvette HMS *La Malouine* rescues *Meyer London*'s crew; another escort vessel rescues the other ship's complement. British rescue tug HMS *Captive* later tows *Thomas G. Masaryk* and beaches her in Maneloa Bay, Libya, where the damaged ship is subsequently written off as a total loss. *Meyer London* sinks.

17 Monday

PACIFIC. Submarines *Barb* (SS 220) and *Steelhead* (SS 280) shell phosphate works on Rasa Island, Okino Daito Jima.

Submarine *Harder* (SS 257), in attack on Japanese convoy, sinks army cargo ship *Matsue Maru* about 150 miles northwest of Woleai, Carolines, 09°30′N, 142°35′E.

Submarine *Searaven* (SS 196) sinks Japanese auxiliary minesweeper *No. 2 Noshiro Maru* 120 miles south of Haha Jima, Bonins, 26°01′N, 142°14′E.

USAAF B-25s sink Japanese lugger *No. 2 Mikage Maru* off Aitape, New Guinea, 02°41′S, 141°18′E.

ATLANTIC. Minesweeper *Swift* (AM 122) and submarine chaser *PC 619* sink German submarine *U 986*, North Atlantic, 50°09′N, 12°51′W.

Destroyer escort *Enright* (DE 216), damaged in collision with Portuguese freighter *Thome* the day before, is towed into New York by salvage tug *Resolute* (NRTS).

U.S. tanker *Pan Pennsylvania*, torpedoed by German submarine *U 550* on 16 April and abandoned, is scuttled at 40°23′20″N, 69°36′30″W.

MEDITERRANEAN. U.S. freighters *James Guthrie* and *Alexander Graham Bell*, in convoy NV 33, are damaged by Allied mines off Isle of Capri, *James Guthrie* at 40°34′10″N, 14°16′50″E, and *Alexander Graham Bell* at 40°34′150″N, 14°17′20″E. *James Guthrie* is abandoned and taken in tow by salvage vessel *Weight* (ARS 35). Towed to Naples, *James Guthrie* is subsequently written off as a total loss. There are no casualties among either the merchant complement or the 28-man Armed Guard. *Alexander Graham Bell* returns to Naples under her own power and is repaired and returned to service. There are no casualties among the 42-man Armed Guard and only two injured from the merchant crew.

18 Tuesday

PACIFIC. PB4Ys (VD 3) conduct long-range reconnaissance of Saipan, Tinian, and Aguijan Islands, Marianas, obtaining complete photographic coverage. USAAF B-24s provide close air support; battle damage forces one B-24 to ditch (see 22 April).

Submarine *Gudgeon* (SS 211) is sunk, probably by Japanese naval aircraft (901st *Kokutai*), southwest of Iwo Jima, 22°44′N, 143°25′E.

Submarine *Tambor* (SS 198) sinks Japanese guardboat *No. 3 Shinko Maru* 300 miles northwest of Wake Island. One of three boats deployed to intercept the patrol vessel, *Tambor* takes one POW and recovers new codes destined for the garrison at Wake.

Second element of Japanese TAKE No. 1 convoy sails from Shanghai and effects rendezvous with the first group that had departed Pusan, Korea, on 16 April.

U.S. freighter *John Straub* hits a mine off Sanak Island, Aleutians, 54°15′N, 163°30′W, and sinks, breaking in two; 14 of the 27-man Armed Guard perish, as do 40 merchant seamen and the ship's solitary passenger. Army coastal freighter *FP 41* rescues the survivors; frigate *Albuquerque* (PF 7) later scuttles the stern half with gunfire.

19 Wednesday

PACIFIC. Operation COCKPIT: Allied naval force (Admiral Sir James F. Somerville, RN, Com-

mander in Chief, British Eastern Fleet), including U.S. carrier *Saratoga* (CV 3) and three U.S. destroyers, strikes Japanese positions and shipping at Sabang, N.E.I., in the first operation in which Pacific Fleet units operate alongside British in offensive action in the Indian Ocean. Planes from *Saratoga* and HMS *Illustrious* sink minelayer *Hatsutaka*, transport *Kunitsu Maru*, and army transport *Haruno Maru*. Pilot of only F6F (VF 12) (from *Saratoga*) shot down by antiaircraft guns is picked up by British submarine HMS *Tactician*, which braves shore battery fire to do so.

Submarine *Finback* (SS 230) sinks Japanese sampan *Ryuho Maru* northwest of Truk, 08°22′N, 151°41′E.

British submarine HMS *Tantalus* sinks tug *Kampung Besar* (nationality unspecified) in Strait of Malacca.

ATLANTIC. TBF (VC 13) from escort carrier *Tripoli* (CVE 64), in TG 21.4, attacks German submarine *U 543* with rockets and depth bombs in the face of heavy antiaircraft fire; *U 543*, however, escapes.

20 Thursday

PACIFIC. Submarine *Seahorse* (SS 304) sinks Japanese submarine *RO 45* off the Marianas, 15°19′N, 145°31′E. *Seahorse*'s sinking of *RO 45* is testimony to effective training. During passage to the patrol area with submarine *Harder* (SS 257), the boats had practiced approaches on each other.

MEDITERRANEAN. German torpedo planes (reported as HE 111s and JU 88s), on the heels of an unsuccessful attack by submarine *U 969*, attack 87-ship convoy UGS 38 off coast of Algeria. Destroyer *Lansdale* (DD 426) is sunk by aerial torpedo about 15 miles northeast of Algiers, 37°03′N, 03°51′E; destroyer escorts *Menges* (DE 320) and *Newell* (DE 322) rescue survivors. Torpedoes narrowly miss Coast Guard cutter *Taney* (WPG 37), destroyer escort *Lowe* (DE 325), and Dutch antiaircraft cruiser *Van Heemskerk*. Not as fortunate is ammunition-carrying U.S. freighter *Paul Hamilton*, which is struck by an aerial torpedo at 36°55′N, 03°54′E, and disintegrates. Search by destroyer escort *Edgar G. Chase* (DE 16) yields no survivors from among the 47-man merchant complement, the 29-man Armed Guard, and the 504 troops. Illuminated by the explosion, freighter *Stephen F. Austin*, at 37°02′N, 03°38′E, is torpedoed and abandoned. Reboarded, the ship receives assistance from British rescue tug HMS *Hengist* and proceeds to Algiers under her own power. British freighters *Samite* and *Royal Star* are also torpedoed, but reach port; *Edgar G. Chase* provides medical treatment to the wounded on board *Stephen F. Austin* and *Royal Star*.

21 Friday

PACIFIC. TF 58 (Vice Admiral Marc A. Mitscher), including carriers, battleships, cruisers, and destroyers, pounds Japanese airfields and defensive positions at Hollandia, Wakde, Sawar, and Sarmi, New Guinea; attacks continue the following day in preparation for Operations PERSECUTION and RECKLESS (see 22 April). Preparatory work by the 5th Air Force, together with the weakness of the Japanese forces and installations in the region, however, means that "not much support from TF 58 was required." Nevertheless, during these operations, Japanese army cargo ship *Kansei Maru* is sunk off Sarmi, as are fishing boats *No. 6 Yoshitoku Maru*, *No. 7 Choei Maru*, and *No. 10 Kompira Maru*; fishing vessels *No. 51 Ume Maru* and *No. 2 Hinode Maru* are sunk off Mapia Island; and fishing boats *Hokushin Maru*, *No. 1 Kaiyo Maru*, and *Kiku Maru* are sunk off Hollandia.

Submarine *Stingray* (SS 186) is sunk when she strikes submerged pinnacle west of the Marianas, 20°30'N, 142°22'E.

MEDITERRANEAN. U.S. freighter *John Armstrong* is damaged by mine at 41°12'N, 12°32'E, while en route from Anzio to Naples. One Armed Guard sailor perishes in the incident, but the ship reaches her original destination unaided.

22 Saturday

PACIFIC. TF 77 (Rear Admiral Daniel E. Barbey) lands two divisions of the I Army Corps (Lieutenant General Robert L. Eichelberger) at Aitape and Tanahmerah Bay in Operation PERSECUTION, and Humboldt Bay, Hollandia, New Guinea, in Operation RECKLESS, 300 miles inside the outer Japanese defensive perimeter. TG 77.1 (Rear Admiral Barbey) lands the 163rd RCT, 41st Infantry Division (Brigadier General Jens A. Doe) at Aitape; TG 77.2 (Rear Admiral William M. Fechteler) lands the 24th Infantry Division (Major General Frederick A. Irving) at Tanahmerah Bay; TG 77.3 (Captain Albert G. Noble) lands the 41st Infantry Division (Major General Irving) at Humboldt Bay. Escort carrier force (TF 78) (Rear Admiral Ralph E. Davison) provides close air support while TF 74 (Rear Admiral Victor A. C. Crutchley, RN) and TF 75 (Rear Admiral Russell S. Berkey) provide gunfire

support for landings that proceed against slight resistance. TF 58 (Vice Admiral Marc A. Mitscher) also provides support. Hollandia becomes a major staging area for the next phase of the New Guinea campaign.

PB4Y sights survivors of USAAF B-24, damaged over the Marianas and ditched on 18 April; PBY sent to rescue the aviators, however, suffers damage in landing and is unable to take off (see 23 April).

Small seaplane tender *Onslow* (AVP 48) and motor minesweeper *YMS 91* support occupation by U.S. Army landing force (Company "I," 3rd Battalion, 111th Infantry) of Ujelang, thus extending U.S. control over the westernmost atoll in the Marshalls.

USAAF B-24s (14th Air Force) attack Japanese Singapore-to-Saigon (SISA 17) convoy at Cape St. Jacques, French Indochina, sinking transport (ex-gunboat) *Nagata Maru*, 10°19'N, 107°05'E, fleet tanker *Koryu Maru*, army cargo vessel *London Maru*, and merchant tanker *No. 3 Sansui Maru*, and damaging tanker *Nisshin Maru*. Sole escort vessel, submarine chaser *Ch 9*, escapes the low-level onslaught unscathed.

PB4Ys sink Japanese transport *Suiten Maru* off Murilo Island, Carolines.[189]

British submarine HMS *Taurus* sinks salvage vessel *Hokuan I-Go* off Malaya, 07°10'N, 99°20'E.

EUROPE. U.S. freighter *George Popham*, in convoy FS 28, is damaged by mine while en route from Methel, Scotland, to London, England, at 51°11'20"N, 01°48'40"E, but reaches her destination under her own power. There are no casualties to the merchant complement or the 29-man Armed Guard.

23 Sunday

PACIFIC. Destroyer *Gansevoort* (DD 608) rescues USAAF B-24 crew, damaged over the Marianas and ditched on 18 April, as well as their would-be rescuers from a PBY, damaged on 22 April.

Submarine *Seadragon* (SS 194) attacks Japanese convoy and sinks freighter *Daiju Maru* off Shiono Misaki, Honshu, 33°26'N, 135°46'E.

Dutch submarine *K XV*, operating under U.S. control for the Netherlands Intelligence Service, sinks a prau and a coaster off New Guinea.

Japanese destroyer *Amagiri* (transporting air base materiel) is sunk by USAAF mine in Makassar Strait about 50 miles south of Balikpapan, 02°12'S, 116°45'E. Heavy cruiser *Aoba* rescues survivors.

24 Monday

PACIFIC. Destroyers *Benham* (DD 796) and *Uhlmann* (DD 687) are damaged in collision during night maneuvers with carriers, south of Oahu, T.H.

Submarine *Robalo* (SS 273) is damaged by aerial bomb off French Indochina, 10°29'N, 109°26'E, but remains on patrol.

Navy aircraft sink Japanese fishing vessel *No. 5 Shinho Maru* and *Mizuno Maru* off north coast of Vogelkop Peninsula, New Guinea.

Japanese army cargo ship *Taka Maru* is sunk by aircraft north of New Guinea, 01°36'S, 138°47'E.

USAAF B-24s damage Japanese fishing vessels *No. 5 Takara Maru* and *No. 25 Sumiyoshi Maru* off western New Guinea.

25 Tuesday

PACIFIC. Submarine *Crevalle* (SS 291) sinks Japanese army cargo ship *Kashiwa Maru* north of Borneo, 07°11'N, 116°46'E.

Submarine *Guavina* (SS 362) sinks Japanese army cargo ship *Tetsuyo Maru* northwest of Chichi Jima, 28°55'N, 140°28'E.

Japanese army cargo ship *Jinsan Maru* is damaged by mine, Saipan, Marianas.

Japanese auxiliary minesweeper *No. 32 Kafuku Maru* is sunk by mine.

MEDITERRANEAN. German mining operations commence off Capreira, Italy; minelayer *TA 23* sinks after striking a mine. *TA 26* and *TA 29* battle U.S. motor torpedo boats *PT 202*, *PT 213*, and *PT 218*.

26 Wednesday

PACIFIC. Destroyer escort *Gilmore* (DE 18) sinks Japanese submarine *I 180*, southwest of Cherikof Island, Aleutians, 55°10'N, 155°40'W.

Submarine *Bonefish* (SS 223) sinks Japanese transport *Tokiwa Maru* at entrance to Davao Gulf, 06°13'N, 125°49'E.

Submarine *Guavina* (SS 362) attacks Japanese convoy and sinks transport *Noshiro Maru I-Go* off Miko Jima, 28°42'N, 141°26'E; attack on cargo ship *No. 2 Asahi Maru* is unsuccessful.

Submarine *Jack* (SS 259) encounters Japanese TAKE No. 1 convoy off west coast of Luzon and sinks army transport *No. 1 Yoshida Maru*, 18°06'N, 119°40'E, and damages army cargo ship *Wales Maru*, 18°14'N, 119°53'E.

Submarine *Sargo* (SS 188) attacks Japanese convoy and sinks army cargo ship *Wazan Maru* (ex-British *Vitorlock*) off Ichiye Saki, Honshu, 33°31'N, 135°24'E.

ATLANTIC. Destroyer escorts *Frost* (DE 144), *Huse* (DE 145), *Barber* (DE 161), and *Snowden* (DE 246) sink German submarine *U 488* west by north of the Canary Islands, 17°54′N, 38°05′W.

27 Thursday

PACIFIC. Cargo ship *Etamin* (AK 93) is damaged by aerial torpedo off Aitape, New Guinea, 03°09′S, 142°24′E.

Japanese TAKE No. 1 convoy reaches Manila.

Submarine *Bluegill* (SS 242) torpedoes Japanese light cruiser *Yubari* west of Sonsorol Island, 05°20′N, 132°16′E; destroyer *Samidare* attempts to tow the crippled ship (see 28 April).

Submarine *Halibut* (SS 232) attacks Japanese convoy and sinks minelayer *Kamome* west of the Nansei Shoto, about 40 miles north of Okinawa, 27°28′N, 128°02′E, and merchant transport *Genbu Maru*, 27°16′N, 128°21′E.

Submarine *Seadragon* (SS 194) damages Japanese freighter *Hawaii Maru* off Shikoku, 33°16′N, 135°48′E.

Submarine *Seahorse* (SS 304) attacks Japanese convoy and sinks transport *Akikawa Maru* about 150 miles west of Saipan, 14°46′N, 143°22′E, and survives depth charging by escorts.

Submarine *Trigger* (SS 237) attacks Japanese convoy about 90 miles north of Palau, 'sinks transport *Mike Maru*, 08°34′N, 134°53′E, and damages escort vessel *Kasado* and army cargo ship *Asosan Maru*, 08°32′N, 134°42′E (see 1 May).

Japanese submarine *I 37* is damaged south of Penang, Malaya, by mine laid by British submarine HMS *Taurus* on 18 April.

USAAF B-24 damages Japanese cargo vessel *Anshu Maru* off Biak, New Guinea.

Japanese auxiliary minesweeper *Hadayoshi Maru* is damaged by mine off Balikpapan, Borneo.

28 Friday

UNITED STATES. Secretary of the Navy William Franklin (Frank) Knox dies in Washington, D.C.

ATLANTIC. German motor torpedo boats *S 100*, *S 130*, *S 136*, *S 138*, *S 140*, *S 142*, *S 143*, *S 145*, and *S 150* (5th and 9th Motor Torpedo Boat Flotillas) attack convoy of eight U.S. tank landing ships entering Lyme Bay, torpedoing and sinking *LST 507* and *LST 531* off Portland Bill, England, 50°28′N, 02°51′W, and damaging *LST 289*.

PACIFIC. Japanese light cruiser *Yubari*, torpedoed by submarine *Bluegill* (SS 242) the previous day, is abandoned, and her crew is taken on board destroyer *Yuzuki*. *Yubari* then sinks off Sonsorol Island, 05°38′N, 131°45′E.

29 Saturday

PACIFIC. TF 58 (Vice Admiral Marc A. Mitscher), including five carriers and seven small carriers, after completing its support of the Hollandia landings, begins two-day attack on Japanese shipping, oil and ammunition dumps, aircraft facilities, and other installations at Truk. Japanese naval aircraft mount strong counterattack on the U.S. formations during which destroyer *Tingey* (DD 539), in TG 58.2, is damaged by friendly fire (see 30 April).

TBF (VT 30) from small carrier *Monterey* (CVL 26), and destroyers *MacDonough* (DD 351) and *Stephen Potter* (DD 538), sink Japanese submarine *I 174* north of Truk, 06°13′N, 151°19′E.

Motor torpedo boats *PT 346* and *PT 347* are accidentally sunk by F4Us (VMF 215) and F6Fs (VF 34), and SBDs and TBFs, respectively, off Cape Lambert, Bismarck Archipelago, 04°13′S, 151°27′E. PBY (VP 91) rescues survivors from the two boats.

Submarines *Bang* (SS 385), *Parche* (SS 384), and *Tinosa* (SS 283) attack Japanese convoy off northwest coast of Luzon. *Bang* sinks army cargo ship *Takegawa Maru* in South China Sea, 19°20′N, 118°50′E, and damages *Yashima Maru* (see 30 April).

Submarine *Flasher* (SS 249) damages Vichy French cargo ship *Song Giang Go* in South China Sea, five miles off Cape Varella, French Indochina, 13°02′N, 109°28′E (see 30 April).

Submarine *Halibut* (SS 232) bombards Japanese installations on Kure Jima, Japan.

Submarine *Pogy* (SS 266) sinks Japanese submarine *I 183*, 30 miles south of Ashizuri Saki, Japan, 32°07′N, 133°03′E.

Japanese transport *Kunikawa Maru* is sunk by mine laid by RAAF Catalinas (mining operations took place on 20, 24, and 27 April) near Balikpapan, Borneo, 01°17′S, 116°49′E.

British submarine HMS *Tantalus* sinks coaster *Pulo Salanama* in Strait of Malacca.

MEDITERRANEAN. USAAF B-17s and B-24s bomb targets in northern Italy and in southern France; during the raid on Toulon, German submarine *U 421* is sunk in harbor.

30 Sunday

PACIFIC. TF 58 air strikes against Japanese installations in the Carolines continue. Reflect-

ing an expected paucity of shipping targets in the area (no large Japanese warships base at Truk), planes from carrier *Lexington* (CV 16) and small carriers *Langley* (CVL 27) and *Monterey* (CVL 26) sink transport *Minsei Maru*, 07°30′N, 134°30′E, and merchant vessel *No. 2 Tenyu Maru*. Planes from small carrier *Cabot* (CVL 28) damage gunboat *No. 2 Hino Maru* at Truk (see 4 May). Planes from *Langley* sink auxiliary submarine chaser *Cha 38* (and the landing barge she is towing) off the south rim of the reef at Truk.

Task force (Rear Admiral Jesse B. Oldendorf) of nine heavy cruisers and eight destroyers detached from TF 58 bombards Japanese positions on Satawan Island in the Namoi Group, Carolines.

Japanese TAKE No. 1 convoy, one group of ships destined for Manokwari, New Guinea, and the other for Halmahera, sails from Manila (see 6 May).

Submarine *Bang* (SS 385) continues attack on convoy engaged the previous night, and sinks Japanese merchant tanker *Nittatsu Maru* off northwest coast of Luzon, 19°04′N, 119°14′E.

Submarine *Flasher* (SS 249) sinks Vichy French gunboat *Tahure* in South China Sea off Cape Varella, French Indochina, 13°02′N, 109°28′E. Damaged Vichy French cargo ship, *Song Giang Go*, torpedoed the day before by *Flasher*, sinks.

ATLANTIC. U.S. freighter *Joseph Warren* grounds on Fenwick Island Shoal, 38°27′N, 74°56′W; tug *Allegheny* (AT 19) and salvage vessel *Relief* (NRTS) proceed to the merchantman's assistance. *Allegheny* refloats the ship and assists her to the Delaware Breakwater.

ARCTIC. U.S. freighter *William S. Thayer*, in convoy RA 59, is torpedoed by German submarine *U 711*, 50 miles south of Bear Island, 73°46′N, 19°10′E, and breaks into thirds; 23 of the 41-man merchant complement perish, as do seven of the 28-man Armed Guard and 20 of the 165 Soviet Navy passengers. Freighter *Robert Eden* and British destroyer HMS *Whitehall* rescue the survivors; escorts scuttle the stern section of the ship with gunfire.

MAY

1 Monday

PACIFIC. Supported by carrier planes from TG 58.1, TG 58.7 (Vice Admiral Willis A. Lee Jr.), consisting of seven battleships screened by 14 destroyers, bombards wharf areas, seaplane base, and other Japanese installations on Ponape, Carolines.

Submarine *Bluegill* (SS 242) sinks Japanese army cargo ship *Asosan Maru,* repaired after her encounter with *Trigger* (SS 237) on 27 April, east of Mindanao, 07°05′N, 130°00′E.

PB4Y damages Japanese cargo vessel *Anshu Maru* off Biak, New Guinea.

District patrol vessel *YP 95* sinks after running aground in Beyer Bay, south shore of Adak, Aleutians, while assisting in a minesweeping mission.

2 Tuesday

PACIFIC. Submarine *Tautog* (SS 199) completes destruction of Japanese army transport *Ryuyo Maru,* grounded 4 March, off Matsuwa Jima, Kurils, 48°04′N, 153°16′E.

ATLANTIC. Destroyer *Parrott* (DD 218) is damaged in collision with U.S. freighter *John Morton* off Norfolk, Virginia, 36°51′N, 76°18′W.

3 Wednesday

PACIFIC. Submarine *Flasher* (SS 249) sinks Japanese freighter *Teisen Maru* in the South China Sea about 300 miles east of Cape Varella, French Indochina, 12°54′N, 114°07′E.

Submarine *Sand Lance* (SS 381) sinks Japanese transport *Kenan Maru* about 15 miles northwest of Saipan, 15°20′N, 145°34′E.

Submarine *Tautog* (SS 199) sinks Japanese army cargo ship *Fushimi Maru* off south coast of Uruppu Island, Kurils, 45°28′N, 149°56′E.

Submarine *Tinosa* (SS 283) sinks Japanese freighter *Toyohi Maru* west of Bashi Channel between Formosa and Luzon, 20°51′N, 118°02′E.

USAAF B-24s (14th Air Force) attack Japanese convoy southwest of Takao, Formosa, sinking cargo ship *Shingu Maru,* 22°05′N, 117°50′E.

INDIAN OCEAN. British submarine HMS *Tantalus* sinks Japanese army cargo ship *Amagi Maru* 40 miles south of Port Blair, 11°00′N, 92°00′E.

ATLANTIC. Destroyer escort *Donnell* (DE 56) is damaged by German submarine *U 765,* 450 miles southwest of Cape Clear, Ireland.

Tugs *Sagamore* (ATO 20) and *Rescue* (NRTS) tow disabled U.S. tanker *Sharpsburg* to New York after the latter had broken down at 39°50′N, 73°07′W.

MEDITERRANEAN. As convoy GUS 38 heads west toward the Straits of Gibraltar, German submarine *U 371* closes in; destroyer escort *Menges* (DE 320) locates the enemy but is torpedoed and damaged by her quarry off

Bougie, Algeria. Consequently, destroyer escorts *Pride* (DE 323) and *Joseph E. Campbell* (DE 70) hunt for *U 371,* joined by British destroyer HMS *Blankney,* French destroyer *L'Alycon* and destroyer escort *Senegalais,* and minesweeper *Sustain* (AM 119). *U 371,* however, escapes (see 4 May).

4 Thursday

PACIFIC. Submarines *Bang* (SS 385), *Parche* (SS 384), and *Tinosa* (SS 283) attack Japanese convoy of freighters in Luzon Strait. *Bang* sinks *Kinrei Maru,* 20°58′N, 117°59′E; *Parche* sinks *Shoryu Maru* and *Taiyoku Maru,* 20°48′N, 118°03′E; and *Tinosa* sinks *Taibu Maru* and *Toyohi Maru,* 20°55′N, 118°12′E.

Submarine *Pargo* (SS 264) sinks Japanese auxiliary netlayer *Eiryu Maru* east of Mindanao, 07°14′N, 129°12′E.

Submarine *Tuna* (SS 203) sinks Japanese guardboat *Tajima Maru* north of Wake Island, 22°06′N, 166°47′E. Lost with *Tajima Maru* are new codes earmarked for delivery to Wake.

At Truk, Japanese guardboat *Sapporo Maru* is sunk by aircraft; gunboat *No. 2 Hino Maru* sinks as the result of damage inflicted by TF 58 planes on 30 April.

Japanese convoy 3503 (10 *Marus* and six escorts) leaves Tateyama, bound for the Marshalls (see 10 and 14 May).

Naval Base and Naval Air Facility, Majuro, Marshalls, are established.

MEDITERRANEAN. While convoy GUS 38 proceeds onward, destroyer escorts *Joseph E. Campbell* (DE 70) and *Pride* (DE 323), French destroyer escort *Senegalais,* and British destroyer HMS *Blankney* continue the hunt for German submarine *U 371* in the western Mediterranean. *Senegalais* attacks the U-boat, 37°49′N, 05°39′E, which is scuttled by her crew and abandoned, but not before *U 371* has torpedoed and damaged *Senegalais.*

5 Friday

PACIFIC. Appointment of Japanese Admiral Toyoda Soemu as Commander in Chief of the Combined Fleet is announced.

U.S. motor torpedo boats blockading the southeastern coast of Bougainville, Solomons, encounter five or more heavily armed Japanese barges. In the ensuing action, the barges and enemy shore batteries on Rantan and Bougainville catch the three PTs in a cross fire, sinking *PT 247,* 06°38′S, 156°01′E.

Submarine *Pogy* (SS 266) attacks Japanese convoy and sinks transport *Shirane Maru* off Shiono Misaki, Honshu, 33°27′N, 135°32′E.

Japanese submarine *I 155* is damaged in collision with fleet tanker/seaplane carrier *Hayasui* in Hiroshima Wan.

MEDITERRANEAN. During convoy GUS 38's continued passage westward, destroyer escort *Laning* (DE 159) locates German submarine *U 967,* but the U-boat torpedoes and sinks destroyer escort *Fechteler* (DE 157) 120 miles northwest of Oran, Algeria, 36°07′N, 02°40′W. *Laning* and tug *Hengist* rescue the survivors.

6 Saturday

PACIFIC. Submarine *Crevalle* (SS 291) attacks Japanese convoy off northern Borneo, sinking fleet tanker *Nisshin Maru* about 40 miles west of Kalutan Island, 07°19′N, 116°52′E.

Submarine *Gurnard* (SS 254) encounters Japanese TAKE No. 1 convoy in the Celebes Sea, sinking Manokwari, New Guinea–bound troop-carrying army cargo ships *Aden Maru, Amatsuzan Maru,* and *Tajima Maru* northwest of Bangka Island, 02°39′N, 124°10′E (see 7 May).

Submarine *Spearfish* (SS 190) attacks Japanese shipping in East China Sea west of Kyushu, and sinks freighter *Toyoura Maru* and damages supply ship *Mamiya,* 32°16′N, 127°08′E.

ATLANTIC. Destroyer escort *Buckley* (DE 51) is damaged when she intentionally rams German submarine *U 66,* which has been harassed by TBMs (VC 55) from escort carrier *Block Island* (CVE 21), about 390 miles west of Cape Verdes. The battle echoes close-quarters fights of the age of sail, as *Buckley's* sailors employ small arms, hand grenades, fists, and even a coffee mug. *U 66* sinks as the result of the multifaceted pounding she has taken in mid-Atlantic, 17°17′N, 32°29′W.

7 Sunday

PACIFIC. Submarines *Bonefish* (SS 223) and *Flasher* (SS 249) damage Japanese army cargo ship *Aobasan Maru* in Sulu Sea off Zamboanga, 07°07′N, 121°50′E.

Submarine *Burrfish* (SS 312) sinks German oiler *Rossbach,* bound for Balikpapan, Borneo, south of Muroto Saki, Japan, 33°15′N, 134°11′E.

Japanese TAKE No. 1 convoy reaches Bangka Island, Celebes, where it will pause before pushing on for Halmahera. Meanwhile, efforts continue to rescue survivors of army cargo ships *Aden Maru, Amatsuzan Maru,* and *Tajima Maru,* sunk by *Gurnard* (SS 254) the previous day (see 9 May).

8 Monday

PACIFIC. Submarine *Hoe* (SS 258) damages Japanese escort vessel *Sado* and army tanker *Akane Maru* in South China Sea west of Luzon Strait, 19°22′N, 120°13′E.

Submarine *Tautog* (SS 199) attacks Japanese convoy in Tsugaru Strait, sinking army cargo ship *Miyazaki Maru* off Ominato, northern Honshu, 41°52′N, 141°12′E.

9 Tuesday

MEDITERRANEAN. Submarine chaser *PC 558* is sunk by German submarine *U 230*, 28 miles northeast by north of Palermo, Sicily.

PACIFIC. Japanese TAKE No. 1 convoy reaches Wasile Bay, Halmahera, having lost four of its original nine *Maru*s during its passage to its destination.

10 Wednesday

PACIFIC. Submarine *Cod* (SS 224) attacks large Japanese convoy off west coast of Luzon, sinking destroyer *Karukaya* and transport *Shohei Maru* about 150 miles northwest of Manila, 15°38′N, 119°32′E.

Submarine *Silversides* (SS 236) attacks Japanese convoy about 120 miles south-southwest of Guam, sinking auxiliary cable ship *Okinawa Maru*, gunboat *No. 2 Choan Maru*, and collier *No. 18 Mikage Maru*, 11°26′N, 143°46′E, and forces the convoy to return whence it came. *Silversides* survives depth charging by one or more of the following ships: escort vessel *Momi*, submarine chaser *Ch 30*, auxiliary submarine chaser *Cha 66*, and auxiliary minelayer *Wa 5*.

Submarine *Tambor* (SS 198) encounters Japanese convoy 3503, torpedoes aircraft transport *Keiyo Maru* about 420 miles northwest of Saipan, 19°26′N, 140°19′E, and survives depth charging by *Coast Defense Vessel No. 24* (see 14 May).

Motor torpedo boat *PT 79* is damaged in collision with PT 80, Cold Bay.

Naval Base, Eniwetok, Marshalls, is established.

MEDITERRANEAN. Off Anzio, submarine chaser *PC 556* is damaged by bomb; destroyers *Charles F. Hughes* (DD 428) and *Hilary P. Jones* (DD 427) bombard German supply dumps.

11 Thursday

PACIFIC. Submarine *Crevalle* (SS 291), returning from a war patrol, evacuates 40 people (including 28 women and children) from Negros, P.I., and picks up intelligence documents believed to be of the highest value. *Crevalle* trans-

Destroyer escort *Ahrens* (DE 575), 13 May 1944, as seen from escort carrier *Bogue* (CVE 9); 16 days later, *Ahrens* and sister ship *Eugene E. Elmore* (DE 686) will sink German submarine *U 549* northwest of the Canary Islands. (NA, 80-G-266487)

fers a limited amount of food, ammunition, and canteen supplies to forces ashore (see 14 May).

Submarine *Sand Lance* (SS 381) attacks Japanese convoy, sinking transport *Mitakesan Maru* off Tinian, 14°57′N, 145°15′E.

Submarine *Sturgeon* (SS 187) attacks Japanese convoy, sinking army cargo ship *Seiryu Maru* about 140 miles north of Chichi Jima, 29°41′N, 141°35′E.

EUROPE. Naval Advanced Amphibious Base, Southhampton, England, is established.

MEDITERRANEAN. Convoy UGS 40 turns away German aerial attack east of Algiers, 37°03′N, 04°12′E. None of the 65 merchantmen under the escort of TF 61 (Commander Jesse C. Sowell) are damaged; among the reasons Commander Sowell enumerates for the successful defense of UGS 40 are living right and that "the Lord is on our side."

ATLANTIC. Covered lighter *YF 415* is destroyed by explosion of undetermined origin in Massachusetts Bay, off Boston, 42°24′N, 70°36′W.

12 Friday

PACIFIC. Submarine *Rasher* (SS 269) attacks Japanese convoy, sinking auxiliary vessel *Choi*

Maru in the Molucca Sea northwest of Boeroe Island, 03°30′S, 126°06′E.

Submarine *Tautog* (SS 199) attacks Japanese convoy, sinking merchant collier *No. 2 Manei Maru* off northeast Honshu, 40°01′N, 141°58′E.

Japanese transport *Kasumi Maru* is sunk by mine (probably Japanese) in Strait of Malacca, 03°50′N, 99°30′E.

Japanese river gunboat *Saga* is damaged (most likely by Chinese B-25s) in South China Sea.

13 Saturday

PACIFIC. F4Us, F6Fs, and SBDs and USAAF B-24s and B-25s bomb Japanese installations at Jaluit, Marshalls; attacks will continue on 14 May.

Submarine *Pogy* (SS 266) sinks Japanese cargo ship *Anbo Maru* off Suruga Bay, Honshu, 34°31′N, 138°33′E.

Japanese landing ships *T.128* and *T.150* are damaged by mines, Palau.

ATLANTIC. Destroyer escort *Francis M. Robinson* (DE 220) sinks Japanese submarine *RO 501* (ex-German *U 1224*), en route to Japan on her maiden voyage, 400 miles south-southwest of the Azores, 18°08′N, 33°13′W.

14 Sunday

PACIFIC. Submarines *Aspro* (SS 309) and *Bowfin* (SS 287) attack Japanese convoy and sink cargo ship *Bisan Maru* about 90 miles northwest of Palau, 08°55′N, 133°42′E.

Submarine *Bonefish* (SS 223) attacks Japanese convoy bound for Sibitu Passage, Borneo, sinking destroyer *Inazuma* near Tawi Tawi, east of Borneo, 05°03′N, 119°36′E, and survives counterattacks by what is most likely destroyer *Hibiki*. *Bonefish* had aimed her initial torpedo at a tanker (*Nichiei Maru*, *Azusa Maru*, or *Tatekawa Maru*) but ended up hitting *Inazuma* instead.

Submarine *Crevalle* (SS 291), with 40 evacuees and intelligence cargo, is damaged by depth charges in the Molucca Passage, off northern Celebes, 00°57′N, 125°51′E. She will, however, safely reach her destination, Darwin, Australia, on 19 May.

Submarine *Sand Lance* (SS 381), encountering that part of convoy 3503 that had been detached to proceed to Guam, sinks army cargo ship *Koho Maru* southwest of Apra Harbor, 13°43′N, 144°42′E, and survives depth chargings by escort vessel *Oki* and torpedo boat *Otori*.

MEDITERRANEAN. German submarine *U 616* attacks convoy GUS 39 off Cape Tenes, Morocco, prompting a search by Oran, Algeria–based U.S. destroyers (Captain Adelbert F. Converse) (see 17 May).

ATLANTIC. Tug *Umpqua* (ATO 25) tows disabled U.S. freighter *Colabee* to Charleston, South Carolina.

15 Monday

PACIFIC. Naval Air Bases, Ebeye and Roi-Namur, Kwajalein Atoll, Marshalls, are established.

During amphibious training exercises in the Hawaiian Operating Area, heavy seas break the moorings of three LCTs carried as deck cargo on board three tank landing craft. *LCT 988* sinks, 20°00′N, 157°00′W; *LCT 984* founders and is scuttled by submarine chaser *PC 1079*; and *LCT 999* is salvaged.

Submarine *Aspro* (SS 309) attacks Japanese convoy, sinking transport *Jokuja Maru* about 175 miles northwest of Palau, 10°10′N, 131°48′E.

MEDITERRANEAN. PBY-5s (VP 63) and British escort vessels HMS *Kilmarnock* and HMS *Blackfly* sink German submarine *U 731* off Tangiers, 35°54′N, 05°45′W.

16 Tuesday

PACIFIC. During exercises, battleship *Colorado* (BB 45) is damaged when she accidentally runs aground on a pinnacle off Kahoolawe, T.H.[190]

Destroyers *Franks* (DD 554), *Haggard* (DD 555), and *Johnston* (DD 557) sink Japanese submarine *I 176*, 150 miles north of Cape Alexander, Solomons, 04°01′S, 156°29′E. *Haggard* suffers slight damage from exploding depth charges. The sinking of *I 176* prompts the Japanese to shift the position of a cordon of submarines ("NA" Operation) in the New Guinea–Carolines area; much radio traffic accompanies the move (see 19 May).

Japanese minelayer *Aotaka* is damaged by mine, Kaoe Bay, Halmahera.

ATLANTIC. Nonrigid airship *K 5* is destroyed in crash into no. 1 hangar, Lakehurst, New Jersey.

17 Wednesday

PACIFIC. Operation STRAIGHTLINE: TF 77 (Rear Admiral William M. Fechteler) lands Army 163rd Regimental Combat Team (Reinforced) in Wakde-Toem area, New Guinea, preceded by bombardment by covering force, TF 74 (Rear Admiral Russell S. Berkey), and eastern attack group, TG 77.2 (Captain Albert G. Noble).

Operation TRANSOM: In an operation timed to coincide with the Wakde landings, planes from an Allied task force (Admiral Sir James F. Somerville, RN), formed around carrier *Saratoga* (CV 3) and British carrier HMS *Illustrious*, bomb Japanese shipping and harbor installations at Surabaya, Java. British planes sink transport *Shinrei Maru*; *Saratoga*'s planes damage *Patrol Boat No. 36*, auxiliary submarine chasers *Cha 107* and *Cha 108*, auxiliary minesweeper *Wa.101* cargo ships *Chuka Maru* and *Tencho Maru*, and tanker *Yosei Maru*.

Destroyers *Frazier* (DD 607) and *Meade* (DD 602) bombard Japanese defenses on Eniben Island, Maloelap Atoll, Marshalls.

Submarines *Sand Lance* (SS 381) and *Tunny* (SS 282) attack convoy 3503, the four *Marus* carrying Japanese soldiers earmarked for service at Yap and Palau, and three escorts. *Sand Lance* sinks transport *Taikoku Maru* about 60 miles west of Saipan, 14°57′N, 144°47′E; *Tunny* sinks army cargo ship *Nichiwa Maru* west of the Marianas, 14°49′N, 142°39′E. *Sand Lance* torpedoes army cargo ship *Fukko Maru*, 14°49′N, 142°23′E, when she stops to pick up *Nichiwa Maru*'s survivors (see 18 May). Although destroyer *Minazuki* and submarine chasers *Ch 31* and *Ch 32* claim the destruction of *Sand Lance* and *Tunny*, both boats survive enemy depth charges.

USAAF P-38s, P-39s, and P-40s carry out sweeps for targets in the Bismarck Archipelago; these operations may account for the sinking of Japanese guardboat *Zuiho Maru* off Duke of York Isle, 04°12′S, 152°20′E.

MEDITERRANEAN. Destroyers *Gleaves* (DD 423), *Hilary P. Jones* (DD 427), *Ellyson* (DD 454), *Hambleton* (DD 455), *Rodman* (DD 456), *Emmons* (DD 457), *Macomb* (DD 458), and *Nields* (DD 616) and RAF Wellington (No. 36 Squadron) sink German submarine *U 616* off coast of Algeria, 37°52′N, 00°11′E. *U 960* attacks *Ellyson* without success (see 19 May).

18 Thursday

PACIFIC. Submarine *Puffer* (SS 268) attacks Japanese convoy in Java Sea, sinking army cargo ship *Shinryu Maru* about 40 miles east-southeast of Surabaya, 07°33′S, 113°16′E.

Japanese merchant tanker *Nichiyoku Maru* is sunk by mine (laid by British submarine HMS *Tally Ho* on 14 May), 03°41′N, 99°04′E.

Japanese army cargo ship *Fukko Maru* sinks as the result of damage inflicted by submarine *Sand Lance* (SS 381) the previous day.

Naval Base and Naval Air Station, Manus Island, Admiralty Islands, are established.

19 Friday

UNITED STATES. James V. Forrestal, Undersecretary of the Navy since 1940, becomes Secretary of the Navy.

PACIFIC. TG 58.6 (Rear Admiral Alfred E. Montgomery) planes bomb Marcus Island.

Japanese radio traffic intercepted by U.S. Navy intelligence allows deductions to be made as to where the new submarine cordon ("NA" Operation) established to intercept American carriers will be; consequently, destroyer escort *England* (DE 635) sinks *I 16* as the latter operates on a resupply run to Buka, 140 miles northeast of Cape Alexander, Solomons, 05°10′S, 158°10′E. *I 16* is the first of five Japanese submarines that *England* will sink in a week's time as U.S. antisubmarine forces work their way down the "NA" line (see 22–24, 26, and 31 May).

Submarine *Skate* (SS 305) sinks Japanese guardboat *Meisho Maru* off Ogasawara Gunto, 28°56′N, 141°38′E.

USAAF B-24s (14th Air Force), on antishipping sweep of the South China Sea, bomb Japanese convoy no. 87, but only succeed in inflicting minor damage on cargo ship *Yamadori Maru* (see 20 May).

USAAF A-20s and P-38s (5th Air Force) attack Japanese shipping and installations at

Manokwari, New Guinea; small cargo vessels *Ogi Maru* and *Juei Maru* are sunk.

USAAF B-25s (11th Air Force) operating against Japanese guardboats off Kamchatka sink *Reiko Maru*, 51°08′N, 159°06′E, and *No. 1 Shinko Maru* and *No. 1 Fukutoku Maru*, 51°08′N, 159°40′E.

Japanese minesweeper *W.8* is damaged by mine, Kaoe Bay, Halmahera.

MEDITERRANEAN. Light cruiser *Brooklyn* (CL 40) shells German supply dumps at Terracina, Sperlonga, and Ganta, Italy.

Destroyers *Niblack* (DD 424) and *Ludlow* (DD 438) and British aircraft sink German submarine *U 960* off Oran, Algeria, 37°20′N, 01°35′E.

Motor torpedo boat *PT 204* is mistakenly torpedoed and damaged by *PT 304* off Vada Rocks, Corsica.

20 Saturday

PACIFIC. TG 58.6 (Rear Admiral Alfred E. Montgomery) planes bomb Marcus Island. Planes from small carrier *San Jacinto* (CVL 30) sink Japanese guardboat *Yawata Maru* 150 miles north of Marcus, 31°22′N, 154°59′E.

TG 53.18 (three light cruisers and eight destroyers) bombards Japanese shore installations on Alu, Poporang, and Morgusia Islands, Shortlands. Enemy return fire damages light cruiser *Montpelier* (CL 57) and straddles light cruiser *Cleveland* (CL 55).

Submarine *Angler* (SS 240) sinks Japanese transport *Otori Maru* (ex-Panamanian *Boyaca*), 05°57′N, 105°12′E, and survives depth charging by escort.

Submarine *Bluegill* (SS 242), despite presence of two escort vessels, sinks Japanese army cargo ship *Miyaura Maru* between Halmahera and Morotai, 02°14′N, 128°05′E; *No. 18 Nitto Maru* rescues survivors.

Submarine *Picuda* (SS 382) is damaged by depth charges, Luzon Strait, 19°00′N, 120°45′E, but remains on patrol.

Submarine *Silversides* (SS 236) sinks Japanese gunboat *Shosei Maru* off Saipan, 13°32′N, 144°36′E.

USAAF B-24s (14th Air Force) bomb Takao, Formosa–bound Japanese convoy no. 88 in South China Sea south of Hong Kong, sinking army cargo ship *Shinju Maru*, 21°20′N, 117°10′E; *No. 1 Shinko Maru* transports survivors to Takao. Freighters *Tsukuba Maru* and *Kori Maru* are damaged. Gunboat *Hashidate* takes the crippled *Tsukuba Maru* in tow; *Kori Maru* reaches Takao unaided. Salvage vessel (ex-Chinese) *Sonjo Maru* is dispatched to aid *Hashidate* (see 22 May).

Other USAAF B-24s (14th Air Force) attack Japanese warships sent to aid convoy no. 87, attacked the previous day, damaging auxiliary submarine chaser *Kinsui Maru* in the South China Sea, 22°00′N, 118°25′E.

Japanese cargo vessel *Wako Maru* is damaged when she runs aground 50 nautical miles north of Batavia, Java, 05°16′S, 106°54′E.

21 Sunday

PACIFIC. In a reprise of the type of raid conducted on Jaluit on 13–14 May, F4Us and PV-1s and USAAF B-24s and B-25s bomb Japanese positions on Wotje, Marshalls. PB2Ys had harassed the atoll the previous night.

Tank landing ship *LST 353* is destroyed by accidental explosion as she is being loaded with mortar ammunition at West Loch, Pearl Harbor. The cataclysmic blast also results in the loss of *LST 39*, *LST 43*, *LST 69*, *LST 179*, and *LST 480*; tank landing craft *LCT 961*, *LCT 963*, and *LCT 983*; 17 tracked landing vehicles (LVT); and eight 155-millimeter guns. *LST 205* and *LST 225* are damaged. During fire-fighting efforts, big harbor tugs *Osceola* (YTB 129) and *Hoga* (YTB 146); medium harbor tug *Geronimo* (YTM 119); little harbor tugs *YTL 233*, *YTL 306*, *YTL 307*, *YTL 308*, *YTL 309*, and *YTL 339*; net tender (tug class) *Tamaha* (YNT 12); and chartered tug *Mikioi* suffer varying degrees of damage in the disaster.[191]

Oiler *Neches* (AO 47) is damaged by mine about 630 miles west of Los Angeles, California.

Submarine *Billfish* (SS 286) attacks Japanese convoy west-southwest of the Marianas; she torpedoes cargo ship *Bokuyo Maru*, 13°42′N, 140°41′E, and survives counterattack by *Coast Defense Vessel No. 12*.

Submarine *Cero* (SS 225), after unsuccessful attack on Japanese transport *Anshu Maru* (*Cero* claims a hit), survives counterattacks by *Anshu Maru* and auxiliary submarine chasers *No. 5 Takunan Maru* and *No. 17 Shonan Maru*, 05°15′N, 128°55′E. Seeing an oil slick, *No. 17 Shonan Maru* resumes escorting *Anshu Maru*; *No. 5 Takunan Maru* remains on the scene to continue countermeasures. *Cero*, however, escapes.

Submarine *Narwhal* (SS 167) attacks, unsuccessfully, 12-ship Japanese H 26 Cebu-to-Wasile convoy, 08°15′N, 127°15′E. Although *Narwhal* claims two hits, no ships are in fact hit (see 22 and 23 May).

22 Monday

PACIFIC. Destroyers *Bancroft* (DD 598) and *Edwards* (DD 619) bombard installations at Wotje Atoll, Marshalls.

Destroyer escort *England* (DE 635), working her way down the "NA" cordon, sinks Japanese submarine *RO 106*, 250 miles north of Kavieng, New Ireland, 01°40′N, 150°31′E (see 23 May).

Submarine *Bluegill* (SS 242) is damaged by aerial bombs off Halmahera, 04°00′N, 128°06′E, but remains on patrol.

Submarine *Picuda* (SS 382), patrolling the South China Sea, comes across Japanese gunboat *Hashidate* towing crippled freighter *Tsukuba Maru* [the latter had been damaged by USAAF B-24s (14th Air Force) on 20 May] accompanied by salvage vessel *Sonjo Maru*. *Picuda* sinks *Hashidate* and *Tsukuba Maru* off Pratas Island, 21°08′N, 117°20′E; *Sonjo Maru* flees in haste and reaches Hong Kong without further incident.

Submarine *Pollack* (SS 180) attacks Japanese convoy no. 4517 and sinks destroyer *Asanagi* 180 miles west-northwest of Chichi Jima, Bonins, 28°19′N, 138°54′E. *Pollack*'s attack on *Coast Defense Vessel No. 18* is not successful.

Submarine *Ray* (SS 271) attacks same Japanese convoy (H 26) intercepted by *Narwhal* (SS 167) the day before, and sinks army cargo ship *Tempei Maru* off south coast of Mindanao, 05°42′N, 127°37′E (see 23 May).

British submarine HMS *Sea Rover* sinks Japanese gunboat *Kosho Maru* off southern entrance to Penang Harbor, Malaya, in Strait of Malacca, 04°52′N, 100°18′E.

23 Tuesday

PACIFIC. TG 58.3 (Rear Admiral Alfred E. Montgomery) planes bomb Japanese installations on Wake Island.

Destroyer escort *England* (DE 635), working her way down the "NA" cordon, sinks Japanese submarine *RO 104*, 250 miles north-northwest of Kavieng, 01°26′N, 149°20′E (see 24 May).

Submarine *Cero* (SS 225) attacks Japanese convoy H 26 and sinks army cargo ship *Taijun Maru*; *Cero* teams with *Ray* (SS 271) to damage army tanker *Kenwa Maru* off Halmahera Island, 02°42′N, 128°08′E.

Submarine *Raton* (SS 270) sinks small Japanese cargo vessels *Kojin Maru*, *Konan Maru*, and *No. 5 Kosei Maru* west of Borneo, 00°25′S, 107°34′E.

PB4Y attacks Japanese cargo vessel *Hakko Maru* near Helen Reef, 02°59′S, 131°31′E.

USAAF A-20s (5th Air Force) bomb Japanese installations and shipping at Biak, New Guinea; fishing boats *No. 2 Genko Maru* and *No. 11 Konpira Maru* are sunk.

MEDITERRANEAN. Light cruiser *Brooklyn* (CL 40) and destroyers *Kearny* (DD 432) and *Ericsson* (DD 440) shell enemy positions in vicinity of Ardea, Italy, with good results. The three ships repeat bombardment of troop concentrations and supply dumps on 24 and 26 May with equal success.

Light cruiser *Philadelphia* (CL 41) and destroyer *Laub* (DD 613) are damaged in collision 20 miles southwest of Nettuno, Italy, 41°11′N, 12°30′E.

Submarine chaser *PC 626* captures German speedboat off Anzio and takes crew prisoner.

24 Wednesday

PACIFIC. Destroyer escort *England* (DE 635), working her way down the "NA" cordon, sinks submarine *RO 116*, 225 miles north-northwest of Kavieng, 00°53′N, 149°14′E (see 26 May).

Submarine *Cabrilla* (SS 288), in northern approaches to Makassar Strait, attacks Japanese underway replenishment vessel *Shioya*, 01°45′N, 121°04′E, and survives counterattacks by her erstwhile quarry and her escort, minesweeper *W.30*, as well as land-based planes.

Submarine *Flying Fish* (SS 229) is damaged by premature explosion of own torpedo, Philippine Sea, 12°54′N, 134°52′E, but remains on patrol (see 25 May).

Submarine *Gurnard* (SS 254), despite presence of escort vessel *No. 1 Toko Maru*, sinks fleet tanker *Tatekawa Maru* off the coast of Mindanao, 05°45′N, 125°43′E.

Submarine *Lapon* (SS 260), in South China Sea, sinks Japanese cargo ship *Bizen Maru*, 07°20′N, 109°20′E, and freighter *Wales Maru*, 07°16′N, 109°04′E.

Submarine *Narwhal* (SS 167) lands men and supplies on Samar, P.I.

Submarine *Perch* (SS 313) attacks Japanese convoy no. 88 in South China Sea, 22°15′N, 118°05′E, but without success. It is the convoy's last adventure with U.S. forces.

Submarine *Raton* (SS 270) attacks Japanese HI 63 convoy about 220 miles east of Singapore and 150 miles west of Sarawak, sinking escort vessel *Iki* and damaging escort vessel *Matsuwa* and oiler *Kyukuho Maru*, 01°17′N, 107°53′E.

Japanese transport *Taichi Maru* is sunk in collision near Chinhai, China, 30°00′N, 116°48′E.

MEDITERRANEAN. U.S. motor torpedo boats *PT 202, PT 213,* and *PT 218* (Lieutenant Commander Robert A. Allan, RNVR) sink German corvette *UJ.2223* (ex-Italian Navy corvette *Maragone*) and damage corvette *UJ.2222* (ex-Italian Navy corvette *Tuffeto*) off Vada Rocks, Corsica.

ATLANTIC. Submarine *Razorback* (SS 394) runs aground at west end of Fisher's Island, Long Island Sound; she is refloated with the assistance of submarine rescue vessel *Falcon* (ASR 2) and tug-class net tenders *Nawat* (YNT 23) and *Cockenoe* (YNT 15), and proceeds on her way under her own power.

25 Thursday

PACIFIC. Submarine *Flying Fish* (SS 229) attacks Japanese convoy, sinking guardboat *Daito Maru* and freighter *Osaka Maru* north of Palau, 11°14′N, 135°12′E.

Japanese cargo ship *Yamamiya Maru* is damaged by mine off Halmahera and returns to port for repairs.

MEDITERRANEAN. Destroyer *Kendrick* (DD 612) shells German positions in the Ardea, Italy, area; enemy shore battery fire improves but inflicts no damage.

26 Friday

PACIFIC. TG 57.8 (destroyers) bombard Japanese shore batteries and installations on Mille Atoll, Marshalls.

Destroyer escort *England* (DE 635), working her way down the "NA" cordon, sinks Japanese submarine *RO 108*, 110 miles northeast of Manus, 00°32′S, 148°35′E (see 31 May).

Submarine *Cabrilla* (SS 288) sinks Japanese transport (ex-seaplane carrier) *Sanyo Maru* about 80 miles north of Menado, Celebes, 02°40′N, 124°35′E.

Submarine *Permit* (SS 178) torpedoes and damages Japanese submarine *I 44* west-southwest of Truk, 07°05′N, 152°00′E.

Submarine *Tambor* (SS 198) sinks Japanese stores ship *Chiyo Maru* west of the Marianas, 20°40′N, 141°50′E.

27 Saturday

PACIFIC. Operation HORLICKS: TF 77 (Rear Admiral William M. Fechteler) lands Army 41st Division (Major General Horace H. Fuller, USA) on Biak in the Schouten Islands off New Guinea. Heavy and light cruisers and destroyers of TG 77.2 (Rear Admiral Victor A. C. Crutchley, RN) and TG 77.3 (Rear Admiral Russell S. Berkey) provide gunfire support.

Motor torpedo boat *PT 339*, damaged by grounding off Pur Pur, western New Guinea, 04°01′S, 144°41′E, is scuttled by her crew to prevent capture.

Submarine chaser *SC 699* is damaged by crashing Japanese plane off western New Guinea, 01°12′S, 136°13′E.

British submarine HMS *Templar* sinks Japanese cargo ship *Tyokai Maru* in Strait of Malacca.

MEDITERRANEAN. U.S. motor torpedo boats attack three German F-lighters in vicinity of Vada Rocks, Corsica, sinking two and damaging one; PTs also attack an enemy motor vessel.

28 Sunday

PACIFIC. Destroyer *Stockton* (DD 646) is damaged by shore battery, Biak Island, Schouten Islands, New Guinea, 01°00′S, 136°00′E.

Submarine *Narwhal* (SS 167) delivers 23-man party and 25 tons of supplies to designated point in Alusan Bay, Samar, 12°14′N, 125°29′E. Subsequent mission, to deliver mail and pick up evacuees and captured documents at Sanco Point, Mindanao, 08°15′N, 126°28′E, is abandoned when contact cannot be made with forces ashore for two successive nights (see 1 June).

PV-1 (VB 148) accidentally bombs submarine *Permit* (SS 178) off Truk, 06°45′N, 151°52′E, but the damage sustained by *Permit* does not prevent her from continuing her war patrol.

MEDITERRANEAN. U.S. motor torpedo boats sink German corvette *UJ.2210* in Ligurian Sea.

29 Monday

PACIFIC. Destroyers (Destroyer Squadron 41) bombard Japanese installations on northern coast of New Ireland, shelling the Medina Plantation area.

Submarine *Rasher* (SS 269) attacks Japanese convoy in the eastern Celebes Sea, damaging gunboat *Anshu Maru* about 110 miles north-northwest of Halmahera, 03°32′N, 127°07′E (see 30 May).

Submarine *Silversides* (SS 236), despite the proximity of four escort vessels and aircraft, sinks Japanese transports *Horaisan Maru* and *Shoken Maru* about 100 miles north-northwest of Saipan, 16°23′N, 144°59′E.

Japanese convoy 3530 sails from Yokohama, bound for Saipan. The seven transports/cargo ships carry men and equipment of the Japanese Army's 118th Infantry (see 4–7 June).

ATLANTIC. German submarine *U 549* sinks escort carrier *Block Island* (CVE 21) and damages destroyer escort *Barr* (DE 576) but is sunk by destroyer escorts *Ahrens* (DE 575) and *Eugene E. Elmore* (DE 686) northwest of the Canary Islands, 31°13′N, 23°03′W.

30 Tuesday

PACIFIC. Submarine *Guitarro* (SS 363), despite proximity of at least three escort vessels, sinks Japanese freighter *Shisen Maru* 60 miles southeast of Keelung, Formosa, 24°32′N, 123°24′E.

Submarine *Pompon* (SS 267) sinks Japanese freighter *Shiga Maru* off Muroto Saki, Japan, 33°15′N, 134°11′E.

Submarine *Rasher* (SS 269) continues attack on Japanese convoy in the eastern Celebes Sea, sinking gunboat *Anshu Maru* about 110 miles north-northwest of Halmahera, 03°40′N, 126°58′E.

USAAF B-25s (11th Air Force) sink Japanese guardboat *Shinyo Maru* northeast of Paramushir, Kurils, and damage guardboat *No. 3 Showa Maru* east of the Kurils.

USAAF B-25s damage Japanese cargo vessel *Nansei Maru* west of Manokwari, New Guinea.

31 Wednesday

PACIFIC. Destroyer escort *England* (DE 635), working her way down the "NA" cordon, assisted by destroyers *McCord* (DD 534) and *Hazelwood* (DD 531) and destroyer escorts *George* (DE 697), *Raby* (DE 698), and *Spangler* (DE 696), sink submarine *RO 105*, 200 miles north-northwest of Kavieng, 00°47′N, 151°30′E.

Submarines *Barb* (SS 220) and *Herring* (SS 233) rendezvous in Sea of Okhotsk about 150 miles west of Matsuwa Island, Kurils, to plan operations against Japanese shipping in the vicinity. Subsequently, *Herring* attacks convoy NE, sinking escort vessel *Ishigaki* and army cargo ship *Hokuyo Maru* west of Matsuwa Island, 48°00′N, 153°00′E (see 1 June); *Barb* comes across convoy NE and sinks army cargo ship *Madras Maru*, 48°21′N, 151°20′E, and transport *Koto Maru* southwest of Paramushir, 47°55′N, 151°42′E.

Japanese river gunboat *Kotaka* is sunk by Chinese aircraft in the Yangtze River.

ATLANTIC. U.S. fishing vessel *Shamrock* breaks down at 42°03′N, 67°28′W; tug *Wandank* (ATO 26) is sent out from Boston, Massachusetts, and Coast Guard cutter *CGC 85001* from Provincetown, while patrol vessel *Migrant* (IX 66) is diverted from her station to assist. *Migrant* tows *Shamrock* until relieved by *Wandank*, which takes the disabled fishing boat to Boston.

JUNE

1 Thursday

PACIFIC. Submarine *Narwhal* (SS 167) lands 16-man party and 25 tons of supplies at Tukuran, on southwest coast of Mindanao, 07°50′N, 123°34′E, and embarks two evacuees for purposes of planning future missions.

Submarine *Herring* (SS 233) continues attacks against Japanese shipping in the Kurils, sinking transport *Iwaki Maru*, the lone surviving ship of convoy NE attacked the previous day by *Herring* and *Barb* (SS 220), and freighter *Hiburi Maru* off Matsuwa Island, 48°00′N, 153°00′E, but is sunk by shore battery (Guards Division 52, Matsuwa Detachment).

Submarine *Pintado* (SS 387) sinks Japanese transport *Toho Maru* about 250 miles northwest of Saipan, 18°08′N, 141°14′E, and damages transport *Kinshu Maru* (see 17 June).

Big harbor tug *Shahaka* (YTB 368) sinks after collision with Section "A" of advance base section dock *ABSD-2*, about midway between the coast of California and the Hawaiian Islands, 27°21′N, 136°29′W.

MEDITERRANEAN. Destroyers *Champlin* (DD 601) and *MacKenzie* (DD 614) shell German strongpoints and shore batteries in the vicinity of Anzio; *Champlin* and *Parker* (DD 604) will alternate covering minesweeping operations west of Anzio and will also do so on 2 and 4 June.

2 Friday

PACIFIC. Submarine *Guitarro* (SS 363), in attack on two Japanese warships carrying out an antisubmarine sweep in advance of convoy east of Formosa, sinks escort vessel *Awaji* near Yasho Island, 22°34′N, 121°51′E. Submarine *Picuda* (SS 382) attacks the same convoy; while her efforts are not successful, her presence prompts the convoy to take evasive action. Cargo vessel *Arimasan Maru* accidentally rams landing ship *Shinshu Maru*, setting off depth charges stowed aft and blowing off *Shinshu Maru*'s stern; the latter ship is towed to Takao for repairs.

Submarine *Shark* (SS 314) attacks Japanese convoy, sinking transport *No. 2 Chiyo Maru* about 600 miles northwest of Saipan, 21°00′N, 140°20′E.

MEDITERRANEAN. Destroyer *MacKenzie* (DD 614) shells German guns in the Partecica de Mari area, near Anzio.

3 Saturday

PACIFIC. Destroyer *Reid* (DD 369) is damaged by dive bomber off western New Guinea, 01°13′S, 136°13′E.

PBY (VPB 52), operating against Japanese shipping off New Guinea, damages torpedo boat *Kiji* 23 miles northwest of Manokwari, 00°40′S, 134°00′E; USAAF A-20s sink fishing boat *No. 96 Banshu Maru* west of Manokwari.

4 Sunday

PACIFIC. Japanese carrier bombers (JUDYs) attack Allied cruiser and destroyer forces TF 74 and TF 75 (Rear Admiral Victor A. C. Crutchley, RN) off Biak, New Guinea; light cruisers *Nashville* (CL 43), 01°05′S, 136°05′E, and *Phoenix* (CL 46), 01°00′S, 136°00′E, are damaged by near-misses. Subsequent torpedo attack by BETTYs is unsuccessful.

Submarine *Flier* (SS 250) sinks Japanese troopship *Hakusan Maru* about 375 miles southwest of Chichi Jima, Bonins, 22°45′N, 136°50′E.

Submarine *Golet* (SS 361) sinks Japanese guardboat *No. 10 Shinko Maru* east of Japan, 35°47′N, 154°54′E.

Coordinated submarine attack group, TG 17.12, makes contact with Japanese convoy 3530. Two of the group's three boats, *Shark* (SS 314) and *Pintado* (SS 387), will obtain favorable attack positions; the third, *Pilotfish* (SS 386), will not. *Shark* sinks army transport *Katsukawa Maru* about 475 miles northwest of Saipan, 19°45′N, 138°15′E (see 5 June).

USAAF B-24s sink Japanese landing ship *T.128*, 110 miles northeast of Morotai, 04°09′N, 129°45′E.

USAAF A-20s (5th Air Force) bomb Manokwari, New Guinea, and Japanese shipping in Geelvink Bay, sinking auxiliary submarine chaser *No. 2 Hakusan Maru* and guardboats *Shimane Maru*, *No. 3 Tokyo Maru*, and *Gongen Maru*.

ATLANTIC. TG 22.3 (Captain Daniel V. Gallery), a hunter-killer group composed of escort carrier *Guadalcanal* (CVE 60) and destroyer escorts *Pillsbury* (DE 133), *Pope* (DE 134), *Flaherty* (DE 135), *Chatelain* (DE 149), and *Jenks* (DE 665), forces German submarine *U 505* to the surface 150 miles off the coast of Rio de Oro, Africa. Lieutenant (j.g.) Albert L. David leads a boarding party from *Pillsbury* (which is damaged in collision with the out-of-control U-boat during salvage operations) that saves the ship despite the dangers posed by scuttling charges. He later assists more well-equipped salvage parties that make the cap-

Boarding party from destroyer escort *Pillsbury* (DE 133) crowds the bow of German submarine *U 505*, 4 June 1944, rigging the boat to be taken in tow. (NA, 80-G-261993)

tured U-boat seaworthy for the tow to Trinidad. For his "gallantry and intrepidity at the risk of life above and beyond the call of duty," David is awarded the Medal of Honor.

5 Monday

PACIFIC. Submarine *Nautilus* (SS 168) lands approximately 90 tons of supplies at Tukuran, Allana Bay, Mindanao, 07°50′30″N, 123°34′30″E, and disembarks Lieutenant John D. Simmons, USNR, to establish communications network.

Submarine *Puffer* (SS 268) attacks Japanese convoy in the Sulu Sea and sinks underway replenishment vessel *Ashizuri* and oiler *Takasaki* and damages tanker *No. 2 Hishi Maru*, northeast of Borneo, 06°44′N, 120°54′E.

TG 17.12 operations against Japanese convoy 3530 continue as submarine *Shark* (SS 314) sinks transport *Tamahime Maru* and army transport *Takaoka Maru* west of the Marianas, 17°37′N, 140°32′E (see 6 June).

EUROPE. Minesweeper *Osprey* (AM 56) is sunk by mine while en route to UTAH beach, Normandy, 50°12′N, 01°20′W; tank landing ship *LST 981* is damaged, 50°45′N, 00°43′E.

6 Tuesday

EUROPE. Allied Expeditionary Force under the supreme command of General Dwight D. Eisenhower, USA, invades Western Europe in Operation OVERLORD. Landings are made on the beaches of Normandy, France, following preinvasion minesweeping and bombardment by Allied warships, and under cover of Allied aircraft and naval gunfire. The invasion fleet of thousands of warships, merchantmen, and landing craft under the command of Admiral Sir Bertram H. Ramsay, RN, is divided into a Western (American) Task Force and an Eastern (British) Task Force. TF 122 (Western Task Force), commanded by Rear Admiral Alan G. Kirk, is composed of two assault forces, TF 124 (Rear Admiral John L. Hall Jr.) and TF 125 (Rear Admiral Don P. Moon), that land the First U.S. Army commanded by Lieutenant General Omar N. Bradley, USA, on OMAHA and UTAH beaches, respectively. Naval gunfire support groups commanded by Rear Admiral Carlton F. Bryant prevent the Germans from moving up reinforcements and cover the Allied troops advancing inland. After the beachheads are established, the primary naval responsibility is the landing of men and supplies. The success of the Normandy land-

ings virtually assures victory in the European theater. The successful movement of so many miscellaneous ships and craft through swept channels traversing unknown waters with strong and variable currents reflects credit upon the planning skills not only of high command levels but of assault force commanders.

Destroyer *Corry* (DD 463), 49°31′N, 01°11′W, is sunk by mine; sister ship *Fitch* (DD 462) rescues *Corry*'s survivors. Mines also account for loss of submarine chaser *PC 1261*, 49°30′N, 01°10′W; landing craft (flotilla flagship) *LC(FF) 31*; tank landing craft *LCT 25*, *LCT 197*, *LCT 294*, *LCT 305*, *LCT 332*, *LCT 362*, *LCT 364*, *LCT 555*, *LCT 593*, *LCT 597*, *LCT 703*, and *LCT 777*; and large infantry landing craft *LCI(L) 85*, *LCI(L) 91*, *LCI(L) 92*, *LCI(L) 232*, and *LCI(L) 497*. *LCT 27* and *LCT 30* sink after running aground. *LCT 362* founders and sinks. *LCT 612*, *LCI(L) 93*, and *LCI(L) 553* are sunk by shore batteries; *LCI(L) 487* is damaged by nearmiss of mortar shell.

Destroyer *Harding* (DD 625) sends armed whaleboat to shore, landing small arms to help the Second Ranger Battalion; the destroyermen relieve a number of soldiers as guards for German POWs, permitting the rangers to reinforce their comrades. Army and Navy beach demolition teams landing in second and third waves remove obstacles and, using bulldozers, push them higher on the beach.

PACIFIC. Submarine *Harder* (SS 257) attacks Japanese convoy in the Celebes Sea, sinking destroyer *Minazuki* 120 miles east-northeast of Tarakan, Borneo, 04°05′N, 119°30′E, and survives counterattacks by destroyer *Wakatsuki* (see 7–9 June).

TG 17.12 operations against Japanese convoy 3530 come to a close as submarine *Pintado* (SS 387) sinks cargo ship *Kashimasan Maru* and army transport *Havre Maru* west-northwest of the Marianas, 16°28′N, 142°16′E (see 7 June).

Submarine *Raton* (SS 270) attacks Japanese convoy and sinks *Coast Defense Vessel No. 15* about 160 miles off Cape St. Jacques, French Indochina, 08°57′N, 109°17′E. *Raton* is damaged by depth charges, but remains on patrol.

USAAF B-24s (5th Air Force) bomb Japanese shipping off Waigeo Island in the northeastern Moluccas Islands; heavy cruiser *Aoba* and light cruiser *Kinu*, however, survive the attacks unscathed.

USAAF A-20s (5th Air Force) attack Japanese shipping off Manokwari, New Guinea, sinking motor sailships *No. 1 Asahi Maru*, *No. 1 Kasuga Maru*, and *No. 5 Taifuku Maru*.

Japanese Truk-bound convoy is attacked by "one large-type enemy plane" (possibly a USAAF B-24 or a USN PB4Y) southwest of Woleai; escorting minelayer *Yurishima* is damaged, 07°46′N, 147°30′E, but torpedo boat *Hiyodori* is not hit. Attacking aircraft also strafes cargo vessels *No. 18 Nissho Maru* and *Shinfoku Maru.*[192]

7 Wednesday

PACIFIC. Submarine *Harder* (SS 257) sinks Japanese destroyer *Hayanami* as the latter patrols south of the Japanese Fleet anchorage at Tawi Tawi, southeast of Sibitu Passage, Borneo, 04°43′N, 120°03′E (see 8 and 9 June).

Submarine *Whale* (SS 239) damages Japanese transports *Shinroku Maru* and *Sugiyama Maru* north-northeast of the Bonins, 31°06′N, 142°34′E.

Remnants of Japanese convoy 3530 reach Saipan, but because of the work of *Shark* (SS 314) and *Pintado* (SS 387), the Imperial Army's 118th Regiment arrives at its destination at half-strength, its weapons and equipment at the bottom of the Pacific.

Naval Advanced Base, Hollandia, New Guinea, is established.

EUROPE. Construction of artificial harbors and sheltered anchorages ("Mulberries") from sunken blockships and concrete caissons begins off Normandy. Off the beachheads minesweeper *Tide* (AM 125) is sunk by a mine. As minesweeper *Pheasant* (AM 61) rescues *Tide*'s survivors, she fouls the stricken minecraft and is damaged, 49°37′N, 01°05′W. Mines also sink transport *Susan B. Anthony* (AP 72) en route to UTAH beach (in an area reported as swept), 49°33′N, 00°49′W, and tank landing craft *LCT 436, LCT 458,* and *LCT 586.* Destroyer *Harding* (DD 625) is damaged when she runs aground, 49°31′N, 00°50′W; destroyer *Jeffers* (DD 621) is damaged by shore battery fire; and motor torpedo boat *PT 505* is damaged by a mine, 49°30′N, 01°09′W. U.S. freighter *Francis Harrington,* in OMAHA beach–bound convoy EMB 2, is damaged by mine at 50°10′N, 00°40′W, but manages to discharge her cargo and disembark the troops she is bringing to the beachhead. Although six of the 515 soldiers perish in the mining, there were no other casualties among the men on board, including the 28-man Armed Guard.

UNITED STATES. Naval Academy Class of 1945 is graduated one year early because of the national emergency.

Army troops crouch inside an LCVP as it heads for OMAHA beach during the invasion of Normandy on 6 June 1944. (NA, 26-G-2340)

Sign atop the crown of Turret II of battleship *Arkansas* (BB 33) off Normandy, 7 June 1944, reflects gunners' optimism: "YOU NAME IT BOSS, WE'LL HIT IT." At top of photo can be partially seen the word's "HITLER'S DOWNFALL" painted on the left and right barrels, respectively. A lull in the action permits crewmen to limber up with a medicine ball (left, background). (NA, 80-G-244214)

8   Thursday

PACIFIC. USAAF B-25s (17th Reconnaissance Squadron), escorted by P-38s (475th Fighter Group), attack Japanese Biak-bound reinforcement convoy (seven destroyers, each towing a large landing barge), sinking *Harusame* 30 miles northwest of Manokwari, 00°05'S, 132°45'E, and damaging *Shiratsuyu* and *Shikinami*; three barges are lost. Later in the day, Allied surface forces, TF 74 and TF 75 (Rear Admiral Victor A. C. Crutchley, RN), including two U.S. light cruisers and accompanying destroyers, intercept the remaining six enemy ships and engage them; the battle continues into 9 June. Although *Hamakaze* claims damage to a U.S. cruiser, none of the Allied ships are damaged; TF 74 and TF 75 gunfire, however, damages *Shigure*, and Crutchley's force turns back the Japanese before they can accomplish their mission.

Submarine *Hake* (SS 256) sinks Japanese destroyer *Kazagumo* at mouth of Davao Gulf, about 20 miles southwest of Cape San Agustin, Mindanao, P.I. 06°04'N, 125°56'E.

Submarine *Harder* (SS 257) evacuates coast-watchers from northeast coast of North Borneo (see 9 June).

Submarine *Rasher* (SS 269), despite presence of escorting submarine chaser *Ch 5*, sinks Japanese underway replenishment vessel *Shioya* northwest of Menado, 03°15'N, 124°03'E.

Submarine *Redfin* (SS 272) disembarks party of six Filipinos (U.S. Army) as well as 6,500 pounds of supplies on Ramos Island, P.I.[193]

Submarine *Whale* (SS 239) is damaged by depth charges north of the Bonins, 31°00'N, 143°55'E, but remains on patrol.

USAAF B-24s sink Japanese army tanker *No. 5 Nippo Maru* off northwest coast of New Guinea, 00°33'S, 132°53'E.

EUROPE. Off Normandy, mines continue to take their toll. Destroyer *Glennon* (DD 620) is damaged by mine, 50°32'N, 01°12'W; destroyer escort *Rich* (DE 695), en route to *Glennon*'s assistance, is sunk by mine, 49°31'N, 01°10'W. Efforts to move *Glennon* from her exposed predicament within range of German artillery are not successful (see 10 June). Tank landing ship *LST 499* is sunk by mine, 49°30'N, 01°10'W. Destroyer *Meredith* (DD 726), damaged by mine, is abandoned, 49°33'N, 01°06'W, and her crew taken off by destroyer *Herndon* (DD 638) (see 9 June). Attack transport *Bayfield* (APA 33) is near-missed by bomb off RED beach. Large infantry landing craft *LCI(L) 495* suffers damage when barrage balloon is shot down directly overhead; the burning wreckage lands atop the LCI(L)'s conning tower.

9   Friday

PACIFIC. Destroyers bombard Japanese repair facilities at Fangelawa Bay, New Ireland.

Submarine *Harder* (SS 257) sinks Japanese destroyer *Tanikaze* in Sibitu Passage, 90 miles southwest of Basilan Island, 04°50'N, 119°40'E. For "gallant and courageous conduct . . . tireless and unselfish devotion to duty, for exemplary steadiness under intense enemy pressure," for "outstanding professional skill, superb judgment and admirable imperturbability" demonstrated during *Harder*'s operations adjacent to the Japanese fleet anchorage at Tawi Tawi between 6 and 9 June, Commander Samuel D. Dealey, *Harder*'s commanding officer, will receive the Medal of Honor posthumously.

Submarine *Swordfish* (SS 193) attacks Japanese convoy east of the Bonins, sinking destroyer *Matsukaze* 55 miles east of Chichi Jima, 27°14'N, 142°55'E.

USAAF A-20s (5th Air Force) bomb Japanese shipping off Manokwari, New Guinea, sinking cargo vessels *No. 10 Fuku Maru*, *No. 12 Fuku Maru*, *Ebisu Maru*, *Fukuda Maru*, *Atarashi Maru*, and *Shosei Maru*.

EUROPE. Off Normandy, destroyer *Meredith* (DD 726) sinks of cumulative damage (bomb and mine), 49°26'N, 01°04'W. German *schnellbootes S 172*, *S 174*, *S 175*, and *S 187* attack convoy in English Channel, torpedoing and sinking tank landing ship *LST 314*, 49°43'N, 00°52'W, and damaging tank landing ship *LST 376*. The latter is later scuttled by escorts, 49°43'N, 00°53'W. Large infantry landing craft *LCI(L) 416* is sunk by mine; motor minesweeper *YMS 305* is damaged by shore battery, 49°31'N, 00°50'W. U.S. freighter *Ezra Weston* is damaged by shore battery fire that kills five and wounds 11 of her 600 embarked troops; there are no other casualties among the ship's complement, including the 26-man Armed Guard. Destroyer escort *Maloy* (DE 791) (flagship for TF 122) is hit by friendly fire during air raid on shipping off the beachhead; attack cargo ship *Achernar* (AKA 53) provides medical assistance to the wounded.

10   Saturday

PACIFIC. PB4Ys (VB 108 and VB 109) sweep ahead of TF 58 (Vice Admiral Marc A. Mitscher) as it approaches the Marianas, to intercept and destroy any Japanese aircraft in the path of the fast carriers. These sweeps will be repeated on 11 June. During these two days of operations, a PB4Y from each squadron will shoot down a Japanese plane at some distance away from the task force. The use of PB4Ys is decided upon because sightings of these long-range planes in that region is a commonplace occurrence and would thus arouse no enemy suspicions that a carrier task force is in the area.

High-speed transport *Talbot* (APD 7) is damaged in collision with battleship *Pennsylvania* (BB 38), en route to the Marianas.

Destroyer *Taylor* (DD 468) sinks Japanese submarine *RO 111*, 210 miles north-northwest of Kavieng, New Ireland, 00°26'N, 149°16'E.

Destroyer escort *Bangust* (DE 739) sinks Japanese submarine *RO 42*, 70 miles northeast of Kwajalein, 10°05'N, 168°22'E.

British submarine HMS *Tantalus* sinks Japanese army cargo ship *Hiyoshi Maru* in Strait of Malacca, 03°05'N, 99°56'E.

USAAF B-25s (5th Air Force) bomb Japanese shipping off Manokwari, New Guinea, sinking auxiliary sailing vessel *Shinei Maru*.

Japanese cargo vessel *Yozan Maru* is damaged by mine off Manila.

Japanese cargo vessel *Kinmon Maru* is sunk by accidental fire, Singapore, 01°17'N, 103°51'E.

EUROPE. Destroyer *Glennon* (DD 620), previously damaged by mine on 8 June, is hit by German artillery fire and sinks off Normandy, 49°32'N, 01°11'W; tank landing craft *LCT 209* sinks after running aground off beachhead. U.S. freighter *Charles Morgan* is damaged by bomb off UTAH beach that kills seven of the 64-man Army stevedore unit on board and one merchant crewman; there are no casualties among the 27-man Armed Guard. Fleet tug *Kiowa* (ATF 72) takes on board the survivors while large infantry landing craft *LCI(L) 319*, one of two specially equipped LCI(L)s for salvage and fire fighting, extinguishes the blaze. *Charles Morgan*, however, despite strenuous efforts to save her, is ultimately declared a total loss.

ATLANTIC. Large infantry landing craft *LCI(L) 691* breaks down off Bay Head, New Jersey; tug *Allegheny* (ATO 19) tows the disabled vessel to Cape May, New Jersey, arriving the following day.

MEDITERRANEAN. Heaviest German air raid since 3 May occurs off Anzio against U.S. shipping off the beachhead. Minesweeper *Symbol* (AM 123), tank landing ship *LST 211*, large infantry landing craft *LCI(L) 41*, and U.S.

freighter *Tarleton Brown* are all damaged by near-misses.

11 Sunday

PACIFIC. F6Fs from TF 58 (Vice Admiral Marc A. Mitscher), 16 from each carrier and 12 from each small carrier, accompanied by a TBF or SB2C from each task group (the latter to lead the fighters in and out), blanket Japanese airfields in the Marianas. This move, which achieves complete surprise, assures control of the air over the Marianas. Combat air patrol F6Fs from TF 58 intercept and splash Japanese planes in the vicinity of TF 58. F6Fs also damage auxiliary submarine chaser *No. 8 Shonan Maru* and aircraft transport *Keiyo Maru* (see 13 June).[194]

Submarine *Barb* (SS 220) sinks Japanese merchant fishing vessels *Chihaya Maru* and *Toten Maru* in Sea of Okhotsk, east of Karafuto, 46°50′N, 144°05′E.

Submarine *Redfin* (SS 272), despite presence of escort vessel, sinks Japanese tanker *Asanagi Maru* west of Jolo, 06°02′N, 120°50′E.

Naval Base, Biak Island, Schouten Islands, is established.

EUROPE. U.S. battleships off Normandy provide gunfire support to U.S. Army forces (101st Airborne) 10 miles inland at Carentan, France (see 12 June).

German motor torpedo boats *S 130*, *S 144*, *S 146*, *S 150,* and *S 167* attack U.S. invasion shipping off Normandy, sinking tank landing ship *LST 496* and tug *Partridge* (ATO 138), 49°30′N, 00°50′N, and damaging *LST 538*, 49°48′N, 00°31′W. During German air attack on shipping off UTAH beach, large infantry landing craft *LCI(L) 219* is near-missed by a bomb that riddles the ship with fragments. Despite efforts by submarine chaser *SC 1291* and the LCI(L)'s crew to keep her afloat, *LCI(L) 219* sinks 90 minutes later. Fleet tug *Bannock* (ATF 81) is damaged when she fouls underwater wreckage off RED beach.

ATLANTIC. TBF (VC 95) from escort carrier *Croatan* (CVE 25) teams with destroyer escorts *Frost* (DE 144), *Huse* (DE 145), and *Inch* (DE 146) to sink German submarine *U 490* midway between Flores Island and Flemish Cap, 42°47′N, 40°08′W.

12 Monday

PACIFIC. TF 58 (Vice Admiral Marc A. Mitscher) works over Japanese air facilities and coast defenses on Saipan, Tinian, Guam, Rota, and Pagan Islands, Marianas. Carrier strikes are repeated on 13 and 14 June in preparation for the landings on Saipan. Aircraft from carrier *Essex* (CV 9) and small carriers *Langley* (CVL 27) and *Cowpens* (CVL 25) (TG 58.4) smash Japanese convoy (which had sailed from Tanapag Harbor for Japan the previous day) northwest of Saipan, sinking torpedo boat *Otori*, 17°32′N, 144°00′E; auxiliary netlayer *Kokku Maru*, 17°32′N, 144°01′E; transports *Batavia Maru*, 17°32′N, 143°17′E, *Hinko Maru*, 17°28′N, 144°19′E, *Kamishima Maru* and *Imizu Maru*, 17°32′N, 144°10′E, *Nitcho Maru*, 17°32′N, 143°10′E, *Reikai Maru*, 17°30′N, 144°00′E, and *Tenryugawa Maru*, 17°32′N, 144°01′E; cargo ship *Bokuyo Maru*; army cargo ships *Fukoku Maru* and *Moji Maru*; and merchant vessel *Tsushima Maru*. Aircraft damage transport *Tatsutakawa Maru* (see 15 June), *Coast Defense Vessel No. 4*, 17°20′N, 144°10′E, submarine chaser *Ch 50*, 17°32′N, 144°10′E, and submarine chasers *Ch 33* and *Ch 51*, auxiliary submarine chaser *Cha 20,* and auxiliary minesweeper *Wa 6*.[195]

Japanese minelayer *Nichiyu Maru*, torpedoed by submarine *Halibut* (SS 232) on 3 March 1943, is further damaged by carrier planes in Apra Harbor, Guam.

Destroyer *Kalk* (DD 611) is damaged by horizontal bomber off western New Guinea, 01°19′S, 136°19′E.

British submarine HMS *Stoic* attacks Japanese convoy and sinks transport *Kainan Maru* off Phuket, Siam, 07°54′N, 98°27′E.

EUROPE. U.S. battleship gunfire supports U.S. Army 101st Airborne as it encircles Carentan, France, and takes the city. Destroyer *Nelson* (DD 623) is torpedoed by German motor torpedo boat *S 138* off OMAHA beach, 49°31′N, 00°50′W; rescue tug *ATR 3* provides assistance to the damaged destroyer.

13 Tuesday

PACIFIC. TF 58 (Vice Admiral Marc A. Mitscher) strikes against Japanese shipping off Saipan continue. Carrier-based planes sink aircraft transport *Keiyo Maru* (which had been damaged in the 11 June fighter sweep) and destroy convoy of small cargo vessels: *No. 11 Shinriki Maru*, *Sekizen Maru*, *Myogawa Maru*, *Shigei Maru,* and *Suwa Maru*. F6Fs attack convoy spotted the previous day and damage fast transport *T.1* southwest of the Marianas, 11°43′N, 140°42′E.

During the strikes, Commander William I. Martin, commanding officer of *Enterprise*'s VT-10, is shot down and parachutes into the sea off RED beach THREE, Saipan. Before he is rescued, he observes that the Japanese have marked the length of the reef offshore with red and white pennants, indicating presited artillery ranges—valuable intelligence information quickly disseminated to the approaching amphibious forces.

TG 58.7 (Vice Admiral Willis A. Lee Jr.) battleships and destroyers conduct an almost day-long bombardment of Japanese installations on Saipan and Tinian.

TF 94 (Rear Admiral Ernest G. Small) cruisers and destroyers bombard Japanese position on Matsuwa Island in the Kurils.

Submarine *Barb* (SS 220) sinks Japanese army transport *Takashima Maru* in Sea of Okhotsk, 50°53′N, 151°12′E, and survives counterattacks by destroyer *Hatsuharu*.

Submarine *Flier* (SS 250) damages Japanese merchant tanker *Marifu Maru* in South China Sea west of Luzon, 15°57′N, 119°42′E (see 6 November).

Submarine *Narwhal* (SS 167) shells oil tanks at Bula, Ceram Island, N.E.I.

Destroyer *Melvin* (DD 680) sinks Japanese submarine *RO 36* between 50 and 75 miles east of Saipan, 15°21′N, 147°00′E.

ATLANTIC. Unarmed U.S. fishing boat *Lark* is shelled and machine gunned by German submarine *U 107* 32 miles off Cape Sable Light, 42°54′N, 65°25′W, and abandoned with the exception of the master and the cook. *Lark* remains afloat as the U-boat leaves the scene, whereupon she rescues every man who had abandoned ship at the approach of the enemy.

14 Wednesday

PACIFIC. Bombardment groups, TG 52.17 (Rear Admiral Jesse B. Oldendorf) and TG 52.18 (Rear Admiral Walden L. Ainsworth), shell Japanese installations on Saipan and Tinian. Enemy shore battery fire damages battleship *California* (BB 44) off Saipan, 15°12′N, 145°42′E, and destroyer *Braine* (DD 630) off Tinian, 15°12′N, 145°42′E; near-misses from shells damage battleship *Tennessee* (BB 43), heavy cruiser *Indianapolis* (CA 35), light cruiser *Birmingham* (CL 62), and destroyer *Remey* (DD 688). Destroyer *Wadleigh* (DD 689) covers withdrawal of Underwater Demolition Team (UDT) 7 after its beach reconnaissance mission.

Submarine *Golet* (SS 361) is probably sunk by Japanese guardboat *Miya Maru*, auxiliary submarine chaser *Bunzan Maru*, and naval aircraft off northern Honshu, 41°04′N, 141°31′E.[196]

Submarine *Rasher* (SS 269), in attack on Japanese convoy in the Celebes Sea, sinks army cargo ship *Koan Maru* about 130 miles south of Mindanao, 04°33′N, 122°23′E.

EUROPE. Tank landing ship *LST 280* is torpedoed by German submarine *U 621* off Normandy, 49°55′N, 00°30′W.

15 Thursday

PACIFIC. Operation FORAGER: TF 52 (Vice Admiral Richmond Kelly Turner) lands Marines (Lieutenant General Holland M. Smith, USMC) on Saipan supported by intensive naval gunfire and carrier-based aircraft. Saipan is the first relatively large and heavily defended land mass in the Central Pacific to be assaulted by American amphibious might. Chengtu, China–based USAAF B-29s (20th Air Force) bomb the Yawata Steel Mills, northern Kyushu, Japan, marking the first time that B-29s are used in distant support of an ongoing amphibious operation. It is also the first time that USAAF planes have bombed the Japanese homeland since the Halsey-Doolittle Raid of 18 April 1942.

Battleship *Tennessee* (BB 43) is damaged by shore battery, northeast of Tinian, 15°02′N, 143°50′E; light cruiser *St. Louis* (CL 49) is damaged by materiel casualty (dropped no. 3 propeller and part of tail shaft), Saipan Channel. Infantry landing craft (gunboat) *LCI(G) 451* and *LCI(G) 726* are damaged by mortar fire off approaches to Saipan landing beaches.

Carrier-based aircraft from TG 58.1 (Rear Admiral Joseph J. Clark) and TG 58.4 (Rear Admiral William K. Harrill) bomb Japanese installations on Iwo Jima, Volcano Islands, and Chichi Jima and Haha Jima in the Bonins; attack on Iwo Jima is repeated on 16 June. Destroyers *Boyd* (DD 544) and *Charrette* (DD 581) sink transport *Tatsutakawa Maru* after she had been damaged by TBFs, TBMs, and F6Fs from small carrier *Bataan* (CVL 29) east of the Bonins, 25°02′N, 144°37′E. TF 58 aircraft sink auxiliary submarine chaser *Cha 54* off Rota Island, Marianas. Destroyer *Halsey Powell* (DD 686) sinks minelayer *Ma 101* (ex-British netlayer HMS *Barlight*, captured at Hong Kong in December 1941) in Tanapag Harbor, Saipan, 15°15′N, 145°45′E.

Japanese submarine chaser *Ch 7* is sunk by mine south of the Palaus, 04°03′N, 135°08′E.

Submarine *Swordfish* (SS 193) attacks Japanese convoy, sinking army cargo ship *Kanseishi Maru* about 150 miles north-northwest of Chichi Jima, 29°30′N, 144°07′E.

Japanese destroyer *Shiratsuyu* is sunk in collision with oiler *Seiyo Maru* west of Mindanao, 09°09′N, 126°51′E.

Japanese cargo vessel *Kanzaki Maru* is stranded and sunk off east coast of Korea, 36°01′N, 129°41′E.

USAAF A-20s, covered by P-38s (5th Air Force), attack Japanese shipping in Kaironi Harbor, near Manokwari, New Guinea, sinking fishing boats *Gyokuto Maru* and *No. 3 Chogyo Maru*, 00°44′S, 133°34′E.

ATLANTIC. TBFs and FM-2s (VC 9) from escort carrier *Solomons* (CVE 67) sink German submarine *U 860* in South Atlantic, 25°27′S, 05°30′W.

EUROPE. Off Normandy, tank landing ships *LST 2*, *LST 266*, *LST 307*, *LST 331*, and *LST 360* are damaged by shore batteries, *LST 133* by mine. Tank landing craft *LCT 447* is damaged by near-miss of bomb during air raid.

MEDITERRANEAN. Motor torpedo boats *PT 552*, *PT 558*, and *PT 559* sink German torpedo boats *TA 26* (ex-Italian Navy *Intrepido*) and *TA 30* (ex-Italian Navy *Dragone*) off the Italian coast between La Spezia and Genoa, 43°58′N, 09°29′E.

UNITED STATES. Admiral Thomas C. Hart, USN (Retired), concludes his inquiry that had begun on 12 February to examine witnesses and record testimony pertinent to the Pearl Harbor attack. The record of the proceedings and exhibits of the "Hart Inquiry" comes to 565 printed pages.

16 Friday

PACIFIC. Battleship, cruiser, and destroyer force (Rear Admiral Walden L. Ainsworth) bombards Japanese installations on Guam.

High-speed transport *Gilmer* (APD 11), on radar picket duty 25 miles west of Saipan, encounters Japanese convoy of small cargo vessels (whose sailors are apparently unaware of the presence of American ships in the Marianas) bound for Saipan, and sinks four: *No. 1 Yusen Maru*, *No. 2 Usen Maru*, *Toa Maru*, and *Tatsutaka Maru*. Destroyer *Shaw* (DD 373), ordered to support *Gilmer*, arrives in time to sink a fifth ship, *No. 17 Yusen Maru*.

Light cruiser *Vincennes* (CL 64) is damaged by materiel casualty (main Kingsbury thrust bearing, no. 3 shaft), at sea with TG 58.4.

Destroyers *Melvin* (DD 680) and *Wadleigh* (DD 689) sink Japanese submarine *RO 114*, 80 miles west of Tinian, 15°02′N, 144°10′E.

Destroyer escort *Burden R. Hastings* (DE 19) sinks Japanese submarine *RO 44*, 110 miles east of Eniwetok, 11°13′N, 164°15′E.

Submarine *Bluefish* (SS 222) attacks Japanese convoy, sinking freighter *Nanshin Maru* in

the Celebes Sea southwest of Tarakan, Borneo, 02°22′N, 118°24′E.

Submarine *Bream* (SS 243) sinks Japanese army cargo ship *Yuki Maru* and damages army cargo ship *Hinode Maru* off Halmahera Island, 02°23′N, 128°43′E; *Coast Defense Vessel No. 2* and submarine chaser *Ch 41* rescue survivors.

17 Saturday

PACIFIC. Japanese carrier bombers (JUDYs) and land attack planes (FRANCESs) attack U.S. carrier force off Tinian, Marianas, damaging escort carrier *Fanshaw Bay* (CVE 70), 15°00′N, 145°00′E. Tank landing ship *LST 84* is damaged by friendly fire, 15°10′N, 145°58′E; infantry landing craft (gunboat) *LCI(G) 468*, damaged by Japanese torpedo planes (JILLs) en route to Saipan, is scuttled by destroyer *Stembel* (DD 644), 13°28′N, 148°18′E. TF 58 aircraft sink Japanese auxiliary submarine chaser *Cha 56* at Rota and transport *Marudai Maru* off Saipan.

PB4Y-1 (VB 109) from Eniwetok sinks Japanese submarine *RO 117* north-northwest of Truk, 11°05′N, 150°31′E.

Submarine *Hake* (SS 256) attacks Japanese convoy as it proceeds from Palau to Davao, and sinks transport *Kinshu Maru* about 65 miles southeast of Davao, 06°10′N, 126°18′E. Later that same day, *Flounder* (SS 251) attacks the same convoy and sinks torpedo recovery ship *Nihonkai Maru* south of Mindanao, 06°36′N, 127°55′E, and survives depth chargings by submarine chasers *Ch 35* and *Ch 64*.

USAAF B-25s (5th Air Force), supported by fighters, work over Japanese shipping in Sorong Harbor, sinking army cargo ships *Minyu Maru* and *No. 12 Sanko Maru* and freighter *Shofuku Maru*, 00°53′N, 131°15′E.

Japanese tanker *Nichiyoko Maru* is damaged by mine off Belawan, Sumatra, N.E.I., 03°40′N, 99°07′E.

EUROPE. Motor minesweeper *YMS 377* is damaged by mine off Normandy, 49°29′N, 01°08′W; tank landing ship *LST 292* is damaged during beaching off RED beach.

ATLANTIC. TBF (VC 95) from escort carrier *Croatan* (CVE 25) damages German submarine *U 853* in the North Atlantic.

MEDITERRANEAN. Allied task force (Rear Admiral Thomas H. Troubridge, RN), including U.S. naval vessels, lands French troops on island of Elba off Italy. U.S. Navy ships participating in the landings include six destroyers, one destroyer escort, five minesweepers, 15 motor minesweepers, 16 submarine chasers, 10 tank landing ships, 20 tank landing craft, and 19 infantry landing craft; one LCI(L) is damaged by shore battery fire. Four U.S. motor torpedo boats sink four German F-lighters loaded with German troops being evacuated from Elba.

18 Sunday

PACIFIC. Destroyer *Phelps* (DD 360), along with infantry landing craft (gunboat) [LCI(G)s] and amphibian tractors [LVT(A)s], oppose between 25 and 30 Japanese landing barges, southward-bound off Garapan, Saipan, sinking 13 and putting the rest to flight. Elsewhere off Saipan, battleship *California* (BB 44) is damaged by friendly fire; *Phelps*, *LCI(G) 371*, and motor minesweeper *YMS 323* are damaged by shore battery off Garapan, 14°58′N, 146°21′E.[197] Japanese naval aircraft bomb U.S. shipping east-northeast of Guam; oilers *Neshanic* (AO 71) and *Saranac* (AO 74) are damaged at 14°45′N, 146°10′E, and oiler *Saugatuck* (AO 75) is near-missed.

Motor torpedo boats *PT 63* and *PT 107* are destroyed by fire after gasoline on the water's surface ignites during refueling at Hamburg Bay, off New Ireland, 01°45′S, 150°01′E.

British submarine HMS *Storm* attacks Japanese convoy off Penang, Malaya, sinking gunboat *Eiko Maru*, 05°59′N, 99°10′E.

19 Monday

PACIFIC. Battle of the Philippine Sea opens as the Japanese Fleet (Vice Admiral Ozawa Jisaburo) contests the landings on Saipan. Japanese carrier-based aircraft attack Fifth Fleet (Admiral Raymond A. Spruance) covering Saipan operation. Despite the combat air patrol and heavy antiaircraft fire, battleship *South Dakota* (BB 57) is damaged by dive bomber, 14°10′N, 143°15′E; battleship *Indiana* (BB 58) is damaged by suicide plane, 14°04′N, 143°23′E; carriers *Bunker Hill* (CV 17), 14°46′N, 143°02′E, and *Wasp* (CV 18), 14°19′N, 143°48′E, are near-missed by dive bombers; heavy cruiser *Minneapolis* (CA 36) is near-missed by horizontal bomber, 14°11′N, 143°09′E; and destroyer *Hudson* (DD 475) is damaged by friendly fire, 14°11′N, 143°09′E. The Japanese lose at least 300 aircraft in what U.S. Navy pilots call the "Marianas Turkey Shoot." Commander David McCampbell, Commander Air Group 15, flying from carrier *Essex* (CV 9), distinguishes himself in aerial combat, splashing at least seven Japanese planes in defense of TF 58 (see 24 October).

Submarine *Albacore* (SS 218) sinks Japanese carrier *Taiho* 180 nautical miles north-north-west of Yap, 12°22′N, 137°04′E; submarine *Cavalla* (SS 244) sinks Japanese carrier *Shokaku* 140 nautical miles north of Yap Island, 11°50′N, 137°57′E. Both boats survive counterattacks by escorts; *Albacore* counts 75 depth charges, *Cavalla* 106.

Motor minesweeper *YMS 323* is damaged by shore battery, as she carries out survey operations off Tanapag Harbor, Saipan, 15°10′N, 145°58′E.

TBM (VT 60) from escort carrier *Suwanee* (CVE 27) sinks Japanese submarine *I 184*, 20 miles south of Guam, 13°01′N, 149°53′E.

USAAF A-20s raid Manokwari, New Guinea, sinking small Japanese cargo vessels *No. 5 Masutuko Maru* and *No. 43 Taigyo Maru*.

EUROPE. Artificial harbor off Normandy installed on 7 June is severely damaged by storm. Elsewhere off the invasion beaches, tank landing ship *LST 523* is sunk by mine, 49°30′N, 01°10′W; rescue tug *ATR 15* is damaged by grounding, 49°22′N, 00°26′W.

20 Tuesday

PACIFIC. Battle of the Philippine Sea concludes as planes from TF 58 (Vice Admiral Marc A. Mitscher), launched late in the afternoon from carriers *Hornet* (CV 12), *Yorktown* (CV 10), *Bunker Hull* (CV 17), and *Lexington* (CV 16) and small carriers *Belleau Wood* (CVL 24), *Monterey* (CVL 26), and *San Jacinto* (CVL 30), strike Japanese fleet in what becomes known as the "Mission Beyond Darkness." TBFs from *Belleau Wood* sink carrier *Hiyo* northwest of Yap Island, 15°30′N, 133°50′E. Fleet tanker *Gen'yo Maru*, damaged by F6Fs, SB2Cs, and TBFs from carrier *Wasp* (CV 18), is scuttled by destroyer *Uzuki*, west of Saipan; likewise, oiler *Seiyo Maru*, damaged by F6Fs, SB2Cs, and TBFs from *Wasp*, is scuttled by destroyer *Yukikaze*, 15°35′N, 133°30′E. TF 58 planes also damage carrier *Zuikaku*, small carriers *Chiyoda* and *Ryuho*, battleship *Haruna*, heavy cruiser *Maya*, destroyers *Samidare* and *Shigure*, and fast fleet tanker/seaplane carrier *Hayasui*. Vice Admiral Mitscher orders the ships of TF 58 to show lights in order to guide returning strike groups home. In the Battle of the Philippine Sea the Japanese Fleet loses 395 (92 percent) of its carrier planes, and 12 floatplanes remain operational. Besides the losses afloat, an estimated 50 land-based Japanese aircraft from Guam are destroyed. The U.S. Fleet loss is 130 planes and 76 pilots and crewmen for the two days, predominantly from the "Mission Beyond Darkness" on 20 June (see 23 June).

Destroyer *Phelps* (DD 360) is damaged by shore battery, Saipan, 15°10′N, 145°58′E.

Submarine *Hake* (SS 256) attacks Japanese convoy off south coast of Mindanao, and sinks army cargo ship *Nichibi Maru* in Saragan Strait, 05°36′N, 125°17′E.

Submarine *Narwhal* (SS 167) lands party of four enlisted men, together with supplies, off north shore of Lipata Point, Panay, P.I., and takes on board 14 evacuees (including one woman).

USAAF A-20s raid New Guinea coastline, sinking Japanese fishing vessels *Shinei Maru* and *No. 3 Kompira Maru* at Manokwari and *No. 31 Taikoko Maru* at Windessi.

21 Wednesday

PACIFIC. Destroyer *Newcomb* (DD 586) and high-speed minesweeper *Chandler* (DMS 9) sink Japanese submarine *I 185*, 90 miles east-northeast of Saipan, 15°50′N, 145°08′E; Japanese guardboat *Kompira Maru* is sunk by gunfire off Tinian.

Submarine *Bluefish* (SS 222), despite presence of escort, sinks Japanese army cargo ship *Kanan Maru* off southern approaches to Makassar Strait, 03°58′S, 116°35′E.

Submarine *Narwhal* (SS 167) sinks Japanese powered sailboat *No. 2 Shinshu Maru* 12 miles southwest of Culasi, 11°22′N, 121°52′E.

Dutch submarine *K 14* damages Japanese minelayer *Tsugaru* between Sorong, New Guinea, and Kau Roads, Moluccas, 01°10′S, 130°30′E.

TBF/Ms and F4Fs (VC 4) from escort carrier *White Plains* (CVE 66) sink Japanese cargo ship *Shoun Maru* off Rota, Saipan, 14°10′N, 145°10′E.

EUROPE. Off Normandy, destroyer *Davis* (DD 395) is damaged by mine, 49°23′N, 00°46′W; Coast Guard cutters *CGC 83415* and *CGC 83471* are sunk by storm.

MEDITERRANEAN. German torpedo boat *TA 25* (ex-Italian Navy *Ardito*), damaged by U.S. motor torpedo boats southwest of Viareggio, Italy, 43°49′N, 10°12′E, is scuttled by German (ex-Italian) torpedo boat *TA 29*.

22 Thursday

PACIFIC. Battleship *Maryland* (BB 46) is damaged by aerial torpedo off Garapan, Saipan, 15°13′N, 145°39′E; tank landing ship *LST 119* is damaged by Tinian shore battery, Saipan, 15°10′N, 145°58′E; and transport *Prince Georges* (AP 165) is damaged by near-miss of bomb off Saipan.

Submarine *Batfish* (SS 310) sinks Japanese freighter *Nagaragawa Maru* off Honshu, 34°36′N, 137°56′E.

Submarine *Flier* (SS 250) torpedoes Japanese army cargo ship *Belgium Maru* west of Mindoro, 13°11′N, 120°27′E.

Submarine *Narwhal* (SS 167) damages Japanese tanker *Itsukushima Maru* in Sulu Sea, 09°00′N, 120°55′E.

Submarine *Nautilus* (SS 168) disembarks party of four Filipino enlisted men and cargo of supplies, and embarks 16 evacuees (including a German POW, four women, and two children), in addition to embarking 18 Malayan natives.

USAAF B-25s attack Japanese shipping off Soprong Island, New Guinea; cargo vessel *Shoyo Maru* is sunk.

EUROPE. U.S. freighter *Cyrus H. K. Curtis* is damaged by mines off SWORD beach, Normandy, but discharges her cargo; there are no casualties among the 43-man merchant complement, the 27-man Armed Guard, or the 250 U.S. troops on board.

23 Friday

PACIFIC. TG 58.1 (Rear Admiral Joseph J. Clark) aircraft bomb Japanese air facilities and shipping in the Marianas, sinking guardboat *Haruta Maru* off Pagan Island.

SB2C crew (VB 14) is rescued by PBM (VH 1); the two men picked up by the flying boat are the last to be recovered in the wake of the "Mission Beyond Darkness" of 20 June. Ironically, the PBM is off course when it finds and recovers the men.

Japanese planes begin night high-level bombing attack on U.S. amphibious shipping off Saipan.

24 Saturday

PACIFIC. Japanese planes conclude night high-level bombing attack on U.S. shipping off Saipan. Battle damage repair ship *Phaon* (ARB 3), submarine chasers *PC(S) 1401* and *PC(S) 1461*, and tank landing craft *LCT 998* are all damaged by near-misses.

TG 58.1 and TG 58.2 (Rear Admiral Joseph J. Clark and Rear Admiral Alfred E. Montgomery, respectively) planes strike Japanese airfields and facilities on Iwo Jima, Volcano Islands, and Pagan Island, Marianas.

Motor torpedo boat *PT 193*, irreparably damaged by grounding, western New Guinea, 00°55′S, 134°52′E, is burned by her crew.

Submarine *Grouper* (SS 214) attacks Japanese convoy off coast of central Japan, and sinks cargo ship *Kumanoyama Maru* and merchant tanker *No. 6 Nanmei Maru* south of Yokosuka, 34°45′N, 139°30′E.

Submarine *Redfin* (SS 272) attacks Japanese convoy off southern coast of Leyte, P.I., and sinks army cargo ship *Aso Maru* southwest of Surigao Strait, 09°51′N, 125°06′E.

Submarine *Tang* (SS 306) attacks Japanese convoy leaving Koshiki Straits and sinks army cargo ships *Tamahoko Maru* and *Kennichi Maru*, merchant tanker *Nasuzan Maru,* and cargo ship *Tainan Maru* outside Nagasaki Harbor, Kyushu, 32°24′N, 129°38′E. *Coast Defense Vessel No. 1* does not prove fast enough to pursue *Tang* to counterattack.

ATLANTIC. TBM (VC 69) from escort carrier *Bogue* (CVE 9) sinks Japanese submarine *I 52*, 800 miles southwest of Fayal, Azores, 15°16′N, 39°55′W.

25 Sunday

PACIFIC. Submarine *Bashaw* (SS 241) attacks Japanese convoy and sinks army cargo ship *Yamamiya Maru* between Taland Island and Halmahera, 03°28′N, 127°06′E.

Submarine *Jack* (SS 259) attacks Japanese convoy and sinks merchant tanker *San Pedro Maru* off northwest coast of Luzon, 16°17′N, 119°40′E.

Japanese minelayer *Nichiyu Maru,* previously damaged on 3 March 1943 and 12 June 1944, is further damaged by naval gunfire in Apra Harbor, Guam.[198]

EUROPE. TF 129 (Rear Admiral Morton L. Deyo) duels German shore batteries and coastal defenses at Cherbourg, France; battleship *Texas* (BB 35) and destroyers *Barton* (DD 722), *Laffey* (DD 724), and *O'Brien* (DD 725) are all damaged by the enemy gunfire.

26 Monday

PACIFIC. TF 94 (Rear Admiral Ernest G. Small) bombards Japanese positions at Kurabu Saki, Paramushir, Kurils.

Infantry landing craft (gunboat) *LCI(G) 438* and *LCI(G) 456* repel attack by Japanese barges (some of which fire torpedoes) off Tanapag Harbor, Saipan, but both gunboats are damaged in the battle. Elsewhere off Saipan, cargo ship *Mercury* (AK 42) is damaged by low-flying Japanese aircraft that flies into cargo boom, and is hit by dud aerial torpedo, 15°10′N, 145°58′E.

British submarine HMS *Truculent* attacks Japanese convoy, sinking cargo ship *Harugiku Maru* about 60 miles southeast of Medan, Sumatra, 03°15′N, 99°46′E.

USAAF P-38s sink Japanese army cargo ship *Hokushin Maru* east of Halmahera Island, 01°03′N, 131°08′E.

USAAF B-25s sink Japanese fishing boat *No. 1 Daisen Maru* off Manokwari, New Guinea.

EUROPE. German garrison at Cherbourg, France, surrenders.

27 Tuesday

PACIFIC. TF 58 planes complete destruction of Japanese water tanker *Kizugawa Maru*, already damaged irreparably by submarine *Seahorse* (SS 304) on 8 April off Guam.

Submarine *Seahorse* (SS 304) attacks Japanese convoy TAMA 23 and sinks merchant tanker *Medan Maru* south-southwest of Formosa, 21°10′N, 120°31′E.

28 Wednesday

PACIFIC. Submarine *Archerfish* (SS 311) sinks Japanese *Coast Defense Vessel No. 24*, 30 miles southwest of Iwo Jima, 24°25′N, 141°20′E, as the enemy warship covers unloading operations by what are most likely landing ships.

Submarine *Pargo* (SS 264) attacks Japanese convoy in Moro Gulf, sinking army cargo ship *Yamagiku Maru* and damaging *Coast Defense Vessel No. 10* about 35 miles east of Zamboanga, 06°50′N, 121°30′E.

Submarine *Sealion* (SS 315), despite presence of escorts, sinks Japanese collier *Sansei Maru* in Tsushima Strait, 33°53′N, 129°01′E.

USAAF B-24s (14th Air Force) attack Japanese convoy MATA 23 southwest of the Pescadores, sinking transport *Ussuri Maru* off Formosa, 23°49′N, 119°02′E; oiler *Rikko Maru* is damaged.

EUROPE. U.S. freighter *Charles W. Eliot* fouls two mines about four miles off JUNO beach, Normandy, and breaks in two; there are no fatalities among the crew (including the 31-man Armed Guard). Survivors are transferred to freighter *George W. Woodward* and later tank landing craft *LCT 527* for transportation to England. *Charles W. Eliot* is subsequently written off as a total loss.

29 Thursday

PACIFIC. Submarine *Bang* (SS 385) damages Japanese fleet tanker *Miru Maru* (see 15 January 1945) and merchant tanker *Sarawak Maru* west of Luzon, 17°13′N, 118°22′E.

Submarine *Darter* (SS 227) attacks Japanese convoy off northern tip of Halmahera Island and sinks minelayer *Tsugaru*, 02°10′N, 128°05′E.

Submarine *Flasher* (SS 249) attacks Japanese convoy, sinking freighter *Nippo Maru* and damaging oiler *Notoro* about 125 miles southeast of Singapore, 00°44′N, 105°45′E; *Ayanami Maru* will tow *Notoro* to Singapore for repairs, escorted by minesweeper *W.17* (see 5 November).

Submarine *Growler* (SS 215), despite presence of three escort vessels, sinks Japanese transport *Katori Maru* in Luzon Strait, 19°00′N, 121°42′E.

Submarine *Sturgeon* (SS 187) attacks Japanese convoy, sinking army cargo ship *Toyama Maru* in the Nansei Shoto, off Taira Jima, 27°47′N, 129°05′E.

ATLANTIC. Coastal minesweeper *Valor* (AMc 108) is sunk in collision with destroyer escort *Richard W. Suesens* (DE 342) off Newport, Rhode Island, 41°128′N, 70°57′W.

EUROPE. German submarine *U 984* attacks OMAHA beach–bound convoy EMC 17 about 30 miles south of the Isle of Wight, torpedoing U.S. freighters *Edward M. House, H. G. Blasdel,* and *James A. Farrell* at 50°07′N, 00°47′W, and *John A. Treutlen* at 50°11′50′N, 00°45′35′W. *Edward M. House* resumes her voyage and reaches the beachhead to discharge cargo and disembark troops; she suffers only two men injured (one of whom is from the 28-man Armed Guard). *H. G. Blasdel* suffers the loss of 76 of her embarked troops (180 are wounded) of the 436 on board; tank landing ship *LST 326* takes off the surviving troops. The ship is later towed to Southampton, England, where she is written off as a total loss. *James A. Farrell* is abandoned, survivors transferring to tank landing ship *LST 50*; four soldiers are killed and 45 wounded from among the 421 embarked on board. There are no casualties among the 42-man merchant complement or the 31-man Armed Guard, but the ship, towed to Spithead, is written off as a total loss. *John A. Treutlen* is abandoned save for a skeleton crew; the merchant complement and 31-man Armed Guard are picked up by Canadian corvette HMCS *Buctouche* and tank landing ship *LST 336*. *John A. Treutlen* is subsequently written off as a total loss.

MEDITERRANEAN. Motor torpedo boats *PT 308* and *PT 309* (Lieutenant John Newell, USNR), patrolling between Cape Falcone on the Italian mainland and the island of Elba, engage two Italian motor torpedo boats, damaging *MAS 562* and forcing its abandonment (see 30 June).

30 Friday

UNITED STATES. Naval ships and craft on hand (all types)—46,032. People: Navy—2,981,365; Marine Corps—472,582; Coast Guard—169,258. Total—3,623,205.

PACIFIC. Submarine *Jack* (SS 259) attacks Japanese convoy about 70 miles west of Manila and sinks army cargo ships *Tsurushima Maru* and *Matsukawa Maru*, 14°15′N, 119°40′E.

Submarine *Plaice* (SS 390), despite a debilitating epidemic of intestinal influenza on board, sinks Japanese gunboat *Hyakafuku Maru* northwest of Chichi Jima, 28°20′N, 141°23′E. Auxiliary netlayer *Kogi Maru*'s counterattack is unsuccessful.

Submarine *Tang* (SS 306) sinks Japanese freighter *Nikkin Maru* in the Yellow Sea off Mokp'o, Korea, 35°05′N, 125°00′E.

Japanese guardboat *Aikoku Maru* is sunk by shore battery off Kwajalein.

EUROPE. Off Normandy during the month of June (exact dates unknown), tank landing craft *LCT 572, LCT 713,* and *LCT 714* are sunk by mines; *LCT 147* sinks after running aground; and *LCT 200, LCT 244,* and *LCT 413* are lost to the rigors of amphibious operations.

MEDITERRANEAN. Motor torpedo boat *PT 306* captures Italian motor torpedo boat *MAS 562* off Elba and tows it into Bastia, Corsica.

JULY

1 Saturday

PACIFIC. Submarine *Batfish* (SS 310) sinks Japanese guardboats *Kamoi Maru* and *No. 5 Isuzugawa Maru* northwest of the Marianas, 31°26′N, 141°11′E.

Submarine *Tang* (SS 306) sinks Japanese fleet tanker *No. 1 Takatori Maru* off Mokp'o, Korea, 34°21′N, 123°55′E, and freighter *No. 2 Taiun Maru*, 34°42′N, 125°25′E.

Japanese freighter *Nikko Maru* is sunk by mine, possibly laid by submarine *Kingfish* (SS 234) on 10 October 1943, off Makassar, 05°38′S, 119°28′E.

2 Sunday

PACIFIC. Operation TABLETENNIS: TF 77 (Rear Admiral William M. Fechteler) lands Army troops (168th Infantry, Reinforced) on Noemfoor Island, to secure the island's three airstrips that will support operations in New Guinea. TF 74 (Commodore John A. Collins, RAN) and TF 75 (Rear Admiral Russell S. Berkey), composed of heavy and light cruisers and destroyers, provide gunfire support.

Japanese landing ship *T.150* is damaged by mine off Amoy, China.

Japanese oiler *Nansei Maru* accidentally rams and sinks oiler *Ceram Maru*, Manila Harbor; *Nansei Maru* is undamaged.

INDIAN OCEAN. U.S. freighter *Jean Nicolet* is torpedoed by Japanese submarine *I 8* at 03°00′S, 74°30′E. *I 8* then shells the ship, setting it afire. Survivors (41-man merchant complement, 28-man Armed Guard, and 30 passengers) are then taken on board the submarine, where their captors search them, bind them, and question them. At least one man is shot; some of the POWs are made to run a gauntlet and some are beaten. In the meantime, the Japanese destroy the lifeboats with gunfire. *I 8* retains the master, radio operator, and a civilian passenger and then submerges, leaving the remainder of the survivors (still bound) topside to drown. Some of the survivors, however, manage to get free and return to the burning *Jean Nicolet* (which sinks the following day) to launch rafts that have escaped destruction (see 4 July).

ATLANTIC. TBM (VC 58) from escort carrier *Wake Island* (CVE 65) sinks German submarine *U 543* southeast of the Azores, 25°34′N, 21°36′W.

Transport *General W. A. Mann* (AP 112), escorted by Brazilian destroyers *Marcilio Dias, Mariz e Barros,* and *Greenhalgh,* sails from Rio de Janeiro, Brazil, with the first elements of the Italy-bound Brazilian Expeditionary Force.

EUROPE. Motor minesweeper *YMS 350* is sunk by mine off Cherbourg, France, 49°38′N, 01°35′W.

3 Monday

PACIFIC. Submarine *Albacore* (SS 218) shells and sinks Japanese steamer *Taimei Maru*, en route from Yap to Palau, 08°10′N, 136°18′E, and takes survivors prisoner.

Submarine *Sturgeon* (SS 187), in attack on Japanese convoy, sinks Japanese army transport *Tairin Maru* north of the Nansei Shoto, 28°58′N, 129°51′E.

Submarine *Tinosa* (SS 283) attacks Japanese Keelung-to-Moji convoy in the East China Sea, and sinks merchant passenger-cargo ship *Kamo Maru* and tanker *Konsan Maru* west of Kyushu, 32°25′N, 128°46′E.

ATLANTIC. Destroyer escorts *Frost* (DE 144) and *Inch* (DE 146) sink German submarine *U 154* off Madeira, 34°00′N, 19°30′W.

4 Tuesday

PACIFIC. Carrier-based aircraft and naval gunfire from two task groups (Rear Admiral Joseph J. Clark and Rear Admiral Ralph E. Davison) hit Japanese installations on Iwo Jima, Volcano Islands, and Chichi Jima and Haha Jima, Bonins. Carrier planes sink submarine chaser *Ch 16* off Chichi Jima; coastal minelayer *Sarushima* (27°10′N, 140°10′E) and auxiliary netlayer *Taiko Maru* off Onagawa Retto; landing ships *T.103*, 108 miles off Chichi Jima, 27°05′N, 140°09′E, and *T.130* off east coast of Iwo Jima, 24°47′N, 140°20′E; minesweeper *W.25* off Chichi Jima, 28°35′N, 141°04′E; auxiliary minesweeper *No. 5 Toshi Maru* off Haha Jima, 26°20′N, 141°50′E; and transports *Shozui Maru*, *Shima Maru*, and *Shinei Maru*, 27°07′N, 142°12′E, and *No. 8 Un'yo Maru*, 27°05′N, 142°09′E, in Takinoura Bay. Landing ship *T.153* and victualling stores ship *Kaiko Maru* are damaged off Ani Jima; submarine chaser *Ch 18* off Chichi Jima.

Destroyer *David W. Taylor* (DD 551) and destroyer escort *Riddle* (DE 185) sink Japanese submarine *I 10*, attempting an evacuation mission to Saipan, 100 miles east-northeast of her destination, 15°26′N, 147°48′E.

Submarine *Guavina* (SS 362), despite presence of four escort vessels, sinks Japanese transport *Tama Maru* 60 miles northwest of Palau, 07°44′N, 133°17′E.

Submarine *Seahorse* (SS 304) attacks Japanese convoy in South China Sea and sinks army cargo ship *Gyoyu Maru*, cargo ship *No. 28 Kyodo Maru*, and freighter *Nitto Maru* about 140 miles south of Hong Kong, 20°18′N, 115°02′E.

Submarine *Tang* (SS 306), operating in the Yellow Sea off the west coast of Korea, sinks Japanese freighters *Asukasan Maru* at 35°22′N, 125°56′E, and *Yamaoka Maru* at 36°05′N, 125°48′E.

RAAF Mitchells damage Japanese cargo vessel *No. 1 Koshu Maru* north of the Kai Islands, 05°05′S, 136°38′E.

Submarine *S 28* (SS 133) is lost to unknown cause during training exercises off Oahu.

INDIAN OCEAN. Indian Navy trawler *Hoxa* rescues survivors (10 of the freighter's merchant complement, 10 Armed Guard sailors, and three passengers) of U.S. freighter *Jean Nicolet*, scourged by Japanese submarine *I 8* on 2 July; 18 of *Jean Nicolet*'s 28-man Armed Guard perish. Of the three Americans taken prisoner and retained on board *I 8*, only one, the passenger, will survive internment.

CARIBBEAN. U.S. tanker *Kittanning* is torpedoed by German submarine *U 539* while returning to Cristobal, C.Z., at 09°50′N, 79°40′W; there are no casualties among the 49-man merchant complement or the 25-man Armed Guard, who are rescued by Coast Guard cutter *Marion* (WPC 145) that, along with cutter *Crawford* (WPC 134), arrives to provide assistance. *Crawford* attempts, unsuccessfully, to tow the crippled ship (see 5 July).

5 Wednesday

PACIFIC. Submarine *Plaice* (SS 390) sinks Japanese auxiliary netlayer *Kogi Maru* off Ototo Jima, 27°43′N, 141°02′E.

Submarine *Sunfish* (SS 281) sinks Japanese merchant passenger-cargo ship *Shinmei Maru* off Paramushir, Kurils, 51°28′N, 156°28′E.

ATLANTIC. Destroyer escorts *Thomas* (DE 102) and *Baker* (DE 190), from TG 22.5, sink German minelayer submarine *U 233* off Halifax, Nova Scotia, 42°16′N, 59°49′W.

EUROPE. U.S. freighter *Sea Porpoise*, en route from UTAH beach, Normandy, to Southampton, England, is torpedoed by German submarine *U 390* at 49°37′N, 00°51′W. There are no fatalities among the 90-man merchant complement, 45-man Armed Guard, and 24 passengers, and the ship is ultimately repaired and returned to service.

CARIBBEAN. U.S. tanker *Kittanning*, torpedoed the previous day by German submarine *U 539*, is taken in tow by tug *Woodcock* (ATO 145) before engine trouble compels the ship to abandon the attempt. Panama Canal tugs *Tavernilla* and *Cardenas*, and, ultimately, Maritime Commission tug *Jupiter Inlet*, bring the damaged vessel to Cristobal, C.Z.

MEDITERRANEAN. USAAF B-17s and B-24s bomb Montpellier and Beziers marshalling yards, as well as submarine pens and harbor installations at Toulon, France; German submarines *U 586* and *U 642* are sunk at the latter port.

6 Thursday

PACIFIC. Carrier-based aircraft commence daily bombings of Japanese coastal and anti-aircraft guns, supply dumps, and airfield installations on Guam and Rota, Marianas.

Submarine *Cobia* (SS 245) sinks Japanese guardboat *Takamiya Maru I-Go* east of Ogasawara Gunto, 28°54′N, 150°50′E.

Submarine *Paddle* (SS 263) attacks Japanese convoy northwest of Halmahera, and sinks destroyer *Hokaze* off Sangi Island, 03°30′N, 125°25′E.

Submarine *Sealion* (SS 315) attacks Japanese convoy in East China Sea and sinks merchant passenger-cargo ship *Setsuzan Maru* off Ningpo, China, 29°55′N, 122°55′E.

Submarine *Tang* (SS 306) sinks Japanese freighter *Dori Maru* in Chosen Bay, 38°50′N, 123°35′E.

CARIBBEAN. U.S. tanker *Esso Harrisburg*, en route from Cartagena, Colombia, to New York, is torpedoed and sunk by German submarine *U 516* at 13°56′N, 70°59′W; four of the 44-man merchant complement and four of the 28-man Armed Guard perish (see 8 July).

7 Friday

PACIFIC. Submarine *Bonefish* (SS 223) shells and sinks Japanese guardboat *Ryuei Maru* at mouth of Tarakan Harbor, Borneo, 02°40′N, 118°22′E.

Submarine *Flasher* (SS 249), despite presence of escort vessel, sinks Japanese transport *No. 2 Koto Maru* off Cape Varella, French Indochina, 13°08′N, 109°28′E.

Submarine *Mingo* (SS 261) sinks Japanese destroyer *Tamanami* 150 miles west-southwest of Manila, 14°16′N, 119°50′E.

Submarine *Skate* (SS 305) attacks Japanese convoy in the southern Sea of Okhotsk, sinking destroyer *Usugumo* and damaging cargo vessel *Kasado Maru* about 160 miles north of Etorofu, Kurils, 47°43′N, 147°55′E.

Submarine *Sunfish* (SS 281) attacks Japanese fishing boats en route from Matsuwa to Uruppu, Kurils, shelling and sinking *No. 105 Hokuyo Maru*, *No. 5 Kannon Maru*, *Ebisu Maru*, and *Kinei Maru*, 47°29′E, 152°29′E.

8 Saturday

PACIFIC. TG 53.18 (Rear Admiral C. Turner Joy) (cruisers and destroyers) begins daily bombardment of Japanese defenses on Guam; battleships join the bombardment group beginning 14 July.

Submarine *Bonefish* (SS 223) sinks Japanese guardboat *Moji Maru* east of Borneo, 02°25′N, 118°14′E.

Submarine *Tautog* (SS 199) sinks Japanese army cargo ship *Matsu Maru* (on her maiden voyage) off Honshu, 41°17′N, 141°30′E.

Japanese guardboats *No. 11 Ebisu Maru*, *No. 3 Fukuei Maru*, *No. 1 Hosei Maru*, *Kofuku Maru*, *No. 1 Kofuku Maru*, *No. 3 Kofuku Maru*, and *No. 3 Sachitaka Maru* are sunk by air raids on shipping off Saipan.

Japanese auxiliary submarine chasers *No. 19 Nitto Maru* and *No. 20 Nitto Maru* are sunk by aircraft off Rabaul.

EUROPE. Tank landing ships *LST 312* and *LST 384* are damaged by V-1 rocket bomb while moored at Naval Advance Amphibious Base, Deptford, England.

CARIBBEAN. Submarine chaser *SC 1299* rescues 18 survivors from U.S. tanker *Esso Harrisburg*, sunk by German submarine *U 516* on 6 July. Dutch escort vessel *Queen Wilhelmina* rescues another 31 survivors. Subsequently, the last group of survivors reaches the Colombian coast.

9 Sunday

PACIFIC. Organized Japanese resistance ceases on Saipan.

Submarine *Dace* (SS 247) carries out unsuccessful attack on Japanese cargo vessel *Gokoku Maru*, 06°22′N, 126°18′E.

Submarine *Nautilus* (SS 168) lands one officer, 22 men, and approximately 10 tons of supplies at rendezvous off mouth of Ammay River, Mindoro, P.I. (see 14 and 16 July).

Submarine *Sunfish* (SS 281) attacks Japanese Kashibawara-bound convoy in the Kurils, sinking army cargo ship *Taihei Maru* north of Araito Island, 51°19′N, 155°43′E; *Kasado Maru* and *Umegawa Maru* survive unscathed.

Submarine *Tautog* (SS 199) sinks Japanese fishing boat *Yawata Maru* southwest of Kushiro, 43°06′N, 144°08′E.

USAAF B-25s (5th Air Force) sink Japanese cargo vessel *Oyashima Maru* near Halmahera Island, 00°34′N, 128°30′E.

Japanese auxiliary submarine chaser *Cha 9* is damaged during air raid on shipping at Rabaul.

MEDITERRANEAN. Minesweeper *Swerve* (AM 121) is sunk by mine about 16 miles southwest of Nettuno, Italy, 41°31′N, 12°285′E.

10 Monday

PACIFIC. Submarine *Tinosa* (SS 283) attacks Japanese fishing boat *No. 5 Shosei Maru* 30 miles west of Danjo Gunto, 32°12′N, 127°00′E.

British submarine HMS *Tally Ho* damages Japanese auxiliary sailing vessel *No. 3 Choun Maru* off Bernam River, Malaya.

RNZAF Corsairs, in strike on Japanese shipping in Keravia Bay, Rabaul, sink auxiliary submarine chaser *Cha 23*, 04°13′S, 152°11′E.

EUROPE. Command designated U.S. Ports and Bases, France (Rear Admiral John Wilkes) is established with headquarters at Cherbourg.

11 Tuesday

PACIFIC. TG 17.16 (Captain William V. O'Regan) (submarine attack group), as it patrols the South China Sea near Formosa, locates the first of five Japanese convoys it will engage in the next two weeks; *Thresher* (SS 200) makes the initial contact with a seven-ship convoy bound from Keelung to the Philippines (see 12 July).

Submarine *Sealion* (SS 315), in the Yellow Sea off the west coast of Korea, near Shosei Jima, sinks Japanese freighters *No. 2 Taiun Maru*, 37°30′N, 124°34′E, and *No. 2 Tsukushi Maru*, 37°24′N, 124°31′E.

U.S. motor torpedo boats sink small Japanese cargo vessel *Yawata Maru* off Babo, 02°33′S, 133°25′E.

Japanese freighter *Senyo Maru* is sunk by aircraft, Yangtze River, China.

12 Wednesday

PACIFIC. TG 17.16 (Captain William V. O'Regan) engages the enemy off north coast of Luzon. Submarine *Apogon* (SS 308) attacks what is most likely army cargo ship *Nichiran Maru* but is damaged when she is rammed by what is probably cargo ship *Mayasan Maru*, 19°51′N, 123°04′E; *Apogon* is forced to terminate her patrol. Submarine *Guardfish* (SS 217) makes no attacks. Later, however, *Piranha* (SS 389) sinks *Nichiran Maru*, 18°50′N, 122°40′E (see 16 July).

ATLANTIC. Convoy UGS 46 is attacked at dawn by 30 German aircraft off Cape Ivi, but no bombs are dropped and only two torpedoes are sighted. Many of the 73 merchantmen in the convoy open fire with automatic weapons on low-flying planes that are heard but not seen amid the protective smoke screens, actions that violate doctrine and instructions. Consequently, U.S. freighter *Toltec* is hit by friendly fire; destroyer escort *Leslie L. B. Knox* (DE 580) provides medical assistance for the six Armed Guard sailors wounded by shell fragments.

Tug *Sagamore* (ATO 20) tows crane ship *AB 1* (ex-*Kearsarge*) from New York Navy Yard to the site of the loss of destroyer *Turner* (DD 648) (sunk off Ambrose Lightship by an internal explosion on 3 January). Attempts to raise *Turner*'s wreck prove unsuccessful (as will a second attempt later in the month), and *Sagamore* tows *AB 1* back to New York.

13 Thursday

PACIFIC. Submarine *Cobia* (SS 245) attacks Japanese convoy, sinking cargo ship *Taishi Maru* about 190 miles northwest of Chichi Jima, Bonins, 27°25′N, 140°30′E. Among the cargo lost on board *Taishi Maru* are 28 tanks (26th Tank Regiment).

USAAF B-25s (Far East Air Force) attack Japanese cargo ships off Halmahera, sinking *Tokai Maru*, 01°25′N, 128°42′E, and damaging *Taimei Maru*, 01°00′N, 128°00′E.

Japanese auxiliary patrol vessel *No. 12 Hamato Maru*, leading a patrol to rendezvous with, and escort, convoy formed around army cargo ship *Umegawa Maru*, collides with auxiliary submarine chaser off Suribachi Wan, Kurils, and sinks.

British submarine HMS *Stoic* sinks Japanese fishing boat *No. 55 Nanyo Maru* 18 miles from Muka Cape, 05°28′N, 100°11′E.

14 Friday

PACIFIC. PB4Ys (VB 109) bomb Iwo Jima in the first strike by land-based planes on that Japanese island base.

Supported by two destroyers and four infantry landing craft (gunboat), Underwater Demolition Team (UDT) 3, in high-speed transport *Dickerson* (APD 21), begins reconnoitering prospective landing beaches at Asan, Guam.

Destroyer escort *William C. Miller* (DE 259) sinks Japanese submarine *RO 48*, 75 miles east of Saipan, 15°18′N, 144°26′E, and teams with high-speed transport *Gilmer* (APD 11) to sink Japanese submarine *I 6*, 70 miles west of Tinian, 15°18′N, 144°26′E.

Submarine *Nautilus* (SS 168) lands party of two men and 30 tons of supplies for Filipino guerrilla forces at rendezvous off Lagoma, Leyte, P.I. (see 16 July).

Submarine *Sand Lance* (SS 381) attacks Japanese convoy in the Banda Sea, sinking gunboat *Taiko Maru* east of Salajar, 05°56′S, 121°34′E.

Japanese *Coast Defense Vessel No. 12* is damaged by aircraft off the Bonins.

15 Saturday

PACIFIC. Submarine *Skate* (SS 305) sinks Japanese crabbing ship *Miho Maru* off Cape Shiretoko, northern Karafuto, Kurils, 48°08′N, 148°06′E. *Miho Maru* takes with her a cargo of canned goods destined for delivery to Hakodate, Japan.

Motor torpedo boat *PT 133* is sunk by Japanese shore battery off eastern New Guinea, 03°28′S, 143°34′E.

16 Sunday

PACIFIC. Infantry landing craft (gunboat) *LCI(G) 469* is damaged by shore battery off Guam, as she supports ongoing UDT operations.

Destroyer *Longshaw* (DD 559) is damaged when she runs aground on submerged reef, Eniwetok.

TG 17.16 (Captain William V. O'Regan) attacks Japanese TAMA 21C Takao-to-Manila convoy in the Luzon Straits. *Piranha* (SS 389) sinks army transport *Seattle Maru*, 19°17′N, 120°15′E.[199] *Guardfish* (SS 217) (flagship for TG 17.16) sinks transport *Mantai Maru* and army cargo ship *Jinsan Maru* off Cape Bojeador, 19°21′N, 119°43′E. *Thresher* (SS 200) sinks army cargo ship *Shozen Maru*, 18°23′N, 119°06′E, and damages freighters *Sainei Maru* and *Nissan Maru*, 18°23′N, 119°32′E (see 17 July).

Submarine *Bonefish* (SS 223) sinks Borneo-bound Japanese cargo vessel *No. 3 Tatsu Maru* in Sulu Sea 10 nautical miles south of Palawan, 10°20′N, 119°50′E.

Submarine *Cabrilla* (SS 288) operates against Japanese convoy off the west coast of Mindanao. In the wake of *Cabrilla*'s unsuccessful attack against transport *Natsukawa Maru*, 08°18′N, 122°49′E, counterattacks by what is most likely submarine chaser *Ch 31* and auxiliary submarine chaser *Cha 64* prove equally unproductive (see 17 July).

Submarine *Nautilus* (SS 168) picks up important intelligence documents from Filipino guerrilla forces at designated spot near Balatong Point, Negros, P.I.[200]

Submarine *Skate* (SS 305) sinks Japanese transport *Nippo Maru*, straggling from convoy east of South Sakhalin, Kurils, 48°29′N, 147°36′E; Soviet ship *Dalstroi* rescues survivors.

RAAF Beaufighters damage Japanese gunboat *Man-Yo Maru*, cargo vessel *Tensho Maru*, and motor sailboat *No. 14 Sakura Maru* off Maumere.

Japanese cargo ship *Hozan Maru* is sunk by accidental gasoline explosion in Manila Harbor, 14°36′N, 120°57′E.

17 Monday

PACIFIC. Underwater demolition teams begin demolishing natural and artificial obstacles on prospective landing beaches on Guam. UDT 4 arrives in high-speed transport *Kane* (APD 18), UDT 6 in high-speed transport *Clemson* (APD 31). Infantry landing craft (gunboat) *LCI(G) 348*, damaged by grounding and Japanese shore battery fire off Guam, is abandoned (see 18 July).

Submarine *Cabrilla* (SS 288) continues attack on Japanese convoy off west coast of Mindanao, sinking army transport *Maya Maru* and damaging transport *Natsukawa Maru*, 07°42′N,

122°05′E; the latter is towed to Zamboanga for repairs.

Submarine *Gabilan* (SS 252) sinks Japanese minesweeper *W.25* northwest of Zenizu, Japan, 33°51′N, 138°35′E.

TG 17.16's attacks on Japanese shipping west of Luzon continue. Submarine *Guardfish* (SS 217) sinks freighter *Hiyama Maru*, 18°21′N, 119°49′E; *Thresher* (SS 200) sinks cargo ship *Nichizan Maru* near Luzon Strait. *Sainei Maru* and *Nissan Maru*, damaged by *Thresher* the previous night, sink.

British submarine HMS *Telemachus* sinks Japanese submarine *I 66* in Strait of Malacca, 02°47′N, 101°03′E.

Japanese motor sailboat *No. 12 Sakura Maru* is sunk by accidental gasoline explosion, Maumere.

Ammunition-carrying U.S. freighter *E. A. Bryan* explodes at the Port Chicago, California, ammunition depot; the adjacent freighter *Quinalt Victory* is also destroyed. Armed Guards on board both vessels are wiped out. Among the casualties are 250 African-American sailors. Survivors refusing to return to work in the wake of the blast are convicted of mutiny. The explosion destroys the greater part of smoke-making material earmarked for shipment to Pearl Harbor for use in amphibious operations, rendering it impossible to provide that material for Operation STALEMATE before the ships leave for the staging area in the Solomons.

18 Tuesday

PACIFIC. Japanese Premier Tojo Hideki and the Japanese cabinet resign; General Koiso Kuniaka forms a new cabinet.

Fleet tug *Apache* (ATF 67) retrieves disabled *LCI(G) 348* from waters off Guam where she had been abandoned the previous day. Cruiser gunfire supports the successful extraction.

Motor gunboat *PGM 7* is damaged in collision in Bismarck Sea, 07°15′S, 155°40′E.

Coordinated submarine attack group, TG 17.3 (Captain Warren D. Wilkin), operating near Luzon Strait, attacks Japanese HI 69 convoy; submarine *Tilefish* (SS 307), trailing *Rock* (SS 274) and *Sawfish* (SS 276), torpedoes *Coast Defense Vessel No. 17*, 21°50′N, 119°55′E, as the latter hunts for *Rock*, whose attack on enemy ships is not successful. *Sawfish* torpedoes oiler *Harima Maru*, 21°56′N, 119°50′E; antisubmarine sweeping ship (ex-training cruiser) *Kashii* carries out counterattack against *Sawfish*.

Submarine *Cobia* (SS 245) sinks Japanese

gunboat *No. 10 Unkai Maru* northwest of Chichi Jima, 29°15′N, 139°10′E, and army cargo ship *Nisshu Maru* west of Chichi Jima, 28°17′N, 139°00′E.

Submarine *Lapon* (SS 260) sinks Japanese auxiliary submarine chaser *Kurama Maru* off southern end of Palawan, 08°22′N, 116°40′E (auxiliary submarine chaser *Kiku Maru* rescues survivors), and survey ship *No. 36 Kyodo Maru* and auxiliary submarine chaser *Kamo Maru* northwest of Labuan, Borneo, 08°22′N, 116°45′E.

Submarine *Plaice* (SS 390) attacks Japanese convoy, sinking submarine chaser *Ch 50*, 200 nautical miles northwest of Chichi Jima, 29°22′N, 139°14′E.

Submarine *Ray* (SS 271) sinks Japanese merchant tanker *Jambi Maru* (ex-Dutch *Djambi*) in the Java Sea north of Bawean Island, 05°21′S, 112°30′E.

USAAF B-24 sinks Japanese transport *No. 3 Kaio Maru* northwest of Morotai, 03°14′N, 127°41′E.

USAAF B-25s sink small Japanese cargo vessel *Yamahama Maru* off Maumere.

19 Wednesday

PACIFIC. Destroyer escort *Wyman* (DE 38) sinks Japanese submarine *I 5*, 360 miles east of Guam, 13°01′N, 151°58′E.

Submarine *Aspro* (SS 309) attacks Japanese Ambon-bound convoy HI 31 and torpedoes *Taiun Maru* at 02°30′S, 129°10′E. *Aspro*'s attack puts the ship out of commission for over a year.

Submarine *Flasher* (SS 249) torpedoes Japanese light cruiser *Oi* in South China Sea west of Manila; escorting destroyer *Shikinami*'s attempt to tow the damaged ship to safety comes to naught when *Oi* breaks in two and sinks, 13°12′N, 114°52′E.

Submarine *Guardfish* (SS 217) attacks Takao-bound Japanese YUTA 09 convoy, and sinks army cargo ship *Teiryu Maru* in South China Sea, southwest of Formosa, 20°00′N, 118°29′E.

Submarine *Tautog* (SS 199) sinks Japanese guardboat *No. 1 Hokuriku Maru* northeast of Tori Jima, 31°30′N, 140°00′E.

RAAF Mitchells attack Japanese shipping, sinking small cargo vessel *No. 53 Ebisu Maru* off southwest coast of Alor Island, and motor sailboat *Bokkai Maru* southwest of Alor, 08°30′S, 124°27′E.

USAAF B-24s (7th Air Force) bomb Japanese installations at Truk; cargo vessel *No. 1 Hokuryu Maru* (listed as lost on this date) may have been sunk during these attacks.

USAAF B-24s damage *Coast Defense Vessel No. 16*, 156 miles southwest of Yap, Carolines.

Japanese cargo ship *Shofuku Maru* is irreparably damaged by accidental explosion, Manila.

20 Thursday

PACIFIC. All beach obstacles on Guam have been removed by underwater demolition teams: 640 on Asan and over 300 on Agat.

Submarine *Cobia* (SS 245) engages three-ship Japanese convoy northwest of Chichi Jima, sinking auxiliary submarine chasers *No. 3 Yusen Maru* and *No. 2 Kaio Maru*, 28°06′N, 141°32′E, and damaging cargo vessel *Shoei Maru*, but not before one of the escorts, however, rams *Cobia*, causing minor damage.

UNITED STATES. Army Pearl Harbor Board (Lieutenant General George Grunert and Major Generals Henry D. Russell and Walter A. Frank), directed to "ascertain and report the facts relating to the attack" of 7 December 1941, begins its work (see 20 October).

21 Friday

PACIFIC. Operation STEVEDORE: TF 53 (Rear Admiral Richard L. Conolly) lands marines (Third Marine Division and First Provisional Marine Brigade) and Army forces (77th Infantry) under Major General Roy S. Geiger, USMC, on Guam. The assault, described as having all the characteristics of "a well-rehearsed play" is preceded by intensive naval gunfire and carrier-based aircraft strikes. Simultaneous employment of naval gunfire and aircraft in the same coastal area marks the first time that the two have been used in this fashion in a Pacific amphibious operation. While enemy opposition is small at the outset, determined resistance develops inland. Submarine chaser *SC 1326* is damaged by mortar fire, Guam, 13°24′N, 144°39′E.

ATLANTIC. Submarine chaser *SC 1505* breaks down off the coast of Georgia, 31°28′N, 79°37′W; submarine chaser *PC 1219* is diverted to help, as is tug *Umpqua* (ATO 25). *PC 1219* tows *SC 1505* until relieved of the task by *Umpqua*, which ultimately brings the disabled patrol vessel to Charleston, South Carolina, the next day.

22 Saturday

PACIFIC. President Roosevelt sails for Hawaii in heavy cruiser *Baltimore* (CA 68) to confer with Admiral Chester W. Nimitz and General Douglas MacArthur, focus attention on the Pacific campaign, and encourage American armed forces that the President is devoting his personal attention to that theater of war, at a time when the European war appears to be attracting the most headlines (see 26 July).

23 Sunday

PACIFIC. Destroyer *Bush* (DD 529) is damaged by premature detonation of 5-inch shell during shore bombardment exercises off Kahoolawe, T.H.

High-speed minesweeper *Chandler* (DMS 9) is damaged by fire off Tinian, Marianas, 15°08′N, 145°28′E.

Japanese guardboat *Wakayoshi Maru* is sunk by mine, Hayatomo Seto, Inland Sea.

Japanese cargo vessel *Takazan Maru* is damaged by RAAF mine in Tiore Strait, Celebes, 04°25′S, 122°17′E.[201]

INDIAN OCEAN. British submarine HMS *Storm* sinks Japanese cargo ship *Kiso Maru* and fishing vessel *Taiho Maru* near Port Owen, 14°00′N, 96°50′E.

ATLANTIC. U.S. freighter *William Gaston* is torpedoed and sunk by German submarine *U 861* while she is en route from Buenos Aires to Baltimore, Maryland, 26°37′S, 46°13′W; there are no casualties among either the merchant or Armed Guard complements (see 25 July).

24 Monday

PACIFIC. TF 52 (Rear Admiral Harry W. Hill) lands Fourth Marine Division (Major General Harry Schmidt, USMC) on Tinian. Landing, which initially encounters light opposition, is supported by naval gunfire, carrier aircraft, and land-based aircraft from Saipan. Shore batteries on Tinian damage battleship *Colorado* (BB 45) and destroyer *Norman Scott* (DD 690) at 15°02′N, 145°50′E, and tank landing ship *LST 481* at 13°24′N, 144°39′E.

USAAF B-24s (5th Air Force) sink Japanese transport *Asahisan Maru* in Kau Bay, Halmahera, 01°10′N, 127°54′E.

ATLANTIC. German submarine *U 861* attacks convoy JT 99 and eludes search aircraft from escort carrier *Solomons* (CVE 67).

UNITED STATES. Navy Court of Inquiry into the Pearl Harbor attack of 7 December 1941, begins its work; Secretary of the Navy James V. Forrestal enjoins the board, consisting of Admiral Orin G. Murfin and Vice Admirals Edward C. Kalbfus and Adolphus Andrews (all retired), to "give its opinion as to whether any offenses have been committed or serious blame incurred on the part of any person or persons in the naval service," and if that is the case, "will specifically recommend what further proceedings should be had" in the matter (see 19 October).

25 Tuesday

PACIFIC. Aircraft from TF 58 (Vice Admiral Marc A. Mitscher) attack Japanese installations and shipping in the western Carolines, at Yap, Ulithi, Fais, Ngulu, Sorol, and Palau; strikes continue until 28 July. F6Fs from small carrier *San Jacinto* (CVL 30) damage destroyer *Samidare* 30 miles north of Babelthuap, Palau, 08°15′N, 134°37′E (see 18 and 26 August). F6Fs from carrier *Bunker Hill* (CV 17) sink guardboat *Ryojin Maru*, 07°30′N, 134°30′E. Guardboat *No. 5 Showa Maru* is also sunk.

USAAF B-25s sink Japanese salvage vessel *Hoshin Maru* 70 nautical miles east of Hong Kong, 22°00′N, 115°50′E.

ATLANTIC. Small seaplane tender *Matagorda* (AVP 22) rescues all 67 survivors of U.S. freighter *William Gaston*, sunk on 23 July by German submarine *U 861* approximately 150 miles southeast of Florianopolis, Brazil.

U.S. freighter *Robin Goodfellow* is torpedoed and sunk by German submarine *U 862* while en route from Cape Town, South Africa, to New York, at 20°03′S, 14°21′W. All hands (including the 27 Armed Guard sailors and the 41-man merchant complement) perish.

EUROPE. U.S. freighter *David Starr Jordan* is bombed and strafed while anchored off UTAH beach, Normandy; two of the 500 soldiers embarked on board are killed by bomb fragments, while 13 other men from among the 43-man merchant complement and 26-man Armed Guard are injured.

26 Wednesday

PACIFIC. Heavy cruiser *Baltimore* (CA 68), with President Roosevelt embarked, arrives at Pearl Harbor, T.H.; the President will meet with Admiral Chester W. Nimitz, Admiral William D. Leahy, and General Douglas MacArthur to discuss Pacific strategy. Ultimately, General MacArthur prevails upon the President and Admiral Nimitz to accord priority to the liberation of the Philippines (see 29 July).

TF 58 strikes against Japanese installations and shipping in western Carolines continue; planes from carrier *Bunker Hill* (CV 17) damage landing ship *T.150* (see 27 July); planes from *Lexington* (CV 16) damage minelayer *Sokuten*, which is then finished off by planes from *Bunker Hill* at 07°20′N, 134°27′E.

U.S. submarines carry out succession of attacks on Japanese convoy HI 68 in South China Sea. *Angler* (SS 240) damages transport

Admiral Chester W. Nimitz points to Japan on a map of the Pacific, while General Douglas MacArthur, President Franklin D. Roosevelt, and Admiral William D. Leahy, look on, during the Chief Executive's visit to Pearl Harbor to discuss Pacific strategy between 26 and 29 July 1944. (NA, 80-G-46221)

(ex-seaplane carrier) *Kiyokawa Maru*, 18°15′N, 118°00′E; *Flasher* (SS 249) sinks merchant tanker *Otoriyama Maru*, 17°56′N, 118°07′E, and teams with *Crevalle* (SS 291) to sink army cargo ship *Tozan Maru*, 18°24′N, 118°02′E. *Crevalle* also sinks transport *Aki Maru*, 18°26′N, 118°02′E.

Submarine *Robalo* (SS 273) is sunk by mine off western Palawan, Balabac Strait, P.I., 08°25′N, 117°53′E.[202]

Submarine *Sawfish* (SS 276) sinks Japanese submarine *I 29* in Balintang Channel, 20°10′N, 121°55′E.

27 Thursday

PACIFIC. TF 58 strikes against Japanese installations and shipping in the western Carolines; Navy carrier planes sink fast transport *T.1* off Palau; planes from carrier *Bunker Hill* (CV 17) sink landing ship *T.150*.

Submarine *Dace* (SS 247) attacks Japanese convoy and sinks fleet tanker *No. 2 Kyoei Maru* about 90 miles south of Zamboanga, 05°25′N, 121°42′E.

USAAF B-24s, B-25s and P-38s (Far East Air Force) work over Japanese shipping near Halmahera Island, damaging motor sailboat *Genjo Maru*.

Japanese escort destroyer *Kunashiri* is damaged (cause unspecified) west of Paramushir, Kurils.

28 Friday

PACIFIC. Destroyer escorts *Wyman* (DE 38) and *Reynolds* (DE 42) sink Japanese submarine *I 55*, 400 miles east of Tinian, 14°26′N, 152°16′E.

Submarine *Aspro* (SS 309) damages previously damaged Japanese gunboat *Peking Maru* aground off Vigan Point, Luzon, 17°33′N, 120°21′E; *Peking Maru* remains aground, a total loss, gutted and abandoned.

Submarine *Crevalle* (SS 291) attacks Japanese convoy off northwestern Luzon, sinking freighter *Hakubasan Maru* off Piedra Point, 16°23′N, 119°40′E.

29 Saturday

PACIFIC. Heavy cruiser *Baltimore* (CA 68), with President Roosevelt embarked, departs Pearl Harbor for Adak, Aleutians (see 3 August).

Tank landing ship *LST 340* is damaged by grounding off east coast of Saipan, 15°10′N, 145°58′E.

Submarine *Balao* (SS 285) shells and sinks Japanese sampan *No. 7 Nissho Maru* about 100

miles off Palau, 09°27′N, 133°19′E; *Drum* (SS 228) sinks sampan *Asahi Maru* with gunfire in the same general area, 09°18′N, 133°20′E, and takes survivor prisoner.

Submarine *Perch* (SS 313) sinks Japanese guardboat *Kannon Maru I-Go* in Philippine Sea, east of Dinagat Island, 10°46′N, 127°13′E.

USAAF P-38s bomb and strafe Japanese shipping off Ambon, N.E.I., damaging auxiliary submarine chaser *Cha 113* and irreparably damaging fishing vessel *No. 5 Yoshie Maru*.

EUROPE. USAAF B-17s (8th Air Force) bomb oil refinery near Bremen; German submarines *U 878* and *U 2323* are lost in bombing raids on this German port city.

30 Sunday

PACIFIC. Operation GLOBETROTTER: TF 77 (Rear Admiral William M. Fechteler) lands Army Sixth Infantry Division (Major General Franklin C. Sibert, USA) near Cape Opmari, northwest New Guinea, and on islands of Amsterdam and Middleburg.

Cargo ship *Adhara* (AK 71) and U.S. freighter *Peter White* are damaged when the latter accidentally rams the Navy ship off Lunga Point, Guadalcanal.

Submarine *Bonefish* (SS 223) sinks Japanese fleet tanker *Kokuyo Maru* about 75 miles northeast of Borneo, 06°07′N, 120°00′E.

USAAF B-25s (Far East Air Force) attack Japanese installations and shipping at Tobele, Halmahera, sinking small cargo vessel *Mansei Maru*.

Open lighter *YC 961* is listed as lost after grounding off Biorka Island, Alaska.

EUROPE. Off Normandy, mines sink motor minesweeper *YMS 304* and damage *YMS 378*, 49°33′N, 01°14′W.

31 Monday

PACIFIC. Operation GLOBETROTTER: TF 77 (Rear Admiral William M. Fechteler) lands Army troops on Cape Sansapor, New Guinea, concluding the New Guinea campaign.

Coordinated submarine attack group TG 17.15 (Commander Lewis S. Parks) carries out succession of attacks on Japanese MI 11 convoy near the Bashi Channel. Submarine *Parche* (SS 384) (flagship) sinks transport *Manko Maru*, 19°08′N, 120°51′E, and merchant tanker *Koei Maru*, 19°00′N, 122°55′E; damages freighter *No. 1 Ogura Maru*, 19°10′N, 120°58′E, and army cargo ship *Fuso Maru*; and teams with *Steelhead* (SS 280) to sink army cargo ship *Yoshino Maru*, 19°05′N, 120°50.5′E. For the heroism he displays in pressing home a daring surface attack, *Parche*'s captain, Commander Lawson P. Ramage, will be awarded the Medal of Honor. *Steelhead* sinks *Fuso Maru*, 19°00'N, 120°55'E, and damages army cargo ship *Dakar Maru*, 19°08'N, 120°51'E, which is towed to San Fernando, Luzon, and abandoned.

Submarine *Dace* (SS 247) sinks small Japanese cargo vessel *Shinju Maru* 20 miles west of Palimban Point, 06°15'N, 124°11'E.

Submarine *Lapon* (SS 260) attacks Japanese convoy, sinking merchant tanker *Tenshin Maru* off the southwest tip of Palawan, 08°50'N, 116°00'E, and damaging weather ship *Hijun Maru*, 08°51'N, 116°45'E.

EUROPE. U.S. freighter *Exmouth* is mined and sunk about 60 miles off the Scottish coast while en route from Hull, England, to Loch Ewe, Scotland, 56°33'N, 01°38'W; there are no casualties among the 43 merchant sailors and the 27-man Armed Guard.

AUGUST

1 Tuesday

PACIFIC. Seventh Amphibious Force (Rear Admiral Daniel E. Barbey) is formed. Group One is to be commanded by Rear Admiral Arthur D. Struble; Group Two by Rear Admiral Charles P. Cecil. Cecil, however, is killed in crash of Naval Air Transport Service PB2Y, Funafuti, Ellice Islands.

Organized Japanese resistance ends on Tinian.

Naval Air Base, Tinian, is established.

Destroyer escort *England* (DE 635) is damaged when she runs aground in Seeadler Harbor, Manus, Admiralty Islands.

Submarine *Puffer* (SS 268) damages Japanese oiler *Sunosaki* northeast of Borneo, 05°08'N, 119°32.5'E.

PBY attacks Japanese convoy, sinking ammunition ship *Seia Maru* in Taliaboe Bay, Soela Island, N.E.I., 01°46'N, 125°32'E. Submarine chasers *Ch 12* and *Ch 53* and auxiliary submarine chaser *Cha 67* rescue survivors.

U.S. freighter *Extavia* is damaged by explosion while en route from New Georgia to the Treasury Islands, but reaches her destination unaided; there are no casualties among the 73-man merchant complement, 81-man Armed Guard, or 845 embarked troops.

ATLANTIC. Tug *Sciota* (ATO 30) is dispatched from Norfolk, Virginia, to provide feed water to Panamanian freighter *El Mundo*, which is experiencing boiler trouble at 34°53'N,

71°52'W. *Sciota* then escorts the merchantman to Norfolk.

2 Wednesday

PACIFIC. Submarine *Tautog* (SS 199) attacks Japanese KO 8801 convoy, sinking army cargo ship *Konei Maru* (ex-Italian *Furiere Consolini*) off Miki Saki, Honshu, 33°57'N, 136°20'E.

Japanese landing ship *T.152* founders in heavy weather between Iwo Jima and Chichi Jima.

ATLANTIC. Destroyer escort *Fiske* (DE 143) is sunk by German submarine *U 804*, 800 miles east of Cape Race, Newfoundland, 47°11'N, 33°29'W.

ATLANTIC. British freighter *Empire Falcon* runs aground off Brigantine Shoal Buoy, 39°24'N, 74°16'W. Although *Empire Falcon* frees herself from her predicament, thus resulting in tug *Allegheny* (ATO 19) being recalled from providing assistance, faulty compasses on board the merchantman means that an escort will be required. Submarine chaser *SC 1015*, in the area at the time, escorts *Empire Falcon* to Cape May, New Jersey. They arrive at their destination the next day.

3 Thursday

UNITED STATES. Office of the General Counsel Navy Department is established; formerly designated Procurement Legal Division, Navy Department.

PACIFIC. Heavy cruiser *Baltimore* (CA 68), with President Roosevelt embarked, arrives at Adak, Aleutians (see 4 August).

Submarine *Cod* (SS 224) sinks Japanese auxiliary netlayer *Seiko Maru* off Mangole, Molucca Sea, 01°47'S, 126°15'E.

Japanese minelayer *Hatsutaka* is damaged by mine laid by British submarine HMS *Truculent* on 24 June, Klang Strait, 02°51'N, 101°15'E.

4 Friday

PACIFIC. While planes from TG 58.3 (Rear Admiral Alfred E. Montgomery) bomb airfields on Iwo Jima, aircraft from TG 58.1 (Rear Admiral Joseph J. Clark), together with four light cruisers and seven destroyers detached from TG 58.1 and TG 58.3 (organized as TU 58.1.6 under Rear Admiral Laurance T. DuBose), attack Japanese convoy 4804 about 25 miles northwest of Muko Jima, Bonins. Ship gunfire sinks escort destroyer *Matsu*, 27°40'N, 141°48'E, and collier *Ryuko Maru*; carrier planes sink transports *No. 7 Unkai Maru*, *Enju*

Maru, *Tonegawa Maru*, and *Shogen Maru*, 27°05'N, 142°11'E, and damage *Coast Defense Vessel No. 4* and *Coast Defense Vessel No. 12*; and ship gunfire and carrier planes combine to sink cargo ship *Hokkai Maru*. Planes from small carrier *Cabot* (CVL 28) damage fast transport *T.4*, 27°07'N, 142°12'E; planes from carriers *Bunker Hill* (CV 17) and *Lexington* (CV 16) sink landing ship *T.133* off coast of Iwo Jima, 24°47'N, 141°20'E.

Heavy cruiser *Baltimore* (CA 68), with President Roosevelt embarked, departs Adak, Aleutians, bound for Kodiak, Alaska (see 7 August).

Submarine *Raton* (SS 270) attacks Japanese freighter *No. 1 Ogura Maru* off coast of Luzon, 16°31'N, 119°44'E, forcing her to take refuge at Santa Cruz.

Submarine *Ray* (SS 271), despite presence of auxiliary submarine chaser *Cha 112*, attacks Makassar-bound Japanese convoy in Celebes Sea, and sinks army cargo ship *Koshu Maru*, 04°05'S, 117°40'E.

Submarine *Sterlet* (SS 392) sinks Japanese guardboats *Miyagi Maru* and *Zensho Maru* northwest of Chichi Jima, 28°11'N, 141°43'E.

PB4Y attacks, but does not damage, Japanese submarine chaser *Ch 12*, 150 miles west of Palau, 07°20'N, 131°34'E.

5 Saturday

PACIFIC. TG 58.1 (Rear Admiral Joseph J. Clark) and TG 58.3 (Rear Admiral Alfred E. Montgomery) planes, as well as cruisers and destroyers (Rear Admiral Laurance T. DuBose), repeat strikes on Japanese installations on Chichi Jima and Haha Jima, Bonins. Planes from carrier *Bunker Hill* (CV 17) inflict further damage upon fast transport *T.4*, 27°07'N, 142°12'E, and damage *T.2* off Chichi Jima, 27°05'N, 142°09'E.

Fast Carrier Task Force is reorganized into First Fast Carrier Task Force, Pacific Fleet (Vice Admiral Marc A. Mitscher) and Second Fast Carrier Task Force, Pacific Fleet (Vice Admiral John S. McCain).

Submarine *Barbel* (SS 316) sinks Japanese merchant passenger-cargo ship *Miyako Maru* off Tokuno Jima, 27°36'N, 128°54'E.

Submarine *Cero* (SS 225) attacks Japanese convoy off Mindanao and sinks oiler *Tsurumi* in Davao Gulf, 05°53'N, 125°41'E.

British submarine HMS *Terrapin* bombards Japanese installations at Gunung Sitoli, Nias Island, off the west coast of Sumatra, engaging shore batteries and guardboat *Shime Maru*.

PBY sinks small Japanese cargo vessel *No. 2 Eiko Maru* off Latoelahat, 03°47′S, 128°06′E.

PVs, attacking Japanese guardboats in the Kurils, damage *Hyuga Maru*, 50°35′N, 159°05′E.

USAAF B-25s (Far East Air Force) sink Japanese army cargo ship *Shirohama Maru* off Boetoeng, Api Island, southern Celebes, 04°40′S, 122°47′E.

MEDITERRANEAN. Rear Admiral Don P. Moon, who had worked tirelessly to develop plans for the assault upon the strongly defended coast of southern France, commits suicide on board his flagship, attack transport *Bayfield* (APA 33); his death is attributed to combat fatigue. Rear Admiral Spencer S. Lewis replaces Moon as task group commander.

6 Sunday

PACIFIC. Submarine *Pintado* (SS 387) attacks Japanese MOTA 22 convoy off southwest coast of Kyushu, sinking army cargo ship *Shonan Maru* (and four large landing barges she carries as deck cargo), 30°53′N, 129°45′E, and damaging escort vessel *Etorofu* east of Kusagaki Jima, 30°51′N, 129°26′E.

Submarine *Rasher* (SS 269) sinks Japanese army cargo ship *Shiroganesan Maru* west of Luzon, 14°10′N, 117°12′E.

Dutch Mitchells sink Japanese army cargo ship *No. 15 Uwajima Maru* in Banda Sea, 04°31′S, 129°53′E.

MEDITERRANEAN. USAAF B-17s and B-24s bomb targets in southeastern France, including submarine pens at Toulon, where they sink German submarines *U 471*, *U 952*, and *U 969*.

EUROPE. Motor torpedo boats *PT 510*, *PT 512*, and *PT 514* engage E-boats of the German 15th Patrol Boat Flotilla and turn them back to Le Havre, France. Battle concludes early the next morning.

U.S. freighter *William L. Marcy* is torpedoed (possibly by a *schnellboote* from the 2nd or 6th Flotillas) off JUNO beach, at 49°23′42″N, 00°26′36″W; although the sole passenger is killed, there are no casualties among the 28-man Armed Guard or the 47-man merchant complement. The ship is later towed to Falmouth, England (17 August), and Swansea, Wales (21 August), where she is written off as a total loss.

7 Monday

PACIFIC. Heavy cruiser *Baltimore* (CA 68), with President Roosevelt embarked, arrives at Kodiak, Alaska, where the Chief Executive transfers to destroyer *Cummings* (DD 365) (see 9 August).

Submarine *Barbel* (SS 316) sinks Japanese cargo vessel *No. 11 Sakura Maru* southwest of Tokuno Jima, 27°36′N, 121°46′E.

Submarine *Bluegill* (SS 242) attacks Japanese convoy, sinking transport *Yamatama Maru* southwest of Mindanao, 06°05′N, 124°23′E.

Submarine *Croaker* (SS 246), despite presence of escort vessel and shore-based air cover, sinks Japanese light cruiser *Nagara* about 35 miles south of Nagasaki, Japan, 32°09′N, 129°53′E.

Submarine *Guitarro* (SS 363) attacks Japanese convoy, sinking escort vessel *Kusagaki* off Capones Island, Luzon, 14°51′N, 119°51′E, and survives depth charging by other escorts (perhaps destroyer *Asakaze*, escort vessel *Yashiro*, and/or *Coast Defense Vessel No. 14*).

Submarine *Puffer* (SS 268) sinks Japanese auxiliary submarine chaser *No. 2 Kyo Maru* off Zamboanga, 07°50′N, 122°07′E.

Submarine *Sailfish* (SS 192) sinks Japanese army cargo ship *Kinshu Maru* in Luzon Strait, 20°09′N, 121°19′E; transport *Shinten Maru* escapes.

Submarine *Sand Lance* (SS 381) is damaged by aerial bombs off northern Celebes, 01°18′N, 121°30′E.

Submarine *Seawolf* (SS 197) lands one officer and five enlisted men (the latter including four radio operators and one weatherman) and 14,538 pounds of supplies, to reinforce intelligence party on Tawi Tawi, P.I. (see 9 August).

Tank landing craft *LCT 182* founders and sinks in heavy weather, Solomon Islands.

USAAF B-24 damages Italian passenger liner *Conte Verde* (scuttled in September 1943), Shanghai.

MEDITERRANEAN. Motor torpedo boats *PT 511*, *PT 520*, and *PT 521* attack German coastal convoy off Cap D'Antifer, France; in the engagement with the 14th Motor Minesweeping Flotilla that lasts into the next day, *PT 520* and *PT 521* are damaged.

8 Tuesday

PACIFIC. Destroyers *Gansevoort* (DD 608) and *Bancroft* (DD 598) and land-based marine aircraft (MAG 13) from Majuro, Marshalls, bombard and bomb Japanese positions on Taroa, Maloelap Atoll.

Submarine *Sterlet* (SS 392) sinks Japanese auxiliary submarine chaser *No. 6 Tama Maru* west of Chichi Jima, 28°11′N, 141°06′E.

EUROPE. U.S. freighter *Ezra Weston*, in convoy EBC 66, is torpedoed by German submarine *U 667* while en route to Falmouth, England, from Avonmouth, at 50°42′N, 05°02′W, and abandoned. British HMS *LCT 24* and French trawler *Jacques Morgand* embark survivors. Canadian corvette HMCS *Regina* stands by the doomed freighter but *U 667* finishes off *Ezra Weston* with another torpedo. There are no casualties among the merchant or Armed Guard complements, or among the passengers.

9 Wednesday

PACIFIC. President Roosevelt reembarks in heavy cruiser *Baltimore* (CA 68) and then shifts to destroyer *Cummings* (DD 365) to visit the Puget Sound (Washington) Navy Yard (see 12 August).

PB4Y (VB 116) crashes on takeoff from Stickell Field, Eniwetok, and burns amid the 340 planes in the carrier aircraft replacement pool area; 106 (F6Fs, FMs, SB2Cs, and TBMs) are destroyed.

Submarine *Barbel* (SS 316) attacks Japanese MI 08 convoy, and sinks army cargo ship *Yagi Maru* and freighter (ex-British *Sagres*) *Boko Maru* north of Okinoshima, 27°56′N, 128°47′E. *Coast Defense Vessel No. 1* and minesweeper *W.17* carry out antisubmarine sweep to no avail.

Submarine *Seawolf* (SS 197) lands one noncommissioned officer, five enlisted men (radiomen and a weather man), and 7,153 pounds of supplies at a new site on northern Palawan, to establish a coastwatcher intelligence station there. *Seawolf* receives "well done" for her "snappy work" on her first two clandestine missions.

British submarine HMS *Trenchant* sinks Japanese fishing boats *No. 2 Hiyoshi Maru* and *No. 111 Boat* off coast of Sumatra, 04°29′S, 102°54′E, and takes survivors prisoner.

USAAF B-25s (Far East Air Force) sink Japanese ship *Tokuyu Maru* and damage fishing boat *No. 6 Meijin Maru* off Halmahera.

Japanese freighter *Hokko Maru* is sunk by aircraft off Shanghai, China.

Japanese cargo ship *Koshin Maru* is sunk by fire, 125 miles northeast of Keelung, Formosa.

ATLANTIC. Motor torpedo boat *PT 509* is sunk in action with German 46th Minesweeping Flotilla and the 2nd Patrol Boat Flotilla off Jersey, English Channel, 49°11′N, 02°15′W.

10 Thursday

PACIFIC. Organized Japanese resistance ends on Guam. Patrols soon begin off northeast coast of the island to prevent escape of enemy forces still present on Guam and to aid marine forces in exterminating or capturing Japanese hidden in caves and brush along the shoreline. Not only do the infantry landing craft employed on this task carry out gunfire support duties but actively pursue measures to induce Japanese to surrender. LCI(G) 466, LCI(G) 469, LCI(G) 471, and LCI(G) 473 convince 157 Japanese to surrender up to the end of September.

Submarine Bowfin (SS 287) sinks Japanese freighter Seiyo Maru off Minami Daito Shima, 25°50′N, 131°12′E.

Submarine Cod (SS 224) sinks Japanese auxiliary submarine chaser Toseki Maru south of the Celebes, 05°15′S, 121°14′E.

Submarine Guitarro (SS 363) attacks Japanese MATA 26 convoy off northwest coast of Luzon, sinking merchant tanker Shinei Maru, 16°15′N, 119°45′E.

Japanese guardboat Sakae Maru is sunk by U.S. aircraft at Rabaul, 04°12′S, 152°15′E.

11 Friday

PACIFIC. Submarine Cod (SS 224) sinks Japanese freighter No. 6 Shinsei Maru south of the Celebes, 05°38′S, 120°37′E.

Submarine Tang (SS 306) attacks Japanese convoy off southern Honshu, and sinks freighter Roko Maru, 33°58′N, 136°18′E.

USAAF B-25s sink Japanese guardboat Daishin Maru east of Paramushir, Kurils, 50°09′N, 157°03′E.

Japanese cargo vessel No. 7 Kyoei Maru is damaged by mine laid by USAAF B-29 (20th Bomber Command) in Musi River, while en route to Palembang, Sumatra.

Japanese tanker Ikuta Maru is sunk by mine off coast of Sumatra.

USAAF planes sink guardboats No. 20 Aiko Maru and No. 32 Ebisu Maru in Kaoe Bay, Halmahera, and Shinyu Maru in Halmahera Bay.

ATLANTIC. Yacht Sylph (PY 12) breaks down about three miles northwest of Block Island, 41°17′N, 71°35′W; rescue tug ATR 14, dispatched from Newport, Rhode Island, to assist, tows the disabled auxiliary vessel to Newport, arriving the next day.

12 Saturday

PACIFIC. President Roosevelt concludes his inspection of naval activities in the Pacific when he departs Puget Sound, Washington, to return to Washington, D.C.

Submarine Pompon (SS 267) attacks Japanese convoy in Sea of Okhotsk, damaging freighter Mayachi Maru east of Sakhalin, 50°35′N, 144°03′E.

Submarine Puffer (SS 268) attacks Japanese convoy off Mindoro, sinking merchant tanker (ex-Winnetou) Teikon Maru off Cape Calavite, 13°26′N, 119°55′E; Puffer also damages tanker Shinpo Maru, which is beached off Golo Island (see 14 August).

Japanese oiler Nichinan Maru is damaged by mine, Palembang; barge Tako Maru is sunk. Tanker Ikuta Maru, which also strikes a mine in the Moesi River, Palembang, is mined and catches fire, leading to her destruction.

13 Sunday

PACIFIC. Submarine Barbel (SS 316) sinks Japanese auxiliary Koan Maru off Amami-O-Shima, 28°31′N, 129°18′E.

Submarine Bluegill (SS 242) attacks Japanese convoy off Cape San Agustin, Mindanao, P.I., and sinks auxiliary submarine chaser Misago Maru and transport Kojun Maru near entrance to Davao Gulf, 06°17′N, 126°10′E.

Submarine Cod (SS 224) attacks Japanese landing ship T.129 with gunfire in the Banda Sea, 05°28′S, 125°08′E, but is driven off by the enemy amphibious ship's accurate return fire (see 14 August).

Submarine Flier (SS 250) is sunk by mine, south of Palawan, Balabac Strait, North Borneo, 09°00′N, 117°15′E (see 31 August).

Submarine Tambor (SS 198) sinks Japanese army cargo ship Toei Maru in southern part of Sea of Okhotsk, 48°35′N, 149°02′E.

Japanese submarine I 365 is damaged by RAAF Fairmile motor gunboats off Biak; a subsequent inspection in drydock at Singapore reveals that "extensive repairs [are] required beyond local facilities."

RAAF Beaufighters sink small Japanese cargo vessel No. 3 Hamayoshi Maru off Kalig Island, 02°14′S, 130°31′E.

Japanese army cargo ship No. 2 Asahi Maru is sunk by aircraft in South China Sea, southeast of Hong Kong, 22°03′N, 114°44′E.

Japanese tanker Busshin Maru is sunk by accidental fire off Ahan Point, Formosa, 20°16′N, 121°52′E.

14 Monday

PACIFIC. Submarine Bluefish (SS 222) sinks Japanese tanker Shinpo Maru, previously damaged by Puffer (SS 268) on 12 August, off Golo Island, 13°39′N, 120°22′E.

Submarine Cod (SS 224), her gun attack frustrated by her quarry's accurate return fire

the previous day, torpedoes and sinks Japanese landing ship T.129 in Banda Sea, about 40 miles south of Boeroe Island and 80 miles southwest of Ambon Bay, 04°17′S, 126°46′E.

Submarine Croaker (SS 246) sinks Japanese gunboat No. 7 Daigen Maru southwest of Inchon, Korea, 37°25′N, 125°12′E.

Submarine Ray (SS 271) attacks Japanese convoy, sinking freighter Zuisho Maru off northwest coast of Borneo, 03°51′N, 112°58′E, and damaging freighter Uga Maru, 03°51′N, 112°58′E (see 21 August).

Japanese cargo ship Mikesan Maru is sunk by mine laid by USAAF B-24 (14th Air Force) off Takao, Formosa, 22°00′N, 120°00′E.

ATLANTIC. Tank landing ship LST 921 is sunk by German submarine U 667 about 11 miles southwest of Hartland Point, England, 51°05′N, 04°47′W.

15 Tuesday

PACIFIC. USAAF B-24s (Far East Air Force) attack Japanese convoy and sink Surabaya-bound army cargo ship Tosho Maru in Banda Sea, southwest of Soena Islands, 04°30′S, 125°26′E; submarine chasers Ch 34 and Ch 35 are dispatched to the scene to rescue survivors.

RAAF Mitchells sink Japanese lugger No. 14 Sakura Maru off north coast of central Timor, N.E.I.

Japanese vessel Kono Maru is sunk by aircraft off Halmahera Island.

MEDITERRANEAN. Operation DRAGOON: Allied troops (Major General Alexander M. Patch, USA) land on coast of southern France between Toulon and Cannes, preceded by heavy naval gunfire and covered by aircraft. The operation is under the command of Vice Admiral H. Kent Hewitt, Naval Commander Western Task Force and Commander Eighth Fleet. Naval gunfire supports the Allied troops. Off RED beach ALPHA, large infantry landing craft LCI(L) 588, LCI(L) 590, LCI(L) 592, and LCI(L) 599 are damaged by mines; tank landing craft LCT 1014 and large infantry landing craft LCI(L) 595 are damaged by German 88-millimeter gunfire; large infantry landing craft LCI(L) 188, LCI(L) 585, LCI(L) 589, LCI(L) 591, and LCI(L) 593 are damaged in varying degrees by underwater obstructions; tank landing craft LCT 452 is damaged by mortar and 88-millimeter shells and underwater obstruction; LCT 1013 is damaged by mortar fire and underwater obstructions; and LCT 1009 is hit by machine gun fire. Off YELLOW beach, large infantry landing craft LCI(L) 943 is damaged by underwater obstruction, and submarine chaser SC 1029 is damaged when APEX (remote control) boat explodes 15 yards from the ship, 43°12′N, 06°41′E; SC 651 provides medical assistance.[203] Off GREEN beach, tank landing ship LST 282, damaged by glider bomb, is beached and abandoned, 43°25′N, 06°50′E; LST 51 and tank landing craft LCT 625 are damaged by artillery fire. U.S. freighter Tarleton Brown is damaged by bomb and near-miss during German air raid on Allied shipping off St. Raphael; there are no fatalities among the merchant crew, the passengers, or the 44-man Armed Guard. Destroyer Somers (DD 381) sinks German ship Esebart and damages corvette Uj 6083 (ex-Italian corvette Capriolo). The latter is captured and then scuttled southwest of Isle Port Cros.

16 Wednesday

PACIFIC. Submarine Croaker (SS 246) sinks Japanese auxiliary minesweeper Taito Maru west of Korea, 36°16′N, 125°49′E.

ATLANTIC. Tank landing ship LST 391 is damaged by mine off Cherbourg, 49°38′N, 01°37′W.

MEDITERRANEAN. Motor torpedo boats PT 202 and PT 218 are sunk by mines, Gulf of Frejus, 43°23′N, 06°43′E; motor minesweeper YMS 24 is sunk by mine, 43°25′N, 06°43′E; submarine chaser SC 525 is damaged; and infantry landing craft LCI 951 is damaged by mine off YELLOW beach. USAAF L-4 Piper Cubs, launched from tank landing ships, spot gunfire for light cruiser Marblehead (CL 12).

17 Thursday

PACIFIC. Submarine Croaker (SS 246) sinks Japanese freighter Yamatero Maru off west coast of Korea, 35°33′N, 126°10′E.

RAAF aircraft sink Japanese cargo vessel No. 2 Jun Maru off south coast of Miscol Island.

Japanese river gunboat Hira is damaged by aircraft at Kiukiang, China.

MEDITERRANEAN. Diversionary assault is carried out with Special Operations Group (TG 80.4) penetrating Baie de Ciotat; destroyer Endicott (DD 495) and two motor torpedo boats bombard western half of the beach area; British river gunboats HMS Aphis and HMS Scarab (whose previous service has ranged from the Danube to the Yangtze) and the 24th Motor Launch Flotilla bombard eastern half. Enemy shore battery fire is heavy but falls short. After group withdraws from beach area, German submarine chasers Uj 6073 and Uj 6081 engage the small task force. Endicott,

Aphis, and Scarab engage them and sink both 13 miles off Cap Croisette Light.

Heavy cruiser Tuscaloosa (CA 37) is near-missed by shore battery off southern France; beachhead screen (TU 80.6.10) engages four German E-boats off southern France; destroyer Harding (DD 625) sinks two, Carmick (DD 493) and Satterlee (DD 626) one apiece. Destroyer Frankford (DD 497), damaged by E-boat, later captures the craft, which sinks subsequently.

ATLANTIC. Coast Guard lighthouse tender Bittersweet (WAGL 389) breaks down en route from Norfolk, Virginia, to the Canal Zone, 50 miles east of Cape Hatteras, North Carolina; accompanying lighthouse tender Bramble (WAGL 392) takes her disabled sister ship in tow (see 18 August).

18 Friday

PACIFIC. Submarine Hardhead (SS 365) sinks Japanese light cruiser Natori about 200 miles east of Samar, P.I., 12°05′N, 129°26′E; accompanying fast transport T.3 continues on for Palau. Destroyers Uranami and Kiyoshimo rescue most of Natori's survivors (see 31 August and 12 September).

U.S. submarines Rasher (SS 269) and Redfish (SS 395) encounter Japanese convoy HI 71 off west coast of Luzon. Rasher sinks escort carrier Taiyo, transport Teia Maru, cargo ship Eishin Maru at 18°16′N, 120°21′E, and oiler Teiyo Maru southwest of Cape Bojeador, 18°09′N, 120°13′E, and damages transport Noshiro Maru southwest of Cape Bojeador, 18°09′N, 119°56′E; Redfish damages merchant tanker Eiyo Maru west of Luzon Strait, 20°28′N, 121°04′E.

Submarine Ray (SS 271) sinks Japanese merchant tanker Nansei Maru off southern tip of Palawan, 08°48′N, 117°02′E.

Dutch submarine Zwaardvisch sinks Japanese vessel Kim Hup Soen in Strait of Malacca, 04°00′N, 99°32′E.

Japanese destroyer Samidare is damaged when she runs aground on Velasco Reef, north of Palau, Carolines (see 26 August).

MEDITERRANEAN. Amphibious force flagship Catoctin (AGC 5) is damaged by JU-88 off southern France, 43°17′N, 06°38′E; the JU-88 had followed closely behind USAAF P-38s and an RAF Beaufighter during an air raid alert. Elsewhere off the beachheads minesweeper Steady (AM 118) suffers damage when a broken fire main floods jamming equipment compartment, and destroyer MacKenzie (DD 614) is disabled by operational casualty

(starboard engine) during attack on submarine contact. U.S. freighter Albert A. Michelson is damaged off St. Tropez by bomb during German air raid; while there are no casualties among the 27-man Armed Guard, five of the 43-man merchant complement are wounded badly enough to warrant their being left in a shoreside hospital for treatment.

ATLANTIC. Coast Guard lighthouse tender Bramble (WAGL 392), with her disabled sister ship Bittersweet (WAGL 389) in tow off Cape Hatteras, North Carolina, is unable to make much headway due to high winds and heavy seas. Big harbor tug Bomazeen (YTB 238) is dispatched from Norfolk, Virginia, to assist; while she is en route, Bramble breaks down as well. Bomazeen tows both Coast Guard vessels to Norfolk, arriving the following day.

19 Saturday

PACIFIC. U.S. submarine attacks on Japanese convoy HI 71, begun the previous day, continue off the west coast of Luzon as Bluefish (SS 222) sinks fast fleet tanker/seaplane carrier Hayasui, 80 nautical miles northwest of Cape Bolinao, 17°34′N, 119°23′E, and damages hospital ship Awa Maru, 17°36′N, 119°38′E.

Submarine Redfin (SS 272) lays mines off Sarawak, Borneo.

Submarine Spadefish (SS 411) sinks Japanese landing craft depot repair ship Tamatsu Maru west of Luzon, 18°48′N, 119°47′E.

MEDITERRANEAN. Battleship Nevada (BB 36), French battleship Lorraine, and heavy cruiser Augusta (CA 31) conduct reconnaissance in force off Toulon to support the U.S. Army's Third Division and French troops making a drive on that port. Escorted by four destroyers, Nevada, Lorraine, and Augusta shell the harbor and batteries at St. Mandrier, the guns for which (nicknamed "Big Willie") consist of turrets removed from battleship Provence (Lorraine's sister ship) and emplaced ashore; heavy cruiser Quincy (CA 71) provides counterbattery fire on Giens, from south of Isle Port Cros.

EUROPE. German submarines U 123 and U 129 are scuttled to avoid capture at Lorient, France.

20 Sunday

PACIFIC. RAAF aircraft damage small Japanese cargo vessel Kairyu Maru, Menado Bay, 00°49′N, 127°38′E.

RAAF Beaufighters sink small Japanese cargo vessel No. 3 Yamada Maru off north coast of Ceram, N.E.I.

USAAF B-24s (14th Air Force) sink Japanese army tanker *Chuko Maru* near Hong Kong, 22°23′N, 115°34′E.

ATLANTIC. TBM and FM-2 (VC 42) from escort carrier *Bogue* (CVE 9) sink German submarine *U 1229* in North Atlantic, 42°20′N, 51°39′W.

MEDITERRANEAN. German submarines *U 178* and *U 188* and *UIT 21* (ex-Italian) are scuttled to avoid capture at Bordeaux, France.

21 Monday

PACIFIC. Off Mindoro, submarines *Guitarro* (SS 363), *Haddo* (SS 255), *Harder* (SS 257), and *Ray* (SS 271) carry out series of attacks on Japanese convoy: *Guitarro* sinks freighter *Uga Maru*, 13°21′N, 120°18′E; *Haddo* sinks freighters *Kinryu Maru* and *Norfolk Maru* and damages merchant tanker *Taiei Maru*, 13°22′N, 120°19′E; and *Ray* sinks merchant tanker *Taketoyo Maru*, 13°23′N, 120°19′E.

Submarine *Muskallunge* (SS 262) attacks Japanese Manila-to-Singapore convoy, sinking army transport *Durban Maru* off Cam Ranh Bay, French Indochina, 11°45′N, 109°46′E.

PB4Ys damage Japanese guardboat *No. 10 Sumiyoshi Maru* and small cargo vessel *Shinyama Maru* northwest of Marcus Island.

PB4Ys damage Japanese cargo vessel *Tateishi Maru* in Davao Harbor.

RAAF Beaufighters and Kittyhawks attack Japanese shipping off Kaimana, 03°40′S, 133°50′E.

Japanese army cargo ship *Tokuhei Maru* is sunk, probably by USAAF aircraft, Tayeh, Yangtze River.

MEDITERRANEAN. Destroyer *Eberle* (DD 430) takes 140 Armenian prisoners from Isle de Proquerolles, France.

22 Tuesday

PACIFIC. Submarine *Bowfin* (SS 287) attacks Japanese convoy, sinking army cargo ship *Tsushima Maru* in the Nansei Shoto, 29°30′N, 129°30′E.

Submarines *Haddo* (SS 255) and *Harder* (SS 257) encounter three Japanese escort vessels off the mouth of Manila Bay. *Haddo* sinks *Sado* 35 miles west of Manila, 14°15′N, 120°05′E; *Harder* sinks *Matsuwa* and *Hiburi* about 50 miles west-southwest of Manila, 14°15′N, 120°05′E. Loss of the trio of escorts in one day prompts the Chief of Staff, First Surface Escort Unit, to lament candidly: "Escort vessels, whose prime duty it is to attack and sink enemy submarines, have themselves been being sunk by enemy subs. This year alone a total of

13 have been sunk and three badly damaged. In addition, the *Kusagaki*, *Matsuwa*, *Sado* and *Hiburi* have been sunk one after the other just recently." The situation mirrors the plight of Japanese antisubmarine operations.

Submarine *Pintado* (SS 387) attacks Japanese convoy, sinking merchant tanker *No. 2 Tonan Maru*, 200 nautical miles southeast of Shanghai, 29°52′N, 125°22′E.

Submarine *Spadefish* (SS 411) attacks Japanese convoy, torpedoing tanker *No. 2 Hakko Maru* in Luzon Strait, 18°48′N, 120°46′E; the damaged tanker takes refuge in Pasaleng Bay, Luzon Strait (see 18 September).

Submarine *Tang* (SS 306) sinks Japanese army cargo ship *No. 2 Nansatsu Maru* off Miki Saki, 34°01′N, 136°21′E.

British submarine HMS *Statesman* sinks Japanese army cargo ship *No. 5 Sugi Maru* (ex-Panamanian *Gran*) off Port Blair, 11°41′N, 92°47′E; escorting torpedo boat *Kari* and submarine chaser *Ch. 9* carry out unsuccessful counterattacks.

Japanese freighter *Kanzaki Maru* is sunk by aircraft off east coast of Korea, 36°01′N, 129°41′E.

23 Wednesday

PACIFIC. Destroyer *Cassin* (DD 372), destroyer escort *Cabana* (DE 260), and infantry landing craft (gunboat) *LCI(G) 346* and *LCI(G) 438* bombard Japanese installations and positions on Aguijan Island, Marianas; ships repeat bombardment [*LCI(G) 348* replaces *LCI(G) 438* on 24 and 25 August] daily until 26 August.

Battleships *Tennessee* (BB 43) and *California* (BB 44) collide while en route from Eniwetok to Espíritu Santo, New Hebrides; damage to *California* will prevent her from participating in upcoming Palau operation.

Submarine *Haddo* (SS 255) torpedoes Japanese destroyer *Asakaze* as the enemy warship is escorting tanker *Niyo Maru*, 20 miles southwest of Cape Bolinao, Luzon, P.I., 16°06′N, 119°44′E. *Asakaze* sinks near Dasol Bay after attempts at salvage fail.

Submarine *Tang* (SS 306) attacks Japanese convoy off Honshu, sinking cargo ship *Tsukushi Maru* off Hamamatsu, 34°37′N, 137°52′E.

PB4Y-1s (VB 102) attack Japanese convoy in the Bonins and sink auxiliary submarine chaser *No. 5 Shonan Maru* northwest of Chichi Jima, 27°07′N, 142°06′E.

MEDITERRANEAN. German garrison on Isle de Proquerolles, France, except isolated stragglers, surrenders to Commander TG 86.3 in

light cruiser *Omaha* (CL 4); the island will then be occupied by Senegalese troops.

High-speed transport *Tattnall* (APD 19) is damaged by collision with underwater object off southern France.

EUROPE. U.S. freighter *Louis Kossuth*, bound for UTAH beach, Normandy, is torpedoed by German submarine *U 989* at 50°16′N, 01°41′30″W. Of the 334 embarked troops, 13 are injured; there are no casualties to either the merchant complement (40 men) or the 28-man Armed Guard. The ship is towed to Cowes, England, by British tug *Empire Winnie*.

24 Thursday

PACIFIC. Submarine *Harder* (SS 257) is sunk by Japanese *Coast Defense Vessel No. 22* off west coast of Luzon, 15°50′N, 119°43′E. Commander Samuel D. Dealey, *Harder*'s aggressive and much-decorated commanding officer (Medal of Honor, four Navy Crosses, and a Silver Star) is lost with his boat.

Submarine *Ronquil* (SS 396) attacks Japanese convoy, sinking army cargo ship *No. 3 Yoshida Maru* off Keelung, Formosa, 25°29′N, 123°15′E, and freighter *Fukurei Maru* off Sankaku Island, 25°13′N, 121°49′E.

Submarine *Sailfish* (SS 192) attacks Japanese convoy in Luzon Strait, sinking transport *Toan Maru*, 21°23′N, 121°37′E.

Submarine *Seal* (SS 183) sinks Japanese freighter *Tosei Maru* off southeast coast of Hokkaido, 42°30′N, 144°05′E.

Submarine chaser *SC 1009* is damaged by grounding off Kahului, Maui, T.H.

British carrier force attacks Padang, Sumatra, sinking Japanese freighter *Shiretoko Maru* off the harbor and damaging *Senko Maru* and *Chisho Maru*.

Japanese minelayer *Itsukushima* is damaged by aircraft off Menado, Celebes, N.E.I.

Japanese auxiliary vessel *Senko Maru* is damaged by aircraft north of Boetoeng Harbor, southern Celebes.

Japanese army cargo ship *No. 21 Kongo Maru* is sunk by aircraft, Philippine location unspecified.

MEDITERRANEAN. Motor torpedo boat *PT 555* is damaged by mine at Cap Couronne buoy; a French vessel attempting to rescue the crew is mined as well, 43°19′N, 05°30′E.

25 Friday

PACIFIC. Submarine *Picuda* (SS 382), in attack on Japanese convoy at the western entrance to the Babuyan Channel, sinks destroyer *Yunagi* 20 miles north-northeast of Cape Bojeador,

P.I., 18°45′N, 120°44′E, and merchant tanker *Kotoku Maru*, 18°46′N, 120°46′E. Later, submarine *Redfish* (SS 395) comes upon the convoy attacked earlier by *Picuda* and damages army cargo ship *Batopaha Maru* north-north-east of Cape Bojeador, 18°31′N, 120°32′E; *Manshu Maru* tows the crippled *Batopaha Maru* to Bangui Bay where she is beached.

Submarine *Tang* (SS 306) sinks Japanese merchant tanker *No. 8 Nanko Maru* off Honshu, 33°55′N, 136°18′E.

General stores issue ship *Talita* (AKS 8) is attacked by accident by U.S. merchant tanker *Amatilla* en route from Eniwetok to Espíritu Santo.

EUROPE. U.S. and French troops liberate Paris, France.

Motor torpedo boats *PT 513*, *PT 516*, and *PT 519* engage German coastal craft off Le Havre; *PT 513* and *PT 516* are damaged.

26 Saturday

PACIFIC. Submarine chaser *PCS 1404* transports a marine reconnaissance party to Aguijan Island, Marianas; after recovering the leathernecks, she bombards the island.

Submarine *Batfish* (SS 310) causes further damage to destroyer *Samidare,* grounded on 18 August, on Velasco Reef, Palau, 08°30′N, 134°37′E. Submariners observe Japanese blowing up the remainder of the wreckage.

Light cruiser *Boise* (CL 47) is damaged when rammed accidentally by harbor tug *Heroine*, Sydney, Australia.

Submarine *S 18* (SS 123) is damaged when accidentally rammed by medium landing ship *LSM 135*, Naval Repair Base, San Diego, California.

Submarine tender *Pelias* (AS 14) is damaged by grounding in San Francisco Bay.

EUROPE. Motor torpedo boats *PT 511*, *PT 514*, and *PT 520* take part in night engagement (that lasts into the following day) that turns back the last German attempt to reinforce the besieged garrison at Le Havre; the PTs sink German artillery ferries *AFP 98* and *AFP 108*.

ATLANTIC. Panamanian freighter *Cloverbrook*, a fire having broken out in a hold, is detached from convoy NG 455 and proceeds to Norfolk, Virginia, with gunboat *Pert* (PG 95) as escort. Tug *Sciota* (ATO 30) is dispatched from Norfolk with a mobile fire-fighting unit embarked, and provides assistance to the merchantman.

27 Sunday

PACIFIC. Submarine *Guitarro* (SS 363) attacks Japanese convoy bound for Coron Bay, P.I., sinking merchant tanker *No. 25 Nanshin Maru*, damaging *No. 3 Nanshin Maru*, and forcing tanker *No. 25 Nanshin Maru* aground, 12°26′N, 119°55′E.

Submarine *Stingray* (SS 186), after being depth charged and "lightly worked over while reconnoitering [the] designated spot" lands party of one Filipino officer, 14 men, and 60 percent of the supplies earmarked for delivery to guerrilla forces at Saddle Rock, Mayaira Point, on northwest shore of Luzon. Heavy Japanese shipping in the vicinity compels *Stingray*'s departure before all stores have been landed (see 31 August).

PVs sink Japanese vessel *Tensho Maru* between Odomari, southwest of Sakhalin, and Onnekotan Island, Kurils.

High-speed minesweeper *Boggs* (DMS 3) and submarine chaser *PC 783* are damaged in collision, San Diego, California.

ATLANTIC. Tank landing ship *LST 327* is damaged by mine while en route from Cherbourg, France, to Southampton, England.

MEDITERRANEAN. Destroyer *Ericsson* (DD 440) captures fishing vessel attempting to escape Toulon, France, and takes 50 German submariners as POWs. Motor torpedo boat *PT 552* sinks four German explosive motorboats at entrance to Toulon Harbor, but control boat escapes.

28 Monday

PACIFIC. USAAF B-25s (11th Air Force) sink auxiliary submarine chaser *Cha 77* at south entrance of Paramushir Straits, Kurils, 50°31′N, 156°12.7′E.

ARABIAN SEA. U.S. freighter *John Barry*, en route from Aden to the Persian Gulf, is torpedoed and sunk by German submarine *U 859* at 15°10′N, 55°18′E. Two members of the merchant crew are lost during the abandonment, but 39 of the 41-man merchant complement and the entire 27-man Armed Guard survive (see 29 August).

MEDITERRANEAN. German garrisons at Marseilles, including outlying islands and St. Mandrier battery (the sole remaining enemy pocket in Toulon), surrender.

29 Tuesday

PACIFIC. Destroyer escort *Conklin* (DE 439) accidentally fires upon U.S. freighter *Dominican Victory* because of unfamiliarity with recognition signals north of the Marshalls.

Infantry landing craft *LCI 566* is damaged by grounding, south of Oahu, 20°56′N, 157°00′E.

Submarine *Jack* (SS 259) attacks Japanese convoy H 3, sinking minesweeper *W.28* and army cargo ship *Mexico Maru* northwest of Menado, Celebes, 02°15′N, 122°50.

PBY sinks Japanese auxiliary sailing vessel *Toyokuni Maru* at entrance to Ambon Bay, 03°22′S, 129°39′E.

Japanese freighter *Koryu Maru* is sunk by aircraft, Kiukiang, China.

Japanese tanker *Kaiko Maru* is damaged by mine in Strait of Malacca, 03°40′N, 100°06′E.

ARABIAN SEA. Dutch freighter *Sanetta* and U.S. freighter *Benjamin Bourn* rescue the 66 survivors from U.S. freighter *John Barry*, sunk by German submarine *U 859* the previous day.

MEDITERRANEAN. Marine detachments from heavy cruiser *Augusta* (CA 31) and light cruiser *Philadelphia* (CL 41) accept the surrender of two German-held islands in Marseilles Harbor and disarm the garrisons.

U.S. motor torpedo boats *PT 302*, *PT 303*, and *PT 304* attack two corvettes and one destroyer off Cap Mele, compelling the enemy ships to reverse course and steam for Genoa, Italy. The PTs will continue their patrol into the next morning but make no further sightings.

30 Wednesday

PACIFIC. Submarine *Narwhal* (SS 167) lands two Filipino officers and 18 men, with about 10 tons of supplies, at a site within Dubut Bay, on east coast of Luzon (see 1 September).

ATLANTIC. U.S. tanker *Jacksonville*, steaming in convoy CU 36, is torpedoed by German submarine *U 482* while en route to Loch Ewe, Scotland, at 55°30′N, 07°30′W; the gasoline cargo explodes, giving little chance for the 49-man merchant complement or the 29-man Armed Guard to abandon the blazing ship, which breaks in two at the second massive explosion. Destroyer escort *Poole* (DE 151) rescues a fireman and one Armed Guard sailor, *Jacksonville*'s only survivors. Escort vessels use depth charges and gunfire to scuttle the after section of the ship; the forward section sinks on its own accord.

31 Thursday

PACIFIC. TG 38.4 (Rear Admiral Ralph E. Davison) attacks Iwo Jima and Chichi Jima (strikes will be repeated on 1 and 2 September) to neutralize Japanese installations there and provide a diversion in advance of planned operations in the Palau, Morotai, and Philippine areas. Off Iwo Jima, F6Fs from carrier *Franklin* (CV 13) sink auxiliary minesweeper *No. 8 Toshi Maru*, 25°00′N, 141°50′E, and freighter *Suruga Maru*, 24°46′N, 141°19′E.

U.S. submarines attack Japanese convoy, bound for Manila, in Luzon Strait. *Barb* (SS 220) sinks auxiliary minesweeper *No. 20 Hinode Maru*, 21°21′N, 121°11′E, and army cargo ship *Okuni Maru*, 21°14′N, 121°22′E. *Queenfish* (SS 393) sinks army tanker *Chiyoda Maru*, 21°21′N, 121°06′E, damages cargo vessel *Tempi Maru*, 21°10′N, 121°04′E, and, along with *Growler* (SS 215), damages army tanker *Rikko Maru*, 21°30′N, 121°19′E; *Sealion* (SS 315) sinks minelayer *Shirataka*, 21°05′N, 121°26′E.

Submarine *Redfin* (SS 272) embarks eight survivors from submarine *Flier* (SS 250) (sunk by mine on 13 August), in addition to two Army enlisted men, a sailor from Patrol Wing 10, four British subjects, one American civilian, and a Finnish citizen, from Palawan, P.I. *Redfin* leaves quantities of small arms, ammunition, and sundry stores and miscellaneous items that can be spared for use ashore by coastwatcher group there.

Submarine *Stingray* (SS 186), en route to Darwin, Australia, rescues one officer and three ratings from Japanese light cruiser *Natori*, sunk on 18 August.

PBYs sink small Japanese cargo vessels *No. 2 Kairyu Maru* and *Kabuchi Maru* off Ceram, N.E.I.

USAAF B-25s and P-38s (14th Air Force) attack Japanese shipping on the Yangtze, sinking transport *Fengyang Maru* and cargo ship *Tokuhei Maru*, and driving *Reizan Maru* aground off Shihweiyao, China, 30°11′N, 115°07′E.

RAAF Mitchells sink small Japanese cargo vessel *No. 8 Sanko Maru* off north coast of Alor Island, Lesser Sunda Islands.

Japanese guardboat *No. 2 Kyoshin Maru* is sunk by U.S. aircraft off Halmahera.

Japanese freighter *Hoyo Maru* is damaged by aircraft, Tayeh, Yangtze River.

Japanese freighter *Tientsin Maru* is sunk by mine off Woosung, China.

SEPTEMBER

1 Friday

PACIFIC. Heavy cruiser *New Orleans* (CA 32), light cruiser *Biloxi* (CL 80), and four destroyers drawn from TG 38.4, bombard Japanese installations at Iwo Jima and Chichi Jima (the bombardment will be repeated the following day). The ships draw no return fire and U.S. gunfire damages landing ship *T.105* off Chichi Jima. Planes from carrier *Enterprise* (CV 6), in TG 38.4, damage fast transport *T.4* at Chichi Jima (see 2 September).

Submarine *Narwhal* (SS 167) lands five Filipino officers and 18 enlisted men, together with about 10 tons of supplies, at site off mouth of the Masanga River, on east coast of Luzon. In addition, she evacuates four U.S. enlisted men.[204]

Submarine *Pilotfish* (SS 386) sinks Japanese auxiliary vessel *Ina Maru* north-northwest of Chichi Jima, 30°32′N, 140°55′E.

Submarine *Tunny* (SS 282) is damaged by aerial bombs, Luzon Strait, 21°50′N, 119°18′E, and is forced to terminate her patrol.

British submarine HMS *Storm* attacks Japanese Mergui-bound convoy with gunfire, sinking auxiliary minesweeper *Wa 4* and damaging auxiliary vessel *Misago Maru*.

Japanese freighter *Sekino Maru* is sunk by aircraft in Celebes Sea, 01°06′N, 122°21′E.

Japanese freighter *Namba Maru* is sunk (by mine laid by 14th Air Force B-24 or by time bomb planted on board prior to sailing) in the Yangtze River about 20 miles below Woosung, China, 31°10′N, 121°50′E.

Naval Operating Base, Saipan, is established.

ARCTIC. Coast guard cutter *Northland* (WPG 49) locates German weather ship *Kehdingen* off Great Koldeyey Island, Greenland, and pursues her through the ice floes. *Kehdingen*, however, is scuttled by her crew to avoid capture. German submarine *U 703*'s attack on *Northland* is thwarted by ice.

MEDITERRANEAN. Motor minesweeper *YMS 21* is sunk by mine off Toulon, France, 43°06′N, 05°54′E.

2 Saturday

PACIFIC. Submarine *Guardfish* (SS 217) sinks Japanese freighter *Shirakami Maru* north of Chichi Jima, 29°48′E, 140°20′E.

Submarine *Finback* (SS 230), while lifeguarding for Chichi Jima strike, rescues Lieutenant (j.g.) George H. W. Bush, A-V(N), USNR, of VT 51; Bush will eventually become the 41st President of the United States. Planes from carrier *Enterprise* (CV 6), in TG 38.4, inflict further damage upon Japanese landing ship *T.4* off Chichi Jima.

British submarine HMS *Sirdar* attacks Japanese convoy and damages guardboat *No. 5 Kaiyo Maru* and *No. 28 Auxiliary Sailing Vessel* off northwestern Sumatra, 03°55′N, 096°20′E;

both patrol craft are driven aground while oiler *Sabang Maru*, which engages the pursuing *Sirdar*, survives the attack undamaged.

British submarine HMS *Strongbow* sinks Japanese army cargo ship *No. 1 Toso Maru* off west coast of Siam, 07°57′N, 98°49′E.

Japanese auxiliary submarine chaser *No. 2 Misago Maru* is sunk by aircraft north of Mindanao.

3 Sunday

PACIFIC. TG 12.5 (Rear Admiral Allan E. Smith), composed of small carrier *Monterey* (CVL 26), three heavy cruisers, and three destroyers, pounds Japanese installations on Wake Island.

Japanese destroyer *Hasu* is damaged by mine off Yangtze estuary, 31°19′N, 121°43′E.

MEDITERRANEAN. Submarine chaser *SC 535* is damaged by storm off Toulon, France, 43°17′N, 06°38′E.

Tank landing craft *LCT 151* is sunk by storm off southwestern coast of Sardinia, 39°22′N, 08°00′E.

4 Monday

PACIFIC. Submarine *Bowfin* (SS 287) sinks Japanese guardboat *No. 6 Hinode Maru* east of the Nanpo Shoto, 31°54′N, 152°05′E.

MEDITERRANEAN. Aviation supply ship *Tackle* (IX 217) is damaged by mine, Port de Buoc, France, while being towed by French tug *Provençal*.

Tank landing ship *LST 659* is damaged when she strikes a submerged wreck off RED beach, southern France.

5 Tuesday

PACIFIC. Submarine *Albacore* (SS 218) sinks Japanese freighter *Shingetsu Maru* south of Muroto Saki, 32°24′N, 134°15′E.

British submarine HMS *Tantivy*, despite presence of escorts, sinks Japanese freighter *Shiretoko Maru* in Semangko Bay, Sunda Strait, 05°44′S, 104°58′E.

Japanese freighter *Kokka Maru* is sunk by mine, Keelung, Formosa.

MEDITERRANEAN. Off southern France invasion beaches, French destroyer *Le Malin* discovers presence of German manned torpedoes and opens fire; destroyer *Ludlow* (DD 438) joins *Le Malin* in dropping depth charges, destroying three torpedoes and capturing the crews who manned them.

6 Wednesday

PACIFIC. TF 38 (Vice Admiral Marc A.

Mitscher) arrives off Palau to begin operations against Japanese airfields and defense installations in the western Carolines; a fighter sweep discloses no aerial opposition and reveals much damage caused by prior strikes. Task groups involved are TGs 38.1, 38.2, and 38.3. TG 38.4 (Rear Admiral Ralph E. Davison), meanwhile, conducts fighter sweep over Yap.

Small carrier *Independence* (CVL 22) begins use of specifically trained air group for night work, marking the first time that a fully equipped night carrier operates with the fast carrier task force.

Destroyers *Ellet* (DD 398) and *Downes* (DD 375) bombard Aguijan Island, Marianas, to destroy gun emplacement located by air reconnaissance.

Submarine *Albacore* (SS 218) sinks Japanese auxiliary minesweeper *No. 3 Eguchi Maru* at entrance to Kii Strait, Japan, 33°29'N, 135°32'E.

Submarine *Hake* (SS 256) torpedoes Japanese destroyer *Hibiki* south-southwest of Cape Bolinao, Luzon, 16°19'N, 119°44'E.

USAAF P-40s sink Japanese fishing boats *Sakae Maru*, *Tairyu Maru*, *Tatsuei Maru*, and *Takuyo Maru* off Kai Island, N.E.I.

Japanese army cargo ship *Eiji Maru*, in convoy TAMA 25, is sunk by mine (laid by 14th Air Force B-24 on 31 August) about 50 miles south of Takao, Formosa, 22°19'N, 120°30'E. *Coast Defense Vessel No. 28* rescues survivors.

7 Thursday

PACIFIC. TGs 38.1, 38.2, and 38.3 conduct full-scale air strikes on Japanese installations throughout the principal Palaus; they will repeat the evolutions (albeit with diminishing force in view of the paucity of targets) the next day. Cruiser Division 14 (Rear Admiral Francis E. M. Whiting) (three light cruisers, screened by four destroyers, drawn from TGs 38.2 and 38.3) bombards Japanese installations on Peleliu, Angaur, and Ngesebus, Palaus, supplementing the carrier air strikes begun the previous day by TF 38. Heavy cruiser *New Orleans* (CA 32), light cruiser *Biloxi* (CL 80), and four destroyers (from TG 38.4) bombard Yap; they will repeat the bombardment the following day. Planes from TG 38.4, meanwhile, on this day and the next will carry out operations against Yap and Ulithi in the Carolines.

U.S. Army forces supported by naval vessels land on Soepiori Island in the Schouten Islands of New Guinea.

Destroyer *Flusser* (DD 368) is damaged by shore battery, Wotje Island, Marshalls, while on a routine patrol to the south of the island.

Submarine *Paddle* (SS 263) attacks Japanese convoy C 076 and sinks transport *Shinyo Maru*, which unbeknown to her attacker has 750 American POWs (from the Davao internment camp) on board (see 29 September), and damages tanker *No. 2 Eiyo Maru* off Sindangan Point, Mindanao, 08°11'N, 122°40'E. *No. 2 Eiyo Maru* is beached at 08°10'N, 122°40'E (see 12 September).

RAAF Beaufighters sink Japanese motor sailboat *Keishin Maru* off southern coast of Ceram.

8 Friday

PACIFIC. Submarine *Bashaw* (SS 241), despite presence of escort vessels, sinks Japanese transport *Yanagigawa Maru* in the Sulu Sea, northwest of Zamboanga, P.I., 08°10'N, 121°48'E.

Submarine *Seal* (SS 183) attacks Japanese convoy KI 505 in the Sea of Okhotsk, torpedoing destroyer *Namikaze* west of Shimushir Island, Kurils, 47°28'N, 148°20'E (see 9 August).

Submarine *Spadefish* (SS 411), in attack on Japanese convoy off Sakishima Gunto, sinks transport *Shokei Maru* and army cargo ship *Shinten Maru*, 24°39'N, 123°31'E, and freighters *Nichiman Maru* and *Nichian Maru*, 24°45'N, 123°26'E. Despite *Spadefish*'s claim of a fifth ship, the other two vessels in the convoy, *No. 1 Toyo Maru* and *Kenjo Maru*, survive unscathed.

USAAF B-24s bomb Japanese shipping off Chichi Jima, Bonins, damaging cargo vessels *Heiwa Maru*, *Toyo Maru*, and *No. 1 Totei Maru*.

ATLANTIC. First German V-2 rocket bomb (485th Artillery Battalion, motorized) lands in London, England.

MEDITERRANEAN. German explosive boats attack destroyer *Hilary P. Jones* (DD 427) off Cap Martin, but inflict no damage; destroyer *Madison* (DD 425) is attacked by German explosive boats but sights them in time to avoid them. U.S. destroyers are attacked by German explosive boats five miles south of Cap Ampeglio; U.S. motor torpedo boats engage an additional four enemy craft.

9 Saturday

PACIFIC. TF 38 (Vice Admiral Marc A. Mitscher) begins strikes against Japanese shipping, facilities, and airfields on Mindanao; carrier-based planes sink transport *Kuniyama Maru* in Sulu Sea, 06°30'N, 121°50'E, and transports *Kurenai Maru* and *Mihara Maru* and cargo ship *Taiyu Maru* in Mindanao Sea, 09°45'N, 125°30'E. Planes from carriers *Essex* (CV 9) and *Lexington* (CV 16) (in TG 38.3) sink

Japanese motor sailboats *No. 6 Asashi Maru*, *No. 2 Chitose Maru*, *No. 2 Eifoku Maru*, *No. 26 Gyosei Maru*, *No. 3 Harunichi Maru*, *No. 7 Kiku Maru*, *No. 1 Sumiyoshi Maru*, *No. 11 Ume Maru*, *No. 8 Takatoshi Maru*, *No. 2 Shinyo Maru*, *Teikoku Maru*, *Yamasa Maru*, and *Ko Maru* at Surigao and Macajalar Bay, Mindanao, 09°45'N, 125°30'E.[205] Light cruisers *Birmingham* (CL 62) and *Santa Fe* (CL 60) and four destroyers detached from TG 58.3 (Rear Admiral Laurance T. DuBose), covered by planes from small carrier *Langley* (CVL 27), demolish coastal convoy consisting of predominantly small ships and craft proceeding down the west coast of Mindanao.

Submarine *Bang* (SS 385) attacks Japanese convoy 3905, en route from Tokyo Bay to Chichi Jima, and sinks transport *Tokiwasan Maru*, 28°53'N, 137°42'E, and freighter *Shoryu Maru*, 28°58'N, 137°45'E.

Submarine *Queenfish* (SS 393) sinks Japanese transport *Toyoka Maru* and merchant passenger-cargo ship *Manshu Maru* and damages torpedo boat *Manazuru* west of the Babuyan Islands, Luzon, 19°45'N, 120°56'E.

Submarine *Seal* (SS 183) continues stalking Japanese convoy KI 505 and, despite presence of escort vessels *Kunajiri* and *Nomi*, sinks army cargo ship *Shonan Maru* in Sea of Okhotsk, north of Etorofu, Kurils, 47°57'N, 148°15'E. All hands are saved from *Shonan Maru* because the ship had been transporting two landing barges (the use of which had been effectively communicated to the crew) and the ship sinks slowly, thus giving them time to deploy the boats that save their lives.

PBY sinks Japanese cargo ship *Kuniyama Maru* off Basilan Island, 06°34'N, 121°50'E.

Japanese auxiliary submarine chasers *Cha 8* and *Cha 9* are sunk by mines (laid on 6–8 July by British submarine HMS *Porpoise*) off mouth of Deli River, Sumatra, 03°54'N, 98°44'E.

Japanese freighter *Tsinan Maru* is sunk by mine (laid by 14th Air Force B-24s) off Woosung, China.

10 Sunday

PACIFIC. TF 38 air strikes against Japanese shipping, facilities, and airfields on Mindanao continue. During these operations, TF 38 planes sink Japanese freighter *No. 7 Unyo Maru* off Mindanao.

Submarine *Sunfish* (SS 281) attacks Japanese convoy at entrance to Tsushima Strait, sinking merchant tanker *Chihaya Maru* off Quelpart Island, 33°47'N, 127°37'E, forcing the convoy to take refuge off Kyokiu Island while escort vessels *Shonan* and *Sagi* protect the anchorage.

Japanese army tanker *Bukun Maru* is sunk by mine (laid by British submarine HMS *Porpoise* on 8 July) in Strait of Malacca, 03°54′N, 98°42′E.

Japanese merchant tanker *No. 2 Hoei Maru* is sunk by mine off Woosung, China.

ANDAMAN SEA. RAF Beaufighters and Hurricanes attack Japanese convoy MR 1 en route to Rangoon, Burma, and sink auxiliary vessel *Misago Maru* (previously damaged by British submarine HMS *Storm* on 1 September); auxiliary minesweeper *Wa 3* is damaged.

EUROPE. Command designated Naval Forces France (Vice Admiral Alan G. Kirk) is established with headquarters at Paris, France.

MEDITERRANEAN. U.S. motor torpedo boat *PT 206* on right flank of southern France beachhead gives chase to German explosive boat unit consisting of a control boat and two drones; one of the latter is destroyed. Minesweeper *Seer* (AM 112) is damaged by mine while sweeping Grande Passe to Rade d'Hyeres, 42°59′N, 06°20′E; fleet tug *Hopi* (ATF 71) tows the damaged ship to Toulon for repairs.

While patrolling between Noli and Genoa, Italy, *PT 559* and British motor torpedo boats attack south-bound convoy, sinking one F-lighter and an ammunition barge. Escorting German patrol craft break off action.

11   Monday

GENERAL. Second Quebec Conference (OCTAGON) between President Roosevelt and British Prime Minister Winston S. Churchill and the Combined Chiefs of Staff begins in Quebec, Canada. The agenda principally concerns the role the Royal Navy will play in the Pacific War.

PACIFIC. Destroyer *Ellet* (DD 398) bombards supply dumps on Aguijan Island, Marianas.

Submarine *Albacore* (SS 218) sinks Japanese auxiliary submarine chaser *Cha 165* off Miyasaki, Kyushu, 32°20′N, 131°50′E.

Submarine *Finback* (SS 230) sinks Japanese army cargo ship *Hassho Maru* and freighter *No. 2 Hakun Maru* north of Chichi Jima, 27°45′N, 140°40′E.

Submarine *Pargo* (SS 264) sinks Japanese auxiliary netlayer *Hinoki Maru* in Java Sea, 06°17′S, 116°24′E.

USAAF B-24s (7th Air Force) bomb Iwo Jima, damaging Japanese cargo vessel *No. 8 Saiwai Maru*; difficulties encountered in attempting to tow the damaged ship result in her being scuttled by gunfire.

Japanese cargo ship *No. 1 Horai Maru* is sunk by aircraft two miles off Palau.

12   Tuesday

GENERAL. Romania signs armistice with the United States, Great Britain, and the Soviet Union.

PACIFIC. TF 38 (Vice Admiral Marc A. Mitscher) begins operations against Japanese shipping and airfields in the Visayas. Planes from three carrier groups (TG 38.1, TG 38.2, and TG 38.3) pound enemy installations on Cebu and shipping offshore, sinking gunboat *Kiso Maru*, auxiliary submarine chasers *Mogami Maru* and *No. 12 Kyo Maru*, auxiliary netlayer *Korei Maru*, auxiliary minesweeper *No. 18 Choun Maru*, guardboats *No. 97 Banshu Maru* and *No. 4 Fukuju Maru*, transports *Bugen Maru* and *Nichiei Maru*, army cargo ships *Keian Maru* and *Genkai Maru*, merchant tanker *Ayazono Maru* and freighters *Toyo Maru*, *No. 2 Shintai Maru*, *No. 5 Shintai Maru*, and *No. 8 Shintai Maru*, 10°20′N, 124°00′E; salvage ship *Miho Maru*, 10°35′N, 124°00′E; transport *Shiramine Maru*, 10°34′N, 124°01′E; transport *Oakita Maru*, 11°21′N, 124°07′E; and transport *Rakuto Maru*, 10°35′N, 124°20′E. TF 38 planes also damage minesweeper *No. 21 Choun Maru* off Cebu, 10°20′N, 124°00′E. Between Biliran and Cebu, TF 38 planes sink auxiliary minesweeper *Takao Maru* and auxiliary submarine chaser *Nan-Ho Maru*; in Bohol Strait, carrier aircraft sink motor torpedo boat *Gyoraitei No. 483*. TF 38 planes also sink submarine chaser *Ch 55* three miles northeast of Cebu, 10°20′N, 124°00′E, as well as tanker *No. 2 Eiyo Maru*, previously damaged by *Paddle* (SS 263) on 7 September, in the Sulu Sea, west by north of Sindangan Point, Mindanao, 08°12′N, 122°37′E. Also lost on this date in the vicinity of the Visayas are *Chowa Maru*, *No. 2 Fuku Maru*, *No. 2 Hatafuku Maru*, *No. 1 Izumo Maru*, *Kaiko Maru*, *Kiho Maru*, *Kito Maru*, *No. 5 Kompira Maru*, *No. 2 Nichinan Maru*, *Sanshu Maru*, *Seiko Maru*, *No. 13 Shoyo Maru*, *Tenko Maru*, and *No. 3 Tosa Maru*.

Ensign Thomas C. Tillar, USNR, a pilot from carrier *Hornet* (CV 12), in TG 38.1, is rescued by Filipinos after his F6F ditches off Apit Island, off the southwestern coast of Leyte. Before Tillar is recovered by SOC from heavy cruiser *Wichita* (CA 45), he learns from his rescuers that the size of the Japanese garrison on Leyte is negligible. That fact, when combined with the lack of aerial opposition encountered and the few airfields that exist on Leyte and Samar, prompts Commander Third Fleet (Admiral William F. Halsey Jr.) to recommend that the planned attack on Yap be abandoned and that the date of the landings on Leyte be advanced from 20 December to 20 October (see 16 September).

Light minelayer *Preble* (DM 20) explodes acoustic mines in the shoals between Angaur and Peleliu, Palaus; she and sister ship *Montgomery* (DM 17) sweep most of the navigable waters by the end of the day. High-speed transport *Noa* (APD 24) is sunk in collision with destroyer *Fullam* (DD 474) off Palau, 07°01′N, 134°30′E; *Fullam* is damaged. Oilers *Millicoma* (AO 73) and *Schuykill* (AO 76) are damaged in collision off the Palaus.

Destroyer *Marshall* (DD 676) captures boat with 44 survivors of Japanese light cruiser *Natori*, sunk on 18 August.

Submarine *Growler* (SS 215) initiates attacks against Japanese HI 72 convoy, sinking escort vessel *Hirado* 250 miles east of Hainan Island, 17°54′N, 114°49′E; she then sinks destroyer *Shikinami* 240 miles south of Hong Kong, 18°25′N, 114°30′E′. *Sealion* (SS 315) sinks transport *Nankai Maru* and freighter *Rakuyo Maru* east of Hainan, 18°42′N, 114°30′E, unaware that the latter carries Allied POWs (see 15 September). *Pampanito* (SS 383) sinks merchant passenger-cargo ship *Kachidoki Maru* (ex-U.S. passenger liner *President Harrison*) and tanker *Zuiho Maru* off Hainan Island, 19°25′N, 112°27′E.

Submarine *Pipefish* (SS 388) sinks Japanese auxiliary vessel *No. 7 Hakutetsu Maru* off Shiono Misaki, Honshu, 33°32′N, 135°56′E.

Submarine *Redfin* (SS 272) carries out unsuccessful attack on Japanese cargo vessel *Tosho Maru* in the Java Sea, south of the Celebes, 05°27′S, 120°28′E, and survives counterattacks by submarine chaser *Ch 53*.

ATLANTIC. U.S. freighter *George Ade*, en route from Mobile, Alabama, to New York, via Key West, Florida, is torpedoed by German submarine *U 518* at 33°30′N, 75°40′W; the ship's Armed Guard fires two rounds at what they believe to be a surfaced submarine. There are no casualties among the 41-man merchant crew or the 27-man Armed Guard. Destroyer *Barton* (DD 722) contacts the stricken ship; rescue tug *ATR 6* takes *George Ade* in tow as weather worsens. Coast Guard cutters *Bedloe* (WPC 128) and *Jackson* (WPC 142) provide escort for the unfolding salvage operation (see 13–16 September).

Destroyer *Warrington* (DD 383), escorting provision stores ship *Hyades* (AF 28), en route from Cape Henry, Virginia, to the Canal

Zone, encounters hurricane off eastern seaboard, 27°57'N, 73°44'W (see 13–16 September).

13 Wednesday

PACIFIC. TG 38.2 (Rear Admiral Gerald F. Bogan) continues operations against Cebu, P.I., supported by TG 38.1 (Vice Admiral John S. McCain) and TG 38.3 (Rear Admiral Frederick C. Sherman), as well as against Japanese targets in the area of Negros, Cebu, and Legaspi. Late that afternoon, TG 38.1 (see 14 September) is detached to provide support for the landings at Morotai.

High-speed minesweeper *Perry* (DMS 17) is sunk by mine, 750 yards off the southeast coast of Angaur, southern Palaus, 06°53'N, 134°10'E.

Submarine *Sunfish* (SS 281), operating in the Yellow Sea, damages Japanese army cargo ship *Gyoku Maru* west of Cheju Strait, 34°32'N, 124°44'E, and sinks army cargo ship *Etajima Maru* off Mokp'o, Korea, 35°04'N, 124°49'E.

USAAF A-20s sink freighter *Akitsushima Maru* off southeastern Ceram, 03°04'S, 128°11'E.

USAAF B-24s sink Japanese cargo ship *Usa Maru* west of Formosa, 23°52'N, 118°56'E.

Japanese landing ship *T.153* is damaged (probably by USAAF aircraft) off Iwo Jima.

ATLANTIC. Worsening weather batters destroyer *Warrington* (DD 383) and escorting provision stores ship *Hyades* (AF 28); rescue tugs ATR 9 and ATR 62, en route from Norfolk, Virginia, to the Canal Zone, are diverted to assist, as is fleet tug *Cherokee* (ATF 66). Meanwhile, salvage vessel *Escape* (ARS 6) joins rescue tug ATR 6 in towing U.S. freighter *George Ade*, torpedoed the previous day, through heavy seas (see 14–16 September).

14 Thursday

PACIFIC. TG 38.2 (Rear Admiral Gerald F. Bogan) attacks Japanese shipping and installations on and around Panay and Negros, P.I., supported by TG 38.3 (Rear Admiral Frederick C. Sherman); during these operations, Navy carrier-based planes damage motor torpedo boat *Gyoraitei No. 482* north of Cebu, 11°00'N, 124°00'E. TG 38.1 (Vice Admiral John S. McCain), en route to support Morotai landings, carries out strikes on Japanese installations on Mindanao; during the course of these operations, SB2Cs (VB 2) sink fast transport *T.5* in Davao Gulf, 06°10'N, 126°00'E.

Destroyers *Farenholt* (DD 491), *McCalla* (DD 488), and *Grayson* (DD 435), detached from TG 38.1, bombard suspected Japanese radar installation on Cape San Augustin, at mouth of Davao Gulf.

Submarine *Pargo* (SS 264) lays mines near Natuna Island, South China Sea.

Japanese escort destroyer *Yashiro* is damaged by mine off Formosa, 22°42'N, 120°12'E.

Japanese cargo ship *Konan Maru* is sunk (marine casualty) off Muroran, Hokkaido, 42°07'N, 140°47'E.

ATLANTIC. U.S. warships and merchant vessels are caught in center of hurricane off the eastern seaboard. Destroyer *Warrington* (DD 383), escorting provision stores ship *Hyades* (AF 28), capsizes 175 miles east-southeast of Great Abaco Island, Bahamas, 27°55'N, 73°42'W; 73 survivors are picked up by searching ships. Rescue tug ATR 9, one of the ships diverted to assist *Warrington* and *Hyades*, suffers storm damage and proceeds to Charleston, South Carolina, for repairs. Meanwhile, U.S. freighter *George Ade*, torpedoed 12 September, breaks loose from ATR 6 and salvage vessel *Escape* (ARS 6) at about 35°55'N, 75°20'W; *George Ade* holds a position off Bodie Island by using her anchors and parted tow cable from ATR 6. Coast Guard cutters *Bedloe* (WPC 128) and *Jackson* (WPC 142), however, escorting *George Ade* and the two salvage vessels, founder in the storm and sink off Cape Hatteras, North Carolina (see 15 and 16 September).

Hurricane also overtakes an NG convoy and scatters the ships assigned to it; Army freighter *FS 315* is disabled by the storm and is taken in tow by British freighter *Silver Star Park*. ATR 7 arrives subsequently and takes over the tow of *FS 315*, bringing the damaged army vessel into Norfolk, Virginia, on 16 September. Motor minesweeper *YMS 409*, assigned duties as an additional escort to the NG convoy scattered by the storm, founders in the hurricane and sinks; *YMS 198* and submarine chaser *PC 1217* suffer storm damage but make port at Miami and Jacksonville, respectively.

Coast Guard *Lightship No. 73*, sinks in storm, Vineyard Sound, Massachusetts.

As storm batters the Tidewater area, frigate *Natchez* (PF 2) (see 18 September) and gunboat *Temptress* (PG 62) (see 21 September) go aground in heavy weather off Lynnhaven Inlet, Virginia, as does U.S. tanker *Brandywine* (see 19 September). District auxiliary vessel *YAG 17* runs aground in Chesapeake Bay off Ocean View, Virginia, 36°57'N, 76°13'W. Efforts to save *YAG 17* prove unavailing, and she is considered beyond salvage.

MEDITERRANEAN. Cruiser-based SOC spots small naval craft off Imperia, Italy, a 300-foot merchantman seven miles to the east, and 14 small craft off Cape Delle Mele; destroyer *Ludlow* (DD 438), with SOC spot and unopposed by enemy shore battery fire, scores at least 12 direct hits on the vessels off Imperia.

15 Friday

PACIFIC. Operation STALEMATE II: First Marine Division (Reinforced) (Major General William H. Rupertus, USMC) lands on Peleliu, Palaus, preceded by several days of intensive carrier-based aircraft bombing and ship gunfire bombardment (TG 32.5, Rear Admiral Jesse B. Oldendorf).

Operation TRADE WIND: TF 77 (Rear Admiral Daniel E. Barbey) lands Army 41st Infantry (Reinforced) (Major General John C. Persons, USA) on Morotai Island, N.E.I., supported by two heavy cruisers, three light cruisers, and 10 destroyers (TG 77.2) (Rear Admiral Russell S. Berkey) and aircraft from six escort carriers (TG 77.1) (Rear Admiral Thomas L. Sprague), screened by eight destroyer escorts. Airfield facilities built on Morotai will be used to support operations against Japanese positions in the Philippines.

Submarine *Guavina* (SS 362) sinks Japanese fast transport *T.3* off Pagubas, southern Mindanao, 05°35'N, 125°24'E.

Submarines *Pampanito* (SS 383) and *Sealion* (SS 315) rescue 73 British and 54 Australian POWs who survived loss of Japanese freighter *Rakuyo Maru* when she was sunk by *Sealion* on 12 September, about 300 miles west of Cape Bojeador, Luzon (see 18 September). There had been 1,300 men in *Rakuyo Maru* when she was torpedoed (see 16 September).

Submarine *Stingray* (SS 186) lands armed reconnaissance party on Majoe Island, Molucca Sea; an air warning party is landed after the place is reconnoitered.

USAAF B-24s sink small Makassar-bound Japanese cargo vessels *Kirishima Maru* and *No. 6 Keinan Maru* off Mongole Island.

RAAF Beaufighters and USAAF A-20s bomb Japanese shipping off southeast coast of Ceram, sinking fishing vessels *No. 3 Hoyu Maru* and *No. 4 Bonan Maru*.

U.S. aircraft sink Japanese guardboats *Kaiko Maru* and *No. 1 Kaza Maru*, Marshalls.

Japanese landing ship *T.104* is damaged when she runs aground during her passage to Iwo Jima.

ATLANTIC. Salvage vessel *Escape* (ARS 6) and rescue tug ATR 6 resume towing U.S. freighter

George Ade, torpedoed 12 September, toward Chesapeake Bay (see 16 September). Tug *Sciota* (ATO 30) and rescue tug *ATR 8* are diverted from relieving *Escape* and *ATR 6* of towing *George Ade* when search plane sights survivors of Coast Guard cutters *Bedloe* (WPC 128) and *Jackson* (WPC 142), sunk in hurricane the previous day. The Coast Guardsmen are consequently picked up and brought to port. An intensive search for further survivors is continued until 18 September, without success.

16 Saturday

GENERAL. Second Quebec Conference (OCTA-GON) attended by President Roosevelt and British Prime Minister Winston S. Churchill ends. Combined Chiefs of Staff approve Admiral William F. Halsey Jr.'s recommendation to advance the invasion of Leyte from 20 December to 20 October.

PACIFIC. Marine Air Wings, Pacific is redesignated Aircraft, Fleet Marine Force, Pacific (Major General Francis P. Mulcahy, USMC) with headquarters at Ewa, Oahu.

Motor torpedo boat operations begin from Morotai, N.E.I., to maintain patrols, break up the movement of Japanese troops in barges, and prevent seaborne counterattacks from Halmahera. Morotai-based *PT 489* and *PT 363* transit 60 miles of mined waters and then run an 11-mile gauntlet of coast defense batteries to rescue Ensign Harold A. Thompson, USNR, from VF 26, a downed pilot from escort carrier *Santee* (CVE 29), in Wasile Bay, Halmahera. Under fire for two and a half hours, both boats receive superficial shrapnel damage in the successful operation that snatches the aviator out of danger. F6Fs from CVEs strafe Japanese gun positions as the PT boats enter the bay while TBMs lay a smoke screen. Lieutenant Arthur M. Preston (Commander, Motor Torpedo Boat Squadron 33), commanding the PTs that pick up Ensign Thompson, will receive the Medal of Honor.

Destroyer *Wadleigh* (DD 689) is damaged by mine off eastern entrance to Kossol Passage, Palau, 07°51′N, 134°39′E.

Submarine *Barb* (SS 220) attacks Japanese Moji-bound convoy, sinking escort carrier *Un'yo* and tanker *Asuza Maru* 220 nautical miles southeast of Hong Kong, 19°08′N, 116°36′E. *Barb* and *Queenfish* (SS 393) pick up an additional 32 British and Australian POWs, survivors of *Rakuyo Maru,* sunk on 12 September by *Sealion* (SS 315). Torpedo boat *Chiburi* and Coast Defense Vessel *No. 27* rescue *Un'yo's* survivors.

Sailors on board submarine *Sealion* (SS 315) help emaciated and oil-covered Australian and British POWs from the waters of the South China Sea, 15 September 1944. (NA, 80-G-281718)

U.S. submarines operate against Japanese convoy MI 14, south of Formosa: *Picuda* (SS 382) sinks army cargo ship *Tokushima Maru* in Bashi Channel, 21°27′N, 121°35′E; *Redfish* (SS 395) sinks fleet tanker *No. 2 Ogura Maru,* 21°24′N, 121°14′E.

Submarine *Sea Devil* (SS 400) sinks Japanese submarine *I 364* off Yokosuka, Japan, 34°30′N, 145°23′E.

Submarine *Shad* (SS 235) attacks Japanese convoy 1915, and although she claims to sink her target, cargo ship *Hakozaki Maru,* off Omae Saki, 34°30′N, 138°25′E, the latter reaches her destination intact.

Japanese army cargo ship *Imaji Maru* (ex-Dutch *De Klerk*) is sunk by Japanese mine, Brunei Bay, Borneo, 05°08′N, 115°05′E.

MEDITERRANEAN. U.S. motor torpedo boats engage German explosive control boat and four drones off Cap Martin.

ATLANTIC. Salvage vessel *Escape* (ARS 6) and rescue tug *ATR 6* bring damaged U.S. freighter *George Ade,* torpedoed 12 September, into Hampton Roads, Virginia; the ship is repaired and returns to active service.

17 Sunday

PACIFIC. TG 32.1 (Rear Admiral William H. P. Blandy) lands Army 81st Infantry (less 323nd

Infantry and reinforced by miscellaneous units) on Angaur, Palaus, supported by carrier-based aircraft and naval gunfire. Airfield facilities on Angaur will be used to support operations against the Philippines.

PBY (FAW 17) sinks Japanese freighter *Shinai Maru* in Staring Bay, Kendari, Celebes, 04°07′S, 122°44′E. One of the PBY's attacks is carried out at such a low level that a foot of wing surface is torn off upon striking one of *Shinai Maru's* kingposts.

Motor torpedo boat *PT 371* is damaged by grounding north by west of Ternate, Halmahera, N.E.I., 02°05′N, 127°51′E (see 19 September).

USAAF P-40s sink Japanese fishing vessel *Hoyo Maru* and damage *No. 5 Kyoei Maru* off eastern Ceram.

Japanese cargo vessel *No. 10 Daigen Maru* sinks after striking a reef off Fukuoka, Kyushu, 33°46′N, 130°22′E.

18 Monday

PACIFIC. Destroyer *Case* (DD 370) and submarine *Sealion* (SS 315) rendezvous about 700 miles west of Saipan to transfer medical officer and medical supplies to treat POWs rescued by the submarine on 15 September.

Submarine *Flasher* (SS 249) attacks Japanese convoy bound for Manila Bay, and sinks auxil-

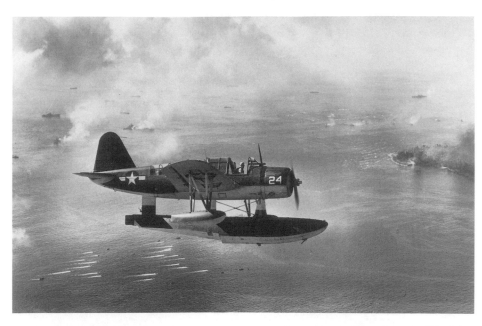

Vought OS2U-3 Kingfisher flown by Lieutenant (j.g.) Paul L. Ferber, USNR, spots the fall of shot upon Japanese positions on Angaur, 17 September 1944. (Author's Collection)

iary gunboat *Saigon Maru* about 60 miles west of Manila, 14°20'N, 120°05'E. Destroyers *Uzuki* and *Yuzuki* carry out hunter-killer operations and rescue survivors.

Submarine *Pipefish* (SS 388) attacks Japanese army transport *Rokko Maru* north of Marcus Island, 32°49'N, 154°22'E.

Submarine *Thresher* (SS 200) attacks Japanese convoy in the Yellow Sea, sinking army cargo ship *Gyoku Maru*, 35°02'N, 124°24'E.

British submarine HMS *Tradewind* attacks Japanese convoy south of Indrapura Point, Sumatra, and sinks army cargo ship *Junyo Maru*, 02°53'S, 101°11'E.

USAAF B-25s damage Japanese auxiliary minesweeper *Wa 5*, salvage tug *Futagami*, and coastal/harbor minesweeper *Ma 3* at Enderby Island, Carolines.

Japanese tanker *No. 2 Hakko Maru*, torpedoed and damaged by submarine *Spadefish* (SS 411) in Luzon Strait on 22 August, breaks in two in heavy swells in Pasaleng Bay, Luzon Strait.

MEDITERRANEAN. Destroyer *Benson* (DD 421) is assigned jammer duties at Toulon; *Livermore* (DD 429) is assigned the same task at Marseilles.

ATLANTIC. Frigate *Natchez* (PF 2), aground off Lynnhaven Roads, Virginia, in hurricane since 14 September, is refloated by tug *Rescue* (NRTS), salvage tug *ATR 74*, and big harbor tug *Bomazeen* (YTB 238).

19 Tuesday

PACIFIC. Infantry landing craft (gunboat) *LCI(G) 459* is sunk by mine off west side of Peleliu reef.

Motor torpedo boat *PT 371*, damaged by grounding off Halmahera on 17 September, is destroyed by demolition charges.

Submarine *Bang* (SS 385) attacks Japanese shipping off east coast of Formosa, sinking tanker *No. 2 Tosei Maru* (*No. 5 Takunan Maru* rescues survivors) and damaging *Coast Defense Vessel No. 30*, 24°54'N, 122°23'E.

Submarine *Redfish* (SS 395) sinks Japanese fishing vessel *Nanko Maru* in Celebes Sea, east by south of Jolo, 05°36'N, 122°16'E, and takes survivor prisoner.

Submarine *Scabbardfish* (SS 397) torpedoes Japanese submarine tender *Jingei* 80 miles northwest of Okinawa, 27°45'N, 127°00'E.

Submarine *Shad* (SS 235) attacks Japanese convoy, sinking coast defense ship *Ioshima* (ex-Chinese cruiser *Ning Hai*) northwest of Hachijo Jima, 33°40'N, 138°18'E.

USAAF B-24s pound Japanese shipping off Chichi Jima, Bonins, damaging landing ship *T.153* and small cargo vessel *Tsukiura Maru*.

ATLANTIC. Salvage vessel *Relief* and salvage tug *Resolute* (NRTS) refloat U.S. tanker *Brandywine*, which went aground one mile east of Lynnhaven Inlet, Virginia, on 14 September.

20 Wednesday

PACIFIC. USAAF B-24s (possibly USN PB4Ys) attack Japanese shipping off Formosa, damaging cargo vessels *Asaka Maru*, *Gokoku Maru*, and *Shinshu Maru*.

21 Thursday

PACIFIC. TF 38 (Vice Admiral Marc A. Mitscher) begins strikes on Japanese shipping in Manila and Subic Bays, Clark and Nichols Fields near Manila, and the Cavite Navy Yard.

At Manila, planes from TG 38.1, TG 38.2, and TG 38.3 sink destroyer *Satsuki*, fleet tanker *Kyokuto Maru*, oilers *Sunosaki* and *Okikawa Maru*, tanker *No. 2 Horai Maru*, army cargo ships *Norway Maru*, *Yozan Maru*, *China Maru*, and *Tsukubusan Maru*, merchant tanker *Niyo Maru*, and cargo ships *Hioki Maru*, *Risshun Maru*, and *Rozan Maru*, 14°35'N, 120°55'E; army cargo ships *Nansei Maru* and *Yamabuki Maru*, 14°45'N, 120°12'E; and army cargo ships *Toyofuko Maru*, *Wakashiro Maru*, *Eikyu Maru*, and *Fukuei Maru*, and cargo ships *Amahi Maru*, *Soerabaja Maru*, and *Yamakaze Maru*.

Planes from carriers *Bunker Hill* (CV 17), *Essex* (CV 9), *Lexington* (CV 16), and *Intrepid* (CV 11) and small carrier *Cabot* (CVL 28) attack Japanese convoy MATA 27 (Manila to Takao) off west coast of Luzon and, despite the efforts of destroyers *Hibiki* and *Yuzuki* and four coast defense ships, sink passenger-cargo ship *Toyofuku Maru*, tanker *No. 1 Ogura Maru*, army cargo ships *Surakarta Maru* and *Yuki Maru*, merchant tanker *Shichiyo Maru*, and army cargo vessel *Nansei Maru* north of Masinloc, 15°25'N, 119°50'E. Of the six escorts, destroyer *Hibiki* is damaged by strafing and by collision while attempting to save *No. 1 Ogura Maru*; *Coast Defense Vessel No. 5* is sunk. Submarine *Lapon* (SS 260) witnesses the end of the attacks at 15°31'N, 119°43'E. Submarine *Haddo* (SS 255), while lifeguarding for TF 38, sinks surveying ship (ex-minelayer) *Katsuriki* 80 miles southwest of Manila, 13°35'N, 119°06'E.

Submarines *Picuda* (SS 382) and *Redfish* (SS 395) attack Japanese TAMA 26 (Takao to Manila) convoy off north coast of Luzon: *Picuda* sinks transport *Awaji Maru*, 18°43'N, 120°53'E; *Redfish* sinks transport *Mizuho Maru*, 18°37'N, 120°43'E.

Submarine *Searaven* (SS 196) attacks Japanese Kurils-bound convoy, sinking army transport *Rizan Maru* in the Sea of Okhotsk, 49°13'N, 145°30'E.

Submarine *Shad* (SS 235) sinks Japanese auxiliary minesweeper *No. 2 Fumi Maru* east of Shinto, 34°45'N, 139°40'E.

TU 33.13.1 (Captain Robley W. Clark), consisting initially of light minelayers *Montgomery* (DM 17) (flagship) and *Preble* (DM 20), four minesweepers, and seven motor minesweepers (YMS), begins minesweeping operations in Ulithi lagoon, Carolines. The sweeps will continue daily until 13 October, after which operations will be conducted on the 17, 27, and 28 October.

ATLANTIC. Salvage vessel *Relief* and salvage tug *Resolute* (NRTS) refloat gunboat *Temptress* (PG 62), which went aground off Lynnhaven Inlet, Virginia, on 14 September.

22 Friday

PACIFIC. TF 38 continues to wreak havoc on Japanese shipping in the Philippines. Off Cebu, Navy carrier-based planes sink gunboat *Onoshi Maru*, auxiliary submarine chaser *No. 16 Yusen Maru*, and auxiliary submarine chaser *No. 7 Shonan Maru* off western tip of Luzon. Off San Fernando, Luzon, carrier planes sink fishery protection gunboat *No. 1 Suzuya Maru*, freighter *Eishin Maru*, and merchant tankers *No. 9 Hammei Maru*, *No. 7 Takasago Maru*, and *No. 24 Nanshin Maru*, as well as army cargo ship *Dakar Maru*, previously damaged by submarine *Steelhead* (SS 280) on 31 July. They also damage auxiliary submarine chaser *No. 2 Suzuya Maru* and army cargo ships *Taishin Maru*, which is run aground to prevent loss, and *Ceram Maru*.

Submarine *Lapon* (SS 260) attacks Japanese convoy off west coast of Luzon, and damages freighter *Jungen Go* off San Antonio, 15°22'N, 119°17'E.

Submarine *Pargo* (SS 264), operating off Balabac, P.I., attacks, unsuccessfully, Japanese cargo vessel *Manshu Maru*, 08°13'N, 117°02'E; counterattack by destroyer *Shiokaze* is likewise unsuccessful.

ATLANTIC. Stores ship *Yukon* (AF 9) is torpedoed by German submarine *U 979* about 43 miles west of Reykjavik, Iceland.

23 Saturday

PACIFIC. TG 33.19 (Rear Admiral William H. P. Blandy) lands 323nd Army RCT (81st Division) on undefended Ulithi Atoll, Carolines. Ulithi will supplant Eniwetok as the foremost advanced base for the Pacific Fleet.

Battleship *West Virginia* (BB 48) reaches Pearl Harbor and rejoins the Pacific Fleet, marking the completion of the program of salvage and reconstruction of the ships damaged at Pearl Harbor on 7 December 1941.

Submarine *Apogon* (SS 308) sinks Japanese guardboat *No. 6 Choyo Maru* north by east of Marcus Island, 34°57'N, 154°44'E.

Submarine *Escolar* (SS 294) departs Midway for first war patrol.[206]

Submarine *Narwhal* (SS 167) lands party of 45 men, together with 35 tons of cargo, at Kiamba, on southwest coast of Mindanao, P.I. (see 27 and 29 September).

British submarine HMS *Trenchant* sinks German submarine *U 859* off Penang, Malaya, 05°46'N, 100°04'E.

PBY sinks Japanese auxiliary vessel *Toshu Maru* in Colono Bay, Celebes, 04°23'S, 122°43'E. Submarine chaser *Ch 53* engages the Catalina but to no avail.

PBY sinks cargo ship *Heiho Maru* in Celebes Sea, 03°40'N, 122°25'E.

Japanese gunboat *Nankai* and transport *Hokkai Maru* are damaged by mines, laid by submarine *Bowfin* (SS 287) on 29 January, off Balikpapan, Borneo, 03°37'S, 116°25'E. Both vessels are towed to Surabaya, Java, for repairs.

24 Sunday

PACIFIC. As Japanese shipping shifts south from Luzon in the wake of the heavy attacks there over the previous days, TF 38 follows, its planes hitting targets ranging from the Calamian group to the Visayas. Aircraft from three task groups (TG 38.1, TG 38.2, and TG 38.3) from TF 38 (Vice Admiral Marc A. Mitscher) participate. Off Calamian Island in Coron Bay, TF 38 planes sink flying boat support ship *Akitsushima*, cargo ship *Kyokusan Maru*, and army cargo ship *Taiei Maru* and damage ammunition ship *Kogyo Maru*, army cargo ship *Olympia Maru*, 11°58'N, 120°03'E, cargo ships *Ekkai Maru* and *Kasagisan Maru*, supply ship *Irako*, oiler *Kamoi*, and small cargo ship *No. 11 Shonan Maru*, 11°59'N, 120°02'E. South of Mindoro, carrier aircraft sink torpedo boat *Hayabusa*, 13°00'N, 122°00'E, and minelayer *Yaeyama* and submarine chaser *Ch 32*, 12°15'N, 121°00'E. Off Masbate, they sink auxiliary submarine chaser *Cha 39* and auxiliary minesweeper *Wa 7*, 12°18'N, 122°46'E, freighter *Shinyo Maru*, 12°21'N, 123°00'E, cargo ships *No. 17 Fukuei Maru* and *No. 2 Koshu Maru*, 11°56'N, 123°08'E, and transport *Siberia Maru*, 11°54'N, 123°10'E. In the Visayan Sea, they sink army cargo ship *Chuka Maru* and tanker *Kenwa Maru*, 11°13'N, 123°11'E. In the South China Sea, they sink tanker *Okigawa Maru*, 14°00'N, 119°00'E.

Hospital ship *Samaritan* (AH 10) is damaged by grounding on Tauu Island Reef, northeast of Bougainville.

Submarine *Barbero* (SS 317) bombards Japanese radar installation on Batag Island off north coast of Samar.

Motor minesweeper *YMS 19* is sunk by mine off southeast coast of Angaur, Palaus, 06°53'N, 134°10'E.

25 Monday

EUROPE. Minelayer *Miantonomah* (CM 10) is sunk by mine off Le Havre, France, 49°27'N, 00°17'E.

PACIFIC. Submarine *Barbel* (SS 316) attacks Japanese convoy in the Nansei Shoto, sinking freighter *Bushu Maru* off Naka No Shima, 29°46'N, 129°40'E; auxiliary submarine chasers *Cha 89* and *Cha 200* rescue survivors.

Submarine *Guardfish* (SS 217) sinks Japanese freighter *No. 2 Miyakawa Maru* in the Yellow Sea off Chinnampo, Korea, 38°30'N, 124°06'E.

Submarine *Nautilus* (SS 168) lands 25 tons of cargo, 20 drums of gasoline, and two drums of oil at designated spot on Cebu, P.I. After accomplishing her mission, however, *Nautilus* runs aground on a shoal. Her crew lightens the stranded boat, burns secret matter, and prepares to demolish equipment, blow up the boat, and evacuate in the event that she cannot be refloated (see 26 and 30 September).

Submarine *Searaven* (SS 196) attacks Japanese small craft off southwest tip of Etorofu, Kurils, sinking *No. 1 Hirota Maru*.

Submarine *Thresher* (SS 200) sinks Japanese freighter *Nissei Maru* in the Yellow Sea, 37°32'N, 124°33'E.

USAAF B-24 (14th Air Force) sinks Japanese cargo ship *Rokkosan Maru* west of Takao, Formosa, 22°28'N, 118°38'E.

MEDITERRANEAN. USAAF B-24s sink German submarines *U 565* and *U 596*, Salamis, Greece.

26 Tuesday

PACIFIC. Destroyer escort *McCoy Reynolds* (DE 440) sinks Japanese submarine *I 175* northeast of Palaus, 09°14'N, 136°40'E.

Submarine *Nautilus* (SS 168), aground off Cebu, frees herself from the shoal upon which she had grounded the previous day, and gets under way to carry out the rest of her clandestine mission (see 30 September).

Submarine *Pargo* (SS 264) sinks Japanese minelayer *Aotaka* west of Balabac Strait, 07°00'N, 116°00'E.

Submarine *Thresher* (SS 200) sinks Japanese freighter *Koetsu Maru* in Yellow Sea, 37°13'N, 123°48'E.

U.S. freighter *Elihu Thompson* is damaged

by mines off Nouméa, New Caledonia, 22°22′10″S, 166°34′E; fleet tug *Apache* (ATF 67) rescues survivors and later beaches the ship to facilitate salvage. Of the 211 troops embarked as passengers, 32 perish in the explosions; there are no casualties among the 42-man merchant complement or 33-man Armed Guard.

Japanese river gunboat *Saga* is damaged by mine, Hong Kong.

27 Wednesday

PACIFIC. Special Air Task Force (STAG 1) (Commander Robert F. Jones) commences operations with TDR-1 drones (controlled from converted TBM-1cs) against Japanese targets in the southwest Pacific. Four TDRs are launched against beached Japanese freighter used as antiaircraft emplacement off Kahili airstrip, Bougainville. Two drones hit the ship, one crashes just short (bomb does not explode), and one is lost en route.

Submarine *Apogon* (SS 308) sinks Japanese cargo ship *Hachirogata Maru* in Sea of Okhotsk off Shimushir Island, 46°32′N, 146°48′E.

Submarine *Bonefish* (SS 223) torpedoes Japanese oiler *Kamoi* 240 miles southwest of Manila, 13°48′N, 148°38′E.

Submarines *Flasher* (SS 249) and *Lapon* (SS 260) attack Japanese MIMA 11 convoy in South China Sea west of Luzon. *Flasher* sinks army transport *Ural Maru* and damages merchant tanker *Tachibana Maru* about 225 miles northwest of Manila, 15°45′N, 117°20′E. *Lapon* torpedoes merchant tanker *Hokki Maru*, 15°50′N, 117°41′E; *Omine Maru* takes the damaged vessel in tow, escorted by submarine chaser *Ch 28*, but salvage efforts prove unsuccessful and *Hokki Maru* is scuttled by gunfire and bombs from reconnaissance floatplane.

Submarine *Narwhal* (SS 167) lands party of three men and 20 tons of cargo at Balingasag, on north coast of Mindanao (see 29 September); submarine *Stingray* (SS 186) discharges 35 tons of cargo at designated spot on that island's east coast (see 30 September).

Submarine *Plaice* (SS 390), attacking Japanese convoy HI 72 west of the Nansei Shoto, sinks Japanese *Coast Defense Vessel No. 10*, 100 miles north-northwest of Amami-O-Shima, 29°26′N, 128°50′E.

Submarine *Searaven* (SS 196) damages Japanese destroyer *Momi* off Etorofu, Kurils, 45°44′N, 148°41′E.

British submarine HMS *Thorough* damages Japanese auxiliary sailing vessel *No. 9 Kashiwa Maru* off north coast of Sumatra.

PBY damages Japanese cargo ship *Tateishi Maru* off Jolo, 06°02′N, 121°29′E; the ship is beached to prevent sinking.

Tank landing craft *LCT 823* sinks after running aground off Palau.

CARIBBEAN. Garbage lighter *YG 39* sinks east by north of Colón, C.Z., 10°10′N, 79°51′W.

MEDITERRANEAN. Motor torpedo boat *PT 559*, with British motor torpedo boats, attacks northbound convoy off Raffallo, Italy.

28 Thursday

PACIFIC. Marines (Third Battalion, Fifth Marines and Company "G," Second Battalion, Fifth Marines) occupy Ngesebus and Kongaruru Islands in the Palaus, covered by naval aircraft and gunfire.

Submarine *Bonefish* (SS 223), despite presence of two escort vessels, sinks Japanese merchant tanker *Anjo Maru* about 75 miles southwest of Manila, 13°10′N, 120°08′E.

PBYs sink Japanese freighter *Tone Maru* in Makassar Strait.

USAAF B-25s sink small Japanese cargo vessel *Keishin Maru* off Ceram.

ATLANTIC. German submarine *U 219* escapes determined attacks by aircraft from escort carrier *Tripoli* (CVE 64) southwest of the Cape Verde Islands.

29 Friday

PACIFIC. Submarine *Narwhal* (SS 167) evacuates 81 Allied POWs (four of whom are badly wounded) who had survived the loss of Japanese transport *Shinyo Maru,* sunk by submarine *Paddle* (SS 263) on 7 September, from Lanboyan Point, Sindangan Bay, Mindanao, P.I.

Submarine *Skate* (SS 305) attacks Japanese convoy north of Okinawa, sinking auxiliary minesweeper *Hoei Maru* and army cargo ship *Ekisan Maru* in the Nansei Shoto, 27°14′N, 128°25′E.

Japanese guardboat *Riki Maru* is sunk by mine off Kota Bharu, Malaya.

ATLANTIC. PB4Ys (VP 107) sink German submarine *U 863*, South Atlantic, 10°45′S, 25°30′W.

ARCTIC. U.S. freighter *Edward H. Crockett*, while proceeding from Archangel, USSR, to Scotland in convoy RA 60, is torpedoed by German submarine *U 310* at 73°00′N, 24°32′E; irreparably damaged, the freighter is scuttled by gunfire from a British destroyer. While there are no casualties to the 27-man Armed Guard, one of the 41-man merchant complement perishes in the explosion of the first torpedo.

MEDITERRANEAN. Motor torpedo boat *PT 310* is damaged when mistakenly strafed by RAF Beaufighter off southern France.

30 Saturday

PACIFIC. Submarine *Nautilus* (SS 168) lands 95 tons of supplies, 70 drums of gasoline, and four drums of oil at designated spot on island of Panay, P.I., and embarks 47 evacuees (seven servicemen, 10 women, five civilian males, and 25 children).[207]

Submarine *Stingray* (SS 186) lands three officers and equipment on east coast of Mindanao.

During Japanese air raid on U.S. shipping off Morotai, N.E.I., freighter *Carl G. Barth* is damaged by strafing; although six of the 118 passengers on board are injured, there are no casualties to either the 52-man merchant complement or the 26-man Armed Guard.

ATLANTIC. Destroyer escort *Fessenden* (DE 142) sinks German submarine *U 1062* southwest of the Cape Verde Islands, 11°36′N, 34°44′W.

MEDITERRANEAN. U.S. motor torpedo boats make two gunnery runs on German explosive boat off San Remo, Italy.

OCTOBER

1 Sunday

UNITED STATES. Office of Deputy Commander in Chief U.S. Fleet and Deputy Chief of Naval Operations (Vice Admiral Richard S. Edwards) is established.

PACIFIC. Special Air Task Force (STAG 1) drone operations continue with two separate attacks on Japanese positions on Bougainville. In the first, four TDRs are launched against antiaircraft gun positions on Ballale and Poporang Islands; one lands in the midst of them, a second detonates within 100 feet of the southwest end of Ballale runway, and two explode on Poporang in the general area of the target. In the second, four TDRs (two allocated to each target) are launched against antiaircraft positions on Kangu Hill, two miles south of Kahili airfield, and the Pororeri River bridge north of Kangu Hill. The first two TDRs hit the lower slope of Kangu Hill, but one does not explode; one TDR crashes (perhaps hit by antiaircraft fire) while the other TDR cannot find the target and explodes north of Kangu Hill.

Destroyer *Bailey* (DD 492) is damaged by strafing off Palau, 06°59′N, 134°13′E.

During minesweeping operations in Ulithi lagoon with TU 33.13.1, motor minesweeper *YMS 385* is sunk by Japanese mine in Zowariyau Channel, 09°52′N, 139°37′E.

Submarine *Cabrilla* (SS 288) attacks Japanese convoy MIMA 11 off northwest coast of Luzon and sinks tankers *Kyokuho Maru* and *Zuiyo Maru*, 16°15′N, 119°43′E. *Coast Defense Ship No. 25* and submarine chaser *Ch 28* rescue survivors.

Submarine *Hammerhead* (SS 364) attacks Japanese convoy MI 18 off northwest coast of Borneo, sinking ore carriers *Kokusei Maru* and *Nichiwa Maru* and cargo ship *Higane Maru*, 06°30′N, 116°11′E, and survives counterattacks by destroyer *Kuretake*.

Submarine *Snapper* (SS 185) attacks Japanese convoy 3927 west of the Bonins, torpedoing transport *Seian Maru*. As the troopship sinks, coastal minelayer *Ajiro* attacks *Snapper*, which survives to sink *Ajiro* as well, 28°20′N, 139°25′E.

Submarine *Trepang* (SS 412) sinks Japanese supply ship *Takunan Maru* north of Ogasawara Gunto, 25°30′N, 142°30′E.

Auxiliary minesweeper *Kaiyo Maru* is sunk by mine off Tsingtao, China.

MEDITERRANEAN. Destroyer *Gleaves* (DD 423) shells German gun positions in Ventimiglia, Italy, area and encounters intense shore battery fire; destroyer *Benson* (DD 421) shells enemy gun emplacement and then destroys two Italian motor torpedo boats (MAS).

Destroyer *Forrest* (DD 461) is damaged in collision with tank landing ship *LST 550* off southern France, 43°20′N, 05°20′E.

2 Monday

PACIFIC. Tank landing ships *LST 129*, *LST 278*, and *LST 661* are damaged by storm, Palau, 06°59′N, 134°13′E.

Submarine *Aspro* (SS 309) attacks Japanese MATA 27 convoy off Cape Bojeador, Luzon, damaging tanker *Oei Maru* and cargo ship *Azuchisan Maru*, 18°26′N, 120°32′E (see 3 October).

Submarine *Pomfret* (SS 391) attacks Japanese convoy TAMA 28 (Takao to Manila) in Luzon Strait, sinking army transport *Tsuyama Maru* about 75 miles southeast of the southern tip of Formosa, 21°21′N, 121°56′E.

Japanese army vessel *Ryochi Maru* is sunk by aircraft off Bantayan Island, north of Cebu.

Japanese cargo ship *Havre Maru* runs aground on a sandbar 2,000 yards east of Jolo, P.I.

MEDITERRANEAN. U.S. freighter *Johns Hopkins*

drags anchor in storm and is mined off Marseilles, France, 43°16′N, 05°08′28″E; destroyer *Hobson* (DD 464) is among the ships that proceeds to the stricken freighter's assistance. Rescue tug *ATR 127* tows the merchantman into Marseilles, where she discharges her cargo and disembarks 466 U.S. and French troops. There are no casualties among the 41-man merchant complement or the 28-man Armed Guard.

3 Tuesday

PACIFIC. Destroyer escort *Shelton* (DE 407) is sunk by Japanese submarine *RO 41* off Morotai, 02°33′N, 129°18′E. During ensuing antisubmarine operations, destroyer escort *Richard M. Rowell* (DE 403), unaware of the proximity of friendly submarines, accidentally sinks submarine *Seawolf* (SS 197), which is transporting U.S. Army personnel to the east coast of Samar, 02°32′N, 129°18′E. There are no survivors.

Destroyer escort *Samuel S. Miles* (DE 183) sinks Japanese submarine *I 177*, 60 miles north-northeast of Angaur, Palaus, 07°48′N, 133°28′E.

Submarine *Aspro* (SS 309) finishes off abandoned Japanese cargo ship *Azuchisan Maru*, damaged the previous day, off northwest coast of Luzon, 18°26′N, 120°32′E.

Submarine *Thresher* (SS 200) sinks Japanese guardboat *No. 28 Nanshin Maru* north-northwest of Marcus Island, 30°49′N, 153°26′E.

Submarine *Tilefish* (SS 307) sinks Japanese motor sailboat *No. 10 Hokko Maru* off Etorofu, Kurils.

Tank landing craft *LCT 1052* is sunk by tropical storm at Ulithi, Carolines.

PBY bombs and damages Japanese minelayer *Itsukushima*, 00°30′N, 120°00′E; *Itsukushima* is taken in tow by another vessel and a course is set for Dangulan.

USAAF aircraft sinks Japanese merchant tanker *No. 14 Nanshin Maru* off Zamboanga, 06°54′N, 122°04′E

Japanese guardboat *No. 16 Tomi Maru*, after rescuing survivors of *Siberia Maru*, sunk on 24 September by TF 38 planes off Masbate, runs aground north of Mactan Island, P.I.

Japanese SAMA 13 convoy, escorted by minesweeper *W.18*, departs Cape St. Jacques, French Indochina. Soon, however, three ships run aground in squall off Britt Bank: *Myogi Maru*, *Heian Maru*, and *Oyo Maru*. *W.18* refloats all three the following day.

MEDITERRANEAN. Destroyer *Niblack* (DD 424) destroys one MAS boat and damages three in

San Remo, Italy, harbor, and then bombards Oneglia harbor. After encountering persistent and accurate fire from German 88-millimeter gun battery, she shifts target to those guns and knocks them out. Destroyer *Plunkett* (DD 431) shells German artillery in Ventimiglia area.

4 Wednesday

PACIFIC. Minelayer *Salem* (CM 11) is damaged by grounding off Tinian, Marianas.

Tank landing craft *LCT 579* is sunk by mine off Palau.

Submarine *Flasher* (SS 249) attacks Japanese TAMA 27 convoy off western Luzon, sinking army cargo ship *Taibin Maru* off Santa Cruz, 15°22′N, 119°51′E. Supply ship *Kurasaki* rescues survivors.

British submarine HMS *Sea Rover* shells Japanese auxiliary sailing vessel *Mie Maru*, 08°05′S, 117°00′E, and drives her aground.

PBY bombs Japanese shipping in Jolo Harbor, sinking cargo ship *Tateishi Maru* and auxiliary sailing vessels *Kigen Maru* and *Kiku Maru*.

USAAF B-25s sink Japanese motor sailship *Man Maru* in Ambon Bay.

ARCTIC. Two-platoon landing force from Coast Guard icebreaker *Eastwind* (WAG 279) captures German weather station at Little Koldeyey, Greenland, 76°41′N, 18°50′W.

MEDITERRANEAN. Destroyer *Niblack* (DD 424) bombards MAS boat pens in San Remo, Italy, harbor and artillery positions in Cap Martin area.

5 Thursday

PACIFIC. Special Air Task Force (STAG 1) operations continue as four TDRs, each carrying a 2,000-pound bomb, are launched against Japanese supply caves in the Keravia Bay, Rabaul, area. One TDR hits in the vicinity of cave entrances; one misses the target area. Two are lost en route due to interference from communications frequency used by motor gunboat (PGM) operating in the waters over which the drones fly.

Submarine *Cod* (SS 224), attacking Japanese convoy in South China Sea, sinks freighter *Tatsuhiro Maru* off west coast of Mindoro, 13°01′N, 120°16′E, and damages cargo ships *Atsuta Maru* and *Araosan Maru*.

6 Friday

PACIFIC. Submarine *Aspro* (SS 309) conducts unsuccessful attack on Japanese convoy off San Fernando, Luzon, missing *Coast Defense Vessel No. 8*; minesweeper *W.20*'s hunt for *Aspro* is likewise unsuccessful (see 7 October).

Submarine *Besugo* (SS 321) engages Japanese guardboat *No. 22 Nanshin Maru* in a surface gunnery action roughly north-northwest of Marcus Island, 30°10'N, 151°00'E; the latter drives off her more heavily armed assailant.

Submarine *Cabrilla* (SS 288), attacking Japanese convoy off northwest coast of Luzon, damages transport *Hokurei Maru* (see 18 October) and sinks tanker *No. 2 Yamamizu Maru*, 17°31'N, 120°21'E.

Submarine *Ray* (SS 271) attacks Japanese oiler *Shiretoko* off entrance to Manila Bay, 13°56'N, 120°00'E; although *Ray* claims to have damaged her, *Shiretoko* is not, in fact, hit. Her reprieve, however, is only temporary (see 7 October).

Submarine *Whale* (SS 239) sinks Japanese merchant tanker *Akane Maru* as the latter straggles from convoy HI 77 under escort of *Coast Defense Vessel No. 21* west of Balintang Channel, 19°40'N, 118°05'E. *Seahorse* (SS 304) then sinks *Coast Defense Vessel No. 21* as the escort ship rescues survivors from *Akane Maru*, 140 miles northwest of Cape Bojeador, Luzon, 19°27'N, 118°08'E (see 7 October).

British submarine HMS *Statesman* shells and sinks Japanese coastal cargo vessels *No. 12 Tosa Maru* and *No. 42 Tachibana Maru* off Go-mai Ya, 09°37'N, 98°27'E, and takes survivors prisoner.

British submarine HMS *Tally Ho* sinks Japanese auxiliary submarine chaser *Cha 2* in a surface gunnery engagement 150 nautical miles west-southwest of Penang, Malaya, 04°20'N, 98°24'E. Auxiliary submarine chaser *Cha 55* rescues survivors and conducts unsuccessful hunt for *Tally Ho*.

Dutch submarine *Zwaardvisch* sinks German submarine *U 168* in Java Sea, 06°20'S, 111°28'E, and takes 27 survivors prisoner.

Japanese gunboat *Saga* is irreparably damaged by mine in Hong Kong Harbor, 22°17'N, 114°10'E. Towed to Taikoo dockyard, *Saga* will never return to active service.

Floating provision storage facility *Asphalt* (IX 153) goes hard aground on a coral reef at Ulithi, Carolines, when her anchor chains part in a storm. She will subsequently be declared a total loss.

EUROPE. U.S. freighter *George Popham* is mined off Normandy but suffers little damage; there are no casualties among the 42-man merchant complement, the 26-man Armed Guard, or the 70 stevedores embarked to work cargo.

MEDITERRANEAN. Destroyer *Niblack* (DD 424) bombards railroad yards on Cape Impeglio. *Niblack* is later damaged when accidentally rammed by destroyer *Jouett* (DD 396) when the latter drags anchor.

U.S. freighter *Elinor Wylie* is mined while en route from Marseilles to Toulon, France, at 42°57'30"N, 05°49'30"E; there are, however, no casualties among the 40-man merchant complement or the 29-man Armed Guard. The ship is towed into Toulon, where she discharges her cargo without further incident.[208]

7 Saturday

PACIFIC. Submarine *Aspro* (SS 309) attacks Japanese convoy as it retires to Yulin, Hainan Island, sinking passenger-cargo ship *Makassar Maru* at 17°46'N, 119°57'E; heavy seas and the fact that the convoy (carrying troops) has already been spotted doom the survivors. Escort vessel *Daito* hunts for *Aspro*.

Submarine *Cabrilla* (SS 288) sinks Japanese transport *No. 8 Shin'yo Maru* off Vigan, Luzon, 17°50'N, 119°37'E.

Submarine *Cod* (SS 224) torpedoes Japanese oiler *Shiretoko* west of Mindoro, 13°40'N, 119°25'E; *Ray* (SS 271) carries out her second attack on the damaged vessel, again without success. *Shiretoko* shapes course for Coron Bay, steering by hand. Japanese planes hunt for *Cod*.

Submarines *Hawkbill* (SS 366) and *Baya* (SS 318) attack Japanese convoy HI 77, attacked the previous day by *Whale* (SS 239) and *Seahorse* (SS 304). Each apparently aware of the other's presence in the area but unaware that they are attacking the same target, *Hawkbill* and *Baya* sink cargo ship *Kinugasa Maru* about 400 miles west of Manila, 14°30'N, 115°48'E.

8 Sunday

PACIFIC. Land-based aircraft from the Marianas increase tempo of air strikes on Iwo Jima.

Submarine *Becuna* (SS 319) damages Japanese seaplane carrier *Kimikawa Maru* in South China Sea, 14°05'N, 115°38'E.

Submarine *Hoe* (SS 258) attacks Japanese convoy off northwestern coast of Luzon, sinking army transport *Kohoku Maru*, 18°40'N, 116°00'E, and damaging *Coast Defense Vessel No. 8*, 18°32'N, 116°13'E. *Coast Defense Vessel No. 25* and submarine chaser *Ch 41* hunt for *Hoe* and rescue survivors.

MEDITERRANEAN. Destroyer *Eberle* (DD 430), with spot provided by aircraft from light cruiser *Brooklyn* (CL 40), bombards vessels in Maurizio Harbor; enemy shore battery fire is accurate in return.

Destroyer *Jouett* (DD 396), patrolling off the coast of Italy, is attacked by six small fast craft;

the ship suffers no damage in the encounter. The next morning *Jouett* will sink several floating mines.

9 Monday

PACIFIC. TG 30.2 (Rear Admiral Allan E. Smith) (three heavy cruisers and six destroyers), in an operation timed to precede fast carrier task force operations against Okinawa, conducts a diversionary bombardment of Japanese installations on Marcus Island. Enemy return fire is intense and accurate at the outset, with Japanese gunners repeatedly straddling the U.S. ships. In related operations, Saipan-based PB4Ys, on interdiction patrols in the path of TF 38 as it approaches the Ryukyus, damage Japanese auxiliary submarine chaser *Sankyo Maru* off Okinawa.

Special Air Task Force (STAG 1) operations continue as four TDRs are launched against Matupi Bridge, Simpson Harbor, Rabaul. Antiaircraft fire, however, downs three of the TDRs; one is lost en route to the target.

One company of the U.S. Army 321st Infantry is landed on Garekayo Island, north of Ngesebus, Palaus, and quickly overruns the island.

In wide-ranging U.S. submarine operations against Japanese shipping in the South China Sea, *Becuna* (SS 319) damages tanker *San Luis Maru*, 12°45'N, 118°00'E, and teams with *Hawkbill* (SS 366) to sink merchant tanker *Tokuwa Maru*, 12°43'N, 118°05'E; *Sawfish* (SS 276) sinks merchant tanker *Tachibana Maru* at 19°33'N, 116°38'E.

Submarine *Croaker* (SS 246) sinks Japanese freighter *Shinki Maru* west of Kyushu, 32°08'N, 129°51'E.

MEDITERRANEAN. Destroyer *Eberle* (DD 430) bombards ammunition dump and buildings; later *Eberle* and destroyer *Jouett* (DD 396), and planes from light cruiser *Brooklyn* (CL 40), destroy several floating mines in the vicinity.

Tank landing craft *LCT 459*, beached off Normandy since 24 September with a broken back, breaks in two and sinks.

10 Tuesday

PACIFIC. TF 38 (Vice Admiral Marc A. Mitscher), in the first occasion since the Marianas campaign in which all four carrier task groups operate together as one unit, pounds Japanese shipping and installations on Okinawa and other islands in the Ryukyus. TF 38 planes sink submarine depot ship *Jingei*, landing ship *T.158*, minelayer *Takashima*, and auxiliary submarine chaser *Cha 87* north-northwest of Okinawa, 26°39′N, 127°52′E. In or near Naha Harbor, carrier-based planes sink auxiliary minesweepers *Shimpo Maru*, 26°13′N, 127°40′E, and *No. 6 Hakata Maru*; guardboats *No. 26 Nansatsu Maru* and *No. 5 Daisei Maru*, 26°13′N, 127°41′E; guardboat *Yuki Maru* and motor torpedo boats *Gyoraitei No. 493*, *Gyoraitei No. 496*, *Gyoraitei No. 498*, *Gyoraitei No. 500*, *Gyoraitei No. 805*, *Gyoraitei No. 806*, *Gyoraitei No. 810*, *Gyoraitei No. 812*, *Gyoraitei No. 813*, *Gyoraitei No. 814*, *Gyoraitei No. 820*, 26°30′N, 128°00′E; army cargo ship *Horai Maru*, 26°38′N, 127°54′E; and freighters *Taikai Maru*, *Fukura Maru*, *Koryu Maru*, *Nanyo Maru*, and *Tetsuzan Maru*, 26°13′N, 127°39′E. Elsewhere in the vicinity, Navy planes sink auxiliary minesweeper *No. 1 Takunan Maru* off Okino Daito Shima, 25°30′N, 131°00′E, and army cargo ship *Hirota Maru* off Miyako Jima, 24°26′N, 125°20′E, and damage *Coast Defense Ship No. 5* and submarine chaser *Ch 58* off Okinawa. Guardboat *No. 6 Daisei Maru*, cargo ship *Toyosaka Maru*, and freighter *No. 7 Takashima Maru* are damaged outside Koniya Harbor.

Motor torpedo boat *PT 368* is damaged by grounding off western New Guinea, 01°59′N, 127°57′E.

Submarine *Barb* (SS 220) sinks Japanese transport *Gokuku Maru* northwest of Hirado Jima, Kyushu, 33°31′N, 129°10′E.

Submarines *Bonefish* (SS 223) and *Lapon* (SS 260) attack Japanese convoy off Cape Bolinao, Luzon. Although success does not crown *Bonefish*'s efforts, *Lapon* torpedoes army transport *Ejiri Maru*, 16°10′N, 119°44′E, which is run aground at 16°53′N, 119°46′E; several large explosions follow. *Kosho Maru* and *Raiei Maru* rescue survivors. *Coast Defense Vessel No. 16* takes on board further survivors the following day.

Dutch submarine *Zwaardvisch* sinks Japanese guardboat *Koei Maru* southwest of Bawean Island, N.E.I., 05°57′S, 112°29′E.

11 Wednesday

PACIFIC. TG 38.1 (Vice Admiral John S. McCain) and TG 38.4 (Rear Admiral Ralph E. Davison), in preparation for strikes against Formosa, attack Japanese airfields and other facilities on the north coast of Luzon; task group planes damage escort destroyer *Yashiro* off San Vicente and cargo vessel *No. 6 Banei Maru* off Aparri.

Submarine *Tang* (SS 306) sinks Japanese freighters *Joshu Go* and *Oita Maru* in Formosa Strait, 25°00′N, 121°00′E.

Smoke mushrooms skyward from explosions as TF 38 planes pound airfield on Formosa, 12 October 1944. (NA, 80-G-281330)

Submarine *Trepang* (SS 412), in attack on Japanese convoy south of Honshu, sinks landing ship *T.105* about 105 miles southwest of Tokyo Bay, 33°07′N, 137°38′E.

British submarine HMS *Strongbow* attacks Japanese convoy off Sabang, N.E.I., without success.

Japanese heavy cruiser *Aoba* and light cruiser *Kinu* are damaged in collision off Lingga Roads, N.E.I.

USAAF B-24 sinks Japanese motor sailship *Hashu Maru* off Tacloban, P.I.

Japanese merchant vessel *Sumiei Maru* is damaged by aircraft, Takao, Formosa.

EUROPE. Tank landing craft *LCT 293* founders and sinks in heavy weather in English Channel.

ATLANTIC. Tug *Wandank* (ATO 26) departs Boston, Massachusetts, with open lighter *YC 762* in tow, and proceeds to Yarmouth, Nova Scotia, where she salvages parts from the crashed airship *K 9*.

12 Thursday

PACIFIC. TF 38 (Vice Admiral Marc A. Mitscher) pounds Japanese shipping, airfields, and industrial plants on Formosa, regarded as the strongest and best-developed base south of the homeland proper, and on northern Luzon. Planes from carriers *Lexington* (CV 16) and *Essex* (CV 9) and small carrier *Langley* (CVL 27) sink transport *Asaka Maru*, cargo ship *Shirotai Maru*, army cargo ship *Mitsuki Maru*, and merchant tankers *No. 6 Horai Maru*, *No. 23 Henshu Maru*, and *No. 26 Nanshin Maru* off the Pescadores, 23°30′N, 119°34′E, as well as transports *Bujo Maru* and *Joshu Maru*; army cargo ship *Yamahagi Maru*; freighters *Gyoun Maru*, *Hakku Maru*, *No. 11 Tenjin Maru*, and *No. 1 Takatomi Maru*; merchant tankers *No. 5 Nanshin Maru*, *No. 11 Nanshin Maru*, and *No. 20 Nanshin Maru*; and dredge *Nitaka Maru*. Tanker *Eiho Maru* and army cargo ship *Shinto Maru* are damaged off Takao, 22°37′N, 119°34′E. Also damaged at Takao are cargo vessels *Teisho Maru* (ex-German freighter *Havenstein*), *Taihoku Maru*, and, at Keelung, *Hakozaki Maru*. USAAF B-24s (14th Air Force) add to the destruction wreaked this day by sinking freighter *Shinan Maru* off Hotei, Formosa, 23°22′N, 120°10′E. Strikes draw heavy Japanese aerial counterattacks during which destroyer *Prichett* (DD 561) is damaged by friendly fire, 22°08′N, 123°19′E. Destruction of Japanese air power in this area paves the way for USAAF B-29 strikes on Formosa's aircraft plants and airfields on 14 and 16 October.

Motor torpedo boat *PT 368*, damaged by grounding, western New Guinea, 01°59'N, 127°57'E, is scuttled by demolition charges.

Submarine *Ray* (SS 271) sinks Japanese transport *Toko Maru* near Cape Calavite, Mindoro, 13°32'N, 120°21'E, and survives counterattacks by torpedo boat *Hiyodori* and *Coast Defense Vessel No. 2*.

Submarine *Trepang* (SS 412) damages Japanese destroyer *Fuyuzuki* off Omae Saki, 33°56'N, 138°09'E.

British submarine HMS *Strongbow* sinks Japanese cargo ship *Manryo Maru* in Strait of Malacca, 02°50'N, 100°50'E.

Japanese cargo ship *Ryusei Maru* sinks after becoming sranded off Tateyama, Honshu, 35°00'N, 140°00'E.

13 Friday

PACIFIC. During Japanese aerial counterattacks in the wake of TF 38 strikes on Formosa the previous day, carrier *Franklin* (CV 13) is damaged when a *kamikaze*, attempting to crash the ship, only succeeds in sliding across her flight deck and crashing close aboard, 22°55'N, 123°12'E; heavy cruiser *Canberra* (CA 70), in TG 38.1, is damaged by aerial torpedo only 85 miles from Formosa, 22°48'N, 123°01'E. While heavy cruiser *Wichita* (CA 45) takes *Canberra* in tow, Cruiser Division 13 (three light cruisers under Rear Admiral Laurance T. DuBose), four destroyers from TG 38.3, and two from TG 38.1 are detached to provide cover. Fleet tug *Munsee* (ATF 107) relieves *Wichita* of towing *Canberra*, and the group sets course for Ulithi, Carolines (see 14 October).

Submarine *Bergall* (SS 320), in attack on Japanese convoy, sinks merchant tanker *Shinshu Maru* off Cam Ranh Bay, French Indochina, 11°52'N, 109°20'E.

British submarine HMS *Sturdy* sinks Japanese coasters *Kosei Maru* and *Hansei Maru* in Gulf of Boni, south of Celebes.

Peleliu Island, Palaus, is secured.

14 Saturday

PACIFIC. While TF 38 remains nearby to provide cover for the ongoing salvage of crippled heavy cruiser *Canberra* (CA 70), damaged the previous day, Japanese aerial counterattacks continue, inflicting damage on carrier *Hancock* (CV 19), 23°30'N, 121°30'E; light cruiser *Reno* (CL 96) (suicide plane); and destroyer *Cassin Young* (DD 793) (strafing), 22°30'N, 124°50'E. Light cruiser *Houston* (CL 81) is damaged by aerial torpedo and destroyer *Cowell* (DD 547)

is damaged when she fouls *Houston* as *Cowell* lies alongside assisting in salvage efforts, 22°27'N, 124°01'E. Heavy cruiser *Boston* (CA 69)—later relieved by fleet tug *Pawnee* (ATF 74)—takes *Houston* in tow (see 15 October). At this juncture, heavy air attacks on TF 38, together with enemy radio propaganda broadcasts that reflect a vast overestimation of the destruction wreaked by attacking Japanese aircraft, prompt Commander Third Fleet (Admiral William F. Halsey Jr.) to withdraw TG 38.2 (Rear Admiral Gerald F. Bogan) and TG 38.3 (Rear Admiral Frederick C. Sherman) to the eastward to set upon any important Japanese fleet units that would attempt to finish off what the enemy propagandists call the "crippled remnants" of TF 38. The Japanese, however, do not take the bait.

During TF 38 operations against Japanese shipping and installations on Formosa, Navy carrier-based planes damage coastal minelayer *Enoshima* and auxiliary submarine chasers *Cha 7* and *Cha 151* off Takao.

Submarine *Angler* (SS 240), in attack on Cebu-bound Japanese convoy C 073 in the Sulu Sea, sinks army transport *Nanrei Maru* about 15 miles north of Panay, P.I., 11°53'N, 121°39'E.

Submarine *Bonefish* (SS 223) sinks Japanese freighter *Fushimi Maru* in South China Sea off Cape Bolinao, Luzon, 16°12'N, 119°45'E.

Submarine *Dace* (SS 247) attacks Japanese convoy in Balabac Strait, sinking merchant tankers *EiKyo Maru* and *Nittetsu Maru*, and damaging ore carrier *Taizen Maru* between Borneo and Palawan, 06°05'N, 115°55'E.

British submarine HMS *Sturdy* sinks Japanese *Communication Vessel No. 128* in Gulf of Boni, south of Celebes.

Carrier *Saratoga* (CV 3) and destroyer escort *Howard F. Clark* (DE 533) are damaged in collision during maneuvers off Oahu.

ATLANTIC. As convoy UGS 56 steams toward Casablanca, French Morocco, U.S. freighter *H. L. Gibson* veers out of formation and accidentally collides with British tanker *George W. McKnight*, 34°07'N, 21°24'W. Fire breaks out immediately, engulfing both ships, fed by the 100-octane gasoline cargo carried in *George W. McKnight*, which is abandoned as the blaze gains headway; five crewmen perish. *H. L. Gibson*'s crew abandons within the hour; two Armed Guard sailors die in the fire or in leaving the burning "Liberty" ship. Destroyer escort *Cronin* (DE 704) rescues 24 British sailors; destroyer escorts *Ahrens* (DE 575) and *Holton* (DE 703) rescue the Americans, and, although

incurring minor topside damage in doing so, quell the flames on board both merchantmen. The DE sailors' arduous work results in both *H. L. Gibson* and *George W. McKnight* getting under way and reaching their destination under their own power.

French submarine *Amazone* runs aground in Fort Pond Bay, 41°02'N, 71°57'W. Tug *Sagamore* (ATO 20) is diverted to the scene; submarine rescue vessels *Falcon* (ASR 2) and *Chewink* (ASR 3) are dispatched from New London, Connecticut (see 16 October).

15 Sunday

PACIFIC. Command designated Minecraft, Pacific Fleet (Rear Admiral Alexander Sharp) is established; Rear Admiral Sharp breaks his flag in minelayer *Terror* (CM 5).

TG 30.3 (Rear Admiral Laurance T. DuBose) is formed to cover the retirement of the crippled heavy cruiser *Canberra* (CA 70) and light cruiser *Houston* (CL 81); an augmented TG 38.1 (Vice Admiral John S. McCain) provides cover while TG 38.2 (Rear Admiral Gerald F. Bogan) and TG 38.3 (Rear Admiral Frederick C. Sherman) take up position to waylay Japanese fleet units that might try to attack the damaged ships. TG 38.4 (Rear Admiral Ralph E. Davison), meanwhile, attacks Japanese installations near Manila, drawing an enemy aerial response that damages carrier *Franklin* (CV 13), 16°29'N, 123°57'E.

Sweep unit (Captain Robley W. Clark) arrives off Ngulu Atoll, western Carolines. Light minelayer *Montgomery* (DM 17) destroys Japanese radio and weather station, and, accompanied by five motor minesweepers (YMS), enters the lagoon to begin minesweeping operations which will continue daily until 23 October.

Special Air Task Force (STAG 1) operations continue: Four TDRs are launched against Matupi Bridge, as part of coordinated attack by other Green Island–based PBJs (VMB 423), F4Us (VMF 218 and VMF 222), and SBDs (VMSB 244 and VMSB 341) against Simpson Harbor, Rabaul. Poor picture reception and pilot error result in none of the TDRs hitting their targets.

USAAF P-38 sinks Japanese auxiliary sailing vessel *No. 5 Yamato Maru* off Bochi Archipelago, 01°10'N, 128°21'E.

Dutch submarine *Zwaardvisch* sinks Japanese oceanographic research vessel *No. 2 Kaiyo Maru* off Surabaya, Java, 06°30'S, 111°35'E.

MEDITERRANEAN. Minesweeping test is conducted in Bay de Ciotat, France, using a blimp; the blimp proves very satisfactory, using loud hailer, VHF radio, and smoke flares to direct attention to mines.

16 Monday

PACIFIC. Japanese torpedo planes attack TG 30.3 (Rear Admiral Laurance T. DuBose) and again damage light cruiser *Houston* (CL 81), 20°54′N, 125°09′E.

Destroyer *Ellet* (DD 398), surveying ship *Bowditch* (AGS 4), two infantry landing craft (gunboat), and a submarine chaser arrive at Ngulu Atoll, western Carolines, and encounter no opposition.

Submarine *Besugo* (SS 321) damages Japanese destroyer *Suzutsuki* off Toi Saki, 32°30′N, 132°36′E.

Submarine *Tilefish* (SS 307) sinks Japanese guardboat *No. 2 Kyowa Maru* five miles north of Matsuwa Jima, 48°07′N, 153°04′E.

Auxiliary minesweeper *No. 6 Hakata Maru* is sunk by U.S. aircraft (perhaps PB4Y) off Minami Daito Jima, 25°30′N, 131°00′E.

USAAF B-24s (14th Air Force) sink Japanese torpedo boat *Hato* and cargo vessel *Tensho Maru*, 130 miles east-southeast of Hong Kong, 21°49′N, 115°50′E. Other USAAF planes damage auxiliary vessel *Santos Maru* and cargo ships *Sagamigawa Maru*, *No. 5 Okinoyama Maru*, and *No. 3 Akatsuki Maru*. Army cargo ship *Bunzan Maru* is destroyed in drydock at Kowloon, 22°17′N, 114°10′E.

USAAF P-38s sink Japanese auxiliary sailing vessel *No. 6 Take Maru* and an unnamed fishing boat off Cagayan, Sulu Archipelago.

RAAF Beaufighters sink Japanese *Communications Vessel No. 135* off Ambon Harbor, N.E.I.

ARCTIC. Coast Guard icebreaker *Eastwind* (WAG 279), supported by sister ship *Southwind* (WAG 280), captures German weather ship *Externsteine* off Cape Borgen, Shannon Island, east coast of Greenland. *Eastwind*'s crew unofficially christens the captured auxiliary "Eastbreeze."[209] Both icebreakers, however, are damaged by pack ice.

ATLANTIC. French submarine *Amazone*, aground in Fort Pond Bay since 14 October, is refloated; tug *Sagamore* (ATO 20) is returned to her previous duties while submarine rescue vessels *Falcon* (ASR 2) and *Chewink* (ASR 3) escort *Amazone* to New London, Connecticut, for examination of the damage.

17 Tuesday

PACIFIC. TG 38.4 (Rear Admiral Ralph E. Davison) attacks Japanese installations at Legaspi and Clark Field, Luzon.

TG 78.3 (Rear Admiral Arthur D. Struble) lands army troops (Sixth Ranger Battalion) on Suluan and Dinagat Islands at the entrance to Leyte Gulf to destroy Japanese installations that could provide early warning of U.S. forces entering the gulf. Unfortunately, the Suluan Island unit transmits a warning, prompting Admiral Toyoda Soemu, Commander in Chief Combined Fleet, to order activation of "SHO 1 GO" Operation plans for defending the Philippines against American invasion and bringing about a decisive battle (see 23–25 October).[210]

Submarine *Narwhal* (SS 167) lands 10 tons of supplies at Tongehatan Point, on northwest coast of Tawi Tawi, P.I. (see 19 October).

Motor minesweeper *YMS 70* is sunk in storm off Leyte, 10°56′N, 125°12′E.

During the third day of sweeping operations in Ngulu Atoll, western Carolines, light minelayer *Montgomery* (DM 17) is damaged by Japanese mine while anchoring, 10°56′N, 125°12′E.

Special Air Task Force (STAG 1) operations continue: Four TDRs are launched against Japanese installations near East Rabaul. One of the four hits the objective, the second hits a target of opportunity, the third is lost due to the failure of a tube in the drone receiver, and the fourth may have been shot down (light and inaccurate antiaircraft fire is noted).

Dutch submarine *Zwaardvisch*, attacking Japanese convoy in the Java Sea, sinks minelayer *Itsukushima* and damages minelayer/netlayer *Wakatake* off Bawean Island, N.E.I., 05°26′S, 113°48′E, and survives counterattacks by submarine chasers *Ch 2* and *Ch 26*.

INDIAN OCEAN. British carrier-based planes sink Japanese collier *Ishikari Maru* in Nancowry Harbor, 08°02′N, 93°32′E.

18 Wednesday

PACIFIC. TG 38.1 (Vice Admiral John S. McCain) and TG 38.4 (Rear Admiral Ralph E. Davison) attack principal Japanese airfields near Manila and shipping in the harbor, sinking passenger-cargo ship *Hoeisan Maru*, 14°35′N, 120°50′E, and army cargo ship *Urato Maru* and freighter *Tempi Maru*, 14°35′N, 120°55′E. Meanwhile, TG 38.2 (Rear Admiral Gerald F. Bogan) pounds enemy shipping off northern Luzon, sinking auxiliary submarine chaser *Cha 95*, transports *Taiho Maru* and *Hokurei Maru* [previously damaged on 6 October by submarine *Cabrilla* (SS 288)], and freighters *Hoten Maru*, *Terukuni Maru*, and *Tsingtao Maru* off Port San Pio Quinto, Cami-

guin Island, 18°54′N, 121°51′E; cargo ship *Shinko Maru* near Babuyan Channel, 18°35′N, 121°40′E; and landing ships *T.135* and *T.136* and minelayer/netlayer *Maeshima* off northeastern Luzon, 17°46′N, 120°25′E. Cargo vessel (ex-Philippine *Zamboanga*) *Yubari Maru* is sunk at Aparri. Cargo ship *No. 3 Taibi Maru* may have also been lost in these attacks at this time.

First bombardment ships begin shelling Japanese installations on Leyte.

Seventh Fleet aircraft, meanwhile, sink Japanese ships *Daikoku Maru*, *No. 2 Gokuku Maru*, *No. 8 Nankai Maru*, *RinKyo Maru*, *Yoto Maru*, and *Zuin Maru* in the Cebu area.

Submarine *Bluegill* (SS 242) and *Raton* (SS 270) attack Japanese convoy in the South China Sea. *Bluegill* sinks army cargo ships *Arabia Maru* and *Chinsei Maru* and freighter *Hakushika Maru*, 14°06′N, 119°40′E; *Raton* sinks army cargo ships *Taikai Maru* and *Shiranesan Maru*, 12°37′N, 118°46′E.

Special Air Task Force (STAG 1) operations continue: Three TDRs are launched against lighthouse on Cape St. George, New Ireland. None hit the target.

ATLANTIC. Naval Advanced Base, Le Havre, France, is established.

MEDITERRANEAN. Motor torpedo boat *PT 558* is damaged in engagement with two German R-boats west of Portofino; while retiring to Leghorn, Italy, *PT 561* is damaged by heavy seas. Tank landing ship *LST 906* drags anchor and is damaged when driven ashore by heavy sea, Leghorn (see 17 January 1945).

19 Thursday

PACIFIC. TG 38.1 (Vice Admiral John S. McCain) and TG 38.4 (Rear Admiral Ralph E. Davison) continue attacks on principal Japanese airfields near Manila and shipping in the harbor. Navy carrier-based planes sink army cargo ship *Belgium Maru* and freighters *Jogu Maru* and *Toshikawa Maru*, 14°35′N, 120°55′E, and *Kurugane Maru* and *Tsukubasan Maru*; damage oiler *Ondo*; and damage cargo ship *Urado Maru* so severely that she is run aground to prevent her sinking. TG 38.1 and TG 38.4 then proceed south to provide direct support for the landings at Leyte. Seventh Fleet planes, meanwhile, sink Japanese ships *Kosei Maru*, *Kafuku Maru*, *Koei Maru*, *No. 8 Kanekichi Maru*, *No. 11 Akita Maru*, and *No. 18 Taigyo Maru* at Cebu. *Havre Maru* is bombed at Jolo, where she has been aground since 2 October.

Off Leyte, destroyer *Ross* (DD 563) is damaged by mine, 10°17′N, 125°40′E; destroyer

Soldiers of the First Cavalry Division, U.S. Army, wade ashore from an LCVP from transport *La Salle* (AP 102) at San Ricardo, near Tacloban, Leyte, 20 October 1944. Visible in the background is a *Fletcher* (DD 445)–class destroyer and at least four infantry landing craft (LCI). (NA, 80-G-59503)

Aulick (DD 569) is damaged by shore battery, 11°13′N, 125°02′E.

Submarine *Narwhal* (SS 167) lands 50 tons of supplies at Calipapa, on southwest coast of Negros, P.I., disembarks a party of six [Filipino mess boy from *Nautilus* (SS 168) and "five prospective mess boys"], and embarks evacuees (20 women and children).

Special Air Task Force (STAG 1) operations continue: Two flights (one TDR each) are launched against Japanese gun positions west of Ballale, Bougainville. In the first, one drone misses its target during its run; in the second, the drone drops part of its bomb load on the target before it crashes.

Destroyer escort *Gilligan* (DE 508) bombards Mille Atoll, Marshalls.

USAAF B-24, searching the northern exit of Makassar Strait, sinks Japanese weather ship *Shonan Maru*.

UNITED STATES. Navy Court of Inquiry into the Pearl Harbor attack of 7 December 1941 (see 24 July for composition) completes its work; 1,397 printed pages encompass the record of its proceedings and its findings.

20 Friday

PACIFIC. Under the overall command of General Douglas MacArthur, who makes good on his promise to "return" to the Philippines, and Vice Admiral Thomas C. Kinkaid, Commander Seventh Fleet, TF 78 (Rear Admiral Daniel E. Barbey) and TF 79 (Vice Admiral Theodore S. Wilkinson) land four divisions of the U.S. Sixth Army (Lieutenant General Walter Krueger) on Leyte. Fast carriers and battleships of the Third Fleet provide support, as do the older battleships (some of which are Pearl Harbor veterans) and escort carriers of the Seventh Fleet.

Japanese aerial counterattacks (horizontal bombers) result in damage to escort carrier *Sangamon* (CVE 26), 10°46′N, 126°23′E, and salvage vessel *Preserver* (ARS 8), 10°50′N, 125°25′E; aerial torpedo damages light cruiser *Honolulu* (CL 48), 11°01′N, 125°07′E. Japanese shore batteries damage destroyer *Bennion* (DD 662), 10°50′N, 125°25′E, and tank landing ship *LST 452*, 11°01′N, 125°01′E.

Submarine *Hammerhead* (SS 364) attacks Japanese convoy SAMA 13 about 15 miles northwest of Miri, Sarawak, and sinks transport *Oyo Maru*, 04°41′N, 113°22′E, and army cargo ship *Ugo Maru*, 04°52′N, 113°24′E.

Special Air Task Force (STAG 1) operations continue: Three TDRs are launched against Japanese gun positions west of Ballale, Bougainville. One is lost, one makes a hit with its

bomb but crashes before it can be directed into its ultimate target (the beached Japanese freighter serving as an antiaircraft gun site off the Kahili airstrip and christened the *"Kahili Maru"*), and the last achieves a bomb hit and crashes into *"Kahili Maru"* as planned.

Naval Operating Base, Guam, is established.

UNITED STATES. Army Pearl Harbor Board (see 20 July for composition) completes its work of reporting "the facts relating to the attack" of 7 December 1941; 3,357 printed pages contain the record of its proceedings and its exhibits.[211]

21 Saturday

PACIFIC. Leyte landings continue. Off invasion beaches, transport *Warhawk* (AP 168) is damaged in collision with battleship *Tennessee* (BB 43), 10°57′N, 125°02′E; mortar fire damages tank landing ships *LST 269*, *LST 483*, and *LST 704*, 10°50′N, 125°25′E.

TG 38.2 (Rear Admiral Gerald F. Bogan) attacks Japanese shipping and installations near Panay, Cebu, Negros, and Masbate. Carrier-based planes sink auxiliary minesweeper *Wa 8*, 11°30′N, 123°20′E; auxiliary submarine chaser *Cha 15*, 12°55′N, 121°35′E; and army tanker *Doko Maru* off east coast of Romblon Island, P.I., 12°35′N, 122°16′E.

British submarine HMS *Tantivy* sinks Japanese freighters *No. 2 Chokyu Maru*, *No. 3 Takasago Maru*, and *Otori Maru* in Makassar Strait.

MEDITERRANEAN. Destroyer *Eberle* (DD 430) bombards targets near San Remo, Italy.

22 Sunday

PACIFIC. TF 38 planes sink Japanese auxiliary submarine chaser *Cha 15* off Cebu, P.I., 11°30′N, 124°00′E.

Japanese oiler *Ryuei Maru* sinks after running aground about 10 miles northwest of the coast of Mindoro, P.I., 13°15′N, 120°19′E.

Submarine *Darter* (SS 227) detects a group of Japanese warships northwest of Borneo, 07°31′N, 115°22′E, and begins trailing them (see 23 October).

Submarine *Sea Dog* (SS 401), in attack on Japanese convoy, sinks supply ship *Muroto* south-southwest of Kagoshima, 29°19′N, 129°44′E, and gunboat *Tomitsu Maru* south of Akuseki Jima, 29°18′N, 129°44′E.

British submarine HMS *Tantivy* sinks Japanese *Communication Ship No. 137* in Makassar Strait.

U.S. freighter *Augustus Thomas* is strafed in

San Pedro Bay, Leyte; one man of the 27-man Armed Guard is wounded.

MEDITERRANEAN. Destroyer *Jouett* (DD 396) conducts two bombardment missions against German positions in the Franco-Italian border regions while destroyer *Madison* (DD 425) supports minesweeping operations in the vicinity.

23 Monday

PACIFIC. Battle for Leyte Gulf (a succession of distinct fleet engagements) opens. While *Darter* (SS 227) continues to trail Japanese ships detected the previous day, submarine *Bream* (SS 243) torpedoes heavy cruiser *Aoba* off Manila Bay, 14°00′N, 119°27′E; light cruiser *Kinu* tows the damaged ship to Cavite. Subsequently, *Darter* and *Dace* (SS 247) attack the First Raiding Force (Vice Admiral Kurita Takeo), one of the three main bodies of the Japanese fleet moving toward Leyte in a major effort to drive U.S. forces from the Philippines. *Dace* sinks heavy cruiser *Maya*, 09°28′N, 117°20′E, while *Darter* (see 24 October) sinks heavy cruiser *Atago* (Vice Admiral Kurita's flagship) and damages her sister ship *Takao*, 09°24′N, 117°11′E, in Palawan Channel, between the northwest coast of Palawan and the extensive area of shoals and reefs known as the "Dangerous Ground." Destroyers *Kishinami* and *Asashimo* rescue *Atago*'s survivors (including Vice Admiral Kurita); *Akishimo* rescues *Maya*'s survivors, transferring them later to battleship *Musashi*.

Destroyer escort *Gilligan* (DE 508) bombards Emidj Island, Jaluit Atoll.

Submarine *Croaker* (SS 246) sinks Japanese freighter *Hakuran Maru* in the Yellow Sea, off west coast of Korea, 35°29′N, 126°05′E.

Submarine *Nautilus* (SS 168) begins mission of landing party of 12 men and 20 tons of equipment on east coast of Luzon (see 24 and 27 October).

Submarine *Sawfish* (SS 276) attacks Japanese convoy, sinking seaplane carrier *Kimikawa Maru* about 100 miles northwest of Luzon, 18°58′N, 118°31′E.

Submarine *Snook* (SS 279) damages Japanese merchant tanker *Kikusui Maru* in South China Sea, west of Luzon Strait, 19°44′N, 118°25′E (see 24 October).

Submarine *Tang* (SS 306) attacks Japanese U 03 convoy, escorted by destroyers *Hasu* and *Tsuga*, northwest of Formosa. Commander Richard H. O'Kane takes *Tang* into the midst of the enemy in a surface torpedo action, sinking cargo ship *Shinju Maru* and transport

Wakatake Maru, 24°49′N, 120°26′E, and damaging freighter *Kori Go*, 24°42′N, 120°21′E, and cargo ship *Toun Maru* (see 24 October).[212]

Special Air Task Force (STAG 1) operations continue in two missions (three TDRs each) flown against beached Japanese ships in Moisuru Bay, Bouganville, and off the south end of the Kahili airstrip. In the first mission, one TDR scores a direct hit on "*Kahili Maru*"; in the second, one TDR scores a direct hit on "*Kahili Maru*" while another hits a beached merchantman in Moisuru Bay.

MEDITERRANEAN. U.S. motor torpedo boats attack German southbound convoy in Ligurian Sea south of Sestri Levanti with no success; a subsequent attack, however, results in the sinking of one F-lighter.

Destroyer *Woolsey* (DD 437) shells German targets in San Remo area; she repeats bombardment mission the next day.

24 Tuesday

PACIFIC. Battle for Leyte Gulf continues as planes from TG 38.2, TG 38.3, and TG 38.4 attack the Japanese First Raiding Force (Vice Admiral Kurita Takeo) in the Sibuyan Sea. Planes from carriers *Enterprise* (CV 6), *Intrepid* (CV 11), and *Franklin* (CV 13) and small carrier *Cabot* (CVL 28) sink battleship *Musashi* south of Luzon, 12°50′N, 122°35′E. Aircraft from the three task groups also damage battleships *Yamato* and *Nagato*, heavy cruisers *Mogami* and *Tone*, and destroyers *Kiyoshimo*, *Fujinami*, and *Uranami*. TG 38.4 planes attack Japanese No. 3 *Butai* of the First Raiding Force (Vice Admiral Nishimura Shoji) and the Second Raiding Force (Vice Admiral Shima Kiyohide) as it proceeds through the Sulu Sea. Planes from *Franklin* sink destroyer *Wakaba* off the west coast of Panay, 11°50′N, 121°25′E; aircraft from *Enterprise* and *Franklin* damage battleships *Fuso* and *Yamashiro*. TG 38.3 (Rear Admiral Frederick C. Sherman) planes attack Mindanao-bound Japanese light cruiser *Kinu* and destroyer *Uranami* between the Bataan Peninsula and Corregidor; SB2Cs (VB 19) from carrier *Lexington* (CV 16) damage *Kinu* by near-misses; and F6Fs (VF 15) from *Essex* (CV 9) strafe the ship. The same strike damages *Uranami*. TF 38 planes also sink army ore carrier *Fuyukawa Maru* off Luzon, 16°30′N, 120°15′E.

Japanese planes, however, attack TG 38.3; combat air patrol and effective use of rain squalls as cover limit the damage to small carrier *Princeton* (CVL 23), hit by bomb from a carrier bomber (JUDY), 15°21′N, 123°31′E. In

trying to save *Princeton*, however, light cruiser *Birmingham* (CL 62) and destroyers *Morrison* (DD 560), *Gatling* (DD 671), and *Irwin* (DD 794) are damaged by rolling against the stricken carrier or by fragments from the cataclysmic explosion when fires touch off *Princeton*'s after magazines. In addition, *Morrison*'s bridge is damaged by a jeep (used to tow aircraft) falling from *Princeton*'s flight deck. *Birmingham* suffers the greatest destruction because she is alongside the carrier when the latter's magazines explode. The cruiser's decks literally run red with blood: 229 men killed, four missing, 211 seriously wounded, and 215 with minor wounds. Ultimately, light cruiser *Reno* (CL 96) and *Irwin* scuttle *Princeton*.

During the aerial action this day, Commander David McCampbell, Commander Air Group 15, flying from *Essex*, again distinguishes himself in combat. With only one wingman, McCampbell attacks what is estimated as over 60 hostile aircraft and downs nine, breaking up the attacking formation before it reaches the fleet. For his "conspicuous gallantry and intrepidity at the risk of his life" on this occasion and on 19 June, McCampbell is awarded the Medal of Honor.

Elsewhere off Leyte, Japanese planes damage destroyer *Leutze* (DD 481), 10°50′N, 125°25′E, tank landing ship *LST 552*, 11°11′N, 125°05′E, and sink infantry landing craft *LCI (L) 1065*. Oiler *Ashtabula* (AO 51) is damaged by aerial torpedo, 11°03′N, 125°22′E. U.S. freighter *Augustus Thomas*, anchored in San Pedro Bay, Leyte, is attacked by a Japanese plane. The ship's Armed Guard gunfire sets the aircraft ablaze, but the *kamikaze* presses home his attack, a wing striking the stack of the nearby tug *Sonoma* (ATO 12) before it crashes the freighter's starboard side. The bombs detonate in the water between the two ships, and the exploding suicider sets *Sonoma* afire. There are no casualties on board *Augustus Thomas* (41-man merchant complement, 27-man Armed Guard, and 480 troop passengers), which is subsequently beached by tugs *Chowanoc* (ATF 100) and *Whippoorwill* (ATO 169). *Sonoma* subsequently sinks off Dio Island, 10°57′N, 125°02′E.

U.S. freighter *David Dudley Field* is damaged by *kamikaze* off Tacloban, Leyte; there are no fatalities among the 40-man merchant complement, 30-man Armed Guard, 50 stevedores embarked to work cargo, and 10 Army passengers. After repairs, the freighter will resume active service.

Coordinated submarine attack group TG 17.15 (Commander Alan B. Banister), meanwhile, operates against Japanese shipping in South China Sea west of Luzon Strait. *Drum* (SS 228) sinks freighter *Shikisan Maru*, 20°27'N, 118°31'E; *Icefish* (SS 367) sinks army cargo ship *Tenshin Maru*, 19°31'N, 118°10'E; and *Seadragon* (SS 194) sinks transport *Eiko Maru* and cargo ship *Daiten Maru*, 20°31'N, 118°33'E, and freighter *Kokuryu Maru*, 20°27'N, 118°31'E. *Snook* (SS 279), operating independently of TG 17.15 but in the same patrol area, sinks army cargo ships *Arisan Maru*, 20°54'N, 118°19'E, and *No. 1 Shinsei Maru*, 20°10'N, 118°17'E; merchant tanker *Kikusui Maru* sinks as the result of damage inflicted by *Snook* the previous day, 19°46'N, 118°30'E. Japanese destroyer *Harukaze*, near the scene of the torpedoing of *Arisan Maru*, attacks a submarine contact. The ensuing 20-meter column of water, followed by a heavy underwater explosion and a profusion of papers and cork amid a spreading oil slick, causes the destroyermen to claim destruction of what proves to be *Shark* (SS 314).[213]

Submarine *Besugo* (SS 321) damages Japanese *Coast Defense Vessel No. 132* south of Ashizuri Saki, Japan, 30°19'N, 132°49'E.

Submarine *Croaker* (SS 246) attacks Japanese convoy in the Yellow Sea, sinking army cargo ship *Mikage Maru* and damaging freighter *Gassan Maru* about 25 miles southwest of Quelpart Island, 33°00'N, 125°49'E.

Submarine *Darter* (SS 227) runs aground on Bombay Shoal, Palawan Passage, P.I., 09°26'N, 116°56'E, and is scuttled by *Nautilus* (SS 168) and *Dace* (SS 247) to prevent *Darter* from falling intact into enemy hands (see 31 October). *Nautilus* completes mission of landing party of 12 men and 20 tons of equipment on east coast of Luzon (see 27 October).

Submarine *Kingfish* (SS 234), despite presence of two escorts, sinks Japanese cargo ship *Ikutagawa Maru* about 30 miles east of Chichi Jima, 27°08'N, 143°13'E.

Submarine *Tang* (SS 306) attacks Japanese convoy in Formosa Strait, and as in the action of the previous day, her captain, Commander Richard H. O'Kane, boldly takes his boat in on the surface to engage the enemy, sinking freighter *Ebara Maru*, 25°03'N, 119°35'E, and damaging tanker *Matsumoto Maru*, 25°04'N, 119°35'E (see 25 October), but is herself sunk by the circular run of one of her own torpedoes, 25°06'N, 119°31'E. For the conspicuous gallantry he displays during *Tang*'s fifth war patrol, O'Kane (who survives the loss of his boat as well as endures imprisonment) will receive the Medal of Honor.

Destroyer escort *Richard M. Rowell* (DE 403) sinks Japanese submarine *I 54*, 70 miles east of Surigao, 09°45'N, 126°45'E.

Japanese submarine *I 56* attacks Humboldt Bay, New Guinea–bound TG 78.1 (Commander Theodore C. Linthicum) and torpedoes tank landing ship *LST 695* west of Mindanao, 08°31'N, 128°34'E. *LST 986* tows her crippled sister ship to Palau; *I 56* survives counterattacks by frigate *Carson City* (PF 50).

Hospital ship *Comfort* (AH 6), fully illuminated in accordance with the dictates of the Geneva Convention, is bombed 22 miles southeast of Leyte.

USAAF B-24s, B-25s, and fighter-bomber aircraft (Far East Air Force), attack Japanese installations and shipping, Sandakan, Borneo; during the air strikes army cargo ship *Taimei Maru* is sunk off Sandakan, 05°50'N, 118°07'E.

Late in the day, Commander Third Fleet (Admiral William F. Halsey Jr.) orders TF 38 (Vice Admiral Marc A. Mitscher) to proceed north to be in position to strike the Japanese Main Force of the Mobile Force (Vice Admiral Ozawa Jisaburo) on the morning of 25 October, but does not inform Commander Seventh Fleet (Vice Admiral Thomas C. Kinkaid) of his action.

Commander Seventh Fleet (Vice Admiral Kinkaid) makes his dispositions to meet the expected enemy onslaught; bombardment and support group TG 77.2 (Rear Admiral Jesse B. Oldendorf) is augmented by close covering group TG 77.3 (Rear Admiral Russell S. Berkey).

Local airfields, however, are not yet ready to base night reconnaissance aircraft, and the only carrier equipped to operate such planes, small carrier *Independence* (CVL 22), is proceeding north with TF 38.

Unbeknown to the Americans, the First Raiding Force (Vice Admiral Kurita Takeo) transits San Bernadino Strait and heads for Leyte Gulf.

MEDITERRANEAN. Motor torpedo boats patrolling off Monte Grosso attack five southbound targets, firing six torpedoes. No definite claims are made.

Destroyer *Woolsey* (DD 437) and British destroyer HMS *Fortune* sink two abandoned German explosive boats 16 miles off Cap Ferrat, France, 43°40'N, 07°20'E; *Woolsey* and minesweeper *Sway* (AM 120) recover prisoners.

25 Wednesday

GENERAL. United States and Great Britain resume diplomatic relations with Italy.

PACIFIC. Battle for Leyte Gulf continues as TG 77.2 (Rear Admiral Jesse B. Oldendorf), augmented by TG 77.3 (Rear Admiral Russell S. Berkey) and TG 70.1 (39 motor torpedo boats), executes the classic maneuver of "crossing the tee" of the Japanese No. 3 *Butai* of the First Raiding Force (Vice Admiral Nishimura Shoji) and the Second Raiding Force (Vice Admiral Shima Kiyohide) in the Battle of Surigao Strait. TG 70.1 begins the action against the Japanese ships. *PT 137* torpedoes light cruiser *Abukuma*, but *PT 493* is sunk by enemy secondary battery gunfire, 10°15'N, 125°23'E. Heavy cruiser *Mogami* turns away attack by *PT 146*, *PT 151*, and *PT 190*; *Abukuma* retires, escorted by destroyer *Ushio* (see 26 October).

Destroyer Squadron 54 (Captain Jesse G. Coward), detached from TF 79, then attacks; *McDermut* (DD 677) sinks destroyer *Yamagumo*, 10°25'N, 125°20'E, and damages destroyers *Asagumo* and *Michisio*. Subsequently, light cruiser *Denver* (CL 58) sinks *Asagumo* at entrance of Surigao Strait, 10°04'N, 125°21'E. Destroyer Squadron 24 (Captain Kenmore M. McManes) enters the fray and *Hutchins* (DD 476) (McManes's flagship) sinks *Michisio*, 10°25'N, 123°25'E. Destroyer Squadron 56 (Captain Roland M. Smoot) attacks; *Albert W. Grant* (DD 649) is damaged by both friendly and Japanese gunfire at this phase of the battle, 10°27'N, 125°25'E. Two Australian warships take part in this fleet action—heavy cruiser HMAS *Shropshire* (in TG 77.3) and destroyer HMAS *Arunta* (in Destroyer Squadron 24)—that sees the destruction of battleships *Fuso* and *Yamashiro*, 10°25'N, 125°20'E. Heavy cruiser *Mogami* and destroyer *Shigure* are damaged, the former most likely by heavy cruisers *Minneapolis* (CA 36) and *Portland* (CA 33) and light cruiser *Columbia* (CL 56). *Mogami*'s travails, however, are not yet over. First, she is damaged in collision with heavy cruiser *Nachi* at about 10°18'N, 125°23'E; she is then further damaged by heavy cruisers *Portland* and *Louisville* (CA 28) and light cruiser *Denver* at about 10°02'N, 125°22'E. *Mogami* then drives off motor torpedo boat *PT 491* (see below).

Meanwhile, First Raiding Force (Vice Admiral Kurita Takeo), which includes four battleships and five heavy cruisers, having passed into the Philippine Sea during the night, surprises TG 77.4 (Rear Admiral Thomas L. Sprague) off Samar. Kurita's force wreaks havoc on the six escort carriers, three destroyers, and four destroyer escorts of TU 77.4.3 (northernmost carrier force) (Rear Admiral Clifton A. F. Sprague). In this battle, which becomes a precipitate flight in the face of an overwhelming enemy force, Kurita's ships inflict severe damage but emerge bloodied by the Homeric efforts of the "small boys" (destroyers and destroyer escorts) and planes from the escort carriers that compel Kurita to retire, inexplicably, without destroying the CVEs and their consorts in detail. "Every conceivable form of plane attack" is employed by the escort carrier planes that are diverted from support missions, "including dummy torpedo runs by planes without torpedoes" (see below). In the Battle off Samar, Japanese gunfire sinks destroyers *Hoel* (DD 533), 11°46′N, 126°33′E, and *Johnston* (DD 557), 11°46′N, 126°09′E, and destroyer escort *Samuel B. Roberts* (DE 413), 11°40′N, 126°20′E, which carry out a daylight torpedo attack ("one of the most gallant and heroic acts of the war") on Japanese battleships and heavy cruisers from ranges from 10,000 to 7,000 yards. Japanese gunfire damages destroyer *Heermann* (DD 523), 11°40′N, 126°15′E, and destroyer escort *Dennis* (DE 405), 11°40′N, 126°20′E. To divert Japanese gunfire away from the lightly armed escort carriers, *Johnston* (Commander Ernest E. Evans) closes the enemy; her gunfire damages light cruiser *Yahagi* and one of her torpedoes damages heavy cruiser *Kumano*. Despite being severely wounded early in the action and his ship heavily damaged, Evans displays courage and fighting spirit that will "live forever in the memory of the officers and men who served with him that day." He is awarded the Medal of Honor posthumously.

Japanese gunfire (either battleship *Haruna* or *Kongo*) also straddles escort carriers *White Plains* (CVE 66), 11°40′N, 126°20′E, *St. Lo* (CVE 63), and *Kitkun Bay* (CVE 71) but scores no direct hits. Heavy cruisers *Chikuma*, *Haguro*, and *Chokai*, light cruiser *Noshiro*, and a destroyer sink escort carrier *Gambier Bay* (CVE 73), 11°31′N, 126°12′E. Japanese gunfire also damages *Fanshaw Bay* (CVE 70) and *Kalinin Bay* (CVE 68), 11°40′N, 126°20′E; the latter claims one hit on a Japanese heavy cruiser (heavy cruiser *Tone* is hit by a 5-inch shell, as is light cruiser *Noshiro*) with her single 5-inch gun. Navy carrier-based aircraft damage battleships *Kongo* (from near-misses) and *Yamato* and heavy cruisers *Chikuma*, *Chokai*, *Haguro*, and *Suzuya* (see below).

Subsequently, Japanese planes attack escort carriers of TU 77.4.1 (Rear Admiral Thomas L. Sprague). *Suwanee* (CVE 27) is damaged by kamikazes, 09°45′N, 126°42′E, and *Santee* (CVE 29) by suicide plane and Japanese sub-

In the desperate Battle off Samar, 25 October 1944, while Japanese shells fall near escort carrier *White Plains* (CVE 66) in the distance, flight deck crewmen prepare General Motors FM-2 Wildcats (VC 5) on board *Kitkun Bay* (CVE 71) for takeoff; a General Motors TBM Avenger (VC 5) sits with wings folded in foreground (left). (NA, 80-G-287497)

marine *I 56*, 09°45′N, 126°20′E. Kamikazes near-miss *Sangamon* (CVE 26), 09°45′N, 126°42′E, and *Petrof Bay* (CVE 80). Destroyer escort *Richard M. Rowell* (DE 403) is damaged by strafing, 10°05′N, 127°10′E.

Following its ordeal off Samar, TU 77.4.3 (Rear Admiral Clifton A. F. Sprague) comes under Japanese air attack. Kamikazes sink *St. Lo*, 11°13′N, 126°05′E, and further damage *Kalinin Bay* and *Kitkun Bay*, 11°10′N, 126°20′E. Damage to the CVEs during this day prompts the use of the partially completed Tacloban airfield; CVE planes land and are serviced and returned to the attack. Thus many pilots and planes are saved that would have had to make water landings if they were unable to reach a carrier deck. "It is remarkable," Vice Admiral Kinkaid (Commander TF 77) writes later, "that in these landings on an unknown and ill-kept field, no serious injuries were sustained by our air personnel, which speaks very highly for their skill."

At the same time, in the battle off Cape Engaño, carrier aircraft from the Third Fleet (Admiral William F. Halsey Jr.) strike the Japanese Main Force of the Mobile Force (Vice Admiral Ozawa Jisaburo). Planes from carriers *Essex* (CV 9) and *Lexington* (CV 16) sink carrier *Zuikaku* 220 nautical miles east-northeast of Cape Engaño, 19°20′N, 125°51′E, and carrier *Chitose* 235 nautical miles east of Cape Engaño, 19°20′N, 125°20′E; carrier *Chiyoda*, damaged by planes from carriers *Lexington* and *Franklin* (CV 13) and small carrier *Langley* (CVL 27), is sunk by heavy cruisers *New Orleans* (CA 32) and *Wichita* (CA 45) and light cruisers *Santa Fe* (CL 60) and *Mobile* (CL 63) 260 nautical miles southeast of Cape Engaño, 18°37′N, 126°45′E. Small carrier *Zuiho* is sunk by planes from *Essex*, *Franklin*, *Lexington*, *Enterprise* (CV 6), and small carrier *San Jacinto* (CVL 30) east-northeast of Cape Engaño, 19°20′N, 125°51′E.

Carrier aircraft damage Japanese battle-

Off Cape Engaño, 25 October 1944, carrier *Zuikaku* lies burning in the distance (right), while small carrier *Zuiho* turns amid near-misses; antiaircraft bursts spatter the sky (center) in this view taken from a plane from carrier *Franklin* (CV 13). (NHC, NH 95786)

ships *Yamato* and *Nagato* and heavy cruiser *Myoko*, torpedoed by TBMs (VT 18) from *Intrepid* (CV 11) or TBMs (VT 29) from small carrier *Cabot* (CVL 28), in San Jose Strait, 12°55′N, 121°52′E; battleship *Haruna*, east of Samar; and light cruiser *Yahagi*, strafed by CVE-based aircraft, and destroyer *Kiyoshimo* off Leyte. Heavy cruiser *Chikuma*, damaged by aerial torpedo fired by a TBM (VC 81) from escort carrier *Natoma Bay* (CVE 62) off Samar, is scuttled by destroyer *Nowaki*, 11°22′N, 126°16′E; heavy cruiser *Suzuya*, damaged by TBMs (TU 77.4.3) off Samar, is scuttled by destroyer *Okinami*, 11°48′N, 126°26′E. Heavy cruisers *Chokai* and *Tone* are bombed by TBMs (VC 5) from escort carrier *Kitkun Bay* off Samar; *Chokai* is scuttled by destroyer *Fujinami*, 11°26′N, 126°15′E. Heavy cruiser *Mogami*, damaged by TBMs (from TU 77.4.1), is scuttled by destroyer *Akebono* southwest of Cape Binit, Panaon Island, 09°40′N, 124°50′E. Light cruiser *Tama* is damaged by TBMs (VT 21) from small carrier *Belleau Wood* (CVL 24) and TBMs (VT 51) from small carrier *San Jacinto* and is then torpedoed and sunk by submarine *Jallao* (SS 368), about 130 miles northeast of Luzon, 21°23′N, 127°19′E. Destroyer *Hatsuzuki* is sunk by the gunfire of

four heavy cruisers and twelve destroyers east northeast of Cape Engaño, 20°24′N, 126°20′E. Submarine *Halibut* (SS 232) sinks destroyer *Akizuki* east-northeast of Cape Engaño, 20°29′N, 126°36′E.

Japanese air attacks continue against shipping off Leyte. U.S. freighter *Adoniram Judson* is attacked by enemy planes off Tacloban; Armed Guard gunners claim splashing six. One bomb explodes close aboard, causing fragmentation damage and wounding two of the embarked stevedores. There are no casualties to the ship's company: 43 merchant seamen and 28 Armed Guards. Freighter *John W. Foster*, anchored in San Pedro Bay, is strafed; seven of the 27-man Armed Guard, three of 170 embarked troops, and one officer are wounded.

Submarine *Cero* (SS 225) arrives off Darigayos Inlet, on west coast of Luzon, to land men and supplies; she fails to make contact with forces ashore on 25, 26, 27, and 28 October, however, and will proceed to an alternate site (see 29 October).

Submarine *Seal* (SS 183), despite presence of escort, sinks Japanese transport *Hakuyo Maru* north of Urup, Kurils, 50°18′N, 150°50′E.

Submarine *Sterlet* (SS 392) attacks Japanese convoy southwest of Kyushu and sinks Japanese merchant tanker *Jinei Maru* about 35 miles west of Yaku Jima, 30°15′N, 129°45′E. Destroyer *Akikaze*, *Coast Defense Vessel No. 31*, and *Coast Defense Vessel No. 43* conduct unsuccessful counterattacks on *Sterlet*.

Japanese fleet tanker *Matsumoto Maru* sinks as the result of damage inflicted by submarine *Tang* (SS 306) in Formosa Strait the previous day, 25°07′N, 119°45′E.

British submarine HMS *Tantivy* sinks Japanese motor sailship *No. 47 Tachibana Maru* in the Flores Sea.

USMC F4Us sink Japanese auxiliary submarine chaser *Cha 52* north of the Palaus, 07°30′N, 134°30′E.

USAAF aircraft sink Japanese merchant tanker *Shoho Maru* in South China Sea, 11°18′N, 114°50′E.

26 Thursday

PACIFIC. Battle for Leyte Gulf concludes as carrier-based planes and USAAF B-24s (Far East Air Force) attack retiring Japanese ships that have survived the previous days' action. TBMs (VC 80 and VC 81) from escort carriers *Manila Bay* (CVE 61) and *Natoma Bay* (CVE 62), respectively, sink light cruiser *Kinu* north of Panay, P.I., 11°46′N, 123°11′E, and destroyer *Uranami* 70 miles north-northeast of Iloilo, Panay, 11°50′N, 123°00′E. F6Fs, TBMs, and SB2Cs from carriers *Hornet* (CV 12) and *Wasp* (CV 18) cripple destroyer *Hayashimo* 40 miles south of Mindoro, 12°05′N, 121°50′E, which is run aground off Semirara Island, out of fuel; sister ship *Okinami* attempts to refuel *Hayashimo* until compelled to push on for Coron Bay by attacking aircraft.[214] F6Fs and TBMs from carrier *Hancock* (CV 19), F6Fs, SB2Cs, and TBMs from *Wasp*, and F6Fs and TBMs from small carrier *Cowpens* (CVL 25) damage light cruiser *Noshiro* west of Panay, 11°35′N, 121°45′E; TBMs (VT 18) and SB2Cs (VB 18) from *Hornet* deliver the coup de grâce at 11°42′N, 121°41′E. Planes from *Hancock* sink landing ship *T.102* in the Guimaras Straits, 11°00′N, 123°00′E. F6Fs, SB2Cs, and TBMs from *Hancock* damage heavy cruiser *Kumano*; destroyer *Okinami* is damaged in the strikes in the Sibuyan Sea. USAAF B-24s (Far East Air Force), in a series of three attacks, sink light cruiser *Abukuma* southwest of Negros Island, 09°20′N, 122°32′E; battleship *Haruna* is damaged by near-misses. TG 34.5 conducts sweep for damaged Japanese ships; light cruisers *Vincennes* (CL 64), *Miami* (CL 89), and *Biloxi*

(CL 80) and destroyers *Miller* (DD 535) and *Owen* (DD 536) sink destroyer *Nowaki* 65 miles south-southeast of Legaspi, Luzon, 13°00′N, 124°54′E. Navy carrier-based aircraft sink merchant tanker *No. 31 Nanshin Maru* near Palawan, 08°22′N, 116°55′E.

Motor torpedo boat *PT 132* is damaged by dive bomber, 09°00′N, 125°00′E.

U.S. freighter *Benjamin Ide Wheeler* is attacked by Japanese plane off Leyte and damaged by near-miss of bomb that wounds three of the ship's embarked troops.

Submarines *Drum* (SS 228) and *Icefish* (SS 367) attack Japanese convoy MOMA 05 off northwestern coast of Luzon, P.I. *Drum* sinks freighter *Taishu Maru* and cargo ship *Taihaku Maru*, 19°21′N, 120°50′E, and damages transports *Aoki Maru* and *Tatsura Maru*, 19°07′N, 120°42′E. *Icefish* sinks freighter *Taiyo Maru* west of Luzon Strait, 19°04′N, 120°36′E, but is damaged by depth charges and is forced to terminate her patrol.

Submarine *Rock* (SS 274), despite presence of escorting minesweeper *W.17*, sinks Japanese merchant tanker *No. 7 Takasago Maru* near Balabac Strait, 10°18′N, 117°47′E.

Japanese begin second phase of reinforcement of their garrisons on Leyte ("TA" Operation) with departure of convoy on this date, bound for Ormoc Bay (see 2 November).

British submarine HMS *Tantivy* shells Japanese motor sailships *No. 2 Katsura Maru* and *No. 3 Matsu Maru* in the Flores Sea, east of Sangean Island, 08°00′S, 119°10′E; the holed *No. 2 Katsura Maru* goes aground as *Tantivy* disengages. The damaged vessel is later towed to Bima, N.E.I., for repairs.

Special Air Task Force (STAG 1) operations in the southwest Pacific conclude as four TDRs are flown against lighthouse on Cape St. George, New Ireland. One of the four demolishes the structure.

USAAF B-24s and B-25s attack Japanese convoy about 160 miles southwest of Hong Kong, sinking freighters *Kaiko Maru* (ex-British *Mary Moller*) and *Doei Maru*, 20°50′N, 111°50′E.

Japanese freighter *Seito Maru* is sunk by mine (laid by RAAF Catalinas between 14–17 September or 11–19 October) off Sumatra, 03°12′S, 116°15′E.

Japanese freighter *Kompira Maru* is sunk by aircraft off Shimushur Island, Kurils.

27 Friday

PACIFIC. TG 38.3 (Rear Admiral Frederick C. Sherman) and TG 38.4 (Rear Admiral Ralph

E. Davison) attack Japanese ships and installations in the Visayas and northern Luzon area. Planes from carrier *Essex* (CV 9) sink destroyer *Fujinami* 80 miles north of Iloilo, Panay, 12°00′N, 122°30′E; planes from *Enterprise* (CV 6) sink destroyer *Shiranui* 80 miles north of Iloilo, Panay, 12°00′N, 122°30′E.[215]

Battleship *California* (BB 44) is damaged by strafing off Leyte, 16°57′N, 125°02′E; submarine chaser (rescue) *PCER 848* is damaged by horizontal bomber, 11°11′N, 125°05′E; and motor torpedo boat *PT 523* is damaged by dive bomber, 11°15′N, 124°59′E.

U.S. freighter *Benjamin Ide Wheeler* is damaged by *kamikaze* that crashes the ship, killing one merchant sailor and one of the 27-man Armed Guard (whose heavy gunfire damages the in-bound suicider) and sets fire to the gasoline cargo; salvage ship *Cable* (ARS 19) comes alongside and extinguishes the blaze while some of the ship's complement and passengers are transferred temporarily to nearby amphibious command ship *Wasatch* (AGC 9).

Damaged heavy cruiser *Canberra* (CA 70) and light cruiser *Houston* (CL 81) reach Ulithi, Carolines, with their supporting ships, their odyssey over.[216]

Submarine *Bergall* (SS 320) attacks Japanese convoy and sinks oiler *Nichiho Maru* and fleet tanker *Itsukushima Maru* west of Balabac Strait, 07°09′N, 116°40′E.

Submarine *Cero* (SS 225) drives Japanese guardboat *No. 3 Kyoei Maru* ashore, Luzon, 17°00′N, 119°00′E.

Submarine *Kingfish* (SS 234) sinks Japanese landing ship *T.138* and army cargo vessel *No. 4 Tokai Maru* 30 miles north-northeast of Iwo Jima, 25°22′N, 141°31′E.

Submarine *Nautilus* (SS 168) lands party of 12 men and 20 tons of cargo at selected spot on east coast of Luzon (see 31 October).

U.S. motor torpedo boats sink Japanese motor sailship *Kyoei Maru* off Ormoc Bay.

USAAF P-38s and P-47s sink Japanese motor sailship *Senshin Maru* off Mactan Island.

USAAF aircraft (14th Air Force) damage Japanese ship *Kashii Maru* in South China Sea, 14°25′N, 110°38′E.

28 Saturday

PACIFIC. TG 38.4 (Rear Admiral Ralph E. Davison) bombs Japanese shipping near Cebu, damaging landing ship *T.101* off Ormoc, Leyte, 11°00′N, 123°00′E.

Destroyer escort *Dempsey* (DE 26), assisted by tank landing craft *LCT 406*, sinks a Japanese torpedo-carrying craft off the main unloading

beach, Peleliu. U.S. freighter *United Victory* is damaged by gunfire from Japanese surface craft; there are no casualties to *United Victory*'s complement, which includes a 27-man Armed Guard.

Destroyer *Helm* (DD 388), assisted by *Gridley* (DD 380) and TBF from small carrier *Belleau Wood* (CVL 24), sinks Japanese submarine *I 46*, 120 miles northeast of Surigao, 10°56′N, 127°13′E.

Light cruiser *Denver* (CL 58) is damaged by *kamikaze* off Leyte, 10°57′N, 125°02′E. During Japanese air attack on U.S. shipping in San Pedro Bay, Leyte, freighter *Cape Romano* is damaged by bombs exploding close aboard; bomb fragments injure two of the 26-man Armed Guard and two of the 47-man merchant complement.

Destroyer escort *Eversole* (DE 404) is sunk by Japanese submarine *I 45* off Leyte, 10°18′N, 127°37′E; *I 45*, however, is, in turn, sunk by destroyer escort *Whitehurst* (DE 634) 120 miles east-northeast of Surigao, 10°10′N, 127°28′E.[217]

Netlaying ship *Viburnum* (AN 57) is damaged by mine at Ulithi, Carolines.

Japanese transport *Sumatra Maru* is sunk by swimmer vehicles ("Chariots") launched from British submarine I IMS *Trenchant*, Phuket Harbor, Siam, 07°54′N, 98°28′E.

Japanese merchant tanker *Baiei Maru* is sunk by Japanese mine in Brunei Bay, Borneo, 05°08′N, 115°05′E.

MEDITERRANEAN. Destroyer *Gleaves* (DD 423), operating off the Franco-Italian frontier, bombards troop concentrations, barracks, and gun emplacements; she achieves excellent results. Enemy shore battery fire is inaccurate.

29 Sunday

PACIFIC. TG 38.2 (Rear Admiral Gerald F. Bogan) attacks Japanese airfields in the Manila area and shipping in Manila Bay, damaging heavy cruiser *Nachi*; sister ship *Ashigara* escapes serious damage (see 5 November). During Japanese air attacks on the fast carriers operating off Leyte, a *kamikaze* crashes *Intrepid* (CV 11), 15°07′N, 124°01′E.

Submarine *Cero* (SS 225) arrives off Santiago Cove, on west coast of Luzon, to land men and supplies; as was the case at Darigayos Inlet (25–28 October), however, she does not make contact with local Filipino forces and shifts to a third site (see 2 November).

Japanese guardboat *No. 3 Kyoei Maru* is lost off Luzon; although the agent of her demise is unspecified, it is most likely Navy carrier-based aircraft, given the level of U.S. naval aviation activity in that area.

PB4Y (VPB 115) sinks Japanese tanker *Itsukushima Maru* off Brunei Bay, 05°04′N, 119°47′E. Destroyer *Shigure* rescues survivors.

Japanese army tanker *Kokko Maru* is sunk by RAAF mine off Balikpapan, Borneo, 01°17′S, 116°48′E.

U.S. aircraft sink Japanese guardboat *No. 16 Kiku Maru* at Rabaul.

U.S. freighter *John A. Johnson* is torpedoed by Japanese submarine *I 12*, 1,000 miles northeast of Oahu, 29°36′30″N, 141°43′W, and is abandoned when she breaks in two. *I 12* surfaces; shells the wreck, setting both halves ablaze; and then bears down on the lifeboats and rafts and fires on them with machine guns and pistols. These brutal actions result in the death of four of the 41 merchant sailors, the Army security officer, and four of the 28-man Armed Guard (see 30 October and 13 November).

Naval Operating Base, Leyte, and Naval Air Station, Samar, are established.

30 Monday

PACIFIC. Carrier *Franklin* (CV 13) and small carrier *Belleau Wood* (CVL 24) are damaged by *kamikazes*, 10°20′N, 126°40′E.

Yacht *Argus* (PY 14) rescues all survivors of U.S. freighter *John A. Johnson*, sunk by Japanese submarine *I 12* the previous day.

Submarine *Salmon* (SS 182) damages Japanese *Coast Defense Vessel No. 22* (one of three in the convoy screen) southwest of Toi Saki, Kyushu, and teams with *Trigger* (SS 237) to damage merchant tanker *Takane Maru*, 30°13′N, 132°49′E. *Salmon*, however, suffers cumulative damage—depth charges exploding close aboard (30°08′N, 132°33′E) and deep submergence—that forces termination of her patrol (see 31 October).

USAAF P-38s (13th Air Force) damage Japanese submarine chaser *Ch 36* near Sibitu Passage, 05°27′N, 119°12′E, and sink merchant tankers *Kosho Maru* and *No. 8 Nanshin Maru* off Sandakan, Borneo, 05°25′N, 119°20′E.

USAAF aircraft sink Japanese ship *Chuko Maru* off Hong Kong.

USAAF B-25s sink Japanese ship *No. 5 Uwa Maru* off Lomblon Island, 08°25′S, 123°25′E.

MEDITERRANEAN. Destroyer *Madison* (DD 425) bombards and destroys German motor convoy, southern France, and sinks floating mines offshore.

31 Tuesday

PACIFIC. Submarine *Gabilan* (SS 252) sinks Japanese oceanographic research vessel *No. 6*

Kaiyo Maru off Muroto Saki, Japan, 32°50′N, 134°21′E.

Submarine *Guitarro* (SS 363) attacks Japanese convoy and sinks cargo ship *Komei Maru* and army cargo ship *Pacific Maru* off Botolan Point, Luzon, 15°17′N, 119°50′E, and although damaged by the concussion generated by the explosion of one of these two ships, remains on patrol.

Submarine *Nautilus* (SS 168), en route to Mios Woendi after completing her clandestine mission (23, 24, and 27 October), finishes the destruction of submarine *Darter* (SS 227), aground on Bombay Shoal (09°26′N, 116°56′E) since 24 October, to prevent the boat from falling into enemy hands.

Submarine *Sterlet* (SS 392) sinks Japanese merchant tanker *Takane Maru*, damaged the day before by *Salmon* (SS 182) and *Trigger* (SS 237), southwest of Kyushu, 30°09′N, 132°45′E.

British submarine HMS *Stoic* sinks two Japanese sailing vessels, 07°40′S, 114°13′E, and bombards warehouses and fuel tanks at Jangka Island.

Motor gunboat *PGM 9* bombards Japanese targets on Aguijan Island, Marianas.

Japanese landing ship *T.131* is damaged by aircraft northeast of Panay; auxiliary submarine chaser *Uruppu Maru* is sunk by aircraft near Mindoro Island.

NOVEMBER

1 Wednesday

PACIFIC. In Leyte Gulf, *kamikazes* sink destroyer *Abner Read* (DD 526), 10°47′N, 125°22′E, and damage destroyers *Anderson* (DD 411), 10°11′N, 125°02′E, and *Claxton* (DD 571) and *Ammen* (DD 527), 10°40′N, 125°20′E. Japanese land attack planes (BETTYs) (702nd *Kokutai*) and FRANCESs damage destroyers *Bush* (DD 529), 10°13′N, 125°21′E, and *Killen* (DD 593), 10°40′N, 125°20′E.

Submarine *Atule* (SS 403) attacks Japanese convoy and sinks transport *Asama Maru* in Luzon Strait, 20°09′N, 117°38′E.

Submarine *Blackfin* (SS 322) attacks Japanese convoy and sinks auxiliary vessel *Caroline Maru* and transport *No. 12 Unkai Maru* in Mindoro Strait, 12°54′N, 120°10′E.[218]

Submarine *Ray* (SS 271) sinks Japanese merchant tanker *No. 7 Horai Maru*, 13°02′N, 120°17′E, and lands party of three men, together with two tons of supplies, at town of Mamburao, on west coast of Mindoro. *Ray* later transfers mail to *Nautilus* (SS 168) and

embarks two aviators and three escaped Allied POWs.

British submarine HMS *Storm* boards Japanese schooner *No. 3 Goenong Perak* in Gulf of Boni, southern Celebes, 04°56′S, 120°59′E; cargo of nickel ore discovered by the boarding party goes to the bottom when the enemy vessel is sunk by demolition charge.

Japanese oiler *Itsukushima Maru* is bombed and sunk by Navy aircraft off Tawi Tawi, 05°04′N, 119°47′E; destroyer *Shigure* rescues survivors.

MEDITERRANEAN. Destroyer *Benson* (DD 421), although troubled by inadequate spotting, fires bombardment mission against railroads and troop concentrations near Toulon, France.

2 Thursday

PACIFIC. Japanese naval land attack planes (701st *Kokutai*) bomb U.S. airstrip and planes on the ground at Tacloban, Leyte.

USAAF B-24s and P-38s (13th Air Force) attack Japanese reinforcement convoy ("TA" Operation, second phase) unloading reinforcements at Ormoc Bay, sinking army cargo ship *Noto Maru*, 10°30′N, 125°00′E. The rest of the convoy, however, returns safely to Manila.

Submarine *Barbero* (SS 317), despite presence of escort *No. 2 Shonan Maru*, sinks Surabaya-bound Japanese army cargo ship *Kuramazan Maru* in Makassar Strait, 04°30′S, 118°20′E.

Submarine *Cero* (SS 225) lands party of 14 men and 20 tons of supplies off the Masanga River, on east coast of Luzon, P.I., and embarks two USN pilots and two other Americans for evacuation. In addition, *Cero* receives important intelligence documents concerning the Philippine situation for urgent transmission to Commander Seventh Fleet.

Submarine *Pomfret* (SS 391) attacks Japanese convoy MOMA 06 in the Bashi Channel, torpedoing transports *Hamburg Maru* and *Atlas Maru*, 20°20′N, 121°30′E, and forces the convoy to seek shelter off Sabtang Island (see 3 November).

British submarine HMS *Shalimar* bombards Malacca, Car Nicobar, 03°16′N, 99°45′E, destroying beached landing barges and numerous other small craft.

British submarine HMS *Storm*, after first taking off the Malayan crews, sinks seven Japanese schooners by gunfire, Celebes, 04°38′S, 121°03′E.

British submarine HMS *Tantalus* attacks Japanese Singapore-to-Manila convoy SIMA 04, sinking cargo ship *Hachijin Maru* and damaging submarine chaser *Ch 1* about 225 miles east of Singapore, 00°48′N, 107°43′E.

British submarine HMS *Terrapin* sinks netlayer *Kumano Maru* in Strait of Malacca, 01°30′N, 103°00′E.

INDIAN OCEAN. U.S. tanker *Fort Lee* is torpedoed and sunk by German submarine *U 181* at 27°35′S, 83°11′E; of the 26-man Armed Guard, at least 10 perish in the loss of the ship (see 7, 9, and 16 November).

ANDAMAN SEA. Japanese army cargo ship *No. 2 Tateyama Maru* is sunk by aircraft off coast of Burma, 13°16′N, 99°46′E.

3 Friday

PACIFIC. Japanese aircraft attack air facilities on Saipan and Tinian as part of a series of strikes on this area from which heavy bombing missions against their home islands are launched.

Japanese planes raid U.S. shipping and airfield facilities at Tacloban, Leyte. U.S. freighter *Matthew P. Deady* is crashed by *kamikaze* that is engaged with intense antiaircraft fire from the Armed Guard; the explosion of the crashing suicider starts a fire in the cargo that threatens the ship. Although fire fighting efforts are successful, two Armed Guard sailors (of the 27-man detachment) and 26 troops (of the 300 on board) perish in the attack.

Light cruiser *Reno* (CL 96) is torpedoed by Japanese submarine *I 41* off Leyte, 13°46′N, 131°27′E. Not since 1942 has a Japanese submarine successfully attacked a ship operating with a fast carrier task force. High winds and heavy seas from a nearby typhoon complicate the task of saving *Reno*, but "skillful seamanship, courage, and the unremitting effort of all of those remaining on board" allow her to reach Ulithi, Carolines, on 11 November.

Submarine *Gurnard* (SS 254) attacks Japanese convoy in the South China Sea and sinks freighter *Taimei Maru* about 275 miles west of Labuan, Borneo, 05°48′N, 111°12′E.

Submarine *Pintado* (SS 387) attacks small detachment of Japanese warships in the South China Sea and sinks destroyer *Akikaze* 160 miles west of Lingayen Gulf, 16°50′N, 117°29′E.

Japanese transport *Hamburg Maru*, torpedoed by submarine *Pomfret* (SS 391) the previous night, sinks off Sabtang Island, 20°18′N, 121°51′E. Transport *Atlas Maru*, also torpedoed by *Pomfret*, is beached; salvage proceeds on *Atlas Maru* until a storm (8–10 November) causes further damage and forces discontinuance of those efforts.

Japanese freighter *Shino Maru* is sunk by aircraft off Palau.

MEDITERRANEAN. Destroyer *Woolsey* (DD 437) shells German troop concentrations near Franco-Italian border.

4 Saturday

PACIFIC. Submarines *Bream* (SS 243), *Guitarro* (SS 363), and *Ray* (SS 271) attack Japanese convoy TAMA 31 off western Luzon; evidence indicates that all three boats, despite presence of escorts (submarine chaser *Ch 5* and *Keishu Maru*), most likely sank transport *Kagu Maru* off Dasol Bay, 15°55′N, 119°44′E.

Submarine *Sailfish* (SS 192) damages Japanese destroyer *Harukaze* and landing ship *T.111* in Luzon Strait, 20°08′N, 121°43′E. Although damaged by aerial bombs, 20°09′N, 121°43′E, *Sailfish* remains on patrol; *Patrol Boat No. 38* takes the damaged *Harukaze* in tow and brings her into port.

British submarine HMS *Terrapin* attacks Japanese convoy in Strait of Malacca and sinks minesweeper *W.5*, 03°14′N, 99°50′E.

U.S. freighter *Frank J. Cuhel* is damaged by friendly fire while anchored off Tacloban, Leyte; the explosion of a shell wounds one of the 500 troops being transported by the ship and two of the 28-man Armed Guard. During Japanese air attack shortly thereafter, freighter *Cape Constance* is damaged when a *kamikaze*, having been hit by the heavy fire being put up by the Armed Guard gunners, explodes over the ship and scatters wreckage. Only the Armed Guard officer is wounded during the attack; there are no other casualties among the 41-man merchant complement and the 28-man Armed Guard.

MEDITERRANEAN. Destroyers *Benson* (DD 421) and *Woolsey* (DD 437) bombard German gun emplacements in Cap Ampeglio area.

5 Sunday

PACIFIC. TF 38 (Vice Admiral John S. McCain) begins two days of carrier strikes on Luzon, targeting Japanese aircraft, airfields, and shipping. TG 38.3 attacks warships and auxiliaries in Manila Bay; chief among the targets are

On board *Ticonderoga* (CV 14), a pilot readies himself to fly a mission against Japanese installations and shipping at Manila, 5 November 1944, in front of a sign chalked on a blackboard that reads: "49 SHOPPING DAYS TILL CHRISTMAS. SEND HOME A 'JAP'." Photograph taken by Lieutenant (j.g.) Wayne Miller. (NA, 80-G-469454)

heavy cruisers *Nachi* and *Ashigara*. Planes from carriers *Lexington* (CV 16) and *Essex* (CV 9) and small carrier *Langley* (CVL 27) sink *Nachi* five nautical miles southwest of Corregidor, 14°23′N, 120°25′E.[219] F6Fs from TG 38.3 sink *Patrol Boat No. 107* [ex-U.S. tug *Genessee* (AT 55)] off Lubang Island, 14°23′N, 120°25′E. Navy carrier-based planes (TG 38.3 hitting targets in Manila Bay, TG 38.1 targets off Santa Cruz) damage destroyer *Akebono* and escort destroyer *Okinawa*, landing ship *T.111*, motor sailship *Tanoguchi Maru,* and cargo ships *Toyu Maru* and *Showa Maru*. During Japanese retaliatory air strikes, *kamikaze* damages carrier *Lexington*, 16°20′N, 123°59′E.

Motor torpedo boat *PT 320* is damaged by aerial bomb off Leyte, 11°11′N, 125°05′E.

USAAF B-29s bomb Singapore, damaging Japanese fleet tanker *Notoro* while she lies in drydock at Selatar, 01°18N, 103°52′E.

Japanese landing ship *T.112* runs aground near Cape Bojeador, Luzon; sister ship *T.151* is ordered to the scene to take aboard the crew and cargo and return to Manila.

Japanese merchant ship *No. 11 Bakshu Maru* is sunk by mine off Penang.

6 Monday

PACIFIC. TF 38 (Vice Admiral John S. McCain) resumes strikes against Luzon; TG 38.3 planes sink Japanese landing ship *T.139*, Silanguin Bay, 14°35′N, 120°55′E. Planes from carrier *Ticonderoga* (CV 14), in TG 38.3, sink tanker *Marifu Maru*, previously damaged by submarine *Flier* (SS 250) on 13 June, in Mariveles Harbor, 14°26′N, 120°29′E.

Submarines *Guitarro* (SS 363), *Bream* (SS 243), *Raton* (SS 270), and *Ray* (SS 271) attack Japanese convoy MATA 31 off Cape Bolinao, Luzon. Although all four attack the previously damaged heavy cruiser *Kumano*, 16°11′N, 119°44′E, only *Ray's* "fish" actually strikes home and causes damage, blowing off the enemy warship's bow. Escorted by *Coast Defense Vessel No. 18*, *Kumano* is towed to Santa Cruz, Luzon, by auxiliary vessel *Doryo Maru* (see 9 November). *Guitarro* is damaged by depth charges at 15°54′N, 119°44′E (submarine chasers *Ch 18* and *Ch 37* and auxiliary submarine chaser *Michiryo Maru* are left at the scene to keep the U.S. boats down), but remains on patrol.

Submarine *Gurnard* (SS 254) lays mines off western Borneo.

Blockading of the Nanpo Shoto, by mining, begins as Project MIKE commences. USAAF B-24s (42nd Bomb Squadron) fly from Guam and stage through Isely Field, Saipan, where the mines are loaded and fuel tanks topped off. The B-24s lay 10 mines off Chichi Jima.

RAAF Mitchells sink Japanese auxiliary submarine chaser *Cha 118* off Soemba Island, N.E.I., 09°38′S, 120°17′E.

MEDITERRANEAN. Destroyer *Plunkett* (DD 431) shells German troop concentrations and pillboxes. She carries out shore bombardment against gun emplacement south of Ventimiglia, Italy.

7 Tuesday

UNITED STATES. President Roosevelt wins an unprecedented fourth term in the White House, defeating Republican challenger Thomas E. Dewey for the second time.

PACIFIC. Submarine *Albacore* (SS 218) is sunk by mine off the northern tip of Honshu, 41°49′N, 141°11′E.

Submarine *Greenling* (SS 213) sinks Japanese transport *No. 8 Kiri Maru* and merchant tanker *Kotai Maru*, 34°34′N, 138°35′E.

Motor torpedo boat *PT 301* is damaged by accidental explosion off western New Guinea, 01°15′S, 136°23′E.

INDIAN OCEAN. British motor vessel *Ernebank* rescues 16 survivors of U.S. tanker *Fort Lee*, torpedoed and sunk by German submarine *U 181* on 2 November (see 9 and 16 November).

8 Wednesday

PACIFIC. Japanese troops, armed with automatic weapons and light mortars, land on Ngeregong Island five miles northeast of Peleliu, under cover of typhoon, and force evacuation (without loss) of men from infantry landing craft (mortar) *LCI(M) 740*, which had been landed there three days before to provide protection for ships utilizing Denges Passage (see 9 November).

Submarine *Growler* (SS 215) is sunk, probably by Japanese destroyer *Shigure*, escort vessel *Chiburi*, and *Coast Defense Vessel No. 19* off Mindoro.

Submarine *Gunnel* (SS 253) attacks Japanese convoy MOMA 06 off west coast of Luzon and sinks torpedo boat *Sagi* about 60 miles west of Lingayen Gulf, 16°09′N, 118°56′E.

Submarine *Hardhead* (SS 365), despite proximity of aircraft and two escorts, sinks Japanese tanker *Manei Maru* about 90 miles southwest of Manila, 13°30′N, 119°25′E.

Submarine *Queenfish* (SS 393) attacks Japanese convoy off southern Kyushu and sinks cargo ship *Hakko Maru* and auxiliary submarine chaser *Ryusei Maru* near Uji Gunto, 31°10′N, 129°39′E.

Submarine *Redfin* (SS 272) attacks Japanese convoy MASI 03 and sinks merchant tanker *No. 2 Nichinan Maru* about 250 miles west of Manila, 14°00′N, 116°48′E (see 9 November).

Submarine *Sea Fox* (SS 402) attacks Japanese convoy TAMO 705 and sinks freighter *Keijo Maru* west of Amami-O-Shima, 29°05′N, 127°40′E.

9 Thursday

PACIFIC. Marine fighters based on Peleliu commence air strikes on Japanese on Ngeregong Island. These strikes, together with bombardment by vessels of LCI(L) Flotilla 13, will continue on 10 November, rendering it untenable for the invaders (see 15 November).

Project MIKE continues as USAAF B-24s (42nd Bomb Squadron) lay 10 mines in Futami Ko, Chichi Jima.

Submarine *Barbero* (SS 317) attacks Japanese convoy MASI 03, attacked the previous day by *Redfin* (SS 272), and sinks merchant tanker *Shimotsu Maru* about 250 miles west of Manila, 14°32′N, 116°53′E.

Submarine *Haddo* (SS 255) sinks Japanese tanker *No. 2 Hishi Maru* in Mindoro Strait, 12°24′N, 120°45′E.

Submarine *Queenfish* (SS 393) attacks Japanese convoy TAMA 28 in East China Sea and sinks gunboat *Chojusan Maru* about 50 miles west of Kyushu, 31°15′N, 129°10′E; *Himejima Maru* rescues survivors.

Japanese cruiser *Kumano*, damaged by U.S. submarines on 6 November, breaks her anchor and drifts aground off Santa Cruz, Luzon.

Japanese "TA" Operation (third phase) convoy reaches Ormoc Bay and unloads men and materiel brought from Manila (see 10 November).

USAAF B-25s and P-38s (13th Air Force) and motor torpedo boats *PT 492*, *PT 497*, *PT 524*, and *PT 525* begin attacks against Japanese convoy in Ormoc Bay, the former damaging escort vessels *Okinawa* and *Shimushu* (see 10 November).

INDIAN OCEAN. U.S. tanker *Tumacacori* rescues 17 survivors of U.S. tanker *Fort Lee*, torpedoed and sunk by German submarine *U 181* on 2 November (see 16 November).

10 Friday

PACIFIC. Ammunition ship *Mount Hood* (AE 11) is destroyed by accidental explosion in Seeadler Harbor, Manus, Admiralty Islands. The cataclysmic blast causes varying degrees of damage to ships in the vicinity: escort carriers *Petrof Bay* (CVE 80) and *Saginaw Bay* (CVE

82); destroyer *Young* (DD 580); destroyer escorts *Kyne* (DE 744), *Lyman* (DE 302), *Walter C. Wann* (DE 412), and *Oberrender* (DE 344); high-speed transport *Talbot* (APD 7); destroyer tender *Piedmont* (AD 17); auxiliary *Argonne* (AG 31); cargo ship *Aries* (AK 51); attack cargo ship *Alhena* (AKA 9); oiler *Cacapon* (AO 52); internal combustion engine repair ships *Cebu* (ARG 6) and *Mindanao* (ARG 3); salvage vessel *Preserver* (ARS 8); fleet tug *Potawatomi* (ATF 109); motor minesweepers *YMS 1*, *YMS 39*, *YMS 49*, *YMS 52*, *YMS 71*, *YMS 81*, *YMS 140*, *YMS 238*, *YMS 243*, *YMS 286*, *YMS 293*, *YMS 319*, *YMS 335*, *YMS 340*, *YMS 341*, and *YMS 342*; unclassified auxiliary *Abarenda* (IX 131); covered lighter *YF 681*; and fuel oil barge *YO 77*. *Mount Hood* has an estimated 3,000 tons of explosives on board, and except for a working party from the ship that is ashore at the time, her entire ship's company perishes. The force of the explosion blasts a trough in the harbor floor longer than the length of a football field and 50 feet wide and 30 to 40 feet deep; some fragments land more than 2,000 yards from where *Mount Hood* lies. Investigators find no fragment of the ship on the ocean floor larger than 16 × 10 feet. In terms of the extent of damage, it ranges from an estimated 48,000 man-hours to repair *Mindanao* (which suffers 23 dead and 174 injured) to "superficial" or "insignificant." In addition to the ships listed above, nine medium landing craft (LCM) and a pontoon barge moored to *Mount Hood* are also destroyed. Thirteen small boats or landing craft are sunk or damaged beyond repair; 33 are damaged but repairable.

Motor torpedo boat *PT 321*, damaged by grounding off Leyte, 11°25′N, 124°19′E, is scuttled.

Submarine *Barb* (SS 220) sinks Japanese transport *Gokoku Maru* seven miles off Koshiki Jima, eastern Kyushu, 33°24′N, 129°04′E.

Submarine *Flounder* (SS 251), apprised four days in advance of her quarry's schedule, sinks German submarine *U 537* in Java Sea, 07°13′S, 115°18′E. *U 537*'s projected 0700 position for this date is 07°12′S, 115°17′E.

Submarine *Greenling* (SS 213) sinks Japanese *Patrol Boat No. 46* (ex-destroyer *Fuji*) southeast of Honshu, 34°30′N, 138°34′E.

Submarine *Steelhead* (SS 280) sinks Japanese repair ship *Yamabiko Maru* south-southwest of Yokosuka, 31°42′N, 137°50′E.

USAAF B-25s, P-47s, and P-38s (13th Air Force) attack Japanese convoy ("TA" Operation, third phase) in Ormoc Bay, hit the previous day, sinking army cargo ships *Kashii Maru* and *Takatsu Maru*, 10°53′N, 124°25′E, and damaging destroyer *Akishimo*, *Coast Defense Vessel No. 13*, and army cargo ship *Kinka Maru*. B-25 attacks drive *Coast Defense Vessel No. 11* aground in Matlang Bay, where she is scuttled and abandoned, 10°54′N, 124°27′E. Nearby fast transports *T.6*, *T.9*, and *T.10*, however, escorted by destroyers *Take* and *Kasumi*, are unmolested. *T.6* and *T.10*, along with destroyers *Naganami* and *Asashimo*, rescue survivors from *Kashii Maru* and *Takatsu Maru*. On their return voyage to Manila, the convoy rescues men from *Celebes Maru*, which has run aground off Bondoc Point, Luzon, earlier that day (see 15 November).

USAAF B-24s attack Surabaya-bound Japanese ships off Soembawa, N.E.I., sinking *No. 21 Tachibana Maru*, *Fuji Maru*, and *Tsukushi Maru* and damaging *Benten Maru*.

11 Saturday

PACIFIC. Aircraft from TG 38.1 (Rear Admiral Alfred E. Montgomery), TG 38.3 (Rear Admiral Frederick C. Sherman), and TG 38.4 (Rear Admiral Ralph E. Davison) set upon Japanese convoy ("TA" Operation, fourth phase) as it enters Ormoc Bay, sinking destroyers *Hamanami*, *Naganami*, *Shimakaze*, and *Wakatsuki*; minesweeper *W.30*; army cargo ships *Mikasa Maru*, *Seiho Maru*, and *Tensho Maru*; and freighter *Taizan Maru* (ex-*St. Quentin*), 10°50′N, 124°35′E.

TG 30.2 (Rear Admiral Allan E. Smith) (three heavy cruisers and five destroyers) bombards airfields and other Japanese shore installations on Iwo Jima; shelling commences shortly before midnight and continues into 12 November. PB4Ys screen the group's approach, spot gunfire, and cover the retirement.

U.S. submarines begin series of attacks on Japanese convoy MOMA 07; *Queenfish* (SS 393) damages transport *Miho Maru* off Mike Harbor, 32°20′N, 128°00′E (see 12 and 14 November).

Submarine *Scamp* (SS 277) is sunk, probably by Japanese *Coast Defense Vessel No. 4* and naval aircraft off Tokyo Bay, 33°38′N, 141°00′E.

Japanese minesweeper *W.22* is sunk by mine off Babelthuap, Palau.

EUROPE. U.S. freighter *Lee S. Overman* is mined off Le Havre, France; outside of one merchant sailor injured, there are no casualties among the 39-man civilian complement and the 27-man Armed Guard. The ship is later written off as a total loss.

12 Sunday

PACIFIC. Landing craft repair ships *Egeria* (ARL 8) and *Achilles* (ARL 41) are damaged by *kamikazes* off Leyte, 11°11′N, 125°05′E. U.S. freighters off Leyte come under attack from Japanese planes as well. *Leonidas Merritt* is crashed by two suiciders off Dulag, Leyte, but her crew controls the fires; one of the 28-man Armed Guard is killed, as are a merchant seaman and one of the embarked stevedores. *Thomas Nelson* is hit by a *kamikaze*, but despite ultimately successful fire-fighting efforts, 133 of the 578 embarked troops are killed, as are three of the 28-man Armed Guard; 88 men are injured. *Jeremiah M. Daily* is struck by a suicider, and the explosion and fires account for the deaths of 100 of the 557 troops on board, in addition to two of the 29-man Armed Guard and four of the 39-man merchant complement; 43 more men are injured and 50 troops jump overboard to escape the flames (they are rescued by nearby boats and craft). *William A. Coulter* is struck by two *kamikazes*, but there are no fatalities among the 41-man merchant complement, 27-man Armed Guard, and four passengers. *Morrison R. Waite* is strafed and then crashed by a Japanese plane, and the resultant fires kill 21 troops and wound 41 (of the 600 embarked at the time); two of the 29-man Armed Guard are wounded in action. *Alexander Majors*'s Armed Guard gunners deflect a *kamikaze* with a well-placed 5-inch round, but the plane strikes the mainmast and, along with its bomb, explodes and showers the forward part of the ship with burning gasoline that compels the Armed Guards at the forward guns to leap overboard to save themselves. Two of the merchant crew are killed and 16 injured, but there are no fatalities among the Armed Guard sailors and the Army passengers. All six of the freighters ultimately return to the west coast of the United States under their own power for repairs.

Destroyer *Nicholas* (DD 449) sinks Japanese submarine *I 37* south of Yap, 08°04′N, 138°03′E.

Submarines *Barb* (SS 220) and *Peto* (SS 265) continue attacks against Japanese convoy MOMA 07 in the East China Sea. *Barb* sinks army cargo ship *Naruo Maru* and damages freighter *Kokuyo Maru*, 31°39′N, 125°36′E; cargo ship *Jinyo Maru* takes the damaged merchantman in tow (see 14 November). *Peto* sinks army cargo ship *Shinshu Maru*, 31°18′N, 125°30′E; army cargo ship *No. 1 Konan Maru* rescues survivors. *Coast Defense Vessel No. 8* conducts unsuccessful hunt for the U.S. boats.

Submarine *Redfin* (SS 272) attacks Japanese convoy, torpedoing freighter *Asogawa Maru* northwest of Palawan, 12°45′N, 118°14′E; submarine chaser *Ch 31* screens the damaged merchantman while *Ch 30* and *Patrol Boat No. 103* [ex-U.S. minesweeper *Finch* (AM 9)] shepherd the rest of the convoy toward Miri, Borneo.

PB4Y carries out low-level attack on Japanese convoy SIMA 04 and sinks freighter *Atsuta Maru* off Malampaya Sound, 11°50′N, 119°19′E.

Japanese auxiliary submarine chaser *Cha 84* is sunk by aircraft off Banggi, North Borneo.

Project MIKE continues as USAAF B-24s (42nd Bomb Squadron), finding cloudy weather at the primary objective, Chichi Jima, opt for the alternative, Haha Jima, and lay 15 mines in effective locations.

USAAF P-51s damage Japanese auxiliary-powered sailing vessel *Namikiri Maru* at entrance to Haiphong River, French Indochina.

ATLANTIC. German battleship *Tirpitz* is sunk by RAF Lancasters, Tromsö Fjord, Norway.

MEDITERRANEAN. Destroyer *Woolsey* (DD 437) shells German howitzer emplacement east of San Remo, Italy, and encounters "fairly accurate" 88-millimeter gunfire in return. Shrapnel showers the ship, but she suffers no casualties.

13 Monday

PACIFIC. Aircraft from three carrier task groups (TG 38.1, TG 38.3, and TG 38.4) of TF 38 (Rear Admiral Frederick C. Sherman, in the temporary absence of Vice Admiral John S. McCain) pound Japanese shipping and port facilities at Manila and in central Luzon. At the former place, TF 38 planes sink light cruiser *Kiso*, destroyers *Hatsuharu* and *Okinami*, and auxiliary submarine chaser *Cha 116*, 14°35′N, 120°50′E, and army cargo ships *Eiwa Maru*, *Kinka Maru*, *Kakogawa Maru*, *Sekiho Maru*, and *Teiyo Maru*, as well as freighters *Taitoku Maru*, *Hatsu Maru*, *Seiwa Maru*, and *Shinkoku Maru*, 14°35′N, 120°55′E; planes damage destroyer *Ushio*. At Cavite, Navy carrier planes sink destroyers *Akebono* and *Akishimo*, fleet tanker *Ondo*, and guardboat *Daito Maru*, 14°29′N, 120°55′E. TF 38 planes also sink army cargo ship *Heian Maru* at Cabcaben and auxiliary submarine chaser *Cha 116* some 20 nautical miles west of Cavite, 14°30′N, 120°45′E.

Minesweeper *Ardent* (AM 340) and frigate *Rockford* (PF 48) sink Japanese submarine *I 12* between San Francisco and Hawaii, 31°55′N, 139°45′W.

Submarine *Seal* (SS 183) sinks Japanese freighter *Gassan Maru* north-northwest of Etorofu, Kurils, 45°35′N, 148°14′E. *Seal's* "lurking off shore" makes it difficult for shipping in the area to proceed independently.

Japanese submarine *I 53* is damaged, cause unspecified, off Marcus Island.

14 Tuesday

PACIFIC. TF 38 (Rear Admiral Frederick C. Sherman) air strikes against Japanese shipping in Philippines continue. At Manila, Navy carrier-based planes sink transport *Tatsura Maru*, merchant tanker *No. 5 Horai Maru*, and freighters *Hatsu Maru* and *Aoki Maru* and damage transport *Tottori Maru* and army cargo ship *Myogi Maru*. Cargo ship *Yukihisa Maru* is sunk just outside Manila Bay, 13°58′N, 120°36′E; light cruiser *Kiso*, sunk the previous day, is bombed again. Off Mindoro, F6Fs from carrier *Yorktown* (CV 10) attack Japanese convoy SIMA 04, sinking merchant tanker *Ayagiri Maru*, 12°40′N, 120°41′E, and damaging army cargo ship *Yutaka Maru* (see 15 November), as well as causing varying degrees of damage to the four submarine chasers (*Ch 1*, *Ch 19*, *Ch 26*, and *Ch 36*) that are escorting the convoy.

Submarine *Halibut* (SS 232) is damaged by depth charges and aerial bombs, Luzon Strait, 20°56′N, 121°33′E, but returns from patrol with no difficulty.

Submarine *Jack* (SS 259) attacks Japanese convoy, sinking freighter *Hinaga Maru* and damaging merchant tanker *No. 2 Yuzan Maru* off Cape Padaran, French Indochina, 11°02′N, 109°02′E (see 15 November).

Submarines *Batfish* (SS 310), *Raton* (SS 270), and *Ray* (SS 271) attack Japanese convoy off the northwest coast of Luzon. *Raton* sinks merchant tanker *No. 5 Unkai Maru*, 17°48′N, 117°58′E; *Ray* sinks *Coast Defense Vessel No. 7*, 65 miles northwest of Cape Bolinao, 17°45′N, 117°45′E (see 15 November).

Submarine *Skipjack* (SS 184) damages Japanese motor sailship *No. 6 Tatsu Maru* off Shimushir, Kurils, 46°40′E, 151°40′E. Strong currents then drive the damaged vessel up on a reef; she is declared a total loss.

Submarine *Spadefish* (SS 411) sinks Japanese freighter *Kokuyo Maru*, previously damaged by *Barb* (SS 220) on 12 November while in convoy MOMA 07, while the damaged merchantman is being towed by cargo ship *Jinyo Maru* toward Singapore, 31°04′N, 123°56′E. *Coast Defense Vessel No. 54* conducts unsuccessful hunt for *Spadefish*.

British submarine HMS *Thorough* shells three Japanese auxiliary sailing vessels in Strait of Malacca, 04°03′N, 100°32′E, sinking one; auxiliary submarine chaser *Cha 113* arrives too late to carry out counterattack.

Project MIKE continues as USAAF B-24s (42nd Bomb Squadron) lay six mines in effective locations off Ani Jima and Haha Jima, Bonins.

During Japanese air raid on U.S. shipping off Leyte, freighter *Floyd B. Olson* is damaged by bomb; there are, however, no casualties among the 43-man merchant complement, the 28-man Armed Guard, and the 409 stevedores embarked to work cargo.

USAAF B-24 sinks Japanese lugger *Kiho Maru* off Sandakan Harbor, Borneo.

Japanese ship *Heiyo* is sunk by mine, Adang Bay, 01°43′S, 116°26′E. *Heiyo's* loss releases minesweeper *W.11* from escort duties.

15 Wednesday

PACIFIC. TG 78.14 (Captain Lord Ashbourne, RN) lands Army troops (31st Division) on Mapia Island, 160 nautical miles northeast of Sansapor, New Guinea.

Marines reoccupy Ngeregong Island (see 9 November), finding that the Japanese have abandoned it after being pounded by USMC aircraft and LCI(L) bombardment.

Submarine *Barbel* (SS 316) attacks Japanese convoy in the South China Sea about 250 miles east of Tourane, French Indochina, sinking transports *Misaki Maru*, 15°10′N, 112°40′E, and *Sugiyama Maru*, 15°14′N, 112°14′E, and escapes search carried out by minesweepers *W.18* and *W.20*.

Submarine *Batfish* (SS 310) continues attack against Japanese convoy off Luzon, sinking supply ship *Kurasaki* north-northwest of Cape Bolinao, 17°41′N, 118°00′E; destroyer *Kuretake* rescues survivors.

Submarine *Guavina* (SS 362) sinks abandoned Japanese army cargo ship *Yutaka Maru*, damaged the previous day by Navy carrier-based aircraft, off Mindoro, 12°25′N, 120°55′E.

Submarine *Jack* (SS 259), operating in the South China Sea, attacks Japanese convoy MI 20, sinking Japanese transports *Nichiei Maru*, 11°11′N, 108°56′E, and *No. 2 Yuzan Maru*, 11°15′N, 108°57′E.

Submarine *Queenfish* (SS 393) attacks Japanese convoy HI 81 and sinks army cargo ship/aircraft transport *Akitsu Maru* at southern entrance of Tsushima Strait, about 60 miles east of Saishu Island, 33°05′N, 128°38′E.

Submarine *Saury* (SS 189) damages Japanese guardboat *Kojo Maru*, northwest of the Bonins, 29°59′N, 139°44′E (see 16 November).

Submarines *Sterlet* (SS 392) and *Silversides*

(SS 236) engage Japanese guardboat *No. 12 Hachiryu Maru* in a spirited surface gunnery action northwest of Ogasawara Gunto, 30°10′N, 137°23′E. *No. 12 Hachiryu Maru* makes port, but will perform no more active service. An account of her battle with *Sterlet* and *Silversides* is broadcast to the Japanese people.

PB4Y completes destruction of Japanese ship *Celebes Maru*, aground since 10 November off Bondoc Point, Luzon, 13°17′N, 112°37′E.

Navy land-based aircraft sink Japanese ship *Harufuji Maru* off Borneo, 06°52′N, 116°51′E.

USAAF P-38s damage Japanese gunboat *Man-Yo Maru* off Balikpapan, Borneo.

RAF Liberators bomb Japanese shipping at Mergui, sinking *No. 3 Tanshin Maru* and communications boat *Kasumi*.

ATLANTIC. Destroyer escort *Frament* (DE 677) is damaged when she accidentally collides with, and sinks, Italian submarine *Luigi Settembrini* 685 miles west of Gibraltar.

16 Thursday

PACIFIC. Submarine *Scabbardfish* (SS 397) sinks Japanese transport *Kisaragi Maru* north by west of Chichi Jima, 29°04′N, 142°12′E.

Submarine *Tambor* (SS 198) engages and sinks Japanese guardboat *Takashiro Maru* in a surface gunnery action southwest of Tori Jima, 30°00′N, 139°30′E, and takes survivors prisoner.

Japanese guardboat *Kojo Maru*, damaged the previous day by submarine *Saury* (SS 189), sinks northwest of the Bonins, 29°59′N, 139°39′E.

USAAF B-24s and P-38s sink fleet tanker *Kyoei Maru* and damage gunboat *Man-yo Maru* off Tarakan, Borneo.

Japanese transport *Amakusa Maru* is damaged when she accidentally rams and sinks cargo vessel *Shinan Maru* near Keelung, Formosa.

INDIAN OCEAN. U.S. freighter *Mary Ball* rescues 17 survivors of U.S. tanker *Fort Lee*, torpedoed and sunk by German submarine *U 181* on 2 November, but not before she has fired on the lifeboat until identifying it as friendly. Fortunately, there are no casualties.

EUROPE. U.S. freighter *Theodore Parker* is mined about 12 miles east of the mouth of the Humber River, 53°33′N, 00°39′E, but returns, under her own power, to the port of Hull, Yorkshire, England, for repairs. There are no casualties to the 42-man merchant complement or the 27-man Armed Guard.

17 Friday

PACIFIC. Attack transport *Alpine* (APA 92) is damaged by *kamikaze* off Leyte, 11°07′N, 125°02′E. Elsewhere, during a Japanese air raid on shipping off RED beach, Leyte, freighter *Benjamin Ide Wheeler* is damaged by bombs; there are no casualties.

TBMs (VC 82) from escort carrier *Anzio* (CVE 57) and destroyer escort *Lawrence C. Taylor* (DE 415) sink Japanese submarine *I 26* in Philippine Sea west of Samar, 12°44′N, 130°42′E.

Submarine *Bluegill* (SS 242) is damaged by depth charges in Makassar Strait, 00°48′N, 118°52′E, but remains on patrol.

Submarines *Burrfish* (SS 312) and *Ronquil* (SS 396) fight a spirited surface gunnery action with Japanese guardboat *Fusa Maru* in heavy weather south of Hachiro Jima, 32°15′N, 140°00′E; American gunfire damages the enemy patrol craft, but not before she in turn damages *Burrfish*. *Ronquil* is damaged by own gunfire (premature explosion of 40-millimeter shell or contact with lifeline stanchion) and is forced to terminate her patrol. *Fusa Maru* makes port but is written off as a total loss. She performs no more active service.

Submarine *Gunnel* (SS 253) attacks Japanese convoy and sinks torpedo boat *Hiyodori* and merchant tanker *Shunten Maru* 130 miles east of Tourane, French Indochina, 16°56′N, 110°30′E, and survives counterattacks by destroyer *Shiokaze* and submarine chaser *Ch 21*.

Submarine *Picuda* (SS 382) sinks Japanese landing ship *Mayasan Maru* and damages merchant tanker *Awagawa Maru* in the Yellow Sea, northwest by north of Okinawa, 33°16′N, 124°43′E.

Submarine *Spadefish* (SS 411) attacks Japanese convoy HI 81 and sinks escort carrier *Shinyo* 140 miles northeast of Shanghai, China, in the Yellow Sea, 33°02′N, 123°33′E, and damages landing ship *Shinshu Maru*.

Submarine *Sunfish* (SS 281) attacks Japanese convoy MI 27 and torpedoes army transport *Edogawa Maru* west of Quelpart Island, 33°40′N, 124°30′E, and survives counterattacks by *Coast Defense Ship No. 61*. *Edogawa Maru* sinks the next day (see 18 November).

Project MIKE continues as USAAF B-24s (42nd Bomb Squadron) lay eight mines in effective locations in Futami Ko, Chichi Jima.

USAAF P-38s sink Japanese ships *Jinko Maru* and *No. 3 Yawata Maru* off Merida, 10°55′N, 124°30′E.

Japanese merchant tanker *Seian Maru* runs aground off entrance to Subic Bay (see 19 November).

MEDITERRANEAN. Destroyer *Woolsey* (DD 437) shells German artillery at Ventimiglia, Italy; shrapnel again showers the ship but she suffers no casualties; destroyer *Benson* (DD 421) bombards barracks in same area.

18 Saturday

PACIFIC. Destroyer escort *Lawrence C. Taylor* (DE 415) and TBM (VC 82) from escort carrier *Anzio* (CVE 57) sink Japanese submarine *I 41* in Philippine Sea east of Samar, 12°44′N, 130°42′E.

Submarine *Blackfin* (SS 322), diverted from her war patrol, picks up captured Japanese cryptographic equipment and other secret documents, in addition to other technical equipment, from spot west of Camurong River, on north coast of Mindoro, P.I.[220]

Submarine *Pampanito* (SS 383) sinks Japanese depot ship *No. 17 Banshu Maru* and freighter *No. 1 Shinko Maru* off Hainan Island, 19°12′N, 110°51′E.

Submarines *Peto* (SS 265), *Spadefish* (SS 411), and *Sunfish* (SS 281) operate against the same Japanese convoy (MI 27) attacked the previous day in the East China Sea west of Saishu Island. *Peto* sinks army cargo ships *Aisakasan Maru*, 33°50′N, 124°44′E, and *Chinkai Maru*, 33°39′N, 124°26′E; *Spadefish* sinks auxiliary submarine chaser *Cha 156*, 33°07′N, 123°19′E; and *Sunfish* sinks army transport *Seisho Maru*, 33°36′N, 124°18′E.

Submarine *Saury* (SS 189) damages Japanese freighter *No. 11 Asahi Maru* north by west of Chichi Jima, 30°50′N, 141°56′E.

Japanese planes raid U.S. shipping off Leyte; freighter *Nicholas J. Sinnott* is near-missed by a *kamikaze*, 11°15′45″N, 125°02′45″E. There are no casualties among the 40-man merchant complement, the 80 Army passengers, or the 26-man Armed Guard. Off Tacloban, Armed Guard gunners on board freighter *Gilbert Stuart* shoot the tail off a *kamikaze* that nevertheless crashes their ship, triggering fires that are ultimately brought under control with the help of fleet tug *Chickasaw* (ATF 83). While five of the 39-man merchant complement perish in the attack, only one of the 29-man Armed Guard is killed in action. Freighter *Cape Romano* is damaged by near-miss of bomb.

Project MIKE continues as USAAF B-24s (42nd Bomb Squadron) lay 12 mines in effective locations in Futami Ko, Chichi Jima. B-24s sink auxiliary sailing vessel *Sumiei Maru* off Haha Jima.

USAAF B-24s bomb Japanese shipping off Labuan, Borneo, damaging escort destroyer *Okinawa*; guardboats *No. 6 Kompira Maru*, *Benten Maru*, and *Eikoku Maru* are sunk by U.S. aircraft off Tarakan.

EUROPE. Tank landing ship *LST 6* is sunk by mine in Seine River, France.

ATLANTIC. Destroyer escort *Camp* (DE 251) is damaged in collision with tanker *Santa Cecilia* off coast of southern Ireland.

MEDITERRANEAN. Motor torpedo boat *PT 311* is sunk by mine off Spezia, Italy, 43°41′N, 09°37′E.

19 Sunday

PACIFIC. TF 38 (Vice Admiral John S. McCain) aircraft attack Japanese shipping off Luzon, in addition to airfields on that island. Navy carrier-based planes attack convoy 10 miles off San Fernando, sinking freighter *Esashi Maru* and damaging escorting submarine chasers *Ch 19* and *Ch 26*, 16°50′N, 120°08′E. Heavy cruiser *Kumano* is strafed by F6Fs.

Elements of TG 78.14 (Captain Lord Ashbourne, RN) land Army troops (31st Division) on Asia Island, 100 nautical miles west of Sansapor, New Guinea.

Destroyer escorts *Conklin* (DE 439) and *McCoy Reynolds* (DE 440) sink Japanese submarine *I 37*, 100 miles west of Palaus, 08°07′N, 134°16′E.[221]

Submarine *Hake* (SS 256) torpedoes Japanese light cruiser *Isuzu* west of Corregidor, 14°22′N, 119°38′E.

British submarine HMS *Stratagem* sinks Japanese merchant tanker *Nichinan Maru* in Strait of Malacca, 01°36′N, 102°53′E.

U.S. freighter *Alcoa Pioneer* is crashed by *kamikaze*, San Pedro Bay, Leyte, killing six of the 28-man Armed Guard. Thirteen other men from among the 46-man merchant complement and two passengers are injured; patrol escort vessel *PCE 851* provides medical assistance. Nearby, a second *kamikaze* crashes Norwegian motor vessel *General Fleischer*, while a third crashes U.S. freighter *Cape Romano*; there are, however, no casualties among *Cape Romano*'s 47-man merchant complement, her two passengers, or the 26-man Armed Guard.

Planes from carrier *Hornet* (CV 12) and small carrier *Monterey* (CVL 26) sink Japanese motor sailship *No. 8 Kyoun Maru* off Mindoro.

Aircraft sink Japanese submarine chaser *Ch 36* and merchant tanker *Seian Maru*, grounded since 17 November, off Subic Bay.

USAAF B-24s damage Japanese transport *Natsukawa Maru* off Brunei Bay, Borneo, 05°20′N, 115°13′E; *Natsukawa Maru*, however, does not return to service, a total loss.

20 Monday

ATLANTIC. Heavy cruiser *Augusta* (CA 31) is damaged by explosion of unknown origin, Boston (Massachusetts) Navy Yard.

PACIFIC. Oiler *Mississinewa* (AO 59) is sunk by *kaiten* (fired by Japanese submarine *I 47* or *I 36*), Ulithi, 10°06′N, 139°43′E.[222]

Japanese planes attack three U.S. tankers proceeding from Ulithi to Eniwetok; near-misses and strafing account for damage to tanker *Fort Dearborn* at 12°00′N, 155°00′E. There are, however, only four men wounded among the ship's 50-man merchant complement, 27-man Armed Guard, and five passengers.

Submarine *Atule* (SS 403) sinks Japanese minesweeper *W.38* southwest of Formosa, 21°21′N, 119°45′E.

USAAF B-25 (14th Air Force) sinks Japanese freighter *Daichi Maru* in Yangtze River northeast of Shanghai, China, 31°57′N, 122°18′E.

USAAF B-25s sink Japanese ship *No. 79 Nanyo Maru* off Timor, N.E.I.

ANDAMAN SEA. British submarine HMS *Tally Ho* sinks Japanese auxiliary minesweeper *Ma 4* 30 miles east of the southern tip of Great Nicobar Island, 06°55′N, 94°15′E.

21 Tuesday

PACIFIC. TF 92 (Rear Admiral John L. McCrea), comprising two light cruisers and nine destroyers, bombards Japanese naval air installations on Matsuwa Island, Kurils.

Submarines *Bashaw* (SS 241) and *Flounder* (SS 251) attack Japanese convoy in the South China Sea, sinking army cargo ship *Gyosan Maru*, 10°36′N, 115°08′E.

Submarine *Scabbardfish* (SS 397) sinks Japanese victualling stores ship *Hokkai Maru* 200 nautical miles south of Tokyo, 33°20′N, 142°00′E.

Submarine *Sealion* (SS 315) attacks Japanese task force (three battleships, a light cruiser, and three destroyers) and sinks battleship *Kongo* and destroyer *Urakaze* about 60 miles north-northwest of Formosa, 26°07′N, 121°36′E.

Japanese oceanographic research vessel *Kaiyo No. 2* is sunk by U.S. aircraft in the Celebes Sea.

USAAF B-24 sinks Japanese ship *Shinsei Maru* in Makassar Strait, 02°04′N, 119°12′E.

Japanese cargo ship *Fukurei Maru* is sunk by

marine casualty off west coast of Korea, 38°08′N, 124°34′E.

22 Wednesday

PACIFIC. TG 38.4 (Rear Admiral Ralph E. Davison) aircraft bomb Japanese air facilities on Yap, Carolines.

Japanese planes raid U.S. air facility at Morotai, N.E.I., destroying 15 bombers and damaging 31.

Submarine *Besugo* (SS 321) sinks Japanese landing ship *T.151* off northern tip of Palawan, 11°22′N, 119°07′E.

Submarine *Guavina* (SS 362) sinks Japanese army cargo ship *Dowa Maru* near Tizard's Bank, northwest of Borneo, 10°22′N, 114°21′E.

Submarine *Scabbardfish* (SS 397) damages Japanese escort vessel *Oki* southeast of Nojima Saki, 33°20′N, 142°00′E.

Japanese auxiliary submarine chaser *Cha 82* is sunk by aircraft off Balabac Island, P.I., 08°00′N, 117°00′E.

USAAF planes damage Japanese cargo ship *Enoshima Maru* at Makassar.

23 Thursday

PACIFIC. Attack transport *James O'Hara* (APA 90) is damaged by *kamikaze* off Leyte, 10°57′N, 125°02′E.

U.S. freighter *Gus W. Darnell* is torpedoed by Japanese plane off Samar Island, P.I., and catches fire. Beached to facilitate salvage, the ship is ultimately declared a total loss. There are no fatalities among the 41-man merchant complement, 27-man Armed Guard, and 15 Army passengers, although 17 men are injured.

Submarines *Bang* (SS 385) and *Redfish* (SS 395) attack Japanese convoy TAKA 206 in the Formosa Strait. *Bang* sinks freighter *Sakae Maru* and transport *Amakusa Maru*, 24°21′N, 122°28′E; *Redfish* sinks freighter *Hozan Maru*, 24°27′N, 122°47′E.

Submarine *Gar* (SS 206), after primary locations are deemed compromised, lands men and supplies at Santiago Cove, Luzon, and on the north coast of Mindoro; she also picks up intelligence documents.

Submarine *Picuda* (SS 382) attacks Japanese convoy TAMO 29 in Tsushima Strait, sinking freighters *Fukuju Maru*, 34°19′N, 128°05′E, and *Shuyo Maru*, 34°19′N, 128°58′E.

GULF OF PANAMA. District patrol vessel *YP 383* is sunk in collision with infantry landing craft *LCI(L) 873*, 08°22′N, 79°29′W.

MEDITERRANEAN. Motor torpedo boat patrol attacks south-bound convoy off Portofino,

Italy, damaging two coasters, while engaged by German shore battery that inflicts no damage on the PTs.

EUROPE. U.S. freighter *William D. Burnham* is torpedoed by German submarine *U 978* about five miles off Barfleur, France; 10 of the 26-man Armed Guard perish, as do eight of the 41-man merchant complement. British escort drifter HMS *Fidget* rescues survivors, transferring most to motor torpedo boat *PT 461*, and the wounded to British destroyer HMS *Vesper*. Salvage tug *ATR 3* later tows *William D. Burnham* to Cherbourg where the freighter is beached and ultimately assessed as a total loss.

24 Friday

PACIFIC. USAAF B-29s based in the Marianas raid Tokyo, Japan, for the first time.

Motor torpedo boats are relieved of patrol duty in the northern Solomons. Infantry landing craft gunboats [LCI(G)] and motor gunboats [PGM] will operate in their stead.

Submarine chaser *PC 1124* and infantry landing craft *LCI 976* are damaged by dive bombers off Leyte, 10°50'N, 125°25'E.

USAAF P-40s and P-47s (13th Air Force) attack one of the groups of ships involved in the fifth phase of "TA" Operation, sinking submarine chaser *Ch 46* and landing ships *T.111*, *T.141*, and *T.160* in Cataingan Bay, Masbate Island, 11°35'N, 124°10'E.

Japanese weather observation ship *Tenkai No. 3* is damaged by aircraft off Balabac, P.I.

25 Saturday

PACIFIC. TG 38.2 (Rear Admiral Gerald F. Bogan) and TG 38.3 (Rear Admiral Frederick C. Sherman) aircraft bomb Japanese shipping off central Luzon. SB2Cs and TBMs from carrier *Ticonderoga* (CV 14) sink heavy cruiser *Kumano* in Santa Cruz Harbor, 15°45'N, 119°48'E. F6Fs, SB2Cs, and TBMs from carriers *Ticonderoga* and *Essex* (CV 9), along with F6Fs and TBMs from small carrier *Langley* (CVL 27), attack convoy about 15 miles southwest of Santa Cruz, on the west coast of Luzon, and sink coast defense ship *Yasojima* (ex-Chinese cruiser *Ping Hai*), 15°45'N, 119°45'E, and landing ships *T.112*, *T.142*, and *T.161*, 15°40'N, 119°45'E. Planes from carrier *Intrepid* (CV 11) sink fast transports *T.6* and *T.10*, and damage fast transport *T.9* and escort destroyer *Take*, Balanacan Harbor, Marinduque Island, 13°25'N, 121°55'E. Planes from *Essex* and *Langley* sink army cargo ship *No. 6 Manei Maru* and damage cargo ship *Kasagisan Maru* off San Fernando, 16°37'N, 120°19'E. Japanese merchant tanker *Ceram Maru* is damaged by aircraft in Manila Bay.

Kamikazes breach the fleet's fighter defenses, however, and press home determined attacks, damaging carriers *Essex, Intrepid,* and *Hancock* (CV 19), 15°47'N, 124°14'E, and small carrier *Cabot* (CVL 28), 15°42'N, 123°09'E. Small carrier *Independence* (CVL 22) is damaged when a VF(N) 41 F6F-5N crashes into the island structure, 15°58'N, 125°14'E.

Motor torpedo boat *PT 363* is sunk by shore battery off Cape Gorango, Halmahera Island, 00°55'N, 127°50'E.

Submarine *Atule* (SS 403) sinks Japanese freighter *Santos Maru* off Sabtang Island, Luzon, 20°12'N, 121°51'E. Although *Atule* claims destruction of escorting submarine chaser *Ch 33*, the latter survives the attack.

Submarine *Cavalla* (SS 244) sinks Japanese destroyer *Shimotsuki* west of Borneo, 02°28'N, 107°20'E.

Submarine *Haddo* (SS 255) torpedoes Japanese escort destroyer *Shimushu* in South China Sea, west-southwest of Manila, 14°00'N, 119°25'E.

Submarine *Hardhead* (SS 365) attacks Japanese convoy about 60 miles west of Manila and sinks *Coast Defense Vessel No. 38* off Bataan Peninsula, 14°33'N, 119°51'E.

Submarine *Mingo* (SS 261) attacks Japanese convoy SIMA 05, sinking army transport *Manila Maru* about 90 miles northwest of Miri, Sarawak, 05°30'N, 113°24'E, and surviving counterattack by escort vessel *Kurahashi*.

Submarine *Pomfret* (SS 391) sinks Japanese *Patrol Boat No. 38* and transport *Shoho Maru*, Luzon Strait, 20°18'N, 121°34'E.

USAAF B-24s (14th Air Force), on night reconnaissance flight over the South China Sea, attack Japanese convoy SATA 02, south of Hainan Island, bombing and strafing *Hida Maru* and escorting minesweepers *W.17* and *W.18*, 16°44'N, 108°24'E, damaging both minecraft. *Hida Maru* takes the crippled *W.18* in tow (see 26 November).

Chinese aircraft attack Japanese river gunboats on the Yangtze near Anking, China, sinking *Fushimi* and damaging *Sumida*.

26 Sunday

PACIFIC. Submarine *Raton* (SS 270) sinks Japanese ammunition ship *Onoe Maru* north of Bismarck Archipelago, 00°40'N, 148°20'E.

Submarine *Pargo* (SS 264) damages Japanese fleet tanker *Yuho Maru* off Miri, Sarawak, 04°55'N, 114°06'E, and although damaged by depth charges from one or both of the auxiliary vessel's escorts, remains on patrol.

U.S. freighter *Howell Lykes* is bombed by Japanese planes, San Pedro Bay, Leyte, and damaged by near-misses; while there are no casualties among the 41-man Armed Guard and 58 Army passengers, two of the ship's 79-man merchant complement are wounded in the attack.

Japanese minesweeper *W.18* sinks as the result of damage inflicted by USAAF B-24s (14th Air Force) the previous night, 16°52'N, 108°38'E.

Chinese planes damage Japanese river gunboats *Hira* and *Hozu* in the Yangtze River near Anking.

27 Monday

PACIFIC. Destroyers bombard Japanese positions at Ormoc Bay, Leyte; firing continues on 28 November. In Leyte Gulf, *kamikazes* sink submarine chaser *SC 744*, 10°44'N, 125°07'E, and damage battleship *Colorado* (BB 45) and light cruisers *St. Louis* (CL 49) and *Montpelier* (CL 57), 10°50'N, 125°25'E.

Japanese planes also strike airfields and aircraft on the ground at Saipan in a surprise mid-day raid, destroying three USAAF B-29s and a P-47 and damaging three B-29s, a B-24, and a P-47.

Organized Japanese resistance on Peleliu ends.

Japanese freighter *Kinko Maru* is sunk by aircraft, Yangtze River.

28 Tuesday

PACIFIC. Destroyers *Saufley* (DD 465), *Waller* (DD 466), *Pringle* (DD 477), and *Renshaw* (DD 499) sink Japanese submarine *I 46* in Leyte Gulf, 10°48'N, 124°35'E.

Submarine *Guavina* (SS 362) attacks Japanese convoy, 12°54'N, 109°21'E, but while success eludes her, she escapes counterattacks by submarine chaser *Ch 43*.

USAAF B-24 (13th Air Force) sinks Japanese merchant tanker *Atago Maru* off Miri, Borneo, 04°29'N, 114°00'E.

29 Wednesday

PACIFIC. In Leyte Gulf, *kamikazes* damage battleship *Maryland* (BB 46), 10°41'N, 125°23'E, and destroyers *Saufley* (DD 465), 10°50'N, 125°25'E, and *Aulick* (DD 569), 10°35'N, 125°40'E.

U.S. freighter *William C. C. Claiborne*, anchored off Leyte, is hit by what is most likely friendly fire that wounds three of the 28-man

Armed Guard and one of the ship's 42-man merchant complement.

Motor torpedo boats attack Japanese shipping in Ormoc Bay. *PT 127* sinks *Patrol Boat No. 105* (ex-Philippine *Arayat*), 10°59′N, 124°33′E; *PT 128* and *PT 191* sink auxiliary minelayer *Kusentai No. 105*.

USAAF B-25s and P-47s (5th Air Force) attack Japanese shipping near Ormoc Bay, sinking submarine chaser *Ch 45*, 10°25′N, 124°00′E. P-40s and P-47s sink army cargo ship *Shinetsu Maru* off Camotes Island, 10°47′N, 124°17′E, and cargo ship *Shinsho Maru* off Ormoc, 11°01′N, 124°36′E.

Submarine *Archerfish* (SS 311) sinks Japanese carrier *Shinano* (on her maiden voyage) 160 nautical miles southwest of Tokyo Bay, Japan, 32°00′N, 137°00′E. *Shinano*, converted from a *Yamato*-class battleship, will be the largest warship sunk by any of the combatants' submarines during World War II. *Archerfish* estimates her victim as a 28,000-ton displacement converted carrier (XCV); *Shinano* displaces at least 64,000.

Submarine *Scabbardfish* (SS 397) sinks Japanese submarine *I 365* east of Honshu, 34°44′N, 141°01′E.

Submarine *Spadefish* (SS 411) sinks Japanese freighter *No. 6 Daiboshi Maru* off the west coast of Korea, 37°17′N, 125°11′E.

British submarine HMS *Sturdy* sinks two Japanese fishing vessels off Bawean Island, 06°20′S, 112°40′E.

30 Thursday

PACIFIC. Submarine *Pipefish* (SS 388) is damaged by aerial bombs in South China Sea off Hainan, 18°07′N, 111°35′E, but remains on patrol.

Submarine *Sunfish* (SS 281) sinks Japanese freighter *Dairen Maru* off western Korea, 38°08′N, 124°35′E.

Japanese bomber, evading a 12-plane combat air patrol, damages floating drydock *ARD 17* with a near-miss, Kossol Roads, Palau.

British submarine HMS *Stratagem* sinks Japanese cargo vessel *Kumano Maru* in Strait of Malacca, 01°30′N, 103°00′E.

British submarine HMS *Strongbow* boards Japanese prau, takes prisoners, and then shells large junk off Priaman, 00°38′S, 100°06′E.

DECEMBER

1 Friday

PACIFIC. Naval Operating Base, Kwajalein, is established.

EUROPE. U.S. freighter *Arizpa* is damaged by mine in the Schelde River, 51°23′N, 03°18′W, but proceeds to Antwerp, her destination, under her own power. There are no casualties among her 41-man merchant complement or the 28-man Armed Guard.

2 Saturday

PACIFIC. Four destroyers (Destroyer Division 44) bombard Japanese positions at Palompon and northern Ormoc Bay, Leyte. Another group of three destroyers (Destroyer Division 120) (Commander John C. Zahm) enters Ormoc Bay at night and battles enemy aircraft, destroyers, and shore batteries (see 3 December).

Submarine *Gunnel* (SS 253) evacuates 11 rescued aviators from Palawan, P.I., and turns over all available stores to Filipino forces ashore before she sets a course for Pearl Harbor.

Submarine *Sea Devil* (SS 400) attacks Japanese convoy MI 29 in the East China Sea, sinking merchant tanker *Akigawa Maru* and passenger-cargo ship *Hawaii Maru* about 80 miles south-southwest of Kyushu, 30°24′N, 128°17′E.

British submarine HMS *Sturdy* sinks Japanese *Communication Ship No. 142* in Makassar Strait, 04°05′S, 119°32′E, by gunfire and demolition charge.

USAAF B-24s sink Japanese gunboat *Bantan Maru* and damage auxiliary minesweeper *Cha 105* and cargo ship *Shoka Maru* 140 nautical miles from Makassar, 03°30′S, 117°30′E.

USAAF P-40s attack Japanese shipping off Palompon, P.I., sinking motor sailship *Kosei Maru*.

3 Sunday

PACIFIC. Destroyer engagement in Ormoc Bay that began late the previous night continues. Destroyer *Cooper* (DD 695) is sunk, possibly by torpedo from escort destroyer *Kuwa*, 10°54′N, 124°36′E, but not before *Cooper*, along with *Allen M. Sumner* (DD 692) and *Moale* (DD 693), sinks *Kuwa* and damages her sister ship *Take*, 10°50′N, 124°35′E. "Black Cat" PBY-5A picks up *Cooper*'s survivors that night and the next day. One PBY carries 56 in addition to its eight-man crew. *Allen M. Sumner* is damaged by horizontal bomber, and *Moale* is damaged (possibly by *Kuwa*) in Ormoc Bay, 10°54′N, 124°36′E.

Hospital ship *Hope* (AH 7), fully illuminated in accordance with the dictates of the Geneva Convention, is attacked by Japanese torpedo planes but not damaged, 125 miles east of Mindanao.

Submarines *Pampanito* (SS 383), *Pipefish*

(SS 388), *Sea Cat* (SS 399), and *Searaven* (SS 196) attack Japanese convoy HI 83 in South China Sea off east coast of Hainan, in heavy seas and poor visibility. *Pipefish* probably sinks *Coast Defense Vessel No. 64*, 18°36′N, 111°54′E; *Pampanito* torpedoes army cargo ship *Seishin Maru*, 18°20′N, 111°52′E; and *Sea Cat* or *Searaven* torpedoes tanker *Harima Maru*. Escort carrier *Kaiyo* and oiler *Kyokun Maru* survive and reach Singapore unscathed.

U.S. Navy land-based aircraft sink Japanese merchant tanker *No. 13 Nanshin Maru* off Balikpapan, 01°22′S, 117°03′E, and merchant tanker *No. 18 Nanshin Maru* off Borneo, 05°55′N, 117°03′E.

EUROPE. U.S. freighter *Francis Asbury* is mined in the Schelde River, 51°22′N, 03°53′W. Of her 41-man merchant complement and 28-man Armed Guard, nine of the former and six of the latter are killed; one merchant sailor and one Armed Guard die later of their injuries. Forty-six from both groups are injured. *Francis Asbury* drifts aground off Ostend, Belgium, where she is sunk by gunfire as a menace to navigation.

MEDITERRANEAN. Tank landing ship *LST 141* is damaged when she runs aground at Bizerte, Tunisia.

4 Monday

PACIFIC. Destroyer *Drayton* (DD 366) is damaged by horizontal bomber off Leyte, 10°00′N, 125°00′E.

Submarine *Flasher* (SS 249) attacks Japanese convoy about 275 miles southwest of Manila, sinking destroyer *Kishinami*, 12°54′N, 116°27′E, and damaging merchant tanker *Hakku Maru*. *Flasher* eludes efforts of the escorting *Yurijima* and *Coast Defense Vessel No. 17*; *Hakku Maru* is later scuttled, 13°12′N, 116°35′E, most likely by *Yurijima* and/or *Coast Defense Vessel No. 17*.

5 Tuesday

PACIFIC. Submarine *Hake* (SS 256) evacuates downed aviators and turns over all supplies that can be spared to Filipino guerrilla forces ashore at Libertad, Panay, P.I.

Tank landing ship *LST 23* and medium landing ship *LSM 20* are damaged by Japanese planes 70 miles northwest of Caiut Point, Leyte, 10°12′N, 125°19′E. *Kamikazes* damage destroyers *Drayton* (DD 366), 10°10′N, 125°20′E, and *Mugford* (DD 389), 10°15′N, 125°20′E.

Japanese planes attack convoy bound for Leyte, torpedoing U.S. freighter *Antoine Saugraine* at 09°42′N, 127°05′E; falling astern of the convoy, the freighter again comes under attack, is torpedoed a second time, and is abandoned. Frigates *San Pedro* (PF 37) and *Coronado* (PF 38) and Army tug *LT 454* rescue the 42-man merchant complement, 26-man Armed Guard, and 376 Army troop passengers between them (see 6 and 7 December). A *kamikaze* crashes freighter *Marcus Daly* in San Pedro Bay, Leyte, 09°34'N, 127°30'E. One of the 27-man Armed Guard is killed, as are two of the 40-man merchant complement and 62 of the 1,200 embarked Army troops; 49 men are wounded. Nearby, Armed Guard gunfire from freighter *John Evans* deflects a *kamikaze* from his suicidal course toward her, but the plane grazes the ship, glancing off the topmast and the stack before splashing close aboard. Bomb fragments cause some topside damage and wound four men (two of the 43-man merchant complement and two of the 26-man Armed Guard).

Medium landing ship *LSM 149* is damaged by grounding off Cape Sansapor, New Guinea.

Japanese escort destroyer *Ikuna* is damaged by aircraft off Formosa.

Naval Base, Tinian, is established.

MEDITERRANEAN. Tank landing craft *LCT 152*, under tow of tank landing ship *LST 141*, is damaged in a gale off Palermo, Sicily. Auxiliary tug *ATA 172* brings *LCT 152* into port.

6 Wednesday

PACIFIC. Submarine *Haddo* (SS 255) attacks small Japanese convoy, escorted by auxiliary submarine chaser *No. 17 Nitto Maru*, in South China Sea west-southwest of Manila, and damages tanker *No. 3 Kyoei Maru*, 14°43'N, 119°39'E; freighter *Kenei Maru* is not hit.

Submarines *Segundo* (SS 398), *Trepang* (SS 412), and *Razorback* (SS 394) attack Japanese convoy TAMA 34, consisting of 10 cargo vessels and four escorts, west of Dalupiri Island, P.I., en route from Takao to Manila. *Trepang* damages army cargo ship *Fukuyo Maru* and freighters *Jinyo Maru* and *Yamakuni Maru*, 18°59'N, 121°05'E; *Segundo* damages freighters *Kanjo Maru*, *Yasukuni Maru*, and *Shinfuku Maru*, 18°57'N, 120°58'E (see 7 December).

Fleet tug *Quapaw* (ATF 110) arrives to assist freighter *Antoine Saugraine*, damaged the previous day by Japanese aerial torpedo off Leyte; she stands ready to tow the freighter if necessary (see 7 December).

Aircraft sink Japanese army cargo ship *Shinto Maru* in South China Sea off Luzon, 18°52'N, 120°57'E.

British submarine HMS *Shalimar* attacks Japanese convoy in Strait of Malacca; she shells merchant tanker *Shinbun Maru* but is forced to break off action and submerge when Japanese Army aircraft appear.

ATLANTIC. Car floats *YCF 41* and *YCF 42* both break in half in heavy seas while in tow of auxiliary tug *ATA 181* (en route from Davisville to the Canal Zone) near Cape Lookout, South Carolina. *ATA 181*, hampered by a steering gear casualty, heads for port with the one remaining car float of the three that she had been towing, *YCF 31*, and the forward section of *YCF 42*. Rescue tug *ATR 74* and Coast Guard tug *Carrabassett* are dispatched from Norfolk, Virginia, to assist in rounding up the errant car float sections (see 10 December).

MEDITERRANEAN. Tank landing ship *LST 906*, aground since 18 October at Leghorn, Italy, is further damaged in gale.

Rescue tug *ATR 1* is damaged in collision in Tyrrhenian Sea, 41°27'N, 12°40'E.

7 Thursday

PACIFIC. TG 78.3 (Rear Admiral Arthur D. Struble) lands Army troops (77th Infantry) on the eastern shore of Ormoc Bay after bombardment by destroyers and LCI(R)s. Within three hours of the first soldiers going ashore, however, enemy air attacks begin. *Kamikazes* damage destroyers *Mahan* (DD 364), 10°50'N, 124°30'E, and *Lamson* (DD 367), 10°28'N,

Destroyer *Lamson* (DD 367), painted in a Measure 32 disruptive color scheme (ocean gray, light gray, and black), shells Japanese positions at Ormoc Bay, 7 December 1944. She will be struck by a Japanese suicide plane soon after this photo was taken. (Author's Collection)

124°41'E. *Mahan* is scuttled by destroyer *Walke* (DD 723); destroyer *Flusser* (DD 368) and rescue tug *ATR 31* extinguish *Lamson*'s fires and she is towed to Leyte Gulf. Other suiciders damage high-speed transports *Ward* (APD 16), 10°51'N, 124°33'E, and *Liddle* (APD 60) 10°57'N, 124°35'E; *Ward* is scuttled by destroyer *O'Brien* (DD 725).[223] Still other *kamikazes* damage tank landing ship *LST 737*, sink medium landing ship *LSM 318*, and damage (by near-misses) *LSM 18* and *LSM 19*.

U.S. freighter *Antoine Saugraine*, damaged on 5 December by Japanese aerial torpedo off Leyte, is torpedoed again during enemy air attack upon shipping at Leyte and sunk.

Japanese planes bomb U.S. airfield on Saipan.

Seaplane tender (destroyer) *Gillis* (AVD 12) is accidentally rammed and damaged by U.S. merchant tanker *Gulf Star* 40 miles off Makapu Point, Oahu.

Submarines *Razorback* (SS 394), *Segundo* (SS 398), and *Trepang* (SS 412) continue their attacks on Japanese convoy TAMA 34, beset the previous day. West of Dalupiri Island, *Razorback* sinks army cargo ship *Kanjo Maru* (damaged the day before by *Segundo*), 18°57'N, 120°58'E. Cargo ship *Yasukuni Maru* runs aground, written off as a total loss, as the consequence of damage inflicted by Navy carrier-based planes and *Segundo* the day before; *Trepang* sinks transport *No. 31 Banshu Maru* north of Luzon, 18°54′N, 120°49′E. Freighter *Jinyo Maru* and army cargo ship *Fukuyo Maru* sink as the result of damage inflicted by *Trepang* the previous day, 18°59′N, 121°05′E.

Opposing the eighth phase of "TA" Operation, USAAF fighter-bombers (5th Air Force) and USMC F4Us (VMF 211, VMF 218, and VMF 313) attack Japanese shipping in San Isidro Bay, Leyte, sinking fast transport *T.11* and army cargo ships *Akagisan Maru*, *No. 5 Shinsei Maru*, *Hakuba Maru*, and *Nichiyo Maru*, and damaging escort destroyers *Ume* and *Sugi*, 11°25′N, 124°20′E.

USAAF P-51s attack Japanese shipping on the Yangtze River near Hankow, China, and sink tug *No. 3 Hojoura Maru*.

8 Friday

PACIFIC. TG 94.9 (Rear Admiral Allan E. Smith) bombards airstrips and shore batteries on Iwo Jima.

Submarines *Paddle* (SS 263) and *Hammerhead* (SS 364), attacking from opposite sides of a Japanese Singapore-to-Manila convoy (SIMA 88), sink merchant tanker *Shoei Maru*, 03°50′N, 111°30′E. *Paddle* escapes the postattack attention of *Coast Defense Vessel No. 43*, one of the convoy's four escorts. Another of the escorts is *Patrol Boat No. 103* [ex-U.S. minesweeper *Finch* (AM 9)].

ATLANTIC. Frigate *Huron* (PF 19) is accidentally rammed and damaged by U.S. freighter *James Fenimore Cooper* about 870 miles northeast of Bermuda.

9 Saturday

PACIFIC. Submarine *Plaice* (SS 390) torpedoes Japanese escort destroyer *Maki* east of Danjo Gunto, 31°57′N, 129°01′E; *Sea Devil* (SS 400) and *Redfish* (SS 395) torpedo carrier *Junyo*, 31°43′N, 129°04′E, and 32°13′N, 129°13′E, respectively.

MEDITERRANEAN. Destroyers *Charles F. Hughes* (DD 428) and *Madison* (DD 425) bombard German coast artillery positions and troop concentrations along the Franco-Italian border.

Motor torpedo boat *PT 307*, en route to Leghorn, Italy, from Maddalena, Sardinia, is damaged by a heavy stern swell off her destination.

10 Sunday

PACIFIC. *Kamikaze* onslaught continues against U.S. ships off Leyte. Destroyer *Hughes* (DD 410) is damaged by *kamikaze*, 10°15′N, 125°10′E; motor torpedo boat *PT 323*, damaged by suicider, 10°33′N, 125°14′E, is

beached and abandoned. South of Dulag, a suicide plane crashes the freighter *Marcus Daly* (previously damaged on 5 December), which is discharging cargo to tank landing craft *LCT 1075* alongside. *LCT 1075* is hit by part of the *kamikaze* and sunk; *Marcus Daly* suffers no fatalities among the embarked complement (38 merchant sailors, 26-man Armed Guard, 60 stevedores, and 124 troops), although eight men are wounded. Nearby freighter *William S. Ladd* is hit by *kamikaze*; there are no fatalities among the 41-man merchant complement, the 29-man Armed Guard, and the 50 stevedores on board to work cargo, although six men are injured. Large infantry landing craft *LCI(L) 543*, *LCI(L) 547*, and *LCI(L) 744* lay alongside to fight the fire, but the flames defy all efforts to extinguish them. The landing craft embark *William S. Ladd*'s people when the uncontrollable blaze nears the hold where the ammunition cargo is stored.

EUROPE. U.S. freighter *Dan Beard* is torpedoed and sunk by German submarine *U 1202* off the coast of Wales, 51°56′N, 05°28′W; 17 of the 40-man merchant complement and 12 of the 27 Armed Guard perish with the ship.

MEDITERRANEAN. Local political and military disturbances result in cancellation of liberty at Piraeus, Greece; Greek snipers wound two crewmen in tank landing ship *LST 74*.

ATLANTIC. Rescue tug *ATR 74* and Coast Guard tug *Carrabassett*, unable to corral car float sections (the after half of *YCF 42* and both halves of *YCF 41* that had broken up on 6 December) and bring them into port, sink them with gunfire to prevent them from becoming hazards to navigation.

11 Monday

PACIFIC. Japanese planes (identified as KATEs) attack Ormoc Bay–bound Resupply Echelon convoy of 13 medium landing ships and large infantry landing craft. Destroyer *Reid* (DD 369) is sunk by *kamikaze* off Leyte, 09°50′N, 124°55′E; medium landing ships *LSM 38* and *LSM 42* and large infantry landing craft *LCI(L) 548* and *LCI(L) 661* rescue survivors. Explosion of *Reid*'s depth charges as she sinks causes casualties among swimmers in the water as well as varying degrees of damage to nearby *LCI(L) 548* and *LCI(L) 753*. *LCI(L) 661* transfers wounded *Reid* survivors to medium landing ship *LSM 42*. Destroyer *Caldwell* (DD 605) is near-missed by a suicider (see 12 December).

USMC F4Us (VMF 211, VMF 218, and VMF 313) repeat mast-head attack on Japanese convoy 30 miles off Leyte, sinking cargo ships *Mino Maru* and *Tasmania Maru*, 11°20′N, 124°10′E.

USAAF B-25s, A-20s, P-38s, and P-40s attack Japanese supply and troop concentrations on the southern shore of Wasile Bay and along the shores of north Halmahera, sinking *No. 2 Sumiyoshi Maru*.

Submarine *Gar* (SS 206) lands 35 tons of supplies at Darigayos Inlet, on west coast of Luzon, and then makes pickup of intelligence documents "of utmost secrecy." She also embarks one naval officer passenger for the return to Mios Woendi.

Submarine *Sea Owl* (SS 405) sinks Japanese auxiliary submarine chaser *Cha 76* in East China Sea, 33°48′N, 128°20′E.

PB4Ys sink Negros Island–bound Japanese freighter *Shonan Maru* north of Banton Island, P.I., 12°42′N, 122°10′E.

ATLANTIC. Submarine chaser *SC 1059* sinks after running aground near the Bahamas.

MEDITERRANEAN. Destroyer *Ludlow* (DD 438) chases German E-boat from a point six miles south of Cap Antibes to 20 miles south of Cap Ampeglio but fails to inflict any damage on the fast-moving (tracked at speeds up to 40 knots) enemy craft.

12 Tuesday

PACIFIC. USMC (MAG 12) and USAAF (13th Air Force) planes thwart last attempt by Japanese to reinforce their Leyte garrison ("TA" Operation, ninth phase) by attacking convoy off the northeastern tip of Panay. Destroyer *Yuzuki* is sunk by USMC planes 65 nautical miles north-northeast of Cebu, 11°20′N, 124°10′E; landing ship *T.159* is sunk by USMC and USAAF planes north of Camotes Island, P.I., 11°20′N, 124°10′E. Escort destroyer *Kiri* and fast tranport *T.15* are damaged by aircraft off Ormoc.

Motor torpedo boats *PT 490* and *PT 492* sink Japanese destroyer *Uzuki* off Canaguayan Point, Leyte, 11°03′N, 124°23′E.

Ormoc Bay Resupply Echelon, attacked by *kamikazes* the previous day, completes unloading and clears the beachhead; it again comes under Japanese air attack. Destroyer *Caldwell* (DD 605) is damaged by *kamikaze*, 10°30′N, 124°42′E; large infantry landing craft *LCI(L) 548* and *LCI(L) 753* rescue men blown overboard from *Caldwell* while *LCI(L) 543* and *LCI(L) 744* proceed alongside to bring fires under control and take off casualties, transporting them to destroyer *Edwards* (DD 619). A VAL intent on crashing into destroyer *Smith* (DD 378) misses and crashes into the sea. Medium landing ships *LSM 42*, *LSM 267*, and *LSM 316* are damaged by near-misses and strafing ZEKEs (Mitsubishi A6M5 Type 0 carrier fighter). *LSM 42* and *LSM 267* suffer further damage during collision later in the day; ultimately, *LSM 42* will tow her disabled sister ship back to San Pedro Bay.

Japanese river gunboat *Katata* is damaged by USAAF aircraft in the Yangtze River near Kiukiang, China.

ATLANTIC. U.S. freighter *Leslie M. Shaw* drops out of convoy and heaves to in heavy weather about 250 miles east-southeast of Norfolk, Virginia, having lost three lifeboats in the storm. She plans to return to port when the weather moderates (see 13 December).

13 Wednesday

PACIFIC. Japanese suicide planes attack U.S. ships operating in Mindanao Sea between Mindanao and Negros, damaging light cruiser *Nashville* (CL 43), 08°57′N, 123°28′E, and destroyer *Haraden* (DD 585), 08°40′N, 122°33′E.[224]

Submarine *Bergall* (SS 320) battles Japanese heavy cruiser *Myoko* off Royalist Bank, South China Sea, 08°08′N, 105°40′E; both ships emerge from the encounter damaged. Although *Bergall* torpedoes and stops her heavier adversary in that brisk fight off French Indochina, she is hit by a dud 8-inch shell from *Myoko* and is forced to terminate her patrol. *Myoko*, however, battles persistent fires that are not extinguished until 15 December (see 15, 16, 18, and 23 December).

Submarine *Pintado* (SS 387) sinks Japanese fast transport *T.12* and landing ship *T.104* in South China Sea, 19°30′N, 118°40′E. Although *Pintado* claims her destruction, the third ship in the convoy, landing ship *T.106*, continues on to Manila (see 15 December).

MEDITERRANEAN. Destroyer *Charles F. Hughes* (DD 428) fires first of three shore bombardment missions, targeting troop concentrations and artillery positions along the Franco-Italian border, that she will carry out between 13 and 16 December.

ATLANTIC. U.S. freighter *Leslie M. Shaw*, hove-to in storm east-southeast of Norfolk, Virginia, begins to founder at 36°25′N, 71°35′W, and requests assistance. Submarine chaser *PC 1087* is detached from convoy GN 174 to pro-

ceed to the merchantman's assistance; tug *Sciota* (ATO 30) is dispatched from Norfolk (see 16 December).

14 Thursday

UNITED STATES. Rank of fleet admiral, U.S. Navy, is established (see 15 December).

PACIFIC. Submarine *Blenny* (SS 324) sinks Japanese *Coast Defense Vessel No. 28* off Dasol Bay, Luzon, about 100 miles northwest of Manila, 15°50′N, 119°45′E, and guardboat *No. 5 Taisho Maru*, 16°27′N, 119°43′E.

Planes from carrier *Hornet* (CV 12) sink Japanese landing ship *T.109* off Vigan, P.I., 17°35′N, 120°20′E.

British submarine HMS *Shalimar* sinks auxiliary minesweeper *No. 7 Choun Maru* off Belawan, Sumatra, 03°55′N, 98°50′E.

Medium landing ship *LSM 151*, en route to Ormoc Bay with the third Resupply Echelon, is damaged by explosion and fire in engine room, and returns to San Pedro Bay, Leyte.

ATLANTIC. U.S. tanker *Edward L. Doheny* begins taking on water at 35°00′N, 74°00′W, and requests assistance. Rescue tug *ATR 6* is dispatched from Morehead City, North Carolina, and gunboat *Might* (PG 94) is diverted from escorting convoy NG 477 to proceed to the scene (see 15 and 16 December).

15 Friday

UNITED STATES. Admirals William D. Leahy (Chairman of the Joint Chiefs of Staff), Ernest J. King (Chief of Naval Operations), and Chester W. Nimitz (Commander in Chief Pacific Fleet) are promoted to the rank of fleet admiral.[225]

PACIFIC. TG 78.3 (Rear Admiral Arthur D. Struble) lands Army forces on southwest coast of Mindoro under cover of carrier-based aircraft (Rear Admiral Felix B. Stump). The Mindoro operation, conceived and undertaken to secure an all-weather airfield to support large-scale landings on Luzon, is regarded as a hazardous venture deep into Japanese-controlled waters. Tank landing ships *LST 472* and *LST 738*, damaged by *kamikazes* off southern tip of Mindoro, 12°19′N, 121°05′E, are scuttled by destroyer *Hall* (DD 583). Elsewhere off Mindoro, suiciders damage escort carrier *Marcus Island* (CVE 77); destroyers *Paul Hamilton* (DD 590) and *Howorth* (DD 592), 12°19′N, 121°02′E; and motor torpedo boat *PT 223*, 12°19′N, 121°05′E.

Miscellaneous auxiliary *Argonne* (AG 31) is damaged by explosion of depth charge acci-

dentally dropped by submarine chaser *SC 702*, Kossol Roads, Palaus.

Submarine *Dragonet* (SS 293) is damaged when she runs aground 12,000 yards off Japanese seaplane base on Matsuwa Island, Kurils.[226]

Submarine *Hawkbill* (SS 366) sinks Japanese destroyer *Momo* west of Luzon, 16°40′N, 117°42′E.

TF 38 planes sink Japanese landing ship *T.106*, which had escaped destruction by submarine *Pintado* (SS 387) on 13 December, in South China Sea off Luzon, 15°30′N, 119°50′E, and damage *Coast Defense Vessel No. 54* north of Calayan Island, Luzon Channel, 19°25′N, 121°25′E.

Japanese auxiliary *Tatebe Maru* takes heavy cruiser *Myoko* (torpedoed and badly damaged on 13 December) in tow and heads for Cape St. Jacques, French Indochina, accompanied by auxiliary submarine chaser *Kaiko Maru* and two auxiliary minesweepers (see 16 December).

EUROPE. Command designated Naval Forces Germany (Vice Admiral Robert L. Ghormley) is established with headquarters at Rosneath, Scotland.

ATLANTIC. Gunboat *Might* (PG 94) makes contact with U.S. tanker *Edward L. Doheny*, damaged the previous day, and begins heading for Norfolk, Virginia (see 16 December).

16 Saturday

PACIFIC. Submarine *Dace* (SS 247) lays mines off French Indochina.

Submarine *Finback* (SS 230), in attack on Japanese convoy, sinks transport *Jusan Maru I-Go* about 50 miles northwest of Chichi Jima, 27°24′N, 141°04′E.

British submarine HMS *Stoic*, despite presence of escort, sinks Japanese gunboat *Shoei Maru* west of Sunda Strait, 05°45′S, 104°43′E.

TF 38 planes sink Japanese freighter *Oryoku Maru*, escorted by destroyer *Momo* and submarine chaser *Ch 60*, in Subic Bay, 14°45′N, 120°13′E; aviators are unaware that *Oryoku Maru* is carrying over 1,600 Allied POWs (one of whom is Commander Francis J. Bridget, former commander of the Naval Battalion on Bataan in 1942, who will be lost). Those POWs who survive the ordeal of the loss of *Oryoku Maru* will be again helpless and unwitting victims of U.S. planes at Takao, Formosa, on 27 December and 9 January 1945. When the draft of POWs reaches its ultimate destination, Moji, Japan, only 497 of the original 1,600+ men remain.

Worsening weather prompts the dispatch

of Japanese destroyers *Kasumi* and *Hatsushimo* to assist auxiliary *Tatebe Maru* in towing damaged heavy cruiser *Myoko* (torpedoed on 13 December) and prompts a change in course from Cape St. Jacques, French Indochina, to Singapore (see 18 December).

MEDITERRANEAN. Destroyer *Niblack* (DD 424), operating in support of the U.S. First Airborne Division along the Franco-Italian frontier, fires first of three shore bombardment missions she will carry out between 16 and 19 December; she targets troop concentrations, rail lines, barracks, and motor convoys. Motor torpedo boat *PT 310*, in company with a British motor torpedo boat, attacks four north-bound F-lighters a mile off Point Sestri; the allied craft claim one F-lighter probably sunk and one damaged.

ATLANTIC. Tug *Sciota* (ATO 30) makes contact with U.S. freighter *Leslie M. Shaw* (foundering since 13 December) 30 miles east of the Chesapeake Swept Channel and tows the merchantman, her main decks awash and her number one hold filled with water, to Norfolk, Virginia.

Rescue tug *ATR 6* makes contact with U.S. tanker *Edward L. Doheny*, damaged on 14 December, and assists the damaged vessel to Norfolk, Virginia. Gunboat *Might* (PG 94) rejoins convoy NG 477.

17 Sunday

PACIFIC. Motor torpedo boat *PT 84* is damaged by suicide plane off Mindoro, P.I., 12°19′N, 121°04′E.

Japanese *Coast Defense Vessel No. 19* is damaged by aircraft south of Cam Ranh Bay, French Indochina.

Japanese heavy cruiser *Myoko* (torpedoed on 13 December) suffers further damage in heavy seas; the ship's damaged stern breaks away while she is being towed by auxiliary vessel *Tatebe Maru* (see 18 December).

MEDITERRANEAN. U.S. and British motor torpedo boats and armed British trawlers attack eight-ship convoy in vicinity of Mesco Point; they claim three F-lighters sunk.

18 Monday

PACIFIC. Third Fleet (Admiral William F. Halsey Jr.) encounters typhoon 180 miles northeast of Samar. Destroyers *Hull* (DD 350), *Monaghan* (DD 354), and *Spence* (DD 512) capsize, 14°57′N, 127°58′E. Destroyer escort *Tabberer* (DE 418), which herself sustains storm damage, rescues 41 *Hull* survivors and 14 from *Spence* (remaining men will be rescued on 20

December). Ships that suffer varying degrees of damage include small carriers *Cowpens* (CVL 25), *Monterey* (CVL 26), *Cabot* (CVL 28), and *San Jacinto* (CVL 30); escort carriers *Altamaha* (CVE 18), *Nehenta Bay* (CVE 74), *Cape Esperance* (CVE 88), and *Kwajalein* (CVE 98); light cruiser *Miami* (CL 89); destroyers *Dewey* (DD 349), *Aylwin* (DD 355), *Buchanan* (DD 484), *Dyson* (DD 572), *Hickox* (DD 673), *Maddox* (DD 731), and *Benham* (DD 796); destroyer escorts *Melvin R. Nawman* (DE 416), *Tabberer*, and *Waterman* (DE 740); oiler *Nantahala* (AO 60); and fleet tug *Jicarilla* (ATF 104).

Motor torpedo boat *PT 300* is damaged by kamikaze off Mindoro, P.I., 12°19′N, 121°05′E.

Japanese auxiliary submarine chaser *Keisho Maru* is sunk by aircraft off Nagoya, Japan.

Towing of damaged Japanese heavy cruiser *Myoko* (torpedoed on 13 December) continues, with destroyer *Kasumi* attempting to take over the job from auxiliary *Tatebe Maru*. Continuing stormy conditions, however, will prevent further towing for the next four days. Meanwhile, heavy cruiser *Haguro*, accompanied by escort vessel *Chiburi*, is sent out from Singapore; they reach *Myoko* and her consorts the next day (see 23 December).

EUROPE. U.S. freighter *Steel Traveller* is mined in the Schelde River and sunk; survivors are rescued by French destroyer *La Combattante*. There are no casualties among the 26-man Armed Guard, but two of the ship's 45-man merchant complement perish.

19 Tuesday

PACIFIC. Submarine *Redfish* (SS 395), despite presence of escorting destroyers, sinks Japanese carrier *Unryu* 200 nautical miles southeast of Shanghai, China, 28°19′N, 124°40′E. *Redfish* is damaged in the resultant depth charging and is forced to terminate her patrol.

PB4Y-1s (VPB 104) attack Japanese convoy in South China Sea and sink transport *Shinfuku Maru*, which had survived attack by submarine *Segundo* (SS 398) on 6 December, 30 miles west of Manila, 13°40′N, 115°50′E.

USAAF P-51s (14th Air Force) attack Japanese shipping at Hong Kong and sink cargo ship *Hida Maru*, 22°17′N, 114°10′E.

Aircraft sink army cargo ship *No. 3 Hiroshi Maru* in Kurils, 44°56′N, 147°39′E.

20 Wednesday

PACIFIC. Organized Japanese resistance ends on Leyte.

Submarine *Sealion* (SS 315) damages San Fernando, Luzon–bound Japanese supply ship

Mamiya in the South China Sea about 450 miles northeast of Cam Ranh Bay, French Indochina, 17°48′N, 114°09′E, and survives counterattacks by destroyer *Kari* and *Coast Defense Vessel No. 17* (see 21 December).

Dutch Mitchells sink Japanese netlayer *Shoeki Maru* in the Flores Sea, 07°00′S, 120°00′E.

ATLANTIC. Tank landing ship *LST 359* is sunk about 440 miles southwest of Cape Finisterre, Spain, 42°04′N, 19°08′W, and destroyer escort *Fogg* (DE 57) is damaged, 43°02′N, 19°19′W, by German submarine *U 870*.

21 Thursday

PACIFIC. Destroyer *Foote* (DD 511), 11°05′N, 121°20′E, and tank landing ships *LST 460* and *LST 749*, 11°13′N, 121°04′E, are damaged by kamikazes off Mindoro, P.I. Off Panay, freighter *Juan de Fuca* is crashed by a suicider; the explosion and resultant fire kills two and wounds 14 of the 65 embarked Army troops and wounds two of the 27-man Armed Guard. *Juan de Fuca*, although damaged, continues on to Mindoro (see 31 December).

Submarine *Sealion* (SS 315) carries out second attack on Japanese supply ship *Mamiya*, and sinks her in the South China Sea, 17°55′N, 114°11′E.

Mine damages Japanese escort vessel *Amakusa* 680 miles from Kanameiwa.

Japanese gunboat *No. 2 Hiyoshi Maru* is damaged by mine off Etorofu, Kurils.

22 Friday

PACIFIC. Destroyer *Bryant* (DD 665) is damaged by kamikaze off Mindoro, P.I., 12°00′N, 121°00′E.

Submarine *Flasher* (SS 249) attacks Japanese convoy HI 82 and sinks fleet tanker *Omurosan Maru* and merchant tankers *Otowasan Maru* and *Arita Maru* about 250 miles north of Cam Ranh Bay, French Indochina, 15°07′N, 109°05′E.

Submarine *Tilefish* (SS 307) sinks Japanese torpedo boat *Chidori* southwest of Omae Saki, 34°33′N, 138°02′E.

Tank landing ship *LST 563* sinks after grounding off Clipperton Island in the eastern Pacific Ocean, 10°17′N, 109°13′W.

USAAF B-24s attack Japanese shipping off north Borneo, sinking small cargo vessels *Nitto Maru*, *Sumiyoshi Maru*, *Kanju Maru*, *Kojin Maru*, and *Hashiro Maru* and damaging *Chosiu Maru*.

RAF and Dutch Mitchells attack Japanese shipping off Koepang, Timor, sinking cargo vessel *Nanyo Maru*.

MEDITERRANEAN. Destroyer *Gleaves* (DD 423) is damaged by shore battery fire as she shells German troop concentrations on the Franco-Italian border.

23 Saturday

PACIFIC. Submarine *Blenny* (SS 324), despite proximity of escort vessel, sinks Japanese merchant tanker *Kenzui Maru* off San Fernando, Luzon, P.I., 16°40′N, 120°16′E.

Moderating weather allows Japanese heavy cruiser *Haguro* to take crippled sister ship *Myoko* in tow; they reach Singapore on 25 December, twelve days after submarine *Bergall* (SS 320) had torpedoed *Myoko* off Royalist Bank. The successful effort to retrieve the ship had involved the deployment of eight ships.

24 Sunday

PACIFIC. TG 94.9 (Rear Admiral Allan E. Smith) follows USAAF bombing raid on Iwo Jima by shelling airstrips and other installations; destroyers *Case* (DD 370) and *Roe* (DD 418) sink Japanese fast transport *T.8*, 25°10′N, 141°00′E, and landing ship *T.157*, 24°47′N, 141°20′E.

Submarine *Barbero* (SS 317) attacks Japanese SIMA 18 convoy, sinking Japanese submarine chaser *Ch 30*, 02°45′N, 110°53′E, and damaging transport *Junpo Maru*, 01°10′N, 108°20′E (see 25 December).

USAAF B-25s sink Japanese fishing boat *Shinei Maru* off Timor.

Aircraft sink Japanese army cargo ship *Goro Maru*, Yangtze River.

Japanese tanker *Ryusho Maru* is damaged by grounding, 14°28′N, 109°07′E.

EUROPE. U.S. freighter *Timothy Bloodworth*, anchored at Antwerp, Belgium, and awaiting formation of a convoy to proceed to the United States, is damaged when one V-1 or V-2 rocket bomb explodes overhead and a second lands nearby. There are, however, no casualties among the 41-man merchant complement, the 26-man Armed Guard, and one passenger.

25 Monday

PACIFIC. Submarine *Barbero* (SS 317) continues attack on Japanese SIMA 18 convoy, sinking transport *Junpo Maru* 130 miles west-southwest of Kuching, Borneo, 00°51′N, 108°08′E.

British submarines HMS *Trenchant* and HMS *Terrapin* sink auxiliary minesweeper *Reisui Maru*, cargo vessel *No. 23 Hinode Maru*, and auxiliary sailing vessel *Wakamiya Maru* in Strait of Malacca, 03°19′N, 99°45′E.

TF 38 aircraft attack Japanese shipping off Masinloc, P.I., sinking landing ship *T.113*, 15°30′N, 119°55′E.

USAAF B-24s sink small Japanese cargo vessels *Chokyu Maru* and *Sumiei Maru* off Sandakan, Borneo, and badly damage *Asahi Maru* and *Nichifuku Maru*.

U.S. freighter *Robert J. Walker* is torpedoed by German submarine *U 862* in the Tasman Sea, 36°35′S, 150°43′E; Armed Guard 20-millimeter gunfire explodes a second torpedo, but a third hits the ship and causes irreparable damage. Two of the ship's 42-man merchant complement are killed. The ship is then abandoned and sinks (see 26 December).

Naval Air Station, Samar, is established.

26 Tuesday

PACIFIC. "REI" Operation: Japanese "San Jose Intrusion Force" (Rear Admiral Kimura Masanori, flag in destroyer *Kasumi*), consisting of heavy cruiser *Ashigara*, light cruiser *Oyodo*, three destroyers, and three escort destroyers, approaches Mindoro to bombard the beachhead. USAAF B-25s, P-38s, P-40s, and P-47s (5th Air Force) and Navy PB4Ys and PBMs successively attack the force. B-25s damage *Ashigara* (near-misses) and *Oyodo*; other ships damaged are destroyers *Asashimo*, *Kiyoshimo*, and *Kasumi* and escort destroyers *Kaya* and *Kashi*. Kimura's force carries out its bombardment mission, then encounters U.S. motor torpedo boats; *PT 77* is damaged, probably accidentally bombed by friendly aircraft. Subsequently, *PT 223* sinks the already damaged *Kiyoshimo* off San Jose, 145 miles south of Manila, 12°20′N, 121°00′E. As the "San Jose Intrusion Force" approaches, U.S. freighter *James H. Breasted* is ordered to seek safety in Ilin Strait; anchoring there she comes under fire, being damaged by shell fragments during the Japanese bombardment. The ship is later bombed by what is probably a U.S. plane, touching off her cargo of gasoline. *James H. Breasted* is abandoned (only one of the 33-man merchant complement requires treatment for injuries; no one is hurt in the 27-man Armed Guard), but the survivors come under friendly fire that (fortunately, in view of their trials and tribulations already) inflicts no further casualties. U.S. motor torpedo boats tow the three boats of survivors toward shore; the ship, battered by friend and foe alike, is later written off as a total loss.

Destroyer *Fanning* (DD 385) sinks Japanese auxiliary submarine chaser *No. 7 Kyo Maru* off Okino Misaki, Bonins.

Submarine *Swordfish* (SS 193) departs Midway for thirteenth war patrol. Contact is made with *Swordfish* on 3 January 1945, but she is never seen again.[227]

USAAF B-24 sinks Japanese cargo vessel *No. 104 Nanyo Maru* off south coast of Boeroe Island, 03°49′S, 126°51′E.

Australian destroyer HMAS *Quickmatch* rescues 40 merchant sailors, one passenger, and the 26-man Armed Guard of freighter *Robert J. Walker*, torpedoed and sunk in the Tasman Sea by German submarine *U 862* the previous day.

27 Wednesday

PACIFIC. TG 94.9 (Rear Admiral Allan E. Smith) follows up USAAF strikes with cruiser and destroyer bombardment of Japanese installations on Iwo Jima and shipping offshore. Destroyer *Dunlap* (DD 384) is damaged by shore battery, but not before she joins *Fanning* (DD 385) and *Cummings* (DD 365) in sinking fast transport *T.7* and landing ship *T.132*, 24°47′N, 141°20′E.

Japanese planes bomb shore positions and auxiliary shipping at Mindoro; attacks are repeated on 28, 29, and 30 December.

Submarine *Baya* (SS 318) locates Japanese heavy cruiser *Ashigara*, light cruiser *Oyodo*, and destroyers *Asashimo* and *Kasumi*, part of the "San Jose Intrusion Force," on its return passage to Cam Ranh Bay, French Indochina. *Baya*'s attack, however, at 12°51′N, 113°27′E, is unsuccessful.

Submarine *Barbero* (SS 317) is damaged by aerial bomb, Lombok Strait, 08°20′S, 115°55′E, and returns to base on her starboard shaft only.

U.S. freighter *Anson Burlingame*, en route from Hollandia, New Guinea, to Bougainville, mistakenly fires upon submarine *Pintado* (SS 387) at 06°50′S, 148°50′E. *Pintado* is not damaged in the encounter that has resulted from Sea Frontier authorities not informing merchant ships, prior to sailing, of projected friendly submarine movements.

Japanese cargo ship *Taicho Maru* is destroyed by accidental munitions explosion at Tanjoeng Priok, Java, 06°06′S, 106°53′E; the blast causes great destruction to nearby harbor and dockyard installations.

28 Thursday

PACIFIC. Japanese air attacks commence against Mindoro-bound TG 77.11 (Captain George F. Mentz); *kamikazes* crash tank landing ship *LST 750* and U.S. freighters *William Sharon* and *John Burke*. *John Burke*, carrying ammunition, explodes; the cataclysmic blast damages auxiliary *Porcupine* (IX 126) and motor torpedo boat *PT 332*. There are no survivors from among *John Burke's* 40-man merchant complement and 28-man Armed Guard. Debris from *John Burke* also hits freighter *Francisco Morozan* 100 yards away, wounding three of that ship's merchant complement. *William Sharon*, set afire by a *kamikaze* and gutted by fires that are ultimately controlled, is abandoned, the survivors transferring to destroyer *Wilson* (DD 408), whose assistance proves invaluable in extinguishing the blaze on board the freighter. Salvage vessel *Grapple* (ARS 7) later tows the gutted merchantman to San Pedro Bay, Leyte, for repairs. *LST 750*, hit subsequently by aerial torpedo, is scuttled by destroyer *Edwards* (DD 619), 09°01′N, 122°30′E. Enemy air attacks continue the following day.

Submarine *Dace* (SS 247) attacks Japanese convoy off Cape Varella, French Indochina, sinking supply ship *Nozaki*, 12°36′N, 109°38′E, and damaging *Chefoo Maru*.

USAAF B-24 sinks Japanese motor sailboat *No. 38 Tachibana Maru* off Flores Island.

ATLANTIC. Attack cargo ship *Trego* (AKA 78) runs aground off Lloyd's Neck, Long Island Sound; rescue tug *ATR 74* assists in refloating the ship at the next high tide.

29 Friday

PACIFIC. Submarine *Hawkbill* (SS 366) sinks Japanese merchant *Lighter No. 130* in Java Sea, 05°35′S, 113°29′E.

ANDAMAN SEA. British submarine HMS *Seascout* shells and destroys grounded Japanese

motor sailships *No. 10 Kashiwa Maru* and *No. 6 Nichitai Maru* in Molucca Bay, Car Nicobar.

EUROPE. German submarine *U 772* attacks convoy TBC 21 in the English Channel, 50°28′N, 02°28′W. Freighter *Arthur Sewall* is torpedoed and the explosion in the engine room kills one man and wounds five; there are no casualties among the 29-man Armed Guard. Towed to Weymouth, England, *Arthur Sewall* is later written off as a total loss. Freighter *Black Hawk* is also a victim of a torpedo from *U 772*; the blast wounds four of the ship's 41-man merchant complement (one of whom dies later), but there are no casualties among the 27-man Armed Guard. *Black Hawk* is abandoned, the survivors being taken on board British corvette HMS *Dahlia*. Towed subsequently to Warboro Bay, England, *Black Hawk* is written off as a total loss.

30 Saturday

PACIFIC. Japanese air attacks continue on Mindoro-bound convoy; *kamikazes* damage destroyers *Pringle* (DD 477), 12°18′N, 121°01′E, and *Gansevoort* (DD 608), 12°21′N, 121°02′E; motor torpedo boat tender *Orestes* (AGP 10), 12°19′N, 121°04′E; and auxiliary *Porcupine* (IX 126), 12°21′N, 121°02′E. *Porcupine* is ultimately scuttled by *Gansevoort*. Freighter *Hobart Baker* is sunk by bombs off Mindoro, 12°17′55″N, 121°04′47″E; two of the 26-man Armed Guard are wounded and of the ship's 38-man merchant complement, there are one dead and one wounded. Also off Mindoro, freighter *Francisco Morozan* is damaged when *kamikaze* is shot down by U.S. fighter and ex-

plodes over the ship; there are, however, no casualties to the 38-man merchant complement and the 29-man Armed Guard.

Submarine *Razorback* (SS 394) attacks Japanese Manila-to-Takao convoy about 60 miles southeast of Formosa, sinking destroyer *Kuretake* in Bashi Channel, 21°00′N, 121°24′E, and damaging cargo ships *Brazil Maru* and *Oi Maru*.

USAAF B-25s, A-20s, and P-40s (5th Air Force) attack Japanese convoy MATA 39 in approaches to Lingayen Gulf, sinking *Coast Defense Vessel No. 20*, 16°30′N, 120°18′E, submarine chaser *Ch 18* off Santiago Island, and army cargo ships *Aobasan Maru*, *Muroran Maru*, and *Teikai Maru* north of San Fernando, 17°18′N, 119°25′E; *Nissho Maru* is damaged.

31 Sunday

PACIFIC. U.S. freighter *Juan de Fuca* is torpedoed by Japanese plane about 20 miles off Mindoro, and runs aground off Ambulong Island; there are no casualties among the 41-man merchant complement and the 27-man Armed Guard, all of whom abandon ship the following day. *Juan de Fuca* is refloated, 24 February 1945. The Navy renames her *Araner* (IX 226), a miscellaneous auxiliary.

ANDAMAN SEA. British submarine HMS *Shakespeare* attacks Japanese convoy and sinks freighter *Unryu Maru* east of Port Blair, 11°40′N, 93°15′E.

EUROPE. USAAF heavy bombers pound Hamburg; in the massive raid, German submarine *U 906*, minesweeper *M 445*, and cargo vessels *Faro*, *Mannheim*, and *Rival* are sunk.

1945

JANUARY

1 Monday

PACIFIC. TU 94.5.10, composed of destroyer escort *Seid* (DE 256), tank landing ship *LST 225,* and three infantry landing craft, land company of Army troops (321st Infantry) on Fais Island (south and east of Ulithi), Carolines, to investigate whether or not it was being used as a Japanese midget submarine base and communications center (see 3 and 4 January).

Submarine *Stingray* (SS 186) delivers 35 tons of supplies to Filipino forces at Tongehatan Point, on north coast of Tawi Tawi, P.I.

U.S. freighter *John M. Clayton* is damaged by bomb dropped by Japanese plane and catches fire off BLUE beach, Mindoro, P.I.; four of the 29-man Armed Guard sailors die of burns.[228]

Japanese cargo vessel *Kyokko Maru* is sunk by mine (laid by British submarine HMS *Tradewind* on 30 October 1944), off Mergui, 12°26′N, 98°39′E.

USAAF planes sink Japanese ships *No. 7 Taiko Maru* and *No. 3 Taiwan Maru* off Masinloc, P.I.

2 Tuesday

EUROPE. Admiral Sir Bertram H. Ramsay, RN, Allied Commander in Chief Expeditionary Force, is killed in airplane accident near Paris, France.

PACIFIC. Submarine *Aspro* (SS 309) torpedoes Japanese landing ship *Shinshu Maru* south of Formosa Strait, 22°42′N, 119°14′E (see 3 January).

Submarine *Becuna* (SS 319) sinks Japanese ship *Daian Maru* east of Madoera Island, N.E.I., 05°50′S, 113°12′E.

USAAF A-20s and P-38s (Far East Air Force) attack Japanese shipping off San Fernando, Luzon, sinking *Coast Defense Vessel No. 138,* transport *Meiryu Maru,* army cargo ship *Shirokawa Maru,* and freighters *Taishin Maru, Hakka Maru, Hishikata Maru,* and *Koryu Maru,* 16°37′N, 120°19′E.

3 Wednesday

PACIFIC. TF 38 (Vice Admiral John S. McCain) begins operations against Japanese airfields and shipping in the Formosa area. Principally along the west coast of Formosa, TF 38 planes, in attack on convoy MATA 04, sink landing ship *Shinshu Maru* [damaged by submarine *Aspro* (SS 309) the day before] and damage army cargo ships *Kibitsu Maru* and *Hyuga Maru;* only escort destroyer *Miyake* and *Coast Defense Vessel No. 39* escape unhit. Nearby, TF 38 aircraft sink cargo ships *Kinrei Maru, No. 2 Ume Maru, No. 22 Kawauchi Maru, Sanni Maru,* and another unidentified *Maru,* and damage army cargo ships *No. 2 Nichiyu Maru, No. 36 Taiwa Maru,* and *Kakuju Maru.*

Occupation of Fais Island, Carolines, continues. Occupying force destroys Japanese radio station found there. Interrogation of natives and Japanese prisoners reveals that Fais had never been used to base ships (see 4 January).

Leading groups of U.S. fleet units bound for Lingayen Gulf make daylight passage of Surigao Strait, where they come under attack from Japanese planes. Oiler *Cowanesque* (AO 79) is damaged by *kamikaze,* 08°56′N, 122°49′E; motor minesweeper *YMS 53* is damaged by near-miss of bomb.

USAAF B-25s (Far East Air Force) on a shipping sweep off Davao, sink Japanese auxiliary submarine chaser *Cha 10*, 07°04′N, 125°37′E.

Escort carrier *Sargent Bay* (CVE 83) and destroyer escort *Robert F. Keller* (DE 419) are damaged in collision during mail delivery exercise, Philippine Islands area.

Submarine *Kingfish* (SS 234), attacking Japanese convoy in the Bonins, sinks Japanese army cargo ship *Shoto Maru* and freighters *Yaei Maru* and *Shibazono Maru* 200 miles north of Chichi Jima, 30°29′N, 142°03′E.

ATLANTIC. U.S. freighter *Henry Miller*, in Hampton Roads, Virginia–bound convoy GUS 63, is torpedoed by German submarine *U 870*, 22 miles southwest of Cape Spartel, 35°51′N, 06°24′W; Coast Guard–manned frigate *Brunswick* (PF 68) takes off most of the crew and armed guard (there are no casualties in either group). The ship, with a reduced complement, reaches Gibraltar under her own power the following day; she is, however, later declared a constructive total loss.

INDIAN OCEAN. British submarine HMS *Shakespeare* and Japanese auxiliary minesweeper *Wa.1* damage each other in surface gun action east of Nancowry Strait, Nicobar Islands.

4 Thursday

PACIFIC. TF 38 continues operations against Japanese airfields and shipping in the Formosa area. Navy planes sink auxiliary submarine chasers *Cha 163*, *Cha 176*, and *Cha 210* and damage escort vessel *Ikuna* and auxiliary submarine chaser *Cha 204* in Formosa Strait; sink auxiliary netlayer *Iwato Maru* northeast of Taiwan; and damage minesweeper *W.41* near Takao.

Japanese air attacks continue against Lingayen Gulf–bound U.S. forces; a *kamikaze* crashes escort carrier *Ommaney Bay* (CVE 79) in the Sulu Sea, irreparably damaging her; another suicider narrowly misses escort carrier *Lunga Point* (CVE 94). Destroyer *Burns* (DD 588) scuttles the irreparably damaged *Ommaney Bay*, 11°25′N, 121°19′E, but not before destroyer *Bell* (DD 587) is damaged by collision with the escort carrier during fire-fighting operations. South of Mindoro, a *kamikaze* crashes U.S. freighter *Lewis L. Dyche* (carrying bombs and fuses), which disintegrates, killing all hands, including the 28-man Armed Guard; debris from the exploding merchantman damages nearby oiler *Pecos* (AO 65) and minelayer *Monadnock* (CM 9), 12°19′N, 121°04′E. Small seaplane tender *Half Moon* (AVP 26) is damaged by near-miss of bomb.

USAAF planes damage Japanese submarine chasers *Ch 17*, *Ch 18*, *Ch 23*, *Ch 37*, and *Ch 38* off San Fernando, Luzon.

Japanese army vessel *No. 15 Horikoshi Maru* is sunk by mine off northeast shore of Mukai Jima, northern Bingo.

Fais Island, Carolines, is formally occupied.

ATLANTIC. Car float *YCF 59*, being towed from New York to Philadelphia, Pennsylvania, fills with water while in tow of rescue tug *ATR 57* and is beached in the Delaware River.

5 Friday

PACIFIC. Japanese air attacks continue against Lingayen Gulf–bound forces in the teeth of heavy antiaircraft fire and combat air patrol. Of the minesweeping group, infantry landing craft (gunboat) *LCI(G) 70* is damaged by *kamikaze*; small seaplane tender *Orca* (AVP 49) and fleet tug *Apache* (ATF 67) are damaged by near-misses of suiciders, 15°36′N, 119°20′E, and 15°53′N, 120°00′E, respectively. *Kamikazes* attacking the bombardment and escort carrier groups damage heavy cruiser *Louisville* (CA 28) and destroyer *Helm* (DD 388), 15°00′N, 119°00′E; escort carriers *Manila Bay* (CVE 61), 14°50′N, 119°10′E, and *Savo Island* (CVE 78), 14°50′N, 119°00′E; and destroyer escort *Stafford* (DE 411), 14°00′N, 120°00′E. Suiciders also crash Australian heavy cruiser HMAS *Australia* (see 8 and 9 January) and destroyer HMAS *Arunta*. Japanese escort destroyers stand toward minesweeping group but turn away at approach of destroyer *Bennion* (DD 662) and Australian frigate HMAS *Gascoyne* and sloop HMAS *Warrego*; subsequently, planes from CVEs of TG 77.4 sink *Momi* 20 miles southwest of entrance to Manila Bay, 14°00′N, 120°20′E, and damage *Hinoki* and *Sugi*. Japanese army cargo submarine *YU 3*, inoperable because of machinery casualty, is scuttled in Lingayen Gulf to avoid capture.

TG 94.9 (Rear Admiral Allan E. Smith), three heavy cruisers and six destroyers, together with USAAF B-24s (escorted by P-38s) jointly pound Japanese shipping and installations on Chichi Jima, Haha Jima, and Iwo Jima, Bonins. Approaching Chichi Jima, destroyers *Dunlap* (DD 384), *Fanning* (DD 385), and *Cummings* (DD 365) damage landing ship *T.107*; *Fanning* sinks her, 26°27′N, 141°11′E. Off Chichi Jima, *David W. Taylor* (DD 551) is damaged by mine, 27°04′N, 142°06′E; destroyer *Fanning* is damaged by gunfire. Off Iwo Jima, *Dunlap*, *Cummings*, *Ellet* (DD 398), and *Roe* (DD 418) sink landing ship *T.154*, 24°27′N, 141°20′E.

PB4Y-1s (VPB 111) sink Japanese midget submarine *Ha 71* two miles southwest of Chichi Jima.

TF 92 (Rear Admiral John L. McCrea), three light cruisers and nine destroyers, bombards Japanese installations (airfield and fish canneries) at Suribachi Wan, Paramushir, Kurils.

Destroyer escort *Edwin A. Howard* (DE 346) is damaged in collision with *Leland E. Thomas* (DE 420) off Mindanao, 09°48′N, 127°15′E.

Minelayer *Monadnock* (CM 9) is damaged by grounding off Ilin Island, Luzon, 12°22′N, 121°01′E.

Submarine *Cavalla* (SS 244) sinks Japanese auxiliary netlayers *Kanko Maru* and *Shunsen Maru* in Java Sea, 05°00′S, 112°16′E.

Destroyer escort *Brackett* (DE 41) shells Japanese installations on Taroa, Marshalls.

ATLANTIC. U.S. freighters *Martin Johnson* and *Frank C. Emerson* collide west of Bermuda, 35°54′N, 68°41′W; rescue tug *ATR 74* is sent to assist the latter ship. Making contact the following day, *ATR 74* assists the damaged merchantman to port.

6 Saturday

PACIFIC. Japanese *kamikaze* attacks intensify against Lingayen Gulf invasion force, damaging battleships *New Mexico* (BB 40) (killing members of an observing British military mission) and *California* (BB 44); light cruiser *Columbia* (CL 56); destroyers *Newcomb* (DD 586) (also hit by friendly fire) and *Richard P. Leary* (DD 664), 16°20′N, 120°10′E; heavy cruiser *Louisville* (CA 28), 16°37′N, 120°17′E;[229] and destroyers *Allen M. Sumner* (DD 692), 16°40′N, 120°10′E, and *O'Brien* (DD 725), 16°23′N, 120°14′E. Destroyer *Lowry* (DD 770) is damaged by friendly fire, 16°40′N, 120°10′E. *Kamikazes* attack minesweeping group, sinking high-speed minesweeper *Long* (DMS 12), 16°12′N, 120°11′E, and damaging sistership *Southard* (DMS 10), 16°11′N, 126°16′E, and high-speed transport *Brooks* (APD 10), 16°20′N, 120°10′E. Destroyer *Walke* (DD 723), on detached duty covering the minesweepers, 16°40′N, 120°10′E, is attacked by four Japanese planes; one crashes the ship's bridge, drenching it with burning gasoline. Mortally wounded, Commander George F. Davis, *Walke*'s commanding officer, remains at the conn amid the wreckage and rallies his crew. Carried below only when assured that his ship would survive, he dies of his wounds within hours. He is awarded the Medal of Honor posthumously.

TF 38 (Vice Admiral John S. McCain), as a consequence of the *kamikaze* attacks, shifts its focus from Formosa to begin operations against Japanese airfields and shipping in the Luzon area. In the South China Sea off northern Luzon, TF 38 planes sink army cargo ship *Kyodo Maru* and merchant tankers *No. 1 Nanko Maru, No. 8 Iyasaka Maru, No. 6 Kyoei Maru, No. 10 Nanshin Maru, No. 10 Kyoei Maru,* and *No. 3 Kyoei Maru.*

Submarine *Besugo* (SS 321) sinks Japanese fleet tanker *Nichei Maru* in Gulf of Thailand, 06°45′N, 102°55′E, and survives counterattack by *Coast Defense Vessel No. 17.*

Submarine *Sea Robin* (SS 407) attacks Japanese convoy and sinks fleet tanker *Tarakan Maru* east of Hainan Island, 19°45′N, 111°25′E.

USAAF B-24s (14th Air Force) bomb targets in vicinity of Cape St. Jacques, French Indochina, sinking auxiliary submarine chaser *Cha 64* off Poulo Condore Island, 08°55′N, 106°30′E, and merchant tanker *No. 3 Iyasaka Maru.*

MEDITERRANEAN. U.S. freighter *Isaac Shelby* is damaged by mine when she straggles from Naples, Italy–bound convoy NV 90; fortunately, there are no casualties to either the merchant complement or the 12-man Armed Guard. The ship, however, is later declared a total loss.

7 Sunday

PACIFIC. Bombardment and fire support group, TG 77.2 (Rear Admiral Jesse B. Oldendorf), and planes from escort carrier group, TG 77.4 (Rear Admiral Calvin T. Durgin), begin pounding Japanese defenses of Lingayen Gulf. Enemy air attacks in the area continue; high-speed minesweeper *Hovey* (DMS 11) is sunk by aerial torpedo and *Palmer* (DMS 5) by bombs, 16°20′N, 120°10′E. *Kamikazes* damage attack transport *Callaway* (APA 35), 17°00′N, 120°00′E, and tank landing ship *LST 912,* 16°20′N, 120°10′E.

Destroyers *Charles Ausburne* (DD 570), *Braine* (DD 630), *Russell* (DD 414), and *Shaw* (DD 373) sink Japanese destroyer *Hinoki* 50 miles west-southwest of Manila Bay, 14°30′N, 119°30′E.

Submarine *Picuda* (SS 382) damages Japanese army tanker *Munakata Maru* 28 miles northwest of Fukikaku, Formosa, 25°42′N, 121°08′E. *Munakata Maru* puts in to Keelung for repairs (see 21 January).

Submarine *Spot* (SS 413) sinks Japanese guardboat *No. 2 Nichei Maru* in the Inland Sea, 31°20′N, 123°40′E.

USAAF B-24s (14th Air Force), attacking Japanese convoy, sink stores ship *Shinsei Maru* in Formosa Strait, 22°40′N, 118°45′E.

8 Monday

PACIFIC. During continuing Japanese aerial onslaught on the Lingayen Gulf invasion force, *kamikazes* damage escort carriers *Kitkun Bay* (CVE 71), 15°48′N, 119°09′E, and *Kadashan Bay* (CVE 76), 15°10′N, 119°08′E. A suicider also crashes close aboard Australian heavy cruiser HMAS *Australia,* ending her support operations for the day (see 9 January).

Infantry landing craft (gunboat) *LCI(G) 404* is damaged by suicide swimmers, Yoo Passage, Palaus.

Submarine *Balao* (SS 285) sinks Japanese freighter *Daigo Maru* southwest of Korea, 34°28′N, 122°39′E.

TG 17.21 (Commander Charles E. Loughlin), coordinated submarine attack group, attacks Japanese MOTA 30 convoy off northwest coast of Formosa. Despite presence of *Coast Defense Vessel No. 26, Coast Defense Vessel No. 36,* and *Coast Defense Vessel No. 134, Barb* (SS 220) sinks freighters *Anyo Maru,* 24°34′N, 120°37′E, and *Shinyo Maru,* 24°55′N, 120°26′E (the latter explodes violently, forcing *Barb* deep and tearing off deck gratings), and merchant tanker *Sanyo Maru,* 24°37′N, 120°31′E, and damages army cargo ship *Meiho Maru,* 24°25′N, 120°29′E. *Picuda* (SS 382) damages cargo ship *Rashin Maru,* 24°41′N, 120°40′E. *Queenfish* (SS 393) damages tanker *Manju Maru,* 24°25′N, 120°28′E. In the confusion generated by TG 17.21′s attack, merchant tanker *Hikoshima Maru* runs aground in Tungshiao Bay, 24°37′N, 120°31′E, where she will be gradually battered apart by heavy seas over ensuing weeks and rendered a total loss to the enemy war effort.

Submarine *Piranha* (SS 389) damages auxiliary netlayer *No. 2 Shinto Maru* in the Nansei Shoto, 29°55′N, 130°05′E.

Japanese ship *No. 22 Seikai Maru* is sunk by mine off Haha Jima, Bonins.

Cargo ship *Malay Maru* is damaged by mine (laid by British submarine HMS *Stoic* on 3 June 1944) off west coast of Malaya, 05°57′N, 100°14′E.

EUROPE. U.S. freighter *Blenheim* is damaged by explosion of German rocket bomb at Antwerp, Belgium; Armed Guard quarters are wrecked and there are 20 casualties among the 44 merchant sailors, 25-man Armed Guard, and one passenger on board at the time.

9 Tuesday

PACIFIC. Operation MUSKETEER MIKE ONE: Under the overall direction of General of the Army Douglas MacArthur, TF 77 (Vice Admiral Thomas C. Kinkaid) lands U.S. Sixth Army troops (Lieutenant General Walter Krueger) at Lingayen Gulf under cover of heavy gunfire from the bombardment force, TG 77.2 (Vice Admiral Jesse B. Oldendorf), and air support from the escort carrier force, TG 77.4 (Rear Admiral Calvin T. Durgin). The troops initially encounter little resistance, but Japanese air attacks and assault demolition boats vex the invasion force off the beaches. *Kamikazes* crash battleship *Mississippi* (BB 41), 16°08′N, 120°18′E; light cruiser *Columbia* (CL 56), 16°08′N, 120°10′E; and destroyer escort *Hodges* (DE 231), 16°22′N, 120°12′E, in addition to Australian heavy cruiser HMAS *Australia,* which is finally sent to the rear areas for repairs. Friendly fire damages battleship *Colorado* (BB 45), 16°08′N, 120°10′E; Japanese assault demolition boats damage transport *War Hawk* (AP 168) and tank landing ships *LST 925* and *LST 1028,* 16°20′N, 120°10′E.

TF 38 (Vice Admiral John S. McCain) supports the landings at Lingayen Gulf with attacks on Japanese airfields and shipping off Formosa, in the Ryukyus, and in the Pescadores. TF 38 planes operating over these areas sink *Coast Defense Vessel No. 3,* 27°10′N, 121°45′E; submarine chaser *Ch 61,* 22°40′N, 120°04′E; fleet tanker *Kuroshio Maru;* merchant tanker *Kaiho Maru,* 22°47′N, 120°11′E; merchant tanker *No. 4 Nanshin Maru* and cargo ship *Fukuyama Maru,* 22°37′N, 120°15′E; and small cargo vessel *No. 21 Ume Maru* and cargo ship *Hisagawa Maru,* 23°04′N, 119°51′E. Escort vessel *Yashiro,* oiler *Kamoi,* escort destroyer *Miyake,* cargo ship *Tainan Maru, Coast Defense Vessel No. 9, Coast Defense Vessel No. 13, Coast Defense Vessel No. 60,* minesweeper *W.102,* and auxiliary submarine chasers *No. 22 Nitto Maru, Cha 161,* and *Kinsui Maru* are all damaged to varying degrees.

Dutch submarine *O 19,* despite presence of escorting submarine chaser *Ch 5,* sinks gunboat *No. 1 Shinko Maru* off Tanjong Puting, Borneo, 03°41′S, 111°57′E.

Japanese freighter *No. 9 Hokoku Maru* is sunk by aircraft off Ishigaki Jima, Sakishima Gunto.

Japanese auxiliary submarine chaser *Cha 216* is damaged by aircraft off Paishatun.

Marshallese scouts are landed on Jaluit to determine the condition of the Japanese garrison there (see 11 January).

ATLANTIC. U.S. freighter *Jonas Lie*, in New York–bound convoy ON 277, is torpedoed by German submarine *U 1055* at the entrance to the Bristol Channel, 51°43′N, 05°25′W. The ship, abandoned, later sinks on 14 January.

10 Wednesday

PACIFIC. Japanese assault demolition boats infiltrate transport areas off Lingayen, sinking infantry landing craft (mortar) *LCI(M) 974*, 16°06′N, 120°14′E, and infantry landing craft (gunboat) *LCI(G) 365*, and damaging destroyers *Robinson* (DD 562) and *Philip* (DD 498), transport *War Hawk* (AP 168), and tank landing ship *LST 610*. Japanese air attacks against the fleet off Lingayen continue, damaging destroyer *Wickes* (DD 578), 16°04′N, 118°55′E. *Kamikaze*s damage destroyer escort *Leray Wilson* (DE 414), 16°20′N, 120°10′E, and attack transport *Dupage* (APA 41), 16°17′N, 120°15′E. Off the west coast of Luzon, high-speed transport *Clemson* (APD 31) and battleship *Pennsylvania* (BB 38) are damaged in collision, 16°20′N, 120°10′E. *Clemson* is also accidentally rammed the same day by attack transport *Latimer* (APA 152), 16°20′N, 120°10′E. Oiler *Guadalupe* (AO 32) is damaged in collision with *Nantahala* (AO 60), 20°06′N, 121°34′E; tank landing ship *LST 567* is damaged in collision with *LST 610*, 16°20′N, 120°10′E.

Submarine *Puffer* (SS 268) sinks Japanese *Coast Defense Vessel No. 42* and damages *Coast Defense Vessel No. 30* in the East China Sea, 26°45′N, 126°11′E.

Japanese merchant vessel *No. 2 Seikai Maru* is damaged by aircraft off Mukai Jima, northern Bingo Nada, Inland Sea.

ATLANTIC. Coast Guard cutter *Nemesis* (WPC 111) collides with U.S. freighter *Felipe de Nueve* off Point Judith; the latter stands by to render assistance. Coast Guard cutter *Kaw* heads to the scene from the Cape Cod Canal, cutter *Hornbeam*, motor minesweeper *YMS 519*, and other small craft from Newport, Rhode Island. *YMS 519* takes on board the injured while *Hornbeam* tows the damaged *Nemesis* to Newport.

11 Thursday

ATLANTIC. Motor minesweeper *YMS 14* is sunk in collision with destroyer *Herndon* (DD 638) in north channel of Boston Harbor, Massachusetts.

PACIFIC. High-speed transport *Belknap* (APD 34) is damaged by *kamikaze* off Luzon, 16°20′N, 120°10′E; tank landing ships *LST 270* and *LST 918* are damaged by shore battery,

16°20′N, 120°10′E; and tank landing ship *LST 700* is damaged by friendly fire, 16°43′N, 119°58′E. U.S. destroyer gunfire sinks Japanese auxiliary minesweeper *Wa.10* south of Vigan, 17°20′N, 120°00′E. Auxiliary minesweeper *No. 56 Banshu Maru* and auxiliary submarine chaser *Hakuyo Maru* are scuttled as blockships at south entrance of Manila Bay, Luzon.

During hunter-killer operations near Yap, Carolines, destroyer *Evans* (DD 552) and destroyer escort *McCoy Reynolds* (DE 440) bombard Japanese defenses; they repeat the operation the following day.

Destroyer escort *Brackett* (DE 41) extracts party of Marshallese scouts from Jaluit, where they had been landed on 9 January to determine the condition of the Japanese garrison there.

Japanese submarines commence "KONGO" Operation, employing suicide torpedoes (*kaitens*). *I 36* launches *kaitens* that damage ammunition ship *Mazama* (AE 9) and large infantry landing craft *LCI(L) 600* at Ulithi, Carolines; salvage vessel *Current* (ARS 22) provides assistance to the torpedoed *Mazama* (see 12 and 20 January).

Japanese freighter *Kinsei Maru* is sunk by marine casualty in Osaka Bay, Japan.

12 Friday

PACIFIC. TF 38 (Vice Admiral John S. McCain) planes pound Japanese shipping, airfields, and other installations in French Indochina. TF 38 planes annihilate HI 86 convoy north of Qui Nhon, sinking antisubmarine sweeping ship (ex-training cruiser) *Kashii*; escort vessel *Chiburi*; *Coast Defense Vessel No. 17*; *Coast Defense Vessel No. 19*; tankers *Ayanami Maru*, *Hoei Maru*, *Akashi Maru*, and *Kumagawa Maru*; and transport *Shinsei Maru*. *Coast Defense Vessel No. 23* and *Coast Defense Vessel No. 51*, transport *Kembu Maru*, army cargo ships *Yushu Maru* and *Kyokun Maru*, tankers *No. 2 Nanryu Maru* and *Shoei Maru*, and cargo ships *Eiman Maru*, *Hotsusan Maru*, *Tatsuhato Maru*, *Otsusan Maru*, *Yujo Maru*, and *No. 63 Banshu Maru* are damaged. Landing ships *T.149* and *T.137*, fleet tankers *San Luis Maru* and *No. 3 Kyoei Maru*, escort vessels *Daito* and *Ukuru*, and *Coast Defense Vessel No. 27* are also damaged. TF 38 planes attack convoy SASI 40. Army cargo ship *France Maru*, merchant tanker *Shingi Maru*, and guardboat *No. 2 Fushimi Maru* are sunk off Vung Tau. Convoy SATA 05 comes under attack by TF 38 planes below Cape Padaran. Submarine chaser *Ch 31*, minesweeper *W.101*, *Patrol Boat No. 103* [ex-U.S. minesweeper *Finch*

(AM 9)], *Coast Defense Vessel No. 35*, *Coast Defense Vessel No. 43*, and the ships they are escorting—tankers *Ayayuki Maru*, *Nagayoshi Maru*, and *Koshin Maru*, cargo ship *Kensei Maru*, and transport *Toyu Maru*—are sunk. Near Cam Ranh Bay, submarine chaser *Ch 43* and auxiliary minesweeper *Otowa Maru* are sunk; submarine chaser *Ch 34* and freighter *Ryuyo Maru* are damaged. At or near Saigon, landing ship *T.140* and victualling stores ship *Ikutagawa Maru*, army cargo ships *Kiyo Maru* and *No. 17 Shinsei Maru*, freighters *Kenei Maru* and *Taikyu Maru*, and tanker *No. 9 Horai Maru* are sunk; landing ship *T.131* and freighters *Chefoo Maru* and *Kanju Maru* are damaged. French ships, due to their proximity to Japanese vessels, also come under attack: light cruiser *Lamotte-Picquet* is sunk, as is surveying vessel *Octant*; steamship *Albert Sarraut* is strafed, as is freighter *Taiposek*.[230]

Off the west coast of Luzon, *kamikazes* damage destroyer escorts *Richard W. Suesens* (DE 342) and *Gilligan* (DE 508), 16°20′N, 120°10′E; attack transport *Zeilin* (APA 3), 15°23′N, 119°25′E; and tank landing ship *LST 700*, 14°04′N, 119°25′E. Suicide pilots also target U.S. merchant ships, damaging freighters *Elmira Victory* (there are no casualties to either the merchant complement or the 27-man Armed Guard), 16°11′N, 120°20′E (friendly fire also causes damage to the ship); *Otis Skinner* (Armed Guard sailors contribute to firefighting efforts), 14°42′N, 119°35′E; *Edward M. Wescott* (10 of the 25-man Armed Guard are wounded by flying debris); *Kyle V. Johnson* (129 of 506 Army troops, being transported, die), 15°12′N, 119°30′E; and *David Dudley Field* (Armed Guard gunfire deflects the *kamikaze* so that it only strikes the ship a glancing blow). In the maelstrom of gunfire put up to splash the attacking planes, friendly fire causes damage to high-speed transport *Sands* (APD 13) and tank landing ships *LST 710* and *LST 778*, 15°00′N, 119°30′E.

"KONGO" Operation continues: Japanese submarine *I 47* launches *kaitens* that damage U.S. freighter *Pontus H. Ross* off Hollandia, New Guinea, 02°33′S, 140°06′W; there are no casualties among the merchant sailors or the 27-man Armed Guard (see 20 January). Success, however, eludes *I 53* at Kossol Roads, Palau; *I 56* at Manus, in the Admiralties; and *I 58* at Apra Harbor, Guam.

13 Saturday

PACIFIC. Japanese *kamikaze* attacks against Lingayen Gulf invasion shipping culminate in suicide plane damaging escort carrier *Sala-maua* (CVE 96), 17°09′N, 119°21′E.

Destroyer escort *Fleming* (DE 32) sinks Japanese submarine *I 362,* 320 miles north-northeast of Truk, 12°08′N, 154°27′E.

Open lighter *YC 912* founders in heavy weather, North Pacific Ocean.

MEDITERRANEAN. Ex-USAAF aircraft rescue boat *P 584,* under administrative control of Office of Strategic Services (OSS) and manned by a navy crew, is destroyed by explosion at Leghorn, Italy, injuring 11 sailors.

14 Sunday

PACIFIC. Submarine *Cobia* (SS 245) sinks Japanese minelayer *Yurijima* off east coast of Malaya, 05°45′N, 103°13′E.

Motor torpedo boat *PT 73,* damaged by grounding off west coast of Mindoro, P.I., 13°50′N, 120°10′E, is beached and abandoned.

USAAF P-51s (14th Air Force) sink Japanese army cargo ship *Akatsuki Maru* in the Yangtze River between Wuhu and Kiukiang, 29°00′N, 116°00′E.

Army freight supply vessel *FS 41* breaks loose from her moorings at Amchitka, Aleutians, in heavy weather, and demolishes 300 feet of an Army dock; fleet tug *Sarsi* (ATF 111) is sent from Adak to go to the ship's assistance.

ATLANTIC. U.S. freighter *Martin Van Buren,* in Nova Scotia–bound convoy BV 141, is torpedoed by German submarine *U 1232* at 44°27′N, 63°26′W; three of the 27-man Armed Guard (members of a 5-inch gun crew) perish when blown overboard. Despite salvage efforts, the ship subsequently drifts ashore and is written off as a total loss.

EUROPE. U.S. freighter *Michael de Kovats* is damaged by explosion of German V-2 rocket bomb at Antwerp, Belgium; none of the 27-man Armed Guard are casualties.

15 Monday

PACIFIC. Escort carrier *Hoggatt Bay* (CVE 75) is damaged by accidental explosion of bombs as TBM (VC 88) lands on board as the ship operates off west coast of Luzon, 17°01′N, 119°20′E.

TF 38 (Vice Admiral John S. McCain) attacks Japanese shipping and aircraft off Formosa and the China coast. TF 38 planes sink destroyer *Hatakaze* and fast transport *T.14* at 22°37′N, 120°15′E; fleet tanker *Miru Maru* and army cargo ship *Enoshima Maru* off Takao; and destroyer *Tsuga* off Mako, 23°33′N, 119°33′E. Auxiliary minelayer *Maroshima* is damaged off Formosa and army cargo ships

Beiju Maru and *Yoshun Maru* are damaged off Keelung.

Destroyer *Swanson* (DD 443) bombards Rota Island, Marianas; she repeats the operation the following day.

Japanese auxiliary minesweeper *No. 1 Kyo Maru* is sunk by mine (laid by British submarine HMS *Porpoise* on 9 January), south of Penang, Malaya, 05°18′N, 100°20′E.

USAAF B-25s, escorted by P-51s and P-40s (14th Air Force), attack Hankow, China, damaging Japanese river gunboat *Narumi.*

Japanese freighter *No. 5 Kujyo Maru* is sunk by aircraft southwest of Paramushir, Kurils.

District patrol vessel *YP 73* sinks after running aground 1,000 yards east of Spruce Cape signal station, Kodiak, Alaska. Coast Guard tender *Bittersweet* (WAG 389) rescues survivors.

MEDITERRANEAN. Destroyers *Boyle* (DD 600) and *McLanahan* (DD 615) support British and American light craft, including U.S. motor torpedo boats, in a night interdiction operation aimed at enemy coastwise shipping.

RAF Spitfire sights one large and one small German escort vessel west of Portofino, Italy; *PT 313* and British *MTB 378* engage a southbound convoy of five flak lighters, sinking one and damaging another. The presence of the escort vessels, however, results in the operation being discontinued.

16 Tuesday

PACIFIC. TF 38 (Vice Admiral John S. McCain) strikes Japanese shipping and installations at Hong Kong, Hainan Island, and along the China coast. Off Hong Kong TF 38 planes sink transport *Hokkai Maru;* merchant tankers *Tenei Maru, Matsushima Maru,* and *Sanko Maru;* and freighter *No. 2 Anri Go.* They also damage oiler *Kamoi,* destroyer *Hasu,* fast transport *T.108,* escort destroyers *Shinnan* and *Nomi,* and *Coast Defense Vessel No. 60.* Off Yulin, TF 38 planes sink merchant tanker *Harima Maru* and damage escort destroyer *Daito.* Guardboat *No. 1 Taiyo Maru* is sunk east of Hainan; merchant tanker *No. 6 Nanryu Maru* is sunk off coast of South China.

ATLANTIC. Destroyer escorts *Otter* (DE 210), *Hubbard* (DE 211), *Hayter* (DE 212), and *Varian* (DE 798) sink German submarine *U 248* north-northeast of the Azores, 47°43′N, 26°37′W.

Non-rigid airship *ZPNK 123* is accidentally deflated at Port Lyautey, French Morocco; the envelope is damaged beyond repair.

EUROPE. U.S. freighter *Marina* is damaged by mine outside of swept channel to Le Havre, France; there are no casualties.

17 Wednesday

PACIFIC. Escort carrier *Nehenta Bay* (CVE 74) is damaged by storm west of Luzon, 17°41′N, 117°33′E.

Submarine *Tautog* (SS 199) sinks Japanese fast transport *T.15* off southern Kyushu, 31°09′N, 130°29′E.

British submarine HMS *Stygian* sinks small Japanese cargo vessel *Nichinan Maru* off Perak, 05°42′N, 98°57′E.

Japanese cargo ship *Minka Maru* is sunk by mine above Kiukiang, China.

MEDITERRANEAN. Tank landing ship *LST 906,* which had been aground at Leghorn, Italy, since 18 October 1944, is refloated.

18 Thursday

PACIFIC. Japanese raiding parties land on Peleliu, Palau Islands. The attempt to damage aircraft on the ground and destroy ammunition is not successful.

Tank landing ship *LST 219* is damaged by grounding off Lingayen, 16°10′N, 120°22′E.

Tank landing ship *LST 752* is damaged in collision off San Ricardo, Leyte, 11°11′N, 125°05′E.

Infantry landing craft (gunboat) *LCI(G) 396* is damaged by mine, Palaus.

Japanese freighter *Reizan Maru* (previously damaged on 31 August 1944 by 14th Air Force planes) is sunk by mine in upper Yangtze.

19 Friday

PACIFIC. Submarine *Spot* (SS 413) sinks Japanese freighter *Usa Maru* off Dairen, Manchuria, 39°07′N, 122°51′E.

ANDAMAN SEA. British submarine HMS *Supreme* damages Japanese auxiliary netlayer *Agata Maru* south of Ross Island, Andaman Islands; submarine chaser *Ch 63,* also damaged in the surface gunnery engagement, is run aground.

20 Saturday

EUROPE. Hungary surrenders to the Allies.

Naval Technical Mission in Europe (Commodore Henry A. Schade) is established with headquarters in Paris, France.

PACIFIC. Submarine *Nautilus* (SS 168) lands supplies on south coast of Mindanao, P.I.

Submarine *Spot* (SS 413) sinks Japanese merchant fishing boat *Tokiwa Maru* off southwestern Korea, 34°45′N, 124°10′E.

Submarine *Tautog* (SS 199) sinks Japanese

torpedo recovery vessel *Shuri Maru* at southern end of Tsushima Strait, 33°37′N, 128°40′E.

"KONGO" Operation concludes with Japanese submarine *I 48* carrying out unsuccessful *kaiten* attack on U.S. shipping at Ulithi, Carolines (see 23 January).

21 Sunday

PACIFIC. TF 38 (Vice Admiral John S. McCain) attacks Japanese shipping and airfields on Formosa and in the Pescadores, as well as in Sakishima Gunto and on Okinawa in the Ryukyus. Japanese planes make concerted counterattacks on the task force ships. *Kamikazes* damage carrier *Ticonderoga* (CV 14), 22°40′N, 122°57′E, and destroyer *Maddox* (DD 731), 23°06′N, 122°43′E; small carrier *Langley* (CVL 27) is damaged by bomb, 22°40′N, 122°51′E. Accidental explosion of bombs carried by TBM (VT 7) damages carrier *Hancock* (CV 19), 22°40′N, 122°30′E. TF 38 planes sink fleet tankers *Eiho Maru* and *Manjo Maru*; cargo ship *Kuroshio Maru*; army cargo ships *Enoura Maru, Asaka Maru, No. 2 Nichiyo Maru,* and *Teifu Maru*; army tankers *Shincho Maru, No. 3 Hoei Maru, No. 5 Hoei Maru,* and *Yamazawa Maru*; fishing boat *Brunei Maru*; and cargo vessels *Daijo Maru* and *Yayoi Maru*. TF 38 planes also damage destroyers *Kashi* and *Sugi*, landing ships *T.114* and *T.143*, freighter *Yulin Maru*, and water supply vessel *Nikko Maru* off Takao, Formosa. Planes from carrier *Yorktown* (CV 10) and small carrier *Cabot* (CVL 28) sink merchant tanker *Munakata Maru* at Keelung; TF 38 planes damage destroyer *Harukaze* off Mako, Formosa.

USAAF B-24s (14th Air Force) sink Japanese salvage vessel *Haruta Maru* at Hong Kong, 22°20′N, 114°10′E.

Submarine *Tautog* (SS 199) sinks Japanese merchant tanker *Zuiun Maru* off western Kyushu, 33°33′N, 129°33′E; auxiliary submarine chaser *Cha 200* and another escort vessel force *Tautog* to go deep.

Landing craft *LCT 253* founders and sinks in heavy weather en route to Tarawa, Gilberts.

ATLANTIC. U.S. freighter *George Hawley*, in convoy TBC 43, is torpedoed and irreparably damaged by German submarine *U 1199* off the Isle of Wight, 49°53′N, 05°44′W.

22 Monday

PACIFIC. TF 38 (Vice Admiral John S. McCain) pounds Japanese shipping, airfields, and other installations in the Ryukyus. TF 38 planes sink motor sailships *No. 1 Iroha Maru* and *Myoei Maru*, fishing boat *No. 1 Waei Maru*, and cargo vessel *Suma Maru* in Gima Harbor, Kume Island; merchant tankers *No. 2 Nanko Maru* and *No. 2 Nanshin Maru* off Miyako Jima; and freighter *Hikosan Maru* in Toguchi Harbor, Okinawa, 26°39′N, 127°53′E. Guardboat *No. 6 Chitose Maru* is sunk, probably by aircraft in the Nansei Shoto.

British submarine HMS *Spirit* sinks Japanese ship *Ryushin Maru* in Java Sea, 06°02′S, 110°41′E.

Japanese submarine chaser *Ch 42* is damaged by mine off Chichi Jima, Bonins.

Japanese river gunboat *Saga* is sunk by aircraft at Hong Kong.

23 Tuesday

ATLANTIC. President Roosevelt embarks in heavy cruiser *Quincy* (CA 71) at Newport News, Virginia, on the beginning of the trip that will include his participation in ARGONAUT Conferences at Malta and Yalta (see 4 February).

PACIFIC. Destroyer escort *Conklin* (DE 439), supported by sisterships *Corbesier* (DE 438) and *Raby* (DE 698), sinks Japanese submarine *I 48* (fresh from her unsuccessful "KONGO" *kaiten* mission to Ulithi), 25 miles off Yap, 09°45′N, 138°20′E.

Submarine *Barb* (SS 220), as an element of TG 17.21 (coordinated attack group), enters Namkwan Harbor, China, and attacks Japanese MOTA 32 convoy. Despite her claim that she sinks three vessels, probably sinks a fourth, and damages two more, she actually destroys only a single ship, freighter *Taikyu Maru*, 27°04′N, 120°27′E.

Submarine *Nautilus* (SS 168) delivers supplies to Filipino forces on the east coast of Mindanao.

Submarine *Sennet* (SS 408) sinks Japanese guardboat *No. 7 Kainan Maru* in Hangchow Bay, 30°00′N, 120°16′E.

Mines laid by RAF Liberators the previous day sink Japanese merchant tanker *No. 1 Hozan Maru* and cargo ship *Nikkaku Maru* south of Sembilan Island, Sumatra, 04°08′N, 98°15′E.

24 Wednesday

PACIFIC. TG 94.9 (Rear Admiral Oscar C. Badger), consisting of battleship *Indiana* (BB 58), three heavy cruisers, seven destroyers, and a light minelayer, and preceded in its approach by a barrier patrol of PB4Ys, bombards Iwo Jima, together with USAAF B-24s (escorted by P-38s). Northeast of Iwo Jima, destroyers *Dun-*

lap (DD 384) and *Fanning* (DD 385) sink Japanese transport *I-Go Yoneyama Maru* and auxiliary minesweepers *Keinan Maru* and *No. 7 Showa Maru*, 24°50′N, 141°22′E, a small three-ship convoy that had just arrived that morning.

Navy land-based planes flying from the Philippines bomb Japanese shipping at Keelung, Formosa, sinking freighter *Beiju Maru* and damaging cargo ship *Taizatsu Maru*, 25°09′N, 121°45′E.

Dock landing ship *Shadwell* (LSD 15) is damaged by aerial torpedo south of Negros Island, P.I., 09°01′N, 123°45′E.

Japanese auxiliary submarine chaser *Shunyo Maru* is sunk by aircraft off Corregidor, P.I.

Submarine *Atule* (SS 403) sinks Japanese freighter *No. 1 Taiman Maru* in the central Yellow Sea, 36°47′N, 123°59′E.

Submarine *Blackfin* (SS 322) sinks Japanese destroyer *Shigure* 160 miles east of Khota Baru, Malaya, 06°00′N, 103°48′E, and teams with *Besugo* (SS 321) to damage merchant tanker *Sarawak Maru* off east coast of Malay Peninsula, 06°00′N, 103°45′E (see 19 March).

Submarine *Guardfish* (SS 217) mistakenly sinks salvage vessel *Extractor* (ARS 15) in Philippine Sea east of Luzon, 15°44′N, 133°29′E.

EUROPE. German planes bomb Antwerp, Belgium, damaging U.S. freighter *Alcoa Banner*; she is later written off as a total loss.

25 Thursday

PACIFIC. Submarine *Greenling* (SS 213) is damaged by depth charges off the Nansei Shoto, 29°27′N, 130°09′E, and is forced to terminate her patrol.

Submarine *Silversides* (SS 236) sinks Japanese army cargo ship *Malay Maru* off Kuro Jima, 31°18′N, 130°08′E, despite presence of auxiliary submarine chasers *Cha 90* and *Cha 168*.

MEDITERRANEAN. Destroyer *McLanahan* (DD 615) shells German command post and then silences shore battery on the Italian Riviera.

ATLANTIC. Norwegian tanker *Britamsea* experiences fire at sea off the Delaware capes, 39°24′N, 72°55′W; rescue tug *ATR 57* (with a mobile fire-fighting unit embarked) is dispatched from Cape May, New Jersey. *ATR 57* firefighters not only succeed in extinguishing the blaze but, forced to remain on board by a delay in the ship being taken in tow, display their versatility by getting the merchantman's engines started with the assistance of the Norwegian engine room force, thus enabling *Britamsea* to proceed to New York under her own power.

26 Friday

PACIFIC. Submarine *Tautog* (SS 199) sinks Japanese merchant sail fishing boat *No. 11 Naga Maru* east by south of Osumi Gunto, 30°00′N, 136°20′E.

Tank landing craft *LCT 1151* founders and sinks off Schouten Islands, 01°00′N, 138°36′E.

Japanese auxiliary submarine chaser *Hakko Maru* is sunk by aircraft off Corregidor.

Japanese freighter *Horai Maru* is sunk by mine near Singapore, 01°20′3″N, 104°06′E.

Japanese auxiliary submarine chaser *No. 13 Kyo Maru* is sunk by mine off Bengeri Point.

Japanese freighter *No. 1 Tamon Maru* is sunk by mine, laid by submarine *Dace* (SS 247) on 16 December 1944, off Gambir Island, French Indochina, 13°36′N, 109°18′E.

27 Saturday

PACIFIC. Submarine *Bergall* (SS 320) sinks Japanese auxiliary minesweeper *Wa. 102* in Lombok Strait, 08°34′S, 115°50′E.

Motor torpedo boat *PT 338* is damaged by grounding off Semimara Island, Luzon, 12°06′N, 121°23′E (see 31 January).

Japanese freighter *Ryuzan Maru* is sunk by USAAF mine near Kiukiang, China, 29°46′N, 116°52′E; cargo ship *Hsin Yang Maru* is sunk by USAAF mine (laid by 14th Air Force B-24 on 19 January) off Kiukiang, 29°55′N, 115°20′E.

Japanese transport *Nagatsu Maru* is damaged by mine off Chichi Jima, Bonins.

ATLANTIC. U.S. freighter *Ruben Dario* is torpedoed and damaged by German submarine, most likely *U 852*, off Saint George's Channel, 52°27′N, 05°21′W. There are no casualties among the 27-man Armed Guard.

28 Sunday

PACIFIC. Submarine *Spadefish* (SS 411) attacks Japanese HI 91 convoy west of Ch'uja Kundo, Korea, and sinks escort vessel *Kume*, 33°50′N, 122°55′E, and transport (ex–seaplane carrier) *Sanuki Maru*, 34°02′N, 123°00′E.

29 Monday

PACIFIC. TG 78.3 (Rear Admiral Arthur D. Struble) lands troops (38th Infantry and 34th RCT of 24th Infantry) near San Antonio, northwest of Subic Bay. They encounter no opposition, move inland rapidly, and seize all initial objectives.

Landing craft repair ship *Amycus* (ARL 2) and medium landing ship *LSM 135* are damaged when accidentally bombed by SBD, Lingayen Gulf, 16°20′N, 120°10′E.

Cargo ship *Serpens* (AK 97) is sunk by explosion of undetermined origin off Guadalcanal, Solomons; the blast damages submarine chasers *PC 588*, *SC 1039*, and *SC 1266*; motor minesweeper *YMS 281*; and district patrol vessel *YP 514*.

Destroyer *Lardner* (DD 487) is damaged when she runs aground off Ngesebus Island, Palaus.

Submarine *Picuda* (SS 382), as part of TG 17.21 (coordinated attack group), attacks Japanese MOTA 23 convoy in Formosa Strait, sinking army cargo ship *Clyde Maru* about 50 miles northwest of Keelung, 25°20′N, 121°06′E.

USAAF B-25s damage Japanese auxiliary submarine chaser *No. 10 Takunan Maru* off Chichi Jima, 27°45′N, 142°00′E. Submarine chaser *Ch 52* tries to tow the ship to safety, but *No. 10 Takunan Maru* sinks early the next morning.

30 Tuesday

PACIFIC. Operation MIKE SEVEN: TG 78.3 (Rear Admiral Arthur D. Struble) lands army troops (38th Infantry) on Grande Island, Subic Bay, against no enemy opposition. Light cruiser *Denver* (CL 58) and destroyers *Fletcher* (DD 445) and *Radford* (DD 446) provide gunfire support. TG 77.4 (Rear Admiral William D. Sample), six CVEs and their screen, provide direct air cover. Attack transport *Cavalier* (APA 37) is torpedoed by Japanese submarine *RO 46* off Subic Bay, 14°48′N, 119°18′E.

Destroyer *Burns* (DD 588) sinks Japanese guardboat *No. 2 Hokoku Maru* off Ojae, 08°42′N, 167°44′E.

Submarine *Bergall* (SS 320) damages Japanese storeship *Arasaki* off north coast of Bali, N.E.I., 08°26′S, 115°40′E.

Submarine *Threadfin* (SS 410) sinks Japanese freighter *Issei Maru* off southern Honshu, 33°30′N, 135°34′E, but although damaged by depth charges from escorts, 33°20′N, 135°30′E, remains on patrol.

British submarine HMS *Tantalus* sinks Japanese fishing boat *No. 12 Taisei Maru* in northern approaches to Bangka Strait, 01°26′S, 105°01′E.

ATLANTIC. Provision stores ship *Pontiac* (AF 20), en route to Halifax, Nova Scotia, in a heavy sea, is damaged by loose paravane and sinks in shallow water off MacNab Island (see 17 February).

31 Wednesday

PACIFIC. Operation MIKE SIX: TG 78.2 (Rear Admiral William M. Fechteler) lands Army troops (two RCTs of the 11th Airborne Division) at Nasugbu, south of the entrance to Manila Bay. TG 77.4 (Rear Admiral William D. Sample) provides cover. A third RCT of the 11th Airborne is airdropped at Tagtaytay Ridge, 14 miles inland, and the three RCTs link up on 3 February. This operation, designed to outflank the enemy forces defending Manila, meets little resistance at the outset; Japanese assault demolition boats attack the screen, however, and sink submarine chaser *PC 1129*, the flagship for the control unit, TU 78.2.7, 14°05′N, 120°30′E.

Submarine *Boarfish* (SS 327) attacks Japanese HI 88 convoy, sinking freighter *Enki Maru* 50 miles southeast of Tourane, French Indochina, 14°55′N, 109°01′E, and damaging cargo ship *Taietsu Maru*, which is run aground 14°56′N, 109°00′E (see 1 February).

Submarine *Pargo* (SS 264) torpedoes Japanese escort vessel *Manju* east-southeast of Cape Padaran, 11°51′N, 109°12′E.

Submarine *Spadefish* (SS 411) unsuccessfully attacks Japanese ship *Nanshin Maru* in Yellow Sea west of Ch'uja Kundo, Korea, 34°14′N, 122°36′E.

Motor torpedo boat *PT 338*, irreparably damaged by grounding on 27 January, is destroyed by demolition squad off Semimara Island, Luzon, 12°06′N, 121°23′E.

USAAF B-25s (Far Eastern Air Force) sink Japanese escort destroyer *Ume* and damage destroyer *Shiokaze* and escort destroyer *Kaede* west of Takao, Formosa, 22°30′N, 12°00′E.

Japanese small cargo vessel *No. 4 Kiri Maru* is sunk by mine off Cape Tavoy, Burma, 13°32′N, 98°10′E.

FEBRUARY

1 Thursday

PACIFIC. Destroyers *Jenkins* (DD 447), *O'Bannon* (DD 450), and *Bell* (DD 587) and destroyer escort *Ulvert M. Moore* (DE 442) sink submarine *RO 115*, 125 miles southwest of Manila, 13°20′N, 119°20′E.

USAAF B-24s (14th Air Force), directed to the scene by *Boarfish* (SS 327), complete the destruction of grounded Japanese cargo ship *Taietsu Maru* (damaged by *Boarfish* the previous day) off the coast of French Indochina, 14°56′N, 109°00′E.

President Franklin D. Roosevelt is flanked by British Prime Minister Winston S. Churchill (left) and Soviet Premier Joseph Stalin at Yalta, February 1945. Two of the President's chief wartime naval advisers are visible here: Fleet Admirals William D. Leahy (directly behind the chief executive) and Ernest J. King (by the pillar behind Leahy). (NA, U.S. Army C-543)

Motor torpedo boats PT 77 and PT 79 are damaged by friendly fire west of Mindoro, 13°55′N, 120°36′E.

USAAF P-51s sink Japanese landing ship T.115 in Luzon Straits, 20°00′N, 121°00′E, and damage escorting submarine chaser Ch 28.

British submarine HMS Spark sinks Japanese towboat No. 203 Katsura Maru and damages motor sailboats Nanyo Maru, Nampo Maru, and No. 80 Tachibana Maru off Jabara, 06°41′S, 110°32′E.

Japanese netlayer No. 16 Nissho Maru is sunk by mine off Hajo Do, Korea, 35°00′N, 125°00′E.

USAAF B-29s (20th Air Force) bomb Japanese shipping and harbor facilities at Singapore, damaging oiler Shiretoko, 01°20′N, 103°50′E.

Japanese tanker No. 26 Nanshin Maru is sunk by mine east of the Nansei Shoto, 30°05′N, 135°15′E; guardboat No. 15 Shinko Maru rescues survivors.

2 Friday

PACIFIC. Submarine Besugo (SS 321), attacking Japanese convoy off Malay Peninsula, sinks Coast Defense Vessel No. 144 off Cape Laguan, 04°32′N, 104°30′E.

Submarine Hardhead (SS 365) sinks Japanese merchant tanker No. 19 Nanshin Maru off east coast of Malaya, 05°40′N, 103°17′E.

USAAF B-24 attacks Japanese tanker Yashima Maru and forces her aground, damaged, off Flores Island, Azores.

Japanese merchant tanker No. 3 Kinyu Maru is sunk by aircraft off Phantiet, French Indochina.

3 Saturday

PACIFIC. Submarine Sea Robin (SS 407) damages Japanese transport Suiten Maru off Bawean Island, N.E.I.

Japanese river gunboat Karatsu [ex-Luzon (PR 7)] is scuttled as blockship at Manila.

Minesweeper W.102 (ex-HMS Waglan) is damaged (cause unspecified) north of Haitan Island, 25°40′N, 119°50′E.

Land-based Navy planes sink Japanese merchant tanker No. 3 Nanryu Maru south of Amoy, China, 24°28′N, 118°13′E.

4 Sunday

GENERAL. Yalta (ARGONAUT) Conference attended by President Roosevelt, British Prime Minister Winston S. Churchill, and Soviet Premier Joseph Stalin begins. Matters discussed include the timing of the Soviet entry into the war against Japan and three postwar issues: the division of Germany, the extent of the Soviet sphere of influence in Europe, and the status of Poland (see 11 February).

PACIFIC. Submarine Barbel (SS 316) is sunk by Japanese naval aircraft in South China Sea between Borneo and Palawan, 07°49.5′N, 116°47.5′E.[231]

Submarine Pargo (SS 264) bombards Woody Island, east of Tourane, French Indochina, destroying Japanese weather station and radio equipment, administration building, a jetty, and several fishing boats.

Submarine Spadefish (SS 411) sinks Japanese freighter Tairai Maru in the Yellow Sea off the west coast of Korea, 37°18′N, 125°22′E.

5 Monday

PACIFIC. Destroyer Bearss (DD 654) suffers minor damage from ammunition hangfire while on exercises in the Aleutians.

Japanese Coast Defense Vessel No. 6 is damaged by marine casualty; minesweeper W.29 is damaged by mine off Chichi Jima, Bonins.

MEDITERRANEAN. Motor torpedo boats PT 308 and PT 313, on a routine patrol from Leghorn, Italy, sight two south-bound KT ships and one escort and engage them a half mile northwest of the swept channel off Portovenere, claiming at least one KT ship sunk.

6 Tuesday

PACIFIC. Submarine Pampanito (SS 383), attacking Japanese convoy, sinks merchant tanker Engen Maru about 200 miles northeast of Singapore, 06°22′N, 106°00′E.

Submarine Spadefish (SS 411) sinks Japanese merchant passenger-cargo ship Shohei Maru off Port Arthur, Korea, 38°46′N, 121°28′E.

PB4Ys attack Japanese convoy in the Sakishima-Okinawa area, sinking small cargo ship No. 77 Ume Maru.

USAAF planes sink Japanese cargo ship No. 3 Kinyu Maru off Cape Padaran, French Indochina, 12°50′N, 109°23′E.

Japanese Coast Defense Vessel No. 12 is damaged by aircraft, 36 miles northwest of Chichi Jima, Bonins.

Japanese tanker Oei Maru is sunk by mine laid by USAAF B-29 (20th Air Force) on 25 January in Johore Strait, 01°09′N, 103°36′E. Battleship/carrier Ise is damaged by mine off Singapore.

INDIAN OCEAN. U.S. freighter Peter Silvester is torpedoed and sunk by German submarine U 862 off the southeast coast of Australia,

34°19′S, 99°37′E; seven of the 26-man Armed Guard perish with the ship (see 9, 13, and 27 February and 10 March).

EUROPE. U.S. freighter *Henry B. Plant*, in Antwerp-bound convoy TAM 71, is torpedoed and sunk by German submarine *U 245* at 51°19′24″N, 01°42′30″W; 7 of the 28-man Armed Guard perish in the abandonment. British minesweeper HMS *Hazard* and HM Trawler *Sir Lancelot* rescue survivors.

7 Wednesday

PACIFIC. Motor torpedo boats *PT 373* and *PT 356* enter Manila Bay for night reconnaissance; these are the first U.S. naval units to enter that body of water since the surrender of Corregidor in 1942.

Destroyer escort *Thomason* (DE 203) sinks Japanese submarine *RO 55* off Iba, Luzon, 15°27′N, 119°25′E.

Submarine *Bergall* (SS 320), attacking Japanese HI 93 convoy off east coast of French Indochina, sinks *Coast Defense Vessel No. 53* and damages merchant tanker *Toho Maru* near Cam Ranh Bay, 11°56′N, 109°18′E. Submarine chaser *Ch 33* engages in rescue work.

Submarine *Guavina* (SS 362), attacking a Japanese convoy, sinks merchant tanker *Taigyo Maru* 250 miles south of Saigon, French Indochina, 06°45′N, 106°00′E.

Submarine *Parche* (SS 384) sinks Japanese army cargo ship *Okinoyama Maru* in Tokara Retto, 29°09′N, 129°45′E.

Submarine *Ronquil* (SS 396) damages Japanese army cargo ship *Kuretake Maru* off Tori Shima, 31°46′N, 140°17′E.

ANDAMAN SEA. British submarine HMS *Subtle* sinks small Japanese cargo vessel *Nanei Maru* east of Nicobar Islands, 07°28′N, 94°56′E.

MEDITERRANEAN. Motor torpedo boats *PT 303* and *PT 304* and British *MTB 422*, patrolling from Golfe Juan, France, engage south-bound enemy convoy off Savona, Italy, and sink at least two vessels.

8 Thursday

MEDITERRANEAN. Destroyer *McLanahan* (DD 615) bombards German outpost on Italian Riviera, shelling troop concentration.

Motor torpedo boat *PT 308*, in company with two British motor torpedo boats, operating from Leghorn, Italy, attacks three northbound flak lighters off Point Moneglia. The MTBs draw fire while *PT 308* scores damage on one flak lighter. A second allied attack is unsuccessful.

PACIFIC. TF 92 (Rear Admiral John L. McCrea), composed of three light cruisers and seven destroyers, sorties from Attu, Aleutians, bound for Matsuwa Island, Kurils.

Submarine *Pampanito* (SS 383) attacks Japanese convoy in Gulf of Siam, sinking gunboat *Eifuku Maru* off Cape Camau, French Indochina, 07°05′N, 104°50′E.

Japanese landing ship *T.143* is run aground and abandoned southeast of the Pescadores, 23°30′N, 119°40′E.

9 Friday

PACIFIC. Navy aircraft sink Japanese army cargo ship *Hekisui Maru* off Mako, Formosa, 23°28′N, 119°40′E.

PV-1 sinks small Japanese cargo vessel *No. 177 Nanshin Maru* in Flores Sea west of Maumere.

Japanese *Coast Defense Vessel No. 61* is damaged by mine, possibly laid by submarine *Ray* (SS 271) on 22 February 1944, 10 miles off Cape St. Jacques, French Indochina, 10°10′N, 106°55′E.[232]

INDIAN OCEAN. U.S. freighter *Cape Edmont* rescues one boatload of survivors from freighter *Peter Silvester*, sunk on 6 February by German submarine *U 862* (see 13 and 27 February and 10 March).

10 Saturday

PACIFIC. Surveying ship *Hydrographer* (AGS 2), as a squall approaches, sights Japanese swimmers approaching her, Schonian Harbor, Palaus, and goes to general quarters. Small arms and machine gun fire dispose of the swimmers; one of their rafts is carrying an explosive charge.

Japanese *Coast Defense Vessel No. 33* and escort destroyer *Mikura* are damaged in collision in Formosa Straits, 23°51′N, 117°52′E.

Japanese battleships *Ise* and *Hyuga* embark oil field exploration engineers. Light cruiser *Oyodo* embarks engineers as well as quantities of tin, zinc, tungsten, mercury, and aviation gasoline; destroyers *Asashimo*, *Kasumi*, and *Hatsushimo* load quantities of rubber and tin. The "Completion Force" sails from Singapore on this date for Kure, Japan. British submarine HMS *Tantalus* sights the Japanese but is unable to attain attack position. Apprised of this force's passage by cryptographic intelligence, 25 U.S. submarines will be deployed along its intended route (see 13 February).

11 Sunday

GENERAL. Yalta (ARGONAUT) Conference attended by President Roosevelt, British Prime Minister Winston S. Churchill, and Soviet Premier Joseph Stalin ends.

PACIFIC. TF 92 (Rear Admiral John L. McCrea), composed of three light cruisers and seven destroyers, arrives off Matsuwa Island, Kurils, to conduct bombardment, but encounters heavy weather that makes high-speed retirement impossible. The operation is accordingly cancelled and the ships return to Attu, Aleutians, on 14 February.

Marianas-based USAAF B-29s carry out extended search missions to look for Japanese guardboats in the path of TF 58 as it steams toward Japan, augmented by Tinian, Marianas–based PB4Ys and planes from the carriers. These searches will be repeated on 12 and 14 February.

Tank landing ship *LST 577*, torpedoed by Japanese submarine *RO 50* while in a reinforcement convoy proceeding from Hollandia to Leyte, 08°05′N, 126°17′E, is scuttled by destroyer *Isherwood* (DD 520). *RO 50* is damaged by gunfire in the encounter with U.S. ships.

Fleet tug *Takelma* (ATF 113) is damaged by collision east of Leyte, P.I., 10°50′N, 125°25′E.

Submarine *Batfish* (SS 310) sinks Japanese submarine *RO 112* off Camiguin, P.I., 18°53′N, 121°50′E.

Submarine *Burrfish* (SS 312) is damaged by depth charges and aerial bombs off Bonins, 27°51′N, 141°55′N, but remains on patrol.

Japanese escort destroyer *Miyake* is damaged by aircraft off Hainan Island, 19°08′N, 108°15′E.

Japanese fast transport *T.13* is damaged by aircraft, Bonins.

USAAF aircraft sink Japanese cargo vessel *Shoto Maru*, Saigon, French Indochina.

MEDITERRANEAN. Destroyer *McLanahan* (DD 615), while withdrawing from bombardment mission off Italian Riviera, is damaged by near-misses from German shore battery at San Remo, Gulf of Genoa.

12 Monday

PACIFIC. Submarine *Hawkbill* (SS 366) sinks small Japanese cargo vessel *Kisaragi Maru* and the two large landing barges she is towing, Lombok Strait, N.E.I.

Japanese merchant ship *Shinko Maru* is sunk by aircraft off coast of Fukien, China, province, 26°57′N, 120°25′E.

13 Tuesday

INDIAN OCEAN. Frigate *Corpus Christi* (PF 44) rescues 102 survivors of U.S. freighter *Peter Sil-*

vester, sunk on 6 February by German submarine *U 862* (see 27 February and 10 March).

PACIFIC. Submarine *Sennet* (SS 408) is damaged by gunfire of Japanese guardboat (*No. 8 Kotoshiro Maru* or *No. 3 Showa Maru*) east by south of Tanega Shima, but administers the coup de grâce to *No. 8 Kotoshiro Maru* after the enemy patrol craft had already been shelled by *Lagarto* (SS 371) and *Haddock* (SS 231), 30°00′N, 136°30′E. *Haddock* then sinks *No. 3 Showa Maru*, which had already been shelled by *Lagarto* and *Sennet*, 30°00′N, 136°30′E (see 14 February).

Submarine *Batfish* (SS 310) sinks Japanese submarine *RO 113* off Babuyan Islands, 19°10′N, 121°23′E.

Submarine *Bergall* (SS 320) attacks Japanese "Completion Force" (see 10 February for composition) southeast of Hainan Island, but fails to score any hits. Later that day, *Blower* (SS 325) fires torpedoes at battleships *Ise* and *Hyuga* and light cruiser *Oyodo*, but, like *Bergall*, fails to score any hits. The Japanese force reaches its destination, Kure, without further incident.

RAAF Liberator sinks Japanese motor sailship *No. 24 Sakura Maru* in Lesser Sundas.

14 Wednesday

PACIFIC. Japanese shore batteries sink motor minesweeper *YMS 48* north of Corregidor, 14°24′N, 120°33′E, and damage destroyers *Fletcher* (DD 445) and *Hopewell* (DD 681) as they support the sweeping of those waters, 14°25′N, 120°30′E, and 14°24′N, 120°33′E, respectively. On board *Fletcher*, Watertender First Class Elmer C. Bigelow, time not permitting his donning a rescue-breathing apparatus, plunges into the acrid powder smoke to extinguish the blaze that had resulted from shell fragments penetrating the no. 1 gun magazine and setting fire to powder cases. Bigelow succumbs to smoke inhalation the following day; for his heroism, he is awarded the Medal of Honor posthumously.

Mines damage destroyers *Radford* (DD 446) and *LaVallette* (DD 448) as they support the sweeping of a channel into Mariveles Harbor, 14°25′N, 120°30′E. Japanese shore batteries sink support landing craft *LCS 26* and *LCS 49* off Luzon.

Submarine *Gato* (SS 212) sinks Japanese *Coast Defense Vessel No. 9* in the Yellow Sea, 34°48′N, 125°28′E.

Submarines *Haddock* (SS 231), *Lagarto* (SS 371), and *Sennet* (SS 408) damage Japanese guardboat *No. 3 Kanno Maru* south of Japan, 29°50′N, 135°31′E.

Submarine *Hawkbill* (SS 366) sinks Japanese auxiliary submarine chasers *Cha 4* and *Cha 114* (ex-Dutch *B 1* class patrol boat) in Java Sea, 08°28′S, 115°45′E.

Japanese army cargo ship *No. 1 Yamanami Maru* is sunk by mine west of Kyushu, Japan.

Japanese hospital ship *Hikawa Maru* is damaged by mine in Singapore Strait.

Japanese auxiliary submarine chaser *Tatsui Maru* is damaged by aircraft in the East China Sea off the coast of China, 27°35′N, 121°16′E.

ARCTIC. U.S. freighter *Horace Gray* is torpedoed by German submarine *U 711* at the entrance to Kola Inlet, 69°21′N, 33°43′W. Beached the following day, *Horace Gray* will subsequently be determined a total loss. There are no casualties to either the merchant complement or the 28-man Armed Guard.

ATLANTIC. Destroyer escort *Durant* (DE 389) tows disabled British freighter *Forthbank* after the latter is detached from convoy after losing her propeller off the Delaware capes, 39°35′N, 73°21′W; rescue tug *ATR 6*, dispatched from New York, relieves the warship of towing duties later that day.

15 Thursday

PACIFIC. TG 78.3 (Rear Admiral Arthur D. Struble) lands army forces (151st Infantry RCT and Third Battalion, 34th RCT) near Mariveles Harbor, Bataan, Luzon; the troops encounter only light opposition and quickly secure the town and the nearby airfield. Medium landing ship *LSM 169* is damaged by mine off Mariveles; motor minesweeper *YMS 46* is damaged by shore battery, 14°23′N, 120°36′E.

TF 58 planes sink Japanese guardboats *No. 3 Choyo Maru* and *No. 2 Santoku Maru* off southern Japan, 30°00′N, 141°00′E, and 30°00′N, 143°00′E, respectively.

Japanese fast transport *T.16* is damaged by aircraft off Iwo Jima.

Japanese auxiliary minesweeper *No. 3 Taihei Maru* is damaged by aircraft off Yonakuni Island, Sakishima Gunto.

16 Friday

PACIFIC. TF 58 (Vice Admiral Marc A. Mitscher), supporting the impending Operation DETACHMENT (invasion of Iwo Jima) achieves complete tactical surprise with initial fighter sweeps and strikes against Japanese installations and shipping in the Tokyo area. TF 58 planes damage *Coast Defense Vessel No. 47* off Yokohama, escort destroyer *Amakusa* off O Shima, auxiliary minesweeper *Hagoromo Maru*

10 miles south of Miyake Jima, and auxiliary submarine chasers *Cha 211*, *Cha 225*, and *Cha 236* off Shimoda (see 17 February).[233] While screening the fast carriers, destroyers *Ingraham* (DD 694) and *Barton* (DD 722) are damaged in collision, 31°45′N, 141°54′E. Meanwhile, fire support ships and CVE-based planes (with the fast carrier task force committed to the Tokyo strikes) begin softening up Iwo Jima as a prelude to Operation DETACHMENT. Oiler *Patuxent* (AO 44), while retiring from the Iwo Jima area, having operated in TU 50.8.2 to replenish the ships in TF 58, is damaged by internal explosion from gasoline vapors. Destroyer escort *Silverstein* (DE 534) accompanies the damaged auxiliary to Saipan.

TF 92 (Rear Admiral John L. McCrea) bombards Japanese installations at Kurabu Saki, Paramushir, Kurils.

Army forces, preceded by naval bombardment and attack by army aircraft, land on Corregidor, Luzon; 503rd Parachute Infantry are airdropped onto the main plateau while the Third Battalion, 24th RCT is lifted to the island in navy medium landing craft (LCM). Support landing craft (large) [LCS(L)] and infantry landing craft (rocket) [LCI(R)] provide covering fire close-in. Motor torpedo boats also support the operation, at one point rescuing stranded Army paratroopers.

Special gunfire support unit of six destroyers (Captain Robert W. Cavenaugh) is formed to provide naval gunfire support for the conquest of Corregidor. Between 16 and 28 February, this unit will deliver pinpoint fire that proves a considerable help to the final elimination of Japanese troops on the island.

Submarine chaser *PC 1119* is damaged by shore battery off Nasugbu, Luzon, 14°23′N, 120°35′E.

Support landing craft *LCS(L) 7* is sunk by Japanese assault demolition boats off entrance to Mariveles Harbor, Bataan, Luzon.

Submarine *Sennet* (SS 408) sinks Japanese minelayer *Naryu* southeast of Honshu, 32°10′N, 135°54′E, but is damaged by depth bombs from enemy aircraft.

PB4Y-1 (VPB 117) sinks Japanese army cargo ship *Ida Maru*, Cape St. Jacques, French Indochina, 10°20′N, 107°06′E; elsewhere off the coast of French Indochina, army cargo ship *No. 23 Yoshitomo Maru* is sunk by aircraft off Qui Nhon, 14°36′N, 109°06′E.

USAAF P-51s (14th Air Force) sink Japanese auxiliary sailing vessel *Minsui Maru* during fighter-bomber strike on river traffic on the Yangtze River near Wuhu, China.

Coast Guard lighthouse tender *Bramble* (WAGL 392) is damaged by grounding on Lockwood Rock, Wrangell Narrows, Aleutians (see 17 February).

MEDITERRANEAN. Motor torpedo boat *PT 303* and two British motor torpedo boats, operating out of Leghorn, Italy, engage two southbound enemy barges off Vernazza with doubtful results.

ATLANTIC. Destroyer *Edison* (DD 439) is damaged when accidentally rammed by British merchant tanker *Benedick* in New York Harbor.

17 Saturday

PACIFIC. TF 58 (Vice Admiral Marc A. Mitscher) continues strikes on Tokyo area; having been spotted and reported by Japanese guardboat, however, TF 58 achieves less surprise than on the previous day. TG 58.1 (Rear Admiral Joseph J. Clark) aircraft bomb Japanese shipping in Yokohama Harbor; planes (CVG 81) from carrier *Wasp* (CV 18) most likely account for the sinking of army cargo ship *Yamashio Maru*. Destroyer *Haynesworth* (DD 700), in the screen of TG 58.3, sinks Japanese guardboat *No. 36 Nanshin Maru* southwest of Mikimoto Light, auxiliary submarine chaser *Wafu Maru* off Omae Saki Light, and a third unnamed vessel in the same general area, capturing 12 prisoners from among the survivors of the three "picket" boats. Once TF 58 has completed its two days of raids on the Tokyo area, it retires toward Iwo Jima to render direct support for Operation DETACHMENT (see 19 February).

Fire support ships, minesweeping units, and underwater demolition teams (UDT) arrive off Iwo Jima and encounter fire from shore batteries. UDT reconnaissance discloses that no underwater obstacles exist, and that the surf and beach conditions are suitable for landings. Infantry landing craft (gunboat) *LCI(G) 474* is sunk by shore battery while supporting UDT operations. Japanese guns also account for damage to battleship *Tennessee* (BB 43), 24°44′N, 141°19′E; heavy cruiser *Pensacola* (CA 24) and destroyer *Leutze* (DD 481), 24°46′N, 141°19′E; as well as to infantry landing craft (gunboats) *LCI(G) 346, LCI(G) 348, LCI(G) 438, LCI(G) 441, LCI(G) 449, LCI(G) 450, LCI(G) 457, LCI(G) 466, LCI(G) 469, LCI(G) 471,* and *LCI(G) 473*. On board the damaged *LCI(G) 449*, Lieutenant Rufus G. Herring, her commanding officer, although badly wounded, personally cons his crippled ship, maintaining her position in support of the unfolding UDT operations until she is able to move to safety.

For his heroism, Herring is awarded the Medal of Honor.

Light cruisers *Phoenix* (CL 46) and *Boise* (CL 47), along with three destroyers, provide call-fire support for continuing operations on Corregidor. Light cruiser *Cleveland* (CL 55) and destroyers *O'Bannon* (DD 450) and *Taylor* (DD 468) bombard the Ternate area, south shore of Manila Bay. Fleet tug *Hidatsa* (ATF 102) is damaged by mine in Mariveles Harbor, 14°25′N, 120°30′E.

Submarine *Bowfin* (SS 287) sinks Japanese Coast Defense Vessel *No. 56* five miles east of Mikura Jima, central Honshu, 33°53′N, 139°43′E. *Bowfin* and aircraft sink guardboat *No. 26 Nanshin Maru* southwest of Mikimoto Light, 30°05′N, 135°15′E.

British submarine HMS *Statesman* attacks Japanese convoy off Ujong Tamiang, 04°26′N, 98°16E, sinking motor sailships *No. 3 Matsujima Maru, No. 19 Nippon Maru, No. 17 Nanyo Maru,* and *No. 14 Nippon Maru*.

USAAF B-24s (Far East Air Force), on an antishipping sweep over the South China Sea, sink Japanese landing ship *T.114* off southern coast of Formosa, 23°04′N, 120°30′E.

USAAF B-24s (7th Air Force) carry out individual snooper strikes against Japanese installations on Chichi Jima; these operations may account for the sinking of tanker *No. 28 Nanshin Maru* northwest of Chichi Jima, 30°00′N, 138°30′E, and freighter *Daibi Maru* off Chichi Jima.

During diving operations in West Loch, Pearl Harbor, on the wreckage of tank landing ships sunk in the ammunition explosions on 21 May 1944, Boatswain's Mate Second Class Owen F. P. Hammerberg risks his own life to save two fellow divers trapped while tunnelling under a wrecked LST. Although Hammerberg's efforts are successful, he suffers mortal injuries in a cave-in, to which he succumbs 18 hours later. For his heroism, Hammerberg is awarded the Medal of Honor posthumously.

District patrol vessel *YP 94*, returning from landing supplies on Chirikof Island, Aleutians, runs aground at the southern end of Tugidak and Sitkinak Islands, Aleutians; rescue tug *ATR 68* is dispatched from Kodiak, Alaska, to render assistance, while air-sea rescue coordination succeeds in rescuing all hands (see 23 February).

Coast Guard cutter *Atalanta* (WPC 102), en route to assist lighthouse tender *Bramble* (WAGL 389), damaged by grounding the previous day, collides with and damages mail

boat *Neptune* near Steamer Point Light, Aleutians. District patrol vessel *YP 251* escorts the damaged *Neptune* to Naval Section Base, Ketchikan, Alaska, while *Atalanta*, undamaged, continues on her mission.

EUROPE. Motor torpedo boat *PT 605* is sunk by striking submerged object off Ostend, Belgium.

ATLANTIC. U.S. freighter *Michael J. Stone*, in convoy UGS 72, is torpedoed by German submarine *U 300*, 27 miles from Gibraltar, 35°55′N, 05°53′W. There are no casualties on board, and the damaged freighter reaches her destination under her own power.

Provision stores ship *Pontiac* (AF 20), which sank in shallow water off MacNab Island while en route to Halifax, Nova Scotia, on 30 January, is raised and towed to Halifax for repairs.[234]

18 Sunday

ATLANTIC. District patrol vessel *YP 94* sinks after running aground off Trinity Islands, 56°32′N, 154°22′W.

PACIFIC. Japanese planes bomb U.S. invasion shipping west-northwest of Iwo Jima: Light minelayer *Gamble* (DM 15) is damaged at 24°55′N, 141°08′E; high-speed transport *Blessman* (APD 48) is damaged at 25°05′N, 141°10′E.

TF 58 (Vice Admiral Marc A. Mitscher) retires from the Tokyo area; destroyers in the screen encounter Japanese patrol vessels. *Waldron* (DD 699) is damaged when she intentionally rams a guardboat at 29°27′N, 141°34′E; *Dortch* (DD 670) sinks auxiliary submarine chaser *Ayukawa Maru* north-northwest of Iwo Jima, 27°35′N, 121°16′E, but is damaged by gunfire in the encounter. *Barton* (DD 722), *Ingraham* (DD 694), and *Moale* (DD 693), operating roughly northwest of Chichi Jima, sink guardboats *No. 35 Nanshin Maru*, 30°00′N, 137°30′E, *No. 3 Kyowa Maru*, 31°00′N, 137°30′E, and *No. 5 Fukuichi Maru*, 30°00′N, 141°00′E.

TG 58.1 (Rear Admiral Joseph J. Clark) carries out fighter sweeps against Japanese guardboats along the latitude 30°N and between longitudes 138° and 142°E, and joins TG 58.4 in launching minor strikes against Japanese installations and shipping at Haha and Chichi Jimas; TG 52.2 (CVEs) also carries out strikes, sinking gunboat *No. 2 Hiyoshi Maru* at Futami, Chichi Jima, 27°05′N, 142°11′E.

TF 58 detaches battleships *North Carolina* (BB 55) and *Washington* (BB 56), heavy cruiser *Indianapolis* (CA 35), two light cruisers, and a

LCVPs head toward the black volcanic sand beaches of Iwo Jima, 19 February 1945; Mount Suribachi looms in the background. Battleship *Texas* (BB 35) lies offshore (left), providing gunfire support; barely discernible on a black and white print because of their monotone Measure 21 (navy blue) color scheme are other fire support ships such as destroyers and light cruisers. Sergeant David G. Christian, USMCR, who takes this photograph, will later be awarded a Bronze Star for heroism. He is critically wounded while carrying out his duties as a combat photographer one week later. (NA, USMC 111904)

destroyer division to augment the fire support group off Iwo Jima. *Washington* and destroyer *Hailey* (DD 556) are damaged in collision.

19 Monday

PACIFIC. Operation DETACHMENT: Preceded by intense naval and air bombardment, Fourth and Fifth Marine Divisions (Lieutenant General Holland M. Smith, USMC) land on Iwo Jima. The operation is under the overall command of Admiral Raymond A. Spruance, Commander Fifth Fleet; Vice Admiral Richmond Kelly Turner is the Joint Expeditionary Force Commander. Naval gunfire and CVE aircraft (TG 52.2) will support the troops ashore during this difficult campaign. TF 58 (Vice Admiral Marc A. Mitscher) augments the air support: TG 58.2 and TG 58.3 furnish pre H-hour support over Iwo Jima and conduct evening fighter sweeps against Haha and Chichi Jimas.

Japanese shore battery on Iwo Jima damages destroyer *John W. Weeks* (DD 701), 25°32′N, 141°01′E; mortar fire damages medium landing ships *LSM 74, LSM 145, LSM*

245, and *LSM 323.* Offshore, collisions account for varying degrees of damage to heavy cruiser *Chester* (CA 27) and amphibious force flagship *Estes* (AGC 12), 24°13′N, 141°25′E; heavy cruiser *Indianapolis* (CA 35) and ammunition ship *Shasta* (AE 6) (during replenishment operations); destroyer escort *Finnegan* (DE 307) and large infantry landing craft *LCI(L) 627,* 22°46′N, 141°19′E; and attack cargo ship *Starr* (AKA 67) and heavy cruiser *Salt Lake City* (CA 25), 24°46′N, 141°19′E. Hospital ship *Samaritan* (AH 10) is hit by friendly fire, 24°46′N, 141°19′E.

Army troops covered by USMC aircraft are landed on the northwest coast of Samar and on Capul Island, P.I., to ensure control of San Bernardino Strait.

Japanese merchant ship *Zuiho Maru* is sunk by aircraft in Yangtze River near Kiukiang, China.

20 Tuesday

PACIFIC. TF 58 (Vice Admiral Marc A. Mitscher) continues to support ongoing operations on Iwo Jima; TG 58.1 and TG 58.4 pro-

vide direct air support, while the latter provides morning and afternoon fighter sweeps against Haha and Chichi Jimas. TG 58.2 and TG 58.3, meanwhile, replenish at sea. Off Iwo Jima, light cruiser *Biloxi* (CL 80) is hit by friendly fire, 25°47′N, 141°15′E; destroyer *Bradford* (DD 545) collides with uncharted submerged wreckage, 24°45.8′N, 141°19.44′E. Attack transports *Napa* (APA 157) and *Logan* (APA 196) are damaged in collision, 24°46′N, 141°19′E; tank landing ship *LST 779* and medium landing ship *LSM 216* are damaged by mortar fire.

Army troops, covered by USMC aircraft, are landed on Biri Island, P.I., to ensure control of San Bernardino Strait.

Submarine *Guavina* (SS 362), attacking Japanese convoy rounding Cape Padaran, French Indochina, damages merchant tanker *Eiyo Maru,* 11°22′N, 109°22′E (see 21 February).

Submarine *Hawkbill* (SS 366), attacking Japanese convoy about 175 miles northwest of Singapore, sinks freighter *Daizen Maru,* 00°42′S, 106°18′E. Although *Hawkbill* claims sinking one other cargo vessel, the two ships in company with the lost freighter, *Kanto Maru* and *Nankai Maru,* survive unscathed.

Submarine *Pargo* (SS 264) sinks Japanese destroyer *Nokaze* off Cape Varella, French Indochina, 12°48′N, 109°38′E, and survives counterattack by destroyer *Kamikaze,* which had been steaming in company with *Nokaze* at the time of *Pargo*'s attack.

Submarine *Pintado* (SS 387) is damaged by aerial bomb, Gulf of Siam, 07°25′N, 111°56′E, but remains on patrol.

Japanese army ship *Rozan Maru* is sunk by mine below Taku, China.

Japanese cargo vessel *No. 34 Kashiwa Maru* is sunk by mine off Surabaya, Java, N.E.I.

21 Wednesday

PACIFIC. Off Iwo Jima, *kamikazes* sink escort carrier *Bismarck Sea* (CVE 95), 24°36′N, 141°48′E, and damage carrier *Saratoga* (CV 3), 24°56′N, 142°01′E (*Saratoga* is also hit by a bomb); escort carrier *Lunga Point* (CVE 94), 24°40′N, 141°44′E; tank landing ships *LST 477,* 24°40′N, 141°44′E, and *LST 809,* 24°08′N, 142°06′E; and net cargo ship *Keokuk* (AKN 4), 24°36′N, 141°48′E. Small carrier *Langley* (CVL 27) is damaged by bomb. Japanese mortar fire damages tank landing ship *LST 390,* 24°46′N, 141°19′E. Collisions account for damage to destroyer *Williamson* (DD 244) and oiler *Suamico* (AO 49), 24°39′N, 142°01′E; destroyer *Bradford* (DD 545) and tank landing ship *LST 812;*

and attack cargo ship *Yancey* (AKA 93) and heavy cruiser *Pensacola* (CA 24), 24°46′N, 141°19′E. Heavy weather damages medium landing ship *LSM 43*.

Navy and USAAF planes bomb and strafe Japanese installations at Truk, Carolines.

Tank landing craft *LCT 175* founders and sinks in heavy weather east-northeast of Morotai, 04°27′N, 133°40′E.

Destroyer *Renshaw* (DD 499) is torpedoed by Japanese submarine *RO 43* south of Siquijor Island, P.I., 24°36′N, 141°48′E. *RO 43* escapes a 10-hour search by destroyers *Waller* (DD 466) and *Shaw* (DD 373) around Siquijor Island.

Submarine *Gato* (SS 212) sinks Japanese freighter *Tairiku Maru* in the Yellow Sea off west coast of Korea, 35°24′N, 125°23′E.

Japanese merchant tanker *Eiyo Maru*, damaged by submarine *Guavina* (SS 362) the previous day, sinks off Cape Padaran, French Indochina, 11°22′N, 109°22′E.

Japanese cargo ship *Fukusei Maru* sinks after running aground off Shira Saki, Honshu, 41°00′N, 142°00′E.

Japanese *Coast Defense Vessel No. 72* and *Coast Defense Vessel No. 150* are damaged in collision off Wenchow, China.

22 Thursday

PACIFIC. Off Iwo Jima, destroyer escort *Melvin R. Nawman* (DE 416) and tank landing ship *LST 807* are damaged in collision, 24°46′N, 141°19′E; tank landing ship *LST 779* is damaged in collision with pontoon barges at 24°46′N, 141°19′E.

Submarine *Becuna* (SS 319), despite presence of two escort vessels, sinks Japanese merchant tanker *Nichiyoku Maru* off Cape Padaran, French Indochina, 11°28′N, 109°06′E.

Japanese fleet tanker *No. 2 Tatekawa Maru* is damaged by USAAF mine (laid by 20th Air Force B-29s) and runs aground in Padaran Bay; USAAF B-25s (Far East Air Force) complete the destruction of *No. 2 Tatekawa Maru* later in the day, 11°08′N, 108°44′E.

Japanese submarine chaser *Ch 41* is damaged by aircraft off Cape St. Jacques, French Indochina, 10°15′N, 107°15′E.

Japanese army ship *Ikuta Maru* is sunk by aircraft off Rabaul, New Britain.

ATLANTIC. U.S. freighter *Charles Brantley Ayecock* accidentally rams and damages Norwegian freighter *Brush* east-northeast of Cape Cod, Massachusetts, 42°36′N, 68°36′E. Coast Guard cutter *Argo* (WPC 100) and tug *Wandank* (ATO 26), dispatched from Boston, assist the Norwegian merchantman to that port.

23 Friday

PACIFIC. Off Iwo Jima, shore batteries damage tank landing ships *LST 684* and *LST 792*, 24°46′N, 141°19′E, and medium landing ships *LSM 46* and *LSM 47*. Operational casualties damage hospital ship *Solace* (AH 5), motor minesweeper *YMS 361*, and medium landing ship *LSM 92*, as well as submarine chaser *PC 877* and tank landing ship *LST 716*, 24°46′N, 141°19′E; friendly fire damages submarine chaser *PCS 1461*, 24°46′N, 141°19′E.

Motor torpedo boats sweep Coron Bay, P.I., destroying launches, lighters, and a lugger and setting fire to a large fuel dump.

Submarine *Hammerhead* (SS 364) intercepts Japanese convoy, sinks escort vessel *Yaku* 15 miles south of Cape Varella, French Indochina, 12°42′N, 109°30′E, and survives counterattack by *Coast Defense Ship No. 31*.

Submarines *Hoe* (SS 258) and *Flounder* (SS 251) collide off the coast of French Indochina. Damage sustained in the underwater encounter compels *Flounder* to shape a course for Subic Bay and repairs; *Hoe*, however, remains on patrol.

USAAF B-25s (Far East Air Force), on antishipping sweep off French Indochina, attack Japanese convoy HI 88G and sink submarine chaser *Ch 35* and damage submarine chaser *Ch 20* and small tanker *No. 35 Nanshin Maru* off Cape Padaran, 10°15′N, 107°31′E.

Japanese freighter *Bizan Maru* is damaged by aircraft off Hong Kong, 23°14′N, 116°49′E.

District patrol vessel *YP 94*, aground and damaged off Tugidak and Sitkinak Islands, Aleutians, since 17 February, breaks in two and sinks.

MEDITERRANEAN. Conversion of tank landing ships into seatrain LSTs is completed at Palermo, Sicily. *LST 32* is to ferry rolling stock from Bizerte, Tunisia, to Reggio, Italy (see 2 March); *LST 140* is to ferry rolling stock from Oran, Algeria, to Marseilles, France.

EUROPE. U.S. freighter *Jane G. Swisshelm* is damaged by explosion of V-2 rocket at Antwerp, Belgium. Only three men of the combined complement of eight officers, 36 enlisted men, 27 Armed Guards, and one passenger report any injuries.

ARCTIC. U.S. freighter *Henry Bacon*, straggling from Scotland-bound convoy RA 64, is sunk by German planes after her Armed Guard puts up a stiff fight against a large number of attacking aircraft, 67°00′N, 07°00′E. Seven of the 26-man Armed Guard die in battle. British destroyers HMS *Opportune*, HMS *Zest*, and HMS *Zambesi* rescue the survivors.

24 Saturday

PACIFIC. Japanese resistance in Manila, P.I., ends.

Off Iwo Jima, destroyers *Heywood L. Edwards* (DD 663) and *Bryant* (DD 665) are damaged by collision, 24°47′N, 141°25′E; heavy weather damages destroyer *Moale* (DD 693), 25°00′N, 141°00′E, and medium landing ships *LSM 202* and *LSM 241*. Tank landing ship *LST 792* is damaged by shore battery fire, 24°46′N, 141°19′E. Operational casualties account for damage to high-speed minesweeper *Howard* (DMS 7) and submarine chaser *SC 1027*.

Submarine *Lagarto* (SS 371) sinks Japanese submarine *I 371* and freighter *Tatsumomo Maru* off Bungo Strait, Kyushu, 32°40′N, 132°33′E.

Submarine *Trepang* (SS 412) sinks Japanese freighter *Uzuki Maru* north-northeast of Miki Saki, 32°40′N, 132°33′E.

Japanese cargo vessel *Kyuryu Maru* is damaged by mine (laid by RAF planes) off Bangkok, Thailand, 13°45′N, 100°35′E; she is later abandoned as a total loss and scuttled.

Japanese escort destroyer *Nomi* is damaged by aircraft, south of Wanshan Island, China Sea.

Japanese freighter *Yulin Maru* sinks after running aground near Qui Nohn, French Indochina, 13°48′N, 109°14′E.

EUROPE. German submarine *U 3007* is sunk by USAAF aircraft, Bremen, Germany.

25 Sunday

PACIFIC. TF 58 (Vice Admiral Marc A. Mitscher) returns to the Tokyo area to pound aircraft factories and airfields. All four task groups carry out fighter strikes and sweeps against their assigned targets. Japanese freighter *Kazusa Maru* is sunk by aircraft off Miyake Jima; auxiliary minesweeper *Wa. 14* is damaged; auxiliary submarine chaser *No. 5 Miyatake Maru* is damaged off Shirahama; and auxiliary submarine chaser *Cha 208* is most likely damaged in the same general area. Heavy weather, however, results in cancellation of the afternoon's strikes; destroyer *Harrison* (DD 573) is damaged in storm south of Honshu, 33°00′N, 141°00′E. TF 58 then passes between Sumisu Jima and Tori Jima to carry out strikes against the Kobe-Nagoya area. TF 58 destroyers encounter seemingly ubiquitous Japanese guardboats off Tori Jima; *Hazelwood* (DD 531) and *Murray* (DD 576) sink *No. 1 Fuji Maru* and *Koki Maru*, 31°06′N, 141°00′E, and *No. 5 Seiun Maru*, 31°00′N, 141°00′E.

Off Iwo Jima, collisions account for damage. Tank landing ship *LST 121* is accidentally rammed by medium landing ship *LSM 140*, 24°46′N, 141°19′E; tank landing ship *LST 928* collides with tank landing ships *LST 764* and *LST 713* and attack transport *Fayette* (APA 43), 24°46′N, 141°19′E; submarine chaser *PC 578* collides with medium landing ship *LSM 207*, 24°46′N, 141°19′E; and attack transport *President Adams* (APA 19) collides with tank landing ship *LST 370*, 24°46′N, 141°19′E. Friendly fire damages seaplane tender *Hamlin* (AV 15), 24°46′N, 141°19′E; Japanese shore battery damages infantry landing craft *LCI 760*.

Motor minesweeper *YMS 275* is damaged by mine off Peleliu, Palaus, 07°20′N, 134°35′E.

Submarine *Flasher* (SS 249) sinks Japanese cargo vessel *Koho Maru* near Hainan, 20°01′N, 111°19′E; USAAF B-24 attacks escorting submarine chaser *Ch 21* while she is rescuing *Koho Maru*'s survivors, but does not damage her.

Submarine *Hoe* (SS 258) attacks Japanese convoy and sinks escort vessel *Shonan* south of Hainan Island, 17°05′N, 110°05′E.

Submarine *Piper* (SS 409) sinks Japanese guardboat *No. 3 Hosen Maru* and sinks freighter *Koho Maru*, 20°04′N, 111°22′E.

British submarine HMS *Trenchant* attacks Japanese convoy in Strait of Malacca, sinking cargo vessel *No. 9 Akiyama Maru*, 03°07′N, 99°56′E; Japanese Army aircraft bomb *Trenchant*, but she escapes unharmed.

26 Monday

PACIFIC. TF 58 (Vice Admiral Marc A. Mitscher) calls off planned operations against targets in the Nagoya-Kobe area because of heavy seas that prevent the force from reaching its objective in time to launch strikes. Consequently, TF 58 retires toward fueling rendezvous. Light cruiser *Pasadena* (CL 65), 31°20′N, 141°15′E, and destroyer *Porterfield* (DD 682), 33°10′N, 143°30′E, are damaged by gunfire when Japanese guardboat penetrates task group formation south of Honshu.

Lieutenant General Millard F. Harmon, Commanding General, USAAF Air Forces, Pacific Area, departs Guam for Oahu, via Kwajalein, Marshalls, in a C-87. The aircraft (its last reported position is 11°15′N, 174°15′E) never reaches its destination. An extensive coordinated search by all services ensues for the next 20 days but fails to locate any trace of the missing transport plane or its passengers.

Off Iwo Jima, storm damages heavy cruiser *San Francisco* (CA 38) and destroyers *Colahan* (DD 658), *Halsey Powell* (DD 686), *Benham* (DD 796), *John W. Weeks* (DD 701), *Stephen Potter* (DD 538), and *Preston* (DD 795); attack cargo ship *Muliphen* (AKA 61) is damaged in collision with heavy cruiser *Salt Lake City* (CA 25), 24°46′N, 141°19′E. Tank landing ships *LST 760* and *LST 884* are damaged by shore batteries, 24°46′N, 141°19′E.

On Iwo Jima, Pharmacist's Mate Second Class George E. Wahlen, USNR, attached to a rifle company in the Second Battalion, 26th Marines, retrieves a wounded leatherneck from in front of his company's lines and carries him to safety. Wahlen, wounded in the left eye before he accomplishes this heroic act, will continue to discharge his duties with similar courage over succeeding days (see 28 February and 3 March).

TBMs (VC 82) from escort carrier *Anzio* (CVE 57), along with her screen providing antisubmarine protection for the forces arrayed against Iwo Jima, sink Japanese submarines *I 368*, 35 miles west of Iwo Jima, 24°43′N, 140°37′E, and *RO 43*, 50 miles west-northwest of Iwo Jima, 25°07′N, 140°19′E.

Destroyer escort *Finnegan* (DE 307) sinks Japanese submarine *I 370*, 120 miles south of Iwo Jima, 22°45′N, 141°27′E.

Minesweeper *Saunter* (AM 295) is damaged by mine off El Fraile Island, Luzon, 14°17′N, 120°38′E.

USAAF planes sink Japanese tanker *No. 9 Takasago Maru* off Hainan Island, 20°01′N, 111°44′E.

Japanese freighter *Zuisho Maru* is damaged by gunfire near Hong Kong.

EUROPE. U.S. freighter *Nashaba*, bound for Ghent, Belgium, in convoy TAM 91, sinks after striking a mine in the Schelde estuary, 51°22′18″N, 02°55′25″E. There are no casualties among the 27-man Armed Guard.

27 Tuesday

PACIFIC. Off Iwo Jima, collisions account for damage to small carrier *San Jacinto* (CVL 30) and oiler *Merrimack* (AO 37), 23°00′N, 139°00′E; destroyer *Colhoun* (DD 801) and attack transport *Knox* (APA 46), 24°49′N, 141°20′E, and *Colhoun*'s collision with attack cargo ship *Libra* (AKA 12) soon thereafter; tank landing ship *LST 121* and attack cargo ship *Starr* (AKA 67), 24°46′N, 141°19′E; and tank landing ships *LST 809* and *LST 224*, 24°46′N, 141°19′E. Japanese shore batteries damage attack cargo ship *Leo* (AKA 60) and tank landing ship *LST 884*; medium landing ship *LSM 92* is damaged by mortar fire.

Submarine *Blenny* (SS 324), attacking Japanese convoy off French Indochina, sinks merchant tanker *Amato Maru* off Cape Padaran, 11°58′N, 109°18′E.

Submarine *Scabbardfish* (SS 397) sinks Japanese guardboat *No. 6 Kikaku Maru*, 100 miles northeast of Keelung, Formosa, 25°45′N, 123°20′W.

Japanese merchant vessel *No. 2 Suma Maru* is sunk by aircraft 80 miles off Amoy, China.

INDIAN OCEAN. British escort carrier HMS *Activity* rescues one boatload of survivors (20 men) from freighter *Peter Silvester*, sunk on 6 February by German submarine *U 862* (see 10 March).

EUROPE. German submarine *U 327* is sunk by PB4Y-1 (VPB 112) and British escort vessels HMS *Labuan*, HMS *Loch Fada*, and HMS *Wild Goose*, English Channel, 49°46′N, 05°47′W.

ATLANTIC. Destroyer *Bainbridge* (DD 246) is damaged by paint locker explosion, 350 miles north of Puerto Rico.

28 Wednesday

PACIFIC. Operation VICTOR THREE: TG 78.2 (Rear Admiral William M. Fechteler) lands Army troops (186th RCT, Reinforced, of the 41st Division) on Puerto Princesa, Palawan Island, P.I.; TG 74.2 (Rear Admiral Ralph S. Riggs), consisting of three light cruisers and four destroyers, provides support. The operation is unopposed.

Off Iwo Jima, destroyer *Bennett* (DD 473) is damaged by aircraft bomb, 24°46′N, 141°19′E; destroyer *Terry* (DD 513) by shore battery, 24°48′N, 141°33′E; and medium landing ship *LSM 42*, by mortar fire. Collisions account for damage to submarine chaser *PCS 1461* (with small craft), 24°46′N, 141°19′E, and tank landing ships *LST 641* and *LST 787*, 24°46′N, 141°19′E.

On Iwo Jima, as the Third Battalion, 27th Marines, battles a Japanese counterattack south of Nishi, Pharmacist's Mate First Class John H. Willis is wounded while administering first aid to casualties. Although evacuated to an aid station, he sneaks back to the front lines and resumes his duties with his assigned platoon. Going to the aid of a wounded man in a shell hole, Willis is treating the casualty when enemy troops lob hand grenades into the position. Willis throws out eight in succession, but a ninth explodes in his hand, killing him. His courageous actions, witnessed by his platoon, prompt them to repulse the Japanese thrust. For his conspicuous gallantry, Willis is awarded the Medal of Honor posthumously.

Elsewhere on Iwo Jima, Pharmacist's Mate Second Class George E. Wahlen, USNR, voluntarily rushes to the aid of an adjacent platoon that has suffered heavy casualties, treating 14 men before returning to his own unit. He braves heavy mortar and rifle fire to do so, actions that, together with that performed on 26 February, establish him as a hero in the eyes of the marines he serves (see 3 March).

Destroyer escort *Major* (DE 796) is damaged when accidentally rammed by U.S. tanker *Apache Canyon*, Balboa, C.Z.

USAAF B-24s attack Japanese convoy in Okinawa area, sinking motor sailship *No. 7 Kokoku Maru*.

ATLANTIC. Destroyer escort *Fowler* (DE 222) and French submarine chaser (ex-U.S. *PC 474*) *L'Indiscret* sink German submarine *U 869* off Morocco, 34°30′N, 08°13′W.

MARCH

1 Thursday

PACIFIC. TF 58 (Vice Admiral Marc A. Mitscher) planes pound Japanese ground installations, airfields, and shipping in the Okinawa area. TF 58 planes sink torpedo boat *Manazuru* off Okinawa, 26°17′N, 127°35′E, and sink minelayer *Tsubame* and damage escort destroyer *Fukue* and auxiliary minesweeper *Nuwajima* off Ishigaki Jima, Sakishima Gunto, 24°23′N, 124°12′E. TF 58 planes sink supply ship *Kinezaki* and army cargo ship *No. 11 Hoshi Maru* in Kuji Bay, 28°10′N, 129°05′E; gunboat *Chohakusan Maru* and freighter *Ryukyu Maru* off Naha; transport *Toyosaka Maru* off Miyako Retto, 24°46′N, 125°30′E; cargo ship *Kinzan Maru* off Okinawa; and freighters *Taiken Maru* off Miyako Jima and *Luzon Maru* off Naze. They also sink cargo ship *Kiku Maru* and damage torpedo boat *Tomozuru* and minesweeper *Seki Maru* off Amami-O-Shima, and damage submarine chaser *Ch 49* off Ishikiri, Suwanose Island. Japanese merchant ships *Dosei Maru* and *Otsu Maru* are sunk in Kuji Bay and off Miyako Jima, respectively. Special bombardment group (Rear Admiral Francis E. M. Whiting), consisting of three light cruisers and eight destroyers, is detached from TG 58.1 to proceed to Okino Daito Jima, Ryukyus (see 2 March).

USAAF B-25s (Far East Air Force) sink Japanese transport *Hokuhi Maru* off Mako, Pescadores, 23°35′N, 119°35′E.

Army troops supported by naval gunfire and USAAF planes land on Lubang Island, P.I.

Task unit consisting of destroyer *Cony* (DD 508), destroyer escort *Formoe* (DE 509), minesweepers *Sentry* (AM 299) and *Salute* (AM 294), and two infantry landing craft (LCI) begins minesweeping and reconnaissance of

Baler Bay and Casiguran Sound, Luzon, to investigate a possible fleet anchorage and determine composition of Japanese forces in the vicinity. Army scouts and interpreters are embarked for deployment ashore.

Submarine *Kete* (SS 369) departs Guam for her second war patrol. Contact will be maintained with her until 20 March, but she is never seen again (see 10 March).[235]

Off Iwo Jima, destroyers *Terry* (DD 513) and *Colhoun* (DD 801) are damaged by shore battery fire, 24°47′N, 141°21′E; medium landing ship *LSM 59* is damaged by operational casualty.

Submarine *Sterlet* (SS 392) sinks Japanese army cargo ship *Tateyama Maru* off Miyake Jima, 34°11′N, 139°44′E.

USAAF B-24s (14th Air Force) attack Japanese convoy, damaging tanker *Terushima Maru* and cargo vessel *Kashima Maru* in Gulf of Tonkin, 19°51′N, 108°50′E. Other B-24s sink merchant tanker *Eisho Maru*, 18°32′N, 108°11′E.

Japanese merchant ship *Daishin Maru* is sunk by aircraft off Manila.

Japanese merchant vessel cargo ship *Eijo Maru* is sunk by grounding off Shantung Peninsula, 36°09′N, 120°30′E.

EUROPE. U.S. freighter *Robert L. Vann*, in convoy ATM 76, sinks after striking a mine off Ostend, Belgium, 51°22′N, 02°53′E. There are no casualties among the 27-man Armed Guard.

2 Friday

PACIFIC. Special bombardment group (Rear Admiral Francis E. M. Whiting) (three light cruisers and eight destroyers) shells Japanese installations on Okino Daito Jima, Ryukyus, and then rejoins TG 58.1.

Destroyer Division 109, detached from TG 58.3, bombards Japanese installations at Parece Vela (Douglas Reef), 20°25′N, 136°05′E.[236]

Off Iwo Jima, light cruiser *Biloxi* (CL 80) is damaged by shore battery fire, and destroyer *Bennett* (DD 473) by dud bomb or torpedo. Collisions account for damage to attack cargo ship *Stokes* (AKA 68), 24°46′N, 141°19′E; tank landing ship *LST 247* [with attack cargo ship *Selinur* (AKA 41)], 24°46′N, 141°19′E; tank landing ship *LST 224* (successive collisions with support landing craft *LCS 52* and tank landing ship *LST 634*), 24°46′N, 141°19′E; tank landing ship *LST 642* (with tank landing ship *LST 784*), 24°46′N, 141°19′E; and attack transport *Berrien* (AP 62). Cargo ship *Hercules* (AK

41) is damaged when she runs aground; tank landing craft *LCT 1029* sinks.

Submarine *Bowfin* (SS 287) sinks Japanese transport *Chokai Maru* northeast of Miyake Jima, 33°50′N, 139°22′E.

British submarine HMS *Terrapin* attacks Japanese Penang-to-Singapore convoy in Strait of Malacca, 03°28′N, 101°00′E, sinking small cargo vessel *Sanko Maru*.

PB4Y-2 (VPB 119) attacks Japanese convoy, sinking transport *Nichirin Maru* in East China Sea about 180 miles east by south of Wenchow, China, 27°12′N, 124°42′E.

Japanese transport *Kasei Maru* is sunk by unknown causes off Shiogama, northern Honshu.

Japanese freighter *Sekiyo Maru* is sunk by aircraft off the Nansei Shoto.

Japanese *Coast Defense Vessel No. 13* is damaged by aircraft east of the Babuyan Islands, 19°47′N, 124°04′E.

USAAF B-25s (Far East Air Force) sink Japanese landing ship *T.143* off Mako, Pescadores, 23°35′N, 121°35′E.

MEDITERRANEAN. Seatrain tank landing ship *LST 32* is damaged when she strikes a submerged wreck at Reggio Calabria on her first lift of 20 railroad cars from Bizerte, Tunisia.

3 Saturday

PACIFIC. Army troops land on Masbate, Burias, and Ticao Islands, P.I., supported by naval gunfire and USMC planes. Only small Japanese garrisons are found, requiring only minimal naval forces for support.

Attack transport *Bolivar* (APA 34) is damaged by shore battery off Iwo Jima, 24°46′N, 141°19′E.

On Iwo Jima, Pharmacist's Mate Second Class George E. Wahlen, USNR, wounded in the back the day before and having already performed heroic acts treating casualties on 26 and 28 February, is wounded a third time as he treats fallen shipmates. Unable to walk, he crawls 50 yards to render aid to a wounded marine. For this and previous acts of valor, Wahlen will be awarded the Medal of Honor.

Elsewhere on Iwo Jima, Pharmacist's Mate Third Class Jack Williams, USNR, while serving as an aid man with a marine rifle company, is thrice wounded as he goes to treat a casualty. Although in a partial state of shock from his wounds, the corpsman shields the marine with his own body as he administers medical care first to the wounded man and then to himself. Instead of going to the rear, Williams remains at the front and tends a sec-

Like a proverbial fish out of water, a U.S. Navy medium landing craft (LCM), its battered bow ramp looking somewhat the worse for wear, is hauled through Maastricht, Holland, on a U.S. Army M-25 tank retriever, 5 March 1945. (NA, SC-206720)

ond wounded marine. As he finally stuggles to the rear to have his own wounds treated, the corpsman is hit a fourth time and killed. For his unwavering determination to carry out his mission, Williams is awarded the Medal of Honor posthumously.

Submarine *Sea Robin* (SS 407) sinks Japanese transport *Suiten Maru* off Malang, Java, 06°34′S, 113°01′E.

Submarine *Trepang* (SS 412) sinks Japanese gunboat *No. 2 Nissho Maru* off southern Honshu, near Mijake Jima, 34°05′N, 139°54′E.

Submarine *Tuna* (SS 203) lands supplies on northeast coast of Borneo.

USAAF B-24s (14th Air Force), on sweep for Japanese shipping, sink Japanese cargo vessel *No. 1 Yaei Maru* in Tonkin Gulf, 20°10′N, 109°31′E, and merchant tanker *No. 1 Iyasaka Maru* off Hainan Island.

RAAF planes lay mines (70 percent U.S. made, 30 percent British) in Yulinakin Bay, Hainan Island; Japanese oiler *Hario* hits a mine and sinks off Cape Bastian, 18°10′N, 109°40′E.

4 Sunday

PACIFIC. Destroyers *Yarnall* (DD 541) and *Ringgold* (DD 500) are damaged in collision while simulating night torpedo attack, 12°15′N, 138°08′E.

Submarine *Baya* (SS 318) attacks Japanese convoy HI 98, sinking merchant tanker *Palembang Maru* off Cape Varella, French Indochina, 12°50′N, 109°30′E (see 5 March).

Submarine *Tilefish* (SS 307) sinks Japanese fishing vessel *Shiko Maru* off Setsuko Saki, 28°15′N, 129°08′E.

British submarine HMS *Clyde* sinks Japanese auxiliary submarine chaser *Kiku Maru* off western Sumatra, N.E.I.

British submarines HMS *Trenchant* and HMS *Terrapin* sink Japanese submarine chaser *Ch 8* in Strait of Malacca, 04°04′N, 110°35′E.

USAAF planes (14th Air Force) lay mines in Yangtze River; Japanese ship *Wan Shih Maru* is sunk north of Shanghai.

RAAF Venturas attack Japanese convoy off Soembawa Island, sinking small cargo vessels *No. 3 Kiri Maru* and *No. 4 Matsu Maru*, 08°17′S, 118°56′E.

5 Monday

PACIFIC. Tank landing ship LST 642 is damaged in collision off Iwo Jima, 24°46′N, 141°19′E.

Submarine *Bashaw* (SS 241) attacks same Japanese convoy (HI 98) vexed by *Baya* (SS 318) the day before, sinking oiler *Ryoei Maru* and army tanker *Seishin Maru* off Tourane, French Indochina, 16°47′N, 108°41′E.

Submarine *Peto* (SS 265) is damaged by aerial bombs in South China Sea off Hainan, 20°57′N, 111°56′E, but remains on patrol.

Submarine *Sea Robin* (SS 407), attacking Japanese convoy in the Java Sea, sinks gunboat *Man-yo Maru*, 05°50′S, 113°46′E; auxiliary netlayer *Nagara Maru*, 05°23′S, 114°00′E; and freighter *Shoyo Maru*, 05°23′S, 114°60′E.

Submarine *Tilefish* (SS 307) damages Japanese minesweeper *W.15* off Akuke Jima, Japan, 29°36′N, 129°45′E. Although run aground by *No. 51 Banshu Maru* to facilitate her salvage, *W.15* is later regarded as a total loss.

USAAF B-25s (Far East Air Force) attack Japanese convoy SAYU 02, sinking auxiliary submarine chasers *Kasuga Maru* and *Ujina Maru* and freighter *Shoto Maru* off coast of French Indochina, 15°32′N, 108°37′E.

USAAF B-24 (Far East Air Force) sinks Japanese auxiliary submarine chaser *Cha 110* in Sape Strait, southeast of the Celebes, 08°36′S, 119°19′E.

Support landing craft LCS 127 sinks after grounding off San Clemente Island, California.

6 Tuesday

PACIFIC. Attack cargo ship *Yancey* (AKA 93) is damaged by collision off Iwo Jima.

USAAF B-24 (possibly a Navy PB4Y) sinks Japanese salvage vessel *Toei Maru* east of Sanmen Wan, 29°00′N, 122°00′E.

USAAF planes attack Japanese convoy at 20°00′N, 112°30′E, and although the airmen believe that they sink a "destroyer," their quarry, actually *Coast Defense Vessel No. 207*, survives undamaged.

Japanese army vessel tanker *Rikko Maru* is stranded and sunk near Keelung, Formosa, 25°09′N, 121°44′E.

Japanese freighter *Hokusui Maru* is sunk (most likely by drifting Japanese mine) off Otabe, Hokkaido, 41°27′N, 140°15′E.

Japanese freighter *No. 22 Suma Maru* is damaged by aircraft, four miles northwest of Fukikaku Light, Formosa.

7 Wednesday

MEDITERRANEAN. Motor torpedo boats *PT 305* and *PT 307* are accidentally bombed (but not damaged) by friendly aircraft while patrolling southwest of Genoa, Italy.

TG 89.9, composed of aviation supply ship

Tackle (IX 217) and fleet tug *Moreno* (ATF 87), departs Naples, Italy, for Odessa, Ukraine, carrying supplies for American POWs liberated from German camps by Soviet troops.

PACIFIC. Navy task unit completes its work in the Baler Bay–Casiguran Sound area of Luzon, having found both bodies of water to afford excellent anchorages; it encounters no mines in Casiguran Sound but sweeps 98 in Baler Bay. Not more than 100 Japanese troops are determined to be in the vicinity.

Japanese submarine chaser *Ch 51* is damaged by aircraft off Hachijo Jima.

Japanese freighter *Enkei Maru* is damaged, most likely by marine casualty, in East China Sea west of Tokara Gunto, 30°42′N, 128°20′E.

8 Thursday

INTERNATIONAL. Inter-American Conference, in session at Mexico City since 21 February, ends.

EUROPE. Submarine chaser *PC 564* engages German minesweepers *M 412*, *M 432*, *M 442*, and *M 452* and nine smaller craft off Chaussey. The Germans are bound for the port of Granville, France (see 9 March).

PACIFIC. Japanese guardboat *No. 3 Daikoku Maru* is sunk by U.S. aircraft east of Ogari Jima.

USAAF B-24s (Far East Air Force) sink Japanese freighter *Ishima Maru* off Hong Kong, 22°34′N, 114°53′E, and guardboat *Hyushin Maru* off St. John Island, 21°42′N, 112°44′E.

USAAF B-24s (14th Air Force) sink Japanese *Coast Defense Vessel No. 69* southeast of Hainan Island, 19°02′N, 111°50′E (see 16 March).

PBMs bomb Japanese convoy, sinking cargo vessel *No. 21 Yusen Maru* in Formosa Strait, 24°27′N, 118°19′E. USAAF aircraft sink landing ship *T.143* off Formosa, 23°35′N, 121°35′E.

USAAF P-51s (14th Air Force) attack Japanese shipping in the Yangtze, off Hankow, sinking cargo vessel *Toyo Maru* (ex-Chinese *Tang Yang*), 30°33′N, 114°17′E.

Japanese cargo vessel *Kwan-Shan Maru* is sunk by mine off Kiangyin, China, 31°55′N, 120°16′E.

Covered lighter *YF 926*, being towed to Pearl Harbor, T.H., founders in heavy weather and sinks.

ANDAMAN SEA. USAAF B-24s (10th Air Force) attack Japanese shipping in Andaman Sea, sinking cargo vessel *Hoyo Maru*, 13°00′N, 98°00′E.

9 Friday

MEDITERRANEAN. Motor torpedo boats *PT 304*, *PT 308*, and *PT 313* engage German flak lighters off Point Mesco, Italy, claiming one sunk, one hit, and one possibly hit; *PT 304* is damaged by shrapnel during the attack. During retirement, however, *PT 308* is damaged when she is accidentally rammed by *PT 304*.

EUROPE. Submarine chaser *PC 564*, outgunned and badly damaged, manages to outrun the German force engaged late on 8 March and is grounded on the French coast at Pierre de Herpin Light. French fishing boats arrive to help the wounded, and the next day, *PC 564* is towed into St. Malo Harbor. Shortly after *PC 564* is knocked out of action, German raiding party assaults Granville, demolishing installations, releasing German POWs held there, and sinking small British freighters *Kyle Castle*, *Nephrite*, and *Parkwood* and Norwegian merchantman *Heien*. The Germans seize collier *Eskwood* and tow her to Jersey, Channel Islands. German minesweeper *M 412* runs aground and is blown up when it is realized that extricating her from her predicament is impossible in the time allowed.

PACIFIC. Japanese present ultimatum to French colonial government in Indochina, demanding that the French military forces submit themselves to Japanese control. French rejection of the ultimatum prompts Japan to put in motion prearranged plans to disarm the French military. Consequently, French colonial sloop *Amiral Charner* shells and sinks river gunboat (ex-subchaser) *Avalanche* at My Tho, French Indochina, to prevent the latter from being captured by the Japanese. River gunboats *Commandant Bordais* and *Vigilante* are scuttled at Haiphong. River gunboat *Francis Garnier* is scuttled in the Mekong River at Kratie, Cambodia (see 10 and 11 March).

PB4Y carries out unsuccessful attack on submarine chaser *Ch 21* off Hong Kong, 22°23′N, 115°03′E.

10 Saturday

PACIFIC. Operation VICTOR FOUR: TG 78.1 (Rear Admiral Forrest B. Royal) lands Army troops [41st Infantry (Reinforced) less 186th RCT] near Zamboanga, Mindanao; landing is supported by naval gunfire and USAAF planes (see 11 March). Japanese shore batteries, however, sink tank landing ships *LST 591* and *LST 626* and infantry landing craft *LCI 710* and *LCI 779*. Attacking troops encounter only light mortar and artillery fire.

Submarine *Kete* (SS 369) attacks Japanese Kagoshima-to-Naha convoy north of Okinawa, sinking transport *Keizan Maru* and army cargo ships *Sanka Maru* and *Dokan Maru* about 100 miles northwest of Amami-O-Shima, 29°48′N, 128°02′E, and survives counterattacks by *Coast Defense Vessel No. 44* and auxiliary minesweeper *No. 2 Shinto Maru*.

USAAF B-25s (Far East Air Force) sink Japanese army tanker *Seishin Maru* off Tourane, French Indochina, 16°01′N, 108°10′E.

French colonial sloop *Amiral Charner* is bombed by Japanese planes at My Tho, French Indochina; deemed beyond repair, she is scuttled to avoid capture, as is old first-class sloop *Marne*. Likewise destroyed at My Tho to prevent their falling into Japanese hands are river gunboats *Mytho* and *Tourane*, the latter at the mouth of the Song Be (see 11 March).

INDIAN OCEAN. Submarine *Rock* (SS 274) rescues the last 15 survivors from U.S. freighter *Peter Silvester*, sunk on 6 February by German submarine *U 862*.

11 Sunday

EUROPE. TU 122.5.1 (Navy landing craft unit) LCVPs go into action 200 miles from the sea, sailors assisting in erecting and maintaining an army pontoon bridge at the Remagen bridgehead. Navy support of the army's crossing the Rhine River proves invaluable and adds greatly to the successful invasion of the German homeland. The movement of the LCVPs and LCMs used in the operation from the Atlantic seaboard to the Rhine River is an undertaking of considerable magnitude.

USAAF heavy bombers (8th Air Force) sink German submarines *U 2515* and *U 2530* during raid on Hamburg, Germany.

PB4Y-1 (VPB 103) sinks German submarine *U 681* southwest of the Scilly Islands, 49°53′N, 06°31′W.

PACIFIC. Army troops landed on 10 March take Zamboanga, Mindanao.

Japanese land attack planes (FRANCESs) (762nd *Kokutai*) flying direct from Kanoya, Japan, attack U.S. fleet anchorage at Ulithi, Carolines; one FRANCES crashes carrier *Randolph* (CV 15), 10°01′N, 139°40′E, another crashes into Sorlen Island. Salvage vessel *Gear* (ARS 34) is damaged by collision with *Randolph* during fire-fighting operations.

Submarine *Segundo* (SS 398) sinks Japanese freighter *Shori Maru* off Shori Do, southern Korea, 34°25′N, 127°54′E.

PBM-3D (VPB 28) attacks Japanese convoy in South China Sea, sinking water carrier *Wayo Maru* about 40 miles southeast of Macao, 21°31′N, 112°28′E.

USAAF B-25s bomb Japanese shipping off Tourane, French Indochina, sinking motor sailships *Kinsei Maru, Namikiri Maru,* and *No. 3 Hinode Maru.*

French surveying vessel *Lapérouse* is scuttled at Cantho, French Indochina, to prevent her from falling into Japanese hands.

Japanese merchant trawler *Koko Maru* is sunk by USAAF mine in Yangtze River, 31°22′N, 121°34′E.

12 Monday

PACIFIC. Japanese guardboats *No. 1 Hinode Maru* and *Shosei Maru* are sunk by U.S. aircraft east of the Ryukyus, 26°54′N, 131°38′E.

13 Tuesday

PACIFIC. USAAF B-24s and B-25s on antishipping sweeps off the China coast between Foochow and Hong Kong attack Japanese convoy KAI 311, sinking cargo vessels *No. 12 Aikoku Maru, No. 37 Kokoku Maru, No. 18 Tarumizu Maru,* and *No. 34 Tarumizu Maru.* B-24s (Far East Air Force) sink *Coast Defense Vessel No. 66* and transport *Masajima Maru* east of Swatow, 23°30′N, 117°10′E.

Army barge *PSB 111* runs aground on northeast side of Seguam Island, Aleutians, but is pulled free by fleet tug *Sarsi* (ATF 111).

14 Wednesday

PACIFIC. Destroyers *Cotten* (DD 669) and *Dortch* (DD 670) sink Japanese guardboats *Futa Maru* and *No. 17 Kaiko Maru* off the Bonins, 30°58′N, 144°54′E.

PVs (VPB 151) begin operating from Iwo Jima's Motoyama airfield no. 1, thus bringing Japanese guardboats operating off the home islands within range of rocket-firing planes.

Submarine *Bream* (SS 243) sinks Japanese auxiliary submarine chaser *Keihin Maru* in Java Sea, south of Borneo, 05°41′S, 114°03′E.

Submarine *Rock* (SS 274) lands supplies on Lombok Island, N.E.I.

Submarine *Trepang* (SS 412) sinks Japanese guardboat *Kaiko Maru* off Inubo Saki, Japan, 35°40′N, 141°00′E.

British submarine HMS *Spirit* sinks Japanese auxiliary sailing vessel *Ryuho Maru* off Massalambo Island, 05°34′S, 114°26′E.

USAAF B-24 on antishipping sweep off south China coast sinks Japanese army cargo ship *No. 3 Taisei Maru,* 03°35′N, 112°10′E. Auxiliary submarine chaser *Yatsushiro Maru* is damaged by aircraft, south of Wenchow, China. Attacks against convoy KAI 311 continue as B-24s and B-25s sink small cargo vessel *No. 15 Gokoku Maru* off south China coast.

USAAF B-29s (274 strong) pound Osaka, Japan; Japanese freighters *Shiraume Maru* and *Shirogane Maru* are sunk in the fire bomb raid that lays waste to the heart of the city.

USAAF B-24s damage Japanese auxiliary submarine chaser *Cha 235* off Mako, Pescadores.

Navy aircraft sink small Japanese cargo vessel *No. 1 Taiki Maru* and damage guardboat *No. 1 Shinya Maru* east of the Ryukyus, 27°10′N, 132°09′E.

Coastal yacht *Amethyst* (PYc 3) is damaged in collision with U.S. merchantman *Platte Park* 150 miles northwest of San Francisco, California.

15 Thursday

PACIFIC. On Iwo Jima, Pharmacist's Mate Second Class Francis J. Pierce, assigned to a marine rifle battalion, is leading a stretcher party to a forward aid station when the group comes under heavy Japanese rifle and machine gun fire that wounds the other corpsman and two of eight stretcher bearers. Pierce takes charge, carries the newly wounded men to shelter, and treats them before he draws his pistol and engages the enemy, covering the litter bearers while they carry three wounded leathernecks to safety. After treating a hemorrhaging casualty who is hit again while the corpsman is taking care of him, Pierce expends the last of his ammunition and kills the enemy soldier who fired on them. Pierce, although exhausted and out of ammmunition, twice carries wounded marines 200 yards over fire-swept terrain (see 16 March).

TF 92 (Rear Admiral John L. McCrea), consisting of light cruisers *Richmond* (CL 9), *Concord* (CL 10), and *Trenton* (CL 11) and seven destroyers, bombards Japanese installations on Matsuwa, Kurils.

Submarine *Bream* (SS 243) is damaged by depth charges off north Borneo, 05°36′N, 114°33′E, and is forced to terminate her patrol.

USAAF B-24s bomb Japanese convoy YUMO 01, which had departed Hong Kong the day before. While the attack on cargo ship *Tatsumiya Maru* proves unsuccessful, the Liberators damage one of the escorts, *Coast Defense Vessel No. 36,* 23°03′N, 116°52′E.

USAAF B-24 sinks Japanese auxiliary powered sailing vessel *Hoseki Maru* in Tonkin Gulf, 18°34′N, 108°37′E.

Japanese submarine chaser *Ch 21* is damaged by marine casualty off the south end of Namoa Island.

Japanese netlayer *Wakamiya Maru* is damaged by marine casualty off Keelung, Formosa.

MEDITERRANEAN. Destroyer *Parker* (DD 604) and three British destroyers carry out antishipping sweep in the Gulf of Genoa, but encounter no enemy vessels.

ATLANTIC. Submarine *Lancetfish* (SS 296) is sunk by accidental improper operation of torpedo tube doors, Boston (Massachusetts) Navy Yard.

16 Friday

PACIFIC. Iwo Jima is declared secured. Nevertheless, this day Pharmacist's Mate Second Class Francis J. Pierce, who distinguished himself the previous day, volunteers to accompany a patrol forward. Shot through the left arm, Pierce directs the treatment of a wounded marine and, refusing to have his own wounds dressed, fires his pistol to draw enemy fire. He remains in that exposed position in the line of fire until the casualty is safely borne away. For his actions this day and on the previous one, Pierce is awarded the Medal of Honor.

Transported in medium landing craft (LCM) and one submarine chaser (SC), and supported by gunfire from three destroyers, two LCI(R), three LCS(L), and 2 LCI(M), Army troops (a reinforced company) land on Basilan Island, Sulu Archipelago, P.I.

Tank landing ship *LST 928* is damaged by grounding off Iwo Jima, 24°46′N, 141°19′E.

Japanese *Coast Defense Vessel No. 69* sinks while in tow, eight miles off Hong Kong, 22°00′N, 113°40′E, as the result of damage inflicted by USAAF B-24s (14th Air Force) on 8 March.

Japanese guardboat *No. 19 Gokoku Maru* is sunk by U.S. aircraft, Kikaiga Jima, Japan.

Japanese merchant tanker *No. 1 Nanryu Maru* is sunk by aircraft off Yangtze estuary, 29°09′N, 122°01′E.

17 Saturday

MEDITERRANEAN. Motor torpedo boats *PT 303* and *PT 305* engage two German F-lighters off Point Mesco, Italy; *PT 303* is damaged when she is accidentally rammed by *PT 305.*

EUROPE. TU 122.5.1 (Navy landing craft unit) LCVPs ferry 2,500 troops across the Rhine River.

PACIFIC. Submarine *Sealion* (SS 315) sinks Bangkok-bound Thai oiler *Samui* off Trengganu coast, 05°18′N, 103°23′E.

Submarine *Spot* (SS 413) attacks Japanese Keelung–to–Shimonoseki, Japan, convoy TAMO 49, escorted by escort vessel *Ikina, Coast Defense Vessel No. 41,* and minesweeper *W.17,* sinking army cargo vessel *Nanking Maru* off Yushiyama Island, 25°28′N, 120°10′E, and damaging cargo ship *Ikomasan Maru*, which is beached off Matsu Island, 26°07′N, 119°57′E, to permit salvage. *Spot* is damaged, however, by gunfire from one or more of the escorts. Later that day, USAAF B-25s further damage *Ikomasan Maru* (see 26 March).

PB4Y attacks Japanese convoy TAMO 49, damaging cargo vessel *Kitakata Maru*, 29°09′N, 122°07′E.

U.S. freighter *Oliver Kelly*, while proceeding through Surigao Strait, is damaged by what is most likely a dud torpedo; Japanese midget submarine activity during this month is recorded from bases on the coast of Cebu, P.I.

Japanese cargo ship *Mansei Maru* is sunk by USAAF mine in the Yangtze, near Shanghai, 31°19′N, 121°42′E.

USAAF B-29s (20th Air Force) bomb Kobe, Japan, damaging Japanese submarine *I 158* and cargo vessels *Enkei Maru* and *Teika Maru* (ex-*Cap Varella*).

18 Sunday

PACIFIC. TF 58 (Vice Admiral Marc A. Mitscher) planes bomb airfields on southern Kyushu and shipping, attacking convoy KATA 504, escorted by *Coast Defense Vessel No. 29* and submarine chaser *Ch 58*, and damaging cargo vessel *Kiyo Maru* and sinking transport *Kenyo Maru*, tanker *No. 1 Nansei Maru*, and Okinawa-bound auxiliary sailing vessels *Kamo Maru* and *Tenjin Maru* off Noma Misaki, 31°24′N, 130°07′E. TF 58 planes sink auxiliary submarine chaser *No. 43 Yusen Maru* 45 miles southwest of Sata Misaki Light; planes from carrier *Hornet* (CV 12) sink merchant vessel *No. 1 Nansei Maru* and damage *Tokuho Maru* and *Asahi Maru* in Yamakawa Harbor. During Japanese retaliatory air strikes off Kyushu, carriers *Enterprise* (CV 6), 30°50′N, 133°42′E, and *Yorktown* (CV 10), 30°40′N, 133°49′E, are damaged by bombs; *Intrepid* (CV 11) is crashed by kamikaze and hit by friendly fire, 30°47′N, 133°50′E.

Operation VICTOR ONE: TG 78.3 (Rear Admiral Arthur D. Struble) lands Army troops (40th Division, less one RCT) on Iloilo, off the southeast coast of Panay, under covering fire of light cruiser *Cleveland* (CL 55) and three destroyers (TU 74.2.2); the troops encounter only token resistance.

PV-1s (VPB 128), on the basis of reports from Filipino guerillas, bomb two Japanese midget submarines in Davao Gulf.

Tank landing ship *LST 635* is damaged by grounding off San Ricardo, Leyte, 11°05′N, 125°05′E.

Submarine *Balao* (SS 285) sinks Japanese merchant trawler *No. 2 Daito Maru* in the Yellow Sea, 35°00′N, 123°51′E.

Submarine *Springer* (SS 414), attacking Japanese convoy, sinks fast transport *T.18* and damages minesweeper *W.17* near Mutsure Jima, Ryukyus, 26°38′N, 127°12′E.

Submarine *Trigger* (SS 237) sinks Japanese army cargo ship *No. 3 Tsukushi Maru* northwest of Okinawa, 28°05′N, 126°44′E.

Japanese landing ship *T.137* is damaged by aircraft, Yaene, Hachijo Jima; freighter *Taiju Maru* is sunk off Hime Jima, Kyushu, by aircraft.

ATLANTIC. Destroyer escorts *Menges* (DE 320), *Mosley* (DE 321), *Pride* (DE 323), and *Lowe* (DE 325) sink German submarine *U 866* south of Nova Scotia, 43°18′N, 61°08′W.

19 Monday

PACIFIC. TF 58 (Vice Admiral Marc A. Mitscher) pounds airfields on Kyushu and Japanese shipping at Kure and Kobe, Honshu, destroying incomplete submarine *I 205* in drydock and damaging battleships *Yamato*, *Hyuga*, and *Haruna*; carriers *Ikoma*, *Katsuragi*, *Ryuho*, and *Amagi*; small carrier *Hosho*; escort carrier *Kaiyo*; heavy cruiser *Tone*; light cruiser *Oyodo*; submarines *I 400* and *RO 67*; and auxiliary submarine chaser *Cha 229* at Kure. TF 58 damages escort destroyer *Kaki* at Osaka; escort destroyer *Shinnan* in Suo Nada, 33°47′N, 131°35′E; landing ship *T.105* near Ujina; and freighter *Rashu Maru* off Uzaki, Hyogo prefecture.

Japanese planes single out carriers for attack. *Wasp* (CV 18) is hit by one bomb, 32°16′N, 134°05′E; friendly fire hits *Essex* (CV 9), 32°10′N, 134°20′E. *Franklin* (CV 13) is hit by two bombs, 32°01′N, 133°57′E; fires sweep across flight and hangar decks. As *Franklin* is rocked by a succession of explosions, Lieutenant Commander Joseph T. O'Callaghan, ChC, the carrier's Roman Catholic chaplain, emerges as a "soul-stirring sight. He seemed to be everywhere," an observer writes later, "giving Extreme Unction to the dead and dying, urging the men on and himself handling hoses, jettisoning ammunition and doing everything he could to help save our ship. He was so conspicuous not only because of the cross daubed with paint across his helmet but because of his seemingly detached air as he went from place to place with head slightly bowed as if in meditation or prayer." Elsewhere on board, Lieutenant (j.g.) Donald A. Gary calms anxious shipmates trapped in a smoke-filled compartment and after repeated

attempts through dark, debris-filled passageways manages to find a way to escape. Later, he organizes and leads fire-fighting parties in the blazing inferno of the hangar deck, and then enters no. 3 fireroom to raise steam in one boiler in the face of extreme hazards. O'Callaghan and Gary will each be awarded the Medal of Honor. Heavy cruiser *Pittsburgh* (CA 72) takes the damaged carrier in tow; light cruiser *Santa Fe* (CL 60) directs salvage and rescue operations. *Santa Fe* and destroyer *Hickox* (DD 673) are damaged while alongside aiding *Franklin*.

Submarine *Balao* (SS 285) attacks Japanese convoy MOTA 43, sinking troopship *Hakozaki Maru* and damaging transport *Tatsuharu Maru* off the Yangtze estuary about 90 miles north-northwest of Shanghai, 33°10′N, 122°10′E, and sinking merchant fishing vessels *No. 1 Katsura Maru*, *No. 1 Eiho Maru*, and *No. 2 Eiho Maru*, 34°40′N, 122°55′E.

Submarine *Bluefish* (SS 222) damages Japanese guardboat *No. 1 Shinya Maru* northnorthwest of Chichi Jima, 31°35′N, 137°50′E.

PV-1s (VPB 128) bomb and damage Japanese midget submarine at Cebu; strike is repeated the next day.

Japanese river gunboat *Suma* is sunk by USAAF mine (laid by 14th Air Force planes on 4 March), in the Yangtze, 51 miles above Kiangyin, China, 32°00′N, 120°00′E. Mine also claims merchant ship *Kozan Maru* below Chinkiang, 32°05′N, 119°56′E.

USAAF mine also sinks Japanese merchant tanker *Sarawak Maru*, repaired after her brush with *Besugo* (SS 321) on 24 January, 10 miles off Horsburgh Light, Singapore, 01°25′N, 104°36′E.

EUROPE. U.S. freighter *Hadley F. Brown*, in convoy TAG 12, is damaged by mine at entrance to Schelde estuary, 51°22′N, 02°53′E. There are no casualties among the 27-man Armed Guard; the ship reaches Flushing, Holland, under tow soon thereafter.

20 Tuesday

MEDITERRANEAN. Destroyer *Parker* (DD 604) shells German mortar positions, supply dumps, dugouts, and buildings on the Franco-Italian border.

PACIFIC. TF 92 (Captain John M. Worthington) (six destroyers) sorties from Attu, Aleutians, to proceed to Paramushir to bombard Japanese installations in the Suribachi Wan area. Heavy ice, however, will cause a cancellation of the operation.

Off Japan, carrier *Enterprise* (CV 6) is dam-

Destroyer *Halsey Powell* (DD 686), working up to full speed to clear the side of carrier *Hancock* (CV 19), is crashed by a *kamikaze*, 20 March 1945. (NA, RG 80)

aged by friendly fire, 30°01′N, 134°30′E, and destroyer *Halsey Powell* (DD 686) is crashed by *kamikaze* at 30°27′N, 134°28′E. TF 58 planes sink Japanese guardboat *No. 1 Kochi Maru* east of Honshu.

Submarine *Blenny* (SS 324) attacks Japanese convoy HI 88I off coast of French Indochina, sinking merchant tankers *No. 21 Nanshin Maru* and *Hosen Maru* and fishing boat *Yamakuni Maru* about 40 miles south of Cam Ranh Bay, 11°18′N, 108°57′E (see 21 March).

Submarine *Devilfish* (SS 292) is damaged by suicide plane off Volcano Islands, 25°36′N, 137°30′E, and is forced to terminate her patrol.

Submarine *Perch* (SS 313) lands men on east coast of Borneo.

Japanese army ship *No. 1 Genzan Maru* is sunk by aircraft off coast of French Indochina.

USAAF B-25s attack Japanese convoy, sinking stores ships *Heishin Maru* and *Fukusei Maru* and damaging torpedo boat *Hatsukari* off Tungshan, China, 23°42′N, 137°15′E.

Japanese *Gyoraitei No. 219* is damaged by aircraft, Toba, 30°06′N, 122°22′E.

ARCTIC. German submarines attack convoy JW 65 off Kola Inlet; *U 995* torpedoes U.S. freighter *Horace Bushnell* 24 miles east of Kilden Light, 69°23′N, 35°17′W. Heavy seas prevent British destroyer HMS *Orwell* from beaching the crippled ship, but the warship embarks the freighter's survivors (including the entire 27-man Armed Guard). Russian tugs later beach the merchantman, which is subsequently declared a total loss. *U 968* torpedoes freighter *Thomas Donaldson* about five miles off Kilden Island, 68°26′30″N, 33°44′20″W. British corvettes HMS *Bamborough Castle*, HMS *Oxlip*, and HMS *Honeysuckle*

rescue survivors; attempt to tow the ship to safety fails and she sinks a half mile from Kilden Island.

21 Wednesday

PACIFIC. Japanese make first known operational use of piloted bombs (*Baka*) in unsuccessful air attack against TF 58.

Patrols land on Guimaras Island, across Iloilo Strait from Iloilo, Panay, and find it clear of Japanese troops.

Two U.S. motor torpedo boats, supported by a British destroyer, attack enemy shipping in Sarawak Harbor, Borneo.

Japanese convoy HI 88I again comes under attack off coast of French Indochina. Submarine *Baya* (SS 318) sinks auxiliary netlayer *Kainan Maru* off Cam Ranh Bay, 12°00′N, 109°17′E, and although damaged by depth charges, 11°55′N, 109°18′E, remains on patrol. USAAF B-25s (Far East Air Force) sink submarine chaser *Ch 33*, cable layer *Tateishi*, and cargo vessels *No. 1 Motoyama Maru*, *No. 2 Fushimi Maru*, and *No. 6 Takasago Maru* and damage submarine chaser *Ch 9* off Nha Trang, 11°50′N, 109°18′E. Surviving vessels, the damaged *Ch 9* and merchant tanker *No. 30 Nanshin Maru*, take refuge at Nha Trang and are assigned to convoy HI 88J.

Japanese gunboat *Okitsu* is damaged by U.S. aircraft near Cape Hung Hua.

22 Thursday

PACIFIC. Patrols land on Inampulugan Island, in Guimaras Strait, and destroy a Japanese mine control station and eliminate the small garrison there.

Japanese planes attack American shipping

in Lingayen Gulf, P.I. During the ensuing anti-aircraft barrage, friendly fire damages U.S. freighter *Ransom A. Moore*; there are, however, no casualties among the merchant crew or the 27-man Armed Guard.

Tank landing ship *LST 727* is damaged by grounding off Iwo Jima, 24°46′N, 141°19′E.

Submarine *Perch* (SS 313) sinks Japanese *Communication Vessel No. 463* en route to Balikpapan, 01°03′S, 117°20′E.

Japanese submarine chaser *Ch 23* is damaged by mine at mouth of Yangtze River.

Covered lighters *YF 724* and *YF 725* founder and sink in heavy weather 380 miles off the Farallones.

EUROPE. German submarines attack Wales-bound convoy TBC 102 and Ghent, Belgium–bound convoy BTC 103. In the former, *U 399* torpedoes and sinks U.S. freighter *John R. Park*, 49°56′N, 05°26′W (all hands are rescued by U.S. freighter *American Press*); in the latter, what is most likely *U 1195* torpedoes and sinks freighter *James Eagan Lane*, 50°13′N, 04°14′W. British freighter *Monkstone* and rescue tug *Flaunt* rescue the survivors. A skeleton crew (including four Armed Guard sailors) reboard the freighter and rig the ship for towing. Tugs *Flaunt* and *Atlas* beach the ship at White-sand Bay, but *James Eagan Lane* is ultimately written off as a total loss.

U.S. freighter *Charles D. McIver* sinks after striking a mine as she leaves Antwerp, Belgium, in convoy ATM 100, 31°22′35″N, 03°05′50″W. British motor minesweeper *BYMS 2279* rescues one of the four boatloads of survivors; the other three boatloads, rescued by a motor torpedo boat, find safety on board tank landing ship *LST 430*. *Charles D. McIver* is later written off as a total loss; there are no casualties among the merchant crew or the 27-man Armed Guard.

23 Friday

EUROPE. TU 122.5.1 (Navy landing craft unit) LCVPs ferry between 4,000 and 4,500 troops from General George S. Patton's U.S. Third Army as it crosses the Rhine at Oppenheim, Germany.

PACIFIC. TF 58 (Vice Admiral Marc A. Mitscher) begins daily strikes against Japanese shipping and installations in the Okinawa area. TF 58 planes sink army cargo ship *Kachosan Maru* 25 miles northwest of Okinawa, 30°23′N, 128°40′E. Cargo vessel *No. 19 Yamato Maru* is also sunk in these strikes. In addition, TF 58 aircrew also claim sinking one midget submarine and damaging another, as well as damaging *Coast Defense Ship No. 29* and submarine chaser *Ch 58* off Sotsuko Saki.

Destroyer *Haggard* (DD 555) is damaged when she rams and sinks Japanese submarine *RO 41* in the Philippine Sea, 22°57′N, 132°19′E.

Submarine *Seahorse* (SS 304) is damaged by aerial bomb off the Ryukyus, 26°00′N, 128°00′E.

Submarine *Spadefish* (SS 411) attacks Japanese Sasebo-to-Ishigaki convoy SAI 05 in the East China Sea about 120 miles north-north-west of Amami-O-Shima, sinking transport *Doryu Maru*, 29°38′N, 127°36′E.

Fleet tug *Zuni* (ATF 95) is damaged by grounding off Iwo Jima, 24°46′N, 141°19′E.

USAAF B-24 (Far East Air Force) sinks Japanese cargo ship *Hokka Go Maru* (ex-Chinese *Peihua*) 110 miles northeast of Wenchow, China, 29°21′N, 122°66′E.

USAAF B-24 attacks Japanese *Coast Defense Vessel No. 40*, 26°58′N, 120°29′E, but although the airmen claim damage to their quarry, she in fact escapes undamaged.

Japanese destroyer *Kuri* is damaged by mine at mouth of Yangtze River.

24 Saturday

EUROPE. Operation FLASHPOINT: TU 122.5.1 (Navy landing craft unit) LCVPs support the U.S. Third Army's crossing of the Rhine, ferrying troops at Boppard, Germany, under heavy enemy 20-millimeter fire. Other navy landing craft from TU 122.5.3 ferry troops of the U.S. Ninth Army across the Rhine south of Wesel, Germany. Medium landing craft (LCM) are used on the Rhine for the first time in this operation.

PACIFIC. TF 59 (Vice Admiral Willis A. Lee Jr.) bombards Okinawa. Japanese sources list two vessels sunk by naval gunfire on this date, perhaps the victims of the battleship bombardment: *Tosan Maru* and *No. 10 Maiko Maru*.

USAAF B-24 (possibly a USN PB4Y) attacks nine-ship Japanese Naha-to-Kagoshima convoy KANA 304 (probably rerouted into the East China Sea because of Allied air activity in the Ryukyus), sinking auxiliary minesweeper *Seki Maru* off Tokara Gunto, 29°12′N, 125°13′E. Planes from TG 58.1—carriers *Bennington* (CV 20) and *Hornet* (CV 12) and small carriers *Belleau Wood* (CVL 24) and *San Jacinto* (CVL 30)—complete the destruction of KANA 304, sinking torpedo boat *Tomozuru*, *Coast Defense Vessel No. 68*, auxiliary minesweepers *Chitose Maru* and *No. 16 Shonan Maru*, army cargo ship *Koshu Maru*, and freighters *Soka Maru*, *Kaijo Maru*, and *No. 3 Tsukushi Maru* about 200

Soldiers of the 89th Division, equipped with M-1 Garands, a Thompson Submachine Gun, and a Browning Automatic Rifle, crouch down in their LCVP as the Navy landing craft transports them across the Rhine at Oberwesel, Germany, 26 March 1945, as photographed by T/5 A.H. Herz, USA. (NA, SC-202464)

miles northwest of Okinawa, 28°25′N, 124°32′E. The same day, TF 58 planes also sink army cargo ship *Seizan Maru* and merchantmen *Sanko Maru* at 29°15′N, 125°13′E, and *Kobe Maru* at 30°00′N, 126°30′E.

USAAF B-24s (Far East Air Force) sink Japanese cargo ship *Koshin Maru* off Boeton Island, Celebes, 05°40′S, 122°49′E.

25 Sunday

PACIFIC. TF 54 (Rear Admiral Morton L. Deyo) battleships, cruisers, and destroyers bombard Kerama Retto and southeast coast of Okinawa, Ryukyus; bombardment will continue daily over ensuing days. Destroyer escort *Sederstrom* (DE 31) is damaged in collision with escort carrier *Sangamon* (CVE 26), 25°00′N, 130°00′E.

Submarine *Tirante* (SS 420) sinks Japanese auxiliary netlayer *Fuji Maru* off Tori Jima, 31°08′N, 130°30′E.

TF 58 planes sink Japanese freighters *No. 5 Okinoyama Maru* and *Chokai Maru* near Naha, Okinawa, 26°13′N, 127°39′E. Auxiliary submarine chaser *Sobun Maru* is damaged between Yaku Jima and Amami-O-Shima.

USAAF B-24s (Far East Air Force) sink Japanese *Kori Go Maru* (ex-Chinese *Houlee*) in

Yangtze estuary near Shanghai, 31°11′N, 122°23′E.

26 Monday

EUROPE. TG 122.5.1 (Navy landing craft unit) ferries U.S. Third Army assault troops across the Rhine at Oberwesel, Germany; medium landing craft (LCM) are used for the first time in the Third Army's Rhine-crossing operation.

PACIFIC. Off Okinawa, destroyer *Halligan* (DD 584) is sunk by mine, 26°10′N, 127°30′E; *kamikazes* damage battleship *Nevada* (BB 36) (near-misses); light cruiser *Biloxi* (CL 80); destroyers *O'Brien* (DD 725), 26°16′N, 127°26′E, *Callaghan* (DD 792), 26°20′N, 127°43′E, and *Kimberley* (DD 521), 26°02′N, 126°54′E; minesweeper *Skirmish* (AM 303), 26°25′N, 127°05′E; light minelayer *Robert H. Smith* (DM 23), 26°00′N, 128°00′E; and high-speed transport *Gilmer* (APD 11), 26°00′N, 127°20′E. High-speed transport *Knudsen* (APD 101) is damaged in air attack, 26°12′N, 127°04′E.

TG 51.1 (Rear Admiral Ingolf N. Kiland) lands U.S. Army force (77th Infantry Division) on Kerama Retto, Ryukyus, under cover of naval bombardment and carrier aircraft.

Operation VICTOR TWO: TG 78.2 (Captain Albert T. Sprague Jr.) lands U.S. Army American Division (Reinforced) less one RCT, on Talisay Point, Cebu, P.I., covered by TG 74.3 (Rear Admiral Russell S. Berkey), consisting of three light cruisers (including Australian HMAS *Hobart*) and six destroyers. The landing is made against only slight resistance. U.S. freighter *Michael J. Owens* Armed Guard gunfire, despite lack of sophisticated fire control equipment, silences Japanese artillery battery on Cebu.

Tank landing craft *LCT 1090* is damaged in amphibious operations off Luzon; submarine chaser *PC 1133* is damaged by grounding, 10°13′N, 123°51′E.

Submarine *Balao* (SS 285) sinks Japanese army stores ship *No. 1 Shinto Maru* in the Yellow Sea, 35°18′N, 123°15′E.

TF 58 planes sink Japanese auxiliary submarine chaser *Nisui Maru* east of Fuku Jima, and cargo ship *Daia Maru* in Kuji Bay, Ryukyus, 20°13′N, 127°16′E.

USAAF B-24s complete destruction of Japanese cargo ship *Ikomasan Maru*, previously damaged by submarine *Spot* (SS 413), then run aground and bombed by USAAF B-25s on 17 March off Matsu Island, 26°07′N, 119°57′E, and sink motor sailships *Koun Maru* and *No. 6 Ebisu Maru*.

USAAF B-24s (Far East Air Force) bomb Japanese shipping in Takao Harbor, sinking cargo vessels *Enoura Maru* and *Kishu Maru*, 22°37′N, 120°15′E.

INDIAN OCEAN. British destroyers annihilate Japanese Port Blair–bound convoy east of Khota Andaman. HMS *Saumarez*, HMS *Volage*, HMS *Vigilant*, and HMS *Virago* sink submarine chasers *Ch 34* and *Ch 63*; HMS *Venus*, HMS *Verulam* and HMS *Virago* sink transport *Risui Maru* and supply ship *Teshio Maru*, 10°38′N, 94°42′E. RAF Liberators contribute to *Risui Maru*'s destruction.

27 Tuesday

EUROPE. TG 122.5.1 (Navy landing craft unit) ferries army troops across the Rhine at Mainz, Germany, in the face of "all the fire power at [the Germans'] disposal," ranging from machine guns and small arms to the deadly 88-millimeter weapons.

PACIFIC. TU 78.9.11 (Commander Selden G. Hooper) supports operation against Caballo Island, near Corregidor. Destroyers *Conway* (DD 507) and *Cony* (DD 508) and three rocket-equipped motor torpedo boats, preceded by an air strike, provide support. Tank landing ship *LST 206* lands U.S. Army 2nd Battalion, 151st Infantry, 38th Division (see 5 April).

Operation STARVATION, the USAAF aerial mining campaign (using Navy-provided mines), commences as 94 B-29s mine the Shimonoseki Straits and the waters of Suo Nada, Japan. This operation and the six that follow are in support of the Okinawa campaign.

High-speed transport *Newman* (APD 59), covering the landings on Cebu, sights and attacks a Japanese midget submarine off Talisay. She is given credit for a "possible" submersible sunk.

Off Okinawa, an aircraft operational casualty damages carrier *Essex* (CV 9), 25°10′N, 132°05′E; *kamikazes* damage light minelayer *Adams* (DM 27), 26°17′N, 127°40′E, high-speed minesweeper *Dorsey* (DMS 1), 26°20′N, 127°18′E, and destroyer *Porterfield* (DD 682). Destroyer *Murray* (DD 576) is damaged by bomb, 26°20′N, 129°46′E.

Submarine *Trigger* (SS 237) sinks Japanese cable layer *Odate* 200 miles southwest of Kyushu, 30°40′N, 127°50′E.

TF 58 planes sink Japanese guardboats *No. 13 Choun Maru* and *No. 27 Yusen Maru* and army cargo ship *No. 28 Suma Maru*, Kuchinoerabu Bay, Osumi Gunto, 30°30′N, 130°05′E, and *No. 12 Myojin Maru*, west of Tori Jima, 30°00′N, 139°30′E.

British submarine HMS *Stygian* damages Japanese minelayer *Wakatake* (previously damaged on 25 March when she encountered a shoal upon leaving Macassar) in Java Sea, south of Kangean Island. Reaching Surabaya on 1 April, *Wakatake* performs no more active service.

USAAF B-24s attack six-ship Japanese convoy off Surabaya, damaging submarine chaser *Ch 5* by near-misses.

Japanese auxiliary minesweeper *Wa.1* is sunk by mine (laid by RAF planes) near the Deli River, Sumatra, 03°52′N, 98°45′E.

28 Wednesday

PACIFIC. Off Okinawa, minesweeper *Skylark* (AM 63) is sunk by mine, 26°20′N, 127°40′E; attack cargo ship *Wyandot* (AKA 92) is damaged by near-misses of bombs, 26°00′N, 127°00′E; medium landing ship (rocket) *LSM(R) 188* is damaged by *kamikaze*; and infantry landing craft (gunboat) *LCI(G) 588* is damaged by assault demolition boat.

Landing craft repair ship *Agenor* (ARL 3) is damaged in collision with landing craft off Iwo Jima, 24°46′N, 141°19′E.

Submarine *Blackfin* (SS 322) is damaged by depth charges off the southeast coast of French Indochina, and is forced to terminate her patrol.

Submarines and USAAF planes begin attacks on Japanese convoy HI 88J moving up the coast of French Indochina; submarine *Bluegill* (SS 242) damages tanker *Honan Maru* (ex-British *War Sirdar*) off Cape Varella, 12°40′N, 109°30′E; *Honan Maru* is beached to permit salvage (see 29 March and 5 April). USAAF B-24 sinks freighter *Asogawa Maru* off Nha Trang, 12°32′N, 109°22′E.

Submarine *Snook* (SS 279) departs Guam for her ninth war patrol; she is contacted by *Tigrone* (SS 419) on 8 April, but is never seen again.[237]

Submarine *Threadfin* (SS 410) sinks Japanese escort vessel *Mikura* off Kyushu, 31°45′N, 131°44′E.

Submarine *Tirante* (SS 420) sinks Japanese fishing boat *Nase Maru* west of Oniki Saki, Kyushu, 32°15′N, 29°55′E.

Submarine *Trigger* (SS 237) is sunk by Japanese patrol vessel *Mikura*, Coast Defense Vessel *No. 33*, and Coast Defense Vessel *No. 59* in the Nansei Shoto, 32°16′N, 132°05′E.[238]

Planes from carrier *Hornet* (CV 12) sink Japanese Coast Defense Vessel *No. 33* south of Kyushu, 31°45′N, 131°45′E.

USAAF B-24s (Far East Air Force) sink Japanese army cargo ship *Meiho Maru* off north coast of Formosa, 25°00′N, 121°00′E; B-24 damages Coast Defense Vessel *No. 102* and Coast Defense Vessel *No. 106* (near-misses) off Keelung, Formosa.

USAAF B-24s (Far East Air Force) attack Japanese shipping in the Celebes, sinking minesweeper *W.11* off Makassar, 05°06′S, 119°14′E, and *Patrol Boat No. 108* off Maniang Island, 04°14′S, 121°28′E.

Japanese auxiliary submarine chasers *Cha 167* and *Cha 175* are sunk by aircraft, east of Fuka Shima, Kyushu.

USAAF B-24 damages Japanese cargo ship *Seito Maru* off North Laut Island, 03°14′S, 116°13′E.

Japanese auxiliary submarine chaser *Cha 178* is sunk by mine, 34°02′N, 130°54′E; cargo ship *Tensei Maru* is sunk by mine in Wakamatsu Harbor, Japan.

Floating workshop *YR 43*, being towed to Kodiak, Alaska, by Army tug *LT 373*, breaks free from her towline and drifts aground two and half miles south of Zaikof Point, Montague Island; rescue tug *ATR 68* and Coast Guard lighthouse tender *Cedar* (WAGL 207) are sent from Kodiak, while tender *Bramble* (WAGL 392) is dispatched from Seward to assist. Army transport *Toloa* brings *YR 43*'s crew on board and takes the men to Dutch Harbor.

ATLANTIC. U.S. tanker *Oklahoma*, bound for Dakar, French West Africa, is torpedoed and sunk by German submarine *U 532* in mid-Atlantic, 13°52′N, 41°17′W; 36 of the 46-man merchant complement and 14 of the 26-man Armed Guard die in the resulting conflagration, as the ship had a cargo of high-octane gasoline and kerosene (see 14 April).

29 Thursday

PACIFIC. TG 58.1 (Rear Admiral Joseph J. Clark) and TG 58.3 (Rear Admiral Frederick C. Sherman) attack airfields and Japanese shipping in the Kagoshima Bay area, Kyushu. Carrier-based planes sink auxiliary submarine chasers *Cha 200* west of Sata Misaki, 31°05′N, 130°39′E, *Chikuto Maru* in Kagoshima Bay, and *Cha 205*, Kuchinoerabu Jima, 30°30′N, 130°10′E, as well as cargo vessels *No. 5 Yusen Maru*, *No. 11 Ebisu Maru*, *Holin Maru*, *Genyo Maru*, *No. 8 Seizan Maru*, *No. 17 Koshin Maru*, *No. 27 Koan Maru*, *No. 32 Koan Maru*, and *Taimokuzan Maru* in Yamagawa Harbor; merchant vessel *No. 3 Yamato Maru* is damaged at the latter place.

TG 78.3 (Rear Admiral Arthur D. Struble), in an operation associated with the taking of Panay, moves Army 185th RCT (40th Division) from Iloilo to Pulupandan Point, northern Negros; the troops encounter no opposition.

Submarine and USAAF attacks continue against Japanese convoy HI 88J: *Bluegill* (SS 242) further damages tanker *Honan Maru* off Cape Varella (see 5 April); *Hammerhead* (SS 364) damages *Coast Defense Vessel No. 84* north of Cape Varella, 14°44′N, 109°16′E. USAAF B-25s (Far East Air Force) sink *Coast Defense Vessel No. 18*, *Coast Defense Vessel No. 130*, and cargo ship *Kaiko Maru*, 15°10′N, 109°26′E. Later the same day, PBMs further damage *Coast Defense Vessel No. 134* south of Hainan.

USAAF B-24 damages Japanese hospital ship *Kazura Maru* off coast of French Indochina, 15°05′N, 109°23′E; submarine chaser *Ch 9* is damaged at 15°10′N, 109°26′E.

USAAF B-24s (Far East Air Force) sink Japanese auxiliary submarine chasers *Cha 156*, *Cha 189*, and *Cha 192* and merchant tanker *Iwakuni Maru* in Takao Harbor, 22°40′N, 120°15′E.

Japanese auxiliary patrol vessel *Pa No. 173* is sunk by mine, Wakamatsu, Japan.

Japanese submarine *I 47* (equipped with *kaitens*) is damaged by Fifth Fleet surface ships/craft off Okinawa and forced to return to Kure for repairs.

ATLANTIC. U.S. freighter *O. B. Martin*, in convoy UGS 80, is damaged by depth charge explosions 25 miles west of Gibraltar; there are no casualties to the merchant crew, passengers, or the 29-man Armed Guard.

30 Friday

EUROPE. Over 1,250 USAAF heavy bombers (8th Air Force) hit U-boat yards and port facilities in Germany, sinking submarines *U 96*, *U 429*, and *U 3508* at Wilhelmshaven; *U 72*, *U 329*, *U 430*, *U 870*, *U 884*, and *U 886* at Bremen; and *U 2340*, *U 348*, *U 350*, and *U 1167* at Hamburg.

PACIFIC. Eighty-seven USAAF B-29s mine the Shimonoseki Straits and the waters off Kure, Hiroshima, and Sasebo, Japan.

High-speed transport *Roper* (APD 20) is damaged in collision with attack transport *Arthur Middleton* (APA 25), Philippine Sea, 20°57′N, 132°05′E.

Submarine *Tirante* (SS 420) sinks Japanese guardboat *Eikichi Maru* off Kagoshima, Japan, 31°11′N, 130°09′E.

Attacks against Japanese convoy HI 88J continue. USAAF B-25s sink auxiliary submarine chaser *Shinan Maru* and damage *Coast Defense Vessel No. 26* off Yulin, Hainan Island, 18°09′N, 109°42′E.

Japanese submarine *I 53* is damaged by mine, Suwo Nada.

31 Saturday

PACIFIC. Off Okinawa, heavy cruiser *Indianapolis* (CA 35) is damaged by *kamikaze*, 26°25′N, 127°30′E; heavy cruiser *Pensacola* (CA 24) is damaged in collision with tank landing ship *LST 277*, 26°10′N, 127°19′E. *Kamikazes* damage light minelayer *Adams* (DM 27), 26°12′N, 127°08′E; attack transport *Hinsdale* (APA 120), 25°54′N, 127°49′E; and tank landing ships *LST 724* and *LST 884*, 25°59′N, 127°50′E.

Small seaplane tender *Coos Bay* (AVP 25) is damaged when rammed accidentally by U.S. merchant ship *Matagorda* west of Eniwetok, 12°07′N, 156°27′E.

U.S. freighter *John C. Fremont* is damaged by mine south of Pier 7, Manila Bay; there are no casualties among the 27-man Armed Guard.

Destroyers *Morrison* (DD 560) and *Stockton* (DD 646) sink Japanese submarine *I 8*, 65 miles southeast of Okinawa, 25°29′N, 128°35′E.

Japanese auxiliary submarine chaser *Cha 233* is sunk by aircraft off Danjo Gunto, 32°19′N, 129°50′E.

USAAF B-24s attack Japanese convoy off Makassar, sinking small cargo vessels *No. 3 Hainan Maru*, *Kanho Maru*, *Manko Maru*, and *Nanho Maru* and damaging *Oshima Maru*, and attack convoy BASU 05 in Makassar Strait off Balkpapan, damaging submarine chaser *Ch 5*.

USAAF B-24s bomb Japanese convoy in harbor at Keelung, damaging hospital ship *Baikal Maru*, cargo vessels *Nikko Maru* and *No. 3 Yamato Maru*, and motor sailship *No. 47 Suma Maru*.

Mines damage Japanese destroyer *Hibiki* off Hime Jima, Kyushu, and escort destroyer *Inagi* off He Saki, Japan.

During March 1945 (exact date indeterminate) car floats *YCF 23*, *YCF 29*, *YCF 36*, and *YCF 37* break up in heavy seas while under tow en route to Eniwetok, Marshall Islands.

APRIL

1 Sunday

PACIFIC. Operation ICEBERG: Marines and Army troops land on Okinawa, Ryukyus, under cover of heavy naval gunfire and aircraft support. The operation is under the overall command of Admiral Raymond A. Spruance, Commander Fifth Fleet. Vice Admiral Richmond Kelly Turner commands the Joint Expeditionary Force; the troops are commanded by Lieutenant General Simon B. Buckner, USA. Off Okinawa, *kamikazes* damage battleship *West Virginia* (BB 48), 26°20′N, 127°40′E, attack transports *Hinsdale* (APA 120) and *Alpine* (APA 92), 26°20′N, 127°41′E, and tank landing ship *LST 884*; battleship *Tennessee* (BB 43) is damaged by shell fragments (possibly friendly fire). *LST 774* is attacked but shoots down her assailant, which sheds its engine on the tank landing ship's deck. Japanese dive bombers damage destroyer *Prichett* (DD 561), 26°38′N, 127°25′E, and minesweeper *Skirmish* (AM 303), 26°33′N, 127°33′E; horizontal bomber damages attack transport *Elmore* (APA 42), 26°20′N, 127°41′E. Destroyer escort *Vammen* (DE 644) is damaged by explosion of undetermined origin (possibly depth charge dropped by assault demolition boat), 26°18′N, 127°29′E. Infantry landing craft (mortar) *LCI(M) 807* is damaged by own mortar explosion; infantry landing craft (rocket) *LCI(R) 704*'s topmast, signal yard, and antennae are shot away by nearby tank landing ship; and medium landing ship (rocket) *LSM(R) 192* is damaged by operational casualty. British ships are not immune from the blowing of the "divine wind" as a *kamikaze* damages fleet carrier HMS *Indefatigable*; destroyer HMS *Ulster* is hit by bomb. *LCI(R) 770* destroys three assault demolition boats beached at Kerama Retto.

In the third of six mine drops carried out in support of ICEBERG, six USAAF B-29s mine the waters off Kure, Japan. Mines sink freighter *Karikawa Maru* off Tsushima, and damage escort vessel *Inagi* southeast of He Saki and auxiliary submarine chaser *Cha 226* in Kii Channel, Japan, 30°04′N, 130°54′E.

TG 78.4 (Captain Homer F. McGee) lands U.S. Army troops (158th RCT) near Legaspi, southern Luzon, under cover of naval gunfire (TU 78.4.1, two destroyers and two destroyer escorts) against light resistance. Opposition intensifies, however, as the troops advance inland.

Submarine *Queenfish* (SS 393) inadvertently sinks Japanese relief ship *Awa Maru* in Formosa Straits, 25°25′N, 120°07′E. *Awa Maru*, a cartel ship, is carrying Red Cross supplies earmarked for distribution to Allied POWs in Singapore. Guaranteed safe conduct by the U.S. government, *Awa Maru* is properly marked and lighted, but *Queenfish*'s commanding officer, Lieutenant Commander Charles E. Loughlin, does not discern the markings in the foggy weather in which his boat encounters the enemy vessel. Loughlin is relieved of his command for the mistake and is court-martialed.

B-24s (Far East Air Force) bomb Japanese shipping at Keelung, Formosa, irreparably damaging *Taiga Maru*.

2 Monday

PACIFIC. TG 76.10 (Captain John D. Murphy) lands U.S. Army 163rd RCT (Reinforced) of the 41st Division, supported by three destroyers, on Sanga Sanga, Sulu Archipelago, P.I., without encountering any resistance. Filipino guerrillas have cleared the island the month before.

Off Okinawa, destroyer *Franks* (DD 554) is damaged in collision with battleship *New Jersey* (BB 62), 25°49′N, 130°01′E; destroyer *Borie* (DD 704) by collision with carrier *Essex* (CV 9), 23°36′N, 131°40′E; and destroyer escort *Foreman* (DE 633) by bomb, 26°10′N, 127°11′E. *Kamikazes* damage attack transports *Henrico* (APA 45), 25°59′N, 127°17′E, and *Goodhue* (APA 107); attack cargo ships *Achernar* (AKA 53), 26°07′N, 127°45′E, and *Tyrrell* (AKA 80), 26°21′N, 127°45′E; high-speed transport *Dickerson* (APD 21); and infantry landing craft (gunboat) *LCI(G) 568*. *LCI(G) 580* is damaged by operational casualty; *LCI(L) 462* is damaged by grounding. Attack transport *Chilton* (APA 38) is damaged by near-miss of *kamikaze*, 25°59′N, 127°17′E; attack cargo

ship *Lacerta* (AKA 29) is damaged by friendly fire, 26°21′N, 127°43′E.

TG 58.4 planes sink Japanese *Coast Defense Vessel No. 186*, fast transport *T.17*, and landing ship *T.145* and damage submarine chaser *Ch 49* and landing ship *T.146* near Amami-O-Shima, 28°07′N, 129°09′E.

Destroyer *Shaw* (DD 373) is damaged by grounding off Negros, 09°36′N, 123°53′E.

Submarine *Hardhead* (SS 365) lays mines off Cape Camau, French Indochina.

Submarine *Sea Devil* (SS 400) attacks Japanese convoy TAMO 51 in the central Yellow Sea, sinking auxiliary vessel *Edogawa Maru*, army cargo ship *Nisshin Maru*, and freighter *Daijo Maru*, 34°18′N, 124°04′E, and damaging freighter *Yamaji Maru*, 34°02′N, 124°00′E.

British submarine HMS *Stygian* sinks Japanese coaster south of Kangean Island, 07°02′S, 115°32′E.

USAAF P-51s damage Japanese river gunboat *Katata* at Shanghai.

USAAF aircraft sink small Japanese cargo vessel *No. 1 Taisei Maru* off Cape St. Jacques, French Indochina, 10°10′N, 106°35′E.

USAAF B-24s bomb Japanese shipping at Hong Kong, sinking freighter *Yokai Maru*.

Ten USAAF B-29s mine the waters off Kure and Hiroshima, Japan.

3 Tuesday

EUROPE. Over 700 USAAF heavy bombers attack U-boat yards at Kiel, Germany, destroying submarines *U 1221*, *U 2542*, and *U 3505*.

PACIFIC. Nine USAAF B-29s mine the waters off Kure and Hiroshima, Japan.

Off Okinawa, escort carrier *Wake Island* (CVE 65) is damaged by near-miss of *kamikaze*, 26°05′N, 128°57′E, as is high speed minesweeper *Hambleton* (DMS 20), 27°00′N, 127°00′E; a *kamikaze* damages tank landing ship *LST 599*, 26°10′N, 127°16′E, and attack transport *Telfair* (APA 210), 25°56′N, 127°17′E. Destroyer *Prichett* (DD 561) is damaged by bomb, 27°17′N, 127°51′E; tank landing ship *LST 554* is damaged by storm, 26°20′N, 127°45′E. Infantry landing craft (rocket) *LCI(R) 762* is stranded off BLUE beach but retracts under own power without damage.

Motor minesweeper *YMS 71* is sunk by mine off Sanga Sanga, 04°59′N, 119°47′E.

TF 58 planes sink Japanese guardboat *No. 1 Taijin Maru;* damage guardboat *No. 2 Hosei Maru* southeast of Japan, 30°00′N, 137°30′E; and sink cargo ship *Imari Maru* off southwestern Kyushu, 33°45′N, 129°42′E. *Coast Defense Vessel No. 32* is damaged at 31°51′N, 124°47′E.

USAAF B-24s (Far East Air Force) bomb Japanese shipping in Hong Kong Harbor, sinking cargo vessels *Heikai Maru* and *Shozan Maru*, and damaging escort vessel *Manju*, 22°17′N, 114°10′E.

USN land-based planes sink Japanese tanker *No. 30 Nanshin Maru* (the only surviving ship of the ill-starred convoy HI 88I), Nha Trang Bay, French Indochina, 12°15′N, 109°10′E.

4 Wednesday

EUROPE. USAAF heavy bombers (939 strong) pound airfields and landing grounds in northern Germany, as well as munitions plant near Ulzen. U-boat yards at Hamburg and Kiel are also bombed, resulting in the destruction of submarines *U 237*, *U 749*, and *U 3003*.

PACIFIC. Off Okinawa, high-speed transport *Dickerson* (APD 21), irreparably damaged by *kamikaze* on 2 April, is towed out to sea and scuttled by salvage crew off Kerama Retto. Infantry landing craft (gunboat) *LCI(G) 82* is irreparably damaged by assault demolition boat, 26°26′N, 128°03′E; sisterships *LCI(G) 79*, *LCI(G) 347*, and *LCI(G) 725* stand by and assist in caring for survivors. *LCI(G) 82* sinks just after being taken in tow by salvage vessel *Gear* (ARS 34). Destroyer *Norman Scott* (DD 690) is damaged in collision with oiler *Cimarron* (AO 22), 23°46′N, 129°25′E. *Kamikaze* damages destroyer *Wilson* (DD 408) off southern end of Kerama Retto; destroyer *Sproston* (DD 577) is damaged by near-miss by bomb, 26°30′N, 127°30′E. Oiler *Cowanesque* (AO 79) is damaged in storm; medium landing ship *LSM 12* founders in heavy weather. Groundings account for damage to tank landing ships *LST 70*, *LST 624*, *LST 675*, and *LST 756*, 26°21′N, 127°45′E; *LST 166*, *LST 689*, and *LST 736*, 26°20′N, 127°45′E; *LST 343*, 26°00′N, 128°00′E; *LST 570*, 26°21′N, 127°44′E, and *LST 781*, 26°23′N, 127°44′E. Tank landing ship *LST 399* is damaged in collision with salvage vessel *Gear* (ARS 34), 26°20′N, 127°45′E.

Japanese escort vessel *Mokuto* is sunk by USAAF mine laid by B-29 (20th Air Force) in Shimonoseki Strait, 33°53′N, 131°03′E; freighter *Hozan Maru* is sunk by mine, 33°45′N, 131°44′E. Submarines *RO 64*, 34°14′N, 132°16′E, and *RO 67*, 34°00′N, 133°00′E, are damaged by USAAF B-29–sown mines in the Inland Sea.[239]

Japanese guardboat *No. 12 Kotoshiro Maru* is sunk by U.S. aircraft off Tori Jima, 30°00′N, 140°00′E.

USAAF B-24s (Far East Air Force) bomb

Japanese shipping at Mako, Pescadores, sinking merchant tanker *No. 2 Kinyu Maru* and cargo vessel *Horei Maru*, 23°32′N, 119°34′E.

Japanese ship *No. 1 Manyu Maru* is sunk by aircraft off Tajin Island.

Japanese hospital ship *Arimasan Maru* is damaged by mine, while en route to Singapore.

British submarine HMS *Spark* attacks Japanese light cruiser *Isuzu*, without success, in the Flores Sea (see 5–7 April).

5 Thursday

PACIFIC. In Japan, the cabinet of Premier Koiso Kuniaki resigns; Admiral Suzuki Kantaro becomes Prime Minister.

Off Okinawa, battleship *Nevada* (BB 36) is damaged by shore battery, 26°13′N, 127°40′E; a dud aerial torpedo damages light minelayer *Harry F. Bauer* (DM 26), 26°30′N, 127°30′E. Collisions account for damage to seaplane tender (destroyer) *Thornton* (AVD 11) and oiler *Escalante* (AO 70), 24°24′N, 128°58′E; landing craft repair ship *Agenor* (ARL 3) and tank landing ship *LST 646*, 24°46′N, 141°19′E; and tank landing ships *LST 273* and *LST 810*, 26°25′N, 127°42′E. Tank landing ship *LST 923* collides with tank landing ship *LST 20*; tank landing ship *LST 940* collides with attack cargo ship *Diphda* (AKA 59), 26°21′N, 127°43′E; and tank landing ship *LST 1000* collides with tank landing ship *LST 20*, 26°21′N, 127°44′E. Tank landing ships suffer varying degrees of damage: *LST 70* when she broaches; *LST 71* in collision; *LST 166*, *LST 625*, *LST 723*, *LST 762*, *LST 782*, and *LST 554* by storm; *LST 608*, *LST 609*, *LST 612*, and *LST 756* by operational casualties incident to beaching; *LST 624*, *LST 675*, and *LST 612* by operational casualties incident to grounding. Infantry landing craft (rocket) *LCI(R) 765* is damaged by operational casualties. U.S. shore battery sinks Japanese auxiliary minelayer *No. 2 Shinto Maru* and damages auxiliary minelayer *Taian Maru* in Naha Harbor, Okinawa, 26°30′N, 128°00′E. Destroyer *Hudson* (DD 475) sinks Japanese submarine *RO 41* off Kerama Retto, 26°22′N, 126°30′E.

Submarine *Besugo* (SS 321) twice attacks Japanese light cruiser *Isuzu* in the Flores Sea (see 6 and 7 April).

Boarding party from submarine *Bluegill* (SS 242) completes destruction of fleet tanker *Honan Maru*, beached and abandoned on 28 March, with demolition charges and incendiaries, near Nha Trang, French Indochina.

Submarine *Hardhead* (SS 365) attacks unescorted Japanese convoy SASI 45, damaging

cargo ship *Araosan Maru* in the Gulf of Siam, 09°37′N, 102°48′E (see 6 April).

PBMs attack Japanese convoy, sinking freighter *No. 2 Tokai Maru* in Pinghai Wan, 22°45′N, 116°10′E; USAAF B-24s, B-26s, and P-38s (Far East Air Force) attack same convoy, sinking cargo ship *Kine Maru*, 22°24′N, 115°28′E.

USAAF B-24s (Far East Air Force) bomb Japanese shipping at Hong Kong, damaging *Coast Defense Vessel No. 52* and *Coast Defense Vessel No. 1;* submarine chasers *Ch 9* and *Ch 20*, 22°45′N, 116°10′E; and fleet oiler *Kamoi*.

Mine laid by USAAF B-29 (20th Air Force) sinks Japanese freighter *No. 13 Nichinan Maru* two miles southeast of He Saki, 33°58′N, 131°02′E. Cargo ship *Iki Maru* is damaged by mine, 33°54′N, 130°53′E.

Army engineers pump diesel fuel into pits and tunnels on Caballo Island, near Corregidor, and ignite it with white phosphorus shells. The process is repeated on 6 and 7 April, and the last defender is killed on 13 April.

Japanese cargo ship *Jozan Maru* is damaged by mine near Singapore, 01°23′N, 104°01′E.

Naval Advanced Air Base, Iwo Jima, is established.

ATLANTIC. U.S. tanker *Atlantic States* is torpedoed by German submarine *U 857* off Cape Cod, 42°07′N, 70°00′42″W; there are no casualties to either the merchant crew or the 12-man Armed Guard. Tug *Wandank* (ATO 26) and rescue tug *ATR 14* are dispatched to the scene from Boston, Massachusetts; *ATR 89* is dispatched from Newport, Rhode Island. Auxiliary *Guinevere* (IX 67) rescues the crew (with the exception of five men, including the Armed Guard officer, who remain on board to keep the ship trimmed) while destroyer escort *Richard S. Bull* (DE 402) stands by to render assistance. Putting a line-handling party on board the damaged tanker, *ATR 14*, together with *ATR 89* and *Wandank*, tows the disabled tanker to Boston, arriving on 7 April.

6 Friday

PACIFIC. Japanese *kamikaze* onslaught against U.S. ships off Okinawa begins. Destroyer *Bush* (DD 529) is sunk, 27°16′N, 127°48′E; four *kamikazes* irreparably damage destroyer *Colhoun* (DD 801), 27°16′N, 127°48′E, which is then scuttled by destroyer *Cassin Young* (DD 793). Tank landing ship *LST 347* is sunk in air attack; destroyer *Rooks* (DD 804) and destroyer escort *Foreman* (DE 633) are damaged. High-speed minesweeper *Emmons* (DMS 22) is

damaged by five suiciders, 26°48′N, 128°04′E, destroyer *Mullany* (DD 528) is damaged by two, 26°24′N, 128°10′E, as is destroyer escort *Witter* (DE 636), 26°04′N, 127°52′E. *Kamikazes* damage destroyers *Morris* (DD 417), 25°55′N, 127°52′E [high-speed transport *Daniel T. Griffin* (APD 38) is damaged by collision with *Morris* as she fights fires alongside, 25°57′N, 127°57′E]; *Leutze* (DD 481) and *Newcomb* (DD 586), 26°38′N, 127°28′E; *Howorth* (DD 592), 26°32′N, 127°40′E; and *Haynesworth* (DD 700), 26°55′N, 129°29′E. *Kamikazes* damage minesweepers *Facility* (AM 233), 26°00′N, 127°00′E; *Defense* (AM 317), 26°38′N, 127°31′E; *Devastator* (AM 318), 26°26′N, 127°40′E; and *Recruit* (AM 285). They also damage destroyer escort *Fieberling* (DE 640), high-speed minesweeper *Rodman* (DMS 21), and minesweeper *Ransom* (AM 283), 26°48′N, 128°04′E; motor minesweepers *YMS 311*, 26°38′N, 127°48′E, and *YMS 321*, 26°00′N, 128°00′E; and tank landing ship *LST 447*, 26°09′N, 127°18′E. Near-misses by *kamikazes* damage small carrier *San Jacinto* (CVL 30), 26°46′N, 129°43′E, and destroyer *Harrison* (DD 573), 27°05′N, 129°22′E. Destroyer *Hyman* (DD 732) is damaged by *kamikaze* and torpedo, 26°45′N, 27°42′E; destroyer *Taussig* (DD 746) is damaged by near-miss of bombs, 27°07′N, 128°39′E; and high-speed minesweeper *Harding* (DMS 28) is damaged by horizontal bomber, 26°00′N, 127°00′E. Friendly fire accounts for damage to battleship *North Carolina* (BB 55), 26°41′N, 129°32′E; light cruiser *Pasadena* (CL 65), 27°00′N, 129°00′E; destroyer *Hutchins* (DD 476), from destroyer *Heywood L. Edwards* (DD 663), 26°00′N, 128°00′E; attack transport *Barnett* (APA 5) and attack cargo ship *Leo* (AKA 60), 26°21′N, 127°43′E; attack transport *Audrain* (APA 59), 26°22′N, 127°43′E; tank landing ships *LST 241*, 26°20′N, 127°45′E, and *LST 1000*, 26°21′N, 127°44′E; and submarine chaser *PCS 1390*, 26°00′N, 128°00′E. Infantry landing craft (rocket) *LCI(R) 1068* is hit by friendly fire of adjacent vessels during antiaircraft action; *LCI(R) 1069* is damaged by fragments when she is near-missed by a *kamikaze*. Tank landing ship *LST 698* is damaged by operational casualty incident to beaching, 26°24′N, 127°45′E; *LST 568*, *LST 570*, and *LST 658* are damaged by operational casualties. U.S. freighter *Logan Victory*, carrying 7,000 tons of ammunition, is irreparably damaged by *kamikaze* off Kerama Retto, 26°10′N, 127°16′E. Survivors are rescued by minesweeper *Strategy* (AM 308) and small craft;

three (including its commander) of the 42-man Armed Guard are killed. The burning merchantman is then scuttled. U.S. freighter *Hobbs Victory*, also carrying ammunition, is attacked by two *kamikazes* northwest of Kerama Retto. Armed Guard gunners shoot down one and damage the second, but the latter manages to crash the freighter and start uncontrollable fires that lead to her abandonment, 26°05′N, 125°14′E. Minesweeper *Success* (AM 310) rescues survivors, transferring them later to attack transport *Gosper* (APA 170). *Hobbs Victory* explodes and sinks the following morning.

Submarine *Besugo* (SS 321) sinks Japanese minesweeper *W.12* in Sape Strait, N.E.I., 08°03′S, 119°14′E.

Submarine *Hardhead* (SS 365) again attacks unescorted Japanese convoy SASI 45, sinking freighter *Araosan Maru* in Gulf of Siam, 09°37′N, 102°48′E.

USAAF B-25s on China coast shipping strike attack Japanese convoy HOMO 03, sinking *Coast Defense Vessel No. 1* and *Coast Defense Vessel No. 134* south-southwest of Amoy, 23°55′N, 117°40′E, and irreparably damaging destroyer *Amatsukaze* five miles east of Amoy, 24°30′N, 118°10′E; while *Amatsukaze*'s crew manages to beach the ship at the entrance to Amoy Harbor, she will perform no more wartime service.

Mines sink Japanese freighters *Koun Maru* in Yangtze near Chinkiang and *Kabuto Maru* at 32°02′N, 119°59′E. Mines laid by USAAF planes on 4 March sink *Hsing Yun Maru* in Yangtze, near Chinkiang, 32°05′N, 119°56′E. Freighter *Fushimi Maru* is sunk by USAAF mine in Shimonoseki Straits, 33°59′N, 130°52′E.

Dutch Mitchells (which claim two hits) and RAAF Liberators (which claim many near-misses) attack Japanese light cruiser *Isuzu* north of Soembawa Island, N.E.I. *Isuzu* proceeds on to disembark troops (see 7 April).

MEDITERRANEAN. Fleet tug *Moreno* (ATF 87) is damaged by striking submerged object off Palermo, Sicily.

ATLANTIC. U.S. fishing boat *Captain Nathaniel B. Palmer* unwittingly snags depth charge in her net about nine miles south-southeast of Block Island; as the charge is being raised to the surface, it explodes, sinking the craft and killing three of the four-man crew. Fishing boat *Mandalay* rescues the sole survivor.

7 Saturday

ATLANTIC. Destroyer escort *Gustafson* (DE 182) sinks German submarine *U 857* off Cape Cod, Massachusetts, 42°22′N, 69°46′W.

U.S. freighter *James W. Nesmith* is torpedoed by German submarine *U 1024* off Holyhead, England, 53°23′N, 04°53′W; Canadian corvette HMCS *Belleville* tows the ship to safety, beaching her off Holyhead the next evening. There are no casualties to either the merchant complement or the 41-man Armed Guard; the ship is later repaired and returned to service.

PACIFIC. TF 58 (Vice Admiral Marc A. Mitscher) attacks Japanese First Diversion Attack Force (located southwest of Kyushu by Kerama Retto–based PBMs and tracked) formed around battleship *Yamato*, moving through East China Sea toward Okinawa. TF 58 planes (numbering 386) sink *Yamato* and light cruiser *Yahagi* west-southwest of Kagoshima, Japan, 30°40′N, 128°03′E; destroyers *Asashimo* in East China Sea, 31°00′N, 128°00′E; *Hamakaze* and *Isokaze* 150 miles southwest of Nagasaki, 30°40′N, 128°03′E; and *Kasumi* in East China Sea, 30°57′N, 127°57′E. TF 58 planes also damage destroyers *Suzutsuki*, *Hatsushimo*, *Yukikaze*, and *Fuyuzuki* in East China Sea, 30°40′N, 128°03′E.[240]

Off Okinawa, high-speed minesweeper *Emmons* (DMS 22), irreparably damaged by five *kamikazes* the previous day, is scuttled by high-speed minesweeper *Ellyson* (DMS 19); tank landing ship *LST 447* sinks as the result of damage inflicted by *kamikaze* the previous day, 26°09′N, 127°18′E. Motor gunboat *PGM 18* is sunk by mine, 26°13′N, 127°55′E; while picking up *PGM 18* survivors, motor minesweeper *YMS 103* is damaged by mine, 26°13′N, 127°54′E. *Kamikazes* damage carrier *Hancock* (CV 19), 27°00′N, 130°00′E; battleship *Maryland* (BB 46), 26°40′N, 127°29′E; destroyers *Longshaw* (DD 559), 26°29′N, 127°41′E, and *Bennett* (DD 473), 27°16′N, 127°48′E; destroyer escort *Wesson* (DE 184), 26°48′N, 127°55′E; and motor minesweeper *YMS 81*, 26°35′N, 127°53′E. Shore battery damages motor minesweeper *YMS 427*, 26°14′N, 127°52′E; tank landing ship *LST 698* is damaged by grounding, 26°24′N, 127°45′E; tank landing ship *LST 890* is damaged in collision with *LST 788*, 26°20′N, 127°45′E; and *PC 462* is damaged by operational casualty. Hospital ship *Comfort* (AH 6) is damaged slightly during air attack.

Submarines *Gabilan* (SS 252) and *Charr* (SS 328) sink Japanese light cruiser *Isuzu* off Soem-

bawa Island, Celebes N.E.I., 07°38′S, 118°09′E.

Submarine *Tirante* (SS 420) sinks Japanese auxiliary submarine chaser *Tama Maru* 10 miles east of Shokokusan Do, southwest of Korea, 34°35′N, 125°20′E.

Japanese fleet tanker *Kamoi* is sunk by aircraft, Hong Kong.

Mine laid by USAAF B-29 (20th Air Force) sinks Japanese freighter *Hatsukari Maru* off Wakamatsu Harbor, 33°55′N, 130°50′E.

Mine damages Japanese naval auxiliary *Shinto Maru* below Woosung, China.

Japanese auxiliary submarine chaser *No. 43 Hino Maru* is damaged by aircraft off Hirado Jima, near Kyushu, Japan.

8 Sunday

PACIFIC. Off Okinawa, destroyer *Gregory* (DD 802) is damaged by *kamikaze*, 27°07′N, 128°39′E; motor minesweeper *YMS 92* is damaged by mine, 26°12′N, 127°53′E; tank landing ship *LST 939* is damaged in collision with tank landing ship *LST 268*, 26°22′N, 127°44′E; tank landing ship *LST 940* is damaged by grounding, 26°20′N, 127°45′E; and infantry landing craft (gunboat) *LCI(G) 580* is damaged by operational casualty incident to grounding.

British submarine HMS *Stygian* unsuccessfully attacks Japanese cargo vessel *Enoshima Maru*, 06°30′S, 113°08′E.

USAAF B-24 (Far East Air Force) attacks Japanese auxiliary submarine chasers southeast of the Celebes, sinking *Cha 101* and damaging *Cha 72*, 04°43′S, 122°17′E.

Mines (laid by USAAF planes) sink Japanese cargo ship *No. 12 Tamon Maru* in Yangtze, near Shanghai, 31°16′N, 121°45′E, and damage escort destroyer *Habushi* below Woosung.

9 Monday

PACIFIC. TG 76.10 (Captain John D. Murphy) lands U.S. Army troops (163rd RCT) supported by three destroyers and USMC planes, on Jolo, Sulu Archipelago, P.I. The Japanese garrison withdraws into the hills.

Twenty USAAF B-29s mine Shimonoseki Straits, Japan.

Off Okinawa, escort carrier *Chenango* (CVE 28) is damaged by crash of F6F (VF 25) on flight deck; destroyer *Charles J. Badger* (DD 657) is damaged by Japanese assault demolition boat, 26°18′N, 127°39′E; *kamikazes* sink tank landing craft *LCT 876* and damage destroyer *Sterett* (DD 407), 26°47′N, 128°42′E; high-speed transport *Hopping* (APD 51) is damaged by shore battery, 26°15′N, 127°55′E, as is tank landing ship *LST 557*, 26°14′N, 127°57′E; and attack cargo ship *Starr* (AKA 67) is damaged by premature explosion of assault demolition boat, 26°20′N, 127°44′E. Tank landing ship *LST 343* and infantry landing craft (mortar) *LCI(M) 354* are damaged by operational casualties. Infantry landing craft (gunboat) *LCI(G) 558* is damaged in air attack.

Destroyers *Mertz* (DD 691) and *Monssen* (DD 798) sink Japanese submarine *RO 56*, 45 miles east of Okinawa, 26°09′N, 130°21′E.

Submarine *Parche* (SS 384) sinks Japanese minesweeper *W.3* as she is escorting transport (ex-armed merchant cruiser) *Ukishima Maru* northeast of Sendai, 39°07′N, 141°57′E. Later, *Sunfish* (SS 281) attacks *Ukishima Maru* at the entrance to Yamada Bay, 39°30′N, 142°05′E. Although *Sunfish* claims to have damaged her, *Ukishima Maru* reaches port undamaged.

Submarine *Spadefish* (SS 411) torpedoes Japanese freighter *Ritsu Maru* off west coast of Korea, 37°21′N, 125°08′E. *Ritsu Maru* attempts to run aground to facilitate salvage, but sinks before she can accomplish her goal.

Submarine *Tirante* (SS 420) attacks Japanese convoy TAMO 53 in the Yellow Sea, sinking army tanker *Nikko Maru* and damaging *Coast Defense Vessel No. 102*, 36°50′N, 123°55′E; transport (ex-seaplane carrier) *Kiyokawa Maru* evades *Tirante* and tows the damaged *Coast Defense Vessel No. 102* to safety.

USN land-based aircraft attack Japanese shipping in Kwangchow Bay, China, sinking cargo vessel *Minko Maru*, 21°26′N, 111°20′E.

Mines damage Japanese training ship (ex-coast defense ship) *Izumo* and fast transport *T.19* off Okurokami Island, Hiroshima Wan.

EUROPE. U.S. freighter *Solomon Juneau*, bound for Cherbourg, France, in convoy TBC 123, is torpedoed by German midget submarine off Dungeness, England, 50°53′15″N, 01°03′45″E. Of the 41-man Armed Guard, one man is blown overboard and lost; a second dies of injuries. None of the 41-man merchant complement are casualties, and the ship is towed to safety.

10 Tuesday

PACIFIC. U.S. Army 27th Division, supported by Eastern Island Attack and Fire Support Group and carrier aircraft, lands on Tsuken Shima off east coast of Okinawa, to begin the search for isolated pockets of Japanese troops.

Off Okinawa, destroyer *Porterfield* (DD 682) is damaged by own gun fire, 26°34′N, 128°28′E; submarine chaser *SC 667* is damaged by grounding, 26°11′N, 127°57′E; motor

minesweeper *YMS 96* is damaged in collision with high-speed minesweeper *Hambleton* (DMS 20), 26°03′N, 127°48′E; and destroyer escort *Manlove* (DE 36) is damaged by strafing, 26°12′N, 127°20′E. Tank landing ship *LST 557* is damaged by shore battery.

Submarine *Crevalle* (SS 291) damages Japanese escort destroyer *Ikuna* southwest of Iki Island, 33°38′N, 129°13′E.

Dutch submarine *O 19* sinks Japanese merchant tanker *Hosei Maru* as the enemy ship proceeds from Balikpapan, Borneo, to Batavia, Japan, 05°30′S, 106°40′E.

Japanese merchant cargo vessel *Maruko Maru* is sunk by mine (laid by USAAF B-29s on 4 and 28 March) in the Yangtze, 31°15′N, 121°29′E. Mines also damage Japanese destroyer *Tsubaki* 58 miles off Woosung, China; gunboat *Uji* and transport *Kotobuki Maru* (ex-Italian liner *Conte Verde*); *Coast Defense Vessel No. 124* near Futaoi Jima; *Coast Defense Vessel No. 156* off Mutsure Light; and minesweeper *W.21* east of the mouth of the Yangtze.

11 Wednesday

PACIFIC. Off Okinawa, *kamikazes* damage battleship *Missouri* (BB 63) and destroyers *Bullard* (DD 660) and *Kidd* (DD 661), 26°00′N, 130°00′E; carrier *Enterprise* (CV 6) (near-miss of two suiciders), 26°00′N, 128°00′E; destroyer escort *Samuel S. Miles* (DE 183), 26°12′N, 127°20′E; and large support landing craft *LCS(L) 36*. Carrier *Essex* (CV 9), 26°50′N, 130°30′E, and destroyer *Hale* (DD 642), 26°00′N, 120°00′E, are damaged by bombs; strafing accounts for damage to destroyers *Black* (DD 666) and *Hank* (DD 702), 27°00′N, 130°00′E. Attack transport *Berrien* (APA 62) is damaged by collision with tank landing ship *LST 808*, 26°22′N, 127°43′E. Friendly fire accounts for damage to destroyer *Trathen* (DD 530), 27°13′N, 130°15′E, and attack cargo ship *Leo* (AKA 60), 26°21′N, 127°43′E. Tank landing ship *LST 399* is damaged by grounding, 26°20′N, 127°45′E; *LST 78* is damaged by air attack. Large support landing craft *LCS(L) 38* is damaged by operational casualty, *LCS(L) 88* by air attack. Infantry landing craft (rocket) *LCI(R) 648* and *LCI(R) 1070* pick up a native boat (containing three women, three men, and 14 children) off Kuro-se, Amami Gunto; the latter vessel delivers them to Hagushi, Okinawa. Tug *Arikara* (ATF 98) is damaged by grounding, as is submarine chaser *SC 667*.

TG 78.3 (Rear Admiral Arthur D. Struble) lands U.S Army battalion combat team of the 164th RCT on Bohol Island, Visayan Islands

(north of Mindanao), from six large infantry landing craft and six medium landing ships. The landings are unopposed by the Japanese and take place over beaches controlled by Filipino guerrillas (Major Ismael P. Ingeniero).[241]

Submarine *Parche* (SS 384) sinks Japanese auxiliary minesweeper *Togo Maru* off Todoga Saki, 38°53′N, 142°05′E.

Submarine *Spadefish* (SS 411) sinks Japanese auxiliary minesweeper *No. 17 Hinode Maru* off Tokckok Kundo, 37°13′N, 125°11′E.

Japanese auxiliary submarine chaser *Cha 215* is sunk by mine off Futaoi Jima, Shimono-seki.

ANDAMAN SEA. RAF Liberators (No. 203 Squadron) sink Japanese submarine chaser *Ch 7* and auxiliary netlayer *Agata Maru*, 08°57′N, 93°38′E.

EUROPE. U.S. freighter *Morgantown Victory*, in convoy VWP 21, strays from swept channel 11 miles off Le Havre, France, 49°46′N, 00°21′E, and is damaged by mine. She is towed to safety; there are no fatalities among the ship's complement (including 14 Armed Guard sailors).

12 Thursday

UNITED STATES. President Franklin Delano Roosevelt dies in Warm Springs, Georgia; Vice President Harry S. Truman succeeds to the presidency.

EUROPE. Tank landing ship *LST 493* sinks after running aground off Plymouth, England, 50°20′N, 04°09′W.

U.S. freighter *Will Rogers*, bound for Antwerp, Belgium, in convoy BB 80, is torpedoed by German submarine *U 1024*, 30 miles southwest of Holyhead, England, 53°45′N, 04°44′W. Beached off that place under her own power, the ship is repaired and returned to active service; she suffers no casualties among the merchant complement or the 27-man Armed Guard.

PACIFIC. Off Okinawa, destroyer *Mannert L. Abele* (DD 733) is sunk by a *Baka*, 27°25′N, 126°59′E; she is the first U.S. Navy ship to be sunk by a piloted bomb. Destroyer *Stanly* (DD 478) is damaged by a *Baka*, 27°12′N, 128°17′E; high-speed minesweeper *Jeffers* (DMS 27) is damaged by a *Baka* and *kamikaze*, 26°50′N, 126°35′E. *Kamikazes* sink large support landing craft *LCS(L) 33* and damage battleship *Idaho* (BB 42), 26°26′N, 127°32′E; battleship *Tennessee* (BB 43), destroyer *Zellars* (DD 777), and destroyer escort *Riddle* (DE 185), 26°00′N, 128°00′E; destroyers *Purdy* (DD 734), 27°16′N,

127°50′E, and *Cassin Young* (DD 793), 27°17′N, 127°50′E; destroyer escorts *Rall* (DE 304), 26°36′N, 127°39′E, *Walter C. Wann* (DE 412), 26°17′N, 127°20′E, and *Whitehurst* (DE 634), 26°04′N, 127°12′E; and light minelayer *Lindsey* (DM 32), 26°28′N, 127°13′E. Minesweeper *Gladiator* (AM 319) is damaged by near-miss of *kamikaze*, 26°05′N, 127°35′E. Japanese air attacks account for damage to light cruiser *Oakland* (CL 95), destroyers *Norman Scott* (DD 690) and *Brush* (DD 745), and destroyer escorts *Conklin* (DE 439) and *Damon E. Cummings* (DE 643). Friendly fire accounts for damage to battleship *New Mexico* (BB 40), 26°31′N, 127°37′E, destroyer *Bennion* (DD 662), and medium landing ship *LSM 279*. Attack cargo ship *Wyandot* (AKA 92) is damaged in collision with medium landing ship *LSM 312*, 26°21′N, 127°44′E; tank landing ship *LST 555* is damaged by grounding, 26°20′N, 127°45′E. Large support landing craft *LCS(L) 57* is damaged by operational casualty (grounding) and three *kamikazes*. One suicide plane attacks U.S. freighter *Minot Victory*, but Armed Guard gunners inflict sufficient damage on the *kamikaze*, so it only strikes the ship a glancing blow and then disintegrates; there are no fatalities on board the merchantman among the 57-man merchant complement, the 27 Armed Guard sailors, and nine passengers.

Submarine *Chub* (SS 329) is damaged by aerial bombs, Java Sea, 06°03′S, 113°56′E, but remains on patrol.

Submarine *Silversides* (SS 236) sinks Japanese auxiliary submarine chaser *Shiratori Maru* east of Tanega Jima, 30°45′N, 131°57′E.

British submarine HMS *Stygian* sinks Japanese auxiliary minesweeper *Wa. 104* and damages auxiliary submarine chasers *Cha 104* and *Cha 114* off north coast of Bali, 08°05′S, 115°06′E.

In the final mining mission carried out in support of the Okinawa campaign, five USAAF B-29s mine Shimonoseki Straits. Previously laid mines sink Japanese submarine *RO 64* off Kobe, 34°14′N, 132°16′E, and freighter *Minatogawa Maru* off Wakamatsu.

B-24 aircraft (service and nationality unspecified) sinks Japanese ship *No. 2 Hakushi Maru* off Badjowe, 04°33′S, 120°23′E.

Fire of undetermined origin destroys buildings and damages Finger Bay dock, Adak Island, Aleutians; the blaze also damages floating drydock *YFD 22* and floating workshop *YR 36*. Gasoline tanker *Ogeechee* (AOG 35) is saved from further damage by escort patrol vessel *PCE 895*, which pulls her out into Finger Bay.

ATLANTIC. U.S. freighter *Mangore* collides with British tanker *Silver Star Park* in dense fog near Hen and Chickens Lightship, Buzzard's Bay; fire breaks out on board the latter and her crew abandons ship. Rescue tugs (NRTS) are dispatched to the scene of the collision, *ATR 89* from Newport, Rhode Island, and *ATR 14* from Boston, Massachusetts (see 13 April).

13 Friday

PACIFIC. Off Okinawa, destroyer escort *Connolly* (DE 306) is damaged by *kamikaze*, 26°55′N, 126°46′E; gasoline tanker *Wabash* (AOG 4) is damaged in collision with small craft, 26°00′N, 128°00′E. Infantry landing craft (rocket) *LCI(R) 651* is damaged by friendly fire; medium landing ship *LSM 320* is damaged by operational casualty.

TU 78.9.16 (Commander Samuel H. Pattie) carries out operation against Fort Drum, the battleship-like citadel constructed on El Fraile Island, Manila Bay. Medium landing ship *LSM 51* lands Company "F," 151st Infantry, who provide cover for army engineers who pump oil into the fortress and then set a demolition fuse before the assault force is withdrawn "to a respectful distance." A series of violent explosions follows, incinerating the Japanese defenders.

Submarine *Parche* (SS 384) sinks Japanese auxiliary minesweeper *No. 1 Misago Maru*, 38°36′N, 141°41′E, and guardboat *No. 2 Kosho Maru*, 38°27′N, 142°13′E, off Todoga Saki.

British submarine HMS *Stygian* sinks auxiliary minesweeper *Wa.104* off Bali, 08°05′S, 115°06′E.

U.S. freighter *Harrington Emerson* is mistakenly bombed and strafed by U.S. aircraft off Borneo, 05°03′N, 119°44′E. The ship is only slightly damaged, and there are no fatalities among the merchant crew, the passengers, stevedores, or the 29 Armed Guards.

Japanese auxiliary submarine chaser *Kaiko Maru* is sunk by aircraft off Hainan Island, 21°25′N, 109°20′E.

Mines laid by USAAF B-29 (20th Air Force) sinks Japanese cargo ship *Shinro Maru* southeast of He Saki Light, 33°53′N, 131°02′E, and damage *Coast Defense Vessel No. 40* off Futaoi Jima. Cargo ship *Kinoto Maru* is sunk by mine off Wada Misaki, 34°39′N, 135°11′E.

USAAF B-24s (Far East Air Force) sink Japanese merchant tanker *No. 12 Nanshin Maru* off southeast coast of Borneo, 04°00′N, 116°20′E.

ATLANTIC. Rescue tug *ATR 14* extinguishes fire on board British tanker *Silver Star Park*, which had been involved in collision with U.S. freighter *Mangore* the previous day in Buz-

zard's Bay. *ATR 14*, together with *ATR 89* and big harbor tug *YTB 179*, assists the damaged tanker to Newport, Rhode Island, arriving the following day.

14 Saturday

PACIFIC. Off Okinawa, *kamikazes* damage battleship *New York* (BB 34), 26°00′N, 128°00′E, and destroyers *Sigsbee* (DD 502), *Dashiell* (DD 659), and *Hunt* (DD 674), 27°15′N, 130°25′E; gunboat *PGM 11* is damaged by grounding, 26°13′N, 127°27′E; and air attack results in minor damage to U.S. freighter *Minot Victory*.

Tank landing ship *LST 241* is damaged in collision west by north of Guam, 14°38′N, 140°19′E.

Submarine *Gabilan* (SS 252) attacks Japanese Surabaya-to-Makassar convoy, sinking cargo vessel *Kako Maru*, 05°19′S, 117°06′E, and auxiliary submarine chaser *No. 1 Shonan Maru*, 05°13′S, 118°12′E.

Submarine *Tirante* (SS 420) attacks Japanese convoy MOSI 02 in the approaches to the Yellow Sea, sinking transport *Jusan Maru*, escort vessel *Nomi*, and *Coast Defense Vessel No. 31* west of Quelpart Island, 33°25′N, 126°15′E. For his skill and daring in carrying out this surface attack through mined and shoal-obstructed waters, Lieutenant Commander George L. Street III, *Tirante*'s captain, will receive the Medal of Honor.

Japanese auxiliary submarine chaser *Cha 11* is sunk by aircraft off coast of French Indochina, 15°45′N, 108°28′E.

Japanese freighter *Kako Go* is sunk by aircraft near Rima Island.

Mines damage Japanese minelayer *Tokiwa* 78 miles off He Saki, Japan, and auxiliary minelayer *Koei Maru* off Hime Jima Lighthouse, Kyushu.

USAAF B-24s (14th Air Force) bomb Japanese shipping at Shanghai, sinking cargo vessel *Takko Maru*, 31°14′N, 121°30′E.

ATLANTIC. U.S. tanker *Delaware*, directed to the scene by a Navy plane, rescues survivors of tanker *Oklahoma* (sunk on 28 March by German submarine *U 532*) at 11°45′N, 66°06′W.

15 Sunday

ATLANTIC. Destroyer escorts *Frost* (DE 144) and *Stanton* (DE 247) sink German submarine *U 1235* north by west of the Azores, 47°54′N, 30°25′W.

PACIFIC. TF 58 (Vice Admiral Marc A. Mitscher) pounds airfields in southern Kyushu, Japan; strikes are repeated on 16 April.

TU 74.3.5 (Captain Jack H. Duncan), consisting of light cruiser *Phoenix* (CL 46) and two destroyers, conducts preparatory bombardment, joined by Army artillery on Luzon, on Carabao Island, the final objective in Manila Bay (see 16 April).

Off Okinawa, *kamikazes* damage destroyer *Laffey* (DD 724), 27°16′N, 127°50′E, and large support landing craft *LCS(L) 51*; Japanese assault demolition boat damages motor minesweeper *YMS 331*, 26°15′N, 127°36′E; attack transport *Berrien* (APA 62) is hit by friendly fire, as is infantry landing craft (rocket) *LCI(R) 649*; and air attack damages medium landing ship (rocket) *LSM(R) 189*. Infantry landing craft (gunboat) *LCI(G) 81*, operating close inshore, grounds on reef. Sister-ship *LCI(G) 442*'s first attempt to tow *LCI(G) 81* fails. Heavy cruiser *Tuscaloosa* (CA 37) stands ready to provide counter-battery fire; *LCI(G) 442*'s second attempt succeeds in refloating *LCI(G) 81*. Infantry landing craft (mortar) *LCI(M) 659* destroys assault demolition boat southwest of Naha (see 16 April).

Submarine *Charr* (SS 328) sows mines off the Malay Peninsula.

Japanese guardboat *No. 2 Hinode Maru* is sunk by U.S. aircraft south of Quelpart Island, 33°19′N, 127°21′E.

Mine laid by USAAF B-29 (20th Air Force) sinks Japanese cargo ship *No. 3 Yamanami Maru* southeast of He Saki, 33°53′N, 131°02′E.

Hulk of Japanese army tanker *Shincho Maru*, sunk by TF 38 planes on 21 January, is scuttled across entrance of Takao Harbor, Formosa.

16 Monday

ATLANTIC. Destroyer escorts *Frost* (DE 144) and *Stanton* (DE 247) sink German submarine *U 880* north-northwest of the Azores, 47°53′N, 30°26′W.

PACIFIC. TU 74.3.5 (Captain Jack H. Duncan), consisting of light cruiser *Phoenix* (CL 46) and two destroyers, conducts bombardment of Carabao Island, Manila Bay, joined by infantry landing craft (rocket) *LCI(R) 224* and *LCI(R) 331*. Six tank landing craft (LCTs) land Army troops (1st Battalion, 151st Infantry) unopposed through the breach blown in the seawall by *Phoenix*'s main battery fire. The soldiers encounter only "one badly shaken pig."[242]

Off Okinawa, *kamikazes* sink destroyer *Pringle* (DD 477), 27°26′N, 126°59′E, and damage carrier *Intrepid* (CV 11), 27°37′N, 131°14′E; battleship *Missouri* (BB 63), 26°00′N, 130°00′E; destroyers *Bryant* (DD 665), 27°05′N, 128°13′E, and *Wilson* (DD 408),

26°03′N, 127°20′E; destroyer escort *Bowers* (DE 637), 26°52′N, 127°52′E; high-speed minesweepers *Hobson* (DMS 26), 27°26′N, 126°59′E, and *Harding* (DMS 28), 26°42′N, 127°25′E; and oiler *Taluga* (AO 62), 26°03′N, 127°26′E. Destroyer *McDermut* (DD 677) is damaged by friendly fire, 27°30′N, 130°20′E. Infantry landing craft (mortar) *LCI(M) 659* destroys second Japanese assault demolition boat southwest of Naha. Infantry landing craft (gunboat) *LCI(G) 407* is attacked by suicide-bent VAL southwest of Naha; the *kamikaze* crashes close aboard, causing minor hull damage. Tank landing ship *LST 449* is damaged by shore battery fire; medium landing ship *LSM 12* founders after broaching, and sinks. Infantry landing craft (mortar) *LCI(M) 754* and submarine chaser *PC 851* are damaged by operational casualties.

Army force (77th Division less the 307th Infantry) lands on the south and southwest coast of Ie Shima, Ryukyus, following preparatory naval gunfire.

Submarine *Sea Dog* (SS 401) sinks Japanese freighter *Toko Maru* off Mikura Jima, 33°31′N, 139°36′E.

Submarine *Sunfish* (SS 281) attacks Japanese convoy emerging from Yamado Harbor, Honshu, and sinks *Coast Defense Vessel No. 73* and transport *Manryu Maru*, 39°35′N, 142°06′E.

Mine laid by USAAF B-29 (20th Air Force) damages Japanese cargo vessel *No. 10 Kaishin Maru* off Shimonoseki, 33°53′N, 131°09′E.

17 Tuesday

PACIFIC. Operation VICTOR FIVE: TG 78.2 (Rear Admiral Albert G. Noble) lands U.S. Army X Corps (Major General Franklin C. Sibert) (24th and 31st Infantry Divisions) near Malabang, Parang, and Cotabato, Mindanao; landings are supported by gunfire of cruisers and destroyers of TG 74.2 (Rear Admiral Ralph S. Riggs). The defenders do not make a determined stand.

Destroyer *Benham* (DD 796) is damaged by *kamikaze* and by friendly fire off Okinawa, 24°01′N, 132°32′E. Medium landing ship (rocket) *LSM(R) 193* is damaged by grounding.

PB4Y (VPB 111) sinks Japanese cargo ship *Gyoyo Maru* off coast of Malaya, 03°27′N, 103°37′E.

Mine laid by USAAF B-29 (20th Air Force) sinks Japanese cargo ship *Sonjo Maru* off Shanghai, 31°13′N, 121°52′E.

Mine laid by USAAF B-29 (21st Air Force) sinks Japanese cargo ship *Tairyu Maru* off Wada Misaki, 34°27′N, 135°11′E. Mine sinks

guardboat *No. 92 Banshu Maru* off Goto Retto, Japan.

18 Wednesday

PACIFIC. Off Okinawa, battleship *New York* (BB 34) is damaged by *kamikaze*; medium landing craft *LSM 28* is damaged in air attack. Light minelayer *Tolman* (DM 28) is damaged by grounding, 26°16′N, 127°32′E; tank landing ship *LST 929* is damaged in collision with tank landing ship *LST 267*, 26°21′N, 127°43′20″E. Infantry landing craft (rocket) *LCI(R) 770*, in attempting to go to the assistance of an LCVP beached on the north shore of Zamami Shima, runs aground (see 19 April).

Destroyers *Heermann* (DD 532), *McCord* (DD 534), *Mertz* (DD 691), and *Collett* (DD 730), assisted by destroyer *Uhlmann* (DD 687) and TBM (VT 47) from small carrier *Bataan* (CVL 29), sink Japanese submarine *I 56*, 150 miles east of Okinawa, 26°42′N, 130°38′E.

Submarine *Seahorse* (SS 304) is damaged by depth charges in Tsushima Strait, 33°45′N, 128°26′E, and is forced to terminate her patrol.

Submarine *Sea Owl* (SS 405) sinks Japanese submarine *RO 46*, 500 yards off Wake Island, 19°17′N, 166°35′E.

Japanese transport *Teizui Maru* (ex-German *Mosel*) is sunk by mine near western entrance to Shimonoseki Strait, 34°04′N, 130°50′E.

ATLANTIC. U.S. freighter *Cyrus H. McCormack*, while in convoy HX 348, is torpedoed and sunk by German submarine *U 1107*, 70 miles southwest of Brest, France, 47°47′N, 06°26′W; British rescue ship *Gothland* picks up the survivors, but two Armed Guard sailors (of the 12-man detachment) are lost along with four of the 40-man merchant crew.

U.S. freighter *Swiftscout* is torpedoed by German submarine *U 548* about 145 miles northeast of Cape Henry, Virginia, 37°30′N, 72°45′W. Rescue tug *ATR 74* is immediately dispatched from Norfolk. Armed Guard gunfire drives *U 548* off, but the U-boat returns to torpedo the ship a second time, sinking her. One merchant seaman is lost and the survivors are rescued by U.S. tanker *Chancellorsville*. *Chancellorsville*'s efficient rescue work eliminates the need for *ATR 74*'s services, and the latter is recalled to Norfolk.

19 Thursday

ATLANTIC. Destroyer escorts *Buckley* (DE 51) and *Reuben James* (DE 153) sink German submarine *U 879* southeast of Halifax, Nova Scotia, 42°19′N, 61°45′W.

PACIFIC. Battleship *Colorado* (BB 45) is damaged by powder explosion off Okinawa, 26°10′N, 127°20′E; light cruiser *Mobile* (CL 63) is damaged by turret explosion, 26°13′N, 127°52′E; minesweeper *Spear* (AM 322) is damaged in air attack; and tank landing ships *LST 267* and *LST 929* are damaged in collision.

Submarine *Cero* (SS 225) sinks Japanese guardboat *No. 3 Isuzu Maru* northwest of Chichi Jima, 30°42′N, 136°42′E.

Submarine *Pogy* (SS 266) is mistakenly attacked by PB4Y (VPB 102) as *Pogy* approaches a Japanese convoy southeast of Honshu, 32°59′E, 139°58′E. Fortunately, the submarine escapes the encounter undamaged and remains on patrol.

Submarine *Sennet* (SS 408), attacking Japanese convoy in Kii Strait off the south coast of Kyushu, sinks auxiliary submarine chaser *Cha 97*, 33°32′N, 135°23′E, and freighter *Hagane Maru*, 33°35′N, 135°23′E.

Submarine *Silversides* (SS 236) sinks Japanese guardboat *Kairyu Maru*, 32°57′N, 145°03′E.

Submarine *Sunfish* (SS 281) attacks Japanese convoy TSO 201 off Hokkaido, sinking gunboat *Kaiho Maru*, 42°22′N, 142°16′E, and freighter *Taisei Maru*, 42°22′N, 142°13′E.

Submarine *Trutta* (SS 421) sinks Japanese merchant vessel *Kaiyo Maru*, 37°52′N, 122°24′E, and merchant fishing boats *Kinshu Maru* and *Mitsuyama Maru*, 37°52′N, 122°24′E.

Infantry landing craft (rocket) *LCI(R) 770*, grounded the day before during attempt to assist beached LCVP off Zamami Shima, is refloated by rescue tug *ATR 80*.

USAAF B-24s bomb Japanese shipping at Saigon, adding further damage to freighters *Kenei Maru* and *Chefoo Maru* (previously damaged in TF 38's 12 January strike).

Japanese tanker *Shonan Maru* sinks after running aground off Belawan, Sumatra, 03°55′N, 98°49′E.

20 Friday

PACIFIC. Escort carrier *Corregidor* (CVE 58), while operating east of the Marianas on antisubmarine patrol in TG 12.3, is damaged in typhoon.

High-speed transports *Bull* (APD 78) and *Kline* (APD 120) are damaged off Okinawa by operational casualty and collision, respectively.

Submarine *Guitarro* (SS 363) lays mines in Berhala Strait off northeast coast of Sumatra, N.E.I.

Submarine chaser *SC 737* is damaged by grounding off Palawan, 09°45′N, 118°44′E.

Mines laid by USAAF B-29s (20th Air Force)

sink Japanese cargo vessels *Yamumitsu Maru* off Nojima, 34°32′N, 128°44′E, and *Sanko Maru* at 33°48′N, 131°00′E, and damage cargo ship *Kitsurin Maru* at western entrance of Shimonoseki Strait.

Army troops supported by naval vessels and USAAF aircraft land on Catanduanes Island, P.I.

ANDAMAN SEA. USAAF P-38s and P-51s attack Japanese shipping off Rangoon, Burma, sinking motor torpedo boat *Gyoraitei No. 412*.

21 Saturday

PACIFIC. Destroyer *Ammen* (DD 527) is damaged by near-miss of bomb off Okinawa, 27°13′N, 128°16′E.

Japanese guardboat *Zenyo Maru* is sunk by U.S. aircraft off Shiono Misaki, 31°30′N, 135°40′E.

Japanese cargo vessel *No. 2 Toshi Maru* is damaged by mine off Singapore.

22 Sunday

ATLANTIC. Destroyer escorts *Carter* (DE 112) and *Neal A. Scott* (DE 769) sink German submarine *U 518* west by south of the Azores, 43°26′N, 38°23′W.

CARIBBEAN. Submarine chaser *SC 1019* sinks after running aground in Yucatan Channel, 22°28′N, 84°30′W.

EUROPE. U.S. freighter *Benjamin H. Bristow*, en route to Southend, England, with convoy ATM 123, is mined off Flushing, Holland, 51°24′30″N, 03°22′E. There are no fatalities among the ship's complement (42 merchant sailors, the 26-man Armed Guard, and a pilot), and the ship is towed to Terneuzen, Holland, for repairs.

PACIFIC. Off Okinawa, large support landing craft *LCS(L) 15* is sunk by aircraft, 27°20′N, 127°10′E. *Kamikazes* sink minesweeper *Swallow* (AM 65), 26°10′N, 127°12′E, and damage destroyers *Hudson* (DD 475), 27°00′N, 127°00′E, and *Wadsworth* (DD 516), 26°10′N, 126°24′E; destroyer *Isherwood* (DD 520) and minesweeper *Ransom* (AM 283), 26°14′N, 127°28′E; and light minelayer *Shea* (DM 30), 26°00′N, 127°00′E. Minesweeper *Gladiator* (AM 319) is damaged by strafing and near-miss of *kamikaze*, 26°21′N, 127°45′E; infantry landing craft (rocket) *LCI(R) 765* is damaged in collision with tank landing ship *LST 484*.

Submarine *Cero* (SS 225) sinks Japanese guardboat *Aji Maru* west of Tori Jima, 31°38′N, 139°00′E, and damages guardboat *No. 9 Takamiya Maru*, 30°04′N, 136°43′E.

Submarine *Hardhead* (SS 365) sinks Japanese cargo vessel *Mankei Maru* off Chimpon, 10°25′N, 99°06′E.

Dutch submarine *O 19* torpedoes Japanese heavy cruiser *Ashigara* as the latter proceeds in company with destroyer *Kamikaze* toward Batavia, 05°37′S, 106°55′E.

Japanese guardboat *Ariake Maru* is sunk by U.S. aircraft in Ise Bay, 34°43′N, 136°43′E.

USAAF P-51s sink Japanese auxiliary submarine chaser *Chikuyu Maru* south of Toshi Jima.

Japanese *Coast Defense Vessel No. 81* is damaged by aircraft off Hangchow Bay, 31°26′N, 123°30′E.

23 Monday

ATLANTIC. Eagle boat *Eagle 56* (PE 56) is sunk by explosion off Portland, Maine. German submarine *U 853* is known to have been in the vicinity at the time; whether or not she conducted the attack that sank the World War I–vintage patrol vessel, however, will never be known (see 6 May).

Norwegian tanker *Katy* is torpedoed by German submarine *U 548* east of Cape Hatteras, North Carolina, 35°56′N, 74°52′W; rescue tug *ATR 74* and salvage tug (NRTS) *Relief* are dispatched from Norfolk, Virginia. A 29-man volunteer crew remains on board the Norwegian ship; *ATR 74* escorts her to Lynnhaven Roads, Virginia.

PACIFIC. Submarine *Besugo* (SS 321) sinks German submarine *U 183* in the Java Sea, 04°57′S, 112°52′E.

PB4Ys (VPB 109) employ "Bat" missiles against Japanese shipping off Balikpapan, Borneo, in the first combat use of the only automatic homing missile to be used in World War II.

Japanese freighter *Tamae Maru* is sunk by accidental ammunition explosion in Sakai Harbor, Japan.

24 Tuesday

ATLANTIC. Destroyer escort *Frederick C. Davis* (DE 136) is torpedoed and sunk by German submarine *U 546*, 570 miles east of Cape Race, Newfoundland, 43°52′N, 40°15′W; *Pillsbury* (DE 133), *Flaherty* (DE 135), *Chatelain* (DE 149), *Neunzer* (DE 150), *Hubbard* (DE 211), *Keith* (DE 241), *Janssen* (DE 396), and *Varian* (DE 798) sink *U 546*, 43°53′N, 40°07′W.

EUROPE. German submarine *U 1223* is sunk by USAAF and British aircraft at Wesermünde, Germany.

PACIFIC. High-speed transport *Stringham* (APD 6) is damaged off Okinawa by operational casualty.

USAAF B-24s sink Japanese motor sailship *Shinyo Maru* off coast of French Indochina.

Japanese tanker *San Diego Maru* is damaged by mine in swept channel, Hiroshima Bay, 34°06′N, 132°25′E.

25 Wednesday

EUROPE. PB4Y (VPB 103) sinks German submarine *U 1107* off Brest, France, 48°12′N, 05°42′W.

PACIFIC. Off Okinawa, escort carrier *Steamer Bay* (CVE 87) and destroyer *Hale* (DD 642) are damaged in collision, 24°48′N, 131°58′E.

High-speed transport *Horace A. Bass* (APD 124) sinks Japanese submarine *RO 109*, 280 miles south-southeast of Okinawa, 21°58′N, 129°35′E.

Submarine *Cod* (SS 224) sinks Japanese minesweeper *W.41* north of Keelung, Formosa, 26°10′N, 121°30′E.

USAAF B-24s bomb Japanese shipping at Saigon, French Indochina, sinking transport *Kaiko Maru*.

USAAF B-24s on antishipping sweep of Makassar Strait sink Japanese *Shuttle Boat No. 302* off Salinguigan Island, 02°19′S, 117°14′E.

Japanese cargo vessel *Sano Maru* is damaged by mine in Yangtze River near Nanking.

26 Thursday

PACIFIC. Attack transport *Barnett* (APA 5) is damaged by friendly fire off Okinawa; destroyer *Hickox* (DD 673) is damaged by air attack.

Submarine *Perch* (SS 313) is damaged by depth charges off North Borneo, 05°32′N, 116°07′E, but remains on patrol.

British submarines HMS *Solent* and HMS *Sleuth* sink Japanese auxiliary minesweeper *Wa.3* in Java Sea west of Kalambau Island, 04°50′S, 115°40′E.

Mines sink Japanese auxiliary minesweeper *Mejima Maru* off Futaoi Light, 34°04′N, 130°47′E, and freighter *Sanko Maru* in Chochiku Channel.

Japanese guardboat *No. 6 Chozan Maru* is sunk by aircraft east of Kammon Strait, off Shimonoseki; freighter *Heiyu Maru* is damaged by aircraft off Tsushima, 34°41′N, 128°54′E.

27 Friday

PACIFIC. Off Okinawa, *kamikazes* damage destroyer *Ralph Talbot* (DD 390), 26°00′N, 128°00′E; destroyer escort *England* (DE 635),

26°40′N, 127°40′E; and high-speed transport *Rathburne* (APD 25), 26°26′N, 127°36′E. Heavy cruiser *Wichita* (CA 45) is damaged by shore battery, 26°14′N, 127°50′E; destroyer *William D. Porter* (DD 579) is damaged by friendly fire, 26°21′N, 127°43′E. Japanese assault demolition boat damages large support landing craft *LCS(L) 37*. A *kamikaze* also crashes U.S. freighter *Canada Victory*, killing one merchant officer and two of the 27-man Armed Guard. *Canada Victory* sinks; survivors swim to nearby attack transport *Lauderdale* (APA 179). Infantry landing craft (rocket) *LCI(R) 763* sinks Japanese assault demolition boat off China Point when the enemy craft attempts to ram the ship. Destroyer *Hutchins* (DD 476) is damaged by depth charge dropped by Japanese assault demolition boat off Okinawa, 26°14′N, 127°49′E.

Japanese auxiliary submarine chaser *No. 31 Yusen Maru* is sunk by aircraft off Amami-O-Shima, Japan.

USAAF mine (laid on 27 March) sinks Japanese cargo vessel *Kaiho Maru* at western entrance of Shimonoseki Strait, 34°00′N, 130°50′E.

28 Saturday

ATLANTIC. Frigate *Huron* (PF 19) accidentally rams and damages French submarine *Argo* off Key West, Florida.

PACIFIC. Off Okinawa, *kamikazes* damage destroyers *Wadsworth* (DD 516), 26°47′N, 126°38′E, *Daly* (DD 519) (near-miss), 27°12′N, 128°16′E, *Twiggs* (DD 591), 27°12′N, 128°16′E, and *Bennion* (DD 662), 27°26′N, 127°51′E; high-speed minesweeper *Butler* (DMS 29) (near-miss), 26°00′N, 127°00′E; hospital ship *Comfort* (AH 6), 25°30′N, 127°40′E; and transport fitted for the evacuation of wounded *Pinkney* (APH 2), 26°00′N, 127°00′E. Destroyer *Brown* (DD 546) is damaged by air attack; destroyer *Lang* (DD 399) is damaged in collision with oiler *Brazos* (AO 4), 26°11′N, 127°20′E. Japanese assault demolition boat causes extensive damage to U.S. freighter *Bozeman Victory*; six men among the 59-man merchant crew, 13 stevedores, and the 27-man Armed Guard suffer injuries. Infantry landing craft (gunboat) *LCI(G) 580* is near-missed by *kamikaze* while en route to Kerama Retto.

Motor minesweeper *YMS 329* is damaged by mine off Tarakan, Borneo, 03°14′N, 117°42′E.

Submarine *Sennet* (SS 408) sinks Japanese cable layer *Hatsushima* off Kii Strait, southeast of Miki Saki, 33°55′N, 136°18′E.

Submarine *Springer* (SS 414) sinks Japanese submarine chaser *Ch 17* west of Kyushu, 32°25′N, 128°46′E, as the latter escorts landing ship *T.146*; later that day, *Trepang* (SS 412) sinks *T.146* off Ose Saki, Japan, 32°24′N, 128°40′E.

British submarine HMS *Tradewind* attacks Japanese convoy off coast of Malaya, sinking merchant tanker *Takasago Maru* 53 miles from Kota Bharu, Malaya, 06°48′N, 101°36′E.

USAAF B-25s and P-38s (Far East Air Force) bomb Japanese shipping at Saigon, sinking tanker *No. 8 Takasago Maru*, 10°49′N, 106°41′E, and motor sailships *No. 10 Shingi Maru*, *No. 9 Nittai Maru*, *No. 1 Kashima Maru*, *Shuttle Boat No. 51*, *Shuttle Boat No. 57*, and *Shuttle Boat No. 74*.

Japanese escort vessel *Uku* and *Patrol Vessel No. 102* [ex-U.S. destroyer *Stewart* (DD 224)] are damaged by aircraft in the Yellow Sea west of Sohuksan Do, 34°52′N, 124°23′E.

USAAF mine sinks Japanese cargo vessel *Gakujo Maru* at western entrance of Shimonoseki Strait, 34°00′N, 130°50′E.

29 Sunday

PACIFIC. Off Okinawa, *kamikazes* damage destroyers *Hazelwood* (DD 531), 27°02′N, 129°59′E, and *Haggard* (DD 555), 27°01′N, 129°40′E, and light minelayers *Shannon* (DM 25), 26°00′N, 127°00′E, and *Harry F. Bauer* (DM 26), 26°47′N, 128°42′E.

Japanese carrier attack planes (KATEs) flying from Truk, Carolines, attack Naval Base, Manus, Admiralty Islands, torpedoing advanced base section docks *ABSD 2* and *ABSD 4* in the belief that the shapes they perceive in the nocturnal strike are aircraft carriers.

Submarine *Besugo* (SS 321) sinks Japanese guardboat *Otome Maru* southeast of Borneo, 05°45′S, 107°30′E.

Submarine *Bream* (SS 243) sinks German minesweeper depot ship *Quito* off Tanjong Puting, Borneo, N.E.I., 04°11′S, 111°17′E.[243]

Submarine *Cero* (SS 225) sinks Japanese freighter *Taishu Maru* off Kamaishi, Japan, 39°15′N, 141°58′E.

Motor minesweeper *YMS 51* is damaged by mine off Tarakan, Borneo, 03°18′N, 117°33′E.

TBM (VC 92) from escort carrier *Tulagi* (CVE 72) sinks Japanese submarine *I 44*, 220 miles southeast of Okinawa, 24°15′N, 131°16′E.

USAAF B-24s on antishipping sweep of Makassar Strait sink Japanese cargo vessel *No. 5 Hirata Maru* in Pamukan Bay, 02°30′S, 116°25′E.

Japanese passenger ferry *No. 2 Kuroshio* (ex-landing ship *T.149*) is damaged by mine during passage from Singapore to Batavia, Java; transport (ex-seaplane carrier) *Kumikawa Maru* is damaged by mine laid by RAAF Catalina off Balikpapan, Borneo. Freighter *No. 1 Aioi Maru* is sunk by mine three miles off Tsunemi.

30 Monday

EUROPE. *Grössadmiral* Karl Doenitz proclaims himself head of the German state by Adolph Hitler's appointment.

Sometime during April 1945 (exact dates indeterminate), USAAF and British aircraft sink German submarines *U 3525* in the Baltic; *U 1131* and *U 1227* at Kiel, Germany; and *U 677*, *U 982*, and *U 2516* at Hamburg, Germany.

ATLANTIC. Destroyer escorts *Thomas* (DE 102), *Bostwick* (DE 103), and *Coffman* (DE 191) and frigate *Natchez* (PF 2) sink German submarine *U 548* off Virginia capes, 36°34′N, 74°00′W.

PBY (VP 63) sinks German submarine *U 1055* west of Brest, France, 48°00′N, 06°30′W.

PACIFIC. Off Okinawa, light minelayer *J. William Ditter* (DM 31) is damaged during Japanese air attack. *Kamikazes* damage minelayer *Terror* (CM 5), 26°10′N, 127°18′E, and U.S. freighter *S. Hall Young* in Nago Bay; infantry landing craft (rocket) *LCI(R) 704* proceeds to the merchantman's assistance and extinguishes the fire. There are no fatalities among the crew, passengers, and 12-man Armed Guard. Large infantry landing craft *LCI(L) 816* is damaged by grounding.

Destroyer *Jenkins* (DD 447) is damaged by mine off Tarakan, Borneo, 03°12′N, 117°37′E.

Submarine *Trepang* (SS 412), despite proximity of three escorting coast defense ships, attacks Japanese convoy MOSI 05, sinking transport *Miho Maru* in the Yellow Sea, 34°27′N, 123°48′E.

Japanese army tanker *Yuno Maru* is sunk by mine, laid by submarine *Guitarro* (SS 363) on 20 April or Dutch submarine *O 19* on 13 April, off east coast of Sumatra, 01°00′S, 104°30′E.

Japanese auxiliary minelayer *Nuwashima* is damaged by aircraft southeast of Dainyu Jima, Saeki.

Japanese freighter *No. 18 Yamabishi Maru* is damaged by mine, off Wakamatsu Light, Japan.

USAAF B-24s (Far East Air Force) sink Japanese transport (ex-seaplane carrier) *Kunikawa Maru* (previously damaged by Australian mine) in Balikpapan Bay, Borneo, 01°15′S, 116°50′E.

MAY

1 Tuesday

PACIFIC. Operation OBOE ONE: TG 78.1 (Rear Admiral Forrest B. Royal) lands 26th Australian Infantry Brigade (Reinforced), 9th Australian Division, on Tarakan Island, Borneo; TG 74.3 (Rear Admiral Russell S. Berkey) provides gunfire support. Vice Admiral Daniel E. Barbey (Commander Seventh Amphibious Force) is attack force commander (see 2 May).

Submarine *Bowfin* (SS 287) sinks Japanese gunboat *Chowa Maru* southeast of Erimo Saki, Hokkaido, Japan, 41°02′N, 144°36′E.

Submarine *Sennet* (SS 408) damages Japanese *Coast Defense Vessel No. 50* off Wakayama, 33°58′N, 136°17′E.

PB4Ys and PBMs (FAW 1) carry out sweeps against Japanese shipping in waters off Korea and in Tsushima Strait, sinking freighters *Kyugkoku Maru*, 34°35′N, 126°00′E, and *Miyatama Maru* and *Komadori Maru* off Mokp'o, 34°11′N, 126°35′E, and damaging freighter *Taruyasu Maru* in the Chochiku Channel.

U.S. freighter *Henry L. Abbott* is damaged by mine, Manila Bay, 14°35′N, 120°58′E. Two of the merchant crew die in the explosion; there are no casualties among the 27-man Armed Guard.

Japanese merchant tanker *No. 2 Iyasaka Maru* is sunk by aircraft off Singapore.

Japanese merchant ship *Richo Go* is sunk by mine off Woosung, China.

2 Wednesday

PACIFIC. Motor minesweeper *YMS 481* is sunk, and *YMS 364* (03°27′N, 117°32′E) and *YMS 334* (03°26′N, 117°40′E) damaged, by Japanese shore batteries as minesweeping operations commence north of Tarakan, Borneo. *YMS 363* is damaged by mine, 03°26′N, 117°32′E.[244] High-speed transport *Cofer* (APD 62) and two support landing craft (LCS) silence the enemy guns.

On Okinawa, Hospital Apprentice Second Class Robert E. Bush, serving as a corpsman with a rifle company with the Second Battalion, Fifth Marines, is administering blood plasma to a wounded marine when the Japanese launch a fierce counterattack against his unit. Steadfastly remaining at the wounded man's side, Bush holds the plasma bottle in one hand and draws his .45 with the other, expending his ammunition at the charging enemy. Seizing a discarded carbine, the battling corpsman, who suffers the loss of an eye among other injuries, kills six Japanese as the marines drive the enemy back. Bush refuses

medical attention for himself until the marine that he had protected is evacuated. Bush then collapses before he himself can reach an aid station. For his selfless heroism, the corpsman is awarded the Medal of Honor.

Submarine *Raton* (SS 270) attacks Japanese convoy SE 3, sinking freighter *Toryu Maru* southeast of the Shantung Peninsula, 37°24′N, 123°50′E.

Submarine *Springer* (SS 414) sinks Japanese escort vessel *Oga* in the Yellow Sea, 33°56′N, 122°49′E (see 3 and 4 May).

Japanese merchant ship *Daian Maru* is sunk by aircraft off Woosung, China.

3 Thursday

PACIFIC. TG 78.2 (Rear Admiral Albert G. Noble) lands Army troops at Santa Cruz, Davao Gulf, P.I.

Phase II of Operation STARVATION commences. In the first of two operations aimed at blockading Japan's industrial centers, 97 USAAF B-29s sow mines in the Shimonoseki Straits and the waters off Kobe, Osaka, and Suo Nada.

Off Okinawa, *kamikazes* sink destroyer *Little* (DD 803), 26°24′N, 126°15′E, and medium landing ship *LSM 195*, and damage destroyer *Bache* (DD 470) and high-speed minesweeper *Macomb* (DMS 23), 26°01′N, 126°53′E, light minelayer *Aaron Ward* (DM 34), 26°24′N, 126°15′E, and large support landing craft *LCS 25*. Cargo ship *Carina* (AK 74) is damaged by assault demolition boat, 26°13′N, 127°50′E. Infantry landing craft *LCI 768* runs aground on reef in Kutaka-Kuchi Channel, southeast of Okinawa; fleet tug *Ute* (ATF 75) pulls her free. U.S. freighter *Sea Flasher* is damaged by friendly fire from battleship *New Mexico* (BB 40); seven men are killed and 47 injured.

Submarine *Lagarto* (SS 371) is sunk by Japanese minelayer *Hatsutaka* in Gulf of Siam, 07°55′N, 102°00′E.

Submarine *Springer* (SS 414) sinks Japanese *Coast Defense Ship No. 25* in the Yellow Sea, 34°56′N, 122°49′E, as that ship proceeds to the scene of the sinking of escort vessel *Oga*, sunk by *Springer* the previous day (see 4 May).

U.S. freighter *Edmund F. Dickens* is damaged by mine, Manila Bay; there are no casualties among the merchant crew or the 27-man Armed Guard.

ANDAMAN SEA. Fall of Rangoon ends campaign in Burma, although isolated pockets of resistance remain west of the Irrawaddy River and between that river and the railway linking Mandalay and Pegu.

4 Friday

PACIFIC. Japanese planes attack Yontan airfield, Okinawa, and U.S. and British ships supporting Okinawa operation. *Kamikaze*s sink destroyers *Luce* (DD 522), 26°35'N, 127°10'E, and *Morrison* (DD 560), 27°10'N, 127°58'E, and medium landing craft *LSM 190* and *LSM 194*. *Kamikaze*s damage light cruiser *Birmingham* (CL 62), 26°19'N, 127°43'E; escort carrier *Sangamon* (CVE 26), 26°01'N, 237°26'E [destroyer *Hudson* (DD 475) collides with *Sangamon* as the destroyer lies alongside, 26°01'N, 127°26'E]; destroyers *Ingraham* (DD 694), 27°10'N, 127°58'E, *Cowell* (DD 547), 26°11'N, 126°35'E, and *Lowry* (DD 770), 27°12'N, 128°17'E; light minelayer *Gwin* (DM 33), 26°13'N, 126°22'E; high-speed minesweeper *Hopkins* (DMS 13), 26°32'N, 126°58'E; motor minesweeper *YMS 331*, 26°32'N, 126°58'E; and British carrier HMS *Formidable* (carrier HMS *Indomitable* is also crashed by a suicider, but her armored deck deflects the attacker into the sea). In addition, light minelayer *Shea* (DM 30) is damaged by a *Baka*, 27°26'N, 126°59'E; minesweeper *Gayety* (AM 239) is damaged by near-misses of *kamikaze* and *Baka*, 26°32'N, 126°58'E; motor minesweeper *YMS 327* is damaged by *kamikaze* and by friendly fire, 26°32'N, 126°58'E; motor minesweeper *YMS 311* is damaged by friendly fire, 26°00'N, 128°00'E; motor gunboat *PGM 17* is damaged by grounding, 26°42'N, 128°01'E, and efforts by fleet tug *Tawakoni* (ATF 114) to free her are unsuccessful; and large support landing craft *LCS 31* and *LCS 57* are damaged by air attack. Coordinated with the air strike, a minor Japanese counterlanding is attempted and repulsed.

Fleet Air Wing 18 (Rear Admiral Marshall R. Greer) is established at Guam for operations in the forward areas.

Submarine *Cero* (SS 225) sinks Japanese freighter *Shinpen Maru* off Yamada Bay, 39°28'N, 142°04'E.

Submarine *Trepang* (SS 412) sinks Japanese minesweeper *W.20* in the Yellow Sea 140 nautical miles southeast of Mokp'o, Korea, 34°16'N, 123°37'E, as *W.20* proceeds to the scene of the sinking of escort vessel *Oga*, sunk by *Springer* (SS 414) on 2 May.

PB4Ys and PBMs (FAW 1) carry out sweeps against Japanese shipping in waters off Korea and in Tsushima Strait, sinking merchant tankers *Koan Maru* and *No. 15 Takasago Maru* off Pusan, 34°40'N, 127°30'E, and damaging cargo vessel *Harukawa Maru* while she is en route from Jinsen to Moji, 34°50'N, 128°30'E.

Destroyer escort *Atherton* (DE 169), the simultaneous explosion of stern track and K-gun–launched depth charges clearly visible, hunts *U 853*, 6 May 1945. *Atherton* is painted in Measure 31/3D camouflage (haze gray, ocean gray, and dull black). (NA, 80-G-453464)

Japanese tanker *No. 2 Yaei Maru* is sunk by USAAF B-29 (20th Air Force)–laid mine off Singapore, 02°00'S, 105°00'E; stores ship *Hayasaki* is damaged by mine, laid by submarine *Guitarro* (SS 363) on 20 April, while en route from Batavia to Singapore, 01°00'S, 104°30'E.

"B-24" (possibly a USN PB4Y-1) attacks Japanese shipping off Cape Camau, French Indochina, sinking auxiliary netlayer *Tokachi Maru*, 08°36'N, 104°43'E.

Tank landing craft *LCT 1358* sinks after running aground off California coast.

5 Saturday

PACIFIC. In the second of two operations aimed at blockading Japan's industrial centers, 98 USAAF B-29s sow mines in the Inland Sea and off Kobe, Osaka, Tokyo, and Nagoya. Army cargo ship *Manshu Maru* is damaged by mine off Wakamatsu, 33°47'N, 131°35'E.

PB4Ys and PBMs (FAW 1) carry out sweeps against Japanese shipping in the waters off Korea and in Tsushima Strait, sinking merchant tankers *No. 5 Takasago Maru* west of Ch'uja Kundo, 34°44'N, 126°16'E, and *No. 11 Takasago Maru* off Yosu; freighters *Washi Maru* (35°33'N, 126°18'E), *Yamatogawa Maru*, and *Naka Maru* off Mokp'o; freighter *No. 9 Taiun*

Maru in Tsushima Strait, 34°00'N, 130°00'E; and freighter *Okusu Maru* off Karatsu, Japan; and damage escort destroyer *Oki* off Inchon, 37°36'N, 126°00'E.

USAAF B-24s (Far East Air Force) raid Japanese shipping and shore installations at Makassar, sinking cargo vessel *Kenzan Maru*.

ATLANTIC. U.S. freighter *Black Point* is torpedoed and sunk by German submarine *U 853* about five miles southeast of Point Judith, Rhode Island, 41°19'02"N, 71°25'01"W. One of the five Armed Guard sailors is killed, as are 11 of the 41-man merchant complement. Yugoslavian freighter *Karman* and Norwegian *Scandanavia*, crash boats from Quonset Point, Rhode Island, and a Coast Guard craft rescue the survivors of the last U.S.-flag merchantman sunk by a U-boat in World War II. *U 853*'s sailors, however, do not get to ponder the significance of their achievement for long (see 6 May).

6 Sunday

ATLANTIC. Destroyer escort *Atherton* (DE 169) and frigate *Moberley* (PF 63) sink German submarine *U 853* off Block Island, 41°13'N, 71°27'W.

Destroyer escort *Farquhar* (DE 139) sinks German submarine *U 881*, North Atlantic,

43°18′N, 47°44′W. *U 881* is the last U-boat sunk by U.S. forces.

PACIFIC. Surveying ship *Pathfinder* (AGS 1) is damaged off Okinawa, 26°38′N, 127°53′E, when *kamikaze* grazes her after gun platform and crashes into the sea. Seaplane tender *St. George* (AV 16) is also damaged by *kamikaze*, 26°10′N, 127°19′E. Japanese planes attack slow convoy 35 miles south of Kerama Retto, bombing and damaging floating drydock *ARD 28*, 25°33′N, 127°27′E. Off Okinawa, battleship *South Dakota* (BB 57) is damaged by explosion of five 16-inch powder tanks in magazine, 26°30′N, 129°30′E.[245]

Destroyer escort *Wintle* (DE 25) and motor minesweeper *YMS 354* cover the evacuation of about 500 Marshallese from Jaluit in large infantry landing craft *LCI(L) 394*, *LCI(L) 479*, and *LCI(L) 481*.

Submarine *Hammerhead* (SS 364) sinks Japanese fleet tanker *Kinrei Maru* in Gulf of Thailand, 08°15′N, 102°00′E.

PB4Ys and PBMs (FAW 1) carry out sweeps against Japanese shipping in the waters off Korea and western Kyushu, sinking merchant tanker *No. 5 Hoei Maru* off Inchon and freighters *Eiko Maru* off Kunsan, 36°26′N, 126°37′E; *Nakagawa Maru* off Yosu, 34°30′N, 127°00′E; *No. 1 Tora Maru* off Mokp'o; *Niosan Maru* north of Kumun Island; and *No. 3 Kinzan Maru* off Kuche Island. Aircraft damage auxiliary minesweeper *Wa. 15* off Mokp'o, auxiliary submarine chaser *Kumi Maru* off Kuche Island, and freighter *Enzan Maru* off Yosu, 34°21′N, 127°24′E.

Japanese cargo ship *Sagamigawa Maru* is sunk by USAAF mine laid by B-29 (20th Air Force), 34°00′N, 130°50′E. Submarine *I 366*, en route to take delivery of *kaitens*, is damaged by mine off Hikari, eastern Bungo Suido.

7 Monday

EUROPE AND ATLANTIC. Germany surrenders unconditionally to the Western Allies and Russia at Reims, France.

PACIFIC. Japanese minesweeper *W.29* and cargo vessel *Kashima Maru* are sunk by mines (laid by USAAF B-29s) in Kanmon Harbor, 34°02′N, 130°54′E; mines also sink freighter *Shofuku Maru* off Dairen, Manchuria, and merchant vessel *Teiko Maru* off Futaoi Jima, Shimonoseki.

USAAF B-24s (Far East Air Force) bomb Japanese shipping and shore installations at Makassar, sinking gunboat *Kenzan Maru* and cargo ship *Hakko Maru*, 05°08′S, 119°35′E.

PBMs or PB2Ys (FAW 1) on sweeps against

Japanese shipping off west coast of Korea and in Tsushima Strait, sink cargo ships *Tatsuchiyo Maru* west of Ch'uja Kundo, 34°00′N, 126°00′E; *No. 2 Kozan Maru* off Mokp'o, 35°16′N, 126°03′E; and *Kaba Maru* and *Hoei Maru* in the eastern channel of Tsushima Strait, 34°00′N, 130°00′E.

Japanese minesweeper *Nuwajima*, damaged by aircraft, is beached, Saeki Bay, Japan.

8 Tuesday

EUROPE AND ATLANTIC. As of 1801 hours, all offensive operations against German land, sea, and air forces cease ("V-E Day").

EUROPE. U.S. freighter *Horace Binney*, in convoy TAM 62, is damaged by mine 15 miles off Ostend, Belgium, 51°21′N, 02°27′E; there are no fatalities among the ship's complement (which includes a 36-man Armed Guard). The ship is towed to Deal, England, and beached, where she is later written off as a total loss.

PACIFIC. Submarine *Bowfin* (SS 287) sinks Japanese fishing boat *No. 3 Daito Maru* east-southeast of Todo Saki, 39°38′N, 142°08′E.

Submarine *Bream* (SS 243) lays mines off Puolo Obi, French Indochina, in the last U.S. Navy submarine mine plant of World War II.

Mines sink Japanese freighter *Shuncho Maru* and damage minesweeper *W.39* south and southeast of Futaoi Light, Shimonoseki, respectively. Transport *Kotobuki Maru* (ex-Italian liner *Conte Verde*) is damaged by mine laid by USAAF B-29 (20th Air Force) off southern Korea, 34°30′N, 126°19′E.

Japanese merchant vessel *No. 6 Kosho Maru* is sunk by aircraft off Hainan Island, 21°51′N, 113°09′E.

9 Wednesday

ATLANTIC. German submarine *U 249* surrenders to PB4Y (FAW 7) off the Scilly Islands, England, becoming the first to do so after hostilities cease in Europe.

PACIFIC. Off Okinawa, *kamikazes* damage destroyer escorts *Oberrender* (DE 344), 26°32′N, 127°30′E, and *England* (DE 635), 26°18′N, 127°13′E, and British carriers HMS *Formidable* and HMS *Victorious*.

Japanese escort vessel *Uku* is damaged by mine off Futaoi Light, Shimonoseki.

FAW 1 planes on sweeps against Japanese shipping off the coast of Korea damage merchant tanker *No. 13 Horai Maru* off Kunsan, 36°10′N, 126°02′E.

10 Thursday

PACIFIC. TG 78.3 (Rear Admiral Arthur D.

Struble) lands Army troops (RCT 108) at Macajalar Bay, Mindanao. The landing is made without opposition; Filipino guerrillas aid in establishing the beachhead.

Off Okinawa, *kamikazes* damage destroyer *Brown* (DD 546), 26°26′N, 127°20′E, and light minelayer *Harry F. Bauer* (DM 26), 26°25′N, 128°31′E.

Mines sink Japanese transport *Tatsuwa Maru* off Imabari, Kurahashi Jima, 34°04′N, 132°26′E, and freighter *Otowa Maru*, 34°38′N, 135°12′E, and damage merchant tugboat *No. 7 Naniwazu Maru* off Wadano Misaki, Japan.

FAW 1 planes sink Japanese merchant tanker *No. 1 Toyu Maru* and cargo ship *No. 2 Yumihari Maru* off west coast of Korea.

11 Friday

PACIFIC. Japanese aircraft attack U.S. ships off Okinawa; two *kamikazes* crash TF 58 flagship, carrier *Bunker Hill* (CV 17), 25°44′N, 129°28′E; light cruiser *Wilkes Barre* (CL 103) and three destroyers provide assistance. Vice Admiral Marc A. Mitscher (Commander TF 58) transfers his flag to destroyer *English* (DD 696), then to carrier *Enterprise* (CV 6) (see 14 May). *Kamikazes* also crash destroyer *Evans* (DD 552), 26°58′N, 127°32′E, and large support landing craft *LCS 88*; destroyer *Hugh W. Hadley* (DD 774) is damaged by a *Baka*, 26°59′N, 127°32′E.

On Okinawa, Pharmacist's Mate Second Class William D. Halyburton Jr., USNR, advances into an open field under fire to treat a casualty. Hit by a bullet while tending to the wounded marine, Halyburton unhesitatingly shields the man with his own body to protect him from further injury. In so doing, the corpsman is mortally wounded. For his heroically saving another man's life at the cost of his own, Halyburton is awarded the Medal of Honor posthumously.

Japanese guardboat *No. 8 Sagami Maru* is sunk by U.S. aircraft off Hong Kong, 21°52′N, 113°08′E.

USAAF B-24s (11th Air Force) sink Japanese army cargo ship *Aitoku Maru* and damage escort destroyer *Hachijo* in Kataoka Harbor, Kurils, 50°42′N, 156°13′E.

PB4Y-2s (VPB 118), operating against Japanese shipping west of Ch'uja Kundo, Korea, sink freighters *Seiri Maru*, 34°17′N, 126°50′E, and *Shinzan Maru*, 34°15′N, 127°10′E. Freighter *Kamiyama Maru* is sunk by aircraft off Mokp'o.

Mines sink Japanese freighter *Kitsurin Maru* and damage two tugboats off Wadano Misaki,

34°39′N, 135°11′E, and damage auxiliary minelayer *Koei Maru* seven miles off Ume Saki.

12 Saturday

PACIFIC. TG 51.24 (Captain Charles A. Buchanan) lands Army troops (reinforced company from the 27th Division) on Tori Shima, to the west of Okinawa, Ryukyus. The island is taken in 15 minutes against no opposition; the only two Japanese seen jump into the sea upon the approach of the landing force.

Battleship *New Mexico* (BB 40) is damaged by *kamikaze* off Okinawa, 26°22′N, 127°43′E; heavy cruiser *Wichita* (CA 45) is damaged by friendly fire, 26°22′N, 127°43′E.

Submarine *Raton* (SS 270) sinks Japanese freighter *Rekizan Maru* in the Yellow Sea off the Shantung Peninsula, 37°25′N, 123°42′E.

Mines laid in Japanese waters by 20th Air Force B-29s sink Japanese army cargo ship *Brazil Maru* off Kobe; freighter *Manbo Maru* off Osaka, 34°30′N, 135°10′E; cargo ship *No. 1 Nissho Maru* off Futaoi Light, Shimonoseki, 34°06′N, 130°47′E; and *No. 1 Nisshin Maru* in Shimonoseki Channel. Mine damages freighter *Hokusei Maru* northwest of Mutsure Jima.

Japanese merchant tanker *No. 13 Takasago Maru* is damaged by aircraft, Kogunsan Kundo.

Navy patrol bombers (TU 50.5.5) damage Japanese merchant ship *Chile Maru*, which is run aground to permit salvage on the north coast of Iki Jima, Tsushima Strait, 34°16′N, 129°40′E. *Chile Maru* is written off, however, as a total loss.

ATLANTIC. Minesweeper *Jubilant* (AM 255) and Italian submarine *Mameli* are damaged when they collide in Casco Bay, Maine.

13 Sunday

PACIFIC. TF 58 (Vice Admiral Marc A. Mitscher) begins two days of strikes on Kyushu airfields. During Japanese retaliatory strikes, small carrier *Bataan* (CVL 29) is damaged by friendly fire, 30°30′N, 132°30′E. Destroyer *Bache* (DD 470), 26°01′N, 126°53′E, and destroyer escort *Bright* (DE 747), 26°21′N, 127°17′E, are damaged by *kamikazes* off Okinawa.

Phase III of Operation STARVATION, a blockade of northwest Honshu and Kyushu, commences as 12 USAAF B-29s mine Shimonoseki Straits and the waters off Niigata, Japan.

Submarine *Baya* (SS 318) attacks Palembang-bound Japanese convoy, sinking tanker *Yosei Maru*, 06°31′S, 111°19′E; guardboat *No. 17 Shonan Maru* carries out unsuccessful coun-

terattack. Although *Baya* claims a second ship sunk, her quarry, tanker *Enoshima Maru*, emerges unscathed.

Submarine *Cero* (SS 225) sinks Japanese freighter *Shinnan Maru* off Todo Saki, Honshu, 39°06′N, 141°57′E.

Submarine *Plaice* (SS 390) attacks Japanese guardboat *Nisshin Maru* southwest of Uruppu Island, 45°30′N, 147°04′E.

British submarine HMS *Trump* sinks Japanese guardboat *No. 15 Shosei Maru* at Sapudi Strait, 07°05′S, 114°13′E.

Navy planes on sweeps against Japanese shipping off coast of Korea sink guardboat *No. 8 Choyo Maru* off Kumun Island, 34°28′N, 127°45′E, and freighter *No. 2 Funakawa Maru* off So Do, 34°00′N, 128°00′E. Freighter *Hakuju Maru* is damaged by aircraft between Kuro Saki and Shirohana.

Mine laid by USAAF B-29 (20th Air Force) sinks Japanese tanker *No. 2 Takasago Maru* off Wadano Misaki, 34°39′N, 135°11′E. Mines sink Japanese freighter *Kinoto Maru* and *Mishima Maru* off Kobe, Japan, and freighter *Magane Maru* (location unspecified). Mines damage auxiliary submarine chaser *Cha 170* off Shodo Jima (laid by USAAF B-24), freighter *Gyoryu Maru* off Kobe, 34°40′N, 135°10′E, and merchant vessel *Miyajima Maru* 129 miles off Ezaki Light, 34°36′N, 134°59′E.

14 Monday

PACIFIC. Carrier *Enterprise* (CV 6) (TF 58 flagship) is damaged by *kamikaze* off Honshu, 30°23′N, 132°36′E; for the second time in a week, Vice Admiral Marc A. Mitscher has to transfer his flag to another carrier, shifting to *Randolph* (CV 15).

Off Okinawa, operational casualties account for damage to tank landing ship *LST 137* and medium landing ship *LSM 137*.

Submarine *Cobia* (SS 245) is damaged by depth charges, Gulf of Siam, 09°35′N, 101°44′E, but remains on patrol.

Submarine *Sand Lance* (SS 381) sinks Japanese auxiliary minesweeper *Yoshino Maru* off Erimo Saki, Hokkaido, 32°00′N, 146°36′E.

Navy aircraft, on sweeps against Japanese freighters off Korea and Kyushu, sink *Kurokamisan Maru* west of Kuche Island, 34°27′N, 127°30′E; off Goto Retto, *Samukaze Maru*, 33°00′N, 129°20′E, and *Kanpu Maru*, 33°02′N, 129°27′E; *Kainan Maru* three miles off Ioshima Light, 32°43′N, 129°46′E; and *Keishin Maru* off Inchon. Aircraft damage *Chofuku Maru* near Hakata Bay, 33°36′N, 130°24′E.

Mine laid by USAAF B-29 (20th Air Force) damages Japanese merchant ship *Miyajima Maru* at Awaji, Japan, 34°28′N, 134°30′E (see 15 May). Mines sink Japanese transport *Anko Maru* off Shimonoseki and merchant tug *No.*

Kawanishi N1K3-J Navy Interceptor Fighter (GEORGE) from the 343rd *Kokutai* recovers from a firing pass below the Martin PBM-5 Mariner (Bureau Number 59046) commanded by Lieutenant (j.g.) John C. Hook, USNR, during the running fight between two PBM-5s from VPB 21 and six to seven N1K3-Js off Goto Retto on 11 May 1945. Photograph taken by Chief Photographer's Mate Donald S. Fruchey. (Author's Collection)

13 *Uwajima Maru* off Hiraiso, 34°30'N, 134°30'E, and damage freighters *Tatsukei Maru*, 34°28'N, 134°45'E, and *No. 6 Kaiyo Maru*, off He Saki, Japan.

UNITED STATES. Admiral H. Kent Hewitt commences "further investigation of facts pertinent to the Japanese attack on Pearl Harbor" in accordance with precept dated 2 May. Secretary of the Navy James V. Forrestal enjoins the admiral to study the proceedings and exhibits of the Hart Inquiry and the Navy Court of Inquiry to determine if "errors of judgment" were made by "certain officers in the Naval Service, both at Pearl Harbor and at Washington" (see 11 July).

15 Tuesday

EUROPE. Commander U.S. Ports and Bases Germany (Rear Admiral Arthur G. Robinson) establishes headquarters at Bremen, Germany.[246]

PACIFIC. Submarine *Hammerhead* (SS 364) sinks Singapore-bound Japanese transport *Tottori Maru* in the Gulf of Siam, 09°12'N, 101°20'E. Escorting minelayer *Hatsutaka* conducts unsuccessful counterattack (see 16 May).

Submarine *Sea Poacher* (SS 406) sinks Japanese army luggers *No. 56 Ume Maru* and *Fukumo Maru* off Etorofu, Kurils, 45°29'N, 149°01'E.

Submarine *Shad* (SS 235) damages Japanese freighter *Mako Maru* southwest of Quelpart Island, 33°42'N, 126°37'E.

USN patrol planes, in wide-ranging sweeps against Japanese shipping, sink freighter *No. 1 Kyodo Maru* off Quelpart Island, 34°15'N, 126°56'E; freighter *Keiun Maru* off Karatsu, western Kyushu, 33°57'N, 129°51'E; and freighter *No. 3 Hakutetsu Maru* off east coast of Korea.

Japanese merchant vessel *Miyajima Maru*, while under tow after being damaged the previous day by a mine, strikes a second mine and sinks, 34°28'N, 134°50'E. *Mishima Maru* is sunk by USAAF mine laid off Kobe on 3 May, 34°30'N, 135°10'E.

16 Wednesday

PACIFIC. Thirty USAAF B-29s mine Shimonoseki Straits and the waters off Miyazu and Maizuru, Japan.

Escort carrier *Shipley Bay* (CVE 85) is damaged in collision with oiler *Cache* (AO 67) off Okinawa, 25°00'N, 130°00'E.

Avengers from British escort carrier HMS *Emperor* sight and attack Japanese heavy cruiser *Haguro* heading into Malacca Strait;

subsequently, British destroyers HMS *Saumarez*, HMS *Venus*, HMS *Verulam*, HMS *Vigilant*, and HMS *Virago* sink *Haguro* 55 nautical miles west-southwest of Penang, Malaya, 04°49'N, 99°42'E, as the enemy ship, in company with destroyer *Kamikaze* (which is damaged in the engagement), is evacuating troops from Port Blair, Andamans, to Singapore.

Submarine *Hawkbill* (SS 366) sinks Japanese minelayer *Hatsutaka* off east coast of Malaya, 04°49'N, 103°31'E.

Submarine *Raton* (SS 270) sinks Japanese freighter *Eiju Maru* in the Yellow Sea off west coast of Korea, 37°34'N, 124°13'E.

Japanese freighter *No. 5 Yamanami Maru* is sunk by mine laid by USAAF B-29s (20th Air Force) off Wadano Misaki, 34°36'N, 135°08'E.

17 Thursday

PACIFIC. Carrier aircraft (Rear Admiral Clifton A. F. Sprague) strike Japanese installations on Taroa Island, Maloelap Atoll, Marshalls.

USAAF 21st Air Force begins operations against airfields on Kyushu and Shikoku from which Japanese kamikaze attacks are launched.

Destroyer *Douglas H. Fox* (DD 779) is damaged by *kamikaze* off Okinawa, 25°59'N, 126°54'E.

Off Wadano Misaki, Japan, USAAF mines sink Japanese transport *Tairyu Maru*, 34°27'N, 135°11'E, and army cargo ship *Koan Maru*, 34°38'N, 135°11'E; mines also sink freighter *Mikazuki Maru* in Yangtze River below Woosung, China, 32°05'N, 119°56'E, and damage *Coast Defense Vessel No. 200* inside Miyazu Harbor, Japan.

Japanese auxiliary submarine chasers *No. 2 Hakusan Maru*, *Wakatake Maru,* and *Yobai Maru* are damaged by aircraft off Ishigaki Jima, Sakishima Gunto.

18 Friday

PACIFIC. Thirty-four USAAF B-29s mine Shimonoseki Straits and the waters off Tsuruya, Japan.

Destroyer *Longshaw* (DD 559), damaged by shore battery off Naha, Okinawa, 26°11'N, 127°37'E, explodes; the wreck is demolished by destroyers *Heywood L. Edwards* (DD 663) and *Picking* (DD 685). Also off Okinawa, high-speed transport *Sims* (APD 50) is damaged by *kamikaze*, 26°00'N, 127°00'E, and tank landing ship *LST 808* by aerial torpedo, 26°42'N, 127°47'E. U.S. freighter *Cornelius Vanderbilt* (carrying gasoline and explosives, as well as general cargo) is bombed by Japanese plane and set afire off Ie Shima, Ryukus, but the 38-man merchant crew, 27-man Armed

Guard, and the 108 stevedores on board working cargo assemble fire-fighting parties and put out the blaze in short order.

Submarine *Shad* (SS 235) sinks Japanese freighter *Chosan Maru* in the Yellow Sea off Gunzan, Korea, 35°41'N, 126°17'E.

Navy land-based aircraft sink Japanese cargo vessel *Enkyo Maru* off coast of Kiangsu, China, 33°14'N, 120°50'E.

Japanese submarine chaser *Ch 57* is damaged by mine (laid by British submarine HMS *Porpoise* on 9 January 1945), south channel into Penang, Malaya, 05°20'N, 100°08'E.

Japanese landing ship *T.137* is damaged by aircraft, 12 miles off Daio Saki, Japan.

Japanese transport *No. 18 Nissho Maru* is damaged by mine in the Inland Sea, off Takamatsu, 34°33'N, 134°47'E.

Japanese auxiliary submarine chaser *No. 3 Takunan Maru* is damaged by aircraft in the East China Sea, northeast of the Yangtze estuary, 32°05'N, 124°40'E.

Japanese freighter *No. 5 Nissen Maru* is damaged by aircraft, 34°43'N, 137°50'E.

19 Saturday

ATLANTIC. Destroyer *Moffett* (DD 362) is damaged when she strikes an unidentified submerged object 65 miles east of Portland, Maine.

PACIFIC. Destroyers bombard Japanese installations on Paramushir, Kurils.

Destroyer escort *Vammen* (DE 644) is damaged in collision with oiler *Cimarron* (AO 22) off Okinawa, 26°24'N, 127°53'E. *Cimarron* is also damaged by grounding, 26°25'N, 127°53'E.

Motor gunboat *PGM 1* is damaged by explosion off Luzon, 14°41'N, 121°46'E.

Japanese army cargo ship *Kaiko Maru* is sunk by aircraft in Keelung Harbor.

Japanese freighter *Daishin Maru* is sunk and light cruiser *Kashima* damaged when the two ships collide in Tsushima Strait, 34°40'N, 128°38'E.

Japanese cargo vessel *Ogishima Maru* is damaged by aircraft, 34°39'N, 137°32'E.

Japanese merchant tanker *Soei Maru* is damaged by mine six kilometers east of Mushima.

20 Sunday

PACIFIC. Thirty USAAF B-29s mine Shimonoseki Straits and the waters off Maizuru and Miyazu, Japan.

Off Okinawa, *kamikazes* damage destroyer *Thatcher* (DD 514), 26°33'N, 127°29'E; destroyer escort *John C. Butler* (DE 339), 26°47'N,

127°52′E; high-speed transports *Chase* (APD 54), 26°18′N, 127°14′E, and *Register* (APD 92), 26°25′N, 127°21′E; and tank landing ship *LST 808*, 26°42′N, 127°47′E. High-speed transport *Tattnall* (APD 19) is damaged by horizontal bomber, 26°00′N, 128°00′E. TBMs from TG 58.3 provide close air support for efforts to take Japanese position holding up the advance of U.S. ground forces northeast of Shuri castle, Okinawa.

Submarine *Cero* (SS 225) sinks Japanese merchant whaler *No. 5 Seki Maru* east-southeast of Kinkazan, 38°06′N, 142°24′E.

Japanese auxiliary submarine chaser *Cha 244* is sunk by aircraft, 22°35′N, 128°51′E.

Japanese army cargo vessel *No. 1 Konan Maru* is sunk by aircraft off Hong Kong.

USAAF B-24s (Far East Air Force) sink Japanese army cargo vessel *Torai Maru* off Keelung, Formosa, 26°00′N, 122°00′E.

Japanese freighter *Nikkan Maru* is sunk by aircraft off Pusan, Korea; merchant refrigerated stores ship *Kanagawa Maru* is sunk by aircraft off south coast of Korea.

Japanese merchant tanker *No. 11 Horai Maru* is damaged by aircraft, location unspecified.

21 Monday

PACIFIC. Submarine *Chub* (SS 329) sinks Japanese minesweeper *W.34* in Java Sea off Kepualuan, 06°15′S, 116°01′E.

Infantry landing craft (rocket) *LCI(R) 1068* is damaged by Japanese shore battery fire off Namumi Saki, Naha, Okinawa.

Japanese freighter *Santen Maru* is sunk by USAAF mine laid by B-29 (20th Air Force) off Niihama, 33°57′N, 133°16′E.

22 Tuesday

PACIFIC. Thirty-two USAAF B-29s mine Shimonoseki Straits.

Planes from carriers *Bennington* (CV 20) and *Hornet* (CV 12) sink Japanese submarine chasers *Ch 37* and *Ch 58* and landing ship *T.173* southwest of Kyushu between Sasebo and Oshima, 29°45′N, 129°10′E.

Mines sink Japanese freighters *No. 25 Uwajima Maru* off Moji, 34°20′N, 134°20′E, and *Sagami Maru* off Wakamatsu, and damage auxiliary submarine chaser *Cha 157* eight miles off Niigata Harbor.

Japanese auxiliary patrol vessel *Pa 25* is damaged by aircraft off Omae Saki, Japan.

Submarine Base, Dutch Harbor, Alaska, is disestablished.

23 Wednesday

PACIFIC. Mines laid by USAAF B-29s (20th Air Force) sink Japanese cargo vessels *Sagami Maru* at 34°00′N, 131°00′E; *No. 2 Shinri Maru* off He Saki, 33°58′N, 131°02′E; and *Kimigayo Maru* west of Hime Jima, 33°06′N, 129°43′E. Mine damages freighter *Iwai Maru* three kilometers southeast of Mushima.

24 Thursday

PACIFIC. TF 58 (Vice Admiral Marc A. Mitscher) strikes airfields on southern Kyushu.

Japanese aircraft attack U.S. positions and ships at Okinawa; strikes continue on 25 May. *Kamikazes* damage destroyer escort *William C. Cole* (DE 641), 26°45′N, 127°52′E; high-speed transport *Sims* (APD 50), 26°00′N, 127°00′E; and large support landing craft *LCS(L) 121*. Friendly fire damages destroyer *Heywood L. Edwards* (DD 663), 26°20′N, 127°43′E. Escort carrier *Suwanee* (CVE 27) is damaged when TBM (VT 40) explodes upon landing, 24°00′N, 124°00′E.

PBMs sink Japanese *Special Coast Defense Ship No. 21* off China coast, 20°58′N, 110°30′E.

Thirty USAAF B-29s mine Shimonoseki Straits and the waters off Niigata, Nanao, and Fushiki, Japan. Mine laid by USAAF B-29 (20th Air Force) sinks Japanese cargo vessel *No. 14 Kaishin Maru* west of the mouth of Kammon Channel, 34°31′N, 130°54′E. Mines sink Japanese freighters *Fukuei Maru* off Shodo Jima, *Kinryuzan Maru* off Moji, *Tatsufuku Maru* off He Saki, *Inaba Maru* west of Oshima, Kagawa prefecture, and (B-29–laid mine) merchant tanker *No. 7 Nanko Maru* off Motoyama Misaki, 33°55′N, 131°20′E. Mines damage transport (ex-seaplane carrier) *Kiyokawa Maru* off Motoyama Misaki and freighters *Nitcho Maru* 44 kilometers southwest of Onna Jima; *Yamazumi Maru* at 34°05′N, 130°51′E; and *No. 2 Tomoe Maru* at 32°52′N, 129°15′E.

25 Friday

PACIFIC. Off Okinawa, *kamikazes* sink high-speed transport *Bates* (APD 47), 26°41′N, 127°47′E, and medium landing ship *LSM 135*, and damage destroyers *Guest* (DD 472), 26°22′N, 127°44′E, and *Stormes* (DD 780), 27°06′N, 127°38′E; destroyer escort *O'Neill* (DE 188), 26°20′N, 127°43′E; high-speed transports *Barry* (APD 29), 26°30′N, 127°00′E (see 21 and 22 June), and *Roper* (APD 20), 26°34′N, 127°36′E; high-speed minesweeper *Butler* (DMS 29), 26°12′N, 127°50′E; and minesweeper *Spectacle* (AM 305), 26°40′N, 127°52′E. Friendly fire damages destroyer *Cowell* (DD 547), 26°41′N, 126°50′E. Japanese

plane torpedoes U.S. freighter *William B. Allison* in Buckner Bay; six merchant sailors and a stevedore die in the explosion. Infantry landing craft (rocket) *LCI(R) 651* lays alongside and, determining the merchant crew to be "in various stages of panic," sends boarding party to take charge of fighting the fire. *LCI(R) 772*, flotilla flagship *LC(FF) 536*, and fleet tug *Tawakoni* (ATF 114) assist, with *LC(FF) 536* evacuating men of the 12th Construction Battalion (Seabees) who had been on board handling cargo. The 34-man merchant complement, 28 Armed Guard sailors, and 150 stevedores later unload the ship's cargo.[247]

Submarine *Blenny* (SS 324) sinks Japanese gunboat *Kairyu Maru*, 06°04′S, 107°27′E.

Submarine *Ray* (SS 271) sinks Japanese schooner *Tsuki Maru* 35 miles east of Kaiyo Island, 39°04′N, 123°06′E.

British submarine HMS *Thorough* sinks Japanese cargo ship *Nittei Maru* off west coast of Borneo, 06°45′S, 112°31′E.

British submarine HMS *Trenchant* sinks Japanese auxiliary minesweeper *Wa. 105* east of Mandalike Island, 06°23′S, 110°55′E.

Mines laid by USAAF B-29s (20th Air Force) sink Japanese cargo vessel *Hikawa Maru* at 33°58′N, 131°02′E, and merchant tanker *No. 3 Toyo Maru* 3.2 kilometers off He Saki, 33°55′N, 131°20′E. Mines also sink transport *Tobi Maru* northwest of Kyushu, 33°58′N, 130°52′E, cargo ship *Matsushima Maru* two miles south of Matsu Saki Island, and freighters *Shiragi Maru* near He Saki and *No. 1 Nissan Maru* off Mutsure. Mines damage destroyers *Sakura* seven kilometers off He Saki Light and *Tsubaki* off Shimonoseki; *Patrol Boat No. 104*, 5.4 kilometers off Futaoi; army cargo ships *Ginsei Maru* and *Ginzan Maru* three kilometers off Mutsure Island; freighters *No. 3 Shinto Maru* off He Saki and *Iyo Maru* east of the mouth of Kammon Channel; and merchant tanker *No. 4 Nanko Maru* 6.5 kilometers off He Saki.

USAAF planes sink Japanese freighter *Amoy Maru* off north coast of Tsushima, 34°46′N, 129°23′E.

Japanese merchant vessel *Kokei Maru* is sunk by aircraft off Pusan, Korea.

Japanese transport *Kamishima Maru* is damaged by stranding off north coast of Java, N.E.I., 06°25′S, 111°00′E.

26 Saturday

PACIFIC. Thirty USAAF B-29s (20th Air Force) mine Shimonoseki Straits and the waters off Fukuoka, Karatsu, and Fushiki, Japan. Mines sink auxiliary submarine chaser *Cha 172* at entrance to Fushiki Harbor, Honshu, 36°48'N, 137°05'E, and freighters *Mogi Maru* south of Hime Jima, 33°43'N, 131°38'E, *Shiokubi Maru* off Motoyama Saki, *No. 9 Kaishin Maru* at 34°00'N, 130°50'E, and *No. 6 Miyakawa Maru* 3.5 kilometers south of He Saki, 33°55'N, 131°02'E. Mines damage gunboat *Hirota Maru*, 34°18'N, 133°32'E; transport *Akeshima Maru* near Moji, 34°47'N, 131°35'E; transport *Inari Maru* off Motoyama Misaki; army cargo ships *Ginzan Maru* off Takenoko signal station and *Igasa Maru* 2.2 kilometers south of He Saki; and freighters *Kunugi Maru* outside Kobe Harbor, 34°39'N, 135°11'E, *Shozan Maru* off Tokuyama, Shimonoseki Strait, 33°57'N, 131°46'E, and *Mitsukisan Maru* at 33°52'N, 131°02'E.

Off Okinawa, *kamikazes* damage high-speed minesweeper *Forrest* (DMS 24), 26°00'N, 128°00'E, and submarine chaser *PC 1603*, 26°25'N, 127°53'E.

Submarine *Billfish* (SS 286) sinks Japanese freighter *No. 7 Kotobuki Maru* off Nagasaki, Japan, 33°19'N, 129°31'E.

Japanese guardboat *Kaishin Maru* is damaged by stranding at north end of Paramushir Island, Kurils.

27 Sunday

PACIFIC. Admiral William F. Halsey Jr., Commander Third Fleet, relieves Admiral Raymond A. Spruance, Commander Fifth Fleet, of operational control at Okinawa. TF 58 thus becomes TF 38, Vice Admiral John S. McCain relieving Vice Admiral Marc A. Mitscher.

Off Okinawa, two *kamikazes* damage destroyer *Braine* (DD 630), 26°25'N, 128°30'E. *Kamikazes* also damage destroyer *Anthony* (DD 515), 26°25'N, 128°30'E; high-speed minesweeper *Southard* (DMS 10), 26°00'N, 127°00'E; high-speed transports *Loy* (APD 56), 26°30'N, 127°30'E, and *Rednour* (APD 102), 26°29'N, 127°21'E; surveying ship *Dutton* (AGS 8), 26°15'N, 127°59'E; and submarine chaser *PCS 1396* and degaussing vessel *YDG 10*, 26°00'N, 128°00'E. Destroyer escort *Gilligan* (DE 508) is damaged by dud torpedo fired by *kaiten* from Japanese submarine *I 367*, 26°47'N, 127°47'E; minesweeper *Gayety* (AM 239) is damaged by near-miss of bomb, 26°00'N, 128°00'E; large support landing craft *LCS 52* is damaged by near-miss of *kamikaze*; and fleet tug *Pakana* (ATF 108) is damaged by strafing, 26°22'N, 127°44'E.

In the final minelaying operation of Phase III of Operation STARVATION, eleven USAAF B-29s (20th Air Force) mine Shimonoseki Straits and the waters off Moji, Japan. B-29–laid mines sink cargo vessels *Chizan Maru* off Wadano Misaki Light, 33°30'N, 130°30'E, and *Kongo Maru* in Shimonoseki Strait off Hakata, 33°41'N, 130°15'E, and merchant tanker *Hojo Maru* off south coast of Yoshimi Island, and damage freighter *Kifune Maru* 1.4 kilometers north of Niigata Light.

Submarine *Tench* (SS 417) sinks Japanese freighter *Kinei Maru* off Kushiro Light, 42°54'N, 144°18'E.

Submarine *Tigrone* (SS 419) sinks Japanese guardboat *No. 3 Yawata Maru* off Tori Jima, 29°24'N, 141°01'E.

Japanese auxiliary minesweeper *No. 3 Misago Maru* is sunk by U.S. aircraft at entrance to Ise Wan, Japan, 34°37'N, 137°19'E.

Japanese naval vessel *Shinho Maru* is sunk by aircraft off Sosa, Chiba prefecture.

Japanese freighter *No. 2 Daito Maru* is sunk by aircraft off Yosu, Korea.

Commanding General, Alaskan Department, requests Navy assistance in evacuating local citizens endangered as Yukon River floods (see 28 and 31 May).

EUROPE. U.S. freighter *John Woolman*, in convoy ATM 167, is damaged by mine 16 miles off Dunkirk, France; there are no fatalities among the ship's complement.

28 Monday

PACIFIC. Off Okinawa, *kamikazes* sink destroyer *Drexler* (DD 741), 27°06'N, 127°38'E, and damage attack transport *Sandoval* (APA 194), 26°15'N, 127°51'E, and large support landing craft *LCS(L) 119*. A suicider (reported as an ALF—a twin-float single-engine biplane) crashes and damages U.S. freighter *Mary A. Livermore* in Buckner Bay, 26°12'N, 127°46'E; the 27 Armed Guards and 75 Construction Battalion sailors on board contribute men to fire-fighting efforts (four Armed Guard sailors, as well as seven merchant seamen, die in the explosion and fires). Another *kamikaze* crashes and damages U.S. freighter *Brown Victory* off Ie Shima; two of the 27 Armed Guards are killed instantly, and 18 injured (one merchant sailor and an Armed Guard sailor die of their wounds later). Still another *kamikaze* crashes U.S. freighter *Josiah Snelling* off Okinawa; Armed Guard gunfire manages to deflect the plane from its suicidal course toward the amidships deckhouse and into a less vulnerable part, saving the ship from worse damage. There are no fatalities on board.

Submarines *Blueback* (SS 326) and *Lamprey* (SS 372) damage Japanese submarine chaser *Ch 1* in a surface gunnery action off Japara, N.E.I., 06°28'S, 110°37'E.

Submarine *Ray* (SS 271) sinks Japanese freighter Biko Maru northwest of Changshan, 38°21'N, 123°58'E.

USAAF B-29-laid mines sink Japanese transport *Akitsu Maru* south of Kure and damage *Coast Defense Vessel No. 29* off Kyushu, 33°07'N, 129°44'E; freighters *Mishimasan Maru* three kilometers off Tateishi Saki and *Annette Fritzen Go* at 33°53'N, 130°05'E; and fishing boat *No. 3 Genei Maru* outside Sasebo Bay.

Commander, Kodiak Sector, Alaskan Sea Frontier, dispatches four PBYs (three from FAW 1 and one from NAS Kodiak) to Fairbanks, via Anchorage, Alaska, to provide assistance in evacuating citizens threatened by rising Yukon River floodwaters (see 31 May).

29 Tuesday

PACIFIC. Off Okinawa, *kamikazes* crash destroyer *Shubrick* (DD 639), 26°38'N, 127°05'E, and high-speed transport *Tatum* (APD 81), 26°40'N, 127°50'E; groundings account for damage to motor minesweeper *YMS 81*, 26°16'N, 127°52'E, and tank landing ship *LST 844*, 26°17'N, 127°51'E.

Mine laid by USAAF B-29 (20th Air Force) sinks Japanese cargo vessel *Umatsu Maru* off Mutsure Jima, 34°00'N, 130°50'E, and damages army cargo ship *No. 6 Unyo Maru* 3.6 miles off He Saki Light, 31°41'N, 129°45'E, and freighter *No. 5 Nissen Maru* off Mutsure Jima.

Japanese freighter *Etsunan Maru* is sunk by RAF-laid mine at 10°30'N, 99°24'E; later that day, submarine *Hawkbill* (SS 366) torpedoes *Kamiyama Maru* as she picks up *Etsunan Maru* survivors and forces the rescuing ship to take refuge at Cape Khokwang.

Submarine *Sterlet* (SS 392), despite proximity of escorting *Coast Defense Ship No. 65*, sinks Japanese army cargo ships *Kuretake Maru* and *Tenryo Maru*, 46°46'N, 144°16'E.

30 Wednesday

PACIFIC. TBM (VC 82) from escort carrier *Anzio* (CVE 57) sinks Japanese submarine *I 361*, 400 miles southeast of Okinawa, 22°22'N, 134°09'E.

Submarine *Blenny* (SS 324) sinks Japanese cargo ship *Hokoku Maru* 40 miles southwest of Banjarmasin, Borneo, 04°09'S, 114°16'E.

Submarine *Croaker* (SS 246), despite proximity of escorting auxiliary submarine chaser *Kenkai Maru*, sinks *No. 154 Shuttle Boat* and *No. 146 Shuttle Boat* at 04°50'S, 113°10'E.

Mines laid by USAAF B-29s (20th Air Force) sink Japanese transport *Hakun Maru* off Hakata, Japan, 33°36′N, 130°25′E, and freighters *Fujitama Maru* off Wadano Misaki Light, 34°30′N, 135°11′E, *Kasumi Maru* 0.8 kilometers off Miji Saki, and *No. 14 Takasago Maru* northwest of Tadotsu, 35°15′N, 133°44′E. Mines damage army cargo ships *Hyuga Maru* 3.6 kilometers south-southeast of Genka Jima and *Shinno Maru* at mouth of Tsuruga Bay.

31 Thursday

PACIFIC. Mines laid by USAAF B-29s (20th Air Force) sink Japanese cargo ship *Man Maru* off He Saki Light, and damage gunboat *Kazan Maru* off Genka Jima, 33°40′N, 129°57′E; army cargo ships *No. 2 Yoro Maru* southeast of He Saki and *Peking Maru* off Onna Jima; and freighter *Jindai Maru* northwest of Mutsure Jima. USAAF B-29–laid mine damages transport *Tensho Maru* at 34°35′N, 135°15′E, but *Tensho Maru* sinks after being towed into Osaka Harbor.

Four PBYs (three from FAW 1 and one from NAS Kodiak) dispatched to Fairbanks, via Anchorage, by Commander Kodiak Sector, Alaskan Sea Frontier, return to Kodiak, their mission of providing assistance in evacuating citizenry threatened by rising Yukon River floodwaters having been completed.

U.S. freighter *American Star* and Soviet freighter *Uzbekistan* are damaged in collision off Dutch Harbor, Alaska; big harbor tug *YTB 191* provides assistance.

JUNE

1 Friday

PACIFIC. USAAF B-29s (458 strong) bomb Osaka; in the course of the raid on that Japanese port city, the B-29s damage army cargo ships *Yamazono Maru* and *Shinwao Maru*, army tankers *Shunsho Maru* and *Eijun Maru*, freighters *No. 2 Kimagayo Maru*, *Daito Maru*, *Hokuju Maru*, *Denshin Maru*, *Biyo Maru*, *Tonegawa Maru*, and merchant tankers *Oyama Maru* and *Encho Maru*.

Mines laid by USAAF B-29s (20th Air Force) sink Japanese army cargo ship *Seishu Maru*, off Shodo Jima; freighters *Abukamagawa Maru* 34°34′N, 134°14′E, and *No. 7 Kenkon Maru* and *Meitei Maru* off Shimonoseki, 34°58′N, 130°56′E; merchant tanker *Yoko Maru*, 34°30′N, 135°15′E; and freighter *Myosei Maru* in Shimonoseki Strait, 33°58′N, 131°03′E. Mines also damage freighters *Kishun Maru* north by east of Moji Saki Light, *Goko Maru* northwest

of Wakamatsu, 33°58′N, 130°41′E, *Unten Maru* west of Seto, Inland Sea, and *Shinano Maru* outside Fushiki Harbor, and cargo vessels *Shinju Maru* 35°42′N, 136°04′E, and *No. 1 Toyo Maru* at entrance of Shimonoseki Strait, 33°57′N, 130°40′E.

Submarine chaser *PC 1599* is damaged by grounding off Hagushi, Okinawa, 26°25′N, 127°43′E. Infantry landing craft (gunboat) *LCI(G) 565* goes aground near Naha (see 2 June).

British submarine HMS *Tiptoe* sinks Japanese cargo ship *Tobi Maru* off Matasiri Island, 04°40′S, 115°32′E.

Naval Air Facility, Peleliu Island, Palaus, is established.

Naval Air Base, Tarawa, is disestablished.

EUROPE. Naval Advanced Base, Bremerhaven, Germany, is established.

2 Saturday

PACIFIC. TF 38 (Vice Admiral John S. McCain) bombs airfields in southern Kyushu, Japan; attacks are repeated on 3 June.

Submarine *Tench* (SS 417) sinks Japanese freighter *Mikamasan Maru* southeast of Shiriya Saki, 41°22′N, 141°28′E.

Infantry landing craft (gunboat) *LCI(G) 565*, grounded the previous day, is refloated by salvage landing craft *LCI(L) 738* off Naha, Okinawa.

Mines laid by USAAF B-29s (20th Air Force) damage Japanese cargo ships *Nissho Maru* two kilometers north of Tateishi Saki, *No. 3 Yubari Maru* west of the mouth of Kammon Strait, *Kashima Maru* at 33°58′N, 130°42′E, *Katsura Maru* between Yoshi Jima and Sanakai Jima, and *No. 1 Toyo Maru* at entrance of Shimonoseki Strait, 33°48′N, 130°42′E.

Japanese cargo vessel *Kojin Maru* is sunk, cause unspecified, near Rabaul, New Britain.

Army coastal cargo vessel *FS 34* reports to District Coast Guard Officer, Ketchikan, Alaska, for temporary duty. *FS 34* will operate out of Dutch Harbor under the Coast Guard for a four-month period, transporting construction materials, fuel, supplies, and workers to expedite the building of direction finder stations on the islands of St. Paul, Unimak, and St. George.

3 Sunday

PACIFIC. TG 31.25 (Rear Admiral Lawrence F. Reifsnider) lands a reinforced RCT (Second Marine Division) on Iheya Shima, Ryukyus.

Off Okinawa, *kamikazes* damage cargo ship *Allegan* (AK 225), 26°00′N, 128°00′E, and large infantry landing craft *LCI(L) 90*.

Submarine *Blueback* (SS 326) sinks unnamed Japanese merchant fishing boat, 05°39′S, 106°47′E.

Submarine *Segundo* (SS 398) sinks Japanese merchantman *No. 94 Anto Maru* off Jinsen, Korea, 36°41′N, 125°23′E.

Mines laid by USAAF B-29s (20th Air Force) sink Japanese naval vessel *No. 15 Hakutetsu Maru* in Inland Sea; army cargo ship *Taiei Maru*, 3.7 kilometers off Motoyama Light, 38°56′N, 137°05′E; and freighters *Osara Maru* off Motoyama Bay, *Konei Maru* outside Karatsu Harbor, 33°33′N, 129°58′E, and *Momo Maru* at 34°35′N, 134°15′E. Mines also damage minelayer *Tokiwa* two kilometers off Bakuchi Saki and freighter *Erimo Maru* off Hime Jima Light, 33°47′N, 131°14′E.

Japanese ship *No. 6 Tankai Maru* is sunk by aircraft, Hitakata, Ibaraki prefecture.

Japanese freighter *Anri Maru* is damaged by aircraft, 34°57′N, 129°13′E.

Japanese freighter *Anjo Maru* is damaged by aircraft off Pusan, Korea.

Destroyer *Porter* (DD 800), operating with TF 92, is damaged in collision with U.S. Army cable ship *Silverado*, the latter being convoyed by escort vessel *PCE 893*, off Kuluk Bay, Adak, Alaska, in "extremely poor" visibility conditions.

4 Monday

EUROPE. U.S. freighter *Colin P. Kelly, Jr.*, bound for Antwerp, Belgium, in convoy TAM 89, is damaged by mine off the Downs, 51°22′48″N, 02°35′E; there are no fatalities among the ship's complement (which includes a 37-man Armed Guard), but the ship is later written off as a total loss.

BLACK SEA. U.S. freighter *New Bern Victory*, en route to Constanta, Romania, is damaged by mine six miles off Odessa, USSR; there are no casualties to the ship's complement and the ship is later repaired and returns to active service.

PACIFIC. District patrol vessel *YP 41* is damaged by operational casualty off Okinawa, 26°18′N, 127°52′E.

Submarine *Billfish* (SS 286) sinks Japanese freighter *Taiu Maru* off Chinnampo, Korea, 38°32′N, 124°45′E.

Submarine *Tench* (SS 417) sinks Japanese transport *Ryujin Maru* off Hachinohe, 40°54′N, 141°29′E.

USAAF B-24s (Far East Air Force) sink Japanese auxiliary submarine chaser *Cha 112* and motor torpedo boat *Gyoraitei No. 162* and damage auxiliary submarine chaser *Kenkai*

Fletcher (DD 445)–class destroyer nearly disappears from view in the typhoon encountered by TF 38, 5 June 1945. (Author's Collection)

Maru in Java Sea off Laut Island, 05°00′S, 116°04′E.

Mines sink Japanese weather observation ship *Hijun Maru* 5.5 miles off He Saki, 33°54′N, 131°06′E; cargo ships *Aichi Maru* (location unspecified) and *Hinode Maru* off Moji; *No. 2 Shiwa Maru* off Taishu Light; unidentified tugboat off south end of Motoyama Saki; and freighters *Kifune Maru* off Niigata and *No. 5 Yamabishi Maru* at 33°44′N, 131°06′E. Mines damage transport *Tsukushi Maru* at 33°50′N, 131°19′E, and freighters *Sawa Maru* two kilometers off Mutsure, 33°54′N, 130°54′E, and *Chikushi Maru* off Motoyama Bay.

Japanese tanker *Hasu Maru* is damaged by mine in Berhala Straits, between Sumatra and Lingga. N.E.I., anchorage.

Japanese freighter *No. 5 Miyakawa Maru* is sunk by marine casualty off Hirado Jima, near Kyushu, Japan.

USAAF planes sink Japanese freighter *Shobu Maru* at 34°20′N, 124°30′E.

Japanese cargo ship *Banshu Maru* is damaged by aircraft, 34°27′N, 129°35′E.

Japanese freighter *No. 1 Taikai Maru* is damaged by aircraft, 31°18′N, 129°24′E.

5 Tuesday

PACIFIC. TF 38 battles typhoon off Okinawa. The storm damages battleships *Indiana* (BB 58), *Massachusetts* (BB 59), *Alabama* (BB 60), and *Missouri* (BB 63); carriers *Hornet* (CV 12) and *Bennington* (CV 20); small carriers *Belleau*

Wood (CVL 24) and *San Jacinto* (CVL 30); escort carriers *Windham Bay* (CVE 92), *Salamaua* (CVE 96), *Bougainville* (CVE 100), and *Attu* (CVE 102); heavy cruisers *Baltimore* (CA 68), *Quincy* (CA 71), and *Pittsburgh* (CA 72); light cruisers *Detroit* (CL 8), *San Juan* (CL 54), *Duluth* (CL 87), and *Atlanta* (CL 104); destroyers *Schroeder* (DD 501), *John Rodgers* (DD 574), *McKee* (DD 575), *Dashiell* (DD 659), *Stockham* (DD 683), *De Haven* (DD 727), *Maddox* (DD 731), *Blue* (DD 744), *Brush* (DD 745), *Taussig* (DD 746), and *Samuel N. Moore* (DD 747); destroyer escorts *Donaldson* (DE 44), *Conklin* (DE 439), and *Hilbert* (DE 742); oilers *Lackawanna* (AO 40) and *Millicoma* (AO 73); and ammunition ship *Shasta* (AE 6).

Off Okinawa, *kamikazes* damage battleship *Mississippi* (BB 41), 26°09′N, 127°35′E, and heavy cruiser *Louisville* (CA 28), 26°07′N, 127°52′E.

Destroyer *Dyson* (DD 572) is damaged when she is accidentally rammed by destroyer escort *Abercrombie* (DE 343) at Kerama Retto, Okinawa, 26°09′N, 127°49′E. Tank landing ship *LST 540* is damaged by operational casualty off Okinawa.

Destroyer escort *French* (DE 367), on antisubmarine screening duties off Peleliu, bombards Malakal and Arakabesan Islands, Palaus.

Minesweeper *Scuffle* (AM 298) is damaged by grounding in Brunei Bay, 08°01′N, 117°13′E.

Gasoline tanker *Sheepscot* (AOG 24) is damaged by grounding off Iwo Jima, 24°46′N, 141°18′E.

Japanese auxiliary submarine chaser *Cha 230* is sunk in collision with army transport *Azusa Maru* one mile south of Sop Do Light, Korea, 34°00′N, 127°18′E. *Azusa Maru* is damaged in the collision.

Japanese guardboat *No. 13 Kintoku Maru* is sunk by U.S. aircraft off Fujinamiohama, Japan.

Mines sink Japanese cargo ship *No. 5 Yawata Maru* off Tsunemi, Moji, and freighter *Taisho Maru* two kilometers off Mutsure Island, 33°54′N, 130°54′E; mines damage destroyer *Yoizuki* 5.8 kilometers northwest of Hime Jima Light, escort destroyer *Shii* in Bungo Straits, army cargo ship *Toyo Maru* near Aohama, freighter *Annette Fritzen Go* off Asa Jima, Fusan, 33°56′N, 131°03′E, and cargo vessel *Toyo Maru* off Shimonoseki, 33°57′N, 131°02′E.

Japanese fast transport *T.9* is damaged by aircraft, north of Chichi Jima, Bonins.

Japanese army cargo ship *Taiko Maru* is damaged by marine casualty off Kannon Saki, Sakishima Gunto.

Japanese freighter *No. 2 Nansei Maru* is damaged by marine casualty, near Moji.

6 Wednesday

PACIFIC. Off Okinawa, minesweepers *Requisite* (AM 109) and *Spear* (AM 322) are damaged in collision, 26°00′N, 127°00′E; light minelayers *Harry F. Bauer* (DM 26) and *J. William Ditter* (DM 31) are damaged by *kamikazes*, 26°14′N, 128°01′E; and landing craft flotilla flagship *LC(FF) 995* is damaged by operational casualty.

Mines sink Japanese auxiliary submarine chaser *Cha 195*, Nanao Bay, Honshu, Japan, 37°10′N, 137°05′E; guardboat *No. 5 Yawata Maru* off Tsurumi; freighter *Gassan Maru* off Moji, 34°00′N, 130°50′E; destroyer *Kaki* off Kominase, 33°46′N, 130°24′E; escort destroyer *Habuto* 1.3 kilometers north of Kannon Saki Light; and cargo ship *No. 18 Tamon Maru* off He Saki Light.

Japanese army cargo ship *No. 20 Hokko Maru* is damaged by marine casualty off east coast of Aomori prefecture.

Auxiliary submarine chaser *Cha 251* (ex-submarine chaser *Ch 51*) is damaged by aircraft, three miles off Aka Shima, near southwestern Kyushu.

UNITED STATES. Naval Academy Class of 1946 graduates one year early because of the national emergency.

7 Thursday

PACIFIC. Phase IV of Operation STARVATION, an intensified blockade of northwestern Honshu and Kyushu, begins as 26 USAAF B-29s mine Shimonoseki Straits and the waters off Fukuoka, Japan.

TG 74.3 (Rear Admiral Russell S. Berkey), composed of three U.S. light cruisers, one Australian light cruiser, and seven destroyers (six U.S. and one Australian), provides close cover and fire support for minesweepers and underwater demolition teams off Brunei Bay, Borneo.

Carrier Randolph (CV 15) is damaged when accidentally crashed by stunting USAAF P-38, Leyte, P.I.

Off Okinawa, kamikazes damage escort carrier Natoma Bay (CVE 62), 24°46'N, 126°37'E, and destroyer Anthony (DD 515), 27°07'N, 127°38'E; operational casualties account for damage to medium landing ship LSM 270, landing craft flotilla flagship LC(FF) 988, and tank landing craft LCT 1054. Tank landing ship LST 540 is damaged by grounding, 26°21'N, 127°45'E; destroyer Beale (DD 471) is damaged in collision with gasoline tanker Yahara (AOG 37) at Kerama Retto, 26°10'N, 127°20'E.

Submarine Blueback (SS 326), operating off Djakarta (formerly Batavia), Java, reports sortie of Japanese heavy cruiser Ashigara (with 1,600 troops embarked) and destroyer Kamikaze for Singapore (see 8 June).

Submarine Shad (SS 235) sinks Japanese army transport Azusa Maru and tanker No. 22 Nanshin Maru 50 miles southwest of Yoso Do, Korea, 33°55'N, 126°50'E.

Submarine Tench (SS 417) sinks Japanese guardboat Hanshin Maru in Sea of Japan, 42°41'N, 143°53'E.

Japanese auxiliary submarine chaser No. 43 Hino Maru is sunk by aircraft off Hirado Jima, Miyanoura.

Mines sink Japanese auxiliary minelayer Hakun Maru near Hong Kong and freighter No. 2 Yubari Maru west of the mouth of Kammon Strait, and damage freighter Taigen Maru outside Fushiki Harbor, Japan.

8 Friday

PACIFIC. TF 38 (Vice Admiral John S. McCain) planes attack Kanoya airfield, Kyushu, Japan.

TG 74.3 (Rear Admiral Russell S. Berkey) bombards Japanese positions in preparation for the landings at Brunei Bay, covering the reconnaissance parties ashore; bombardment is repeated on 9 June. TG 74.2 (Rear Admiral Ralph S. Riggs) operates as distant cover for the operation (see 11 June). During sweeping operations in Brunei Bay, minesweeper Salute (AM 294) is sunk by mine, 05°08'N, 115°05'E.

As fighting continues on Okinawa, Hospital Apprentice First Class Fred F. Lester, serving with a rifle platoon, sees a wounded marine beyond the front lines. As he advances under heavy fire, Lester is hit and severely wounded. He attempts unaided to drag the wounded marine to safety, but is hit again. Although paralyzed on his right side, Lester succeeds in dragging the marine to cover. Realizing he has been mortally wounded, the corpsman, spurning medical attention for himself, directs marines to treat the casualty he had brought to safety, thus saving that man's life. Lester devotes his last efforts to directing the treatment of two other wounded marines before he dies. For his courage "above and beyond the call of duty," Lester is awarded the Medal of Honor posthumously.

British submarines HMS Stygian and HMS Trenchant, under the operational control of Commander Submarines Seventh Fleet, patrol northern entrance of Bangka Strait, N.E.I., having been informed of the departure of Japanese heavy cruiser Ashigara and destroyer Kamikaze from Batavia the day before. Kamikaze detects Trenchant, which summons Stygian to help. Stygian's attack on Kamikaze is unsuccessful; the destroyer counterattacks with depth charges and damages the British boat. Ashigara, assuming that only one Allied submarine has been involved (and that disposed of by Kamikaze), sets a straight course through northern Bangka Strait. HMS Trenchant, however, sinks Ashigara 14 nautical miles west-southwest of Muntok, 01°59'S, 104°56'E. Kamikaze rescues survivors; nearly three-quarters of the 1,600 troops embarked at Batavia, however, have gone down with the ship.

Submarine Cobia (SS 245) sinks Japanese transport Hakusa Maru and tanker No. 22 Nanshin Maru off French Indochina, 08°56'N, 105°37'E.

Japanese submarine tender Chogei is damaged by mine 1.6 kilometers southwest of Bakuchi Saki, Nansei Shoto.

Japanese freighter Ojima Maru is damaged by aircraft between Ainoura, Japan, 33°12'N, 129°39'E, and Taino Saki.

USAAF B-24s bomb Japanese shipping near Banjarmasin, Borneo, sinking Shuttle Boat No. 466 and damaging Shuttle Boat No. 423 near mouth of Barita River.

9 Saturday

PACIFIC. TG 31.25 (Rear Admiral Lawrence F. Reifsnider) lands a reinforced RCT (Second Marine Division) on Aguni Shima, Ryukyus.

TG 38.4 (Rear Admiral Arthur W. Radford) strikes Japanese installations on Okino Daito Shima, Ryukyus.

Twenty-seven USAAF B-29s mine Shimonoseki Straits.

Submarine Sea Owl (SS 405) sinks Japanese Coast Defense Vessel No. 41 in Tsushima Strait, southeast of Mokp'o, Korea, 34°22'N, 128°11'E.

Coordinated submarine attack group (Commander Earl T. Hydeman), consisting of three individual units of three boats apiece, commences operations in the Sea of Japan. TG 17.21 (Commander Hydeman) begins offensive operations off northwest coast of Honshu; Crevalle (SS 291) sinks Japanese freighter Hokuto Maru in western approaches to Tsugaru Strait, 40°54'N, 139°48'E, and Sea Dog (SS 401) (flagship for TG 17.21) sinks freighters Sagawa Maru and Shoyo Maru, 38°10'N, 138°20'E. TG 17.23 (Commander Robert D. Risser) commences offensive operations off east coast of Korea; Tinosa (SS 283) sinks freighter Wakatama Maru 37°32'N, 129°10'E.

Submarine Tench (SS 417) sinks Japanese transport Kamishika Maru off southern Hokkaido, 41°49'N, 141°11'E.

Mines laid by USAAF B-29s (20th Air Force) sink Japanese freighters No. 35 Banshu Maru, 36°19'N, 136°12'E, and Inaura Maru, 0.7 kilometers off Takase Light, 34°00'N, 131°00'E.

PB4Ys or PBMs sink Japanese freighter No. 5 Kaishin Maru at 37°05'N, 129°08'E.

USAAF B-24s bomb Japanese shipping off Banjarmasin, Borneo, sinking cargo vessel Koryu Maru, No. 423 Shuttle Boat, and No. 444 Shuttle Boat and damaging cargo vessel No. 8 Nippo Maru.

10 Sunday

PACIFIC. Operation OBOE SIX: TG 78.1 (Rear Admiral Forrest B. Royal) lands two brigades of the 9th Australian Division (Reinforced) at Brunei Bay, Borneo. TG 74.3 (Rear Admiral Russell S. Berkey) (three U.S. light cruisers, Australian light cruiser HMAS Hobart, six U.S. destroyers, and HMAS Arunta) carries out heavy pre-landing bombardment. USAAF Far East Air Force (13th Air Force) and RAAF 1st Tactical Air Force provide air cover.

TG 38.1 (Rear Admiral Joseph J. Clark) bombs and bombards enemy airfield and other installations on Minami Daito Shima, Ryukyus.

Off Okinawa, destroyer escort *Gendreau* (DE 639) is damaged by shore battery, 26°03′N, 127°12′E. Destroyer *William D. Porter* (DD 579) is sunk by *kamikaze*, 27°06′N, 127°38′E; despite the fires and exploding ammunition, Lieutenant Richard M. McCool Jr. unhesitatingly places his ship, large support landing craft *LCS(L) 122,* alongside the sinking warship to take off her survivors (see 11 June).

TG 17.21 (Commander Earl T. Hydeman), submarine attack group, operates against Japanese shipping. *Crevalle* (SS 291) sinks army cargo ship *Daiki Maru* in western approaches to Tsugaru Strait, 40°44′N, 139°48′E; *Spadefish* (SS 411) sinks freighter *No. 2 Taigen Maru* off Otaru, 43°23′N, 140°39′E, transport *No. 8 Unkai Maru* off Shakotan Misaki, 43°55′N, 141°13′E, and cargo ship *Jintsu Maru,* 43°28′N, 140°28′E. TG 17.22 (Commander George E. Pierce) operates off southern coast of Honshu; *Skate* (SS 305) sinks submarine *I 122* in Sea of Japan, six miles off Rokugo Saki, 37°30′N, 137°24′E. TG 17.23 (Commander Robert D. Risser) operates off east coast of Korea; *Flying Fish* (SS 229) sinks army cargo ship *Taga Maru* off Seishin, 41°42′N, 129°34′E.

Submarine *Dace* (SS 247) attacks Japanese convoy, sinking freighter *Hakuyo Maru* in Sea of Okhotsk, about 120 miles west of Shimushu Island, 47°21′N, 149°07′E.

Submarine *Tench* (SS 417) sinks Japanese merchant tanker *No. 6 Shoei Maru,* 41°15′N, 141°31′E.

PB4Y-2s (VPB 118), flying from Okinawa, commence mining waters of the Korean Archipelago. The intent is to drive Japanese shipping, forced by the work of PB4Ys and PBMs to carry out nocturnal operations (sheltering by day in small protected anchorages), out into the open sea to facilitate mast-head attacks. The mines thus planted could sink undiverted shipping and place an additional burden on the already overtaxed Japanese minesweeping force. On this initial mission, the first aerial mining using Privateers, however, the PB4Ys encounter intense antiaircraft fire from Japanese warships in Tsushima Strait during the run-in to the objective, Pusan Harbor. The PB4Ys mine the waters along the Korean coast between Shinchi Do and Seigan Do instead (see 11 June–1 July).

Japanese auxiliary submarine chaser *Cha 63* is sunk in collision west of Mokp'o, Korea, 34°50′N, 126°10′E.

Mines damage Japanese escort destroyer *Habuto* 2.6 kilometers north of Kannon Saki, Sakishima Gunto, and guardboat *Choei Maru* off Shinminato.

PB4Ys (VB 102) sink Japanese merchant tanker *Tado Maru* off west coast of Korea, 36°00′N, 125°00′E.

ATLANTIC. Brazilian freighter *Ayuruoca* and Norwegian freighter *General Fleischer* collide near Buoy "E," New York Channel; submarine chaser *SC 1057* and Coast Guard cutter *Icarus* (WPC 110) are diverted to the scene, and rescue tug *ATR 57* is dispatched from New York. *SC 1057* takes off 65 men from *Ayuruoca*; the Brazilian merchantman sinks soon thereafter.

11 Monday

PACIFIC. Off Okinawa, Japanese air attacks continue against ships on radar picket stations; large support landing craft *LCS(L) 122* is damaged when *kamikaze* crashes near her conning tower. Her commanding officer, Lieutenant Richard M. McCool Jr., although wounded at the outset, releases men trapped in a burning compartment, suffering further injuries in so doing. For courageously saving the lives of his men and inspiring his crew to save their ship, in addition to his actions the previous day in rescuing survivors of destroyer *William D. Porter* (DD 579), McCool is awarded the Medal of Honor.

Elsewhere off Okinawa, a *kamikaze* crashes alongside U.S. freighter *Walter Colton;* the ship receives additional damage from friendly fire of nearby ships in the anchorage. Of the combined complement of 41 merchant sailors, 29 Armed Guards, and 11 Construction Battalion men, only three men suffer injuries. Dock landing ship *Lindenwald* (LSD 6) is also damaged by friendly fire, 26°17′N, 127°53′E. Infantry landing craft (gunboat) *LCI(G) 567,* investigating a radar echo close to the reefs off Naha, finds the contact to be a lone swimmer, the sole survivor of a boat that had capsized seeking to escape from Itoman, Okinawa. *LCI(G) 567* chases the swimmer, shoots over his head, and throws life rings at him for 30 minutes, finally convincing him to come on board as a POW.

Elimination of Japanese heavy cruiser *Ashigara* (sunk on 8 June by British submarine HMS *Trenchant*) as a possible threat to the unfolding operations at Brunei Bay, Borneo, coupled with the fact that the landings have taken place on schedule against light opposition, results in the release of TG 74.2 (Rear Admiral Ralph S. Riggs) from its distant cover assignment.

TF 92 (Rear Admiral John H. Brown Jr.), consisting of light cruisers *Richmond* (CL 9) and *Trenton* (CL 11) and five destroyers, bombards Japanese installations on Matsuwa, Kurils.

Twenty-six USAAF B-29s mine Shimonoseki Straits and the waters off Tsuruga, Japan. Japanese freighter *Hiwaka Maru* is sunk by mine, 34°44′N, 125°52′E.

Okinawa-based PB4Y-2s (VPB 118) fly second aerial mining mission into the Korean Archipelago, but fog, blanketing the objective, compels the Privateers to jettison their ordnance en route back to base.

Coordinated submarine attack group (Commander Earl T. Hydeman) continues operations against Japanese shipping. TG 17.21 (Commander Hydeman) operates off northwest coast of Honshu; *Crevalle* (SS 291) sinks gunboat *No. 5 Hakusan Maru* off Henashi Saki, 40°43′N, 139°51′E, and *Sea Dog* (SS 401) sinks freighter *Kofuku Maru,* 40°28′N, 139°47′E. TG 17.23 (Commander Robert E. Risser) operates off east coast of Korea; *Bowfin* (SS 287) sinks freighter *No. 3 Shinyo Maru* off Genzan, 39°24′N, 128°59′E; and *Flying Fish* (SS 229) sinks cargo ship *Meisei Maru* off Rashin, 41°47′N, 131°44′E.

Submarine *Segundo* (SS 398) sinks Japanese freighter *No. 2 Fukui Maru* in the Yellow Sea off the Shantung Peninsula, 37°11′N, 123°23′E.

Submarine *Tirante* (SS 420) enters Ha Jima Harbor and sinks Japanese freighter *Hakuju Maru,* southern Kyushu, 42°37′N, 129°45′E.

PB4Y-2 sinks Japanese auxiliary submarine chaser *Cha 237* at entrance to Ise Bay, 34°30′N, 137°06′E; the explosion of the enemy patrol vessel, however, heavily damages the attacking Privateer.

Japanese guardboat *No. 5 Nichiei Maru* is sunk by U.S. aircraft southwest of Paramushir, Kurils, 50°00′N, 155°00′E.

Japanese cargo ship *Kimi Maru* is sunk by aircraft off west coast of Aomori prefecture.

12 Tuesday

PACIFIC. Off Okinawa, light cruiser *Vicksburg* (CL 86) is damaged when own shell bursts as it leaves muzzle, 26°10′N, 127°20′E.

Coordinated submarine attack group (Commander Earl T. Hydeman) continues operations against Japanese shipping. TG 17.21 (Commander Hydeman) operates off northwest coast of Honshu and Hokkaido; *Sea Dog* (SS 401) sinks freighters *Shinsen Maru* and *Kaiwa Maru* off Nyudo Saki, 40°11′N, 139°46′E, and *Spadefish* (SS 411) sinks guardboat *Daido Maru* west of Wakkanai, Hokkaido, 45°08′N, 141°10′E. From TG 17.22 (Commander George E. Pierce), operating off the southern coast of Honshu, *Skate* (SS 305) sinks freighters *Yozan*

Maru, Kenjo Maru, and *Zuiko Maru* and damages *Kankyo Maru* in Togi Harbor, 37°08′N, 136°42′E. From TG 17.23 (Commander Robert D. Risser), operating off east coast of Korea, *Tinosa* (SS 283) sinks freighter *Keito Maru* off Kyoga'ri, 37°30′N, 129°20′E.

Japanese submarine chaser *Ch 57* and passenger ferry *No. 2 Kuroshio* (ex-landing ship *T.149*) are sunk by British destroyers HMS *Tartar,* HMS *Eskimo,* and HMS *Nubian* (10th Destroyer Flotilla), 20 miles north of Sabang, Sumatra, 06°20′N, 94°45′E, as the enemy is engaged in withdrawing his troops from the Andamans.

Japanese auxiliary submarine chaser *Myoken Maru* is sunk by aircraft, Atsuta dockyard, 43°25′N, 142°24′E.

Okinawa-based PB4Y-2s (VPB 118), using radar, mine the waters off Chin Do, Korean Archipelago. The same waters are mined again the following day.

Mines laid by USAAF B-29s sink Japanese army cargo ship *Aizan Maru* in Hakata Bay, 33°38′N, 130°22′E; freighters *Sagami Maru,* 25 miles off Kabura Saki, and *Fumitsuki Maru* off Shirasu, 33°57′N, 130°44′E; and liaison ship *Shimonoseki Maru* at 36°30′N, 130°19′E. Mines damage army tanker *Yamadono Maru* 2.5 kilometers off Manabe Island.

13 Wednesday

PACIFIC. Large infantry landing craft *LCI(L) 871,* on routine patrol along the east coast of Urukthapel Island, Palaus, engages Japanese artillery and mortar batteries.

APDs land Fleet Marine Force Reconnaissance Battalion on Kume Shima, in rubber boats. The marines find the island, located 50 miles west of Okinawa, virtually undefended contrary to earlier intelligence estimates (see 26 June).

Twenty-nine USAAF B-29s (20th Air Force) mine Shimonoseki Straits and the waters off Niigata, Japan. Mines laid in these and previous plants by B-29s sink freighters *Matsuo Maru* 3.4 kilometers south of Motoyama; *Hiyoshi Maru* and *No. 8 Nissho Maru* off He Saki, 33°54′N, 131°07′E; and *Koryu Maru* off He Saki, 33°55′N, 131°07′E. Mines damage escort destroyer *Io* 1.7 kilometers southeast of Kannon Saki and freighters *Kinyo Maru,* Kyoken Saki, Kammon Strait; *Kannon Maru* (unspecified location); *Hakujitsu Maru* at 33°37′N, 130°44′E; *Takakurasan Maru* at 37°07′N, 137°03′E; and *No. 2 Kofuku Maru,* 37°07′N, 137°03′E.

Off Okinawa, battleship *Idaho* (BB 42) is damaged by grounding, 26°14′N, 127°57′E.

Submarine *Bergall* (SS 320) is damaged by mine (U.S. or British proximity-fused) in Gulf of Siam, 11°45′N, 99°50′E, and is forced to terminate her patrol.

Coordinated submarine attack group (Commander Earl T. Hydeman) continues operations against Japanese shipping. TG 17.21 (Commander Hydeman) operates off northwest coast of Honshu and Hokkaido; *Spadefish* (SS 411) mistakenly sinks Soviet cargo ship *Transbalt* west by north of Le Pérouse Strait, 45°44′N, 140°48′E. From TG 17.22 (Commander George E. Pierce), *Bonefish* (SS 223) sinks cargo ship *Oshikasan Maru* northwest of Suzu Misaki, Honshu, 38°30′N, 136°58′E, and *Skate* (SS 305) sinks freighter *Hattenzan Maru,* 37°20′N, 134°28′E.

Submarine *Bowfin* (SS 287) sinks Japanese freighter *Meiho Maru* in Sea of Japan off Kojo, Korea, 39°00′N, 128°05′E.

PBMs (FAW 1), on sweep against Japanese shipping off southwestern Korea coast, sink freighter *Kaisho Maru* off Mokp'o, 35°49′N, 126°23′E.

Mines laid by USAAF B-24s (14th Air Force) sink Japanese freighter *Koun Maru* off Macao, 23°30′N, 113°30′E.

14 Thursday

PACIFIC. British TG 111.2 (Rear Admiral Eric J. P. Brind, RN), composed of fleet carrier HMS *Implacable,* escort carrier HMS *Ruler,* four light cruisers, and five destroyers, attacks Truk Atoll to neutralize Japanese air bases there (see 15 June).

Motor gunboat *PGM 24* is damaged when accidentally rammed by light minelayer *Thomas E. Fraser* (DM 24) off Okinawa, 25°30′N, 126°00′E.

Submarine *Sea Devil* (SS 400), despite presence of two escorts, sinks Japanese transport *Wakamiyasan Maru* in the northern Yellow Sea, 37°35′N, 123°30′E.

Coordinated submarine attack group (Commander Earl T. Hydeman) continues operations against Japanese shipping. From TG 17.21, *Spadefish* (SS 411) sinks freighter *Seizan Maru* off western Sakhalin, 47°03′N, 142°01′E.

PB4Y-2s (VPB 118), flying from Okinawa, mine waters between Gyuji Do, Toso Do, and Jobai Do, Korean Archipelago, encountering antiaircraft fire from nearby anchored shipping. The same waters are mined each day over the next three days, but the Privateers encounter no further antiaircraft fire on those occasions.

Mine laid by USAAF B-29s sinks Japanese army cargo ship *No. 18 Umajima Maru* at

33°39′N, 130°15′E.

PB4Y bombs Japanese shipping off Banjarmasin, Borneo, sinking *No. 470 Shuttle Vessel.*

BLACK SEA. U.S. freighter *Attleboro Victory,* en route to Constanta, Romania, is damaged by mine in the Black Sea, 44°59′N, 30°54′E. There are no casualties to the ship's complement (which includes 12 Armed Guard sailors), and the ship is later repaired and returns to active service.

15 Friday

PACIFIC. British TG 111.2 (Rear Admiral Eric J. P. Brind, RN), bombards Japanese installations, Truk Atoll.

Fifteen motor minesweepers (YMS), accompanied by the high-speed transport *Cofer* (APD 62) and landing craft equipped with light minesweeping gear, arrive off Balikpapan, Borneo, to begin mine clearance operations.

Thirty USAAF B-29s mine Shimonoseki Straits and the waters off Fushiki, Fukuoka, and Karatsu, Japan.

Destroyer escort *O'Flaherty* (DE 340) is damaged in collision with escort carrier *Block Island* (CVE 106) off Okinawa, 26°00′N, 128°00′E.

Coordinated submarine attack group (Commander Earl T. Hydeman) continues operations against Japanese shipping. From TG 17.21, operating off northwest coast of Honshu, *Sea Dog* (SS 401) sinks freighter *Koan Maru,* off Sakata, 39°53′N, 139°40′E.

Japanese guardboats *Gion Maru* and *Jinko Maru* are sunk by U.S. aircraft, Cam Ranh Bay, French Indochina.

Japanese freighter *No. 2 Tanshin Maru* is sunk by marine casualty off Malay Peninsula.

USAAF B-24s (10th Air Force) attack Japanese convoy in Gulf of Siam, damaging destroyer *Kamikaze* and minesweeper *W.4* and sinking merchant tanker *Toho Maru* off Samui Island, 09°25′N, 99°54′E.

Japanese freighter *Heiryu Maru* sinks after colliding with submerged wreck southwest of Shinshin Island, Korea, 36°39′N, 126°07′E.

Japanese cargo vessel *Junkawa Maru* is sunk by mine off Tanjong Lumut, Sumatra, 04°41′S, 106°13′E.

16 Saturday

UNITED STATES. Naval Air Test Center, Patuxent River, Maryland, is established.

PACIFIC. Off Okinawa, destroyer *Twiggs* (DD 591) is sunk by aerial torpedo, 26°08′N, 137°35′E; infantry landing craft (rocket)

LCI(R) 650 participates in rescue operations, closing to the edge of burning oil to do so. Escort carrier *Steamer Bay* (CVE 87) is damaged by aircraft operational casualty, 24°00′N, 128°00′E.

Submarine *Piranha* (SS 389) sinks Japanese freighter *Eiso Maru* off Esan Saki, Hokkaido, 41°57′N, 140°56′E.

British submarine HMS *Taciturn* sinks Japanese auxiliary submarine chaser *Cha 105* and unnamed air warning picket hulk (ex-Dutch submarine *K-XVIII*) off Surabaya, Java.

Japanese auxiliary submarine chaser *Wakatake Maru* is sunk by aircraft, Keelung Harbor.

Japanese army cargo ship *Taikyu Maru* is sunk by mine west of the mouth of Kammon Channel; freighter *No. 35 Banshu Maru* is sunk by mine off eastern end of Shimonoseki Strait, 33°57′N, 130°43′E.

Japanese freighter *Takeshima Maru* is sunk by aircraft off Sohuksan Do, Korea, 34°35′N, 125°58′E.

Japanese destroyer *Natsuzuki* is damaged 3.1 kilometers off Mutsure Island, Japan.

17 Sunday

PACIFIC. Twenty-seven USAAF B-29s mine Shimonoseki Straits and the waters off Kobe, Japan.

Gasoline tanker *Chestatee* (AOG 49) is damaged in collision with U.S. tanker *Sinclair Superflame* off Luzon, 07°04′N, 122°06′E.

Coordinated submarine attack group (Commander Earl T. Hydeman) continues operations against Japanese shipping. From TG 17.21, operating off Hokkaido, *Spadefish* (SS 411) attacks Japanese convoy, sinking auxiliary minelayer *Eijo Maru* off Matsuta Misaki, 42°38′N, 139°49′E.

Submarine chaser *PC 794* is damaged when she strikes an uncharted rock off Theodore Point, Otter Island, Alaska, 52°45′10″N, 172°53′20″E.

Japanese cargo ship *Kongo Maru* is sunk by aircraft, north of Shumushu Island, Kurils.

Japanese fast transport *T.16* is damaged by aircraft, 15 miles off Oshima.

Japanese *Coast Defense Vessel No. 46* is damaged by marine casualty north of Tsingtao, China.

Japanese naval vessel *Bingo Maru* is damaged by marine casualty two kilometers off Paekyong Do, Korea; freighter *Jintsugawa Maru* is sunk by marine casualty off Najin, Korea.

18 Monday

PACIFIC. Lieutenant General Simon B. Buckner, USA, commander of the U.S. Tenth Army, is killed while observing front line operations on Okinawa; Major General (later Lieutenant General) Roy S. Geiger, USMC, assumes temporary command of the Tenth Army to direct its final combat operations on the island.

TG 96.1, composed of battleship *Nevada* (BB 36) and two destroyers (Captain Homer L. Grosskopf), en route from Pearl Harbor to Saipan, bombards shore installations on Emidj Island, Jaluit Atoll, Marshalls, coordinated with bombing by land-based planes from U.S. bases in the Marshalls.

Rear Admiral Forrest B. Royal, Commander Amphibious Group 6, dies of coronary thrombosis, on board amphibious force flagship *Rocky Mount* (AGC 3), en route to Leyte following the successful conclusion of the Brunei Bay landings.

Motor minesweeper *YMS 50*, damaged by Allied mine off Balikpapan, Borneo, 01°18′S, 116°49′E, is scuttled by light cruiser *Denver* (CL 58).

Submarine *Apogon* (SS 308), attacking Japanese convoy RU, sinks transport *Hakuai Maru* and guardboat *No. 2 Kusonoki Maru* southwest of Paramushir, Kurils, 50°30′N, 155°01′E (see 19 June).

Coordinated submarine attack group (Commander Earl T. Hydeman) continues operations against Japanese shipping in Sea of Japan. From TG 17.22 (Commander George E. Pierce), operating off southern coast of Honshu, *Bonefish* (SS 223), after conferring with *Tunny* (SS 282) at 37°02′N, 135°32′E, sinks cargo ship *Konzan Maru*, 37°13′N, 137°18′E. *Bonefish*, however, is later sunk by the combined efforts of escort destroyer *Okinawa*, *Coast Defense Vessel No. 63*, *Coast Defense Vessel No. 75*, *Coast Defense Vessel No. 158*, and *Coast Defense Vessel No. 207*, 37°18′N, 137°55′E.[248] From TG 17.23 (Commander Robert D. Risser), operating off eastern coast of Korea, *Tinosa* (SS 283) sinks freighter *Wakae Maru* off Kansong, 38°25′N, 128°34′E.

Submarine *Bullhead* (SS 332) sinks Japanese auxiliary sailing vessel *No. 58 Sakura Maru* in Sunda Strait, off Merak, 05°35′S, 106°02′E.

Submarine *Dentuda* (SS 335) sinks Japanese guardboats *Reiko Maru* and *Heiwa Maru* in East China Sea west of Tokara Gunto, 30°45′N, 126°00′E.

PB4Y-2s (VPB 118) continue aerial mining of waters in Korean Archipelago, sowing mines in the waters north of Roka Do.

Mines sink Japanese transport *Shintai Maru* west of Noto Hanto, 36°50′N, 134°36′E, auxiliary submarine chaser *Cha 197*, 1.48 kilometers southwest of Moji Saki, and freighters *Nissho Maru* off Moji and *Bizan Maru* at 33°58′N, 130°44′E. Mines damage naval vessel *Shintai Maru* at 36°59′N, 136°43′E.

Marine casualties damage Japanese freighters *No. 1 Oshima Maru* east of Tachang Shan Island, *Shinko Maru* one kilometer off Nisshin, and *Hazuki Maru* off Kuzuiwa.

Japanese *Motor Gunboat No. 54* is sunk by aircraft off Port Arthur.

19 Tuesday

PACIFIC. Destroyer *Dunlap* (DD 384), while patrolling north of Chichi Jima, Borneo, sinks Japanese luggers *Gorgen Maru* and *Legaspi Maru* and cargo ship *Kasidori Maru*; the enemy vessels are en route to evacuate noncombatants from Chichi Jima to the Japanese home islands, and to take off supplies of gasoline.

Twenty-eight USAAF B-29s mine Shimonoseki Straits and the waters off Niigata, Miyazu, and Maizuru, Japan.

PB4Y-2s (VPB 118) continue aerial mining of waters in Korean Archipelago, sowing mines in the waters north of Roka Do, in a repeat of the mission flown the previous day. On this occasion, however, all planes are damaged by antiaircraft fire when they strafe a ship encountered in the vicinity.

Submarine *Bullhead* (SS 332) sinks Japanese auxiliary sailing vessel *No. 57 Tachibana Maru* in Sunda Strait, off Merak, 05°56′S, 106°00′E.

Submarine *Cabezon* (SS 334), attacking Japanese convoy beset by *Apogon* (SS 308) the previous day, sinks freighter *Zaosan Maru* southwest of Paramushir, Kurils, 50°39′N, 154°38′E.

Coordinated submarine attack group (Commander Earl T. Hydeman) continues operations against Japanese shipping in Sea of Japan. From TG 17.21 (Commander Hydeman), *Sea Dog* (SS 401) attacks convoy off northwest coast of Hokkaido, sinking army cargo ship *Kokai Maru* and freighter *No. 3 Shinhei Maru*, and damaging freighter *Naga Maru*, 43°12′N, 140°19′E.

Japanese auxiliary submarine chaser *Koshun Maru* is lost to marine casualty 4.5 kilometers off Yura Saki, eastern Bungo Suido.

Japanese freighter *Hattenzan Maru* is sunk by aircraft off Masan, Korea; freighter *Heian Maru* is damaged by marine casualty off Hunghae, 36°03′N, 129°35′E.

Japanese merchant tanker *No. 1 Nanki Maru*

is sunk by mine off Aki Nada, in the western part of the Inland Sea; guardboat *No. 3 Kaigyo Maru* is damaged by mine 1.9 kilometers off He Saki, Japan.

ATLANTIC. U.S. freighter *Calvin Coolidge*, en route from Le Havre, France, to Boston, Massachusetts, is damaged by mine, 49°50′N, 04°57′W. There are no casualties among the 56-man merchant crew, 31 Armed Guard sailors, and 457 embarked troops.

20 Wednesday

PACIFIC. TG 12.4, en route from Pearl Harbor to Leyte, attacks Wake Island; planes from carriers *Hancock* (CV 19) and *Lexington* (CV 16) and small carrier *Cowpens* (CVL 25) (Rear Admiral Ralph E. Jennings) bomb Japanese installations.

Tank landing ship *LST 562* is damaged when accidentally rammed by tank landing craft *LCT 1310*, Brunei Bay, Borneo, 04°29′N, 114°01′E. Motor minesweeper *YMS 368* is damaged by mine off Balikpapan, 01°19′S, 116°58′E.

Minesweepers *Device* (AM 220) and *Dour* (AM 223) are damaged in collision off Okinawa, 26°00′N, 127°00′E. Tank landing ship *LST 288* is damaged by operational casualty.

Submarine *Kraken* (SS 370) sinks Japanese auxiliary sailing vessel *No. 58 Tachibana Maru* in Sunda Strait, off Merak, 05°56′S, 106°00′E.

Coordinated submarine attack group (Commander Earl T. Hydeman) continues operations against Japanese shipping in Sea of Japan. From TG 17.23 (Commander Robert D. Risser), operating off eastern coast of Korea, *Tinosa* (SS 283) sinks army cargo ship *Taito Maru*, 36°04′N, 130°26′E, and freighter *Kaisei Maru*, 35°39′N, 130°29′E.

Japanese merchant tanker *Nanshin Maru* is sunk by mine, possibly laid by submarine *Ray* (SS 271) on 22 February 1944, off Cape St. Jacques, French Indochina.

Mine sinks Japanese freighter *Kenan Maru* in north Kyushu Channel, 33°59′N, 130°48′E; mines laid by USAAF B-29 (20th Air Force) sink merchant tanker *No. 1 Nanki Maru* off Aki Nada, 33°58′N, 131°01′E, and damage freighters *Nitto Maru* 5.7 kilometers off Tateishi Light and *Keizan Maru* seven kilometers southeast of Motoyama Saki. Cargo ship *Huashan Maru* is sunk by B-29-laid mine near Fukuoka, Kyushu, 33°38′N, 130°22′E.

Japanese freighter *Kamome Maru* is sunk by aircraft between Pusan, Korea, and Yosu, Korea.

USAAF B-24s (Far East Air Force), on ship-ping sweep off coast of Korea, sink cargo ship *Keijo Maru* off Mokp'o, 34°47′N, 126°23′E.

PB4Y-2s (VPB 118) continue aerial mining of waters of Korean Archipelago in a repeat of the mission of the previous day, but on this occasion encounter heavy antiaircraft fire from Japanese warships in the vicinity.

21 Thursday

PACIFIC. Okinawa is declared secured 82 days after the initial landings; capture of Okinawa provides U.S. forces with air and naval bases within 350 miles of Kyushu. Japanese air attacks on U.S. ships offshore, however, continue. *Kamikazes* damage destroyer escort *Halloran* (DE 305), 26°00′N, 128°00′E, and sink medium landing ship *LSM 59* while she is escorting fleet tug *Lipan* (ATF 85) and high-speed transport *Barry* (APD 29). *Barry* (previously damaged by *kamikaze* on 25 May) and in tow of *Lipan*, is en route to Ie Shima (see 22 June).[249] In addition, suiciders damage seaplane tenders *Curtiss* (AV 4) and *Kenneth Whiting* (AV 14), 26°10′N, 127°18′E.

Twenty-seven USAAF B-29s mine the waters off Oura, Senzaki, Nanao, Fushiki, and Osaka, Japan.

PB4Y-2s (VPB 118), flying from Okinawa, continue aerial mining of waters of Korean Archipelago, sowing mines in waters in channel between Hikin Do, Iion Do, and Gantai Do; one plane encounters antiaircraft fire from Japanese warship in vicinity. Waters north of Roka Do are mined again as well.

Landing craft repair ship *Endymion* (ARL 9) is torpedoed by Japanese submarine *I 36* north of Truk, 12°41′N, 156°20′E. Three hunter-killer groups are formed to hunt for *I 36* (see 28 June).

Motor minesweeper *YMS 335* is damaged by shore battery, Balikpapan, Borneo, 01°18′S, 116°50′E.

Submarine *Parche* (SS 384) sinks Japanese freighter *Hizen Maru* in Tsugaru Strait, 41°19′N, 141°28′E.

Submarine *Piranha* (SS 389) damages Japanese freighter *Shirogane Maru* off northeastern coast of Honshu, 39°28′N, 142°10′E.

ATLANTIC. District patrol vessel *YP 13* is damaged in collision with U.S. freighter *Warrior* near Buoy "E," New York Channel; rescue tug *ATR 6* tows *YP 13* to New York; *Warrior* proceeds without assistance.

22 Friday

PACIFIC. High-speed transport *Barry* (APD 29), damaged by *kamikazes* (on 25 May and 21 June), sinks as the result of damage received the previous day.

Off Okinawa, *kamikazes* damage high-speed minesweeper *Ellyson* (DMS 19), 26°04′N, 127°55′E, and tank landing ship *LST 534*, 26°18′N, 127°49′E; medium landing ship *LSM 213* is damaged by operational casualty.

Motor minesweeper *YMS 10* is damaged by shore battery, Balikpapan, Borneo, 01°18′S, 116°51′E.

USAAF B-29s (162 strong) bomb naval facility at Kure, Japan, destroying the incomplete submarines *I 204* and *I 352* and damaging escort destroyer *Nire* and submarine *RO 67*.

Coordinated submarine attack group (Commander Earl T. Hydeman) continues operations against Japanese shipping in Sea of Japan. From TG 17.21 (Commander Hydeman), operating off Hokkaido and Karafuto, Kurils, *Crevalle* (SS 291) torpedoes escort destroyer *Kasado*, 43°23′N, 139°47′E.

Submarine *Parche* (SS 384) sinks unnamed Japanese fishing boat off Hokkaido, 42°08′N, 140°58′E.

Submarine *Piranha* (SS 389) damages *Coast Defense Vessel No. 196* off eastern Honshu, 39°32′N, 142°11′E.

Mines laid by USAAF B-29s (20th Air Force) sink Japanese freighters *Yubu Maru* in Kammon Channel, 34°00′N, 131°00′E; *Tokasegawa Maru* off Tsutura, in Kammon Channel, 33°55′N, 131°20′E; *Taigen Maru* near Kammon Channel, 34°00′N, 130°30′E; and *Ungetsu Maru* north of Mutsure, Japan, as well as damage transport *Tatsumiya Maru* one kilometer off Ganryu Jima Light.

PB4Y-2s (VPB 118), flying from Okinawa, continue aerial mining of waters of Korean Archipelago, sowing mines in waters in channel between Hikin Do, Iion Do, and Gantai Do.

PBMs bomb lighthouse and Japanese shipping off south coast of Korea, 36°55′N, 125°47′E.

MEDITERRANEAN. U.S. freighter *Pierre Gibault*, en route from Izmir, Turkey, to Oran, Algeria, is damaged by mine off Kythera Island, 36°04′30″N, 26°06′30″E. Greek destroyer escort *Themosticles* takes off the wounded (seven Armed Guard sailors) and dead (two merchant sailors and two Armed Guards) soon thereafter. The ship, beached on 26 June off Kythera Island, is subsequently written off as a total loss.

23 Saturday

PACIFIC. Twenty-six USAAF B-29s mine the waters off Karatsu, Fukuoka, Sakai, and Niigata, Japan.

PB4Y-2s (VPB 118), flying from Okinawa, continue aerial mining of waters of Korean Archipelago, sowing mines in waters in channel north of Iion Do and Gantai Do, and off Ninshi Do and Chi Do.

Coordinated submarine attack groups TG 17.21 (Commander Earl T. Hydeman), TG 17.22 (Commander George E. Pierce), and TG 17.23 (Commander Robert D. Risser) rendezvous and exit Sea of Japan through Le Pérouse Strait; the eight boats will then proceed to Midway.

Motor minesweeper YMS 364 is damaged by shore battery, Balikpapan, Borneo, 01°19′S, 116°52′E.

Submarine Hardhead (SS 365) sinks Japanese auxiliary submarine chaser Cha 42 in Java Sea, 05°44′S, 114°16′E, and after undergoing counterattack by auxiliary submarine chaser Cha 113, sinks Cha 113 and No. 833 Shuttle Boat, 05°45′S, 114°16′E.

Submarine Tirante (SS 420) sinks Japanese sailing junk No. 293 Antung Maru off west coast of Korea, 37°54′N, 125°34′E.

Mines sink Japanese freighter Goshu Maru off Mutsure Light, Japan, and damage freighter Kocho Maru 1.5 kilometers off Takenoko Light.

Japanese freighter Shingishu Maru is damaged by aircraft off Pusan, Korea.

24 Sunday

PACIFIC. Destroyer escort Neuendorf (DE 200) is damaged in collision off Panay, P.I., 10°41′N, 122°35′E.

Motor minesweeper YMS 339 is damaged, accidentally, by U.S. aircraft off Balikpapan, Borneo, 01°19′S, 116°52′E.

Submarine Tirante (SS 420) sinks Japanese sailing junk No. 284 Antung Maru off west coast of Korea, 38°36′N, 124°40′E.

British submarine HMS Statesman damages Japanese submarine depot ship Komahashi off northern Sumatra.

British submarine HMS Torbay sinks unnamed merchant coaster (motor sailboat) in Malacca Strait.

Mines sink Japanese freighters Katsura Maru, 34°19′N, 133°35′E, No. 8 Kenkon Maru 2.4 kilometers off Mutsure Light, and Tatsukaba Maru at mouth of Karatsu Bay and damage freighters Tsurukawa Maru, 33°55′N, 131°05′E, and Unzen Maru, 35°33′N, 133°17′E.

PB4Y-2s (VPB 118), flying from Okinawa in a repeat of mission carried out the previous day, continue aerial mining of waters of Korean Archipelago, sowing mines in waters north of Iion Do and Gantai Do, and off Ninshi Do and Chi Do. The Privateers, upon completion of the mining operation, strafe targets of opportunity that include railroad facilities, airports, and Japanese shipping, sinking merchant ship Pluto Go off Mokp'o.

Japanese freighter Wakamatsu Maru is damaged by aircraft, 33°47′N, 131°31′E.

25 Monday

PACIFIC. PB4Y-2s (VPB 118), flying from Okinawa, continue aerial mining of waters of Korean Archipelago, sowing mines in waters north of Chin Do. Upon completion of the mining operation, the Privateers strafe targets of opportunity that include lighthouses and Japanese shipping.

Twenty-six USAAF B-29s mine Shimonoseki Straits and the waters off Tsuruga and Ohama, Japan. Mines sink Japanese freighters Anri Go off Mutsure and Kozan Maru off Wakamatsu and damage escort destroyer Kuga in Fukagawa Bay.

Underwater demolition teams, covered by aircraft, begin operations on the beaches at Balikpapan, Borneo, in advance of landings slated to begin there.

Japanese freighter Katori Maru is sunk by aircraft off Cape Changgi, Korea, 36°02′N, 129°25′E.

Japanese freighter No. 5 Ise Maru is sunk by aircraft, outside Sakito, 33°01′N, 129°33′E.

26 Tuesday

PACIFIC. TG 31.24 (Captain Charles A. Buchanan) lands assault troops from Fleet Marine Force Reconnaissance Battalion, in addition to a reinforced rifle company from the First Marine Division on Kume Shima, Ryukyus.

Underwater demolition teams at Balikpapan, Borneo, continue operations to clear obstacles, covered by close support unit (an element of TG 78.2) composed of 10 support landing craft (large) [LCS(L)], eight rocket-equipped infantry landing craft [LCI(R)], and six infantry landing craft (gunboats) [LCI(G)].

PB4Y-2s (VPB 118), flying from Okinawa, continue aerial mining of waters of Korean Archipelago, sowing mines in waters north of Chin Do and north of Iion Do and Gantai Do.

Destroyer escort Halloran (DE 305) is strafed by Japanese aircraft in Davao Gulf, P.I.

Off Balikpapan, motor minesweeper YMS 39 is sunk by mine, 01°19′S, 116°49′E; motor minesweeper YMS 365, damaged by mine, 01°18′S, 116°50′E, is scuttled by U.S. forces.

Off Okinawa, small seaplane tender Suisun (AVP 53) is damaged when accidentally rammed by tank landing craft LCT 1407, 26°10′N, 127°19′E.

Destroyers Bearss (DD 654), John Hood (DD 655), Jarvis (DD 799), and Porter (DD 800) sink Japanese auxiliary submarine chasers Cha 73, Cha 206, and Cha 209 and guardboat No. 2 Kusunoki Maru, and damage auxiliary submarine chaser Cha 198, south of Onekotan, Kurils, 49°40′N, 155°30′E.

Submarine Parche (SS 384), attacking Japanese convoy, sinks gunboat Kamitsu Maru and freighter Eikan Maru seven miles off Todo Saki, southern Honshu, 39°25′N, 142°04′E, but although damaged by depth charges, remains on patrol.

Japanese escort destroyer Enoki is sunk by mine, Obama Wan, Fukui, 35°28′N, 135°44′E. Destroyer Hatsuume is damaged by mine off Maizuru, Japan.

Japanese freighter Kisei Go is sunk by aircraft off Tong Do, Korea, 34°43′N, 127°15′E.

Japanese submarine I 162 is damaged by marine casualty off south coast of Korea.

Japanese naval vessel Bingo Maru is damaged by aircraft, East China Sea.

Japanese cargo ship Nadamitsu Maru is damaged by aircraft off Yodoe, Tottori prefecture.

Japanese cargo ship No. 11 Shinsei Maru is damaged by marine casualty east of Kamoi Saki.

27 Wednesday

PACIFIC. Twenty-nine USAAF B-29s mine the waters off Hagi, Niigata, Kobe, and Osaka, Japan.

PB4Y-2s (VPB 118), flying from Okinawa, continue aerial mining of waters of Korean Archipelago, sowing mines in fields off Chin Do and northwest of Roka Do.

Destroyer Caldwell (DD 605) is damaged by mine in Brunei Bay, Borneo, 05°07′N, 115°06′E.

Submarine Blueback (SS 326) sinks Japanese submarine chaser Ch 2 north of Lombok, Java Sea, 07°25′S, 116°00′E.

PV-1 (VPB 142) sinks Japanese submarine I 165, 450 miles east of Saipan, Marianas, 15°28′N, 153°39′E.

Japanese auxiliary minelayer Kyushu Maru is sunk by U.S. aircraft east of Otsu, Japan.

Mines sink Japanese freighters *Mifuku Maru* outside Nanao Harbor, 37°06′N, 137°02′E, and *No. 7 Kaishin Maru* off Mutsure, Japan, and damage escort destroyer *Sakito*, 34°13′N, 126°36′E, Army cargo ship *Maoka Maru* 0.3 kilometer off Niigata Light, and freighters *Yuzuki Maru* off Moji and *Mifunesan Maru* off Harima-Nada.

Japanese army cargo ship *Hozu Maru* is sunk by aircraft, near Rabaul, New Britain.

Japanese submarine chaser *Ch 19* is damaged by aircraft, south of Korea; freighter *Keisei Maru* is damaged by aircraft, near Mokp'o, Korea.

Navy land-based aircraft damage Japanese cargo vessel *Keijo Maru*, 34°19′N, 126°27′E.

Japanese freighter *No. 7 Nichiyu Maru* is damaged by marine casualty, 36°53′N, 129°26′E.

28 Thursday

PACIFIC. Japanese submarine *I 36* carries out unsuccessful *kaiten* attack on general stores issue ship *Antares* (AKS 3) as the latter is en route from Saipan to Pearl Harbor, 13°10′N, 154°57′E; destroyer *Sproston* (DD 577) comes to *Antares*'s aid, sinking one *kaiten* and damaging *I 36*, 12°50′N, 154°50′E.

Off Balikpapan, Borneo, motor minesweeper *YMS 47* is damaged by mine, 01°19′S, 116°55′E; motor minesweeper *YMS 49* is damaged by shore battery, 01°00′S, 117°00′E.

PB4Y-2s (VPB 118), flying from Okinawa, continue aerial mining of waters of Korean Archipelago in a repeat of mission the previous day, sowing mines off Chin Do and northwest of Roka Do. Although fighter opposition materializes, the Privateers "after considerable sparring" drive off the enemy without loss.

Mines sink Japanese freighter *Daikokusan Maru* off Moji, Japan, and damage cable ship *Osei Maru* three kilometers southeast of Jizo Saki and freighter *Yahiko Maru*, 34°21′N, 130°56′E.

Japanese naval vessel *Toyokawa Maru* is damaged by marine casualty 450 meters southeast of Hiko Shima, near Shimonoseki.

29 Friday

PACIFIC. Twenty-five USAAF B-29s (20th Air Force) mine Shimonoseki Straits and the waters off Maizuru and Sakata, Japan. Mines laid by B-29s in these and previous plants sink freighter *Kyokuto Maru* off Mutsure, and damage naval vessel *Soshu Maru* two kilometers off Tsuruga Light, 35°41′N, 136°05′E, and freighters *Akizuki Maru* in Tsuruga Harbor,

No. 1 Nichiyu Maru at 34°04′N, 130°52′E, and *Hiyoriyama Maru* outside Sakai Harbor.

PB4Y-2s (VPB 118), flying from Okinawa, continue aerial mining of waters of Korean Archipelago, sowing mines in fields off Gyuji Do, Jobai Do, and Toso Do.

30 Saturday

Naval vessels on hand (all types)—67,952. People: Navy—3,383,196; Marine Corps—476,709; Coast Guard—171,192. Total—4,031,097.

PACIFIC. PB4Y-2s (VPB 118), flying from Okinawa, continue aerial mining of waters of Korean Archipelago, sowing mines in fields off the south central coast.

Off Balikpapan, Borneo, destroyer *Smith* (DD 378) is damaged by shore battery, 01°17′S, 116°53′E; minesweeper *YMS 314* is damaged by mine, 01°18′S, 116°51′E.

Submarines *Baya* (SS 318) and *Capitaine* (SS 336) attack Japanese Makassar-to-Surabaya convoy MASU 705, engaging escorting submarine chaser *Ch 5* and sinking cargo vessel *Bandai Maru*, 06°27′S, 117°13′E.

Japanese army cargo ship *Hokushin Maru* is lost to unknown cause in South China Sea, 15°00′N, 115°00′E.[250]

Japanese freighter *No. 1 Ryuho Maru* is sunk by aircraft, 35°01′N, 140°10′E.

Mines damage Japanese escort destroyer *Nara* six miles west-southwest of Shimonoseki, Japan, 33°54′N, 130°49′E; *Coast Defense Vessel No. 154*, 2.8 kilometers off He Saki Light; and freighters *Chikuma Maru*, 15 kilometers off Hime Jima, *Taruyasu Maru*, 37°07′N, 137°04′E, and *Taisei Maru*, 35°00′N, 133°00′E.

Japanese *Coast Defense Vessel No. 215* is damaged 2.8 kilometers off Iwa Saki.

Japanese freighter *No. 1 Taiyu Maru* is damaged by aircraft, Moji Harbor.

Open lighter *YC 1272*, beached on south side of Cerritos Channel, San Pedro, California, is lost during June (date indeterminate).

JULY

1 Sunday

PACIFIC. TG 78.2 (Rear Admiral Albert G. Noble) lands 7th Australian Division (Reinforced) (less one brigade) at Balikpapan, Borneo; landing is covered by Allied naval gunfire and aircraft. This, the final major amphibious assault of the Borneo campaign, is unopposed.

Over 530 USAAF B-29s firebomb Ube, Kure, Shimonoseki, and Kumamoto, Japan;

auxiliary minelayer *Himetaka Maru* is damaged at Kure.

PB4Y-2s (VPB 118), flying from Okinawa, conclude aerial mining of waters of Korean Archipelago, sowing mines in fields off Chin Do. VPB 118 wraps up mining operations this date, having sown 195. The aircrew notice the absence of shipping in the areas mined, leading to the conclusion that the effort "has effectively stopped the movement of enemy ships in the inner channels around the southwest coast of Korea."

Twenty-four USAAF B-29s mine Shimonoseki Straits and the waters off Nanao and Fushiki, Japan. Mines sink Japanese freighters *Tenyu Maru* at entrance of Niigata Harbor and *Naoshima Maru* three miles north of Shodo Jima, and damage freighters *Yamaji Maru* 34°28′N, 135°08′E, and *Eijun Maru*, off Moji.

Submarine *Haddo* (SS 255) sinks Japanese *Coast Defense Vessel No. 72* and freighters *Konri Maru*, *No. 1 Taiun Maru*, and *No. 2 Taiun Maru* in the Yellow Sea off the west coast of Korea, 38°08′N, 124°38′E.

Japanese minesweeper depot ship *Chohei Maru* and freighter *Koa Maru* are damaged by U.S. aircraft, Woosung, China.

Japanese freighter *Mitakesan Maru* is damaged by aircraft, 34°20′N, 129°24′E.

USAAF planes (Far East Air Force) sink Japanese freighter *Shinneisho Maru* at mouth of Yangtze River, 31°21′N, 121°38′E.

2 Monday

PACIFIC. Japanese planes attack fleet units patrolling off Okinawa; high-speed transport *Scribner* (APD 122) is narrowly missed by aerial torpedo.

Submarine *Apogon* (SS 308) damages Japanese auxiliary submarine chasers *Cha 58* and *Cha 65*, 49°28′N, 154°19′E.

Submarine *Barb* (SS 220) employs rockets in bombardment of Japanese shore installations at Kaiyho Island off the east coast of Karafuto, Kurils; this is the first successful use of these weapons against shore positions by a U.S. submarine.

Submarines *Haddo* (SS 255) and *Paddle* (SS 263) attack Japanese shipping in the Yellow Sea off Inchon, Korea, sinking one unnamed cargo vessel and leaving another drifting, 37°55′N, 124°58′E.

Mines sink Japanese auxiliary submarine chaser *Cha 188* in Sea of Japan, off Mutsure Light, 33°59′N, 130°52′E, and damage army motor sailer *Nanko Maru* off Kammon Light.

Japanese merchant tanker *No. 5 Nanki Maru*

is sunk by marine casualty, 34°18′N, 141°25′E. Marine casualties (most likely groundings or storms) account for damage to cargo ship *Awa Maru* between Hakodate and Yokohama, and cargo vessel *Annette Fritzen* at entrance to Pusan Harbor, Korea.

USAAF B-29s (20th Air Force) bomb Japanese shipping and installations at Kure, sinking cargo vessel *Himetaka Maru*, 34°11′N, 132°31′E.

PB4Ys (FAW 1) sink Japanese sailing vessel *Nishima Maru* off Mokp'o, Korea, 35°50′N, 126°30′E, and cargo ship *No. 12 Shima Maru* at 35°43′N, 126°32′E.

3 Tuesday

EUROPE. Commander, U.S. Naval Forces, Germany (Vice Admiral Robert L. Ghormley) establishes headquarters at Frankfurt am Main, Germany.

PACIFIC. Over 560 USAAF Air Force B-29s firebomb Kochi, Himeji, Takamatsu, and Tokushima, Japan, concluding the raid early the following morning (see 4 July).

Final mine plant of Phase IV of Operation STARVATION: 31 USAAF B-29s mine Shimonoseki Straits and the waters off Maizuru and Funakawa, Japan.

PB4Ys (FAW 1) sink Japanese army cargo ship *Hoei Maru* off Mokp'o, Korea, 34°22′N, 126°25′E.

USAAF B-24s bomb Japanese shipping at Banjarmasin, Borneo, sinking cargo vessel *No. 3 Misaki Maru*.

Japanese merchant tanker *No. 5 Nanko Maru* is sunk by marine casualty, Seto, Inland Sea.

4 Wednesday

PACIFIC. TF 32 (Rear Admiral Jesse B. Oldendorf), consisting of three battleships, two heavy cruisers, one light cruiser, four escort carriers, 11 destroyers, and four destroyer escorts, departs Buckner Bay, Okinawa, to provide cover for the minesweeping operation slated to begin the following day (see 5 July).[251]

Destroyer *Murray* (DD 576) intercepts Japanese hospital ship *Takasago Maru* as she evacuates sick and wounded members of Wake Island garrison. *Murray* reports that isolation and bombardment have reduced life on the atoll to a mere struggle for survival.

Submarine *Tirante* (SS 420) sinks Japanese guardboats *Koshe Maru* and *Mashuye Maru* in the Yellow Sea, east of Tsingtao, China, 37°15′N, 123°19′E.

Japanese auxiliary patrol vessel *Pa No. 177* is

destroyed by fire, following raid that began the day before by USAAF B-29s on Tokushima, Japan.

Mines sink Japanese transport *Tsukushi Maru* southeast of Shimonoseki, 33°50′N, 131°19′E, and damage army cargo ship *Taiko Maru* off Bakuchi Saki and freighter *Sagami Maru* off Osaka.

Marine casualties account for damage to Japanese freighters *Hiyoriyama Maru* outside Sakai Harbor and *Unzen Maru* three miles south of Taki Harbor, Yaku Shima, Nansei Shoto.

5 Thursday

PACIFIC. General of the Army Douglas MacArthur announces the liberation of the Philippines.

TF 39 (Rear Admiral Alexander Sharp), composed of seven light minelayers (DM), 52 minesweepers (AM), six high-speed minesweepers (DMS), 49 motor minesweepers (YMS), and seven netlayers, begins minesweeping operations in the East China Sea.

Destroyer *Smith* (DD 378) is accidentally damaged by depth charge off Balikpapan, Borneo, 01°00′S, 117°00′E.

Submarine *Barb* (SS 220) sinks Japanese freighter *No. 11 Sapporo Maru* outside Odomari Harbor, southwest of Sakhalin, 46°04′N, 142°14′E.

Submarines *Lizardfish* (SS 373) and *Puffer* (SS 268) bombard Japanese port facilities and shipping at Chelukan Buwang, Bali. *Lizardfish* sinks auxiliary submarine chaser *Cha 37* and *No. 153 Shuttle Vessel*, in addition to barges and landing craft, 08°10′S, 114°50′E; fires ignited by the shelling destroy small cargo vessel *Hino Maru*. *Puffer* sinks cargo vessels *Heiyo Maru* and *Nihon Maru* in Bulelong Roads, 08°04′S, 115°05′E.

Mines sink Japanese transport *Toyokawa Maru* near Mutsure Jima, 33°56′N, 130°53′E, and merchant tanker *No. 1 Tosei Maru* 1.7 kilometers off Niigata Harbor and damage freighters *Miurasan Maru* at 34°47′N, 128°49′E, *Enho Maru* at 33°29′N, 130°15′E, and *Take Maru* near Moji, Japan.

Japanese landing ship *T.147* is damaged by aircraft off Hachijo Jima.

Japanese freighter *Awa Maru* is damaged by aircraft 20 miles off Katsura Light, Saeki Bay.

Japanese freighter *Hirano Maru* is damaged by aircraft off Fukuyama, Hokkaido, 41°11′N, 140°04′E.

USAAF planes sink Japanese cargo vessel *Tone Maru* off Banjarmasin, Borneo, 03°20′S, 114°35′E.

Japanese *Coast Defense Vessel No. 95* is damaged by marine casualty, Tsurumi Harbor.

6 Friday

PACIFIC. Mines sink Japanese merchant cable ship *Toyo Maru* 73 miles northeast of Tobigasuhana and freighters *Shori Maru* off Ogushi, *No. 5 Tokai Maru* off Mutsure Light, 33°59′N, 130°52′E, and *Shinei Maru* near Shimonoseki, 33°54′N, 131°01′E. Mines damage auxiliary submarine chaser *Cha 153* off Niigata Harbor; army cargo ships *Ujina Maru*, 120 meters north of Niigata Light, and *Nissho Maru*, at mouth of Senzaki Bay; and freighter *Sakaki Maru* 3.1 kilometers south of Motoyama Light.[252]

Japanese freighter *Mitsuminesan Maru* is damaged by marine casualty near Chinhae, Korea.

7 Saturday

ATLANTIC. President Truman, Secretary of State James F. Byrnes, and Fleet Admiral William D. Leahy embark in heavy cruiser *Augusta* (CA 31) for Antwerp, Belgium, on the first leg of their trip that will ultimately take them to Potsdam.

PACIFIC. Submarine *Trepang* (SS 412) sinks Japanese freighter *No. 2 Koun Maru*, 42°21′N, 141°28′E.

Mines sink Japanese freighters *Meizan Maru* at mouth of Mokp'o Harbor and *Nachizan Maru* in Kammon Strait, and damage merchant tanker *No. 10 Kinyu Maru*, Osaka Harbor, and cargo ships *Tairi Maru* off Hime Jima and *Taiju Maru* and *No. 5 Tokai Maru* (location unspecified).

8 Sunday

PACIFIC. Submarine *Cod* (SS 224) rescues crew of Dutch submarine *O 19*, stranded on Ladd Reef in South China Sea, 300 miles northwest of Brunei Bay, and scuttles *O 19* with torpedoes and gunfire.

Submarine *Sea Robin* (SS 407) sinks Japanese auxiliary submarine chaser *Cha 85* off Quelpart Island, 33°50′N, 126°42′E.

Submarine *Tirante* (SS 420) sinks Japanese merchant passenger-cargo ship *Saitsu Maru* near Dairen, Korea, 38°48′N, 121°25′E.

Japanese freighter *Mikunisan Maru* is sunk by aircraft at mouth of Mokp'o Harbor, Korea.

Japanese freighter *Sumera Maru* is damaged by aircraft near Sakito Saki.

Japanese *Coast Defense Vessel No. 95* is damaged by mine inside Yokosuka Harbor.

Japanese army cargo ship *Tensho Maru* and freighter *Koshin Maru* are damaged by collision in Sea of Japan, east by north of Hungnam, Korea, 40°14'N, 131°42'E.

9 Monday

PACIFIC. USAAF B-29s (475 strong) firebomb Sendai, Sakai, Gifu, and Wakayama, Japan, concluding the raid early the following morning; 61 B-29s bomb the oil refinery at Yokkaichi.

Phase V of Operation STARVATION, aimed at the total blockade of the Japanese home islands, begins as 30 USAAF B-29s mine Shimonoseki Straits and the waters off Niigata and Nanao. Mines sink cargo ship *Nippu Maru* outside Wakamatsu Harbor and damage cargo ships *Kamishima Maru* off Wakamatsu and *Gakujo Maru* at 33°57'N, 130°43'E; freighters *Shinto Maru* outside Wakamatsu Harbor and *Sanzen Maru* five kilometers southeast of Genkai Jima Light; and merchant tanker *Mitsu Maru* in Kobe Harbor.

Motor minesweeper *YMS 84* is sunk by mine off Balikpapan, Borneo, 01°19'S, 116°48'E.

Submarine *Bluefish* (SS 222) sinks Japanese auxiliary submarine chaser *Cha 50* off east coast of Malaya, 02°13'N, 105°03'E.

Japanese merchant tanker *Tenwa Maru* is damaged by marine casualty in Kobe Harbor, Japan.

10 Tuesday

PACIFIC. TF 38 (Vice Admiral John S. McCain) launches strikes against Japanese airfields on the Tokyo plain.

Submarine chaser *SC 521* founders and sinks, east by south of San Cristobal, Solomons, 11°03'S, 164°50'E.

Tank landing ship *LST 1107* is damaged by grounding off Okinawa, 26°21'N, 126°47'E.

Submarine *Hammerhead* (SS 364) sinks Japanese cargo ship *Sakura Maru* and merchant tanker *No. 5 Nanmei Maru* in Gulf of Siam, off Malay Peninsula, 09°38'N, 101°31'E.

Submarine *Lionfish* (SS 298) attacks Japanese submarine *I 162* south of Ashisuri Saki, 32°31'N, 131°54'E. Although *Lionfish* claims two hits and to have sunk her quarry, *I 162* escapes undamaged.

Submarine *Moray* (SS 300) sinks Japanese merchant whaler *No. 6 Fumi Maru* east of Kinkazan, 38°11'N, 142°15'E.

Submarine *Runner* (SS 476) sinks Japanese minesweeper *W.27* off Tado Saki, Honshu, 39°20'N, 142°07'E.

Submarine *Sea Robin* (SS 407) sinks Japanese army cargo ship *Sakishima Maru* north of Quelpart Island, 33°39'N, 126°40'E.

Japanese guardboat *No. 3 Kashima Maru* and freighter *No. 10 Hachiryu Maru* are sunk by U.S. aircraft 40 miles north of the mouth of the Yangtze.

Mine laid by USAAF B-29 (20th Air Force) sinks Japanese cargo ship *Nippu Maru* outside Wakamatsu Harbor, 33°06'N, 129°43'E; freighter *Chikuma Maru* is sunk by mine 18 kilometers off Moji Saki; and merchant vessel *Tsukuba Maru* is damaged by mine 4.5 miles west of Osaka Harbor.

11 Wednesday

PACIFIC. Twenty-seven USAAF B-29s mine Shimonoseki Straits and the waters off Najin and Pusan, Korea (marking the first mining operation in Korean waters by B-29s), and off Maizuru, Japan. Mines sink Japanese escort destroyer *Sakura* off Osaka, 35°50'N, 135°20'E, and freighter *No. 3 Takechi Maru* near Shodo Jima, and damage merchant vessel *Tatsutyuyu Maru* off Sensaki.

Submarine *Barb* (SS 220) sinks Japanese guardboat *No. 15 Seiho Maru* and merchant diesel sampan *No. 15 Seiho Maru* off Hokkaido, 44°03'N, 146°30'E.

Submarine *Kingfish* (SS 234) sinks Japanese fishing boat *Inari Maru* off Maedate, Japan, 38°03'N, 142°29'E.

UNITED STATES. Admiral H. Kent Hewitt concludes his "investigation of facts pertinent to the Japanese attack on Pearl Harbor." The record of the proceedings and exhibits of this inquiry cover 1,342 printed pages.

12 Thursday

PACIFIC. Submarine chaser *PC 582* is damaged by grounding in Maglagabon Bay, Samar, P.I., 11°05'N, 125°20'E.

Mines sink Japanese salvage ship *Nasu Maru* near Niigata, Japan, cargo vessel *No. 3 Fukushin Maru* off Osaka Harbor Lighthouse, freighter *Kojun Maru* 180 miles east of Niigata, 37°57'N, 139°04'E, and tanker *Mitsu Maru* in Akashi Strait, 33°38'N, 135°03'E, and damage freighters *Takarasan Maru* outside Wakamatsu Harbor and *Nasu Maru* off Niigata.

Japanese freighter *Hakara Maru* is damaged by aircraft off Hekata.

Japanese freighter *Kashi Maru* is damaged by marine casualty off south end of Chizen Misaki.

13 Friday

PACIFIC. TF 95 (Rear Admiral Francis S. Low), composed of large cruisers *Alaska* (CB 1) and *Guam* (CB 2), four light cruisers, and nine destroyers, sorties from Leyte Gulf to conduct antishipping sweeps in the East China Sea.[253]

TF 93 (Rear Admiral John H. Brown Jr.), composed of light cruisers *Richmond* (CL 9) and *Concord* (CL 10) and five destroyers, commences an antishipping sweep; these ships will pass down the Kuril chain and into the Sea of Okhotsk. Although shadowed by Japanese planes, TF 93 will not be attacked.

Thirty-one USAAF B-29s mine Shimonoseki Straits and the waters off Masan, Reisui, and Chongjin, Korea, and Fukuoka, Japan. Mines (laid this day and on previous occasions) sink freighters *No. 7 Agata Maru* and *No. 13 Yamabishi Maru*, Wakamatsu Harbor, and damage freighter *Hayahi Maru* 10 kilometers north of Mutsure Light and cargo ship *Korasan Maru* in Shimonoseki Strait, 33°56'N, 130°56'E.

Japanese guardboats *No. 7 Myojin Maru* and *No. 6 Sakae Maru* are sunk by U.S. aircraft off Chichi Jima, 27°04'N, 142°11'E.

British submarine HMS *Trenchant* sinks unnamed Japanese schooner, western Celebes, 03°10'S, 118°50'S.

GENERAL. Italy declares war on Japan.

14 Saturday

PACIFIC. TF 38 (Vice Admiral John S. McCain), since bad weather prevents attacks on the primary targets (airfields in northern Honshu and Hokkaido), strikes shipping, rail facilities, and ground installations in those areas instead; attack is repeated on 15 July. TF 38 planes sink escort destroyer *Tachibana* and *Coast Defense Vessel No. 219* in Hakodate Harbor, Hokkaido, 41°48'N, 140°41'E; *Coast Defense Vessel No. 65* and *Coast Defense Vessel No. 74*, 15 miles south of Muroran, Hokkaido, 42°21'N, 140°59'E; submarine chaser *Ch 48*, 2.1 kilometers off Nakanegishi; auxiliary minesweepers *No. 2 Choyo Maru* five miles off Kikonai, 41°38'N, 140°35'E, *No. 3 Keijin Maru* northeast of Shiriya Saki, 41°30'N, 141°30'E, *Sonobe Maru* off Hiro, Hokkaido, 42°11'N, 143°36'E, and *No. 2 Tamazono Maru*, Kushiro Pier, Hokkaido, 42°58'N, 144°25'E; guardboats *Chitose Maru* four miles off Kayabe, Hokkaido, *No. 18 Eikoku Maru* off Shiobuki Saki, Hokkaido, *No. 2 Meiji Maru* off Hakodate, and *Ojima Maru* off Shiriya Saki, 41°30'N, 141°40'E; gunboat *Hokoku Maru* off Omae Saki, Tsugaru Strait, 41°33'N, 141°08'E;

OFFICIAL PHOTOGRAPH
NOT TO BE RELEASED
FOR PUBLICATION
NAVY YARD MARE ISLAND, CALIF

RESTRICTED

5270-45
PLAN VIEW FORWARD.
MARE ISLAND, CAL.
12 JULY 19
(CA-35)

Heavy cruiser *Indianapolis* (CA 35), painted in Measure 22 camouflage (navy blue and haze gray), at Mare Island Navy Yard, 12 July 1945, shortly before her last voyage. Circled areas in the photo indicate recent alterations. *Cleveland* (CL 55)–class light cruiser is visible in background (right), with open lighter *YC 283* alongside. (NA, 19-N-86915)

transport *No. 1 Un'yo Maru* off Muroran, Hokkaido, 42°21′N, 140°59′E; army cargo vessel *No. 6 Nissen Maru* near Tsugaru Strait; freighters *Taisei Maru* and *Shimofusa Maru* at west entrance of Tsugaru Strait, *Osaki Maru* off Hakodate, *Shichiyo Maru*, 43°47′N, 141°12′E, *Imizu Maru* off Furubiba, Otaru Bay, *Setagawa Maru* off Yongtok, *Eiho Maru* and *No. 5 Kaisei Maru* off Hakodate and *Saito Maru* off east coast of Korea; train ferries *No. 2 Seikan Maru*, *No. 3 Seikan Maru*, *No. 4 Seikan Maru*, *No. 10 Seikan Maru*, *Tsugaru Maru*, *Shoho Maru*, and *Hiran Maru*, and freighters *Senzan Maru* and *Awa Maru* in Aomori-Hakodate area.[254] In addition, TF 38 planes damage destroyer *Yanagi* in Tsugaru Strait; *Coast Defense Vessel*

No. 205 outside Otaru Harbor and *Coast Defense Vessel No. 215* in Hakodate Harbor; auxiliary submarine chaser *Cha 72* and auxiliary minesweeper *Minakami Maru* off Usujiri; guardboat *Miya Maru* off the eastern end of Tsugaru Strait; auxiliary minesweeper *No. 1 Tamazono Maru* at Kushiro Pier, Hokkaido, 42°58′N, 144°25′E; army vessels *Kaizan Maru* outside Hachinohe Harbor and *Sachi Maru* off Otaru; army cargo ship *Taisho Maru* (location unspecified); train ferries *No. 6 Seikan Maru*, *No. 8 Seikan Maru*, and *Matsumae Maru* in Aomori-Hakodate area; freighters *Eitoku Maru*, *Hanasaki Maru*, and *Kenkoku Maru* in Hakodate Harbor; freighters *Taka Maru*, *No. 23 Hokuryu Maru*, *Eireki Maru*, and *No. 3 Koun*

Maru off Muroran; merchant vessel *Hokushin Maru* in Tsugaru Strait; freighters *Shoho Maru* off Yobetsu; *Hirano Maru* (beached) in Miuyama Bay, *Kotsu Maru* and *No. 13 Kyodo Maru* off Otaru, *Shunko Maru* (location unspecified), *Hachirei Maru* nine miles off Iwanai, and *Toyo Maru* off Cape Temma; merchant tankers *No. 5 Kyoei Maru* (beached off Matsumae), and *No. 6 Shoun Maru* (beached off Akashi); and dredger *Kushiro Maru* (location unspecified).

TU 34.8.1 (Rear Admiral John F. Shafroth), consisting of three battleships, two heavy cruisers, and nine destroyers, bombards coastal city of Kamaishi, Honshu, in the first naval gunfire bombardment of the Japanese homeland. The primary target is the Japan Ironworks plant.

Tank landing ships *LST 684* and *LST 826* are damaged by grounding off Okinawa, 26°12′N, 127°57′E.

Mines sink Japanese freighters *Senju Maru* off Moji, Japan, and *Kiukiang Maru* at 35°06′N, 129°43′E.

15 Sunday

PACIFIC. TU 34.8.2 (Rear Admiral Oscar C. Badger), consisting of three battleships, two light cruisers, and eight destroyers, bombards steel and iron works at Muroran on southern coast of Hokkaido, primarily targeting the large Nihon Steel Company and Wanishi Iron and Steel Manufacturing Company.

TF 38 (Vice Admiral John S. McCain), repeating the attacks of the previous day, sinks Japanese minesweeper *W.24* off Tsugaru, 41°38′N, 141°00′E; *Coast Defense Vessel No. 219* off northern Honshu, 41°48′N, 140°41′E; auxiliary submarine chaser *Bunzan Maru* off Hachinoe, Honshu; guardboat *Shinei Maru* off Shirojiri, Hokkaido; freighters *Shoka Maru* off Otaru, *Tokai Maru* at entrance to Sutsu Bay, *No. 5 Seikai Maru* off Mutsure, *Urakawa Maru* and *Toyu Maru* off Nemuro, Japan, and *Shinko Maru* at 40°48′N, 140°05′E; merchant train ferry *No. 1 Seikan Maru* near Miumaya; and merchant fishing boat *No. 15 Taisho Maru* off Ofuyo. TF 38 planes damage freighter *Rijo Maru* off Aomori; escort destroyer *Kasado*, *Coast Defense Vessel No. 47*, and *Coast Defense Vessel No. 55* off Otaru; escort destroyers *Io* and *Fukue* and auxiliary submarine chasers *Cha 81* and *Yaryu Maru* in Hachinoe Harbor, Honshu; *Coast Defense Vessel No. 215* at Fukushima anchorage; *Coast Defense Vessel No. 221* at entrance to Tsugaru Strait; and submarine chaser *Ch 47* at Yamada anchorage. Auxiliary minesweeper *Fuji Maru* is stranded after bomb damage off Hakodate, Hokkaido.

Twenty-seven USAAF B-29s mine the waters off Najin, Wonsan, Hungnam, and Pusan, Korea, and off Naoetsu and Niigata, Japan. Japanese cargo ship *Sorachi Maru* is damaged by mine in Rashin Harbor, Korea; freighter *No. 5 Nichiyu Maru* is damaged by mine off Tomita.

Light minelayer *Thomas E. Fraser* (DM 24) is damaged in collision with miscellaneous auxiliary *Elk* (IX 115) off Okinawa, 26°13′N, 127°50′E.

Submarine *Bluefish* (SS 222) sinks Japanese submarine *I 351*, 100 miles east-northeast of Natuna Besar, Borneo, 05°44′N, 110°06′E.

Submarine *Skate* (SS 305) sinks Japanese transport *Miho Maru* east of south Sakhalin, Kurils, 48°29′N, 147°36′E.

16 Monday

UNITED STATES. First atomic bomb test is held at Alamogordo, New Mexico.

PACIFIC. TF 37, British fast carrier task force (Vice Admiral Henry B. Rawlings, RN), composed of one battleship, four aircraft carriers, eight light cruisers, and 18 destroyers, joins Third Fleet. The British force will operate as part of the U.S. Third Fleet until hostilities end.

TBM (VC 13) from escort carrier *Anzio* (CVE 57) teams with destroyer escort *Lawrence C. Taylor* (DE 415) to sink Japanese submarine *I 13*, 540 miles east of Yokohama, Japan, 34°28′N, 150°55′E.

Submarine *Baya* (SS 318) sinks Ambon-bound Japanese torpedo boat *Kari* in Java Sea, 05°48′S, 115°53′E.

Submarine *Blenny* (SS 324) sinks Japanese gunboat *Nankai* west of Surabaya, Java, N.E.I., 05°26′S, 110°33′E.

Mines sink Japanese auxiliary submarine chaser *Byoritsu Maru* at entrance to Chongjin Bay; freighters *Nanjin Maru* off Wakamatsu, *Nissho Maru* off Mutsure, and *Taikosan Maru* off Motoyama Misaki; and merchant cargo vessel *Rijo Maru* off Ube. Mine irreparably damages submarine depot ship *Nachi Maru* north of Kyushu, off Mutsure Jima, 33°59′N, 130°52′E.

Japanese merchant tanker *No. 6 Toyu Maru* is damaged by aircraft, Kudamatsu, western Inland Sea, Japan.

17 Tuesday

EUROPE. Potsdam (TERMINAL) Conference begins. Attended by President Truman, British Prime Minister Winston S. Churchill, and Soviet Premier Joseph Stalin, this will be the last wartime meeting of the heads of state of those respective powers.

Battleship *Indiana* (BB 58), painted in Measure 22 camouflage (navy blue and haze gray), bombards Kamaishi, 14 July 1945, as seen from *South Dakota* (BB 57). (NA, 80-G-490145)

PACIFIC. TF 38 (Vice Admiral John S. McCain) and British TF 37 (Vice Admiral Henry B. Rawlings, RN) launch strikes against airfields in the Tokyo area.

TU 34.8.2 (Rear Admiral Oscar C. Badger), consisting of five battleships, two light cruisers, and 10 destroyers, bombards heavily industrialized Mito-Hitachi area of Honshu. British battleship HMS *King George V* and two destroyers are attached to the force, making this the first joint U.S.-British bombardment of the Japanese homeland. Carrier *Bon Homme Richard* (CV 31) provides night combat air patrol to cover the operation.

Twenty-eight USAAF B-29s mine Shimonoseki Straits and the waters off Chongjin, Korea, and Nanao and Fushiki, Japan.

Over 200 USAAF B-24s, B-25s, A-26s, and P-47s attack Kiangwan airfield, Shanghai, which contains the largest concentration of Japanese aircraft in China.

Japanese *Coast Defense Vessel No. 204* is damaged by marine casualty, Senzaki Bay, Japan.

MEDITERRANEAN. U.S. freighter *John H. Hammond* is damaged by mine off Elba, 42°55′30″N, 10°08′00″E; the three Armed Guard sailors are uninjured in the incident, but three merchant sailors die and four are injured. The ship is subsequently towed to Piombino, Italy.

18 Wednesday

PACIFIC. TF 38 (Vice Admiral John S. McCain) strikes Yokosuka Naval Base and airfields in the Tokyo area. Primary target at the former place is battleship *Nagato*, which is damaged. TF 38 planes also sink training ship (ex-armored cruiser) *Kasuga*, escort destroyer *Yaezakura* (60 percent completed), submarine *I 372*, submarine chaser *Harushima*, and auxiliary patrol vessels *Pa No. 37*, *Pa No. 110*, and *Pa No. 122* at Yokosuka.[255] TF 37 and TF 38 planes sink Japanese motor torpedo boat *Gyoraitei No. 28* at Yokosuka and damage battleship *Nagato*, motor torpedo boat *Gyoraitei No. 256*, landing ship *T.110*, target ship *Yakaze*, and auxiliary submarine chaser *Cha 225*.

TG 35.4 (Rear Admiral Carl F. Holden), composed of four light cruisers and the destroyers of Destroyer Squadron 62, detached from TG 38.1, conduct antishipping sweep off the entrance to Sagami Nada and bombard Japanese radar installations at Nojima Saki, Honshu (see 19 July). En route to the objective, destroyers *Hank* (DD 702) and *Wallace L. Lind* (DD 703), detached to take a radar contact under fire, mistakenly shell (but do not damage) submarine *Gabilan* (SS 252).

Planes from carrier *Wasp* (CV 18) bomb Japanese installations on Wake Island.

Submarine *Barb* (SS 220) sinks Japanese *Coast Defense Vessel No. 112* south of Sakhalin, Japan, 46°04′N, 142°16′E.

Submarine *Cero* (SS 225) is damaged by aerial bomb off Kurils, 45°14′N, 148°41′E, and is forced to terminate her patrol.

Submarine *Hawkbill* (SS 366) is damaged by depth charges off Malaya, 04°41′N, 103°30′E, and is forced to terminate her patrol.

British submarine HMS *Trenchant* attacks Japanese convoy, sinking army shuttle vessel *Hayabusa Maru* and damaging cargo vessels *No. 3 Taikyo Maru, No. 3 Nichiei Maru,* and *No. 2 Saiwai Maru* northwest of Lombok Island, 08°22′S, 116°02′E.

USN land-based planes sink Japanese merchant cargo vessels *Chishima Maru* off Kawajiri at 34°36′N, 125°00′E, *Shintai Maru* at 34°25′N, 130°40′E, and *Tagami Maru* off Tsushima, 34°47′N, 137°02′E.

Japanese escort carrier *Kaiyo* is damaged by mine 135 miles northwest of Sata Misaki, Kyushu, 30°59′N, 130°40′E.

Japanese freighter *Tenyo Maru* is sunk (cause unknown), north of Honshu.

Japanese fast transport *T.9* is damaged by aircraft four miles east of Hatsushima, Japan.

Japanese merchant tanker *No. 8 Horai Maru* is damaged by marine casualty, Atsuta, north of Ishikari.

19 Thursday

PACIFIC. Twenty-nine USAAF B-29s mine the waters off the Japanese ports of Niigata, Kobe, Osaka, Maizuru, and Miyazu, Japan, and the Korean ports of Wonsan and Hungnam.

TF 38 planes damage Japanese carriers *Amagi* and *Katsuragi* and battleship *Haruna* at Kure, Japan.

TG 35.4 (Rear Admiral Carl F. Holden) concludes its bombardment of Japanese radar installations at Nojima Saki, Honshu.

Carrier *Antietam* (CV 36) is damaged by premature explosion of 5-inch shell during gunnery exercises, Hawaiian Operating Area.

Japanese planes attack U.S. fleet units off Okinawa; one *kamikaze* crashes and damages destroyer *Thatcher* (DD 514), 26°15′N, 127°50′E; another nearly crashes destroyer *Charles J. Badger* (DD 657).

Submarine *Bumper* (SS 333), attacking Japanese convoy in Gulf of Siam, sinks fleet tanker *No. 3 Kyoei Maru.*

Mine sinks Japanese merchant dredger *Daikoku Maru* inside Niigata Harbor.

20 Friday

PACIFIC. Submarine *Bumper* (SS 333) attacks Japanese convoy in Gulf of Siam, sinking guardboat *No. 3 Kyoraku Maru,* 08°08′N, 103°40′E.

Submarine *Threadfin* (SS 410) sinks Japanese minesweeper *W.39* northwest of Mokp'o, Korea, 35°01′N, 125°42′E.

Japanese freighter *Tatsutagawa Maru* is sunk by mine, Shimonoseki Strait.

21 Saturday

PACIFIC. Submarine *Sea Robin* (SS 407) sinks Japanese cargo vessels *Chio Maru* and *Yoshi Maru* 30 kilometers east of Shinishi Island, 33°45′N, 126°25′E.

Mines sink Japanese freighter *Nichiyo Maru* in Tomita Harbor and damage army cargo ship *Kazura Maru* off Pusan, Korea.

Japanese freighter *Meiyu Maru* is damaged by aircraft 5.4 kilometers off Makino Jima Light.

22 Sunday

PACIFIC. TF 93 (Rear Admiral John H. Brown Jr.), consisting of light cruisers *Richmond* (CL 9) and *Concord* (CL 10) and five destroyers, conducts unopposed bombardment of installations at Suribachi, Paramushir, Kurils.

Destroyer Squadron 61, on antishipping sweep in vicinity of Sagami Bay, Japan, picks up on its radar screens a four-ship Japanese convoy about five miles west of Nojima Saki and engages it (see 23 July).

Japanese attack U.S. shipping off Okinawa; attack transport *Marathon* (APA 200) is damaged by aerial torpedo, 26°13′N, 127°50′E.

Twenty-six USAAF B-29s mine Shimonoseki Straits and the waters off Najin, Pusan, and Masan, Korea.

Japanese auxiliary minesweeper *No. 7 Toshi Maru* is wrecked off Sata Misaki, Japan, 31°00′N, 130°40′E.

Mines sink Japanese freighter *Katori Maru* off Niigata and unnamed merchant motor sailer 1.5 kilometers off Cape Motoyama. Mines damage auxiliary submarine chaser *Cha 20* off Kobe; freighters *Kojo Maru* off Niigata, *Choyo Maru* off Najin, and *Daikoku Maru,* Hagi Harbor; and merchant tanker *Yuyo Maru* 1.6 kilometers off Mushima Light.

Japanese merchant ship *Hokko Go* is sunk by aircraft, 35°10′N, 129°30′E.

Japanese freighter *No. 3 Manei Maru* is sunk by USAAF mine laid by B-29 (20th Air Force) 10 kilometers west of Funagawa, Honshu, 39°53′N, 139°52′E.

Japanese merchant fishing boat *No. 58 Nanshin Maru* is damaged by aircraft, 35°20′N, 130°00′E.

23 Monday

PACIFIC. Destroyer Squadron 61 concludes its engagement with a Japanese convoy, encountered the previous day, off Sagami Bay, sinking *No. 3 Hakutetsu Maru* off Mora, Chiba prefecture, 34°54′N, 139°50′E.

Submarine *Barb* (SS 220) lands an eight-man commando party, which blows up a Japanese train on east coast of Karafuto.

Submarine *Hardhead* (SS 365) sinks Japanese auxiliary submarine chaser *Cha 117* off Java, N.E.I., 08°10′S, 115°29′E.

Submarine *Sea Poacher* (SS 406) sinks Japanese guardboat *No. 2 Kiri Maru* between Ono Saki and Shoya Saki, Japan, 37°16′N, 141°04′E.

Mines sink Japanese guardboat *No. 2 Taisho Maru* off Chinhae, Korea; merchant tug *Kaiko Maru* and cargo ship *Shoko Maru* off Niigata; freighters *No. 1 Taiha Maru* and *No. 2 Taishin Maru* off Moji, *No. 6 Nissho Maru* off Kammon Strait, *Yamadori Maru* outside Wakamatsu Harbor, and *No. 2 Tsurukawa Maru* off Wakamatsu; and merchant vessel *Kocho Maru* off Mutsure. Mine damages freighter *Gizan Maru* near Moji.

USAAF B-24s (Far East Air Force), on antishipping sweep off south coast of Korea, sink Japanese merchant tanker *No. 15 Horai Maru* off Hokko, 36°02′N, 129°23′E.

Japanese freighter *No. 5 Adaka Maru* is damaged by aircraft, 34°36′N, 130°55′E.

24 Tuesday

PACIFIC. TF 38 launches strikes against the Inland Sea area, Japan, striking Kure Naval Base and airfields at Nagoya, Osaka, and Miho. TF 38 planes sink battleship-carrier *Hyuga* in Hiro Bay, Kure, 34°10′N, 132°33′E; heavy cruiser *Tone* (direct hits and near-misses), 34°14′N, 132°27′E (she is pushed aground at Nomi Jima to facilitate salvage); training ship (ex-coast defense ship) *Iwate* off Eta Jima, 34°14′N, 132°30′E; target ship (ex-battleship) *Settsu* at Kure; and guardboat *Kaiwa Maru* north of Hime Jima, Kyushu. Aircraft damage carrier *Ryuho* and battleship-carrier *Ise* at Kure; battleship *Haruna* and light cruiser *Oyodo* off Eta Jima; heavy cruiser *Aoba* at Kure Navy Yard; escort destroyer *Hagi* and fast transport *T.19* at Kure; torpedo cruiser *Kitakami* (near-misses and strafing) and destroyers *Yoizuki* and *Hari* near Kure; escort destroyer *Kaba* off Osaka; escort destroyer *Tsubaki* near Okayama, 34°38′N, 133°50′E;

Coast Defense Vessel No. 190 in Tanabe Harbor; and Coast Defense Vessel No. 4 off Toba. Transport (ex-seaplane carrier) Kiyokawa Maru is beached at Shida, Shimonoseki Straits; carrier Amagi is hit by only one rocket off Kurahashi Jima, Kure, 34°11′N, 132°30′E, but its passage close by the commanding officer so unnerves the captain that he unhesitatingly orders the ship abandoned.

Japanese escort carrier Kaiyo is damaged by planes from British carriers HMS Formidable, HMS Indefatigable, and HMS Victorious. Kaiyo's travails, however, do not end there. She is damaged by USAAF mine (laid by a 20th Air Force B-29) off Beppu, Japan, 33°18′N, 131°30′E. Destroyer Yukaze takes the wounded warship in tow (see 29 July).

Aircraft (service unspecified) sink Japanese freighters Ito Maru off Kominase Light, Inari Maru in Moji Harbor, Komyo Maru off Okinoshima Light, No. 2 Ise Maru off Mihoga Saki, and Kinokawa Maru off Yoshiura; merchant tankers No. 9 Kinyu Maru off Tsuru Jima, Sabang Maru off Okurokami Island, and Kanatsu Maru in Awa Jima anchorage; merchant tug Mutsurejima Maru off Kagaji, Oita prefecture; and merchant vessels Sugamada Maru, Jinzai Harbor, and Sen Maru off Hakodate.

Aircraft (service unspecified) damage Japanese freighter Kurogane Maru, Kobe, Japan, and merchant tanker Gyokuei Maru, 33°55′N, 131°45′E.

Guardboats No. 3 Seisho Maru and Taiko Maru are sunk by U.S. aircraft at Kobe, Japan.

Auxiliary submarine chaser Cha 98 is sunk by aircraft off Moji, Japan.

Japanese transport No. 11 Kaishin Maru is sunk by aircraft south of Tsushima, 33°31′N, 129°47′E.

TG 35.3 (Rear Admiral J. Cary Jones Jr.), consisting of four light cruisers (from TG 38.3) and six destroyers (from TG 38.4), conducts high-speed antishipping sweep across Kii Strait, Japan. Destroyer Colahan (DD 658) fires upon only surface contact, which proves to be submarine Toro (SS 422), on lifeguard station south of Shikoku. Fortunately, Toro is not damaged in this case of mistaken identity (see 25 July).

Escort carrier Vella Gulf (CVE 111), as TU 19.6.1, carries out air strikes on Pagan, one of the two remaining bases in the Marianas. She carries out strikes against Rota (the other base) two days later.

Destroyer escort Underhill (DE 682), damaged by kaitens from Japanese submarine I 53 off Luzon, 19°20′N, 126°42′E, is scuttled by

submarine chasers PC 803 and PC 804 and escort patrol vessel PCE 872.

Submarine Chub (SS 329) sinks Japanese tug (ex-Dutch Ginah) off Java, 07°46′S, 114°24′E.

Japanese auxiliary minesweeper Wa. 3 is sunk by aircraft, Surabaya, Java, N.E.I.

Mines sink Japanese freighters Koichi Maru, Wonsan Harbor, Korea, and Himekawa Maru four kilometers off Hime Jima, Kyushu, and damage auxiliary submarine chaser Cha 226 off Moji and merchant tanker Tatsukusu Maru, Hagi.

Japanese merchant tanker No. 6 Nanki Maru is damaged by marine casualty, 38°18′N, 141°25′E.

25 Wednesday

PACIFIC. TF 38 continues air strikes on targets of opportunity in the Inland Sea area. TF 38 planes sink Japanese guardboats No. 10 Dairi Maru and No. 2 Kompira Maru off Moji and No. 10 Fukuei Maru in Bungo Strait, 33°00′N, 132°10′E; army tanker Kaisoku Maru off Hiro; freighter Daio Maru at 35°06′N, 129°40′E; and merchant tankers No. 6 Ryuei Maru off eastern part of Okurokami Island and No. 6 Kinyu Maru off east coast of Ani Jima. In addition, they damage heavy cruiser Aoba, Kure, 34°13′N, 132°31′E; Coast Defense Vessel No. 4, Toba; freighters No. 6 Tokai Maru and No. 5 Shokai Maru off Shimane Peninsula, and Meiho Maru, Agenosho; and merchant tanker Tenwa Maru, Kanoya.

TG 35.3 (Rear Admiral J. Cary Jones Jr.), consisting of four light cruisers (from TG 38.3) and six destroyers (from TG 38.4), bombards Kushimoto Seaplane Base airfield near Shiono Misaki, Honshu, and adjacent facilities.

Thirty USAAF B-29s (20th Air Force) mine the waters off Chongjin and Pusan, Korea, and Fushiki, Nanao, Ohama, and Tsuruga, Japan. Mines laid by B-29s sink Japanese freighters Hoshi Maru at mouth of Maizuru Bay, 34°35′N, 135°21′E, and Eian Maru off Tottori, Honshu, 35°33′N, 133°14′E.

Submarine Barb (SS 220) bombards lumber mill and sampan building yard at Shibetoro, destroying 35 sampans under construction.

British submarine HMS Stubborn sinks Makassar-bound Japanese Patrol Boat No. 2 (ex-destroyer Nadakaze) in Java Sea, 07°06′S, 115°42′E.

26 Thursday

PACIFIC. Destroyer Lowry (DD 770) is damaged by on-board tetrachlorethane (chemical) explosion, Philippine Sea, 19°30′N, 128°00′E.

U.S. aircraft sink Japanese auxiliary minesweepers No. 18 Hinode Maru and Rikuzen Maru off Haeju-Won, Korea, 37°58′N, 126°40′E, and 37°58′N, 125°40′E, respectively.

Aircraft (service unspecified) sink Japanese merchant tanker Seria Maru near Aioi, 34°01′N, 131°25′E; freighter Mishima Maru near Hizen, O Shima; and merchant fishing vessel No. 40 Misago Maru off Uketo.

Japanese target ship (ex-battleship) Settsu is damaged by marine casualty, Eta Jima Harbor, northwest of Kure.

Japanese freighter Annette Fritzen Go is damaged by mine off Pusan, Korea.

Cargo ship Spica (AK 16) and U.S. freighters Jonathan Harrington and Enos A. Mills depart Dutch Harbor, Alaska, for Point Barrow, transporting men and supplies for Navy Petroleum Reserve 4 (see 3, 8, 10, 22, 24, and 25 August).

27 Friday

PACIFIC. Potsdam Declaration calling for unconditional surrender is delivered to the Japanese government. The Japanese, however, ignore the ultimatum, prompting President Truman to approve plans to drop atomic weapons on Japan.

Twenty-five USAAF B-29s (20th Air Force) mine Shimonoseki Straits and the waters off Niigata, Miyazu, Maizuru, and Senzaki, Japan. Mines laid by USAAF B-29s sink Japanese army cargo ship Unten Maru off Suo Nada, 33°56′N, 131°11′E, and freighters Meiko Maru off Kokushi, Yamaguchi prefecture, 34°10′N, 130°55′E, and No. 55 Banshu Maru, Odo Strait, Shimonoseki; mines damage freighters Jintsugawa Maru off Fushiki and Tatsumaki Maru off Wakamatsu.

Cargo ship Ganymede (AK 104) is damaged in collision with Army barge BKP 42 (346th Harbor Craft Company), P.I., 11°11′N, 125°05′E.

U.S. freighter John A. Rawlins is damaged by Japanese aerial torpedo in Naha Harbor, Okinawa; in addition to the 39-man merchant crew, 28 Armed Guards and 191 Construction Battalion men are on board at this time. Of those men, only three are injured; the ship, however, will ultimately be written off as a total loss. U.S. freighter Pratt Victory is damaged by aerial torpedo south of Ie Shima, Ryukyus; the blast sinks tank landing craft LCT 1050 alongside discharging cargo. There are no fatalities among the 27-man Armed Guard on board Pratt Victory, which offloads the remainder of her cargo without further incident.

Submarine *Pargo* (SS 264) is damaged by depth charges and aerial bombs off northern Celebes, 01°35′N, 125°20′E, but remains on patrol.

Submarine *Pogy* (SS 266) sinks Japanese freighter *Chikuzen Maru* southwest of Kyoga Saki, about 90 miles north of Tottori, Honshu, 37°00′N, 134°02′E.

British submarine HMS *Tudor* sinks Japanese fishing vessel at 06°15′S, 108°08′E.

USAAF planes (Far East Air Force) sink Japanese landing ship *T.176* off southern Kyushu, 31°00′N, 130°33′E.

Japanese transport *Doshi Maru* is sunk by aircraft off Nishitomari, east of O Shima.

Japanese auxiliary submarine chaser *No. 40 Giso Maru* is sunk by aircraft off Urajiri.

Aircraft damage Japanese auxiliary submarine chaser *No. 11 Shonan Maru* inside Chefoo Harbor, China, and damage merchant tanker *No. 2 Seiko Maru* off Osaka.

28 Saturday

PACIFIC. TF 38 (Vice Admiral John S. McCain) strikes Inland Sea area between Nagoya and northern Kyushu, principally targeting the Kure Naval Base. TF 38 planes sink battleship *Haruna* off Eta Jima, eight miles northwest of Kure, 34°15′N, 132°29′E; battleship-carrier *Ise*, five miles northwest of Kure, 34°12′N, 132°31′E; training ship (ex-coast defense vessel) *Izumo* off Eta Jima, 34°14′N, 132°30′E; heavy cruiser *Aoba*, Kure Navy Yard, 34°13′N, 132°31′E; light cruiser *Oyodo* off Eta Jima (by near-misses), 34°13′N, 132°25′E; submarine *I 404*, Kure; escort destroyer *Nashi*, Mitajiri Saki, Kure, 34°14′N, 132°30′E; guardboat *No. 5 Fukuju Maru* at Kujukurihama, Chiba prefecture; guardboats *No. 2 Fukusei Maru* and *No. 2 Inari Maru*, Kobe; submarine depot ship *Komahashi*, victualling stores ship *Kosho Maru*, and auxiliary minesweeper *No. 18 Banshu Maru*, Owase; guardboat *No. 2 Han'ei Maru*, Aomori; naval auxiliary *Koryu Maru*, Innoshima dockyard; freighters *Kinzan Maru* four miles east of Ogashima and *Kiyotada Maru* in Ube Harbor; freighters *No. 11 Kyowa Maru* in Kobe Harbor and *No. 3 Mikage Maru* off Otaru; and merchant tankers *No. 4 Kinyu Maru* 34°48′N, 134°28′E, and *No. 6 Kinyu Maru* at 34°23′N, 134°50′E. British carrier planes (TF 37) sink *Coast Defense Vessel No. 4* in Ise Bay, 34°43′N, 136°43′E, and *Coast Defense Vessel No. 30* off Yura.

TF 38 planes also damage carrier *Katsuragi* and training carrier *Hosho*, Kure; torpedo cruiser (ex-light cruiser) *Kitakami* in Hi-roshima Bay; submarine *I 205* (repaired after damage inflicted by TF 58 aircraft on 19 March) in drydock, Kure; destroyer *Asagao* west of Bisan-Seto; *Coast Defense Vessel No. 45* and submarine chaser *Ch 14* near Yokosuka; escort destroyer *Habushi* and *Coast Defense Vessel No. 44*, Sasebo; *Coast Defense Vessel No. 190* in Yura Straits; guardboats *No. 2 Kainan Maru* and *No. 2 Inari Maru*, Kobe Harbor; motor torpedo boat *Gyoraitei No. 823*, Yokosuka; auxiliary minesweepers *No. 10 Showa Maru* and *No. 1 Kyojin Maru* off Owase, Japan, as well as merchant passenger ship *Tenzan Maru*, 35°42′N, 132°42′E; freighters *No. 8 Shinto Maru*, 35°06′N, 129°45′E, and *Nagasaki Maru* off south side of Osagi Jima; merchant tankers *No. 18 Nissho Maru* and *No. 2 Seiko Maru*, Osaka, and *Shingi Maru*, Kobe; and freighter *Taigen Maru*, in dock at Innoshima.

TF 32 (Rear Admiral Jesse B. Oldendorf) provides cover for the ongoing minesweeping operations in the East China Sea (Rear Admiral Alexander Sharp). TF 32 CVEs launch planes to conduct strikes on shipping off the mouth of the Yangtze River; no targets, however, are found.

Destroyer *Callaghan* (DD 792) is sunk by *kamikaze*, on radar picket station approximately 50 miles southwest of Okinawa, 25°43′N, 126°55′E; she is the last Allied vessel to be lost to that weapon. Destroyer *Prichett* (DD 561) is damaged by near-miss of suicide plane, 25°43′N, 126°56′E, as she assists the mortally damaged *Callaghan*. Reflecting the depth of desperation reached by the Japanese, *Callaghan*'s assailant is a bomb-carrying WILLOW (primary training biplane).

Submarine *Hardhead* (SS 365) damages Japanese *No. 165 Shuttle Boat*, 09°09′S, 115°25′E.

Submarine *Sennet* (SS 408), attacking Japanese convoy off western Honshu, sinks freighters *Hagikawa Maru*, eight miles west of Noshiro Harbor, 40°17′N, 139°50′E, and *No. 15 Unkai Maru* and *Hakuei Maru* off Sakata, 39°49′N, 139°47′E.

Japanese auxiliary minesweeper *No. 1 Keijin Maru* sinks after running aground off Owase, Japan, 34°05′N, 136°14′E.

Japanese army cargo ship *Hitora Maru* is damaged by marine casualty, Innoshima dockyard, Japan.

Japanese transport *Teiritsu Maru*, damaged by mine sown by USAAF B-29s (20th Air Force), is run aground 0.2 kilometer southwest of Bakuchi Saki, 35°32′N, 135°20′E (see 30 July).

29 Sunday

PACIFIC. TU 34.8.1 (Rear Admiral John F. Shafroth), consisting of three battleships, four heavy cruisers, and 10 destroyers, begins bombardment of shops, aircraft factory, and other facilities at Hamamatsu, Honshu. British battleship HMS *King George V* and three destroyers operate independently but join in the bombardment. Carrier *Bon Homme Richard* (CV 31) supplies precautionary night combat air patrols and spotter aircraft.

Twenty-six USAAF B-29s (20th Air Force) mine Shimonoseki Straits and the waters off Najin, Korea, and Fukuoka, Japan. Freighter *Tatsukashi Maru*, damaged by mine, is beached off Pusan, Korea.

Destroyer *Cassin Young* (DD 793) and high-speed transport *Horace A. Bass* (APD 124) are damaged by suicide planes off Okinawa, 26°08′N, 127°58′E, and 26°17′N, 127°34′E, respectively.

USAAF P-47s (7th Air Force), on sweep for targets of opportunity in the Nagasaki, Japan, area, sink auxiliary submarine chaser *Cha 207*, 32°00′N, 130°00′E. A-26s damage merchant tanker *No. 5 Yamamizu Maru* off Nagasaki.

USAAF B-25s (Far East Air Force) damage Japanese escort carrier *Kaiyo* in Hiji Harbor, Beppu Wan, 33°20′N, 131°32′E.

USAAF B-25s and P-51s, on antishipping sweep off coast of Korea, sink Japanese army cargo ships *Hokusei Maru* off Kuryungpo and *No. 18 Ono Maru* off Ulsan; freighter *Seishin Maru*, 35°32′N, 127°30′E; and tanker *Yushin Maru* and cargo vessel *Shoryu Maru*, 35°32′N, 127°30′E. In addition, they damage freighters *No. 12 Reisui Maru* in western channel of Tsushima Strait, 34°59′N, 128°59′E, and *Kokyu Maru* off Pusan. Japanese freighter *Tangetsu Maru* is also sunk off Ulsan, Korea; merchant passenger ship *Tenzan Maru* is sunk, 35°40′N, 132°39′E.

Marine casualties sink Japanese freighter *Sumioyoshi Maru* outside Kamaishi Harbor, Japan, and damage freighters *Miesan Maru* near Shira Jima and *No. 2 Mitsu Maru* south of Wakamiya Saki, Iki Island, and also result in the loss of guardboats *Asahi Maru* east of Pusan, Korea, and *No. 6 Kaiyo Maru* off Wakamiya Saki, Korean Strait.

30 Monday

PACIFIC. Heavy cruiser *Indianapolis* (CA 35) is sunk by Japanese submarine *I 58* northeast of Leyte, 12°02′N, 134°48′E (see 2 August). TF 38 (Vice Admiral John S. McCain) launches strikes against airfields and industrial targets in central Honshu and sweeps against Japanese shipping in Maizuru Bay. TF 38 planes sink escort vessel *Okinawa* six miles north-northwest of Maizuru, 35°30′N, 135°21′E; submarine chaser *Ch 26* in Korea Strait, 34°47′N, 128°27′E; minelayer *Toshima* off Maizuru; auxiliary submarine chasers *Keisho Maru* and *Chikuzen Maru* and guardboat *No. 12 Kogyo Maru* at Imaura; auxiliary submarine chasers *No. 2 Nippon Maru* in Usami Bay and *No. 53 Banshu Maru* off Obama; guardboat *No. 10 Sumiyoshi Maru* eight miles north of Kohi Jima; freighters *Kashi Maru* off Tsuruga, 35°30′N, 135°21′E, and *Taruyasu Maru* off Maizuru; and merchant ship *Kamogawa Maru* off Ullung Island, 35°20′N, 130°30′E. TF 38 planes damage escort destroyer *Takane* near Maizuru; submarine depot ship *Chogei*, submarines *I 153* and *I 202*, Coast Defense Vessel No. 2, and minelayer *Tatsumiya Maru* off Maizuru; Coast Defense Vessel No. 27 in Korea Strait, 34°47′N, 128°27′E; auxiliary submarine chaser *Cha 182* off Ito; and guardboat *No. 18 Sumiyoshi Maru* (damaged and run aground) north of Kohi Jima. TF 38 planes also damage freighter *Shotai Maru* and merchant vessel *Fukuan Maru* off Maizuru. British carrier planes from TF 37 complete the destruction of transport *Teiritsu Maru*, aground off Maizuru since 28 July, 35°32′N, 135°20′E.

TU 34.8.1 (Rear Admiral John F. Shafroth), consisting of three battleships, four heavy cruisers, and 10 destroyers, completes bombardment of shops, aircraft factory, and other facilities at Hamamatsu, Honshu, Japan. One British battleship and three destroyers take part in this effort as well.

Task force (Rear Admiral Alexander Sharp) completes minesweeping operations in the East China Sea; his ships sweep approximately 7,300 square miles and destroy 404 mines without casualty.

British midget submarines *XE 1* (towed to the area by submarine HMS *Spark*) and *XE 3* (towed by HMS *Stygian*) penetrate defenses of Singapore Harbor to attack Japanese heavy cruisers *Myoko* and *Takao*, respectively (see 31 July).

Submarine *Sennet* (SS 408) sinks Japanese freighter *Yuzan Maru* near Mutsuta Misaki, western Hokkaido, 42°36′N, 139°49′E.

Mines laid by USAAF B-29s (20th Air Force) sink destroyer *Hatsushimo* inside Miyazu Bay, 12 miles west-northwest of Maizuru, Japan, 35°33′N, 135°12′E, and passenger-cargo vessel *Shokei Maru* at 42°36′N, 139°48′E, and damage destroyer *Yukikaze* near Miyazu.

Aircraft sink Japanese army cargo ship *Gessan Maru* off Ulsan, Korea; merchant passenger ship *Shokei Maru* in Miyazu Bay; freighters *No. 2 Shozan Maru* off Ulgi and *Koshin Maru* off Pang-O-Jin; and freighter *Shinko Maru* off Choshi. Aircraft also damage freighters *Choko Maru* off Himo; *Shoko Maru* in Wakasa Bay, western coast of Honshu, Japan; and *No. 5 Kenkon Maru* at 35°44′N, 124°57′E; merchant tug *Hokusan Maru*, Pusan, Korea; and freighter *Nissho Maru* off Tsuruga, Japan.

Japanese freighter *Matsura Maru* is damaged by marine casualty, beached, at mouth of Yujin Harbor.

Japanese freighter *No. 15 Yamabishi Maru* is lost to marine casualty, Wakasa Bay, western coast of Honshu, Japan.

31 Tuesday

PACIFIC. Destroyers of Destroyer Squadron 25, conducting antishipping sweep in Suguru Gulf, bombard railroad yards and industrial area of Shimuzu, Japan.

PB4Ys (FAW 1), operating from Yontan Field, Okinawa, destroy a span of the Seisen River bridge, severing the main north-south double track railroad line in Korea.

Destroyer *Bancroft* (DD 598) is damaged in collision with miscellaneous auxiliary *Carondelet* (IX 136) off Luzon, 14°50′N, 120°15′E.

Submarine *Thornback* (SS 418) damages Japanese submarine chaser *Ch 42* five miles off Osaki, Japan, 38°53′N, 141°35′E.

Japanese heavy cruiser *Takao* is damaged by charges, placed by British midget submarines *XE 3* and *XE 1* the night before, at Singapore.[256]

Mines sink Japanese guardboat *No. 5 Teru Maru* off Wonsan, Korea, and naval auxiliary *No. 5 Matsumae Maru* off Pusan.

Auxiliary submarine chaser *No. 9 Kamoi Maru* is damaged by grounding, Ukushima.

Japanese naval vessels sunk during July 1945 (exact date unspecified): guardboats *No. 51 Tama Maru*, by U.S. aircraft, at mouth of Yangtze River; *No. 3 Kaigyo Maru*, by mine, east of the mouth of Kammon Strait, Japan; and *No. 5 Shinshu Maru*, by U.S. aircraft, off Japan (exact location unspecified); and auxiliary minesweeper *No. 2 Keijin Maru*, by aircraft, four kilometers north of Shiriya, Japan.

Japanese merchant vessels damaged during July 1945 (exact date unspecified): cargo ships *Shojun Maru*, agent unknown, near Masan, Korea; *Imazugawa Maru*, by aircraft, location unspecified; *No. 8 Hino Maru*, agent unknown, at northern entrance of Kammon Strait; and

No. 1 Shinyo Maru, agent and location of loss/damage unspecified; and tanker *No. 11 Yoshitomo Maru*, agent and location of loss/damage unspecified.

AUGUST

1 Wednesday

PACIFIC. TG 12.3 attacks Wake Island. Planes from small carrier *Cabot* (CVL 28) bomb installations. Battleship *Pennsylvania* (BB 38) bombards the atoll but is damaged by shore battery, 19°20′N, 166°30′E.

TG 95.2 (Rear Admiral Francis S. Low), a fast striking group consisting of large cruisers *Alaska* (CB 1) and *Guam* (CB 2), four light cruisers, and nine destroyers, departs Okinawa and proceeds into the East China Sea to conduct antishipping sweeps off Shanghai, China.

TG 95.3 (Vice Admiral Jesse B. Oldendorf), consisting of three battleships, a heavy cruiser, a light cruiser, three escort carriers, six destroyers, and three destroyer escorts, accompanies TG 95.2 to furnish covering support.

Heaviest USAAF B-29 raid to date: 774 planes drop 6,632 tons of bombs on five different targets in Japan. Additionally, in what will be the largest operation of its kind, 42 USAAF B-29s mine Shimonoseki Straits and the waters off Najin and Chongjin, Korea, and Hamada, Japan. Japanese escort vessel *Ikura* is damaged by mine in Oguchi Channel, Nanao.

USAAF B-24s (Far East Air Force) bomb Nagasaki dockyard area, damaging motor torpedo boat *Gyoraitei No. 102*; USAAF B-25s and fighter-bomber aircraft (Far East Air Force) bomb shipping in Nagasaki Harbor, damaging freighter *Kinko Maru* and tanker *Tada Maru*. Other USAAF (Far East Air Force) planes sink freighter *Hayabusa Maru* near Eboshi Light, 33°41′N, 129°59′E.

Japanese merchant tanker *Chokai Maru* is damaged by marine casualty in Kii Strait, 34°38′N, 134°56′E.

British submarines HMS *Thorough* and HMS *Taciturn* attack Japanese shipping in Buleleng Roads, N.E.I.; while *Taciturn* engages shore batteries, *Thorough* sinks cargo vessels *Hino Maru* and *Shoei Maru* and shells warehouses.

Submarine chaser *PC 784* collides with Army tug *LT 666* in a dense fog off entrance to Amchitka, Alaska, harbor; both vessels suffer damage, but there are no injuries to either crew.

2 Thursday

EUROPE. Potsdam (TERMINAL) Conference, attended by President Truman, British Prime Minister Clement Attlee (who had replaced Winston S. Churchill as prime minister in the July general elections in Britain), and Soviet Premier Joseph Stalin, ends.

PACIFIC. PV-1 (VPB 52), flying from Peleliu, sights first survivors from heavy cruiser *Indianapolis* (CA 35) at 11°30′N, 133°30′E. Rescue efforts, involving ships and planes, begin this day and continue until 8 August.

Destroyers *Conner* (DD 582) and *Charrette* (DD 581) intercept and search Japanese hospital ship *Tachibana Maru*, which is found to be carrying arms and ammunition in boxes marked with red crosses; the destroyers place prize crew of 80 marines and sailors on board. *Tachibana Maru* is then taken to Morotai, N.E.I., for examination.

Submarine *Bugara* (SS 331), operating against Japanese coastal shipping off the Malay Peninsula, sinks schooner with gunfire and takes on board crew. One lifeboat, however, sinks and fouls the submarine's port screw, damaging it, 06°40′N, 101°51′E. Later, *Bugara* happens across Malay pirates attacking Chinese-manned Japanese schooner en route to Singapore, 06°21′N, 102°15′E. The brigands flee upon *Bugara*'s approach. After taking off the Chinese crew (who are grateful for the submarine's timely arrival, the Malayan cutthroats having already killed two crewmen) and sinking the schooner, *Bugara* then pursues the pirates and destroys them. Later, *Bugara*'s divers, working in the dark, repair the screw damaged earlier in the day.

Army tender *TP 122* grounds off East Cape, Amchitka, Alaska, near Irakin Point; rescue tug *ATR 32* is sent to the scene to assist.

USAAF mines sink Japanese freighter *Santo Maru* off Niigata, Japan, 37°57′N, 139°04′E, and damage minesweeper *W.17* south of Chinhae, Korea, 36°06′N, 128°40′E.

3 Friday

PACIFIC. Mines laid by USAAF B-29s (20th Air Force) sink Japanese freighters *No. 3 Kamikage Maru* outside Najin Harbor, Korea, and *Tairetsu Maru* in Kobe Harbor, 34°39′N, 135°12′E, and transport *Aga Maru* off Takatakao, 38°55′N, 139°45′E. Mines damage army ship *Osho Maru* off Tsuruga, 35°40′N, 136°04′E, and freighters *Kokuyo Maru* east of He Saki and *Shotai Maru* in Fushiki Harbor, Japan.

Japanese cargo ship *Taii Maru* is damaged,

agent unspecified, 5.6 kilometers off Karasu Jima Islet, north of Sa Shima Light.

British submarines HMS *Trump* and HMS *Tiptoe* attack Japanese Batavia-to-Singapore convoy escorted by *Patrol Boat No. 109*, sinking army cargo vessel *Tencho Maru*, 05°07′S, 106°05′E.

Navy Petroleum Reserve 4 Expedition, formed around cargo ship *Spica* (AK 16) and U.S. freighters *Jonathan Harrington* and *Enos A. Mills*, anchors off Icy Cape, Alaska. There it will remain until ice conditions improve at Point Barrow, its ultimate destination (see 8, 10, 22, 24, and 25 August).

4 Saturday

PACIFIC. Japanese merchant tanker *Koshin Maru* is sunk by mine in Osaka Harbor, 34°37′N, 135°18′E. Mines also damage army cargo ship *Tensho Maru* outside Najin Harbor, Korea, and merchant tanker *No. 4 Nanko Maru* near He Saki, Japan.

PBMs sink Japanese vessel *No. 1 Hanshin Maru* off China coast, 32°57′N, 117°26′E.

ADRIATIC. U.S. freighter *William J. Palmer* is sunk by mine five miles out of Trieste, Italy, 45°34′15″N, 13°36′15″E.

5 Sunday

PACIFIC. Twenty-eight USAAF B-29s mine the waters off Najin, Korea, and Geijitsu, Tsuruga, Oura, and Hagi, Japan.

Destroyer escort *Earl V. Johnson* (DE 702) is damaged by explosion (possibly a near-miss of *kaiten* fired by submarine *I 53*), Philippine Sea, 20°17′N, 128°07′E.

Destroyer *Bristol* (DD 857) is damaged in collision with oiler *Ashtabula* (AO 51) off Iwo Jima, 29°00′N, 142°00′E.

Submarine *Aspro* (SS 309) rescues shot-down USAAF P-51 pilot deep in Sagami Wan, Honshu, covered by PB4Ys that splash four of 12 Japanese planes that try to interfere with the extraction.

Submarine *Billfish* (SS 286), attacking Japanese convoy in the Yellow Sea, sinks freighter *Kori Maru* off the Kwantung Peninsula, 38°51′N, 121°59′E.

Submarine *Pogy* (SS 266) sinks Japanese freighter *Kotohirasan Maru* in the Japan Sea about 30 miles west of Akita, Honshu, 39°52′N, 138°52′E.

Mines damage Japanese fast transport *T.20* four miles off Koiwai Jima, Japan, and damage freighter *Nissho Maru* in vicinity of Nanao and Oguchi and merchant tanker *No. 32 Yoshitomo Maru* 5.5 kilometers off Genkai Jima.

Japanese freighter *Iki Maru* is damaged by aircraft off Hamada Island, Japan.

RAAF Liberator sinks Japanese ship *No. 15 Eigyo Maru* off western Flores Island, Azores.

Japanese auxiliary submarine chaser *No. 25 Hino Maru* sinks after running aground in Bungo Strait off Hino Misaki.

6 Monday

PACIFIC. USAAF B-29 "Enola Gay" (509th Composite Group) drops atomic bomb on Hiroshima, Honshu; Commander William S. Parsons is the weaponeer on this mission.

TG 95.3 planes, from escort carriers *Lunga Point* (CVE 94), *Makin Island* (CVE 93), and *Cape Gloucester* (CVE 109) (Vice Admiral Jesse B. Oldendorf), strike enemy shipping in Tinghai Harbor, China.

Air group from carrier *Intrepid* (CV 11) bombs Japanese installations on Wake Island, as the ship is en route from Pearl Harbor to join TF 38 in the western Pacific.

TF 58 planes damage Japanese *Coast Defense Vessel No. 37* and small minelayer/netlayer *Kyosai* east of Nojima Saki, 34°52′N, 139°58′E.

Submarine *Bugara* (SS 331) comes across British submarine HMS *Sleuth* and four Japanese junks. *Bugara*, in display of Anglo-American cooperation, assists the British boat by sinking two of the enemy craft by gunfire, 06°51′N, 101°44′E.

Submarine *Bullhead* (SS 332) is sunk, probably by Japanese Army aircraft (73rd *Chutai*) in Java Sea, off Bali, 08°20′S, 115°42′E.

USAAF B-25s and P-51s (Far East Air Force) attack Japanese shipping in Tsushima Strait, sinking freighters *No. 7 Shintai Maru* and *Kowa Maru* five miles east of Tsuno Jima, 34°26′N, 129°16′E.

USAAF mines sink Japanese freighters *No. 2 Chokai Maru* off Fushiki Light, 38°49′N, 137°04′E; *Isojima Maru* in south channel of Kammon Strait, 33°56′N, 130°56′E; and *No. 2 Kozan Maru* at 33°53′N, 132°00′E.

Japanese auxiliary minelayer *Kinjo Maru* and auxiliary netlayer *Kosei Maru* are damaged by aircraft, near Kujukuruhama.

7 Tuesday

PACIFIC. Submarine *Pargo* (SS 264), attacking Japanese convoy off northeastern Korea, sinks freighter *Rashin Maru*, 41°15′N, 131°19′E.

Thirty USAAF B-29s mine Shimonoseki Straits and the waters off Maizuru and Sakai, Japan, and Najin, Korea.

USAAF B-29s (20th Air Force), on shakedown flight, bomb Japanese installations at

Truk, Carolines, sinking auxiliary submarine chaser *Cha 66,* 07°23′N, 151°53′E.

Japanese auxiliary submarine chaser *Rumoe Maru* is sunk by aircraft near My Tho, French Indochina.

USAAF B-25s (Far East Air Force) attack Japanese convoy off Fusan, Korea, sinking *Coast Defense Vessel No. 39* at 35°06′N, 129°03′E, and merchant tankers *No. 7 Kinyu Maru* and *No. 9 Nanki Maru* near Koje-Do, 34°55′N, 128°44′E.

Japanese army cargo ship *Kibitsu Maru* is sunk by mine 250 meters east of Hiraiso, 34°37′N, 135°03′E.

Japanese merchant ship *Keizan Maru* is damaged by aircraft 13 miles south-southwest of Hime Jima Light, Kyushu.

Japanese freighters *Daigen Maru* and *Chiyotama Maru* are damaged when they collide four miles south of Funagawa pier, Honshu.

8 Wednesday

PACIFIC. Crew from destroyer *Cassin* (DD 372) boards Japanese hospital ship *Kiku Maru,* about 250 miles northwest of Marcus Island, and after observing no violations, permits the vessel to proceed to Yokosuka.

Submarine *Muskallunge* (SS 262) is damaged by machine gun fire while engaging Japanese "sea trucks" off the Kurils, 46°41′N, 151°43′E, but remains on patrol.

U.S. freighter *Casimir Pulaski* is damaged when nearby dredging operations detonate mine or bomb off the ship's port bow as she lies alongside Pier 13, Manila, P.I.; the blast injures two of the 28-man Armed Guard.

PB4Ys attack Japanese shipping off Pusan, Korea, sinking *No. 7 Yamabishi Maru* and *Kagoshima Maru* off that port and guardboat *No. 63 Hino Maru* east of Kyosaitoo.

Japanese cargo vessel *Shinten Maru* is damaged by mine off Wada Misaki, southwestern end of Kobe, Japan, harbor.

USAAF B-24s, B-25s, A-26s, P-51s, and P-47s (Far East Air Force) carry out strikes against targets on Kyushu, and Japanese shipping between Kyushu and Korea, sinking freighter *Shokai Maru* off Pusan and *Megami Maru* off Shodo Jima; *Kainan Maru* is damaged.

Japanese freighter *Tenzan Maru* is damaged by marine casualty northeast of Kamaishi, Japan.

Navy Petroleum Reserve 4 Expedition, formed around cargo ship *Spica* (AK 16) and U.S. freighters *Jonathan Harrington* and *Enos A. Mills,* departs Icy Cape, Alaska, for Point Barrow (see 10, 22, 24, and 25 August).

9 Thursday

PACIFIC. USAAF B-29 "Bock's Car" (509th Composite Group) drops atomic bomb on Nagasaki, Kyushu; Commander Frederick W. Ashworth is the weaponeer on this mission. In the nuclear devastation unleashed upon that Japanese port city, merchant tanker *Tsuruoka Maru* is damaged.

TF 38 (Vice Admiral John S. McCain) pounds Japanese shipping and airfields ranging from northern Honshu and Hokkaido to the coast of Korea, sinking auxiliary submarine chasers *Shintohoku Maru; No. 2 Kongo Maru,* and *No. 6 Takunan Maru;* minesweepers *W.1* and *W.33;* fleet tanker *Juko Maru;* and freighter *No. 36 Banshu Maru* off Hamada, 39°30′N, 142°04′E. USN (TF 38) and British carrier aircraft (TF 37) sink escort vessels *Amakusa* and *Inagi* off Onagawa.

Off Honshu, retaliatory air strikes by Japanese planes result in friendly fire damage to destroyer *John W. Weeks* (DD 701), 35°00′N, 143°00′E; *kamikaze* damages destroyer *Borie* (DD 704) at 37°21′N, 143°45′E.

TU 12.5.6—battleship *New Jersey* (BB 62), light cruiser *Biloxi* (CL 80), and four destroyers—bombards Wake Island while en route from Pearl Harbor to Eniwetok, Marshalls.

TU 34.8.1, consisting of battleships and cruisers (Rear Admiral John F. Shafroth), shells industrial targets at Kamaishi, Honshu. Two British light cruisers participate in the bombardment as well.

Soviet forces enter Korea. Soviet planes sink Japanese *Coast Defense Vessel No. 82* north of Joshin, Korea, 41°21′N, 131°12′E, and merchant vessels *Kasado Maru* and *No. 2 Ryuho Maru* off Kamchatka, Sea of Okhotsk.

Submarine *Hawkbill* (SS 366) shells Tambelan Island, 230 miles east of Singapore, destroying Japanese radio station.

Destroyer escort *Johnnie Hutchins* (DE 360), carrying out an antisubmarine sweep on the convoy route between Leyte and Okinawa, sinks what may have been *kaitens* launched by *I 58,* known to have been in the area at that time.

USAAF B-25s, on antishipping sweeps against Japanese shipping traffic off the coast of Korea, sink auxiliary submarine chaser *No. 63 Hino Maru* west of Koje-do; freighter *No. 7 Yamabishi Maru* off Tsushima, 35°09′N, 129°30′E; and army cargo ship *Daito Maru,* 15 miles off Chongjin. Freighters *Edamitsu Maru* and *Sotsu Go* and tanker *Empo Maru* are sunk by aircraft off Najin. Freighter *Senko Maru* is sunk by aircraft off Chongjin; *Tensho Maru* is

damaged. Freighters *Kagoshima Maru* and *Toyoshima Maru* are sunk by aircraft off Pusan.

Japanese freighter *Izu Maru* is sunk by aircraft, Shiogama Harbor, Honshu.

Japanese freighter *No. 7 Yamanami Maru* is sunk by U.S. aircraft, 25°15′N, 138°44′E.

Japanese freighter *No. 2 Ryuho Maru* is sunk by aircraft off Utka.

Japanese freighter *No. 6 Banshu Maru* is damaged by aircraft off Hamada, Japan.

Japanese destroyer *Yanagi* and minelayer *Tokiwa* are damaged by aircraft, Ominato, Japan.

Japanese escort vessel *Yashiro,* Coast Defense Vessel No. 87, army cargo ship *Ryuwa Maru,* and freighter *Meiyu Maru* are damaged by aircraft off Unggi, Korea.

USAAF B-25s (Far East Air Force) damage Japanese fast transport *T.21* off Tsuwa Jima, 33°59′N, 132°31′E. Although *T.21* is run aground to permit salvage, she never returns to active service (see 10 August).

Mines damage Japanese freighters *Enoshima Maru* in Oguchi Channel, Nanao, *Genyo Maru,* 35°51′N, 131°15′E, and *Shinri Go,* 34°06′N, 131°19′E, and merchant vessel *Okita Maru* near Sumoto.

10 Friday

PACIFIC. TF 38 (Vice Admiral John S. McCain) pounds Japanese shipping, airfields, and railroads in northern Honshu. Planes from British TF 37 participate as well. TF 38 planes sink submarine chaser *Ch 42* and minesweeper *W.1* in Yamada Bay, 38°26′N, 141°30′E; auxiliary minesweeper *No. 2 Kongo Maru* off Onagawa, 38°30′N, 141°29′E; freighter *Masayoshi Maru* and tanker *No. 3 Nanki Maru* in Sakata Harbor, 38°55′N, 139°49′E; freighter *No. 14 Horai Maru* off east coast of Korea, 37°00′N, 130°24′E; freighter *No. 5 Nishiki Maru* off Hachinohe Harbor; and cargo ship *Chichibu Maru* in Keelung Harbor, Formosa, 42°20′N, 130°24′E. TF 37 or TF 38 planes sink auxiliary submarine chaser *No. 6 Takunan Maru* off Onagawa. TF 38 planes damage auxiliary minelayer *Koei Maru* off Ominato and freighter *Toyotama Maru* off Sakata, 38°15′N, 139°22′E.

USAAF B-25s (Far East Air Force) carry out sweeps against Japanese shipping off Korea and Kyushu, sinking army cargo ship *Ujina Maru* and freighters *Manei Maru* and *No. 7 Hosei Maru,* and damaging auxiliary patrol vessel *Pa No. 84,* army cargo ship *Yorihime Maru,* and freighter *No. 7 Manei Maru,* and, in Tsugaru Strait, liaison vessel *Aniwa Maru.* In antishipping sweeps off the Korean coast, planes sink cargo ships *Taishun Maru* and *Awakawa Maru* off Chongjin, 41°26′N, 129°49′E; merchant cargo vessels *Taiko Maru*, *Erimo Maru*, and *Kari Go* in or off Najin Harbor, and army cargo ship *Isshin Maru* off Ulsan. In Tsushima Strait, planes sink freighter *Shofuko Maru*, 34°43′N, 129°50′E, and damage *Coast Defense Vessel No. 194*, *Coast Defense Vessel No. 198*, and army cargo ship *Tairetsu Maru*, 34°42′N, 130°13′E.

Thirty-one USAAF B-29s (20th Air Force) mine Shimonoseki Straits and the waters off Hagi and Yuyawan, Japan, and Wonsan, Korea. Mines sink freighter *Shinjo Maru* off Hime Jima and damage *Coast Defense Vessel No. 63* in Nanao Bay, 37°08′N, 136°50′E; freighters *Harada Maru* at 34°23′N, 134°57′E, *Tsushima Maru* (location unspecified), and *No. 12 Nissho Maru* 1.6 kilometers off Echizen Saki; and merchant tanker *No. 8 Kinyu Maru* in Maizuru Harbor.

Soviet forces enter Korea. Soviet planes sink Japanese *Coast Defense Vessel No. 82* north of Joshin, Korea, 41°21′N, 131°12′E, and merchant vessels *Kasado Maru* and *No. 2 Ryuho Maru* off Kamchatka Peninsula, in Sea of Okhotsk.

Submarine *Hawkbill* (SS 366) shells and destroys Japanese radio station on Djemadja Island, 150 miles northeast of Singapore.

Navy Petroleum Reserve 4 Expedition, formed around cargo ship *Spica* (AK 16) and U.S. freighters *Jonathan Harrington* and *Enos A. Mills*, reaches Point Barrow, Alaska, and discharges some tonnage until ice and weather conditions force a halt in operations (see 22, 24, and 25 August).

U.S. freighter *Jack Singer* is torpedoed by Japanese plane off Naha, Okinawa. None of the 29-man Armed Guard are injured, and only one merchant seaman reports any injuries suffered in the incident. The ship is later written off as a total loss.

Japanese fast transport *T.21* sinks as the result of damage suffered the previous day off Tsuwa Jima, 33°59′N, 132°31′E.

11 Saturday

PACIFIC. TG 95.4 (Captain Henry J. Armstrong Jr.), composed of four light minelayers (DM), 40 minesweepers (AM), 10 motor minesweepers (YMS), and various supporting vessels, departs Buckner Bay, Okinawa, to proceed into the East China Sea to conduct minesweeping operations.

TF 38 planes damage Japanese destroyer *Kaba* and submarines *I 36*, *I 159*, and *I 402* at Kure, Japan.

Destroyer *McDermut* (DD 677) is damaged by small-caliber naval gunfire in Kurils, 49°30′N, 155°01′E.

Submarine *Chub* (SS 329) sinks Japanese army auxiliary sailing vessel *No. 32 Sakura Maru* in the Java Sea, north of Bali, 06°40′S, 115°44′E.

Submarine *Hawkbill* (SS 366) puts landing party and Australian commandoes ashore at Terampah Harbor, Matak Island, Anambas Islands, that destroys a gasoline dump, captures intelligence documents, and rescues an Indian POW.

Submarine *Jallao* (SS 368) sinks Japanese freighter *Teihoku Maru* in the Sea of Japan, north of Oki Gunto, 38°03′N, 133°12′E.

Mines laid by USAAF B-29s (20th Air Force) sink Japanese freighter *No. 2 Nisshin Maru* eight kilometers off Wakamatsu Light, 33°45′N, 131°30′E, and damage landing ship *T.153* two miles east-northeast of Kanawaiwa, Japan.

Japanese merchant vessel *Wajun Go* is damaged by marine casualty near Funagawa, Honshu.

12 Sunday

PACIFIC. TF 92, composed of two light cruisers and 12 destroyers (Rear Admiral John H. Brown Jr.), bombards Japanese installations on Matsuwa Island and at Kurabu Cape and Suribachi Bay, Paramushir, Kurils. A prebombardment sweep of the Sea of Okhotsk results in the destruction of 10 trawlers.

Battleship *Pennsylvania* (BB 38) is damaged by aerial torpedo, Buckner Bay, Okinawa, 26°14′N, 127°50′E.

Japanese submarine *I 58* conducts unsuccessful *kaiten* attack on dock landing ship *Oak Hill* (LSD 7) while she is en route from Okinawa to Leyte Gulf accompanied by destroyer escort *Thomas F. Nickel* (DE 587).

USAAF B-25s and fighter-bomber aircraft (Far East Air Force) conduct sweeps against Japanese shipping off Korea and Kyushu, sinking auxiliary patrol vessel *Pa 166* five miles southeast of Urasaki, Japan, and freighter *Hozugawa Maru* off the east coast of Korea, 35°00′N, 126°00′E, and damaging *Kitanami Maru* off Mishima Light.

Mines sink Japanese freighter *No. 1 Shinyo Maru* north of Kyushu, and damage freighter *Yurakawa Maru* eight kilometers off Wakamatsu Light and army cargo ship *No. 16 Tamon Maru* in Koguchi Channel, Nanao, 37°07′N, 137°02′E.

13 Monday

PACIFIC. TF 38 (Vice Admiral John S. McCain) attacks targets in the vicinity of Tokyo. In the aftermath of the strike, USAAF OA-10A extracts a TBM crew (VT 87) from carrier *Ticonderoga* (CV 14) from the inner reaches of Tokyo Bay midway between Yokohama and Kizarazu, marking the first time that a U.S. plane has accomplished a rescue in those waters.

Attack transport *Lagrange* (APA 124) is crashed by suicide plane, Buckner Bay, Okinawa, 26°14′N, 127°52′E.

Submarine *Atule* (SS 403) sinks Japanese *Coast Defense Vessel No. 6* and damages *Coast Defense Vessel No. 16* off south coast of Hokkaido, 42°16′N, 142°12′E.

Submarine *Torsk* (SS 423) sinks Japanese freighter *Kaiho Maru* off Anto Saki, Honshu, 36°17′N, 136°09′E.

USAAF B-24s and B-25s (Far East Air Force) on wide-ranging sweeps against Japanese shipping off Korea and Kyushu sink guardboat *Ayanami Maru* at 34°50′N, 131°10′E, and damage freighters *Tatsukiri Maru* at 34°35′N, 131°23′E, and *No. 11 Tosei Maru* off Hakata, 33°36′N, 130°24′E.

Japanese army tanker *No. 10 Nitto Maru* is damaged by mine off O Shima, Japan, 34°22′N, 130°54′E.

14 Tuesday

PACIFIC. Japan accepts the provisions of the Potsdam Declaration and agrees to surrender ("V-J Day"). General of the Army Douglas MacArthur is named Supreme Allied Commander to receive the enemy's capitulation and conduct the occupation of the Japanese homeland.

Thirty-five USAAF B-29s (20th Air Force) mine Shimonoseki Straits and the waters off Nanao, Maizuru, and Hamada, Japan, in the final B-29 minelaying operations of the war. Mines laid earlier by B-29s sink gunboat *Hirota Maru* off Mutsure, Japan, 33°59′N, 130°52′E; cargo ship *Mikamasan Maru* at 39°18′N, 126°28′E; and freighters *Yojo Maru* in Osaka Harbor, 34°38′N, 135°28′E, and *Kashima Maru* off coast of Korea, 35°10′N, 129°00′E.

Submarine *Spikefish* (SS 404) sinks Japanese submarine *I 373*, en route from Sasebo to Takao, 190 miles southeast of Shanghai, China, 29°00′N, 124°00′E.

Submarine *Torsk* (SS 423), operating in the Sea of Japan, sinks *Coast Defense Vessel No. 13* at 35°44′N, 134°38′E, and *Coast Defense Vessel No. 47* at 35°41′N, 134°38′E.

Marine casualties account for damage to Japanese merchant tankers *No. 8 Nankai Maru* at 36°54′N, 126°12.5′E, and tanker *Nanki Maru* 300 miles off Bontensen.

Aircraft (nationality and type unidentified) sink Japanese freighter *No. 6 Hatokama Maru* off Tanoura, Kyushu, and damage freighters *No. 5 Shinko Maru* at 34°35′N, 131°23′E, and *Tatsusugi Maru* at 34°12′N, 129°46′E. Freighter *No. 3 Takakawa Maru*, damaged by aircraft, is beached north of Hirato Jima off Kyushu, Japan.

ATLANTIC. Auxiliary *Avery Island* (AG 76) runs aground about six miles off Cape Henry, Virginia; salvage tug *Relief* (NRTS), rescue tug *ATR 74,* and tug *Sciota* (ATO 30) refloat the ship.

15 Wednesday

PACIFIC. Before receiving the announcement of the end of hostilities, planes from fast carrier task force (Vice Admiral John S. McCain) raid airfields in the vicinity of Tokyo, encountering heavy aerial opposition. Second strike is cancelled while it is en route to objectives; pilots jettison their ordnance and return to their carriers.

TG 30.6 (Commodore Rodger W. Simpson) is formed to liberate, evacuate, and care for Allied POWs in Japan.

Japanese escort vessel *Kanju* is sunk by Soviet naval aircraft off Wonsan, Korea, 39°10′N, 127°27′E.

Japanese auxiliary submarine chaser *Cha 167* is sunk by accident, Kure.

Japanese freighter *No. 12 Yamabishi Maru* is damaged by aircraft southwest of Ko Saki, Tsushima, 34°41.5′N, 129°36′E.

MEDITERRANEAN. U.S. freighter *William D. Byron* is damaged by two mines off Savona, Italy, 44°00′N, 09°00′E; one of four Armed Guard sailors is injured.

16 Thursday

PACIFIC. Destroyer *Healy* (DD 672) makes sonar contact with underwater object about 100 miles east of Iwo Jima and carries out depth charge attack.

Submarine *Piper* (SS 409) is attacked in Japan Sea by unknown assailant.

17 Friday

PACIFIC. General Prince Higashikuni Naruhiko becomes Prime Minister of Japan and forms a new cabinet.

Japanese *Coast Defense Vessel No. 46* is sunk by mine off Mokp'o, Korea, 34°51′N, 126°02′E.

The blackboard tells the story: "WAR OVER," while the X-ed out directive for plane captains to wash the planes has obviously been rendered unnecessary by the end of hostilities. Pilots at Naval Air Station, Kaneohe Bay, T.H., rejoice over the victory in the Pacific, 14 August 1945. Bureau numbers listed on the board are for Eastern FM-2 Wildcats. (Author's Collection)

19 Sunday

PACIFIC. Formation of fleet marine and bluejacket landing forces from officers and men afloat begins; these men are transferred, at sea, to transports for the impending occupation of Yokosuka under Commander, TF 31 (see 20 August).

Japanese delegates arrive in Manila to receive surrender instructions.

Japanese escort vessel *Oki* is damaged by mine off Pusan, Korea.

20 Monday

PACIFIC. TF 31 (Rear Admiral Oscar C. Badger) is formed to assume responsibility for the occupation of Yokosuka Naval Base.

Navy patrol planes reconnoiter Indochina and south China coasts; Japanese fighters attempt to intercept them.

21 Tuesday

PACIFIC. Two Chinese junks (Lieutenant Livingston Swentzel Jr., USNR), manned by seven Americans and 20 Chinese guerrillas, are attacked by Japanese junk (with a crew of 83 men) while en route from Haimen to Shanghai, China. In a 45-minute action, the Chinese craft, directed by Lieutenant Swentzel, engage the enemy with bazookas, machine guns, and grenades. Upon boarding the Japanese craft, the Allied force finds 45 dead and 35 wounded; the victory has been achieved at the cost of four Chinese killed, and one American and five Chinese wounded. For his heroism above and beyond the call of duty, Lieutenant Swentzel is awarded the Navy Cross in what probably proves to be the last surface action of World War II.

Japanese escort vessel *Miyake* is damaged by mine near Moji, Japan, 33°58′N, 131°00′E.

Tenth Army security patrols on Okinawa by this point have captured 69 Japanese and killed 218 since the island is declared secure.

Asiatic Wing, Naval Air Transport Service, is established at Oakland, California.

22 Wednesday

PACIFIC. Captain Harold B. Grow, Atoll Commander, Majuro, accepts surrender of Mille Atoll, Marshalls (the first Japanese garrison to capitulate in the Pacific) on board destroyer escort *Levy* (DE 162).

Navy Petroleum Reserve 4 Expedition, formed around cargo ship *Spica* (AK 16) and U.S. freighters *Jonathan Harrington* and *Enos A. Mills*, discharges remainder of tonnage at Point Barrow, Alaska (see 24 and 25 August).

Japanese antiaircraft batteries near Hong Kong fire upon navy patrol planes over China coast.

Japanese destroyer *Asagao* is damaged by mine in Shimonoseki Straits.

23 Thursday

PACIFIC. TG 38.4 (Rear Admiral Arthur W. Radford) planes search for Japanese shipping between Hachijo Jima and the Bonins. Such movement would have been contrary to surrender instructions, but the searching aircraft report no violations.

24 Friday

PACIFIC. U.S. freighters *Jonathan Harrington* and *Enos A. Mills*, of the Navy Petroleum Reserve 4 Expedition, are damaged by ice floes off Point Barrow, Alaska (see 25 August).

25 Saturday

PACIFIC. TF 38 aircraft begin daily flights over Japan to patrol airfields, shipping movements

and to locate and supply prisoner of war camps; operation continues until 2 September. Carrier *Wasp* (CV 18) and destroyer *Chauncey* (DD 667) are damaged by typhoon.

TG 95.4 (Captain Henry J. Armstrong Jr.) returns to Buckner Bay, Okinawa, having completed its mine clearance work in the East China Sea and destroyed 578 mines during 11 days of sweeping.

Chief of Naval Operations accords Navy Petroleum Reserve 4 Expedition a "well done" for accomplishing its mission "in an expeditious and seamanlike manner in spite of fog and ice."

27 Monday

PACIFIC. Third Fleet (Admiral William F. Halsey Jr.) stands into Sagami Wan, the outer bay to Tokyo, Japan.

Japanese submarine *I 14* surrenders to destroyers *Murray* (DD 576) and *Dashiell* (DD 659) east of northern Honshu. Prize crew from destroyer escort *Bangust* (DE 739) boards *I 14* about 450 miles east of Nojima Saki.

Japanese submarine *I 400* surrenders to destroyers *Blue* (DD 744) and *Mansfield* (DD 728) east of northern Honshu; destroyer escort *Weaver* (DE 741) places boarding party on board *I 400*.

PB4Y (FAW 18) lands at Atsugi airfield, 14 miles from Tokyo because of mechanical difficulties. No Japanese approach the plane, which returns to Iwo Jima the same day.

28 Tuesday

PACIFIC. USAAF technicians land at Atsugi airfield, near Tokyo; these are the first American troops to land in Japan.

Administrative and operational control of the Seventh Fleet (Admiral Thomas C. Kinkaid) passes from Commander in Chief Southwest Pacific Area (General of the Army Douglas MacArthur) to Commander in Chief Pacific Fleet (Fleet Admiral Chester W. Nimitz).

29 Wednesday

PACIFIC. Fleet Admiral Chester W. Nimitz, Commander in Chief Pacific Fleet, arrives in Tokyo Bay on board PB2Y, and breaks his flag in battleship *South Dakota* (BB 57).

Submarine *Segundo* (SS 398) encounters Japanese submarine *I 401* off northeast coast of Honshu, and "after considerable negotiation," places prize crew on board.

TG 30.6 (Commodore Rodger W. Simpson) arrives in Tokyo Bay to undertake emergency evacuation of Allied POWs in waterfront ar-

eas. Guided by TBMs from small carrier *Cowpens* (CVL 25) and taken to the scene by LCVPs from high-speed transport *Gosselin* (APD 126), Commodore Simpson carries out his orders. The appearance of the LCVPs off the camp at Omori (the first liberated) triggers "an indescribable scene of jubilation and emotion" by the former captives, some of whom swim out to the approaching landing craft.

Japanese garrisons on Halmahera and Morotai, N.E.I., surrender.

30 Thursday

PACIFIC. Landings by the occupation forces begin in the Tokyo Bay area under cover of guns of the Third Fleet plus naval and USAAF aircraft.

Rear Admiral Robert B. Carney and Rear Admiral Oscar C. Badger accept surrender of Yokosuka Naval Base. Headquarters of Commander Third Fleet is established there.

Conference is held on board destroyer *Stack* (DD 406) at Truk, Carolines, to discuss the surrender of that Japanese base. Brigadier General Leo D. Hermle, USMC, is the leader of U.S. representatives.

Four motor torpedo boats transport 50 Japanese troops from Miti Island to Morotai, N.E.I., to contact scattered units there to effect a complete surrender.

U.S. freighter *Peter White* is damaged by mine 50 miles from Mauban, Luzon, 14°37′N, 122°26′E; only four men of the ship's total complement (52 merchant sailors, one passenger, and 17 Armed Guards) are injured, and the ship reaches Leyte.

31 Friday

PACIFIC. Rear Admiral Francis E. M. Whiting accepts surrender of Marcus Island on board destroyer *Bagley* (DD 386).

Marines (Company "L," Third Battalion, Fourth Marines) land at Tateyama Naval Base, Honshu, on the northeast shore of Sagami Wan, and accept its surrender. They will reconnoiter the beach approaches and cover the landing of Army's 112th Cavalry.

Japanese submarine *I 401* surrenders to submarine *Segundo* (SS 398) at entrance to Tokyo Bay.

U.S. freighter *Joseph Carrigan* is damaged by mine in Brunei Bay, Borneo.

Japanese merchant vessels sunk/damaged during August 1945 (exact dates indeterminate): refrigerated cargo ship *Banshu Maru*, agent unknown, location unspecified; cargo ship *Eito Maru*, by aircraft, off Murotsu, approximately 34°46′N, 134°30′E; and cargo ship *No. 1 Taikai Maru*, by aircraft, location unspecified.

Japanese merchant vessel damaged during August 1945 (exact date indeterminate): cargo ship *Shincho Maru*, by mine, off Ube, Japan.

SEPTEMBER

1 Saturday
PACIFIC. Two civilian internment camps are located in Tokyo area; internees are evacuated in hospital ship *Benevolence* (AH 13).

2 Sunday
PACIFIC. Japanese surrender documents are signed on board battleship *Missouri* (BB 63) at anchor in Tokyo Bay. General of the Army Douglas MacArthur signs for the Allied Powers; Fleet Admiral Chester W. Nimitz signs for the United States.

TF 33 (Rear Admiral John L. Hall Jr.) lands army forces at Yokohama.

Japanese surrender Palau Islands in ceremony on board destroyer escort *Amick* (DE 168).

Japanese surrender Truk in ceremony on board heavy cruiser *Portland* (CA 33).

Japanese surrender Pagan Island, northern Marianas, on board destroyer *Rhind* (DD 404).

Japanese surrender Rota, Marianas, in ceremony on board destroyer escort *Heyliger* (DE 510).

3, Monday
PACIFIC. Japanese surrender Wake Island in ceremony on board destroyer escort *Levy* (DE 162).

Escort carrier *Anzio* (CVE 57) is damaged in collision with oiler *Suamico* (AO 49) while fueling off Okinawa.

4 Tuesday
PACIFIC. Japanese surrender Aguijan Island, Marianas, in ceremony on board Coast Guard cutter *CGC 83425*.

5 Wednesday
PACIFIC. Japanese surrender Yap Island, Carolines, in ceremony on board destroyer *Tillman* (DD 641).

6 Thursday
PACIFIC. Japanese surrender Maleolap Atoll, Marshalls, in ceremony on board destroyer escort *Wingfield* (DE 194).

U.S. troops begin return to United States as

Fleet Admiral Chester W. Nimitz signs the surrender accords for the United States, on board battleship *Missouri* (BB 63), Tokyo Bay, 2 September 1945, while General of the Army Douglas MacArthur, Admiral William F. Halsey Jr., and Rear Admiral Forrest Sherman (left) look on. Among those standing in the front row (background) is Vice Admiral John S. McCain, who dies four days later. (NA, 80-G-701293)

General Motors TBM Avenger (VT 94) from carrier *Lexington* (CV 16) roars low over POW camp at Narumi, southeastern Honshu, 3 September 1945, to drop supplies. (Author's Collection)

TF 11 (Vice Admiral Frederick C. Sherman) sails from Tokyo Bay for the West Coast.

11 Tuesday

Operation MAGIC CARPET begins.

11 September to 31 December 1945

Between the signing of the capitulation documents on board battleship *Missouri* (BB 63) and the end of the year, Japanese garrisons on the Asiatic mainland and on bypassed islands scattered throughout the western Pacific surrender. Occupation of Japan progresses and the administrative organization of the U.S. naval forces in the area is adjusted where necessary to enable the Navy to carry out occupation and demilitarization duties. Naval combat strength shrinks as demobilization procedures are set in motion. On 10 October 1945 Headquarters of the Commander in Chief U.S. Fleet (Fleet Admiral Ernest J. King) is disestablished.

APPENDIX

PRINCIPAL CIVILIAN OFFICIALS AND NAVAL OFFICERS IN COMMAND
7 DECEMBER 1941–2 SEPTEMBER 1945
Note: Command changes occurring between 1 September 1939 and 7 December 1941 can be found in the text for that period. Rank shown for a military officer is highest rank held while in assignment indicated. [a] Acting. [b] Temporary.

SECRETARY OF THE NAVY
Frank Knox, 7 December 1941–28 April 1944
James V. Forrestal (A), 28 April 1944–19 May 1944
James V. Forrestal, 19 May 1944–2 September 1945

UNDERSECRETARY OF THE NAVY
James V. Forrestal, 7 December 1941–19 May 1944
Ralph A. Bard, 24 June 1944–30 June 1945
Artemus L. Gates, 3 July 1945–2 September 1945

ASSISTANT SECRETARY OF THE NAVY
Ralph A. Bard, 7 December 1941–24 June 1944
H. Struve Hensel, 30 January 1945–2 September 1945

ASSISTANT SECRETARY OF THE NAVY FOR AIR
Artemus L. Gates, 7 December 1941–30 June 1945
John L. Sullivan, 1 July 1945–2 September 1945

CHIEF OF NAVAL OPERATIONS
Adm. Harold R. Stark, 7 December 1941–26 March 1942
Fleet Admiral Ernest J. King, 26 March 1942–2 September 1945

VICE CHIEF OF NAVAL OPERATIONS   *Established 12 March 1942.*
Adm. Frederick J. Horne, 26 March 1942–2 September 1945

JOINT CHIEFS OF STAFF   *Established 9 February 1942.*
Chairman:
Fleet Admiral William D. Leahy, 20 July 1942–2 September 1945
Navy:
Adm. Harold R. Stark, 9 February 1942–26 March 1942
Fleet Admiral Ernest J. King, 9 February 1942–2 September 1945

Army:
General of the Army George C. Marshall, 9 February 1942–
2 September 1945
Army Air Forces:
General of the Army Henry H. Arnold,
9 February 1942–2 September 1945

CHIEF OF STAFF TO THE COMMANDER IN CHIEF OF THE ARMY AND NAVY OF THE UNITED STATES *Established 20 July 1942.*
Fleet Admiral William D. Leahy, 20 July 1942–2 September 1945

CHAIRMAN OF THE GENERAL BOARD
Rear Adm. Walton R. Sexton, 7 December 1941–10 August 1942
Adm. Arthur J. Hepburn (Ret.), 11 August 1942–2 September 1945

COMMANDANT, UNITED STATES MARINE CORPS
Lt. Gen. Thomas Holcomb, 7 December 1941–31 December 1943
Gen. Alexander A. Vandegrift, 1 January 1944–2 September 1945

COMMANDANT, UNITED STATES COAST GUARD
Adm. Russell R. Waesche, 7 December 1941–2 September 1945

BUREAU CHIEFS
BUREAU OF AERONAUTICS
Rear Adm. John H. Towers, 7 December 1941–7 October 1942
Rear Adm. John S. McCain, 9 October 1942–6 August 1943
Rear Adm. DeWitt C. Ramsey, 6 August 1943–1 June 1945
Rear Adm. Harold B. Sallada, 1 June 1945–2 September 1945

BUREAU OF MEDICINE AND SURGERY
Vice Adm. Ross T. McIntyre, 7 December 1941–2 September 1945.

BUREAU OF NAVIGATION
Became BUREAU OF PERSONNEL 12 May 1942.
Rear Adm. Chester W. Nimitz, 7 December 1941–19 December 1941
Vice Adm. Randall Jacobs, 19 December 1941–13 May 1942

BUREAU OF NAVAL PERSONNEL
Vice Adm. Randall Jacobs, 13 May 1942–2 September 1945

BUREAU OF ORDNANCE
Rear Adm. William H. P. Blandy, 7 December 1941–9 December 1943
Vice Adm. George F. Hussey, 10 December 1943–2 September 1945

BUREAU OF SHIPS
Rear Adm. Samuel M. Robinson, 7 December 1941–31 January 1942
Rear Adm. Alexander H. Van Keuren, 1 February 1942–2 November 1942
Vice Adm. Edward L. Cochrane, 2 November 1942–2 September 1945

BUREAU OF SUPPLIES AND ACCOUNTS
Rear Adm. Ray Spear, 7 December 1941–31 May 1942
Rear Adm. William B. Young, 1 June 1942–8 March 1945
Rear Adm. William J. Carter, 8 March 1945–2 September 1945

BUREAU OF YARDS AND DOCKS
Vice Adm. Ben Moreell, 7 December 1941–2 September 1945

COMMANDANTS, NAVAL DISTRICTS AND RIVER COMMANDS

FIRST NAVAL DISTRICT
Rear Adm. William T. Tarrant, 7 December 1941–15 July 1942
Vice Adm. Wilson Brown Jr., 15 July 1942–8 February 1943
Rear Adm. Robert A. Theobald, 9 February 1943–28 October 1944
Rear Adm. Felix X. Gygax, 28 October 1944–2 September 1945

THIRD NAVAL DISTRICT
Rear Adm. Adolphus Andrews, 7 December 1941–16 March 1942
Rear Adm. Edward J. Marquart, 17 March 1942–31 March 1944
Rear Adm. William R. Munroe, 31 March 1944–6 November 1944
Rear Adm. Monroe Kelly, 6 November 1944–2 September 1945

FOURTH NAVAL DISTRICT
Rear Adm. Adolphus E. Watson, 7 December 1941–30 August 1942
Rear Adm. Milo F. Draemel, 30 August 1942–2 September 1945

FIFTH NAVAL DISTRICT
Rear Adm. Manley H. Simons, 7 December 1941–31 May 1943
Rear Adm. H. Fairfax Leary, 1 June 1943–30 October 1943
Rear Adm. David M. LeBreton, 30 October 1943–20 August 1945
Rear Adm. Walden L. Ainsworth, 20 August 1945–2 September 1945

SIXTH NAVAL DISTRICT
Rear Adm. William H. Allen, 7 December 1941–2 June 1942
Rear Adm. William A. Glassford, Jr., 2 June 1942–14 May 1943
Rear Adm. Jules James, 14 May 1943–2 September 1945

SEVENTH NAVAL DISTRICT
Combined with Sixth until 1 February 1942.
Capt. Russell S. Crenshaw,[a] 1 February 1942–3 June 1942
Rear Adm. James L. Kauffman, 3 June 1942–3 February 1943
Capt. Howard H. J. Benson,[a] 3 February 1943–1 April 1943
Rear Adm. William R. Munroe, 1 April 1943–25 March 1944
Capt. Howard H. J. Benson,[a] 25 March 1944–17 July 1944
Vice Adm. Walter S. Anderson, 17 July 1944–2 September 1945

EIGHTH NAVAL DISTRICT
Capt. Thaddeus A. Thomson,[a] 7 December 1941–22 April 1942
Rear Adm. Frank T. Leighton, 22 April 1942–18 March 1943
Capt. Eugene T. Oates,[a] 18 March 1943–14 June 1943
Rear Adm. Andrew C. Bennett, 14 June 1943–2 September 1945

NINTH NAVAL DISTRICT
Rear Adm. John Downes, 7 December 1941–3 January 1944
Vice Adm. Arthur S. Carpender, 3 January 1944–2 September 1945

TENTH NAVAL DISTRICT
Vice Adm. John H. Hoover, 7 December 1941–12 August 1943
Vice Adm. Arthur B. Cook, 12 August 1943–14 May 1944
Vice Adm. Robert C. Giffen, 14 May 1944–20 August 1945
Vice Adm. William R. Munroe, 20 August 1945–2 September 1945

ELEVENTH NAVAL DISTRICT
Rear Adm. Charles A. Blakely, 7–9 December 1941
Rear Adm. John S. McCain,[a] 9–22 December 1941

Rear Adm. Ralston S. Holmes, 22 December 1941–31 December 1942
Capt. George M. Ravenscroft,[a] 31 December 1942–30 March 1943
Rear Adm. David W. Bagley, 30 March 1943–31 January 1944
Rear Adm. Wilhelm L. Friedell, 31 January 1944–2 September 1945

TWELFTH NAVAL DISTRICT
Vice Adm. John W. Greenslade, 7 December 1941–1 February 1944
Rear Adm. Carlton H. Wright, 1 February 1944–2 September 1945

THIRTEENTH NAVAL DISTRICT
Vice Adm. Charles S. Freeman, 7 December 1941–21 November 1942
Vice Adm. Frank Jack Fletcher, 21 November 1942–12 October 1943
Rear Adm. Sherwoode A. Taffinder, 12 October 1943–15 December 1944
Rear Adm. Robert M. Griffin, 15 December 1944–2 September 1945

FOURTEENTH NAVAL DISTRICT
Rear Adm. Claude C. Bloch, 7 December 1941–4 April 1942
Rear Adm. David W. Bagley, 4 April 1942–17 February 1943
Vice Adm. Robert L. Ghormley, 17 February 1943–25 October 1944
Rear Adm. William R. Furlong,[a] 25 October 1944–28 November 1944
Vice Adm. David W. Bagley, 28 November 1944–25 July 1945
Vice Adm. Sherwoode A. Taffinder, 25 July 1945–2 September 1945

FIFTEENTH NAVAL DISTRICT
Rear Adm. Frank H. Sadler, 7 December 1941–15 April 1942
Rear Adm. Clifford E. Van Hook, 15 April 1942–14 October 1943
Rear Adm. Harold C. Train, 14 October 1943–10 June 1944
Capt. Ellis S. Stone,[a] 10 June 1944–3 November 1944
Rear Adm. Howard F. Kingman, 3 November 1944–9 July 1945
Capt. Schuyler Mills,[a] 9 July 1945–23 August 1945
Rear Adm. John R. Beardall, 23 August 1945–2 September 1945

SIXTEENTH NAVAL DISTRICT   *Disestablished on 6 May 1942.*
Rear Adm. Francis W. Rockwell, 7 December 1941–18 March 1942
Capt. Kenneth M. Hoeffel, 18 March 1942–6 May 1942

SEVENTEENTH NAVAL DISTRICT   *Established on 15 April 1944.*
Rear Adm. Francis E. M. Whiting, 15 April 1944–12 August 1944
Rear Adm. Allan E. Smith,[b] 12 August 1944–24 August 1944
Rear Adm. Ralph F. Wood, 24 August 1944–2 September 1945

POTOMAC RIVER NAVAL COMMAND   *Established 8 December 1941.*
Rear Adm. George T. Pettengill (Ret.), 8 December 1941–15 September 1942
Rear Adm. Ferdinand L. Reichmuth, 15 September 1942–2 September 1945

SEVERN RIVER NAVAL COMMAND   *Established 8 December 1941.*
Rear Adm. Russell Willson, 8–30 December 1941
Capt. Thomas S. King,[a] 30 December 1941–31 January 1942
Rear Adm. John R. Beardall, 31 January 1942–8 August 1945
Vice Adm. Aubrey W. Fitch, 8 August 1945–2 September 1945

SEA FRONTIER COMMANDERS
ALASKAN   *Established 15 April 1944.*
Vice Adm. Frank Jack Fletcher, 15 April 1944–2 September 1945

CARIBBEAN   *Naval Coastal Frontier until 6 February 1942.*
Vice Adm. John H. Hoover, 7 December 1941–12 August 1943
Vice Adm. Arthur B. Cook, 12 August 1943–14 May 1944
Vice Adm. Robert C. Giffen, 14 May 1944–20 August 1945
Vice Adm. William R. Munroe, 20 August 1945–2 September 1945

EASTERN   *North Atlantic Naval Coastal Frontier until 6 February 1942.*
Vice Adm. Adolphus Andrews, 7 December 1941–1 November 1943
Vice Adm. H. Fairfax Leary, 1 November 1943–2 September 1945

GULF   *Southern Naval Coastal Frontier until 6 February 1942.*
Rear Adm. William H. Allen, 7 December 1941–3 February 1942
Capt. Russell S. Crenshaw,[a] 3 February 1942–3 June 1942
Rear Adm. James L. Kauffman, 3 June 1942–3 February 1943
Capt. Howard H. J. Benson,[a] 3 February 1943–1 April 1943
Rear Adm. William R. Munroe, 1 April 1943–25 March 1944
Capt. Howard H. J. Benson,[a] 25 March 1944–17 July 1944
Rear Adm. Walter S. Anderson, 17 July 1944–2 September 1945

HAWAIIAN   *Naval Coastal Frontier until 6 February 1942.*
Rear Adm. Claude C. Bloch, 7 December 1941–2 April 1942
Rear Adm. David W. Bagley, 2 April 1942–17 February 1943
Vice Adm. Robert L. Ghormley, 17 February 1943–25 October 1944
Commo. Marion C. Robertson,[a] 25 October 1944–28 November 1944
Vice Adm. David W. Bagley, 28 November 1944–25 July 1945
Vice Adm. Sherwoode A. Taffinder, 25 July 1945–2 September 1945

MOROCCAN   *Established as Sea Frontier Forces, Western Task Force, 19 November 1942. Became MOROCCAN 17 February 1943. Disestablished 1 August 1945.*
Rear Adm. John L. Hall, 19 November 1942–9 February 1943
Capt. Chester L. Nichols,[b] 9 February 1943–19 February 1943
Rear Adm. Frank J. Lowry, 19 February 1943–20 September 1943
Capt. Chester L. Nichols,[b] 20 September 1943–13 October 1943
Commo. Benjamin V. McCandlish, 13 October 1943–1 August 1945

NORTHWEST   *Pacific-Northern Naval Coastal Frontier until 6 February 1942. Disestablished 15 April 1944.*
Vice Adm. Charles S. Freeman, 7 December 1941–21 November 1942
Vice Adm. Frank Jack Fletcher, 21 November 1942–15 April 1944

PANAMA   *Naval Coastal Frontier until 6 February 1942.*
Rear Adm. Frank H. Sadler, 7 December 1941–15 April 1942
Rear Adm. Clifford E. Van Hook, 15 April 1942–14 October 1943
Rear Adm. Harold C. Train, 14 October 1943–10 June 1944
Capt. Ellis S. Stone,[a] 11 June 1944–3 November 1944
Rear Adm. Howard F. Kingman, 3 November 1944–9 July 1945
Capt. Schuyler Mills,[a] 9 July 1945–23 August 1945
Rear Adm. John R. Beardall, 23 August 1945–2 September 1945

PHILIPPINE   *Naval Coastal Frontier until 6 February 1942. Inactive from 6 May 1942 to 13 November 1944.*
Rear Adm. Francis W. Rockwell, 7 December 1941–18 March 1942

Capt. Kenneth M. Hoeffel, 18 March 1942–6 May 1942
Vice Adm. James L. Kauffman, 13 November 1944–2 September 1945

WESTERN   *Pacific-Southern Naval Coastal Frontier until 6 February 1942.*
Vice Adm. John W. Greenslade, 7 December 1941–1 February 1944
Vice Adm. David W. Bagley, 1 February 1944–17 November 1944
Adm. Royal E. Ingersoll, 17 November 1944–2 September 1945

FLEET COMMANDERS

Note: Only fleets comprising ships are listed. Those with fleet designations for administrative purposes only (i.e., First Fleet, Ninth Fleet) have been omitted.

UNITED STATES FLEET

Adm. Ernest J. King was designated Commander in Chief United States Fleet 20 December 1941. King assumed the duties and established his headquarters in the Navy Department, Washington, on 30 December 1941.
Adm. Husband E. Kimmel, 7 December 1941–17 December 1941
Fleet Admiral Ernest J. King, 30 December 1941–2 September 1945

ATLANTIC FLEET   *Additionally designated Second Fleet, 15 March 1943.*
Adm. Ernest J. King, 7 – 31 December 1941
Adm. Royal E. Ingersoll, 1 January 1942–15 November 1944
Adm. Jonas H. Ingram, 15 November 1944–2 September 1945

PACIFIC FLEET
Adm. Husband E. Kimmel, 7 December 1941–17 December 1941
Vice Adm. William S. Pye,[b] 17 December 1941–31 December 1941
Fleet Admiral Chester W. Nimitz, 31 December 1941 – 2 September 1945

ASIATIC FLEET   *Disestablished on 4 February 1942.*
Adm. Thomas C. Hart, 7 December 1941–4 February 1942

THIRD FLEET   *Established 15 March 1943, formerly South Pacific Force.*
South Pacific Force   *(Established 20 April 1942)*
Vice Adm. Robert L. Ghormley, 19 June 1942–18 October 1942
Adm. William F. Halsey Jr., 18 October 1942–15 March 1943
Third Fleet
Adm. William F. Halsey Jr., 15 March 1943–2 September 1945

FOURTH FLEET   *Established 15 March 1943, formerly South Atlantic Force, originally Task Force 23, Atlantic Fleet. Disestablished 15 April 1945.*
Task Force 23
Vice Adm. Jonas H. Ingram, 7 December 1941–15 September 1942
South Atlantic Force   *(Established 15 September 1942)*
Vice Adm. Jonas H. Ingram, 15 September 1942–15 March 1943
Fourth Fleet
Vice Adm. Jonas H. Ingram, 15 March 1943–11 November 1944
Vice Adm. William R. Munroe, 11 November 1944–15 April 1945

FIFTH FLEET   *Established 5 August as Central Pacific Force. Became FIFTH FLEET 26 April 1944.*
Adm. Raymond A. Spruance, 5 August 1943–2 September 1945

SEVENTH FLEET   *Established 19 February 1943, formerly Southwest Pacific Force, Southwest Pacific Force absorbed U.S. Naval Forces Southwest Pacific, on 20 April 1942, which in turn had succeeded Asiatic Fleet on 4 February 1942.*
United States Naval Forces Southwest Pacific   *Designated 4 February 1942*
Vice Adm. William A. Glassford, 4 February 1942–2 April 1942
Rear Adm. William R. Purnell, 2 April 1942–20 April 1942
Southwest Pacific Force   *Combined with United States Naval Forces, Southwest Pacific, on 20 April 1942.*
Vice Adm. H. Fairfax Leary, 20 April 1942–11 September 1942
Vice Adm. Arthur S. Carpender, 11 September 1942–19 February 1943
Seventh Fleet
Vice Adm. Arthur S. Carpender, 19 February 1943–26 November 1943
Adm. Thomas C. Kinkaid, 26 November 1943–2 September 1945

EIGHTH FLEET   *Established 15 March 1943, and disestablished on 15 April 1945; forces became part of Twelfth Fleet.*
Adm. H. Kent Hewitt, 29 March 1943–11 April 1945
Vice Adm. William A. Glassford Jr., 11 April 1945–15 April 1945

TENTH FLEET   *All United States antisubmarine activities and forces in Atlantic coordinated and controlled by Tenth Fleet. Established on 20 May 1943; disestablished on 12 June 1945.*
Fleet Admiral Ernest J. King, 20 May 1943–12 June 1945

TWELFTH FLEET   *Established 15 March 1943, previously Naval Forces, Europe, which was formed 30 April 1942.*
Adm. Harold R. Stark, 15 March 1943–15 August 1945
Adm. H. Kent Hewitt, 16 August 1945–2 September 1945

AREA COMMANDERS

PACIFIC OCEAN AREAS   *Established 3 April 1942.*
Fleet Admiral Chester W. Nimitz, 8 May 1942–2 September 1945

NORTH PACIFIC AREA   *Established 17 May 1942.*
Rear Adm. Robert A. Theobald, 17 May 1942–4 January 1943
Vice Adm. Thomas C. Kinkaid, 4 January 1943–11 October 1943
Vice Adm. Frank Jack Fletcher, 11 October 1943–2 September 1945

SOUTH PACIFIC AREA   *Established 20 April 1942.*
Vice Adm. Robert L. Ghormley, 19 June 1942–18 October 1942
Adm. William F. Halsey Jr., 18 October 1942–15 June 1944
Vice Adm. John H. Newton, 15 June 1944–13 March 1945
Vice Adm. William L. Calhoun, 13 March 1945–2 September 1945

SOUTHEAST PACIFIC AREA   *Established 8 December 1941.*
Rear Adm. Abel T. Bidwell, 8 December 1941–6 January 1942
Rear Adm. John F. Shafroth, 6 January 1942–25 December 1942
Rear Adm. Francis E. M. Whiting, 25 December 1942–12 October 1943
Rear Adm. Harold C. Train, 12 October 1943–8 June 1944
Capt. Ellis S. Stone,[a] 8 June 1944–3 November 1944
Rear Adm. Howard F. Kingman, 3 November 1944–9 July 1945
Capt. Schuyler Mills,[a] 9 July 1945–23 August 1945
Rear Adm. John R. Beardall, 23 August 1945–2 September 1945

SOUTHWEST PACIFIC AREA *Established 18 April 1942.*
General of the Army Douglas MacArthur, 18 April 1942–
2 September 1945

TYPE COMMANDERS
AIR FORCE ATLANTIC FLEET *Established 1 January 1943 by combining
Carriers Atlantic Fleet (formerly Aircraft Atlantic Fleet) and Fleet Air
Wings, Atlantic Fleet (formerly Patrol Wings Atlantic Fleet).*
Aircraft Atlantic Fleet
Rear Adm. Arthur B. Cook, 7 December 1941–6 April 1942
Carriers, Atlantic Fleet *(Established 6 April 1942)*
Rear Adm. Ernest D. McWhorter, 6 April 1942–1 January 1943
Patrol Wings Atlantic Fleet
Rear Adm. Ernest D. McWhorter, 7 December 1941–3 April 1942
Rear Adm. Alva D. Bernhard, 10 April 1942–1 November 1942
Fleet Air Wings, Atlantic Fleet *(Established 1 November 1942)*
Rear Adm. Alva D. Bernhard, 1 November 1942–1 January 1943
Air Force, Atlantic Fleet
Rear Adm. Alva D. Bernhard, 1 January 1943–8 March 1943
Capt. Thomas L. Sprague,[a] 8 March 1943–20 March 1943
Vice Adm. Patrick N. L. Bellinger, 20 March 1943–2 September 1945

AMPHIBIOUS FORCE ATLANTIC FLEET *Established 14 March 1942,
deleted from Atlantic Fleet organization 18 October 1943.*
Rear Adm. Roland M. Brainard, 14 March 1942–18 April 1942
Capt. Robert R. M. Emmett,[a] 18 April 1942–28 April 1942
Vice Adm. H. Kent Hewitt, 28 April 1942–28 February 1943
Rear Adm. Alan G. Kirk, 28 February 1943–18 October 1943

BATTLESHIPS ATLANTIC FLEET *Functions of type commander trans-
ferred on 1 November 1943 to Commander Fleet Operational Training
Command, Atlantic Fleet.*
Rear Adm. John W. Wilcox, 7 December 1941–27 March 1942
Rear Adm. Alexander Sharp, 27 March 1942–22 August 1942
Rear Adm. Monroe Kelly, 22 August 1942–8 May 1943
Rear Adm. Olaf M. Hustvedt, 8 May 1943–1 November 1943

CRUISERS ATLANTIC FLEET *No type commander assigned from 28 April
1942 to 1 November 1943 when functions of type commander were assumed
by Commander Fleet Operational Training Command, Atlantic Fleet.*
Rear Adm. H. Kent Hewitt, 7 December 1941–28 April 1942

DESTROYERS ATLANTIC FLEET
Rear Adm. Ferdinand L. Reichmuth, 7 December 1941–
22 December 1941
Rear Adm. Arthur S. Carpender, 22 December 1941–3 June 1942
Rear Adm. Oscar C. Badger, 3 June 1942–14 December 1942
Rear Adm. Morton L. Deyo, 14 December 1942–1 January 1944
Rear Adm. James C. Jones, 1 January 1944–20 September 1944
Rear Adm. Oliver M. Read, 20 September 1944–2 September 1945

SERVICE FORCE ATLANTIC FLEET *Established 1 March 1942, formerly
Train, Atlantic Fleet.*
Train, Atlantic Fleet
Rear Adm. Randall Jacobs, 7 December 1941–17 December 1941
Vice Adm. Ferdinand L. Reichmuth, 17 December 1941–1 March 1942

Service Force Atlantic Fleet
Vice Adm. Ferdinand L. Reichmuth, 1 March 1942–22 August 1942
Vice Adm. Alexander Sharp, 22 August 1942–11 October 1944
Commo. Charlton E. Battle,[a] 11 October 1944–23 December 1944
Vice Adm. Sherwoode A. Taffinder, 23 December 1944–15 July 1945
Commo. Charlton E. Battle,[a] 15 July 1945–26 August 1945
Vice Adm. Robert C. Giffen, 26 August 1945–2 September 1945

SUBMARINES ATLANTIC FLEET
Rear Adm. Richard S. Edwards, 7 December 1941–3 January 1942
Capt. Elwin F. Cutts,[a] 3 January 1942–30 March 1942
Rear Adm. Freeland A. Daubin, 30 March 1942–25 November 1944
Rear Adm. Charles W. Styer, 25 November 1944–2 September 1945

AIR FORCE PACIFIC FLEET *Established 1 September 1942 combining
Carriers Pacific Fleet (formerly Aircraft Battle Force, Pacific Fleet) and
Patrol Wings, Pacific Fleet (formerly Aircraft Scouting Force, Pacific Fleet).*
Aircraft, Battle Force, Pacific Fleet
Vice Adm. William F. Halsey Jr., 7 December 1941–10 April 1942
Carriers, Pacific Fleet *(Established 10 April 1942)*
Vice Adm. William F. Halsey Jr., 10 April 1942–11 July 1942
Rear Adm. Aubrey W. Fitch, 11 July 1942–31 August 1942
Aircraft, Scouting Force, Pacific Fleet
Rear Adm. John S. McCain, 7 December 1941–10 April 1942
Patrol Wings, Pacific Fleet *(Established 10 April 1942)*
Rear Adm. John S. McCain, 10 April 1942–1 May 1942
Rear Adm. Patrick N. L. Bellinger, 1 May 1942–9 August 1942
Rear Adm. Aubrey W. Fitch, 9 August 1942–31 August 1942
Air Force, Pacific Fleet
Rear Adm. Aubrey W. Fitch, 1 September 1942–15 September 1942
Rear Adm. Leigh Noyes,[a] 15 September 1942–15 October 1942
Vice Adm. John H. Towers, 15 October 1942–28 February 1944
Rear Adm. Charles A. Pownall, 28 February 1944–16 August 1944
Vice Adm. George D. Murray, 16 August 1944–20 July 1945
Vice Adm. Alfred E. Montgomery, 20 July 1945–2 September 1945

AMPHIBIOUS FORCE PACIFIC FLEET *Established 20 February 1942.*
Maj. Gen. Clayton B. Vogel, USMC, 20 February 1942–10 April 1942
Vice Adm. Wilson Brown Jr., 10 April 1942–1 July 1942
Rear Adm. Milo F. Draemel, 1 July 1942–10 August 1942
Capt. Frank A. Braisted,[a] 10 August 1942–23 August 1942
Rear Adm. Francis W. Rockwell, 23 August 1942–15 August 1943
Adm. Richmond K. Turner, 15 August 1943–2 September 1945

BATTLESHIPS PACIFIC FLEET *Established 10 April 1942, formerly Bat-
tleships Battle Force. Type command divided into two Battleship Squad-
rons on 15 December 1944.*
Battleships Battle Force
Rear Adm. Walter S. Anderson, 7 December 1941–10 April 1942
Battleships Pacific Fleet
Rear Adm. Walter S. Anderson, 10 April 1942–28 September 1942
Vice Adm. H. Fairfax Leary, 28 September 1942–16 April 1943
Vice Adm. Willis A. Lee, 16 April 1943–15 December 1944
Battleship Squadron ONE
Vice Adm. Jesse B. Oldendorf, 15 December 1944–2 September 1945

Battleship Squadron TWO
Vice Adm. Willis A. Lee, 15 December 1944–16 June 1945
Rear Adm. John F. Shafroth, 16 June 1945–2 September 1945

CRUISERS PACIFIC FLEET   *Established 10 April 1942 by combining Cruisers Battle Force, Pacific Fleet, with Cruisers Scouting Force, Pacific Fleet.*

CRUISERS BATTLE FORCE, PACIFIC FLEET
Rear Adm. H. Fairfax Leary, 7 December 1941–6 February 1942
Rear Adm. Frank Jack Fletcher, 6 February 1942–10 April 1942
Cruisers Scouting Force, Pacific Fleet
Rear Adm. John H. Newton, 7 December 1941–31 December 1941
Rear Adm. Frank Jack Fletcher, 31 December 1941–10 April 1942
Cruisers Pacific Fleet
Vice Adm. Frank Jack Fletcher, 10 April 1942–29 October 1942
Rear Adm. Thomas C. Kinkaid, 29 October 1942–31 March 1943
Rear Adm. Mahlon S. Tisdale, 1 April 1943–2 January 1944
Rear Adm. John L. Kauffman, 2 January 1944–31 October 1944
Rear Adm. Walden L. Ainsworth, 31 October 1944–13 July 1945
Rear Adm. William H. P. Blandy, 13 July 1945–2 September 1945

DESTROYERS PACIFIC FLEET   *Established 10 April 1942 from Destroyers Battle Force, Pacific Fleet.*
Destroyers Battle Force, Pacific Fleet
Rear Adm. Milo F. Draemel, 7 December 1941–30 December 1941
Rear Adm. Robert A. Theobald, 30 December 1941–10 April 1942
Destroyers Pacific Fleet
Rear Adm. Robert A. Theobald, 10 April 1942–4 July 1942
Rear Adm. Walden L. Ainsworth, 4 July 1942–8 January 1943
Rear Adm. Mahlon S. Tisdale, 8 January 1943–2 January 1944
Rear Adm. John L. Kauffman, 2 January 1944–31 October 1944
Rear Adm. Walden L. Ainsworth, 31 October 1944–13 July 1945
Rear Adm. William H. P. Blandy, 13 July 1945–2 September 1945

MINECRAFT PACIFIC FLEET   *Established 15 October 1944.*
Rear Adm. Alexander Sharp, 15 October 1944–30 August 1945
Rear Adm. Arthur D. Struble, 30 August 1945–2 September 1945

MOTOR TORPEDO BOAT SQUADRONS PACIFIC FLEET   *Established 1 February 1944.*
Commo. Edward J. Moran, 9 March 1944–3 April 1945
Commo. Richard W. Bates, 20 May 1945–2 September 1945

SERVICE FORCE PACIFIC FLEET   *Established 27 February 1942, formerly Base Force, Pacific Fleet.*
Base Force, Pacific Fleet
Rear Adm. William L. Calhoun, 7 December 1941–27 February 1942
Service Force, Pacific Fleet
Vice Adm. William L. Calhoun, 27 February 1942–6 March 1945
Vice Adm. William W. Smith, 6 March 1945–2 September 1945

SUBMARINE FORCE PACIFIC FLEET   *Established 10 September 1942, formerly Submarines Pacific Fleet, originally Submarines, Scouting Force Pacific Fleet.*
Submarines Scouting Force, Pacific Fleet
Rear Adm. Thomas Withers, 7 December 1941–1 January 1942
Submarines Pacific Fleet   *(Established 1 January 1942)*
Rear Adm. Thomas Withers, 1 January 1942–14 May 1942
Rear Adm. Robert H. English, 14 May 1942–20 September 1942
Submarine Force, Pacific Fleet
Rear Adm. Robert H. English, 20 September 1942–21 January 1943
Capt. John H. Brown Jr.,[a] 21 January 1943–14 February 1943
Vice Adm. Charles A. Lockwood, 14 February 1943–
    2 September 1945

COMMANDER SOUTH CHINA PATROL   *Inactivated 10 December 1941.*
Capt. Lester J. Hudson, 7 December 1941–10 December 1941

NOTES

1939

1. Within a fortnight, *U 30* is herself a victim, when she is bombed by Skuas from British carrier HMS *Ark Royal* on 14 September 1939. With a slightly damaged bow and two torpedo tubes out of action, *U 30* puts in to Reykjavik, Iceland, on 19 September to land a seriously wounded man before she returns to sea.

2. Publicly, Germany will continue to deny responsibility for the sinking of *Athenia* until the postwar Nuremburg Trials bring the truth to light.

3. The U.S. Navy originally acquired *Bear*, built in Scotland for the sealing trade, to rescue the survivors of the ill-fated Greeley Arctic Expedition in 1884. The Navy transferred the ship to the U.S. Treasury Department in 1885 for deployment in the Revenue Cutter Service (later U.S. Coast Guard). In 1929, the Coast Guard transferred her to private ownership. Rear Admiral Richard E. Byrd, USN (Retired), acquired *Bear* in 1932 for use in Antarctic exploration.

4. She is decommissioned on 15 November 1939, renamed *Sailfish* (SS 192) on 9 February 1940, and recommissioned on 15 May 1940.

5. The ship is later acquired by the Navy on 8 July 1940 and converted to the seaplane tender *Tangier* (AV 8).

6. Dutch minesweeper *Willem van Ewijck* was lost off Terschelling on 8 September to a Dutch mine.

7. The destroyers find the going rough on the Grand Banks; they will be replaced by 327-foot Coast Guard cutters that will be administratively assigned to Destroyer Division 18.

8. Vessels listed as "in service" include some used for USNR or Naval Militia training. Vessels not in commission include those loaned to the states of Pennsylvania, California, New York, and Massachusetts for use as maritime school ships, the Maritime Commission, and the Sea Scouts, as well as "relics" like the Civil War vintage *Hartford*, the Spanish-American War prize *Reina Mercedes*, and Spanish-American War veterans *Olympia* and *Oregon*. Interestingly, the 1 October 1939 list contains the river gunboat *Panay* (PR 5), bombed and sunk by Japanese naval aircraft in the Yangtze River near Nanking, China, on 12 December 1937.

9. *Iroquois* will later be acquired by the Navy on 22 July 1940 and will be converted to a hospital ship. As *Solace* (AH 5) she will play an important role in treating casualties at Pearl Harbor on 7 December 1941.

10. The cargo is held at Alexandria for about two weeks and then reloaded on board steamship *President Polk*. The president of the shipping concern involved (American President Lines) subsequently requests the Department of State to protest methods employed by the British naval authorities at Port Said and Alexandria in searching that company's vessels. "The fact that [the] British . . . allowed this eventual delivery," the shipping executive complains, "indicates that [the] shipment ought never have been interfered with in [the] first place."

11. *Yarnall* had only been in commission since 4 October.

12. The U.S. Navy studies the Battle of the River Plate from a perspective of drilling gunners to maintain fire by local (rather than a centralized director) control. To this end, a scenario similar to the River Plate engagement is included in an exercise in 1940. In addition, the Director of Fleet Training considers the "proper use of smoke either as a defense measure or as a means of covering movements of an attacking force" extremely important, and points out the demonstrable effectiveness of a smoke screen "as a means of protection for light forces" employed by Commodore Harwood in the battle with *Admiral Graf Spee*.

13. The Americans maintain such a close and persistent surveillance of the Australian warship that *Perth*'s commanding officer, Captain Harold B. Farncomb, RAN, is said to have remarked in exasperation, "Queer idea of 'neutrality' these Americans have!"

14. The provisions include flour, sugar, potatoes, matches, lard, gasoline, and lubricating oil. The supplies will be replaced in New Zealand with funds turned over to Rear Admiral Richard E. Byrd, USN (Retired), by the Chief Magistrate.

15. *Admiral Graf Spee* had sunk nine British merchantmen during her cruise, totaling 50,089 tons of shipping. Not a single life had been lost in the process. In World War I, the famed German raider *Emden* had sunk 16 ships of 66,146 tons before her demise under the guns of Australian cruiser HMS *Sydney*.

16. The U.S. Navy eventually commissions *Arauca* as refrigerated stores ship *Saturn* (AF 40).

1940

17. U.S. Ambassador to Brazil Jefferson Caffery reports to Secretary of State Cordell Hull on 20 March that the Brazilian government's protesting *Dorsetshire's* stopping *Wakama* had not pleased the British. The British maintained that they were protecting Brazilian commerce. "Indeed you are not," the Brazilian Minister for Foreign Affairs Oswaldo Aranha retorts, "you are definitely not protecting our commerce by maintaining your warships off our coast. It is apparent to me that your blockade of Germany is plainly ineffective. If it were effective, you could stop the German boats [sic] on the other side before they entered German ports."

18. *Hannover* will ultimately be converted into escort carrier HMS *Audacity*.

19. *Mimi Horn* is scuttled to avoid capture in Denmark Strait on 28 March; *Seattle* is lost during the early phases of the invasion of Norway on 8–9 April.

20. Among the individuals who take part in this operation in a volunteer capacity is Charles Herbert Lightoller, the former second officer of the ill-fated British passenger liner *Titanic*.

21. This is not the first time a cruiser is dispatched on a mission of this kind. Light cruisers *Nashville* (CL 43) and *Honolulu* (CL 48) brought back $25 million in gold, stabilization funds lent to the Bank of England but returned because of wartime fears in the late summer/early autumn of 1938. The money was delivered to the Federal Reserve Bank in New York on 11 October 1938.

22. The warm generosity with which the United States meets the British request for ships contrasts markedly with the cold response to the Uruguayan government's request to purchase three destroyers. U.S. Minister to Uruguay Edwin C. Wilson recounts (2 October) an interview with "a leading Uruguayan" who complains: "Having been exhorted to cooperate in continental defense, we want to build up our pitifully non-existent Navy, and we ask you to let us have two or three old destroyers that have been lying useless in your ports since the last war. You handed over fifty of these destroyers to Great Britain, and we see pictures reproduced in the papers of quantities of these ships tied up in your ports, looking like so many toy vessels in a shop window. Yet, you tell us that you find it impossible to let us have even a single one of these." Secretary of State Cordell Hull confidentially informs Minister Wilson (13 September) that the Navy Department believes "that the strategic situation in the North Atlantic does not permit the disposal of any destroyers to Uruguay at the present time, the more so as this would inevitably lead to similar requests from other American republics for [the] purchase of destroyers."

23. The timely goodwill visit comes in the wake of an extensive cabinet shakeup by the Haitian president the previous day. Rear Admiral Ellis later writes that *Rhind's* visit had a "very soothing effect on the minds of the people" in the Haitian port.

24. *Littorio* returns to service by 9 March 1941, *Caio Duilio* by 15 May 1941. Only *Conte de Cavour* is never again operational.

25. Admiral Smeallie's worsening condition results in his being ordered to Naval Hospital, Mare Island, California, for further treatment, and ultimately to the naval hospital in Washington, D.C.

1941

26. Purportedly, the surreptitious photographs snapped of *Atlantis* by *Life* magazine photographer Carl Mydans, who is among the passengers, will prove helpful in providing the Royal Navy with a record of the auxiliary cruiser's appearance.

27. German submarine torpedoes had wreaked great destruction against HX 126. *U 94* had sunk British steamers *Harpagus* and *Norman Monarch* and Norwegian motor tanker *John P. Pederson*, *U 556* had damaged British motor tanker *San Felix* and sunk British motor tanker *British Security* and motorship *Darlington Court*, *U 111* had sunk British steamer *Cockaponset*, *U 98* had sunk British steamer *Rothermere*, *U 109* had sunk British steamer *Marconi*, and *U 93* had sunk Dutch motor tanker *Elusa*.

28. One of the pursuing ships is British battleship HMS *Rodney*, en route to the United States for a refit at Boston when she is rerouted to participate in the hunt for *Bismarck*; on board is U.S. Naval Observer Lieutenant Commander Joseph H. Wellings, who witnesses the ensuing battle from that unique vantage point.

29. U.S. Ambassador to the United Kingdom John Winant reports on 11 July 1941 that of the 27 American Red Cross nurses traveling to serve in England, nine had arrived safely, 10 had been rescued (four in serious condition), and eight were missing.

30. "O God, Our Help in Ages Past" was also sung during the funeral service for the late Lord Lothian, the British Ambassador to the United States, at the National Cathedral in Washington, D.C., on 15 December 1940.

31. The freighter's assailant is unknown.

32. The Royal Navy thoroughly evaluates the submarine, the first to be captured intact for intensive study; the U-boat serves as HMS *Graph* until it is wrecked in 1944. Among the ships that capture the submarine is Canadian destroyer HMCS *Niagara*, formerly U.S. destroyer *Thatcher* (DD 162), one of the 50 transferred in the destroyers-for-bases agreement of 3 September 1940.

33. As can be seen, the name "Avenger" is assigned well before either Pearl Harbor (7 December 1941) or the slaughter of torpedo planes at the Battle of Midway (4 June 1942). These two events are commonly believed to have motivated the assignment of this particular nickname to the TBF/TBM series. The name "Seagull" is also applied unofficially to the Curtiss SOC series which is in use in cruiser-based observation squadrons. Ironically, the SO3C proves a failure in service, and the SOC it was designed to replace serves on.

34. The Dutch freighter's crew, however, is apparently rescued by another ship, for the *Lloyd's List of Shipping Losses: World War II* lists only one man missing from among the complement of 35.

35. Lost on board the British flush-decker are two survivors from *Erviken* and nine from *W. C. Teagle*.

36. There she will undergo repairs alongside repair ship *Vulcan* (AR 5) and eventually return to the United States.

37. *Oahu* (PR 6) is the sister ship of river gunboat *Panay* (PR 5), which had been bombed and sunk by Japanese naval aircraft near Nanking, China, on 12 December 1937.

38. Schooner *Lanikai* is acquired and commissioned, but the start of the war results in her planned mission being cancelled. The third vessel, schooner *Molly Moore*, is selected for the mission but is never taken over. *Lanikai's* civilian career had seen her used as a "prop" in the filming of motion picture *Hurricane* that starred Dorothy Lamour and Jon Hall.

39. *Sonoma*, armed with only two .30-caliber machine guns, will eventually reach Honolulu on 15 December with her tows.

40. Bennion's falling in action sets in motion a chain of events that will result in Mess Attendant Second Class Doris Miller becoming the first African-American to be awarded the Navy Cross. Miller, a brawny, broad-shouldered former high school football player, is recruited to carry the mortally wounded captain from the bridge. Their egress temporarily blocked by fires, however, the men are compelled to remain on the bridge. Miller mans a .50-caliber machine gun. "It wasn't hard," he told interviewers later. "I just pulled the trigger and she worked fine. I had watched the others with these guns. I guess I fired her for about fifteen minutes. I think I got one of those Jap planes. They were diving pretty close to us." Sadly, Miller will not survive the war; he will perish with escort carrier *Liscome Bay* (CVE 56) on 24 November 1943 off the Gilberts.

41. Contrary to some secondary accounts, *Utah* (a converted battleship) is not attacked because she resembled an aircraft carrier. She is attacked because, in the excitement of the moment, she looked sufficiently like the capital ship she once had been. Of the other sunken ships, *California*, *West Virginia*, *Oglala*, and *Sotoyomo* are raised and repaired; *Cassin* and *Downes* are rebuilt around their surviving machinery; all are returned to service. *Oklahoma*, although raised after monumental effort, is never repaired, and ultimately sinks while under tow to the west coast to be broken up for scrap. The hulks of *Arizona* and *Utah* remain at Pearl as memorials.

42. This particular Type A may have been the one whose periscope harbor tug *YT 153* attempts to ram early in the attack.

43. *Thresher* mistakes *Gamble* for destroyer *Litchfield* (DD 336) (the latter ship assigned to work with submarines in the Hawaiian Operating Area), the ship with which she is to rendezvous. *Gamble*, converted from a flush-deck, four-pipe destroyer, resembles *Litchfield*. Sadly, the delay occasioned by the mistaken identity proves fatal to a seriously injured sailor on board the submarine, who dies four hours before the boat finally reaches port on the eighth, of multiple injuries suffered on 6 December 1941 when heavy seas wash him against the signal deck rail.

44. One particular family tragedy prompts concern in the Bureau of Navigation (later Bureau of Naval Personnel) on the matter of brothers serving in the same ship, a common peacetime practice in the U.S. Navy. Firemen First Class Malcolm J. Barber and LeRoy K. Barber, and Fireman Second Class Randolph H. Barber, are all lost when battleship *Oklahoma* (BB 37) capsizes. The Bureau considers it in the "individual family interest that brothers not be put on the same ship in war time, as the loss of such a ship may result in the loss of two or more members of the family, which might be avoided if brothers are separated." The Bureau, however, stops short of specifically forbidding the practice. On 3 February 1942, it issues instructions concerning the impracticality of authorizing transfers of men directly from recruit training to ships in which relatives are serving, and urges that brothers then serving together be advised of the undesirability of their con-

tinuing to do so. Authorizing commanding officers to approve requests for transfers to facilitate separation, the Bureau directs in July 1942 that commanding officers of ships not forward requests for brothers to serve in the same ship or station. This is too late, however, to prevent the five Sullivan brothers from serving in light cruiser *Juneau* (CL 52) (see 13 November 1942).

45. Among the civilians who distinguish themselves this day is Tai Sing Loo, the yard photographer, who has a scheduled appointment to take a picture of the marine Main Gate guards. During the attack, he helps the marines of the Navy Yard fire department fight fires in Drydock No. 1 and later, in the wake of the morning's devastation, delivers food to famished leathernecks.

46. *Wake*, the only U.S. Navy ship to surrender during World War II, is renamed *Tatara* and serves under the Rising Sun for the rest of the war.

47. Repaired and refloated, *President Harrison* is renamed *Kakko Maru* and later, *Kachidoki Maru* (see 12 September 1944). Among the baggage awaiting shipment out of occupied China along with the North China marines are the priceless remains of *Peking Man* (Sinanthropus pekingensis), which are never seen again. Their fate remains a mystery to this day.

48. Another individual who somehow fails to get a seat on the outgoing flying boat is an official from the Bureau of the Budget who was on Wake to go over construction costs.

49. *Robert L. Barnes*, maintained in reduced commission as a floating oil depot, her seaworthiness reduced by age and deterioration, had served since 1 July 1937 as the training ship for Guamanian mess attendants recruited on the island.

50. Utter, as a commander, will later coordinate the carrier air strikes that lead to the destruction of Japanese battleship *Yamato* (see 7 April 1945).

51. The B-17 is probably the one flown by Captain Colin P. Kelly Jr., who is awarded the Distinguished Service Cross posthumously for heroism when Japanese fighters attack his bomber over Clark Field as he returns from his mission over Aparri.

52. Plane is flown by a VS 6 pilot.

53. Possible candidates for having carried out the shelling are *I 2, I 3, I 4, I 5, I 6,* or *I 7*.

54. The squadron had been embarked in *Lexington* (CV 2) when the outbreak of war cancelled the projected ferry mission on 7 December 1941.

55. Dr. Jürgen Rohwer, in his volume on Axis submarine successes, attributes the sinking to a mine laid by Japanese submarine *I 124* on 8 December 1941 off Corregidor, P.I. Corregidor was formerly the British seaplane carrier HMS *Engadine*, which took part in the Battle of Jutland in 1916.

56. *Marechal Joffre* will be formally acquired by the Navy on 20 April 1942, and will serve as the transport *Rochambeau* (AP 63).

57. The merchantman is salvaged, however, and is renamed *Tatsutama Maru*.

58. *Hirondelle* is renamed *Gyonan Maru* and will survive the war. *Argus* is refitted and commissioned in the Japanese Navy as the gunboat *Hong Kong Maru*; for her fate under her new owners, see 19 and 21 June 1943.

59. *Finch* repeats the procedure on 1 January 1942, but since the crew never returns to the damaged merchantman, *Don Jose* is never salvaged.

60. She sinks on 2 January 1942.

1942

61. All but two crewmen survive internment.

62. The sinking of the minesweepers has dire consequences for the Dutch artillerymen. Since the action occurs after the garrison had surrendered, the Japanese execute the gunners.

63. The unsung efforts to keep the gunboat supplied at her isolated station at one point involved the employment of a rotation of three U.S. Navy trucks to bring stores from Haiphong, French Indochina, to Chungking. The perilous route went through bandit-infested territory over roads often bombed by the Japanese. The driving occasioned much wear and tear on the vehicles and many hardships for the men who operated them.

64. Destroyer *Jacob Jones* (DD 130), originally part of TU 4.1.2, runs low on fuel during the passage and puts in to Iceland to refuel. She thus does not make the voyage to Londonderry.

65. Japanese source is unclear; records of the U.S. Army Air Force units engaged that day refer only to attacks on Japanese ships off Balikpapan, not Kendari.

66. *Florence Luckenbach*'s 38-man crew will ultimately return to the United States in transport *Wakefield* (AP 21).

67. The ships will then proceed to Batavia, Java, N.E.I., and thence on to Colombo, Ceylon. An additional passenger will join *West Point* en route to Ceylon when one of the pregnant passengers gives birth to a baby boy on 4 February.

68. *Van Cloon* is later salvaged by the Japanese and serves as *Kembu Maru* (see 12 January 1945).

69. *Kurama Maru*'s assailant is unknown, for no U.S. submarines carry out attacks in latitude 28°N on either 9 or 10 February. *Trout*, the only boat active north of Formosa at that time, reports attacking only *Chuwa Maru* on 9 February.

70. *R 5*'s captain is Lieutenant Commander Dudley W. Morton, who will later gain fame commanding submarine *Wahoo* (SS 238).

71. Ultimately, after repeated and arduous attempts to float the ship, she is declared a total loss on 8 May 1942.

72. The raft is on display in the U.S. Naval Academy Museum, Annapolis, Maryland.

73. *Horai Maru* and *Tatsuno Maru* are salvaged. For *Tatsuno Maru*'s ultimate fate, see 15 January 1944; *Horai Maru*, although raised and towed to Singapore for repairs, never returns to operational service. *Shinshu Maru* (sometimes apparently known as *Ryujo Maru* for security reasons) is also refloated and repaired.

74. *Pope*'s survivors, like those from the two British men-of-war, will become POWs. *Pope*'s executive officer, Lieutenant Richard N. Antrim, will, in April 1942 at Kendari, N.E.I., interpose himself between a brutal Japanese guard and a fellow POW being beaten by the enemy soldier, a selfless act that, along with other instances of heroism evidenced during his captivity, will earn Antrim the Medal of Honor.

75. Scuttling charges complete what is thought to be destruction of the ship, but *Stewart* is raised, repaired, and placed in service by the Japanese as *Patrol Boat No. 102*. She will remain in service through "V-J Day."

76. Six men, however, will perish as a result of mistreatment and malnutrition in POW camps during the war.

77. One SBD (VS 6) is shot down and its crew taken prisoner; unlike the SBD crew captured at Wake, however, the two men captured off Marcus will survive their captivity.

78. The downed plane is one of the two prototype Kawanishi H8K1 Type 2 flying boats, a type later given the nickname EMILY.

79. The submariners do not know that *Chichibu Maru* has on board the two-man crew of an *Enterprise* SBD (VS 6), captured after their plane was shot down during the 24 February strike on Wake Island. Although nearby ships rescue survivors, the two Americans are not among those picked up.

80. The tanker is written off as a constructive total loss and towed to Hampton Roads, Virginia, by tug *Resolute* and thence to Baltimore, Maryland. She is then rebuilt and renamed *Sweep*. The Navy subsequently acquires the ship on 12 July 1944. Renamed *Silver Cloud* (IX 143), she serves as a floating storage tanker into December 1945.

81. Renamed *Mei Yuan* ("of American origin"), the ship will be formally transferred to the Chinese government on 17 February 1948.

82. *Acme* is ultimately repaired and eventually resumes active service.

83. Tug *Wellfleet* (NRTS) will eventually tow the stern section from Morehead City, North Carolina, to Baltimore, Maryland. With a new bow, *Esso Nashville* returns to active service.

84. The hull numbers AK 100 and AK 101 are assigned to disguise the true nature of the ships' "Q-ship" mission.

85. *Liebre* is later acquired by the Navy and renamed *Meredosia* (IX 193).

86. After the fall of the Philippines, the Japanese will raise *Finch* and refit her, commissioning her as *Patrol Boat No. 103*. For her ultimate fate, see 12 January 1945.

87. *Harry F. Sinclair Jr.* undergoes repairs and returns to active service as *Annibal*.

88. The story of the *City of New York*'s Armed Guard, commanded by Ensign Regis J. Schaefer, USNR, is illustrative of the privations faced by these small groups of sailors. Seaman First Class John A. McGinnis, ill and confined in sick bay when the ship comes under attack, enters a lifeboat with 19 other men. Over the next 13 days, eight men die of exposure; the rest suffer frostbite to varying degrees. McGinnis not only takes his turn on the oars but pulls when others refuse to; when the others are unable to do so, he forces himself to hoist the sail himself. "Even just a few hours before his death," his subsequent letter of commendation states, "he crawled over and tugged at the sail to hoist it." John McGinnis dies two hours after the boat is sighted. "During the thirteen days we spent in that lifeboat," one witness writes later, "his conduct was an example to everyone in it, and certainly reflected credit on the naval service." The detachment commander, Ensign Schaefer, goes on to command the Armed Guard on board Dutch motorship *Chant* (see 15 June).

89. Among the decorations Nimitz presents is a Distinguished Flying Cross to one of the four pilots involved in shooting down the Japanese flying boat on 10 March. Sadly, the aviator is killed in the Battle of Midway on 4 June.

90. The two-man crew, though, reaches Guadalcanal and ultimately sails to the New Hebrides.

91. *Genesee*'s career, however, is not over. The Japa-

nese raise her and commission her as the unnamed *Patrol Boat No. 107*. For her ultimate fate, see 5 November 1944.

92. The ship is later renamed *Kerry Patch*.

93. *Luzon*, like *Finch* and *Genesee*, will be given a second career by the victors, who raise her and commission her as gunboat *Karatsu* (see 1944 and 1945).

94. *Quail's* intrepid sailors eventually reach Darwin, Australia, on 6 June.

95. *YO 64*, built in 1886 as *Atlas*, was acquired by the Navy in April 1898, and served with distinction in the Spanish-American War as the armed tug *Wompatuck*. Struck from the naval vessel register on 11 February 1938 and slated for disposal, she was reinstated and reclassified on 9 October 1941, apparently in response to a need for auxiliary craft with the expansion of the Navy to meet the national emergency—ironically, the same kind of situation that had led to her original acquisition in 1898.

96. Still later, *Jamestown* is acquired by the Navy and will serve as *Mariveles* (IX 197).

97. On 21 May *Nashville* breaks radio silence in accordance with the radio deception plan in her operations orders, but the next day her orders are changed and she is rerouted to Dutch Harbor.

98. The lifeboat makes landfall at Cape Corrientes, Cuba, the next morning; the rafts are recovered by a Cuban gunboat.

99. Seaplane tender (destroyer) *Ballard* (AVD 10) relieves *Thornton* on 4 June.

100. Commander John Ford, USNR, the famed motion picture director, is a passenger in *Ballard*. Footage that Ford and an assistant will shoot on Midway before, during, and after the battle is incorporated into a documentary, *The Battle of Midway*. Ford will assemble a second documentary from film shot on board carrier *Hornet* (CV 8), covering Torpedo Squadron (VT) 8. While *The Battle of Midway* is for public distribution (and will win an Academy Award), tragic circumstances will dictate that the documentary about VT 8 be distributed privately to only the families of the men who fly from *Hornet* that momentous morning (see 4 June).

101. Due to the emergency nature of *Yorktown's* deployment, men from VF 42 and VT 5, two squadrons whose planes are transferred off the ship, remain on board as well to service VF-3's F4Fs and VT-3's TBDs.

102. *Chant's* Armed Guard commander, Ensign Regis J. Schaefer, USNR, who remains on board to supervise the abandonment of the ship and is among the last men over the side, survives the loss of his second ship in three months. He had been commander of the Armed Guard unit on board U.S. steamship *City of New York*, sunk on 29 March.

103. *Robert C. Tuttle*, towed to Lynnhaven Roads by tug *Keshena* (NRTS) is ultimately written off as a total loss; tug *Keshena* tows *Esso Augusta* into Hampton Roads, and the latter is returned to service.

104. Tug *Samson* replaces *John R. Williams* and will operate out of Cape May and New York.

105. Tug *Cumco* will replace *Keshena* and will operate out of Little Creek.

106. Ironically, *Astoria* is the ship in which the ashes of Japanese Ambassador to the U.S. Saito Hiroshi were returned to Japan in the spring of 1939. *Astoria's* commanding officer for this diplomatic voyage was then-Captain Richmond Kelly Turner, the same man who directs the American amphibious forces off Guadalcanal.

107. Nine leathernecks, however, either inadvertently left on Makin or unable to get back to the submarines, are subsequently captured by the Japanese and taken to Kwajalein, where they are executed on 16 October.

108. *Wandank* (AT 26) and *Sagamore* (AT 20), and civilian tugs *Samson* and *Foundation Franklin* will tow *Wakefield* to Boston for permanent repairs. The transport will not return to service until February 1944.

109. *Kashino* was specifically designed and built to service the 18.1-inch gunned *Yamato*-class battleships.

110. Captain James Fife, Commander Submarine Squadron 2, writes that he "hoped that [Lipes's] success will not encourage others to take unnecessary risks" in such cases in the future (see 14, 15, and 22 December).

111. *Wichita* almost figured in an international incident in 1937. She left the east coast of the United States in August of that year with 19 Bellanca planes earmarked for delivery to Hong Kong, and small arms and ammunition consigned to Shanghai and Saigon. That material, however, is offloaded at San Pedro in September before the ship sails on her transpacific voyage. It is highly unlikely that the Japanese, knowing of the ship's cargo, would permit her to continue on to China, a country with which they were (albeit undeclared) at war. The U.S. government was not prepared to provide naval escort for ships transporting arms to China in the autumn of 1937.

112. The other crewman who dies of his wounds is Coxswain Samuel B. Roberts Jr., USNR. The Navy honors his memory by naming a destroyer escort for him. The ship earns fame and adds further luster to the name (see 25 October 1944).

113. Ensign Willett just missed the opening of World War II in the Pacific; detached from battleship *California* (BB 44), he was west coast–bound in passenger liner *Lurline* when she departed Honolulu on 5 December 1941.

114. *U 512's* only survivor is rescued by destroyer *Ellis* (DD 154) 10 days later at 07°52'N, 56°05'W.

115. The plane carrying out the attack is the PBY flying boat assigned not to an individual squadron but to Commander Aircraft South Pacific Force and is flown by his assigned pilot. It is bringing out "exhausted pilots" from Henderson Field at the time.

116. Some Japanese sources list the ship sunk by *Drum* as *Hachimanzan Maru*.

117. USAAF A-29 and B-18 bombers attacked submarines on 9 October off Trinidad, but the attacks yield no positive indications of damage.

118. The PBY carries out a daylight torpedo attack on the Japanese transport force, a near-suicidal feat that earns its pilot, Major Jack Cram, USMC, the Navy Cross. Reports indicate that Cram may have scored the hit on *Sasago Maru*.

119. *Vireo* and *PAB No. 6*, escorted by *Hovey* and destroyer *Grayson* (DD 435), arrive at Espíritu Santo on 26 October.

120. *Daniel Boone* is later acquired by the Navy for use as a cargo ship and is renamed *Ara* (AK 136).

121. *President Coolidge's* sister ship, *President Hoover*, had suffered a similar ignominious fate when she ran aground off Formosa in December 1937.

122. The action on the night of 12–13 November also proves the setting for heroism by Mess Attendant First Class Leonard R. Harmon, on board *San Francisco*, who is attending to the needs of the ship's executive officer, Commander Mark H. Crouter, who, though wounded when the Japanese land attack plane

crashes the after superstructure of the cruiser on 12 November, stubbornly refuses evacuation and remains on board. Both men are killed when a shell demolishes Crouter's cabin. Harmon is awarded a posthumous Navy Cross. The destroyer escort *Harmon* (DE 678), commissioned on 31 August 1943, is the first U.S. Navy ship named for an African-American sailor.

123. The haste with which *Enterprise* is sent out once more against the enemy is reflected in the fact that on board engaged in making repairs are Seabees of the 20th Naval Construction Battalion.

124. Among the lost sailors of *Juneau's* complement are the five Sullivan brothers; the loss to the family saddens the entire nation.

125. Some records give the name of the ship sunk as *Kara Maru*.

126. *Caddo's* master dies in a prison camp; the other officer survives, making a total of only seven men who live through the ordeal of the loss of the ship.

1943

127. When U.S. troops enter Bizerte on 7 May, they identify a number of sunken merchantmen, victims of the frequent Allied bombings of the port and scuttling by retreating Axis forces. The two merchant vessels claimed hit by the B-17s on 2 January are most likely from the following group of ships: French cargo vessels *Moron*, *Roubaisien*, and *Divona*; passenger ship (transport) *Gouveneur Général De Guydon*; trawler *Gascogne*; steamer *Raviguan*; German freighter *Brott*; or Italian freighter *Sivigliano*.

128. Assigning credit for the hit is difficult, since the action takes place at night and several boats are involved. *PT 40*, *PT 46*, and *PT 112* each claim at least one hit apiece.

129. *Arthur Middleton* is refloated on 6 April.

130. Sadly, Lieutenant John R. Borum, Armed Guard officer, and J. Cameron, Junior Third Officer, who had been instrumental in saving the ship on 18 November 1942 when she was torpedoed, are both lost.

131. Two scenarios exist to explain *Grampus's* disappearance: she is sunk by (1) Japanese destroyer *Minegumo* in Blackett Strait on the night of 5–6 March or (2) Japanese naval aircraft (958th *Kokutai*) southeast of New Britain on 19 February. She is listed as overdue, presumed lost, on 22 March 1943.

132. *Amberjack* is listed as overdue, presumed lost, on 22 March 1943.

133. *Albacore* is also credited with an unnamed 750-ton frigate-type ship. Japanese records, however, do not list such a patrol vessel lost on that date.

134. Submarine *Permit* (SS 178) records a hit on a freighter on this date, but the position of the attack is 150 miles away from where *Hokuto Maru* is sunk.

135. Japanese submarines *I 17* and *I 26* rescue some survivors on 6 March; *I 26* rescues more on the eighth from an islet west of Goodenough Island.

136. Two possible scenarios exist to explain *Triton's* loss: she is sunk by (1) Japanese destroyer *Satsuki* north of the Admiralties on 15 March or (2) submarine chaser *Ch 24* on the same day. She is listed as overdue, presumed lost, on 10 April 1943.

137. Naval historian Dr. Jürgen Rohwer maintains that *U 163* most likely falls victim to Canadian escort vessel HMCS *Prescott* on 13 March. *U 163*, which has departed Lorient, France, on 10 March, is listed as "missing" after 15 March 1943.

138. *L'Audacieux* had been badly damaged in battle with Australian heavy cruiser HMAS *Australia* off Dakar on 23 September 1940 and had been beached. Refloated, *L'Audacieux* is taken to Bizerte, Tunisia, for repairs.

139. The freighter is ultimately sunk as part of the artificial harbor created off the coast of France beginning 7 June 1944.

140. The agent of factory ship *No. 2 Nissho Maru's* destruction is a mystery, since neither U.S. nor British submarines chronicle an attack on that day. Those who analyze the loss likewise dismiss the possibilities of Japanese or Soviet submarines. *Seawolf* (SS 197) comes across a derelict vessel approximately *No. 2 Nissho Maru's* size six days later; her attempt to administer the coup de grâce, however, fails when her last torpedo misses its target.

141. *William Williams* is ultimately acquired by the Navy under bareboat charter, renamed *Venus*, and classified as a cargo ship, AK 135. Converted at Sydney, Australia, she is commissioned on 26 September 1944 and serves until decommissioned on 18 April 1946.

142. Significantly, the sinking of *U 569* enables the convoy being covered by *Bogue* to proceed unhindered by U-boats.

143. The other boats being transported on board *Stanvac Manila*—*PT 167*, *PT 171*, *PT 172*, and *PT 174*—are damaged, but are repairable.

144. The exact cause of *Runner's* loss may never be determined with certainty. One probable explanation is that she strikes a mine off Honshu between 8 June and 4 July; possible explanations include her sinking (1) on 6 June off northeastern Honshu by the auxiliary guardboat *Minakami Maru* and naval aircraft, (2) on 16 June by destroyer *Nokaze* and naval aircraft, or (3) on 22 or 23 June off northeastern Honshu by the concerted efforts of naval aircraft, minelayer *Shirakami*, and auxiliary guardboats *Kaiwa Maru*, *Minakami Maru*, and *Miya Maru*. However, *Runner* is most likely the agent of destruction for *Seinan Maru* on 11 June, given the boat's assigned patrol area off Honshu in which she encounters the freighter; thus, the latter two explanations might hold. Ominato *Kokutai* planes, however, attack the submarine that sank *Seinan Maru* on 11 June, giving perhaps yet another explanation for *Runner's* demise. In any event, she is listed as overdue, presumed lost, on 20 July 1943.

145. Reed does not survive the war. He is transferred to Japanese custody and perishes while in their hands.

146. *U 758* is the first U-boat to be equipped with a quadruple-mount 20-millimeter gun mount to give the submarine a fighting chance in the event of attack on the surface by aircraft.

147. The wreck of the I-boat is destroyed by USAAF bombers on 5 July.

148. *Harder* later observes *Sagara Maru* 50 miles northeast of this attack position on 29 June, beached and well down in the water with decks awash.

149. *Hulbert* is eventually refloated on 21 July.

150. *S. B. Hunt* is later acquired by the Navy for use as a floating oil storage facility and is renamed *Flambeau* (IX 192).

151. That same day, VC 29 planes attack another U-boat in the vicinity (perhaps *U 168*), without success.

152. TBFs from VC 29 attack what is perhaps *U 532* that same day, without success.

153. Among the passengers who perish in the loss of the tank landing ship is Lieutenant Commander Mc-

Clelland Barclay, USNR, a noted contemporary artist and illustrator called to the colors.

154. Among the survivors is the U-boat's commanding officer, *Kapitänleutnant* Friedrich Guggenberger, who commanded *U 81* when she torpedoed and sunk British carrier HMS *Ark Royal* in the Mediterranean in November 1941.

155. The damage prevents *U 37* from laying mines off Wadi Sebou, French Morocco, and compels her to return to France for repairs.

156. F-lighters are German craft similar in size to a U.S. Navy LCT (tank landing craft), 170 feet long with a cargo capacity of 120 tons; their extensive compartmentation makes them virtually resistant to gunfire but not to a direct hit with a torpedo.

157. A future President of the United States, Lieutenant (j.g.) John F. (Jack) Kennedy, USNR, is commanding officer of *PT 109*.

158. *U 117* was a milch cow submarine and had rendezvoused with *U 66*, attacked by VC 1 planes on 3 August.

159. The Navy acquires the ship. Renamed *Zebra*, she is initially classified as a miscellaneous auxiliary IX 107, but is later reclassified as a net cargo ship, AKN 5.

160. *Francis W. Pettygrove* reaches Gibraltar on 15 August; beached on 12 October she will be adjudged a total loss.

161. Two scenarios exist to explain her loss: (1) she strikes a mine between 29 August and 27 September off northern Honshu or (2) she is sunk by the concerted effort of Japanese aircraft and the minelayer *Ashikazi* off northeastern Honshu on 17 September. *Pompano* is listed as overdue, presumed lost, on 15 October 1943.

162. According to intercepted diplomatic message traffic, the Japanese had apparently arranged to take over *Ada* (a 5,248-ton ship) and had even assigned her the name *Ataka Maru*; *Paddle* may have interrupted that transfer.

163. Among the 36 survivors rescued by destroyer *Barker* (DD 213) are nine men from the hapless *U 604*, scuttled on 11 August 1943.

164. *Grayling* is listed as overdue, presumed lost, on 30 September 1943.

165. Submarine chasers *SC 690* and *SC 977* and Dutch gunboat *Flores* are detached to escort the damaged monitor to Palermo.

166. *Biscayne* retains her original seaplane tender designation until she is formally reclassified from AVP 11 to AGC 18 on 10 October 1944.

167. The drydock, however, will be swept ashore by high winds; *PT 219* will be eventually scrapped as beyond salvage.

168. *Santo Maru* is repaired, reclassified as a transport, and renamed *Sansei Maru* (see 8 December).

169. There are at least four possible explanations to account for *Dorado's* disappearance: (1) she is sunk in error by a Guantánamo-based flying boat on 13 October in the Caribbean at 15°21′N, 73°13′W; (2) she strikes a mine laid by German submarine *U 214* off Colón on 8 October; (3) she strikes a mine laid by *U 214* on 13 or 14 October east of the Antilles; or (4) she is the victim of an unreported enemy attack. In any event, *Dorado* is listed as overdue, presumed lost, on 24 October 1943.

170. *Wahoo* is listed as overdue, presumed lost, on 9 November 1943.

171. She eventually sails for the United States two days before Christmas 1943 and ends her days as part

of the artificial harbor created off Normandy beginning 7 June 1944.

172. Submarine *Guardfish* (SS 217) had conducted valuable preinvasion work, investigating reefs and shoals, selecting an approach lane for the transports, and checking the position of Cape Torokina "with remarkable accuracy" (since the cape's position varied as much as seven miles on existing charts).

173. JANAC study attributes the damage to surveying ship *Tsukushi* and transport *Ryosan Maru*, however, to Australian-laid mines.

174. *Corvina* is listed as overdue, presumed lost, on 23 December 1943.

175. Speculation exists that the ship could have chanced upon a mine laid by submarine *Sunfish* (SS 281) between 14 and 17 December 1942.

176. The explanation of *Capelin's* loss may never be determined for certain: (1) she is sunk on 23 November off Kaoe Bay, Celebes Sea (01°34′N, 123°07′E) by Japanese aircraft (934th *Kokutai*) and minelayer *Wakatake*; (2) hull defects, reported prior to her departure from Darwin on her final voyage, cause her demise; or (3) she strikes a mine in Japanese field laid along the northern coast of the Celebes in *Capelin's* designated operating area. She is listed as overdue, presumed lost, on 18 March 1944.

177. Among the other 53 officers and 648 men either killed or listed as missing is Ship's Cook Third Class Doris Miller, one of the first African-American heroes of World War II, who had earned a Navy Cross for heroism at Pearl Harbor on 7 December 1941.

178. In the same area the next day a PV-1 from VP 140 attacks a Japanese submarine that may have been *I 177* as well.

1944

179. The most probable cause of *Scorpion's* loss is her striking a mine, in either the Yellow or East China Seas. She is listed as overdue, presumed lost, on 6 March 1944.

180. During the last half of February, ZP 42 blimps, operating from Brazilian bases, locate and aid in the recovery of some 450 tons of baled rubber, part of *Rio Grande's* cargo.

181. Service Squadron 10 is based at Majuro (February–May 1944), Eniwetok (June–September 1944), Ulithi (October 1944–April 1945), and Leyte-Samar, P.I. (May–August 1945), during the war. At the height of its activities, the squadron controls 609 vessels at five fleet anchorages.

182. *Delhi Maru* is on her maiden voyage as a "Q-ship," her conversion having been completed 14 January.

183. *U 129* and *U 516* are surprised at this fueling rendezvous as well, but both escape.

184. *Bowfin* identifies the escort for the tanker as what she believes to be ex-U.S. destroyer *Stewart* (DD 224), which had been salvaged by the Japanese and commissioned as the unnamed *Patrol Vessel No. 102*.

185. *Grayback* is listed as overdue, presumed lost, on 30 March 1944. If the Japanese account for a definite "kill" on that date is accepted, then the attribution for the sinking of naval transport *Ceylon Maru* on 27 February at 31°45′N, 127°45′E, for *Pogy* (SS 266) is questionable. Commonly given credit for the sinking, *Pogy* did not report any such attack in her patrol report for that date. *Grayback* could have been damaged and con-

tinued her patrol, sunk *Ceylon Maru*, and then succumbed to the effects of the damage inflicted on 26 February.

186. *Trout* is reported as overdue, presumed lost, on 17 April 1944.

187. *Karatsu* will never return to active service. She is one of four ships intentionally sunk to block the channel through the entrance of the breakwater off Manila in February 1945.

188. When ordered by Rear Admiral Sakonju (who flies his flag in heavy cruiser *Aoba*) to retain a minimum of POWs on board and "dispose of" the rest, *Tone's* commanding officer, Captain Mayuzumi Haruo, refuses. Subsequently, on 15 March the ship disembarks 32 men at Batavia, Java; 72 remain on board *Tone* when she sails for Singapore three days later. That night (18–19 March), *Tone's* crew executes every POW on board. Ultimately, War Crimes Tribunal sentences Sakonju to death, Mayuzumi to seven years' imprisonment.

189. *Suiten Maru* is raised on 12 July and reenters active service.

190. She is repaired in time to participate in the Marianas campaign.

191. Fortunately, five LSTs in the Hawaiian Operating Area were uncommitted to other operations and were assigned to the force that would invade the Marianas in mid-June.

192. The exact identity of the attacking aircraft is not known, since no Allied claim apparently matches the damage reported in Japanese dispatches. Possible candidates are USAAF B-24s, which harass Truk regularly between 5 and 7 June.

193. Practice in Exmouth Gulf, Australia, on 29 May enables *Redfin* to disembark the men and discharge the cargo in three hours' time.

194. *No. 8 Shonan Maru* escapes from Saipan on 23 June and reaches Manila on 1 July.

195. Only one merchantman, *Inari Maru*, reaches Japan.

196. *Golet* is listed as overdue, presumed lost, on 26 July 1944.

197. *Phelps* moors alongside the battle damage repair ship *Phaon* (ARB 3) soon thereafter, in such a manner to permit the destroyer to continue to carry out her fire support duties.

198. After U.S. forces capture Guam, the wreck of *Nichiyu Maru* is demolished with explosives sometime between 27 and 30 July.

199. Although the Japanese claim *Seattle Maru* is a hospital ship, she is unlighted and in convoy when she is torpedoed by *Piranha*. Recognition that *Seattle Maru* is serving in a more warlike capacity comes when no protest accompanies her loss.

200. *Nautilus* is unable to carry out one mission during this cruise into the Philippines, when the Japanese occupation of Bohol, Visayan Islands (north of Mindanao), renders it impossible to land the party of men and approximately 30 tons of supplies earmarked to be dropped off at a rendezvous off Canauayon Islet, Mindanao, P.I.

201. Later damage at an indeterminate date, inflicted by what are most likely USAAF planes, results in her ultimate sinking by 5 October.

202. Among those lost with *Robalo* is her commanding officer, Lieutenant Commander Manning M. Kimmel, one of the sons of Rear Admiral Husband E. Kimmel, who had been Commander in Chief Pacific Fleet on 7 December 1941.

203. As *SC 651* nears the badly damaged *SC 1029*, the former's commanding officer, Lieutenant (j.g.) Joseph W. Barr, USNR, sees an act of determination that inspires those who witness it: an enlisted man picks himself up off the deck and looks for the national ensign, which had been blown away by the force of the explosion. That sailor "who looked to be in pain . . . with the blank expression of shock still on his face," Barr writes, "scrambled around to find that ensign and then hoisted it immediately. It was apparently the first act in setting the ship to rights."

204. *Narwhal* subsequently picks up one Filipino officer and mail off San Roque, Cateel Bay, on east coast of Mindanao.

205. In addition, there are 12 other small cargo vessels destroyed during the strikes, but their names are either garbled in message traffic or otherwise unrecoverable.

206. Submarine *Perch* (SS 313) loses contact with *Escolar* on 17 October, after which point *Escolar* is never heard from again. The most likely cause of *Escolar's* loss is her striking a Japanese mine about 17 October between 33°44′N, 127°33′E, and 33°44′N, 129°06′E, the site of minefields laid in 1943 and 1944. She is listed as overdue, presumed lost, on 27 November 1944.

207. A third task for *Nautilus* during this series of special missions—discharging cargo, gasoline, and oil at a designated spot near the mouth of the Pola River—is cancelled and the boat directed to proceed to Mios Woendi.

208. Subsequently, the Navy charters the ship and renames her *Triana* (IX 223), and she is used as a floating storage facility.

209. *Externsteine* is taken into U.S. Navy service and commissioned 24 January 1945 as miscellaneous auxiliary *Callao* (IX 205). The Bureau of Ships uses the ship for experimental work into 1950.

210. "SHO 1 GO" is one of four contingency plans in existence at this time: "SHO 2 GO" deals with the Formosa, the Nansei Shoto, and southern Kyushu areas; "SHO 3 GO" with Kyushu, Shikoku, Honshu, and the Bonins; "SHO 4 GO" with Hokkaido.

211. There were two further War Department Pearl Harbor–related investigations: the Clarke Inquiry (conducted by Colonel Carter C. Clark into top secret communications matters), 14–16 September 1944 and 13 July–4 August 1945, and the Clausen Investigation (conducted by Major Henry C. Clausen), 23 November 1944–12 September 1945.

212. *Toun Maru* will be towed to Takao for repairs but will never return to active service.

213. *Shark* is listed as overdue, presumed lost, on 27 November 1944.

214. Some of *Hayashimo's* survivors land on a nearby isolated island and name it for their ship.

215. *Fujinami* is lost with all hands, including the survivors of heavy cruiser *Chokai*, rescued on 25 October.

216. *Houston's* career proves short after her repairs, lasting from March to October 1945; decommissioned on 15 December 1947, she never returns to active service. *Canberra*, converted and reclassified as a guided missile heavy cruiser (CAG 2), will participate in the Vietnam War (1965–1968).

217. *Whitehurst* will portray the fictional "USS Haynes" in the 1957 motion picture *The Enemy Below*. Among the realistic footage that can be seen in this fine film are depth charge attacks similar to those that sunk *I 45*.

218. Submarine *Ray* (SS 271) may have torpedoed *Caroline Maru* as well.

219. Divers from salvage vessel *Chanticleer* (ARS 7) investigate the wreck (March–April 1945), which lies in shallow water, and retrieve valuable intelligence documents.

220. *Blackfin's* trove of enemy documents will ultimately be transported by 13th Air Force aircraft to the Seventh Fleet Intelligence Center (SEFIC) at Hollandia.

221. *I 37* is on a *kaiten* mission at the time, bound for the Palaus, when she is reported missing on 20 November.

222. Since both submarines expended five *kaitens* between them (four from *I 47* and one from *I 36*) and none of the *kaiten* crews survived, no possibility exists of confirming which submarine should be credited with sinking *Mississinewa*.

223. Three years—to the day—earlier, *Ward* (Lieutenant William W. Outerbridge) fired on a Japanese midget submarine attempting to gain entrance into Pearl Harbor. In a remarkable coincidence, *O'Brien's* commanding officer when she scuttles *Ward* is Commander Outerbridge.

224. Rear Admiral Arthur D. Struble, commanding TG 78.3, will shift his flag from the damaged *Nashville* to destroyer *Dashiell* (DD 659).

225. Admiral William F. Halsey Jr. will be promoted to fleet admiral after the conclusion of hostilities.

226. *Dragonet*, on her maiden war patrol, eventually manages to clear the reef, and after a passage fraught with difficulty (including, at one point, a 63-degree port list), reaches Midway on 20 December.

227. Lack of evidence militates against establishing the definite cause for *Swordfish's* loss. She (1) is sunk by *Coast Defense Vessel No. 4* on 5 January 1945 off Tori Jima, Bonins, 29°25′N, 141°07′E, or (2) strikes a mine after 9 January 1945 in the Okinawa area (12,000 had been laid in four fields in that area between January and June 1944). She is listed as overdue, presumed lost, on 15 February 1945.

1945

228. The "Liberty" ship is beached the next day to prevent further damage; the Navy subsequently repairs her. She is renamed *Harcourt* and classified as a miscellaneous auxiliary (IX 225).

229. Rear Admiral Theodore E. Chandler, Commander Cruiser Division 4, who, as a captain, had commanded light cruiser *Omaha* (CL 4) when she seized German blockade runner *Odenwald* on 6 November 1941, is fatally wounded in the attack on *Louisville*.

230. Six USN and USMC airmen shot down during the raids on the Saigon region are interned under international law. The Governor of Cochin China, Ernest Hoeffel, has them removed from confinement near Saigon to an internment camp in the northern part of French Indochina. Hoeffel's "initiative and friendly cooperation" protect the Americans from apprehension by the Japanese in March, and the fliers are subsequently transferred to U.S. forces in Kunming, China. Hoeffel will ultimately be awarded the Medal of Freedom from a grateful United States in 1953.

231. *Barbel* is reported as overdue, presumed lost, on 16 February 1945.

232. She is towed to Saigon, but is never repaired, and is ultimately broken up there.

233. *No. 2 Nagaoka Maru* (a Japanese ship or craft of unknown tonnage) is sunk off Hachijo Jima on this date; she is in the vicinity of TF 58 and may have been accounted for by its planes.

234. Proceeding thence to Norfolk, Virginia, *Pontiac* is decommissioned there on 20 May and is returned to the Maritime Commission the next day.

235. Plausible scenarios for *Kete*'s disappearance: (1) She strikes a mine about 20 March in a field sown by minelayer *Tokiwa* and auxiliary minelayer *Koei Maru* less than a month before (27 February) or (2) she is sunk by one of four Japanese submarines, *Ro 41* (the most likely suspect), *Ro 49*, *Ro 56*, or *I 8* (all of which are lost soon thereafter), believed to be in the vicinity east of Okinawa between 20 and 23 March. In any event, *Kete* is listed as overdue, presumed lost, on 16 April 1945.

236. During the retirement phase, destroyer *Preston* (DD 795) rescues eight survivors from a downed USAAF B-29; the downed airmen had been spotted by a search plane from carrier *Bunker Hill* (CV 17), in TG 58.3.

237. There are three plausible explanations for *Snook*'s loss: she is sunk by (1) Japanese naval aircraft (256th, 453rd, and 951st *Kokutais*) on 9 April near the Shuzan Islands; (2) escort vessel *Okinawa*, Coast Defense Vessel No. 8, Coast Defense Vessel No. 32, and Coast Defense Vessel No. 52 after being detected by planes from the aforementioned naval air groups; or (3) submarine *I 56* while she carries out her last assignment, lifeguarding, in the Nansei Shoto. In any event, *Snook* is listed as overdue, presumed lost, on 16 May 1945.

238. *Trigger* is listed as overdue, presumed lost, on 1 May 1945.

239. *RO 67* is ultimately decommissioned 20 July and used as a pontoon at Sasebo.

240. *Yamato* carries only enough fuel for a one-way voyage. Plans call for the massive battleship to be beached off Okinawa to employ her 18.1-inch guns as coast artillery.

241. Japanese forces are located on 15 April and fighting continues until 23 April. Survivors of the Japanese garrison remained "hunted and harried" until hostilities end in August.

242. "The disposition of the pig they [the Japanese garrison] left behind is not noted in the records," writes Robert Ross Smith in *Triumph in the Philippines*, "but it would not be unreasonable to assume that some of the men of the 1st Battalion, 151st Infantry, had fresh pork chops for supper on 16 April 1945."

243. Some sources list *Bream*'s victim as *Teishu Maru*; ULTRA material, however, uses the German name and refers to communications between Tokyo and Berlin concerning her loss.

244. Minesweeping is particularly difficult at Tarakan, not only because of the shore batteries that fire upon the minecraft, but because of the various types of mines that have to be swept: magnetic, acoustic, and contact. These mines also have various national origins: British, American, Japanese, and possibly even Dutch.

245. "Superb damage control measures and fire fighting," *South Dakota*'s war diarist notes, "quickly brought the fire under control and narrowly averted a major disaster." *South Dakota* lay alongside ammunition ship *Wrangell* (AE 12) at the moment the first tank exploded.

246. Robinson had, as a captain, commanded light cruiser *Marblehead* (CL 12) during the early months of the war.

247. Fleet tug *Tenino* (ATF 115) later tows *William B. Allison*, written off by the War Shipping Administration as a total loss, to Kerama Retto, Okinawa, where she undergoes repairs and is taken over by the Navy for use as a mobile storehouse for lubricants and drummed petroleum products. Classified as a miscellaneous auxiliary (IX 117), she is renamed *Gamage*.

248. *Bonefish* is reported as overdue, presumed lost, on 30 July 1945.

249. *Barry*, decommissioned that morning, sails loaded with empty powder cases, shell cases, ammunition tanks, and empty oil drums, being employed to a picket station off Okinawa as a decoy to "absorb several suiciders." Irreparably damaged submarine chaser *PC 1603* is earmarked for the same purpose.

250. Probable agent of destruction is submarine *Lagarto* (SS 371), which is assigned to patrol the South China Sea at that time. *Lagarto* does not return from her war patrol. She is listed as overdue, presumed lost, on 10 August 1945.

251. This force will operate approximately 150 miles northwest of Okinawa.

252. *Japanese Monograph No. 116* lists two army vessels (unspecified as to type) identified only by number (No. 94 and No. 1491) that are damaged by aircraft off Quelpart Island.

253. Those operations, carried out between 21 and 23 July, yield a paucity of targets, since no Japanese shipping larger than sampans (several of which are sunk) is encountered.

254. The sinking of the seven train ferries on 14 July and one the following day, together with the damage inflicted upon three additional vessels of this type, is deemed a severe blow to transportation facilities between Hokkaido and the main island of Honshu, virtually cutting off important agricultural and mineral supplies of the northern island.

255. Submarine chaser *Harushima* had originally been the U.S. Army cable ship *Colonel G. F. E. Harrison*, salvaged from Mariveles Bay, Luzon, P.I., in 1942.

256. *XE 1* had been earmarked to attack Japanese heavy cruiser *Myoko*, also at Singapore, but could not find her and ended up joining *XE 3* in attacking *Takao*.

GLOSSARY

A-20	Douglas A-20 Boston (USAAF)
A-24	Douglas A-24 Dauntless (USAAF variant of SBD)
A-26	Douglas A-26 Invader (USAAF)
A-28	Lockheed A-28 Hudson (USAAF variant of PBO)
A-29	Lockheed A-29 Hudson (USAAF variant of PBO)
ABC	American-British-Canadian
ABDA	Australian-British-Dutch-American
ACV	Auxiliary aircraft carrier (USN)
AEDO	Aeronautical Engineering Duty Only (U.S.)
Albacore	Fairey Albacore torpedo/strike aircraft (FAA)
ALF	Kawanishi E7K Type 94 reconnaissance seaplane (Japanese)
APEX	twin-float single-engine biplane (Japanese)
AR 196	Arado AR 196 floatplane (German)
AT	United States–United Kingdom convoy
AVG	American Volunteer Group ("Flying Tigers"); also aircraft escort vessel
B-17	Boeing B-17 Flying Fortress (USAAF)
B-18	Douglas B-18 Bolo (USAAF)
B-24	Consolidated B-24 Liberator (USAAF variant of PB4Y)
B-25	North American B-25 Mitchell (USAAF)
B-26	Martin B-26 Marauder (USAAF)
B-29	Boeing B-29 Superfortress (USAAF)
B.C.C.	British Crown Colony
Beaufighter	Bristol Beaufighter torpedo/strike/fighter (RAF/RAAF)
Beaufort	Bristol Beaufort light/torpedo bomber (RAF/RAAF)
BETTY	Mitsubishi G4M Type 1 land attack plane (Japanese)
Boston	Export variant of Douglas A-20 (RAAF/RAF)
Brewster B 339	Export variant of Brewster F2A Buffalo (Dutch/RAF/RAAF/RNZAF)
BT	Bahia (Brazil)-Trinidad convoy
B.W.I.	British West Indies
C-87	Consolidated C-87 Liberator (cargo variant of B-24)
CAMCO	Central Aircraft Manufacturing Company
Catalina	Consolidated PBY Catalina (RAF/RAAF)
CB	Construction Battalion (or large cruiser)
CEAG	Commander, *Enterprise* Air Group
C.Z.	Canal Zone (Panama)
DO 24	Dornier 24 flying boat (Dutch)
EDO	Engineering Duty Only (USN)
F2A	Brewster F2A Buffalo (USN/USMC)
F4F	Grumman F4F Wildcat (USN/USMC)
F4U	Vought F4U Corsair (USN/USMC)

F6F	Grumman F6F Hellcat (USN/USMC)	OS2N	Naval Aircraft Factory OS2N Kingfisher (USN)
FAA	Fleet Air Arm	OS2U	Vought OS2U Kingfisher (USN)
FAW	Fleet Air Wing	OSS	Office of Strategic Services (U.S.)
FIDO	homing torpedo	P-35	Seversky P-35 (no nickname) (USAAF)
FM	General Motors FM Wildcat (USN)	P-36	Curtiss P-36 Hawk (USAAF)
FRANCES	Yokosuka P1Y bomber (Japanese)	P-39	Bell P-39 Airacobra (USAAF)
GEORGE	Kawanishi N1K3-J Navy Interceptor Fighter (Japanese)	P-40	Curtiss P-40 Kittyhawk/Warhawk (USAAF)
		P-51	North American P-51 Mustang (USAAF)
GHQ	General Headquarters	P-400	Bell P-400 Airacobra (export P-39) (USAAF)
HE 111	Heinkel HE 111 medium/torpedo bomber (German)	P2Y	Consolidated P2Y flying boat (USN)
HE 115	Heinkel HE 115 floatplane (German)	PA	Persian Gulf–Aden convoy
HMAS	His Majesty's Australian Ship	PB2Y	Consolidated PB2Y Coronado (USN)
HMCS	His Majesty's Canadian Ship	PB4Y-1	Consolidated PB4Y-1 Liberator (USN/USMC)
HMNZ	His Majesty's New Zealand Ship	PB4Y-2	Consolidated PB4Y-2 Privateer (USN)
HMS	His Majesty's Ship	PBM	Martin PBM Mariner (USN)
HS 123	Hispano-Suiza HS 123L (license-built variant of Italian Fiat CR 32 fighter) (Spanish)	PBO	Lockheed PBO Hudson (USN)
		PBY	Consolidated PBY Catalina (USN/USMC)
Hudson	Lockheed Hudson (export variant of PBO) (RAF/RAAF/RNZAF)	PETE	Mitsubishi F1M Type 0 observation seaplane (Japanese)
HX	Halifax–New York convoy	PG	Panama-Guantanamo convoy
JAKE	Aichi E13A Type 0 reconnaissance seaplane (Japanese)	PH-3	Hall PH-3 (USCG seaplane)
		P.I.	Philippine Islands
JANAC	Joint Army-Navy Assessment Committee	POW	Prisoner of war
JF	Grumman JF Duck amphibian (USCG/USN/USMC)	PQ	Iceland–North Russia convoy
JILL	Nakajima B6N carrier attack bomber (Japanese)	PT-13	Primary trainer (USAAF)
JU 87	Junkers JU 87 dive bomber (*Stuka*) (German)	PV-1	Lockheed PV-1 Ventura (USN/RNZAF)
JU 88	Junkers JU 88 medium bomber (German)	PV-2	Lockheed PV-2 Harpoon (USN)
JUDY	Yokosuka D4Y carrier bomber (Japanese)	QP	North Russia–Iceland convoy
KATE	Nakajima B5N carrier attack plane (Japanese)	R3D	Douglas R3D (no nickname) (USMC)
KMS	United Kingdom–Mediterranean (Slow) convoy	R4C	Curtiss R4C Condor (USN)
Kokutai	Japanese term for land-based naval air group	R4D	Douglas R4D Skytrain/Skytrooper (USN/USMC)
Lancaster	Avro Lancaster heavy bomber (RAF)	RA	Kola Fjord–Loch Ewe (Scotland) convoy
LB-30	Consolidated LB-30 Liberator (export variant of B-24)	RAAF	Royal Australian Air Force
MAD	Magnetic Anomoly Detection	RAF	Royal Air Force
MAG	Marine Aircraft Group (U.S. Marine Corps)	RAN	Royal Australian Navy
Martin 139	Export variant of Douglas B-10 bomber (Dutch)	RCAF	Royal Canadian Air Force
M.I.	Mariana Islands	RCT	Regimental Combat Team
MKS	Mediterranean–United Kingdom (Slow) convoy	RD	Douglas RD flying boat
MOMP	Mid-Ocean Meeting Point	RFA	Royal Fleet Auxiliary (RN)
NA	National Archives	RINS	Royal Indian Navy Ship
NAS	Naval Air Station (U.S.)	RN	Royal Navy
NASM	National Air and Space Museum.	RNN	Royal Netherlands Navy
NATS	Naval Air Transport Service (U.S.)	RNVR	Royal Navy Volunteer Reserve
N.E.I.	Netherlands East Indies	RNZAF	Royal New Zealand Air Force
NELL	Mitsubishi G3M2 Type 96 land attack plane (Japanese)	SAAF	South African Air Force
		SACO	Sino-American Cooperative Organization
NHC	Naval Historical Center	SB2C	Curtiss SB2C Helldiver (USN)
NHF	Naval Historical Foundation	SB2U	Vought SB2U Vindicator (USN/USMC)
NRTS	Navy Rescue Tug Service	SBC	Curtiss SBC Helldiver (USN)
N.W.I.	Netherlands West Indies	SBD	Douglas SBD Dauntless (USN/USMC)
O-47	North American O-47 observation plane (USAAF)	SC	Sydney (Nova Scotia)–United Kingdom convoy
		SG	Sydney (Nova Scotia)–Greenland convoy
OA-10	Consolidated OA-10 Catalina (USAAF variant of PBY)	SKUA	Blackburn fighter/dive-bomber (FAA)
		SM 79	Savoia-Marchetti SM 79 medium/torpedo bomber (Italian)
OB	United Kingdom–North America convoy		
ON	United Kingdom–North America convoy	SOC	Curtiss SOC Seagull (USN)
ONS	United Kingdom–North America (Slow) convoy	SON	Naval Aircraft Factory SON Seagull (USN)
OPM	Office of Production Management (U.S.)	STAG	Special Air Task Force (USN)

Swordfish	Fairey Swordfish torpedo/strike aircraft (FAA)	VB	Bombing Squadron (carrier- and land-based)
TA	United Kingdom–United States convoy	VC	Composite Squadron
TAG	Trinidad-Aruba-Guantanamo convoy	VCS	Cruiser Scouting Squadron
TB	Trinidad–Bahia convoy	VF	Fighting Squadron
TBD	Douglas TBD Devastator (USN)	VGS	Scouting Squadron (aircraft escort vessel)
TBF	Grumman TBF Avenger (USN/USMC)	VHF	Very High Frequency
TBM	General Motors TBM Avenger (USN)	Vildebeest	Vickers Vildebeest torpedo/strike aircraft (RAF)
TF	Task Force	VJ	Utility Squadron
TG	Task Group	VMF	Marine Fighting Squadron
T.H.	Territory of Hawaii	VMO	Marine Observation Squadron
TJ	Trinidad–Rio de Janeiro convoy	VMSB	Marine Scout Bombing Squadron
TSR	Torpedo spotting reconnaissance (British plane type)	VMTB	Marine Torpedo Bombing Squadron
TU	Task Unit	VOS	Observation Squadron (battleship-based)
UC	United Kingdom–Caribbean convoy	VP	Patrol Squadron
UDT	Underwater Demolition Team	VPB	Patrol Bombing Squadron
UGF	United States–Gibraltar (Fast) convoy	VR	Transport Squadron
UGS	United States–Gibraltar (Slow) convoy	VS	Scouting Squadron
USA	United States Army	VT	Torpedo Squadron
USAAC	United States Army Air Corps (pre-July 1941)	WILLOW	Yokosuka K5Y Type 95 intermediate trainer (Japanese)
USAAF	United States Army Air Force (post-July 1941)	WS	United Kingdom–Middle East ("Winston [Churchill]'s Specials") convoy
USCG	United States Coast Guard		
USMC	United States Marine Corps	WSA	War Shipping Administration (U.S.)
USN	United States Navy	XPBS	Sikorsky XPBS flying boat (USN)
USNR	United States Naval Reserve	ZEKE	Mitsubishi A6M5 Type 0 carrier fighter
USSR	Union of Soviet Socialist Republics	ZERO	Mitsubishi A6M2 Type 0 carrier fighter (Japanese)
UT	United States–United Kingdom convoy		
VAL	Aichi D3A1 Type 99 carrier bomber (Japanese)		

BIBLIOGRAPHY

PRIMARY SOURCES

While the original published text of the *United States Naval Chronology, World War II* served as the basic skeletal framework for this edition, I discovered through experience that I could take almost nothing for granted. There was no recourse but to seek primary documents in the Operational Archives Branch. Owing to the massive number of action reports and war diaries (for ships, squadrons, task forces, task groups, fleets, et cetera) consulted to verify the actions covered by this new chronology, footnotes would easily account for another book of like size. The World War II records consulted are now located at the National Archives and Records Administration facility at College Park, Maryland, in Record Group (RG) 45 (Office of Naval Records and Library). Two Special Research Histories (SRH) contained in the records of the National Security Agency (RG-457, also located at College Park) proved invaluable: SRH-168 [*Agenda, Minutes/Assessments of the Joint Army-Navy Assessment Committee (JANAC)*] and SRH-184 [*CNO, Pacific Intelligence Section, Allied Claims and Enemy Confirmation of Damage to Japanese Ships (January 1943–September 1945)*].

SECONDARY SOURCES

Abbazia, Patrick. *Mr. Roosevelt's Navy: The Private War of the U.S. Atlantic Fleet, 1939–1942.* Annapolis, Md.: Naval Institute Press, 1975.

Adamson, Hans C., and George F. Kosco. *Halsey's Typhoons: A Firsthand Account of How Two Typhoons, More Powerful Than the Japanese, Dealt Death and Destruction to Admiral Halsey's Third Fleet.* New York: Crown, 1967.

Alden, John D. *U.S. Submarine Attacks during World War II (Including Allied Submarine Attacks in the Pacific Theater).* Annapolis, Md.: Naval Institute Press, 1989.

Bailey, Thomas A., and Paul B. Ryan. *Hitler vs. Roosevelt: the Undeclared Naval War.* New York: Free Press, 1979.

Ballantine, Duncan S. *U.S. Naval Logistics in the Second World War.* Princeton, N.J.: Princeton University Press, 1947.

Barbey, Daniel E. *MacArthur's Amphibious Navy: Seventh Amphibious Force Operations, 1943–1945.* Annapolis, Md.: Naval Institute Press, 1969.

Belote, James H., and William M. Belote. *Titans of the Seas: The Development and Operations of Japanese and American Carrier Task Forces During World War II.* New York: Harper and Row, 1975.

Blair, Clay, Jr. *Silent Victory: The U.S. Submarine War Against Japan.* Philadelphia: Lippincott, 1975.

Borg, Dorothy. *The United States and the Far Eastern Crisis of 1933–1938: From the Manchurian Incident Through the Initial Stage of the Undeclared Sino-Japanese War.* Cambridge, Mass.: Harvard University Press, 1964.

Borg, Dorothy, and Shumpei Okamoto, eds. *Pearl Harbor as History: Japanese-American Relations, 1931–1941.* New York: Columbia University Press, 1973.

Boyd, Carl, and Akihiko Yoshida. *The Japanese Submarine Force and World War II.* Annapolis, Md.: Naval Institute Press, 1995.

Bragadin, Marc' Antonio. *The Italian Navy in World War II.* Annapolis, Md.: Naval Institute Press, 1957.

Browning, Robert M., Jr. *U.S. Merchant Vessel Casualties of World War II.* Annapolis, Md.: Naval Institute Press, 1996.

Buell, Thomas B. *Master of Sea Power: A Biography of Fleet Admiral Ernest J. King.* Boston: Little, Brown, 1980.

———, *The Quiet Warrior: A Biography of Admiral Raymond A. Spruance.* Boston: Little Brown, 1974.

Bulkley, Robert J. *At Close Quarters: PT Boats in the United States Navy.* Washington, D.C.: Government Printing Office, 1962.

Calhoun, C. Raymond. *Typhoon, The Other Enemy: The Third Fleet and the Pacific Storm of December 1944.* Annapolis, Md.: Naval Institute Press, 1981.

Carter, Worral Reed. *Beans, Bullets, and Black Oil: The Story of Fleet Logistics Afloat in the Pacific During World War II.* Washington, D.C.: Government Printing Office, 1953.

Carter, Worral Reed, and Elmer E. Duvall. *Ships, Salvage, and Sinews of War: The Story of Fleet Logistics Afloat in Atlantic and Mediterranean Waters During World War II.* Washington, D.C.: Government Printing Office, 1954.

Connery, Robert H. *The Navy and Industrial Mobilization in World War II.* Princeton, N.J.: Princeton University Press, 1951.

Cook, Charles. *The Battle of Cape Esperance: Strategic Encounter at Guadalcanal.* New York: Crowell, 1968.

Costello, John. *The Pacific War.* New York: Rawson, Wade, 1981.

Cressman, Robert J., et al., *A Glorious Page in Our History, The Battle of Midway, 4–6 June 1942.* Missoula, Mont.: Pictorial Histories Publishing Co., 1991.

Cressman, Robert J. *"A Magnificent Fight": The Battle for Wake Island.* Annapolis, Md.: Naval Institute Press, 1995.

Cressman, Robert J., and J. Michael Wenger. *Steady Nerves and Stout Hearts: The Enterprise (CV-6) Air Group and Pearl Harbor, 7 December 1941.* Missoula, Mont.: Pictorial Histories Publishing Co., 1990.

Cunningham, Winfield S., with Lydel Sims. *Wake Island Command.* Boston: Little, Brown, 1961.

Dull, Paul S. *A Battle History of the Imperial Japanese Navy, 1941–1945.* Annapolis, Md.: Naval Institute Press, 1978.

Dyer, George Carroll. *The Amphibians Came to Conquer: The Story of Admiral Richmond Kelly Turner,* 2 vols. Washington, D.C.: Government Printing Office, 1972.

Feis, Herbert. *The Road to Pearl Harbor: The Coming of the War Between the United States and Japan.* Princeton, N.J.: Princeton University Press, 1950.

Frank, Richard B. *Guadalcanal.* New York: Random House, 1990.

Friedlander, Saul. *Prelude to Downfall: Hitler and the United States, 1939–41.* New York, Knopf, 1967.

Fuchida, Mitsuo, and Okumiya Masatake. *Midway: The Battle That Doomed Japan.* Edited by Clarke Kawakami and Roger Pineau. Annapolis, Md.: Naval Institute Press, 1955.

Gable, Christopher R. *The U.S. Army GHQ Maneuvers of 1941.* Washington, D.C.: Center of Military History, 1991.

Gannon, Michael. *Operation Drumbeat: The Dramatic Story of Germany's First U-Boat Attacks Along the American Coast in World War II.* New York: Harper and Row, 1990.

Garfield, Brian W. *The Thousand-Mile War: World War II in Alaska and the Aleutians.* Garden City, N.Y.: Doubleday, 1969.

Gilbert, Martin. *The Second World War: A Complete History.* New York: Henry Holt, 1989.

Goldstein, Donald M., Katherine V. Dillon, and J. Michael Wenger. *The Way It Was: Pearl Harbor, The Original Photographs.* Washington, D.C.: Brassey's, 1991.

Goldstein, Donald M., and Katherine V. Dillon, eds. *Fading Victory: The Diary of Admiral Matome Ugaki, 1941–1945.* Translated by Masataka Chihaya. Pittsburgh: University of Pittsburgh Press, 1991.

Griffith, Samuel B. *The Battle for Guadalcanal.* New York: Lippincott, 1963.

Hart, B. H. Liddell. *History of the Second World War.* New York: G. P. Putnam, 1971.

Hayes, Grace P. *The History of the Joint Chiefs of Staff in World War II: The War Against Japan.* Annapolis, Md.: Naval Institute Press, 1982.

Holmes, Wilfred J. *Undersea Victory: The Influence of Submarine Operations on the War in the Pacific.* Garden City, N.Y.: Doubleday and Co., Inc., 1966.

———. *Double-Edged Secrets: U.S. Naval Intelligence Operations in the Pacific During World War II.* Annapolis, Md.: Naval Institute Press, 1979.

Hough, Frank Olney. *The Island War; The United States Marine Corps in the Pacific.* Philadelphia: J. B. Lippincott, 1947.

Hoyt, Edwin P. *How They Won the War in the Pacific: Nimitz and His Admirals.* New York: Weybright and Talley, 1970.

Hughes, Terry, and John Costello. *The Battle of the Atlantic.* New York: The Dial Press, 1977.

Isely, Jeter A., and Philip A. Crowl. *The U.S. Marines and Amphibious War: Its Theory and Its Practice in the Pacific.* Princeton, N.J.: Princeton University Press, 1951.

Jentschura, Hansgeorg, Dieter Jung, and Peter Mickel. *Warships of the Imperial Japanese Navy, 1869–1945.* Annapolis, Md.: Naval Institute Press, 1977.

Johnson, Ellis A., and David A. Katcher. *Mines Against Japan.* Silver Spring, Md.: Naval Ordnance Laboratory, 1973.

Kahn, David. *Seizing the Enigma: The Race to Break the U-boat Codes, 1939–1943.* Boston: Houghton Mifflin, 1991.

Keegan, John. *The Second World War.* New York: Viking Books, 1990.

———, ed. *The Times Atlas of the Second World War.* New York: Harper & Row, 1989.

King, Ernest J. *U.S. Navy at War, 1941–45: Official Reports to the Secretary of the Navy.* Washington, D.C.: United States Navy Department, 1946.

King, Ernest J., and Walter M. Whitehill. *Fleet Admiral King, a Naval Record.* New York: Norton, 1952.

Lane, Frederic Chapin. *Ships for Victory: A History of Shipbuilding Under the United States Maritime Commission in World War II.* Baltimore: Johns Hopkins Press, 1951.

Langer, William L., and S. Everett Gleason. *The Undeclared War, 1940–41.* New York: Harper & Row, 1953.

Leahy, William D. *I Was There: The Personal Story of the Chief of Staff to Presidents Roosevelt and Truman, Based on His Notes and Diaries Made at the Time.* New York: McGraw-Hill, 1950.

Leutze, James R. *Bargaining for Supremacy: Anglo-American Naval Collaboration, 1937–1941.* Chapel Hill, N.C.: University of North Carolina Press, 1977.

———. *A Different Kind of Victory: A Biography of Admiral Thomas C. Hart.* Annapolis, Md.: Naval Institute Press, 1981.

Lewin, Ronald. *The American Magic: Codes, Ciphers, and the Defeat of Japan.* New York: Farrar Straus Giroux, 1982.

Lloyd's of London. *Lloyd's War Losses: The Second World War, 3 September 1939–14 August 1945.* Vol. 1. *British, Allied, and Neutral Merchant Vessels Sunk or Destroyed by War Causes.* London: Lloyd's of London Press, Ltd., 1989; Vol. 2. *Statistics Showing Monthly Losses of British, Allied, and Neutral Merchant Vessels, etc.* London: Lloyd's of London Press, Ltd., 1991.

Lockwood, Charles A. *Sink 'Em All: Submarine Warfare in the Pacific.* New York: Dutton, 1951.

Lockwood, Charles A., and Hans Christian Adamson. *Battles of the Philippine Sea.* New York: Crowell, 1967.

Lord, Walter. *Day of Infamy.* New York: Holt, 1957.

———. *Incredible Victory.* New York: Harper and Row, 1967.

———. *Lonely Vigil: Coastwatchers in the Solomons.* New York: Viking Press, 1977.

Lorelli, John A. *The Battle of the Komandorski Islands, March 1943.* Annapolis, Md.: Naval Institute Press, 1984.

Loxton, Bruce, with Chris Coulthard-Clark. *The Shame of Savo: Anatomy of a Naval Disaster.* Annapolis, Md.: Naval Institute Press, 1994.

Lundstrom, John B. *The First South Pacific Campaign: Pacific Fleet Strategy, December 1941 – June 1942.* Annapolis, Md.: Naval Institute Press, 1976.

———. *The First Team: Pacific Naval Air Combat from Pearl Harbor to Midway.* Annapolis, Md.: Naval Institute Press, 1984.

———. *The First Team and the Guadalcanal Campaign: Naval Fighter Combat from August to November 1942.* Annapolis, Md.: Naval Institute Press, 1994.

Marder, Arthur J. *Old Friends, New Enemies: The Royal Navy and the Imperial Japanese Navy, 1936–1945.* Vol. 1. *Strategic Illusions, 1936–1941.* Oxford: Clarendon Press, 1981.

Marder, Arthur J., Mark Jacobsen, and John Horsfield. *Old Friends, New Enemies: The Royal Navy and the Imperial Japanese Navy, 1936–1945.* Vol. 2. *The Pacific War, 1942–1945.* New York: Oxford University Press, 1990.

Miles, Milton E. *A Different Kind of War: The Little-Known Story of the Combined Guerrilla Forces Created in China by the U.S. Navy and the Chinese During World War II.* Garden City, N.Y.: Doubleday, 1967.

Miller, Edward S. *War Plan Orange: The U.S. Strategy to Defeat Japan, 1897–1945.* Annapolis, Md.: Naval Institute Press, 1991.

Moore, Arthur R. *"A Careless Word—a Needless Sinking" : A History of the Staggering Losses Suffered by the U.S. Merchant Marine, Both in Ships and Personnel, During World War II,* rev. ed., with addendum. Kings Point, N.Y.: American Merchant Marine Museum, 1985.

Morison, Samuel Eliot. *History of United States Naval Operations in World War II.* 15 vols. Boston: Little, Brown, 1962.

Nelson, Curtis L. *Hunters in the Shallows: A History of the PT Boat.* Washington, D.C. and London: Brassey's, 1998.

Newcomb, Richard F. *Iwo Jima*. New York: Holt, Rinehart, and Winston, 1965.

Nichols, Charles S., and Henry I. Shaw Jr. *Okinawa: Victory in the Pacific*. Rutland, Vt.: Charles E. Tuttle Co., 1955.

O'Connor, Raymond G. *Perilous Equilibrium: The Failure of the Second London Naval Conference and the Onset of World War II*. Cambridge, Mass.: Harvard University Press, 1974.

Parillo, Mark P. *The Japanese Merchant Marine in World War II*. Annapolis, Md.: Naval Institute Press, 1993.

Parker, Frederick D. *A Priceless Advantage: U.S. Navy Communications Intelligence and the Battles of Coral Sea, Midway, and the Aleutians*. Fort George G. Meade, Md.: National Security Agency, Center for Cryptologic History, 1993.

Prange, Gordon, with Donald M. Goldstein and Katherine V. Dillon. *At Dawn We Slept: The Untold Story of Pearl Harbor*. New York: McGraw-Hill, 1981.

Prange, Gordon, with Donald M. Goldstein and Katherine V. Dillon. *Miracle at Midway*. New York: McGraw-Hill, 1982.

Prange, Gordon, with Donald M. Goldstein and Katherine V. Dillon. *December 7, 1941: The Day the Japanese Attacked Pearl Harbor*. New York: McGraw-Hill, 1987.

Prange, Gordon, with Donald M. Goldstein and Katherine V. Dillon. *Pearl Harbor: The Verdict of History*. New York: McGraw-Hill, 1986.

Reynolds, Clark G. *The Fast Carriers: The Forging of an Air Navy*. Huntington: Robert E. Krieger, 1978.

Richardson, James O. *On the Treadmill to Pearl Harbor: The Memoirs of Admiral James O. Richardson, USN (Retired) as told to Vice Admiral George C. Dyer, USN (Retired)*. Washington, D.C.: Naval History Division, 1973.

Rohwer, Jürgen. *Axis Submarine Successes, 1939–1945*. Annapolis, Md.: Naval Institute Press, 1983.

———. *The Critical Convoy Battles of March 1943: The Battle for HX.229/SC.122*. Annapolis, Md.: Naval Institute Press, 1977.

Roscoe, Theodore. *United States Destroyer Operations in World War II*. Annapolis, Md.: Naval Institute Press, 1953.

———. *United States Submarine Operations in World War II*. Annapolis, Md.: Naval Institute Press, 1949.

Roskill, Stephen W. *Naval Policy Between the Wars*. 2 vols. New York: Walker, 1968.

Rowland, Buford, and William Boyd. *U.S. Navy Bureau of Ordnance in World War II*. Washington, D.C.: Government Printing Office, 1953.

Sadkovich, James J. *The Italian Navy in World War II*. Westport, Conn.: Greenwood Press, 1994.

Schoenfeld, Max. *Stalking the U-Boat: USAAF Offensive Antisubmarine Operations in World War II*. Washington, D.C.: Smithsonian Institution Press, 1995.

Sherrod, Robert L. *History of Marine Corps Aviation in World War II*. Washington, D.C.: Combat Forces Press, 1952.

Smith, William W. *Midway: Turning Point of the Pacific*. New York: Crowell, 1966.

Stephen, John J. *Hawaii Under the Rising Sun: Japan's Plans for Conquest After Pearl Harbor*. Honolulu: University of Hawaii Press, 1984.

Stillwell, Paul, ed. *Air Raid: Pearl Harbor! Recollections of a Day of Infamy*. Annapolis, Md.: Naval Institute Press, 1981.

Thomas, David A. *The Battle of the Java Sea*. London: Deutsch, 1968.

Thorne, Christopher. *Allies of a Kind: The United States, Britain and the War Against Japan, 1941–1945*. New York: Oxford University Press, 1978.

Toland, John. *But Not in Shame: The Six Months After Pearl Harbor*. New York: Random House, 1961.

———. *The Rising Sun: The Decline and Fall of the Japanese Empire, 1936–1945*. New York: Random House, 1970.

U.S. Army, Far East Command. *The Imperial Japanese Navy in World War II: A Graphic Presentation of the Japanese Naval Organization and List of Combatant and Non-Combatant Vessels Lost or Damaged in the War*. Japanese Operational Monograph Series, No. 116. Tokyo: Military History Section, Special Staff, General Headquarters, Far East Command, 1952.

U.S. Navy Department. *General Instructions for Commanding Officers of Naval Armed Guards on Merchant Ships, 1942*. Washington, D.C.: Government Printing Office, 1942.

Utley, Jonathan G. *Going to War with Japan, 1937–1941*. Knoxville, Tenn.: University of Tennessee Press, 1985.

van Oosten, F. C. *The Battle of the Java Sea*. Annapolis, Md.: Naval Institute Press, 1976.

Wallin, Homer N. *Pearl Harbor: Why, How, Fleet Salvage, and Final Appraisal*. Washington, D.C.: Naval History Division, 1968.

Warner, Denis A., and Peggy Warner, with Sadao Seno. *Disaster in the Pacific: New Light on the Battle of Savo Island*. Annapolis, Md.: Naval Institute Press, 1992.

Williams, Mary H., comp., *Chronology: 1941–1945* in *United States Army in World War II: Special Studies*. Washington, D.C.: Office of the Chief of Military History, 1960.

Willmott, H. P. *The Barrier and the Javelin: Japanese and Allied Pacific Strategies, February to June 1942*. Annapolis, Md.: Naval Institute Press, 1983.

———. *Empires in the Balance: Japanese and Allied Pacific Strategies to April 1942*. Annapolis, Md.: Naval Institute Press, 1982.

———. *The Great Crusade: A New Complete History of the Second World War*. New York: Free Press, 1990.

Y'Blood, William T. *The Little Giants: U.S. Escort Carriers Against Japan*. Annapolis, Md.: Naval Institute Press, 1987.

———. *Red Sun Setting: The Battle of the Philippine Sea*. Annapolis, Md.: Naval Institute Press, 1981.

———. *Hunter-Killer: U.S. Escort Carriers in the Battle of the Atlantic*. Annapolis, Md.: Naval Institute Press, 1983.

ABOUT THE AUTHOR

Robert J. Cressman is a historian in the Contemporary History Branch of the Naval Historical Center in Washington, D.C. He is a graduate of the University of Maryland, where he earned a B.A. and M.A. while studying under the late Gordon W. Prange. In addition to writing numerous articles for magazines and journals, Cressman is the author of several books including *A Magnificent Fight: The Battle for Wake Island* published by the Naval Institute Press. He is married and lives in Rockville, Maryland.